Encyclopedia of World Cultures

Volume X

INDEXES

ENCYCLOPEDIA OF WORLD CULTURES

David Levinson
Editor in Chief

North America
Oceania
South Asia
Europe (Central, Western, and Southeastern Europe)
East and Southeast Asia
Russia and Eurasia / China
South America
Middle America and the Caribbean
Africa and the Middle East
Indexes

The *Encyclopedia of World Cultures* was prepared under the auspices and with the support of the Human Relations Area Files at Yale University. HRAF, the foremost international research organization in the field of cultural anthropology, is a not-for-profit consortium of twenty-three sponsoring members and 300 participating member institutions in twenty-five countries. The HRAF archive, established in 1949, contains nearly one million pages of information on the cultures of the world.

Encyclopedia of World Cultures

Volume X

INDEXES

David Levinson
Volume Editor

G.K. Hall & Co.
Boston, Massachusetts

MEASUREMENT CONVERSIONS

When You Know	Multiply By	To Find
LENGTH		
inches	2.54	centimeters
feet	30	centimeters
yards	0.9	meters
miles	1.6	kilometers
millimeters	0.04	inches
centimeters	0.4	inches
meters	3.3	feet
meters	1.1	yards
kilometers	0.6	miles
AREA		
square feet	0.09	square meters
square yards	0.8	square meters
square miles	2.6	square kilometers
acres	0.4	hectares
hectares	2.5	acres
square meters	1.2	square yards
square kilometers	0.4	square miles

TEMPERATURE

$$°C = (°F - 32) \div 1.8$$
$$°F = (°C \times 1.8) + 32$$

© 1996 by the Human Relations Area Files, Inc.

First published 1996
by G.K. Hall & Co., an imprint of Simon & Schuster Macmillan
866 Third Avenue
New York, NY 10022

10 9 8 7 6 5 4 3 2 1

Library of Congress Cataloging-in-Publication Data
(Revised for volume 10)

Encyclopedia of world cultures.

Includes bibliographical references, filmographies, and indexes.
Contents: v. 1. North America / Timothy J. O'Leary, David Levinson, volume editors—v. 10. Index / David Levinson, volume editor.
1. Ethnology—Encyclopedias. I. Levinson, David, 1947-
GN307.E53 1991   306'.097   90-49123
ISBN 0-8161-1840–X (set : alk. paper)
ISBN 0-8161-1808–6 (v. 1 : alk. paper)

The paper used in this publication meets the minimum requirements of American National Standard for Information Sciences—Permanence of Paper for Printed Library Materials. ANSI Z39.48-1984.   ∞™
MANUFACTURED IN THE UNITED STATES OF AMERICA

Contents

Project Staff   vi

Preface   vii

Introduction *by Paul Hockings*   xiii

The Task of Ethnography   xv

List of Cultures by Country   1

Ethnonym Index   17

Subject Index   79

Preface

This project began in 1987 with the goal of assembling a basic reference source that provides accurate, clear, and concise descriptions of the cultures of the world. We wanted to be as comprehensive and authoritative as possible: comprehensive, by providing descriptions of all the cultures of each region of the world or by describing a representative sample of cultures for regions where full coverage is impossible, and authoritative by providing accurate descriptions of the cultures for both the past and the present.

The publication of the *Encyclopedia of World Cultures* in the last decade of the twentieth century is especially timely. The political, economic, and social changes of the past fifty years have produced a world more complex and fluid than at any time in human history. Three sweeping transformations of the worldwide cultural landscape are especially significant.

First is what some social scientists are calling the "New Diaspora"—the dispersal of cultural groups to new locations across the world. This dispersal affects all nations and takes a wide variety of forms: in East African nations, the formation of new towns inhabited by people from dozens of different ethnic groups; in Micronesia and Polynesia, the movement of islanders to cities in New Zealand and the United States; in North America, the replacement by Asians and Latin Americans of Europeans as the most numerous immigrants; in Europe, the increased reliance on workers from the Middle East and North Africa; and so on.

Second, and related to this dispersal, is the internal division of what were once single, unified cultural groups into two or more relatively distinct groups. This pattern of internal division is most dramatic among indigenous or third or fourth world cultures whose traditional ways of life have been altered by contact with the outside world. Underlying this division are both the population dispersion mentioned above and sustained contact with the economically developed world. The result is that groups who at one time saw themselves and were seen by others as single cultural groups have been transformed into two or more distinct groups. Thus, in many cultural groups, we find deep and probably permanent divisions between those who live in the country and those who live in cities, those who follow the traditional religion and those who have converted to Christianity, those who live inland and those who live on the seacoast, and those who live by means of a subsistence economy and those now enmeshed in a cash economy.

The third important transformation of the worldwide cultural landscape is the revival of ethnic nationalism, with many peoples claiming and fighting for political freedom and territorial integrity on the basis of ethnic solidarity and ethnic-based claims to their traditional homeland. Although most attention has focused recently on ethnic nationalism in Eastern Europe and the former Soviet Union, the trend is nonetheless a worldwide phenomenon involving, for example, American Indian cultures in North and South America, the Basques in Spain and France, the Tamil and Sinhalese in Sri Lanka, and the Tutsi and Hutu in Burundi, among others.

To be informed citizens of our rapidly changing multicultural world we must understand the ways of life of people from cultures different from our own. "We" is used here in the broadest sense, to include not just scholars who study the cultures of the world and businesspeople and government officials who work in the world community but also the average citizen who reads or hears about multicultural events in the news every day and young people who are growing up in this complex cultural world. For all of these people—which means all of us—there is a pressing need for information on the cultures of the world. This encyclopedia provides this information in two ways. First, its descriptions of the traditional ways of life of the world's cultures can serve as a baseline against which cultural change can be measured and understood. Second, it acquaints the reader with the contemporary ways of life throughout the world.

We are able to provide this information largely through the efforts of the volume editors and the nearly one thousand contributors who wrote the cultural summaries that are the heart of the book. The contributors are social scientists (anthropologists, sociologists, historians, and geographers) as well as educators, government officials, and missionaries who usually have firsthand research-based knowledge of the cultures they write about. In many cases they are the major expert or one of the leading experts on the culture, and some are themselves members of the cultures. As experts, they are able to provide accurate, up-to-date information. This is crucial for many parts of the world where indigenous cultures may be overlooked by official information seekers such as government census takers. These experts have often lived among the people they write about, conducting participant-observations with them and speaking their language. Thus they are able to provide integrated, holistic descriptions of the cultures, not just a list of facts. Their portraits of the cultures leave the reader with a real sense of what it means to be a "Taos" or a "Rom" or a "Sicilian."

Those summaries not written by an expert on the culture have usually been written by a researcher at the Human Relations Area Files, Inc., working from primary source materials.

The Human Relations Area Files, an international educational and research institute, is recognized by professionals in the social and behavioral sciences, humanities, and medical sciences as a major source of information on the cultures of the world.

Uses of the Encyclopedia

This encyclopedia is meant to be used by a variety of people for a variety of purposes. It can be used both to gain a general understanding of a culture and to find a specific piece of information by looking it up under the relevant subheading in a summary. It can also be used to learn about a particular region or subregion of the world and the social, economic, and political forces that have shaped the cultures in that region. The encyclopedia is also a resource guide that leads readers who want a deeper understanding of particular cultures to additional sources of information. Resource guides in the encyclopedia include ethnonyms listed in each summary, which can be used as entry points into the social science literature where the culture may sometimes be identified by a different name; a bibliography at the end of each summary, which lists books and articles about the culture; and a filmography at the end of each volume, which lists films and videos on many of the cultures.

Beyond being a basic reference resource, the encyclopedia also serves readers with more focused needs. For researchers interested in comparing cultures, the encyclopedia serves as the most complete and up-to-date sampling frame from which to select cultures for further study. For those interested in international studies, the encyclopedia leads one quickly into the relevant social science literature as well as providing a state-of-the-art assessment of our knowledge of the cultures of a particular region. For curriculum developers and teachers seeking to internationalize their curriculum, the encyclopedia is itself a basic reference and educational resource as well as a directory to other materials. For government officials, it is a repository of information not likely to be available in any other single publication or, in some cases, not available at all. For students, from high school through graduate school, it provides background and bibliographic information for term papers and class projects. And for travelers, it provides an introduction into the ways of life of the indigenous peoples in the area of the world they will be visiting.

Format of the Encyclopedia

The encyclopedia comprises ten volumes, ordered by geographical regions of the world. The order of publication is not meant to represent any sort of priority. Volumes 1 through 9 contain a total of about fifteen hundred summaries along with maps, glossaries, and indexes of alternate names for the cultural groups. The tenth and final volume contains cumulative lists of the cultures of the world, their alternate names, and a bibliography of selected publications pertaining to those groups.

North America covers the cultures of Canada, Greenland, and the United States of America.
Oceania covers the cultures of Australia, New Zealand, Melanesia, Micronesia, and Polynesia.
South Asia covers the cultures of Bangladesh, India, Pakistan, Sri Lanka and other South Asian islands, and the Himalayan states.
Europe covers the cultures of Europe.

East and Southeast Asia covers the cultures of Japan, Korea, mainland and insular Southeast Asia, and Taiwan.
Russia and Eurasia / China covers the cultures of Mongolia, the People's Republic of China, and the former Union of Soviet Socialist Republics.
South America covers the cultures of South America.
Middle America and the Caribbean covers the cultures of Central America, Mexico, and the Caribbean islands.
Africa and the Middle East covers the cultures of Madagascar and sub-Saharan Africa, North Africa, the Middle East, and south-central Asia.

Format of the Volumes

Each volume contains this preface, an introductory essay by the volume editor, the cultural summaries ranging from a few lines to several pages each, maps pinpointing the location of the cultures, a filmography, an ethnonym index of alternate names for the cultures, and a glossary of scientific and technical terms. All entries are listed in alphabetical order and are extensively cross-referenced.

Cultures Covered

A central issue in selecting cultures for coverage in the encyclopedia has been how to define what we mean by a cultural group. The questions of what a culture is and what criteria can be used to classify a particular social group (such as a religious group, ethnic group, nationality, or territorial group) as a cultural group have long perplexed social scientists and have yet to be answered to everyone's satisfaction. Two realities account for why the questions cannot be answered definitively. First, a wide variety of different types of cultures exist around the world. Among common types are national cultures, regional cultures, ethnic groups, indigenous societies, religious groups, and unassimilated immigrant groups. No single criterion or marker of cultural uniqueness can consistently distinguish among the hundreds of cultures that fit into these general types. Second, as noted above, single cultures or what were at one time identified as single cultures can and do vary internally over time and place. Thus a marker that may identify a specific group as a culture in one location or at one time may not work for that culture in another place or at another time. For example, use of the Yiddish language would have been a marker of Jewish cultural identity in Eastern Europe in the nineteenth century, but it would not serve as a marker for Jews in the twentieth-century United States, where most speak English. Similarly, residence on one of the Cook Islands in Polynesia would have been a marker of Cook Islander identity in the eighteenth century, but not in the twentieth century when two-thirds of Cook Islanders live in New Zealand and elsewhere.

Given these considerations, no attempt has been made to develop and use a single definition of a cultural unit or to develop and use a fixed list of criteria for identifying cultural units. Instead, the task of selecting cultures was left to the volume editors, and the criteria and procedures they used are discussed in their introductory essays. In general, however, six criteria were used, sometimes alone and sometimes in combination to classify social groups as cultural groups: (1) geographical localization, (2) identification in the social science literature as a distinct group, (3) distinct language, (4) shared traditions, religion, folklore, or values, (5) maintenance of group identity in the face of strong assimilative pressures, and (6) previous listing in an inventory of the world's cultures such as *Ethnographic Atlas* (Murdock 1967) or the *Outline of World Cultures* (Murdock 1983).

In general, we have been "lumpers" rather than "splitters" in writing the summaries. That is, if there is some question about whether a particular group is really one culture or two related cultures, we have more often than not treated it as a single culture, with internal differences noted in the summary. Similarly, we have sometimes chosen to describe a number of very similar cultures in a single summary rather than in a series of summaries that would be mostly redundant. There is, however, some variation from one region to another in this approach, and the rationale for each region is discussed in the volume editor's essay.

Two categories of cultures are usually not covered in the encyclopedia. First, extinct cultures, especially those that have not existed as distinct cultural units for some time, are usually not described. Cultural extinction is often, though certainly not always, indicated by the disappearance of the culture's language. So, for example, the Aztec are not covered, although living descendants of the Aztec, the Nahuatl-speakers of central Mexico, are described.

Second, the ways of life of immigrant groups are usually not described in much detail, unless there is a long history of resistance to assimilation and the group has maintained its distinct identity, as have the Amish in North America. These cultures are, however, described in the location where they traditionally lived and, for the most part, continue to live, and migration patterns are noted. For example, the Hmong in Laos are described in the Southeast Asia volume, but the refugee communities in the United States and Canada are covered only in the general summaries on Southeast Asians in those two countries in the North America volume. Although it would be ideal to provide descriptions of all the immigrant cultures or communities of the world, that is an undertaking well beyond the scope of this encyclopedia, for there are probably more than five thousand such communities in the world.

Finally, it should be noted that not all nationalities are covered, only those that are also distinct cultures as well as political entities. For example, the Vietnamese and Burmese are included but Indians (citizens of the Republic of India) are not, because the latter is a political entity made up of a great mix of cultural groups. In the case of nations whose populations include a number of different, relatively unassimilated groups or cultural regions, each of the groups is described separately. For example, there is no summary for Italians as such in the Europe volume, but there are summaries for the regional cultures of Italy, such as the Tuscans, Sicilians, and Tirolians, and other cultures such as the Sinti Piemontese.

Cultural Summaries

The heart of this encyclopedia is the descriptive summaries of the cultures, which range from a few lines to five or six pages in length. They provide a mix of demographic, historical, social, economic, political, and religious information on the cultures. Their emphasis or flavor is cultural; that is, they focus on the ways of life of the people—both past and present—and the factors that have caused the culture to change over time and place.

A key issue has been how to decide which cultures should be described by longer summaries and which by shorter ones. This decision was made by the volume editors, who had to balance a number of intellectual and practical considerations. Again, the rationale for these decisions is discussed in their essays. But among the factors that were considered by all the editors were the total number of cultures in their region, the availability of experts to write summaries, the availability of information on the cultures, the degree of similarity between cultures, and the importance of a culture in a scientific or political sense.

The summary authors followed a standardized outline so that each summary provides information on a core list of topics. The authors, however, had some leeway in deciding how much attention was to be given each topic and whether additional information should be included. Summaries usually provide information on the following topics:

CULTURE NAME: The name used most often in the social science literature to refer to the culture or the name the group uses for itself.

ETHNONYMS: Alternate names for the culture including names used by outsiders, the self-name, and alternate spellings, within reasonable limits.

ORIENTATION
Identification. Location of the culture and the derivation of its name and ethnonyms.
Location. Where the culture is located and a description of the physical environment.
Demography. Population history and the most recent reliable population figures or estimates.
Linguistic Affiliation. The name of the language spoken and/or written by the culture, its place in an international language classification system, and internal variation in language use.

HISTORY AND CULTURAL RELATIONS: A tracing of the origins and history of the culture and the past and current nature of relationships with other groups.

SETTLEMENTS: The location of settlements, types of settlements, types of structures, housing design and materials.

ECONOMY
Subsistence and Commercial Activities. The primary methods of obtaining, consuming, and distributing money, food, and other necessities.
Industrial Arts. Implements and objects produced by the culture either for its own use or for sale or trade.
Trade. Products traded and patterns of trade with other groups.
Division of Labor. How basic economic tasks are assigned by age, sex, ability, occupational specialization, or status.
Land Tenure. Rules and practices concerning the allocation of land and land-use rights to members of the culture and to outsiders.

KINSHIP
Kin Groups and Descent. Rules and practices concerning kin-based features of social organization such as lineages and clans and alliances between these groups.
Kinship Terminology. Classification of the kinship terminological system on the basis of either cousin terms or genera-

tion, and information about any unique aspects of kinship terminology.

MARRIAGE AND FAMILY

Marriage. Rules and practices concerning reasons for marriage, types of marriage, economic aspects of marriage, post-marital residence, divorce, and remarriage.

Domestic Unit. Description of the basic household unit including type, size, and composition.

Inheritance. Rules and practices concerning the inheritance of property.

Socialization. Rules and practices concerning child rearing including caretakers, values inculcated, child-rearing methods, initiation rites, and education.

SOCIOPOLITICAL ORGANIZATION

Social Organization. Rules and practices concerning the internal organization of the culture, including social status, primary and secondary groups, and social stratification.

Political Organization. Rules and practices concerning leadership, politics, governmental organizations, and decision making.

Social Control. The sources of conflict within the culture and informal and formal social control mechanisms.

Conflict. The sources of conflict with other groups and informal and formal means of resolving conflicts.

RELIGION AND EXPRESSIVE CULTURE

Religious Beliefs. The nature of religious beliefs including beliefs in supernatural entities, traditional beliefs, and the effects of major religions.

Religious Practitioners. The types, sources of power, and activities of religious specialists such as shamans and priests.

Ceremonies. The nature, type, and frequency of religious and other ceremonies and rites.

Arts. The nature, types, and characteristics of artistic activities including literature, music, dance, carving, and so on.

Medicine. The nature of traditional medical beliefs and practices and the influence of scientific medicine.

Death and Afterlife. The nature of beliefs and practices concerning death, the deceased, funerals, and the afterlife.

BIBLIOGRAPHY: A selected list of publications about the culture. The list usually includes publications that describe both the traditional and the contemporary culture.

AUTHOR'S NAME: The name of the summary author.

Maps

Each regional volume contains maps pinpointing the current location of the cultures described in that volume. The first map in each volume is usually an overview, showing the countries in that region. The other maps provide more detail by marking the locations of the cultures in four or five subregions.

Filmography

Each volume contains a list of films and videos about cultures covered in that volume. This list is provided as a service and in no way indicates an endorsement by the editor, the volume editor, or the summary authors. Addresses of distributors are provided so that information about availability and prices can be readily obtained.

Ethnonym Index

Each volume contains an ethnonym index for the cultures covered in that volume. As mentioned above, ethnonyms are alternative names for the culture—that is, names different from those used here as the summary headings. Ethnonyms may be alternative spellings of the culture name, a totally different name used by outsiders, a name used in the past but no longer used, or the name in another language. It is not unusual that some ethnonyms are considered degrading and insulting by the people to whom they refer. These names may nevertheless be included here because they do identify the group and may help some users locate the summary or additional information on the culture in other sources. Ethnonyms are cross-referenced to the culture name in the index.

Glossary

Each volume contains a glossary of technical and scientific terms found in the summaries. Both general social science terms and region-specific terms are included.

Special Considerations

In a project of this magnitude, decisions had to be made about the handling of some information that cannot easily be standardized for all areas of the world. The two most troublesome matters concerned population figures and units of measure.

Population Figures

We have tried to be as up-to-date and as accurate as possible in reporting population figures. This is no easy task, as some groups are not counted in official government censuses, some groups are very likely undercounted, and in some cases the definition of a cultural group used by the census takers differs from the definition we have used. In general, we have relied on population figures supplied by the summary authors. When other population data sources have been used in a volume, they are so noted by the volume editor. If the reported figure is from an earlier date—say, the 1970s—it is usually because it is the most accurate figure that could be found.

Units of Measure

In an international encyclopedia, editors encounter the problem of how to report distances, units of space, and temperature. In much of the world, the metric system is used, but scientists prefer the International System of Units (similar to the metric system), and in Great Britain and North America the English system is usually used. We decided to use English measures in the North America volume and metric measures in the other volumes. Each volume contains a conversion table.

Acknowledgments

In a project of this size, there are many people to acknowledge and thank for their contributions. In its planning stages, members of the research staff of the Human Relations Area Files provided many useful ideas. These included Timothy J. O'Leary, Marlene Martin, John Beierle, Gerald Reid, Delores Walters, Richard Wagner, and Christopher Latham. The advisory editors, of course, also played a major role in planning the project, and not just for their own volumes but also for the project as a whole. Timothy O'Leary, Terence Hays, and Paul Hockings deserve special thanks for their comments on this preface and the glossary, as does Melvin Ember, president of the Human Relations Area Files. Members of the office and technical staff also must be thanked for so quickly and carefully attending to the many tasks a project of this size inevitably generates. They are Erlinda Maramba, Abraham Maramba, Victoria Crocco, Nancy Gratton, and Douglas Black. At Macmillan and G.K. Hall, the encyclopedia has benefited from the wise and careful editorial management of Elly Dickason, Elizabeth Kubik, and Elizabeth Holthaus, and the editorial and production management of Ara Salibian.

Finally, I would like to thank Melvin Ember and the board of directors of the Human Relations Area Files for their administrative and intellectual support for this project.

DAVID LEVINSON

References

Murdock, George Peter (1967). *Ethnographic Atlas*. Pittsburgh: University of Pittsburgh Press.

Murdock, George Peter (1983). *Outline of World Cultures*. 6th rev. ed. New Haven: Human Relations Area Files.

Introduction

It has taken ten years of work to produce this ten-volume Encyclopedia of World Cultures. Thirteen editors, six associate editors, 800 contributors, 20 translators, and the staffs of the Human Relations Area Files, G. K. Hall and Co., and Macmillan Library Reference have been involved in the process. In keeping with the global scope of the subject matter, the 800 contributors represent 52 different nations, with the majority writing from the United States, Great Britain, and Canada. Some 150 articles were translated from Russia, Spanish, Portuguese, French, Ukrainian, Kazakh, and Chinese for inclusion in the Encyclopedia. That so many nations are represented reflects the time-consuming and costly effort by the volume editors to involve anthropologists from other nations in this project.

Our work has produced some 1,430 articles covering 1,800 cultures and three appendices covering an additional 1,200 cultures. Thus, these ten volumes provide descriptive information on 3,000 cultures around the world. While some of the cultures described here are only a few hundred people strong, at the other extreme one finds the Han Chinese who number over one billion but as the world's largest ethnic group are described in a single article.

The years during which we worked on the Encyclopedia were ones of enormous global political, social, and economic change. That these changes have influenced cultures around the world and relations among cultures is well documented in many of the articles. These global changes also influenced our work on the Encyclopedia. The break-up of the former Soviet Union made it possible for anthropologists in Russia and formerly Soviet but now newly independent republics to contribute to the Encyclopedia. That their contributions contain much information on material culture and folklore but little on kinship and political organization tells as much about how anthropological research was controlled during the years of Soviet rule. Continuing political and cultural repression in China, on the other hand, made it difficult to find scholars who would be allowed to write for a Western audience and, in fact, ultimately determined what cultures in China we could cover.

Indigenous rights movements influenced our definition of a culture and also the names we gave to specific cultures. More and more as the project progressed, we found contributors choosing the name the indigenous people now prefer for themselves in place of a name conventionally used in anthropology or by colonial powers in the past. Any possible confu-

sion these changes or inconsistencies in naming might cause the reader are eliminated by the ethnonym indexes in each volume and the complete ethnonym index in this volume, which list alternative names for cultures.

Our work was also influenced by the attention paid by different governments to cultural variation within their borders. The Indonesian government, for example, in an effort to build a pan-Indonesian national culture, downplays the considerable cultural diversity within its borders and does not enumerate its population by cultural group. Thus, we had to construct our own list of cultures in Indonesia and rely on older data for population estimates. The Vietnamese, by contrast, in their last census produced a detailed list of all cultural groups, with standardized spellings and population figures. Finally, the migration of millions of people each year (both as emigrants and as refugees) kept alive for us the question of how to cover migrant communities outside their homeland. In general, we adhered to the policy established in Volume 1: to give immigrant groups less attention than indigenous groups.

Another type of cultural group given less than full attention in some volumes is the regional culture. Regional cultures, which are a worldwide phenomenon, are cultures whose members are defined simultaneously as members of a broader, usually national culture and as members of a more narrowly defined regional culture. Examples include Wessexmen or Yorkshiremen in England, New Englanders in the United States, and Central Mountain peasants in Norway. Our coverage of regional cultures has varied from volume to volume and even from nation to nation within volumes. When we have opted to give more attention to regional cultures—such as the Highland Scots in Scotland, Catalans in Spain, Bretons in France, or Sicilians in Italy, it is because they speak or until quite recently spoke a distinct language, are a political or quasi-political entity, or are clearly defined by themselves and others as a distinct culture. Many of these regional cultures are being absorbed into the national cultures, but some, such as Bretons and Catalans, are resisting, while others, such as the Cornish, are seeking to reestablish themselves as distinct cultural regions.

How to Use the Encyclopedia

Each of the nine volumes of text of the *Encyclopedia of World Cultures* deals with the cultures of a particular geographic area, and within each volume the cultures are arranged alphabetically. All entries present the information on different aspects of the culture—location, economy, kinship and family, religion, et cetera—in the same order, which makes it easy to locate the answer to specific questions.

An index to these volumes might therefore be perceived as a superfluous tool. However, we have designed an index that will make possible what the individual volumes cannot do, namely, cross-cultural comparisons. In the index each expression of culture—from family rites to religion and form of government—is broken down into different manifestations of these traditions, and under these headings the Index then lists the cultures practicing these customs. The Index is therefore the place to start if one is interested in types of culture and how they might compare with other types. Of course, the Index also lists each individual culture.

The study of particular countries is facilitated by the List of Cultures by Country, beginning on page 1. An Ethnonym Index, a complete list of all cultures covered in the Encyclopedia as well as alternate names by which they may be known, follows on page 17. The Index proper starts on page 17.

The Task of Ethnography

The word *ethnography*, created from two Greek words meaning "to describe a people" by the German pedagogue J. H. Campe in 1807, first appeared in English in 1834. This was on the eve of the earliest attempts to establish a science of anthropology. Not coincidentally, the word came into use at a time when educated Westerners, especially Christian believers, became interested in the characteristics and spiritual welfare of those they categorized as "savages," in connection with the mounting opposition to the immoral practice of slavery and the possibility of new realms for evangelization. In fact, the English word emerged a year after the British Parliament had abolished slavery. It was a period, too, when the systematic colonization of Australia, New Zealand, and Canada began to bring tens of thousands of Europeans into direct contact with peoples who had no idea what or where Europe was, and whose languages were unknown.

Robert H. Lowie (1953) grandly summed up the aim of ethnography as "the complete description of all cultural phenomena everywhere and at all periods." Most ethnographers, however, have confined their attention to contemporary societies. In recent years *ethnography* has taken on three closely related meanings: (1) the total scientific knowledge of the culture of a particular people; (2) the methodical acquisition of this knowledge; and (3) a published account of a culture and society. Some writers, especially French anthropologists, equate the term with "ethnology." In this Encyclopedia the authors and editors have employed all three of the above senses.

Early Forms of Ethnography

The proto-ethnography, if we may coin a word, has a very long history. It is not unusual today for histories of anthropology to begin with a bow toward Herodotus (c. 484–420 BCE), who did indeed attempt a methodical account of his known world (Blanco 1992). Through the subsequent centuries numerous Chinese writers, the Arab traveler al-Biruni, and many European explorers and travelers attempted to describe unknown cultures and peoples for the edification of the readers at home. Some of these authors were more critical of their sources than others, and the best no doubt made some serious intellectual efforts to get their facts straight. Today we would have to classify such people as travel writers whose work was essentially uninformed by any overall theory of society. (Herodotus was the exception, for he did have a theory about climate determining cultures.) In general they were caught up in the extraordinary nature of their exotic subject material, or even in the mere emotional effect of their travels. Witness the following paragraph from a nineteenth-century British account of a visit to a Hindu temple:

> The drums are beating *violently* as he approaches, and *wild* music of *strange* sorts is issuing from the *equally strange* building before him. He is admitted (after he has taken off his shoes), and beholds a sight as *extraordinary* as is the *noise* that accompanies it. On the walls of the room are *hideous* images, carved in stone and daubed in red paint, one representing a monkey, one a creature with a fat human belly, and an elephant's head, each with an offering of yellow marigolds before it.

I have italicized the words used to convey the emotional effect on the writer, apparently his major concern. That style of writing never contributed anything to anthropology.

This is not the place to survey the thousands of volumes produced, especially in the eighteenth and nineteenth centuries, by what may seem like armies of explorers, colonial officials, military officers, planters, traders, itinerant journalists, and Christian missionaries. Their colorful accounts are often well worth reading (albeit with a good deal of skepticism), and may contain highly revelatory illustrations and—after 1870—photographs. Anthropologists preparing for a bout of fieldwork in a particular territory are well advised to pay some attention to its earlier descriptive literature, however biased or inadequate it may appear. Yet it will only provide them with a shallow background, for almost never can it answer theoretical questions.

The Development of Modern Methods

Up to about World War I anthropology had developed through a division of labor. It was amateurs who discovered the early remnants of fossil man and some of the most famous Paleolithic living sites. Distinguished professors of human anatomy then studied the specimens in their laboratories and wrote their textbooks on human evolution. And in ethnology it was mostly amateurs too—travelers, colonial officials, and missionaries in particular—who wrote some of the earliest ethnographic descriptions of non-Western cultures and societies. These were later digested, and in the process given a new context, by such famed armchair anthropologists as Sir James Frazer or Sir Herbert Spencer, to be presented in altered format as the latest theories about mankind. These denizens of the great scholarly libraries usually had no first-hand experience of daily life in any non-Western society. For them ethnology and ethnography were almost two separate sciences, the one generalizing into grand theory from the specific field observations of the other.

Yet in the first two decades of the twentieth century several British and American scholars, among them Franz Boas, Bronislaw Malinowski, A. R. Radcliffe-Brown, and W. H. R. Rivers, accomplished the feat of bestriding these two tendencies by producing some of the earliest social theory to be grounded in *their own* field observations of non-Western peoples. The particular peoples chosen for study by this handful of men were exotic, small, marginal societies that up to that time few scholars knew anything about. But now there were men in the universities who, like the explorers of centuries past, had first-hand knowledge of these strangely different cultures; and it was knowledge based on such a long familiarity that their published accounts showed the "natives" or "savages" to be not as strange or different as might have been expected: There was pattern to their lives, a continuity and purpose, and even a sense of family, God, and history where scarcely any had been expected.

It was also fortunate that what we now view as the first scientific ethnographies by the early professional anthropologists covered such a broad range of territories and economic types. Boas had worked with the Baffin Island Inuit (1883–1884) and the Kwakiutl of British Columbia (1885–1935). His student A. L. Kroeber worked with the remaining tribes of California (1901–1939). Malinowski found himself among the Trobriand Islanders of New Guinea during World War I (1915–1917), and made great strides in field methodology through his mastery of the language. Rivers pioneered in the study of kinship with his work on the South Indian Todas (1902), and repeatedly worked in Melanesia (1898–1915). A. R. Radcliffe-Brown studied the Andaman Islanders in the Bay of Bengal in 1906–1908, and then developed a broad acquaintance with Australian aboriginal tribes from 1910 to 1931. If we were to look at other parts of the world we could identify several others who did sterling ethnographic work: yet it was the above men who did most to establish the groundwork of social theory and fieldwork procedure in anthropology.

This statement is not to be taken as meaning that social theory is only an Anglo-American product. The work of other European social theoreticians is not to be slighted, especially the seminal studies of two French sociologists, Émile Durkheim and his student Marcel Mauss, and of the great German sociologists Max Weber and Karl Marx. Social anthropology has always acknowledged its debt to these figures. Yet they were sociologists and they did no fieldwork among non-Western peoples. So while Weber's study of ancient Jewish, Hindu, Buddhist, Taoist, and Confucian civilizations and Durkheim's study of Australian aboriginal religion were immensely influential, it was left to ethnographers such as Radcliffe-Brown and A. P. Elkin to check the facts and incorporate these studies into their own work.

Today there is no sense that ethnography is a science separable from other aspects of sociocultural anthropology. For many it has become almost a literary style, while for others it is viewed as the basic accumulation of cultural facts upon which sociocultural theory is built. Since the middle of the twentieth century, ethnographies have tended to narrow their scope as compared with the "classics" of the earlier masters. So where these latter wrote all-encompassing works with titles like *The Todas* (Rivers 1906) or *The Veddas* (Seligman and Seligman 1911), the past half-century has been marked by such contributions as *Migrant Labour and Tribal Life* (Schapera 1947), *The Dynamics of Clanship Among the Tallensi* (Fortes

1945), or *Rank and Religion in Tikopia* (Firth 1970). These are no less ethnographies than their predecessors, but they chose a narrower scope and filled in the details with more intimacy and understanding than had previously been possible.

Before Rivers, Boas, and Malinowski revolutionized fieldwork, data collection had often been restricted to the acquisition of material artifacts for museums, along with some necessary word lists. But after World War I we find a greater variety of approaches in participant observation, including the recording of life histories, the administration of objective tests, and the shooting of film. In 1938 George P. Murdock edited the first edition of *An Outline of Cultural Materials* to help organize the vast accumulation of field data from around the world and to serve as an index to field observations.

In 1968 Harold C. Conklin outlined what the ethnographic enterprise involves:

> The ethnographer tries not to rely upon published outlines and questionnaires; he shuns interviews with informants carried out in artificial settings; and he avoids premature quantification or overdifferentiated measurement. Initially, at least, flexibility, curiosity, patience, and experimentation with many alternative devices and procedures are desirable. In everyday conversations between field worker and informant, for example, attention to and use of such verbal techniques as the following have been used profitably, although not always with equal success: recording and using natural question and comment frames (i.e., the ways in which information is normally solicited and transmitted in the local language); noting and using question-response sequences and implications; testing by intentional substitution of acceptable and incongruent references; testing by paraphrase; testing by reference to hypothetical situations; testing by experimental extensions of reference; and testing by switching styles, channels, code signals, message content, and roles (by reference or impersonation). Similarly, in the making of visual and nonverbal observations initial experimentation and flexibility help to determine focuses and boundaries of scenes, scheduled events, key roles, etc. Graphic and plastic modeling media have provided additional dimensions for the exploration of actual or hypothetical situations otherwise not easily investigated. Furthermore, ethnomodels, often ignored or treated anecdotally, may clarify and facilitate field observation. When local systems have been qualitatively established, other procedures such as scaling techniques may be applied to increase the range of observations and provide some basis for quantification by various kinds of discrete, direct, or indirect measures [p. 175].

Conklin goes on to discuss how "the observer becomes a part of . . . the observed universe," a matter which has received much consideration in recent years.

Recent Trends in Ethnography

Since the 1970s a dozen trends can be discerned, to judge from the journal articles and academic books dealing with ethnography:

1. Many publications have been devoted to a self-conscious concern with ethics and what is called "reflexivity," including a variety of autobiographical essays. Many

ethnographers today find themselves involved in the promotion and advocacy (or otherwise) of local causes. This practice raises questions about the objectivity of the data that they are simultaneously gathering in a community.

2. Field observations are being quantified in preparation for increasingly sophisticated analyses by computer.

3. There is much focus on urban social systems, at home and abroad, and on "postpeasants," neither of which was a major concern of earlier ethnography.

4. Modernization and social change are omnipresent, so the early concern with describing "static" societies in equilibrium (e.g., Rivers on the Todas) has disappeared.

5. Anthropologists continue to identify with "their people," but are now more likely to enter into formal partnerships with them, either for economic improvement or for better recording the old traditions that will be passed down to a literate posterity. Much academic and museum research is now published for very different audiences. It is recognized that a community providing data to an anthropologist has intellectual rights in that material.

6. While not all of the world's cultures are adequately known, and some broad ethnographics are still being published, the tendency is to devote a book to what may seem very narrow and specialized or esoteric—but nonetheless interesting and potentially important—issues.

7. Recognition of the relevance of ecological factors is no longer the mark of one particular "school" of anthropology, but is fundamental in the intellectual background of ethnographers.

8. By focusing on pervasive processes like modernization, industrialization, urbanization, and cultural change generally, ethnographers are relying less on data gathered from just one or at most a handful of reliable "key informants" and more on survey approaches with a population sample.

9 Although the early concern with kinship persists, there is now more research on networks that link individuals not only to their relatives but also to political powers, work opportunities, and ecological issues.

10. The study of a selected community remains popular, although many anthropologists now work with heterogeneous regions or with intercommunity issues involving some ethnic diversity.

11. While research teams larger than two people were highly unusual in social anthropology (though common in bioanthropology and archaeology), multiperson and even interdisciplinary teams are now being deployed in the field. This reflects recognition of the artificiality of disciplinary boundaries and of the relevance of findings in economics, demography, and psychology to the investigation of modern social processes.

Ethnicity and Subcultural Variation

Although the Greek word _ethnos_ at the root of ethnicity, ethnography, and related words had the meaning of "a people," the sense in modern anthropological terms is of a people's _culture_, their habits, customs, beliefs, and ways of making a living and organizing their social relationships; it is definitely not concerned with their physical organisms.

Not all of the cultures that are the subject of articles in the Encyclopedia can be equated with "societies." The latter term has been defined in many ways to denote the largest organization of groups of persons sharing a similar culture. Admittedly there is a good deal of unavoidable flexibility in the way social scientists use that term, yet it is clear that many of the entries in the Encyclopedia deal not with societies but with part-societies (e.g., Peripatetics, Volume 3) or a religious cult (e.g., Bengali Shakta, Volume 3) or a caste-block (e.g., Vellala, Volume 3) or an ethnic group that finds itself embedded in a larger, encompassing society (e.g., Cornish, Volume 4). The variety of types of social unit raises the question whether the material in different entries is strictly comparable.

This Encyclopedia deals with the specific cultures of perhaps 1,800 "peoples," large and small, regardless of the type of social unit they represent and how they are best defined. Some of the tribes or island groups are only a few hundred people strong. At the other extreme we find the Han (more commonly referred to as Chinese), who are described in a single article covering over one billion people. Some cultures may appear very similar to their neighbors, while others are quite distinctive and strive to maintain that distinctiveness. When two or more cultures share a similar history, inhabit contiguous territories, and have a common language and religion and similar economic, political, and family institutions, they may look so similar—both on paper and on the ground—that a question can easily arise as to whether they are really two cultures or just subcultural variations of the same one. The more serious theoretical question centers on how anthropologists define a culture and demarcate its boundaries. Do they perhaps reify and make more contained something that is in fact rather fluid? Do they see social boundaries where in fact these are of little or no importance?

The term _subculture_ is a useful one here, yet it appears in the indexes of few textbooks and remains generally undefined. There are indeed _subsystems_ within all cultures, made up of the divergent patterns of the two sexes, the often varying patterns among different age-sets, and, in stratified societies, the normative behavior characterizing the various classes or castes. Beyond this, though, a culture that is not highly localized in a tiny social group tends to develop regional subvarieties which it would be appropriate to call subcultures, too. Yet there is a difference here. For example, British national culture cannot and would never survive without the part-cultures of the two genders; the adolescents, the middle-aged, and the elderly; and the distinctive behavioral patterns of the several social classes. On the other hand, it could survive quite well without the subculture of Ulster, even though Northern Ireland is a constituent part of the United Kingdom. What is the difference here? The point is that regional variations can be amalgamated or lost depending on fluctuating political and military conditions. Ulster could well become a regional variation of Irish culture (for many, it already is), whereas Protestants in Ulster insist it is a regional variant of British culture.

One study that has focused on such issues has been Fredrik Barth's early work on the Pathans of the border zone between Pakistan and Afghanistan, Pathans, or Pakhtuns (Volume 3), share the use of some of that land with Kohistanis and Gujjars, two other ethnic groups with very different economic adaptations to this mountainous area. Barth (1969) makes the universally valid point that:

> Though the members of such an ethnic group may carry a firm conviction of identity, their knowledge of distant communities who claim to share this identity will be

limited; and intercommunication within the ethnic group—though it forms an uninterrupted network—cannot lightly be assumed to disseminate adequate information to maintain a shared body of values and understanding through time. Thus, even if we can show that the maintenance of Pathan identity is an overt goal, for all members of the group, this will be a goal pursued within the limited perspective of highly discrepant local settings. Consequently the aggregate result will not automatically be the persistence of an undivided and distinctive, single ethnic group [p. 117].

Individuals can even *shift* their ethnic identity depending on where they are and what they want to do. A Pathan on entering Peshawar City becomes a Baluch-, Panjabi-, or Persian-speaking townsman, changing his ethnic label to avoid the costs of failure at being assimilated (Barth 1969, p. 133).

There is no doubt that the boundaries of most subcultures are highly permeable and thus that change is inevitable. Television and other mass media, employment mobility, the motorways, overseas vacations, and perhaps an enhanced sense of "belonging in Europe," have all played their part in the late twentieth century to make one's personal identity as a Cornishman—and indeed the very use of the term—a quaint thing of the past. It is important to realize that what has already happened in this corner of England is also in process of happening with most, if not all, of the ethnic groups that form the subjects of the entries throughout this Encyclopedia.

PAUL HOCKINGS

Bibliography on Ethnographic Methods

Asch, Timothy, and Patsy Asch (1995). "Film in Ethnographic Research." In *Principles of Visual Anthropology*, 2nd edition, edited by Paul Hockings, 335–360. Berlin: Mouton de Gruyter.

Atkinson, Paul (1990). *The Ethnographic Imagination: Textual Constructions of Reality*. London and New York: Routledge.

Atkinson, Paul (1992). *Understanding Ethnographic Texts*. Newbury Park, Calif.: Sage Publications.

Barth, Fredrik (1969). *Ethnic Groups and Boundaries: The Social Organization of Culture Difference*. Boston: Little, Brown.

Barth, Fredrik (1981). "Models of Social Organization III." In *Process and Form in Social Life, Selected Essays of Fredrik Barth*. Vol 1. London: Routledge & Kegan Paul.

Bernard, H. Russell (1988). *Research Methods in Cultural Anthropology*. Newbury Park, Calif.: Sage Publications.

Berreman, Gerald D. (1962). *Behind Many Masks: Ethnography and Impression Management in a Himalayan Village*. Ithaca, N.Y.: Society for Applied Anthropology.

Béteille, André, and T. N. Madan (1975). *Encounter and Experience: Personal Accounts of Fieldwork*. New Delhi: Vikas Publishing House.

Blanco, Walter, ed. and trans. (1992). *Herodotus: The Histories; New Translation, Selections, Backgrounds, Commentaries*. New York: W. W. Norton.

Boissevain, Jeremy (1981). "Ethnographic Fieldwork." In *The Social Science Encyclopedia*, edited by Adam Kuper and Jessica Kuper, 272–273. London and New York: Routledge.

Bowen, Elenore Smith (pseud. of Laura Bohannan). (1954) *Return to Laughter*. London: Gollancz; New York: Doubleday & Co.

Chagnon, Napoleon A. (1974). *Studying the Yąnomamö*. New York: Holt, Rinehart and Winston.

Conklin, Harold C. (1968). "Ethnography." In *International Encyclopedia of the Social Sciences*, edited by David L. Sills, 5: 172–178. New York: Macmillan and the Free Press; London: Collier-Macmillan Publishers.

de Brigard, Emilie (1995). "The History of Ethnographic Film." In *Principles of Visual Anthropology*, 2nd edition, edited by Paul Hockings, 13–43. Berlin: Mouton de Gruyter.

Durkheim, Émile (1912). *Les Formes élémentaires de la vie religeuse*. Paris. Translated as *Elementary Forms of the Religious Life* in many editions.

Edgerton, Robert B., and L. L. Langness (1974). *Methods and Styles in the Study of Culture*. San Francisco: Chandler & Sharp Publishers.

Epstein, A. L., ed. (1967). *The Craft of Social Anthropology*. London: Tavistock Publications.

Firth, Raymond William (1970). *Rank and Religion in Tikopia: A Study in Polynesian Paganism and Conversion to Christianity*. Boston: Beacon Press.

Fortes, Meyer (1945). *Dynamics of Clanship among the Tallensi . . .* London: Oxford University Press.

Foster, George, Thayer Scudder, Elizabeth Colson, and Robert V. Kemper, eds. (1979). *Long-Term Field Research in Social Anthropology*. New York: Academic Press.

Freilich, Morris, ed. (1970). *Marginal Natives: Anthropologists at Work*. New York: Harper & Row, Publishers.

Georges, Robert A., and Michael O. Jones (1980). *People Studying People: The Human Element in Fieldwork*. Berkeley and Los Angeles: University of California Press.

Golde, Peggy, ed. (1986). *Women in the Field: Anthropological Experiences*. 2nd edition. Berkeley and Los Angeles: University of California Press.

Gopāla Śarana (1975). *The Methodology of Anthropological Comparisons: An Analysis of Comparative Methods in Social and Cultural Anthropology*. Viking Fund Publications in Anthropology, 53. Tucson: University of Arizona Press.

Hammersley, Martyn, and Paul Atkinson (1983). *Ethnography: Principles in Practice*. London and New York: Tavistock Publications.

Hanson, F. Allan (1973). _Meaning in Culture._ London: Routledge & Kegan Paul.

Harris, Marvin (1968). _The Rise of Anthropological Theory._ New York: Thomas Y. Crowell Co.

Heider, Karl G. (1976). _Ethnographic Film._ Austin and London: University of Texas Press.

Henry, Frances, and Satish Saberwal, eds. (1969). _Stress and Response in Fieldwork._ New York: Holt, Rinehart and Winston.

Hockings, Paul (1995). "Conclusion: Ethnographic Filming and Anthropological Theory." In _Principles of Visual Anthropology,_ 2nd edition, edited by Paul Hockings, 507–529. Berlin: Mouton de Gruyter.

Jackson, Bruce (1987). _Fieldwork._ Urbana and Chicago: University of Illinois Press.

Jongmans, D. G., and Peter C. W. Gutkind, eds. (1967). _Anthropologists in the Field._ New York: Humanities Press, Publishers.

Kaplan, David, and Robert A. Manners (1972). _Culture Theory._ Englewood Cliffs, N.J.: Prentice-Hall, Inc.

Kroeber, Alfred L. (1948). _Anthropology: Race • Language • Culture • Psychology • Prehistory._ London: George G. Harrap & Co. Ltd.

Lawless, Robert, Vinson H. Sutlive, and Mario D. Zamora, eds. (1983). _Fieldwork: The Human Experience._ New York: Gordon and Breach Science Publishers.

Lebeuf, Jean-Paul (1968). "L'Enquête orale en ethnographie." In _Ethnologie générale,_ edited by Jean Poirier, 180–199. Paris: Éditions Gallimard.

Lofland, John (1971). _Analyzing Social Settings: A Guide to Qualitative Observation and Analysis._ Belmont, Calif.: Wadsworth Publishing Company.

Lowie, Robert H. (1953). "Ethnography, Cultural and Social Anthropology." _American Anthropologist_ 55 (4).

Maget, Marcel (1968). "Problèmes d'ethnographie européenne." In _Ethnologie générale,_ edited by Jean Poirier, 1247–1338. Paris: Éditions Gallimard.

Mauss, Marcel (1967). _Manuel d'Ethnographie,_ 2nd edition. Paris: Payot.

Murdock, George P., _et al.,_ eds. (1982). _Outline of Cultural Materials,_ 5th revised edition. New Haven: Human Relations Area Files.

Naroll, Raoul, and Ronald Cohen, eds. (1970). _A Handbook of Method in Cultural Anthropology._ New York and London: Columbia University Press.

Noblit, George W., and R. Dwight Hare (1988). _Meta-Ethnography: Synthesizing Qualitative Studies._ Newbury Park, Calif.: Sage Publications.

Pelto, Pertti J., and Gretel H. Pelto (1973). "Ethnography: The Fieldwork Enterprise." In _Handbook of Social and Cultural Anthropology,_ edited by John J. Honigmann, 241–288. Chicago: Rand McNally and Company.

Pelto, Pertti J., and Gretel H. Pelto (1978). _Anthropological Research: The Structure of Inquiry._ Cambridge: Cambridge University Press.

Powdermaker, Hortense (1966). _Stranger and Friend: The Way of an Anthropologist._ New York: W. W. Norton & Company.

Rivers, William H. R. (1906). _The Todas._ London: Macmillan.

Sanjek, Roger (1990). _Fieldnotes: The Makings of Anthropology._ Ithaca and London: Cornell University Press.

Schapera, Isaac (1947). _Migrant Labour and Tribal Life: A Study of Conditions in the Bechuanaland Protectorate._ London: Oxford University Press.

Scherer, Joanna C. (1995). "Ethnographic Photography in Anthropological Research." In _Principles of Visual Anthropology,_ 2nd edition, edited by Paul Hockings, 201–216. Berlin: Mouton de Gruyter.

Seligman, Charles Gabriel, and Brenda Z. Seligman (1911). _The Veddas._ Cambridge: Cambridge University Press.

Spindler, George D., ed. (1970). _Being an Anthropologist: Fieldwork in Eleven Cultures._ New York: Holt, Rinehart and Winston.

Spradley, James P. (1980). _Participant Observation._ New York: Holt, Rinehart and Winston.

Srinivas, M. N., A. M. Shah, and E. A. Ramaswamy, eds. (1979). _The Fieldworker and the Field: Problems and Challenges in Sociological Investigation._ New Delhi: Oxford University Press.

Wax, Rosalie H. (1971). _Doing Fieldwork: Warnings and Advice._ Chicago and London: University of Chicago Press.

Werner, Oswald, and G. Mark Schoepfle (1987). _Systematic Fieldwork._ 2 vols. Newbury Park, Calif.: Sage Publications.

Williams, Thomas Rhys (1967). _Field Methods in the Study of Culture._ New York: Holt, Rinehart and Winston.

List of Cultures by Country

Aegean Islands
Cyclades, **4:**75-78
Afghanistan
Aimaq, **9:**10
Baluchi, **3:**22-24
Ghorbat, **9:**105-107
Hazara, **9:**114-115
Jews of the Middle East, **9:**147-148
Karakalpaks, **6:**165-169
Kohistani, **3:**128
Kyrgyz, **6:**228-232
Nuristanis, **9:**250-251
Pamir peoples, **6:**302-306
Pashai, **9:**267
Pathan, **3:**230-233
peripatetics, **9:**274-276
Qizilbash, **9:**287-288
refugees in Pakistan, **3:**250
Tajiks, **6:**351-354
Turkmens, **6:**368-372
Albania
Albanians, **4:**3-8
Algeria
Arabs, **9:**22-25
Jews, **9:**137-138
peripatetics of the Maghreb, **9:**278
Tuareg, **9:**366-369
Alsace
Alsatians, **4:**8-9
Ashkenazic Jews, **4:**16
Angola
Kongo, **9:**166-168
Lunda, **9:**195-199
Ndembu, **9:**238-241
Pende, **9:**271-274
San-speaking peoples, **9:**300-304
Anguilla
Anguillans, **8:**7
Antigua
Antigua and Barbuda, **8:**7-10
Antilles. *See* French Antilles; Netherlands Antilles
Aomoro Islands
Swahili, **9:**327-329
Arctic
Eskimo, **1:**107

Netsilik Inuit, **1:**254
Saami, **4:**220-223
Argentina
Araucanians, **7:**51-55
Chiriguano, **7:**119-122
Chorote, **7:**124-126
Japanese, **7:**59
Mataco, **7:**227-230
Mennonites, **7:**239-240
Mocoví, **7:**240-241
Nivaclé, **7:**248-251
Old Believers, **6:**290-294
Sephardic Jews, **4:**229
Toba, **7:**330-334
Armenia
Armenians, **6:**27-31
Greeks, **6:**140-144
Kurds, **6:**224-227
Yezidis, **6:**407-411
Aruba
Arubans, **8:**11-14
Australia
Anglo-Indian, **3:**12
Aranda, **2:**16-19
Ashkenazic Jews, **4:**17
Dieri, **2:**49
Hindu, **3:**102
Kamilaroi, **2:**104
Karadjeri, **2:**111
Kariera, **2:**111-112
Latvians, **6:**235-238
Mardudjara, **2:**179-182
Murngin, **2:**223-227
Ngatatjara, **2:**238-241
Old Believers, **6:**290-294
Pintupi, **2:**264-267
Romanians, **4:**212-215
Siberian Estonians, **6:**335-337
Tasmanians, **2:**315-317
Tiwi, **2:**327-330
Torres Strait Islanders, **2:**345-348
Ukrainians, **6:**388-395
Vietnamese, **5:**284-287
Warlpiri, **2:**373-375
Wik Mungkan, **2:**376-379
Wongaibon, **2:**385

Yir Yoront, **2:**394-395
Yungar, **2:**395
Austria
Ashkenazic Jews, **4:**16, 17
Austrians, **4:**18-21
Germans, **4:**121, 122
peripatetics, **4:**195-197
Tiroleans, **4:**263-264
Xoraxané Romá, **4:**281
Azerbaijan
Armenians, **6:**27-31
Azerbaijani Turks, **6:**47-51
Ingilos, **6:**149-151
Khinalughs, **6:**197-202
Kurds, **6:**224-227
Mountain Jews, **6:**270-274
Nestorians, **9:**241-244
Shahsevan, **9:**307-310
Talysh, **6:**354-357
Tats, **6:**357-361
Tsakhurs, **6:**364-368
Udis, **6:**375-378
Yezidis, **6:**407-411

Bahama Islands
Bahamians, **8:**17-20
Bahrain
Arabs, **9:**22-25
Baltic countries. *See* Estonia; Latvia; Lithuania
Bangladesh
Aryan, **3:**12-13
Baul, **3:**25-26
Bengali, **3:**29-34
Chakma, **3:**58-61
Chinese of South Asia, **3:**68
Munda, **3:**181-184
Muslim, **3:**184-186
refugees in India, **3:**250
Santal, **3:**252-255
Sheikh, **3:**257
Zamindar, **3:**306-307
Barbados
Barbadians, **8:**20-24

1

Barbuda
  Antigua and Barbuda, 8:7-10
Belarus
  Ashkenazic Jews, 4:17
  Ashkenazim, 6:31-37
  Belarussians, 6:57-62
  Germans, 6:137-140
  Gypsies, 6:145-148
  Poles, 6:306-309
Belau, 2:24-27
Belgium
  Belgians, 4:35
  Flemish, 4:105-109
  peripatetics, 4:195-197
  Walloons, 4:276-278
  Xoraxané Romá, 4:281
Belize
  Creoles, 8:82
  Garifuna, 8:113-115
  Mopan, 8:182
  Q'eqchi', 8:226-227
Benin
  Ewe and Fon, 9:83-88
  Sonhay, 9:319-320
  Yoruba, 9:390-391
Bermuda
  Bermudians, 8:24-25
Bhutan
  Bhutanese, 3:45-46
  Munda, 3:181-184
  Neo-Buddhist, 3:200
  Rai, 3:249
  Tibetans, 6:493-496
Bolivia
  Afro-Bolivians, 7:7-10
  Aymara, 7:65-68
  Ayoreo, 7:69-72
  Baure, 7:86
  Callahuaya, 7:87-90
  Chácobo, 7:104-107
  Chimane, 7:111-113
  Chipaya, 7:114-117
  Chiquitano, 7:117-119
  Chiriguano, 7:119-122
  Guarayu, 7:174-175
  Huarayo, 7:176-179
  Itonama, 7:179
  Jamináwa, 7:180
  Japanese, 7:59-60
  Mataco, 7:227-230
  Mennonites, 7:239-240
  Mojo, 7:241-242
  Moré, 7:242-243
  Movima, 7:243
  Nivaclé, 7:248-251
  Pauserna, 7:270
  Sirionó, 7:309-311
  Tacana, 7:317-318
  Toba, 7:330-334
  Yuqui, 7:390-395
  Yuracaré, 7:395-396

Bosnia-Hercegovina
  Bosnian Muslims, 4:36
  Croats, 4:72-75
  Serbs, 4:230
  Xoraxané Romá, 4:281
Botswana
  Herero, 9:115-118
  San-speaking peoples, 9:300-304
  Tswana, 9:360-364
Brazil
  Afro-Brazilians, 7:10-14
  Amahuaca, 7:33-36
  Anambé, 7:40-43
  Apalai, 7:44-47
  Apiaká, 7:48-51
  Araweté, 7:55-58
  Asians in South America, 7:58-60
  Asurini, 7:61-62
  Azoreans, 4:26
  Bakairi, 7:73-75
  Baniwa-Curripaco-Wakuenai, 7:76-80
  Bororo, 7:86-87
  Campa, 7:90-91
  Canela, 7:94-98
  Chinese, 7:58
  Chiquitano, 7:117-119
  Cinta Larga, 7:127-129
  Cocama, 7:130
  Craho, 7:135-138
  Culina, 7:145-148
  Desana, 7:152-154
  Fulniô, 7:161
  Gagauz, 6:124-126
  Gorotire, 7:161-163
  Guajajára, 7:166-167
  Jamináwa, 7:180
  Japanese, 7:59
  Kadiwéu, 7:183
  Kagwahiv, 7:184-186
  Kaingáng, 7:186
  Kalapalo, 7:187
  Karajá, 7:187-191
  Kashinawa, 7:194-197
  Koreans, 7:60
  Krikati/Pukobye, 7:203-206
  Kuikuru, 7:206-209
  Makushi, 7:218-219
  Marubo, 7:220-223
  Maxakali, 7:233
  Mayoruna, 7:233-235
  Mehinaku, 7:235-239
  Mennonites, 7:239-240
  Mundurucu, 7:243-246
  Nambicuara, 7:246-247
  Old Believers, 6:290-294
  Otavalo, 7:252-255
  Paï-Tavytera, 7:259-260
  Palikur, 7:260-264
  Paresí, 7:268-270
  Pemon, 7:270-273
  Piro, 7:278-281

  Puinave, 7:281-282
  Rikbaktsa, 7:286-288
  Sephardic Jews, 4:229
  Sharanahua, 7:299
  Shavante, 7:300-301
  Sherente, 7:302-303
  Suruí, 7:312-314
  Suya, 7:314-317
  Tapirapé, 7:320-322
  Terena, 7:324-327
  Ticuna, 7:327-330
  Trio, 7:334-337
  Waimiri-Atroari, 7:341-345
  Wáiwai, 7:345-348
  Wanano, 7:348-351
  Wapisiana, 7:354-356
  Waurá, 7:360
  Wayãpi, 7:360-364
  Witoto, 7:364-365
  Xikrin, 7:366-369
  Xokléng, 7:370-371
  Yanomamö, 7:374-377
  Yawalapití, 7:377-380
British Guyana. *See* Guyana
British Isles. *See* England; Ireland;
    Northern Ireland; Scotland; Wales;
    United Kingdom
Brunei
  Hindu, 3:102
  Penan, 5:209-210
Bukovina
  Ashkenazic Jews, 4:17
Bulgaria
  Bulgarian Gypsies, 4:40-42
  Bulgarians, 4:42-45
  Gagauz, 4:118;6:124-126
  Old Believers, 6:290-294
  peripatetics, 4:195-197
  Pomaks, 4:204-205
  Vlachs, 4:273-275
Burkina Faso
  Dyula, 9:75-78
  Lobi-Dagarti peoples, 9:182-186
  Mande, 9:215-216
  Mossi, 9:227-231
Burma. *See* Myanmar
Burundi
  tropical-forest foragers, 9:356-357

Cambodia
  Brao, 5:47
  Buddhist, 5:47-48
  Cham, 5:72-74
  Chinese in Southeast Asia, 5:74-78
  Chong, 5:78
  Khmer, 5:134-138
  Kui, 5:150
  Mon, 5:188-189
  Pear, 5:209
  Rhadé, 5:211-212

Saoch, 5:224-225
Vietnamese, 5:284-287
Cameroon
Bamiléké, 9:36-40
Fali, 9:93-97
Kanuri, 9:151-153
tropical-forest foragers, 9:356-357
Canada
Abenaki, 1:1-6
Acadians, 1:6-9
Albanians, 1:119
Algonkin, 1:16-17
Amish, 1:18-21
Anglo-Indian, 3:12
Armenians, 1:119
Ashkenazic Jews, 4:16, 17
Asian Indians, 1:321
Assiniboin, 1:27
Austrians, 1:119
Baffinland Inuit, 1:28-31
Bangladeshi, 1:321
Basques, 1:31-35
Bearlake Indians, 1:35
Beaver, 1:35
Belgians, 1:119
Bellabella, 1:36
Bella Coola, 1:36
Blackfoot, 1:40-42
Blacks, 1:43-44
Byelorussians, 1:119
Caribou Inuit, 1:51
Carrier, 1:52
Chilcotin, 1:67
Chinese, 1:321
Chipewyan, 1:67-69
Comox, 1:75-76
Copper Eskimo, 1:76-79
Cowichan, 1:79
Cree, Western Woods, 1:79-82
Croats (Croatians), 1:120
Czechs, 1:120
Danes, 1:120
Dogrib, 1:87-90
Doukhobors, 1:90-93
Druze, 9:74-75
Dutch, 1:120-121
East Asians, 1:94-98
English, 1:121
Eskimo, 1:107
Estonians, 6:111-115
European-Canadians, 1:119-127
Finns, 1:121
French Canadians, 1:131-133
Gagauz, 6:124-126
Germans, 1:121-122
Greeks, 1:122
Gros Ventre, 1:134
Haida, 1:135-136
Haitians, 1:137-138
Han, 1:139
Hare, 1:139-142

Hasidim, 1:142-145
Hindu, 3:102
Huron, 1:152
Hutterites, 1:153-155
Icelanders, 1:123
Iglulik Inuit, 1:155
Irish, 1:123
Iroquois, 1:164-167
Italians, 1:123-124
Jews, 1:168-171
Kaska, 1:178
Klallam, 1:189-190
Kmhmu, 5:138-141
Koreans, 5:144-149
Kutchin, 1:196
Kutenai, 1:197
Kwakiutl, 1:197-200
Labrador Inuit, 1:201-202
Lake, 1:202
Latvians, 1:124;6:235-238
Lillooet, 1:206-207
Lithuanians, 1:124
Maliseet, 1:210-213
Mennonites, 1:216-220
Metis of Western Canada, 1:226-229
Micmac, 1:233-235
Micronesians, 1:235-239
Mohawk, 1:242
Montagnais-Naskapi, 1:243-246
Mountain, 1:249
Netsilik Inuit, 1:254
Nootka, 1:255-258
Northern Metis, 1:261-262
Norwegians, 1:124
Ojibwa, 1:268-272
Okanagon, 1:271-272
Old Believers, 1:272-275;6:290-294
Oneida, 1:275-276
Onondaga, 1:276
Ottawa, 1:279-280
Pakistani, 1:321
Poles, 1:124-125
Portuguese, 1:125
Potawatomi, 1:296-297
Rom, 1:303-306
Romanians, 1:125;4:212-215
Russians, 1:125-126
Sarsi, 1:307-308
Scots, 1:126
Sekani, 1.311; _see also_ Beaver
Serbs, 1:126
Shuswap, 1:318
Siberian Estonians, 6:335-337
Sikhs, 1:322, 323, 324
Slavey, 1:318-320
Slovaks, 1:126
Slovenes (Slovenians), 1:127
South and Southeast Asians, 1:321-324
Spaniards, 1:127
Sri Lankans, 1:321
Swedes, 1:127

Swiss, 1:127
Tahltan, 1:334
Teton, 1:343-346
Thompson, 1:350
Tsimshian, 1:354-355
Tuscarora, 1:356
Tutchone, 1:356
Ukrainians, 1:357-359;6:388-395
Vietnamese, 1:321;5:284-287
Welsh, 1:127
Canary Islands
Canarians, 4:50-53
Cape Verde Islands
Cape Verdeans, 4:53-57
Cayman Islands
Cayman Islanders, 8:45-48
Central African Republic
tropical-forest foragers, 9:356-357
Zande, 9:397-400
Chad
Arabs, 9:22-25
Bagirmi, 9:32-35
Kanuri, 9:151-153
Sara, 9:304-307
Teda, 9:339
Chile
Araucanians, 7:51-55
Aymara, 7:65-68
Easter Island, 2:53-55
China
Abor, 3:3-5
Achang, 6:417-418
Akha, 5:11-13
Bai, 6:419-421
Blang, 6:421-422
Bonan, 6:422
Bouyei, 6:422-423
Buddhist, 5:47-48
Buriats, 6:65-68
Central Thai, 5:69-72
Dai, 6:423-428
Daur, 6:428-429
De'ang, 6:429-431
Dong, 6:431
Dongxiang, 6:431-432
Drung, 6:432-433
Evenki (Northern Tungus), 6:120-124
Ewenki, 6:433-435
Gelao, 6:435
Hakka, 6:436-439
Han, 6:439-449
Hani, 6:449-451
Hezhen, 6:452
Hui, 6:452-454
Jing, 6:454
Jingpo, 6:454-459
Jino, 6:459-460
Kachin, 5:114-119
Kazak, 6:460-461
Kirgiz, 6:461
Kmhmu, 5:138-141

China (cont'd)
  Koreans, **5:**144-149;**6:**204-207
  Kyrgyz, **6:**228-232
  Lahu, **5:**150-154;**6:**462-464
  Lhoba, **6:**464
  Li, **6:**464
  Lisu, **5:**163-166;**6:**465-466
  Manchu, **6:**466-468
  Maonan, **6:**468-469
  Miao, **6:**469-473
  Moinba, **6:**473
  Mongols, **6:**473-476
  Mulam, **6:**476-477
  Naxi, **6:**477-480
  Nu, **6:**480-481
  Oroqen, **6:**482-483
  Pamir peoples, **6:**302-306
  Pumi, **6:**483-484
  Qiang, **6:**484-488
  Salar, **6:**488
  Shan, **5:**239-241
  She, **6:**488-491
  Shui, **6:**491
  Tai Lue, **5:**252-256
  Tajiks, **6:**351-354, 492
  Tatars, **6:**492-493
  Tibetans, **6:**493-496
  Tu, **6:**496-497
  Tujia, **6:**497-499
  Uighur, **6:**381-385
  Uigur, **6:**499-500
  Uzbeks, **6:**500
  Wa, **6:**501-504
  Xibe, **6:**504
  Yao, **6:**505
  Yi, **6:**505-508
  Yugur, **6:**508-509
  Zhuang, **6:**509-512
  see also Taiwan
Colombia
  Afro-Colombians, **7:**14-18
  Afro-Hispanic Pacific Lowlanders,
    7:19-23
  Awá Kwaiker, **7:**62-65
  Baniwa-Curripaco-Wakuenai, **7:**76-80
  Barí, **7:**82-85
  Chimila, **7:**114
  Chocó, **7:**122-123
  Cocama, **7:**130
  Cubeo, **7:**139-142
  Cuiva, **7:**142-145
  Cuna, **7:**148-151
  Desana, **7:**152-154
  Emberá, **7:**154-158;**8:**108-111
  Guahibo-Sikuani, **7:**164-166
  Guajiro, **7:**167-170
  Guambiano, **7:**170-173
  Karihona, **7:**191-194
  Ka'wiari, **7:**197-200
  Kogi, **7:**200-203
  Macuna, **7:**212-215

  Noanamá, **7:**251-252
  Otavalo, **7:**252-255
  Páez, **7:**256-258
  Piapoco, **7:**274
  Piaroa, **7:**275-278
  Puinave, **7:**281-282
  Saliva, **7:**291-293
  Siona-Secoya, **7:**306-309
  Tanimuka, **7:**318-320
  Tatuyo, **7:**322-324
  Ticuna, **7:**327-330
  Tunebo, **7:**337-339
  Wanano, **7:**348-351
  Witoto, **7:**364-365
  Wounaan, **8:**108-111
  Yukpa, **7:**382-385
  Yukuna, **7:**385-390
Congo
  Kongo, **9:**166-168
  tropical-forest foragers, **9:**356-357
Cook Islands
  Cook Islanders, **2:**40-42
  Manihiki, **2:**172-173
  Pukapuka, **2:**270-273
  Tongareva, **2:**339-341
Corsica
  Corsicans, **4:**65-68
Costa Rica
  Blacks of Costa Rica, **8:**25-26
  Boruca, Bribri, Cabécar, **8:**26-30
  Chinese of Costa Rica, **8:**59-62
  Costa Ricans, **8:**78-82
  Creoles, **8:**82
  Maleku, **8:**157
Crete
  Cretans, **4:**68-71
Croatia
  Croats, **4:**72-75
  Dalmatians, **4:**85-87
  Serbs, **4:**230
  Vlachs, **4:**273-275
Cuba
  Cubans, **8:**86-90
Curaçao
  Curaçao, **8:**95-98
Cyprus
  Cypriots, **4:**79-81
  Maronites, **9:**218-220
Czech and Slovak Federative Republic
  Czechs, **4:**82-84
  peripatetics, **4:**195-197
  Rom, **4:**217-219
  Slovaks, **4:**242-246
  Vlach Gypsies of Hungary, **4:**270-273
  see also Slovakia

Denmark
  Danes, **4:**88-90
  Faroe Islanders, **4:**98-100
  peripatetics, **4:**195-197

  Scandinavian peripatetics, **4:**228-229
  Xoraxané Romá, **4:**281
  see also Greenland
Djibouti
  Afar, **9:**7-9
Dominica
  Carib of Dominica, **8:**37-40
  Creoles, **8:**82
  Garifuna, **8:**113-115
Dominican Republic
  Dominicans, **8:**98-103
Dutch Guiana. *See* Suriname
Dutch Leeward Islands
  Arubans, **8:**11-14

East African coastline
  Swahili, **9:**327-329
East Bengal. *See* Bangladesh
East Germany. *See* Germany
Ecuador
  Afro-Hispanic Pacific Lowlanders,
    7:19-23
  Awá Kwaiker, **7:**62-65
  Canelos Quichua, **7:**98-102
  Colorado, **7:**131
  Cotopaxi Quichua, **7:**132-135
  Emberá, **7:**154-158
  Jivaro, **7:**182-183
  Otavalo, **7:**252-255
  Salasaca, **7:**289-291
  Saraguro, **7:**293-295
  Siona-Secoya, **7:**306-309
  Waorani, **7:**351-353
Egypt
  Albanians, **4:**3-8
  Arabs, **9:**22-25
  Bedouin, **9:**42-46
  Copts, **9:**68-69
  Jews, Arabic-speaking, **9:**134-136
  Karaites, **6:**162-165
  Maronites, **9:**218-220
  Nubians, **9:**245-248
  Palestinians, **9:**262-266
  peripatetics, **9:**276-277
El Salvador
  Lenca, **8:**155-156
  Pipil, **8:**215
  Poqomam, **8:**217-219
England
  Cornish, **4:**64-65
  English, **4:**95-97
  Irish Travellers, **4:**154-157
  Rominche, **4:**216-217
Equatorial Guinea
  tropical-forest foragers, **8:**356-357
Eritrea
  Tigray, **9:**346-349
Estonia
  Estonians, **6:**111-115
  Old Believers, **6:**290-294

Ethiopia
Afar, **9:**7-9
Amhara, **9:**15-21
Anuak, **9:**21-22
Falasha, **9:**89-93
Fulani, **9:**100-103
Konso, **9:**169-172
Suri, **9:**323-327
Tigray, **9:**346-349

Faroe Islands
Faroe Islanders, **4:**98-100
Fiji
Bau, **2:**22-24
Hindu, **3:**102
Lau, **2:**143-145
Rotuma, **2:**280-283
Finland
Finns, **4:**101-104
Karelians, **6:**169-172
peripatetics, **4:**195-197
Saami, **4:**220-223
Scandinavian peripatetics, **4:**228-229
France
Ajië, **2:**6-10
Alsatians, **4:**8-9
Aquitaine, **4:**13-15
Ashkenazic Jews, **4:**16, 17
Auvergnats, **4:**21-23
Aveyronnais, **4:**23-26
Basques, **4:**29-32
Bretons, **4:**37-40
Burgundians, **4:**46-47
Catalans, **4:**61-64
Corsicans, **4:**65-68
Flemish, **4:**105-109
French, **4:**109
Futuna, **2:**65-68
Jews of Algeria, **9:**137-138
Kalmyks, **6:**154-158
Kmhmu, **5:**138-141
Loyalty Islands, **2:**148
Mangareva, **2:**172
Marquesas Islands, **2:**188-191
Occitans, **4:**182-185
Provençal, **4:**209-211
Rapa, **2:**273-276
Raroia, **2:**276-277
Sephardic Jews, **4:**229
Tahiti, **2:**305-307
Uvea, **2:**363-364
Vietnamese, **5:**284-287
Xoraxané Romá, **4:**281
French Antilles
French Antillians, **8:**112
French Guiana
Emerillon, **7:**158-159
Maroni Carib, **7:**220
Palikur, **7:**260-264
Wayãpi, **7:**360-364

Gabon
tropical-forest foragers, **9:**356-357
Gambia
Fulani, **9:**100-103
Mande, **9:**215-216
Georgia, Republic of
Abkhazians, **6:**5-10
Ajarians, **6:**12-15
Armenians, **6:**27-31
Georgians, **6:**129-137
Greeks, **6:**140-144
Jews, **6:**126-128
Jews of the Middle East, **9:**147-148
Khevsur, **6:**193-197
Kurds, **6:**224-227
Laz, **6:**238-241
Meskhetians, **6:**259-262
Mingrelians, **6:**262-265
Ossetes, **6:**297-302
Svans, **6:**343-347
Udis, **6:**375-378
Yezidis, **6:**407-411
Germany
Alsatians, **4:**8-9
Ashkenazic Jews, **4:**15, 16, 17
Bavarians, **4:**32-35
Estonians, **6:**111-115
Frisians, **4:**109
Germans, **4:**121-124
Old Believers, **6:**290-294
peripatetics, **4:**195-197
Silesians, **4:**237-238
Sorbs, **4:**252-254
Xoraxané Romá, **4:**281
Ghana
Akan, **9:**11-12
Ewe and Fon, **9:**83-88
Lobi-Dagarti peoples, **9:**182-186
Mamprusi, **9:**210-215
Mande, **9:**215-216
Mossi, **9:**227-231
Songhay, **9:**319-320
Goa
Anglo-Indian, **3:**12
Great Britain. _See_ England; Scotland;
    Northern Ireland; Wales; United
    Kingdom
Greece
Albanians, **4:**3-8
Cretans, **4:**68-71
Cyclades, **4:**75-78
Cypriots, **4:**79-81
Gagauz, **4:**118;**6:**124-126
Greeks, **4:**131-134
Greek-speaking Jews, **4:**134-136
Ionians, **4:**148-150
Mount Athos, **4:**174-177
Peloponnesians, **4:**191-194
peripatetics, **4:**195-197
Pomaks, **4:**204-205
Sarakatsani, **4:**223-225

Sephardic Jews, **4:**229
Tasakonians, **4:**269
Vlachs, **4:**273-275
Greenland
East Greenland Inuit, **1:**106
Eskimo, **1:**107
Inughuit, **1:**159-161
West Greenland Inuit, **1:**376-379
Grenada
Grenadians, **8:**115-116
Grenadines
Creoles, **8:**82
Guadeloupe
Guadeloupians, **8:**116
Guatemala
Awakateko, **8:**14-17
Ch'orti', **8:**69-70
Chuj, **8:**70-74
Garifuna, **8:**113-115
Itza', **8:**132-135
Ixil, **8:**136
Jakalteko, **8:**136
Kaqchikel, **8:**140
K'iche', **8:**140-142
Ladinos, **8:**151-153
Mam, **8:**157-160
Mopan, **8:**182
Poqomam, **8:**217-219
Poqomchi', **8:**219-220
Q'anjob'al, **8:**224-225
Q'eqchi', **8:**226-227
Sipakapense, **8:**235
Tojolab'al, **8:**260-263
Tz'utujil, **8:**296-298
Uspantec, **8:**299
Xinca, **8:**305
Guinea
Kpelle, **9:**172-174
Mande, **9:**215-216
Guinea Bisseau
Mande, **9:**215-216
Guyana
Akawaio, **7:**30-33
Barama River Carib, **7:**80-82
Chinese in the English-speaking
    Caribbean, **8:**55-58
Hindu, **3:**102
Makushi, **7:**218-219
Wáiwai, **7:**345-348
Wapisiana, **7:**354-356

Haiti
Haitians, **8:**120-123
Holland. _See_ Netherlands
Honduras
Garifuna, **8:**113-115
Jicaque, **8:**140
Ladinos, **8:**151-153
Lenca, **8:**155-156
Miskito, **8:**170-172

Honduras (cont'd)
Nicaragua, 8:236-239
Paya, 8:209
Hong Kong
Hakka, 6:436-439
Hindu, 3:102
Hungary
Ashkenazic Jews, 4:17
Hungarians, 4:143-145
peripatetics, 4:195-197
Vlach Gypsies, 4:270-273

Iberian Peninsula. *See* Spain; Portugal
Iceland
Icelanders, 4:146-148
India
Abor, 3:3-5
Agaria, 3:6
Ahir, 3:7
Anavil Brahman, 3:7-8
Andamanese, 3:8-12
Anglo-Indian, 3:12
Aryan, 3:12-13
Assamese, 3:13-14
Badaga, 3:14-18
Baiga, 3:18-21
Bania, 3:24-25
Baul, 3:25-26
Bene Israel, 3:27-28
Bengali, 3:29-34
Bengali Shakta, 3:35-36
Bengali Vaishnava, 3:36-37
Bhil, 3:37-42
Bhuiya, 3:42-45
Bhutanese, 3:45-46
Bihari, 3:46
Bohra, 3:46-47
Bondo, 3:48-51
Brahman, 3:51
British, 3:79, 80
Castes, Hindu, 3:57
Chenchu, 3:61-62
Chin, 3:62-67
Chinese of South Asia, 3:68
Chitpavan Brahman, 3:68-70
Cochin Jew, 3:71-73
Coorg, 3:73-74
Divehi, 3|75-78
Europeans in South Asia, 3:79-80
French, 3:80
Garia, 3:81
Garo, 3:81-84
Gond, 3:84-87
Grasia, 3:87-88
Gujar, 3:88-89
Gujarati, 3:89-92
Hijra, 3:96-98
Hill Pandaram, 3:98-100
Hill tribes, 3:101
Hindu, 3:102
Indian Christians, 3:103

Irula, 3:104-109
Jain, 3:109-110
Jat, 3:110-113
Jatav, 3:113-115
Kachin, 5:114-119
Kanarese, 3:116-117
Kanbi, 3:117-118
Kanjar, 3:118-121
Kashmiri, 3:122
Khasi, 3:122-126
Khoja, 3:127-128
Kol, 3:129-131
Koli, 3:131-132
Kond, 3:132-133
Korku, 3:133-134
Kota, 3:134-138
Koya, 3:139-142
Kshatriya, 3:142
Kurumbas, 3:142-143
Labbai, 3:144
Lakher, 3:144-148
Lepcha, 3:148-149
Lingayat, 3:151-153
Lisu, 5:163-166
Magar, 3:154-162
Mahar, 3:163-165
Malayali, 3:165-166
Mappila, 3:166-167
Maratha, 3:168-170
Meo, 3:174
Mikir, 3:174-176
Mizo, 3:177-179
Mogul, 3:179-180
Munda, 3:181-184
Muslim, 3:184-186
Nagas, 3:186-191
Nambudiri Brahman, 3:192-194
Nayaka, 3:194-196
Nayar, 3:196-200
Neo-Buddhist, 3:200
Nicobarese, 3:208-210
Okkaliga, 3:214
Oraon, 3:214-215
Oriya, 3:215-218
Pahari, 3:219-223
Pandit of Kashmir, 3:224-226
Paniyan, 3:227
Parsi, 3:227-230
peripatetics, 3:233-236
Punjabi, 3:236-242
Purum, 3:242-244
Qalandar, 3:245-248
Rai, 3:249
Rajput, 3:249
Reddi, 3:249-250
refugees in, 3:250
Sadhu, 3:251-252
Santal, 3:252-255
Sayyid, 3:256
Scheduled Castes/Scheduled Tribes, 3:256-257
Sheikh, 3:257

Sidi, 3:260-261
Sikh, 3:261
Sora, 3:268-270
Sudra, 3:271
Syriacs, 9:334-335
Syrian Christian of Kerala, 3:271-275
Tamil, 3:275-279
Telugu, 3:284-287
Thadou, 3:287-289
Thakur, 3:292-293
Thug, 3:294
Tibetans, 6:493-496
Toda, 3:294-298
Untouchables, 3:299
Vaisya, 3:300
Vellala, 3:303-306
Zamindar, 3:306-307
Indonesia
Acehnese, 5:3-4
Alorese, 5:14-16
Ambonese, 5:16-19
Asmat, 2:19-21
Ata Sikka, 5:19-22
Ata Tana 'Ai, 5:22-26
Atoni, 5:26-29
Bajau, 5:30-35
Balantak, 5:35
Balinese, 5:35-38
Banggai, 5:38
Batak, 5:38-41
Baweanese, 5:41-42
Bolaang Mongondow, 5:43
Bonerate, 5:43-46
Bugis, 5:48-52
Butonese, 5:66-69
Chinese in Southeast Asia, 5:74-78
Dani, 2:43-46
Eipo, 2:55-58
Endenese, 5:84-86
Gayo, 5:88-90
Gorontalese, 5:90
Hindu, 3:102
Iban, 5:96-99
Indonesian, 5:102-103
Irianese, 5:103
Javanese, 5:111-114
Kalimantan Dayaks, 5:120
Kapauku, 2:104-107
Kédang, 5:131-133
Kerintji, 5:134
Kubu, 5:150
Laki, 5:154
Lamaholot, 5:154-157
Madurese, 5:167-168
Makassar, 5:171-174
Manggarai, 5:176
Marind-anim, 2:182-184
Mejbrat, 2:195-197
Mentaweian, 5:181
Mimika, 2:206-208
Minahasans, 5:181
Minangkabau, 5:181-184

Modang, **5**:185-187
Moluccans—North, **5**:188
Moluccans—Southeast, **5**:188
Muna, **5**:189
Muyu, **2**:227-230
Ndaonese, **5**:194
Nias, **5**:194-197
Ogan-Besemah, **5**:197-199
Palu'e, **5**:204-209
Penan, **5**:209-210
Rotinese, **5**:212-215
Saluan, **5**:217
Samal, **5**:217-221
Sangir, **5**:224
Sasak, **5**:225-227
South Asians in Southeast Asia,
    5:243
Sundanese, **5**:246-247
Ternatan/Tidorese, **5**:273
Tetum, **5**:276-277
Tidong, **5**:277
Toala, **5**:280
Tobelorese, **5**:280
Tomini, **5**:280
Tor, **2**:342-344
Toradja, **5**:280-281
Toraja, **5**:281-283
Waropen, **2**:376
Ionian Islands
Ionians, **4**:148-150
Iran
Aimaq, **9**:10
Arabs, **9**:22-25
Assyrians, **9**:27-28
Azerbaijani Turks, **6**:47-51
Baha'is, **9**:35
Bakhtiari, **9**:35-36
Baluchi, **3**:22-24
Basseri, **9**:41-42
Chaldeans, **9**:63-64
Georgians, **6**:129-137
Jews of Iran, **9**:138-141
Jews of Kurdistan, **9**:144-147
Karakalpaks, **6**:165-169
Kurds, **9**:174-177
Lur, **9**:201-202
Mandaeans, **9**:214-215
Nestorians, **9**:241-244
peripatetics, **9**:274-276
Persians, **9**:278-280
Qashqa'i, **9**:284-287
Qizilbash, **9**:287-288
refugees in Pakistan, **3**:250
Syriacs, **9**:334-335
Talysh, **6**:354-357
Zoroastrians, **9**:406-410
Iraq
Arabs, **9**:22-25
Assyrians, **9**:27-28
Chaldeans, **9**:63-64
Jews, Arabic-speaking, **9**:134-136
Jews of Kurdistan, **9**:144-147

Kurds, **9**:174-177
Mandaeans, **9**:214-215
Nestorians, **9**:241-244
Palestinians, **9**:262-266
peripatetics, **9**:276-277
refugees in Pakistan, **3**:250
Sleb, **9**:315
Turkmens, **6**:368-372
Yezidis, **6**:407-411
Ireland
Gaels (Irish), **4**:114-117
Irish, **4**:151-154
Irish Travellers, **4**:154-157
Northern Irish, **4**:177-180
peripatetics, **4**:195-197
Tory Islanders, **4**:264-266
see also Northern Ireland
Isle of Man
Manx, **4**:169-171
Israel
Ashkenazic Jews, **4**:16, 17
Bene Israel, **3**:27-28
Bukharan Jews, **6**:62-65
Circassians, **6**:85-91;**9**:65-68
Cochin Jews, **3**:71-73
Druze, **9**:74-75
Falasha, **9**:89-93
Jews of Algeria, **9**:137-138
Jews of Israel, **9**:141-144
Jews of Yemen, **9**:149-150
Karaites, **6**:162-165;**9**:153-156
Krymchaks, **6**:213-216
Lithuanian Jews, **6**:243-248
Maronites, **9**:218-220
Mountain Jews, **6**:270-274
Palestinians, **9**:262-266
peripatetics, **9**:276-277
Samaritans, **9**:300
Sephardic Jews, **4**:229
Italy
Albanians, **4**:3-8
Bergamasco, **4**:36
Calabrese, **4**:48-50
Friuli, **4**:112-114
Italians, **4**:157
Ladin, **4**:160
peripatetics, **4**:195-197
Piemontese, **4**:198-199
Piemontese Sinti, **4**:199-201
Sardinians, **4**:225-227
Sephardic Jews, **4**:229
Sicilians, **4**:235-237
Slovensko Roma, **4**:249-251
Tuscans, **4**:269-270
Xoraxané Romá, **4**:281-283
Ivory Coast
Akan, **9**:11-12
Dyula, **9**:75-78
Lobi-Dagarti peoples, **9**:182-186
Mande, **9**:215-216
Mossi, **9**:227-231
Songhay, **9**:319-320

Jamaica
Chinese in the English-speaking
    Caribbean, **8**:55-58
Hindu, **3**:102
Jamaicans, **8**:136-140
Rastafarians, **8**:228-229
Japan
Ainu, **5**:7-10;**6**:11
Buddhist, **5**:47-48
Burakumin, **5**:58-63, 149
Japanese, **5**:104-111
Koreans, **5**:144-149, 149-150;**6**:204-207
Okinawans, **5**:199-200
Jordan
Arabs, **9**:22-25
Chechen-Ingush, **6**:71-76
Circassians, **6**:85-91;**9**:65-68
Druze, **9**:74-75
Palestinians, **9**:262-266
peripatetics, **9**:276-277
Samaritans, **9**:300
Sleb, **9**:315

Kazakhstan
Balkars, **6**:51-54
Dungans, **6**:107-111
Gagauz, **4**:118
Germans, **6**:137-140
Greeks, **6**:140-144
Gypsies, **6**:145-148
Kazak, **6**:460-461
Kazakhs, **6**:172-183
Koreans, **6**:204-207
Kurds, **6**:224-227
Meskhetians, **6**:259-262
Poles, **6**:306-309
Uighur, **6**:381-385
Volga Tatars, **6**:399-403
Kenya
Asians of Africa, **9**:25-26
Fulani, **9**:100-103
Gusii, **9**:107-111
Hindu, **3**:102
Iteso, **9**:127-130
Kikuyu, **9**:161-162
Kipsigis, **9**:163-165
Luo, **9**:200
Luyia, **9**:202-206
Maasai, **9**:207-210
Mbeere, **9**:220-223
Mijikenda, **9**:224-225
Nandi and other Kalenjin peoples,
    9:231-234
Okiek, **9**:258-262
Pokot, **9**:280-283
Turkana, **9**:370-373
Kiribati, 2:120-123
Korea
Buddhist, **5**:47-48
Kolisuch'ŏk, **5**:141-144
Koreans, **5**:144-149

Kuwait
Arabs, **9:**22-25
Palestinians, **9:**262-266
Sleb, **9:**315

Kyrgyzstan
Dungans, **6:**107-111
Germans, **6:**137-140
Kirgiz, **6:**461
Koreans, **6:**204-207
Kurds, **6:**224-227
Kyrgyz, **6:**228-232
Meskhetians, **6:**259-262
Uighur, **6:**381-385
Volga Tatars, **6:**399-403

Laos
Akha, **5:**11-13
Alak, **5:**13
Brao, **5:**47
Bru, **5:**47
Buddhist, **5:**47-48
Chinese in Southeast Asia, **5:**74-78
Duane, **5:**79
Hani, **6:**449-451
Hmong, **5:**92-95
Kasseng, **5:**130
Kattang, **5:**131
Katu, **5:**131
Khua, **5:**138
Kmhmu, **5:**138-141
Kui, **5:**150
Lahu, **5:**150-154
Lamet, **5:**157
Lao, **5:**157-160
Loven, **5:**166
May, **5:**177
Ngeh, **5:**194
Oy, **5:**200
Pacoh, **5:**200
P'u Noi, **5:**211
Sek, **5:**230
So, **5:**242
Sork, **5:**242
Sou, **5:**243
Tau-Oi, **5:**261
T'in, **5:**277-280
Vietnamese, **5:**284-287
Yumbri, **5:**294

Latvia
Gypsies, **6:**145-148
Latvians, **6:**235-238
Old Believers, **6:**290-294
Poles, **6:**306-309

Lebanon
Arabs, **9:**22-25
Chaldeans, **9:**63-64
Druze, **9:**74-75
Jews, Arabic-speaking, **9:**134-136
Maronites, **9:**218-220
Palestinians, **9:**262-266

peripatetics, **9:**276-277
Syriacs, **9:**334-335

Leeward Islands
Antigua and Barbuda, **8:**7-10
Arubans, **8:**11-14

Liberia
Kpelle, **9:**172-174
Mande, **9:**215-216

Libya
Arabs, **9:**22-25
Bedouin, **9:**42-46
Palestinians, **9:**262-266
Tuareg, **9:**366-369

Lithuania
Ashkenazic Jews, **4:**17
Gypsies, **6:**145-148
Lithuanian Jews, **6:**243-248
Lithuanians, **6:**248-252
Old Believers, **6:**290-294
Poles, **6:**306-309

Luxembourg
Luxembourgeois, **4:**163

Macedonia
Slav Macedonians, **4:**238-241
Vlachs, **4:**273-275

Madagascar
Betsileo, **9:**53-57
Sakalava, **9:**292-299
Swahili, **9:**327-329
Tandroy, **9:**335-338
Tsimihety, **9:**357-359

Madeira Archipelago
Madeirans, **4:**164-166

Mafia Island
Swahili, 327-329

Majorca
Sephardic Jews, **4:**229

Malawi
Asians of Africa, **9:**26

Malaysia
Bajau, **5:**30-35
Bisaya, **5:**42-43
Chinese in Southeast Asia, **5:**74-78
Dusun, **5:**79-84
Hindu, **3:**102
Iban, **5:**96-99
Kalimantan Dayaks, **5:**120
Kenyah-Kayan-Kajang, **5:**133-134
Malay, **5:**174-176
Melanau, **5:**177-181
Murut, **5:**192-193
Penan, **5:**209-210
Samal, **5:**217-221
Sea Nomads of the Andaman, **5:**227-229
Selung/Moken, **5:**230-233
Semang, **5:**233-236
Senoi, **5:**236-239
South Asians in Southeast Asia, **5:**243

Temiar, **5:**265-273
Tidong, **5:**277

Maldives, Republic of
Divehi, **3:**75-78
Europeans in South Asia, **3:**79-80

Mali
Dogon, **9:**71-74
Dyula, **9:**75-78
Mande, **9:**215-216
Sonhay, **9:**319-320
Tuareg, **9:**366-369

Maliku Island (India)
Divehi, **3:**75-78

Maltese Archipelago
Maltese, **4:**166-169

Marshall Islands
Bikini, **2:**27-28
Marshall Islanders, **2:**191-194

Martinique
Martiniquais, **8:**161-164

Mauritania
Arabs, **9:**22-25
Fulani, **9:**100-103

Mauritius
Hindu, **3:**102
Mauritian, **3:**170-173

Mexico
African Mexicans, **8:**3
Amuzgo, **8:**3-6
Cahita, **8:**34-37
Cattle Ranchers of the Huasteca, **8:**40-44
Chatino, **8:**48-52
Chinantec, **8:**52-55
Chiricahua, **1:**70
Chocho, **8:**62-63
Ch'ol, **8:**63-66
Chontal of Tabasco, **8:**66-69
Cocopa, **1:**74
Cora, **8:**74-77
Cuicatec, **8:**90-93
Guarijío, **8:**117-120
Huave, **8:**123
Huichol, **8:**124-128
Indians of Baja California, **8:**129
Italian Mexicans, **8:**129-132
Kickapoo, **1:**182-186
Kikapu, **8:**143-145
Ladinos, **8:**151-153
Lakandon, **8:**153-154
Lipan Apache, **1:**207-208
Mam, **8:**157-160
Mazahua, **8:**164-166
Mazatec, **8:**167-169
Mixe, **8:**172-176
Mixtec, **8:**176-178
Nahua of Huasteca, **8:**184-187
Nahua of the State of Mexico, **8:**188-190
Nahua peoples, **8:**182-183

Nahuat of the Sierra de Puebla, 8:190-193
Opata, 8:199-200
Otomí of the Sierra, 8:200-203
Otomí of the Valley of Mezquital, 8:203-206
Pame, 8:207-208
Pima Bajo, 8:209-214
Pima-Papago, 1:287-290
Popoloca, 8:215-216
Popoluca, 8:216-217
Potawatomi, 1:296-297
Rom, 1:303-306
Sephardic Jews, 4:229
Seri, 8:232-235
Tarahumara, 8:240-242
Tarascans, 8:243-245
Tepehua, 8:247-250
Tepehuan of Chihuahua, 8:250-254
Tepehuan of Durango, 8:254-258
Tequistlatec, 8:259
Tlapanec, 8:259
Tojolab'al, 8:260-263
Totonac, 8:263-266
Triqui, 8:270-272
Tzeltal, 8:273-274
Tzotzil and Tzeltal of Pantelhó, 8:274-278
Tzotzil of Chamula, 8:278-281
Tzotzil of San Andrés Larraínzar, 8:282-285
Tzotzil of San Bartolomé de los Llanos, 8:286
Tzotzil of Zinacantan, 8:291-294
Wasteko, 8:300-304
Yaqui, 8:305-307
Yukateko, 8:308-310
Zapotec, 8:311-314
Zoque, 8:314-317
Micronesia, Federated States of
Kapingamarangi, 2:108-111
Kosrae, 2:128-130
Nomoi, 2:252-253
Pohnpei, 2:267-270
Truk, 2:351-354
Ulithi, 2:358-360
Woleai, 2:382-384
Yap, 2:391-394
Moldova
Gagauz, 4:118;6:124-126
Germans, 6:137-140
Gypsies, 6:145-148
Moldovans, 6:265-270
Old Believers, 6:290-294
Mongolia
Buddhist, 5:47-48
Buriats, 6:65-68
Evenki (Northern Tungus), 6:120-124
Mongols, 6:473-476

Montenegro
Montenegrins, 4:171-174
Serbs, 4:230
Montserrat
Montserratians, 8:179-182
Morocco
Arabs, 9:22-25
Bedouin, 9:42-46
Berbers, 9:48-52
Jews of the Middle East, 9:147-148
peripatetics of the Maghreb, 9:278
Sephardic Jews, 4:229
Mount Athos (autonomous republic)
Hagiorites, 4:174-177
Mozambique
Lozi, 9:187-190
Shona, 9:312-314
Swazi, 9:329-333
Myanmar (Burma)
Akha, 5:11-13
Buddhist, 5:47-48
Burmese, 5:64-66
Chin, 3:62-67
Chinese of South Asia, 3:68
Hani, 6:449-451
Hindu, 3:102
Hmong, 5:92-95
Kachin, 5:114-119
Karen, 5:124-130
Lahu, 5:150-154
Lisu, 5:163-166;6:465-466
Mon, 5:188-189
Nagas, 3:186-191
Palaung, 5:200-204
Purum, 3:242-244
Sea Nomads of the Andaman, 5:227-229
Selung/Moken, 5:230-233
Shan, 5:239-241
South Asians in Southeast Asia, 5:242
Wa, 6:501-504

Namibia
Herero, 9:115-118
Khoi, 9:157-160
San-speaking peoples, 9:300-304
Tswana, 9:360-364
Nauru
Nauruan, 2:236-238
Nepal
Aryan, 3:12-13
Bhutanese, 3:45-46
Brahman and Chhetri, 3:51-54
Europeans in South Asia, 3:79-80
Gurkha, 3:92-93
Gurung, 3:93-95
Hindu, 3:102
Jain, 3:109-110
Limbu, 3:149-151
Magar, 3:154-162

Munda (Satar), 3:181-184
Neo-Buddhist, 3:200
Nepali, 3:201-205
Newar, 3:205-208
Nyinba, 3:210-213
Rai, 3:249
refugees in, 3:250
Santal, 3:252-255
Satar, 3:181-184
Sherpa, 3:257-260
Sunwar, 3:271
Tamang, 3:275
Thakali, 3:289-292
Tharu, 3:293
Tibetans, 6:493-496
Netherlands
Ambonese, 5:16-19
Dutch, 4:91-94
Frisians, 4:109-112
Gypsies and caravan dwellers, 4:136-138
Hindu, 3:102
peripatetics, 4:195-197
Xoraxané Romá, 4:281
Netherlands Antilles
Curaçao, 8:95-98
Netherlands Antillians, 8:193-194
Netherlands Guiana. _See_ Suriname
New Caledonia
Vietnamese, 5:284-287
New Guinea. _See_ Papua New Guinea
New Zealand
Maori, 2:176-178
Old Believers, 6:290-294
Tokelau, 2:330-333
Nicaragua
Creoles, 8:82
Creoles of Nicaragua, 8:82-86
Garifuna, 8:113-115
Miskito, 8:170-172
Rama, 8:227-228
Sumu, 8:236-239
Niger
Hausa, 9:111-114
Kanuri, 9:151-153
Sonhay, 9:319-320
Tuareg, 9:366-369
Zarma, 9:403-406
Nigeria
Edo, 9:78-82
Hausa, 9:111-114
Ibibio, 9:119-120
Igbo, 9:120-123
Kanuri, 9:151-153
Rukuba, 9:288-291
Songhay, 9:319-320
Tiv, 9:349-351
Yakö, 9:382-387
Yoruba, 9:390-391
Northern Ireland
Irish, 4:151-154

Northern Ireland (cont'd)
Irish Travellers, **4:**154-157
Northern Irish, **4:**177-180
North Korea. *See* Korea
Norway
Norwegians, **4:**180-182
peripatetics, **4:**195-197
Saami, **4:**220-223
Scandinavian peripatetics, **4:**228-229

Oman
Arabs, **9:**22-25
Orkney Islands
Orcadians, **4:**186-188

Pakistan
Aryan, **3:**12-13
Baluchi, **3:**22-24
Brahui, **3:**54
Burusho, **3:**54-56
Chinese of South Asia, **3:**68
Dard, **3:**75
Europeans in South Asia, **3:**79-80
Hazara, 114-115
Jat, **3:**110-113
Kalasha, **3:**116
Kanjar, **3:**118-121
Karakalpaks, **6:**165-169
Kashmiri, **3:**122
Khoja, **3:**127-128
Kohistani, **3:**128
Kyrgyz, **6:**228-232
Mogul, **3:**179-180
Muslim, **3:**184-186
Pamir peoples, **6:**302-306
Pathan, **3:**230-233
Punjabi, **3:**236-242
Qalandar, **3:**245-248
Qizilbash, **9:**287-288
refugees in, **3:**250
Sayyid, **3:**256
Sheikh, **3:**257
Sidi, **3:**260-261
Sindhi, **3:**263-264
Palestine. *See* Israel
Panama
Bugle, **8:**31-34
Chocó, **7:**122-123
Emberá, **7:**154-158;**8:**108-111
Kuna, **8:**146-150
Ngawbe, **8:**194-198
Noanamá, **7:**251-252
Teribe, **8:**259
Wounaan, **8:**108-111
Papua New Guinea
Abelam, **2:**3-6
Banaro, **2:**21
Boazi, **2:**28-31
Chambri, **2:**31-33
Chimbu, **2:**34-37

Daribi, **2:**46-48
Dobu, **2:**49-52
Foi, **2:**59-62
Fore, **2:**62-65
Futuna, **2:**68-70
Gahuku-Gama
Gainj, **2:**71-73
Garia, **2:**73-76
Gebusi, **2:**76-79
Gnau, **2:**80-82
Gogodala, **2:**82-85
Goodenough Island, **2:**85-88
Gururumba, **2:**92-94
Iatmul, **2:**98-100
Kaluli, **2:**101-104
Keraki, **2:**112-114
Kewa, **2:**114-117
Kilenge, **2:**118-120
Kiwai, **2:**124-127
Koiari, **2:**127
Kurtatchi, **2:**131-133
Kwoma, **2:**133-136
Lak, **2:**137-139
Lakalai, **2:**139-142
Lesu, **2:**145-147
Mae Enga, **2:**148-151
Mafulu, **2:**151-153
Mailu, **2:**154-157
Maisin, **2:**157-160
Manam, **2:**167-169
Mandak, **2:**169-172
Manus, **2:**173-176
Maring, **2:**185-188
Mekeo, **2:**197-200
Melpa, **2:**200-202
Mendi, **2:**203-205
Miyanmin, **2:**209-212
Motu, **2:**212-215
Mountain Arapesh, **2:**215-218
Mundugumor, **2:**218-220
Murik, **2:**220-223
Namau, **2:**230-232
Nasioi, **2:**233-235
Ningerum, **2:**245-248
Nissan, **2:**248-251
Orokaiva, **2:**255-258
Orokolo, **2:**258-261
Rossel Island, **2:**277-280
Sambia, **2:**284-286
Selepet, **2:**292-295
Sengseng, **2:**295-298
Siane, **2:**298-299
Sio, **2:**299-301
Siwai, **2:**301-304
Tairora, **2:**307-310
Tangu, **2:**310-313
Tauade, **2:**317-320
Telefolmin, **2:**321-323
Tolai, **2:**333-336
Trobriand Islands, **2:**348-351
Usino, **2:**360-363
Wamira, **2:**364-367

Wantoat, **2:**367-370
Wape, **2:**370-372
Wogeo, **2:**380-382
Wovan, **2:**385-387
Yangoru Boiken, **2:**388-391
Paraguay
Ache, **7:**3-7
Angaité, **7:**43-44
Asians in South America, **7:**58-60
Ayoreo, **7:**69-72
Chamacoco, **7:**107-110
Chinese, **7:**58
Chiriguano, **7:**119-122
Chorote, **7:**124-126
Japanese, **7:**59
Koreans, **7:**59
Lengua, **7:**210-211
Maká, **7:**215-218
Mennonites, **7:**239-240
Nivaclé, **7:**248-251
Paï-Tavytera, **7:**259-260
Toba, **7:**330-334
Pembar Island
Swahili, 327-329
Peru
Aguaruna, **7:**29-30
Amahuaca, **7:**33-36
Amuesha, **7:**37-39
Asians in South America, **7:**58-60
Aymara, **7:**65-68
Campa, **7:**90-91
Candoshi, **7:**92-94
Cashibo, **7:**103-104
Chayahuita, **7:**110-111
Chinese, **7:**58-59
Cocama, **7:**130
Culina, **7:**145-148
Huarayo, **7:**176-179
Jamináwa, **7:**180
Japanese, **7:**59, 60
Jebero, **7:**181
Kashinawa, **7:**194-197
Marinahua, **7:**219-220
Mashco, **7:**224-227
Matsigenka, **7:**230-233
Mayoruna, **7:**233-235
Piro, **7:**278-281
Sharanahua, **7:**299
Shipibo, **7:**303-306
Siona-Secoya, **7:**306-309
Ticuna, **7:**327-330
Witoto, **7:**364-365
Yagua, **7:**371-374
Philippines
Agta, **5:**4-6
Bagobo, **5:**29
Bajau, **5:**30-35
Bilaan, **5:**42
Bontok, **5:**46-47
Bukidnon, **5:**52-55
Chinese in Southeast Asia, **5:**74-78
Cotabato Manobo, **5:**78-79

Filipino, **5:**86-87
Gaddang, **5:**87
Hanunóo, **5:**90-91
Ibaloi, **5:**95
Ifugao, **5:**99-101
Ilanon, **5:**101
Ilongot, **5:**101-102
Isneg, **5:**103
Itneg, **5:**103
Kalagan, **5:**119
Kalibugan, **5:**120
Kalingas, **5:**121-123
Kankanai, **5:**124
Maguindanao, **5:**168-171
Maranao, **5:**177
Palawan, **5:**204
Philippine Negritos, **5:**210-211
Sagada Igorot, **5:**215-217
Samal, **5:**217-221
Samal Moro, **5:**221-224
Sangir, **5:**224
South Asians in Southeast Asia, **5:**243
Subananun, **5:**243-246
Sulod, **5:**246
Tagalog, **5:**248-251
Tagbanuwa, **5:**251-252
Tasaday, **5:**259-261
Tausug, **5:**261-265
Visayan, **5:**287-288
Yakan, **5:**288-291
Poland
Ashkenazic Jews, **4:**16, 17
Carpatho-Rusyns, **6:**69-71
Kashubians, **4:**158-159
Old Believers, **6:**290-294
Poles, **4:**201-204
Silesians, **4:**237-238
Portugal
Azoreans, **4:**26-29
Cape Verdeans, **4:**53-57
Madeirans, **4:**164-166
Portuguese, **4:**206-208
Sephardic Jews, **4:**228, 229
Portuguese Guinea. *See* Guinea Bisseau
Prussia. *See* Germany
Puerto Rico
Puerto Ricans, **8:**220-224

Qatar
Arabs, **9:**22-25

Réunion
Hindu, **3:**102
Romania
Ashkenazic Jews, **4:**17
Gagauz, **4:**118;**6:**124-126
Nogays, **6:**286-290
Old Believers, **6:**290-294
peripatetics, **4:**195-197
Romanians, **4:**212-215

Transylvanian ethnic groups, **4:**266-269
Vlach Gypsies of Hungary, **4:**270-273
Vlachs, **4:**273-275
Rumania. *See* Romania
Russia
Aghuls, **6:**10-11
Ainu, **5:**7-10;**6:**11
Albanians, **4:**3-8
Aleuts, **6:**15-19
Altaians, **6:**19-23
Andis, **6:**23-27
Ashkenazic Jews, **4:**16, 17
Ashkenazim, **6:**31-37
Asiatic Eskimos, **6:**37-42
Avars, **6:**43-47
Balkars, **6:**51-54
Bashkirs, **6:**55-57
Buriats, **6:**65-68
Chechen-Ingush, **6:**71-76
Chukchee, **6:**76-79
Chuvans, **6:**79-83
Chuvash, **6:**83-85
Dargins, **6:**95-99
Dolgan, **6:**99-103
Don Cossacks, **6:**103-107
Even, **6:**115-119
Evenki (Northern Tungus), **6:**120-124
Gagauz, **6:**124-126
Germans, **4:**121;**6:**137-140
Greeks, **6:**140-144
Gypsies, **6:**145-148
Hezhen, **6:**452
Itelmen, **6:**151-154
Kalmyks, **6:**154-158
Karachays, **6:**158-162
Karaites, **6:**162-165
Karelians, **6:**169-172
Ket, **6:**183-185
Khakas, **6:**186-188
Khanty, **6:**189-192
Komi, **6:**202-204
Koryaks and Kerek, **6:**207-210
Kriashen Tatars, **6:**210-213
Kubachins, **6:**216-219
Kumyks, **6:**220-224
Kurds, **9:**174-177
Laks, **6:**232-235
Lezgins, **6:**241-243
Mansi, **6:**252-255
Maris, **6:**255-258
Mongols, **6:**473-476
Mountain Jews, **6:**270-274
Nanai, **6:**274-276
Nenets, **6:**276-279
Nganasan, **6:**280-283
Nivkh, **6:**283-286
Nogays, **6:**286-290
Old Believers, **6:**290-294
Orochi, **6:**294-295
Orok, **6:**296-297
Ossetes, **6:**297-302

Poles, **6:**306-309
Russian peasants, **6:**309-313
Russians, **6:**313-317
Rutuls, **6:**318-321
Saami, **6:**322-324
Selkup, **6:**325-328
Shors, **6:**328-331
Siberiaki, **6:**331-335
Siberian Estonians, **6:**335-337
Siberian Germans, **6:**337-340
Siberian Tatars, **6:**340-342
Tabasarans, **6:**347-351
Tats, **6:**357-361
Tofalar, **6:**361-364
Tsakhurs, **6:**364-368
Tuvans, **6:**372-375
Udmurt, **6:**378-381
Volga Tatars, **6:**399-403
Yakut, **6:**404-407
Yukagir, **6:**411-414
Rwanda
tropical-forest foragers, **9:**356-357

Saint Kitts and Nevis
Kittsians and Nevisians, **8:**145-146
Saint Lawrence Island
Yuit, **1:**389-393
Saint Lucia
Saint Lucians, **8:**229-232
Saint Vincent
Garifuna, **8:**113-115
Sardinia
Sardinians, **4:**225-227
Xoraxané Romá, **4:**281-283
Saudi Arabia
Arabs, **9:**22-25
Palestinians, **9:**262-266
Sleb, **9:**315
Scandinavia. *See* Denmark; Norway; Finland; Sweden
Scotland
Highland Scots, **4:**139-142
Irish Travellers, **4:**154-157
Lowland Scots, **4:**162-163
Orcadians, **4:**186-188
Shetlanders, **4:**232-234
Senegal
Fulani, **9:**100-103
Mande, **9:**215-216
Wolof, **9:**377-380
Serbia, Republic of
Albanians, **4:**3-8
Croats, **4:**72-75
Vlachs, **4:**273-275
Yugoslavia, **4:**229-232
Shetland Islands
Shetlanders, **4:**232-234
Siberia
Yuit, **1:**389-393
Sicily
Albanians, **4:**3-8

Sicily (cont'd)
Sicilians, **4:**235-237
Xoraxané Romá, **4:**281-283
Sierra Leone
Mande, **9:**215-216
Mende, **9:**223
Temne, **9:**341-345
Sikkim
Sikkimese, **3:**262
Silesia
Silesians, **4:**237-238
Singapore
Chinese in Southeast Asia, **5:**74-78
Han, **6:**439-449
Hindu, **3:**102
Selung/Moken, **5:**230-233
Singaporeans, **5:**242
South Asians in Southeast Asia, **5:**243
Slovakia
Carpatho-Rusyns, **6:**69-71
peripatetics, **4:**195-197
Rom of Czechoslovakia, **4:**217-219
Slovaks, **4:**242-246
see also Czech and Slovak Federative
Republic
Slovenia
Croats, **4:**71-75
Slovenes, **4:**246-249
Solomon Islands
Anuta, **2:**13-15
Choiseul Island, **2:**37-40
Guadalcanal, **2:**88-91
Malaita, **2:**160-163
New Georgia, **2:**238
Ontong Java, **2:**253-255
Rennell Island, **2:**277
San Cristobal, **2:**289
Santa Cruz, **2:**290-292
Tikopia, **2:**324-326
Somalia
Somalis, **9:**315-318
South Africa
Ashkenazic Jews, **4:**17
Asians of Africa, **9:**26
Cape Coloureds, **9:**58-60
Hindu, **3:**102
Khoi, **9:**157-160
Lithuanian Jews, **6:**243-248
Ndebele, **9:**235-238
Pedi, **9:**268-271
Swazi, **9:**329-333
Tswana, **9:**360-364
Xhosa, **9:**380-381
Zulu, **9:**411-412
South Korea. *See* Korea
Soviet Union. *See* Russia; *specific republics*
Spain
Andalusians, **4:**9-12
Balearics, **4:**29
Basques, **4:**29-32
Canarians, **4:**50-53

Castilians, **4:**57-61
Catalans, **4:**61-64
Galicians, **4:**118-121
Gitanos, **4:**127-130
Leonese, **4:**160-162
Otavalo, **7:**252-255
Pasiegos, **4:**188-191
peripatetics, **4:**195-197
Sephardic Jews, **4:**228-229
Spaniards, **4:**254-255
Spanish Rom, **4:**254-255
Sri Lanka
Chinese of South Asia, **3:**68
Europeans in South Asia, **3:**79-80
Moor, **3:**180-181
refugees in India, **3:**250
Sinhalese, **3:**264-267
Tamil, **3:**280-284
Vedda, **3:**300-303
Sudan
Acholi, **9:**3-6
Anuak, **9:**21-22
Arabs, **9:**22-25
Baggara, **9:**28-32
Bedouin, **9:**42-46
Copts, **9:**68-69
Dinka, **9:**69-71
Fulani, **9:**100-103
Nubians, **9:**245-248
Nuer, **9:**249-250
peripatetics, **9:**276-277
Shilluk, **9:**310-311
Suri, **9:**323-327
Zande, **9:**397-400
Suriname
Chinese in the English-speaking
Caribbean, **8:**55-58
Hindu, **3:**102
Maroni Carib, **7:**220
Saramaka, **7:**296-298
Trio, **7:**334-337
Swaziland
Swazi, **9:**329-333
Sweden
Estonians, **6:**111-115
peripatetics, **4:**195-197
Saami, **4:**220-223
Scandinavian peripatetics, **4:**228-229
Siberian Estonians, **6:**335-337
Swedes, **4:**256-258
Switzerland
German Swiss, **4:**124-127
Jurassians, **4:**157-158
peripatetics, **4:**195-197
Romansch, **4:**215-216
Swiss, **4:**259
Swiss, Italian, **4:**259-262
Syria
Arabs, **9:**22-25
Chaldeans, **9:**63-64
Chechen-Ingush, **6:**71-76
Circassians, **6:**85-91;**9:**65-68

Druze, **9:**74-75
Jacobites, **9:**131-133
Jews, Arabic-speaking, **9:**134-136
Kurds, **9:**174-177
Maronites, **9:**218-220
Palestinians, **9:**262-266
peripatetics, **9:**276-277

Taiwan
Bunun, **5:**55-58
Hakka, **6:**436-439
Han, **6:**439-449
Hui, **6:**452-454
Taiwan aboriginal peoples, **5:**256-258
Taiwanese, **5:**258-259
Tajikistan
Bukharan Jews, **6:**62-65
Germans, **6:**137-140
Jews of the Middle East, **9:**147-148
Koreans, **6:**204-207
Kurds, **6:**224-227
Pamir peoples, **6:**302-306
Tajiks, **6:**351-354, 492
Turkmens, **6:**368-372
Uighur, **6:**381-385
Tanzania
Asians of Africa, **9:**26
Chagga, **9:**60-62
Fipa, **9:**98-100
Hindu, **3:**102
Iraqw, **9:**124-126
Luo, **9:**200
Maasai, **9:**207-210
Nyakyusa and Ngonde, **9:**251-254
Nyamwezi and Sukuma, **9:**255-258
Okiek, **9:**258-262
Zaramo, **9:**400-403
Thailand
Akha, **5:**11-13
Buddhist, **5:**47-48
Central Thai, **5:**69-72
Chaobon, **5:**74
Chinese in Southeast Asia, **5:**74-78
Chong, **5:**78
Hani, **6:**449-451
Hindu, **3:**102
Hmong, **5:**92-95
Karen, **5:**124-130
Kmhmu, **5:**138-141
Kui, **5:**150
Lahu, **5:**150-154
Lao, **5:**157-160
Lao Isan, **5:**160-163
Lawa, **5:**163
Lisu, **5:**163-166;**6:**465-466
Mon, **5:**188-189
Pak Thai, **5:**200
Sea Nomads of the Andaman, **5:**227-229
Sek, **5:**230
Selung/Moken, **5:**230-233

Semang, **5:**233-236
Shan, **5:**239-241
So, **5:**242
South Asians in Southeast Asia, **5:**243
T'in, **5:**277-280
Vietnamese, **5:**284-287
Yao of Thailand, **5:**291-293
Yuan, **5:**293-294
Yumbri, **5:**294
Tibet
Abor, **3:**3-5
Buddhist, **5:**47-48
refugees in India/Nepal, **3:**250
Togo
Ewe and Fon, **9:**83-88
Songhay, **9:**319-320
Yoruba, **9:**390-391
Tonga
Niue, **2:**251-252
Tonga, **2:**336-339
Tory Island
Tory Islanders, **4:**264-266
Transylvania
ethnic groups, **4:**266-269
Trinidad and Tobago
Chinese in the English-speaking
    Caribbean, **8:**55-58
East Indians in Trinidad, **8:**104-107
Garifuna, **8:**113-115
Hindu, **3:**102
Trinidadians and Tobagonians, **8:**266-
    269
Tunisia
Arabs, **9:**22-25
Bedouin, **9:**42-46
Turkey
Abkhazians, **6:**5-10
Albanians, **4:**3-8
Arabs, **9:**22-25
Assyrians, **9:**27-28
Chaldeans, **9:**63-64
Chechen-Ingush, **6:**71-76
Circassians, **6:**85-91;**9:**65-68
Gagauz, **6:**124-126
Georgians, **6:**129-137
Jacobites, **9:**131-133
Jews of Kurdistan, **9:**144-147
Karakalpaks, **6:**165-169
Kurds, **9:**174-177
Laz, **6:**238-241
Nestorians, **9:**241-244
Nogays, **6:**286-290
Ossetes, **6:**297-302
peripatetics, **9:**274-276
Pomaks, **4:**204-205
Sephardic Jews, **4:**228, 229
Syriacs, **9:**334-335
Turkmens, **6:**368-372
Turks, **9:**373-376
Yezidis, **6:**407-411
Yörük, **9:**393-396
see also Cyprus

Turkmenistan
Greeks, **6:**140-144
Koreans, **6:**204-207
Kurds, **6:**224-227
Turkmens, **6:**368-372
Uighur, **6:**381-385
Yezidis, **6:**407-411
Turks and Caicos Islands
Turks and Caicos islanders, **8:**272-273
Tuvalu
Tuvaluans, **2:**354-357

Uganda
Acholi, **9:**3-6
Alur, **9:**13-15
Asians of Africa, **9:**26
Ganda, **9:**104-105
Iteso, **9:**127-130
Karamojong, **9:**156-157
Lango, **9:**178-182
Lugbara, **9:**193-195
Luyia, **9:**202-206
Nandi and other Kalenjin peoples,
    9:231-234
Pokot, **9:**280-283
tropical-forest foragers, **9:**356-357
Ukraine
Ashkenazic Jews, **4:**17
Ashkenazim, **6:**31-37
Carpatho-Rusyns, **6:**69-71
Crimean Tatars, **6:**91-95
Evenki (Northern Tungus), **6:**120-
    124
Gagauz, **4:**118
Germans, **4:**121;**6:**137-140
Greeks, **6:**140-144
Gypsies, **6:**145-148
Krymchaks, **6:**213-216
Old Believers, **6:**290-294
Poles, **6:**306-309
Romanians, **4:**212-215
Ukrainian peasants, **6:**385-388
Ukrainians, **6:**388-395
Ulster. *See* Northern Ireland
United Arab Emirates
Arabs, **9:**22-25
United Kingdom
Anglo-Indians, **3:**12
Copts, **9:**68-69
Cornish, **4:**64-65
English, **4:**95-97
Highland Scots, **4:**139-142
Hindu, **3:**102
Irish, **4:**151-154
Irish Travellers, **4:**154-157
Lowland Scots, **4:**162-163
Northern Irish, **4:**177-180
Orcadians, **4:**186-188
peripatetics, **4:**195-197
Rominche, **4:**216-217
Welsh, **4:**278-280

United States of America
Abenaki, **1:**1-6
Achumawi, **1:**9-10
Acoma, **1:**298
African Americans, **1:**10-13
Ahtna, **1:**14
Alabama, **1:**14
Albanians, **1:**107;**4:**3-8
Aleuts, **1:**14-16;**6:**15-19
American Isolates, **1:**17-18
Amish, **1:**18-21
Appalachians, **1:**21-23
Arab Americans, **1:**23-25
Arapaho, **1:**16
Arikara, **1:**16
Armenians, **1:**107-108
Ashkenazic Jews, **4:**16, 17
Asian Indians, **1:**325, 326
Assiniboin, **1:**16
Assyrians, **9:**27-28
Austrians, **1:**108
Bangladeshis, **1:**325, 326-327
Bannock, **1:**31
Basques, **1:**31-35
Belgians, **1:**108
Bhutanese, **1:**327
Black Creoles of Louisiana, **1:**36-40
Blackfoot, **1:**40-42
Black West Indians, **1:**44-46
Bruneians, **1:**327
Bukharan Jews, **6:**62-65
Burmese, **1:**327
Byelorussians, **1:**108
Caddo, **1:**47
Cahuilla, **1:**47-48
Cajuns, **1:**48-51
Cambodians, **1:**327
Cape Verdeans, **4:**53, 54
Carpatho-Rusyns, **1:**108-109
Catawba, **1:**52-55
Cayuga, **1:**55
Cayuse, **1:**55
Central Yup'ik Eskimos, **1:**55-59
Chamorros, **2:**34
Chastacosta, **1:**59
Chehalis, **1:**59-60
Chemehuevi, **1:**329-333
Cherokee, **1:**60-62
Cheyenne, **1:**63-66
Chickasaw, **1:**66
Chinook, **1:**67
Chiricahua, **1:**70
Chitimacha, **1:**70
Choctaw, **1:**70-73
Chuj, **8:**70-74
Chumash, **1:**73
Circassians, **6:**85-91
Coast Miwok, **1:**73
Cochiti, **1:**298
Cocopa, **1:**74
Coeur d'Alène, **1:**74
Columbia, **1:**74

United States of America (cont'd)
Comanche, 1:75
Copts, 68-69
Creek, 1:82-83
Croats (Croatians), 1:109
Crow, 1:83
Czechs, 1:109
Danes, 1:109
Delaware, 1:84-87
Druze, 74-75
Dutch, 1:110
East Asians, 1:98-103
Eastern Shoshone, 1:104-106
English, 1:110
Eskimo, 1:107
Estonians, 1:110;6:111-115
European-Americans, 1:107-118
Finns, 1:110
Flathead, 1:128
Fox, 1:128-130
French, 1:111
Garifuna, 8:113-115
Germans, 1:111
Gosiute, 1:134
Greeks, 1:112
Gros Ventre, 1:134
Gypsies, 6:145-148
Haida, 1:135-136
Haitians, 1:137-138
Halchidhoma, 1:139
Han, 1:139
Hasidim, 1:142-145
Havasupai, 1:145
Hawaiians, 2:95-97
Hidatsa, 1:145-148
Hindu, 3:102
Hmong, 5:92-95
Hopi, 1:148-151
Hopi-Tewa, 1:151
Huma, 1:151
Hungarians, 1:112
Hupa, 1:152
Hutterites, 1:153-155
Illinois, 1:156
Indians of Baja California, 8:129
Indonesians, 1:327
Ingalik, 1:156-159
Iowa, 1:162
Irish, 1:112-113
Irish Travelers, 1:162-164
Iroquois, 1:164-167
Italians, 1:113
Jemez, 1:299
Jews, 1:168-171
Jicarilla, 1:171-174
Kalapuya, 1:175
Kalispel, 1:175
Kalmyks, 6:154-158
Kansa, 1:175
Karaites, 6:162-165;9:153-156
Karok, 1:175-177
Kawaiisu, 1:178

Keres Pueblo Indians, 1:179-182
Kickapoo, 1:182-186
Kikapu, 8:143-145
Kiowa, 1:186-189
Kiowa Apache, 1:189
Klallam, 1:189-190
Klamath, 1:190-192
Klikitat, 1:192
Kmhmu, 5:138-141
Koreans, 5:144-149;6:204-207
Koyukon, 1:193
Krymchaks, 6:213-216
Kumeyaay, 1:193-196
Kutchin, 1:196
Kutenai, 1:197
Laguna, 1:298
Lake, 1:202
Laotians, 1:327-328
Latinos, 1:202-206
Latvians, 1:114;6:235-238
Lipan Apache, 1:207-208
Lithuanian Jews, 6:243-248
Lithuanians, 1:114
Luiseño, 1:208
Lumbee, 1:208-209
Mahican, 1:209
Maidu, 1:209
Malaysians, 1:328
Maldivians, 1:327
Maliseet, 1:210-213
Mandan, 1:213-215
Maricopa, 1:216
Massachuset, 1:216
Mennonites, 1:216-220
Menominee, 1:220-222
Mescalero Apache, 1:222-225
Metoac, 1:230
Miami, 1:230-232
Micronesians, 1:235-239
Missouri, 1:239
Miwok, 1:239-240
Mohave, 1:240-242
Mohawk, 1:242
Mohegan, 1:242
Moldovans, 6:265-270
Molokans, 1:243
Mono, 1:243
Mormons, 1:246-249
Nabesna, 1.250; *see also* Tanana
Nambe, 1:298-299
Nanticoke, 1:250
Navajo, 1:250-253
Nepalese, 1:327
Nez Percé, 1:254-255
North Alaskan Eskimos, 1:258-261
Northern Metis, 1:261-262
Northern Paiute, 1:262-265
Northern Shoshone and Bannock, 1:265-268
Norwegians, 1:114
Ojibwa, 1:268-272
Okanagon, 1:271-272

Old Believers, 1:272-275;6:290-294
Omaha, 1:275
Oneida, 1:275-276
Onondaga, 1:276
Osage, 1:276-279
Oto, 1:279
Ottawa, 1:279-280
Ozarks, 1:280-282
Pacific Eskimo, 1:282-283
Pakistanis, 1:328
Palestinians, 262-266;1:325
Passamaquoddy, 1.283; *see also* Maliseet
Pawnee, 1:283-286
Pennacook, 1:286
Pennsylvania Dutch, 1:114-115
Penobscot, 1.286; *see also* Abenaki
peripatetics, 1:286-287
Pima Bajo, 8:209-214
Pima-Papago, 1:287-290
Poles, 1:115
Polynesians, 1:290-292
Pomo, 1:292-296
Ponca, 1:296
Portuguese, 1:115
Potawatomi, 1:296-297
Powhatan, 1:297
Pueblo Indians, 1:297-299
Quapaw, 1:300
Quechan, 1:300-302
Quileute, 1:303
Quinault, 1:303
Rom, 1:303-306
Romanians, 1:115-116;4:212-215
Russians, 1:116
Samoa, 2:286-289
Sandia, 1:299
San Felipe, 1:298
Sanpoil, 1:307
Santa Ana, 1:298
Santee, 1:307
Santo Domingo, 1:298
Sauk, 1.308; *see also* Fox
Scots, 1:116
Sea Islanders, 1:308-311
Seminole of Florida, 1:311-314
Seminole of Oklahoma, 1:314-315
Seneca, 1:315
Sephardic Jews, 4:229
Serbs, 1:116
Serrano, 1:315
Shakers, 1:316
Shasta, 1:317
Shawnee, 1:317
Siberian Estonians, 6:335-337
Slovaks, 1:117;4:242
Slovenes (Slovenians), 1:117
Snoqualmie, 1:320-321
Sorbs, 1:117
South and Southeast Asians, 1:324-327
Southern Paiute (and Chemehuevi), 1:329-333

Spaniards, **1:**117
Spokane, **1:**333
Sri Lankans, **1:**325, 328
Swedes, **1:**117-118
Swiss, **1:**118
Tanaina, **1:**334-337
Tanana, **1:**337-340
Taos, **1:**340-343
Tenino, **1:**343
Teton, **1:**343-346
Tewa Pueblos, **1:**347-350
Thais, **1:**328-329
Tigua, **1:**299
Tillamook, **1:**351
Tlingit, **1:**351-353
Tolowa, **1:**353
Tonkawa, **1:**354
Tubatulabal, **1:**355
Tunica, **1:**355-356
Tuscarora, **1:**356
Twana, **1:**356
Ukrainians, **1:**118;**6:**388-395
Umatilla, **1:**359
Ute, **1:**360-363
Vietnamese, **1:**325, 329;**5:**284-287
Wailaki, **1:**363
Walapai, **1:**363-366
Wallawalla, **1:**366
Wappo, **1:**366
Washoe, **1:**366-370
Welsh, **1:**118
Western Apache, **1:**371-373
Western Shoshone, **1:**374-375
Wichita, **1:**379
Winnebago, **1:**379-382
Wintun, **1:**383
Wishram, **1:**383
Wiyot, **1:**383-385
Yakima, **1:**386
Yankton, **1:**386
Yaqui, **8:**305-307
Yavapai, **1:**386
Yokuts, **1:**387-389
Yuchi, **1:**389
Yuit, **1:**389-393
Yuki, **1:**393
Yurok, **1:**393-396
Zia, **1:**298
Zuni, **1:**396-400
Uruguay
Mennonites, **7:**239-240
Uzbekistan
Bukharan Jews, **6:**62-65
Dungans, **6:**107-111
Germans, **6:**137-140
Greeks, **6:**140-144
Gypsies, **6:**145-148
Jews of the Middle East, **9:**147-148
Karakalpaks, **6:**165-169
Koreans, **6:**204-207
Kurds, **6:**224-227
Meskhetians, **6:**259-262

Tajiks, **6:**351-354
Turkmens, **6:**368-372
Uighur, **6:**381-385
Uzbeks, **6:**395-399, 500
Volga Tatars, **6:**399-403

Vanuatu
Ambae, **2:**10-13
Malekula, **2:**164-166
Nguna, **2:**242-244
Pentecost, **2:**261-264
Tanna, **2:**313-315
Venezuela
Afro-Venezuelans, **7:**24-29
Akawaio, **7:**30-33
Baniwa-Curripaco-Wakuenai, **7:**76-80
Barí, **7:**82-85
Cariña, **7:**102-103
Cuiva, **7:**142-145
Guahibo-Sikuani, **7:**164-166
Guajiro, **7:**167-170
Hoti, **7:**175-176
Otavalo, **7:**252-255
Panare, **7:**264-267
Paraujano, **7:**267-268
Pemon, **7:**270-273
Piapoco, **7:**274
Piaroa, **7:**275-278
Puinave, **7:**281-282
Pume, **7:**282-285
Saliva, **7:**291-293
Tunebo, **7:**337-339
Warao, **7:**357-359
Yanomamö, **7:**374-377
Yekuana, **7:**380-382
Yukpa, **7:**382-385
Vietnam
Akha, **5:**11-13
Bahnar, **5:**30
Bru, **5:**47
Buddhist, **5:**47-48
Cham, **5:**72-74
Chinese in Southeast Asia, **5:**74-78
Chrau, **5:**78
Cua, **5:**79
Duane, **5:**79
Halang Doan, **5:**90
Hani, **6:**449-451
Hmong, **5:**92-95
Hre, **5:**95
Katu, **5:**131
Khua, **5:**138
Kmhmu, **5:**138-141
Lahu, **5:**150-154
Ma, **5:**167
May, **5:**177
Mnong, **5:**184-185
Mon, **5:**188-189
Monom, **5:**189
Muong, **5:**189-192
Pacoh, **5:**200

Rengao, **5:**211
Rhadé, **5:**211-212
Sedang, **5:**229-230
South Asians in Southeast Asia, **5:**243
Tay, **5:**265
Vietnamese, **5:**284-287
Virgin Islands
Virgin Islanders, **8:**299-300

Wales
Irish Travellers, **4:**154-157
Rominich, **4:**216-217
Welsh, **4:**278-280
West Bengal. *See* India
Western Samoa
Samoa, **2:**286-289
West Germany. *See* Germany

Yemen
Arabs, **9:**22-25
Hindu, **3:**102
Jews of Yemen, **9:**149-150
peripatetics, **9:**276-277
Yemenis, **9:**388-390
Yugoslavia
Albanians, **4:**3-8
Bosnian Muslims, **4:**36
Circassians, **6:**85-91
Croats, **4:**72-75
Dalmatians, **4:**85-87
Montenegrins, **4:**171-174
peripatetics, **4:**195-197
Romanians, **4:**212-215
Serbs, **4:**229-232
Slav Macedonians, **4:**238-241
Slovenes, **4:**246-249
Vlachs, **4:**273-275
Xoraxané Romá, **4:**281-283
see also Bosnia-Hercegovina; Croatia;
    Macedonia; Serbia; Slovenia

Zaire
Alur, **9:**13-15
Kongo, **9:**166-168
Luba of Shaba, **9:**190-193
Lugbara, **9:**193-195
Lunda, **9:**195-199
Mangbetu, **9:**216-217
Mongo, **9:**225-227
Ndembu, **9:**238-241
Pende, **9:**271-274
Suku, **9:**320-323
tropical-forest foragers, **9:**356-357
Zande, **9:**397-400
Zambia
Asians in South America of Africa,
    9:26
Bemba, **9:**46-47
Lozi, **9:**187-190

Zambia (cont'd)
  Lunda, **9:**195-199
  Ndembu, **9:**238-241
  Tonga, **9:**352-355

Zanzibar
  Swahili, 327-329
Zimbabwe
  Lozi, **9:**187-190

  Shona, **9:**312-314
  Tonga, **9:**352-355
  Tswana, **9:**360-364

Ethnonym Index

This index provides some of the alternative names and the names of major subgroups for cultures covered in the nine text volumes of the encyclopedia. The culture names that are entry titles are in boldface. The letter a following a volume number indicates a listing in the appendix to that volume. For volume 6, the symbol (R) indicates that the article is to be found in Part One, Russia and Eurasia; (C) indicates that the article is in Part Two, China.

Aaingáng, 7: **Kaingáng**
A Bai, 2: **Ambae**
Abaka Tatars, 6(R): **Khakas**
Abans, 6(R): **Shors**
Abagusii, 9: **Gusii**
Abaluhya, 9: **Luyia**
Abaluyia, 9: **Luyia**
Abazintsy, 6(R): **Abkhazians**
Abbe, 9a
Abdal, 9: **Peripatetics of Afghanistan, Iran, and Turkey (Turkey)**
Abé, 9a: **Abbe**
Abelam, 2
Abenaki, 1
Abenaque, 1: **Abenaki**
Abenaquioicts, 1: **Abenaki**
Abenaquois, 1: **Abenaki**
Abidji, 9a
Abkhazians, 6(R)
Abkhazy, 6(R): **Abkhazians**
Abnaki, 1: **Abenaki**
Abo, 9a: **Toposa**
Abor, 3
Abron, 9a
Absarokee, 1: **Crow**
Abuan, 9a
Abui, 7a: **Hishkariana**
Abuit, 3: **Abor**
Abulas, 2: **Abelam**
Abu Sharib, 9a
Acadians, 1
Acadians of Louisiana, 1: **Cajuns**
Acadiens, 1: **Acadians**
Acaguayo, 7: **Akawaio**
Acari, 3a: **Navandanna**

Acauayo, 7: **Akawaio**
Acawai, 7: **Akawaio**
Accawai, 7: **Akawaio**
Acehnese, 5
Acha, 6(C): **Jingpo**
Achagua, 7a: **Achawa**
Achang, 6(C)
Acharaj, 3a: **Mahabrahman**
Ach'areli, 6(R): **Ajarians**
Achari, 3a: **Kammalan**
Acharji, 3a: **Kammalan**
Achawa, 7a
Achawa, 9a: **Yao**
Ache, 7
Achehnese, 5: **Acehnese**
Achik, 3: **Garo**
Achinese, 5: **Acehnese**
Acholi, 9
Achomawi, 1: **Achumawi**
Achumano, 7: **Chimane**
Achumawi, 1
Acolapissa, 1a
Acoli, 9: **Acholi**
Acoma, 1: **Keres Pueblo Indians; Pueblo Indians**
Acooli, 9: **Acholi**
Acquewyen, 7: **Akawaio**
Acra, 9a: **Ga-Adandme-Krobo**
Acuria, 7a: **Akurio**
Adal, 9: **Afar**
Adamstown Indians, 1: **American Isolates**
Adare, 9a: **Harari**
Addo, 9a: **Edo-Speaking Peoples**
Adhola, 9a: **Padhola**

Adi, 3a
Adi, 3: **Abor**
Adi-Dravida, 3: **Untouchables**
Adi-Dravida, 3a: **Holeya**
Adigal, 3a: **Adiyan**
Adikal, 3a: **Ambalavasi**
Adioukrou, 9a
Adivasis, 3: **Scheduled Castes and Scheduled Tribes**
Adivichanchar, 3a: **Pardhi**
Advichincher, 3a: **Pardhi**
Adiyan, 3a
Adiyar, 3a: **Adiyan**
Adiye, 9a: **Hadiyya**
Adja, 9a
Adole, 7: **Piaroa**
Adyge, 9: **Circassians**
Adyghe, 6(R): **Circassians**
Aents, 7: **Aguaruna; Jivaro**
Aeta, 5: **Philippine Negritos**
Afango, 9a: **Birom**
Afar, 9
Afenmai, 9a: **Etsako**
Afghan, 3: **Pathan**
Afipa, 9: **Fipa**
Afnu, 9: **Hausa**
Aframerindians, 1: **American Isolates**
African Americans, 1
African-Canadians, 1: **Blacks in Canada**
African Mexicans, 8
African Negroes, 7: **Afro–South Americans**
Afrikaners, 9
Afro-Americans, 1: **African Americans; 7: Afro–South Americans**

Afro-Bolivians, 7
Afro-Brazilians, 7
Afro-Colombianos, 7: Afro-Hispanic
    Pacific Lowlanders of Ecuador and
    Colombia
Afro-Colombians, 7
Afro-Ecuatorianos, 7: Afro-Hispanic
    Pacific Lowlanders of Ecuador and
    Colombia
Afro-French, 1: Black Creoles of
    Louisiana
Afro-Hispanic Pacific Lowlanders of
    Ecuador and Colombia
Afro–South Americans, 7
Afro-Venezolanos, 7: Afro-Venezuelans
Afro-Venezuelans, 7
Afunu, 9: Hausa
Agah've, 7: Yawalapití
Agamudaiyan, 3a
Agari, 3a: Agri
Agaria, 3
Agaria, 3a: Agri
Agariya, 3: Agaria
Agarwal, 3: Bania
Agarwala, 3: Bania
Agarwal Marwadi, 3: Bania
Agasa, 3a
Agaw, 9a: Awi
Ager, 3a: Agri
Agesaru, 3a: Dhobi
Aggarwal, 3: Bania
Agharia, 3: Agaria
Aghem, 9: Bamiléké
Aghorapanthi, 3a: Aghori
Aghori, 3a
Aghoripanthi, 3a: Aghori
Aghuls, 6(R)
Agiryama, 9a: Giriama
Agle, 3a: Agri
Aglurmiut, 1: Central Yup'ik Eskimos
Agni, 9a
Agni Honnappana Matadavaru, 3a:
    Hasalar
Agnihotri, 3a
Agnikula, 3a: Palli
Agouti, 7: Marinahua
Agrahari, 3a
Agrawal, 3: Bania
Agrehri, 3a: Agrahari
Agsali, 3a: Sonar
Agri, 3a
Agta, 5
Aguacateco, 8: Awakateko
Aguahun, 7: Aguaruna
Aguajun, 7: Aguaruna
Aguano, 7a: Awano
Aguaruna, 7
Aguateca, 8: Awakateko
Aguri, 3a
Agutchaninnewug, 1: Hidatsa
Aguti, 7: Marinahua
A-ha-chae, 1: Osage

Ahaggar Tuareg, 9: Berbers of Morocco
Ahar, 3a: Ahar
Ahari, 3a: Ahar
Aharia, 3a: Sesodia Rajput
Ahariya, 3a: Sesodia Rajput
Ahban, 3a
Aheri, 3a: Ahar; Aheriya; Thori
Aheria, 3a: Aheriya
Aheriya, 3a
Ahir, 3
Ahiwasi, 3a
Ahl al-Muzaiyad, 9: Peripatetics of Iraq
    . . . Yemen (Yemen)
Ahl al-Nawwaḥ, 9: Peripatetics of Iraq
    . . . Yemen (Yemen)
Ahl-i-Hadi, 3a: Wahabi
Ahni, 6(C): Hani
Ahtena, 1: Ahtna
Ahtna, 1
Ahtnakotana, 1: Ahtna
Ahuahun, 7: Aguaruna
Aiaho, 1: Chiricahua
Aiga, 2: Orokaiva
Aikaná, 7a
Aimaq, 9
Aimol, 3a: Kuki
Aini, 5: Akha; 6(C): Hani
Aino, 5: Ainu
Ainu, 5; 6(R)
Aiome Pygmies, 2: Gainj
Aivilingmiut, 1: Iglulik Inuit
Aizo, 9a
Aja-Gbe, 9a: Adja
Ajagyak Brahman, 3a: Babhan
Ajaju, 7: Karihona
Ajana, 7a: Wayana
Ajarians, 6(R)
Aji, 6(C): Jingpo
Ajibba, 9a: Murle
Ajië, 2
ajNenton, 8: Chuj
ajSan Matéyo, 8: Chuj
ajSan Sabastyán, 8: Chuj
Ajudhyabasi, 3a: Audhiya
Ajukru, 9a: Adioukrou
Ajuru, 7a: Wayoró
Aka, 3a
Aka, 5: Akha
Ak'a, 5: Akha
Aka, 9: Tropical-Forest Foragers
Aka-Bala-wa, 3a: Aka-Bale
Aka-Bale, 3a
Aka-Bea, 3a
Aka-Bo, 3a
Aka-Bojig-yab, 3a: A-Pucikwar
Aka-Cari, 3a
Aka-Jeru, 3a
Aka-Kede, 3a
Aka-Kol, 3a
Aka-Kora, 3a
Akali, 3a
Akan, 9

Akansa, 1: Quapaw
Akapotuval, 3a: Mussad
Akawai, 7: Akawaio
Akawaio, 7
Akawoio, 7: Akawaio
Akeroa, 9a: Toposa
Akha, 5
Akha, 6(C): Hani
Akhuni, 2: Dani
Aki, 5: Banggai
Akimel O'Odham, 1: Pima-Papago
Akka, 5: Akha
Ak Nogays (White Nogays), 6(R):
    Nogays
Akokolemu, 9a: Kuman
Akosa, 9: Lunda
Aksali, 3a: Sonar
Aksulik, 6(C): Uigur
Akuapem, 9: Akan
Akuáwa-Asurini, 7: Asurini
Akuliyo, 7a: Akurio
Akulmiut, 1: Central Yup'ik Eskimos
Akum, 9a: Kuman
Akurio, 7a
Akwa, 9a: Nyakwai
Akwamu, 9: Akan
Akwawa, 7a: Parakanã
Akwaya, 7: Asurini
Akwẽ, 7: Sherente
Akwén, 7: Shavante
Akwén, 7a: Shakriabá
Akwẽ-Shavante, 7: Shavante
Akyem, 9: Akan
Alaba, 9a
Alabama, 1
Alabama-Coushatta, 1: Alabama
Alacaluf, 7a: Kawe'skar
Alada, 9a: Goun
Alagia, 9a: Alladian
Ala Igbo, 9: Igbo
Alak, 5
Alakong, 5: Bahnar
Alama, 7: Canelos Quichua
Alan, 6(R): Balkars
Alante, 9a: Balante
Alaqeband, 3a: Patwa
Alas, 6(R): Laz
Albanians, 4
Albanians, 1: European-Americans;
    European-Canadians
Albanois, 4: Albanians
Alcojolados, 7: Paraujano
Alemanes, 4: Germans
Alequa, 1: Yurok
Aleut, 1
Aleut, 1: Pacific Eskimo
Aleutian, 1: Aleut
Aleuts, 6(R)
Algonkin, 1
Algonquin, 1: Algonkin
Alia, 3a: Chasa
Alibamu, 1: Alabama

Alifura, 5: **Ambonese**
A-Liko, 5: **Melanau**
Aliles, 7: **Paraujano**
Aliquois, 1: **Yurok**
Alishan, 5: **Taiwan Aboriginal Peoples**
Alitkar, 3a: **Khatik**
Alkari, 3a
Alladian, 9a
Allar, 3a
Allemands, 4: **Germans**
Alliklik, 1: **Serrano**
Alliouagana, 8: **Montserratians**
Alomwe, 9a: **Macua-Lomue**
A Long, 6(C): **Nu**
Aloreezen, 5: **Alorese**
Alorese, 5
Alsatians, 4
Alsea, 1a
Alta, 5: **Agta**
Alta, 6(R): **Altaians**
Altai, 6(R): **Altaians**
Altaians, 6(R)
Altai Turks, 6(R): **Altaians**
Altays, 6(R): **Altaians**
Alucuyana, 7a: **Wayana**
Alu-Kurumbas, 3: **Kurumbas**
Alur, 9
Alutiiq, 1: **Pacific Eskimo**
Aluunda, 9: **Lunda**
Alyoot, 1: **Aleut**
Amage, 7: **Amuesha**
Amaguaca, 7: **Amahuaca**
Amahuaca, 7
Amajo, 7: **Amuesha**
Amajuaca, 7: **Amahuaca**
Amamijin, 5: **Okinawans**
Amanajé, 7a: **Amanayé**
Amanayé, 7: **Anambé**
Amanayé, 7a
Amandebele, 9: **Ndebele**
Amangbetu, 9: **Mangbetu**
Amar, 9a: **Haner**
Amara, 9: **Amhara**
Amat, 3a
Amath, 3a: **Amat**
Amawaka, 7: **Amahuaca**
Amba, 9a
Ambae, 2
Ambalakkaran, 3a
Ambalavasi, 3a
Ambastha, 3a: **Baidya**
Ambattan, 3a
Ambekar, 3a: **Besta**
Ambelam, 2: **Abelam**
Ambelas, 2: **Abelam**
Ambi, 3a: **Besta**
Ambig, 3a: **Besta**
Ambiga, 3a: **Besta**
Ambo, 9a: **Ovambo**
Ambonese, 5
Ambulas, 2: **Abelam**
Amelecite, 1: **Maliseet**

'Amer, 9: **Peripatetics of the Maghreb** (Algeria)
American Isolates, 1
Americo-Liberians, 9
Ameshe, 1: **Hidatsa**
Amhara, 9
Ami, 5: **Taiwan Aboriginal Peoples**
Amia, 5: **Taiwan Aboriginal Peoples**
Amina, 9a: **Ga-Adandme-Krobo**
Amish, 1
Amma Coorg, 3a: **Amma Coorg**
Amma Kodagi, 3a: **Amma Coorg**
Amniapé, 7a: **Mekē**
Amojave, 1: **Mohave**
Amókebeit, 7: **Mocoví**
Ampika, 9a: **Bolewa**
Amueixa, 7: **Amuesha**
Amuesha, 7
Amuetamo, 7: **Amuesha**
Amuzgo, 8
Anaang, 9a
Anabaptists, 1: **Mennonites**
Anabaptosts, 7: **Mennonites**
Anago, 9: **Yoruba**
Anal, 3a: **Kuki**
Anambé, 7
Anambe, 7: **Anambé**
A-nan, 6(C): **Maonan**
Anangai, 2: **Woleai**
Anavil Brahman, 3
Ancutere, 7: **Siona-Secoya**
Andal, 6(R): **Andis**
Andalucians, 4: **Andalusians**
Andalusians, 4
Andamanese, 3
Ande, 7: **Campa**
Andh, 3a
Andhra, 3: **Telugu**
Andhra Brahman, 3a
Andiitsy, 6(R): **Andis**
Andirá, 7a: **Mawé**
Andis, 6(R)
Andoa, 7a
Andoke, 7a
Andoque, 7a: **Andoke**
Andresero, 8: **Tzotzil of San Andrés Larraínzar**
Ang, 6(C): **De'ang**
Angai Tagaro, 2: **Ambae**
Angaité, 7
Angaité, 7a: **Maskoi**
Angal, 2: **Mendi**
Angami, 3: **Nagas**
Anganen, 2: **Mendi**
Angarakudu, 3a: **Mangala**
Angate, 7: **Angaité**
Angkola-Sipirok, 5: **Batak**
Anglo-Indian, 3
Anglo-Irish, 4: **Northern Irish**
Anglophones of Cameroon
Angoni, 9a: **Ngoni**
Angotero, 7: **Siona-Secoya**

Anguillans, 8
Angutero, 7: **Siona-Secoya**
Ani Igbo, 9: **Igbo**
‖Anikhoe, 9a
Anishinabe, 1: **Ojibwa**
Anitakwa, 1: **Catawba**
Ankole, 9a
Ankwe, 9a
Annakaza, 9a
Annamese, 5: **Vietnamese**
Antandroy, 9: **Tandroy**
Anti, 7: **Campa; Matsigenka**
Antigua and Barbuda, 8
Antyaja, 3a: **Madiga**
Antyaja, 3a: **Mala**
A Nu, 6(C): **Nu**
Añu, 7: **Paraujano**
Anuak, 9
Anung, 5: **Lisu**
Anuta, 2
Anuu, 7: **Paraujano**
Anyi, 9: **Akan**
Anyin, 9a: **Agni**
Ao, 3: **Nagas**
Aoaqui, 7a: **Urak**
Aoba, 2: **Ambae**
Apaches de Cuartelejo, 1: **Mescalero Apache**
Apaches de Nabaju, 1: **Navajo**
Apaches del Rio Grande, 1: **Mescalero Apache**
Apaches-Mohaves, 1: **Yavapai**
Apachi, 1: **Mescalero Apache**
Apalachee, 1a
Apalai, 7
Apalakiri, 7: **Kalapalo**
Apalaquiri, 7: **Kalapalo**
Aparahya, 7: **Apalai**
Aparai, 7: **Apalai**
Aparay, 7: **Apalai**
Apa Tani, 3a
Apayao, 5: **Isneg**
Apiaká, 7
Apiaká del Rio Tocantin, 7a: **Arára Pariri**
Apichum, 7a: **Wayoró**
Apinayé, 7a
Appa, 9a: **Yergam**
Appalachians, 1
Appareille, 7: **Apalai**
Appiroi, 7: **Appalai**
Apsaalooke, 1: **Crow**
Apsaroke, 1: **Crow**
Apswa, 6(R): **Abkhazians**
A-Pucikwar, 3a
Aquitaine, 4
A'raab, 9: **Bedouin**
Arab Americans, 1
Arabci, 9: **Peripatetics of Afghanistan, Iran, and Turkey (Turkey)**
Arabela, 7a
Arab Muslims, 1: **Arab Americans**

Arabophone Jews, 9: **Jews, Arabic-Speaking**
Arabs, 9
Aradhi, 3a: **Bhute**
Aradhya, 3a
Aradhya Brahman, 3a: **Aradhya**
Araibayba, 7: **Guarayu; Pauserna**
Arain, 3a
Arakh, 3a
Aramasen Chuuk, 2: **Truk**
Aranadan, 3a
Aranda, 2
Arandan, 3a: **Aranadan**
Arandeuara, 7a: **Amanayé**
Araona, 7a
Arapaho, 1
Arapahoe, 1: **Arapaho**
Arapaso, 7a
Arapaso, 7a: **Tucano**
Arapaso-Tapuya, 7a: **Arapaso**
Arapesh, 2: **Mountain Arapesh**
Arapium, 7a: **Mawé**
Arara, 7a: **Arára Pariri; Koayá**
Arará do Para, 7a: **Arára Pariri**
Arára Pariri, 7a
Arasario, 7a: **Malayo**
Arasu, 3a
Araucanians, 7
Arauirá, 7: **Bororo**
Arawak, 7a: **Lokono**
Arawako, 7a: **Bintukua**
Arawaté, 7
Arawe, 2: **Sengseng**
Arbëresh, 4: **Albanians**
Arctic Highlanders, 1: **Inughuit**
'Are'are, 2: **Malaita**
Arecuna, 7: **Pemon**
Are Katika, 3a: **Kasai**
Arekuna, 7: **Pemon**
Arenakotte, 7a: **Patamona**
Areneno, 1: **Pima-Papago**
Arewaru, 3a: **Kasai**
Argobba, 9a
Argobbinya, 9a: **Argobba**
Arhuaco, 7a: **Bintukua**
Ari, 9a: **Abidji**
Aricours, 7: **Palikur**
Arihini-Baré, 7a: **Baré**
Arikapú, 7a: **Jabutí**
Arikara, 1
Arindrano, 9: **Betsileo**
Arisan, 5: **Taiwan Aboriginal Peoples**
Ariti, 7: **Paresí**
Arkansas, 1: **Quapaw**
Arleng, 3: **Mikir**
Arlija, 4: **Xoraxané Romá**
Armenians, 6(R)
Armenians, 1: **European-Americans; European-Canadians**
Armyanin, 6(R): **Armenians**
Arna, 9: **Hausa**
Arna, 9a

Arnauts, 4: **Albanians**
Arnuta, 4: **Xoraxané Romá**
Aromans, 4: **Romanians**
Aromuni, 4: **Vlachs**
Arora, 3a
Arouaques-Kaggaba, 7: **Kogi**
Arra-Arra, 1: **Karok**
Arrernte, 2: **Aranda**
Arta, 5: **Agta**
Aruá, 7a
Aruã, 7a: **Marworna**
Arubans, 8
Arunta, 2: **Aranda**
Arupá, 7a: **Urupá**
Arusi-Guji, 9a: **Oromo**
Arut, 5: **Kalimantan Dayaks**
Aruund, 9: **Lunda**
Arvanits, 4: **Albanians**
Arveqtormiut, 1: **Netsilik Inuit**
Arvernes, 4: **Auvergnats**
Aryan, 3
Arya Samaj, 3a
Arya Somavansi Kshatriya, 3a: **Mochi**
Asaga, 3a: **Agasa**
Asal Paharia, 3a: **Maler**
Asan, 3a: **Kaniyan**
Asante, 9: **Akan**
Asaro, 2: **Gururumba**
Asengseng, 2: **Sengseng**
Asháninca, 7: **Campa**
Ashaninka, 7: **Matsigenka**
Asheq, 9: **Peripatetics of Afghanistan, Iran, and Turkey** (Iran)
Ashing, 3: **Abor**
Ashiwi, 1: **Zuni**
Ashkenazic Jews, 4
Ashkenazim, 6(R)
Ashkenazim, 1: **Jews**
Ashlushlai, 7: **Nivaclé**
Ashochimi, 1: **Wappo**
Asi, 6(R): **Balkars**
As-iakh, 6(R): **Khanty**
Asian Indians, 1: **South and Southeast Asians of Canada; South and Southeast Asians of the United States**
Asians in South America, 7
Asians of Africa, 9
Asiat, 6(R): **Balkars**
Asiatic Eskimos, 1: **Yuit**
Asiatic Eskimos, 6(R)
Asiáticos, 7: **Asians in South America**
Askinarmiut, 1: **Central Yup'ik Eskimos**
Asmat, 2
Asmat-ow, 2: **Asmat**
Assamese, 3
Assamese Muslims, 3: **Garia**
Assiniboin, 1
Assiniboine, 1: **Assiniboin**
Assinipwat, 1: **Assiniboin**
Assurniní, 7: **Asurini**

Assyrians, 9
Asua, 9: **Tropical-Forest Foragers**
Asur, 3a
Asur, 3: **Munda**
Asurini, 7
Asurini, 7a: **Awaete**
Ata Bi'ang, 5: **Ata Sikka**
Atacameño, 7a: **Atakama**
'Ata Ende, 5: **Endenese**
Atahori Rote, 5: **Rotinese**
Ata 'Iwang, 5: **Ata Tana 'Ai**
'Ata Jaö, 5: **Endenese**
Atakama, 7a
Ata Kangae, 5: **Ata Tana 'Ai**
Atakapa, 1a
Ata Kiwan, 5: **Lamaholot**
Ata Krowé, 5: **Ata Sikka; Ata Tana 'Ai**
Ata Manggarai, 5: **Manggarai**
Ata Nuha, 5: **Palu'e**
Ata Nusa, 5: **Palu'e**
Ata Pulo, 5: **Palu'e**
Atari, 3a
Ata Sikka, 5
Ata Tana 'Ai, 5
Atayal, 5: **Taiwan Aboriginal Peoples**
Atazan, 5: **Taiwan Aboriginal Peoples**
Atchinese, 5: **Acehnese**
Ateso, 9a: **Teso**
Athi, 9: **Okiek**
Athonite Monks, 4: **Mount Athos**
Atikū, 7a
Atimopiskay, 1: **Dogrib**
Atjehnese, 5: **Acehnese**
Atoin Meto, 5: **Atoni**
Atoin Pah Meto, 5: **Atoni**
Atoni, 5
Atonoxó, 7: **Maxakali**
Atrato, 7: **Chocó**
Atroahi, 7: **Waimiri-Atroari**
Atroahí, 7a: **Atroarí**
Atroahy, 7: **Waimiri-Atroari**
Atroarí, 7a
Atrohai, 7: **Waimiri-Atroari**
Atruahí, 7: **Waimiri-Atroari**
Atruahí, 7a: **Atroarí**
Atsa, 6(C): **Jingpo**
Atsina, 1: **Gros Ventre**
Atta, 5: **Philippine Negritos**
Attayes, 1: **Tenino**
Attie, 9a
Attie, 9: **Akan**
Ature, 7: **Piaroa**
Auca, 7: **Waorani**
Auca, 7a: **Wao**
Audhalia, 3a: **Audhelia**
Audhelia, 3a
Audhiya, 3a
Audhya, 3a: **Audhiya**
Aughar, 3a: **Aghori**
Aukuyene, 7: **Palikur**

Aura, 7: Waurá
Aussa, 9: Hausa
Austral Islands, 2: Rapa
Australian Aborigines, 2: Aranda;
    Dieri; Kamilaroi; Karadjeri' Kari-
    era; Mardudjara; Murngin; Ngatat-
    jara; Pintupi; Tasmanians; Tiwi;
    Warlpiri; Wik Mungkan; Wongai-
    bon; Yir Yoront; Yungar
Austrians, 4
Austrians, 1: European-Americans;
    European-Canadians
Auvergnats, 4
A va, 6(C): Wa
Ava, 7: Chiriguano; Paï-Tavytera
Avá-Canoeiro, 7a
Avadhapuri, 3a: Audhiya
Avanersuarmiut, 1: Inughuit
Avars, 6(R)
Aveyronnais, 4
Avikam, 9a
Avam, 6(R): Nganasan
A vo, 6(C): Wa
Awá Cuaiquer, 7: Awá Kwaiker
Awá Kwaiker, 7
Awá, 7: Awá Kwaiker
Awaete, 7a
Awake, 7a: Urak
Awaketeco, 8: Awakateko
Awan, 3a
Awano, 7a
Awara, 2: Wantoat
Awareté, 7a: Parakanã
Awaruna, 7: Aguaruna
A'wé, 7: Shavante
Aweikoma, 7: Kaingáng; Xokléng
Aweke, 7a: Urak
Awetí, 7a
Awi, 9a
Awigaza, 1: Mandan
Awngi, 9a: Awi
Awori, 9: Yoruba
A'wwadat, 9: Peripatetics of Iraq . . .
    Yemen (Egypt)
Axe, 7: Ache
Axi, 6(C): Yi
Ayan, 9a: Bassari
A Yia, 6(C): Nu
Ayisyens, 8: Haitians
Aymara, 7
Ayo, 9a: Yao
Ayoreo, 7
Ayoreóde, 7: Ayoreo
Ayuuk, 8: Mixe
Ayyawar, 3a: Satani
Azande, 9: Zande
Azerbaijanis, 6(R): Azerbaijani
    Turks
Azerbaijani Turks, 6(R)
Azeris, 6(R): Azerbaijani Turks
Azna, 9: Hausa

Azoreans, 4
Aztec, 8: Nahua of the Huasteca

Ba'ale Mikra, 6(R): Karaites; 9:
    Karaites
Baatpétam_e, 7: Cinta Larga
Baba, 3: Sadhu
Babadjou, 9: Bamiléké
Babemba, 9: Bemba
Babhan, 3a
Baboo, 3: Bengali
Baboute, 9a
Babria, 3a
Babui, 7a: Hishkariana
Bacaeri, 7: Bakairi
Bacaery, 7: Bakairi
Bacairi, 7: Bakairi
Bacayri, 7: Bakairi
Bache, 9: Rukuba; 9a: Rukuba
Bachgoti, 3a
Bachhal, 3a: Bachhil
Bachhil, 3a
Backward Classes, 3: Scheduled Castes
    and Scheduled Tribes
Bacongo, 9a: Kongo
Badacar, 3: Badaga
Badaga, 3
Badager, 3: Badaga
Badahäla, 3a
Badahela, 3a: Badahäla
Baḏʾḏʾaaʾh, 9: Peripatetics of Iraq . . .
    Yemen (Egypt)
Baddagher, 3: Badaga
Baden, 9a: Kunema
Badhak, 3a
Badhi, 3a: Barhai
Badhik, 3a: Badhak
Badhoyi, 3a
Badi, 3a: Nat
Badjaw, 5: Bajau; Samal
Badondo, 9a: Kongo
Badyanesin, 9: Peripatetics of
    Afghanistan, Iran, and Turkey
    (Afghanistan)
Badyaranke, 9a
Bafang, 9: Bamiléké
Baffinland Inuit, 1
Bafou, 9: Bamiléké
Bafoussam, 9: Bamiléké
Baga, 9a
Baga-Binari, 9a: Baga
Baga Holeya, 3a: Bakkaru
Baga-Koga, 9a: Baga
Bagam, 9: Bamiléké
Bagata, 3a
Bagde Thakar, 3a: Thakar
Bagdi, 3a
Baggara, 9
Baggaru, 3a: Bakkaru
Baghdadi Jew, 3a
Baghel Rajput, 3a
Bagirmi, 9

Bagri, 3a: Badhak
Bagri, 3a: Bagdi
Bagri Rajput, 3a
Bagtit, 3a: Bagdi
Baha'is, 9
Bahalawan, 9: Peripatetics of Iraq . . .
    Yemen (Egypt and Sudan)
Bahamians, 8
Bahamians, 1: Black West Indians in
    the United States
Bahelia, 3a: Pardhi
Baheliya, 3a: Pardhi
Bahellia, 3a: Pardhi
Bahia Brazilians, 7: Afro–South
    Americans
Bahna, 3a
Bahrot, 3a: Bhatraja
Bahrot, 3a: Charan
Bahun, 3: Brahman and Chhetri of
    Nepal
Bahurupya, 3a: Telaga
Bai, 6(C)
Bai, 3a: Bai Rajput
Bāī, 9a: Beri
Bāī Cieguaje, 7: Siona-Secoya
Baidya, 3a
Baiga, 3
Baihong, 6(C): Hani
Baihuo, 6(C): Bai
Baikar, 3a: Gorait
Bailadeira, 3a: Devadasi
Bailne Kumbar, 3a: Ghisadi
Baima, 6(C): Qiang
Bai Man, 6(C): Bai
Bai Miao, 6(C) Miao
Baini, 6(C): Bai
Bairagi, 3a: Telaga
Bai Rajput, 3a
Baiswar, 3a
Baiti Kamara, 3a: Ghisadi
Baiyi, 6(C): Dai
Baizi, 6(C): Bai
Baizu, 6(C): Bai
Bagobo, 5
Bahau, 5: Kenyah-Kayan-Kajang
Bahnar, 5
Bahr, 5: Pear
Bai-yi, 5: Tai Lue
Bajania, 3a
Bajantri, 3a: Mangala
Bajao, 5: Samal
Bajau, 5
Bajau, 5: Samal; Selung/Moken
Bajau Laut, 5: Bajau
Bajg, 3a: Nat
Bajo, 5: Bajau
Baka, 9a
Baka, 9: Tropical-Forest Foragers
Bakaeri, 7: Bakairi
Bakaery, 7: Bakairi
Bakaire, 7: Bakairi
Bakairi, 7

Bakedi, **9a: Teso**
Bakhayo, 9a
Bakhayo, **9: Luyia**
Bakhtiari, 9
Bakkaru, 3a
Bakongo, **9: Kongo**
Bakta, **3a: Bagata**
Balagai, **3a: Holeya**
Balahar, **3a: Basor**
Balahi, 3a
Balai, **3a: Balahi**
Bala-Jangam, **3a: Mailari**
Balamiha, **8: Awakateko**
Balantak, 5
Balante, 9a
Balasantosha, **3a: Telaga**
Balatumani, **9: Peripatetics of
    Afghanistan, Iran, and Turkey**
    (Afghanistan)
Balé, **7a: Baré**
Bale, **9: Suri; 9a: Lendu**
Balearics, 4
Balija, 3a
Balinese, 5
Balji, **3a: Balija**
Balkars, 6(R)
Baloum, **9: Bamiléké**
Baloundou-Mbo, 9a
Balqar, **6(R): Balkars**
Balsapuertino, **7: Chayahuita**
Balte, **3a: Kuki**
Baluba, **9: Loba of Shaba**
Baluch, **3: Baluchi; 9: Peripatetics of
    Afghanistan, Iran, and Turkey**
    (Afghanistan)
Baluchi, 3
Balud, **5: Bilaan**
Baluga, **5: Agta; Philippine Negritos**
Balumbila, **9: Tonga**
Baluyia, **9: Luyia**
Bamaha, **9: Bamiléké**
Bamana, **9a: Bambara**
Bamaroteng, **9: Pedi**
Bambara, 9a
Bamcha, **3a: Bavacha**
Bamdendjina, **9: Bamiléké**
Bamendjou, **9: Bamiléké**
Bamenkoumbit, **9: Bamiléké**
Bamenyam, **9: Bamiléké**
Bamia, **9: Iteso**
Bamiléké, 9
Bamileke, 9a
Bam-Margi, 3a
Bamoun, 9a
Bana, **9: Bamiléké**
Banac, **1: Bannock**
Banajiga, **3a: Balija**
Banakwut, **1: Bannock**
Banana, **9a: Massa**
Banaphar, 3a
Banar, **2: Banaro**
Banara, **2: Banaro**

Banaro, 2
Banavá-Jafí, **7a: Banawá**
Banawá, 7a
Banda, 9a
Banda, **3a: Mondaru**
Bandar, **3a: Kadera**
Bandarwālā, **3: Qalandar**
Bandhalgoti, 3a
Bandhara, 3a
Bandhilgoti, **3a: Bandhalgoti**
Bandhugoti, **3a: Bandhalgoti**
Bandi, 3a
Bandi, 9a
Bandjoun, **9: Bamiléké**
Bang, **9a: Mambila**
Bangali, 3a
Bangali, **3: Bengali**
Bangangté, **9: Bamiléké**
Banggai, 5
Bangladeshi, **3: Bengali**
Bangladeshis, **1: South and Southeast
    Asians of the United States**
Bangoua, **9: Bamiléké**
Bangwa, **9: Bamiléké**
Bangwa-Fontem, **9: Bamiléké**
Bani, **3: Bania**
Bania, 3
Bania, **3a: Komati**
Banik, **3: Bania**
Banikar, **3: Bania**
Baniwa-Curripaco-Wakuenai, 7
Baniya, **3: Bania**
Banjara, 3a
Banjari, **3a: Banjara**
Banjhilgoti, **3a: Bandhalgoti**
Banjig, **3: Bania**
Bannock, **1: Northern Shoshone and
    Bannock**
Bansberia, **3a: Beria**
Bansi, **3a: Suraj-Bansi**
Bansphod, **3a: Basor**
Bansphor, **3a: Basor**
Bant, 3a
Bantu, **3a: Mutrasi**
Bantu Kavirondo, **9: Luyia**
Banua, **3a: Buna**
Banu Sasan, **9: Peripatetics of Iraq . . .
    Yemen** (Egypt)
Banyala, 9a
Banyala, **9: Luyia**
Banyamwezi, **9: Nyamwezi and Sukuma**
Banyaruanda, **9a: Nyaruanda**
Banyore, 9a
Banyore, **9: Luyia**
Banziri, 9a
Baori, **3a: Bawariya**
Baoria, **3a: Badhak**
Baoule, 9a
Bapedi, **9: Pedi**
Bapi, **9: Bamiléké**
Baqal, **3a: Komati**
Baqqara, **9: Baggara**

Baraan, **5: Bilaan**
Barahatta, **3a: Charan**
Barai, **3a: Tamdi**
Baraik, **3a: Ganda**
Baraiya, **3a: Tamdi**
Barama River Carib, 7
Bara Mohmand, **3a: Mohmand**
Barasana, 7a
Barasána, **7a: Barasana**
Barasono, **7a: Barasana**
Barath, **3a: Charan**
Baraua, **3a: Bhoi**
Barazana, **7a: Barasana**
Barbadians, 8
Barbari, **9: Aimaq**
Barchain, **3a: Chain**
Baré, 7a
Bare, **7a: Baré**
Barea, **9a: Nara**
Barekari, **3a: Besta**
Barelas, **3: Bhil**
Baretha, **3a: Dhobi**
Bargah, **3a: Bari**
Bargaha, **3a: Bari**
Bargahi, **3a: Bari**
Bargandi, **3a: Korava**
Bargi Dhangar, **3a: Hatkar**
Bargu, **9a: Bariba**
Bargujar, 3a
Barhai, 3a
Barhi, **3a: Barhai**
Bari, 3a
Barí, 7
Bari, **7: Barí; 9a: Beri**
Bariba, 9a
Barida, **7: Barí**
Barka, **9a: Baga**
Barkar, **3a: Besta**
Barma, 9a
Barmaki, **9: Peripatetics of Iraq . . .
    Yemen** (Egypt)
Barnaré, **7: Wayãpi**
Barnik, **3: Bania**
Barodia, **3a: Vitolana**
Barotse, **9: Lozi**
Barozi, **9: Lozi**
Barthapalya, **3: Nyinba**
Bartle Bay, **2: Wamira**
Baru, **5: Bru**
Barua Magh, **3a: Marma**
Barui, **3a: Tamdi**
Barutse, **9: Lozi**
Barwala, **3a: Batwal**
Barwar, 3a
Bascos, **1: Basques**
Basdewa, 3a
Bashilele, **9a: Lele**
Bashkirs, 6(R)
Bashkort, **6(R): Bashkirs**
Basiani, **6(R): Balkars**
Basman, **6(R): Balkars**
Basogna, 9a

Basonga, 9: Luyia
Basor, 3a
Basotho, 9: Pedi
Basques, 1; 4
Bassa, 9a
Bassari, 9a
Basseri, 9
Basters, 9: Cape Coloureds
Basuku, 9: Suku
Basukuma, 9: Nyamwezi and Sukuma
Basundi, 9a: Kongo
Batak, 5
Batak, 5: Philippine Negritos
Batatiyeh, 9: Peripatetics of Iraq . . .
    Yemen (Egypt)
Batawat, 1: Wiyot
Batcham, 9: Bamiléké
Batchingou, 9: Bamiléké
Batèk De', 5: Semang
Batèk Nòng, 5: Semang
Batgam, 3a
Bathudi, 3a: Bottada
Bathurst Islanders, 2: Tiwi
Bati, 9: Bamiléké
Batié, 9: Bamiléké
Batoka, 9: Tonga
Batonga, 9: Tonga
Batonu, 9a: Bariba
Batsotso, 9a
Batsotso, 9: Luyia
Batswana, 9: Tswana
Batta, 3: Pandit of Kashmir
Battu Turaka, 3a: Bhatraja
Batuku, 9a: Tuku
Batwal, 3a
Batzi Krisanoetike, 8: Tzotzil of
    Chamula
Batz'i vinik, 8: Tzotzil of San Andrés
    Larraínzar
Bau, 2
Baudó, 8: Emberá and Wounaan
Baul, 3
Baule, 9: Akan
Baure, 7
Bauri, 3a: Bawariya
Bauri, 3a: Bhoi
Bauria, 3a: Bawariya
Baurio, 3a: Bavuri
Bavacha, 3a
Bavarians, 4
Bavina, 3a: Bhavin
Bavuri, 3a
Bawaria, 3a: Badhak
Bawaria, 3a: Bawariya
Bawariya, 3a
Bawe, 9: Tonga
Baweanese, 5
Bawean Islanders, 5: Baweanese
Baya, 9a
Bayaka, 9: Suku
Baynawa, 9a: Guidar
Bayogoula, 1a

Baza, 9a: Kunema
Baza, 9a: Ngbandi
Bazigar, 3a: Nat
Bbadha, 9a: Lendu
Bearlake Indians, 1
Beaš, 4: Peripatetics
Beaver, 1
Bechuana, 9: Tswana
Bed, 3a: Bedar
Bedar, 3a
Bedawiye, 9a: Beja
Bedea, 3a: Bedar
Bedea, 7: Chocó
Bedia, 3a: Bedar
Bedia, 3a: Beria
Bediya, 3a: Bedar
Bediya, 3a: Beria
Bedouin, 9
Bedu, 9: Bedouin
Beesti, 3a: Bhishti
Beglopopovtsy, 6(R): Old Believers
Begundy, 6(R): Old Believers
Behara, 3a: Bhoi
Behna, 3a: Dhuniya
Beiço do Pau, 7a: Tapayuna
Beicos de Pau, 7: Suya
Beir, 9a: Murle
Beiyi, 6(C): Dai
Beja, 9a
Bejea, 3a: Bedar
Bejia, 3a: Bedar
Béké, 8: Martiniquais
Belarussians, 6(R)
Belarussian Siberians, 6(R): Siberiaki
Belau, 2
Beldar, 3a
Beldar, 3a: Upparwar
Belgians, 4
Belgians, 1: European-Americans;
    European-Canadians; 4: Flemish;
    Walloons
Belhoola, 1: Bella Coola
Believers, 1: Shakers
Belkyur, 6(R): Balkars
Bellabella, 1
Bella Coola, 1
Bellacoola, 1: Bella Coola
Bellacoola, 1: Bella Coola
Belokrinitsy, 6(R): Old Believers
Belorussians, 1: European-Americans;
    European-Canadians; 6(R):
    Belarussians
Belu, 5: Tetum
Bemba, 9; 9a
Bembe, 9: Kongo; 9a: Kongo
Bena, 9a
Bendar, 3a: Bedar; Madiga
Bendiren, 6(C): Mulam
Bendyapá, 7a
Bene Israel, 3
Benei Yisrael, 9: Samaritans
Bengalee, 3: Bengali
Bengali, 3

Bengali, 3a: Bangali
Bengali Shakta, 3
Bengali Vaishnava, 3
Benguetano, 5: Ibaloi
Benguet Igorot, 5: Ibaloi
Beni, 9a: Berta
Beni 'Ades, 9: Peripatetics of the
    Maghreb (Algeria)
Beni-Amer, 9a
Beni-Amer, 9a: Beja
Beni Bacchar, 9: Peripatetics of the
    Maghreb (Morocco)
Beni Hami, 9: Peripatetics of the
    Maghreb (Morocco)
Beni Israel, 3: Bene Israel
Benlong, 6(C): De'ang
Benren, 6(C): Wa
Bentbansi, 3a: Dharkar
Ben 'Zaa, 8: Zapotec
Beothuk, 1a
Berad, 3a: Bedar
Berava, 3a
Berba, 9a: Bariba
Berbers of Morocco, 9
Bergamasco, 4
Bergie, 3: Badaga
Beri, 9a
Beria, 3a
Beria, 3a: Bedar
Beriberi, 9: Aimaq
Beri-beri, 9: Kanuri
Beri Chetti, 3a
Beri Chuba, 5: Senoi
Berik, 2: Tor
Bering Sea Eskimos, 1: Central Yup'ik
    Eskimos
Beriya, 3a: Bedar
Beriya, 3a: Beria
Bermudians, 8
Berta, 9a
Berti, 9a
Bespopovtsy, 6(R): Old Believers
Besta, 3a
Bestha, 3a: Besta
Besuni, 9: Peripatetics of Iraq . . .
    Yemen (Sudan)
Beta Esráel, 9: Falasha
Bete, 9a
Betsileo, 9
Betta Kuruba, 3a: Urali
Betta Kurumba, 3a: Urali
Betta-Kurumbas, 3: Kurumbas
Bettu Kurumba, 3a: Urali
Bez-Carne, 9: Peripatetics of the
    Maghreb (Morocco)
Bhabra, 3a
Bhadauriya, 3a
Bhadbhunja, 3a: Bharbhunja
Bhadrapad, 3a: Viramushti
Bhadri, 3a: Joshi
Bhagalia, 3: Bhil
Bhagat, 3a

Bhagwat, **3a: Telaga**
Bhaina, 3a
Bhakat, **3a: Bhagat**
Bhakta, **3a: Bagata**
Bhaktollu, **3a: Pichakuntala**
Bhale Sultan, 3a
Bhaluwālā, **3: Qalandar**
Bhamta, 3a
Bhamtya, **3a: Bhamta**
Bhand, **3a: Bhandari**
Bhandari, 3a
Bhandari, **3a: Nai**
Bhangi, 3a
Bhangia, **3a: Bhangi**
Bhanr, **3a: Bhandari**
Bhaosar, **3a: Chhipa**
Bhar, 3a
Bhar, **3a: Bharia**
Bharadi, **3a: Davre Jogi**
Bharadwaj, **3a: Bhar**
Bharai, 3a
Bharat, **3a: Bhar**
Bharbhunja, 3a
Bharia-Bhumia, **3a: Bharia**
Bharewa, **3a: Tamera**
Bharia, 3a
Bharpatwa, **3a: Bhar**
Bharvad, **3a: Gadaria**
Bhat, 3a
Bhat, **3a: Bhatraja**
Bhatia, 3a
Bhatiya, **3a: Bhatia**
Bhatiyara, 3a
Bhat Murti, **3a: Bhatraja**
Bhato, **3a: Bhatraja**
Bhatra, 3a
Bhatra, **3a: Ramaiya**
Bhatraja, 3a
Bhatraju, **3a: Bhatraja**
Bhatrazu, **3a: Bhat; Bhatraja**
Bhatt, **3a: Bhat**
Bhatta, **3: Pandit of Kashmir**
Bhattadiripad, **3: Nambudiri Brahman**
Bhatti, 3a
Bhattra, **3a: Bhatra**
Bhatwandlu, **3a: Bhatraja**
Bhausagar, **3a: Chhipa**
Bhavaguna, **3a: Bhandari**
Bhavaiya, 3a
Bhavasagari, **3a: Chhipa**
Bhavaya, **3a: Bhandari**
Bhavin, 3a
Bhavsar, **3a: Chhipa**
Bhenrihar, **3a: Gadaria**
Bhiksha Kunte, **3a: Kunte**
Bhikshuk, **3a: Deshastha Brahman**
Bhil, 3
Bhilala, 3a
Bhilala, **3: Bhil**
Bhil-Grasia Bhomia, **3: Grasia**
Bhillakabberu, **3a: Besta**
Bhil Mina, **3a: Mina**

Bhind, **3a: Bind**
Bhisak, **3a: Baidya**
Bhishti, 3a
Bhisti, **3a: Bhishti**
Bhod, **3a: Bhutia**
Bhogam, **3a: Devadasi**
Bhoi, 3a
Bhoir, 3a: Bhoyar
Bhoksa, 3a
Bholia, **3a: Bhulia**
Bholwa, **3a: Bhulia**
Bhondari, **3a: Bhandari**
Bhopa, **3a: Rabari**
Bhope, **3a: Bhute**
Bhoriya, **3a: Bhulia**
Bhot, **3a: Bhutia**
Bhote, **3: Bhutanese**
Bhotia, **3: Bhutanese; Nyinba; 3a:**
    Bhutia; 6(C): Tibetans
Bhotiya, **3a: Bhutia**
Bhottada, **3a: Bottada**
Bhoyar, 3a
Bhui, **3: Bhuiya**
Bhuihar, **3: Bhuiya**
Bhuimali, **3a: Bhuinmali; Hari**
Bhuinhar, **3a: Babhan**
Bhuinmali, 3a
Bhuiya, 3
Bhuiya, **3: Baiga**
Bhuiya Magh, **3a: Marma**
Bhuiyar, **3: Bhuiya**
Bhuj, **3a: Bharbhunja**
Bhujari, **3a: Bharbhunja**
Bhujua, **3a: Bharbhunja**
Bhuksa, **3a: Bhoksa**
Bhulia, 3a
Bhumanchi Reddi, **3: Reddi**
Bhumia, 3: Baiga, Bhuiya
Bhumiaraja, **3: Baiga**
Bhumij, **3: Baiga, Munda**
Bhumija, **3: Baiga**
Bhumijan, **3: Baiga**
Bhumiya, **3: Bhuiya**
Bhunjia, 3a
Bhurji, **3a: Bharbhunja**
Bhusundar, **3a: Bhuinmali**
Bhutanese, 3
Bhutanese, **1: South and Southeast**
    Asians of the United States
Bhute, 3a
Bhutia, 3a
Bhutia, **3: Bhutanese; Nyinba**
Biadju, **5: Kalimantan Dayaks**
Bianco Cabécar, **8: Boruca, Bribri, and**
    Cabécar
Biar, 3a
Bias, **3a: Gujarati Brahman**
Biate, **3a: Kuki**
Bibo, **2: Gebusi**
Bidakamtata, **1: Pomo**
Bidayuh, **5: Kalimantan Dayaks**
Bïdé, **7: Arawaté**

Bideyat, **9a: Beri**
Bidur, **3a: Vidur**
Biete, **3a: Kuki**
Bihari, 3
Bijishti, **3a: Bhishti**
Bikini, 2
Bikini, **2: Marshall Islands**
Bikyek, **9a: Bassa**
Bilaan, 5
Bilanes, **5: Bilaan**
Bileki, **2: Lak**
Bilen, 9a
Bilimagga, **3a: Bili Maggar**
Bili Maggar, 3a
Billava, 3a
Billava, **3a: Hale Paika**
Billoru, **3a: Billava**
Billoru, **3a: Hale Paika**
Billuvaru, **3a: Hale Paika**
Biloxi, **1a**
Bilqula, **1: Bella Coola**
Bin, **3a: Bind**
Binandele, **2: Orokaiva**
Bind, 3a
Bindu, **3a: Bind**
Binei Mikra, **6(R): Karaites; 9:**
    Karaites
Binga, 9a
Bini, **9: Edo; 9a: Edo-Speaking Peoples**
Binii Gula'sa', **8: Zapotec**
Binjhal, **3a: Binjhwar**
Binjhia, **3a: Binjhwar**
Binjhoa, **3a: Binjhwar**
Binjhwar, 3a
Binna, **9a: Yungur**
Binokid, **5: Bukidnon**
Bintukua, 7a
Binukid, **5: Bukidnon**
Biotu, **9a: Isoko**
Biotu, **9a: Urhobo**
Biraan, **5: Bilaan**
Birar, **6(R): Evenki**
Birhor, 3a
Birhor, **3: Munda**
Birhul, **3a: Birhor**
Birifor, **9: Lobi-Dagarti Peoples**
Birjia, **3a: Binjhwar**
Birom, 9a
Bisaya, 5
Bisaya, **5: Visayan**
Bisayan, **5: Visayan**
Bisen, 3a
Bishnoi, 3a
Bitso, **6(C): Dai**
Biwat, **2: Mundugumor**
Biyar, **3a: Biar**
Biyue, **6(C): Hani**
Bizika, **6(C): Tujia**
Bizka, **6(C): Tujia**
Black Americans, **1: African Americans**
Black Benglong, **6(C): De'ang**
Black Brazilians, **7: Afro-Brazilians**

Black Carib, 8: Garifuna
Black Coes, 1: American Isolates
Black Creoles, 1: Black Creoles of
    Louisiana
Black Creoles of Louisiana, 1
Blackfoot, 1
Black French, 1: Black Creoles of
    Louisiana
Black Indians, 7: Afro–South
    Americans
Black Jews, 3: Cochin Jew
Black Lisu, 6(C): Lisu
Black Maures, 9a
Black Portuguese, 4: Cape Verdeans
Blacks, 1: Blacks in Canada; 7:
    Afro–South Americans
Blacks in Canada, 1
Blacks of Costa Rica, 8
Blacksmith Tatars, 6(C): Shors
**Black West Indians in the United
    States, 1**
Blan, 3: Mauritian
Blang, 6(C)
Blann, 5: Bilaan
Blimo, 2: Miyanmin
Blood, 1: Blackfoot
Blue Muds, 1: Nez Percé
Bngala, 9a
Bo, 6(C): Bai
Boadzi, 2: Boazi
Boanari, 7: Waimiri-Atroari
Boazi, 2
Bobo, 9a
Bobo Dioula, 9a: Bobo
Bobo Fing, 9a: Bobo
Bodo, 3a: Kachari
Bodpa, 6(C): Tibetans
Boe, 7: Bororo
Boeginneezen, 5: Bugis
Bofi, 9: Tropical-Forest Foragers
Bogam, 3a: Devadasi
Bogos, 9a: Bilen
Bogotá, 8: Bugle
Bohémiens, 4: Peripatetics
Bohora, 3a
Bohora, 3: Bohra
Bohra, 3
Bohra, 3a: Bohora
Bois Brulé, 1: Metis of Western Canada
Bokar, 3: Abor
Boker, 3a: Adi
Bokhi Ludi, 1: Doukhobors
Boko, 9a: Busa
Bokobaru, 9a: Busa
Bokoruge, 9a: Daju
Bokotá, 8: Bugle
Bola, 9a: Mancagne
Bolaang Mongondow, 5
Bole, 9a: Bolewa
Bolewa, 9a
Bolongan, 5: Tidong
Boloven, 5: Loven

Boma-Kasai, 9a: Boma-Sakata
Bomalatavallu, 3a: Killekyata
Boma-Murle, 9a: Murle
Boma-Sakata, 9a
Bombe Atadavaru, 3a: Killekyata
Bonan, 6(C)
Bonari, 7: Waimiri-Atroari
Bondei, 9a
Bondo, 3
Bondo Gadaba, 3: Bondo
Bone Indians, 1: Osage
Bonerate, 5
Bonerif, 2: Tor
Bonga, 9a: Mboshi
Bongo, 9a
Bongo, 9: Tropical-Forest Foragers
Bonom, 5: Bahnar; Monom
Bonthuk, 3a
Bonthuk Savareau, 3a: Bonthuk
Bontoc, 5: Bontok
Bontoc Igorot, 5: Bontok
Bontok, 5
Boolaang-Mongondonese, 5: Bolaang
    Mongondow
Bora, 7a
Boran, 9a
Borana, 9a: Oromo
Borekar, 3a: Gopal
Bori, 3: Abor
Bori, 3a: Adi
Bornu, 9: Kanuri
Boro, 7a: Bora
Boro-Boro, 3a: Kachari
Borodda, 9a: Wolayta
Boro Muinane, 7a: Bora
Bororo, 7
Bororodjis, 9a
Bororo'en, 9: Fulani
Bororo Fulani, 9a: Bororodjis
Boruca, 7a: Payawá
Boruca, 8: Boruca, Bribri, and Cabécar
Boruca, Bribri, and Cabécar, 8
Borul, 3a
Bosavi, 2: Kaluli
Bosha, 9: Peripatetics of Afghanistan,
    Iran, and Turkey (Turkey)
Bosnian Muslims, 4
Bot, 3a: Bhutia
Botocudos, 7: Xokléng
Bottada, 3a
Boubangui, 9a: Mboshi
Boumpe, 9: Mende; 9a: Mende
Bourguignons, 4: Burgundians
Bouyei, 6(C)
Boya, 1: Pomo; 3a: Bedar; 9a:
    Longarim
Boyanese, 5: Baweanese
Boyar, 3a
Boyi, 6(C): Dai
Bozi, 6(C): Bai
Braba, 1: Taos
Brahma Kshatri, 3a

Brahman, 3
Brahman, 3: Pandit of Kashmir
Brahman and Chhetri of Nepal, 3
Brahui, 3
Brame, 9a: Mancagne
Brancararú, 7a: Pankararú
Brandywine, 1: American Isolates
Brao, 5
Brassa, 9a: Balante
Brass Ankles, 1: American Isolates
Brat, 2: Mejbrat; 6(R): Buriats
Bratsk, 6(R): Buriats
Brava, 4: Cape Verdeans
Brazilian Negroes, 7: Afro-Brazilians
Breizhiz, 4: Bretons
Bretoned, 4: Bretons
Bretons, 4
Briars, 1: Appalachians
Bribri, 8: Boruca, Bribri, and Cabécar
Bribriwak Bribri, 8: Boruca, Bribri, and
    Cabécar
Brijia, 3a: Binjhwar
Brinjara, 3a: Banjara
British, 4: Northern Irish
Brong, 9: Akan; 9a: Abron
Brotherton, 1: Mahican
Brown People, 1: American Isolates
Bru, 5
B'ru, 5: Bru
Bruinmense, 9: Cape Coloureds
Brunca Boruca, 8: Boruca, Bribri, and
    Cabécar
Bruneians, 1: South and Southeast
    Asians of the United States
Brunka Boruca, 8: Boruca, Bribri, and
    Cabécar
Buban, 6(C): Zhuang
Bube Ediya, 9a: Bubis
Bubis, 9a
Budaga, 3: Badaga
Budai, 6(C): Zhuang
Budbudki, 3a: Joshi
Buddager, 3: Badaga
Buddagur, 3: Badaga
Buddhist, 5
Budip, 5: Stieng
Budong, 6(C): Zhuang
Budubudiki, 3a: Joshi
Budubudikke, 3a: Joshi
Budubudukala, 3a: Joshi
Budubudukki, 3a: Joshi
Buduma, 9a
Buganda, 9: Ganda
Buginese, 5: Bugis
Bugis, 5
Bugle, 8
Buglere, 8: Bugle
Bugré, 7: Xokléng
Bui, 3: Bhuiya
Buitenlandse Zigeuners, 4: Gypsies
    and Caravan Dwellers in the
    Netherlands

Buka, 2: Kurtatchi
Bukekari, 3a: Atari
Bukharan Jews, 6(R)
Bukharskie Evrei, 6(R): Bukharan Jews
Buki, 5: Sulod
Bukidnon, 5
Bukidnon, 5: Sulod
Bukiyip, 2: Mountain Arapesh
Bukovynians, 1: Ukrainians of Canada
Bukueta, 8: Bugle
Bukusu, 9a
Bukusu, 9: Luyia
Bulahar, 3a: Basor
Bulalakao, 5: Hanunóo
Bulanda, 9a: Balante
Bulebule, 9a: Amba
Bulgar, 6(R): Balkars
Bulgarian Gypsies, 4
Bulgarian Muslims, 4: Pomaks
Bulgarians, 4
Bulgarini, 4: Bulgarians
Bulgaro-Mohamedanin, 4: Pomaks
Bulgars, 4: Bulgarians
Bulghar, 6(R): Volga Tatars
Bulibuzi, 9a
Bulong, 6(C): Zhuang
Buluan, 5: Bilaan
Buman, 6(C): Zhuang
Bumin, 6(C): Zhuang
Buna, 3a
Buna, 6(C): Zhuang
Bundela Rajput, 3a
Bundeli Bhoi, 3a: Bhoi
Bungee, 1: Ojibwa
Bungi, 1: Ojibwa
Bungu, 9a: Bongo
Bunjawa, 9: Hausa
Bunlap, 2: Pentecost
Buno, 3a: Buna
Bunong, 6(C): Zhuang
Bunt, 3a: Bant
Bunun, 5
Bupian, 6(C): Zhuang
Burakumin, 5
Burga, 3: Badaga
Burgenländer, 4: Austrians
Burgher, 3: Badaga
Burgundians, 4
Buriaad, 6(R): Buriats
Buriat-Mongol, 6(R): Buriats
Buriats, 6(R)
Burkeneji, 9a: Samburu
Burmans, 5: Burmese
Burmese, 5
Burmese, 1: South and Southeast
     Asians of the United States
Burmese Shan, 5: Shan
Burol, 3a: Borul
Buruburá, 7a: Puruborá
Burud, 3a: Basor
Burum, 3: Purum
Burun, 9a: Uduk

Burusho, 3
Busa, 9a
Bush Cree, 1: Cree, Western Woods
Bushenege, 7: Afro–South Amerians
Bush Mekeo, 2: Mekeo
Bush Negroes, 7: Afro–South
     Americans; Saramaka
Bushuang, 6(C): Zhuang
Bushwhackers, 1: American Isolates
Butam, 2: Lak
Bute, 9a: Baboute
Butia, 3a: Bhutia
Butona, 2: Ambae
Butonese, 5
Butu, 6(C): Zhuang
Buyang, 6(C): Zhuang
Buyue, 6(C): Zhuang
Bwaidoka, 2: Goodenough Island
Byas Brahman, 3a: Gujarati Brahman
Byau Min, 6(C): Yao
Byelorussians, 1: European-Americans;
     European-Canadians; 6(R):
     Belarussians

Caaguá, 7: Paï-Tavytera
Cabécar, 8: Boruca, Bribri, and
     Cabécar
Cabeças Secas, 7a: Gavião
Cabiyari, 7: Ka'wiari
Cacataibo, 7: Cashibo
Caca Weranos, 7: Chimila
Cachibo, 7: Cashibo
Cacibo, 7: Cashibo
Caddo, 1
Caddoquis, 1: Caddo
Cadiguebo, 7: Kadiwéu
Caduveo, 7: Kadiwéu
Caduvéo, 7: Kadiwéu
Caduví, 7: Kadiwéu
Caffre, 9: Xhosa
Cafre, 9: Xhosa
Cafucos, 7: Afro–South Americans
Cágaba, 7: Kogi
Caguachi, 7: Yagua
Cahahaguillas, 1: Cahuilla
Cahita, 8
Cahita, 8: Yaqui
Cahivo, 7: Cashibo
Cahto, 1: Wailaki
Cahuapa, 7: Chayahuita
Cahuarano, 7a: Kawarano
Cahuilla, 1
Cahunari, 7: Yagua
Caiapô, 7: Gorotire
Caigua, 1: Kiowa
Caimbé, 7a: Kaimbé
Caingáng, 7: Kaingáng
Caingang of Santa Catarina, 7: Xokléng
Caingua, 7: Paï-Tavytera
Caiwá, 7: Paï-Tavytera
Cajans, 1: American Isolates
Cajuns, 1

Cakchiquel, 8: Kaqchikel
Calabar, 9a: Efik
Calabrese, 4
Calabrians, 4: Calabrese
Calagan, 5: Kalagan
Calamox, 1: Tillamook
Calapooya, 1: Kalapuya
Calavantina, 3a: Devadasi
Calender, 3a: Chhipa
Caliana, 7a: Sapé
Calinga, 5: Kalingas
Callagaes, 7: Toba
Callahuaya, 7
Callawaya, 7: Callahuaya
Calusa, 1a
Camaragoto, 7: Pemon
Camayura, 7a: Kamayurá
Camba, 7: Campa
Cambodian, 5: Khmer
Cambodians, 1: South and Southeast
     Asians of Canada; South and
     Southeast Asians of the United
     States
Camileroi, 2: Kamilaroi
Camminanti, 4: Peripatetics
Campa, 7
Campa del Alto Perené, 7: Campa
Campa del Pichis, 7: Campa
Campiti, 7: Campa
Camsa, 7a: Kamsá
Camucones, 5: Tidong
Canamari, 7a: Kanamarí
Canaque, 2: Ajië
Canarese, 3: Kanarese
Canarians, 4
Canary Islanders, 4: Canarians
Candoshi, 7
Canela, 7
Canella, 7: Canela
Canelo, 7: Canelos Quichua
Canelos, 7: Canelos Quichua
Canelos Quichua, 7
Canineqmiut, 1: Central Yup'ik
     Eskimos
Canoê, 7a: Kanoé
Canoe Indians, 1: Mahican
Canoeiro, 7: Rikbaktsa; 7a: Avá-
     Canoeiro
Canpo piyapi, 7a: Chayawita
los Cantoneses, 8: Chinese of Costa
     Rica
Capanahua, 7a: Kapanawa
Capapacho, 7: Cashibo
Cape Coloureds, 9
Cape Indians, 1: Massachuset
Cape Verdeans, 4
Cape York Inuit, 1: Inughuit
Capiekrans, 7: Canela
Capishana, 7a: Kanoé
Capohn, 7: Akawaio
Caposhó, 7: Maxakali
Capuruchano, 7: Pume

Caquinte, **7: Campa**
Carabayo, **7a: Karabayo**
Carabere, **7: Guarayu; Pauserna**
Caracaty, **7: Krikati/Pukobye**
Carajá, **7: Karajá**
Carajuwa, **7a: Oyampi**
Carapana, **7a: Karapana**
Carapoto, **7a: Tingi**
Caratiana, **7a: Karitiana**
Caravaya, **7a: Kayuvava**
Carib, **7: Barama River Carib; Cariña; 7a: Galibí**
Caribe, **7: Cariña**
Carib of Dominica, 8
Caribou Inuit, 1
Carifuna, **8: Carib of Domninica**
Carijona, **7: Karihona**
Cariña, 7
Carinña, **7: Maroni Carib**
Carinya, **7: Cariña**
Cariri, **7a: Kiriri**
Carmel Indians, **1: American Isolates**
Carnijó, **7: Fulniô**
Carolinians, **1: Micronesians**
Carpatho-Russians, **1: European-Americans**
Carpatho-Rusyns, 6(R)
Carpatho-Rusyns, **1: European-Americans**
Carpatho-Ukrainians, **1: European-Americans**
Carrier, 1
Casca, **1: Kaska**
Cashibo, 7
Cashinahua, **7: Kashinawa**
Cashiniti, **7a: Paresí**
Cashquiha, **7a: Chane**
Casibo, **7: Cashibo**
Cassia, **3: Khasi**
Cassubians, **4: Kashubians**
Castee, **3: Anglo-Indian**
Castilians
Castors, **1: Beaver**
Catalans (Països Catalans), 4
Catalonians, **4: Catalans (Països Catalans)**
Catarinos, **8: Tzotzil and Tzeltal of Pantelhó**
Catauixi, **7a: Katawishí**
Catawba, 1
Catio, **7: Chocó**
Catío, **7: Emberá; 8: Emberá and Wounaan**
Catru, **8: Emberá and Wounaan**
Cattle Ranchers of the Huasteca, 8
Catuquina, **7a: Katukina**
Cau Ma, **5: Ma**
Caumari, **7: Yagua**
Cauwachi, **7: Yagua**
Cavachi, **7: Yagua**
Caviña, **7a: Kavinenya**
Caxibo, **7: Cashibo**

Cayabí, **7a: Kayabí**
Cayapa, **7a: Kayapa**
Cayapô, **7: Gorotire**
Cayapo del Sur, **7: Xokléng**
Cayman Islanders, 8
Cayua, **7: Kadiwéu**
Cayubaba, **7a: Kayuvava**
Cayuga, 1
Cayuse, 1; 1a
Cěch, **4: Czechs**
Celtic, **4: Highland Scots**
Celts, **4: Gaels (Irish); Highland Scots; Northern Irish**
Ceni, **1: Caddo**
Central Americans, **1: Latinos**
Central Kankanaey, **5: Kankanai**
Central Liba, **9: Luba of Shaba**
Central Moluccans, **5: Ambonese**
Central Thai, 5
Central Togo, 9a
Central Yup'ik Eskimos, 1
Cere, **8: Seri**
Čergaša, **4: Xoraxané Romá**
Ceri, **8: Seri**
Cerracuna, **7: Cuna**
Češi, **4: Czechs**
Chaai, **9: Suri**
Chachi, **7a: Kayapa**
Chacktaws, **1: Choctaw**
Chácobo, 7
Chadar, 3a
Chaga, **9: Chagga**
Chagga, 9
Chahar Aimaq, **9: Aimaq**
Chai, **3a: Chain**
Chain, 3a
Chaini, **3a: Chain**
Chakala, **3a: Dhobi**
Chakes, **7: Yukpa**
Chaki, **3a: Teli**
Chakkan, 3a
Chakkiliyan, 3a
Chakkiyar, **3a: Ambalavasi**
Chakla, **3a: Dhobi**
Chakma, 3
Chalaque, **1: Cherokee**
Chalavadi, **3a: Holeya**
Chaldeans, 9
Chaldeans, **1: Arab Americans; 9: Assyrians**
Chalia, **3a: Salagama**
Chaliyan, 3a
Challi, **9: Peripatetics of Afghanistan, Iran, and Turkey (Iran)**
Chalu, **9: Peripatetics of Afghanistan, Iran, and Turkey (Afghanistan)**
Chalvadi, **3a: Holeya**
Cham, 5
Chama, **7: Shipibo**
Chamacoco, 7
Chamano, **7: Chimane**

Chamar, **3: Jatav**
Chamar Gaur, **3a: Gaur Rajput**
Chamba, 9a
Chambhar, **3a: Madiga; Mochi**
Chambira, **7a: Urarina**
Chambri, 2
Chambuli, **2: Chambri**
Chamí, **7: Emberá; 7a: Tadó**
Chami, **8: Emberá and Wounaan**
Chamikuro, 7a
Chamila, **7: Chimila**
Chammar, **3a: Mochi**
Chamo', **8: Tzotzil of Chamula**
Chamorros, 2
Chamorros, **1: Micronesians**
Chamula, **8: Tzotzil of Chamula**
Chanabal, **8: Tojolab'al**
Chañabal, **8: Tojolab'al**
Chanco, **7: Chocó; Noanamá**
Chandal, 3a
Chandal, **3a: Madiga**
Chandala, **3a: Chandal**
Chandel Rajput, 3a
Chandos, **3a: Durava**
Chandravedi, **3a: Sanaurhia**
Chane, 7a
Chaneabal, **8: Tojolab'al**
Chang, **3a: Chandal**
Chang, **3: Nagas**
Changar, **9: Peripatetics of Afghanistan, Iran, and Turkey (Afghanistan)**
Changi, **9: Peripatetics of Afghanistan, Iran, and Turkey (Iran)**
Changma, **3: Chakma**
Changsan, **3a: Kuki**
Ch'ani, **6(R): Laz**
Channewar, **3a: Padma Sale**
Chanral, **3a: Chandal**
Chanura Malla, **3a: Jetti**
Chaobon, 5
Chao Dol, **5: T'in**
Chaolay, **5: Sea Nomads of the Andaman**
Chaouanons, **1: Shawnee**
Chapara, **7: Candoshi**
Chaplintsy, **6(R): Asiatic Eskimos**
Chapparband, **3a: Chhapparband**
Chapra, **7: Candoshi**
Chaqi, **3a: Teli**
Chaquita, **1: Choctaw**
Charan, 3a
Charandasi, 3a
Chareshmal, **9: Peripatetics of Afghanistan, Iran, and Turkey (Iran)**
Charfarda, 9a
Charhoa, **3a: Chhipa**
Chasa, 3a
Chasadhoba, 3a
Chasadhopa, **3a: Chasadhoba**

Chascosa, 7: Campa
Chashan, 6(C): Jingpo
Chasi, 3a: Pod
Chasi-Das, 3a: Kewat
Chasovennye, 6(R): Old Believers
Chassidim, 1: Hasidim
Chastacosta, 1; 1a
Chatali, 3a: Satani
Chatani, 3a: Satani
Chatino, 8
Chat-Kas, 1: Choctaw
Chatla, 3a
Cha'tno, 8: Chatino
Chattri, 3a: Kawar
Chaudhri, 3a
Chaudriji, 3a: Babhan
Chauhan, 3a
Chauhan Rajput, 3a
Chavante, 7: Shavante
Chavash, 6(R): Chuvash
Chavchuvans, 6(R): Koryaks and
    Kerek
Chawaska, 1a
Chawí, 7: Chayahuita
Chawiyana, 7a: Hishkariana
Chayabita, 7: Chayahuita
Chayahuita, 7
Chayavita, 7: Chayahuita
Chayawita, 7a
Chayawita, 7: Chayahuita
Chayenne, 1: Cheyenne
Chayhuita, 7: Chayahuita
Chebero, 7: Jebero
Chechen, 6(R): Chechen-Ingush
Chechen-Ingush, 6(R)
Che'e Foka, 1: Pomo
Cheenook, 1: Cheyenne
Chehalis, 1
Cheke, 9a: Gude
Chelan, 1: Columbia
Chelofes, 9: Wolof
Chemehuevi, 1: Southern Paiute (and
    Chemehuevi)
Chenanesmá, 7: Angaité
Chenchu, 3
Che-nung, 5: Lisu
Chenva, 3a: Sindhava
Cheraqui, 1: Cherokee
Cheremis, 6(R): Maris
Cherente, 7: Sherente
Cherkess, 6(R): Circassians
Chernyye klobuki, 6(R): Karakalpaks
Chero, 3a
Cherokee, 1
Cherokees, 1: Lumbee
Cherry Island, 2: Anuta
Cheru, 3a: Chero
Cheruma, 3a: Cheruman
Cheruman, 3a
Cherumukkal, 3a: Cheruman
Cherwa, 3a: Kawar
Chet-Rami, 3a

Chetti, 3a
Chetti, 3a: Komati
Chetty, 3a: Chetti; Komati
Chewa, 9a
Chewaere, 1: Oto
Chewara, 3a: Kawar
Che Wong, 5: Senoi
Cheyenne, 1
Chhalapdar, 3a
Chhalya, 3a: Kuki
Chhapagar, 3a: Chhipa
Chhapgar, 3a: Chhipa
Chhapparband, 3a
Chhatri, 3a: Khatri; Killekyata
Chhazang, 3a
Chhetri, 3a: Khetri
Chhimba, 3a: Chhipa
Chhimpi, 3a: Chhipa
Chhipa, 3a
Chhipi, 3a: Chhipa; Darzi
Chhota Sahib, 3: Europeans in South
    Asia
Chhutar, 3a: Sutradhar
Chibcha, 7a
Chibemba, 9: Bemba; 9a: Bemba
Chibh, 3a
Chicana, 7: Hoti
Chicano, 7: Hoti
Chicanos, 1: Latinos
Chicao, 7a: Chikão; Txikão
Chickahominy Indians, 1: American
    Isolates
Chickasaw, 1
Chicots, 1: Metis of Western Canada
Chicri, 7: Xikrin
Chien, 1: Cheyenne
Chighalbf, 9: Peripatetics of
    Afghanistan, Iran, and Turkey
    (Afghanistan)
Chigogo, 9a: Gogo
Chik, 3a: Ganda
Chikano, 7: Hoti
Chikão, 7a
Chikão, 7a: Txikão
Chikáon, 7a: Txikão
Chikapu, 8: Kikapu
Chikito, 7: Chiquitano
Chikitsak, 3a: Baidya
Ch'i-lao, 6(C): Gelao
Chil-Baraik, 3a: Ganda
Chilcotin, 1
Chiluvale, 9a: Lovalle
Chimakonde, 9a: Makonde
Chimane, 7
Chimanis, 7: Chimane
Chimanisa, 7: Chimane
Chimariko, 1a
Chimatengo, 9a: Matengo
Chimaviha, 9a: Mawia
Chimbu, 2
Chimere, 7: Saliva
Chimero, 7: Saliva

Chimila, 7
Chimile, 7: Chimila
Chimmesyan, 1: Tsimshian
Chimnisin, 7: Chimane
Chimwera, 9a: Mwera
Chin, 3
Chinantec, 8
Chinbok, 3: Chin
Chinbon, 3: Chin
Chinese, 1: East Asian of Canada; East
    Asians of the United States; 6(C):
    Han; 7: Asians in South America
Chinese in the English-Speaking
    Caribbean, 8
Chinese in Southeast Asia, 5
Chinese Muslims, 6(C): Hui
Chinese of Costa Rica, 8
Chinese of South Asia, 3
Chinese of Southeast Asia, 1: South and
    Southeast Asians of Canada;
    South and Southeast Asians of the
    United States
Chinese Royal, 8: Chinese in the
    English-Speaking Caribbean
Chinese Shan, 5: Shan
Chingana, 9: Peripatetics of Iraq . . .
    Yemen (Egypt)
Chingathan, 3a
Ching-po, 3a: Singpho
Chini, 3: Chinese of South Asia
Chin Nation, 1: Lillooet
Chinook, 1
los Chinos, 8: Chinese of Costa Rica
Chinyanja, 9a: Nyanja
Chipaya, 7
Chipayne, 1: Lipan Apache
Chipeo, 7: Shipibo
Chipewyan, 1
Chipolgolo, 9a: Pogoro
Chipollu, 3a: Darzi
Chippewa, 1: Ojibwa
Chiquimitica, 7: Baure
Chiquitano, 7
Chirauánga, 7a: Siriano
Chiriabá, 7a: Shakriabá
Chiricahua, 1
Chiricoa, 7: Guahibo-Sikuani
Chiriguano, 7
Chiriguano, 7: Guarayu
Chiru, 3a: Kuki
Chisena, 9a: Sena
Chishti, 3a
Chishtiya, 3a: Chishti
Chita Pardhi, 3a: Pardhi
Chitari, 3a: Jingar
Chiter, 3a: Jingar
Chitevari, 3a: Mochi
Chitimacha, 1; 1a
Chitpavan Brahman, 3
Chitra-Gottineke, 1: Mountain
Chitrakar, 3a: Jingar; Mochi
Chitrakathi, 3a

Chitrali, 3a
Chívari, 7: Jivaro
Chiwaro, 7: Jivaro
Chiwemba, 9: Bemba
Chocama, 7: Chocó; Noanamá; 8: Emberá and Wounaan
Chocho, 8
Chochol, 8: Chocho
Chocholteca, 8: Chocho
Chochón, 8: Chocho
Chocho-Popolocan, 8: Chocho
Chochoteco, 8: Chocho
Chocó, 7
Chocó, 7: Emberá; 7a: Shokó; 8: Emberá and Wounaan
Choctaw, 1
Chodhara, 3a: Chodhra
Chodhra, 3a
Choiseul Island, 2
Choko, 7a: Tadó; 8: Emberá and Wounaan
Chokwe, 9a
Ch'ol, 8
Chol, 8: Ch'ol
Cholo, 7: Chocó; Emberá
Cholotí, 8: Ch'orti'
Chong, 5
Chongloi, 3a: Kuki
Chono, 8: Chocho
Chontal, 8: Tequistlatec
Chontales, 8: Chontal of Tabasco
Chontal Maya, 8: Chontal of Tabasco
Chontal Mayan, 8: Chontal of Tabasco
Chontal of Oaxaca, 8: Tequistlatec
Chontal of Tabasco, 8
Chontalpa, 8: Tequistlatec
Chonyi, 9: Mijikenda
Chopi, 9a
Chopunnish, 1: Nez Percé
Chori, 7: Siriono; Yuki
Chorote, 7
Choroti, 7: Chorote
Chorté, 8: Ch'orti'
Ch'orti', 8
Chortí, 8: Ch'orti'
Chosŏn, 5: Korean
Chothe, 3a: Kuki
Chrau, 5
Christians of St. Thomas, 3: Syrian Christian of Kerala
Chucho, 8: Chocho
Chuchón, 8: Chocho
Chuckler, 3a: Chakkiliyan
Chudbudki Joshi, 3a: Joshi
Chuhra, 3a: Bhangi
Chuj, 8
Chukchee, 6(R)
Chukchi, 6(R): Chukchee
Chulikata Mishmi, 3a: Mishmi
Chulupí, 7: Nivaclé
Chumane, 7: Chimane
Chumash, 1

Chunara, 3a: Kadia
Chuncho, 7: Campa; Huarayo; Mashco
Chunkar, 3a: Beldar
Chunnar, 3a: Upparwary
Churahi, 3a
Churapa, 7: Chiquitano
Churihar, 3a: Kachera
Churu, 3a: Chero
Churumatas, 7: Mataco
Churupí, 7: Nivaclé
Chutia, 3a
Chuukese, 1: Micronesians
Chuvans, 6(R)
Chuvantsky, 6(R): Chuvans
Chuvash, 6(R)
Chysh Kizhi, 6(R): Shors
Ciawani, 7: Warao
Cibola, 1: Zuni
Cicaque, 8: Jicaque
Cigani, 4: Peripatetics
Cikán, 4: Rom of Czechoslovakia
Cikitano, 7: Chiquitano
Cincari, 4: Vlachs
Cingaros, 4: Peripatetics
Çingene, 9: Peripatetics of Afghanistan, Iran, and Turkey (Turkey)
Cinta Larga, 7
Circassians, 6(R); 9
Citarâ, 7: Emberá
Citará, 8: Emberá and Wounaan
Clallam, 1: Klallam
Clamath, 1: Klamath
Cloud People, 8: Mixtec
Coahuillas, 1: Cahuilla
Coahuilteco, 1a
Coaiquer, 7: Awá Kwaiker
Coast Miwok, 1
Coast Salish, 1: Comox
Coast Yuki, 1: Yuki
Cocama, 7
Cocapa, 1: Cocopa
Cochaboth, 7: Maká
Coche, 7a: Kamsá
Cochinese, 5: Vietnamese
Cochinis, 3: Cochin Jew
Cochin Jew, 3
Cochiti, 1: Keres Pueblo Indians; Pueblo Indians
Cocomaricopa, 1: Maricopa
Coconino, 1: Havasupai
Cocopa, 1
Cocopa, 8: Indians of Baja California
Cocopah, 1: Cocopa
Coe Clan, 1: American Isolates
Coeur D'Alène, 1
Cogi, 7: Kogi
Cogui, 7: Kogi
Cohatur, 3: Kota
Collo, 9: Shilluk
la Colonia China, 8: Chinese of Costa Rica

Colorado, 7
Colored, 1: African Americans
Colored Chinese, 8: Chinese in the English-Speaking Caribbean
Coloureds, 9: Cape Coloureds
Columbia, 1
Colville, 1: Sanpoil
Colvonta, 3a: Devadasi
Comanche, 1
Comcaac, 8: Seri
Comox, 1
Concow, 1: Maidu
Conestoga, 1a
Congo, 9a: Kongo
Coniagui, 9a
Conibo, 7: Shipibo
Conis, 7: Yuracaré
Conoy, 1: Nanticoke
Cooch, 3a: Kochh
Cook Islanders, 1: Polynesians; 2: Cook Islands
Cook Islands, 2
Cook Islands Maoris, 2: Cook Islands
Coorg, 3
Coorgi, 3: Coorg
Coos, 1a
Copalis, 1: Chehalis
Copper Eskimo, 1
Copts, 9
Copts, 1: Arab Americans
Coquille, 1: Chastacosta
Cora, 8
Coras-nayaritas, 8: Cora
Corchaug, 1: Metoac
Coreguaje, 7a: Korewahe
Corinchee, 5: Kerintji
Cornish, 4
Coroado, 7: Kaingáng
Coroados, 7: Kaingáng
Coroasos, 7: Kaingáng
Coronados, 7: Mataco
Coropo, 7a: Patashó
Corses, 4: Corsicans
Corsi, 4: Corsicans
Corsicans, 4
Corumbiar, 7a: Aikaná
Cossacks, 6(R): Don Cossacks
Cossyah, 3: Khasi
Costano, 1a
Costa Ricans, 8
Costeños, 7: Afro-Colombians; Afro-Hispanic Pacific Lowlanders of Ecuador and Colombia
Co Sung, 5: Lahu
Cotabato Manobo, 5
Coto, 7a: Payawá
Cotopaxi Quichua, 7
Cò Tu, 5: Katu
Courtes Oreilles, 1: Ottawa
Covari, 7: Tunebo
Cowela, 1: Cahuilla
Cowichan, 1

Cowlitz, 1: Chehalis
Cowrie Shell Miao, 6(C): Miao
Coxodoa, 7a: Himarimã
Co Xung, 5: Lahu
Coyaviti, 7: Angaité
Coyukon, 1: Koyukon
Cozárini, 7a: Paresí
Craho, 7
Craô, 7: Craho
Cree, Western Woods, 1
Creek, 1
Creole Chinese, 8: Chinese in the
    English-Speaking Caribbean
Creoles, 8; 9a
Creoles, 1: American Isolates; Black
    Creoles of Lousiana; 3: Mauritian;
    7: Afro–South Americans; 8:
    Martiniquais
Créoles, 1: Black Creoles of Louisiana;
    3: Mauritian
Créoles Noirs, 1: Black Creoles of
    Louisiana
Creoles of Color, 1: Black Creoles of
    Louisiana
Creoles of Nicaragua
Cretans, 4
Crevas, 1: Osage
Crichanás, 7: Waimiri-Atroari
Crimean Jews, 6(R): Krymchaks
Crimean Tatar, 6(R)
Criollos, 7: Afro-Venezuelans; 8:
    Creoles of Nicaragua
Crioul, 4: Cape Verdeans
Crioulo, 9a: Creoles
Crisca, 7: Shavante
Crixá, 7: Shavante
Crnogorci, 4: Montenegrins
Croatans, 1: Lumbee
Croatians, 1: European-Americans;
    European-Canadians; 4: Croats
Croats, 4
Croats, 1: European-Americans;
    European-Canadians
Crow, 1
Cruzados, 1: Yavapai
Cua, 5
Cuacua, 7a: Wanaí
Cuajala, 1: Southern Paiute (and
    Chemehuevi)
Cuaiquer, 7: Awá Kwaiker
Cuan, 6(C): Bai
Cuban Americans, 1: Latinos
Cubans, 8
Cubeo, 7
Cucapá, 1: Cocopa
Cuchan, 1: Quechan
Cuchano, 1: Quechan
Cuchi, 7: Yuracaré
Cuextecatl, 8: Wasteko
Cuiba, 7: Cuiva; Guahibo-Sikuani
Cuibos, 7: Cuiva
Cuicatec, 8

Cuicuru, 7: Kuikuru
Cuicutl, 7: Kuikuru
Cuipoco, 7: Piapoco
Cuiva, 7
Cujareño, 7a
Cujibi, 7a: Kujubi
Culina, 7
Cumanashó, 7: Maxakali
Çumul'-kup, 6(R): Selkup
Cuna, 7
Cuna, 8: Kuna
Cuna-Cuna, 7: Cuna
Cuna Tule, 7: Cuna
Cuñi, 1: Zuni
Cunibo, 7: Shipibo
Cunimia, 7: Guahibo-Sikuani
Cunza, 7a: Atakama
Curaçao, 8
Curaçaoënaar, 8: Curaçao
Curashicuna, 7a: Yavarana
Curasicana, 7a: Yavarana
Curina, 7a: Katukina; Kutakina Acre
Curripcao, 7: Baniwa-Curripaco-
    Wakuenai
Cusabo, 1a
Cushan, 1: Quechan
Cussu, 9a
Cutashó, 7a: Patashó
Cutchi Memon, 3a: Kachi Meman
Cutchwaha Rajput, 3a: Kachhwaha
    Rajput
Cutler Indians, 1: American Isolates
Cutukina, 7a: Kutakina Acre
Cuybas, 7: Cuiva
Cyclades, 4
Cymry, 4: Welsh
Cypriots, 4
Czechs, 4
Czechs, 1: European-Americans;
    European-Canadians

Daba, 9a
Dabeiba, 8: Emberá and Wounaan
Dabgar, 3a
Dacoit, 3: Thug
Dacoo, 3: Thug
Dadibi, 2: Daribi
Dadupanthi, 3a
Dafali, 3a
Dafla, 3a
DagaaWiili, 9: Lobi-Dagarti Peoples
Dagara, 9: Lobi-Dagarti Peoples
Dagarti, 9: Lobi-Dagarti Peoples
Dagbamba, 9: Mamprusi; 9a: Dagomba
Dagbani, 9a: Dagomba
Dagchifut, 6(R): Mountain Jews
Dagomba, 9a
Daguer, 6(C): Daur
Dahait, 3a
Dahar, 3a: Daharia
Daharia, 3a
Dahayat, 3a: Dahait

Dahomeans, 9: Ewe and Fon; 9a: Ewe
    and Fon
Dahuer, 6(C): Daur
Dai, 3a; 6(C)
Dai, 3: Chin; 5: Shan; Tai Lue
Daija, 6(C): Dai
Dailü, 6(C): Dai
Daina, 6(C): Dai
Dairi-Pakpak, 5: Batak
Daisa, 6(C): Achang
Dajak, 5: Kalimantan Dayaks
Daju, 9a
Dakarkari, 9a
Dakaut, 3a
Da ka va, 6(C): Wa
Dakota, 1: Santee; Teton
Dak-putra, 3a: Dakaut
Dalmatians, 4
Dalsingar, 3a: Jingar
Dama, 9: Herero; 9a: Dasanec
Damara, 9: Herero
Damot, 9a: Awi
Damugat, 5: Agta
Dan, 9a
Danakil, 9: Afar
Dancers, 1: Cahuilla
Dandasi, 3a
Dandawa, 9a: Dendi
Dandewala, 3a: Beria
Danes, 4
Danes, 1: European-Americans;
    European-Canadians
Dang, 5: Palaung
Dang-Charha, 3a: Nat
Dangerous Islands, 2: Raroia
Dangi, 3a
Dangri, 3a
Dani, 2
Dani, 7a: Dení
Daphla, 3a: Dafla
Darbania, 3a: Kotwal
Dard, 3
Dard, 3: Kohistani
Darganti, 6(R): Dargins
Dargi, 6(R): Dargins, 6(R)
Dargins, 6(R)
Dargwa, 6(R): Dargins
Daribi, 2
Darién, 7: Chocó
Dariena, 7: Chocó
Darji, 3a: Darzi; Jingar
Darke County Group, 1: American
    Isolates
Darkhan, 3a: Tarkhan
Dar Massenya, 9: Bagirmi
Darshani, 3a: Kanphata
Darwesh, 3a: Dafali
Darzi, 3a
Dasa, 3a
Dasanec, 9a
Dasari, 3a: Dasri
Dashan, 5: Kachin; 6(C): Jingpo

Dasi, 3a: Devadasi
Dasri, 3a
Datiyal Kachari, 3a: Rabha
Datog, 9a: Taturu
Dätsana-Desana, 7
Datuana, 7a: Retuna
Daudi Bohra, 3: Bohra
Daur, 6(C)
Daur, 3a: Dauri
Daure Gosavi, 3a: Davre Jogi
Dauri, 3a
Da Vach, 5: Hre
Davak, 5: Hre
Davre Gosavi, 3a: Davre Jogi
Davre Jogi, 3a
Dawari, 3a: Dauri
Dawashin, 9: Peripatetics of Iraq . . .
      Yemen (Yemen)
Dawoer, 6(C): Daur
Daya, 5: Kalimantan Dayaks
Dayak, 5: Iban
Dayerrie, 2: Dieri
De'ang, 6(C)
De'arua, 7: Piaroa
Dearuwa, 7: Piaroa
De'ath-īʰā, 7: Piaroa
Deerie, 2: Dieri
Deg Hit'an, 1: Ingalik
Dehghaot'ine, 1: Slavey
Dehu, 2: Loyalty Islands
Deja, 7: Piapoco
Delang, 5: Kalimantan Dayaks
Delaware, 1
Demala-Gattara, 3a
Dempo, 5: Ogan-Besemah
Dena'ina, 1: Tanaina
Dendi, 9a
Dene, 1: Slavey
Dení, 7a
Deni-Jamamadi, 7a: Dení
Depala, 3a
Depressed caste, 3: Untouchables
Derung, 6(C): Drung
Desana, 7
Desâna, 7: Desana
Desano, 7: Desana
Deshasth, 3a: Deshastha Brahman
Deshastha Brahman, 3a
Desi, 3a: Kochh
Deswali, 3a: Mina
Deti, 9a
Deuri-Chutiya, 3a: Chutia
Deutschen, 4: Germans
Deutschen Shweiz, 4: German Swiss
Devadasi, 3a
Devadig, 3a: Suppalig
Devadiga, 3a: Suppalig
Devang, 3a: Devanga
Devanga, 3a
Devangalu, 3a: Devanga
Devanga Sale, 3a: Devanga
Devli, 3a: Bhavin

Devra, 3a: Devanga
Dewar, 3a
Dewoi, 9a: Dey
Dewoin, 9a: Dey
Dey, 9a
Dghwede, 9a
Dhakar, 3a
Dhamang, 3: Tamang
Dhanak, 3a: Dhanuk
Dhangad, 3a: Domara; Golla; Oraon
Dhangar, 3: Golla; Oraon
Dhangar Mahratta, 3a: Golla
Dhanka, 3a: Gamit; Golla
Dhankas, 3: Bhil; Oraon
Dhanuhar, 3a: Dhanwar
Dhanuk, 3a
Dhanwar, 3a
Dhaonsi, 3a: Dakaut
Dharhi, 3a: Dosadh
Dhari, 3a: Dosadh
Dharkar, 3a
Dharua, 3a: Dhurwa
Dhebra, 3a: Bhoi
Dhed, 3a: Dheda
Dheda, 3a
Dheda, 3a: Meghval
Dhedha, 3a: Meghval
Dhemal, 3a: Dhimal
Dhenuar, 3a: Dhanwar
Dher, 3a: Madiga; Mala
Dhimal, 3a
Dhimar, 3a: Bhoi
Dhivar, 3a: Mangela
Dhivara, 3a: Kewat
Dhoba, 3a
Dhoba, 3a: Dhobi
Dhobhi, 3a: Dhobi
Dhobi, 3a
Dhoby, 3a: Hena
Dhoddiyan, 3a: Yogi
Dhodi, 3a: Dhodia
Dhodia, 3a
Dholi, 3: Bhil; 3a: Bajania; Mirasi
Dholuo, 9: Luo
Dhondphoda, 3a: Beldar
Dhopadhola, 9a: Padhola
Dhor, 3a
Dhotada, 3a: Bottada
Dhuldhoya, 3a
Dhulia, 3a: Basor
Dhuna, 3a: Dhuniya
Dhund, 3a
Dhundia, 3a: Dhodia
Dhunia, 3a: Bahna
Dhuniya, 3a
Dhupi, 3a: Dhobi
Dhuri, 3a
Dhuru, 3a: Dhurwa
Dhurwa, 3a
Di, 6(C): Qiang
Diafouba, 9a: Dan
Diakkane, 9a: Jahanka

Diakonovtsy, 6(R): Old Believers
Dialonke, 9a
Dian, 9a
Diankhanke, 9a
Diari, 2: Dieri
Dibongiya, 3a: Chutia
Dida, 9a
Didayi, 3a
Didinga, 9a
Diegueño, 1: Kumeyaay
Dieri, 2
Dieyerie, 2: Dieri
Dieyrie, 2: Dieri
Diggers, 1: Western Shoshone
Digo, 9a
Digo, 9: Mijikenda
Digor, 6(R): Ossetes
Digueño, 8: Indians of Baja California
Digwan, 3a: Jingar
Diila, 9a: Kunema
Dikhit, 3a: Dikshit
Dikhshit, 3a: Dikshit
Dikshit, 3a
Dilzhę'é, 1: Western Apache
Dimasa, 3a: Kachari
Dimasa Kachari, 3a: Kachari
Dindjié, 1: Kutchin
Dine, 1: Navajo
Dineh, 1: Navajo
Dinka, 9
Dinneh, 1: Navajo
Diola, 9a
Diore, 7: Xikrin
Divaru, 3a: Hale Paika
Divehi, 3
Divehin, 3: Divehi
Dives, 3: Divehi
Diyeri, 2: Dieri
Diyhup, 7a: Yahup
Djagada, 9a
Djapa, 7a: Bendyapá
Djao, 9a: Yao
Djedi, 9a: Fon
Djerma, 9
Djerma, 9: Zarma
Djermis, 9: Zarma
Djoheina, 9a
Djok, 9a: Chokwe
Dobocubí, 7: Barí
Dobu, 2
Dochkafuara, 7a: Tuyuka
Dodoth, 9a
Dogar, 3a
Dogba, 9a: Guiziga
Dog Eaters, 1: Arapaho
Dogom, 9: Dogon
Dogon, 9
Dogono, 9: Dogon
Dogra, 3a
Dogrib, 1
Dohká-poára, 7a: Tuyuka
Dohor, 3a: Dhor

Dok Acoli, 9a: Acholi
Dolgan, 6(R)
Dolomites, 4: Ladin
Doluva, 3a
Dom, 3a: Bhangi
Dom, 3a: Domara; Mirasi
Doma, 9a: Abron
Domahra, 3a: Domara
Domar, 3a: Domara
Domara, 3a
Domban, 3a: Domara
Dombar, 3a: Domara
Dombara, 3a: Domara
Dombari, 3a: Domara
Dombe, 9a
Dombo, 3a: Domara
Dome, 3a: Domara
Dominicans, 8
Dominicans, 1: Latinos
Dominickers, 1: American Isolates
Dom Mirasi, 3a: Mirasi
Dom-Patni, 3a: Patni
Domra, 3a: Domara
Domri, 3a: Domara
Don Cossacks, 6(R)
Dondo, 9a: Kongo
Done, 1: Dogrib
Dong, 6(C)
Donga Dasari, 3a
Dongore, 3a: Gavli
Dongxiang, 6(C)
Doom, 3a: Domara
Doopgesinden, 1: Mennonites
Dophla, 3a: Dafla
Dor, 9a: Bongo
Dorla, 3a
Dorla, 3: Koya
Dorobo, 9: Okiek
Dorossié, 9a
Dorossié, 9: Lobi-Dagarti Peoples
Dosadh, 3a
Dosadha, 3a: Dosadh
Doukhobors, 1
Doungel, 3a: Kuki
Dourou, 9a
Douvangar, 9a: Mofou
Doza, 9a
Dreadlocks, 8: Rastafarians
Dreads, 8: Rastafarians
Drio, 7: Trio
Drung, 6(C)
Druze, 9
Druze, 1: Arab Americans
Dschagga, 9: Chagga
Dschang, 9: Bamiléké
Dthee-eri, 2: Dieri
Duane, 5
Duasen, 6(R): Yezidis
Duba, 2: Rossel Island
Dubaduba, 3a: Joshi
Duberwal, 3: Kohistani
Dubla, 3a

Dublas, 3: Bhil
Dubo, 6(R): Tuvans
Dudekula, 3a
Dudwala, 3a
Dui, 9a: Dourou
Duka, 9a: Coniagui; Dukawa
Dukaiya, 7a: Okaina
Dukawa, 9a
Dulia, 3a: Basor
Dulangan, 5: Cotobato Manobo
Dulongzu, 6(C): Drung
Dum, 3a: Domara
Dumagat, 5: Philippine Negritos
Dumal, 3a
Duman, 9: Peripatetics of Iraq . . .
     Yemen (Iraq)
Dumar, 3a: Domara
Dumi, 9: Peripatetics of Afghanistan,
     Iran, and Turkey (Iran)
Dum Mirasi, 3a: Mirasi
Dummna, 3a: Domara
Dungan, 6(C): Hui
Dungans, 6(R)
Dungri, 3: Bhil
Dungri-Grasia, 3: Grasia
Durava, 3a
Durayi, 3a: Panna
Durba, 3a: Babria
Durga Murgi, 3a: Besta
Duru, 9a: Dourou
Duruma, 9: Mijikenda
Dusadh, 3a
Dusadh, 3a: Dosadh
Du-Sulatelu, 1: Wiyot
Dusun, 5
Dutch, 4
Dutch, 1: European-Americans;
     European-Canadians
Dutchmen and Dutchwomen, 4: Dutch
Dwamish, 1a
Dyabarma, 9: Zarma
Dyak, 5: Iban
Dyamate, 9a: Diola
Dyarma, 9: Zarma
Dyerma, 9: Zarma
Dzah-hmi, 8: Chinantec
Dzase, 7: Piapoco
Dzaze, 7: Piapoco
Dzhigets, 6(R): Circassians
Dził ghạ'i, 1: Western Apache
Dził t'aadń, 1: Western Apache

East Asians of Canada, 1
East Asians of the United States, 1
Easter Island, 2
Eastern Dakota, 1: Santee
Eastern Indians, 1: Abenaki
Eastern Luba, 9a: Hemba
Eastern Lunda, 9: Lunda
Eastern Mono, 1: Mono
Eastern Shoshone, 1
Eastern Timbira, 7: Candoshi

East Futuna, 2: Futuna
East Greenland Inuit, 1
East Indian, 3a
East Indian, 3: Anglo-Indian
East Indians, 1: South and Southeast
     Asians of Canada; South and
     Southeast Asians of the United
     States
East Indians in Trinidad, 8
East Main Cree, 1: Montagnais-Naskapi
East Syrians, 9: Syriacs
East Toraja, 5: Toala
East Uvean, 2: Uvea
Ebantfu ba kwa Ngwane, 9: Swazi
Ebera, 7: Chocó
Eberá, 7: Chocó
Ebira, 9a: Igbira
Ebrie, 9a
Ebuna, 9a: Yungur
Ebwe, 9a: Ewe
Eceeje, 7: Huarayo
Ece'je, 7: Huarayo
Echeloots, 1: Wishram
Echijita, 9a: Jita
Echoja, 7: Huarayo
Ecuadorian Quichua, 7: Cotopaxi
     Quichua
Edanadan Chetti, 3a
Édang, 5: Kédang
Edaw, 5: Akha
E-De, 5: Rhadé
E Dê, 5: Rhadé
Ede Nago, 9a: Nagot
Edinoverie, 6(R): Old Believers
Edisto, 1a
Edo, 9
Edo-Speaking Peoples, 9a
Edugaura, 2: Dobu
Eesti, 6(R): Estonians
Eestlased, 6(R): Siberian Estonians
Efate, 2: Nguna
Efe, 9: Tropical-Forest Foragers; 9a:
     Ewe
Efik, 9a
Eftanissiotes, 4: Ionians
Egamik, 6(R): Pamir Peoples
Egba, 9: Yoruba
Egbado, 9: Yoruba
Eggon, 9a
Egun, 9a: Goun
Egyptian Nubians, 9: Nubians
Ehnek, 1: Karok
Eipo, 2
Eipodumanang, 2: Eipo
Eireanneach, 4: Irish
Ejagham, 9a
Ekagi, 2: Kapauku
Ekari, 2: Kapauku
Ekaw, 6(C): Hani
Eket, 9a
Ekibena, 9a: Bena
Ekihaya, 9a: Haya

Ekiti, 9: Yoruba
Ekoi, 9a: Ejagham
Ekokoma, 9a: Mbembe
Elama, 3a: Velama
Elayad, 3a: Ambalavasi
Elema, 2: Orokolo
Elkbasumh, 1: Bellabella
Ellice Islands, 2: Tuvalu
Ellines, 4: Greeks
Elma, 3a
El Salvadorians, 1: Latinos
emaSwati, 9: Swazi
emaSwazi, 9: Swazi
Emba, 9a: Hemba
Embatteo, 3a: Panikki
Embena, 7: Chocó
Embená, 8: Emberá and Wounaan
Emberá, 7
Emberá, 7: Chocó
Emberá and Wounaan, 8
Emberak, 7: Chocó
Embran, 3a: Havik Brahman
Embu, 9: Mbeere
Emereñon, 7: Emerillon
Emerillon, 7
Emerilon, 7: Emerillon
Emerion, 7: Emerillon
Emischi, 5: Ainu
Emñreke Pinz Makñ, 7: Tatuyo
Empená, 8: Emberá and Wounaan
Empera, 7: Chocó
Emperá, 8: Emberá and Wounaan
Enaawenê-nawê, 7a: Salumã
Enagua, 7: Piapoco
'Enata, 2: Marquesas Islands
Encabellado, 7: Siona-Secoya
Endenese, 5
Endo, 9a
Endo, 9: Nandi and Other Kalenjin
    Peoples
Enelhit, 7: Lengua; 7a: Chane
Enenslet, 7: Angaité
E'ñepa, 7: Panare
Enetes, 7: Yuracaré
Enewetak, 2: Marshall Islands
Engl, 4: English
English, 4
English, 1: European-Americans;
    European-Canadians
Enimacá, 7: Maká
Enimagá, 7: Maká
Enlhit, 7: Lengua
Enlhiy, 7a: Maskoi
Enlit, 7: Angaité
Enslit, 7: Angaité
Eoni, 6(C): Hani
Eotile, 9a: Mekyibo
Epera, 7: Chocó; 8: Emberá and
    Wounaan
Épined, 7: Puinave
Erakala, 3a
Eranadan, 3a: Aranadan

Eravallan, 3a
Eravallar, 3a: Eravallan
Eravallen, 3a: Eravallan
Erdiha, 9a
Erie, 1a
Erilagaru, 3: Irula
Ersu, 6(C): Qiang
Erudandi, 3a: Gangeddu
Esa, 9a: Ishan
Esaw, 1: Catawba
Escholtz Islands, 2: Bikini
Ese Éjas, 7: Huarayo
Ese Ejja, 7: Huarayo
Ese-Exa, 7: Huarayo
Eskimo, 1
Eskualdunak, 1: Basques; 4: Basques
Esquimaux, 1: Eskimo
Esquimox, 1: Eskimo
Esráelotch, 9: Falasha
Estonians, 6(R)
Estonians, 1: European-Americans;
    European-Canadians
Eta, 5: Burakumin
Etaboslé, 7: Maká
Etalena, 7: Terena
Etall, 5: Taiwan Aboriginal Peoples
Etchareottine, 1: Slavey
Etechemin, 1: Maliseet
Etel, 6(R): Chuvans
Ethelená, 7: Terena
Ethun, 9a: Dukawa
Etone, 7: Terena
Etsako, 9a
Ettiwandlu, 3a: Madiga
Euahlayi, 2: Kamilaroi
Eunuch, 3: Hijra
Eurasian, 3: Anglo-Indian
Eurocs, 1: Yurok
European-Americans, 1
European-Canadians, 1
Europeans in South America, 7
Europeans in South Asia, 3
Euskaldunak, 1: Basques; 4: Basques
Eutah, 1: Ute
Even, 6(R)
Evenki, 6(R)
Ewe, 9a
Ewe and Fon, 9
Ewenki, 6(C)
External caste, 3: Untouchables
Eyabida, 7: Chocó
Ezhuva, 3a
Ezo, 5: Ainu

Fakir, 3a
Falasha, 9
Falasha, 9a: Awi
Fali, 9; 9a
Fall Indians, 1: Gros Ventre
Fang, 9a
Fante, 9a
Fante, 9: Akan

Faqir, 3a: Fakir
Faraones, 1: Mescalero Apache
Faroe Islanders, 4
Faruaru, 7a: Hishkariana
Fataleka, 2: Malaita
Fe'e Fe'e, 9: Bamiléké
Fehemi, 9: Peripatetics of Iraq . . .
    Yemen (Egypt and Sudan)
Felasha, 9: Falasha
Fellaata, 9: Fulani
Fellah, 9: Fulani
Fenni, 4: Saami
Feodoseevtsy, 6(R): Old Believers
Ferangi, 3: Europeans in South Asia
Feuj, 9: Peripatetics of Afghanistan,
    Iran, and Turkey (Iran)
Filani, 9: Fulani
Filastinyoun, 9: Palestinians
Filipino, 5
Filippovtsy, 6(R): Old Believers
Finn, 4: Saami
Finnish Kaale, 4: Scandinavian
    Peripatetics
Finns, 4
Fipa, 9
Fitita, 7: Witoto
Fiji, 2: Bau, Lau, Rotuma
Filipinos, 1: East Asians of Canada;
    East Asians of the United States
Finns, 1: European-Americans;
    European-Canadians
Firaste Mang, 3a: Mang-Garori
Fish-Eaters, 1: Assiniboin
Fishkin Tatars, 6(C): Hezhen
Five Nations, 1: Iroquois
Fiwaga, 2: Foi
Flamencos, 4: Flemish
Flanders, 4: Flemish
Flathead, 1
Flechas de Palo Apaches, 1: Lipan
    Apache
Flemings, 4: Flemish
Flemish, 4
Flowery Lisu, 6(C): Lisu
Foe, 2: Foi
Fogbo, 9a: Fon
Foi, 2
Foi'i, 2: Foi
Fomopea, 9: Bamiléké
Fon, 9a
Fon, 9: Ewe and Fon
Fongondeng, 9: Bamiléké
Fongoro, 9a
Fora, 9a: Fur
Fordunga, 9a: Fur
Fore, 2
Foredafa, 7a: Morunawa
Formosans, 5: Taiwan Aboriginal
    Peoples
Forniô, 7: Fulniô
Føroyingar, 4: Faroe Islanders
Foto, 9: Bamiléké

Fotouni, **9:** Bamiléké
Fox, 1
Franco-Mauriciens, **3:** Mauritian
Franco-Mauritians, **3:** Mauritian
Francophones, **1:** French Canadians
Frase, **9a:** Balante
French, 4
French, **1:** European-Americans
French Antillians, 8
French Canadians, 1
French-Flemish, **4:** Flemish
French of India, 3
French Polynesians, **1:** Polynesians
French Tamils, **3:** French of India
Frentones, **7:** Mocoví; Toba; **7a:**
    Maskoi
Frisians, 4
Friulano, **4:** Friuli
Friulans, **4:** Friuli
Friuli, 4
Friulians, **4:** Friuli
Frysk, **4:** Frisians
Fula, **9:** Fulani
Fulani, 9
Fulata, **9:** Fulani
Fulbe, **9:** Fulani
Fulero, **9a:** Furiiru
Fulniô, 7
Fun, **3a:** Kuki
Funj, 9a
Fur, 9a
Furiiru, 9a
Furniô, **7:** Fulniô
Futuna, 2
Fuyuge, **2:** Mafulu
Fuyughé, **2:** Mafulu

Ga-Adandme-Krobo, 9a
Gabar, **9:** Zoroastrians
Gabit, 3a
Gabr, **9:** Zoroastrians
Gadaba, **3:** Munda; **3a:** Gadba
Gadan, **5:** Gaddang
Ga'dang, **5:** Gaddang
Gadaria, 3a
Gadariya, **3a:** Gadaria
Gadba, 3a
Gaddanes, **5:** Gaddang
Gaddang, 5
Gaddi, 3a
Gaderiya, **3a:** Gadaria
Gadhavi, **3a:** Charan
Gadi, **3a:** Gaddi
Gadit, **3a:** Dudwala
Gadri, **3a:** Gadaria
Gaduliya Lohar, 3a
Gaeda, 9a
Gaedhils, **4:** Gaels (Irish)
Gaels (Irish), 4
Gagauz, 4; 6(R)
Gagou, 9a
Gahadawala, **3a:** Gaharwar Rajput

Gahala-Berava, 3a
Gaharwar Rajput, 3a
Gahlot, **3a:** Sesodia Rajput
Gahuku, **2:** Gahuku-Gama
Gahuku-Gama, 2
Gain, **9a:** Ga-Adandme-Krobo
Gainj, 2
Gajra, **3:** Ahir
Gajo, **5:** Gayo
Gakkhar, 3a
Galasqo, **1:** Wishram
Gal Bhoi, **3a:** Raikari
Galego, **4:** Galicians
Galiara, **3a:** Bandhara
Galibí, 7a
Galibí, **7:** Cariña
Galibi, **7:** Maroni Carib
Galice, **1:** Chastacosta
Galicians, 4
Galicians, **1:** Ukrainians of Canada
Galla, **9a:** Oromo
Gallego, **4:** Galicians
Gallinas, 9a
Gallinas, **9a:** Vai
Gallinomero, **1:** Pomo
Gallong, **3:** Abor; **3a:** Adi
Galofes, **9:** Wolof
Gama, 9a
Gamadi, 3a
Gamalhou, **3a:** Kuki
Gambier Islands, **2:** Mangareva
Gamgauda, **3a:** Gam Vakkal
Gamit, 3a
Gamit, **3:** Bhil
Gammala, 3a
Gamo-Gofa, 9a
Gamta, **3a:** Gamit
Gam Vakkal, 3a
Gan, **9:** Lobi-Dagarti Peoples
Gǁana, **9:** San-Speaking Peoples
Ganda, 3a; 9; 9a
Gandhabania, **3a:** Gandhabanik
Gandhabanik, 3a
Gandharb, **3a:** Gandharv
Gandharia, 3a
Gandharv, 3a
Gandhi, **3a:** Atari
Gandhmali, 3a
Gandi, **3a:** Ganda
Gandia, **3a:** Ganda
Gandla, **3a:** Ganiga; Teli
Ganeshia, **3a:** Meghval
Gang, **9a:** Acholi
Gangadikāra Okkalu, **3:** Okkaliga
Gangari, 3a
Gangauta, **3a:** Gangota
Gangeddu, 3a
Gangeddulu, **3a:** Gangeddu
Gangemakkalu, **3a:** Besta
Gangimakkalu, **3a:** Besta
Gangota, 3a
Gangte, **3a:** Kuki

Gani, **9:** Acholi
Ganig, **3a:** Teli
Ganiga, 3a
Ganiga, **3a:** Teli
Ganigaru, **3a:** Teli
Ganikan, **3a:** Kaniyan
Ganrar, 3a
Ganreriya, **3a:** Gadaria
Ganthachor, **3a:** Bhamta
Gants, **2:** Gainj
Ganz, **2:** Gainj
Gao borey, **9:** Songhay
Gaolan, **3:** Ahir
Gaolan Nongan, **6(C):** Zhuang
Gaoli, **3:** Ahir
Gara, **3:** Grasia
Garaba, **3a:** Gadba
Garadjui, **2:** Karadjeri
Garariya, **3a:** Gadaria
Garasia, **3:** Bhil, Grasia
Gareri, **3a:** Gadaria
Garfuku, **2:** Gahuku-Gama
Garia, 2; 3
Garifuna, 8
Garifuna, **8:** Carib of Dominica
Garinagu, **8:** Garifuna
Garo, 3
Garpagari, 3a
Garudi, **3a:** Nat
Gaspesians, **1:** Micmac
Gataq, **3:** Munda
Gauda, 3a
Gauda, **3a:** Gaur
Gauda, **3a:** Nador
Gauda Chitrakara, **3a:** Gudikara
Gauddes, **3a:** Gauda
Gaudo, 3a
Gaudo, **3a:** Gauda
Gauliga, **3a:** Gavli
Gauliga, **3a:** Golla
Gaur, 3a
Gauria, 3a
Gaur Rajput, 3a
Gavada, 3a
Gavada, **3a:** Golla
Gavali, **3a:** Golla
Gavandi, **3a:** Gamadi
Gavara, **3a:** Komati
Gavião, 7a
Gaviões, **7:** Krikati/Pukobye; **7a:**
    Pukobyé
Gavit, **3a:** Gamit
Gavli, 3a
Gäwändi, **9:** Peripatetics of
    Afghanistan, Iran, and Turkey
    (Turkey)
Gayo, 5
Gbagyi, 9a
G'ban, **9a:** Gagou
Gbandere, **9a:** Banziri
Gbang, **9a:** Birom
Gbari, 9a

Gbaya, 9a: Ngabaka
Gbaya Mandjia, 9a
Gbe, 9a: Ewe
Gbuhwe, 9a: Lamang
Gebusi, 2
Gekoyo, 9: Kikuyu; 9a: Kikuyu
Gelao, 6(C)
Geleba, 9a: Dasanec
Gelo, 6(C): Gelao
Gens de couleur, 3: Mauritian
Gens des Buttes, 1: Tanana
Gens des Lacs, 1: Lake
Gens des Puants, 1: Winnebago
Gens du Lac d'Ours, 1: Bearlake Indians
Gens du Voyage, 4: Peripatetics
Gente de Color, 7: Afro-Colombians
Gente Morenas, 7: Afro-Hispanic
    Pacific Lowlanders of Ecuador
    and Colombia
Gente Negra, 7: Afro-Colombians;
    Afro-Hispanic Pacific Lowlanders
    of Ecuador and Colombia
Gentoo, 3: Hindu
Georgian Jews, 6(R)
Georgians, 6(R)
Gerala, 3: Ahir
Germans, 4; 6(R)
Germans, 1: European-Americans;
    European-Canadians
German Swiss, 4
Gerse, 9: Kpelle
Gesinan, 9a: Harari
Gewhassi, 9: Peripatetics of Iraq . . .
    Yemen (Sudan)
Ghache, 3a: Basor
Ghadi, 3a
Ghadshi, 3a
Ghaijo, 3a: Nai
Ghajar, 9: Peripatetics of Iraq . . .
    Yemen (Egypt and Sudan);
    Peripatetics of Afghanistan, Iran,
    and Turkey (Iran)
Ghalbelbaf, 9: Peripatetics of
    Afghanistan, Iran, and Turkey
    (Afghanistan)
Ghalghay, 6(R): Chechen-Ingush
Ghanche, 3a: Basor
Ghanchi, 3a: Basor
Ghanchi, 3a: Teli
Ghantichor, 3a: Bhamta
Ghantra, 3a: Lohar
Ghara, 3a: Gauria
Ghardera, 3a: Babria
Ghasi, 3a: Ghasia
Ghasia, 3a
Ghasiya, 3a: Ghasia
Ghawazi, 9: Peripatetics of Iraq . . .
    Yemen (Egypt)
Ghazi Kumukh, 6(R): Laks
Ghenanema, 9: Peripatetics of the
    Maghreb (Morocco)
Ghermedi, 3a

Gherwal Rajput, 3a: Gaharwar Rajput
Ghirth, 3a
Ghisadi, 3a
Ghisari, 3a: Lohar
Ghor, 3a: Banjara
Ghorbat, 9
Ghorbat, 9: Peripatetics of
    Afghanistan, Iran, and Turkey
    (Afghanistan)
Ghorbati, 9: Peripatetics of
    Afghanistan, Turkey, and Iran
    (Turkey and Iran)
Ghosi, 3a
Ghumar, 3a: Kumhar
Ghumiar, 3a: Kumhar
Ghuraba, 9: Peripatetics of Iraq . . .
    Yemen (Sudan)
Ghurbat, 9: Peripatetics of Iraq . . .
    Yemen (Syria and Egypt)
Ghurradin, 9: Peripatetics of Iraq . . .
    Yemen (Egypt)
Ghvanal, 6(R): Andis
Gian, 9: Lobi-Dagarti Peoples
Gíbari, 7: Jivaro
Gibidki, 3a: Joshi
Gigikuyu, 9: Kikuyu
Giha, 9a: Ha
Gikiyu, 9: Kikuyu; 9a: Kikuyu
Gilbertese, 1: Micronesians; 2: Kiribati
Gileno, 1: Pima-Papago
Giliak, 6(R): Nivkh
Gillamooks, 1: Tillamook
Gilyak, 6(R): Nivkh
Gin, 6(C): Jing
Girara, 2: Gogodala
Girhasth Brahman, 3a: Babhan
Giriama, 9a
Giriama, 9: Mijikenda
Girisia, 3: Grasia
Giriya(a)ku, 6(R): Nivkh
Gisu, 9a
Gitanos, 4
Gitanos, 4: Peripatetics
Gitans, 4: Peripatetics
Givari, 7: Jivaro
Gívaro, 7: Jivaro
G'ivri, 6(R): Mountain Jews
Glavda, 9a
Gnau, 2
Goa Chetti, 3a: Kudumi Chetti
Goajivo, 7: Guahibo-Sikuani
Goala, 3: Ahir
Goan, 3a
Goanese, 3: Anglo-Indian; 3a: Goan
Gogo, 9a
Gogodala, 2
Gogodara, 2: Gogodala
Gohar Herkeri, 3a: Banjara
Goilala, 2: Mafulu, Tauade
Gokulashta Gusain, 3a: Vallabacharya
Gol, 3a: Golla
Gola, 3a; 9a

Gola, 3a: Golla; Khava; 9a:
    Badyaranke
Golak Brahman, 3a
Golalare, 3a: Alkari
Golandaz, 3a: Kadera
Golapurab, 3a
Golar, 3a: Golla
Gold, 6(C): Hezhen
Goliath, 2: Eipo
Golkar, 3: Ahir; 3a: Golla
Golla, 3a
Gollakulam, 3a: Pichakuntala
Gollam, 3a: Golla
Gollarajulu, 3a: Golla
Gollewar, 3a: Golla
Gond, 3
Gondaliga, 3a: Gondhali
Gond-Gowari, 3a
Gondhali, 3a
Gond Majhwar, 3a: Majhwar
Gone, 3a
Goniga, 3a: Gone
Gonja, 9a
Gonr, 3a: Bharbhunja
Gonsavi, 3a
Goodenough Island, 2
Gopal, 3a
Gorait, 3a
Gorakhnathi, 3a: Kanphata
Gorokans, 2: Gahuku-Gama
Gorontalese, 5
Gorontalo, 5: Gorontalese
Goroti, 7: Gorotire
Gorotire, 7
Gorpalwad, 3a: Telaga
Gorum, 3: Munda
Gosain, 3a
Gosangi, 3a: Madiga
Gosayi, 3a: Gosain
Goshute, 1: Gosiute
Gosiute, 1
Goswami, 3a: Gosain
Gouda, 3a: Goundala
Gouldtowners, 1: American Isolates
Gouli, 3a: Gavli
Goun, 9a
Goundala, 3a
Gourhi, 3a: Mallah
Gourounsi, 9a
Gourous, 9a
Gouru, 9a
Govardhan, 3a: Golak Brahman
Gowari, 3a
Gowder, 3a: Gauda
Goyigama, 3a
Gradahô, 7: Gorotire
Gradau, 7: Gorotire
Grasia, 3
Grass Koiari, 2: Koiari
Graubunden, 4: Swiss, Italian
Great Andamanese, 3: Andamanese
Great Russians, 6(R): Russian Peasants

Grebo, 9a
Greeks, 4; 6(R)
Greeks, 1: European-Americans;
    European-Canadians
Greek-Speaking Jews of Greece, 4
Green Island, 2: Nissan
Green River Snakes, 1: Eastern
    Shoshone
Grenadians, 8
Grhastha Brahman, 3: Anavil Brahman
Griegos, 4: Greek-Speaking Jews of
    Greece
Grigioni Italiano, 4: Swiss, Italian
Grihastha, 3a: Deshastha Brahman
Grihasth Brahman, 3a: Babhan
Gros Ventre, 1
Gros Ventre of the Prairie, 1: Gros
    Ventre
Gros Ventres of the Missouri, 1: Hidatsa
Grusi, 9a
Gu, 9a
Guabi, 8: Huave
Guacururre, 7a: Pilagá
Guadalcanal, 2
Guadalcanar, 2: Guadalcanal
Guadeloupians, 8
Guahibo, 7: Guahibo-Sikuani
Guahibo-Sikuani, 7
Guaiapi, 7: Wayãpi
Guaica, 7: Akawaio; Yanomamö
Guʿaidiyah, 9: Peripatetics of Iraq . . .
    Yemen (Iraq and Syria)
Guaipujinave, 7: Puinave
Guaipuño, 7: Puinave
Guajá, 7a
Guajajára, 7
Guajaribo, 7: Yanomamö
Guajiro, 7
Guamaca, 7a: Malayo
Guamanians, 1: Micronesians
Guambiano, 7
Guan, 9a
Guaná, 7a: Chane
Guanano, 7: Wanano
Guanches, 4: Canarians
Guanting, 6(C): Tu
Guaque, 7: Karihona; 7a: Wayana
Guaradjara, 2: Karadjeri
Guaraní, 7a: Tapieté
Guaraniete, 7: Guarayu
Guarasug'we, 7: Pauserna
Guaraúnos, 7: Warao
Guarayo, 7: Guarayu; Huarayo
Guarayu, 7
Guarayuta, 7: Pauserna
Guarequena, 7a: Warekena
Guaríba, 7a: Wariva
Guarijío, 8
Guarijio, 8: Guarijío
Guarogíos, 8: Guarijío
Guasurango, 7a: Tapieté
Guatemalans, 1: Latinos

Guató, 7a
Guatuso, 8: Maleku
Guatuzo, 8: Maleku
Guayabero, 7: Guahibo-Sikuani
Guayagui, 7: Ache
Guayaki, 7: Ache
Guayaná, 7: Kaingáng
Guayba, 7: Guahibo-Sikuani
Guayca, 7: Akawaio
Guayma, 8: Seri
Guaymí, 8: Ngawbe
Guaymí-Sabanero, 8: Bugle
Guazazara, 7: Guajajára
Gude, 9a
Gudeilla, 9a: Hadiyya
Gudella, 9a: Haner
Gudigar, 3a: Gudikara
Gudigara, 3a: Gudikara
Gudikara, 3a
Guebre, 9: Zoroastrians
Guentusé, 7: Nivaclé
Guere, 9a
Guerze, 9: Kpelle
Guguwãlã, 3: Kanjar
Guianes, 5: Bontok
Guicuru, 7: Kuikuru
Guidar, 9a
Guineas, 1: American Isolates
Guiolof, 9: Wolof
Guite, 3a: Kuki
Guitoto, 7: Witoto
Guiziga, 9a
Gujar, 3
Gujarati, 3
Gujarati Brahman, 3a
Gujaratis, 1: South and Southeast
    Asians of Canada; South and
    Southeast Asians of the United
    States
Gujareta, 3: Gujar
Gujjar, 3: Gujar
Gujjara, 3: Gujar
Gujrati Brahman, 3a: Gujarati Brahman
Gula, 9a: Gola
Gulgulia, 3a
Gulla, 3a: Golla
Gullah-Speaking African Americans, 1:
    Sea Islanders
Gullar, 3a: Golla
Gungawa, 9a: Reshawa
Gun-Gbe, 9a: Goun; Gu
Gunilroy, 2: Kamilaroi
Gunlodu, 3a
Gunrhi, 3a: Mallah
Guozhou, 5: Lahu
Gurage, 9a
Guramalum, 2: Lak
Gurani, 9: Peripatetics of Afghanistan,
    Iran, and Turkey (Iran)
Gurao, 3a
Gurav, 3a: Gurao
Gurava, 3a

Gurbet, 9: Ghorbat
Gurbéti, 4: Xoraxané Romá
Guriya, 3a: Mallah
Gurjara Brahman, 3a: Gujarati
    Brahman
Gurjar Brahman, 3a: Gujarati Brahman
Gurkha, 3
Gurkhali, 3: Gurkha
Gurma, 9a
Gurukkal, 3a: Ambalavasi
Guruku, 9a: Safwa
Gurung, 3
Gurupá, 7a: Urupá
Gururumba, 2
Gurusthulu, 3a: Balija
Gusain, 3a: Gosain
Gusii, 9
Guyanese, 1: Black West Indians in the
    United States
Gwamba, 9a: Tsonga
Gwari Matai, 9a: Gbagyi
Gwari Yamma, 9a: Gbari
Gwe, 9a
Gwere, 9a
G!wi, 9a
G!wi, 9: San-Speaking Peoples
Gwich'in, 1: Kutchin
Gyloffes, 9: Wolof
Gypsies, 6(R)
Gypsies, 1: Peripatetics; Rom; 3:
    Peripatetics; 4: Peripatetics
Gypsies and Caravan Dwellers in the
    Netherlands, 4

Ha, 9a
Haarat, 7: Tupari
Habashi, 3a: Sidi
Habbe, 9: Dogon
Habenapo, 1: Pomo
Habshi, 3: Sidi; 3a: Sidi
Habura, 3a
Haddad, 9a
Haddad, 9: Peripatetics of Afghanistan,
    Iran, and Turkey (Iran)
Haddi, 3a
Hadi, 3a: Haddi
Hadiya, 9a: Haner
Hadiyya, 9a
Hageners, 2: Melpa
Hagiorites, 4: Mount Athos
Hagueti, 7: Cashibo
Ha Ha Hae, 7a: HãHãHãi
HãHãHãi, 7a
Haibulu, 6(R): Avars
Haida, 1
Haidah, 1: Haida
Haiga, 3a: Havik Brahman
Haihaivansi, 3a: Haihaya Rajput
Haihaya Rajput, 3a
Haillom, 9a
Hai|lom, 9: San-Speaking Peoples
Haitians, 1; 8

Haïtiens, 8: Haitians
Hajala, 9: Peripatetics of Iraq . . .
    Yemen (Egypt)
Hajam, 3a: Nai
Hajango, 3a: Kuki
Hajjam, 3a: Nai
Hajuri, 3a: Khava
Hakka, 6(C)
Hakkipikki, 3a: Hale Paika
Haknyin, 6(C): Hakka
Hakuru, 3a: Vahumpura
Halab, 9: Peripatetics of Iraq . . .
    Yemen (Sudan)
Halaba, 3a: Pentiya; 9a: Alaba
Ḥalabi, 9: Peripatetics of
    Iraq . . . Yemen (Egypt)
Halagama, 3a: Salagama
Halakwalip, 7a: Kawe'skar
Halang Doan, 5
Halba, 3a
Halba, 3a: Pentiya
Halbi, 3a: Halba
Halchidhoma, 1
Halepaik, 3a: Hale Paika
Hale Paika, 3a
Halfans, 9: Nubians
Half-Breeds, 1: American Isolates
Halfbreeds, 1: Metis of Western Canada
Halia-Das, 3a: Kewat
Haliti, 7: Paresí
Halití, 7a: Paresí
Haliwa Indians, 1: American Isolates
Halkomelem, 1: Cowichan
Halleer, 3a: Hallir
Hallikar, 3a
Hallikararu, 3a: Hallikar
Hallikar Okkaliga, 3a: Hallikar
Hallir, 3a
Halpati, 3a: Dubla
Halpularen, 9a: Tocouleur
Halvakki Vakkal, 3a
Halwai, 3a
Hämäläaiset, 4: Finns
Hamba, 9a: Amba
Hambbe, 9: Dogon
Hamer, 9a
Hampangan, 5: Hanunóo
Han, 1; 6(C)
Han Baiyi, 6(C): Dai
Hanbar, 3a: Golla
Han Chinese, 6(C): Han
Han Dai, 6(C): Dai
Hande Kuruba, 3a: Kuruba
Hande Vazir, 3a: Kuruba
Handichikka, 3a: Handi Jogi
Handi Jogi, 3a
Handisew, 6(R): Andis
Hanena, 7a: Barasana
Haner-Banna, 9a: Hamer
Hangaza, 9a
Han'guk, 5: Korean
Hanhui, 6(C): Hui

Hani, 6(C)
Hani, 5: Akha
Hankutchin, 1: Han
Hannali, 3a
Hanneng, 3a: Kuki
Hanono-o, 5: Hanunóo
Hansa, 6(C): Achang
Hanti, 6(R): Khanty
Hantrika, 4: Peripatetics
Hanunóo, 5
Haokip, 3a: Kuki
Haolai, 3a: Kuki
Haoni, 6(C): Hani
Haoussa, 9: Hausa
Haqui, 8: Cahita
Harakantra, 3a
Harákmbet, 7: Mashco
Harákmbut, 7a: Toyoneri
Harari, 9a
Harbola, 3a: Basdewa
Hardas, 3a: Chitrakathi
Hare, 1
Hareri, 9a: Harari
Ha[rh] ndea[ng], 5: Sedang
Hari, 3a
Hari, 3a: Bhangi
Harijan, 3: Untouchables
Harni, 3a
Har-Santan, 3a: Hari
Haruai, 2: Wovan
Hasala, 3a: Hasalar
Hasalar, 3a
Hasalaru, 3a: Hasalar
Hasidim, 1
Haslar, 3a: Hasalar
Hassaniya, 9a: Maures
Hassouna, 9a
Hasula, 3a: Hasalar
Hataholi Lote, 5: Rotinese
Hata Lu'a, 5: Palu'e
Hata Rua, 5: Palu'e
Hatgar, 3a: Hatkar
Hati, 3a
Hatkar, 3a
Hatkar, 3a: Devanga
Haupit, 3a: Kuki
Hausa, 9
al Hausin, 9: Hausa
Haut-Katanga, 9a
Havasupai, 1
Havig, 3a: Havik Brahman
Havika, 3a: Havik Brahman
Havik Brahman, 3a
Hawaidar, 3a: Kadera
Hawaiian Islanders, 2: Hawaiians
Hawaiians, 2
Ḥawee, 9: Peripatetics of Iraq . . .
    Yemen (Egypt)
Haxluit, 1: Wishram
Hay, 6(R): Armenians
Haya, 9a
Haytians, 8: Haitians

Hazara, 9
Hazaragi, 9: Hazara
Hebbe-Gauda, 3a: Mukri
Hebrews, 1: Jews
Hehe, 9a
Heiltsuk, 1: Bellabella
Hei Miao, 6(C): Miao
Helav, 3a: Helava
Helava, 3a
Hellenes, 4: Greeks
Heman, 6(C): Hani
Hemba, 9a
Ḥemmeli, 9: Peripatetics of Iraq . . .
    Yemen (Egypt)
Hena, 3a
Henaya, 3a: Hena
Hengna, 3a: Kuki
Heni, 6(C): Hani
Hepetineri, 7: Amahuaca
Herati, 9: Peripatetics of Afghanistan,
    Iran, and Turkey (Afghanistan)
Herders of southern Africa, 9: Khoi
Herero, 9
Heri, 3a: Ahar; 8: Seri
Heruriwa, 7: Yukuna
Héta, 7a
Hetland, 4: Shetlanders
Hevero, 7: Jebero
Hewaktokto, 1: Hidatsa
el Heweidat, 9: Peripatetics of Iraq . . .
    Yemen (Egypt)
Hezareh, 9: Hazara
Hezare'i, 9: Hazara
Hezhe, 6(C): Hezhen
Hezhen, 6(C)
Hiaupiri, 7: Waimiri-Atroari
Híbaro, 7: Jivaro
Hicaque, 8: Jicaque
Hidatsa, 1
Higaonan, 5: Bukidnon
Higaunen, 5: Bukidnon
Highlander, 4: Highland Scots
Highlanders, 1: Appalachians
Highland Scots, 4
Hijra, 3
Hilani, 9: Fulani
Hillbillies, 1: Appalachians; Ozarks
Hill Kolis, 3: Koli
Hill Miri, 3a: Miri
Hill Pandaram, 3
Hill Pulaya, 3a: Pulluvan
Hill Tribes, 3
Hima, 9a
Hima, 9a: Nkore
Himarimã, 7a
Himberá, 8: Emberá and Wounaan
Hindoo, 3: Hindu
Hindous, 3: Mauritian
Hindu, 3
Hindus, 3: Mauritian
Hinin, 5: Burakumin
Hinna, 3a

Hipandis, 1: **Lipan Apache**
Hishkariana, 7a
Hispanics, 1: **Latinos**
Hitänwoiv, 1: **Arapaho**
Hitchiti, 1a
Hitnu, 7: **Guahibo-Sikuani**
Hitote, 7: **Witoto**
Hitunena, 1: **Gros Ventre**
Hjaltland, 4: **Shetlanders**
Hkamti Shan, 5: **Shan**
Hlikhin, 6(C): **Naxi**
Hmong, 5
Hmong, 1: **South and Southeast Asians of the United States**; 6(C): **Miao**
Hñahñu/Hñąhñų, 8: **Otomí of the Sierra**; **Otomí of the Valley of Mezquital**
Ho, 3a
Ho, 3: **Munda**
Hocangra, 1: **Winnebago**
Hochón, 8: **Chocho**
Hoctatas, 1: **Oto**
Ho Drong, 5: **Bahnar**
Hohe, 1: **Assiniboin**
Hokkaidō Ainu, 5: **Ainu**
Holar, 3a: **Holeya**
Holaya, 3a: **Holeya**
Holeya, 3a
Holia, 3a
Hollanders, 4: **Dutch**
Holli, 9a
Holo, 5: **Lamaholot**
Holontalo, 5: **Gorontalese**
Holuva, 3a: **Pentiya**
Holva, 3a: **Pentiya**
Homalco, 1: **Comox**
Hon-dyapá, 7a: **Bendyapá**
Hongsungh, 3a: **Kuki**
Hon-Potdar, 3a: **Sonar**
Hoopa, 1: **Hupa**
Hoorn Islands, 2: **Futuna**
Hopi, 1
Hopi-Tewa, 1
Hor, 3: **Munda**
Horahane, 4: **Bulgarian Gypsies**
Horn Islands, 2: **Futuna**
Hororo, 9a
Horudahua, 7a: **Morunawa**
Horunahua, 7: **Marinahua**
Hosadevara Okkalu, 3a: **Morasu Okkalu**
Hoti, 7
Houaïlou, 2: **Ajië**
Houma, 1: **Huma**
Houni, 5: **Akha**
Howihar, 9: **Peripatetics of Afghanistan, Iran, and Turkey (Iran)**
Hōzāyē, 9: **Jews of Kurdistan**
Hrangkhwal, 3a: **Kuki**
Hre, 5
H.Rê, 5: **Hre**

Hrusso, 3a: **Aka**
Hrvati, 4: **Croats**
Htin, 5: **T'in**
Hua, 6(C): **Han**
Huabi, 8: **Huave**
Huachipaire, 7a: **Wachipaeri**
Hualapai, 1: **Walapai**
Hua Miao, 6(C): **Miao**
Huaorani, 7: **Waorani**
Huaqiao, 5: **Chinese in Southeast Asia**
Huarayo
Huaren, 5: **Chinese in Southeast Asia**
Huarí, 7a: **Aikaná**
Huarijio, 8: **Guarijío**
Huastec, 8: **Wasteko**
Huaugrani, 7: **Waorani**
Huaque, 7a: **Karihona**
Huave, 8
Huavi, 8: **Huave**
Huazontecos, 8: **Huave**
Huba, 9a: **Kilba**
Huchnom, 1: **Yuki**
Hūdāyē, 9: **Jews of Kurdistan**
Hude, 9a: **Dghwede**
Huei, 5: **Oy**
Hughchee, 1: **Yuchi**
Huhmei, 8: **Chinantec**
Hui, 6(C)
Huichol, 8
Huichole, 8: **Huichol**
Huihui, 6(C): **Hui**
Huilliche, 7: **Araucanians**
Huitata, 7: **Witoto**
Huito, 7: **Witoto**
Huitoto, 7: **Witoto**
Huitoto Meneca, 7a: **Meneka**
Hulo, 9: **Mende**; 9a: **Mende**
Hulontalo, 5: **Gorontalese**
Hulsavar, 3a: **Hasalar**
Huma, 1
Huma, 9a: **Toposa**
Humai, 5: **Palaung**
Humaluh, 1: **Cowichan**
Humba, 9a: **Ovambo**
Humberá, 8: **Emberá and Wounaan**
Humptulip, 1: **Chehalis**
Hunde, 9a
Hune, 9a: **Dukawa**
Hungarians, 4
Hungarians, 1: **European-Americans**; **European-Canadians**
Hungaros, 4: **Spanish Rom**
Hung Miao, 6(C): **Miao**
Hunjara, 2: **Orokaiva**
Hunu, 3a
Hunzukuts, 3: **Burusho**
Huo, 7: **Piaroa**
Hupa, 1
Hupda, 7a
Huriní, 7: **Asurini**
Huron, 1

Huron of Lorette, 1: **Huron**
Hurumi, 7: **Yukuna**
Husaini Brahman, 3a
Hutanga, 1: **Kansa**
Hutterite Brethren, 1: **Hutterites**
Hutterites, 1
Hutu, 9a
Hutu, 9a: **Nyaruanda**
Huzaas, 1: **Osage**
Huzhu, 6(C): **Tu**
Hwach'ŏk, 5: **Kolisuch'ŏk**
Hydah, 1: **Haida**
Hyder, 1: **Haida**

Iaai, 2: **Loyalty Islands**
Ialofes, 9: **Wolof**
Iamin␣áwa, 7: **Jamin␣áwa**
Iatê, 7: **Fulniô**
Iatmul, 2
Iaualapití, 7: **Yawalapití**
Iauanauá, 7a: **Yawanawa**
Ibadan, 9: **Yoruba**
Ibali, 9a: **Teke**
Ibaloi, 5
Ibaloy, 5: **Ibaloi**
Iban, 5
Ibibio, 9; 9a
Ibilao, 5: **Ilongot**
Ibilaw, 5: **Ilongot**
Ibo, 9: **Igbo**
Ibo'tsa, 7a: **Okaina**
Ica, 7a: **Bintukua**
Icaguate, 7: **Siona-Secoya**
Icelanders, 4
Icelanders, 1: **European-Canadians**
Ichibemba, 9: **Bemba**
Ichikile, 7a: **Shukurú**
Ichilamba, 9a: **Lamba**
Idäan, 5: **Dusun**
Idafan, 9a: **Irigwe**
Idahan Murut, 5: **Murut**
Idaiyan, 3a
Idiga, 3a
Idiga, 3a: **Goundala**
Idigar, 3a: **Idiga**
Idakho, 9: **Luyia**
Idoma, 9a
Idu-Mishmi, 3a: **Mishmi**
Iduna, 2: **Goodenough Island**
Ife, 9: **Yoruba**
Ifonyin, 9: **Yoruba**
Ifugao, 5
Ifugaw, 5: **Ifugao**
Igabu, 1: **Kickapoo**
Igala, 9a
Igbira, 9a
Igbo, 9
Igbomina, 9: **Yoruba**
Iglulik Inuit, 1
Iglulingmiut, 1: **Iglulik Inuit**
Ignacio, 7: **Mojo**
Igodor, 5: **Ibaloi**

Igorot, 5: Bontok; Kankanai; Sagada
  Igorot
Iguanito, 7a: Wanaí
Ihka, 7a: Bintukua
Iiqhy, 6(R): Tsakhurs
Ijaw, 9a
Ijca, 7a: Bintukua
Ijebu, 9: Yoruba
Ijesha, 9: Yoruba
Ijka, 7a: Bintukua
Ijo, 9a: Ijaw
Ik, 9a
Ikake, 8: Jicaque
Ikaw, 5: Akha
Ikho, 5: Akha
Ikiha, 9a: Ha
Ikikuria, 9a: Kuria
I-Kiribati, 1: Micronesians; 2:
  Kiribati
Ikito, 7a
Ikokolemu, 9a: Kuman
Ikõrõ, 7a: Gavião
Iksonawa, 7a
Ikwere, 9a
Ilakeband, 3a: Patwa
Ilanon, 5
Ilanum, 5: Ilanon
Ilanun, 5: Ilanon
Ilaqeband, 3a: Patwa
Ilayatu, 3a: Ambalavasi
Ile, 6(R): Evenki
Ilhéus, 4: Azoreans
Illanun, 5: Ilanon
Illavan, 3a: Ezhuva
Illinois, 1
Illyrians, 4: Albanians
Ilmaasai, 9: Maasai
Ilongot, 5
Ilpirra, 2: Warlpiri
Ilungut, 5: Ilongot
Ilyongut, 5: Ilongot
Imacas, 7: Maká
Imajeghen, 9: Berbers of Morocco
Imazighen, 9: Berbers of Morocco
Imbangala, 9: Lunda
Imike, 7: Yukuna
Imzabiyen, 9: Berbers of Morocco
Inchazi, 9a: Rukuba
Indian Chinese, 3: Chinese of South
  Asia
Indian Christian, 3
Indians, 1: South and Southeast
  Asians of Canada; South and
  Southeast Asians of the United
  States
Indians of Baja California, 8
Indians of Robeson County, 1:
  Lumbee
Indians of Venustiano Carranza, 8:
  Tzotzil of San Bartolomé de los
  Llanos
Indígenas, 7: Saraguro

Indochinese, 1: South and Southeast
  Asians of Canada; South and
  Southeast Asians of the United
  States
Indo-Mauriciens, 3: Mauritian
Indo-Mauritians, 3: Mauritian
Indonesian, 5
Indonesians, 1: South and Southeast
  Asians of the United States
Indos, 1: South and Southeast Asians
  of the United States
Indo-Trinidadians, 8: East Indians in
  Trinidad
Indra Sudra, 3a: Kuruba
Ineme, 9a
Ingain, 7: Kaingáng
Ingalik, 1
Ingalikó, 7a: Ingarikó
Ingarico, 7: Akawaio
Ingarikó, 7a
Ingelete, 1: Ingalik
Ingessana, 9a
Ingilos, 6(R)
Ingush, 6(R): Chechen-Ingush
Inhini-Baré, 7a: Baré
Inibaloi, 5: Ibaloi
Inibaloy, 5: Ibaloi
Inibioi, 5: Inbaloi
Inimacá, 7: Maká
Injhwar, 3a
Inkality, 1: Ingalik
Inkariko, 7: Akawaio
Inkiliki, 1: Ingalik
Inkilikiiugel'nut, 1: Ingalik
Inkongo, 9a: Kuba
Insular Portuguese, 4: Azoreans;
  Madeirans
Inughuit. _See_ Eskimo
Inuit, 1
Inuit of Quebec, 1: Labrador Inuit
Inuñaina, 1: Arapaho
Iñupiat, 1: North Alaskan Eskimos
Iolof, 9: Wolof
Ionians, 4
Ioniennes, 4: Ionians
Iowa, 1
Ipai, 1: Kumeyaay
Ipande, 1: Lipan Apache
Ipare, 2: Tanna
Ipetinere, 7: Amahuaca
Ipewi, 7a: Kreen Akerôre
Ipi, 2: Orokolo
Ipugao, 5: Ifugao
Iqba'iliyen, 9: Berbers of Morocco
Iquito, 7a: Ikito
Ir, 6(R): Ossetes
Ira-an, 5: Palawan
Iraki, 3a: Iraqi
Iraligar, 3: Irula
Iramba, 9a
Iranche, 7a: Iranshe
Irangi, 9a: Rangi

Irani, 3a
Iranians, 9: Persians
Iranon, 5: Ilanon
Iranshe, 7a
Iraqi, 3a
Iraqw, 9
Irátxe, 7a: Iranshe
Irava, 3a: Ezhuva
Iraya, 5: Gaddang Irianese
Irifiyen, 9: Berbers of Morocco
Irigwe, 9a
Irish, 4
Irish, 1: European-Americans;
  European-Canadians
Irish Countrymen and Countrywomen,
  4: Gaels (Irish)
Irish Gypsies, 1: Irish Travelers
Irish Travelers, 1
Irish Travelers, 1: Peripatetics
Irish Travellers, 4
Irobmkateye, 7: Krikati/Pukobye
Iroquois, 1
Iron, 6(R): Ossetes
Iru, 9a: Nkore
Irula, 3
Irulan, 3: Irula
Isa, 9a: Ishan
Isanyati, 1: Santee
Iscobaquebu, 7a: Iksonawa
Isconahua, 7a: Iksonawa
Isekiri, 9a
Ishan, 9a
Ishawiyen, 9: Berbers of Morocco
Ishilhayen, 9: Berbers of Morocco
Ishindi Lunda, 9: Lunda
Ishír, 7: Chamacoco
Isixhosa, 9: Xhosa
Isla de Pascua, 2: Easter Island
Island Carib, 8: Carib of Dominica;
  Garifuna
Isleta, 1: Pueblo Indians
Isnag, 5: Isneg
Isned, 5: Isneg
Isneg, 5
Isoko, 9a
Isonkuaíli, 1: Okanagon
Israel, 6(R): Bukharan Jews
Israelite Karaites, 9: Karaites
Isroil', 6(R): Mountain Jews
Issa, 1: Catawba
Issei, 7: Asians in South America
Issues, 1: American Isolates
Is-te Semihn-ole, 1: Seminole
Istica-ti, 1: Seminole
Istopa, 1: Mandan
Isukha, 9: Luyia
Italiani in Svizzera, 4: Swiss, Italian
Italian Mexicans, 8
Italians, 4
Italians, 1: European-Americans;
  European-Canadians
Itanere, 1: Inughuit

Itatin, 7: Guarayu; Pauserna
Ite'chi, 7a: Taushiro
Iteghe, 9a: Teke
Itelmen, 6(R)
Itén, 7: Moré
Iténe, 7: Moré
Iteneo, 7: Moré
Iténez, 7: Moré
Iteso, 9
Itesyo, 9: Iteso
Itinerants, 4: Irish Travellers
Itneg, 5
Itonama, 7
Itucaliu, 7a: Urarina
Itza', 8
Itzá, 8: Itza'
Itzaj Maya, 8: Itza'
Itzá Maya, 8: Itza'
Iu Mian, 5: Yao of Thailand
Iuwana, 7a: Wanaí
Ivaparé, 7a: Héta
Ixcatec-Chocho, 8: Chocho
Ixil, 8
Iyala, 9a
Iyemi, 7a: Tariana
Iyich, 1: Tenino
Iz(e)di, 6(R): Yezidis
Izhava, 3a: Ezhuva
Izhuva, 3a: Ezhuva
Izoceño, 7: Chiriguano

Jaavotí, 7a: Jabutí
Jabarti, 9a
Jabutí, 7a
Jacalteco, 8: Jakalteko
Jackson Whites, 1: American Isolates
Jacobites, 9
Jad, 3a: Besta; Devanga
Jadam, 3a
Jadar, 3a: Jingar
Jadav, 3: Jatav
Jadon, 3a: Yadu Rajput
Jadua-Brahman, 3a
Jaduah-Brahman, 3a: Jadua-Brahman
Jaga, 3a: Basdewa
Jaguallapai, 1: Walapai
Jahai, 5: Semang
Jahanka, 9a
Jah Hut, 5: Senoi
Jaika, 8: Maleku
Jain, 3
Jaintia, 3a
Jaiswar, 3a: Bhatti
Jakalteko, 8
Jalagadugu, 3a: Sonjhara
Jalap, 3a
Jalali, 9: Peripatetics of Afghanistan,
    Iran, and Turkey (Afghanistan)
Jalari, 3a
Jalia Kaibarta, 3a: Kewat
Jalia Kaibartta, 3a: Kewat
Jaliya, 3a: Kewat

Jallad, 3: Kanjar
Jallonke, 9a: Dialonke
Jalo, 3a: Kewat
Jalof, 9: Wolof
Jalwa, 3a: Kewat
Jamaicans, 8
Jamaicans, 1: Black West Indians in the
    United States
Jamajabs, 1: Mohave
Jamamadí, 7a
Jambinahua, 7: Jamináwa
Jaminaua, 7: Jamináwa
Jamináwa, 7
Jaminawá, 7: Jamináwa
Janappan, 3a
Jangal Jati, 3a: Kuruvikkaran
Jangam, 3a: Jangama
Jangama, 3a
Janganah, 9: Peripatetics of Iraq . . .
    Yemen (Iraq)
Jangtei, 3a: Kuki
Janhanka, 9a: Diankhanke
Janjua, 3a
Japanese, 5
Japanese, 1: East Asians of Canada;
    East Asians of the United States;
    7: Asians in South America
Jar, 9a: Jarawa
Jarawa, 3a; 9a
Jari, 7a: Yarí
Jarú, 7a: Urupá
Jarwas, 3: Andamanese
Jasondhi, 3a: Bhat
Jat, 3
Jat, 9: Peripatetics of Afghanistan,
    Iran, and Turkey (Afghanistan)
Jatav, 3
Jatava, 3a: Jatav
Jat-Baluch, 9: Peripatetics of
    Afghanistan, Iran, and Turkey
    (Afghanistan)
Jathikarta, 3a: Telaga
Jati, 3a
Jatua, 3: Jatav
Jauaperí, 7: Waimiri-Atroari
Jaunas, 7: Ticuna
Jaunsari, 3a
Javahé, 7: Karajá
Javanese, 5
Javeri, 3a: Johari
Javheri, 3a: Johari
Jawa, 7: Yagua
Jayantia, 3a: Jaintia
Jebero, 7
Jecuches, 1: Cahuilla
Jekri, 9a: Isekiri
Jele, 3a: Kewat
Jeliya, 3a: Kewat
Jemadar, 3a: Kotwal
Jemez, 1: Pueblo Indians
Jenischen, 4: Peripatetics
Jenu-Kurumbas, 3: Kurumbas, Nayaka

Jenu-Nayaka, 3: Nayaka
Jerawa, 9a
Jetti, 3a
Jews, 1
Jews, 4: Ashkenazic Jews; Greek-
    Speaking Jews of Greece;
    Sephardic Jews
Jews, Arabic-Speaking, 9
Jews of Algeria, 9
Jews of Iran, 9
Jews of Islam, 9: Jews of the Middle
    East
Jews of Israel, 9
Jews of Kurdistan, 9
Jews of Lite, 6(R): Lithuanian Jews
Jews of South America, 7
Jews of the Middle East, 9
Jews of Yemen, 9
Jhadi Telenga, 3a
Jhalo, 3a: Malo
Jhalo Malo, 3a: Malo
Jhara, 3a: Sonjhara
Jhinwar, 3a
Jhir, 3a: Jhinwar
Jhira, 3a: Sonjhara
Jhiwar, 3a: Jhinwar
Jhora, 3a: Sonjhara
Jiarong, 6(C): Qiang
Jibana, 9: Mijikenda
Jibaro, 7: Jivaro
Jicaque, 8
Jicarilla, 1
Jie, 9a
Jigalong, 2: Mardudjara
Jildgar, 3a: Mochi
Jimdar, 3a: Khambu
Jin, 6(C): Mulam
Jing, 6(C)
Jingar, 3a
Jingar, 3a: Mochi
Jinghpaw, 5: Kachin; 6(C): Jingpo
Jingpo, 6(C)
Jino, 6(C)
Jirayat, 3a: Mochi
Jiripancoh, 7a: Pankararé
Jirjoront, 2: Yir Yoront
Jita, 9a
Jívara, 7: Jivaro
Jivaro, 7
Jívira, 7: Jivaro
Jiwi, 7: Guahibo-Sikuani
Jiye, 9a
Jju, 9a: Kaje
Jo Akwa, 9a: Nyakwai
Jocolabal, 8: Tojolab'al
Jogi, 3: Sadhu; 3a: Jugi; Yogi; 9:
    Peripatetics of Afghanistan, Iran,
    and Turkey (Afghanistan)
Johari, 3a
Joharia, 3a: Johari
John Day, 1: Tenino
Joiya, 3a

Jojolabal, 8: Tojolab'al
Jola, 9: Peripatetics of Afghanistan,
    Iran, and Turkey (Afghanistan)
Jolaha, 3a: Julaha
Jo Lango, 9: Lango
Jolha, 3a: Julaha
Joloanos, 5: Tausug
Jolof, 9: Wolof
Jolo Moros, 5: Tausug
Jo Long, 5: Bahnar
Jonam, 9a
Jongbe, 3a: Kuki
Joshi, 3a
Jotgi, 3a: Dakaut
Joti, 7: Hoti
Jouhari, 3a: Johari
Juaneño, 1: Luiseño
Juang, 3a
Juang, 3: Munda
Juave, 8: Huave
Juberí, 7a: Paumarí
Jugar, 6(R): Bukharan Jews
Jugi, 3a
Jūhū, 9: Jews of Kurdistan
Jukaghir Odul, 6(R): Yukagir
Juki, 9: Peripatetics of Iraq . . . Yemen
    (Syria and Lebanon); Peripatetics
    of Afghanistan, Iran, and Turkey
    (Iran)
Jukun, 9a
Julaha, 3a
Julaha, 3a: Padma Sale
Julahe, 3a: Julaha
Jumano, 1a
Jumia Magh, 3a: Marma
Jundu, 9a: Kamaku
Jungle people, 3: Chenchu
Jupda, 7a: Hupda
Jurassians, 4
Jurchen, 6(C): Manchu
Juríes, 7: Toba
Juriti, 7a: Jurití
Jurúna, 7a
Jyandra, 3a: Devanga
Jyntia, 3a: Jaintia
Jyotishi, 3a: Joshi

Kaana Masala, 9a: Masalit
Kaa'wa, 7: Paï-Tavytera
Kabbaligar, 3a: Besta
Kabber, 3a: Besta
Kabbera, 3a: Besta
Kabekirwak Cabécar, 8: Boruca, Bribri,
    and Cabécar
Kabher, 3a: Besta
Kabillary, 7: Ka'wiari
Kabiraj, 3a: Baidya
Kabiri, 2: Gogodala
Kabir-Panthi, 3a
Kabiyari, 7: Ka'wiari
Kabuli, 3a
Kabras, 9a

Kabras, 9: Luyia
Kabuliwallah, 3a: Kabuli
Kabutari, 3a: Beria
Kabyles, 9: Berbers of Morocco
Kacha, 3: Nagas
Kacha Gauliga, 3a: Golla
Kachara, 3a: Kachera
Kachari, 3a
Kache, 9a: Kaje
Kachera, 3a
Kachhi, 3a
Kachhi, 3a: Kachi Meman
Kachhia, 3a
Kachhwaha Rajput, 3a
Kachi Meman, 3a
Kachin, 5
Kada, 9a: Guidar
Kadan, 3a: Kadar
Kadapau, 1: Catawba
Kadar, 3a
Kadawapuritana, 7a: Warekena
Kadazan, 5: Dusun
Kader, 3a
Kadera, 3a
Kadhera, 3a: Kadera
Kadia, 3a
Kadir, 3a: Kadar
Kadiveu, 7: Kadiwéu
Kadiweu, 7: Kadiwéu
Kadiwéu, 7
Kadiya, 3a: Kadia
Kado, 9: Songhay
Kadu Golla, 3a
Kadu Kuruba, 3a
Kaduo, 6(C): Hani
Kadupattan, 3a
Kaduveo, 7: Kadiwéu
Kaele, 9a: Moundang
Kaet, 3a: Kayasth
Kaeth, 3a: Kayasth
Kaffer, 9: 7Xhosa
Kafficho, 9a: Kefa Mocha
Kaffir, 9: Xhosa; Zulu
Kafir, 3a
Kágaba, 7: Kogi
Kagan, 5: Kalagan
Kaghzi, 3a
Kagu, 9a: Gu
Kagulu, 9a: Kaguru
Kaguru, 9a
Kagwahiv, 7
Kahar, 3a: Bhoi; Jhinwar
Kahar Bhoi, 3a: Bhoi
Kahar Bhui, 3a: Bhoi
Kah-cho-tinneh, 1: Hare
Kahtar, 3a: Khattar
Kahut, 3a
Kahuilla, 1: Cahuilla
Kai, 2: Ningerum
Kaiapo, 7: Gorotire
Kaibartta, 3a: Kewat
Kaibartta-Das, 3a: Kewat

Kaikadi, 3a: Erakala; Korava
Kaikara, 3a: Kavikara
Kaikari, 3a: Korava
Kaikkoolar, 3a: Kaikolan
Kaikolan, 3a
Kaileuna, 2: Trobriand Islands
Kaimbé, 7a
Kain, 3a: Sonar
Kainah, 1: Blackfoot
Kainantu, 2: Tairora
Kaingáng, 7
Kaingangue, 7: Kaingáng
Kainguá, 7: Paï-Tavytera
Kainya, 3a: Sonar
Kaiowá, 7: Paï-Tavytera
Kait, 3a: Kayasth
Kaith, 3a: Kayasth
Kaiwa, 7: Kadiwéu
Kaiwá, 7: Paï-Tavytera
Kaiyuhkhotana, 1: Ingalik
Kajabí, 7a: Kayabí
Kaja-kaja, 2: Marind-anim
Kaje, 9a
Kakchiquel, 8: Kaqchikel
Kakhen, 3a: Singpho
Kakka Kuravan, 3a: Kakkalan
Kakkalan, 3a
Kakkan, 3a: Kakkalan
Kakwa, 9a
Kalaallit, 1: West Greenland Inuit
Kalachuri, 3a: Haihaya Rajput
Kalagan, 5
Kalal, 3a: Goundala; Iraqi; Kalar
Kalamantan, 5: Dusun
Kalanady, 3a
Kalanga, 3a
Kalapalo, 7
Kalapalu, 7: Kalapalo
Kalapuya, 1
Kalar, 3a
Kalari Panikkan, 3a: Kaniyan
Kalasha, 3
Kalash Kafir, 3: Kalasha
Kalauna, 2: Goodenough Island
Kalavant, 3a: Bhavin
Kalawant, 3a: Devadasi; Mirasi
Kalderash, 1: Rom
Kale, 1: Pomo; 4: Peripatetics
Kaliana, 7a: Sapé
Kalibugan, 5
Kalimantan Dayaks, 5
Kalina', 5: Isneg
Kalina, 7a: Gailbí
Kalingas, 5
Kalingga, 5: Kalingas
Kalingi, 3a: Kalanga
Kalingulu, 3a: Kalanga
Kalinji, 3a: Kalanga
Kalinya, 7: Cariña
Kalispel, 1
Kalkola, 3a: Beldar
Kalladi-mangam, 3a: Mondaru

Kalladi-siddhan, 3a: **Mondaru**
Kallan, 3a: **Kallar**
Kallar, 3a
Kallawaya, 7: **Callahuaya**
Kalmyks, 6(R)
Kalpaks, 6(R): **Karakalpaks**
Kalu, 3a: **Teli**
Kaluli, 2
Kalum, 9a: **Baga**
Kaluvadi, 3a: **Kudubi**
Kalwar, 3a: **Kalar**
Kalyanakulam, 3a: **Mangala**
Kalyo-kengyu, 3: **Nagas**
Kamadja, 9a
Kamakan, 7a: **Patashó**
Kamaku, 9a
Kaman Mishmi, 3a: **Mishmi**
Kamar, 3a
Kamarakoto, 7: **Pemon**
Kamathi, 3a: **Madiga**
Kamayurá, 7a
Kamba, 9a
Kambari, 9a
Kambatta, 9a: **Kembats**
Kambe, 9: **Mijikenda**
Kambeba, 7a: **Omawa**
Kambiwá, 7a
Kamboh, 3a
Kamchadals, 6(R): **Itelmen**
Kameheya, 7: **Yukuna**
Kamenshchiki, 6(R): **Siberiaki**
Kami, 3a
Kamia, 1a
Kamia, 1: **Kumeyaay**; 3a: **Kami**
Kamilaroi, 2
Kamma, 3a
Kammala, 3a: **Kammalan**
Kammalan, 3a
Kammara, 3a: **Kammalan**
Kammu, 5: **Kmhmu**
Kamoro, 2: **Mimika**
Kampa, 7: **Campa**
Kampuchean, 5: **Khmer**
Kamsá, 7a
Kamsala, 3a: **Kammalan**
Kamsale, 3a: **Kammalan**
Kamsé, 7a: **Kamsá**
Kanada Brahman, 3a
Kanak, 2: **Ajië**
Kanaka, 2: **Ajië**
Kanakajatiyavaru, 3a: **Kuruba**
Kanakkan, 3a
Kanakkan, 3a: **Kanikkar**
Kanaladi, 3a
Kanamantí, 7a
Kanamarí, 7a
Kanapulaya, 3a: **Pulluvan**
Kanarese, 3
Kanaujia Brahman, 3a: **Kanyakubja Brahman**
Kanaujiya, 3a: **Bhar; Kanyakubja Brahman**

Kanaura, 3a: **Kanet**
Kanaurese, 3a: **Kanet**
Kanbi, 3
Kanbi, 3: **Maratha**
Kanchan, 3a: **Devadasi**
Kanchaviralu, 3a: **Mailari**
Kancho, 1: **Hare**
Kandera, 3a: **Dhuniya; Kadera**
Kandeyo, 3a: **Vahumpura**
Kandh, 3: **Kond**
Kandha, 3a
Kandha Ganda, 3a: **Kandha**
Kandoazi, 7: **Candoshi**
Kandu, 3a: **Bharbhunja**
Kanela, 7: **Canela**
Kanembu, 9a
Kanet, 3a
Kang, 6(C): **Jingpo**
Kangra Brahman, 3a
Kanhobal, 8: **Q'anjob'al**
Kani, 3a: **Kanikkar**
Kanialanath Raval, 3a: **Raval Jogi**
Kaniang, 5: **Karen**
Kanikar, 3a: **Kanikkar**
Kanikaran, 3a: **Kanikkar**
Kanikkar, 3a
Kanikkaran, 3a: **Kanikkar**
Kanina, 1: **Havasupai**
Kani Razu, 3a: **Bhatraja**
Kanisan, 3a: **Kaniyan**
Kanishana, 7a: **Kanoé**
Kaniyan, 3a
Kanjar, 3
Kanjari, 3: **Kanjar**
Kanjobal, 8: **Q'anjob'al**
Kankanaey, 5: **Kankanai**
Kankanai, 5
Kankanay, 5: **Kankanai; Sagada Igorot**
Kannadiga, 3: **Kanarese**
Kannadiyan, 3a
Kannaji Bhat, 3a: **Bhatraja**
Kanoé, 7a
Kanongesha Lunda, 9: **Lunda**
Kanphata, 3a
Kansabanik, 3a: **Tamera**
Kansar, 3a: **Tamera**
Kansara, 3a: **Tamera**
Kansari, 3a: **Tamera**
Kansa, 1
Kantaha, 3a: **Mahabrahman**
Kantana, 9a: **Mama**
Kanu, 3a: **Bharbhunja**
Kanuck, 1: **Yurok**
Kanuri, 9; 9a
Kanwar, 3a: **Kawar**
Kanyakubja Brahman, 3a
Kanyan, 3a: **Kaniyan**
Kaoka, 2: **Guadalcanal**
Kaonde, 9a
Kaora, 3a: **Khairwar**
Kaowerawedj, 2: **Tor**

Kapali, 3a
Kapanawa, 7a
Kaparia, 3a: **Basdewa**
Kapariya, 3a
Kapauku, 2
Kapdi, 3a: **Basdewa**
Kapewar, 3a: **Munur**
Kapinga, 2: **Kapingamarangi**
Kapingaramarangi, 2
Kapiwana, 7a
Kapohn, 7: **Akawaio**
Kapon, 7: **Akawaio**
Kapong, 7: **Akawaio**
Kapóng, 7a: **Ingarikó; Patamona**
Kaposhó, 7: **Maxakali**
Kappiliyan, 3a
Kapsiki, 9a
Kapu, 3: **Reddi**
Kap Yorkere, 1: **Inughuit**
Kaqchikel, 8
Karabayo, 7a
Karachays, 6(R)
Karachi, 9: **Peripatetics of Afghanistan, Iran, and Turkey (Iran)**
Karadjari, 2: **Karadjeri**
Karadjeri, 2
Karagan, 5: **Kalagan**
Karagas, 6(R): **Tofalar**
Karagir, 3a: **Nai**
Karaïb, 7: **Maroni Carib**
Karaim, 6(R): **Karaites**; 9: **Karaites**
Karaite Jews, 9: **Karaites**
Karaites, 6(R); 9
Karaiyan, 3a: **Pattanavan**
Karaj, 9: **Peripatetics of Iraq . . . Yemen (Iraq)**
Karajá, 7
Karakalpaki, 6(R): **Karakalpaks**
Karakalpaks, 6(R)
Karalpaks, 6(R): **Karakalpaks**
Karamojong, 9; 9a
Karan, 3a
Karana, 3a: **Karan**
Karanga, 3a: **Korava**; 9: **Shona**
Karanjkar, 3a: **Jingar**
Karankawa, 1a
Karapana, 7a
Karaphuna, 8: **Garifuna**
Karataha, 3a: **Mahabrahman**
Karau, 2: **Murik**
Karava, 3a
Karavazhi, 3a
Karavlachs, 4: **Romanians**
Karbardians, 6(R): **Circassians**
Kare, 9a: **Toposa**
Kareang, 5: **Karen**
Karelians, 6(R)
Karelians, 4: **Finns**
Karen, 5
Karenga, 3a: **Korava**
Kare Okkalu, 3a
Karhada Brahman, 3a

Karhade Brahman, 3a: **Karhada
Brahman**
Karhataka Brahman, 3a: **Karhada
Brahman**
Kariang, 5: **Karen**
Kariera, 2
Karigar, 3a: **Beldar**
Karihona, 7
Karimbalan, 3a: **Karimpalan**
Karimojong, 9: **Karamojong**
Karimpalan, 3a
Karimui, 2: **Daribi**
Kariña, 7: **Cariña**
Karinya, 7: **Cariña**
Karipúna-Palikúr, 7: **Palikur**
Karitiana, 7a
Karjalaiset, 4: **Finns**; 6(R): **Karelians**
Karko, 3: **Abor**
Karmakar, 3a: **Kamar**
Karnam, 3a: **Karan**
Karna Sale, 3a
Karnati, 3a: **Nat**
Karnatic Brahman, 3a: **Kanada
Brahman**
Karnijô, 7: **Fulniô**
Karo, 5: **Batak**
Karok, 1
Karral, 3a: **Chandal**
Karthus Half-Breeds, 1: **American
Isolates**
Kärtner, 4: **Austrians**
Kartveli, 6(R): **Georgians**
Karuk, 1: **Karok**
Karumpuraththal, 3a: **Kappiliyan**
Karunjra, 3a: **Kunjra**
Kasa, 1: **Kaska**
Kasaba, 3: **Irula**
Kasai, 3a
Kasar, 3a: **Bohora; Tamera**
Kasava, 3: **Irula**
Kasban, 3a: **Devadasi**
Kasbi, 3a: **Devadasi**
Kaseng, 5: **Kasseng**
Kasera, 3a: **Tamera**
Kasharaí, 7a
Kashaya, 1: **Pomo**
Kashgarlik, 6(C): **Uigur**
Kashibo, 7: **Cashibo**
Kashikapdi, 3a: **Tirmali**
Kashinawa, 7
Kashiniti, 7a: **Paresí**
Kashmiri, 3
Kashubians, 4
Kasia, 3: **Khasi**
Kaska, 1
Kaskija, 7a: **Chane**
Kassab, 3a: **Kasai**
Kasseng, 5
Kassia, 3: **Khasi**
Kassya, 3: **Khasi**
Kasta Brahman, 3a
Kasuba, 3: **Irula**

Kasupá, 7a: **Aikaná**
Kastha, 3a
Kasya, 3: **Khasi**
Kaszubs, 4: **Kashubians**
Katab, 9a
Katabu, 3a: **Killekyata**
Kataha, 3a: **Mahabrahman**
Katakoti, 3a: **Katalarayan**
Katalarayan, 3a
Katang, 5: **Kattang**
Katangnang, 5: **Sagada Igorot**
Katawishí, 7a
Katawixi, 7a: **Katawishí**
Katbo, 3a: **Telaga**
K'atchô-gottinè, 1: **Hare**
Katera, 3a: **Dhuniya**
Kathak, 3a
Kathar, 3a: **Khattar**
Kathi, 3a
Kathia, 3a: **Kathi**
Kathik, 3a: **Kathak**
Kathiyara, 3a
Kathkari, 3a: **Katkari**
Kathodi, 3a: **Katkari**
Kathodia, 3a: **Katkari**
Katia, 3a
Katibaglodu, 3a: **Telaga**
Katika, 3a: **Kasai**
Katike, 3a
Katikilu, 3a: **Katike**
Katin, 5: **T'in**
Katio, 7: **Chocó**; 7a: **Tadó**
Katío, 8: **Emberá and Wounaan**
Katipappla, 3a: **Telaga**
Kätish, 6(R): **Khinalughs**
Katkari, 3a
Kato, 1
Kato, 5: **Katu**
Kattalan, 3a: **Ulladan**
Kattan, 3a: **Ulladan**
Kattang, 5
Katti Bomalawaru, 3a: **Telaga**
Kättid, 6(R): **Khinalughs**
Kattu Mahrati, 3a: **Kuruvikkaran**
Kattu Naikr, 3: **Nayaka**
Kattu Nayaka, 3: **Nayaka**
Katu, 5
Ka-Tu, 5: **Katu**
Katua, 3a: **Katia**
Katuema, 7a: **Hishkariana**
Katukina, 7a
Katwa, 3a: **Katia**
Kauguia, 7: **Kogi**
Kauiyari, 7: **Ka'wiari**
Kauli(a), 9: **Peripatetics of Iraq . . .
Yemen** (Iraq and Syria)
Kauma, 9: **Mijikenda**
Kaup, 2: **Murik**
Kaur, 3a: **Kawar**
Ka va, 6(C): **Wa**
Kavara, 3a
Kavarai, 3a: **Balija**

Kavikara, 3a
Kavinenya, 7a
Kaw, 1: **Kansa**; 5: **Akha**; 6(C): **Hani**
Kawahib, 7a: **Ntogapíd**
Kawaiisu, 1
Kawapana, 7a: **Chayawita**
Kawar
Kawarano, 7a
Kawchodinne, 1: **Hare**
Kawe'skar, 7a
Kawia, 1: **Cahuilla**
Ka'wiari, 7
Kawichan, 1: **Cowichan**
Kawillary, 7: **Ka'wiari**
Kawonde, 9a: **Kaonde**
Kaxararí, 7a: **Kashararí**
Kaxinaua, 7: **Kashinawa**
Kaxinawa, 7: **Kashinawa**
Kaya, 3a: **Kayasth**
Kayabí, 7a
Kayalan, 3a
Kayapa, 7a
Kayapo del Sur, 7: **Kaingáng; Xokléng**
Kayapo-Gorotire, 7: **Gorotire**
Kayapwe, 7a: **Andoa**
Kayashta, 3a: **Kayasth**
Kayasth, 3a
Kayath, 3a: **Kayasth**
Kayin, 5: **Karen**
Kayla, 9: **Falasha**
Kayova, 7: **Paï-Tavytera**
Kayuvava, 7a
Kazak, 6(C)
Kazakh, 6(C): **Kazak**
Kazakhs, 6(R)
Kazaks, 6(R): **Kazakhs**
Kazanlï, 6(R): **Volga Tatars**
Kazembe Mutanda Lunda, 9: **Lunda**
Keating Mountain Group, 1: **American
Isolates**
Kebahan, 5: **Kalimantan Dayaks**
Kebu, 9a
Kecherda, 9a
K'e-chia, 6(C): **Hakka**
Kédang, 5
Kefa-Mocha, 9a
Keffa, 9a: **Kefa Mocha**
Kekamba, 9a: **Kamba**
Keiyo, 9a
Keiyo, 9: **Nandi and Other Kalenjin
Peoples**
Kejia, 6(C): **Hakka**
Kelabit, 5: **Murut**
Kelangi, 9a: **Rangi**
Kel Tagelmust, 9: **Tuareg**
Kel Tamacheq, 9: **Tuareg**
Keer, 3a: **Kir**
Kehal, 3a
Kekchí, 8: **Q'eqchi'**
K'ekchí, 8: **Q'eqchi'**
Kelasi, 3a: **Nai**
Kelefomin, 2: **Telefolmin**

Kelefoten, 2: Telefolmin
Kelemantan, 5: Melanau
Kelts, 4: Gaels (Irish)
Kemaloh Kelabit, 5: Murut
Kemata, 9a: Kembats
Kembats, 9a
Kenai, 1: Tanaina
Kenaiakhotana, 1: Tanaina
Kenaitze, 1: Tanaina
Kenchli, 9: Peripatetics of Afghanistan,
    Iran, and Turkey (Iran)
Kensiu, 5: Semang
Kenyah-Kayan-Kajang, 5
Kenyi, 9a
Keot, 3a: Kewat
Keraki, 2
Keralite, 3: Malayali
Kerek, 6(R): Koryaks and Kerek
Keren, 6(C): Hakka
Keresans, 1: Keres Pueblo Indians
Keres Pueblo Indians, 1
Kerinchi, 5: Kerintji
Kerintji, 5
Kernow, 4: Cornish
Kern River Indians, 1: Tubatulabal
Ket, 6(R)
Kettle Falls Indians, 1: Sanpoil
Ketu, 9: Yoruba
Kewa, 2
Kewapi, 2: Kewa
Kewat, 3a
Keyot, 3a: Kewat
Khaa, 3a: Kho
Kha Ché, 5: T'in
Khadri Vaishnava, 3a: Satani
Khaka, 6(R): Dolgan
Khakas, 6(R)
Khae Lisaw, 5: Lisu
Khae Liso, 5: Lisu
Khagar, 3a: Kotwal
Khaira, 3a: Khairwar
Khairwa, 3a: Khairwar
Khairwar, 3a
Kha Kho, 5: Akha
Kha Ko, 5: Akha
Kha Lamet, 5: Lamet
Khal'mg, 6(R): Kalmyks
Khambu, 3a
Khamti, 3a
Khamu, 5: Kmhmu
Khānābādōsh, 3: Kanjar; Qalandar
Khand, 3: Kond
Khandait, 3a
Khandayat, 3a: Khandait
Khang, 5: Kachin
Khangar, 3a: Kotwal
Khant, 3a
Khanty, 6(R)
Kha P'ai, 5: P'u Noi
Kha Pai, 5: T'in
Khapariya, 3a: Kapariya
Kha Quy, 5: Lahu

Kharadi, 3a: Barhai
Kharak, 3a
Khareng, 3a: Kuki
Kharia, 3a
Kharia, 3: Munda; Lodhi
Kharian, 3a: Kharia
Kharpatil, 3a: Agri
Kharral, 3a
Kharria, 3a: Kharia
Kharva, 3a
Kharvi, 3a: Kharva
Kharwar, 3a
Kharwar, 3a: Khairwar
Khasa, 3a: Khasiya
Khasi, 3
Khasía, 3: Khasi
Khasiah, 3: Khasi
Khasiya, 3a
Khasiya Rajput, 3a: Dusadh
Khas Pakho, 5: Pacoh
Khassia, 3: Khasi
Khassu, 3: Khasi
Khatak, 3a: Khattak
Khati, 3a: Lohar
Khatik, 3a
Khatik, 3a: Kasai
Kha T'in, 5: T'in
Khatri, 3a
Khatriya, 3a: Satani
Khattak, 3a
Khattar, 3a
Khattri, 3a: Khatri
Khava, 3a
Khawathlang, 3a: Kuki
Khawchung, 3a: Kuki
Khayra, 3a: Khairwar
Khazak, 6(C): Kazak
Khelma, 3a: Kuki
Khephong, 3a: Kuki
Kheria, 3a: Kharia; Lodhi
Kherwar, 3a: Khairwar; Kharwar
Khetri, 3a
Khevsur, 6(R)
Khevsuri, 6(R): Khevsur
Khewat, 3a: Kewat
Khinalughs, 6(R)
Khoi, 9
Khoikhoi Hottentots, 9: Khoi
Khoisan, 9: Khoi
Khojem, 6(C): Hui
Khmae, 5: Khmer
Khmer, 5
Khmer, 1: South and Southeast Asians
    of Canada; South and Southeast
    Asians of the United States
Khmu, 5: Kmhmu
Kho, 3a
Khodalo, 3a: Bavuri
Khoja, 3
Khokar, 3a
Kho Ko, 5: Akha
Khokur, 3a: Khokar

Kholhou, 3a: Kuki
Kho' Mu, 5: Kmhmu
Khond, 3: Kond
Khon Thai, 5: Central Thai
Khosia, 3: Khasi
Khothalong, 3a: Kuki
Khua, 5
Khua, 5: Cua
Khubar, 3a: Kumhar
Khuhar, 3a: Kumhar
Khundzi, 6(R): Avars
Khu Xung, 5: Lahu
Khyan, 3a: Kewat
Kiam, 5: Cham
Kiatagmiut, 1: Central Yup'ik Eskimos
Kiaus, 5: Dusun
Kibera, 9a: Amba
Kibo, 9a: Birom
Kiboma, 9a: Boma-Sakata
Kibushy, 9: Sakalava
K'iche', 8
Kickapoo, 1
Kickapoo, 8: Kikapu
Kidigo, 9a: Digo
Kidlineks, 1: Copper Eskimo
Kiemba, 9a: Hemba
Kietas, 2: Nasioi
Kifuliiru, 9a: Furiiru
Kiga, 9a
Kikapu, 8
Kikapu, 1: Kickapoo
Ki Khási, 3: Khasi
Kik-Kun, 6(R): Kyrgyz
Kikongo, 9a: Kongo
Kikuyu, 9; 9a
Kilba, 9a
Kilega, 9a: Lega
Kilemoka, 7a
Kilendu, 9a: Lendu
Kilenge, 2
Kiliket, 3a: Killekyata
Kilivila, 2: Trobriand Islands
Kiliwi, 8: Indians of Baja California
Killekyata, 3a
Killekyatha, 3a: Killekyata
Killikiyata, 3a: Killekyata
Killinirmiut, 1: Copper Eskimo
Killiwal, 3: Kohistani
Kil Reddi, 3: Reddi
Kimakua, 9a: Makua
Kimanda, 9a: Nyasa
Kimatumbi, 9a: Matumbi
Kimbundu, 9a
Kimi, 9a: Krim
Kim Mun, 6(C): Yao
Kimyal, 2: Eipo
Kinalinga, 5: Kalingas
Kinga, 9a
Kingariya, 3a: Kingriya
Kingbetu, 9: Mangbetu; 9a: Mangbetu
Kingengereko, 9a: Ndengereko

Kingoni, 9a: Ngoni
Kingriha, 3a: Kingriya
Kingriya, 3a
Kingulu, 9a: Nguu
Kinh, 5: Vietnamese
Kiningo, 9a: Kaguru
Kinnara, 3a
Kinnara, 3a: Kanet
Kinnaurese, 3a: Kanet
Kinnepatoo, 1: Caribou Inuit
Kinner, 3a: Kanet
Kintak, 5: Semang
Kinyasa, 9a: Nyasa
Kinyika, 9a: Giriama
Kiot, 3a: Kewat
Kiowa, 1
Kiowa Apache, 1
Kioway, 1: Kiowa
Kipgen, 3a: Kuki
Kipsigis, 9
Kir, 3a
Kir, 9a: Mandari
Kirad, 3a: Kirar
Kiranti, 3
Kirar, 3a
Kirdi, 9: Sara
Kirgiz, 6(C) Kirgiz; 6(R): Kyrgyz
Kirgiz, 6(C)
Kiribati, 2
Kiriniti, 2: Kapingamarangi
Kiriri, 7a
Kiriri-Xuco, 7a: Kiriri
Kiriwina, 2: Trobriand Islands
Kirwo, 9a: Meru
Kisa, 9a
Kisa, 9: Luyia
Kisada, 3a: Nagasia
Kisan, 3: Oraon; 3a: Nagasia
Kishambala, 9a: Shanbaa
Kisii, 9: Gusii
Kissi, 9a
Kisutu, 9a: Ngoni
Kitanemuk, 1: Serrano
Kitava, 2: Trobriand Islands
Kiteke, 9a: Teke
Kitonaqa, 1: Kutenai
Kittim, 9a: Krim
Kittitians, 8: Kittsians and Nevisians
Kittsians and Nevisians, 8
Kivwanji, 9a: Wanji
Kiwai, 2
Kiwegapaw, 1: Kickapoo
Kiwikapawa, 1: Kickapoo
Kiyanzi, 9a: Yans-Mbun
Kiyombe, 9a: Yombe
Kizhakkan Pulaya, 3a: Pulluvan
Kizhi, 6(R): Altaians
Kk ayttchare Ottine, 1: Hare
'kKxou, 3: Chin
Klahoose, 1: Comox
Klallam, 1
Klamath, 1

Klickitat, 1: Klikitat
Klikitat, 1; 1a
Kmhmu, 5
Kmhmu', 5: Kmhmu
Knife, 1: Thompson
Ko, 3a: Kho
Koayá, 7a
Kobewa, 7: Cubeo
Kocch, 3a: Kochh
Koch, 3a: Kochh
Kochh, 3a
Koch-Mandai, 3a: Kochh
Kochuvelan, 3a
Kochuvelanmar, 3a: Kochuvelan
Kodara, 3: Coorg
Kodikkalkaran, 3: Labbai
Koeboe, 5: Kubu
Koeri, 3a: Koiri
Kofán, 7a
Kofyar, 9a
Kogapakori, 7: Matsigenka
Köggaba, 7: Kogi
Kogi, 7
Kohatur, 3: Kota
Kohistani, 3
Kohistanis, 9: Pashai
Kohli, 3a
Koi, 3: Gond; Koya
Koiari, 2
Koil Pantala, 3a: Koil Tampuran
Koil Tampuran, 3a
Koirao, 3a: Kuki
Koireng, 3a: Kuki
Koiri, 3a
Kokama, 7: Cocama
Koka-mungin, 2: Yir Yoront
Kokna, 3a: Konkna
Kokni, 3a: Konkna
Koko, 9a: Bassa
Koko Manjoen, 2: Yir Yoront
Kokomindjan, 2: Yir Yoront
Kokonino, 1: Havasupai
Kokorda, 9a
Kokwapá, 1: Cocopa
Kol, 3
Kol, 3: Munda
Kola, 9: Tropical-Forest Foragers
Kolam, 3a
Kolarian, 3: Munda
Kolcha, 3a: Kolgha
Kolchan-Teneyna, 1: Koyukon
Kolela, 9a: Dakarkari
Kolgha, 3a
Kolhati, 3a: Beria; Domara; Nat
Koli, 3
Koli, 3a: Mutrasi
Kolibugan, 5: Kalibugan
Koli Christian, 3a: East Indian
Koli Dhor, 3a: Kolgha
Koli Machhi, 3a: Macchi
Kolisuch'ök, 5
Kolita, 3a: Kolta

Koliyan, 3a
Kollia, 3a
Kololo, 9: Lozi; 9a: Lozi
Kolta, 3a
Kom, 3a: Kuki
Komarpaik, 3a
Komati, 3a
Komi, 6(R)
Komparía, 7: Campa
Komti, 3a: Komati
Konai, 3a: Mochi
Konambo, 7a: Andoa
Kond, 3
Konda, 2: Dani
Konda Dora, 3a
Kondadora, 3a: Konda Dora
Konda Kapu, 3a: Konda Dora
Konde, 9a: Makonde; 9a: Ngonde
Kondl, 3: Kond
Kondoma, 6(R): Shors
Konga Malayan, 3a
Konga Vellala, 3a
Kongo, 9; 9a
Konhomtata, 1: Pomo
Konjara, 9a: Fur
Konjo, 9a
Konkanastha, 3: Chitpavan Brahman
Konkani Brahman, 3a
Konkani Maratha, 3a: Gabit
Konkani Sudra, 3a: Kudumi Chetti
Konkau, 1: Maidu
Konkna, 3a
Kon Ko De, 5: Bahnar
Konkone, 1: Tonkawa
Konkow, 1: Maidu
Kono, 9a
Konso, 9
Kontum, 5: Bahnar
Konyak, 3: Nagas
Konzo, 9a: Konjo
Koo, 3a: Kho
!Koõ, 9a
!Koõ, 9: San-Speaking Peoples
Kooch Band, 3a: Kuchband
Koodan, 3a: Kudan
Koonarie, 2: Dieri
Koosa, 9: Xhosa; 9a: Xhosa
Kootan, 3a: Kudan
Kootchin, 1: Kutchin
Kootenay, 1: Kutenai
Kopu, 6(C): Gelao
Kora, 3: Munda; 3a: Khairwar;
    Korava
Koracha, 3a: Korava
Koraga, 3a: Korava
Koragar, 3a: Korava
Korait, 3a: Gorait
Korama, 3a: Korava
Koranga, 3a: Korava
Koranko, 9a
Korar, 3a: Korava
Korara, 9a: Uduk

Korashi, 9: Pashai
Korava, 3a
Koravan, 3a: Panan
Korchar, 3a: Korava
Korean, 5
Koreans, 6(R)
Koreans, 1: East Asians of Canada;
    East Asians of the United States;
    7: Asians in South America
Koreans in Japan, 5
Korewahe, 7a
Korga, 3a: Korava
Korgar, 3a: Korava
Kori, 3a
Koriki, 2: Namau
Korinchi, 5: Kerintji
Koring, 9a: Orri
Korka, 3a: Adi
Korku, 3
Korku, 3: Munda
Kormar, 3a: Korava
Korner, 4: Peripatetics
Koro, 9a
Koroa, 1: Tunica
Korsou, 8: Curaçao
Korua, 3a: Korava; Korwa
Korubo, 7a
Korumbiara, 7a: Aikaná
Korva, 3a: Korava
Korwa, 3a
Korwa, 3: Munda
Korwah, 3a: Erakala
Koryaks and Kerek, 6(R)
Koryo, 6(R): Koreans
Koshta, 3a: Koshti
Koshti, 3a
Koshti, 3a: Devanga
Kosian, 5: Balantak
Kosirau, 2: Maisin
Kosirava, 2: Maisin
Kosrae, 2
Kosraeans, 1: Micronesians
Kossa, 9: Mende; 9a: Mende
Kosso, 9: Mende
Kossowa, 9: Gusii
Kota, 3
Kotal, 3a: Kotwal
Kotar, 3: Kota
Koter, 3: Kota
Kothur, 3: Kota
Kotitia, 7: Wanano
Koto, 7a: Payawá
Kotoko, 9a
Kotokori, 9a: Igbira
Kottai Vellala, 3a
Kotte Okkalu, 3a
Kotsuny, 7a: Uru
Kot Vakkal, 3a: Kotte Okkalu
Kotwal, 3a
Kotwar, 3a: Chadar; Kotwal
Kougni, 9a: Kongo
Koulango, 9a

Kouli, 9: Peripatetics of Afghanistan,
    Iran, and Turkey (Afghanistan)
Koupui, 3a
Kouyou, 9a: Mboshi
Kowatingok, 7a: Ingarikó
Kowli, 9: Peripatetics of Afghanistan,
    Iran, and Turkey (Iran)
Kowohan, 3a: Kurichchian
Koya, 3
Koyukon, 1
Koyyo-Nayaka, 3: Nayaka
Kpe, 9a
Kpelle, 9
Kpese, 9: Kpelle
Kpilakpila, 9a: Pila-Pila
Krahn, 9a
Krahó, 7: Craho
Krahô, 7: Craho
Krainisch, 4: Slovenes
Kraô, 7: Craho
Kräshenlär, 6(R): Kriashen Tatars
Kreda, 9a
Kreen Akerôre, 7a
Krem, 5: Bahnar
Krenjé, 7a: Pukobyé
Kreol, 3: Mauritian
Krepi, 9a: Ewe
Kreshchenye Tatary, 6(R): Kriashen
    Tatars
Kriashen Tatars, 6(R)
Krīkateye, 7: Krikati/Pukobye
Krīkatí, 7: Krikati/Pukobye
Krikati/Pukobye, 7
Krim, 9a
Krio, 9a: Creoles
Krishna Golla, 3a: Golla
Krishna-kula, 3a: Golla
Krishnakuladavaru, 3a: Kadu Golla
Krishnavakakkar, 3a
Krites, 4: Cretans
Kritiči, 4: Cretans
Kritiki, 4: Cretans
Krixaná, 7: Waimiri-Atroari
Kroo, 9a: Kru
Krou of Bas Cavally, 9a
Krowé, 5: Ata Tana 'Ai
Kru, 9a
Krumen, 9a: Kru
Krymchaks, 6(R)
Krymskie, 6(R): Crimean Tatars
K'rymtatarlar, 6(R): Crimean Tatars
Kryvians, 1: European-Americans;
    European-Canadians
Kshatriya, 3
Kshaurak, 3a: Nai
Kuaghe, 2: New Georgia
Kuaiquer, 7: Awá Kwaiker
Kuba, 9a
Kubachins, 6(R)
Kubachintsy, 6(R): Kubachins
Kubar, 3a: Kumhar
Kubhar, 3a: Kumhar

Kubu, 5
Kubuna, 2: Bau
Kubutar, 3a: Nat
Kuchband, 3a
Kuchbandhia, 3a: Kuchband
Kuche, 9a: Rukuba
Kucong, 5: Lahu
Kuda, 3: Oraon
Kudan, 3a
Kudavakkal, 3a
Kudiya, 3a
Kudubi, 3a
Kudumata, 9a: Diola
Kudumi, 3a: Kudumi Chetti
Kudumi Chetti, 3a
Kudumikkar, 3a: Kudumi Chetti
Kudumo, 3a
Kuhlanapo, 1: Pomo
Kui, 5
Kui, 3: Kond
Kuiba, 7: Cuiva
Kuigpagmiut, 1: Central Yup'ik
    Eskimos
Kuikuro, 7: Kuikuru
Kuikuru, 7
Kuisítapúya, 7a: Warekena
Kujubi, 7a
Kukamba, 9a: Amba
Kuki, 3a
Kukna, 3a: Konkna
Kuku, 9a
Kuku, 3: Chin
Kukwe, 9a: Ngonde
Kulavadi, 3a: Holeya
Kulina, 7: Culina
Kulleespelm, 1: Kalispel
Kulsekharam, 3a: Satani
Kulta, 3a: Kolta
Kumam, 9a: Kuman
Kuman, 9a
Kuman, 2: Chimbu
Kumar, 3a: Kumhar
Kumbara, 3a: Kumhar
Kumbaran, 3a: Kumhar
Kumbaro, 3a: Kumhar
Kumbhakar, 3a: Kumhar
Kumbhar, 3a: Kumhar
Kumeyaay, 1
Kumhar, 3a
Kummara, 3a: Kumhar
Kumuinu, 1: Nez Percé
Kumyks, 6(R)
Kuna, 8
Kunari, 2: Dieri
Kunawara, 3a: Kanet
Kunbi, 3: Maratha
Kunchati Okkalu, 3a: Kunchitiga
Kunchigar, 3a: Kunchitiga
Kunchiliyan, 3a: Kunchitiga
Kunchitiga, 3a
Kundu Vadiyan, 3a
Kunduvatiyan, 3a: Kundu Vadiyan

Kunema, 9a
!Kung, 9a
Kungmiut, 1: Netsilik Inuit
Kunjra, 3a
Kunkara, 3a: Kachhia
Kunloi, 5: Palaung
Kunnuva, 3a
Kunsa, 7a: Atakama
Kunte, 3a
Kuntei, 3a: Kuki
Kunyi, 9: Kongo
Kuoy, 5: Kui
Kuppesaz, 3a: Dabgar
Kur, 3a: Kawar
Kuramwar, 3a: Kuruba
Kurasoleño, 8: Curaçao
Kurava, 3a: Kuruba
Kuravan, 3a: Korava
Kuraver, 3a: Korava
Kurdim, 9: Jews of Kurdistan
Kurds, 6(R); 9
Kuri, 3a: Mayara
Kuria, 9a
Kuricchiyan, 3a: Kurichchian
Kurichchan, 3a: Kurichchian
Kurichchian, 3a
Kurichiya, 3a: Kurichchian
Kurichiyan, 3a: Kurichchian
Kurichiyar, 3a: Kurichchian
Kurile Ainu, 5: Ainu
Kurintji, 5: Kerintji
Kurmandz, 6(R): Kurds
Kurtatchi, 2
Kuruba, 3a
Kurubas, 3: Kurumbas
Kuruchan, 3a: Kurichchian
Kurukh, 3: Oraon
Kurukkal, 3a: Ambalavasi
Kurukwa, 7: Yuqui
Kuruma, 3a: Kuruba
Kuruman, 3a: Kuruba
Kurumba, 3a: Kuruba
Kurumbas, 3
Kurumo, 3a: Kudumo
Kurunkh, 3: Oraon
Kurup, 3a: Kaniyan
Kuruparía, 7: Campa
Kuruvikkaran, 3a
Kuruvina Banajiga, 3a: Bili Maggar
Kuruvinna Setti, 3a: Bili Maggar
Kusaie, 2: Kosrae
Kuseri, 9a: Kotoko
Kusikia, 7a
Kusquqvagmiut, 1: Central Yup'ik
    Eskimos
Kusuvar, 3a
Kutakina Acre, 7a
Kutana, 3a: Bhangi
Kuṭaṇa, 9: Peripatetics of Afghanistan,
    Iran, and Turkey (Afghanistan)
Kutchin, 1
Kutenai, 1

Kuttawa, 1: Carrier
Kutubuans, 2: Foi
Kutzovlachs, 4: Romanians
Kuvoko, 9a: Lamang
Kuznets Tatars, 6(R): Shors
Kwaara borey, 9: Songhay
Kwagulth, 1: Kwakiutl
Kwahu, 9: Akan
Kwakwak, 9a: Kakwa
Kwaiailk, 1: Chehalis
Kwaiker, 7: Awá Kwaiker
Kwaio, 2: Malaita
Kwajalein, 2: Marshall Islands
Kwakiool, 1: Kwakiutl
Kwakiutl, 1
Kwalhiokwa, 1a
Kwangali-Gcikuru, 9a
Kwanim Pa, 9a: Uduk
Kwanyama, 9a: Ovambo
Kwapa, 1: Quapaw
Kwara, 9: Yoruba
Kwara'ae, 2: Malaita
Kwarra, 9a: Mama
Kwawkewlth, 1: Kwakiutl
Kwawkwakawakw, 1: Kwakiutl
KwaZulu, 9: Zulu
Kweni, 9a: Gouru
Kwerba, 2: Tor
Kwi, 5: Lahu
Kwoll, 9a: Irigwe
Kwoma, 2
Kxoe, 9a
Kxoe, 9: San-Speaking Peoples
Kyenga, 9a: Shangawa
Kyinnaa, 1: Yurok
Kyoma, 7: Angaité
Kypriotes, 4: Cypriots
Kyrghyz, 6(C): Kirgiz
Kyrgyz, 6(R)
Kyrgyz, 6(C): Kirgiz

La, 6(C): Wa
Laban, 3a: Banjara
Labana, 3a
Labana, 3a: Banjara
Labbai, 3
Labhana, 3a: Banjara
Labrador Eskimo, 1: Labrador Inuit
Labrador Inuit, 1
Labwor, 9a
Lacandon, 8: Lakandon
Lacandone, 8: Lakandon
Lachi, 6(C): Jingpo
Lad, 3a: Ladar
Ladakhi, 3a
Ladar, 3a
Ladin, 4
Ladinos, 8
Ladinos, 4: Ladin
Lad Kasab, 3a: Kasai
La-eng, 5: Palaung
Lafquenche, 7: Araucanians

Laget, 2: Lak
Lagoon Cluster, 9a
Lagoon Islands, 2: Tuvalu
Laguna, 1: Keres Pueblo Indians;
    Pueblo Indians
Lahaula, 3a: Lahula
Lahauli, 3a: Lahula
Laheri, 3a: Lakhera
Lahu, 5; 6(C)
Lahula, 3a
Lahuli, 3a: Lahula
Lahuna, 6(C): Lahu
Lahupa, 6(C): Lahu
Lahuxi, 6(C): Lahu
Lai, 3: Chin
Laifang, 3a: Kuki
Lairen, 6(C): Hakka
Laizo, 3: Chin
Lajjhar, 3a: Rajjhar
Lak, 2
Lakalai, 2
Lakandon, 8
Lake, 1
Lake Miwok, 1: Coast Miwok
Lakher, 3
Lakhera, 3a
Lakheri, 3a: Lakhera
Laki, 5
Lakk, 6(R): Laks
Lakota, 1: Teton
Laks, 6(R)
Lala, 3a: Kayasth
Lalaki, 5: Laki
Lalang, 6(C): Jingpo
Lalawa, 9a: Dakarkari
Lalbegi, 3a
Lal Dasi, 3a
Lali, 9a: Kongo
Lalung, 3a
Lama, 3a
Lama, 3: Tamang
Lamadu, 5: Kalimantan Dayaks
Lamaholot, 5
Lamane, 3a: Banjara
Lamang, 9a
Lamani, 3a: Banjara
Lamba, 9a
Lambadi, 3a: Banjara
Lambani, 3a: Banjara
Lambel, 2: Lak
Lamet, 5
Lamgang, 3a: Kuki
Lamuts, 6(R): Even
L'añagashik, 7: Toba
Lanatai, 5: Yuan
Landa, 3a: Mondaru
Landawadu, 3a: Mondaru
Land Dayaks, 5: Kalimantan Dayaks
Landlord, 3: Zamindar
Landogo, 9a: Lokko
Landouma, 9a
Landouman, 9a: Landouma

Langalanga, 2: Malaita
Langha, 3a: Mirasi
Langi, 9a
Langi, 9: Lango; 9a: Rangi
Lango, 9
Lango, 9: Acholi; 9a: Didinga; Langi
Langoli Pardhi, 3a: Pardhi
Langshu, 6(C): Jingpo
Langwo, 6(C): Jingpo
Lanòh, 5: Semang
Lanon, 5: Ilanon
Lao, 5
Lao, 1: South and Southeast Asians of
    Canada; South and Southeast
    Asians of the United States; 5:
    Yuan
Laoc, 5: Kalagan
Lao Isan, 5
Lao Loum, 5: Lao
Lao Meui, 5: Lao
Lao Neua, 5: Lao
Lao Phuan, 5: Lao
Lao Theung, 5: Kmhmu
Lao Yuon, 5: Lao
Lapalapa, 7a: Leko
Lapp, 4: Saami
Lapps, 6(R): Saami
Larhia, 3a: Beldar
Larim, 9a: Longarim
Larka Kol, 3a: Ho
Larka Kolh, 3a: Ho
La Sam, 6(C): Dai
Lasaw, 5: Lisu
Lashi, 5: Lisu; 6(C): Jingpo
Lasi, 5: Lisu
Lassik, 1: Wailaki
Latechelechí-Maiceros, 7: Nivaclé
Latinos, 1
Latter-Day Saints, 1: Mormons
Latvians, 6(R)
Latvians, 1: European-Americans;
    European-Canadians
Latvieši, 6(R): Latvians
Latvji, 6(R): Latvians
Lau, 2
Lau, 2: Malaita
Lauru, 2: Choiseul Island
Laus, 2: Malekula
Lava, 5: Lawa
Lavana, 3a: Lohana
Lave, 5: Brao
Laven, 5: Loven
Lavu'a, 5: Lawa
Lawa, 5
Lawa, 5: Tai Lue; T'in
Lawangan, 5: Kalimantan Dayaks
Lawani, 9: Peripatetics of Afghanistan,
    Iran, and Turkey (Afghanistan)
La-wor-a, 5: Lawa
Laya, 3a: Maulik
Laz, 6(R)
Lazoi, 6(R): Laz

LDS, 1: Mormons
League of the Iroquois, 1: Iroquois
Lebanese, 1: Arab Americans
Lebou, 9a
Leco, 7a: Leko
Lega, 9a
Leko, 7a
Lela, 9a: Dakarkari
Lele, 9a
Le-Met, 5: Lamet
Lemki, 6(R): Capartho-Rusyns
Lenape, 1: Delaware
Lenca, 8
Lendien, 3: Mauritian
Lendu, 9a
Lendu, 3: Mauritian
Lengola, 9a
Lengthang, 3a: Kuki
Lengua, 7
Lengua, 7: Maká
Lengua-Maskoi, 7: Lengua
Lengua-Sur, 7: Lengua
Lenti, 3a: Kuki
Leonese, 4
Lepanto Igorot, 5: Sagada Igorot
Lepcha, 3
Leper's Island, 2: Ambae
Le Shu O-op'a, 5: Lisu
Lesu, 2
Lesuo, 5: Lisu
Letoama, 7a: Retuna
Letten, 6(R): Latvians
Letts, 6(R): Latvians
Leu, 5: Bru
Leur Seur, 5: Lisu
Le va, 6(C): Wa
Lezgi, 6(R): Lezgins
Lezgins, 6(R)
Lhangum, 3a: Kuki
Lho, 5: Lahu
Lhoba, 6(C)
Lhote, 3: Nagas
Lhoujem, 3a: Kuki
Lhouvun, 3a: Kuki
Li, 6(C)
Li, 5: Lisu
Liang, 6(C): De'ang
Libres, 7: Afro-Colombians; Afro-
    Hispanic Pacific Lowlanders
    of Ecuadorand Colombia;
    Afro–South Americans
Lietuva, 6(R): Lithuanians
Lihsaw, 5: Lisu
Likouala, 9a: Mboshi
Lillooet, 1
Lilowat, 1: Lillooet
Lil'wat, 1: Lillooet
Limba, 9a
Limba, 9a: Ngabaka
Limbu, 3
Ling, 6(C): Mulam
Linga Balija, 3a: Balija

Linga Banajiga, 3a: Balija
Lingayat, 3
Lingotes, 5: Ilongot
Lip'a, 5: Lisu
Lipan Apache, 1
Lipane, 1: Lipan Apache
Lipianis, 1: Lipan Apache
Lipo, 5: Lisu
Lip'o, 5: Lisu
Lipyane, 1: Lipan Apache
Lisaw, 5: Lisu
Li-shaw, 5: Lisu
Lishu, 5: Lisu
Liso, 5: Lisu
Lisu, 5; 6(C)
Litawen, 6(R): Lithuanians
Lithuanian Jews, 6(R)
Lithuanians, 6(R)
Lithuanians, 1: European-Americans;
    European-Canadians
Litva, 6(R): Lithuanians
Litvaks, 6(R): Lithuanian Jews
Litwa, 6(R): Lithuanians
Liyuwa, 9a
Llawa, 7: Yagua
Lleeengit, 1: Tlingit
Lo, 9a: Gouru
Lobi-Dagarti Peoples, 9
Lobirifor, 9a
LoBirifor, 9: Lobi-Dagarti Peoples
LoDagaa, 9: Lobi-Dagarti Peoples
Lodha, 3a: Lodhi
Lodhe, 3a: Lodhi
Lodhi, 3a
Lo-Gang, 9: Acholi
Logoli, 9a
Logoli, 9: Luyia
Logone, 9a: Kotoko
Logwari, 9: Lugbara
Lohana, 3a
Lohar, 3a
Lohar, 3a: Jingar
Lohara, 3a: Lorha
Lohei, 5: Lahu
Lohra, 3a: Lorha
Loinan, 5: Saluan
Loinanezen, 5: Saluan
Loindang, 5: Saluan
Loisu, 5: Lisu
Lokko, 9a
Lokono, 7a
Lokop, 9a: Samburu
Lolaki, 5: Laki
Lolo, 6(C): Yi; 9a: Lomwe; Macua-
    Lomue
Lom, 6(R): Gypsies
Lombaha, 2: Ambae
Lomomgo, 9: Mongo
Lomongo, 9: Mongo
Lomwe, 9a
Lonari, 3a
Lonaria, 3a: Lonari

Longana, 2: **Ambae**
Longarim, 9a
Long Belah, 5: **Modang**
Long Glit, 5: **Modang**
Long Island Indians, 1: **Metoac**
Long Way, 5: **Modang**
Lonkar, 3a: **Lonari**
Lonmali, 3a: **Lonari**
Loochoo Islanders, 5: **Okinawans**
Lopari, 6(R): **Saami**
LoPiel, 9: **Lobi-Dagarti Peoples**
Lor, 9: **Lur**
Lord Howe, 2: **Ontong Java**
Lord Howe's Group, 2: **Ontong Java**
Lorenzano, 7: **Mojo**
Lorenzo, 7: **Amuesha**
Lorha, 3a
Lori, 9: **Lur**
LoSaala, 9: **Lobi-Dagarti Peoples**
Lotia, 3: **Bohra**
Lotilla Murle, 9a
Loucheux, 1: **Kutchin**
Lovale, 9a: **Lwena**
Lovalle, 9a
Love, 5: **Brao**
Loven, 5
Lower Chehalis, 1: **Chehalis**
Lower Lillooet, 1: **Lillooet**
Lower Nubians, 9: **Nubians**
Lower Pima, 8: **Pima Bajo**
Lower Rogue River Indians, 1: **Chastacosta**
Lower Zambezi, 9a
LoWiili, 9: **Lobi-Dagarti Peoples**
Lowland Scots, 4
Loyalty Islands, 2
Lozi, 9; 9a
Lü, 5: **Tai Lue**
Lua, 5: **Lawa**
Lua', 5: **Tai Lue**
Luaʔ, 5: **T'in**
Luangiua, 2: **Ontong Java**
Luapula Lunda, 9: **Lunda**
Luba Kaonde, 9a: **Kaonde**
Luba Katanga, 9: **Luba of Shaba**
Lubale, 9a: **Lwena**
Luba Lomami, 9: **Luba of Shaba**
Luba of Shaba, 9
Luba Samba, 9: **Luba of Shaba**
Luba Shankagi, 9: **Luba of Shaba**
Lucians, 8: **Saint Lucians**
Ludars, 1: **Peripatetics**
Lue, 5: **Tai Lue**
Luena, 9a: **Lovalle**
Luganda, 9: **Ganda**; 9a: **Ganda**
Lugbara, 9
Lugosa, 9a: **Soga**
Luhar, 3a: **Lohar**
Luiseño, 1
Lukenyi, 9a: **Soga**
Luli, 9: **Peripatetics of Afghanistan, Iran, and Turkey** (Iran)

Luli Mogat, 9: **Peripatetics of Afghanistan, Iran, and Turkey** (Afghanistan)
Lumbee, 1
Lumbwa, 9: **Kipsigis**
Lummi, 1: **Klallam**
Luna, 7: **Tunebo**; 9a: **Kuba**
Lun Bawang, 5: **Murut**
Lunda, 9
Lunda, 9: **Ndembu**; 3a: **Khava**
Lunda-Kazembe (Cazembe), 9: **Lunda**
Lunda-Ndembu, 9: **Lunda**
Lun Daya, 5: **Murut**
Lun Daye, 5: **Murut**
Lunia, 3a: **Nunia**
Luniya, 3a: **Nunia**
Lunyole, 9a: **Nyoro**
Luo, 9
Luoluo, 6(C): **Yi**
Luoravetlan, 6(R): **Chukchee**
Lupheng, 3a: **Kuki**
Lur, 9
Lusatians, 4: **Sorbs**
Lusatian Serbs, 4: **Sorbs**
Lushai, 3: **Mizo**
Luso-Indian, 3a: **Goan**
Lusu, 5: **Lisu**
Luti, 9: **Peripatetics of Afghanistan, Iran, and Turkey** (Iran)
Lutuami, 1: **Klamath**
Lu-tzu, 5: **Lisu**
Luunda, 9: **Lunda**
Luvana, 3a: **Lohana**
Luwa, 5: **Lawa**
Luwa'an, 5: **Bajau**
Luwu, 5: **Toala**
Luxembourgeois, 4
Luxembourgers, 4: **Luxembourgeois**
Luxi, 6(C): **Naxi**
Luyia, 9
Lwaʔ, 5: **T'in**
Lwena, 9a
Lwo, 9: **Acholi; Anuak**
Lypanes, 1: **Lipan Apache**

Ma, 5
Maa, 9: **Maasai**
Maai, 7a: **Payawá**
Maalemin, 9: **Peripatetics of the Maghreb** (Mauritania)
Maanyan Dayaks, 5: **Kalimantan Dayaks**
Maarulal, 6(R): **Avars**
Maasai, 9
Máasehual, 8: **Yukateko**
Maatpétamãe, 7: **Cinta Larga**
Maba, 9a
Ma'ba, 9a: **Ngabaka**
Mabiha, 9a: **Mawia**
Macaguaje, 7: **Siona-Secoya**
Macaguane, 7: **Guahibo-Sikuani**
Macassarese, 5: **Makassar**

Maccá, 7: **Maká**
Macchi, 3a
Macedonians, 4: **Slav Macedonians**
Macedoromans, 4: **Romanians**
Mācēhualmeh, 8: **Nahuat of the Sierra de Puebla**
Machchhi, 3a: **Macchi**
Machhandar, 3a: **Bhoi**
Machhi, 3a: **Macchi**
Machhua, 3a: **Mallah; Tiyar**
Machigar, 3a: **Mochi**
Machiguenga, 7: **Matsigenka**
Machinde Bhoi, 3a: **Macchi**
Machoto, 7: **Itonama**
Machwaya, 1: **Rom**
Mackenzie Inuit, 1a
Maco, 7: **Piaroa**
Maconde, 9a
Macoushi, 7: **Makushi**
Macú, 7a: **Karabayo; Máku**
Macua-Lomue, 9a
Macuchi, 7: **Makushi**
Macuna, 7
Macuní, 7: **Maxakali**
Macurap, 7a
Macusa, 7a: **Karabayo**
Macusari, 7: **Jivaro**
Macusi, 7: **Makushi**
Macuxi, 7: **Makushi**
Mada, 9a
Mada Eggoni, 9a: **Eggon**
Madak, 2: **Mandak**; 3a: **Madhunapit**
Madari, 3a
Madeirans, 4
Madeirense, 4: **Madeirans**
Madi, 9a
Madi, 5: **Saluan**
Ma'diti, 9a: **Madi**
Madgi, 3a: **Madiga**
Madhunapit, 3a
Madig, 3a: **Mang**
Madiga, 3a
Madigaru, 3a: **Madiga**
Madigowd, 3a: **Madiga**
Madiha, 7: **Culina**
Madija, 7: **Culina**
Madiwal, 3a: **Agasa**
Madiyal, 3a: **Dhobi**
Madkar, 3a: **Bhandari**
Madru, 3a: **Madiga**
Madurese, 5
Mae Enga, 2
Mafa, 9a: **Matakam**
Mafulu, 2
Mag, 3a: **Marma**
Magada, 3a: **Bhatraja**
Magahaya Brahman, 3a: **Babhan**
Magar, 3
Magi, 2: **Mailu**
Magindanao, 5: **Maguindanao**
Magindanaw, 5: **Maguindanao**
Magh, 3a: **Marma**

Magha, 3: **Lakher**
Maghrebi Jews, 9: **Jews of Algeria**
Magpie Miao, 6(C): **Miao**
Maguindanao, 5
Maguindanaon, 5: **Maguindanao**
Maguindanau, 5: **Maguindanao**
Maguzawa, 9: **Hausa**
Magyarok, 4: **Hungarians; Transylvanian Ethnic Groups**
Magyars, 1: **European-Americans; European-Canadians; 4: Hungarians**
Mah, 5: **Senoi**
Maha, 1: **Omaha**
Mahâ, 7: **Tatuyo**
Mahabrahman, 3a
Maha-Brahman, 3a: **Acharaj**
Mahajan, 3: **Bania**
Mahakul, 3: **Ahir**
Mahali, 3a: **Mahli; Nai**
Maha Malasar, 3a: **Malasar**
Mahanti, 3a: **Karan**
Mahanubhao, 3a: **Manbhao**
Mahapatra, 3a: **Mahabrahman**
Mahar, 3
Mahara, 3a: **Koshti**
Maharana, 3a: **Jingar**
Mahatma, 3: **Sadhu**
Mahatmana, 3a: **Manbhao**
Mahato, 3a: **Ganda**
Mahdavia Musalman, 3a
Mahesari Marwadi, 3a
Mahesri, 3a: **Mahesari Marwadi**
Maheswari, 3a: **Mahesari Marwadi**
Mahi, 9a
Mahia, 3a
Mahibarez, 7: **Nambicuara**
Mahican, 1
Mahigir, 3a: **Bhoi**
Mahili, 3a: **Mahli**
Mahli, 3a
Mahmand, 3a: **Mohmand**
Mahommedan, 3: **Muslim**
Mahra, 3a: **Bhoi; Jhinwar**
Mahratta, 3: **Maratha**
Mahtam, 3a
Mahton, 3a
Mai, 5: **Senoi**
Maí, 5: **T'in**
Maidu, 1
Mailari, 3a
Mailu, 2
Maina, 3a: **Mina**
Mainu, 7: **Jivaro**
Maipura, 7a: **Tariana**
Maira, 3a: **Mayara**
Maisin, 2
Maisina, 2: **Maisin**
Majhi, 3a: **Majhwar**
Majhia, 3a: **Majhwar**
Majhwar, 3a
Majuro, 2: **Marshall Islands**
Maká, 7

Mak'á, 7: **Maká**
Makassar, 5
Makassaren, 5: **Makassar**
Makassarese, 5: **Makassar**
Makbe, 9: **Dogon**
Makira, 2: **San Cristobal**
Makiritare, 7: **Yekuana**
Makká, 7: **Maká**
Maklaks, 1: **Klamath**
Mako, 7a: **Máku**
Makonde, 9a
Makoua, 9a: **Mboshi**
Maku, 7: **Piaroa; 7a: Hupda; Yahup**
Máku, 7a
Ma Ku, 5: **Yumbri**
Makú, 7a: **Yahup**
Makua, 9a
Makú Gauriba, 7a: **Wariva**
Makurap, 7a
Makuschi, 7: **Makushi**
Makushi, 7
Makuxi, 7: **Makushi**
Mal, 3a: **Mala; Maler**
Mala, 3a
Mala Adiyar, 3a: **Malayadiar**
Mala Arayan, 3a
Malabari, 3: **Malayali**
Malabar Jews, 3: **Cochin Jew**
Malacharivan Malasar, 3a: **Malasar**
Malai Arayan, 3a: **Mala Arayan**
Malai Malasar, 3a: **Malasar**
Malai Pandaram, 3: **Hill Pandaram**
Malaita, 2
Malai Vedam, 3a: **Mala Vedan**
Malai Vedan, 3a: **Mala Vedan**
Malakar, 3a: **Mali**
Malakkaran, 3a
Malakkuravan, 3a: **Mala Kuravan**
Mala Koravan, 3a: **Mala Kuravan**
Mala Kuravan, 3a
Mala Malasar, 3a: **Malasar**
Malankudi, 3a: **Vishavan**
Malankuravan, 3a: **Mala Kuravan**
Malanow, 5: **Melanau**
Mala Panickkar, 3a: **Mala Panikkar**
Mala Panikkar, 3a
Malapaṇṭāram, 3: **Hill Pandaram**
Malapulaya, 3a
Mala Pulayan, 3a: **Malapulaya**
Malasar, 3a
Mala Ulladan, 3a: **Ulladan**
Malavara, 3a: **Kavikara**
Mala Vedan, 3a
Malaveder, 3a: **Mala Vedan**
Malavetan, 3a: **Mala Vedan**
Mala Vettuvan, 3a: **Mala Vedan**
Malay, 5
Malayadiar, 3a
Malayalar, 3a
Malayalee, 3: **Malayali**
Malayali, 3
Malayali Kshatriya, 3a

Malayan, 3a
Malayan, 5: **Malay**
Malayarayan, 3a: **Kanikkar; Mala Arayan**
Malayarayar, 3a: **Mala Arayan**
Malayo, 7a
Malays, 1: **South and Southeast Asians of the United States**
Malaysian, 5: **Malay**
Malaysians, 1: **South and Southeast Asians of the United States**
Maldivians, 1: **South and Southeast Asians of the United States; 3: Divehi**
Male, 3a: **Maler**
Malecite, 1: **Maliseet**
Maleku, 8
Male Kudia, 3a: **Kudiya**
Male Kudiya, 3a: **Kudiya**
Malekula, 2
Malemiut, 1: **North Alaskan Eskimos**
Maler, 3a
Maleru, 3a: **Maler**
Malha, 3a: **Mallah**
Malha Malasar, 3a: **Malasar**
Mali, 3a
Mali Gujarati, 3a
Malinke, 9a
Malinke, 9a: **Manding**
Malinke, 9a
Maliseet, 1
Malkan, 6(R): **Balkars**
Malkars, 6(R): **Balkars**
Mallabhatlu, 3a: **Helava**
Mallah, 3a
Malla Kshatriya, 3a: **Jetti**
Mallige Madevi Vakkalu, 3a: **Agasa**
Malo, 3a
Malo-Patni, 3a: **Malo**
Mal Paharia, 3a: **Maler**
Malqat, 6(R): **Balkars**
Maltese, 4
il-Maltin, 4: **Maltese**
Mam, 8
Mama, 9a
Mamah Darat, 5: **Kalimantan Dayaks**
Mamanwa, 5: **Philippine Negritos**
Mambare, 2: **Orokaiva**
Mambere, 9a: **Mambila**
Mambetto, 9: **Mangbetu**
Mambila, 9a
Mambule, 2: **Mafulu**
Mambyuara, 7: **Nambicuara**
Mames, 8: **Mam**
Mam Maya, 8: **Mam**
Mamorí, 7a
Mamoria, 7a: **Mamorí**
Mampa, 9a: **Sherbro**
Mamprusi, 9
Man, 5: **Hmong; Yao of Thailand**
Maʿn, 9: **Peripatetics of Iraq . . . Yemen (Yemen)**
Mana, 3a

Managua, 7: Cashibo
Manajo, 7a: Amanayé
Manala-Ndebele, 9: Ndebele
Manam, 2
Mananyé, 7a: Amanayé
Manare, 7: Tunebo
Manasi, 7: Chiquitano
Manbhao, 3a
Manbhav, 3a: Manbhao
Mancagne, 9a
Manchu, 6(C)
Mand, 3a: Mer
Manda, 9a: Nyasa
Manda Buchawad, 3a: Telaga
Mandadan Chetti, 3a
Mandaeans, 9
Mandailing, 5: Batak
Mandak, 2
Mandan, 1
Mandara, 9a
Mandari, 9a
Mandatan Chetti, 3a: Mandadan Chetti
Mandaya, 5: Isneg
Mande, 9
Mande, 9a: Mande-Speaking Peoples
Mande, 9a: Mandinka-Mory
Mandenyi, 9a: Mmani
Mander, 2: Tor
Manding, 9a
Manding, 9: Mande
Mandingo, 9a
Mandingo, 9a: Manding
Mandingue, 9: Mande
Mandinka, 9a: Mandingo
Mandinka-Mory, 9a
Mandjaque, 9a
Mandula Gollalu, 3a: Handi Jogi
Mandula Jogi, 3a: Handi Jogi
Manegir, 6(R): Evenki
Mang, 3a
Manga, 9a
Manga, 3a: Mang
Mangala, 3a
Mangala, 3a: Nai
Mangan, 3a: Charan
Mangareva, 2
Mangati, 9a: Taturu
Mangbettu, 9: Mangbetu
Mangbetu, 9
Mangbetu, 9a
Mangela, 3a
Mangela, 3a: Mang
Manggarai, 5
Mang Garodi, 3a: Mang-Garori
Mang-Garori, 3a
Mang Garudi, 3a: Mang-Garori
Mangjel, 3a: Kuki
Mangkasaren, 5: Makassar
Mang Raut, 3a: Mang
Mangyan, 5: Hanunóo
Manhasset, 1: Metoac
Manianga, 9: Kongo

Manihar, 3a: Kachera
Manihiki, 2
Manipuri, 3a
Manjhi, 3a: Majhwar
Mankar, 3: Bhil
Manks, 4: Manx
Mannan, 3a
Mannewar, 3a
Manoan, 6(C)
Manobo, 5: Bagobo
Manoot, 5: Selung/Moken
Manrhoat, 1: Kiowa
Mansi, 6(R)
Manso, 1a
Mantannes, 1: Mandan
Manteran, 1: Cherokee
Manus, 2
Manuš, 4: Peripatetics
Manusian, 2: Manus
Manuvu, 5: Bagobo
Manyari, 3a: Johari
Manx, 4
Manya, 9a: Mandingo
Manya-Kan, 9a: Mandingo
Manzi, 6(C): Qiang
Maori, 2
Mapayo, 7a: Wanaí
Mapoggers, 9: Ndebele
Mappila, 3
Mappilla, 3: Mappila
Mapuche, 7: Araucanians
Mapuda, 9a: Gude
Mar, 6(R): Maris
Mara, 3: Chin, Lakher
Marachi, 9a
Marachi, 9: Luyia
Maragua, 7a: Mawé
Marajona, 7a
Marakkala, 3: Moor of Sri Lanka
Marakkayar, 3a
Marakwet, 9a
Marakwet, 9: Nandi and Other Kalenjin Peoples
Maral, 3a: Mali
Marama, 9a
Marama, 9: Luyia
Maramagri, 3a: Marma
Maran, 3a: Ambalavasi
Maranao, 5
Marar, 3a: Ambalavasi; Mali
Maratha, 3
Maratha Bhoi, 3a
Marati, 3a
Maravan, 3a
Maravi, 9a
Marayan, 3a: Ambalavasi
Marayarmiut, 1: Central Yup'ik Eskimos
Mardudjara, 2
Mardujarra, 2: Mardudjara
Mareños, 8: Huave
Māre Roma, 4: Slovensko Roma

Māre Romora, 4: Slovensko Roma
Margali, 6(R): Mingrelians
Marginal Peoples, 1: American Isolates
Mari, 6(R): Maris
Maricopa, 1
Marielitos, 1: Latinos
Marinahua, 7
Marinawa, 7: Marinahua
Marind-anim, 2
Maring, 2
Mariposan, 1: Yokuts
Maris, 6(R)
Marisiz, 1: Maliseet
Mariyari, 3a: Muriari
Marka, 9a: Soninké
Marma, 3a
Marocasero, 7a: Malayo
Maroni Carib, 7
Maronites, 9
Maroons, 7: Afro–South Americans
Marota, 9: Pedi
Marotse, 9: Lozi
Marovo, 2: New Georgia
Marquesans, 2: Marquesas Islands
Marquesas Islands, 2
Marshallese, 1: Micronesians
Marshall Islands, 2
Martiniquais, 8
Maru, 6(C): Jingpo
Marubo, 7
Marúbo, 7: Marubo
Marutse, 9: Lozi
Marwadi Bania, 3: Bania
Marwadi Brahman, 3a
Marwari, 3: Bania
Marwari Shravak, 3a
Marwat, 3a
Marworna, 7a
Marworna, 7a: Galibí
Masai, 9: Maasai
Masaka, 7a: Aikaná
Masalib, 9: Peripatetics of Iraq . . . Yemen (Egypt)
Masalit, 9a
Masan Jogi, 3a: Telaga
Mashacalí, 7: Maxakali
Mashacari, 7: Maxakali
Masha'iliyyah, 9: Peripatetics of Iraq . . . Yemen (Egypt)
Mashakali, 7: Maxakali
Mashco, 7
Mashi, 9a
Mashki, 3a: Bhishti
Maskegan, 1: Cree, Western Woods
Maskoi, 7a
Maskurahi, 9: Peripatetics of Afghanistan, Iran, and Turkey (Afghanistan)
Maspo, 7: Amahuaca
Massa, 9a
Massachuset, 1

Massur, 5: Lahu
Mastanahua, 7a: Mastanawa
Mastanawa, 7a
Mata, 6(R): Evenki
Matabele, 9a: Ndebele
Mataco, 7
Mataco-Güisnay, 7: Mataco
Mataco-Noctenes, 7: Mataco
Mataco-Véjoz, 7: Mataco
Matadi, 3a: Upparwar
Mataguayo, 7: Mataco
Matakam, 9a
Matam, 3a: Mahtam
Matambwe, 9a: Makonde
Matanawí, 7a
Matangi Makallu, 3a: Madiga
Matengo, 9a
Matha, 3a
Mathelá, 7: Nivaclé
Matia Kanbi
Matial, 3a: Mochi
Matipuhi, 7a
Matipuhy, 7a: Matapuhi
Matipui, 7a: Matapuhi
Matis, 7a
Matisana, 7: Wapisiana
Matko, 3a: Nai
Matkuda, 3a: Beldar
Mato, 9a: Macua-Lomue; 9a: Makua
Matses, 7: Mayoruna
Matsigenka, 7
Mattole, 1: Wailaki
Matumbi, 9a
Mauáua, 7: Waimiri-Atroari
Maué, 7a: Mawé
Maulik, 3a
Maulik, 3a: Dhimal
Maumee, 1: Miami
Mauntadan Chetty, 3a: Mandadan
    Chetti
Maure, 7: Baure
Maures, 9a
Mauriciens, 3: Mauritian
Mauritian, 3
Mavchi, 3: Bhil; 3a: Gamit
Mavilan, 3a
Mavillon, 3a: Mavilan
Mawawa, 7: Waimiri-Atroari
Mawé, 7a
Mawia, 9a
Mawooshen, 1: Abenaki
Maxakali, 7
Maxi-Gbe, 9a: Mahi
Maxirna, 7: Mayoruna
May, 5
Maya, 7a
Maya, 8: Awakateko; Ch'ol; Chontal of
    Tabasco; Cho'rti'; Chuj; Itza';
    Ixil; Jakalteko; Kaqchikel;
    Ki'che'; Lakandon; Mam; Mopan;
    Poqomam; Poqomchi'; Q'anjob'al;
    Q'eqchi'; Sipakapense; Tojolab'al;

Tzeltal; Tzotzil and Tzeltal of Pan-
    telhó; Tzotzil of Chamula; Tzotzil
    of San Andrés Larraínzar; Tzotzil
    of San Bartolomé de los Llanos;
    Tzotzil of Zinacantan; Tz'utujil;
    Uspanteko; Wasteko; Yukateko
Mayan, 3: Kohistani
Mayangna, 8: Sumu
Mayara, 3a
Mayero, 8: Itza'; Yukateko
Mayet, 2: Murik
Mayiruna, 7: Mayoruna
Mayo, 7: Mayoruna; 8: Cahita
Mayombe, 9a: Yombe
Mayoruna, 7
Mayr, 3: Kohistani
Mazahua, 8
Mazatec, 8
Mbaka, 9a: Baka
Mbanja, 9a
Mbati, 9a: Ngbandi
Mbato, 9a
Mbau, 2: Bau
Mbayá-Guaikuru, 7: Kadiwéu
Mbeere, 9
Mbembe, 9a
Mbere, 9: Mbeere
Mbia, 7: Yuqui
Mbila, 9a: Safwa
Mbocobí, 7: Mocoví
Mboma, 9: Kongo
M'Bororo, 9a
Mboshi, 9a
Mbouda, 9: Bamiléké
Mboum, 9a
Mboumtiba, 9a: Mboum
Mbowamb, 2: Melpa
Mbui, 9a
Mbulu, 9: Iraqw
Mbundu, 9a
Mbundu, 9a: Ovimbundu
Mbuti, 9: Tropical-Forest Foragers
Mdariya, 3a: Madari
Me, 2: Kapauku
Mebengokre, 7: Gorotire
Mech, 3a
Mechi, 3a: Mech
Medar, 3a: Basor
Medara, 3a: Basor
Medarakaran, 3a: Basor
Medare, 3a: Basor
Medarlu, 3a: Basor
Meddaḥin, 9: Peripatetics of Iraq . . .
    Yemen (Egypt)
Medlpa, 2: Melpa
Medzan, 9: Tropical-Forest Foragers
Meerolu, 3a: Darzi
Megh, 3a: Meghval
Meghval, 3a
Meghwal, 3a: Meghval
Megloromans, 4: Romanians
Megong, 9a: Eggon

Megreli, 6(R): Mingrelians
Mehar, 3a: Bhulia
Mehinaco, 7: Mehinaku
Mehinacu, 7: Mehinaku
Mehinaku, 7
Mehtar, 3: Mahar; 3a: Bhangi; 9:
    Peripatetics of Afghanistan, Iran,
    and Turkey (Iran)
Meidob, 9a
Meinaco, 7: Mehinaku
Meinacu, 7: Mehinaku
Meithi, 3a
Mejbrat, 2
Mejprat, 2: Mejbrat
Mek, 2: Eipo
Mekĕ, 7a
Mekeo, 2
Mekinsẽji, 7: Suya
Mekyibo, 9a
Melakkaran, 3a
Melakudi, 3a: Kudiya
Melanau, 5
Melanu, 5: Melanau
Melayu, 5: Malay
Meleno, 5: Melanau
Melilema, 1: Tenino
Melpa, 2
Melungeons, 1: American Isolates
Melville Islanders, 2: Tiwi
Memar, 3a: Upparwar
Meme, 7: Emberá
Memsahib, 3: Europeans in South Asia
Menangkabau, 5: Minangkabau
Mende, 9; 9a
Mendi, 2
Mendicant Telega, 3a: Telaga
Mendriq, 5: Semang
Meneka, 7a
Meng, 3a: Meghval
Menggaè, 5: Modang
Menggu, 6(C): Mongols
Menghvar, 3a: Meghval
Menghwal, 3a: Meghval
Mengsa, 6(C): Achang
Mengsa-shan, 6(C): Achang
Mening, 9a
Mennists, 1: Mennonites; 7:
    Mennonites
Mennonists, 1: Mennonites
Mennonites, 1; 7
Mennonites, 1: Amish
Menominee, 1
Menomini, 1: Menominee
Mentaweian, 5
Mentaweier, 5: Mentaweian
Meo, 3
Meo, 5: Hmong
Mer, 3a
Merai, 3a: Darzi
Merdu, 9a: Mursi
Mereyo, 7: Emerillon
Mereyon, 2: Woleai

Méridionaux, 4: Occitans
Merile, 9a: Dasanec
Meritu, 9a: Mursi
Meru, 9a
Merule, 9a: Murle
Mesaya, 7: Karihona
Mescalero Apache, 1
Meskhetians, 6(R)
Meskhetian Turks, 6(R): Meskhetians
Meskhetinskie Turki, 6(R):
    Meskhetians
Mesquakie, 1: Fox
Mesri Marwadi, 3a: Mahesari
    Marwadi
Mesticos, 9a
mestizo rancheros, 8: Cattle Ranchers
    of the Huasteca
Mestizos, 1: American Isolates
Mestri, 3a: Panan
Methow, 1: Columbia
Métis, 1: Metis of Western Canada
Metis of Western Canada, 1
Metoac, 1
Metoko, 9a
Metropolitans, 8: Martiniquais
Mewa-farosh, 3a: Kunjra
Mewasi, 3: Bhil
Mewāti, 3: Meo
Mewun, 2: Malekula
Mexica, 8: Nahuat of the Sierra de
    Peubla
Mexican Americans, 1: Latinos
Mexicano, 8: Nahua Peoples; Nahua of
    the Huasteca; Nahua of the State
    of Mexico; Nahuat of the Sierra de
    Puebla
Mexijcatl, 8: Nahua of the Huasteca
Meybrat, 2: Mejbrat
Mezcaleros, 1: Mescalero Apache
Mfantse, 9a: Fante
Mhali, 3a: Nai
Mhar, 3: Mahar
Mhed, 3a: Mer
Mher, 3a: Mer
Mi, 5: Muong
Miá, 7: Sirionó
Miami, 1
Miamiouek, 1: Miami
Mian, 3a
Mian, 5: Yao of Thailand
Mian Balantak, 5: Balantak
Mian Banggai, 5: Banggai
Miango, 9a: Irigwe
Mianmin, 2: Miyanmin
Mian Sea-Sea, 5: Banggai
Miao, 6(C)
Miao, 5: Hmong
Mical, 1: Klikitat
Michif, 1: Metis of Western Canada
Michuguaca, 8: Tarascans
Mickmakiques, 1: Micmac
Micmac, 1

Micronesian Americans, 1:
    Micronesians
Micronesians, 1
Micro-Races, 1: American Isolates
Middle Columbia Salish, 1: Columbia
Middle Peoples, 1: American Isolates
Midis, 4: Occitans
Mien, 6(C): Yao
Migmagi, 1: Micmac
Migueleno, 7a: Kujubi
Mihavane, 9a: Lomwe; Macua-Lomue
Mihir, 3a: Bhulia
Mihngh, 3a: Meghval
Mihtar, 3a: Hari
Mije, 8: Mixe
Mijikenda, 9; 9a
Mikaru, 2: Daribi
Mikhifore, 9a
Mikir, 3
Mikmaw, 1: Micmac
Milan, 3: Abor
Milano, 5: Melanau
Milat, 3: Mauritian
Milbank Sound Indians, 1: Bellabella
Mima-Mimi, 9a
Mi Marva, 9a: Guiziga
Mimika, 2
Mina, 3a
Mina, 3: Meo; 5: Muna
Minahasans, 5
Minahasser, 5: Minahasans
Mina Meo, 3: Meo
Minangende, 9a: Ngabaka
Minangkabau, 5
Minceir, 4: Peripatetics
Mincopie, 3: Andamanese
Mingrelets, 6(R): Mingrelians
Mingrelians, 6(R)
Minitari, 1: Hidatsa
Minjia, 6(C): Bai
Minnetarees of Fort de Prairie, 1: Gros
    Ventre
Mintil, 5: Semang
Minyong, 3: Abor; 3a: Adi
Mir, 3a: Mirasi
Miraña, 7a: Bora
Mirana, 7a: Miranya
Mirane, 7a: Miranya
Miranya, 7a
Mirasi, 3a
Miri, 3a
Mirimã, 7a: Himarimã
Miriti, 7a: Neenoã
Miriti-Tapuia, 7a: Neenoã
Mirshikar, 3a: Pardhi
Miruma, 2: Gururumba
Misaba, 6(C): Yi
Misao, 3a: Kuki
Mishär, 6(R): Volga Tatars
Mi-shing, 3a: Miri
Mishmi, 3a
Miskito, 8

Miskito Coast Creoles, 8: Creoles of
    Nicaragua
Miskitu, 8: Miskito
Mississauga, 1: Ojibwa
Mississippi Sioux, 1: Santee
Missouri, 1
Mistri, 3a: Barhai
Mith Gavada, 3a: Gavada
Mithiya, 3a: Halwai
Mitro, 6(C): Dai
Miwok, 1
Miwuyt, 2: Murngin
Mixe, 8
Mixtec, 8
Miyadar, 3a: Basor
Miyanmin, 2
Mizel, 3a: Kuki
Mizilman, 3: Mauritian
Mizo, 3
Mmani, 9a
Mnong, 5
M.Nông, 5: Mnong
Mnong Gar, 5: Mnong
Noai, 5: Muong
Moal, 5: Muong
Moamiami, 5: Taiwan Aboriginal
    Peoples
Moasham, 1: Abenaki
Mobi, 2: Foi
Mobile, 1a
Mochavaru, 3a: Mochi
Mochi, 3a
Mochigar, 3a: Mochi
Mocobí, 7: Mocoví
Mocoví, 7
Modak, 3a: Mayara
Modaliyar, 3a: Mudaliyar
Modang, 5
Modi-Raj, 3a: Mutrasi
Moenane, 7a: Muinane
Moenanezen, 5: Muna
Mofa, 9a: Matakam
Mofou, 9a
Moger, 3a
Mogh, 3a: Marma
Mogha, 3a: Rabari
Moghia, 3a: Pardhi
Moghul, 3: Mogul
Mogosnae, 7: Mocoví
Mogul, 3
Mohammedan, 3: Muslim
Mohave, 1
Mohave-Apache, 1: Yavapai
Mohawk, 1
Mohegan, 1
Mohmand, 3a
Moi, 5: Muong
Moili, 3a: Suppalig
Moinba, 6(C)
Moinjaang, 9: Dinka
Mojeno, 7: Baure
Mojo, 7

Moken, **5**: Sea Nomads of the
    Andaman; Selung/Moken
Mokoit, **7**: Mocoví
Mol, **5**: Muong
Molala, 1a
Moldavians, **4**: Romanians
Moldovans, 6(R)
Moldovians, **6(R)**: Moldovans
Mole-Dagbane, 9a
Molé-Dagbane, **9a**: Mossi
Molesalam, 3a
Molokans, 1
Moluccans, North, 5
Moluccans, Southeast, 5
Mombe, **9a**: Ngonde
Momin, 3a
Momin, **3a**: Julaha
Momna, **3a**: Momin
Monache, **1**: Mono
Monaxó, **7**: Maxakali
Mondaru, 3a
Mondé, 7a
Mondi, **3a**: Mondaru
Mondiwadu, **3a**: Mondaru
Mondo, **5**: Sulod
Mong, **5**: Hmong
Monggol, **6(C)**: Mongols
Mongo, 9
Mongols, 6(C)
Mongols, **6(C)**: Tu
Mongondow, **5**: Bolaang Mongondow
Mongondu, **5**: Bolaang Mongondow
Monguor, **6(C)**: Tu
Mongwandi, **9a**: Ngbandi
Mono, 1
Monochó, **7**: Maxakali
Monom, 5
Mono-Pi-Utes, **1**: Northern Paiute
Montagnais, **1**: Montagnais-Naskapi
Montagnais-Naskapi, 1
Montagnard, **5**: Muong; **9a**: Mandara
Montauk, 1a
Montauk, **1**: Metoac
Montenegrins, 4
Montero, **7a**: Yavarana
Montese, **7**: Paï-Tavytera
Montserratians, 8
Moor of Sri Lanka, 3
Moors, **1**: American Isolates; **9a**:
    Maures
Moose, **9**: Mossi
Mopan, 8
Mopane, **8**: Mopan
Mopanero, **8**: Mopan
Mopán Maya, **8**: Mopan
Moperequoa, **7**: Guarayu
Moplah, **3**: Mappila
Mopoi, **7a**: Wanaí
Mo-quami, **5**: Taiwan Aboriginal
    Peoples
Moqui, **1**: Hopi
Morasu, **3a**: Morasu Okkalu

Morasu Okkalu, 3a
Morata, **2**: Goodenough Island
Moravané, **4**: Czechs
Moré, 7
Morehead, **2**: Keraki
Morenos, **7**: Afro-Bolivians; Afro-
    Colombians; Afro-Hispanic
    Pacific Lowlanders of Ecuador and
    Colombia; Afro–South Americans;
    Afro-Venezuelans; **8**: Creoles of
    Nicaragua
Morerebí, **7a**: Matanawí
Morisien, **3**: Mauritian
Mormons, 1
Moro, **7**: Ayoreo
Morochos, **7**: Afro-Colombians
Mortlock Islands, **2**: Nomoi
Morunahwa, **7**: Marinahua
Morunawa, 7a
Morung, **3a**: Tripura
Mösaälman, **6(R)**: Volga Tatars
Mosca, **7a**: Chibcha
Moshi, **9**: Mossi
Mosi, **9**: Mossi
Moskito, **8**: Miskito
Moslem, **3**: Muslim
Moso, **6(C)**: Naxi
Mosobiae, **7**: Mocoví
Mosopelea, 1a
Mosqueto, **8**: Miskito
Mosquito, **8**: Miskito
Mossi, 9; 9a
Motad Reddi, **3**: Reddi
Motcare, **3a**: Gonsavi
Moterequoa, **7**: Pauserna
Motilones, **7**: Yukpa
Motilones Bravos, **7**: Barí
Motilones del Sur, **7**: Barí
Motu, 2
Moundang, 9a
Mountain, 1
Mountain Arapesh, 2
Mountaineers, **1**: Appalachians
Mountain Jews, 6(R)
Mountain Shors, **6(R)**: Shors
Mountain Tatars, **6(R)**: Balkars
Mountain Whites, **1**: Appalachians
Mount Athos, 4
Mourdia, **9a**
Mousgoum, 9a
Moustique, **8**: Miskito
Move, **8**: Ngawbe
Movere, **8**: Ngawbe
Movima, 7
Movina, **7**: Movima
Mowar, 3a
Moxa, **7**: Baure
Moxo, **7**: Baure; Mojo
Moyili, **3a**: Suppalig
Mpangu, **9**: Kongo
Mrassa, **6(R)**: Shors
Mro, **3a**: Tripura

Mru, **3a**: Tripura
Mrung, **3a**: Tripura
Mser, **9a**: Kotoko
Mua'meratijjeh, **9**: Peripatetics of
    Iraq . . . Yemen (Egypt)
Muamin, **3a**: Kachi Meman
Mubi, **2**: Foi; **9a**: Gude
Muchi, **3a**: Mochi
Mudaliar, **3**: Vellala
Mudaliyar, 3a
Mudi, **3a**: Bagdi
Muduga, 3a
Mudugar, **3a**: Muduga
Mudugas, **3**: Kurumbas
Mudukkan, **3a**: Muduga
Muduvan, **3a**: Muduga
Muduvar, **3a**: Muduga
Muexcas, **7a**: Chibcha
Mug, **3a**: Marma
Mugaba, **2**: Rennel Island
Mugal, **3**: Mogul
Mughal, **3**: Mogul
Mugulasha, 1a
Muhial, 3a
Muica, **7a**: Chibcha
Muinane, 7a
Mujawar, **3a**: Chhalapdar
Muka Dora, **3a**: Konda Dora
Mukeri, **3a**: Banjara
Mükhadar, **6(R)**: Rutuls
Mukkava, **3a**: Mukkuvan
Mukkuvan, 3a
Mukri, 3a
Muku, **2**: Lakalai
Mulam, 6(C)
Mulao, **6(C)**: Mulam
Mulaozu, **6(C)**: Mulam
Mulatos (Mullatos), **7**: Afro-Bolivians;
    Afro-Colombians; Afro-Hispanic
    Pacific Lowlanders of Ecuador and
    Colombia; Afro–South Americans;
    Afro-Venezuelans
Mulattoes, **1**: American Isolates
Mulla Kuruman, **3a**: Mullukurumba
Mulla-Kurumbas, **3**: Kurumbas
Mullakurumber, **3a**: Mullukurumba
Mullukurumba, 3a
Multani, **3a**: Mochi
Mulwi, **9a**: Mousgoum
Mumin, **6(C)**: Hui
Muna, 5
Munchi, **9**: Tiv
Munda, 3
Mundé, **7a**: Aikaná
Mundo, **5**: Sulod
Mundokuma, **2**: Mundugumor
Mundugamor, **2**: Mundugumor
Mundugumor, 2
Mundurucu, 7
Munduruku, **7**: Mundurucu
Munggan, **2**: Wik Mungkan
Munggava, **2**: Rennel Island

Muni, 3: Sadhu
Munichi, 7a
Munjuk, 9a: Mousgoum
Münkü, 7a
Münkü, 7a: Iranshe
Munnud Kapu, 3a: Munur
Munnur, 3a: **Munur**
Munnurwad, 3a: Munur
Munsee, 1: Delaware
Munur, 3a
Munurwar, 3a: Beldar; Munur
Muong, 5
Mupun, 9a: Sura
Mura, 7a
Murao, 3a: Koiri
Mura-Piraha, 7a: **Mura**
Múra-Pirahã, 7a: **Pirahã**
Murciélagos, 7: **Karihona**
Murha, 3a
Muri, 8: Bugle
Muria Huitoto, 7: Witoto
Muriari, 3a
Murik, 2
Murire, 8: Bugle
Murle, 9a
Murli, 3a: Waghya
Murli Joshi, 3a: Waghya
Murmi, 3: Tamang
Murngin, 2
Mursi, 9a
Murut, 5
Musabir, 3a: Mochi
Musahar, 3a
Musalli, 3a: **Bhangi**; 9: **Peripatetics of Afghanistan, Iran, and Turkey** (Afghanistan)
Musalman, 3: **Moor of Sri Lanka; Muslim**
Musalman Brahman, 3a: **Husaini Brahman**
Musavi, 6(R): **Balkars**
Muscogee, 1: Creek
Musembani, 9a: Moundang
Mushahar, 3a: Musahar
Mushera, 3a: Musahar
Mushwæn, 6(R): Svans
Musilin, 6(C): Hui
Muskogee, 1: Creek
Muslim, 3
Muslims, 3: Mauritian
Muslim Samalan, 5: **Samal Moro**
Musokantanda Lunda, 9: **Lunda**
Mussad, 3a
Mustalainen, 4: **Peripatetics**
Mustee, 3: **Anglo-Indian**
Mustigar, 3a: Khetri
Musuk, 9a: Mousgoum
Musulmans, 3: **Mauritian**
Mûtea, 7a: Karapana
Muthrasi, 3a: Mutrasi
Muthuvan, 3a: Muduga
Muthuwan, 3a: **Muduga**

Mutracha, 3a: Mutrasi
Mut-Raj, 3a: Mutrasi
Mutrasa, 3a: Mutrasi
Mutrasi, 3a
Mutratcha, 3a: Mutrasi
Muttan, 3a
Muttaracha, 3a: Mutrasi
Muttarasan, 3a: Mutrasi
Muttatu, 3a: Ambalavasi; Mussad
Muttirajulu, 3a: Mutrasi
Muttiriyan, 3a: Mutrasi
Muya, 6(C): Qiang
Muyami, 6(C): Qiang
Muyu, 2
Mvele, 9a: Bassa
Mvuba, 9a
Mwaghavul, 9a: Sura
Mwela, 9a: Mwera
Mwenga, 9a: Lega
Mwera, 9a
Mwiska, 7a: Chibcha
Mwüska, 7a: Chibcha
Myadar, 3a: Basor
Myam-ma, 3a: Marma
Myanmarese, 5: Burmese
Myasa Beda, 3a
Myasa Nayakar, 3a: Myasa Beda
Myatari, 3a: Devanga
Mynky, 7a: Iranshe; Münkü

Naath, 9: Nuer
Nabajo, 1: Navajo
Nabaju, 1: Navajo
Nabaloi, 5: Ibaloi
Nabei, 6(C): Hezhen
Nabesna, 1
Nabesnatana, 1: Nabesna
Nabiltse, 1: Hupa
Naddaf, 3a: Dhuniya
Nadi, 3a: Ulladan
Nadig, 3a: Nai
Nador, 3a
Nadu Gauda, 3a: Nador
Nafukua, 7a: Nahukuá
Nagala, 3: Chin
Nagarakulam, 3a: Nagartha
Nagarata, 3a: Nagartha
Nagarattar, 3a: Nagartha
Nagar Brahman, 3a
Nagartha, 3a
Nagas, 3
Nagasia, 3a
Nagbansi, 3a
Nagesar, 3a: Nagasia
Nagesia, 3a: Nagasia
Nagori, 3a
Nagot, 9a
Nagyuktogmiut, 1: Copper Eskimo
Nahal, 3a
Nahane, 1: Kaska
Nahani, 1: Kaska
Naherna, 3a: Nai

Nahua of the Huasteca, 8
Nahua of the State of Mexico, 8
Nahua Peoples, 8
Nahuat of the Sierra de Puebla, 8
Nahukuá, 7a
Nahukwa, 7: Kalapalo
Nahul, 3a: Nahal
Nai, 3a
Naicken, 3: Nayaka
Naidu, 3a: Balija
Naik, 3a: Bhavin
Naik, 3a: Mutrasi; Ramosi
Naiken, 3: Nayaka
Naikin, 3a: Bhavin
Naiklok, 3a: Ramosi
Naikr, 3: Nayaka
Nair, 3: Nayar
Nakanai, 2: Lakalai
Nakash Maistri, 3a: Jingar
Nakes Rengma, 3: Nagas
Nakhi, 6(C): Naxi
Nakkalvandlu, 3a: Kuruvikkaran
Nakota, 1: Yankton
Naksia, 3a: Nagasia
Nalakeyava, 3a: Nalke
Nalke, 3a
Nalou, 9a
Nalu, 9a: Nalou
Nama, 3a: Chandal
Namaká, 7: Maká
Nama-Sudra, 3a: Chandal
Namau, 2
Nambe, 1: Pueblo Indians; Tewa Pueblos
Nambiar, 3a: Ambalavasi
Nambicuara, 7
Nambidi, 3a: Ambalavasi
Nambikwara, 7: Nambicuara
Nambiquara, 7: Nambicuara
Nambiyar, 3a: Ambalavasi
Nambiyassan, 3a: Ambalavasi
Namboodiri Brahman, 3: **Nambudiri Brahman**
Namboodiripad, 3: **Nambudiri Brahman**
Nambu, 2: Keraki
Nambudiri Brahman, 3
Nampati, 3a: Ambalavasi
Namte, 3a: Kuki
Namuyi, 6(C): Qiang
Nanai, 6(R)
Nanai, 6(C): Hezhen
Nanakpanthi, 3a
Nanakputra, 3a: Udasi
Nanakshahi, 3a: Nanakpanthi
Nanay, 6(R): Nanai
Nanchinad Vellala, 3a
Nandi and Other Kalenjin Peoples, 9
Nangia-Napore, 9a
Nani, 6(R): Orochi
Naniao, 6(C): Hezhen
Nanku Parisha, 3a: Kammalan
Nanticoke, 1

Nanticoke, 1: American Isolates
Ñãn̦u, 8: Otomí of the Sierra
Nao, 3a: Nai
Naoda, 3a
Napik, 3a: Nai
Napit, 3a: Nai
Naqqal, 3a: Bhandari
Nara, 9a
Nari, 6(C): Naxi
Narragansett, 1: Mohegan
Naru, 3a
Nasioi, 2
Naskapi, 1: Montagnais-Naskapi
Nat, 3a
Natage, 1: Mescalero Apache
Natahene, 1: Mescalero Apache
Natano, 1: Hupa
Natchez, 1a
Natchitoches, 1: American Isolates
Natick, 1: Massachuset
Nati Dread, 8: Rastafarians
Nation of the Willows, 1: Havasupai
Natmandsfolk, 4: Scandinavian
    Peripatetics
Nattukottai Chetti, 3a
Nattu Malasar, 3a: Malasar
Nattu Malayan, 3a: Malasar
Nattuvan, 3a
Nau, 3a: Nai
Naua, 3a: Nai
Naukantsy, 6(R): Asiatic Eskimos
Naumuslim, 3a
Nauru, 2
Nauruans, 1: Micronesians
Nausar, 9: Peripatetics of Afghanistan,
    Iran, and Turkey (Afghanistan)
Nauset, 1: Massachuset
Navaho, 1: Navajo
Navajo, 1
Navandanna, 3a
Navayat, 3a: Quraishi
Navdigar, 3a: Nat
Navodo, 2: Nauru
Nawa, 7a: Kapanawa
Nawar, 9: Peripatetics of Iraq . . .
    Yemen (Syria, Jordan, Israel, and
    Egypt)
Nawazi-Moñtji, 7: Chimane
Nawodo, 2: Nauru
Naxi, 6(C)
Naya, 3a: Maulik
Nayadaru, 3a: Nai
Nayadi, 3a
Nayadi, 3a: Ulladan
Nayady, 3a: Nayadi
Nayaka, 3
Nayar, 3
Nayares, 8: Cora
Nayaritas, 8: Cora
Nayinda, 3a: Nai
Nazarani, 3: Syrian Christian of Kerala
Nbule, 9a: Baboute

Nda, 9a: Moundang
Ndali, 9a
Ndani, 2: Dani
Ndaonese, 5
Ndara, 9a: Mandara
Ndau Ndau, 5: Ndaonese
Ndebele, 9; 9a
Ndeé, 1: Western Apache
Ndembu, 9
Ndengereko, 9a
Nderobo, 9a
Ndibu, 9: Kongo
Ndi Igbo, 9: Igbo
Ndirma, 9a: Kilba
Ndorobo, 9: Okiek
Nduindui, 2: Ambae
Ndumba, 2: Tairora
Ndzunda, 9: Ndebele
Ndzunda-Ndebele, 9: Ndebele
Nederlandse Zigeuners, 4: Gypsies and
    Caravan Dwellers in the
    Netherlands
Neenoã, 7a
Negres, 7: Afro–South Americans
Negritos, 5: Agta; Semang; 7: Afro-
    Bolivians
Negro, 1: African Americans
Negro Brazilians, 7: Afro-Brazilians
Negroes, 7: Afro–South Americans
Negros, 7: Afro-Bolivians; Afro-
    Colombians; Afro-Hispanic
    Pacific Lowlanders of Ecuador and
    Colombia; Afro-Venezuelans; 8:
    Creoles of Nicaragua
Nehalem, 1: Tillamook
Nehantic, 1: Mohegan
Nemangbetu, 9: Mangbetu; 9a:
    Mangbetu
Nembi, 2: Mendi
Nendö, 2: Santa Cruz
Nenets, 6(R)
Nengone, 2: Loyalty Islands
Nengres, 7: Afro–South Americans
Nentego, 1: Nanticoke
Neo-Buddhist, 3
Nepalese, 1: South and Southeast
    Asians of the United States;
    Nepali
Nepali, 3
Nepoyo, 7a: Wanaí
Nesilextcin, 1: Sanpoil
Nespelem, 1: Sanpoil
Nestorians, 9
Nestorians, 9: Assyrians
Nestucca, 1: Tillamook
Netherlands Antillians, 8
Netsilik Inuit, 1
Neutral, 1a
Nevuga Yupiga, 6(R): Asiatic Eskimos
Newã, 3: Newar
Newar, 3
Newār, 3: Newar

New Georgia, 2
New Halfa, 9: Nubians
Newiki, 7a: Tariana
New Kuki, 3: Thadou
New Nubia, 9: Nubians
Neyigeyavaru, 3a: Thakar
Nez Percé, 1
Ngaavi, 5: Dusun
Ngaayatjara, 2: Ngatatjara
Ngabaka, 9a
Ngäbe, 8: Ngawbe
Ngadadjara, 2: Ngatatjara
Ngadju Dayaks, 5: Kalimantan Dayaks
Ngai, 6(C): Hakka
Ngakarimonjong, 9: Karamojong
Ngakarimonjong, 9a: Karamojong
Nganasan, 6(R)
Ngatatjara, 2
Nga Tikopia, 2: Tikopia
Ngawbe, 8
Ngawbére, 8: Ngawbe
Ngbandi, 9a
Ngbanyito, 9a: Gonja
Ngeh, 5
Nghe, 5: Ngeh
Ngiaw, 5: Shan
Ngio, 5: Shan
Ngiturkan, 9: Turkana
Ngóbe, 8: Ngawbe
Ngonde, 9a
Ngonde, 9: Nyakyusa and Ngonde
Ngoni, 9a
Ngoni cluster, 9a
Ngò Pa, 5: Semang
Ngulu, 9a: Lomwe; Macua-Lomue;
    Nguu
Nguna, 2
Ngunese, 2: Nguna
Ngungwel, 9a: Teke
Nguoi Cham-pa, 5: Cham
Nguru, 9a: Lomwe
Nguu, 9a
Ngwandi, 9a: Ngbandi
Nhandéva, 7a: Tapieté
Nharo, 9a
Nharo, 9: San-Speaking Peoples
Nhavi, 3a: Nai
Niakuoll, 5: Choabon
Niam-Niam, 9: Zande
Niang, 6(C): De'ang
Niantic, 1: Mohegan
Nias, 5
Niasan, 5: Nias
Niasser, 5: Nias
Nibuhi, 6(R): Nivkh
Nicaraguans, 1: Latinos
Nicobarese, 3
Nicola, 1a
Nidula, 2: Goodenough Island
Niederösterreicher, 4: Austrians
Nigger-Hill People, 1: American
    Isolates

Nihal, 3a: Nahal
Nihamwo, 7: Yagua
Nihang, 3a: Akali
Nihonjin, 5: Japanese
Nika, 9a: Giriama
Nikkei, 1: East Asians of Canada
Nikubun, 6(R): Nivkh
Nikumbh, 3a
Nilamba, 9a: Iramba
Nilari, 3a: Chhipa
Nilbandhu, 3a: Gunlodu
Nilgar, 3a: Chhipa
Nilotic Kavirondo, 9: Luo
Nimaqá, 7: Maká
Nimenim, 1: Comanche
Nimi, 1: Bannock; Northern Shoshone
Nimipu, 1: Nez Percé
Ningerum, 2
Ninggiroem, 2: Ningerum
Ninggirum, 2: Ningerum
Ñiose, 7: Sirionó
Nipmuc, 1a
Nipmuc, 1: Massachuset
Nipo-Brasileiros, 7: Asians in South
    America
Nipo-Latinos, 7: Asians in South
    America
Nipponjin, 5: Japanese
Nirali, 3a: Chhipa
Nirle, 3: Bhil
Nisenan, 1: Maidu
Nishad, 3a: Chandal
Nishi, 3a: Dafla
Nishinam, 1: Maidu
Nissan, 2
Nissei, 7: Asians in South America
Niue, 2
Niuean, 2: Niue
Niuefekai, 2: Niue
Niutachi, 1: Missouri
Nivaclé, 7
Nivkh, 6(R)
Njembe, 9a
Njimaqá, 7: Maká
Njomaqá, 7: Maká
Nkore, 9a
Nlaka'pamux, 1: Thompson
n'Men, 3: Chin
Noanabs, 8: Emberá and Wounaan
Noanamá, 7
Noanama, 7: Chocó
Noanamá, 8: Emberá and Wounaan
Noanes, 8: Emberá and Wounaan
Noarma, 9a
Noche, 1: Yokuts
Noenama, 7: Chocó; Noanamá
Nogays, 6(R)
Noghaylar, 6(R): Nogays
Noires, 7: Afro–South Americans
Nokhchiy, 6(R): Chechen-Ingush
Nomad River Peoples, 2: Gebusi
Nomatsigenka, 7: Mataco

Nomatsiguenga, 7: Campa
Nomoi, 2
Nonama, 7: Chocó; Noanamá
Nonamá, 8: Emberá and Wounaan
Nonameño, 8: Emberá and Wounaan
Nongatl, 1: Wailaki
Noniar, 3a: Nunia
Noniyan, 3a: Nunia
Nonpastoral nomads, 3: Peripatetics
Nonukan, 5: Tidong
Nootka, 1
Nootsack, 1: Klallam
Nor Tagrbo, 9a: Mambila
North African Jews, 9: Jews of Algeria
North Alaskan Eskimos, 1
Northeastern Thai, 5: Lao Isan
Northern Belgians, 4: Flemish
Northern Blackfoot, 1: Blackfoot
Northern Emberá, 7: Chocó
Northern Irish, 4
Northern Kankanai, 5: Sagada Igorot
Northern Kwakiutl, 1: Bellabella
Northern Lunda, 9: Lunda
Northern Mbene, 9a: Bassa
Northern Metis, 1
Northern Ojibwa, 1: Ojibwa
Northern Paiute, 1
Northern Sagala, 9a: Kaguru
Northern Sekai, 5: Temiar
Northern Shoshone and Bannock, 1
Northern Shoshoni, 1: Northern
    Shoshone and Bannock
Northern Sotho, 9: Pedi
Northern Tepehuan, 8: Tepehuan of
    Chihuahua
Northern Tonto, 1: Western Apache
Northern Tsou, 5: Taiwan Aboriginal
    Peoples
North Mbukushu, 9a
Norwegians, 4
Norwegians, 1: European-Americans;
    European-Canadians
Nosu, 6(C): Yi
Notsi, 2: Lesu
Nova Scotia Micmac, 1: Micmac
Novita, 7a: Tadó
N'Puchle, 1: Sanpoil
(N)Sandi, 9: Kongo
Ntalkyapamuk, 1: Thompson
Ntandu, 9: Kongo
Ntocoit, 7: Toba
Ntogapíd, 7a
Nu, 6(C)
Nuba, 9a
Nubi, 9a
Nubians, 9
Nuer, 9
Nufawa, 9a: Nupe
Nugum, 2: Yangoru Boiken
Ņuhų, 8: Otomí of the Sierra
Nuitadi, 1: Mandan
Nukuini, 7a

Nukuma, 2: Kwoma
Nukumairaro, 2: Anuta
Numa, 1: Northern Paiute; Southern
    Paiute (and Chemehuevi)
Numangkake, 1: Mandan
Numbiai, 7a
Numinu, 1: Comanche
Numu, 1: Comanche
Nunamiut, 1: North Alaskan Eskimos
Nunia, 3a
Nunivaarmiut, 1: Central Yup'ik
    Eskimos
Nuniya, 3a: Nunia
Nupe, 9a
Nupenchi, 9a: Nupe
Nuptadi, 1: Mandan
Nuptare, 1: Mandan
Nuquencaibo, 7a: Kapanawa
Nuristanis, 9
Nusu, 6(C): Nu
Nut, 3a: Nat
Ñuu Savi, 8: Mixtec
Nuzhen, 6(C): Manchu
Nya, 6(R): Nganasan
Nyag Dii, 9a: Dourou
Nyakwai, 9a
Nyakyusa and Ngonde, 9
Nyakyusa-Ngonde, 9a: Ngonde
Nyamwezi, 9a
Nyamwezi and Sukuma, 9
Nyandeva, 7: Guarayu
Nyaneka, 9a
Nyangatom, 9a
Nyanja, 9a
Nyankore, 9a: Nkore
Nyaruanda, 9a
Nyasa, 9a
Nyiha, 9a
Nyika, 9a
Nyika, 9: Mijikenda
Nyikoròma, 9: Suri
Nyinba, 3
Nyixa, 9a: Nyiha
Nykole, 9a: Nkore
Nymylan, 6(R): Koryaks and Kerek
Nyole, 9a: Nyuli
Nyoole, 9a: Nyoro
Nyore, 9a: Nyuli
Nyoro, 9a
Nytipai, 1: Kumeyaay
Nytuk, 9a: Samburu
N'yūhū, 8: Otomí of the Sierra
Nyuli, 9a
Nyuli, 9a: Nyoro
Nzakara, 9: Zande
Nzak Mbay, 9a: Mboum
Nzima, 9a

Oaiampi, 7a: Oyampi
Oasis dwellers of the Algerian Mzab, 9:
    Berbers of Morocco
Oba, 2: Ambae

Obbo, 5: Bagobo
Obenaki, 1: Abenaki
Oberösterreicher, 4: Austrians
Obo, 5: Bagobo
Ocaine, 7a: Okaina
Occhan, 3a
Occitans, 4
Occowyes, 7: Akawaio
Ockotikana, 7: Wanano
Octatas, 1: Oto
Od, 3a: Beldar
Ódami, 8: Tepehuan of Chihuahua
Odawa, 1: Ottawa
Odde, 3a: Beldar
Odden, 3a: Beldar
Ode, 3a: Beldar
Odewandlu, 3a: Beldar
Odeya, 3a: Vader
Odh, 3a: Beldar
Odia, 3: Oriya
Odissi, 3: Oriya
Odiya, 3: Oriya
Ofayé, 7a
Ogan-Besemah, 5
Ohlwa, 8: Sumu
Oi, 5: Oy
Oilean Thoraighe, 4: Tory Islanders
Oirats, 6(R): Kalmyks
Oirubae, 8: Arubans
Oja, 3a: Konda Dora
Ojana, 7a: Wayana
Ojha, 3a
Ojibwa, 1
Ojuli, 9: Peripatetics of Afghanistan,
    Iran, and Turkey (Iran)
Okaina, 7a
Okam, 9a: Mbembe
Okanagon, 1
Okelousa, 1a
Okiek, 9
Okinagan, 1: Okanagon
Okinaken, 1: Okanagon
Okinawajin, 5: Okinawans
Okinawans, 5
Okkaliga, 3
Okodyiua, 7: Wanano
Oko-Juwoi, 3a
O·χ, 3: Toda
Olah Cigany, 4: Vlach Gypsies of
    Hungary
Olamentke, 1: Coast Miwok
Old Believers, 1; 6(R)
Old Ritualists, 1: Old Believers
Oleai, 2: Woleai
Olee, 3a: Oli
Olgana, 3a: Bhangi
Oli, 3a
Oliya, 3a: Oli
Ollares, 3a: Allar
Olnea, 2: Woleai
Olo, 2: Wape
Olof, 9: Wolof

Olua, 8: Sumu
Olugwere, 9a: Gwere
Olunyole, 9a: Nyuli
Omage, 7: Amuesha
Omaha, 1
Omaito, 3a: Omanaito
Omanaito, 3a
Omanatya, 3a: Omanaito
Omaua, 7: Karihona
Omawa, 7a
Omba, 2: Ambae
Ometo, 9a: Wolayta
Omia, 9: Iteso
Ommura, 2: Tairora
Omogua, 7a: Omawa
Omo-Murle, 9a
Ondo, 9: Yoruba
Oneida, 1
Onge, 3a
Onge, 3: Andamanese
Ongee, 3a: Onge
Onian, 9a: Bassari
Onicoin, 7: Marinahua; Sharanahua
Ono Niha, 5: Nias
Onondaga, 1
Onotos, 7: Paraujano
Ontarahronon, 1: Kickapoo
Ontong Java, 2
Onufrievtsy, 6(R): Old Believers
Óob, 8: Pima Bajo
O'odham, 1: Pima-Papago
Ó Odham, 8: Pima Bajo
'O'odham, 8: Pima Bajo
Oorali Curumaru, 3a: Urali
Opa, 2: Ambae
Opaina, 7: Tanimuka
Oparo, 2: Rapa
Opata, 8
Ópata, 8: Opata
Opatoro, 8: Lenca
Openango, 1: Abenaki
Orakzai, 3a
Oran Boyan, 5: Baweanese
Orang Ambon, 5: Ambonese
Orang Asli, 5: Semang
Orang Babian, 5: Baweanese
Orang Bawean, 5: Baweanese
Orang Bonerate, 5: Bonerate
Orang Boyan, 5: Baweanese
Orang Bri, 5: Senoi
Orang Bukit, 5: Senoi
Orang Buton, 5: Butonese
Orang Butung, 5: Butonese
Orang Butuni, 5: Butonese
Orang Darat, 5: Kubu; Senoi
Orang Djawa, 5: Javanese
Orang Ende, 5: Endenese
Orang Hutan, 5: Senoi
Orang Laut, 5: Selung/Moken
Orang Madura, 5: Madurese
Orang Maluku, 5: Moluccans, North;
    Moluccans, Southeast

Orang Mantawei, 5: Mentaweian
Orang Nias, 5: Nias
Orang Palu'e, 5: Palu'e
Orang Pesukuan, 5: Selung/Moken
Orang Rayat, 5: Selung/Moken
Orang Rih, 5: Senoi
Orang Seraq, 5: Senoi
Orang Seroq, 5: Senoi
Orang Sunda, 5: Sundanese
Orang Ternate, 5: Ternatan/Tidorese
Orang Tidore, 5: Ternatan/Tidorese
Orang Timor Asli, 5: Atoni
Orang Tobelo, 5: Tobelorese
Orang Ulu, 5: Senoi
Orao, 3: Oraon
Oraon, 3
Ora Oubao, 8: Arubans
Orcadians, 4
Orchipoins, 1: Chipewyan
Orcocoyana, 7a: Wayana
Oregon Snakes, 1: Northern Paiute
Orejon, 7a: Payawá
Orelha de Pau, 7a: Numbiai
Oréva, 7: Guarayu
Orientales, 7: Asians in South America
Oriental Jews, 4: Sephardic Jews; 9:
    Jews of the Middle East
Orientals, 1: East Asians of Canada;
    East Asians of the United States
Orientas, 7: Asians in South America
Orissi, 3: Oriya
Oriya, 3
Orkney Islanders, 4: Orcadians
Oro, 9a: Oron
Orochen, 6(R): Evenki
Orochi, 6(R)
Orochisel, 6(R): Orochi
Orogo, 2: Kaluli
Orok, 6(R)
Orokaiva, 2
Orokolo, 2
Oromo, 9a
Oron, 9a
Oropoi, 9a: Oropom
Oropom, 9a
Oroqen, 6(C)
Oro Ubo, 8: Arubans
Orowari, 7a: Wari
Orri, 9a
Orringorrin, 9a: Orri
Othan, 9a: Uduk
Orthodox Coptic Christians, 9: Copts
Osage, 1
Ossetes, 6(R)
Osson, 6(R): Balkars
Ostiak of the Yenisei, 6(R): Ket
Ostyak, 6(R): Khanty; Selkup
Ostyak-Samoyeds, 6(R): Selkup
Oswal, 3: Bania
Otan, 3a
Otari, 3a
Otchipiweons, 1: Chipewyan

Ot Danum Dayaks, 5: Kalimantan
    Dayaks
Oto, 1
Otomí of the Sierra, 8
Otomí of the Sierra Norte de Puebla, 8:
    Otomí of the Sierra
Otomí of the Southern Huasteca, 8:
    Otomí of the Sierra
Otomí of the Valley of Mezquital, 8
Ottawa, 1
Ouassoulounke, 9a
Ouayampis, 7: Way_pi
Ouayeoue, 7: Wáiwai
Oubenaki, 1: Abenaki
Oubykhs, 6(R): Circassians
Ouchage, 1: Osage
Ouled Sliman, 9a
Oumami, 1: Miami
Ounia, 9a
Ouobe, 9a
Ouoloff, 9: Wolof
Outagami, 1: Fox
Outcaste, 5: Burakumin
Ovambo, 9a
Overseas Chinese, 5: Chinese in
    SoutheastAsia
Overseas Indians, 8: East Indians in
    Trinidad
Ovimbundu, 9a
Ovoiba, 9a: Edo-Speaking Peoples
Ovsi, 6(R): Balkars
Owens Valley Paiute, 1: Mono
Owo, 9: Yoruba
Oy, 5
Oyadagahroene, 1: Catawba
Oyampi, 7a
Oyampi, 7: Wayãpi
Oyampik, 7: Wayãpi
Oyampiques, 7: Wayãpi
Oyaricoulet, 7a: Akurio
Oyata'ge Ronon, 1: Cherokee
Oyhut, 1: Chehalis
Oyo, 9: Yoruba
Ozarks, 1

Paáiáha, 7a: Andoke
Pa-ang, 5: Palaung
Pab, 3a: Ganda
Pacaguara, 7: Chácobo
Pacaguara de Ivon, 7: Chácobo
Pacanawa, 7a: Poyanawa
Paca Nova, 7a: Wari
Pachhima Brahman, 3a: Babhan
Pachuara, 7: Chácobo
Pacific Eskimo, 1
Pacific Gulf Eskimo, 1: Pacific Eskimo
Pacific Islanders, 1: Micronesians;
    Polynesians
Pacific Yup'ik Eskimo, 1: Pacific Eskimo
Pacoh, 5
Padam, 3: Abor; 3a: Adi
Padhola, 9a

Padiga Raju, 3a: Bhatraja
Padinjaran Pulaya, 3a: Pulluvan
Padmaraj, 3a: Pod
Padma Sale, 3a
Padouca, 1: Comanche
Padti, 3a
Padu, 3a: Batgam
Padvi, 3a: Gamit
Paekchŏng, 5: Kolisuch'ŏk
Páez, 7
Paez, 7: Páez
Pagan Gaddang, 5: Gaddang
Pahari, 3
Paharia, 3a: Maler
Pahaya, 8: Paya
Pahilwan, 3a: Mang-Garori
Pahlad Bansi, 3a: Bishnoi
Pahodja, 1: Iowa
Pahouin, 9a
Pahouin, 9a: Fang
Pah-Utes, 1: Southern Paiute (and
    Chemehuevi)
Pai, 5: T'in
P'ai, 5: T'in
Paï, 7: Paï-Tavytera
Pãï, 7: Siona-Sceoya
Paica, 7: Chiquitano
Paï-Cayuä, 7: Paï-Tavytera
Paicogês, 7: Krikati/Pukobye
Paidi, 3a
Paik, 3a
Pailibo, 3: Abor
Paingua, 7: Paï-Tavytera
Paipai, 8: Indians of Baja California
Paï-Tavytera, 7
Paï-Tavyterä, 7: Paï-Tavytera
Paite, 3a: Kuki
Paiter, 7: Suruí
Paitu, 3a: Kuki
Paiute, 1: Northern Paiute; Southern
    Paiute (and Chemehuevi)
Paiwan-Rukai, 5: Taiwan Aborigi-
    nalPeoples
Pai Yao, 6(C): Yao
Pai-Yi, 5: Tai Lue
Pajade, 9a: Badyaranke
Pajonalino, 7: Campa
Pakanati Jogi, 3a: Handi Jogi
Pakawara, 7a
Pakhali, 3a: Bhishti
Pakhawaji, 3a: Mirasi
Pakhtun, 3: Pathan
Pakistanis, 1: South and Southeast
    Asians of Canada; South and
    Southeast Asians of the United
    States
Pakiut'lema, 1: Yakima
Paknat Reddi, 3: Reddi
Pak Thai, 5
Pala'au, 5: Bajau
Palaiyakkaran, 3a: Mutrasi

Palatola, 7: Cuna
Palau, 2: Belau
Palauans, 1: Micronesians
Palaung, 5
Palawan, 5
Palawanin, 5: Palawan
Palawano, 5: Palawan
Palawanon, 5: Palawan
Palayakkaran, 3a: Polegar
Palayan, 3a: Palliyar
Palee, 3a: Pali
Palestinians, 9
Palestinians, 1: Arab Americans
Palewar, 3a: Bhoi
Pali, 3a
Palie, 3a: Pali
Palikur, 7
Paliwar, 3a: Palwar
Paliya, 3a: Kochh; Pali
Paliyan, 3a: Palliyar
Pallan, 3a
Palle, 3a: Palli
Palleyan, 3a: Palliyar
Palli, 3a
Pallilu, 3a: Palli
Palliyan, 3a: Palliyar
Palliyar, 3a
Palong, 5: Palaung
Palouse, 1: Wallawalla
Paluanes, 5: Palawan
Palu'e, 5
Palu-Kurumbas, 3: Kurumbas
Paluo, 9a
Palus, 1: Wallawalla
Palvada Kotwalia, 3a: Vitolana
Palwar, 3a
Pame, 8
Pamirians, 6(R): Pamir Peoples
Pamirian Tajiks, 6(R): Pamir Peoples
Pamir Peoples, 6(R)
Pamlico, 1a
Pampadeque, 7: Cocama
Pamunkey, 1a
Pan, 3a: Ganda; Pano; 7: Paï-Tavytera
Pan'akwati, 1: Bannock
Panal, 3a: Pardhan
Panama Emberá, 7: Chocó
Panamaka, 8: Sumu
Panan, 3a
Panapanayan, 5: Taiwan
    AboriginalPeoples
Panara, 3a: Nalke
Panare, 7
Panchadayi, 3a: Kammalan
Panchal, 3a: Kammalan; Lohar
Panchala, 3a: Kammalan
Panchalan, 3a: Kammalan
Panchama, 3: Untouchables; 3a: Mala
Pancham Banajigaru, 3a: Balija
Panchamollu, 3a: Madiga
Panchkalshi, 3a
Panda, 3a: Dakaut

Pandabequeo, 7: Cocama
Pandani, 1: Arikara
Pandaram, 3: Vellala; 3a: Valluvan
Pandava Reddi, 3: Reddi
Pandi Jogulu, 3a: Handi Jogi
Pandit of Kashmir, 3
Pando, 3a
Pandula Gollalu, 3a: Handi Jogi
Panduro-Tadó, 7a
Pangan, 5: Semang
Pangi, 3: Abor
Pangtash, 5: Taiwan Aboriginal Peoples
Pangul, 3a
Pangwal, 3a
Pangwala, 3a: Pangwal
Pangwe, 9a: Fang
Pani, 1: Pawnee
Pania, 3: Paniyan
Panika, 3a: Ganda
Panikkan, 3a: Kaniyan
Panikki, 3a
Panimaha, 1: Arikara
Panisavan, 3a
Paniya, 3: Paniyan
Paniyan, 3
Panjabi, 3: Punjabi
Panjari, 3a: Dudekula
Panjukotti, 3a: Dudekula
Panka, 3a: Ganda
Pankararé, 7a
Pankararú, 7a
Panna, 3a
Panna-Durayi, 3a: Panna
Pannaitti, 1: Bannock
Pano, 3a
Panoteca, 8: Wasteko
Panr, 3a: Ganda
Pansari, 3a: Tamdi
Panta Reddi, 3: Reddi
Panthay, 6(C): Hui
Pantia, 3a: Pentiya
Panue, 9a: Fang
Panumapa, 7: Wanano
Panwa, 3a: Ganda
Panwale, 3a: Bari
Panwar Rajput, 3a
Panya, 3: Paniyan
Panzas, 1: Pawnee
Pao, 3a: Ganda
Paoli, 3a: Julaha
Papabota, 1: Pima-Papago
Papago, 1: Pima-Papago
Papatsje, 1: Maricopa
Papavô, 7a
Papurí-uara, 7: Desana
Paracha, 3a
Parachagi, 3a: Paracha
Parachi, 3a: Paracha
Paradesi, 3a
Paradesi Jews, 3: Cochin Jew
Parahaiya, 3a: Parahiya
Parahiya, 3a

Parahujano, 7: Paraujano
Paraicha, 3a: Paracha
Paraichi, 3a: Paracha
Paraiya, 3a
Paraiyan, 3a: Paraiya
Parakanã, 7a
Paramuna, 7a: Patamona
Paranapura, 7: Chayahuita
Parancha, 3a: Paracha
Parangiperja, 3a: Poraja
Paraogwan, 7: Paraujano
Paraokan, 7: Paraujano
Paraqwan, 7: Paraujano
Parasar-Das, 3a: Kewat
Parauano, 7: Paraujano
Paraujano, 7
Pa rauk, 6(C): Wa
Parava, 3a: Paravan
Paravan, 3a
Parawkan, 7: Paraujano
Parayan, 3a: Paraiya
Parbhu, 3a: Prabhu
Pardeshi Alitkar, 3a: Khatik
Pardhan, 3a
Pardhi, 3a
Pardos, 7: Afro-Brazilians; Afro–South
     Americans; Afro-Venezuelans
Parecí, 7: Paresí
Parene, 7a: Yavitero
Paresí, 7: 7a
Paressí, 7: Paresí
Paretí, 7: Paresí
Pargha, 3a
Parhaiya, 3a: Parahiya
Parhowka, 7: Paraujano
Paria, 3a: Paraiya
Pariah, 3: Untouchables; 3a: Paraiya
Paricura, 7: Palikur
Paricuri, 7: Palikur
Parigha, 3a: Pargha
Parihar, 3a
Parikwenê, 7: Palikur
Parintintin, 7: Kagwahiv
Parit, 3a: Dhobi
Parivar, 3a: Bhoi
Parivara, 3a: Besta
Parivaram, 3a
Parja, 3a: Poraja
Parkitiwaru, 3a: Besta
Paroja, 3a: Poraja
Parsai, 3a: Joshi
Parsee, 3: Parsi
Parsi, 3
Parucuria, 7: Palikur
Parukoto, 7a: Hishkariana
Parwari, 3: Mahar
Pasemah, 5: Ogan-Besemah
Pashai, 9
Pashtun, 3: Pathan
Pasi, 3a
Pasi, 3: Abor; 3a: Adi
Pasiegos, 4

Passamaquoddy, 1
Passi, 3a: Pasi
Pastagia, 3a: Kachhia
Pastaza Quichua, 7: Canelos Quichua
Pastulirmiut, 1: Central Yup'ik Eskimos
Patamona, 7a
Patanwal, 3: Kohistani
Patar, 3a: Devadasi
Patari, 3a
Patashó, 7a
Patashó, 7a: HãHãHãi
Patauni, 3a: Patni
Patawát, 1: Wiyot
Patel, 3: Kanbi
Patelia, 3: Bhil
Patchogue, 1: Metoac
Pathan, 3
Pathari, 3a: Pardhan; Patari
Patharvat, 3a
Pathia, 3: Bhil
Pathiyan, 3a: Pathiyar
Pathiyar, 3a
Pathrot, 3a: Beldar
Pathura Dawaru, 3a: Devadasi
Patidar, 3: Kanbi
Patni, 3a
Patnulkaran, 3a
Patoriva, 3a: Devadasi
Patra, 3a: Patwa
Patsoka, 7a: Jurutí
Pattanavan, 3a
Pattar, 3a: Sonar
Patua, 3a: Juang; Patwa
Patuni, 3a: Patni
Patur, 3a: Devadasi
Paturiya, 3a: Devadasi
Patvegar, 3a: Patwa
Patvekari, 3a: Patwa
Patwa, 3a
Patwi, 3a: Patwa
Patwin, 1a
Pau Cerna, 7: Pauserna
Paumarí, 7a
Paumotu, 2: Raroia
Paumuca, 7: Chiquitano
Paungar, 3a: Chhipa
Pauserna, 7
Pauserna-Guarasug'we, 7: Pauserna
Pavada, 3: Bhil
Pavé, 4: Peripatetics
Paviotso, 1: Northern Paiute
Pawi, 3a
Pawnaka, 7a
Pawnee, 1
Pawnee Picts, 1: Pawnee
Pawnee Piques, 1: Pawnee
Pawni, 1: Pawnee
Pawra, 3: Bhil
Pawyer, 8: Paya
Paxas Novas, 7a: Wari
Paya, 8
Payao, 5: Isneg

Payawá, 7a
Pear, 5
Pea Ridge Group, 1: American Isolates
Peaux de Lievre, 1: Hare
Peba, 7: Yagua
Pebo, 7: Kogi
Pech, 8: Paya
Peddintiwandlu, 3a: Madiga
Pedi, 9
Pehtsik, 1: Karok
Pehua, 7: Yagua
Pehuenche, 7: Araucanians
Pei Er Mi, 6(C): Pumi
Peigan, 1: Blackfoot
Peimi, 6(C): Pumi
Pelam, 5: Taiwan Aboriginal Peoples
Pelew, 2: Belau
Pelly Bay Eskimo, 1: Netsilik Inuit
Peloponnesians, 4
Pemon, 7
Penan, 5
Pende, 9
Pendhari, 3a: Pindari
Pendhari Mang, 3a: Mang-Garori
Pend d'Oreilles, 1: Kalispel
Pennacook, 1; 1a
Pennan, 5: Penan
Pennsylvania Dutch, 1: Amish;
    European-Americans; Mennonites
Pennsylvania Germans, 1: Amish
Penobscot, 1
Penoquiquia, 7: Chiquitano
Penrhyn, 2: Tongareva
Penta, 3a
Pentecost, 2
Pentia, 3a: Pentiya
Pentiya, 3a
People of Color, 1: Blacks in Canada
People of Nevis, 8: Kittsians and
    Nevisians
People of Saint Kitts, 8: Kittsians and
    Nevisians
Peoria, 1a
Pequot, 1: Mohegan
Perika, 3a
Perike, 3a: Perika
Perike Shetti, 3a: Perika
Periki, 3a: Perika
Peripatetics, 1; 3; 4
Peripatetics of Afghanistan, Iran, and
    Turkey, 9
Peripatetics of Iraq, Syria, Lebanon,
    Jordan, Israel, Egypt, Sudan,
    Yemen, 9
Peripatetics of the Maghreb, 9
Perka, 3a: Perika
Perki, 3a: Perika
Persians, 9
Person County Indians, 1: American
    Isolates
Perumal Madukkaran, 3a: Gangeddu
Pesch, 8: Paya

Pesegem, 2: Dani
Pessy, 9: Kpelle
Petén Maya, 8: Itza'
Peul, 9: Fulani
Peva, 7: Yagua
Phanse Pardhi, 3a: Pardhi
Phanseegur, 3: Thug
Phansigar, 3: Thug
Phans-Pardhi, 3a: Pardhi
Phii Bree, 5: Mnong
Philippine Negritos, 5
Phi Tong Luang, 5: Yumbri
Phorhépicha, 8: Tarascans
Phudgi, 3a
Phulari, 3a: Tamdi
Phunoi, 5: P'u Noi
Phurhépecha, 8: Tarascans
Piadoco, 7: Piapoco
Piapoco, 7
Piapóko, 7: Piapoco
Piaroa, 7
Piasau Id'an, 5: Dusun
Pichagunta, 3a: Pichakuntala
Pichai, 3a: Pichakuntala
Pichakuntala, 3a
Pichchuguntavallu, 3a: Helava
Pichigunta, 3a: Pichakuntala
Picunche, 7: Araucanians
Picuris, 1: Pueblo Indians
Pidá-Djapá, 7a: Katukina
Piedmontese, 4: Piemontese
Pieds-Noirs, 9: Jews of Algeria
Piegan, 1: Blackfoot
Piemontese, 4
Piemontese Sinti, 4
Pierced Noses, 1: Nez Percé
Pikraj, 9: Peripatetics of Afghanistan,
    Iran, and Turkey (Afghanistan)
Pikuni, 1: Blackfoot
Pilagá, 7a
Pilam, 5: Taiwan Aboriginal Peoples
Pila-Pila, 9a
Pilipino, 5: Tagalog
Pillaimar, 3: Vellala
Pima, 1: Pima-Papago
Pima Bajo, 8
Pima-Papago, 1
Pinaren, 7a: Tembé
Pindara, 3a: Pindari
Pindari, 3a
Pinjara, 3a: Bahna
Pinjari, 3a: Bahna
Piñoca, 7: Chiquitano
Pintado, 5: Visayan
Pintubi, 2: Pintupi
Pintupi, 2
Pioché, 7: Siona-Secoya
Piocobgêz, 7: Krikati/Pukobye
Piojé, 7: Siona-Secoya
Pipavasi, 3a: Darzi
Pipil, 8
Pirá, 7a

Pirahã, 7a
Pirataguari, 7: Guarayu
Piratapuia, 7a: Pirá
Pirhain, 3a: Bharai
Pirixi, 7a: Wayana
Piro, 1a; 7
Pisabo, 7a
Piscataway, 1: Nanticoke
Pisharati, 3a: Ambalavasi
Pisharodi, 3a: Ambalavasi
Pisharoti, 3a: Ambalavasi
Pisquibo, 7: Shipibo
Pitjantjatjara, 2: Ngatatjara
Pito-O-Te Henua, 2: Easter Island
Pit River Indians, 1: Achumawi
Pitsobu, 7a: Pisabo
Pitt River Indians, 1: Achumawi
Piuma, 5: Taiwan Aboriginal Peoples
Piya, 9a: Wurkum
Piyoti, 7: Yukuna
Plain Folks, 1: Appalachians
Plain People, 1: Mennonites; 7:
    Mennonites
Plains Ojibwa, 1: Ojibwa
Plains Shoshone, 1: Eastern Shoshone
Ple, 5: Temiar
Pleasant Island, 2: Nauru
Ple-Temiar, 5: Temiar
Pnar, 3a: Jaintia
Pocomám, 8: Poqomam
Pocomán, 8: Poqomam
Poconchí, 8: Poqomchi'
Pod, 3a
Poduval, 3a: Mussad
Poenan, 5: Penan
Poggy-Islander, 5: Mentaweian
Pogolu, 9a: Pogoro
Pogoro, 9a
Pohnpei, 2
Pohnpeians, 1: Micronesians
Pohr, 5: Pear
Poi, 3a: Pawi
Pojoaque, 1: Pueblo Indians; Tewa
    Pueblos
Põkateye, 7: Krikati/Pukobye
Poké, 7: Terena
Pokomám, 8: Poqomam
Pokomán, 8: Poqomam
Pokomchí, 8: Poqomchi'
Pokonchi, 8: Poqomchi'
Pokot, 9
Pola, 3a: Kochh
Polacy, 4: Poles
Polak, 6(R): Poles
Polak/Polka, 4: Poles
Polar Eskimo, 1: Inughuit
Polareskimoer, 1: Inughuit
Polargroenlaendere, 1: Inughuit
Pole, 2: Kewa
Polegar, 3a
Polen, 4: Poles
Poles, 4; Poles, 6(R)

Poles, 1: European-Americans; European-Canadians
Poleya, 3a: Holeya
Polia, 3a: Kochh
Poliak, 4: Poles
Poliane, 4: Poles
Poligar, 3a: Polegar
Polikla, 1: Yurok
Polyak, 4: Poles
Polynesians, 1
Pomaks, 4
Pomo, 1
Pomortsy, 6(R): Old Believers
Ponape, 2: Pohnpei
Ponasht, 1: Northern Shoshone and Bannock
Pondichériens, 3: French of India
Pondicherry, 3: French of India
Ponca, 1
Pondo, 9a
Pontian Greeks, 6(R): Greeks
Pontic, 4
Pontic Greeks, 6(R): Greeks
Ponwar, 3a: Panwar Rajput
Poojaree, 3a: Pujari
Pooles, 1: American Isolates
Poonan, 5: Penan
Põpekateye, 7: Krikati/Pukobye
Popo, 9a: Ewe
Popoloca, 8
Popoluca, 8
Popovtsy, 6(R): Old Believers
su Populu Sardu, 4: Sardinians
Popya, 8: Paya
Poqomam, 8
Poqomchi', 8
Poraja, 3a
Poraja, 3: Bondo
Porja, 3: Bondo; 3a: Poraja
Pornowol, 2: Pentecost
Poroja, 3a: Poraja
Portuguese, 4
Portuguese, 1: European-Americans; European-Canadians
Potadar, 3a: Sonar
Potawatomi, 1
Pothuval, 3a: Ambalavasi
Potiguara, 7a
Potomac Indians, 1: American Isolates
Potuval, 3a: Mussad
Pouhatan, 1: Powhatan
Poumotu, 2: Raroia
Pounan, 5: Penan
Poundra, 3a: Pod
Powhatan, 1
Poya, 8: Paya
Poyai, 8: Paya
Poyanawa, 7a
Poyer, 8: Paya
Prabhu, 3a
Pral, 5: T'in
Prairie Apache, 1: Kiowa Apache

Pramalai Kallar, 3a: Kallar
Pramara Rajput, 3a: Panwar Rajput
Prathama Sudra, 3a: Kuruba
Praying Indians, 1: Massachuset
Prêtos, 7: Afro-Brazilians; Afro–South Americans
Primi, 6(C): Pumi
Priulians, 4: Friuli
Provencal, 4
Promaucae, 7: Araucanians
P'u, 5: T'in
Puar, 3a: Panwar Rajput
Pucari, 3a: Pujari
Pueblo Indians, 1
Puerto Ricans, 8
Puerto Ricans, 1: Latinos
Puertorriqueños, 8: Puerto Ricans
Pugusch, 2: Lak
Pugut, 5: Agta; Philippine Negritos
Püimiwã, 7a: Siriano
Puinabe, 7: Puinave
Puinabi, 7: Puinave
Puinabo, 7: Puinave
Puinahua, 7: Puinave
Puinave, 7
Pujari, 3a
Pujunan, 1: Maidu
Pukapuka, 2
Pukhtun, 3: Pathan
Pukobyé, 7a
Pulaya, 3a: Pulluvan; Cheruman; Malapulaya; Pulluvan
Pulluvan, 3a
Pume, 7
Pumi, 6(C)
Pumi, 6(C): Qiang
Punan, 5: Penan
Punjabi, 3
Punnush, 1: Bannock
P'u Noi, 5
Pu Noi, 5: P'u Noi
Punyavachan, 3a: Kammalan
Puquina, 7: Chipaya
Purepecha, 8: Tarascans
Purépecha, 8: Tarascans
Puruborá, 7a
Purukarôt, 7: Xikrin
Purum, 3
Puru-Purú, 7a: Paumarí
Pushkarna, 3a
Putian, 5: Sulod
Putuli, 3a: Gandhabanik
Puyuma, 5: Taiwan Aboriginal Peoples
Pwo, 5: Karen
Pygmies, 9: Tropical-Forest Foragers
Pyuma, 5: Taiwan Aboriginal Peoples
Py-utes, 1: Northern Paiute

Qalandar, 3
Q'anjob'al, 8
Qarachaylï, 6(R): Karachays

Qaraites, 9: Karaites
Qara Nogays (Black Nogays), 6:(R) Nogays
Qarbalband, 9: Peripatetics of Afghanistan, Iran, and Turkey (Iran)
Qarrad, 9: Peripatetics of Iraq . . . Yemen (Egypt)
Qashqa'i, 9
Qassab, 3a
Qassai, 3a: Qassab
Qawal, 9: Peripatetics of Afghanistan, Iran, and Turkey (Afghanistan)
Qawashqar, 7a: Kawe'skar
Qawwal, 3a: Mirasi
Qazi Qumukh, 6(R): Laks
Q'eqchi', 8
Qeraçi, 9: Peripatetics of Afghanistan, Iran, and Turkey (Turkey)
Qevsur, 6(R): Khevsur
Qiang, 6(C)
Qing Miao, 6(C): Miao
Qiren, 6(C): Manchu
Qiu, 6(C): Drung
Qizilbash, 9
Qollahuaya, 7: Callahuaya
Qollawaya, 7: Callahuaya
Qom, 7: Toba
Qoml'ek, 7: Toba
Qompi, 7: Toba
Qorbat, 9: Ghorbat
Qqueres, 1: Keres Pueblo Indians
Quaitso, 1: Quinault
Qualuyaarmiut, 1: Central Yup'ik Eskimos
Quapaw, 1
Quasi-Indians, 1: American Isolates
Quebec Micmac, 1: Micmac
Québecois, 1: French Canadians
Quechan, 1
Quechua, 7
Queets, 1: Quinault
Quemaya, 1: Kumeyaay
Querechos, 1: Mescalero Apache
Queres, 1: Keres Pueblo Indians
Queresans, 1: Keres Pueblo Indians
Quiché, 8: K'iche'
Quijos, 7: Canelos Quichua
Quileute, 1
Quiliniks, 1: Copper Eskimo
Quillayute, 1: Quileute
Quinaelt, 1: Quinault
Quinaielt, 1: Quinault
Quinault, 1
Quini, 1: Zuni
Quinipissa, 1a
Quinquis, 4: Peripatetics
Quiva, 7: Cuiva
Qumïq, 6(R): Kumyks
Quoratem, 1: Karok
Quraish, 3a: Quraishi
Quraishi, 3a

Qureshi, **3a: Quraishi**
Qurungua, **7: Sirionó**
Qwulhhwaipum, **1: Klikitat**

Rabai, **9: Mijikenda**
Rabari, 3a
Rabbit Skins, **1: Hare**
Rabha, 3a
Rachewar, **3a: Rajwar**
Rachi, **3a: Paracha**
Racial Islands, **1: American Isolates**
Racial Isolates, **1: American Isolates**
Rada, **3a: Hena**
Raday, **5: Rhadé**
Raddi, 3a
Ra-Deo, 3a
Radha, **3a: Bhagat**
Raewari, **3a: Rahbari**
Raghbansi, **3a: Raghuvansi**
Raghubansi, **3a: Raghuvansi**
Raghuvansi, 3a
Raghvi, **3a: Raghuvansi**
Rahbari, 3a
Rahwari, **3a: Rahbari**
Rai, 3
Rai, **3a: Khambu**
Raika, **3a: Rabari**
Raikari, 3a
Raikwar, 3a
Rain, **3a: Arain**
Raj, **3a: Beldar**
Raja Deo, **3a: Ra-Deo**
Rajak, **3a: Dhobi**
Rajanaka, **3a: Rana**
Raja Reddi, **3: Reddi**
Rajaur, **3a: Rajjhar**
Rajawar, **3a: Rajwar**
Rajbanshi, **3a: Tiyar**
Rajbansi, **3a: Kochh; Tiyar**
Rajbansi Morma, **3a: Marma**
Rajbhar, **3a: Bhar; Rajjhar**
Raji, 3a
Raji, **3: Rai**
Rajjhar, 3a
Rajpinde, **3a: Arasu**
Rajput, 3
Raju, **3a: Razu**
Rajuar, **3a: Rajwar**
Rajwar, 3a
Rajwar, **3a: Rajjhar**
Rakhia, **3a: Meghval**
Raki, **3a: Iraqi**
Ralámuli, **8: Tarahumara**
Rālik, 2: Marshall Islands
Rama, 8
Ramadiya, **9: Peripatetics of Iraq . . . Yemen (Egypt)**
Ramaiya, 3a
Ramano, **7: Chimane**
Ramapo Mountain People, **1: American Isolates**
Ramayye, **3a: Johari**

Ramdu, **3a: Dhobi**
Ramkókamekra, **7: Canela**
Ramo, **3: Abor**
Ramoshi, **3a: Ramosi**
Ramosi, 3a
Ramps, **1: American Isolates**
Rana, 3a
Rana, **3a: Gola**
Rancheros, **8: Cattle Ranchers of the Huasteca**
Randhawa, 3a
Rangari, **3a: Chhipa; Rangrez**
Rangchan, **3a: Kuki**
Rangi, 9a
Rangidas Garodi, **3a: Mang-Garori**
Rangkhol, **3a: Kuki**
Rangkhote, **3a: Kuki**
Rangrez, 3a
Ranki, **3a: Iraqi**
Rao, **3a: Bhat**
Rapa, 2
Rapa-Iti, **2: Rapa**
Rapa Nui, **2: Easter Island**
Rapides Indians, **1: American Isolates**
Rapid Indians, **1: Gros Ventre**
Rappahannock Indians, **1: American Isolates**
Rarámuri, **8: Tarahumara**
Raroia, 2
Rasende, **4: Peripatetics**
Raskol'niks, **1: Old Believers**
Rastafari, **8: Rastafarians**
Rastafarians, 8
Rastas, **8: Rastafarians**
Rastaogi, 3a
Rastaugi, **3a: Rastaogi**
Ratak, **2: Marshall Islands**
Rathakara, **3a: Gudikara**
Rathaur Rajput, **3a: Rathor Rajput**
Rathi, 3a
Rathia, **3: Bhil**
Rathia Tanwar, **3a: Kawar**
Rathor Rajput, 3a
Raul Jogi, **3a: Raval Jogi**
Raunia, **3a: Nunia**
Rauniar, **3a: Nunia**
Rauru, **2: Choiseul Island**
Rautia, 3a
Raval, **3a: Raval Jogi**
Ravalia, **3a: Raval Jogi**
Raval Jogi
Rawal, **3: Bhil; 3a: Raval Jogi**
Rawat, **3: Ahir; 3a: Raji**
Rayat Laut, **5: Selung/Moken**
Razu, 3a
Red Benglong, **6(C): De'ang**
Red Bones, **1: American Isolates**
Reddi, 3
Reddi Dhora, **3a: Domara**
Reddi Domara, **3a: Domara**
Redwoods, **1: Yuki**
Ree, **1: Arikara**

Refugees in South Asia, **3**
Rega, **9a: Lega**
Remo, 7a
Remo, **3: Bondo**
Rena, **3a: Rona**
Rendille, 9a
Rengao, 5
Rengma, **3: Nagas**
Rennel Island, 2
Rennellese, **2: Rennel Island**
Republican Chinese, **5: Taiwanese**
Reshawa, 9a
Reshe, **9a: Reshawa**
Retuna, 7a
Re Ulithi, **2: Ulithi**
Reungao, **5: Rengao Rhadé**
Rhaetians, **4: Romansch**
Rheno, **7a: Remo**
Riang, **3a: Kuki**
Ribe, **9: Mijikenda**
Ricaree, **1: Arikara**
Ricari, **1: Arikara**
Rickahochan, **1: Cherokee**
Rifaʿiyya, **9: Peripatetics of Iraq . . . Yemen (Egypt)**
Rifians, **9: Berbers of Morocco**
Rikbaktsa, 7
Rikhia, **3a: Meghval**
Río Verde, 8: Emberá and Wounaan
Rishi, **3a: Mochi**
Rishia, **3a: Meghval**
River Indians, **1: Delaware; Mahican**
Riwari, **3a: Rahbari**
Rma, **6(C): Qiang**
Roang Magh, **3a: Marma**
Rockaway, **1: Metoac**
Rockingham Surry Group, **1: American Isolates**
Rocky Cree, **1: Cree, Western Woods**
Rodi, 3a
Rodiya, **3a: Rodi**
Roghangar, **3a: Teli**
Roghankash, **3a: Teli**
Rohilla, **3: Pathan**
Roissy, **2: Wogeo**
Rom, 1
Rom, **1: Peripatetics; 4: Peripatetics**
Roma, **4: Bulgarian Gypsies; Slovensko Roma; Xoraxané Romá; 6(R): Gypsies**
Rômâni (Romanians), **4: Transylvanian Ethnic Groups**
Romani, **9: Peripatetics of the Maghreb (Morocco and Egypt)**
Romanians, 4
Romanians, **1: European-Americans; European-Canadians**
Romaničel, **4: Peripatetics**
Romanies, **4: Peripatetics; Rominsche**
Romaniotes, **4: Greek-Speaking Jews of Greece**
Romansch, 4

Roma Sloveni, **4: Slovensko Roma**
Rominchels, **1: Peripatetics**
Rominsche, 4
Rom of Czechoslovakia, 4
Romora, **4: Slovensko Roma**
Rona, 3a
Rong, **6(C): Qiang**
Rongao, **5: Rengao**
Ro-ngao, **5: Rengao**
Root-Diggers, **1: Western Shoshone**
Rora, **3a: Arora**
Roshania, 3a
Ross, **6(R): Russians**
Rossel Island, 2
Rotinese, 5
Rotse, **9: Lozi**
Rotuma, 2
Rouergats, **4: Aveyronnais**
Roumanians, **1: European-Americans; European-Canadians; 4: Romanians**
Rourou, **6(C): Nu**
Rova, **2: Rossel Island**
Roviana, **2: New Georgia**
Rozi, **9: Lozi; 9a: Lozi**
Rudari, **4: Peripatetics**
Ruhaya, **9a: Haya**
Rukonjo, **9a: Konjo**
Rukuba, 9; 9a
Rumai, **5: Palaung**
Rumanians, **1: European-Americans; European-Canadians; 4: Romanians**
Runapura, **7: Canelos Quichua**
Runas, **7: Saraguro**
Rundi, 9a
Rus', **6(R): Russians**
Rusnaks, **1: European-Americans**
Rusnatsi, **6(R): Capartho-Rusyns**
Russian Peasants, 6(R)
Russians, 6(R)
Russians, **1: European-Americans; European-Canadians**
Russian Siberians, **6(R): Siberiaki**
Russkiy, **6(R): Russians**
Rusyny, **6(R): Capartho-Rusyns**
Ruthenians, **1: European-Americans; Ukrainians of Canada**
Ruthens, **6(R): Ukrainians**
Rutse, **9: Lozi**
Rutuls, 6(R)
Ruund, **9: Lunda**
Rwo, **9a: Meru**
Ryuku Islanders, **5: Okinawans**
Ryūkyūjin, **5: Okinawans**

Sa, **2: Pentecost**
Sa'a, **2: Malaita**
Saam', **6(R): Saami**
Saami, 4; 6(R)
Sabah Murut, **5: Murut**
Sabanero, **8: Bugle**

Sabaot, 9a
Sabine, **1: Huma**
Sabines, **1: American Isolates**
Sabzaki, **9: Peripatetics of Afghanistan, Iran, and Turkey (Afghanistan)**
Sabz-farosh, **3a: Kunjra**
Sabzi-farosh, **3a: Kunjra**
Sac, **1: Sauk**
Sachsen (Saxons), **4: Transylvanian Ethnic Groups**
Saclave, **9: Sakalava**
Sada, 3a
Sada, **5: Toala**
Sadama, 9a
Sa'dan Toraja, **5: Toraja**
Sadaru, **3a: Sada**
Sadgop, **3a: Chasa**
Sadh, 3a
Sadhu, 3
Sadi, **8: Seri**
Sadu, **9: Peripatetics of Afghanistan, Iran, and Turkey (Afghanistan)**
Saek, **5: Sek**
Safi, **9: Pashai**
Safwa, 9a
Sagada Igorot, 5
Sagar, 3a
Sagar, **3a: Upparwar**
Sagarollu, **3a: Upparwar**
Saghais, **5: Dusun**
Sahara, **3: Sora**
Saharia, **3a: Sahariya**
Sahariya, 3a
Saharya, **3a: Sahariya**
Sahib, **3: Europeans in South Asia**
Saho, 9a
Sahte, **3a: Kuki**
Sahtú gotine, **1: Bearlake Indians**
Sahukar, **3: Bania; 3a: Komati**
Ṣaʿideh, **9: Peripatetics of Iraq . . . Yemen (Egypt)**
Saija, **8: Emberá and Wounaan**
St. Landry Mulattoes, **1: American Isolates**
Saint Lucians, 8
Saints, **1: Mormons**
Sairhem, **3a: Kuki**
Sais, **3a: Darzi; Ghasia**
Saiset, **5: Taiwan Aboriginal Peoples**
Saisiat, **5: Taiwan Aboriginal Peoples**
Saisirat, **5: Taiwan Aboriginal Peoples**
Saisiyat, **5: Taiwan Aboriginal Peoples**
Sai Sutar, **3a: Darzi**
Saka, **5: Kalagan**
Sakadwipi, 3a
Sakai, **5: Semang; Senoi**
Sakaka, **7a: Hishkariana**
Sakala, **3a: Dhobi**
Sakalava, 9
Sakalave, **9: Sakalava**
Sakaldwipi, **3a: Sakadwipi**

Sakartvelo, **6(R): Georgians**
Sakha, **6(R): Dolgan; Yakut**
Sakhalin Ainu, **5: Ainu**
Sakishimajin, **5: Okinawans**
Sala, **6(C): Salar**
Salagama, 3a
Salahuva Vakkalu, 3a
Salamay, **7a: Mondé**
Salapu Kapulu, **3a: Salahuva Vakkalu**
Salar, 6(C)
Salasaca, 7
Salat, 3a
Salayar, **5: Bonerate**
Sale, 3a
Sale, **3a: Padma Sale**
Salewar, **3a: Koshti**
Salewar, **3a: Padma Sale**
Sali, **3a: Devanga; 3a: Sale**
Salīb, **9: Sleb**
Saliba, **7: Saliva**
Salineros, **8: Seri**
Salish, **1: Flathead**
Saliua, **7: Saliva**
Saliva, 7
Saliyan, **3a: Sale**
Salnam, **3a: Kuki**
Salon, **5: Selung/Moken**
Salsette Christian, **3a: East Indian**
Salt Pomo, **1: Pomo**
Saluan, 5
Salumã, 7a
Salvi, **3a: Sale**
Salzburger, **4: Austrians**
Sama, **5: Bajau; Samal; Samal Moro**
Samaale, **9: Somalis**
Sama Dilaut, **5: Bajau**
Samah, **5: Samal**
Samaʿina, **9: Peripatetics of Iraq . . . Yemen (Egypt)**
Samal, 5
Samal, **5: Samal Moro**
Samal Moro, 5
Samantan, 3a
Samanthan, **3a: Ambalavasi**
Samaria Mal, **3a: Maler**
Samaritans, 9
Sambara, **9a: Shanbaa**
Sambavar, **3a: Paraiya**
Sambia, 2
Samburu, 9a
Same, **6(R): Saami**
Sameraya, **3a: Satani**
Samgar, **3a: Mochi**
Sámi, **4: Saami**
Samia, 9a
Samia, **9: Luyia**
Samiamoo, **1: Klallam**
Samil Paharia, **3a: Maler**
Samish, **1: Klallam**
Samoa, 2
Samoans, **1: Polynesians**
Samot, **2: Asmat**

Samoyed, 6(R): Nenets; Nganasan; Selkup
Sampur, 9a: Samburu
Samvedi Christian, 3a: East Indian
Sanadh, 3a
Sanadhya, 3a: Basdewa
Sanaiwad, 3a: Bhandari
Sanaurhia, 3a
Sanaurhiya, 3a: Sanaurhia
Sanauria Brahman, 3a: Basdewa
San Bartoleños, 8: Tzotzil of San Bartolomé de los Llanos
San Carlos, 1: Western Apache
Sanco, 7a: Malayo
San Cristobal, 2
Sand Hill Indians, 1: American Isolates
Sandia, 1: Pueblo Indians
Sand Papago, 1: Pima-Papago
San Felipe, 1: Keres Pueblo Indians; Pueblo Indians
Sangar, 3a
San Geronimo de Taos, 1: Taos
Sangha, 9a
Sangi, 3a: Maler
Sangir, 5
Sangirezen, 5: Sangir
Sangley, 5: Chinese in Southeast Asia
Sango, 9a
Sangtam, 3: Nagas
Sani, 6(C): Yi
Saniʿa, 9: Peripatetics of Iraq . . . Yemen (Egypt)
Sanish, 1: Arikara
Sanja, 7a: Malayo
San Jorge, 7: Chimila; 8: Emberá and Wounaan
San Joseños, 8: Itzaʾ
San Juan, 1: Pueblo Indians; Tewa Pueblos
San Juan Chamula, 8: Tzotzil of Chamula
Sanka, 1: Kutenai
Sankhabanik, 3a: Sankhari
Sankhakar, 3a: Sankhari
Sankhari, 3a
Sanmukh, 3a: Nai
Sannoi, 6(R): Laz
Sanorhiya, 3a: Sanaurhia
Sanpoil, 1
Sansei, 7: Asians in South America
Sansei-neto, 7: Asians in South America
Sansi, 3a: Sansia
Sansia, 3a
Sansiya, 3a: Sansia
San-Speaking Peoples, 9
Sant, 3: Sadhu
Santa Ana, 1: Keres Pueblo Indians; Pueblo Indians
Santa Barbara Indians, 1: Chumash
Santa Catarina Pantelhó, 8: Tzotzil and Tzeltal of Pantelhó

Santa Clara, 1: Pueblo Indians; Tewa Pueblos
Santa Cruz, 2
Santal, 3
Santa María, 7: Siona-Secoya
Santee, 1
San Teli, 3a: Teli
Santhal, 3: Santal
Santo Domingo, 1: Keres Pueblo Indians; Pueblo Indians
Sanyasi, 3: Sadhu
Saoch, 5
Saonsi, 3a: Sansia
Saonta, 3: Santal
Saonthal, 3: Santal
Saora, 3: Sora
Saparo, 7a: Andoa
Sapáro, 7a: Arabela
Sapé, 7a
Sapei, 9a: Sebei
Sapera, 3a: Nat
Sapmi, 4: Saami
Sar, 9a: Warjawa
Sara, 9
Saraguro, 7
Sarakatsani, 4
Sarakole, 9a: Soninké
Saramacca, 7: Saramaka
Saramaka, 7
Saramaka Bush Negroes, 7: Saramaka
Saramaka Maroons, 7: Saramaka
Saramo, 7: Itonama
Saranahua, 7: Sharanahua
Saraswat, 3: Pandit of Kashmir
Saraveka, 7a
Sarawak Murut, 5: Murut
Sarcee, 1: Sarsi
Saraf, 3a: Sonar
Sarai, 3a
Sarak, 3a
Saraswat Brahman, 3a: Saraswati
Saraswati, 3a
Sardarji, 3: Sikh
Sardi, 4: Sardinians
Sardinians, 4
Sare, 9: Pashai
Sarnabanik, 3: Bania
Saroti, 3a: Pardhan
Sarsi, 1
Sarsut, 3a: Saraswati
Saruro, 7: Pume
Sarvade, 3a
Sarvade Joshi, 3a: Sarvade
Sarwaria, 3a: Sultani
Sarwariya, 3a
Sasak, 5
Sasi, 9a: Shashi
Sassak, 5: Sasak
Satana, 1: Shawnee
Satani, 3a
Satere, 7a: Mawé
Satgop, 3a: Chasa

Sathvara, 3a: Sathwara
Sathwara, 3a
Satnami, 3a: Sadh
Satsop, 1: Chehalis
Sattadavil, 3a: Satani
Satudene, 1: Bearlake Indians
Sauk, 1
Saulteaux, 1: Ojibwa
Saundika, 3a: Sundi
Saunta, 3: Santal
Saur, 3a: Sahariya
Saura, 3: Sora
Sauria, 3a: Maler
Sauria Paharia, 3a: Maler
Savar, 3: Sora
Savara, 3: Sora
Savar Paharia, 3a: Maler
Saviar, 6(R): Balkars
Sawar, 3: Sora
Sawara, 3: Sora
Sawasi, 3a: Ganda; Pano
Sayaco, 7: Amahuaca
Sayawa, 9a
Sayyid, 3
Sazandeh, 9: Peripatetics of Afghanistan, Iran, and Turkey (Iran)
Scandinavian Peripatetics, 4
Scandinavians, 4: Danes; Faroe Islanders; Finns; Icelanders; Norwegians; Swedes
Scheduled Caste, 3: Untouchables
Scheduled Castes and Scheduled Tribes, 3
Scheduled Tribe, 3: Hill Tribes
Schian, 1: Cheyenne
Schiripuno, 7: Waorani
Schitzui, 1: Coeur D'Alène
Schlesien, 4: Silesians
Schwaben (Swabians), 4: Transylvanian Ethnic Groups
Schweiz, 4: German Swiss
Scotch, 4: Highland Scots
Scots, 1: European-Americans; European-Canadians; 4: Highland Scots; Lowland Scots
Scots Irish, 4: Northern Irish
Scottish, 4: Highland Scots; Lowland Scots
Scottish Travelers, 1: Peripatetics
Scuffletonians, 1: Lumbee
Sea Dayak, 5: Iban
Sea Gypsies, 5: Sea Nomads of the Andaman
Sea Islanders, 1
Sea Kolis, 3: Koli
Sea Nomads of the Andaman, 5
Sebei, 9a
Sebei, 9: Nandi and Other Kalenjin Peoples
Séclave, 9: Sakalava
Seco, 8: Paya

Secotan, 1a
Secoya, 7: Siona-Secoya
Sedang, 5
Seex, 9a: Serer
Segidi, 3a
Seharia, 3a: Sahariya
Sehria, 3a: Sahariya
Se'ie Bribri, 8: Boruca, Bribri, and
    Cabécar
Seiyara, 9a: Sayawa
Sejwari, 3a
Sek, 5
Sekani, 1
Sekoya, 7: Siona-Secoya
Selayar, 5: Bonerate
Selemo, 9a: Isekiri
Selepet, 2
Selish, 1: Flathead
Selkup, 6(R)
Selon, 5: Selung/Moken
Selong, 5: Selung/Moken
Selung, 5: Selung/Moken
Selung/Moken, 5
Sema, 3: Nagas
Semang, 5
Semat, 1: Kiowa Apache
Sembadavan, 3a
Semeiski, 6(R): Siberiaki
Semelai, 5: Senoi
Semigae, 7a: Andoa
Seminole, 1
Seminole of Oklahoma, 1
Semoq, 5: Senoi
Semsa, 3a: Kachari
Sena, 9a
Seneca, 1
Sengar Rajput, 3a
Sengseng, 2
Sengunthar Mudaliyar, 3a: Kaikolan
Seniang, 2: Malekula
Senijextee, 1: Lake
Seniyan, 3a: Karna Sale
Senoi, 5
Senoufo, 9a
Sentinelese, 3: Andamanese
Senva, 3a: Sindhava
Sephardic Jews, 4
Sephardic Jews, 9: Jews of Algeria
Sephardim, 1: Jews
Sepoy, 3a: Sipahi
Serbs, 4
Serbs, 1: European-Americans;
    European-Canadians
Seregong, 7: Akawaio
Serekon, 7: Akawaio
Serekong, 7: Akawaio
Serente, 7: Sherente
Serer, 9a
Seri, 8
Serracong, 7: Akawaio
Serrakong, 7: Akawaio
Serrano, 1

Sesake, 2: Nguna
Sesodia Rajput, 3a
Sesotho, 9a: Suto
Setá, 7a: Héta
Setebo, 7: Shipibo
Seth, 3: Bania, Zamindar
Setti, 3a: Chetti; Komati
Settlers, 1: Labrador Inuit
Seven Cities of Cibola, 1: Zuni
Sewara, 3a: Jati
Seya, 9a: Sayawa
Sfardim, 9: Jews of Algeria
Sgaw, 5: Karen
Shabar, 3a: Lodhi
Shabe, 9: Yoruba
Shadibaz, 9: Peripatetics of
    Afghanistan, Iran, and Turkey
    (Afghanistan)
Shaha, 3a: Sundi
Shah'aini, 9: Peripatetics of Iraq . . .
    Yemen (Egypt)
Shahaini, 9: Peripatetics of Iraq . . .
    Yemen (Sudan)
Sha-hi'ye-la, 1: Cheyennne
Shahsevan, 9
Shaikh, 3: Sheikh
Shakekahquah, 1: Kickapoo
Shakers, 1
Shakriabá, 7a
Shambioá, 7: Karajá
Shamerim, 9: Samaritans
Shamsi, 3a: Sonar
Shamya, 9a: Sinyar
Shan, 5
Shanan, 3a
Shanar, 3a: Shanan
Shanbaa, 9a
Shangawa, 9a
Shangul, 9a: Berta
Shanha, 6(C): She
Shanwar, 3: Bene Israel
Shapra, 7: Candoshi
Sharadakani, 3a: Telaga
Sharanahua, 7
Sharánahua, 7: Sharanahua
Shar pa, 3: Sherpa
Shashi, 9a
Shasta, 1; 1a
Shavante, 7
Shawanah, 1: Shawnee
Shawano, 1: Shawnee
Shawanwa, 1: Shawnee
Shawiya, 9: Berbers of Morocco
Shawnee, 1
Shayabit, 7: Chayahuita
She, 6(C)
Sheikh, 3
Sheikh Mohammadi, 9: Peripatetics of
    Afghanistan, Iran, and Turkey
    (Afghanistan)
Shemin, 6(C): She
Shenavi, 3a: Saraswati

Shendu, 3: Lakher
Shenva, 3a: Sindhava
Sheoran, 3a
Sheorani, 3a: Shiranni
Sherani, 3a: Shiranni
Sherbro, 9a
Sherdukpen, 3a
Sherente, 7
Sherkeri, 9a: Isekiri
Sherpa, 3
Shet, 3a: Sonar
Shetá, 7a: Héta
Shetinasha, 1: Chitimacha
Shetlanders, 4
Shia, 1: Arab Americans
Shiba, 9a: Sherbro
Shidishana, 7: Yanomamö
Shidong, 6(C): Jingpo
Shiho, 9a: Saho
Shihwapmukh, 1: Shuswap
Shikana, 7: Hoti
Shikapo, 1: Kickapoo
Shikari, 3a: Pardhi
Shillekyata, 3a: Killekyata
Shilluk, 9
Shimacu, 7a: Urarina
Shimagae, 7a: Andoa
Shimizya, 7: Chimila
Shimong, 3: Abor; 3a: Adi
Shimpi, 3a: Darzi
Shin, 3a
Shingade, 3a: Bhandari
Shin-Heimin, 5: Burakumin
Shinnecock, 1a
Shinnecock, 1: Metoac
Shinyiha, 9a: Nyiha
Shioko, 9a: Chokwe
Shipibo, 7
Shipiwo, 7: Shipibo
Shiptare, 4: Albanians
Shir, 9a: Mandari
Shirani, 3a: Shiranni
Shiranni, 3a
Shirazi, 9a
Shiriana, 7: Yanomamö
Shishagar, 3a
Shisham, 5: Lisu
Shiva Brahman, 3a: Tamdi
Shivachandi Thakur, 3a: Bhat
Shiva Gurava, 3a: Gurava
Shivarchaka, 3a: Tamdi
Shiv Jogi, 3a: Raval Jogi
Shiwila, 7: Jebero
Shluh, 9: Berbers of Morocco
Shoalwater Salish, 1: Chehalis
Shoeiha, 9: Peripatetics of Iraq . . .
    Yemen (Egypt)
Shoho, 9a: Saho
Shokleng, 7: Xokléng
Shokó, 7a
Shokó, 7: Xokléng
Shokó-Kariri, 7a

Shokowa, 1: Pomo
Sholaga, 3a: Sholiga
Shola-Nayaka, 3: Nayaka
Sholega, 3a: Sholiga
Sholiga, 3a
Shomeronim, 9: Samaritans
Shom-Pen, 3a
Shona, 9
Shonga, 9a: Shangawa
Shoodra, 3: Sudra
Shori, 7: Yanomamö
Shors, 6(R)
Shortsy, 6(R): Shors
Shoshocoes, 1: Western Shoshone
Shravagi, 3a: Alkari
Shuar, 7: Jivaro
Shuara, 7: Jivaro
Shudra, 3: Sudra; 3a: Sudir
Shui, 6(C)
Shui Bai-yi, 5: Tai Lue
Shui Baiyi, 6(C): Dai
Shui Dai, 5: Tai Lue; 6(C): Dai
Shukurú, 7a
Shukurú-Kariri, 7a
Shuli, 9a: Acholi
Shuswap, 1
Shuta enima, 8: Mazatec
Shuuli, 9: Acholi
Shwæn, 6(R): Svans
Shyenne, 1: Cheyenne
Sia, 1: Keres Pueblo Indians
Sial, 3a
Siam, 6(C): Dai
Siamese Tai, 5: Central Thai
Siane, 2
Siar, 2: Lak
Siarra, 2: Lak
Sibe, 6(C): Xibe
Siberiachi, 6(R): Siberiaki
Siberiaki, 6(R)
Siberian Cossacks, 6(R):
    Siberiaki
Siberian Estonians, 6(R)
Siberian Germans, 6(R)
Siberian Tatars, 6(R)
Sibiriaki, 6(R): Siberiaki
Sibtatars, 6(R): Siberian Tatars
Sibundoy, 7a: Kamsá
Siciliani, 4: Sicilians
Sicilians, 4
Sidamo, 9a: Sadama
Siddi, 3a: Sidi
Sidi, 3; 3a
Sierra Blanca Apaches, 1: Mescalero
    Apache
Sierra Nahuat, 8: Nahuat of the Sierra
    de Puebla
Sigaba, 2: Sio
Sigawa, 2: Sio
Sika, 5: Ata Sikka
Sikanee, 1: Sekani
Sikh, 3

Sikhs, 1: South and Southeast Asians
    of Canada; South and Southeast
    Asians of the United States
Sikka, 5: Ata Sikka
Sikkanese, 5: Ata Sikka
Sikkimese, 3
Siksika, 1: Blackfoot
Sikuani, 7: Guahibo-Sikuani
Silesians, 4
Silésie, 4: Silesians
Siletz, 1: Tillamook
Silozi, 9: Lozi
Silti, 9a: Gurage
Silung, 5: Selung/Moken
Silveños, 7: Guambiano
Simano-li, 1: Seminole
Simba, 7: Chiriguano
Simbu, 2: Chimbu
Simelungun, 5: Batak
Simiza, 7: Chimila
Simpi, 3a: Darzi
Simza, 7: Chimila
Sinai, 3a: Rabari
Sinama, 5: Samal
Sinamaicas, 7: Paraujano
Sindhava, 3a
Sindhi, 3
Sindhu, 3a
Sindhva, 3a: Sindhava
Sindi, 3: Sindhi
Sine-Saloum, 9a: Serer
Sine-Sine, 9a: Serer
Singaporean, 5
Singe, 3a
Singhalese, 3: Sinhalese
Singhinem Yupiga, 6(R): Asiatic
    Eskimos
Singhpo, 5: Kachin
Singpho, 3a
Singson, 3a: Kuki
Sinhala, 3: Sinhalese
Sinhalese, 3
Sini Svobodi, 1: Doukhobors
Sinkakaius, 1: Columbia
Sinkiuse, 1: Columbia
Sinkyone, 1: Wailaki
Sino-Mauriciens, 3: Mauritian
Sino-Mauritians, 3: Mauritian
Sinte, 4: Peripatetics
Sin-teng, 3a: Jaintia
Sinti, 4: Peripatetics
Sinti Piemontese, 4: Piemontese Sinti
Sinti Pimuntezi, 4: Piemontese Sinti
Sinumiut, 1: Netsilik Inuit
Sinwa, 3: Mauritian
Sinyar, 9a
Sio, 2
Siona, 7: Siona-Secoya
Siona-Secoya, 7
Sioní, 7: Siona-Secoya
Sioux, 1: Santee; Teton; Yankton
Sipacapa Quiché, 8: Sipakapense

Sipacapeño, 8: Sipakapense
Sipacapense, 8: Sipakapense
Sipahi, 3a
Sipakapense, 8
Sipibo, 7: Shipibo
Sipulotes, 5: Dusun
Sireniktsy, 6(R): Asiatic Eskimos
Siriana, 7a: Siriano
Siriano, 7a
Sirionó, 7
Sisodiya, 3a: Sesodia Rajput
Sitlhou, 3a: Kuki
Siuai, 2: Siwai
Siuslaw, 1a
Sivabhaktaru, 3a: Balija
Sivugam Yupiga, 6(R): Asiatic Eskimos
Siwai, 2
Síwaro, 7: Jivaro
Six Nations, 1: Iroquois
Siyahpayak, 9: Peripatetics of
    Afghanistan, Iran, and Turkey
    (Afghanistan)
Sizaki, 9a: Shashi
Skeena, 1: Tsimshian
Skitswish, 1: Coeur D'Alène
Skokomish, 1: Twana
Skopje Slavs, 4: Slav Macedonians
Skoylpeli, 1: Sanpoil
Slask, 4: Silesians
Slave, 1: Slavey
Slavey, 1
Slavey, 9: Sleb
Slavic Siberians, 6(R): Siberiaki
Slav Macedonians, 4
Sleb, 9
Ṣlêb, 9: Sleb
Sleyb, 9: Sleb
Slezko, 4: Silesians
Sliammon, 1: Comox
Slováci, 4: Slovaks
Slovák, 4: Slovaks
Slovaks, 4
Slovaks, 1: European-Americans;
    European-Canadians
Slovenec, 4: Slovenes
Slovenes, 4
Slovenes, 1: European-Americans;
    European-Canadians
Slovenian, 4: Slovenes
Slovenians, 1: European-Americans;
    European-Canadians
Slovenski, 4: Slovenes
Slovensko Roma, 4
Small Nambas, 2: Malekula
Smaq, 5: Senoi
Smith Sound Inuit, 1: Inughuit
Smoo, 8: Sumu
Smu, 8: Sumu
Snake, 1: Northern Shoshone and
    Bannock
Snake Indians, 1: Comanche
Snare, 1: Thompson

Snoqualamuke, 1: Snoqualmie
Snoqualmick, 1: Snoqualmie
Snoqualmie, 1
Snoqualmoo, 1: Snoqualmie
Snoqualmu, 1: Snoqualmie
Snuqualmi, 1: Snoqualmie
So, 5
Soai, 5: Kui
Soba, 1: Pima-Papago
Sobaipuri, 1: Pima-Papago
Sobo, 9a: Isoko; 9a: Urhobo
Sochile, 9a: Ngonde
Society Islands, 2: Tahiti
Socré, 7: Xokléng
Sodia, 3a: Jhinwar
Soeri, 3a
Soga, 9a
Soioty, 6(R): Tuvans
Soiri, 3a: Soeri
Sok, 5: Sork
Solaga, 3a: Sholiga
Sola Nayaka, 3: Nayaka
Soliga, 3a: Sholiga
Soligaru, 3a: Sholiga
Solongo, 9: Kongo
Solor, 5: Lamaholot
Solorese, 5: Lamaholot
Solot, 5: Lamaholot
Soloti, 7: Chorote
So-lot-luk, 1: Wiyot
Solubba, 9: Sleb
Somalis, 9
Somba, 9a
Sombansi, 3a
Somekhi, 6(R): Armenians
Somoo, 8: Sumu
Somvanshi Kshatriya Pathare, 3a:
    Panchkalshi
Sona, 3a: Sonar
Sonakar, 3: Moor of Sri Lanka
Sonar, 3a
Sonar, 3: Moor of Sri Lanka
Sonarbania, 3: Bania
Sondhi, 3a: Sundi
Sondi, 3a: Sundi
Songhay, 9
Songhoi, 9: Songhay
Songhrai, 9: Songhay
Songish, 1: Klallam
Songwe, 9a: Safwa
Soni, 3a: Sonar
Soninké, 9a
Sonjhara, 3a
Sonkar, 3a: Beldar
Son Kolis, 3: Koli
Sonr, 3a: Sonar
Sons of the Celestial Anaconda, 7:
    Tatuyo
Sooke, 1: Klallam
Soo-lah-te-luk, 1: Wiyot
Soomaali, 9: Somalis
Soques, 8: Zoque

Sor, 3a: Sahariya
Sora, 3
Sora, 3: Munda
Sorbs, 4
Sorbs, 1: European-Americans
Sori, 8: Seri
Sork, 5
Soromaja, 2: Tor
Sosia, 3a: Sahariya
Sotho, 9a
Sotirgaik, 7: Nivaclé
Soto, 7: Yekuana
Sotz'leb, 8: Tzotzil of Zinacantan
Sou, 5
Sou, 6(C): Bai
Souk, 5: Sou
Sounti, 3a: Sundi
Souriquois, 1: Micmac
Soussou, 9a: Susu
South Alaskan Eskimo, 1: Pacific
    Eskimo
South and Southeast Asians of
    Canada, 1
South and Southeast Asians of the
    United States, 1
South Asians in Southeast Asia, 5
Southern Appalachians, 1:
    Appalachians
Southern Bullom, 9a: Sherbro
Southern Cayapo, 7: Xokléng
Southern Dutch, 4: Flemish
Southern Kankanai, 5: Kankanai
Southern Kayapo, 7: Kaingáng;
    Xokléng
Southern Kwakiutl, 1: Kwakiutl
Southern Lunda, 9: Lunda; Ndembu
Southern Maidu, 1: Maidu
Southern Mestizos, 1: American
    Isolates
Southern Murut, 5: Murut
Southern Ndebele, 9: Ndebele
Southern Nguni, 9: Xhosa
Southern Paiute (and Chemehuevi), 1
Southern Pulaya, 3a: Pulluvan
Southern Thai, 5: Pak Thai
Southern Tonto, 1: Western Apache
Southhampton Inuit, 1a
South Koreans, 7: Asians in South
    America
South Mbukushu, 9a
South Mendi, 2: Kewa
South Moluccans, 5: Ambonese
South Ragans, 2: Pentecost
South Toraja, 5: Toraja
Southwest Alaska Eskimos, 1: Central
    Yup'ik Eskimos
Southwestern Chippewa, 1: Ojibwa
Southwestern Ojibwa, 1: Ojibwa
Sowar, 3a: Komati
Sowcar, 3: Bania
Soyopas, 1: Mohave
Spaniards, 4

Spaniards, 1: European-Americans;
    European-Canadians
Spanish Rom, 4
Spasovtsy, 6(R): Old Believers
Spiritual Christians, 1: Molokans
Spokan, 1: Spokane
Spokane, 1
Spukanees, 1: Spokane
Srawak, 3a: Sarak
Srbi, 4: Serbs; Transylvanian Ethnic
    Groups
Sredneziatskie Evrei, 6(R): Bukharan-
    Jews
Sri Lankans, 1: South and Southeast
    Asians of the United States
Sri Vaishnava Brahman, 3a
Ssabela, 7: Waorani
Ssipipo, 7: Shipibo
Starokreshchenye Tatary, 6(R):
    KriashenTatars
Staroobriadtsy, 6(R): Old Believers
Starovery, 6(R): Old Believers
Starrahhe, 1: Arikara
Steierer, 4: Austrians
Stieng, 5
Stockbridge-Munsee, 1: Mahican
Stone Tower Culture, 6(C): Qiang
Stoneys, 1: Assiniboin
Stonies, 1: Assiniboin
Stranniki, 6(R): Old Believers
Strong's Island, 2: Kosrae
Subanen, 5: Subanun
Subano, 5: Subanun
Subanon, 5: Subanun
Subanun, 5
Subarnbanik, 3: Bania
Submerged Races, 1: American
    Isolates
Suda, 3a: Sudh
Sudanese Nubians, 9: Nubians
Sudh, 3a
Sudha, 3a: Sudh
Sudho, 3a: Sudh
Sudir, 3a
Sudra, 3
Sudugadu Siddha, 3a
Sugali, 3a: Banjara
Suhín, 7: Nivaclé
Suiá, 7: Suya
Suiás, 7: Suya
Suis, 3a: Darzi
Suji, 3a: Darzi
Suk, 9: Pokot
Sukali, 3a: Banjara
Suki, 2: Boazi
Sukte, 3a: Kuti
Suku, 9
Sukuma, 9: Nyamwezi and Sukuma
Suku Ternate, 5: Ternatan/Tidorese
Suku Tidore, 5: Ternatan/Tidorese
Suku Tobelo, 5: Tobelorese
Ṣulaib, 9: Sleb

Sulaka, **9a: Maures**
Suláteluk, **1: Wiyot**
Suleib, **9: Sleb**
Ṣuleyb, **9: Peripatetics of Iraq . . .**
      Yemen (Syria)
Sulod, 5
Sultani, 3a
Sultania, **3a: Sultani**
Sultankar, **3a: Khatik**
Ṣulubba, **9: Sleb**
Suluk, **5: Tausug**
Sulu Moros, **5: Tausug**
Sulun, **6(C): Ewenki**
Sulus, **5: Tausug**
Sumau, **2: Garia**
Sumi, **1: Zuni**
Summoo, **8: Sumu**
Sumo, **8: Sumu**
Sumoo, **8: Sumu**
Sumu, 8
Sunar, **3a: Sonar**
Sunara, **3a: Sonar**
Sunbar, **3: Sunwar**
Sundaka, **3a: Sundi**
Sundanese, 5
Sundhi, **3a: Sundi**
Sundi, 3a
Sundi, **9a: Kongo**
Sundyak, **5: Dusun**
Sunera, **3a: Sonar**
Sungar, **3a: Besta**
Suniar, **3a: Sonar**
Suniari, **3a: Sonar**
Sunnakallu Bestha, **3a: Besta**
Sun People, **1: Spokane**
Sunri, **3a: Sundi**
Sunuwar, **3: Sunwar**
Sunwar, 3
Sunwari, **3: Sunwar**
Suomalaiset, **4: Finns**
Supai, **1: Havasupai**
Suppalig, 3a
Sura, 9a
Surajbans, **3a: Suraj-Bansi**
Suraj-Bansi, 3a
Surayi, **9: Assyrians**
Suretika, **1: Arapaho**
Suri, 9
Suriní, **7: Asurini**
Surir, **3a: Soeri**
Suris, **7: Toba**
Suriyani Christiani, **3: Syrian Christian**
      of Kerala
Surma, **9: Suri**
Suruí, 7
Surutiyeh, **9: Peripatetics of Iraq . . .**
      Yemen (Egypt)
Suryachelad, **3a: Kasai**
Suryâné, **9: Syriacs**
Suryavanisa, **3: Reddi**
Suryâyé, **9: Syriacs**
Sushen, **6(C): Hezhen**

Susi, **9: Peripatetics of the Maghreb**
      (Morocco)
Susmani, **9: Peripatetics of**
      Afghanistan, Iran, and Turkey
      (Turkey)
Susquehanna, **1a**
Süsse-kum, **6(R): Selkup**
Susu, **9a**
Sutar, **3a: Barhai**
Suthar, **3a: Barhai; Sutradhar**
Suthra Shahi, 3a
Suto, **9a**
Sutradhar, 3a
Suxwapmux, **1: Shuswap**
Suya, 7
Suyá, **7: Suya**
Suzmani, **9: Peripatetics of**
      Afghanistan, Iran, and Turkey
      (Iran)
Svans, 6(R)
Svizzera Meridionale, **4: Swiss, Italian**
Svizzeri Italiani, **4: Swiss, Italian**
Svobodniki, **1: Doukhobors**
Swahili, 9
Swami, **3: Sadhu**
Swasa, **9: Berbers of Morocco**
Swati, **9: Swazi**
Swazi, 9
Swedes, 4
Swedes, **1: European-Americans**
Swiss, 4
Swiss, **1: European-Americans;**
      European-Canadians; 4: German
      Swiss; Jurassians; Romansch;
      Swiss, Italian
Swiss-Brethren, **1: Mennonites**
Swiss, Italian, 4
Syal, **3a: Sial**
Syam, **5: Central Thai**
Syce, **3a: Ghasia**
Syriacs, 9
Syrian Christian of Kerala, 3
Syrian Jacobites, **9: Syriacs**
Syrians, **1: Arab Americans**
Syrjäne, **6(R): Komi**
Szleb, **9: Sleb**

Ta-ang, **5: Palaung**
Ta'au, **5: Selung/Moken**
Tabasarans, 6(R)
Tabassarans, **6(R): Tabasarans**
Tacana, 7
Tachoni, 9a
Tachoni, **9: Luyia**
Tadan, **3a: Dasri**
Tadar, **6(R): Khakas**
Tadjik, **6(C): Tajik; 6(R)Tajiks**
Tadó, 7a
Tadó, **8: Emberá and Wounaan**
Tadvi, **3: Bhil; 3a: Gamit**
Tadzhiks, **6(R): Tajiks**
Tadzik, **6(C): Tajik**

Tae' Toraja, **5: Toraja**
Taga, 3a
Tagakaolo, **5: Kalagan**
Tagal, **5: Murut**
Tagalagad, **5: Bilaan**
Tagalog, 5
Tagata Samoa, **2: Samoa**
Tagbanoua, **5: Tagbanuwa**
Tagbanua, **5: Tagbanuwa**
Tagbanuwa, 5
Taggal, **5: Murut**
Tagol, **5: Murut**
Tagore, **3: Thakur**
Tagul, **5: Murut**
Tahamí, **7: Emberá**
Tahiti, 2
Tah-le-wah, **1: Tolowa**
Tahltan, 1
Ta Hoi, **5: Tau-Oi**
Tahtacı, **9: Peripatetics of Afghanistan,**
      Iran, and Turkey (Turkey)
Tahuajca, **8: Sumu**
Ṭahwaĝiya, **9: Peripatetics of Iraq . . .**
      Yemen (Egypt)
Tai, 3a
Tai, **3a: Khamti; 5: Central Thai; Tai**
      Lue; 6(C): Dai
T'ai, **5: Central Thai**
Taia, **8: Paya**
Taidnapam, **1: Klikitat**
Tai Khun, **5: Shan**
Tailakar, **3a: Teli**
Taili, **3a: Teli**
Tailika, **3a: Teli**
Tai Long, **5: Shan**
Tailpal, **3a: Teli**
Tai Lu, **5: Shan**
Tai Lue, 5
Tai Mao, **5: Shan**
Tai Nu, **5: Shan**
Taiora, **2: Tairora**
Tairora, 2
Taiwan Aboriginal Peoples, 5
Taiwanese, 5
Taiwanese, **7: Asians in South America**
Taiwano, **7a: Barasana**
Taiyal, **5: Taiwan Aboriginal Peoples**
Tajik, **6(C)**
Tajik, **9: Pashai**
Tajiks, 6(R)
Takana, **7: Tacana; 7a: Araona**
Takankar, **3a: Pardhi**
Takara, **3: Thakur; 3a: Beldar**
Takari, **3a: Beldar; Bhamta**
Takelma, 1a
Takhan, **3a: Tarkhan**
Takia, **3a: Pardhi**
Takogan, **5: Bilaan**
Takshik, **7: Toba**
Takulli, **1: Carrier**
Takur, **3: Thakur**

Talamanca Bribri, 8: Boruca, Bribri, and Cabécar
Talaoerezen, 5: Sangir
Talavia, 3: Bhil; 3a: Dubla
Talawa, 1: Tolowa
Taliaseri, 7a: Tariana
Talïsh, 6(R): Talysh
Talïshlar, 6(R): Talysh
Tallige', 1: Cherokee
Taltushtuntude, 1: Chastacosta
Talushon, 6(R): Talysh
Talysh, 6(R)
Tama, 7a: Korewahe
Tamacheq, 9: Tuareg
Tamacoci, 7: Chiquitano
Tamang, 3
Tamang, 3: Nyinba; Thakali
Tama-Speaking Peoples, 9a
Tambala, 3a: Tamdi
Tambat, 3a: Tamera
Tambatkar, 3a: Jingar; Tamera
Tamboli, 3a: Tamdi
Tambuli, 3a: Tamdi
Tambunaus, 5: Dusun
Tambunwhas, 5: Dusun
Tamdi, 3a
Tame, 7: Tunebo
Tamera, 3a
Tamhera, 3a: Tamera
Tamil, 3
Tamiḷar, 3: Tamil
Tamiḷarkaḷ, 3: Tamil of Sri Lanka
Tamil Brahman, 3a: Paradesi
Tamilian, 3: Tamil, Tamil of Sri Lanka
Tamil of Sri Lanka, 3
Tamils, 1: South and Southeast Asians of the United States
Tamli, 3a: Tamdi
Tamliwandlu, 3a: Tamdi
Tamokomes, 7a: Oyampi
Tamoli, 3a: Tamdi
Tampa, 7: Campa
Tamu, 3: Thakali
Tamuan, 5: Kalimantan Dayaks
Tamuli, 3a: Tamdi
Tana, 2: Tanna
Tanaina, 1
Tanaka, 9a
Tanana, 1
Tä-nä-tinne, 1: Hare
Tandan, 3a
Tandel, 3a: Macchi; Mangela
Tandroy, 9
Tandy-Uriankhai, 6(R): Tuvans
Tangale, 9a
Tangam, 3: Abor
Tangin, 3: Abor
Tangipahoa, 1a
Tangkhul, 3: Nagas
Tangren, 5: Chinese in Southeast Asia
Tangsa, 3a
Tangu, 2

Tani, 3: Abor
Tanimbarese, 5: Moluccans, Southeast
Tanimboka, 7: Tanimuka
Tanimuca, 7a: Retuna
Tanimuco, 7: Tanimuka
Tanimuka, 7
Tanimuko, 7: Tanimuka
Tanna, 2
Tannese, 2: Tanna
Tannin-kootchin, 1: Tanana
Tannu-Uriankhaitsy, 6(R): Tuvans
Tano, 1: Hopi-Tewa; Tewa Pueblos
Tano-Tewa, 1: Tewa Pueblos
Tanti, 3a
Tanti, 3a: Ganda
Tantrabaya, 3a: Tanti
Tantubaya, 3a: Tanti
Tantunayakadu, 3a: Padma Sale
Tantwa, 3a: Tanti
Tao, 7: Chiquitano
Taoajka, 8: Sumu
Tà ôi, 5: Tau-Oi
Taonla, 3a
Taos, 1
Tapacua, 7: Shavante
Tapasi, 3: Sadhu
Tapayuna, 7a
Tapayuna, 7: Suya
Tapeba, 7a
Tapieté, 7a
Tapirapé, 7
Tapiro, 2: Kapauku
Tapsawi, 3: Sadhu
Tapueyocuaca, 7a: Arabela
Tapui, 7: Chiriguano
Tara-Baaka, 9a: Baka
Tarahumar, 8: Tarahumara
Tarahumara, 8
Tarahumari, 8: Tarahumara
Tarakan, 3a
Tarakan, 5: Tidong
Tarapecosi, 7: Chiquitano
Tarascans, 8
Tarascos, 8: Tarascans
Taraumar, 8: Tarahumara
Tarëno, 7: Trio
Targala, 3a: Bhandari; Bhavaiya
Targui, 9: Tuareg
Tariana, 7a
Tariba, 2: Usino
Tariurmiut, 1: North Alaskan Eskimos
Tarkhan, 3a
Tarkhan, 3a: Barhai
Tarkhanr, 3a: Tarkhan
Tarkihar, 3a
Tarlyk, 6(R): Siberian Tatars
Tarok, 9a: Yergam
Tarrantines, 1: Micmac
Taru, 3a
Tarvgi-Samoyeds, 6(R): Nganasan
Tasa, 3a: Chasa
Tasaday, 5

Tasioteños, 8: Seri
Taskara, 3: Thakur
Tasmanians, 2
Tat, 9: Peripatetics of Afghanistan, Iran, and Turkey (Iran)
Tatar, 6(R): Volga Tatars
T'at'ar, 9: Peripatetics of Iraq . . . Yemen (Egypt)
Tataren, 4: Peripatetics
Tatari, 9: Peripatetics of the Maghreb (Mauritania)
Tatar Jews, 6(R): Krymchaks
Tatars, 6(C)
Tatary, 6(R): Crimean Tatars
Tatchila, 7: Colorado
Tatere, 4: Scandinavian Peripatetics
Tatoga, 9a: Taturu
Tats, 6(R)
Tátskan wátitch, 1: Tonkawa
Tattar, 3a: Paracha
Tattare, 4: Scandinavian Peripatetics
Taturu, 9a
Tatuyo, 7
Tatwa, 3a: Tanti
Tauade, 2
Tauata, 2: Tauade
Taufgesinnten, 1: Mennonites
Taulipang, 7: Pemon
Taulu, 6(R): Balkars
Tau-Oi, 5
Taupane, 8: Jicaque
Taurepan, 7: Pemon
Taushiro, 7a
Tausug, 5
Tavastians, 4: Finns
Tavgi, 6(R): Nganasan
Tavricheskie, 6(R): Crimean Tatars
Tavyters, 7: Paï-Tavytera
Tawahka, 8: Sumu
Tawaif, 3a: Devadasi
TawaLáj Lawós, 7: Maká
Tawari, 7a: Kanamarí
Ṭawayifa, 9: Peripatetics of Iraq . . . Yemen (Egypt)
Tawka, 8: Paya
Taw Sug, 5: Tausug
Taya, 8: Paya
Tay, 5
Tày, 5: Tay
Taya, 8: Paya
Tayal, 5: Taiwan Aboriginal Peoples
Tayberon, 1: Taos
Tchambuli, 2: Chambri
Tchame, 5: Cham
Tchams, 5: Cham
Tchatakes, 1: Choctaw
Tchere, 9a: Guiziga
Tchiactas, 1: Choctaw
Tchinouks, 1: Chinook
Te-bot-e-lob-e-lay, 1: Tubatulabal
Tebou, 9: Teda
Tebu, 9: Teda
Teco, 7: Emerillon

Teda, 9
Teda-Tou, 9a
Tedong, 5: **Tidong**
Te'enana, 2: **Marquesas Islands**
Teenek, 8: **Wasteko**
Teguas, 1: **Tewa Pueblos**
Teguessie, 9a
Tehueco, 8: **Cahita**
Tehuelche, 7a: **Tewelche**
Teitete, 7a: **Teteté**
Teja, 1: **Caddo**
Tejuca, 7a: **Tuyuka**
Teke, 9a
Tekuna, 7: **Ticuna**
Telaga, 3a
Telaga, 3a: **Mutrasi**
Telangi Sadar Bhoi, 3a: **Mala**
Telefol, 2: **Telefolmin**
Telefolmin, 2
Telefomin, 2: **Telefolmin**
Telgaund, 3a: **Mutrasi**
Teli, 3a
Teli, 3: **Bene Israel**
Telli, 3a: **Teli**
Telugu, 3
Telugu Brahman, 3a: **Andhra Brahman**
Telugu Dher, 3a: **Mala**
Telugu Kummaravadu, 3a: **Kumhar**
Telu Limpoe, 5: **Toala**
Te Maori, 2: **Maori**
Tembé, 7a
Tembé, 5: **Temiar**
Tembeta, 7: **Chiriguano**
Temer, 5: **Temiar**
Temiar, 5
Temne, 9; 9a
Ten'a, 1: **Ingalik**
Tenan-kutchin, 1: **Tanana**
Tenda, 9a: **Bassari**; 9a: **Coniagui**
Tende, 9a: **Kuria**
Tenetehara, 7a: **Amanayé**
Tenetehára, 7: **Guajajára**; 7a: **Tembé**
Teneteher, 7: **Guajajára**
Tengalai Sri Vaishnava, 3a: **Sri Vaishnava Brahman**
Tengaud, 3a: **Mutrasi**
Tenik, 9a
Tenino, 1
Tennankutchin, 1: **Tanana**
Tennan-tnu-kokhtana, 1: **Tanana**
Ten Vanniya, 3: **Irula**
Tepehua, 8
Tepehuan of Chihuahua, 8
Tepehuan of Durango, 8
Tepes, 9a: **Tepeth**
Tepeth, 9a
Tepoca, 8: **Seri**
Tequistlatec, 8
Tequistlateco, 8: **Tequistlatec**
Tera, 9a
Terena, 7
Terenoá, 7: **Terena**

Terenos, 7: **Terena**
Terenue, 7: **Terena**
Teribe, 8
Terik, 9: **Nandi and Other Kalenjin Peoples**
Ternatan/Tidorese, 5
Terraba, 8: **Teribe**
Teso, 9a
Tesuque, 1: **Pueblo Indians**; **Tewa Pueblos**
Tetaria, 3a: **Gamit**
Tête Pelée, 1: **Comanche**
Teteté, 7a
Teto, 5: **Tetum**
Teton, 1
Teton Sioux, 1: **Teton**
Tetum, 5
Tetun, 5: **Tetum**
Teuso, 9a
Teuso, 9a: **Ik**
Tevi, 8: **Huichol**
Tew, 9a: **Tumbuka**
Tewa Pueblos, 1
Tewelche, 7a
Teyas, 1: **Mescalero Apache**
Teymanim, 9: **Jews of Yemen**
Thacchanaden, 3a: **Thachanaden**
Thachanaden, 3a
Thachanad Muppan, 3a: **Thachanaden**
Thadou, 3
Thadu, 3: **Thadou**
Thaggappanmargal, 3a: **Muduga**
Thai, 5: **Central Thai**
Thai Lao, 5: **Lao Isan**
Thais, 1: **South and Southeast Asians of the United States**
Thai Yai, 5: **Shan**
Thakali, 3
Thakar, 3a
Thakara, 3: **Thakur**
Thakkar, 3: **Thakur**
Thakkura, 3: **Thakur**
Thakoor, 3: **Thakur**
Thakur, 3
Thakur, 3a: **Bhat**
Thalavadi, 3a: **Darzi**
Thammadi, 3a: **Tamdi**
Thampa, 7: **Campa**
Thanapati, 3a: **Gandhmali**
Thanda Pulayan, 3a: **Pulluvan**
Thangluya, 3a: **Kuki**
Thangngen, 3a: **Kuki**
Thantapulaya, 3a: **Pulluvan**
Thapatkari, 3a: **Beldar**
Tharu, 3
Thathera, 3a: **Tamera**
Thecannies, 1: **Sekani**
Theinbaw, 5: **Kachin**
Thiame, 5: **Cham**
Thīhā, 7: **Piaroa**
Thin, 5: **T'in**
Thirteen Island, 2: **Woleai**

Thlingchadinne, 1: **Dogrib**
Thlinget, 1: **Tlingit**
Thlinkets, 1: **Tlingit**
Tho, 5: **Tay**
Thompson, 1
Thompson River Indians, 1: **Thompson**
Thongcha, 3a: **Marma**
Thongtha, 3a: **Marma**
Thori, 3a
Thu, 5: **Tay**
Thug, 3
Thuleeskimoer, 1: **Inughuit**
Thulegroenlaendere, 1: **Inughuit**
Tiadje, 5: **Tomini**
Tialo, 5: **Tomini**
Tiamath, 1: **Yurok**
Tiar, 3a: **Tiyar**
Ti:ari, 2: **Dieri**
Tiatinagua, 7: **Huarayo**
Tibbu, 9: **Teda**
Tibetan, 3a
Tibetans, 6(C)
Tiburone, 8: **Seri**
Ticino, 4: **Swiss, Italian**
Tico, 8: **Costa Ricans**
Ticuna, 7
Tiddi, 9a: **Meidob**
Tidoeng, 5: **Tidong**
Tidong, 5
Tidorese, 5: **Ternatan/Tidorese**
Tidung, 5: **Tidong**
Tiê, 5: **T'in**
Tigala, 3a
Tigray, 9
Tigre, 9: **Tigray**
Tigua, 1: **Pueblo Indians**
Tihuakuna, 7: **Waorani**
Tijang Djawi, 5: **Javanese**
Tijang Madura, 5: **Madurese**
Tikar, 9a
Tikopia, 2
Tikuna, 7: **Ticuna**
Tilgar, 3a: **Tigala**
Tilghatak, 3a: **Teli**
Tili, 3a: **Teli**
Tillamook, 1; 1a
Tilvai, 3a: **Tigala**
Tilwan, 3a: **Teli**
Timaoán, 7a: **Tapayuna**
Timbaro, 9a
Timbé, 7a: **Tembé**
Timmannee, 9: **Temne**; 9a: **Temne**
Timorese, 5: **Atoni**
Timputs, 2: **Kurtatchi**
Timucua, 1a
T'in, 5
Tin, 5: **T'in**
Tingi, 7a
Tinde, 1: **Jicarilla**
Tinkers, 4: **Irish Travellers**
Tinputz, 2: **Kurtatchi**
Tio, 9a

Tior, 3a: **Tiyar**
Tiou, 1: **Tunica**
Tioux, 1: **Tunica**
Tipai, 1: **Kumeyaay**; 8: **Indians of Baja California**
Tipai-Ipai, 1: **Kumeyaay**
Tipituni, 7: **Waorani**
Tippera, 3a: **Tripura**
Tipperah, 3a: **Tripura**
Tipra, 3a: **Tripura**
Tipuna, 7: **Ticuna**
Tiran, 5: **Tidong**
Tirbanda, 3a: **Tirgar**
Tirgar, 3a
Tirgul Brahman, 3a
Tiriki, 9a
Tiriki, 9: **Luyia**
Tirinié, 7: **Sirionó**
Tirío, 7: **Trio**
Tiriyo, 7: **Trio**; 7a: **Akurio**
Tiriyó, 7: **Trio**
Tïrïyo, 7: **Trio**
Tirma, 9: **Suri**
Tirmali, 3a
Tiroleans, 4
Tiroler, 4: **Austrians**
Tirones, 5: **Tidong**
Tiroon, 5: **Tidong**
Titunwan, 1: **Teton**
Tiuitiuas, 7: **Warao**
Tiv, 9
Tivi, 9: **Tiv**
Tiwi, 2
Tiyan, 3a
Tiyar, 3a
Tjamoro, 2: **Chamorros**
Tlakluit, 1: **Wishram**
Tlalem, 1: **Klallam**
Tlapanec, 8
Tlatskanai, 1a
Tlicho, 1: Dogrib
Tlingit, 1
Tlinkit, 1: **Tlingit**
Tlokeang, 1: **Wailaki**
Tmiir, 5: **Temiar**
Tnaina, 1: **Tanaina**
Tngui-Boto, 7a: **Tingi**
To'aba'ita, 2: **Malaita**
Toala, 5
To Ale, 5: **Toala**
Toanhooches, 1: **Twana**
Toas, 7: **Paraujano**
Toba, 7
Toba, 5: **Batak**
Toba-Pilagá, 7a: **Pilagá**
Tobelorese, 5
Tobolik, 6(R): **Siberian Tatars**
To Bugi, 5: **Bugis**
Tocouleur, 9a
Toda, 3
Toda, 9: **Teda**
Todaga, 9: **Teda**

Todava, 3: **Toda**
Toderichroone, 1: **Catawba**
Tocunas, 7: **Ticuna**
Todga, 9: **Teda**
Tofa, 6(R): **Tofalar**
Tofalar, 6(R)
Togalubombeyavaru, 3a: **Killekyata**
Togata, 3a: **Thakar**
Tohono O'odham, 1: **Pima-Papago**
Toi, 9a: **Didinga**
Tojolab'al, 8
Tojolabal, 8: **Tojolab'al**
Toka, 9: **Tonga**
Tokelau, 2
Tokre Kolcha, 3a: **Kolgha**
Tokuna, 7: **Ticuna**
Tokushu Burakumin, 5: **Burakumin**
Tol, 8: **Jicaque**
Tolai, 2
To Laki, 5: **Laki**
Tolpan, 8: **Jicaque**
Toli-toli, 5: **Tomini**
Tolo, 5: **Bahnar**
To Loinang, 5: **Saluan**
Tolowa, 1; 1a
Tolubomalawaru, 3a: **Telaga**
Tomar, 3a: **Tomara Rajput**
Tomara Rajput, 3a
Tombalu, 5: **Minahasans**
Tombo, 9: **Dogon**
Tombucas, 9a: **Tumbuka**
Tombula, 5: **Minahasans**
Tombulu, 5: **Minahasans**
Tominers, 5: **Tomini**
Tomini, 5
Tom-Kuznets Tatars, 6(R): **Shors**
Tommo, 9: **Dogon**
To Muna, 5: **Muna**
Ton, 3: **Toda**
Tonga, 2; 9
Tongans, 1: **Polynesians**
Tongareva, 2
Tonkawa, 1
Tonkinese, 5: **Vietnamese**
Toori, 3a: **Turi**
Toposa, 9a
Tor, 2
Torá, 7a
Toraa, 5: **Toraja**
Torach, 4: **Tory Islanders**
Toradja, 5
Toraja, 5
Toraya, 5: **Toraja**
Torea, 3a: **Besta**
Toreya, 3a: **Besta**
Tor Inis, 4: **Tory Islanders**
Toro, 9a
Toro, 9: **Dogon**
Torobbo, 9: **Okiek**
Toroobe, 9: **Fulani**
Torres Strait Islanders, 2
Torrupan, 8: **Jicaque**

Tory Islanders, 4
Toshmal, 9: **Peripatetics of Afghanistan, Iran, and Turkey** (Iran)
To Sung, 5: **Bahnar**
Totiketik, 8: **Tzotzil of San Bartolomé de los Llanos**
Totiques, 8: **Tzotzil of San Bartolomé de los Llanos**
Toto, 3a
Totoimo, 7a: **Hishkariana**
Totonac, 8
Totonaca, 8: **Totonac**
Totonaco, 8: **Totonac**
Tottiyan, 3a
Tottiyan, 3a: **Yogi**
Toubakai, 9a: **Soninké**
Toubou, 9a
Toubou, 9: **Teda**
Toubouri, 9a
To Ugi', 5: **Bugis**
Towcka, 8: **Sumu**
TowoLi, 7: **Maká**
To Wugi', 5: **Bugis**
Toyoneri, 7a
Toyori, 7a: **Toyoneri**
Tozui, 9: **Lozi**
Trans-Fly, 2: **Keraki**
Transylvanian Ethnic Groups, 4
Travancorean, 3: **Malayali**
Travelers, 1: **Irish Travelers**; 4: **Peripatetics**; **Rominsche**
Traveller Gypsies, 4: **Rominsche**
Travellers, 4: Peripatetics
Travelling People, 4: **Irish Travellers**
Trekkers, 9: **Afrikaners**
Tremembé, 7a
Trigarth, 3a: **Tirgul Brahman**
Trigueños, 7: **Afro–South Americans**
Trigul Brahman, 3a: **Tirgul Brahman**
Trinidadians, 1: **Black West Indians in the United States**
Trinidadians and Tobagonians, 8
Trinitario, 7: **Mojo**
Trinity Indians, 1: **Hupa**
Trio, 7
Tripra, 3a: **Tripura**
Tripura, 3a
Tripuri, 3a: **Tripura**
Triques, 8: **Triqui**
Triqui, 8
Tri-Racial Isolates, 1: **American Isolates**
Tri-Racials, 1: **American Isolates**
Trobriand Islands, 2
Tropical-Forest Foragers, 9
Truk, 2
Truka, 7a
Trukese, 1: **Micronesians**
Trumai, 7a
Tsáchela, 7: **Colorado**
Tsakala, 3a: **Dhobi**
Tsakhi, 6(R): **Tsakhurs**

Tsakhurs, 6(R)
Tsakonians, 4
Tsa'lagi', 1: Cherokee
Tsannoi, 6(R): Laz
Tsapotecatl, 8: Zapotec
Tsa'ragi, 1: Cherokee
Tsarisen, 5: Taiwan Aboriginal Peoples
Tsase, 7: Piapoco
Tsatchela, 7: Colorado
Tsattine, 1: Beaver
Tscham, 5: Cham
Tscherkess, 6(R): Circassians
Tsethaottine, 1: Mountain
Tsetsaut, 1a
Tshaahui, 7: Chayahuita
Tsiam, 5: Cham
Tsigan, 9: Peripatetics of Afghanistan,
    Iran, and Turkey (Turkey)
Tsiganes, 4: Peripatetics
Tsigani, 4: Bulgarian Gypsies
Tsilkotin, 1: Chilcotin
Tsimihety, 9
Tsimshian, 1
Tsirakaua, 7: Ayoreo
Tsniuk, 1: Chinook
Tsolote, 7: Chorote
Tsonga, 9a
Tsoop-Nit-Pa-Loo, 1: Nez Percé
Tsoque, 8: Zoque
Tsou, 5: Taiwan Aboriginal Peoples
Tsuou, 5: Taiwan Aboriginal Peoples
Tsutpeli, 1: Nez Percé
Tsu'u, 5: Taiwan Aboriginal Peoples
Tswana, 9
Tsygane, 6(R): Gypsies
Ttö,ja, 7: Piaroa
Tu, 6(C)
Tual, 6(R): Ossetes
Tuamotu, 2: Raroia
Tuar, 3a: Tomara Rajput
Tuareg, 9
Tuba, 6(R): Tofalar
Tubal, 6(R): Mingrelians
Tubatulabal, 1
Tubu, 9: Teda
Tubuai Archipelago, 2: Rapa
Tucano, 7a
Tucuna, 7: Ticuna; 7a: Tucanol
Tucundiapa, 7a: Bendyapá
Tuda, 9: Teda
Tudag, 5: Cotabato Manobo
Tudaga, 9: Teda
Tuding, 6(C): Tujia
Tugen, 9a
Tugen, 9: Nandi and Other Kalenjin
    Peoples
Tugeri, 2: Marind-anim
Tuhun, 5: Dusun
Tui Kaba, 2: Bau
Tujen, 6(C): Tujia
Tujia, 6(C)
Tukano, 7a: Tucano

Túkedákenei, 7a: Warekena
Tukolor, 9a: Tocouleur
Tukomi, 3: Nagas
Tukspuch, 1: Tenino
Tuku, 9a
Tukuna, 7: Ticuna; 7a: Tucano
Tukun-Dyapá, 7a: Bendyapá
Tulao, 6(C): Zhuang
Tularosa Apache, 1: Mescalero Apache
Tule, 7: Cuna; 8: Kuna
Tulemala, 8: Kuna
Tulong, 6(C): Drung
Tulu Brahman, 3a: Havik Brahman
Tumanao, 5: Bilaan
Tumbuka, 9a
Tumin, 6(C): Tujia
Tummior, 5: Temiar
Tunaha, 1: Kutenai
Tundjung, 5: Kalimantan Dayaks
Tunebo, 7
Tunevo, 7: Tunebo
Tungaru, 2: Kiribati
Tungus, 6(R): Even; Evenki; 6(C):
    Ewenki
Tunica, 1; 1a
Tunjur, 9a
Tunumiut, 1: East Greenland Inuit
Tununirmiut, 1: Iglulik Inuit
Tunwar, 3a: Tomara Rajput
Tupari, 7
Tupen, 9a: Bassa
Tupinakî, 7a: Tupinikin
Tupinikin, 7a
Tupy, 7: Kaingáng
Turcomans, 6(R): Turkmens
Turfanlik, 6(C): Uigur
Turi, 3a
Turi, 3: Munda
Turijene', 5: Bajau
Turiwara, 7: Anambé
Turk, 9: Qashqa'i
Turkana, 9
Türken, 9: Turks
Turkey Tribe, 1: Delaware
Turki Hajam, 3a: Nai
Turkish Nomadic Pastoralists, 9: Yörük
Turkish-Speaking Bulgars, 6(R): Gagauz
Türkler, 9: Turks
Turkmens, 6(R)
Türkmens, 6(R): Turkmens
Turks, 9
Turks, 1: American Isolates; 6(C):
    Tatars; 6(R): Meskhetians
Turks and Caicos Islanders, 8
Tusayan, 1: Hopi
Tuscans, 4
Tuscarora, 1
Tushá, 7a
Tutavar, 3: Toda
Tutchone, 1
Tutchonekutchin, 1: Tutchone
Tutelo, 1a

Tütsch Swiss, 4: German Swiss
Tutsi, 9a
Tutsi, 9a: Nyaruanda
Tutuni, 1: Chastacosta
Tuvalu, 2
Tuvans, 6(R)
Tuvintsy, 6(R): Tuvans
Tuyoneiri, 7a: Toyoneri
Tuyuka, 7a
Tuyurymiut, 1: Central Yup'ik Eskimos
Tuzemnye, 6(R): Bukharan Jews
Twa, 9a
Twahka, 8: Sumu
Twaka, 8: Sumu
Twana, 1
Twanka, 8: Sumu
Twashta Kasar, 3a: Tamera
Twaxha, 8: Sumu
Twightwees, 1: Miami
Txikão, 7a
Txikao, 7a: Chikão
Tya, 6(R): Dolgan
Tya Kikhi, 6(R): Dolgan
Tyapi, 9a: Landouma
Tygh, 1: Tenino
Tyigh, 1: Tenino
Tyroleans, 4: Tiroleans
Tyva, 6(R): Tuvans
Tzakonians, 4: Tsakonians
Tzeltal, 8
Tzo, 5: Taiwan Aboriginal Peoples
Tzoques, 8: Zoque
Tzotzil and Tzeltal of Pantelhó, 8
Tzotziles, 8: Tzotzil of San Bartolomé
    de los Llanos
Tzotzil of Chamula, 8
Tzotzil of San Andrés Larraínzar, 8
Tzotzil of San Bartolomé de los
    Llanos, 8
Tzotzil of Zinacantan, 8
Tzun Huan Djapá, 7a: Bendyapá
Tz'utujil, 8

Uabui, 7a: Hishkariana
U-ah-miri, 7: Waimiri-Atroari
Uaicama, 7a: Pirá
Uaimeris, 7: Waimiri-Atroari
Uaimirys, 7: Waimiri-Atroari
Uaipí, 7: Puinave
Uaiuai, 7: Wáiwai
Uajibo, 7: Guahibo-Sikuani
Ualamo, 9a: Wolayta
Ualan, 2: Kosrae
Uamerys, 7: Waimiri-Atroari
Uanano, 7: Wanano
Uap, 2: Yap
Uarekena, 7a: Warekena
Uari, 7a: Aikaná
Uassahy, 7: Waimiri-Atroari
Uaura, 7: Waurá
Uba, 9a: Wolayta
Ubde-Nahèrn, 7a: Hupda

Ubde Tukano, **7a: Hupda**
Ubykhs, **6(R): Circassians**
Ucayali, **7: Cocama**
Ucayalino, **7: Campa**
Uchla, **3a: Bhamta**
Uchlia, **3a: Bhamta**
Uchi, **1: Yuchi**
Ud, **3a: Beldar**
Udaiyan, 3a
Udasi, 3a
Udins, **6(R): Udis**
Udis, 6(R)
Udmurt, 6(R)
Uduk, 9a
Ufaina, **7: Tanimuka**
Ugbug, **6(R): Kubachins**
Ugbugan, **6(R): Kubachins**
Ugyuligmiut, **1: Netsilik Inuit**
Uhro-Rusyns, **1: European-Americans**
Uibuh, **3a: Kuki**
Uighur, 6(R)
Uighur, **6(C): Uigur**
Uigur, 6(C)
Uigur, **6(R): Uighur**
Uilta, **6(R): Orok**
Ukhotnom, **1: Yuki**
Ukrainian-Canadians, **1: Ukrainians of Canada**
Ukrainian Peasants, 6(R)
Ukrainians, 6(R)
Ukrainians, **1: European-Americans**
Ukrainian Siberians, **6(R): Siberiaki**
Ukrainians of Canada, 1
Uleai, **2: Woleai**
Ulithi, 2
Ulladan, 3a
Ullatan, **3a: Ulladan**
Ulrucks, **1: Yurok**
Ulster Irish, **4: Northern Irish**
Ulster Scots, **4: Northern Irish**
Ul'ta, **6(B): Orok**
Ulúa, **8: Sumu**
Ulwa, **8: Sumu**
Umatilla, 1
Umaua, **7: Karihona**
Umpqua, 1a
Umpqua, **1: Chastacosta**
Unaliqmiut, **1: Central Yup'ik Eskimos**
Unami, **1: Delaware**
Unangan, **6(R): Aleuts**
Ungazim Yupiga, **6(R): Asiatic Eskimos**
Uni, **7: Cashibo**
Union Islands, **2: Tokelau**
Unni, **3a: Ambalavasi**
Untouchables, 3
Upanguayma, **8: Seri**
Uppaliga, **3a: Uppar; Upparwar**
Uppar, 3a
Uppara, **3a: Uppar; Upparwar**
Upparwar, 3a
Upper Chehalis, **1: Chehalis**
Upper Chinook, **1: Wishram**

Upper Pimas, **1: Pima-Papago**
Upper Tanana, **1: Nabesna**
Uppiliyan, **3a: Upparwar**
Urak, 7a
Urali, 3a
Urali Kuruman, **3a: Urali**
Urali Kurumaru, **3a: Urali**
Urali Kurumba, **3a: Urali**
Urali-Kurumbas, **3: Kurumbas**
Urali Kurumber, **3a: Urali**
Uraly, **3a: Urali**
Urang Gayo, **5: Gayo**
Urangkhai Sakha, **6(R): Yakut**
Urang Prijangan, **5: Sundanese**
Urang Sunda, **5: Sundanese**
Uraon, **3: Oraon**
Urarina, 7a
Ureung Aceh, **5: Acehnese**
Ureung Baroh, **5: Acehnese**
Ureung Tunong, **5: Acehnese**
Urhobo, 9a
Uria, **3a: Sansia**
Uriankhai, **6(R): Tuvans**
Uriankhi, **6(R): Tuvans**
Uridavan, **3a: Uridavan Gowdalu**
Uridavan Gowdalu, 3a
Uriní, **7: Asurini**
Uro, **7a: Uru**
Urohima, **9a: Hima**
Urrominna, **2: Dieri**
Uru, 7a
Uru, **7: Chipaya**
Urubu-Kaapor, 7a
Urueuwawáu, 7a
Uru Golla, **3a: Golla**
Urukuena, **7a: Wayana**
Urumí, **7a: Ntogapíd**
Urupá, 7a
Ushery, **1: Catawba**
Usilele, **9a: Lele**
Usino, 2
Uspantec, **8: Uspanteko**
Uspanteco, **8: Uspanteko**
Uspanteko, 8
Utah, **1: Ute**
Utaw, **1: Ute**
Ute, 1
Uti, **6(R): Udis**
Uua, **7: Tunebo**
Uvea, 2
Uvean, **2: Uvea**
U'wa, **7: Tunebo**
Uwaiwa, **7: Guahibo-Sikuani**
Uwotjuja, **7: Piaroa**
Uyghur, **6(R): Uighur**
Uygur, **6(C): Uigur**
Uzbeks, 6(C), (R)

Va, **6(C): Wa**
Vada, 3a
Vadaca, **3: Badaga**
Vadacar, **3: Badaga**

Vadagalai Sri Vaishnava, **3a: Sri Vaishnava Brahman**
Vadda, **3: Vedda**
Vaddar, **3a: Beldar**
Vaddo, **3: Vedda**
Vader, 3a
Vadval, **3a: East Indian**
Vaghe, 3a: Waghya
Vagher, 3a
Vaghri, 3a
Vahumpura, 3a
Vai, 9a
Vaidu, 3a
Vaidya, **3a: Baidya**
Vaidyan, **3a: Baidya**
Vaiphei, **3a: Kuki**
Vaiphui, **3a: Kuki**
Vais, **3a: Nagbansi**
Vaishya, **3: Vaisya; 3a: Komati**
Vaisya, 3
Vaiti, 3a
Vajir, **3a: Khava**
Vakuta, **2: Trobriand Islands**
Valaf, **9: Wolof**
Valaiyan, 3a
Valan, **3a: Valaiyan**
Valand, **3a: Nai**
Valer, **3a: Holeya**
Vallabacharya, 3a
Vallamban, 3a
Vallodolid, **1: Taos**
Valluvan, 3a
Valluva Pandaram, **3a: Valluvan**
Valluva Pulaya, **3a: Pulluvan**
Valuvan, **3a: Valluvan**
Valvi, **3a: Gamit**
Vana Palli, **3: Irula**
Van Duzen Indians, **1: Wailaki**
Vangawala, **9: Peripatetics of Afghanistan, Iran, and Turkey (Afghanistan)**
Vani, **3: Bania**
Vania, **3: Bania**
Vaniyan, 3a
Vanjari, **3a: Banjara**
Vanjha, 3a
Vannan, 3a
Vanneru, **3a: Tigala**
Vannikuladavaru, **3a: Tigala**
Vanniya, **3a: Palli**
Vanniyan, **3a: Palli**
Vanyume, **1: Serrano**
Vapidiana, **7: Wapisiana**
Vaqueros, **1: Mescalero Apache**
Varaich, 3a
Varangana, **3a: Devadasi**
Vardar Slavs, **4: Slav Macedonians**
Varik, **3a: Nai**
Variyar, **3a: Ambalavasi**
Varli, 3a
Varohío, **8: Guarijío**
Varohíos, **8: Guarijío**

Varojíos, 8: Guarijío
Vasava, 3: Bhil; 3a: Gamit
Vasave, 3: Bhil; 3a: Gamit
Vascos, 1: Basques; 4: Basques
Vastad, 3a: Viramushti
Vasudeva Joshi, 3a
Vavdichaski, 3a: Nai
Vayasa, 3a: Nagbansi
Vedan, 3a
Vedda, 3
Veddah, 3: Vedda
Veddha, 3: Vedda
Vedic Indians, 3: Aryan
Ved-Patr, 3a
Veiao, 9a: Yao
Velalar, 3: Vellala
Velama, 3a
Velan, 3a
Velikorusskiy, 6(R): Russians
Vellala, 3
Velli-Durayi, 3a
Vellutedan, 3a
Venda, 9a
Vere, 9a
Vetere, 9a: Mekyibo
Vetta Kuruman, 3a: Urali
Vettuvan, 3a: Mala Vedan
Vettuva Pulayan, 3a: Mala Vedan
Vettuvarn, 3a: Mala Vedan
Viajeros, 4: Peripatetics
Viard, 1: Wiyot
Viceita Bribri, 8: Boruca, Bribri, and
    Cabécar
Vidur, 3a
Vidur Brahman, 3a: Vidur
Vietnamese, 5
Vietnamese, 1: South and Southeast
    Asians of Canada; South and
    Southeast Asians of the United
    States
Vigha, 3a: Satani
Vilanes, 5: Bilaan
Vilela, 7a
Vili, 9: Kongo
Vilkurup, 3a
Villaya, 3: Irula
Villu Vedan, 3a: Eravallan
Vinton County Group, 1: American
    Isolates
Vinuk, 8: Tz'utujil
Vipranoru, 3a: Telaga
Vir, 3a: Viramushti
Virabhat, 3a: Viramushti
Virabhatalu, 3a: Mailari
Viraghata Madivala, 3a: Agasa
Viramushti, 3a
Virasaiva, 3: Lingayat
Vira Vaishnava, 3a: Satani
Virgin Islanders, 8
Visayan, 5
Vishavan, 3a
Vishnu Archaka, 3a: Satani

Vishotar, 3a: Rabari
Vishva Brahman, 3a: Kammalan
Vitola, 3a: Vitolana
Vitolana, 3a
Vitolia, 3a: Vitolana
Vitoria, 3a: Vitolana
Vlaamingen, 4: Flemish
Vlach Gypsies of Hungary, 4
Vlachs, 4
Vlachs, 4: Romanians; Sarakatsani
Vlamisch, 4: Flemish
Vlasi, 4: Vlachs
Vlatzii, 4: Romanians
Vodda, 3a: Beldar
Vodden, 3a: Beldar
Voguls, 6(R): Mansi
Vohora, 3: Bohra
Vokeo, 2: Wogeo
Vokkaliga, 3: Okkaliga
Volga Tatars, 6(R)
Volof, 9: Wolof
Vonoma, 9a
Vorarlberger, 4: Austrians
Votyak, 6(R): Udmurt
Voutere, 9a: Baboute
Voyageurs, 4: Peripatetics
Vuddaghur, 3: Badaga
Vulkan Islanders, 2: Manam
Vute, 9a: Baboute

Wðlasðkwiyðk, 1: Maliseet
Wa, 6(C)
Wa'a, 9a: Dghwede
Wabi, 8: Huave
Wabnaki, 1: Abenaki
Wabui, 7a: Hishkariana
Wacawaio, 7: Akawaio
Wa-chaga, 9: Chagga
Wachipaeri, 7a
Waddar, 3a: Beldar; Sansia
Wadewar, 3a: Sansia
Wadul, 6(R): Yukagir
Wadu Rajlu, 3a: Beldar
Wafipa, 9: Fipa
Wagarabai, 2: Miyanmin
Wageva, 2: Wogeo
Wagga, 9a: Waja
Waghe Joshi, 3a: Waghya
Waghya, 3a
Wagrani, 7: Waorani
Wahabi, 3a
Wa-hmi, 8: Chinantec
Wahoya Pāï, 7: Siona-Secoya
Wahyára, 7a: Jurutí
Wah-shoes, 1: Washoe
Wahshoo, 1: Washoe
Waiam, 1: Tenino
Waiampí, 7a: Oyampi
Waiano, 7a: Wayana
Waiapi, 7: Wayãapi
Waibuk, 2: Wovan
Waica, 7: Akawaio; Yanomamö

Waika, 7: Yanomamö; 7a: Patamona
Waikána, 7a: Pirá
Waikino, 7a: Pirá
Wailaki, 1
Wailatpa, 1: Cayuse
Wailatpu, 1: Cayuse
Wailpiri, 2: Warlpiri
Waimare, 7a: Paresí
Waimiri-Atroari, 7
Waimirys, 7: Waimiri-Atroari
Wainad Chetti, 3a: Wynadan Chetti
Waiwa, 7: Guahibo-Sikuani
Wáiwai, 7
Waiwe, 7: Wáiwai
Waja, 9a
Wakaki, 9a: Jukun
Wakande, 9a: Mbembe
Wakaraü, 7: Tupari
Wakawai, 7: Akawaio
Wakisii, 9: Gusii
Wakore, 9a: Soninké
Waktu Lima, 5: Sasak
Wakuenai, 7: Baniwa-Curripaco-
    Wakuenai
Wala, 9a
Walapai, 1
Walãpi, 7: Wayãpi
Walatola, 7: Cuna
Walbiri, 2: Warlpiri
Waled Abu Tenna, 9: Peripatetics of
    Iraq . . . Yemen (Egypt)
Walia, 9a: Massa
Walkers, 1: Western Shoshone
Wallachs, 4: Romanians
Wallawalla, 1
Wallis Island, 2: Uvea
Walloons, 4
Walpiri, 2: Warlpiri
Walula, 1: Wallawalla
Waluli, 2: Kaluli
Waluriki, 2: Ambae
Wama, 7a: Akurio
Wamaka, 7a: Malayo
Wambulu, 9: Iraqw
Wambutu, 9a: Mangbetu
Wamia, 9: Iteso; 9a: Teso
Wamira, 2
Wampanoag, 1: Massachuset
Wampi-misamera, 7: Guambiano
Wanaí, 7a
Wanama, 7a: Akurio
Wanano, 7
Wandala, 9a: Mandara
Wandorobo, 9: Okiek
Wanga, 9a
Wanga, 9: Luyia
Wanináwa, 7a: Kutakina Acre
Wanjara, 3a: Banjara
Wanjari, 3a: Banjara
Wanji, 9a
Wannekar, 3a: Chhipa
Wansphoda, 3a: Vitolana

Wantoat, 2
Wanukeyena, 1: Hidatsa
Wao, 7a
Wao, 7: Waorani
Waodani, 7: Waorani
Waog, 7: Waorani
Waograni, 7: Waorani
Waorani, 7
Wapa, 9a: Jukun
Wape, 2
Wapë, 2: Wape
Wapei, 2: Wape
Wapi, 2: Wape
Wapishana, 7: Wapisiana
Wapisiana, 7
Wapixana, 7: Wapisiana
Wappinger, 1a
Wappo, 1; 1a
Wapu, 2: Wantoat
Warani, 7: Waorani
Warao, 7
Warathi, 3a: Dhobi
Waraweete, 7: Warao
Warekena, 7a
Wari, 7a
Warijío, 8: Guarijío
Warijíos, 8: Guarijío
Warik, 3a: Nai
Warjawa, 9a
Warji, 9a: Warjawa
Wariva, 7a
Warli, 3a: Varli
Warlpiri, 2
Warm Springs Sahaptin, 1: Tenino
Waropen, 2
Warthi, 3a: Dhobi
Wasashe, 1: Osage
Wasbasha, 1: Osage
Waschagga, 9: Chagga
Wasco, 1: Wishram
Washa, 1a
Washakie's Band, 1: Eastern
    Shoshone
Washaws, 1: Washoe
Washew, 1: Washoe
Washo, 1: Washoe
Washoe, 1
Washoo, 1: Washoe
Washkuk, 2: Kwoma
Wasida, 2: Orokaiva
Wasio, 2: Kurtatchi
Waskuk, 2: Kwoma
Wasteko, 8
Wasu, 7a
Wasudeo, 3a: Basdewa
Wasulunka, 9a: Ouassoulounke
Watapahato, 1: Kiowa
Watari, 3a: Otari
Watkari, 3a: Otari
Wattu, 3a
Waunama, 8: Emberá and Wounaan
Waunan, 8: Emberá and Wounaan

Waunana, 7: Chocó; Noanamá; 8:
    Emberá and Wounaan
Waurá, 7
Wauru, 7: Waruá
Wauyukma, 1: Wallawalla
Wayaculé, 7a: Akurio
Wayam, 1: Tenino
Wayampam, 1: Tenino
Wayampi, 7: Wayãpi
Wayampí, 7a: Oyampi
Wayana, 7a
Wayãpi, 7
Wayca, 7: Akawaio
Wayoró, 7a
Wayuu, 7: Guajiro
Wazir, 3a
Wedau, 2: Wamira
Wee, 9a: Guere
Wehèa, 5: Modang
Weits-pek, 1: Yurok
Welamo, 9a: Wolayta
Weleya, 2: Woleai
Welsh, 4
Welsh, 1: European-Americans;
    European-Canadians
Wemba, 9: Bemba; 9a: Bemba
Wená, 7: Desana
Wenatchi, 1: Columbia
Wendat, 1: Huron
Wendisch, 4: Slovenes
Wends, 1: European-Americans; 4:
    Sorbs
Wenhayek, 7: Mataco
Wenrohonron, 1a
Wentusij, 7: Nivaclé
Were, 9a: Vere
Werekena, 7a: Warekena
Wesorts, 1: American Isolates
West Alaska Eskimos, 1: Central Yup'ik
    Eskimos
West Britons, 4: Northern Irish
West Coast People, 1: Nootka
Western Abenaki, 1: Pennacook
Western Apache, 1
Western Bontok, 5: Sagada Igorot
Western Central Enga, 2: Mae Enga
Western Desert Aborigines, 2:
    Ngatatjara
Western Elema, 2: Orokolo
Westerners, 9a: Anglophones of
    Cameroon
Western Lunda, 9: Lunda
Western Mongols, 6(R): Kalmyks
Western Mono, 1: Mono
Western Nahane, 1: Tahltan
Western Shoshone, 1
Western Sioux, 1: Teton
West Greenland Inuit, 1
West Indians, 1: Black West Indians in
    the United States
West Nakanai, 2: Lakalai
West Ouvean, 2: Loyalty Islands

Wetawit, 9a: Berta
Wetitsaan, 1: Hidatsa
Wetu Telu, 5: Sasak
Whale Sound Inuit, 1: Inughuit
White Clay People, 1: Gros Ventre
White Jews, 3: Cochin Jew
White Lisu, 6(C): Lisu
White Mongols, 6(C): Tu
White Mountain, 1: Western Apache
White Russians, 1: European-
    Americans; European-Canadians;
    6(R): Belarussians
White Ruthenians, 1: European-
    Americans; European-Canadians
Wianu, 2: Yangoru Boiken
Wichi, 7: Mataco
Wichita, 1
Wiciyela, 1: Yankton
Widekum, 9a
Wiedertaufer, 1: Mennonites
Wiener, 4: Austrians
Wihinaitti, 1: Northern Shoshone
Wik, 2: Wik Mungkan
Wikí, 1: Wiyot
Wik Mungkan, 2
Wikmunkan, 2: Wik Mungkan
Wikye', 7: Mataco
Wikyi', 7: Mataco
Wild Nuchen, 6(C): Hezhen
Wilta, 6(R): Orok
Winave, 7: Puinave
Windisch, 4: Slovenes
Wind River Shoshone, 1: Eastern
    Shoshone
Winnebago, 1
Wintu, 1: Wintun
Wintun, 1
Wirá, 7: Desana
Wirá-pora, 7: Desana
Wisaesi, 2: Kaluli
Wishosk, 1: Wiyot
Wishram, 1
Witoto, 7
Wíyat, 1: Wiyot
Wiyaw, 2: Wovan
Wiyot, 1
Wizarika, 8: Huichol
Wo, 9a: Bassari
Wobe
Wocowaio, 7: Akawaio
Wodeya, 3a: Vader
Wogeo, 2
Wokiare, 7a: Yavarana
Wokkaliga, 3: Okkaliga
Wola, 2: Mendi
Wolayta, 9a
Woleai, 2
Wollufs, 9: Wolof
Wolof, 9
Wombunger, 2: Wongaibon
Wongaibon, 2
Wongai-bun, 2: Wongaibon

Wong Djawa, 5: **Javanese**
Wonghi, 2: **Wongaibon**
Wonghibon, 2: **Wongaibon**
Wongkadieri, 2: **Dieri**
Wong Madura, 5: **Madurese**
Woni, 5: **Akha**; 6(C): **Hani**
Wonkadieri, 2: **Dieri**
Wonti, 2: **Waropen**
Woolwa, 8: **Sumu**
Woonwagenbewoners, 4: **Gypsies and Caravan Dwellers in the Netherlands; Peripatetics**
Woowa, 8: **Sumu**
Wopu, 2: **Wantoat**
Worpen, 2: **Waropen**
Wõth-ĩʰã, 7: **Piaroa**
Wóthuha, 7: **Piaroa**
Wounaan, 7: **Chocó; Noanamá; 8: Emberá and Wounaan**
Wounan, 8: **Emberá and Wounaan**
Woun Meu, 7: **Chocó; Noanamá**
Wovan, 2
Woyawai, 7: **Wáiwai**
Wrukzai, 3a: **Orakzai**
Wuaiamares, 7: **Waimiri-Atroari**
Wudder, 3a: **Beldar**
Wuddghur, 3: **Badaga**
Wulamba, 2: **Murngin**
Wulwa, 8: **Sumu**
Wuna, 9a: **Mboum**
Wurkum, 9a
Wuya, 9a: **Waja**
Wyandot, 1: **Huron**
Wynaadan Chetti, 3a: **Wynadan Chetti**
Wynadan Chetti, 3a

Xagua, 7a: **Achawa**
Xakléng, 7: **Xokléng**
Xakriabá, 7a: **Shakriabá**
Xambioá, 7: **Karajá**
Xaroxa, 9a: **Didinga**
Xavante, 7: **Shavante**
Xebero, 7: **Jebero**
Xerente, 7: **Sherente**
Xetá, 7a: **Héta**
Xevero, 7: **Jebero**
Xhosa, 9
Xhosa, 9a
Xiao ka va, 6(C): **Wa**
Xiaoshan, 6(C): **Jingpo**
Xibba, 9a: **Kilba**
Xibe, 6(C)
Xibitaona, 7: **Cocama**
Xicaque, 8: **Jicaque**
Xifan, 6(C): **Pumi**
Xihuila, 7: **Jebero**
Xikrin, 7
Xinca, 8
Xingu, 7a: **Awaete**
Xinren, 6(C): **Hakka**
Xipibo, 7: **Shipibo**
Xiriana, 7: **Yanomamö**

Xívari, 7: **Jivaro**
Xivaro, 7: **Jivaro**
Xó dâng, 5: **Sedang**
Xogléng, 7: **Xokléng**
Xokléng, 7
Xoko, 7a: **Shokó**
Xoko-Kariri, 7a: **Shokó-Kariri**
Xokré, 7: **Xokléng**
Xokréng, 7: **Xokléng**
Xolota, 7: **Chorote**
Xong, 5: **Chong**
Xonkléng, 7: **Xokléng**
Xoraxané Romá, 4
Xosa, 9: **Xhosa**
X. Tiêng, 5: **Stieng**
Xu, 9: **San-Speaking Peoples**
Xuɛįdzŭ, 6(R): **Dungans**
Xukuru, 7a: **Shukurú**
Xukuru-Kariri, 7a: **Shukurú-Kariri**

Yabotí, 7a: **Jabutí**
Yachumi, 3: **Nagas**
Yacouba, 9a: **Dan**
Yadava, 3a: **Yadu Rajput**
Yadava-kula, 3a: **Golla**
Yadavakuladavaru, 3a: **Kadu Golla**
Yadu-Bhatti, 3a: **Yadu Rajput**
Yadu Rajput, 3a
Yagan, 7a: **Yamána**
Yagham, 7a: **Yamána**
Yagua, 7
Yaguaperí, 7: **Waimiri-Atroari**
Yaguin, 1: **Kumeyaay**
Yahua, 7: **Yagua**
Yahud awlad al-ʿarab, 9: **Jews, Arabic-Speaking**
Yahudi, 6(R): **Bukharan Jews**
Yahudim, 9: **Jews of Israel**
Yahuna, 7: **Tanimuka**
Yahundai, 9: **Jews of Iran**
Yahup, 7a
Yahval lum, 8: **Tzotzil of San Andrés Larraínzar**
Yaka, 9: **Suku**
Yakan, 5
Yakima, 1
Yakö, 9
Yakoma, 9a
Yakurr, 9: **Yakö**
Yakut, 6(R)
Yakut, 6(C): **Ewenki**
Yakutians, 6(R): **Yakut**
Yala, 9a: **Iyala**
Yalatola, 7: **Cuna**
Yaloffs, 9: **Wolof**
Yalunka, 9a: **Dialonke**
Yamamawa, 7: **Jamináwa**
Yamána, 7a
Yamasee, 1a
Yamináhua, 7: **Jamináwa**
Yaminahua, 7a: **Jamamadí**
Yaminaua, 7: **Jamináwa**

Yampai, 1: **Walapai**
Yana, 1a
Yanadi, 3a
Yande, 7: **Sirionó**
Yanesha, 7: **Amuesha**
Yang, 5: **Karen**
Yangoru, 2: **Yangoru Boiken**
Yangoru Boiken, 2
Yangsuch'ŏk, 5: **Kolisuch'ŏk**
Yankton, 1
Yanoama, 7: **Yanomamö**
Yanomama, 7: **Yanomamö**
Yanomami, 7: **Yanomamö**
Yanomamö, 7
Yans-Mbun, 9a
Yanzi, 9a: **Yans-Mbun**
Yao, 6(C); **9a**
Yao Min, 6(C): **Yao**
Yao of Thailand, 5
Yaoyen, 5: **Lisu**
Yap, 2
Yapaco, 7: **Piapoco**
Yapese, 1: **Micronesians**
Yaqui, 8
Yaqui, 8: **Cahita**
Yarí, 7a
Yaruro, 7: **Pume**
Yarussa, 6(R): **Avars**
Yata, 3a
Yatê, 7: **Fulniô**
Yati, 3: **Sadhu; 3a: Jati**
Ya-tkitisci, 1: **Seminole**
Yatmul, 2: **Iatmul**
Yauaiti Tapiiya, 7a: **Parakanã**
Yauaperi, 7: **Waimiri-Atroari**
Yauaperí, 7: **Waimiri-Atroari**
Yauarana, 7a: **Yavarana**
Yaúna, 7: **Tanimuka**
Yavapai, 1
Yavarana, 7a
Yavarete, 7a: **Yavitero**
Yavi, 7a: **Tariana**
Yavitano, 7a: **Yavitero**
Yavitero, 7a
Yawalap'h, 7: **Yawalapití**
Yawalapití, 7
Yawanawa, 7a
Yawaveřesha, 7: **Yawalapití**
Yawarawiti, 7: **Yawalapití**
Yawyen, 5: **Lisu**
Yayuna, 7: **Tanimuka**
Yazĭdĭ, 6(R): **Yezidis**
Yazoo, 1: **Tunica**
Ycahuate, 7: **Siona-Secoya**
Yealtland, 4: **Shetlanders**
Yedina, 9a: **Buduma**
Yeh-jen, 5: **Lisu**
Yehudei Teyman, 9: **Jews of Yemen**
Yekhee, 9a: **Etsako**
Yekuana, 7
Yekwana, 7: **Yekuana**
Yela, 2: **Rossel Island**

Yelama, 3a: Velama
Yelma, 3a: Velama
Yemenis, 9
Yemenis, 1: Arab Americans
Yenadi, 3a: Yanadi
Yenisei Kirghiz, 6(R): Khakas
Yenisey Ostyak, 6(R): Ket
Yerava, 3a
Yeravallar, 3a: Eravallan
Yergam, 9a
Yerukala, 3a: Erakala
Yerukula, 3a: Erakala
Yerwa, 9: Kanuri
Yetland, 4: Shetlanders
Yevrei, 6(R): Ashkenazim
Yezidis, 6(R)
Yfugao, 5: Ifugao
Yi, 6(C)
Yihudi, 9a: Awi
Yimbe, 9a: Limba
Yir Yoront, 2
Yisraelim, 9: Jews of Israel
Yocotan, 8: Chontal of Tabasco
Yoeme, 8: Yaqui
Yofuaha, 7: Chorote
Yogi, 3a
Yogi, 3: Sadhu
Yokaya, 1: Pomo
Yokot'an, 8: Chontal of Tabasco
Yokuts, 1
Yolngu, 2: Murngin
Yolof, 9: Wolof
Yom, 9a: Pila-Pila
Yombe, 9a
Yombe, 9: Kongo
Yoreme, 8: Yaqui
Yoruba, 9
Yörük, 9
Youanne, 5: Yuan
Youon, 5: Yuan
Youruk, 1: Yurok
Yowana, 7: Hoti
Yowuxua, 7: Chorote
Yoxuaxa, 7: Chorote
Ypande, 1: Lipan Apache
Yrraya, 5: Gaddang
Yu, 6(C): She
Yuan, 5
Yuana, 7: Hoti
Yuapín, 7: Pume
Yuberí, 7a: Paumarí
Yuchi, 1; 1a
Yu di Korsou, 8: Curaçao
Yuezu, 6(C): Jing
Yugur, 6(C): Yi
Yuit, 1
Yukaghir, 6(R): Yukagir

Yukagir, 6(R)
Yukateko, 8
Yuki, 1; 1a
Yuki, 7: Yuqui
Yuko, 7: Yukpa
Yukpa, 7
Yukuna, 7
Yum, 1: Quechan
Yuma, 1: Quechan
Yumbo, 7: Canelos Quichua
Yumbri, 5
Yumináwa, 7: Jamináwa
Yun, 5: Yuan
Yungar, 2
Yungur, 9a
Yupa, 7: Yukpa
Yu'pa, 7: Yukpa
Yupibu, 6(C): Hezhen
Yupik, 6(R): Asiatic Eskimos
Yuqui, 7
Yuracaré, 7
Yurak, 6(R): Nenets
Yurak-Samoyeds, 6(R): Nenets
Yurock, 1: Yurok
Yurok, 1
Yurukarika, 7a
Yuruná, 7a: Jurúna
Yuruti, 7a: Jurutí
Yuta Payuchis, 1: Southern Paiute (and
   Chemehuevi)
Yuulngu, 2: Murngin

Za, 8: Zapotec
Zaa, 9a: Dourou
Zabarmas, 9: Zarma
Zabermas, 9: Zarma
Zabirmawa, 9: Zarma
Zabramas, 9: Zarma
Zabrima, 9: Zarma
Zaghawa, 9a: Berti
Zaghvana, 9a: Dghwede
Zaiwa, 6(C): Jingpo
Zalamo, 9: Zaramo
Zalamu, 9: Zaramo
Zambos, 7: Afro-Bolivians; Afro-
   Hispanic Pacific Lowlanders
   of Ecuador and Colombia;
   Afro–South Americans; Afro-
   Venezuelans
Zamindar, 3
Zamindar, 3a: Babhan
Zamindar Brahman, 3a: Babhan
Zamuco, 7: Ayoreo; Mojo
Zanar, 6(R): Mingrelians
Zande, 9
Zápara, 7a: Andoa
Zaparas, 7: Paraujano

Zaparo, 7a: Arabela
Zapotec, 8
Zapoteco, 8: Zapotec
Zara, 9a: Bobo
Zaramo, 9
Zaramu, 9: Zaramo
Zardoshti, 9: Zoroastrians
Zargar, 3a: Sonar
Zarma, 9
Zaruro, 7: Pume
Zatchila, 7: Colorado
Zaveri, 3a: Johari
Zawa, 7: Yagua
Zedong, 5: Tidong
Zegua, 9a: Zingua
Zemindar, 3: Zamindar
Zerma, 9: Zarma
Zhch'uch'ur, 6(R): Mountain Jews
Zhongguo ren, 6(C): Han
Zhuang, 6(C)
Zhulõasi, 9: San-Speaking Peoples
Zia, 1: Keres Pueblo Indians; Pueblo
   Indians
Ziba, 9a: Haya
Zíbaro, 7: Jivaro
Zigani, 9: Peripatetics of the Maghreb
   (Morocco)
Zigeuner, 4: Peripatetics
Zigula, 9a: Zingua
Zinacantecos, 8: Tzotzil of Zinacantan
Zinacantecs, 8: Tzotzil of Zinacantan
Zingari, 4: Peripatetics
Zingaros, 4: Spanish Rom
Zingua, 9a
Ziryene, 6(R): Komi
Zo, 3: Chin
Zoc, 8: Zoque
Zogui, 3a: Gonsavi
Zomi, 3: Chin; Mizo
Zoque, 8
Zoró, 7a: Gavião
Zoroastrian, 3: Parsi
Zoroastrians, 9
Zúbaca, 7: Chiquitano
Zugweya, 9a: Busa
Zulu, 9
Zumbagua/Guangaje, 7: Cotopaxi
   Quichua
Zumo, 8: Sumu
Zuni, 1
Zuruahã, 7a
Zutt, 9: Peripatetics of Iraq . . . Yemen
   (Iraq and Syria)
Zwolle-Ebard People, 1: American
   Isolates
Zyrian, 6(R): Komi
Zyryan, 6(R): Komi

Subject Index

Ababinili (supreme being)
　Chickasaw, **1**:66
Abaca growing
　Bukidnon, **5**:53
Abalone pendants
　Pomo, **1**:294
Abandonment
　of abnormal children
　　Comanche, **1**:75
　of disabled
　　Kiowa, **1**:189
　fears of
　　Danes, **4**:90
　marital
　　Madeirans, **4**:165
　　Nepali, **3**:204
　of old and weak
　　Qalandar, **3**:248
　as social control threat
　　Central Yup'ik Eskimos, **1**:58
Abduction, marriage by. *See* Marriage, by
　abduction
Abominable Snowman legend
　Lepcha, **3**:149
Abortion
　as birth control
　　Amahuaca, **7**:35
　　Don Cossacks, **6**:106
　　Greeks, **4**:134
　　Maori, **2**:177
　　Mingrelians, **6**:264
　　Ossetes, **6**:301
　　Serbs, **4**:231
　　Siberiaki, **6**:333
　　Tuvans, **6**:374
　　Ukrainian peasants, **6**:387
　　Yap, **2**:391
　　Yuracaré, **7**:396
　forbidden
　　Irish, **4**:153
　　Micmac, **1**:235
　　Zoroastrians, **9**:408
　illegal but practiced
　　Maltese, **4**:168
　legal
　　Carpatho-Rusyns, **6**:70
　　Czechs, **4**:83
　　English, **4**:97
　　Kalmyks, **6**:156
　　Serbs, **4**:231

　plant abortifacients
　　Cinta Larga, **7**:129
　　Tauade, **2**:320
　after premarital relations
　　Rukuba, **9**:290
　prevalent
　　Greeks, **4**:134
　　Lithuanians, **6**:251
　　Tasmanians, **2**:316
　　Yuracaré, **7**:396
　　see also subhead as birth control
　　　above
　social policy conflict
　　Flemish, **4**:108
　unheard of
　　Azerbaijani Turks, **6**:49
Above-ground funerary structures. *See*
　Mortuary practices
Above Old Man (supreme deity)
　Wiyot, **1**:385
Absentee landlords. *See* Leaseholds; Tenant
　farming; Sharecropping
Abulation. *See* Bathing
Accidental deaths
　high rate
　　Irish Travellers, **4**:154
　taboos
　　Hill Pandaram, **3**:100
Accordian playing. *See under* Musical
　instruments
Accountants. *See* Financial services
Acorn gathering
　Karok, **1**:176
　Kumeyaay, **1**:194
　Luiseño, **1**:164
　Miwok, **1**:239, 240
　Pomo, **1**:294
　Tolowa, **1**:353
　Tubatulabal, **1**:355
　Western Apache, **1**:371
　Wintun, **1**:383
　Wiyot, **1**:384
　Yokuts, **1**:387
　Yurok, **1**:394
Acrobatics
　Kyrgyz, **6**:231
　Laks, **6**:234
　see also Entertainers
Acupuncture. *See under* Medical practices and
　treatments

Adelphic polyandry
　Jat, **3**:112
Adolescence
　sexual relations, **8**:138
Adolescents
　labor duty
　　Estonian, **6**:113
　latitude in free time
　　Manx, **4**:171
　long training period for adulthood
　　Lillooet, **1**:207
　organized protests against authority
　　Dutch, **4**:94
　sexual relations
　　Mohave, **1**:241
　　Norwegians, **4**:181
　　see also Premarital sex
　tooth pointing
　　tropical-forest foragers, **9**:357
　see also Coming of age; Menstruation;
　　Puberty rites
Adoption practices
　Abelam, **2**:5
　Abkhazians, **6**:7, 8
　Aleuts, **6**:18
　Amahuaca, **7**:35
　Amhara, **9**:19
　Andamanese, **3**:10
　Anuta, **2**:14
　Apiaká, **7**:50
　Asmat, **2**:19, 20, 21
　Baffinland Inuit, **1**:30
　Bai, **6**:420
　Bakairi, **7**:74
　Barí, **7**:84
　Belarussians, **6**:61
　Belau, **2**:26
　Blackfoot, **1**:42
　Chechen-Ingush, **6**:74
　Chipaya, **7**:116
　Chuvans, **6**:82
　Copper Eskimo, **1**:78
　Dobu, **2**:50, 51
　Dolgan, **6**:101
　Dong, **6**:431
　Ewenki, **6**:434
　Fali, **9**:96
　Fore, **2**:63
　Fox, **1**:130
　Georgians, **6**:133

Adoption practices (cont'd)
  Han, **6:**444
  Hawaiians, **2:**96
  Huarayo, **7:**178
  Iban, **5:**97
  Kaingáng, **7:**186
  Keres Pueblo Indians, **1:**180
  Ket, **6:**184
  Kewa, **2:**116
  Kickapoo, **1:**186
  Kilenge, **2:**119
  Kiowa, **1:**187
  Kiwai, **2:**126
  Kol, **3:**130
  Kolisuch'ok, **5:**143
  Koreans in the United States, **1:**102
  Kosrae, **2:**129
  Malay, **5:**175
  Malekula, **2:**165
  Manam, **2:**168
  Mandak, **2:**171
  Maori, **2:**177
  Maratha, **3:**169
  Marshall Islands, **2:**193
  Martiniquais, **8:**162
  Mayoruna, **7:**234
  Meskhetians, **6:**260
  Miami, **1:**231, 232
  Micronesians, **1:**237
  Modang, **5:**186
  Mountain Arapesh, **2:**216
  Murik, **2:**222
  Nagas, **3:**189
  Nauru, **2:**237
  Nogays, **6:**288
  Nomoi, **2:**252
  Nuristanis, **9:**251
  Palu'e, **5:**206
  Parsi, **3:**228
  Pohnpei, **2:**269
  Pukapuka, **2:**272
  Russians, **6:**316
  Saint Lucians, **8:**231
  Sea Islanders, **1:**310
  Seminole, **1:**313
  Sengseng, **2:**296
  Sherpa, **3:**259
  Somalis, **9:**318
  Svans, **6:**344, 345
  Tonga, **2:**338
  Tongareva, **2:**340
  Toraja, **5:**282
  Tuareg, **9:**368
  Tuvalu, **2:**356
  Ulithi, **2:**359
  Winnebago, **1:**381
  Wogeo, **2:**381
  Woleai, **2:**383
  Xokléng, **7:**371
  Yao, **6:**505
  Yao of Thailand, **5:**292
  see also Fosterage
Adult baptism
  Amish, **1:**18
  Hutterites, **1:**153, 154-155
  Mennonites, **1:**219
Adultery
  accepted in disparate-age marriages

  Bondo, **3:**49
  as annulment ground
    Piemontese, **4:**198
  blood revenge
    Madurese, **5:**167
  casual attitude toward
    She, **6:**490
  childbirth
    Lakalai, **2:**141
  commented on as if no longer happening
    Apiaká, **7:**50
  common
    Ache, **7:**5
    Arubans, **8:**12
    Canela, **7:**96
    Eipo, **2:**57
    Flemish, **4:**107
    Gorotire, **7:**163
    Guarijío, **8:**118
    Jamaicans, **8:**138
    Kanbi, **3:**118
    Sakalava, **9:**296
    Suya, **7:**316
    Tapirapé, **7:**321
    Tauade, **2:**319
    Temiar, **5:**269
    Toba, **7:**332
    Wamira, **2:**366
    Wogeo, **2:**381
    Yuqui, **7:**393
  condemned as antisocial
    Dutch, **4:**93
  condemned strongly
    Castilians, **4:**60
    Danes, **4:**89
    Gond, **3:**85
    Karen, **5:**128
    Koryaks and Kerek, **6:**209
    Mae Enga, **2:**150
    Mailu, **1:**255;**2:**156
    Sagada Igorot, **5:**216
  court system for women suspects
    Nambudiri Brahman, **3:**192
  as divorce ground. See under Divorce
    grounds
  double standard
    Bahamians, **8:**19
    Hani, **6:**450
    Mailu, **2:**155, 156
    Mongo, **9:**226
    Rom of Czechoslovakia, **4:**219
  husband receives compensation
    Limbu, **3:**150
    Nyamwezi and Sukuma, **9:**256
    Tauade, **2:**319
  legally only committed by women
    Piemontese, **4:**198
  as marriage type
    Limbu, **3:**150
  punished by ancestral spirits
    Gond, **3:**85
  punishments
    Amahuaca, **7:**36
    Baluchi, **3:**23
    Blackfoot, **1:**42
    Bugle, **8:**33
    Candoshi, **7:**94
    Fali, **9:**96

  Gnau, **2:**82
  Koryaks and Kerek, **6:**209
  Lango, **9:**181
  Mailu, **2:**155, 156
  Malekula, **2:**166
  Mojo, **7:**242
  Mongo, **9:**226
  Namau, **2:**232
  Ojibwa, **1:**270
  Pathan, **3:**233
  Piro, **7:**280
  Purum, **3:**241
  Rom of Czechoslovakia, **4:**219
  Saramaka, **7:**297
  Shipibo, **7:**305
  Yawalapití, **7:**379
  Zande, **9:**399
  as social conflict source
    Gebusi, **2:**78
    Guadalcanal, **2:**91
    Malekula, **2:**166
    Mekeo, **2:**199
    Sambia, **2:**285
    Trobriand Islands, **2:**350
    Truk, **2:**353
    Wanano, **7:**350
    Yurok, **1:**395
  uncommon by women
    Tikopia, **2:**325
  upper-class male liasons with lower-status
    woman
    Trinidadians and Tobagonians, **8:**268
  wife's violent reaction to husband's
    Tikopia, **2:**325
  see also Concubinage
Adulthood
  attained at marriage
    Kalmyks, **6:**156
    Manx, **4:**170
    Munda, **3:**184
    Nias, **5:**196
    Otavalo, **7:**254
    Sicilians, **4:**236
    Tiroleans, **4:**263
    Welsh, **4:**280
  marking
    Dargins, **6:**98
  red warpaint
    Miami, **1:**231
  see also Initiation rites
Adventists. See Seventh-Day Adventists
Affinial relations. See under Family; Mother-
    in-law
Affirmative action
  Scheduled Castes and Scheduled Tribes,
    3:256-257
Affluence. See Wealth
African religions
  Guadeloupians, **8:**116
  Jamaicans, **8:**139
  Tswana, **9:**364
Afrocentric movement
  African Americans, **1:**12, 15
Afterlife
  administrator deity feeds on dead
    San-speaking peoples, **9:**304
  as all imaginable pleasures
    Iban, **5:**99

as all objects animate
  Iban, **5**:98
ancestors interact with living
  Awakateko, **8**:17
  Chagga, **9**:62
  Chontal of Tabasco, **8**:69
  Dinka, **9**:71
  Edo, **9**:82
  Garifuna, **8**:115
  Iraqw, **9**:126
  Lango, **9**:182
  Lunda, **9**:198, 199
  Luyia, **9**:205, 206
  Mbeere, **9**:223
  Miskito, **8**:172
  Montserratians, **8**:182
  Mossi, **9**:231
  Motu, **2**:215
  Nuer, **9**:250
  Nyamwezi and Sukuma, **9**:258
  Okiek, **9**:262
  Pomo, **1**:296
  Shilluk, **9**:311
  Suku, **9**:323
  Temne, **9**:345
  Tsimihety, **9**:359
  Tzotzil and Tzeltal of Pantelhó, **8**:278
  Tzotzil of Chamula, **8**:281
  Tzotzil of Zinacantan, **8**:294
  Vlachs, **4**:275
  Zoroastrians, **9**:410
ancestors take form of hyena
  Iraqw, **9**:126
as ancestral land
  Cubeo, **7**:142
  Saramaka, **7**:298
  Walapai, **1**:366
angel interactions
  Jews, Arabic-speaking, **9**:136
angels record good/bad deeds
  Berbers of Morocco, **9**:52
bad and good spheres. _See subhead_ duality
    based on past deeds _below_
bad ghosts stay on earth
  Wiyot, **1**:385
bad lives bound to tree
  Kikapu, **8**:145
as beautiful place of plenty and happiness
  Karihona, **7**:193-194
  Miami, **1**:232
  Pentecost, **2**:264
  Quechan, **1**:302
as bureaucracy
  Hmong, **5**:94
camp of the dead
  Cheyenne, **1**:66
children ascend directly to heaven as angels
  Afro-Colombians, **7**:18
  Afro-Venezuelans, **7**:28
  Otavalo, **7**:255
  Otomí of the Sierra, **8**:203
children's spirits return to mother's womb
    to be reborn
  Tonga, **9**:355
crossing river by boat to underwater world
  Yurok, **1**:396
crossing river of death aided by ferryman
  Lobi-Dagarti peoples, **9**:186

crossing river to sky of the dead
  Yukuna, **7**:390
deeper afterworld if no connection with
    living
  Luba of Shaba, **9**:193
delayed until personal road is traversed
  Zuni, **1**:400
as depths of Blue Lake
  Taos, **1**:343
determined by one's descendants
  Chechen-Ingush, **6**:75
disbelief in
  Ache, **7**:7
  Acholi, **9**:6
  Gahuku-Gama, **2**:70
  Lingayat, **3**:153
  Norwegians, **4**:182
  Suri, **9**:327
  Tahiti, **2**:307
diseased or cowardly travel to village of
    spirits in south
  Pawnee, **1**:286
duality based on past deeds
  Berbers of Morocco, **9**:52
  Betsileo, **9**:57
  Bretons, **4**:40
  Creoles of Nicaragua, **8**:86
  Cuna, **7**:151
  Dyula, **9**:78
  Faroe Islanders, **4**:100
  Futuna, **2**:67-68
  Greeks, **4**:134
  Hakka, **6**:439
  Hausa, **9**:114
  Kashubians, **4**:159
  Kikapu, **8**:145
  Korean, **5**:148
  Lakandon, **8**:154
  Latinos, **1**:206
  Makassar, **5**:174
  Micronesians, **1**:239
  Nagas, **3**:191
  Nahuat of the Sierra de Puebla, **8**:193
  Newar, **3**:208
  Nivaclé, **7**:251
  Old Believers, **1**:275
  Oriya, **3**:218
  Otomí of the Sierra, **8**:203
  Palikur, **7**:264
  Parsi, **3**:229, 230
  Purum, **3**:244
  Qashqa'i, **9**:287
  Rikbaktsa, **7**:288
  Salasaca, **7**:291
  Somalis, **9**:318
  Tarascans, **8**:246
  Tigray, **9**:349
  Turks, **9**:376
  Tuvalu, **2**:357
  Ulithi, **2**:360
  Yemenis, **9**:390
  Zapotec, **8**:314
elders become ancestors
  Tswana, **9**:364
as eternal retribution
  Javanese, **5**:114
as eternal summer with abundance of beer,
    dancing, and sex

Nivaclé, **7**:251
fate determined by type of death
  Bunun, **5**:58
  Mixtec, **8**:178
  Nahua of the Huasteca, **8**:187
  Tepehua, **8**:250
  West Greenland Inuit, **1**:379
  Wolof, **9**:380
  Zapotec, **8**:314
as flower garden situated at the sunset
  Temiar, **5**:273
formal trial
  Kashubians, **4**:159
gender-specific places
  Karihona, **7**:193
ghost and soul separated from body Bondo,
    3:50
ghost rides around on night swallow
  Karihona, **7**:194
ghosts become progressively smaller animals
  Canela, **7**:97-98
  Mataco, **7**:229-230
ghosts go "East" five days after burial
  Wiyot, **1**:385
ghosts haunt dreams of living
  Guajiro, **7**:169
ghosts inspire fear in living
  Piro, **7**:280
ghosts seek vengeance on living
  Anuak, **9**:22
  Tswana, **9**:364
as Golden Mountain
  Tepehua, **8**:249
good half returns to source of life while bad
    half lingers around living
  Barama River Carib, **7**:82
good soul becomes star in heaven
  Pawnee, **1**:286
halfway house on way to spirit world
  Lozi, **9**:190
heaven and hell. _See subhead_ duality based
    on past deeds _above_
heaven and hell as summer or winter
  Belarussians, **6**:61
heaven, hell, or purgatory
  Acadians, **1**:9
  Central Thai, **5**:71
  Dalmatians, **4**:87
  Gaels (Irish), **4**:117
  Parsi, **3**:230
  Popoloca, **8**:216
  Sicilians, **4**:237
heaven levels based on moral respectability
  Tlingit, **1**:353
hell as glacial
  Bretons, **4**:40
as hunting grounds
  West Greenland Inuit, **1**:379
as idealized version of pre-colonial life
  Nandi and other Kalenjin peoples, **9**:234
as idealized version of real world
  Winnebago, **1**:382
immortality of soul
  Costa Ricans, **8**:81
  Jain, **3**:109
  Parsi, **3**:230
  Powhatan, **1**:297
  Santal, **3**:255

Afterlife (cont'd)
    Semang, **5:**236
    see also Reincarnation beliefs
immortality of yogi
    Santal, **3:**255
infants become wandering spirits
    Lobi-Dagarti peoples, **9:**186
as inversion of living world
    Kongo, **9:**168
as journey
    Balinese, **5:**37
    Bonerate, **5:**46
    Bulgarians, **4:**45
    Chinese in Southeast Asia, **5:**78
    Hmong, **5:**95
    Kaluli, **2:**103
    Khevsur, **6:**197
    Melanau, **5:**180
    Modang, **5:**187
    Moldovans, **6:**269
    Naxi, **6:**480
    Nguna, **2:**244
    Subanun, **5:**246
    Ukrainian peasants, **6:**388
    Yakan, **5:**290
as joyless existence
    Chamacoco, **7:**110
judgment
    Bengali Muslims, **3:**34
    Greeks, **4:**134
    Muong, **5:**192
    Old Believers, **1:**274
    Parsi, **3:**230
    Pathan, **3:**233
    Somalis, **9:**318
    Tajiks, **6:**354
    Tigray, **9:**349
    Tikopia, **2:**326
    Yemenis, **9:**390
    Zoroastrians, **9:**410
judgment day in Jerusalem
    Palestinians, **9:**266
judgment on two levels
    Nubians, **9:**248
as kachina village heaven
    Zuni, **1:**400
Land of the Coyote
    Western Shoshone, **1:**375
Land of the Dead
    Central Yup'ik Eskimos, **1:**59
    Chin, **3:**64
    Guahibo-Sikuani, **7:**166
    Mohave, **1:**242
    Pima-Papago, **1:**290
    Quechan, **1:**302
    Toda, **3:**297, 298
Land of the Souls
    Haida, **1:**136
as land where everything is clean and no
        suffering exists
    Pume, **7:**285
Land of Wolf and Coyote
    Northern Shoshone and Bannock,
        1:268
life essence regenerated in decendants
    Tz'utujil, **8:**298
life flows backwards
    Selkup, **6:**328

life force returns symbolically to mother's
        womb
    Warao, **7:**359
lower world with similar life to ordinary
        world
    Tanaina, **1:**337
as many-storied white building
    Khevsur, **6:**197
Milky Way as path to peninsula of the
        dead
    Guajiro, **7:**170
Milky Way as path to Spirit Village, **1:**346
as minor concern
    Faroe Islanders, **4:**100
mirroring living world
    Ewe and Fon, **9:**88
    Igbo, **9:**123
    Iraqw, **9:**126
as modern city with golden commodities
    Cuna, **7:**151
multiple
    Ata Sikka, **5:**22
    Ata Tana 'Ai, **5:**26
    Bugis, **5:**51
    Dobu, **2:**52
    Garia, **2:**76
    Marquesas Islands, **2:**191
    Palu'e, **5:**209
    Siwai, **2:**304
    Tikopia, **2:**326
    see also subhead heaven, hell, or purgatory
        above
multiple soul resides in sky or is reincar-
        nated
    Yoruba, **9:**393
narrow road leading to Paradise
    Nagas, **3:**191
as negative deity
    Chorote, **7:**126
as neither desirable nor happy
    Navajo, **1:**253
as next life
    Awá Kwaiker, **7:**65
    Kuna, **8:**150
nine steps to underworld
    Chatino, **8:**52
as nothingness
    Tahiti, **2:**307
only for disciplined community members
    Mennonites, **1:**220
on other side of body of water
    Kongo, **9:**168
passage through four layers to land of plenty
        far to south
    Quechan, **1:**302
pass into spiritual realm
    San-speaking peoples, **9:**304
pictoral representations
    Yukateko, **8:**310
as place of abundance with no strife nor
        need to work
    Mehinaku, **7:**239
as place where people lived before being
        born
    Tatuyo, **7:**324
purgatory followed by upper world irregard-
        less of past conduct
    Palikur, **7:**264

purification by flame prior journey to
        heaven
    Mixe, **8:**175
as reality
    Mescalero Apache, **1:**225
as recycling of soul
    Iban, **5:**99
reincarnation. *See* Reincarnation beliefs
replicates ordinary world
    Barí, **7:**85
    Dusun, **5:**83
    Evenki (Northern Tungus), **6:**123
    Han, **6:**447
    Itelmen, **6:**154
    Kalingas, **5:**123
    Kwakiutl, **1:**200
    Luba of Shaba, **9:**193
    Manchu, **6:**468
    Mataco, **7:**229
    Melanau, **5:**180
    Mixtec, **8:**178
    Miyanmin, **2:**212
    Nganasan, **6:**282
    Nias, **5:**197
    Rutuls, **6:**321
    Seri, **8:**235
    Svans, **6:**346
    Tabasarans, **6:**351
    Tairora, **2:**310
    Tasmanians, **2:**317
    Tiwi, **2:**329
    Ute, **1:**362
    Waorani, **7:**353
    Xikrin, **7:**369
    Yukpa, **7:**385
replicates ordinary world (but pleasant and
        peaceful)
    Karihona, **7:**193-194
    Pima-Papago, **1:**290
    Southern Paiute (and Chemehuevi),
        1:333
replicates ordinary world (but with plenty
        of hunting, drinking, and feasting)
    Nagas, **3:**191
as residence with Supreme Being
    Candoshi, **7:**94
resurrection
    Falasha, **9:**92
resurrection after long wait
    Turks, **9:**376
as return to house of father
    Mehinaku, **7:**239
as reunification with loved ones
    Gaels (Irish), **4:**117
as reunion with ancestors
    Apalai, **7:**47
as reversal of ordinary world
    Koryaks and Kerek, **6:**210
    Southern Paiute (and Chemehuevi),
        1:332
    Tauade, **2:**320
    Tofalar, **6:**363
    Wovan, **2:**387
rewards
    Fulani, **9:**103
    Santal, **3:**255
shadow roams earth until controlled by
        shaman

Emberá, 7:158
in sky
  Herero, 9:118
  Ojibwa, 1:271
in sky with happy place for rich people
  Karak, 1:177
soul accompanied by cattle
  Tandroy, 9:338
soul accompanied by souls of grave goods
  Micmac, 1:235
soul and shade distinction
  Amuesha, 7:39
  Amuzgo, 8:6
  Maká, 7:218
  Tanaina, 1:337
  Wayãpi, 7:364
soul assists sun
  Tz'utujil, 8:298
soul asumes shape of insect
  Bretons, 4:40
soul becomes bird
  Guarijío, 8:119
soul becomes ghost
  Zande, 9:399, 400
soul crosses bridge
  Zoroastrians, 9:410
soul free to roam
  Tuareg, 9:369
soul journeys west
  Cuicatec, 8:93
soul journeys to west or northwest
  Yokuts, 1:389
soul reenters pregnant woman's womb
  Rukuba, 9:291
soul remains with body
  Abkhazians, 6:9
soul retraces life
  Huichol, 8:128
soul roams near grave
  Tuareg, 9:369
souls come down to earth
  Otomí of the Valley of Mezquital, 8:206
soul separates from body
  Zoque, 8:317
soul stays in shooting star
  Rukuba, 9:291
soul takes year to reach God
  Greeks, 4:134
soul travels long distance on dangerous road
    fraught with temptations
  Guarayu, 7:174-175
special region for shamans
  Karihona, 7:194
specific ordinary location
  Bukidnon, 5:55
  Choiseul Island, 2:40
  Endenese, 5:86
  Goodenough Island, 2:88
  Kiribati, 2:123
  Rossel Island, 2:280
  Rotuma, 2:283
  Tairora, 2:310
  Trobriand Islands, 2:351
  Yangoru Boiken, 2:390
spirit endures emotional and material
    deprivation
  Sora, 3:270
spirit guides to final resting place

Tanana, 1:340
spirit in heart becomes jaguar
  Waorani, 7:353
spirit hovers about village and maintains
    interest in life there
  Bhil, 3:42
spirit instructed on arduous journey to next
    world
  Winnebago, 1:382
spirit interacts with living
  Bhil, 1:42
  Koya, 3:142
  Menominee, 1:222
  Rom of Czechoslovakia, 4:219
  Sea Islanders, 1:311
  Sora, 3:270
  Suku, 9:323
  Vedda, 3:303
spirit lingers near or in village
  Koya, 3:142
spirit purified by shaman to enter world of
    the dead
  Guambiano, 7:173
spirit reflects qualities in life
  Bhil, 3:42
spirits continue to exist
  Acholi, 9:6
  Creoles of Nicaragua, 8:86
spirits dwell near former home
  Mixe, 8:175
spirits roam earth retracing steps traveled in
    life
  Rom, 1:306
spirits roams in forest until annual celebra-
    tion returns to community of spirits
  Nayaka, 3:196
spirit takes on snake form
  Swazi, 9:333
spiritual realm where deceased become
    dimly remembered ancestors
  Kpelle, 9:174
  Lango, 9:182
  Lobi-Dagarti peoples, 9:186
  Tonga, 9:355
as stars
  Tongareva, 2:341
for suicides. _See_ Suicide, beliefs about
three types depending on past life
  Yurok, 1:396
  see also subhead heaven, hell, or purgatory
    above
as timeless/spaceless relationship with God
  English, 4:97
as torture
  Tor, 2:344
as transfer to new residence
  Finns, 4:104
as transition to ultimate reincarnation
  Tlingit, 1:353
two souls
  Ibibio, 9:120
two spirits
  Betsileo, 9:57
underwater
  Yurok, 1:396
underworld
  Ajië, 2:10
  Chamorros, 2:34

Fipa, 9:100
Ingalik, 1:159
Malekula, 2:166
Maori, 2:178
Mikir, 3:176
Mimika, 2:208
Nivkh, 6:285
Saami, 4:222
Telefolmin, 2:323
Washoe, 1:370
underworld (with pleasures denied in upper
    world)
  Pukapuka, 2:273
vague
  Agta, 5:6
  Alorese, 5:16
  Cotopaxi Quichua, 7:135
  Korean, 5:148
  Melanau, 5:180
  Orokolo, 2:260
  Pintupi, 2:267
  Senoi, 5:239
  Western Apache, 1:373
village of the dead
  Thadou, 3:289
walking down road filled with obstacles to
    beautiful country
  Miami, 1:232
as well-stocked room
  Circassians, 6:91
as westward land of the dead
  Maricopa, 1:216
  Montagnais-Naskapi, 1:246
  Ojibwa, 1:271
  Terena, 7:327
as wilderness where spirits sing nocturnally
  Mbeere, 9:223
  see also Ancestral spirits; Dead, the; Ghosts;
    Mortuary practices; Reincarnation
    beliefs; Soul
Agama Nunusaku (religion)
  Ambonese, 5:19
Agastya (mythical sage)
  Malayali, 3:166
Agave. _See_ Mescal gathering
Age disparity, marital. _See_ Gerontogamy
Aged. _See_ Elderly
Age-grade. _See under_ Associations, clubs, and
    societies; _under_ Hierarchical society
Age trials _See_ Initiation rites
Aggressiveness
as basis of society
  Albanians, 4:6
  Irish Travellers, 4:156
as desirable trait
  Cretans, 4:70
  Eastern Shoshone, 1:105
  Vlach Gypsies of Hungary, 4:272
political and parochial competition
  Maltese, 4:168
toleration of
  Pasiegos, 4:191
as undesirable trait
  Central Yup'ik Eskimos, 1:61
  Cherokee, 1:61-62
  Choctaw, 1:72
  Danes, 4:90
  Divehi, 3:77, 78

Aggressiveness (cont'd)
   Kogi, 7:202
   Pima-Papago, 1:289
   Washoe, 1:369
   West Greenland Inuit, 1:377, 378
   Zuni, 1:398
   see also Avoidance
   see also Warfare; Warriors
Agha Khan followers
   Khoja, 3:127, 128
Aglipayan Church
   Tagalog, 5:250
Agnatic descent. *See* Descent, agnatic
Agnosticism
   Czechs, 4:84
   Kanjar, 3:121
   Qalandar, 3:248
   see also Atheism
Agrarian reform. *See* Landholding, land redistribution
Agriculte
   slash-and-burn
     Itza', 8:134
Agriculture
   astronomically/meteorologically based
     Ayoreo, 7:69-70
     Piapoco, 7:274
     Puinave, 7:281
   bachelors
     Finns, 4:103
     Gaels (Irish), 4:116
   burn-beating
     Finns, 4:102
   canal systems
     Mennonites, 1:217
   ceremonies and festivals. *See* Ceremonies,
     agricultural
   chateau-farms
     Walloons, 4:276
   chemical fertilizer
     Nubians, 9:247
   collective
     Poles, 4:203
     Romanians, 4:213
     Slovaks, 4:243, 244, 245
   commercial specialized
     Dutch, 4:92
   cooperatives
     Albanians, 4:4
     Bulgarians, 4:43, 44
     Czechs, 4:83
     Danes, 4:89
     Hungarians, 4:144
     Portuguese, 4:207
     Slav Macedonians, 4:240
     Slovenes, 4:247-248
   crofting work cycle
     Highland Scots, 4:139-140
     Shetlanders, 4:233
     Tory Islanders, 4:265
   crop cultivation by gender
     Kikuyu, 9:161
     Tonga, 9:353
     Tsimihety, 9:358
   crop rotation
     Anuta, 2:14
     Araucanians, 7:52
     Kashubians, 4:158

     Ndembu, 9:239
     Rotuma, 2:281
     Rukuba, 9:289
     Shetlanders, 4:233
     Slovenes, 4:247
     Tangu, 2:311
   dibble stick
     Nahua of the Huasteca, 8:185
     Tepehuan of Chihuahua, 8:252
   digging stick
     Konso, 9:169
     Miami, 1:231
     Popoluca, 8:216
     Q'anjob'al, 8:225
     Tzotzil and Tzeltal of Pantelhó, 8:276
     Yukateko, 8:309
     Zapotec, 8:312
   double-cropping
     Hausa, 9:112
     Lisu, 5:164
     Malay, 5:175
   dry cultivation
     Bondo, 3:49
     Castilians, 4:59
     Cyclades, 4:77
     Persians, 9:279
     Sicilians, 4:236
   ecozone diversificiation
     Aymara, 7:66
   encierros
     Amuzgo, 8:5
   estate farms
     Andalusians, 4:10
     Basques, 4:31
     Cape Verdeans, 4:55
     Occitans, 4:184
     Orcadians, 4:187
     Sicilians, 4:235, 236
   exclusively male labor
     Cypriots, 4:80
   export
     Costa Ricans, 8:79
   fallowing
     Nyakyusa and Ngonde, 9:253
     Tunebo, 7:337
   "feminization of"
     Serbs, 4:231
   fertilizing
     Lisu, 5:164
   flood cultivation
     Bagirmi, 9:33
     Nubians, 9:246
   food shortages
     Cubans, 8:88
   gardens. *See* Gardening
   Green revolution
     Punjabi, 3:238
     Sinhalese, 3:265
   hand cultivation
     Acholi, 9:4
     Chin, 3:63
   high-altitude
     Nepali, 3:202
     Nyinba, 3:211
   hoe use
     Acholi, 9:4
     Bamiléké, 9:38
     Chin, 3:63

     Garo, 3:82
     Gusii, 9:108
     Hausa, 9:112
     Irula, 3:104, 105
     Kanuri, 9:151
     Lakher, 3:145
     Lobi-Dagarti peoples, 9:183
     Lozi, 9:187
     Luyia, 9:204
     Mende, 9:223
     Nagas, 3:188
     Ndembu, 9:239
     Newar, 3:206
     Nyamwezi and Sukuma, 9:256
     Thadou, 3:288
     Tonga, 9:353
     Yakö, 9:384
     Yoruba, 9:391
   human fertilizer
     Lobi-Dagarti peoples, 9:183
   intercropping
     Hausa, 9:112
     Iraqw, 9:125
     Kuna, 8:147
     Yoruba, 9:391
     Zarma, 9:404
   irrigation
     Ajië, 2:7
     Akha, 5:11
     Assyrians, 9:27
     Balinese, 5:36
     Bonan, 6:422
     Bontok, 5:46
     Dani, 2:43
     Drung, 6:432
     Han, 6:442
     Hani, 6:450
     Hawaiians, 2:96
     Hmong, 5:93
     Jino, 6:460
     Kalingas, 5:122
     Lisu, 5:164
     Ma, 5:167
     Makassar, 5:172
     Malay, 5:175
     Maonan, 6:468
     Meskhetians, 6:259
     Miao, 6:470
     Mohave, 1:241
     Mongols, 6:474
     Mormons, 1:247-248
     Pamir peoples, 6:305
     Sasak, 5:226
     She, 6:489
     Southern Paiute (and Chemehuevi),
       1:331
     Tabasarans, 6:348
     Tairora, 2:308
     Tewa Pueblos, 1:348
     Tibetans, 6:494
     Tuvans, 6:373
     Uighur, 6:382, 499
     Uvea, 2:364
     Uzbeks, 6:396
     Walapai, 1:364
     Wamira, 2:365
     Western Apache, 1:372
     Zuni, 1:397

isolated family farms
    Ozarks, 1:281
luxury items
    Flemish, 4:106
machete use
    Mende, 9:223
machinery
    Poles, 4:203
milpa plots
    Nahuat of the Sierra de Puebla, 8:191
    Poqomam, 8:218
    Q'anjob'al, 8:225
    Q'eqchi', 8:226
    Tzotzil of Chamula, 8:279
    Tzotzil of San Andrés Larraínzar, 8:284
    Wasteko, 8:302
mixed cropping
    Provencal, 4:210
    Salasaca, 7:289
open field system
    Danes, 4:89
plantation
    Cape Verdeans, 4:55
    Haitians, 8:121-122
    Irula, 3:104, 105
    Jamaicans, 8:137, 138
    Mauritian, 3:171
    Montserratians, 8:180
    Puerto Ricans, 8:222
    Syrian Christian of Keral, 3:273
planting stick
    Mohave, 1:241
plow
    Amhara, 9:18
    Berbers of Morocco, 9:49
    Chocho, 8:63
    Cyclades, 4:77
    Falasha, 9:91
    Fali, 9:94
    Gusii, 9:108
    Iteso, 9:128
    Konso, 9:169
    Korku, 3:133
    Mixtec, 8:176
    Nahua of the Huasteca, 8:185
    Nandi and other Kalenjin peoples, 9:232
    Nyamwezi and Sukuma, 9:256
    Oriya, 3:216
    Pedi, 9:269
    Sara, 9:305
    Sherpa, 3:258
    Shetlanders, 4:233
    Sinhalese, 3:265
    Tamil, 3:276, 277
    Telugu, 3:285
    Tepehuan of Chihuahua, 8:252
    Tequistlatec, 8:259
    Tigray, 9:347
    Tonga, 9:353
    Tswana, 9:361
    Yemenis, 9:388
    Zapotec, 8:312
related industries
    Flemish, 4:106
rites and rituals. _See_ Ceremonies agricul-
    tural
river-bottom plots
    Hidatsa, 1:146

Mandan, 1:214
Mohave, 1:240-241
Quechan, 1:301
romanticism of
    Austria, 4:21
scattered-plot
    Cypriots, 4:80
    Hungarians, 4:143
    Leonese, 4:161
    Occitans, 4:184, 185
    Poles, 4:203
    Portuguese, 4:207
    Swedes, 4:257
sharecropping. _See_ Sharecropping
shifting
    Bemba, 9:46
    Lunda, 9:197
    Mongo, 9:226
sickle use
    Magar, 3:156
    Nagas, 3:188
slash-and-burn
    Abelam, 2:4
    Abor, 3:3, 5
    Agta, 5:5
    Aguaruna, 7:29
    Ajië, 2:7
    Akawaio, 7:31
    Akha, 5:11
    Alak, 5:13
    Algonkin, 1:17
    Alorese, 5:14
    Ambae, 2:11
    Amhara, 9:18
    Amuesha, 7:37
    Amuzgo, 8:5
    Apalai, 7:45
    Apiaká, 7:48
    Araweté, 7:56
    Atoni, 5:27
    Badaga, 3:15
    Bagirmi, 9:33
    Bagobo, 5:29
    Baiga, 3:19
    Bakairi, 7:74
    Balantak, 5:35
    Banggai, 5:38
    Baniwa-Curripaco-Wakuenai, 7:77
    Barama River Carib, 7:81
    Bau, 2:22
    Bhil, 3:38
    Bhuiya, 3:43
    Bilaan, 5:42
    Bisaya, 5:42
    Bondo, 3:49
    Bonerate, 5:44
    Brao, 5:47
    Bukidnon, 5:53
    Burmese, 5:64
    Cashibo, 7:104
    cattle ranchers of Huasteca, 8:42
    Chácobo, 7:105
    Chakma, 3:59
    Cherokee, 1:61
    Chin, 3:63
    Chinantec, 8:53
    Chiriguano, 7:120
    Chocó, 7:122

Choiseul Island, 2:38
Chontal of Tabasco, 8:68
Cinta Larga, 7:127
Cocama, 7:130
Craho, 7:136
Cubeo, 7:140
Culina, 7:146
Cuna, 7:149
Dani, 2:43
Daribi, 2:47
Desana, 7:152
Dobu, 2:50
Drung, 6:432
Emberá and Wounaan, 8:109
Endenese, 5:85
Fore, 2:63
Gainj, 2:71
Garo, 3:82, 83, 84
Gnau, 2:80
Gond, 3:85
Gorontalese, 5:90
Guadalcanal, 2:89
Guajajára, 7:166
Guarijío, 8:117
Gururumba, 2:92
Hani, 6:450
Hanunóo, 5:91
Hoti, 7:175
Huarayo, 7:177
Huichol, 8:125
Iban, 5:96
Ilongot, 5:101
Iroquois, 1:165
Irula, 3:104, 105
Isneg, 5:103
Itza', 8:134
Ixil, 8:136
Jamináwa, 7:180
Jingpo, 6:456
Jino, 6:460
Jivaro, 7:182
Kachin, 5:115
Kalagan, 5:119
Kalimantan Dayaks, 5:120
Kalingas, 5:122
Karajá, 7:188
Karen, 5:125
Kashinawa, 7:195
Kattang, 5:131
Katu, 5:131
Ka'wiari, 7:198
Kédang, 5:131
Keraki, 2:112, 114
K'iche', 8:141
Kilenge, 2:118
Kmhmu, 5:139
Koya, 3:140
Kpelle, 9:173
Krikati/Pukobye, 7:204
Kuikuru, 7:207
Kuna, 8:147
Kurtatchi, 2:131
Kurumbas, 3:143
Lahu, 5:151, 152;6:462
Lakher, 3:145
Lamaholot, 5:155
Lamet, 5:157
Lesu, 2:146

Agriculture (cont'd)
Lisu, 5:163, 164;6:465
Loven, 5:166
Luba of Shaba, 9:191
Ma, 5:167
Macuna, 7:212
Mae Enga, 2:149
Mafulu, 2:152
Maisin, 2:158
Malekula, 2:164
Manam, 2:167
Manggarai, 5:176
Manus, 2:173
Marinahua, 7:220
Maring, 2:185
Maroni Carib, 7:220
Marubo, 7:222
Mataco, 7:228
Matsigenka, 7:231
May, 5:177
Mayoruna, 7:234
Mehinaku, 7:236
Mekeo, 2:198
Miao, 6:470
Mikir, 3:175
Mimika, 2:206
Mixe, 8:173
Mixtec, 8:176, 177
Mizo, 3:178
Mnong, 5:184
Modang, 5:186
Moré, 7:242
Mountain Arapesh, 2:216
Muna, 5:189
Mundurucu, 7:244
Murut, 5:193
Muyu, 2:228
Nagas, 3:188
Nahua of the Huasteca, 8:185
Nambicuara, 7:247
Nasioi, 2:233
Ngawbe, 8:195
Nias, 5:195
Nissan, 2:249
Noanamá, 7:251
Nu, 6:480
Oraon, 3:215
Orokaiva, 2:256
Páez, 7:257
Paï-Tavytera, 7:259
Palaung, 5:201
Panare, 7:265
Paresí, 7:269
Paya, 8:209
Pemon, 7:271
Pentecost, 2:262
Piapoco, 7:274
Pima Bajo, 8:211
Popoluca, 8:216
Puinave, 7:281
Pume, 7:283
Purum, 3:243
Q'anjob'al, 8:225
Q'eqchi', 8:226
Qiang, 6:486
Rhadé, 5:212
Rikbaktsa, 7:287
Rossel Island, 2:278

Sakalava, 9:293
Salasaca, 7:289
Saliva, 7:292
Sambia, 2:284
Samoa, 2:287
Santa Cruz, 2:290
Santal, 3:253
Sara, 9:305
Saramaka, 7:296
Sedang, 5:230
Semang, 5:234
Senoi, 5:236, 237
Shan, 5:240
She, 6:489
Shipibo, 7:304
Siane, 2:298
Siona-Secoya, 7:307
Sora, 3:268-269
Stieng, 5:243
Subanun, 5:244
Suku, 9:321
Sumu, 8:237
Suruí, 7:312
Suya, 7:315
Taiwan aboriginal peoples, 5:257
Tangu, 2:311
Tanimuka, 7:318
Tanna, 2:313
Tatuyo, 7:322
Tauade, 2:318
Tau-Oi, 5:261
Tay, 5:265
Telefolmin, 2:321
Temiar, 5:266, 267
Tepehuan of Chihuahua, 8:252
Tetum, 5:276
Ticuna, 7:328
T'in, 5:278
Toda, 3:297
Tolai, 2:334
Torres Strait Islanders, 2:346
Trio, 7:335
Trobriand Islands, 2:349
Truk, 2:352
Tupari, 7:339
Tzotzil and Tzeltal of Pantelhó, 8:276
Tzotzil of San Andrés Larraínzar, 8:284
Tzotzil of Zinacantan, 8:292
Tz'utujil, 8:297
Udmurt, 6:380
Vedda, 3:301, 302
Wa, 6:502
Waimiri-Atroari, 7:343
Wáiwai, 7:346
Wamira, 2:365
Wapisiana, 7:354
Wasteko, 8:302
Waurá, 7:360
Wayapi, 7:361
Witoto, 7:364
Wogeo, 2:380
Wovan, 2:385
Xikrin, 7:367
Yagua, 7:372
Yangoru Boiken, 2:388
Yanomamö, 7:375
Yao, 6:505
Yawalapití, 7:378

Yekuana, 7:381
Yi, 6:506
Yoruba, 9:391
Yukateko, 8:309
Yukpa, 7:383
Yukuna, 7:386
slash-and-mulch
Afro-Hispanic Pacific Lowlanders, 7:20
Chocó, 7:122
Waorani, 7:352
small-plot
Galicians, 4:119, 120
Greeks, 4:132
Irish, 4:152
Montserratians, 8:180
Northern Irish, 4:178, 179
Piemontese, 4:198
Provencal, 4:210
Sicilians, 4:236
Tory Islanders, 4:265
Welsh, 4:279
spade cultivation
Shetlanders, 4:233
Tandroy, 9:336
state farms
Poles, 4:203
Romanians, 4:213
state subsidies
Germans, 4:122
subsistence
Aimaq, 9:10
Amhara, 9:18
Anuak, 9:21
Awakateko, 8:15
Bagirmi, 9:33
Bahamians, 8:18
Bamiléké, 9:38
Berbers of Morocco, 9:49
Boruca, Bribri, Cabécar, 8:27
Bugle, 8:32
Cahita, 8:35
Caquinte, 7:91
Ch'ol, 8:64
Chontal of Tabasco, 8:68
Chuj, 8:71
Cora, 8:76
Costa Ricans, 8:79
Cotopaxi Quichua, 7:133
Creoles of Nicaragua, 8:83-84
Cuicatec, 8:91
Edo, 9:79
Emberá and Wounaan, 8:109
Ewe and Fon, 9:84
Falasha, 9:91
Fali, 9:94
Fipa, 9:98
Gales (Irish), 4:115
Ganda, 9:104
Guarayu, 7:174
Guarijío, 8:117
Gusii, 9:108
Haitians, 8:121
Hazara, 9:115
Huichol, 8:125
Ibibio, 9:119
Igbo, 9:121
Iteso, 9:128
Itonama, 7:179

Konso, **9**:169
Lenca, **8**:155
Leonese, **4**:160-161
Lozi, **9**:187
Lunda, **9**:196
Makushi, **7**:218
Mam, **8**:158
Mamprusi, **9**:211
Mande, **9**:215
Mazatec, **8**:168
Mongo, **9**:226
Mount Athos, **4**:175
Movima, **7**:243
Nahua of the Huasteca, **8**:185
Nubians, **9**:246
Nuristanis, **9**:250
Nyakyusa and Ngonde, **9**:253
Nyamwezi and Sukuma, **9**:256
Okiek, **9**:259
Otavalo, **7**:253
Otomí of the Sierra, **8**:201
Ozarks, **1**:281
Pame, **8**:207
Pashai, **9**:267
Persians, **9**:279
Qashqa'i, **9**:285
Sardinians, **4**:226
Serbs, **4**:230
Shetlanders, **4**:233
Swazi, **9**:330
Tandroy, **9**:336
Tequistlatec, **8**:259
Tiv, **9**:350
Tojolab'al, **8**:261
Tory Islanders, **4**:265
Tswana, **9**:361
Tzeltal, **8**:273
Ucayalino, **7**:91
Western Apache, **1**:372
Wolof, **9**:378
Yakö, **9**:383
Yoruba, **9**:391
YörÜk, **9**:394
Zulu, **9**:411
subsistence/cash
    Wasteko, **8**:302
    Zapotec, **8**:312
swidden. _See subhead_ slash-and-burn _above_
tenant farming. _See_ Tenant farming
terraced
    Anuta, **2**:14
    Avars, **6**:44, 45
    Azoreans, **4**:27
    Basques, **4**:30-31
    Batak, **5**:39
    Bondo, **3**:49
    Burusho, **3**:55
    Chakma, **3**:58-59
    Dalmatians, **4**:86
    Ifugao, **5**:99
    Jingpo, **6**:455, 456
    Kogi, **7**:201
    Kota, **3**:136
    Lisu, **5**:164
    Magar, **3**:155
    Miao, **6**:470
    Mizo, **3**:178
    Nagas, **3**:188

Nepali, **3**:202
Pahari, **3**:219, 220
Santal, **3**:253
She, **6**:489
three-field system
    Araucanians, **7**:52
use plot
    Romanians, **4**:213
wet cultivation
    Bondo, **3**:49
    Nagas, **3**:188
    Pandit of Kashmir, **3**:224
    Santal, **3**:253
    Sinhalese, **3**:264, 265
    Sora, **3**:269
    Tamil, **3**:276, 277
    Tharu, **3**:293
    Vedda, **3**:301
    Vellala, **3**:304
see also Dairy products; Landholding;
    Livestock raising; _specific crops_
Agro-romanticism
    Austria, **4**:21
Agrotown
    Calabrese, **4**:49
Ahimsa
    Jain, **3**:109-110
Ahura Mazda (creator)
    Parsi, **3**:229
AIDS virus
    Haitians, **1**:137
    Lango, **9**:182
Alchemy
    Burmese, **5**:65
Alcohol
    abstention
        Bania, **3**:25
        Bohra, **3**:47
        Old Believers, **1**:274
    abuse
        Austrians, **4**:21
        Azoreans, **4**:29
        Highland Scots, **4**:141, 142
        Irish Travelers, **1**:164
        Irish Travellers, **4**:154
        Khanty, **6**:191
        Kikapu, **8**:145
        Kota, **3**:135
        Kutenai, **1**:197
        Lithuanians, **6**:251
        Madeirans, **4**:166
        Mescalero Apache, **1**:225
        Micmac, **1**:235
        Micronesians, **1**:238
        Montagnais-Naskapi, **1**:244
        Nguna, **2**:244
        Ojibwa, **1**:270
        Pintupi, **2**:266
        Russian peasants, **6**:313
        Russians, **6**:316
        Sea Nomads of the Andaman, **5**:229
        Shetlanders, **4**:234
        Siberiaki, **6**:334
        Tlingit, **1**:353
        Tonga, **9**:355
        Warlpiri, **2**:374
        West Greenland Inuit, **1**:378
        Wik Mungkan, **2**:379

Yap, **2**:393
aguardiente drinking
    Galicians, **4**:121
banana beer drinking
    Chagga, **9**:61
beer brewing
    Danes, **4**:89
    Santal, **3**:253
beer for circumcision initiation
    Iraqw, **9**:125
beer drinking
    Bavarians, **4**:33
    Walloons, **4**:276
beer offered to shades
    Pedi, **9**:270
beer offered to spirits
    Luba of Shaba, **9**:192
    Tonga, **9**:355
beer parties as social events
    Iteso, **9**:128
brandy making
    Romanians, **4**:213
cassava spirits
    Barama River Carib, **7**:82
    Zande, **9**:398
contraband activities
    Cotopaxi Quichua, **7**:133
drinking and dancing festival
    Piaroa, **7**:278
drinking and vomiting manioc beer cere-
        mony, **7**:148
drinking during fiestas
    Tlapanec, **8**:259
drinking as part of funeral
    Orcadians, **4**:188
drinking as ritual
    Awá Kwaiker, **7**:65
    Don Cossacks, **6**:106
    Garifuna, **8**:115
    K'iche', **8**:142
    Maká, **7**:218
    Paï-Tavytera, **7**:259, 260
    Panare, **7**:267
    Pemon, **7**:273
    Sakalava, **9**:298
    Spanish Rom, **4**:255
    Trio, **7**:336
    Yawalapití, **7**:380
drunkenness as inappropriate
    Canarians, **4**:52
as excuse for inappropriate behavior
    Culina, **7**:147
    Pume, **7**:284
gin drinking
    Walloons, **4**:276
gin production
    Ndembu, **9**:239
haoma drink
    Zoroastrians, **9**:409, 410
heavy drinking at funerals
    Araucanians, **7**:55
home-brewed beer
    San-speaking peoples, **9**:302
honey beer
    Kikuyu, **9**:161
    Mbeere, **9**:221
    Okiek, **9**:260
honey mead

Alcohol (cont'd)
    Sakalava, 9:298
  maize beer
    Lugbara, 9:194
  manioc beer drinking
    Culina, 7:148
    Mashco, 7:227
    Yagua, 7:373
  millet beer
    Fipa, 9:98
    Luba of Shaba, 9:191
    Shona, 9:313, 314
  millet beverages
    Lunda, 9:196
  missionary critics of
    Mbeere, 9:222
  palm wine
    Mijikenda, 9:224
    Suku, 9:321
    Yakö, 9:383
    Zande, 9:398
  production
    Ata Tana 'Ai, 5:23
    Guadeloupians, 8:116
    Kachin, 5:116
    Khevsur, 6:194
    Lisu, 6:465
    Svans, 6:346
    Tatars, 6:492
    Zapotec, 8:312
  prohibition
    Doukhobors, 1:92
    Mormons, 1:248
    Ngawbe, 8:197
    Palu'e, 5:206
  pub importance
    Gaels (Irish), 4:115
  rice drinks
    Lisu, 5:165
    Subanun, 5:244
    T'in, 5:279
  ritual beer
    Mbeere, 9:222
    Ndebele, 9:237
  social drinking
    K'iche', 8:142
  sorghum beer
    Lobi-Dagarti peoples, 9:183
    Luba of Shaba, 9:191
    Mossi, 9:228
  sorghum beverages
    Lunda, 9:196
  sugarcane beer
    Kikuyu, 9:161
  sugarcane rum
    Kpelle, 9:173
  susceptibility to commercial products
    Pume, 7:284
  toasting
    Georgians, 6:134
    Mountain Jews, 6:272
  use of
    Kshatriya, 3:142
    Limbu, 3:151
    Rajput, 3:249
  violence caused by
    Culina, 7:147
    Mescalero Apache, 1:225

    Micmac, 1:235
    Micronesians, 1:238
    Ngawbe, 8:197
    Pume, 7:284
    Shetlanders, 4:234
    Tonga, 9:355
    Tzotzil and Tzeltal of Pantelhó, 8:277
    Tzotzil of Chamula, 8:280
    West Greenland Inuit, 1:378
  whiskey distillation
    Tory Islanders, 4:265
  see also Wine making
Alcoholism. *See* Alcohol, abuse
Alienation
  Austrian, 4:21
  Keres Pueblo Indians, 1:181
Allopathic medicine. *See under* Medical practices and treatments
All Saints' Day
  Black Creoles of Louisiana, 1:40
  Cahita, 8:37
  Chuj, 8:74
  Mam, 8:160
  Mixtec, 8:178
  Poles, 6:309
  Portuguese, 4:208
  Saint Lucians, 8:232
  Tzotzil of Zinacantan, 8:294
  Walloons, 4:278
  Zapotec, 8:313
All Souls' Day
  Cahita, 8:37
  Cuicatec, 8:93
  Maltese, 4:169
All Souls' Eve
  Itza', 8:135
  Tory Islanders, 4:266
Alms. *See* Begging; Charitable giving
Alpaca herding
  Callahuaya, 7:88
Alphabets
  Avars, 6:44
  Azerbaijani Turks, 6:47-48
  Balkars, 6:52
  Belarussians, 6:58
  Circassians, 6:86
  Dargins, 6:96
  Dong, 6:431
  Dongxiang, 6:431
  Dungans, 6:108, 111
  Evenki (Northern Tungus), 6:124
  Georgians, 6:129
  Gypsies, 6:145
  Japanese, 5:104-105
  Kalmyks, 6:155
  Karachays, 6:158
  Kirgiz, 6:461
  Komi, 6:203
  Krymchaks, 6:213
  Kumyks, 6:220
  Kurds, 6:225
  Kyrgyz, 6:228
  Laks, 6:233
  Latvians, 6:235
  Lezgins, 6:242
  Lisu, 6:465
  Lithuanians, 6:249
  Mansi, 6:252

  Moldovans, 6:266
  Mongols, 6:474
  Mountain Jews, 6:272
  Nivkh, 6:283
  Ossetes, 6:298
  Siberian Tatars, 6:341
  Talysh, 6:355
  Tofalar, 6:361
  Tsakhurs, 6:364
  Turkmens, 6:369
  Tuvans, 6:372
  Udis, 6:375
  Udmurt, 6:379
  Uighur, 6:381, 382
  Uzbeks, 6:396
  Volga Tatars, 6:399
  Yakut, 6:404
  Yukagir, 6:411
  Zhuang, 6:509
Alternate generations principle
  Santal, 3:253
Amahuaca, 7:34
Ambilineal descent. *See* Descent, ambilineal
Amo'tken (deity)
  Flathead, 1:128
Amte'p (deity)
  Flathead, 1:128
Amulets
  Albanians, 4:6, 7
  Andamanese, 3:11
  Baffinland Inuit, 1:31
  Bedoin, 9:46
  Bengali, 3:34
  Callahuaya, 7:90
  Chagga, 9:62
  Cyclades, 4:78
  Fulani, 9:102
  Galicians, 4:120
  Hare, 1:142
  Ingalik, 1:158
  Inughuit, 1:161
  Jews of Iran, 9:141
  Jews of Kurdistan, 9:146
  Kanjar, 3:121
  Kanuri, 9:153
  Karaites, 9:155
  Lozi, 9:189
  Mikir, 3:176
  North Alaskan Eskimos, 1:261
  Pathan, 3:233
  Qalandar, 3:248
  Sadhu, 3:251
  Sherpa, 3:260
  Sora, 3:270
  Suri, 9:326
  Tamil, 3:279
  Tanana, 1:340
  Tsimihety, 9:359
  Tswana, 9:364
  Ute, 1:362
  Walapai, 1:366
  Wolof, 9:380
  Yuit, 1:392
  Zaramo, 9:403
Anabaptists
  Amish, 1:18
  Hutterites, 1:153, 154-155
  see also Mennonites

Anacona (supernatural)
  Apalai, **7:**47
  Cubeo, **7:**141
  Ka'wiari, **7:**199
  Macuna, **7:**214
  Tatuyo, **7:**323, 324
Anambé, **7:**41
Ancestor cult
  Kazakhs, **6:**181
  Kurds, **6:**227
  Kurumbas, **3:**143
  Orochi, **6:**295
  Udis, **6:**378
Ancestor pot
  Koya, **3:**139
Ancestor reincarnation
  Munda, **3:**184
Ancestor worship
  Akan, **9:**12
  Akha, **5:**13
  Ambonese, **5:**19
  Anuta, **2:**15
  Araucanians, **7:**54
  Atoni, **5:**28
  Awakateko, **8:**16, 17
  Bai, **6:**420, 421
  Balantak, **5:**35
  Bamiléké, **9:**39
  Bau, **2:**24
  Cariña, **7:**103
  Chamorros, **2:**34
  Chechen-Ingush, **6:**75
  Chinese in Canada, **1:**97
  Chinese in Southeast Asia, **5:**77
  Chinese in the United States, **1:**103
  Chukchee, **6:**77
  Coorg, **3:**74
  Dogon, **9:**73
  Endenese, **5:**86
  Ewenki, **6:**434
  Fali, **9:**96
  Gelao, **6:**435
  Haitians, **8:**122
  Hakka, **6:**438
  Han, **6:**447
  Hani, **6:**451
  Ibaloi, **5:**95
  Ibibio, **9:**120
  Jamaicans, **8:**139
  Jino, **6:**460
  Kazakhs, **6:**181
  Kerintji, **5:**134
  Khasi, **3:**125
  Korean, **5:**148
  Koreans, **6:**206
  Koryaks and Kerek, **6:**208, 209
  Koya, **3:**141
  Kriashen Tatars, **6:**212
  Lau, **2:**145
  Li, **6:**464
  Lobi-Dagarti peoples, **9:**185
  Lugbara, **9:**195
  Luo, **9:**200
  Magar, **3:**161, 162
  Manchu, **6:**468
  Mansi, **6:**254
  Maonan, **6:**468
  Maring, **2:**187

  Maris, **6:**257
  Mendi, **2:**205
  Mongo, **9:**226-227
  Mulam, **6:**477
  Munda, **3:**184
  Muong, **5:**192
  Nepali, **3:**205
  Newar, **3:**208
  Nias, **5:**197
  Nomoi, **2:**252
  Nyamwezi and Sukuma, **9:**257
  Nyinga, **3:**213
  Oriya, **3:**216
  Orochi, **6:**295
  Oroquen, **6:**483
  Pandit of Kashmir, **3:**226
  Pedi, **9:**270
  Pende, **9:**273-274
  Rennell Island, **2:**277
  Rotuma, **2:**283
  Sakalava, **9:**297-298
  Saluan, **5:**217
  Samoa, **2:**288
  San Cristobal, **2:**289
  Santal, **3:**255
  Saramaka, **7:**298
  Sasak, **5:**225, 227
  Selepet, **2:**294-295
  Shona, **9:**314
  Sio, **2:**301
  South and Southeast Asians of Canada, **1:**324
  Swazi, **9:**332
  Taiwan aboriginal peoples, **5:**258
  Tanna, **2:**315
  Toraja, **5:**283
  Triqui, **8:**272
  Tswana, **9:**363
  Tujia, **6:**498
  Tuvalu, **2:**356, 357
  Ukrainian peasants, **6:**387, 388
  Ukrainians, **6:**394
  Vedda, **3:**302, 303
  Vietnamese, **5:**286
  Wa, **6:**503
  Warao, **7:**359
  Waropen, **2:**376
  Xibe, **6:**504
  Yukuna, **7:**389
  Zande, **9:**399
  Zhuang, **6:**511
  Zulu, **9:**412
  see also Afterlife; Ceremonies, ancestor; Sacrifice, for ancestors; Spirits, ancestral
Ancestral house
  Coorg, **3:**74
Ancestral landholding. _See_ Landholding, ancestral claims
Ancestral shrine and platform
  Coorg, **3:**74
Ancestral spirits
  Achang, **6:**418
  Anuta, **2:**15
  Asmat, **2:**20
  Baiga, **3:**21
  Balinese, **5:**37
  Banggai, **5:**38
  Bhil, **3:**41

  Bhuiya, **3:**45
  Chambri, **2:**32
  Chimbu, **2:**37
  Dai, **6:**427
  Eipo, **2:**58
  Fore, **2:**64
  Gainj, **2:**73
  Garia, **2:**76
  Gnau, **2:**82
  Gond, **3:**85, 86, 87
  Goodenough Island, **2:**88
  Guadalcanal, **2:**91
  Hawaiians, **2:**97
  Hill Pandaram, **3:**100
  Hmong, **5:**94
  Irula, **3:**105, 108, 109
  Jingpo, **6:**459
  Kachin, **5:**118
  Kewa, **2:**117
  Khmer, **5:**136
  Kickapoo, **1:**186
  Kmhmu, **5:**141
  Koryaks and Kerek, **6:**209
  Lisu, **5:**166
  Magar, **3:**162
  Mailu, **2:**156
  Makassar, **5:**173
  Malaita, **2:**163
  Manggarai, **5:**176
  Manus, **2:**175
  Maring, **2:**187, 188
  Maris, **6:**258
  Marshall Islands, **2:**194
  Mekeo, **2:**199
  Mendi, **2:**205
  Mnong, **5:**185
  Moluccans—South, **5:**188
  Motu, **2:**215
  Mountain Arapesh, **2:**217
  Murik, **2:**222
  Muyu, **2:**229, 230
  Namau, **2:**232
  Nayaka, **3:**196
  Nias, **5:**196
  Ontong Java, **2:**255
  Oriya, **3:**218
  Pahari, **3:**223
  Pamir Peoples, **6:**304
  Pentecost, **2:**264
  Qiang, **6:**487
  Rotinese, **5:**214
  Rotuma, **2:**283
  Sagada Igorot, **5:**217
  Samal, **5:**221
  Sasak, **5:**227
  Siberiaki, **6:**334
  Sora, **3:**269, 270
  Subanun, **5:**246
  Tikopia, **2:**326
  T'in, **5:**279, 280
  Trobriand Islands, **2:**349
  Ulithi, **2:**360
  Vietnamese, **5:**287
  Wantoat, **2:**370
  Wape, **2:**372
  Warlpiri, **2:**374
  Yangoru Boiken, **2:**390
  see also Ghosts

Ancestry
  belief in common. *See* Apical ancestry
  mythical
    Abor, **3**:4
Anchovy fishing
  Basques, **4**:31
Anger repression
  Kuikuru, **7**:208
Anglicanism
  Ambae, **2**:11
  Antigua and Barbuda, **8**:9, 10
  Anuta, **2**:15
  Baffinland Inuit, **1**:31
  Barbadians, **8**:23
  Black West Indians in the United States,
      1:46
  Cape Coloureds, **9**:59
  Chinese in Caribbean, **8**:58
  Chorote, **7**:126
  English, **4**:97
  English-Canadians, **1**:121
  Gainj, **2**:71
  Grenadians, **8**:116
  Guadalcanal, **2**:89
  Indian Christians, **3**:103
  Japanese in Canada, **1**:98
  Kittsians and Nevisians, **8**:145
  Kwakiutl, **1**:198, 199
  Lowland Scots, **4**:163
  Maisin, **2**:157, 159
  Malaita, **2**:163
  Manx, **4**:171
  Mataco, **7**:229
  Mbeere, **9**:222
  Montserratians, **8**:181
  North Alaskan Eskimos, **1**:261
  Northern Shoshone and Bannock, **1**:267
  Ojibwa, **1**:270
  Orokaiva, **2**:257
  Ottawa, **1**:280
  Palestinians, **9**:266
  Pentecost, **2**:261, 262
  Santa Cruz, **2**:290
  Syrian Christians of Keral, **3**:274
  Tanana, **1**:338, 340
  Toda, **3**:297
  Torres Strait Islanders, **2**:345, 347
  Trinidadians and Tobagonians, **8**:269
  Turks and Caicos Islanders, **8**:273
  Wamira, **2**:365
  Welsh, **4**:280
  Wovan, **2**:385
  Yir Yoront, **2**:395
Animal actors
  Southern Paiute (and Chemehuevi), **1**:332
Animal breeding. *See specific kinds of animals*
Animal clan names
  Miami, **1**:231
  Winnebago, **1**:382
Animal dealers
  peripatetics of Afghanistan, Iran, and
      Turkey, **9**:275
  peripatetics of the Maghreb, **9**:278
  see also Horse trading
Animal husbandry. *See* Livestock raising;
    specific kinds of animals
Animal nicknames
  Maliseet, **1**:211

Animal offerings. *See* Sacrifice, animal
Animal reverence
  Ahir, **3**:7
  Bania, **3**:25
  Chin, **3**:64
  Croats, **4**:74
  Gujarati, **3**:92
  Kalasha, **3**:116
  Kiowa, **1**:188
  Mangbetu, **9**:217
  Pandit of Kashmir, **3**:224-225
  Toda, **3**:297, 298
  see also Taboos, animal; Vegetarianism;
      Zootheism
Animals
  appeasement before and after hunt
    Yuit, **1**:392
  chicken divination
    Nyamwezi and Sukuma, **9**:257
  demonic
    Mataco, **7**:227
  domestication
    Acholi, **9**:4
    Basseri, **9**:41
    Dogon, **9**:72
    Edo, **9**:79
    Kongo, **9**:167
    Kurds, **9**:175
    Lakandon, **8**:154
    Lenca, **8**:155
    Lozi, **9**:187
    Luba of Shaba, **9**:191
    North Alaskan Eskimos, **1**:259
    Seri, **8**:233
    Shahsevan, **9**:308
    Suku, **9**:321
    Sumu, **8**:237
    Tepehuan of Durango, **8**:256
    Wolof, **9**:378
    Yakö, **9**:383
    Zande, **9**:398
    see also Livestock; *specific animals*
  having human attributes in past
    Pomo, **1**:295
  as human ancestors
    Northern Paiute, **1**:265
  human transformation into
    Osage, **1**:278
  medicinal use of parts
    Nagas, **3**:191
  mythical with human traits
    Ute, **1**:362
    Yukagir, **6**:413
  possessing souls
    Cuna, **7**:151
    West Greenland Inuit, **1**:378
    Yuit, **1**:392
  possessing spirit
    Montagnais-Naskapi, **1**:246
  as protectors or spirits
    Choctaw, **1**:73
    Comanche, **1**:75
    Cree, **1**:82
    Dogrib, **1**:89
    Hopi, **1**:150
    Jicarilla, **1**:174
    Kiowa, **1**:188
    Koya, **1**:340

    Kumeyaay, **1**:195
    Labrador Inuit, **1**:202
    Maliseet, **1**:212, 213
    Mazatec, **8**:169
    Mixe, **8**:175
    Nubians, **9**:248
    Pame, **8**:208
    Slavey, **1**:320
    Tanaina, **1**:336
    Tanana, **1**:349
    Teton, **1**:346
    Thompson, **1**:350
    Tubatulabal, **1**:355
    Tzotzil of San Andrés Larraínzar, **8**:285
    Washoe, **1**:370
    Winnebago, **1**:382
    Zapotec, **8**:313
    Zoque, **8**:316
  in religious beliefs
    Cuna, **7**:151
    Guahibo-Sikuani, **7**:166
    Huarayo, **7**:178
    Macuna, **7**:214
    Mashco, **7**:226, 227
    Matsigenka, **7**:232
    Netsilik Inuit, **1**:254
    Northern Shoshone and Bannock, **1**:267
    Piaroa, **7**:278
    Piro, **7**:280
    Rikbaktsa, **7**:288
    Salasaca, **7**:291
    Saramaka, **7**:298
    Suya, **7**:317
    Tanana, **1**:340
    Tupari, **7**:340
    Waimiri-Atroari, **7**:344
    Wanano, **7**:350
    Waorani, **7**:353
    Wapisiana, **7**:356
    Yukpa, **7**:384
    Yukuna, **7**:389
    Yuqui, **7**:394
    see also Animal reverence; Sacrifice,
        animal; Zootheism
  separation of sea and land
    Copper Eskimo, **1**:78
  supernatural
    Northern Paiute, **1**:264
  witch manipulation of
    Iraqw, **9**:126
  see also Hunting; *specific animals*
Animal sacrifice. *See* Sacrifice, animal
Animal spirits. *See* Animals, as protectors or
    spirits
Animal taboos. *See* Taboos, animal
Animal totems
  Abenaki, **1**:4
  Caribou Inuit, **1**:51
  Cocopa, **1**:74
  Hare, **1**:142
  Ingalik, **1**:158
  Jicarilla, **1**:174
  Kiowa, **1**:188
  Kumeyaay, **1**:195
  Lobi-Dagarti peoples, **9**:184
  Maratha, **3**:169
  Mossi, **9**:229
  Ndebele, **9**:236

Animal trainers
    Bulgarian Gypsies, 4:41
    Gypsies and caravan dwellers in the
        Netherlands, 4:137
    peripatetics, 1:287
    Qalandar, 3:245, 246, 247
Animal worship. _See_ Zootheism
Animism
    Abor, 3:5
    Agta, 5:6
    Akha, 5:13
    Alak, 5:13
    Andamanese, 3:11
    Asmat, 2:20
    Azerbaijani Turks, 6:50
    Balinese, 5:37
    Baul, 3:26
    Bhil, 3:41
    Bisaya, 5:43
    Central Thai, 5:71
    Chaobon, 5:74
    Chechen-Ingush, 6:75
    Chukchee, 6:78-79
    Comanche, 1:75
    Cree, 1:82
    Delaware, 1:86
    Drung, 6:432
    Dusun, 5:83
    Eastern Shoshone, 1:106
    Even, 6:119
    Ewenki, 6:434
    Filipino, 5:86, 87
    Fox, 1:130
    Gond, 3:86
    Goodenough Island, 2:88
    Gujarati, 3:92
    Hani, 6:451
    Hare, 1:141
    Hidsata, 1:147
    Hill Pandaram, 3:100
    Huron, 1:152
    Ingalik, 1:158
    Inughuit, 1:161
    Irula, 3:104
    Jino, 6:460
    Karelians, 6:172
    Karen, 5:128, 129
    Kashubians, 4:159
    Kerintji, 5:134
    Khmer, 5:137
    Kickapoo, 1:185
    Kikapu, 8:145
    Kiowa, 1:188
    Komi, 6:204
    Korean, 5:148
    Kpelle, 9:174
    Kriashen Tatars, 6:211
    Kumeyaay, 1:195
    Kwakiutl, 1:199
    Kyrgyz, 6:229
    Lakher, 3:147
    Lao, 5:157, 158, 159
    Lawa, 5:163
    Li, 6:464
    Limbu, 3:150-151
    Loven, 5:166
    Mae Enga, 2:150
    Malay, 5:176

    Mandan, 1:215
    Maris, 6:258
    Menominee, 1:222
    Mescalero Apache, 1:225
    Micronesians, 1:238
    Mikir, 3:176
    Moluccans—North, 5:188
    Mongols, 6:476
    Montagnais-Naskapi, 1:246
    Mulam, 6:477
    Munda, 3:184
    Muong, 5:191
    Nagas, 3:190
    Nanai, 6:276
    Navajo, 1:253
    Naxi, 6:479
    Nayaka, 3:196
    Nepali, 3:205
    Nez Percé, 1:254
    Nicobarese, 3:210
    Nivkh, 6:285
    Nogays, 6:289
    North Alaskan Eskimos, 1:261
    Northern Paiute, 1:264
    Okanagon, 1:272
    Orokaiva, 2:257
    Orokolo, 2:260
    Oroquen, 6:483
    Ossetes, 6:301
    Paniyan, 3:227
    Philippine Negritos, 5:210
    Pomo, 1:295
    Ponca, 1:296
    Powhatan, 1:297
    Qiang, 6:487
    Rotuma, 2:283
    Saami, 4:222
    Sambia, 2:285
    Santal, 3:254-255
    Sea Nomads of the Andaman, 5:228
    Selung/Moken, 5:232
    Seminole, 1:313
    Senoi, 5:238
    Shors, 6:331
    Shuswap, 1:318
    Slavey, 1:320
    Southern Paiute (and Chemehuevi), 1:332
    Swedes, 4:258
    Tajik, 6:492
    Tanaina, 1:336
    Taos, 1:343
    Temiar, 5:271
    Teton, 1:346
    Tewa Pueblos, 1:349
    Thakali, 3:291, 292
    Tlingit, 1:353
    Toda, 3:297
    Tomini, 5:280
    Tuvalu, 2:357
    Ukrainians, 6:394
    Vietnamese, 5:286
    Wa, 6:503
    Walapai, 1:365
    Washoe, 1:370
    Western Apache, 1:373
    Western Shoshone, 1:375
    West Greenland Inuit, 1:378
    Wichita, 1:379

    Winnebago, 1:382
    Woleai, 2:384
    Yakut, 6:406
    Yap, 2:394
    Yuit, 1:392
    see also Anthropomorphic beings; Nature
        spirits; Nature worship
Ankou (death figure)
    Bretons, 4:40
Annulment
    Bhil, 3:40
    Macuna, 7:213
    Piemontese, 4:198
Antelope hunting
    Jicarilla, 1:172
    Tubatulabal, 1:355
    Western Shoshone, 1:374
Anthropomorphic beings
    Bunun, 5:57-58
    Choctaw, 1:72
    Goodenough Island, 2:88
    Klamath, 1:192
    Miami, 1:232
    Northern Paiute, 1:264
    Southern Paiute (and Chemehuevi), 1:332
    Tairora, 2:309
    Western Apache, 1:373
    see also Animism; Nature spirits
Antiaggressiveness. _See_ Aggression, as unde-
    sirable trait
Anticlericism
    Orcadians, 4:188
    Portuguese, 4:208
Antiques trade
    Manx, 4:170
    Vlach Gypsies of Hungary, 4:271
Anugraha belief
    Pandit of Kashmir, 3:226
Aowasa (ceremony)
    Dai, 6:427
Aphorism use
    Bretons, 4:39
Apical ancestry. _See_ Descent, apical
Apocalypse belief. _See_ Ghost Dance;
    Millenarianism beliefs
Apostolic groups
    Tonga, 9:355
Apparel. _See_ Clothing
Appearance, distinctive
    Andamanese, 3:11
    Kond, 3:133
    Sikh, 3:261
    see also Clothing, distinctive
Appearances, keeping up. _See_ Public
    esteem
Appetite suppression
    Goodenough Island, 2:88
Appi (creator deity)
    Northern Shoshone and Bannock, 1:267
Appliqué
    Bukidnon, 5:55
    Lahu, 5:154
Appliqué work
    Oriya, 3:218
Apprenticeship
    Flemish, 4:107
    German Swiss, 4:125
    Torres Strait Islanders, 2:347

Apricot growing
  Pahari, 3:220
  willing of trees
    Burusho, 3:56
Arbitration. See under Conflict resolution
Archaeological sites
  Aleut, 1:14-15
Architecture
  Andis, 6:24
  Armenians, 6:28
  Avars, 6:44
  Azerbaijani Turks, 6:48
  Belarussians, 6:59
  Bengali, 3:34
  Bretons, 4:40
  Castilians, 4:61
  Chechen-Ingush, 6:75
  Croats, 4:75
  Dargins, 6:98
  Dong, 6:431
  English, 4:97
  Finns, 4:104
  Flemish, 4:106
  Frisians, 4:110, 111, 112
  German Swiss, 4:125
  Iatmul, 2:98
  Khmer, 5:138
  Lao Isan, 5:163
  Lithuanians, 6:251
  Madeirans, 4:164-165, 166
  Minangkabau, 5:184
  Mormons, 1:247
  Muslim, 3:185
  Newar, 3:208
  Nias, 5:195
  Oriya, 3:218
  Pahari, 3:223
  Punjabi, 3:242
  Rajput, 3:249
  Sambia, 2:286
  Tabasarans, 6:350
  Tamil, 3:279
  Tsakhurs, 6:367
  Uighur, 6:384
  Uzbeks, 6:396
  Vietnamese, 5:287
  Volga Tatars, 6:400
  see also Decorative arts; Houses and housing
Arctic environment
  Baffinland Inuit, 1:28, 29
  Caribou Inuit, 1:51
  Copper Eskimo, 1:76
  Eskimo, 1:107
  Netsilik Inuit, 1:254
  Saami, 4:220-221
Arctic hysteria
  Evenki (Northern Tungus), 6:123
Aristocracy. See Hierarchical society
Armenian Apostolic Church
  Armenians, 4:81;6:28
Armenian Catholic Church
  Armenians, 6:28
Armenian Christian Church
  Armenians, 6:28, 31
Armeno-Gregorian (religion)
  Tats, 6:360
  Udis, 6:375, 378
Arms industry. See Weapons industry

Army. See Military service
Arnapkapfaluk (Copper Eskimo deity), 1:78
Arranged marriage. See under Marriage
Arrowroot
  Marshall Islands, 2:192
  Niue, 2:251
  Wamira, 2:365
Art. See Decorative art; Paintings; Sculpture;
    Visual arts
Arthurian legend
  Cornish, 4:64
Artisans. See Decorative arts; specific crafts and
    specialties
Asceticism
  Baul, 3:26
  Bengali Shakta, 3:35
  Bengali Vaishnava, 3:36
  Jain, 3:109-110
  Sadhu, 3:252-252
Ashaninca (Campa group), 7:91
Ashrams
  Baul, 3:26
  Bengali Shakta, 3:35
  Pandit of Kashmir, 3:226
Ashura (ceremony)
  Azerbaijani Turks, 6:50
Assembly
  Santal, 3:254
Assembly of God
  Mamprusi, 9:214
  Nyakyusa and Ngonde, 9:254
  Washoe, 1:370
  Western Apache, 1:373
Assembly industries
  Dominicans, 8:101
Assimilation
  Armenian-Americans, 1:108
  Austrian-Americans, 1:108
  Coeur d'Alène, 1:74
  German-Americans, 1:111
  Han, 1:139
  Illinois, 1:156
  Jews of Algeria, 9:137-138
  Kalispel, 1:175
  Kansa, 1:175
  Klallam, 1:190
  Klamath, 1:190, 191
  Klikitat, 1:192
  Lake, 1:202
  Lepcha, 3:148
  Metoac, 1:230
  Miami, 1:230, 231
  Missouri, 1:239
  Polynesians, 1:291
  Spanish-Canadians, 1:127
  Swedish-Canadians, 1:127
  Swiss-Canadians, 1:127
  into Vellala, 3:303
  Vlachs, 4:273, 274
Assimilation, government programs
  for Bulgarian Gypsies, 4:41
  for Gitanos, 4:128, 129
  for Irish Travellers, 4:155
  for Ladin, 4:160
  for peripatetics, 4:196
  for Piemontese Sinti, 4:200
  for Pomaks, 4:205
  for Rom of Czechoslovakia, 4:218

  for Saami, 4:220
  for Slovaks, 4:242
  for Slovensko Roma, 4:250
  for Ukrainians of Canada, 1:357
  for Xoraxané Romá, 4:281
Associations, clubs, and societies
  age-graded
    Blackfoot, 1:42
    Gros Ventre, 1:134
  brotherhoods
    Afro-Venezuelans, 7:27
    Albanians, 4:6
    Andalusians, 4:12
    Cheyenne, 1:65
    Mennonites, 1:219
    Portuguese, 4:208
    Tewa Pueblos, 1:349
    Vlach Gypsies of Hungary, 4:271, 277
  Canarians, 4:52
  ceremonial
    Hopi, 1:150
    Kwakiutl, 1:200
    Menominee, 1:222
    Sarsi, 1:308
    see also Kachinas
  cultural identity
    Castilians, 4:60
    Chinese in Southeast Asia, 5:76-77
    Czech-Canadians, 1:120
    East Asians of Canada, 1:97
    East Asians of the United States, 1:102
    Greek-speaking Jews of Greece, 4:135
    Jews, 1:169-170
    Klingit, 1:352
    Micronesians, 1:238
    Northern Irish, 4:179
    Polish-Canadians, 1:125
    Serbian-Canadians, 1:126
    Slovene-Americans, 1:117
    Sorbs, 4:253
    South and Southeast Asians of Canada,
      1:323
    Swiss, Italian, 4:261
    Ukrainians of Canada, 1:358
  to emulate upper-caste behavior
    Jatav, 3:115
  fraternal orders
    Andalusians, 4:12
    Castilians, 4:60
  freemasonry
    Flemish, 4:108
    Jatav, 3:114
    Mahar, 3:164
  funeral
    Laks, 6:234
    Rapa, 2:275
  hunters and warriors
    Pawnee, 1:285
  medicine men
    Pawnee, 1:285
  men's
    Blackfoot, 1:42
    Cheyenne, 1:65
    Eipo, 2:56, 57
    Gorotire, 7:163
    Hopi, 1:150
    Kurtatchi, 2:131, 132
    Kwoma, 2:134

Lak, **2:**137, 138
Mandan, **1:**214, 215
Pamir peoples, **6:**304
Rutuls, **6:**318, 320
Sambia, **2:**285
Santa Cruz, **2:**291
Sindhi, **3:**263
Sio, **2:**300, 301
Siwai, **2:**302
Wamira, **2:**367
Xikrin, **7:**369
military and social
Crow, **1:**83
Gros Ventre, **1:**134
special interests
Fox, **1:**129
military police
Pawnee, **1:**285
mutual-aid societies
Aveyronnais, **4:**24
religious
Tiroleans, **4:**264
religious social
Mormons, **1:**248
Tewa Pueblos, **1:**349
secret
Ambonese, **5:**17
Bamiléké, **9:**40
Chinese in Southeast Asia, **5:**77
East Asians of the United States, **1:**102
Keres Pueblo Indians, **1:**181
Kpelle, 173;**9:**174
Lobi-Dagarti peoples, **9:**185-186
Mende, **9:**223
sectarian
Northern Irish, **4:**179
shamans
Pawnee, **1:**286
sodalities. _See subhead_ brotherhoods _above_
sorcerers
Potawatomi, **1:**297
trade
Belau, **2:**27
voluntary common-interest
Danes, **4:**89, 90
Germans, **4:**123
Norwegians, **4:**181
Slovaks, **4:**245
Walloons, **4:**277
war society
Yakö, **9:**386
women's
Blackfoot, **1:**42
Cheyenne, **1:**65
Gorotire, **7:**163
Hopi, **1:**150
Mandan, **1:**215
Wamira, **2:**367
Xikrin, **7:**369
young men's
Belau, **2:**26
Garia, **2:**75
Kubachins, **6:**218
Mikir, **3:**176
Rapa, **2:**275
Romanians, **4:**214
Wamira, **2:**367
youth

African Americans, **1:**12
Arab Americans, **1:**24
Miao, **6:**471
Ukrainian peasants, **6:**387
see also Dormitories
Astrology
Betsileo, **9:**57
Brahman and Chhetri of Nepal, **3:**52
Burmese, **5:**65
Divehi, **3:**78
Han, **6:**447
Kalmyks, **6:**156
Nepali, **3:**205
Oriya, **3:**218
Pandit of Kashmir, **3:**226
Punjabi, **3:**241
Sadhu, **3:**251
Tamil of Sri Lanka, **3:**283-284
Vietnamese, **5:**286
Yao of Thailand, **5:**292
Zhuang, **6:**511
Astronomy
Ayoreo, **7:**69-70
Muslim, **3:**185
Piapoco, **7:**274
Puinave, **7:**281
Winnebago, **1:**381
Yi, **6:**508
Asymmetrical alliance. _See under_ Marriage
Atheism
Abkhazians, **6:**9
Ajarians, **6:**14
Albanians, **4:**7
Bulgarians, **4:**45
Chuvash, **6:**85
Czechs, **4:**84
Germans, **6:**140
Gypsies, **6:**148
Itelmen, **6:**153
Kalmyks, **6:**157
Karakalpaks, **6:**168
Koreans, **6:**206
Latvians, **6:**238
Nganasan, **6:**282
Nivkh, **6:**285
Poles, **6:**308
Turkmens, **6:**371
Ukrainian peasants, **6:**386, 387
Vietnamese, **5:**286
Atlatls
Cocama, **7:**130
Jivaro, **7:**182
Movima, **7:**243
Auctions
Tamil, **3:**277
Aunt, paternal
Mejbrat, **2:**196
Murik, **2:**222
Tikopia, **2:**325
Torres Strait Islanders, **2:**346
Authoritarianism
Madeirans, **4:**166
Sinhalese, **3:**266
Tamil of Sri Lanka, **3:**83, 282
Automobile
manufacturing
Germans, **4:**122
Piemontese, **4:**198

Swedes, **4:**257
second-hand car dealing
peripatetics, **1:**287
Piemontese Sinti, **4:**200
Rom, **1:**304
Slovensko Roma, **4:**250
Vlach Gypsies of Hungary, **4:**271
Autonomist movement. _See_ Nationalist
movements
Autonomy. _See_ Individual autonomy
Aveyronnais, **4:**23-24
Aviation industry
Germans, **4:**122
Avocado growing
Cretans, **4:**70
Avoidance
of conflict or confrontation
Andamanese, **3:**10
Azoreans, **4:**28
Delaware, **1:**86
Dogrib, **1:**89
Faroe Islanders, **4:**100
Han, **6:**446-447
Hare, **1:**141
Hill Pandaram, **3:**100
Iban, **5:**98
Irula, **3:**107
Javanese, **5:**113
Mehinaku, **7:**238
Nayaka, **3:**196
Norwegians, **4:**182
Pemon, **7:**273
Pima-Papago, **1:**289
Piro, **7:**280
Purum, **3:**244
Rom, **1:**305
Rom of Czechoslovakia, **4:**219
Sherpa, **3:**259
Tanana, **1:**340
Ternatan/Tidorese, **5:**276
Tewa Pueblos, **1:**349
Trio, **7:**336
Wáiwai, **7:**348
Washoe, **1:**369
Western Apache, **1:**373
West Greenland Inuit, **1:**378
see also Nonviolence
as social control
Circassians, **9:**67
Itza', **8:**135
Siwai, **2:**304
Tanna, **2:**314
Tauade, **2:**319
Telefolmin, **2:**323
Avoidance (kinship). _See under_ Family; _under_
Marriage; Mother-in-law avoidance
Avuncular marriage. _See_ Marriage, avun-
cular
Avunculocal residency. _See under_ Residence
(newly married)
Axe
handle manufacture
Micmac, **1:**233
use
Araweté, **7:**56
Chin, **3:**63
Lakher, **3:**145
Nagas, **3:**188

Ayahuasca use (hallucinogen)
  Cocama, 7:130
  Guahibo-Sikuani, 7:166
  Huarayo, 7:178
  Matsigenka, 7:232
  Piro, 7:280
  Shipibo, 7:306
  Siona-Secoya, 7:309
  Tatuyo, 7:324
  Waorani, 7:353
Aya system
  Lingayat, 3:151
Ayllu (social unit)
  Callahuaya, 7:89
  Canelos Quichua, 7:99-100
  Chipaya, 7:116
Ayurvedic medicine. See under Medical treat-
      ments and practices
Azerbaijani Turks, 6:49

Baby houses (jungle houses)
  Sora, 3:268, 269
Bachelors. See Single people
Bachelors' dormitories. See Dormitories
      (single male or female)
Bagpipes. See under Musical instruments
Baha'i faith
  Baha'is, 9:35
  Boruca, Bribri, Cabécar, 8:29, 30
  Cook Islands, 2:42
  Temiar, 5:272
  Zoroastrians, 9:409
Bai (ancestral spirit)
  Magar, 3:162
Bai (ceremony)
  Dai, 6:427
Baidyo. See Healer
Baki. See Shamanism
Ballads. See Bards; Oral tradition
Bamboo uses
  Baiga, 3:19
  Chakma, 3:58, 61
  Chenchu, 3:61
  Garo, 3:84
  Grasia, 3:88
  Hill Pandaram, 3:99
  Khasi, 3:123
  Kuna, 8:147
  Lakher, 3:145
  Nagas, 3:188
  Nayaka, 3:195
Banana growing and uses
  Afro-Bolivians, 7:8
  Afro-Columbians, 7:17
  Ajië, 2:7
  Akawaio, 7:31
  Amahuaca, 7:34
  Ambae, 2:11
  Anambé, 7:41
  Apiaká, 7:48
  Asurini, 7:61
  Bakairi, 7:74
  Barí, 7:83
  Blacks of Costa Rica, 8:25
  Bugle, 8:32
  Canarians, 4:51
  Canelos Quichua, 7:99
  Cape Verdeans, 4:55

Carib of Dominica, 8:38
Cariña, 7:102
Cashibo, 7:104
Chácobo, 7:105
Chagga, 9:61
Chimane, 7:112
Chocó, 7:122
Choiseul Island, 2:38
Cocama, 7:130
Cotabato Manobo, 5:79
Cretans, 4:70
Culina, 7:146
Emberá, 7:155
Emberá and Wounaan, 8:109
Emerillon, 7:159
Ganda, 9:104
Gebusi, 2:77
Guadalcanal, 2:89
Guadeloupians, 8:116
Guajajára, 7:166
Guarayu, 7:174
Hoti, 7:175
Jamaicans, 8:137
Jebero, 7:181
Jivaro, 7:182
Karajá, 7:188
Karihona, 7:192
Kikuyu, 9:161
Kosrae, 2:128
Krikati/Pukobye, 7:204
Kwoma, 2:134
Macuna, 7:212
Mailu, 2:154
Marinahua, 7:220
Marind-anim, 2:183
Maroni Carib, 7:220
Marquesas Islands, 2:189
Marubo, 7:222
Mayoruna, 7:234
Mnong, 5:184
Mojo, 7:242
Mongo, 9:226
Moré, 7:242
Motu, 2:213
Mundugumor, 2:218
Mundurucu, 7:244
Murut, 5:193
Muyu, 2:228
Ningerum, 2:246
Noanamá, 7:251
Nyakyusa and Ngonde, 9:253
Paï-Tavytera, 7:259
Paraujano, 7:267
Pemon, 7:271
Piapoco, 7:274
Piaroa, 7:276
Pukapuka, 2:270
Rennell Island, 2:277
Rikbaktsa, 7:287
Saint Lucians, 8:230
Saramaka, 7:296
Sharanahua, 7:299
Shavante, 7:300
Shipibo, 7:304
Sio, 2:300
Somalis, 9:316
Sumu, 8:237
Suruí, 7:312

Suya, 7:315
Tacana, 7:318
Tangu, 2:311
Tanimuka, 7:318
Tapirapé, 7:320
Ticuna, 7:328
Tolai, 2:334
Trio, 7:335
Tunebo, 7:338
Tupari, 7:339
Tuvalu, 2:355
Usino, 2:361
Waimiri-Atroari, 7:343
Wamira, 2:365
Warao, 7:357
Wayapi, 7:361
Witoto, 7:364
Wogeo, 2:380
Xikrin, 7:367
Yagua, 7:372
Yanomamö, 7:375
Yekuana, 7:381
Yuracaré, 7:395
Bananas
  as male property
    Chagga, 9:61
    Kikuyu, 9:161
Band
  Apache, 1:371
  Baffinland Inuit, 1:30
  Blackfoot, 1:41
  Carrier, 1:51
  Cheyenne, 1:65
  Chipewyan, 1:69
  Chiricahua, 1:70
  Comanche, 1:75
  Cree, 1:81, 82
  Delaware, 1:85, 86
  Eastern Shoshone, 1:105
  Flathead, 1:128
  Gros Ventre, 1:134
  Hare, 1:141
  Havasupai, 1:145
  Jicarilla, 1:173
  Kaska, 1:178
  Kickapoo, 1:182, 183, 185
  Kiowa, 1:187, 188
  Kiowa Apache, 1:189
  Kumeyaay, 1:193, 194, 195
  Kutchin, 1:196
  Kutenai, 1:197
  Kwakiutl, 1:198, 199
  Lillooet, 1:206
  Lipan Apache, 1:208
  Maliseet, 1:210, 211
  Menominee, 1:221
  Micmac, 1:234, 235
  Mohave, 1:241
  Montagnais-Naskapi, 1:245
  Navajo, 1:252
  Nayaka, 3:196
  Nootka, 1:255, 257
  Northern Shoshone and Bannock, 1:267
  Ojibwa, 1:269, 270
  Okanagon, 1:272
  Osage, 1:277, 278
  Pawnee, 1:285
  peripatetics, 1:286;3:236

Pima-Papago, 1:289
Ponca, 1:296
Rom, 1:305
Sarsi, 1:308
Seminole of Oklahoma, 1:314
Shuswap, 1:317
Slavey, 1:319, 320
Slovensko Roma, 4:250
Spokane, 1:333
Tanana, 1:338, 339-240
Teton, 1:344
Tonkawaa, 1:354
Tsimshian, 1:354
Tubatulabal, 1:355
Ute, 1:360, 361-362
Walapai, 1:365
Washoe, 1:368
Western Apache, 1:372
Yankton, 1:386
Yavapai, 1:386
Banditry. _See_ Brigandage
Bango council (Abor), 3:5
Banishment. _See under_ Punishment
Banking. _See under_ Financial services
Banshee
Gaels (Irish), 4:117
Baptism
adult
Amish, 1:18
Hutterites, 1:153, 154-155
Mennonites, 1:219
collective ceremony for children
Yukuna, 7:388
importance of
Khevsur, 6:196
Mandaeans, 9:215
Micronesians, 1:238
Moldovans, 6:268
Old Believers, 1:274
Poles, 6:308
Siberian Estonians, 6:336-337
Siberian Germans, 6:339
Ukrainian peasants, 6:387
Yezidis, 6:410
rebaptism
Copts, 9:69
Baptists
Bamiléké, 9:39
Carib of Dominica, 8:40
Cayman Islanders, 8:47
Cherokee, 1:62
Cubans, 8:90
Czech-Canadians, 1:120
Germans, 6:140
Haitians, 1:138
Karen, 5:129
Khakas, 6:188
Kittsians and Nevisians, 8:145
Komi, 6:204
Lumbee, 1:209
Mamprusi, 9:214
Micronesians, 1:238
Miyanmin, 2:212
Mundurucu, 7:245
Northern Shoshone and Bannock, 1:267
Osage, 1:279
Ottawa, 1:280
Pacific Eskimo, 1:283

Sea Islanders, 1:310
Selung/Moken, 5:231
Seminole, 1:314
Seminole of Oklahoma, 1:315
Telefolmin, 2:323
Transylvanian ethnic groups, 4:268
Turks and Caicos Islanders, 8:273
Washoe, 1:370
Welsh, 4:280
Western Apache, 1:373
Barbasco (fishing poison)
Amahuaca, 7:34
Baniwa-Curripaco-Wakuenai, 7:77
Chocó, 7:123
Colorado, 7:131
Cuna, 7:149
Hoti, 7:175
Huarayo, 7:177
Ka'wiari, 7:198
Mashco, 7:225
Matsigenka, 7:231
Mayoruna, 7:234
Puinave, 7:281
Sirionó, 7:310
Tunebo, 7:338
Tupari, 7:340
Yekuana, 7:381
Yuqui, 7:392
Bards
Iban, 5:98
Kikuyu, 9:162
Koya, 3:140
Lowland Scots, 4:163
Occitans, 4:185
peripatetics of the Maghreb, 9:278
Rajput, 3:249
Shahsevan, 9:310
Bare breastedness. _See_ Nudity, breast baring
Barley growing
Aghuls, 6:11
Altaians, 6:21
Bavarians, 4:33
Belarussians, 6:60
Berbers of Morocco, 9:49
Castilians, 4:59
Cyclades, 4:77
Cypriots, 4:80
Dargins, 6:96
Don Cossacks, 6:104
Dungans, 6:109
Hazara, 9:115
Hutterites, 1:153
Karachays, 6:159
Khevsur, 6:194
Khinalughs, 6:199
Konso, 9:169
Korean, 5:146
Kurds, 9:175
Laks, 6:234
Latvians, 6:236
Leonese, 4:161
Lezgins, 6:242
Lisu, 5:164
Lur, 9:202
Maris, 6:257
Miao, 6:470
Moldovans, 6:266
Mongols, 6:474

Montenegrins, 4:172
Nepali, 3:202
Nu, 6:480
Nubians, 9:246
Orcadians, 4:186
Ossetes, 6:299
Pahari, 3:220
Pathan, 3:231
Persians, 9:279
Poles, 4:203
Pomaks, 4:205
Qiang, 6:485
Rutuls, 6:319
Salar, 6:488
Selkup, 6:326
Serbs, 4:230
Sherpa, 3:258
Shetlanders, 4:233
Shors, 6:329, 330
Sunwar, 3:271
Svans, 6:344
Tajik, 6:492
Talysh, 6:355
Tats, 6:358
Thakali, 3:290
Tibetans, 6:494
Tigray, 9:347
Tory Islanders, 4:265
Tsakhurs, 6:365
Tuvans, 6:373
Udis, 6:376
Volga Tatars, 6:401
Welsh, 4:279
Bar mitzvah ceremony
Ashkenazim, 6:36
Bene Israel, 3:28
Karaites, 9:155
Barn style
Frisians, 4:110, 111, 112
Barrio (neighborhood)
Latinos, 1:204
Barter
Abor, 3:4
Apiaká, 7:49
Burusho, 3:55
Chin, 3:64
Chipaya, 7:116
Garo, 3:83
Irish Travelers, 1:163
Irish Travellers, 4:155
Irula, 3:106
Jews of Kurdistan, 9:145
Kanjar, 3:119, 120
Kashinawa, 7:195
Khasi, 3:123
Kuikuru, 7:207
Kumeyaay, 1:194
Kwakiutl, 1:198
Lingayat, 3:151
Maliseet, 1:211
Matsigenka, 7:231
Motu, 2:213
Munducuru, 7:244
Nagas, 3:188
Nayaka, 3:194, 195
Páez, 7:257
Pokot, 9:282
Pume, 7:283

Barter (cont'd)
Saami, **4:**221
Salasaca, **7:**290
Slovaks, **4:**243
Slovensko Roma, **4:**250
Thakali, **3:**290
Vlachs, **4:**274
Washoe, **1:**368
West Greenland Inuit, **1:**377
see also Exchange
Barter (labor for goods)
Aymara, **7:**66-67
Matsigenka, **7:**231
Mayoruna, **7:**235
Yukuna, **7:**386-387
Basava (deity)
Lingayat, **3:**151
Baserria (farm)
Basques, **4:**31
Basketry
Abenaki, **1:**4
Achumawi, **1:**10
Akawaio, **7:**33
Aleut, **1:**15, 16
Aleuts, **6:**18
Anambé, **7:**42
Araweté, **7:**56
Atoni, **5:**28
Awá Kwaiker, **7:**63
Baiga, **3:**19, 21
Bhuiya, **3:**43
Bulgarian Gypsies, **4:**41
Cahuilla, **1:**47
Canarians, **4:**51
Central Yup'ik Eskimos, **1:**57
Cherokee, **1:**61
Chocó, **7:**123
Choctaw, **1:**71
Craho, **7:**136, 138
Cree, **1:**81
Cuna, **7:**149
Delaware, **1:**85
Desana, **7:**152
Emberá, **7:**156
Friuli, **4:**113
Fulniô, **7:**161
Garo, **3:**84
Guahibo-Sikuani, **7:**165
Haida, **1:**135
Hanunóo, **5:**91
Hopi, **1:**149
Huarayo, **7:**177
Jicarilla, **1:**172
Karok, **1:**176, 177
Kashinawa, **7:**195
Klamath, **1:**191, 192
Kmhmu, **5:**139
Kolisuch'ok, **5:**144
Kota, **3:**135
Koya, **3:**140
Krikati/Pukobye, **7:**204
Kumeyaay, **1:**194
Kurumbas, **3:**143
Kwakiutl, **1:**198
Lahu, **5:**154
Lakher, **3:**145
Lamaholot, **5:**156
Magar, **3:**156

Maguindanao, **5:**169
Maliseet, **1:**211
Mandan, **1:**214
Maris, **6:**257
Mehinaku, **7:**236
Menominee, **1:**221
Micmac, **1:**233, 235
Mingrelians, **6:**263
Mizo, **3:**178
Modang, **5:**187
Mundurucu, **7:**244, 245
Nagas, **3:**188
Navajo, **1:**251
Nayaka, **3:**195
Nez Percé, **1:**254
Noanamá, **7:**252
Nootka, **1:**256
North Alaskan Eskimos, **1:**259
Northern Paiute, **1:**263
Northern Shoshone and Bannock, **1:**266
Palikur, **7:**262
Panare, **7:**265
Paraujano, **7:**267
Pemon, **7:**273
peripatetics, **1:**287
Piemontese Sinti, **4:**200
Pima-Papago, **1:**288
Pomo, **1:**294, 295
Purum, **3:**243
Rotinese, **5:**213
Saami, **4:**221
Santal, **3:**253
Sea Islanders, **1:**310
Seminole, **1:**312
Senoi, **5:**237
Shakers, **1:**316
Shavante, **7:**301
Siberiaki, **6:**334
Siwai, **2:**302
Southern Paiute (and Chemehuevi), **1:**331
Tai Lue, **5:**256
Tanaina, **1:**335
Tanana, **1:**339
Temiar, **5:**268
Thompson, **1:**359
Ticuna, **7:**328
Tlingit, **1:**351
Trio, **7:**335
Tubatulabal, **1:**355
Ute, **1:**361
Waimiri-Atroari, **7:**343, 345
Wáiwai, **7:**346, 348
Walapai, **1:**364-365
Wanano, **7:**350
Washoe, **1:**368, 370
Wayapi, **7:**361, 363
Western Shoshone, **1:**375
Wiyot, **1:**384
Yawalapití, **7:**378
Yokuts, **1:**388, 389
Yurok, **1:**394
Zuni, **1:**397
Basque, **4:**31
Bastardy. *See* Illegitimacy
Bathing
ceremonial
Azerbaijani Turks, **6:**50
Baiga, **3:**20

Bengali Muslims, **3:**34
Bukharan Jews, **6:**64
Cochin Jews, **3:**73
Gujarati, **3:**92
Jews of Yemen, **9:**149
Nayar, **3:**200
Nicobarese, **3:**209
as initiation rite
Lesu, **2:**147
Paraujano, **7:**268
ritual after childbirth
Sakalava, **9:**296
ritualized
Finns, **4:**104
Maris, **6:**258
Waimiri-Atroari, **7:**345
Yokuts, **1:**388
see also Foot washing; *under* Medical practices and treatments; Sauna
Batik
Bouyei, **6:**422
Ewe and Fon, **9:**88
Miao, **6:**471
Zhuang, **6:**510
Bat mitzvah (ceremony)
Ashkenazim, **6:**36
Bauxite mining
Akan, **9:**11
Dalmatians, **4:**86
Jamaicans, **8:**137, 138
Beads. *See under* Money and wealth
Beadwork
Abenaki, **1:**5-6
Akawaio, **7:**33
Chocó, **7:**123
Dogrib, **1:**88
Fox, **1:**130
Hare, **1:**140
Hidatsa, **1:**146
Kickapoo, **1:**184
Maliseet, **1:**211
Marubo, **7:**222, 223
Ndebele, **9:**238
Northern Paiute, **1:**263
Nubians, **9:**248
Ojibwa, **1:**271
Osage, **1:**277
Pokot, **9:**283
Pomo, **1:**294
Quechan, **1:**301
San-speaking peoples, **9:**303
Saraguro, **7:**294
Shipibo, **7:**304
Tanaina, **1:**337
Tanana, **1:**339
Teton, **1:**345
Tlingit, **1:**351
Tswana, **9:**364
Waimiri-Atroari, **7:**343
Wáiwai, **7:**348
Washoe, **1:**370
Western Apache, **1:**372
West Greenland Inuit, **1:**377
Wiyot, **1:**384
Zuni, **1:**397, 398
Bean growing
Algonkin, **1:**17
Anuak, **9:**21

Arikara, **1:**26
Baggara, **9:**30
Blang, **6:**421
Boruca, **8:**27
Choctaw, **1:**71
Ch'ol, **8:**64
Cocopa, **1:**74
Creek, **1:**83
Drung, **6:**432
Falasha, **9:**91
Georgians, **6:**132
Guarijío, **8:**117
Hani, **6:**450
Hazara, **9:**115
Hidatsa, **1:**146
Hopi-Tewa, **1:**151
Ifugao, **5:**99
Iraqw, **9:**125
Iroquois, **1:**165
Kédang, **5:**133
Khinalughs, **6:**199
Lenca, **8:**155
Luyia, **9:**204
Mam, **8:**158
Mandan, **1:**214
Maricopa, **1:**216
Mazahua, **8:**165
Miami, **1:**231
Mohave, **1:**240
Nahuat of the Sierra de Puebla, **8:**191
Ojibwa, **1:**269
Omaha, **1:**275
Opata, **8:**199
Osage, **1:**277
Otomí of the Valley of Mezquital, **8:**204
Ottawa, **1:**279
Palu'e, **5:**205
Pame, **8:**207
Pawnee, **1:**284
Paya, **8:**209
Pima Bajo, **8:**211
Popoluca, **8:**216
Poqomam, **8:**218
Potawatomi, **1:**297
Powhatan, **1:**297
Q'anjob'al, **8:**225
Quechan, **1:**301
Santee, **1:**307
Shawnee, **1:**317
Taos, **1:**341
Tepehuan of Chihuahua, **8:**252
Tepehuan of Durango, **8:**256
Tewa Pueblos, **1:**348
Tlapanec, **8:**259
Torres Strait Islanders, **2:**346
Tzotzil and Tzeltal of Pantelhó, **8:**276
Tzotzil of Chamula, **8:**279
Tzotzil of San Andrés Larraínzar, **8:**284
Tzotzil of San Bartolomé de los Llanos,
    8:287
Tzotzil of Zinacantan, **8:**292
Walapai, **1:**364
Wichita, **1:**379
Winnebago, **1:**380
Yoruba, **9:**391
Yukateko, **8:**309
Zapotec, **8:**312
Zoque, **8:**315

Zuni, **1:**397
see also Maize; Squash growing
Bear ceremonialism. _See_ Ceremonies, bear
Bear Clan
    Winnebago, **1:**382
Bear cult
    orochi, **6:**295
Bear Dance
    Southern Paiute (and Chemehuevi), **1:**332
    Ute, **1:**362
Bear hunting
    Cree, **1:**80
    Kalapuya, **1:**175
    Micmac, **1:**233
    Montagnais, **1:**244
    Ojibwa, **1:**269
    Osage, **1:**277
    Potawatomi, **1:**297
    Tanaina, **1:**335
    see also Polar bear hunting
Bear protector
    Tanaina, **1:**336
Bear trainers
    Bulgarian Gypsies, **4:**41
    Gypsies and caravan dwellers in the
        Netherlands, **4:**137
    peripatetics, **1:**287
    Qalandar, **3:**245, 246, 247
Beast Gods
    Zuni, **1:**399
Beating (as initiation rite)
    Kiwai, **2:**127
    Tauade, **2:**319, 320
Beatings. _See_ Child discipline, corporal pun-
    ishment; _under_ Punishment
Beaver bundles
    Blackfoot, **1:**42
Beaver Ceremony
    Comanche, **1:**75
Beaver hunting and trapping
    Kalapuya, **1:**175
    Montagnais-Naskapi, **1:**244
Beds
    heated
        Dungans, **6:**111
        Nanai, **6:**275
        Orochi, **6:**294
        Tajik, **6:**492
Beef production. _See_ Cattle raising
Beekeeping
    Belarussians, **6:**60
    Ionians, **4:**149
    Khasi, **3:**123
    Maris, **6:**257
    Moldovans, **6:**266
    Shors, **6:**330
    Svans, **6:**344
    Udmurt, **6:**379, 380
    Ukrainian peasants, **6:**386
    see also Honey gathering
Beer drinking. _See under_ Alcohol
Beet growing
    Persians, **9:**279
Begging
    Hijra, **3:**96
    Irish Travellers, **4:**155
    Kanjar, **3:**120
    peripatetics, **3:**234-235, 236

Piemontese Sinti, **4:**200
Qalandar, **3:**246, 247
Sadhu, **3:**251-252
Sidi, **3:**260
Slovensko Roma, **4:**250
Xoraxané Romá, **4:**281-282
Bell-metal objects
    Oriya, **3:**216
"Beloved" men (Choctaw leaders), **1:**72
Below-ground burial. _See_ Mortuary
    practices
Belt weaving
    Zuni, **1:**397, 398
Beluga whaling
    Baffinland Inuit, **1:**29
Bengali kinship terminology. _See under_
    Kinship terminology
Bengal tiger ritual
    Chin, **3:**64
Benji Bama (spirit)
    Abor, **3:**5
Berdache. _See_ Transsexuality
Betel
    Kachin, **5:**116
    Li, **6:**464
    Lisu, **5:**165
    Mekeo, **2:**198
    Mundugumor, **2:**218
    Nicobarese, **3:**209
    Rotinese, **5:**213
    T'in, **5:**278
Betrothal. _See_ Child betrothal; Courtship;
    Marriage, arranged
Betrothal, childhood. _See_ Child betrothal
Bhagat. _See_ Shamanism
Bhagavan (creator-god)
    Baiga, **3:**21
    Telugu, **3:**287
Bhagwan (deity)
    Bhil, **3:**41
Bhikkus (Buddhist monk)
    Sinhalese, **3:**267
Bicycle manufacturing
    Punjabi, **3:**238
Bifurcate kinship terminology. _See under_
    Kinship terminology
Big houses. _See_ Houses and housing, long-
    houses
Bilateral descent. _See under_ Descent
Bilingualism. _See under_ Language
Bilocal residency. _See under_ Residence
Biniou (bagpipe)
    Bretons, **4:**40
Biradari (kinship group)
    Kanjar, **3:**120
    Zamindar, **3:**307
Birchbark objects
    Cree, **1:**81
    Dogrib, **1:**88
    Ingalik, **1:**157
    Maliseet, **1:**211
    North Alaskan Eskimos, **1:**259
    Ojibwa, **1:**269
    Swedes, **4:**258
    Tanaina, **1:**335
    Tanana, **1:**339
    Thompson, **1:**350
    see also Canoe building

Bird guardian spirits
  Teton, **1**:346
Birinda (social unit)
  Sora, **3**:269
Birth. *See* Childbirth
Birth control
  contraception
    Amahuaca, **7**:35
    Desana, **7**:153
    Maltese, **4**:168
  discouraged
    Mormons, **1**:249-250
  herbal medicine for
    Garo, **3**:84
  to limit family size
    Bretons, **4**:39
    Burgundians, **4**:47
    Oriya, **3**:217
  prohibited
    Hasidim, **1**:144
    Piemontese, **4**:198
  pronatalist policies
    Romanians, **4**:213
  public limitation policies
    Khevsur, **6**:195
  see also Abortion; Infanticide
Birth huts. *See under* Childbirth
Birthrate
  decline
    Irish, **4**:151
    Maltese, **4**:167
  high
    Irish Travellers, **4**:154
    Mormons, **1**:247
    Rom of Czechoslovakia, **4**:218
    Tory Islanders, **4**:264
  low
    Bulgarians, **4**:42
    German Swiss, **4**:126
    Parsi, **3**:227, 228
Birth-related practices. *See* Childbirth
Bison hunting
  Arapaho, **1**:26
  Arikara, **1**:26, 214
  Assiniboin, **1**:27
  Cheyenne, **1**:64
  Comanche, **1**:75
  Crow, **1**:83
  Eastern Shoshone, **1**:104, 105
  Flathead, **1**:128
  Gros Ventre, **1**:134
  Hidatsa, **1**:146, 214
  Jicarilla, **1**:172
  Kickapoo, **1**:183
  Kiowa, **1**:187
  Lipan Apache, **1**:207
  Mandan, **1**:214
  Metis of Western Canada, **1**:226, 227, 229
  Miami, **1**:231
  Nez Percé, **1**:254
  Northern Shoshone and Bannock, **1**:266, 267
  Ojibwa, **1**:269
  Omaha, **1**:275
  Osage, **1**:277
  Pawnee, **1**:284, 285
  Ponca, **1**:296
  Santee, **1**:307

Sarsi, **1**:308
Teton, **1**:344, 346
Tonkawa, **1**:354
Ute, **1**:360
Wichita, **1**:379
Winnebago, **1**:381
Yankton, **1**:386
Bison reverence
  Kiowa, **1**:188
Blackbirding (impressment)
  Guadalcanal, **2**:89
  Lak, **2**:137
  Lakalai, **2**:140
  Mijikenda, **9**:225
  Pukapuka, **2**:270
  Santa Cruz, **2**:290
  Trobriand Islands, **2**:348
  Tuvalu, **2**:354
  see also Slavery
Black market
  Bulgarian Gypsies, **4**:41
  Slovaks, **4**:243
  Vlach Gypsies of Hungary, **4**:272
Black Medicine (sacred being)
  Mandan, **1**:215
Black moiety
  Fox, **1**:129
Black Monday
  Arubans, **8**:14
Black mourning. *See under* Mourning
Black Mouth (men's society)
  Hidsata, **1**:147
  Mandan, **1**:215
Black-on-black pottery
  Tewa Pueblos, **1**:349
Blacksmith
  design skills
    Lozi, **9**:187-188
  as inherited trade
    Luyia, **9**:204
    Swazi, **9**:330
  low caste status
    Berbers of Morocco, **9**:49
    Maasai, **9**:207
    Mossi, **9**:228
    Teda, **9**:340
  as medicine man/ritual leader
    Kpelle, **9**:173
  taboos
    Swazi, **9**:330
Blacksmithing trade
  Achang, **6**:417
  Bulgarian Gypsies, **4**:41
  Chuvans, **6**:81
  Gypsies, **6**:146
  Hakka, **6**:437
  Hani, **6**:450
  Hanunóo, **5**:91
  Hmong, **5**:93
  Jino, **6**:460
  Kalimantan Dayaks, **5**:120
  Kenyah-Kayan-Kajang, **5**:133
  Khasi, **3**:123
  Kota, **3**:135
  Koya, **3**:140
  Lahu, **5**:152;**6**:462
  Lamaholot, **5**:155
  Lisu, **5**:165

Makassar, **5**:172
Maonan, **6**:468
Mbeere, **9**:221
Minangkabau, **5**:182
Modang, **5**:187
Mulam, **6**:476
Nagas, **3**:188
Nivkh, **6**:284
Rom of Czechoslovakia, **4**:218, 219
Selkup, **6**:326
Shetlanders, **4**:233
Shors, **6**:328
Siberiaki, **6**:333
Siberian Germans, **6**:339
Slovensko Roma, **4**:250
Swedes, **4**:258
Vlach Gypsies of Hungary, **4**:271
Volga Tatars, **6**:401
Yakut, **6**:406
Yao of Thailand, **5**:291
Black-topping trade
  peripatetics, **1**:287
Blanket weaving
  Kwakiutl, **1**:198
  Navajo, **1**:251
  Taos, **1**:342
  Tlingit, **1**:351, 353
  Tsimshian, **1**:355
  Zuni, **1**:397
Bleeding cure. *See under* Medical practices and treatments
Blood brotherhood
  Albanians, **4**:6
  Corsicans, **4**:67
  Don Cossacks, **6**:105
  Georgians, **6**:133
  Laz, **6**:240
  Mingrelians, **6**:263
  Montenegrins, **4**:173
  Sakalava, **9**:295
  Serbs, **4**:231
  Vlachs, **4**:274
Blood feud
  Albanian-Americans, **1**:107
  Albanians, **4**:5, 6-7, 8
  Appalachian, **1**:22
  Baluchi, **3**:23
  cattle ranchers of Huasteca, **8**:44
  Chatino, **8**:52
  Chin, **3**:66
  Copper Eskimo, **1**:78
  Corsicans, **4**:67, 68
  Cretans, **4**:71
  Greeks, **4**:133
  Ingalik, **1**:158
  Karok, **1**:177
  Klamath, **1**:192
  Montenegrins, **4**:173
  North Alaskan Eskimos, **1**:260
  Pasiegos, **4**:191
  Pomo, **1**:295
  Sardinians, **4**:227
  Sinhalese, **3**:267
  Slovensko Roma, **4**:251
  Vedda, **3**:302
  Vlachs, **4**:275
  Western Apaches, **1**:373
  Xoraxané Romá, **4**:282, 283

Yurok, **1:**395
see also Feuding
Bloodletting (as initiation)
Chambri, **2:**32
Chimbu, **2:**36
Fore, **2:**65
Gnau, **2:**82
Bloodletting (medical). *See* Medical practices
and treatments, bleeding
Blood sacrifice. *See* Sacrifice *headings*
Blood sucking (evil spirit)
Kashubians, **4:**159
Blood vengeance. *See under* Conflict reso-
lution
Blowguns
Akawaio, **7:**31
Baniwa-Curripaco-Wakuenai, **7:**77
Canelos Quichua, **7:**101
Chayahuita, **7:**111
Chocó, **7:**123
Emberá, **7:**156
Hoti, **7:**175
Jebero, **7:**181
Jivaro, **7:**182
Karihona, **7:**192
Ka'wiari, **7:**198
Mayoruna, **7:**234
Noanamá, **7:**251
Panare, **7:**265
Piaroa, **7:**276
Puinave, **7:**281
Siona-Secoya, **7:**307
Tatuyo, **7:**323
Ticuna, **7:**328, 329
Waorani, **7:**352
Witoto, **7:**365
Yagua, **7:**372
Boat building
Bajau, **5:**32
Bonerate, **5:**44
Butonese, **5:**67
Divehi, **3:**76
Old Believers, **1:**273
Orcadians, **4:**187
Palu'e, **5:**205, 206
Rapa, **2:**274
Samal, **5:**219
Samal Moro, **5:**222
Samoa, **2:**287
Selung/Moken, **5:**232
Shetlanders, **4:**233
Tory Islanders, **4:**265
Yakan, **5:**289
Yurok, **1:**394
see also Canoe building; Shipbuilding
industry
Boat nomads
Bajau, **5:**30-35
sea nomads of the Adaman, **5:**227-229
Selung/Moken, **5:**230
Body
God's existence believed within each
human
Baul, **3:**26
representation
Nagas, **3:**191
rings. *See* Earrings; Nose rings
see also Nudity

Body branding
Oraon, **3:**215
Santal, **3:**254
see also Tattooing
Body cutting. *See* Body scarification
Body painting and ornamentation
Ache, **7:**7
Agta, **5:**6
Andamanese, **3:**11
Apalai, **7:**47
Asurini, **7:**62
Baniwa-Curripaco-Wakuenai, **7:**79
Chácobo, **7:**106
Chamacoco, **7:**110
Chayahuita, **7:**111
Chimbu, **2:**37
Chocó, **7:**123
Colorado, **7:**131
Cree, **1:**82
Cubeo, **7:**142
Cuiva, **7:**145
Emberá, **7:**158
Fore, **2:**65
Fox, **1:**130
Gahuku-Gama, **2:**70
Gainj, **2:**73
Garia, **2:**76
Guarayu, **7:**174
Haida, **1:**136
Huarayo, **7:**178
Ingalik, **1:**158
Kalapuya, **1:**175
Karajá, **7:**189
Karok, **1:**177
Ka'wiari, **7:**200
Kewa, **2:**117
Kosrae, **2:**130
Lakalai, **2:**142
Lesu, **2:**147
Macuna, **7:**215
Maká, **7:**218
Marind-anim, **2:**184
Maring, **2:**188
Marubo, **7:**223
Mashco, **7:**227
Mehinaku, **7:**239
Melpa, **2:**202
Mendi, **2:**205
Miami, **1:**231
Murik, **2:**223
Ngatatjara, **2:**241
Ningerum, **2:**248
Nivaclé, **7:**251
Rikbaktsa, **7:**288
Sadhu, **3:**251
Saliva, **7:**292
Sambia, **2:**286
Santa Cruz, **2:**292
Shavante, **7:**301
Sherente, **7:**303
Siona-Secoya, **7:**309
Suri, **9:**326
Suya, **7:**317
Tanimuka, **7:**319
Tanna, **2:**315
Tasmanians, **2:**317
Tiwi, **2:**329
Trio, **7:**336

Usino, **2:**363
Ute, **1:**361
Visayan, **5:**287
Wáiwai, **7:**348
Waorani, **7:**353
Washoe, **1:**370
Waurá, **7:**360
Witoto, **7:**365
Xikrin, **7:**368, 369
Yekuana, **7:**381
Yukuna, **7:**390
Yuqui, **7:**392, 394
see also Face painting; Tattooing
Body piercing
ears
Amahuaca, **7:**36
Bakairi, **7:**75
Cotopaxi Quichua, **7:**134
Dobu, **2:**51
Fulani, **9:**102
Kiwai, **2:**126
Krikati/Pukobye, **7:**205
Mafulu, **2:**153
Mailu, **2:**155
Mehinaku, **7:**238
Nagas, **3:**190
Okiek, **9:**261
peripatetics of Iraq, Syria, Lebanon,
Jordan, Israel, Egypt, Sudan, and
Yemen, **9:**277
Rikbaktsa, **7:**287, 288
Selepet, **2:**294
Shavante, **7:**301
Sherente, **7:**302
Taiorora, **2:**310
Taiwan aboriginal peoples, **5:**257
Waropen, **2:**376
Waurá, **7:**360
Wogeo, **2:**381
Yawalapití, **7:**380
Yekuana, **7:**381
lips
Ache, **7:**7
Asurini, **7:**62
Cinta Larga, **7:**128
Karajá, **7:**190
Lobi-Dagarti peoples, **9:**186
Mayoruna, **7:**235
Paï-Tavytera, **7:**259
Xokléng, **7:**371
nose
Amahuaca, **7:**36
Chácobo, **7:**106
Colorado, **7:**131
Cuna, **7:**150, 151
Dobu, **2:**51
Irula, **3:**108
Kiwai, **2:**126
Kuna, **8:**150
Mafulu, **2:**153
Mardudjara, **2:**181
Mayoruna, **7:**235
Mimika, **2:**208
Paresí, **7:**269
peripatetics of Iraq, Syria, Lebanon,
Jordan, Israel, Egypt, Sudan, and
Yemen, **9:**277
Quechan, **1:**301

Body piercing (cont'd)
  Tairora, 2:310
  Waropen, 2:376
  penis
    Wogeo, 2:381
Body scarification
  Ache, 7:6, 7
  Dieri, 2:49
  Guadalcanal, 2:90
  Guarayu, 7:174
  Iatmul, 2:99, 100
  Kpelle, 9:173
  Lugbara, 9:194
  Mossi, 9:231
  Pauserna, 7:270
  Pokot, 9:283
  San-speaking peoples, 9:303
  Saramaka, 7:298
  Sirionó, 7:310, 311
  Swazi, 9:331
  Tapirapé, 7:321
  Tasmanians, 2:317
  Tigray, 9:348
  Toba, 7:333
  Wapisiana, 7:355
  Wogeo, 2:381
  Xikrin, 7:369
  Yawalapití, 7:380
  see also Face scarification
Bogey man threats
  Copper Eskimo, 1:78
  Maliseet, 1:212
Bogum bokang (conflict resolution)
  Abor, 3:5
Bogumilism
  Slav Macedonians, 4:241
Bolas (weapon)
  bolas
    Chipaya, 7:115
    Itonama, 7:179
    Lengua, 7:210
    Mocoví, 7:240
Bole-Maru
  Pomo, 1:295
Bombarde (wind instrument)
  Bretons, 4:40
Bon (Tibet shamanism)
  Bhutanese, 3:46
Bonded labor. See under Labor
Bone carving. See Carved objects, bone
Bones
  crumbling as ideal death
    Winnebago, 1:382
  disinterment. See under Mortuary practices
  feeding
    Santal, 3:255
  gathering ritual
    Santal, 3:255
Bon Kate (feast)
  Cham, 5:73
Boo (ceremony)
  Kapingamarangi, 2:110
"Boogers" threats
  Cherokee, 1:61
Boogie Man kachinas
  Zuni, 1:398
Born for Water (culture hero)
  Mescalero Apache, 1:225

Bosnian Muslims, 4:36
Bound labor. See Labor, bonded
Bow priesthood
  Zuni, 1:398-399, 400
Brahman
  Aryan, 3:13
  Bengali, 3:33
  Bengali Shakta, 3:35
  Brahaman, 3:51
  Chitpavan, 3:68-70
  East Indians in Trinidad, 8:107
  Hindu, 3:102
  Nepalese, 3:52-54
  Pahari, 3:222
  see also Hinduism
Brahman attributes, 3:51, 222
Branding. See Body branding
Brass work
  Edo, 9:82
  Ewe and Fon, 9:88
  Garia, 3:81
  Nagas, 3:188
  Newar, 3:206
  Oriya, 3:216
  Tamil, 3:277
Bratstvo (clan)
  Montenegrins, 4:173
Bravery (as admired trait)
  Kiowa, 1:188
Breadfruit
  Kosrae, 2:128
  Mangareva, 2:172
  Marquesas Islands, 2:189
  Mekeo, 2:198
  Muyu, 2:228
  Nomoi, 2:252
  Pohnpei, 2:268
  Samoa, 2:287
  Tonga, 2:337
  Truk, 2:352
  Ulithi, 2:358
  Uvea, 2:364
  Woleai, 2:383
Breast-baring. See under Nudity
Breast-feeding
  casual approach to
    Afro-Hispanic Pacific Lowlanders, 7:22
  ceremonial simulation
    Amhara, 9:19
  duration
    Amhara, 9:19
    Badaga, 3:16
    Baiga, 3:20
    Bhil, 3:40
    East Indians in Trinidad, 8:106
    Edo, 9:80
    Fulani, 9:102
    Guarijío, 8:118
    Hausa, 9:113
    Ingalik, 1:157
    Iteso, 9:129
    Itza', 8:134
    Luba of Shaba, 9:192
    Magar, 3:158
    Matsigenka, 7:232
    Mbeere, 9:222
    Menominee, 1:221
    Nagas, 3:190

Ndembu, 9:240
Nepali, 3:204
Newar, 3:207
Otomí of the Sierra, 8:201
Pahari, 3:221
Piemontese Sinti, 4:201
Sakalava, 9:296
Santal, 3:254
Sora, 3:270
Suku, 9:322
Tamil, 3:278
Tarascans, 8:246
Terena, 7:326
Toda, 3:296
Tory Islanders, 4:266
Tswana, 9:363
Wayapi, 7:362
Wolof, 9:379
Yukuna, 7:388
Zaramo, 9:402
  malnourishment of mother
    Wasteko, 8:303
  sexual intercourse taboo during years of
    Suku, 9:322
  shared
    Mixtec, 8:177
  until child walks and talks
    Lobi-Dagarti peoples, 9:184
  until mother's next pregnancy
    Lango, 9:180
  weaning abruptly
    Yanomamö, 7:376
  weaning between three to six months
    Austrians, 4:20
  weaning with bitter herb
    Nahuat of the Sierra de Puebla, 8:192
  weaning gradually after extended duration
    Mehinaku, 7:237
  wet nurse
    Khevsur, 6:195
Bretons, 4:37, 39
Bride-price
  Abelam, 2:5
  Acehnese, 5:3
  Acholi, 9:5
  Agaria, 3:6
  Albanians, 4:5
  Aleuts, 6:18
  Alur, 9:13
  Ambae, 2:12
  Ambonese, 5:18
  Arabs, 9:24
  Araucanians, 7:53
  Asmat, 2:20
  Ata Sikka, 5:21
  Atoni, 5:27-28
  Awakateko, 8:16
  Badaga, 3:16
  Baggara, 9:30
  Bagirmi, 9:34
  Bagobo, 5:29
  Bai, 6:420
  Baiga, 3:20
  Bajau, 5:33
  Baluchi, 3:23
  Bamiléké, 9:38-39
  Banaro, 2:21
  Basseri, 9:42

Batak, 5:40
Berbers of Morocco, 9:50-51
Bhil, 3:39
Bonerate, 5:45
Bugis, 5:50
Bukharan Jews, 6:64
Buriats, 6:67
Burusho, 3:55
Castilians, 4:60
Chagga, 9:62
Chambri, 2:32
Chechen-Ingush, 6:74
Chimbu, 2:36
Chin, 3:65, 66
Choiseul Island, 2:39
Chuj, 8:72
Chuvash, 6:84
Circassians, 6:88
Craho, 7:137
Dai, 6:425, 426
Daribi, 2:47
Daur, 6:429
De'ang, 6:430
Dinka, 9:70
Dobu, 2:51
Dolgan, 6:101
Don Cossacks, 6:105
Dungans, 6:109
Dusun, 5:82
Endenese, 5:85
Even, 6:119
Evenki (Northern Tungus), 6:122
Ewe and Fon, 9:86
Fipa, 9:99
Foi, 2:60, 62
Fore, 2:63
Gahuku-Gama, 2:69
Gainj, 2:71, 72
Garia, 2:74, 75
Gayo, 5:89
Ghorbat, 9:107
Gnau, 2:81
Gond, 3:85
Goodenough Island, 2:87
Grasia, 3:88
Guadalcanal, 2:89, 90
Guajiro, 7:168
Gujar, 3:89
Gurung, 3:94
Gusii, 9:109
Gypsies, 6:147
Han, 6:444, 445
Hausa, 9:113
Hidatsa, 1:147
Hmong, 5:93, 94
Ibibio, 9:120
Ilongot, 5:101, 102
Ingilos, 6:150
Iraqw, 9:125
Irula, 3:106, 107
Iteso, 9:129
Jews of Kurdistan, 9:146
Jingpo, 6:457
Jivaro, 7:183
Kachin, 5:117
Kaluli, 2:102
Kanjar, 3:120, 121
Kanuri, 9:152

Kapauku, 2:106
Karachays, 6:160
Karaites, 6:165;9:155
Karakalpaks, 6:167
Karamojong, 9:157
Karok, 1:176
Kazak, 6:460
Kazakhs, 6:179, 180
Kenyah-Kayan-Kajang, 5:134
Ket, 6:185
Kewa, 2:116
Khanty, 6:192
Khinalughs, 6:200
Khmer, 5:136
Kikuyu, 9:162
Kilenge, 2:118, 119
Kiwai, 2:125
Kmhmu, 5:140
Kol, 3:130
Konso, 9:170
Korku, 3:134
Koya, 3:141
Kpelle, 9:173
Kriashen Tatars, 6:212
Kuikuru, 7:208
Kumyks, 6:222
Kurds, 9:176
Kurtatchi, 2:132
Kyrgyz, 6:230
Lak, 2:138, 139
Lakalai, 2:141
Lakandon, 8:154
Lakher, 3:146
Laks, 6:234
Lango, 9:179, 180
Lao, 5:158
Lepcha, 3:149
Lezgins, 6:243
Li, 6:464
Limbu, 3:150
Lisu, 5:165
Lobi-Dagarti peoples, 9:184
Lozi, 9:188
Luba of Shaba, 9:192
Lugbara, 9:194
Lunda, 9:197
Luyia, 9:204-205
Madurese, 5:167
Mafulu, 2:152
Maguindanao, 5:170
Mailu, 2:155
Maisin, 2:158
Makassar, 5:173
Malaita, 2:161, 162
Malay, 5:175
Malekula, 2:165
Manam, 2:168
Manchu, 6:467
Mandak, 2:171
Mansi, 6:253
Manus, 2:174, 175
Maratha, 3:69
Maring, 2:186, 188
Maris, 6:257
Mayoruna, 7:234
Mbeere, 9:221
Mejbrat, 2:196
Mekeo, 2:199

Melanau, 5:179
Melpa, 2:201
Meskhetians, 6:260
Miami, 1:231
Mimika, 2:207
Mixtec, 8:177
Mizo, 3:178
Mocoví, 7:241
Modang, 5:186
Motu, 2:214
Mountain Arapesh, 2:216
Mountain Jews, 6:272
Mulam, 6:476
Munda, 3:183
Muong, 5:191
Murik, 2:222
Murut, 5:193
Muyu, 2:228
Nagas, 3:189
Namau, 2:231, 232
Nandi and other Kalenjin peoples, 9:233
Ndebele, 9:236
Nepali, 3:203, 204
Nguna, 2:243
Nias, 5:194, 195, 196
Ningerum, 2:247
Nissan, 2:250
Nivkh, 6:284
Nogays, 6:288
Nu, 6:481
Nuer, 9:250
Nyamwezi and Sukuma, 9:256
Ogan-Besemah, 5:198
Okiek, 9:260
Orok, 6:296
Orokaiva, 2:257
Orokolo, 2:259
Oroquen, 6:483
Ossetes, 6:300
Pahari, 3:221
Palu'e, 5:206
Pathan, 3:232
Penan, 5:210
Pentecost, 2:263
peripatetics, 3:235
peripatetics of Iraq, Syria, Lebanon, Jordan,
    Israel, Egypt, Sudan, and Yemen,
    9:277
Popoloca, 8:216
Pumi, 6:484
Qalandar, 3:247
Q'anjob'al, 8:225
Q'eqchi', 8:226
Qiang, 6:486
Rom, 1:305
Rossel Island, 2:279
Rotinese, 5:213
Salar, 6:488
Samal, 5:220
Sambia, 2:285
San Cristobal, 2:289
Santa Cruz, 2:291
Santal, 3:253
Sara, 9:306
Selepet, 2:294
Selkup, 6:327
Selung/Moken, 5:232
Sengseng, 2:297

Bride-price (cont'd)
Senoi, **5:**238
Seri, **8:**234
Shilluk, **9:**311
Shona, **9:**313
Siberian Tatars, **6:**342
Sio, **2:**300
Spanish Rom, **4:**255
Subanun, **5:**245
Swahili, **9:**328
Swazi, **9:**331
Tairora, **2:**309
Taiwan aboriginal peoples, **5:**257, 258
Tajik, **6:**353, 492
Talysh, **6:**356
Tanaina, **1:**336
Tats, **6:**359
Tauade, **2:**319
Telefolmin, **2:**321, 322
Temne, **9:**343
Tetum, **5:**276
Thadou, **3:**288
Tiv, **9:**351
Tofalar, **6:**363
Tolai, **2:**335
Torres Strait Islanders, **2:**346
Totonac, **8:**265
Tsimihety, **9:**358
Tswana, **9:**362
Tuareg, **9:**368
Tujia, **6:**498
Tupari, **7:**340
Turkana, **9:**372
Turkmens, **6:**370
Tzotzil and Tzeltal of Pantelhó, **8:**277
Tzotzil of San Andrés Larraínzar, **8:**285
Usino, **2:**362
Uzbeks, **6:**397
Wa, **6:**502
Wantoat, **2:**369
Wape, **2:**371
Waropen, **2:**376
Western Shoshone, **1:**375
Wiyot, **1:**384
Wovan, **2:**386
Xoraxané Romá, **4:**282
Yakan, **5:**289
Yangoru Boiken, **2:**389
Yao, **6:**505
Yao of Thailand, **5:**292
Yawalapití, **7:**379
Yemenis, **9:**389
Yezidis, **6:**409
Yi, **6:**507
Yoruba, **9:**392
Yukpa, **7:**384
Yukuna, **7:**387
Yuracaré, **7:**396
Yurok, **1:**395
Zande, **9:**398
Zaramo, **9:**402
Bride-service
Aimaq, **9:**10
Akawaio, **7:**32
Aleuts, **6:**18
Amahuaca, **7:**35
Amuesha, **7:**38
Aranda, **2:**17

Asiatic Eskimos, **6:**41
Bakairi, **7:**74
Baniwa-Curripaco-Wakuenai, **7:**78
Barama River Carib, **7:**81
Betsileo, **9:**56
Boazi, **2:**30
Bukidnon, **5:**54
Candoshi, **7:**93
Chácobo, **7:**106
Chamacoco, **7:**109
Chamorros, **2:**34
Chiquitano, **7:**118
Cocama, **7:**130
Cuna, **7:**150
Dai, **6:**425
Dobu, **2:**50
Drung, **6:**432
Evenki (Northern Tungus), **6:**122
Ewe and Fon, **9:**86
Fipa, **9:**99
Gayo, **5:**89
Goodenough Island, **2:**87
Guahibo-Sikuani, **7:**165
Hanunóo, **5:**91
Hare, **1:**141
Huarayo, **7:**177
Ibibio, **9:**120
Itelmen, **6:**153
Jebero, **7:**181
Jivaro, **7:**183
Kagwahiv, **7:**185
Karihona, **7:**192
Kashinawa, **7:**196
Kenyah-Kayan-Kajang, **5:**134
Khanty, **6:**191
Khoi, **9:**159
Kickapoo, **1:**184
Kiwai, **2:**126
Kmhmu, **5:**140
Koya, **3:**141
Kpelle, **9:**173
Kuikuru, **7:**208
Lahu, **5:**152;**6:**463
Lak, **2:**138
Li, **6:**464
Lisu, **5:**165
Lobi-Dagarti peoples, **9:**184
Lunda, **9:**197
Maliseet, **1:**211
Mansi, **6:**253
Mataco, **7:**229
Matsigenka, **7:**231
Mayoruna, **7:**234
Mehinaku, **7:**237
Mejbrat, **2:**196
Micmacs, **1:**234
Mixtec, **8:**177
Miyanmin, **2:**210
Murik, **2:**222
Murngin, **2:**225
Northern Paiute, **1:**264
Nyakyusa and Ngonde, **9:**253
Nyamwezi and Sukuma, **9:**256-257
Palikur, **7:**262
Pemon, **7:**272
Piapoco, **7:**274
Piaroa, **7:**277
Piro, **7:**280

Popoluca, **8:**217
Puinave, **7:**281
Purum, **3:**243
Qiang, **6:**486
Rotinese, **5:**213
Sambia, **2:**285
Santal, **3:**253
Semang, **5:**235
Shona, **9:**313
Siona-Secoya, **7:**308
Southern Paiute (and Chemehuevi), **1:**331
Subanun, **5:**245
Taiwan aboriginal peoples, **5:**257
Tanaina, **1:**336
Tangu, **2:**311
Tatuyo, **7:**323
Tetum, **5:**276
Tigray, **9:**348
T'in, **5:**278, 279
tropical-forest foragers, **9:**357
Waimiri-Atroari, **7:**344
Wáiwai, **7:**347
Wapisiana, **7:**355
Yagua, **7:**372
Yakut, **6:**406
Yanomamö, **7:**375
Yao of Thailand, **5:**292
Yawalapití, **7:**379
Yukuna, **7:**387
Bride theft. *See* Marriage, by abduction
Bride-wealth. *See* Bride-price
Bridge-building
German Swiss, **4:**127
Brigandage
Calabrese, **4:**49
Slav Macedonians, **4:**241
Thug, **3:**294
see also Piracy
Bronze work
Newar, **3:**206, 207
Broom-making
Shakers, **1:**316
Brotherhood. *See* Blood brotherhood; Milk
    brotherhood; Siblings
Brotherhood societies. *See under* Associations,
    clubs, and societies
Brother of husband, marriage to. *See* Levirate
    marriage
Brothers, fictive
Yuit, **1:**391
Brother-sister relations. *See* Siblings; Uncle,
    maternal
Brothers, marriage to several at same time. *See*
    Polyandry (fraternal)
Bruderschaft. *See* Brotherhood societies
"Brush dances"
Yurok, **1:**395
Buckwheat growing
Bai, **6:**419
Daur, **6:**429
Hmong, **5:**93
Lahu, **6:**462
Lisu, **6:**465
Nu, **6:**480
Nyinba, **3:**211
Pamir peoples, **6:**304
Qiang, **6:**485
Salar, **6:**488

Tay, **5:**265
Thakali, **3:**290
Tibetans, **6:**494
Yi, **6:**506
Buddha's enlightenment (ceremony)
  Lao, **5:**159
Buddhism
  Acehnese, **5:**3
  Bai, **6:**421
  Balinese, **5:**35
  Bengali, **3:**29
  Bhutanese, **3:**45, 46
  Bugis, **5:**51
  Burgundians, **4:**47
  Chakma, **3:**60, 61
  Chaobon, **5:**74
  Chinese in Southeast Asia, **5:**75, 77
  Chinese of Costa Rica, **8:**62
  Don Cossacks, **6:**107
  Dusun, **5:**80
  East Asians in the United States, **1:**103
  Gayo, **5:**89
  Gurung, **3:**95
  Hakka, **6:**438, 439
  Indonesian, **5:**103
  Japanese, **5:**104, 109
  Jatav, **3:**115
  Javanese, **5:**111, 113
  Jing, **6:**454
  Jingpo, **6:**458
  Kachin, **5:**115, 118
  Karen, **5:**128, 129
  Kmhmu, **5:**141
  Kolisuch'ok, **5:**141, 142, 143, 144
  Korean, **5:**148
  Kui, **5:**150
  Kyrgyz, **6:**228
  Lamaholot, **5:**155
  Lawa, **5:**163
  Loven, **5:**166
  Mahar, **3:**163, 164, 165
  Manchu, **6:**468
  Maonan, **6:**468
  Mauritian, **3:**173
  Miao, **6:**472
  Mulam, **6:**477
  Muong, **5:**192
  Naxi, **6:**479
  Neo-Buddhist, **3:**200
  Nepalis, **3:**204-205
  Newar, **3:**206-207, 208
  Nyinba, **3:**211, 213
  Oy, **5:**200
  Pak Thai, **5:**200
  Pamir peoples, **6:**303
  P'u Noi, **5:**211
  Qiang, **6:**487
  Selung/Moken, **5:**232
  Sherpa, **3:**258, 259
  Sinhalese, **3:**264, 267
  South and Southeast Asians of Canada, **1:**324
  Sunwar, **3:**271
  Tamang, **3:**275
  Thakali, **3:**291, 292
  T'in, **5:**277
  Uighur, **6:**382, 384, 499, 500
  Untouchable converts, **3:**200, 299
  Vedda, **3:**302, 303
  Yi, **6:**507
  Zhuang, **6:**511
Buddhism (Gelygpa)
  Buriats, **6:**68
Buddhism (Hinayana)
  Dai, **6:**427
Buddhism (Mahayana)
  Bhutanese, **3:**46
  Chinese in Southeast Asia, **5:**75
  Han, **6:**447-448
  Lahu, **5:**153, 154;**6:**462, 463
  Newar, **3:**208
  Sherpa, **3:**259
  Singaporean, **5:**242
  Temiar, **5:**266
  Vietnamese, **5:**285, 286
Buddhism (Nichirenshu)
  Burakumin, **5:**63
Buddhism (Shinshu)
  Burakumin, **5:**63
Buddhism (Theravada)
  Achang, **6:**418
  Blang, **6:**422
  Brao, **5:**47-48
  Burmese, **5:**64, 65
  Cambodians in the United States, **1:**327
  Central Thai, **5:**69, 71
  Chakma, **3:**60
  Dai, **6:**424, 426, 427, 428
  De'ang, **6:**431
  Khmer, **5:**135, 137
  Lahu, **5:**153
  Lao, **5:**157, 159
  Lao Isan, **5:**160, 161, 162, 163
  Mon, **5:**189
  Newar, **3:**208
  Palaung, **5:**201, 202, 203
  Shan, **5:**241
  Sinhalese, **3:**264, 267
  South and Southeast Asians of Canada, **1:**324
  Tai Lue, **5:**253, 255, 256
Buddhism (Tibetan)
  Daur, **6:**429
  Ewenki, **6:**434
  Kalmyks, **6:**157
  Lepcha, **3:**149
  Moinba, **6:**473
  Mongols, **6:**475, 476
  Naxi, **6:**479
  Nu, **6:**481
  Nyinba, **3:**213
  Pumi, **6:**484
  Qiang, **6:**487
  Sherpa, **3:**259, 260
  Tamang, **3:**275
  Thakali, **3:**291, 292
  Tibetans, **6:**493, 495-496
  Tu, **6:**497
  Tuvans, **6:**374
  Yugur, **6:**509
Buffalo. _See_ Water buffalo
Buffalo Dance
  Kickapoo, **1:**186
Buffalo doctors
  Kiowa, **1:**188, 189
Buffalo hunting. _See_ Bison hunting
Buhuchara Mata (deity)
  Hijra, **3:**96, 97, 98
Building trades. _See_ Carpentry; Construction industry
Buleka (ceremony)
  Manam, **2:**169
Bullfighting
  Andalusians, **4:**12
  Castilians, **4:**61
  Salasaca, **7:**290
Bunches (family compounds)
  Washoe, **1:**368
Bundle societies
  Kickapoo, **1:**184, 185, 186
Bundles. _See_ Medicine bundles
Bundling (courting)
  Finns, **4:**103
Bungla ingu (ceremony)
  Chimbu, **2:**37
Bun Khao saak (festival)
  Lao Isan, **5:**163
Bunphrawes (festival)
  Lao Isan, **5:**162, 163
Bura Deo (supreme being)
  Agaria, **3:**6
  Kond, **3:**133
Bureaucracy
  Austrians, **4:**20
  Aveyronnais, **4:**26
  Czechs, **4:**84
  Germans, **4:**123
  Nayar, **3:**199
Burial. _See_ Mortuary practices
Burning (as initiation)
  Kiwai, **2:**127
Bush knife
  Chin, **3:**63
Business ownership. _See_ Entrepreneurs; Shopkeeping
Busk Dance. _See_ Green Corn Dance
Butchers
  Kolisuch'ok, **5:**143, 144
  Untouchables, **3:**299
Butterfly Festival
  Bai, **6:**421
Butter tub manufacture
  Micmac, **1:**233
Butter Week (festival)
  Old Believers, **6:**294
Buttock-baring. _See under_ Nudity

Cabapizca ceremony
  Guarijío, **8:**119
Cabbage growing
  Badaga, **3:**15
  Pasiegos, **4:**189
  Shetlanders, **4:**233
  Toda, **3:**295
Cabildo (governmental body)
  Canarians, **4:**52
  Canelos Quichua, **7:**100
  Páez, **7:**257-258
Cacao. _See_ Cocoa growing
Cactus gathering
  Western Shoshone, **1:**374
Caitanya (saint deity)
  Bengali Vaishnava, **3:**36-37

Calabash carving
  Ewe and Fon, 9:88
Calabrese, 4:48
Calendar
  African American, 1:13
  Amuzgo, 8:6
  Jews, 1:171
  Mam, 8:160
  Pathan, 3:233
  see also Ceremonies, calendrical
Calendar histories
  Kiowa, 1:189
Calligraphy
  Han, 6:448
  Japanese, 5:110
  Tajiks, 6:354
  Uzbeks, 6:398
  Volga Tatars, 6:402
Calumet Dance
  Miami, 1:232
Calvinism
  Afrikaners, 9:9
  Bamiléké, 9:39
  Dutch-Americans, 1:110
  Frisians, 4:111
  Highland Scots, 4:141-142
  Swazi, 9:332
  Transylvanian ethnic groups, 4:268
  Welsh, 4:279, 280
  see also Congregationalism; Dutch Re-
    formed Church; Presbyterianism
Calypso music
  Antigua and Barbuda, 8:10
  Chinese in Caribbean, 8:58
  Creoles of Nicaragua, 8:86
  Mauritian, 3:173
  Trinidadians and Tobagonians,
    8:269
Camels
  breeding
    Sleb, 9:315
  breeding and driving
    Jat, 3:111, 112
  herding
    Somalis, 9:316
    Teda, 9:340
    Turkana, 9:371
  raising
    Kalmyks, 6:155
    Kazakhs, 6:177
    Turkmens, 6:369
  transport
    Berbers of Morocco, 9:49
    Tuareg, 9:367
    Yörük, 9:394
Camote growing
  Yakan, 5:288
Canarians, 4:51
Candlemas
  Orcadians, 4:188
Candomblé
  Afro-Brazilians, 7:13
Cane swallowing (as initiation)
  Fore, 2:65
Cane work
  Khasi, 3:123
Canneries
  Bulgarians, 4:43

Kwakiul, 1:198
  Pacific Eskimo, 1:282, 283
  Tanaina, 1:335
Cannibal giant (mythological figure)
  Cree, 1:82
Cannibalism
  Apiaká, 7:50
  Asmat, 2:20
  Boazi, 2:30
  Cashibo, 7:104
  Desana, 7:153
  Dobu, 2:49
  Eipo, 2:58
  Emerillon, 7:159
  Fore, 2:62
  Gebusi, 2:79
  Goodenough Island, 2:85, 87
  Jebero, 7:181
  Kachin, 5:118
  Kagwahiv, 7:185
  Kaluli, 2:103
  Karihona, 7:193
  Lak, 2:139
  Mafulu, 2:153
  Malaita, 2:162
  Maori, 2:178
  Miami, 1:232
  Miyanmin, 2:211
  Namau, 2:230, 232
  Nguna, 2:242
  Nissan, 2:250
  Noanamá, 7:251
  Orokaiva, 2:257
  Rossel Island, 2:279, 280
  Suruí, 7:313
  Tanimuka, 7:319
  Tanna, 2:315
  Tauade, 2:320
  Tongareva, 2:339
  Wamira, 2:367
  Wayapi, 7:363
  Witoto, 7:365
Canoe building
  Abenaki, 1:4
  Anambé, 7:42
  Awá Kwaiker, 7:63
  Belau, 2:27
  Chukchee, 6:77
  Cuna, 7:149
  Desana, 7:152
  Dogrib, 1:88
  Guadalcanal, 2:89
  Kalimantan Dayaks, 5:120
  Kenyah-Kayan-Kajang, 5:133
  Kiwai, 2:125
  Klallam, 1:190
  Kosrae, 2:128
  Lakalai, 2:140
  Lau, 2:143
  Maliseet, 1:211
  Manam, 2:168
  Menominee, 1:221
  Mimika, 2:207
  Montagnais-Naskapi, 1:244
  Nicobarese, 3:209
  Nissan, 2:249
  Noanamá, 7:251-252
  Nootka, 1:257

Okanagon, 1:272
  Pohnpei, 2:269
  Saliva, 7:292
  San Cristobal, 2:289
  Santa Cruz, 2:290
  Sio, 2:300
  Tanaina, 1:335
  Thompson, 1:350
  Tikopia, 2:325
  Tokelau, 2:331
  Tonga, 2:337
  Tongareva, 2:340
  Tor, 2:342
  Torres Strait Islanders, 2:346
  Trobriand Islands, 2:349
  Warao, 7:358
  Wayapi, 7:361
  Wiyot, 1:384
  Wogeo, 2:380
  Yuracaré, 7:395
  see also Boat building
Canoe-launching ceremony
  Andamanese, 3:11
Canton (political division)
  German Swiss, 4:126
Cantors
  Jews, 1:171
Cao Dai (religion)
  Vietnamese, 5:286
Cape Verdeans, 4:54, 55
Capital punishment. See under Punishment
Capture, marriage by. See Abduction,
    marriage by
Caravan housing. See under Houses and
    housing
Cardamon growing
  Lepcha, 3:148, 149
  Syrian Christian of Kerala, 3:273
Cardiovascular disease
  Saami, 4:222
Career training
  Parsi, 3:228
"Car" festival
  Tamil of Sri Lanka, 3:284
Cargo cults
  Asmat, 2:21
  Dani, 2:45
  Eipo, 2:58
  Garia, 2:74, 76
  Goodenough Island, 2:85, 88
  Lakalai, 2:140, 142
  Manam, 2:167
  Maring, 2:185
  Mekeo, 2:198
  Mountain Arapesh, 2:216
  Muyu, 2:229
  Nasioi, 2:235
  Nguna, 2:244
  Orokolo, 2:258
  Sengseng, 2:296
  Tangu, 2:310
  Tanna, 2:313
  Usino, 2:361, 363
Cargo system
  Amuzgo, 8:5
  Chinantec, 8:54
  Ch'ol, 8:65
  Chuj, 8:73

Guarijío, 8:118
Mam, 8:159
Nahua of the State of Mexico, 8:190
Nahuat of the Sierra de Puebla, 8:193
Otomí of the Sierra, 8:202, 203
Totonac, 8:266
Triqui, 8:272
Tzotzil and Tzeltal of Pantelhó, 8:278
Tzotzil of Chamula, 8:281
Tzotzil of Zinacantan, 8:294
Zapotec, 8:313
Zoque, 8:316
Caribou hunting
    Baffinland Inuit, 1:29
    Caribou Inuit, 1:51
    Chipewyan, 1:68
    Copper Eskimo, 1:76, 77, 78
    Cree, 1:80
    Dogrib, 1:88
    Hare, 1:140
    Iglulik Inuit, 1:155
    Ingalik, 1:157
    Labrador Inuit, 1:201
    Maliseet, 1:211
    Micmac, 1:233
    Naskapi, 1:244
    Netsilik Inuit, 1:254
    North Alaskan Eskimos, 1:259
    Tanaina, 1:335
    Tanana, 1:338
    West Greenland Inuit, 1:377, 379
Carnival (festival)
    Antigua and Barbuda, 8:10
    Arubans, 8:14
    Bavarians, 4:35
    Black Creoles of Louisiana, 1:39-40
    Cajuns, 1:50
    Canarians, 4:52
    Chinese in Caribbean, 8:58
    Ch'ol, 8:65
    Croats, 4:74
    East Indians in Trinidad, 8:107
    Germans, 4:123
    German Swiss, 4:127
    Mixtec, 8:178
    Nahua of the Huasteca, 8:187
    Peloponnesians, 4:194
    Provencal, 4:211
    Trinidadians and Tobagonians, 8:269
    Tzotzil and Tzeltal of Pantelhó, 8:278
    Walloons, 4:278
    Zoque, 8:317
Carnival workers
    Kanjar, 3:119, 120, 121
    peripatetics, 1:287
Carob growing
    Cretans, 4:70
Carpatho-Rusyns, 6:70
Carpentry
    Black Creoles of Louisiana, 1:38
    Cretans, 4:70
    Kota, 3:135
    Lepcha, 3:149
    Mizo, 3:178
    Pahari, 3:223
    Santal, 3:253
    see also Woodworking
Carpet weaving. See Rug weaving

Carrot growing
    Toda, 3:295
Cars. See Automobile
Cartwrights and carting
    Metis of Western Canada, 1:228
Carved objects
    bone
        Ainu, 5:8
        Aleuts, 6:18
        Asiatic Eskimos, 6:42
        bone
            Tanaina, 1:335
        Chukchee, 6:78
        Dani, 2:44
        Eipo, 2:56
        Even, 6:119
        Evenki (Northern Tungus), 6:124
        West Greenland Inuit, 1:377
        Wiyot, 1:384
    calabash
        Ewe and Fon, 9:88
    canoes
        Wiyot, 1:384
    coconut shell
        Cape Verdeans, 4:55
    fetishes
        Zuni, 1:397, 400
    flint
        North Alaskan Eskimos, 1:259
    horn
        Kashubians, 4:159
    ivory
        Aleuts, 6:18
        Bau, 2:23
        Central Yup'ik Eskimos, 1:57
        Khanty, 6:192
        North Alaskan Eskimos, 1:259
        Sinhalese, 3:267
        Yakut, 6:407
        Yuit, 1:390, 392
    jet
        Pume, 7:284-285
    rock
        Baniwa-Curripaco-Wakuenai, 7:79
        Cubeo, 7:142
        Dalmatians, 4:87
        Macuna, 7:215
        Yuit, 1:390
    shell
        Choiseul Island, 2:38
    shells
        Wiyot, 1:384
    soapstone
        Callahuaya, 7:88
        Gusii, 9:110
        West Greenland Inuit, 1:377
    stone
        Maliseet, 1:211
        Northern Paiute, 1:263
        Pahari, 3:223
        Shona, 9:314
    varied
        Andamanese, 3:9
        Bhil, 3:41, 42
        Kwakiutl, 1:198
        Saami, 4:221
        Sinhalese, 3:267
    see also Mask carving

whalebone
    Azoreans, 4:27
    Cape Verdeans, 4:55
wood
    Abkhazians, 6:7
    Achang, 6:418
    Ainu, 5:10
    Akan, 9:11
    Albanians, 4:4
    Aleuts, 6:18
    Asmat, 2:19, 21
    Bamiléké, 9:39-40
    Bashkirs, 6:56
    Belarussians, 6:61
    Belau, 2:27
    Burusho, 3:56
    Canelos Quichua, 7:101-102
    Central Yup'ik Eskimos, 1:57
    Chechen-Ingush, 6:75
    Chocó, 7:123
    Chuvash, 6:85
    Circassians, 6:91
    Cretans, 4:71
    Croats, 4:75
    Cuna, 7:151
    Dai, 6:428
    Dalmatians, 4:87
    Delaware, 1:85
    dolls
        Fali, 9:95
    Doukhobors, 1:93
    Easter Island, 2:55
    Emberá, 7:156
    Emberá and Wounaan, 8:109
    Even, 6:119
    Evenki (Northern Tungus), 6:124
    Ewe and Fon, 9:88
    Ewenki, 6:434
    Garo, 3:84
    Georgians, 6:136
    Gogodala, 2:83, 84
    Goodenough Island, 2:88
    Gujarati, 3:92
    Hawaiians, 2:97
    Iatmul, 2:99, 100
    Ibibio, 9:119
    Ifugao, 5:99
    Igbo, 9:121
    Ingalik, 1:158
    Karajá, 7:188, 189
    Karok, 1:176
    Kashubians, 4:159
    Khanty, 6:192
    Komi, 6:204
    Krikati/Pukobye, 7:204
    Kubachins, 6:217
    Kumyks, 6:223
    Kwoma, 2:136
    Latinos, 1:204, 206
    Lesu, 2:146, 147
    Lobi-Dagarti peoples, 9:186
    Luba of Shaba, 9:193
    Lunda, 9:199
    Madeirans, 4:165
    Mailu, 2:156
    Maonan, 6:468
    Maori, 2:178
    Mimika, 2:207, 208

Carved objects (cont'd)
Minangkabau, 5:182
Modang, 5:187
Mossi, 9:231
Munda, 3:184
Murik, 2:221, 223
Murngin, 2:224
Nagas, 3:188, 191
Namau, 2:231
Ndembu, 9:241
Nepali, 3:202
Newar, 3:208
Nguna, 2:243
Nias, 5:197
Noanamá, 7:252
Nootka, 1:256, 257
Orochi, 6:295
Orokolo, 2:260
Pahari, 3:223
Romanians, 4:214
Russian peasants, 6:311, 313
Rutuls, 6:321
Samal, 5:221
Santal, 3:253, 255
Saracatsani, 4:225
Saramaka, 7:298
Shipibo, 7:304
Shona, 9:314
Siberiaki, 6:334
Siberian Estonians, 6:336
Sio, 2:301
Siona-Secoya, 7:307
Slovaks, 4:243, 245
Swahili, 9:329
Tabasarans, 6:349
Tagalog, 5:249
Taiwan aboriginal peoples, 5:257
Tetum, 5:276
Tewa Pueblos, 1:348
T'in, 5:277
Tlingit, 1:353
Tor, 2:343
Trobriand Islands, 2:348, 349
Usino, 2:361
Uzbeks, 6:397
Vlachs, 4:274
Wik Mungkan, 2:379
Yakut, 6:405, 407
Yawalapití, 7:378
see also Totem poles; Woodworking
Casa (coresident kinship group)
Andalusians, 4:11
Cash-based economy. *See* Money economy
Cashews
growing
Zaramo, 9:401
processing
Syrian Christian of Kerala, 3:273
Cassava growing
Alur, 9:13
Ambonese, 5:17
Ata Sikka, 5:20
Bajau, 5:32
Bau, 2:22
Bonerate, 5:44
Candoshi, 7:93
Edo, 9:79
Endenese, 5:85

Filipino, 5:87
Ibibio, 9:119
Igbo, 9:121
Iteso, 9:128
Luba of Shaba, 9:191
Lugbara, 9:194
Lunda, 9:196
Makassar, 5:172
Malekula, 2:164
Manam, 2:167
Mataco, 7:228
Nambicuara, 7:247
Ndembu, 9:239
Nias, 5:195
Paya, 8:209
Samal, 5:219
Samal Moro, 5:222
Saramaka, 7:296
Sasak, 5:226
Semang, 5:234
Suruí, 7:312
Tausug, 5:262
Temiar, 5:267
Terena, 7:325
Ternatan/Tidorese, 5:274
Tobelorese, 5:280
Toraja, 5:281
Trio, 7:335
Wapisiana, 7:354, 355
Wayapi, 7:361
Yakan, 5:288
Yakö, 9:383
Zande, 9:397
Cassava spirits
Barama River Carib, 7:82
Zande, 9:398
Castes
Agaria, 3:6
Ahir, 3:7
Anavil Brahman, 3:7-8
Assamese, 3:14
Balinese, 5:37
Bania, 3:24
Bene Israel, 3:27, 28
Bengali, 3:31, 32-33
Bhil, 3:40
Bihari, 3:46
Brahman, 3:51, 52, 53, 224
Chhetri, 3:52, 53
Chitpavan Brahman, 3:68, 70
Circassians, 6:89
Cochin Jew, 3:71-72, 73
Coorg, 3:73-74
Divehi, 3:77-78
East Indians in Trinidad, 8:105
Garia, 3:81
Gond, 3:86
Gujar, 3:88-89
Gujarati, 3:90
hijra, 3:96-97
Hill Pandaram, 3:98-100
Hindu, 3:57, 102
Irula, 3:106, 107
Jamaicans, 8:138
Jat, 3:110, 111
Jatav, 3:113, 114, 115
Kanbi, 3:117, 118
Khoja, 3:127, 128

Kshatriya, 3:142
Lhoba, 6:464
Magar, 3:154, 159
Mande, 9:215
Mappila, 3:167
Maratha, 3:168
Moluccans—South, 5:188
Moor of Sri Lanka, 3:181
Muslim, 3:185
Nambudiri Brahman, 3:192-194
Nayar, 3:196, 199, 200
Nepali, 3:201, 202, 203, 204, 305
Newar, 3:206-207, 208
Nuristanis, 9:251
Okkaliga, 3:213
Oriya, 3:216, 217
Pahari, 3:219, 220, 221-222, 223
Pandit of Kashmir, 3:224-226
peripatetics, 3:234, 235
Punjabi, 3:237, 239, 241
Rom of Czechoslovakia, 4:217, 219
Sadhu, 3:251
Sasak, 5:226
Scheduled, 3:256-257
Sidi, 3:260, 261
Sinhalese, 3:265, 266
Sora, 3:270
Sudra, 3:271
Syrian Christian of Kerala, 3:271, 274
Tamang, 3:275
Tamil, 3:277, 278, 279
Tamil of Sri Lanka, 3:280, 281, 282-283
Teda, 9:340
Telugu, 3:285, 286
Tharu, 3:293
Toda, 3:296-297
Turkmens, 6:370
Untouchables, 3:299
Vaisya, 3:300
Vedda, 3:302
Vellala relationship with other, 3:303, 304, 305
Wolof, 9:379
Yezidis, 6:408, 409
Zamindar, 3:306, 307
see also Hereditary occupations; Outcastes
Castration. *See* Emasculation ritual
Cat domestication
Burusho, 3:55
Pandit of Kashmir, 3:225
Catharism heresy
Occitans, 4:185
Catholicism. *See* Roman Catholicism; Uniate Catholicism
Cattle
ceremony
Cahita, 8:35
Fulani, 9:101
as focus of life
Xhosa, 9:381
representing status and wealth
Karamojong, 9:157
see also Sacrifice, livestock
Cattle herding
Iteso, 9:128
Khoi, 9:159
Maasai, 9:207
Nuer, 9:249

Nyakyusa and Ngonde, 9:253
Pashai, 9:267
Pokot, 9:282
San-speaking peoples, 9:302
Shilluk, 9:311
Somalis, 9:316
Suri, 9:324
Turkana, 9:371
Cattle lending
    Chagga, 9:61
    Iraqw, 9:125
Cattle raising
    Abkhazians, 6:7
    Acehnese, 5:3
    Aghuls, 6:11
    Ahir, 3:7
    Ajarians, 6:13
    Altaians, 6:21
    Alur, 9:13
    Amuesha, 7:37
    Aveyronnais, 4:25
    Azerbaijani Turks, 6:49
    Baggara, 9:29-30
    Bakairi, 7:74
    Balkars, 6:53
    Barí, 7:84
    Belarussians, 6:60
    Betsileo, 9:54
    Bolaang Mongondow, 5:43
    Buriats, 6:66
    Cajuns, 1:49
    Canelos Quichua, 7:99
    cattle ranchers of the Huasteca, 8:42
    Central Thai, 5:70
    Circassians, 6:88
    Cora, 8:76
    Daur, 6:429
    Dinka, 9:70
    Dominicans, 8:102
    Don Cossacks, 6:104
    Drung, 6:432
    Finns, 4:102
    Fulani, 9:101
    Georgians, 6:132
    Greeks, 6:142
    Guahibo-Sikuani, 7:165
    Guajiro, 7:168
    Gusii, 9:108
    Herero, 9:116-117
    Hidatsa, 1:146
    Irula, 3:105
    Itonama, 7:179
    Jingpo, 6:456
    Karachays, 6:159
    Karakalpaks, 6:167
    Karelians, 6:170
    Kazak, 6:460
    Kazakhs, 6:177
    Khakas, 6:187, 188
    Khanty, 6:190
    Khevsur, 6:194
    Khinalughs, 6:198
    Khmer, 5:136
    Kikapu, 8:144
    Kipsigis, 9:164
    Kirgiz, 6:461
    Kriashen Tatars, 6:211
    Kumyks, 6:221

    Kurds, 6:226
    Kyrgyz, 6:229
    Lao, 5:158
    Lao Isan, 5:161
    Laz, 6:240
    Lengua, 7:210
    Lithuanians, 6:250
    Luyia, 9:204
    Madurese, 5:167
    Makassar, 5:172
    Maonan, 6:468
    Maris, 6:257
    Mazahua, 8:165
    Meskhetians, 6:259
    Mingrelians, 6:263
    Mixtec, 8:177
    Moldovans, 6:266
    Montserratians, 8:180
    Murut, 5:193
    Naxi, 6:478
    Ndebele, 9:236
    Ndembu, 9:239
    Nivkh, 6:284
    Nogays, 6:287
    Northern Irish, 4:178
    Northern Paiute, 1:263
    Nu, 6:481
    Nyamwezi and Sukuma, 9:256
    Orcadians, 4:186, 187
    Ossetes, 6:299
    Otavalo, 7:253
    Otomí of the Valley of Mezquital, 8:204
    Pak Thai, 5:200
    Pamir peoples, 6:304
    Pasiegos, 4:189-190
    Piapoco, 7:274
    Piro, 7:279
    Portuguese, 4:206
    Pueblo Indians, 1:298
    Pumi, 6:483
    Qiang, 6:485
    Rutuls, 6:318, 319
    Sakalava, 9:293
    Shetlanders, 4:233
    Shona, 9:312
    Shors, 6:329
    Siberiaki, 6:333
    Siberian Estonians, 6:336
    Svans, 6:344
    Swazi, 9:330
    Swedes, 4:257
    Swiss, Italian, 4:261
    Tabasarans, 6:348
    Tacana, 7:318
    Tai Lue, 5:253
    Talysh, 6:355
    Tats, 6:358
    Tausug, 5:262
    Terena, 7:325
    Tibetans, 6:494
    Tigray, 9:347
    Tiroleans, 4:263
    Tonga, 9:353
    Tsakhurs, 6:365
    Tsimihety, 9:358
    Tswana, 9:361
    Tuvans, 6:373
    Udis, 6:376

    Udmurt, 6:380
    Ukrainians, 6:392
    Uzbeks, 6:396
    Vlachs, 4:274
    Volga Tatars, 6:401
    Waimiri-Atroari, 7:343
    Walapai, 1:364
    Wapisiana, 7:355
    Welsh, 4:279
    Western Apache, 1:371-372
    Xhosa, 9:381
    Yakan, 5:289
    Yakut, 6:405, 406
    Yaqui, 8:306
    Yi, 6:506
    Zulu, 9:411
    Zuni, 1:397
    see also Dairy products
Cave burial. _See_ Mortuary practices, burial in
    cave
Cave dwellers
    Mount Athos, 4:175, 176
    Tasaday, 5:259-261
    Western Shoshone, 1:374
Caviar production
    Azerbaijani Turks, 6:49
Cedar wood use
    Klallam, 1:190
Celibacy
    Northern Irish, 4:179
    Old Believers, 6:291, 292
    Shakers, 1:316
    Sherpa, 3:259
    Siberiaki, 6:334
Celtic church
    Cornish, 4:65
Celtic harp
    Bretons, 4:40
Cement making
    Dalmatians, 4:84
Cemeteries
    All-Saints' Day ceremonies
        Black Creoles of Louisiana, 1:40
    grave decoration
        Abor, 3:4
        Albanians, 4:8
        Bhil, 3:41, 42
        Bondo, 3:51
        Gitanos, 4:130
    gravehouse
        Haida, 1:136
    importance of
        Austrians, 4:21
        Azoreans, 4:29
        Bavarians, 4:35
        Bulgarians, 4:45
        Canarians, 4:53
        Pasiegos, 4:191
        Romanians, 4:215
        Slovensko Roma, 4:251
    maintenance
        Walloons, 4:278
    maintenance and visitation
        Peloponnesians, 4:194
    national
        Flemish, 4:109
    see also Grave markers; Mortuary
        practices

Cenobitism
  Mount Athos, **4:**176
Censorship
  Azoreans, **4:**28
  Hasidim, **1:**144
Ceramic manufacture
  Burgundians, **4:**47
  Czechs, **4:**83
  Madeirans, **4:**165
  Sicilians, **4:**236
  Slovaks, **4:**243
  Swedes, **4:**258
Ceramics (craft). *See* Pottery
Cereal farming
  Andalusians, **4:**10
  Bosnian Muslims, **4:**36
  Bulgarians, **4:**43
  Burgundians, **4:**46
  Nuristanis, **9:**250
  Occitans, **4:**183, 184
  Peloponnesians, **4:**193
  Portuguese, **4:**206
  Provencal, **4:**210
  Swedes, **4:**257
  see also specific grains
Ceremonial chambers. *See* Kiva groups
Ceremonial dressing (as initiation rite)
  Kilenge, **2:**119
Ceremonial kinship
  Cypriots, **4:**80
  see also Fictive kin
Ceremonies
  absence of
    Western Shoshone, **1:**375
  age set rituals
    Maasai, **9:**209
  agricultural
    Abelam, **2:**4
    Acehnese, **5:**4
    Acholi, **9:**6
    Akha, **5:**13
    Amahuaca, **7:**36
    Aquitaine, **4:**15
    Araucanians, **7:**54
    Asurini, **7:**62
    Atoni, **5:**28
    Bavarians, **4:**35
    Bhil, **3:**41
    Callahuaya, **7:**90
    Chácobo, **7:**107
    Chiriguano, **7:**122
    Chocó, **7:**123
    Divehi, **3:**78
    Dobu, **2:**51
    Dogon, **9:**73
    Dusun, **5:**83
    Emberá, **7:**158
    Endenese, **5:**86
    Friuli, **4:**113
    Garia, **2:**74
    Germans, **4:**123
    Gnau, **2:**82
    Goodenough Island, **2:**86, 88
    Guadalcanal, **2:**90
    Iban, **5:**96
    Iraqw, **9:**126
    Kashubians, **4:**159
    Ka'wiari, **7:**200

  Kiwai, **2:**125
  Lak, **2:**138
  Lobi-Dagarti peoples, **9:**185
  Mandan, **1:**215
  Marubo, **7:**223
  Mekeo, **2:**200
  Mossi, **9:**231
  Munda, **3:**184
  Nagas, **3:**190, 191
  Ningerum, **2:**247
  Oraon, **3:**215
  Orokolo, **2:**260
  Punjabi, **3:**241
  Rennell Island, **2:**277
  Rukuba, **9:**291
  Santal, **3:**255
  Sara, **9:**307
  Sengseng, **2:**297, 298
  Siwai, **2:**303
  Sora, **3:**270
  Sorbs, **4:**253
  Suruí, **7:**314
  Terena, **7:**327
  Thadou, **3:**289
  Warao, **7:**359
  Wayapi, **7:**363
  Xikrin, **7:**369
  Yakö, **9:**387
  Yukpa, **7:**384
  Yukuna, **7:**389
  Zulu, **9:**411
  see also subhead harvest; *subhead* planting
    below
agricultural cycle
  Cuicatec, **8:**93
  Finns, **4:**104
  German Swiss, **4:**127
ancestor
  Awá Kwaiker, **7:**65
  Betsileo, **9:**57
  Chinese of Costa Rica, **8:**62
  Kwaiker, **7:**65
  Mamprusi, **9:**214
  Mossi, **9:**230
  Saint Lucians, **8:**232
  see also Sacrifice, for ancestors
annual cycle. *See subhead* calendrical *below*
annual mourning. *See* Mourning
ayllu
  Callahuaya, **7:**90
  Canelos Quichua, **7:**101
bathing. *See* Bathing, ceremonial
bear
  Ainu, **5:**9-10
  Evenki (Northern Tungus), **6:**124
  Ewenki, **6:**434
  Finns, **4:**104
  Ket, **6:**184
  Khanty, **6:**192
  Kiowa, **1:**188
  Mansi, **6:**255
  Nivkh, **6:**284, 285
  Orochi, **6:**295
  Orok, **6:**296
  Oroquen, **6:**483
  Saami, **4:**222
  Selkup, **6:**328
  Shors, **6:**331

  Ute, **1:**362
"big drinking" ceremony
  Shipibo, **7:**306
Blue Lake pilgrimage
  Taos, **1:**343
calendrical
  Amhara, **9:**20
  Central Yup'ik Eskimos, **1:**59
  Cherokee, **1:**62
  Chuj, **8:**73-74
  East Indians in Trinidad, **8:**106
  Jews, Arabic-speaking, **9:**136
  Pawnee, **1:**285
  Pomo, **1:**295
  Sakalava, **9:**298
  Seminole of Oklahoma, **1:**314
  Sorbs, **4:**253
  Southern Paiute (and Chemehuevi),
    1:332
  Tepehuan of Chihuahua, **8:**254
  Tewa Pueblos, **1:**349
  see also subhead seasonal *below*
carob
  Chorote, **7:**126
  Toba, **7:**333
cattle
  Cahita, **8:**35
  Fulani, **9:**102
chief inauguration/mourning
  Mehinaku, **7:**239
childbirth
  Ache, **7:**6-7
  Chinantec, **8:**55
  Hawaiians, **2:**96
  Kipsigis, **9:**165
  Nambicuara, **7:**247
  Nivaclé, **7:**251
  Nyakyusa and Ngonde, **9:**253, 254
  Nyamwezi and Sukuma, **9:**257
  Suku, **9:**322
  Tairora, **2:**310
clothing. *See* Clothing, ceremonial
confirmation
  Danes, **4:**90
corn
  Bakairi, **7:**75
dance. *See* Dance, ceremonial
divination. *See* Divination
divine kingship
  Bagirmi, **9:**34
drinking. *See* Alcohol
ear-piercing
  Amahuaca, **7:**36
  Bakairi, **7:**75
  Okiek, **9:**261
  Rikbaktsa, **7:**288
  Shavante, **7:**301
end of fasting
  Nubians, **9:**248
enemy soul pacification
  Karajá, **7:**191
ethnic festivals
  Jews of Israel, **9:**144
exchange. *See* Exchange, ceremonial
fertility
  Chipaya, **7:**117
  Foi, **2:**60, 61
  Gahuku-Gama, **2:**70

Kashinawa, 7:197
Maasai, 9:209
Pima Bajo, 8:213
Santal, 3:255
Selepet, 2:295
Sorbs, 4:253
Ukrainian peasants, 6:387
Ute, 1:362
Wáiwai, 7:348
Warao, 7:359
Yakut, 6:407
first-fruit rites
  Yokuts, 1:388-389
fishing
  Kapingamarangi, 2:110
  Northern Shoshone and Bannock, 1:267
  Thompson, 1:350
  Tolowa, 1:353
flood-related
  Lozi, 9:189
flower
  Otomí of the Sierra, 8:202
  Saint Lucians, 8:232
games and competitions. _See_ Games
gender roles
  Mandan, 1:214
gift exchange. _See_ Gift exchange
godfatherhood
  Montenegrins, 4:173-174
  see also Fictive kin
good luck
  Callahuaya, 7:90
harmony with supernaturals
  Navajo, 1:253
harvest
  Bugle, 8:33-34
  Catawba, 1:54-55
  Germans, 4:123
  Huichol, 8:127
  Washoe, 1:370
harvest purification
  Zaramo, 9:402
healing
  Callahuaya, 7:90
  Canela, 7:97
  Foi, 2:60, 61
  Kagwahiv, 7:185
hereditary privileges
  Nootka, 1:256
historical commemorations
  Galicians, 4:120
honoring dead
  Kuikuru, 7:209
  Palikur, 7:263
  Sherente, 7:303
house completion
  Kipsigis, 9:165
hunting
  Culina, 7:148
  Ka'wiari, 7:200
  Mandan, 1:215
  North Alaskan Eskimos, 1:261
  Pawnee, 1:285
  Yuit, 1:392
hunting vs. horticulture ritualization
  Culina, 7:148
increase
  Goodenough Island, 2:88

Wik Mungkan, 2:379
initiation. _See_ Initiation rites
insect-stinging
  Amahuaca, 7:36
  Apalai, 7:46
  Cariña, 7:103
  Karihona, 7:193
  Wapisiana, 7:355
  Wayapi, 7:363
  Xikrin, 7:369
  Yekuana, 7:381
kar'úk
  Quechan, 1:302
king's ancestors
  Edo, 9:82
king's enthronement
  Luba of Shaba, 9:193
kingship annual ritual
  Swazi, 9:332
krun rituals
  Ngawbe, 8:197-198
land diving
  Pentecost, 2:264
land purification
  Konso, 9:171
leg-spreading
  Chuj, 8:72, 73
life-cycle. _See_ Life-cycle rituals
life-stage transitions. _See_ Rites of passage
lightning god
  Triqui, 8:272
lip-piercing
  Ache, 7:7
  Asurini, 7:62
  Cinta Larga, 7:128
  Karajá, 7:190
male chivalry
  Dalmatians, 4:87
manhood tests
  Piaroa, 7:278
Medicine Dance
  Ojibwa, 1:271
men-only gatherings
  Vlach Gypsies of Hungary, 4:272
men-women separation
  Shahsevan, 9:309
merit-making
  Yao of Thailand, 5:293
model Viking ship procession
  Shetlanders, 4:234
name day
  Dalmatians, 4:87
naming. _See under_ Names
new drum
  Marubo, 7:223
new house
  Bugle, 8:34
  Chocó, 7:123
  Somalis, 9:318
  Yukuna, 7:389
new year
  Ghorbat, 9:107
  Kurds, 9:177
  Nubians, 9:248
  Zoroastrians, 9:410
new year purification of town
  Swahili, 9:329
nose-piercing

Amahuaca, 7:36
Cuna, 7:151
pastoral
  Kurds, 9:177
  Tepehuan of Chihuahua, 8:254
patron saint. _See_ Patron saint
peace-making
  Murngin, 2:226
pig
  Nicobarese, 3:210
pilgrimage festivals
  Mount Athos, 4:176
pilgrimages. _See_ Pilgrimages
placenta disposal
  Chinantec, 8:55
planting
  Q'eqchi', 8:227
  Sorbs, 4:253
  Tepehua, 8:249
  Tzotzil and Tzeltal of Pantelhó, 8:278
possession
  Sakalava, 9:298
processions. _See_ Processions
promotion to next grade
  Konso, 9:171
propitiatory
  Lahu, 5:154
puja
  East Indians in Trinidad, 8:107
purification
  Akan, 9:12
  Japanese, 5:109
  Kédang, 5:133
  Khevsur, 6:196, 197
  Konso, 9:172
  Nyakyusa and Ngonde, 9:254
  Talysh, 6:356
quarantine
  Tuvalu, 2:357
rain
  Andis, 6:27
  Ayoreo, 7:72
  Ojibwa, 1:272
  Santal, 3:255
  Tabasarans, 6:350
  Yukateko, 8:310
  Zapotec, 8:313
  see also Sacrifice, rain; Sun Dance
rainy-season dueling contests
  Suri, 9:325
religious
  Afro-Colombians, 7:18
  Afro-Hispanic Pacific Lowlanders, 7:23
  Afro-Venezuelans, 7:28
  Bakairi, 7:75
  Chamacoco, 7:110
  Cotopaxi Quichua, 7:135
  Guarayu, 7:174
  Old Believers, 1:274
  Otavalo, 7:255
  Páez, 7:258
  Salasaca, 7:291
  Teton, 1:344
  see also Patron saint; _specific holidays_
religious ecstaticism
  Baul, 3:27
  Shakers, 1:316
renewal rituals

Ceremonies (cont'd)
    Gururumba, 2:93
    Ute, 1:362
return from battle
    Mocoví, 7:241
revitalization of society rite
    Suku, 9:323
rites of passage. See Rites of passage
ritual contest
    Yaqui, 8:307
ritual-sibling
    Ngawbe, 8:198
royal bath
    Sakalava, 9:294
royal circumcision
    Sakalava, 9:294, 296, 298
sacred-secular combination
    Portuguese, 4:208
saint exchange
    Mam, 8:160
saints. See Saints
salmon
    Karok, 1:176
    Tanaina, 1:337
    Yurok, 1:395
seasonal
    Chimila, 7:114
    Huichol, 8:127
    Karajá, 7:191
    Kogi, 7:202
    Krikati/Pukobye, 7:205
    Madeirans, 4:166
    Mbeere, 9:222
    Nahua of the Huasteca, 8:187
    Osage, 1:279
    Otavalo, 7:255
    Tanimuka, 7:319
seasonal home change
    Kikapu, 8:145
secret
    Kiwai, 2:126
    Lak, 2:138, 139
    Lobi-Dagarti peoples, 9:185-186
    Sambia, 2:284
Shalako
    Zuni, 1:399
skill acquisition
    Iatmul, 2:99
slaughtering feasts
    Chagga, 9:61
spirit-related
    Acholi, 9:6
    Candoshi, 7:94
    Chocó, 7:123
    Macuna, 7:214
    Mehinaku, 7:238-239
    Ndembu, 9:240-241
    Palikur, 7:263
    Pume, 7:284
    Songhay, 9:320
    Suruí, 7:313-314
    Zarma, 9:406
spring
    She, 6:491
    Slave Macedonians, 4:241
    Tabasarans, 6:350
"Striking the pole"
    Miami, 1:232

thanksgiving
    Cree, 1:82
    Southern Paiute (and Chemehuevi),
        1:332
    Yuit, 1:392
trance during
    Ewe and Fon, 9:86, 88
trophy
    Kagwahiv, 7:185
    Nivaclé, 7:251
unity
    Kashinawa, 7:197
visitor
    Barí, 7:85
    Marubo, 7:223
war bundles
    Winnebago, 1:382
warfare
    Mandan, 1:215
warriors promoted to elders
    Maasai, 9:209
wi:gita
    Pima-papago, 1:289, 290
witch doctor séances
    Zande, 9:399
women's
    Chitpavan Brahman, 3:70
    Toda, 3:297
women's fertility
    Maasai, 9:209
see also Initiation rites; Sacrifice; specific
    ceremonies and events
Chaan (second house)
    Pahari, 3:220
Chaldeans
    Arab Americans, 1:24, 25
    Assyrians, 9:27
    Chaldeans, 9:63-64
Chandi (deity)
    Magar, 3:160
Changha (festival)
    Jing, 6:454
Changing Season (rite of passage)
    African Americans, 1:12
Changing Woman (deity). See Spider Woman
Chanting
    Amahuaca, 7:36
    Angaité, 7:44
    Ayoreo, 7:72
    Bakairi, 7:75
    Baniwa-Curripaco-Wakuenai, 7:79
    Chácobo, 7:107
    Chimane, 7:113
    Chorote, 7:126
    Cinta Larga, 7:129
    Delaware, 1:86
    Desana, 7:154
    Huarayo, 7:178
    Jews, 1:171
    Karajá, 7:191
    Kuna, 8:150
    Lengua, 7:211
    Macuna, 7:215
    Marubo, 7:223
    Mashco, 7:227
    Mataco, 7:227
    Nambicuara, 7:247
    Nivaclé, 7:251

    Panare, 7:267
    Sherpa, 3:260
    Shipibo, 7:306
    Suruí, 7:313
    Trio, 7:336
    Tupari, 7:341
    Wanano, 7:350
    Waorani, 7:353
    Yanomamö, 7:377
    Yawalapití, 7:380
    Yekuana, 7:381
    Yuqui, 7:394, 395
Charcoal production
    Montserratians, 8:180
    Poqomam, 8:218
    Vlachs, 4:274
Charismatic Catholicism
    Black Creoles of Louisiana, 1:39
Charismatic leadership. See under Leadership
    qualities
Charitable giving
    Andalusians, 4:12
    Muslim, 3:185
    Newar, 3:208
    Parsi, 3:228
Charms. See Amulets
Charred Body (culture hero)
    Hidatsa, 1:147
Chastity. See Celibacy; Virginity
Chatchi exogamy, rule of
    Garo, 3:83
Cheese making
    Auvergnats, 4:22
    Aveyronnais, 4:25
    German Swiss, 4:125
    Sardinians, 4:226
    Swiss, Italian, 4:261
    Walloons, 4:276
Chemical industry
    Bulgarians, 4:43
    Catalans, 4:62
    Germans, 4:122
    German Swiss, 4:125
    Poles, 4:203
    Slovaks, 4:243
    Slovenes, 4:247
    Tuscans, 4:269
    Welsh, 4:279
Chestnuts (as staples)
    Aveyronnais, 4:25
    Corsicans, 4:66
Chicken raising
    Afro-Hispanic Pacific Lowlanders, 7:20
    Afro-Venezuelans, 7:26
    Awá Kwaiker, 7:63
    Batak, 5:39
    Bilaan, 5:42
    Bisaya, 5:42
    Bontok, 5:46
    Bugis, 5:49
    Central Thai, 5:70
    Chayahuita, 7:111
    Circassians, 6:88
    Dusun, 5:81
    Emberá, 7:155
    Endenese, 5:85
    Gayo, 5:88
    Georgians, 6:132

Greeks, **6**:142
Guahibo-Sikuani, **7**:165
Iban, **5**:97
Ilongot, **5**:101
Kalimantan Dayaks, **5**:120
Kashubians, **4**:158
Kédang, **5**:131
Lahu, **5**:152;**6**:462
Lamaholot, **5**:155
Lisu, **5**:164
Maguindanao, **5**:169
Mansi, **6**:253
Minahasans, **5**:181
Mnong, **5**:184
Ndaonese, **5**:194
Northern Irish, **4**:170
Orcadians, **4**:187
Otavalo, **7**:253
Pukapuka, **2**:271
Sagada Igorot, **5**:216
Saluan, **5**:217
Samal Moro, **5**:222
Selung/Moken, **5**:231
Senoi, **5**:237
Subanun, **5**:244
Taiwan aboriginal peoples, **5**:257
Tausug, **5**:262
Temiar, **5**:267
Ternatan/Tidorese, **5**:275
Tetum, **5**:276
Toraja, **5**:281
Tujia, **6**:498
Udis, **6**:376
Ulithi, **2**:358
Vietnamese, **5**:285
Volga Tatars, **6**:401
Wapisiana, **7**:355
Welsh, **4**:279
Woleai, **2**:383
Yakan, **5**:289
Yao of Thailand, **5**:291
Zhuang, **6**:510
Chicken ritual
Popoloca, **8**:216
Tzotzil of San Bartolomé de los Llanos,
8:291
Tzotzil of Zinacantan, **8**:292, 294
see also Sacrifice, chickens
Chickpea growing
Falasha, **9**:91
Chicle industry
Itza', **8**:134
Chiefdom
Ache, **7**:6
Acholi, **9**:5
Arikara, **1**:26
Ayoreo, **7**:71
Badaga, **3**:17
Bakhtiari, **9**:36
Baure, **7**:86
Bemba, **9**:46-47
Bhil, **3**:39, 40
Canela, **7**:96
Cariña, **7**:103
Chácobo, **7**:106
Chagga, **9**:62
Chakma, **3**:60
Chamacoco, **7**:109

Chin, **3**:64, 65, 66
Chiriguano, **7**:121
Choctaw, **1**:72
Chorote, **7**:125
Corg, **3**:73
Dyula, **9**:77
Flathead, **1**:128
Fulniô, **7**:161
Haida, **1**:136
Havasupai, **1**:145
Hidsata, **1**:147
Highland Scots, **4**:141
Hopi, **1**:149-150
Huron, **1**:152
Jat, **3**:112
Karajá, **7**:190
Khasi, **3**:125, 126
Khoi, **9**:160
Kickapoo, **1**:185
Kiowa, **1**:188
Klallam, **1**:190
Klamath, **1**:192
Kpelle, **9**:174
Kuikuru, **7**:208
Kutchin, **1**:196
Kutenai, **1**:197
Lakher, **3**:145-146, 147
Luba of Shaba, **9**:192
Luiseño, **1**:208
Lur, **9**:202
Magar, **3**:160
Makushi, **7**:219
Maliseet, **1**:212
Maricopa, **1**:216
Maroni Carib, **7**:220
Mashco, **7**:226
Mehinaku, **7**:238
Menominee, **1**:221
Miami, **1**:231
Micmac, **1**:234
Mikir, **3**:176
Miwok, **1**:240
Mohave, **1**:241
Mojo, **7**:242
Nagas, **3**:190
Nambicuara, **7**:247
Ndembu, **9**:240
Nez Percé, **1**:254
Nicobarese, **3**:210
Noanamá, **7**:251
Nootka, **1**:256
Northern Shoshone and Bannock, **1**:267
Nuer, **9**:250
Nyakyusa and Ngonde, **9**:253-254
Ojibwa, **1**:270
Okanagon, **1**:272
Omaha, **1**:275
Osage, **1**:278
Pacific Eskimo, **1**:283
Palikur, **7**:263
Paresí, **7**:269
Pawnee, **1**:285
Pende, **9**:273-274
peripatetics of Afghanistan, Iran, and
Turkey, **9**:276
Piro, **7**:280
Pomo, **1**:292
Rukuba, **9**:290

Santal, **3**:254
Sara, **9**:306
Saramaka, **7**:297
Seminole of Oklahoma, **1**:314
Shawnee, **1**:317
Sherente, **7**:303
Shilluk, **9**:311
Shona, **9**:313
Sirionó, **7**:310, 311
Snoqualmie, **1**:321
Songhay, **9**:319
Sora, **3**:268
Tacana, **7**:318
Tanana, **1**:339
Temne, **9**:344
Terena, **7**:326
Thadou, **3**:288, 289
Tharu, **3**:293
Toba, **7**:332
Tonkawa, **1**:354
Tubatulabal, **1**:355
Tupari, **7**:340
Ute, **1**:361-362
Walapai, **1**:365
Winnebago, **1**:382
Wintun, **1**:383
Wolof, **9**:379
Xokléng, **7**:370-371
Yagua, **7**:373
Yankton, **1**:386
Yawalapití, **7**:379
Yoruba, **9**:392
Yukpa, **7**:384
Zarma, **9**:405
see also War chief
Chiefdom, female. *See* Women political
leaders
Chief of the Dead (deity)
Thompson, **1**:350
Child betrothal
Albanians, **4**:5
Amahuaca, **7**:35
Bai, **6**:420
Bashkirs, **6**:56
Betsileo, **9**:56
Bisaya, **5**:43
Bukharan Jews, **6**:64
Bukidnon, **5**:54
Chipewyan, **1**:68
Copper Eskimo, **1**:78
Daribi, **2**:47
Daur, **6**:429
Easter Island, **2**:54
Fore, **2**:63
Greeks, **6**:143
Haida, **1**:136
Hani, **6**:450
Ibibio, **9**:120
Itonama, **7**:179
Jingpo, **6**:457
Kalmyks, **6**:156
Karachays, **6**:160
Karakalpaks, **6**:167
Kazakhs, **6**:180
Khevsur, **6**:195
Khinalughs, **6**:200
Kirgiz, **6**:461
Kurtatchi, **2**:132

Child betrothal (cont'd)
  Mafulu, **2:**152
  Maori, **2:**177
  Mardudjara, **2:**180
  Mayoruna, **7:**234
  Meskhetians, **6:**260
  Mingrelians, **6:**264
  Motu, **2:**214
  Mountain Arapesh, **2:**216
  Namau, **2:**231
  Nasioi, **2:**234
  Naxi, **6:**479
  Nu, **6:**481
  Pentecost, **2:**263
  Pohnpei, **2:**269
  Rutuls, **6:**320
  Sambia, **2:**285
  Siberiaki, **6:**333
  Svans, **6:**345
  Tabasarans, **6:**349
  Tahiti, **2:**306
  Tats, **6:**359
  Tauade, **2:**319
  Toda, **3:**296, 297
  Tongareva, **2:**340
  Warlpiri, **2:**374
  Yuit, **1:**391
Childbirth
  attended by men
    Ache, **7:**5, 6
  bathing ritual following
    Sakalava, **9:**296
  birth hut
    Kota, **3:**137
  birth huts
    Nicobarese, **3:**209
  celebrations
    Baggara, **9:**31
  contamination belief
    Lakalai, **2:**141
    Sambia, **2:**285
    Ukrainians, **6:**393
  crouching position
    Popoloca, **8:**216
    Tzotzil of Zinacantan, **8:**293
  elaborate postbirth ritual
    Nagas, **3:**190
  extramarital
    Lakalai, **2:**141
  father treated as if he gave birth. *See subhead* couvade observed *above*
  fertility
    Buriats, **6:**68
  in forest
    Chocó, **7:**123
    Tacana, **7:**318
  in garden
    Yukuna, **7:**388
  in hammock
    Asurini, **7:**62
  hijra's ritualized dancing and singing, **3:**96, 98
  in home
    Maroni Carib, **7:**220
  husband assists
    Popoloca, **8:**216
  importance attached to
    Ute, **1:**361

kneeling or sitting on bench
    Popoluca, **8:**217
  magical cure for difficult
    Cuna, **7:**151
  maternal uncle receives ceremonial payment from paternal family
    Ata Sikka, **5:**21
  men excluded
    Asurini, **7:**62
    Chocó, **7:**123
  mother and child considered polluting until eleventh day
    Brahman and Chhetri of Nepal, **3:**53
    Magar, **3:**157
  mother's death during
    Mojo, **7:**242
    West Greenland Inuit, **1:**379
  parental dietary and other restrictions and taboos
    Nootka, **1:**256
  placenta disposal
    Arabs, **9:**24
    Bamiléké, **9:**39
    Chinantec, **8:**55
  postpartum confinement
    Otavalo, **7:**255
    Tarascans, **8:**246
    Tswana, **9:**364
    Zaramo, **9:**402
    see also subhead seclusion following *below*
  postpartum sexual abstinence duration
    Chiquitano, **7:**118
    Dani, **2:**44
    Hausa, **9:**113
    Krikati/Pukobye, **7:**205
    Lango, **9:**180
    Maori, **2:**177
    Tapirapé, **7:**321
    Zaramo, **9:**402
  postpartum synagogue entry forbidden
    Karaites, **9:**155
  premarital
    Jino, **6:**460
    Kapauku, **2:**106
    Khevsur, **6:**195
    Lithuanians, **6:**251
    Nganasan, **6:**281
    Tofalar, **6:**363
    see also Illegitimacy
  private
    Nootka, **1:**256
  protective rites against evil spells
    Gond, **3:**86
  religious ceremonies
    Tzotzil of Chamula, **8:**281
  return to natal village for first birth
    Shilluk, **9:**311
  return to parental home for first birth
    Maratha, **3:**169
  return to parental home from seventh month through delivery
    Irula, **3:**104, 106
  rituals to insulate baby from dangerous spirits
    Wayapi, **7:**362
  in sauna
    Finns, **4:**104
  seclusion

Eipo, **2:**56
  Fore, **2:**63
  Khevsur, **6:**193, 196
  Nivkh, **6:**284
  Oroquen, **6:**483
  Rossel Island, **2:**278
  Sengseng, **2:**296
  Svans, **6:**345
  Tairora, **2:**308
  Tausug, **5:**263
  Trobriand Islands, **2:**351
  seclusion before and after
    Toda, **3:**297
  seclusion during and after
    Miami, **1:**231
  seclusion following
    Bedouin, **9:**45
    Karihona, **7:**193, 193
    Otavalo, **7:**255, 255
    Páez, **7:**257, 257
    Sakalava, **9:**296
    Suruí, **7:**313, 313
    Wayapi, **7:**362, 362
    Yukuna, **7:**388
    see also subhead couvade observed *above*
  sixth-day ceremony with firecrackers
    Khoja, **3:**127
  taboos. *See under* Taboos
  unsanitary conditions
    Wasteko, **8:**303
  see also Breast-feeding; Child-rearing philosophy; Infanticide; Infants
Child care
  by au pairs
    Icelanders, **4:**147
  by community
    Baggara, **9:**31
    Ewe and Fon, **9:**86
    Hutterites, **1:**154
    Tandroy, **9:**337
  day care outside home
    Czechs, **4:**84
    Icelanders, **4:**147
    Irula, **3:**107
    Swedes, **4:**258
    Walloons, **4:**277
  by designated individual
    Saramaka, **7:**297
  by elderly and handicapped
    Western Shoshone, **1:**375
  by elders
    Quechan, **1:**301
  by entire household
    Basques, **4:**31
  by extended family
    Bedouin, **9:**44
    Emberá, **7:**157
    Karajá, **7:**189-190
    Kashinawa, **7:**196
    Ozarks, **1:**281
    Pume, **7:**284
    Suya, **7:**316
    Vlachs, **4:**274
    Yawalapití, **7:**379
  by female family members
    Azoreans, **4:**28
    Faroe Islanders, **4:**99
    Gaels (Irish), **4:**116

Hungarians, 4:144
Rom, 1:305
Waimiri-Atroari, 7:344
by female neighbor or relative
Kongo, 9:167
gender-shared
Abor, 3:4
Andamanese, 3:10
Baiga, 3:20
Chakma, 3:59
Chin, 3:65
German Swiss, 4:126
Koya, 3:140
Nicobarese, 3:209
Romanians, 4:213
by grandmother
Tswana, 9:363
by grandparents
Austrians, 4:20
Baffinland Inuit, 1:30
Bakairi, 7:74
Barí, 7:85
Blackfoot, 1:42
Candoshi, 7:93
Chakma, 3:59-60
Chinese in Canada, 1:96
Chiriguano, 7:121
Chorote, 7:125
Comanche, 1:75
Cyclades, 4:78
Czechs, 4:84
Dalmatians, 4:87
Irula, 3:107
Jicarilla, 1:173
Kashinawa, 7:196
Kumeyaay, 1:195
Latinos, 1:205
Lunda, 9:197
Mescalero Apache, 1:225
Ndebele, 9:237
Nivaclé, 7:249
Northern Paiute, 1:264
Oriya, 3:217
Pandit of Kashmir, 3:225
Pawnee, 1:285
Poles, 4:203
Pomo, 1:294
Santal, 3:254
Sea Islanders, 1:310
Southern Paiute (nd Chemehuevi), 1:331
Swedes, 4:258
Taos, 1:342
Ute, 1:361
Vlach Gypsies of Hungary, 4:272
by men
Kanjar, 3:120
Mescalero Apache, 1:224
Tewa Pueblos, 1:348
by mother and father, 1:348, 349
Occitans, 4:185
by mother and female household members
Cypriots, 4:80
Czechs, 4:84
Leonese, 4:161
by mother and female relatives
Faroe Islanders, 4:99
Shetlanders, 4:234

by mother and grandmother
Orcadians, 4:187
Slovaks, 4:244
by mother and maternal relatives
Mescalero Apache, 1:225
by mother primarily
Afro-Bolivians, 7:9
Andalusians, 4:11
Castilians, 4:60
Catalans, 4:63
Friuli, 4:113
Miami Miami, 1:231
Piemontese, 4:198
Piemontese Sinti, 4:201
by multiple caregivers
Mbeere, 9:222
by neighbors
Flemish, 4:107
by older siblings
Barí, 7:85
Bengali, 3:32
Calabrese, 4:49
Chakma, 3:59
Chin, 3:65
Cyclades, 4:78
Flemish, 4:107
Garo, 3:83
Gurung, 3:94
Huarayo, 7:178
Hungarians, 4:144
Irula, 3:107
Jatav, 3:114
Kanjar, 3:120
Kashinawa, 7:159
Koya, 3:141
Mehinaku, 7:237
Montagnais-Naskapi, 1:245
Nyinba, 3:212
Orcadians, 4:187
Oriya, 3:217
Rominche, 4:217
Shetlanders, 4:234
Sora, 3:270
Tzotzil of San Bartolomé de los Llanos, 8:289
Ute, 1:361
Warao, 7:358
Yukuna, 7:388
by opposite-sex sibling
Acholi, 9:5
public health nurse checks on
Icelanders, 4:147
by young adolescent girls
Micronesians, 1:237-238
see also Child discipline; Child-rearing philosophy; Infants
Child-care philosophy
indulgent
tropical-forest foragers, 9:357
Child custody
extended family
Toba, 7:332
family of either parent
Wiyot, 1:384
father
Bhuiya, 3:44
Kanuri, 9:152
Luyia, 9:205

father and his family
Irula, 3:107
Kota, 3:137
Pahari, 3:221
father in bride-wealth marriage
Nyamwezi and Sukuma, 9:256
father gets older children and mother keeps babies
Kol, 3:130
father keeps weaned children
Hausa, 9:113
father's clan
Yuit, 1:391
father's rights supercede mother's
Yemenis, 9:389
maternal
Emberá and Wounaan, 8:110
Iroquois, 1:166
Kashinawa, 7:195
Pume, 7:284
Rominche, 4:216
Ute, 1:361
maternal, but returned to birth father after age five if mother remarries
Rukuba, 9:290
maternal compensation to father
Yurok, 1:395
maternal matrilineal clan, 1:398
mother keeps infant until father demands it
Mizo, 3:178
mother keeps nursing children
Fali, 9:95
Tiv, 9:351
mother keeps younger children
Yakö, 9:385
mother keeps youngest child
Dogon, 9:72
mother returns to natal home without children
Luyia, 9:205
paternal grandparents
East Indians in Trinidad, 8:106
Child discipline
advice as
Northern Paiute, 1:264
boys severely disciplined by father
Shahsevan, 9:309
cold water immersion
Menominee, 1:221
corporal punishment
Abkhazians, 6:8
Alorese, 5:15
Amhara, 9:19
Amuesha, 7:38
Arabs, 9:24
Atoni, 5:28
Bagirmi, 9:34
Bakairi, 7:74
Barí, 7:85
Bavarians, 4:34
Bhil, 3:40
Bohra, 3:47
Bugis, 5:50
Carib of Dominica, 8:39
Chatino, 8:51
Cheynne, 1:65
Cretans, 4:71
Eipo, 2:57

Child discipline (cont'd)
    Falasha, 9:92
    Goodenough Island, 2:87
    Haitians, 8:122
    Hungarians, 4:144
    Italian Mexicans, 8:131
    Jamaicans, 8:138
    Javanese, 5:112
    Khasi, 3:125
    Makassar, 5:173
    Marubo, 7:223
    Mendi, 2:204
    Mikir, 3:176
    Montenegrins, 4:173
    Nandi and other Kalenjin peoples, 9:233
    Nguna, 2:243
    Old Believers, 6:293
    Oriya, 3:217
    Orokaiva, 2:257
    Piro, 7:280
    Poles, 4:203
    Pukapuka, 2:272
    Romanians, 4:214
    San-speaking peoples, 9:303
    Seminole, 1:313
    Serbs, 4:231
    Siberiaki, 6:333
    Tairora, 2:309
    Tandroy, 9:338
    Ticuna, 7:329
    Tuvalu, 2:356
    Tzotzil of San Bartolomé de los Llanos,
        8:289
    Usino, 2:362
    Vlachs, 4:274
    Welsh, 4:280
    Yanomamö, 7:376
    Yoruba, 9:392
    Yuqui, 7:393
corporal punishment discouraged
    Norwegians, 4:182
corporal punishment forbidden
    Awakateko, 8:16
    East Indians in Trinidad, 8:106
    English, 4:97
    Faroe Islanders, 4:99
    Ghorbat, 9:107
    Manx, 4:171
    Menominee, 1:221
    Suri, 9:326
    Teton, 1:345
corporal punishment frequent
    Kpelle, 9:173
corporal punishment rare
    Fipa, 9:99
    Jews of Iran, 9:140
    Puerto Ricans, 8:222
    Wolof, 9:379
corporal punishment in schools
    Jews, Arabic-speaking, 9:135
corporal punishment for severe infractions
    Yemenis, 9:389
corporal punishment sparing
    Itza', 8:134
criticism
    Czechs, 4:84
denial
    Vlachs, 1:274

by designated individual
    Mandan, 1:215
    Nivaclé, 7:249
    Washoe, 1:369
fasting
    Fox, 1:129
by father
    Poles, 4:203
harsh
    Popoloca, 8:216
harshness followed by cuddling and
        comforting
    Amahuaca, 7:35
lenient
    Slavey, 1:320
mild remonstrance
    Mohave, 1:241
mockery
    West Greenland Inuit, 1:377
by mother
    Mescalero Apache, 1:225
by mother or mother's brother
    Konso, 9:170
by mother's brother
    Seminole, 1:313
    Zuni, 1:398
by older siblings
    Chatino, 8:51
ostracism
    Metis of Western Canada, 1:228
    West Greenland Inuit, 1:377
parents never punish
    Mandan, 1:215
physical punishment. See subhead corporal
        punishment above
punishment increases with age
    Luba of Shaba, 9:192
rare occurences
    Fulani, 9:102
    Ojibwa, 1:270
reasoning
    Norwegians, 4:182
    Piemontese Sinti, 4:201
rewards
    Osage, 1:278
ridicule
    Amahuaca, 7:35
    Navajo, 1:252
    Osage, 1:278
    Pukapuka, 2:272
    San-speaking peoples, 9:303
    Tanaina, 1:336
    Teton, 1:345
    Ulithi, 2:359
    Ute, 1:361
    Yoruba, 9:392
as right of any older person
    Mescalero Apache, 1:225
scolding
    Amhara, 9:19
    Bagirmi, 9:34
    Baniwa-Curripaco-Wakuenai, 7:78
    Matsigenka, 7:232
    Menominee, 1:221
    Piaroa, 7:277
    Quechan, 1:302
    Ticuna, 7:329
scratching with garfish teeth

    Seminole, 1:313
shaming
    Candoshi, 7:93
    Emberá, 7:157
    Gayo, 5:89
    Metis of Western Canada, 1:228
    Navajo, 1:252
    Nissan, 2:250
    Nootka, 1:256
    Ogan-Besemah, 5:199
    Tanna, 2:314
    Tausug, 5:263
strong social pressure
    Montagnais-Naskapi, 1:245
teasing
    Samal Moro, 5:223
threats
    Pomo, 1:294
    West Greenland Inuit, 1:377
threats of harm by supernatural creatures
    Cherokee, 1:61
    Copper Eskimo, 1:78
    Maliseet, 1:212
    Menominee, 1:221
    Metis of Western Canada, 1:228
    Pomo, 1:294
    Washoe, 1:369
    Zuni, 1:398
    see also Child-rearing philosophy
Childhood ceremonies
    Albanians, 4:6
    Badaga, 3:16
    Bosnian Muslims, 4:36
    Brahman and Chhetri of Nepal, 3:53
    Flemish, 4:108
    Swazi, 9:331
    Tamil of Sri Lanka, 3:282
    Toda, 3:297
Childhood rituals
    Chuj, 8:72, 73
    Luyia, 9:206
Child indenture. See Labor, bonded
Child labor. See Child tasks; under Labor
Childlessness
    as couple preference
        Czechs, 4:83
    as divorce ground
        Inughuit, 1:160
Child marriage. See Marriage, youth
Child-price
    Usino, 2:362
Child-rearing philosophy
    adult-centered
        Tiroleans, 4:263
    adult companionionship emphasized
        Wapisiana, 7:355
    adult role models
        Afro-Hispanic Pacific Lowlanders, 7:22
        Afro-Venezuelans, 7:27
        Akawaio, 7:32
        Amahuaca, 7:35
        Apalai, 7:46
        Baniwa-Curripaco-Wakuenai, 7:78
        Bulgarians, 4:44
        Catawba, 1:54
        Central Yup'ik Eskimos, 1:58
        Chácobo, 7:106
        Culina, 7:147

Emberá, 7:157
Ingalik, 1:157
Kuikuru, 7:208
Lakher, 3:146
Macuna, 7:213-214
Maká, 7:217
Maliseet, 1:212
Mataco, 7:229
Matsigenka, 7:231, 232
Mescalero Apache, 1:225
Mundurucu, 7:245
Norwegians, 4:182
Panare, 7:266
Paraujano, 7:268
Pemon, 7:272
Piaroa, 7:277
Saami, 4:222
Saraguro, 7:294
Saramaka, 7:297
Warao, 7:358
Wayapi, 7:362
Winnebago, 1:381
Xikrin, 7:368
Yagua, 7:373
Yawalapití, 7:379
Yuqui, 7:393
affectionate
    Bengali, 3:32
    Cape Verdeans, 4:55
    Hare, 1:141
    Ingalik, 1:157
    Jatav, 3:114
    Kiowa, 1:188
    Magar, 3:158-159
    Miami, 1:231
    Micmac, 1:234
    Nayaga, 3:195-196
    Newar, 3:207
    Nicobarese, 3:209
    Nootka, 1:256
    Sora, 3:270
    Tamil, 3:278
    Tamil of Sri Lanka, 3:282
    Toda, 3:296
affection seldom shown
    Circassians, 9:57
    Gusii, 9:109
    Kipsigis, 9:165
aggressiveness condemned
    Danes, 4:90
aggressiveness discouraged
    Pima-Papago, 1:289
    West Greenland Inuit, 1:377
    Zuni, 1:398
aggressiveness encouraged
    Fore, 2:64
    Maori, 2:178
    Sengseng, 2:297
    Vlach Gypsies of Hungary, 4:272
amiability emphasized
    Kuikuru, 7:208
assertiveness emphasized
    Cinta Larga, 7:128
    Yanomamö, 7:376
aunts and uncles play important roles
    Qashqa'i, 9:286
authoritarian
    Dobu, 2:51

Samoa, 2:288
Tokelau, 2:331
Tolai, 2:335
behavior rules well-defined
    Osage, 1:278
boys and girls compete
    Ewenki, 6:434
boys and girls conditioned differently
    Teton, 1:345
    Tewa Pueblos, 1:349
    Vlach Gypsies of Hungary, 4:272
boys and girls preferred equally
    Danes, 4:90
boys and girls treated alike
    Cotopaxi Quichua, 7:134
boys dressed as girls to ward off evil spirits
    Arabs, 9:24
boys favored
    Arabs, 9:24
    Jews of Iran, 9:140
boys given preferential treatment
    Vlach Gypsies of Hungary, 4:272
boys less restricted than girls
    Sephardic Jews, 4:228
boys more protected than girls
    Vlachs, 4:274
boys preferred
    East Indians in Trinidad, 8:106
carefree childhood emphasized
    Flemish, 4:107
child-centered
    Abenaki, 1:5
    Acholi, 9:5
    African American, 1:12
    Arab Americans, 1:24
    Arabs, 9:24
    Comanche, 1:75
    Copper Eskimo, 1:78
    Flemish, 4:107
    Hungarians, 4:144
    Kiowa, 1:188
    Maltese, 4:168
    Menominee, 1:221
    Rom, 1:305
    Romanians, 4:214
    Saint Lucians, 8:231
    Shona, 9:313
    Taos, 1:342
    Ute, 1:361
    Vlach Gypsies of Hungary, 4:272
    West Greenland Inuit, 1:377
child's individuality recognized
    Dutch, 4:93
    Mescalero Apache, 1:225
    Navajo, 1:252
    Norwegians, 4:182
    Piemontese Sinti, 4:201
    Saami, 4:222
    Western Apache, 1:372
child's responsibility for own actions
        emphasized
    Northern Paiute, 1:264
close mother-child ties
    Ionians, 4:150
    Tory Islanders, 4:266
collaborative learning
    Guahibo-Sikuani, 7:165
communal well-being emphasized

Yukuna, 7:388
conformity to local values emphasized
    Hungarians, 4:144
    Madeirans, 4:165
constant maternal contact
    Afro-Bolivians, 7:9
    Callahuaya, 7:89
    Cinta Larga, 7:128
    Miami, 1:231
    Piemontese Sinti, 4:201
    Wáiwai, 7:347
    Wanano, 7:350
    Waorani, 7:353
    Wayapi, 7:362
    Yanomamö, 7:376
    Yukuna, 7:388
criticism emphasized
    Czechs, 4:84
economic activity participation. _See_ Child
        tasks
education. _See_ Education
emotional restraint emphasized
    Bonerate, 5:45
    Slavey, 1:320
family dependency encouraged
    Rom, 1:305
family honor emphasized
    Tausug, 5:263
family solidarity emphasized
    Vietnamese, 5:285
father responsible for training
    Candoshi, 7:93
firstborn-parental avoidance
    Zarma, 9:405
frustration avoidance emphasized
    Piemontese Sinti, 4:201
full involvement in adult society
    Rominche, 4:217
genealogy emphasized
    Ozarks, 1:281
generosity emphasized
    Slavey, 1:320
girl avoids and fears father and elders
    Maasai, 9:208
girls preferred
    Seri, 8:234
    Zaramo, 9:402
godparent involvement
    Greeks, 4:133
harsh
    Albanians, 4:6
    Bavarians, 4:34
    Bhil, 3:40
hostility and violence discouraged
    Washoe, 1:369
    Zuni, 1:398
humility emphasized
    Old Believers, 1:274
    Tanana, 1:339
imitative learning. _See subhead_ adult role
        models _above_
independence valued
    Boazi, 2:30
    Central Thai, 5:71
    Chipaya, 7:116
    Finns, 4:103
    Hungarians, 4:144
    Kalingas, 5:122

Child-rearing philosophy (cont'd)
  Kiribati, 2:122
  Kwoma, 2:135
  Mailu, 2:155
  Melanau, 5:179
  Murik, 2:222
  Muyu, 2:229
  Poles, 4:203
  Pume, 7:280
  Semang, 5:235
  Tanana, 1:339
  Temiar, 5:270
  Vlach Gypsies of Hungary, 4:272
  individual autonomy emphasized
    Slavey, 1:320
  individual rights respected
    Mescalero Apache, 1:225
  indulgent
    Aranda, 2:17
    Ata Tana 'Ai, 5:24
    Bulgarians, 4:44
    Flemish, 4:107
    Garia, 2:75
    Gebusi, 2:78
    Goodenough Island, 2:87
    Javanese, 5:112
    Kaingáng, 7:186
    Keraki, 2:113
    Kiribati, 2:122
    Korean, 5:147
    Lahu, 5:153
    Lak, 2:138
    Malay, 5:175
    Maltese, 4:168
    Mardudjara, 2:181
    Mendi, 2:204
    Micronesians, 1:237
    Mohave, 1:241
    Muong, 5:191
    Murngin, 2:225
    Nootka, 1:256
    Orokolo, 2:259
    Rom, 1:305
    Siwai, 2:303
    Tahiti, 2:306
    Tasmanians, 2:316
    Tauade, 2:319
    Tigray, 9:348
    Tikopia, 2:326
    tropical-forest foragers, 9:357
    Ulithi, 2:359
    Ute, 1:361
    Wantoat, 2:369
    Warlpiri, 2:374
    Western Apache, 1:372
    Wik Mungkan, 2:378
    Yuqui, 7:393
    see also subhead permissive/indulgent
      below
  industriousness emphasized
    Dargins, 6:98
    Slavey, 1:320
  infant always near mother or another
      woman's body
    Amhara, 9:19
  intergenerational dependency valued
    Dalmatians, 4:87
    Sicilians, 4:236

  interpersonal skills emphasized
    Bukidnon, 5:54
    Japanese, 5:108
    Kwoma, 2:135
    Malekula, 2:165
    Melanau, 5:180
    Mountain Arapesh, 2:217
    Rossel Island, 2:279
    Samal Moro, 5:223
  "knowing one's place" emphasized
    Romanians, 4:214
  learning by observation. See subhead adult
      role models above
  manners and etiquette emphasized
    Poles, 4:203
  maternal-paternal division of responsibilities
    Mescalero Apache, 1:225
  maternal uncle role
    Yagua, 7:373
  "merriness" and "alertness" emphasized
    Yurok, 1:395
  moral conduct seen reflecting on mother
    Sardinians, 4:227
  morality and religion emphasized
    Welsh, 4:280
  no role for father
    Kumyks, 6:223
  nurturing
    Washoe, 1:369
  patriotism inculcated
    Poles, 4:203
  permissive
    Aleut, 1:15-16
    Amahuaca, 7:35
    Baiga, 3:20
    Blackfoot, 1:42
    Catawba, 1:54
    Cherokee, 1:61-62
    Cheyenne, 1:65
    Choctaw, 1:72
    Cree, 1:81
    Delaware, 1:86
    Divehi, 3:77
    Faroe Islanders, 4:99
    Gond, 3:86
    Hidatsa, 1:147
    Hopi, 1:149
    Jews, 1:169
    Kickapoo, 1:185
    Kwakiutl, 1:199
    Maliseet, 1:212
    Metis of Western Canada, 1:228
    Miami, 1:231
    Micmac, 1:234
    Mohave, 1:241
    Navajo, 1:252
    Nayaga, 3:195-196
    Nepali, 3:204
    Ojibwa, 1:270
    Pahari, 3:221
    Pomo, 1:294
    Quechan, 1:301
    Seminole, 1:313
    Sherpa, 3:259
    Slavey, 1:320
    Southern Paiute (and Chemehuevi),
      1:331
    Tanaina, 1:336

    Tewa Pueblos, 1:348
    Thadou, 3:288
    Ute, 1:361
    Washoe, 1:369
    West Greenland Inuit, 1:377
    Yuit, 1:391
    Zuni, 1:398
  permissive/indulgent
    Ache, 7:5
    Amuesha, 7:38
    Araweté, 7:57
    Barama River Carib, 7:82
    Canela, 7:96
    Canelos Quichua, 7:100
    Chamacoco, 7:109
    Chiriguano, 7:121
    Chorote, 7:125
    Colorado, 7:131
    Cotopaxi Quichua, 7:134
    Cubeo, 7:141
    Culina, 7:147
    Cuna, 7:150
    Dani, 2:44
    Desana, 7:153
    Emberá, 7:157
    Evenki (Northern Tungus), 6:122
    Flemish, 4:107
    Gogodala, 2:84
    Guahibo-Sikuani, 7:165
    Guajiro, 7:169
    Iban, 5:98
    Kuikuru, 7:208
    Macuna, 7:213
    Ningerum, 2:247
    Otavalo, 7:254
    Piemontese Sinti, 4:200
    Saraguro, 7:294
    Shipibo, 7:305
    Siona-Secoya, 7:308
    Terena, 7:326
    Ticuna, 7:329
    Toba, 7:332
    Vietnamese, 5:285
    Waorani, 7:353
    Wapisiana, 7:355-356
    Xokléng, 7:371
    Yagua, 7:373
    see also subhead indulgent above
  perseverance valued
    Finns, 4:103
  praise and encouragement emphasized
    Mandan, 1:215
    Qalandar, 3:247
  protective
    Futuna, 2:67
    Rom, 1:305
  public displays of affection avoided
    Khevsur, 6:196
  relaxed
    Tory Islanders, 4:266
  reputation within community emphasized
    Sardinians, 4:227
  resourcefulness valued
    Flemish, 4:107
  respect emphasized
    Apiaká, 7:49
    Aymara, 7:67
    Hungarians, 4:144

Kogi, **7:**202
Maltese, **4:**168
Micronesians, **1:**237
Serbs, **4:**231
Tiroleans, **4:**263
Vlachs, **4:**274
respect for others valued
Finns, **4:**103
restraint emphasized
Menominee, **1:**221
self-confidence and self-reliance emphasized
Yuit, **1:**391
self-control emphasized
German Swiss, **4:**127
Menominee, **1:**221
West Greenland Inuit, **1:**377-378
self-effacement emphasized, **1:**289
self-reliance emphasized
Poles, **4:**203
social role emphasized
Sardinians, **4:**227
spoiling of child. *See subhead* indulgent;
    subhead permissive/indulgent *above*
storytelling as training
Menominee, **1:**221
Mescalero Apache, **1:**225
Orcadians, **4:**187
Pomo, **1:**294
Winnebago, **1:**381
strictness
Bavarians, **4:**34
Central Yup'ik Eskimos, **1:**58
Chamacoco, **7:**109
Desana, **7:**153
Kogi, **7:**202
Kumeyaay, **1:**195
Oriya, **3:**217
Pawnee, **1:**285
Sinhalese, **3:**266
Tamil of Sri Lanka, **3:**282
strong parental bonds
Chin, **3:**66
Gond, **3:**85, 86
tolerant
Micmac, **1:**234
toughness emphasized
Poles, **4:**203
versatility rewarded
Saami, **4:**222
willfulness allowed
Flemish, **4:**107
work ethic emphasized
Old Believers, **1:**274
see also Child discipline Children; Infants
Children
adoption of. *See* Adoption practices
afterlife of. *See under* Afterlife
beggars
Xoraxané Romá, **4:**281, 282
belief in rebirth of
Tamil, **3:**279
believed to have close supernatural
    associations
Menominee, **1:**221
clan recruitment
Daribi, **2:**47
cultural denial of sexuality of
Rominche, **4:**217

death caused by Bad Dead
Yakö, **9:**387
diet. *See under* Food
as economic investment
Barbadians, **8:**22-23
foster. *See* Fosterage
four minimum per family to replace grand-
    parents
Kikuyu, **9:**162
freedom to choose where to live
Mescalero Apache, **1:**225
Rapa, **2:**275
funerary practices. *See under* Mortuary
    practices
handicapped
Hani, **6:**451
illegitimate. *See* Illegitimacy
infantile sexual manifestations punished,
    7:202
interethnic
Okinawans, **5:**200
latchkey
Cayman Islanders, **8:**47
live with grandparents in preteen years
Lunda, **9:**197
mortality rate. *See* Infant and child
    mortality rates
peer influence
English, **4:**97
Frisians, **4:**111
popular culture influence
English, **4:**97
presentation to ancestors
Fali, **9:**96
property rights
Korku, **3:**134
punishment. *See* Child discipline
relationship with parents
Belau, **2:**26
Chambri, **2:**32
Gahuku-Gama, **2:**69
Gogodala, **2:**84
religious fasting required
Old Believers, **6:**293
sexual expression allowed
Araweté, **7:**57
sleep away from parents at young age
Gusii, **9:**110
sleep with other children or grandparents
Ndembu, **9:**240
soul acquisition
Selkup, **6:**327
"spouses" for spirits
Ewe and Fon, **9:**86
as status for parents
Martiniquais, **8:**163
toys
Orcadians, **4:**187
toys out of scraps
Tswana, **9:**361
trance during possession ceremony
Ewe and Fon, **9:**86
valued. *See* Child-rearing philosophy, child-
    centered
see also Adolescents; Infants
Child tasks (family economic activity par-
    ticipation)
Awá Kwaiker, **7:**64

Bulgarians, **4:**43
Callahuaya, **7:**89
Craho, **7:**138
Danes, **4:**90
Flemish, **4:**107
Gaels (Irish), **4:**116
Guajiro, **7:**169
Irish Travellers, **4:**155
Kashubians, **4:**158, 159
Koya, **3:**140
Madeirans, **4:**165
Manx, **4:**171
Montagnais-Naskapi, **1:**245
Newar, **3:**207
Nyinba, **3:**212
Otavalo, **7:**254
Pahari, **3:**221
Pasiegos, **4:**190
Pemon, **7:**272
Qalandar, **3:**247
Rikbaktsa, **7:**287
Rom, **1:**304
Rominche, **4:**217
Salasaca, **7:**290
Santal, **3:**254
Sherpa, **3:**259
Sinhalese, **3:**266
Slovaks, **4:**244
Suya, **7:**316
Swedes, **4:**257, 258
Tamil, **3:**278
Tiroleans, **4:**263
Trio, **7:**336
Wanano, **7:**350
Xoraxané Romá, **4:**281, 282
Yanomamö, **7:**376
Yuit, **1:**391
Yukuna, **7:**388
Yurok, **1:**394
Child of Water (deity)
Western Apache, **1:**373
Chilie cultivation
Lahu, **5:**152
Mazahua, **8:**165
Telugu, **3:**285
Tepehuan of Chihuahua, **8:**252
Tlapanec, **8:**259
Vedda, **3:**301
Chilkat blanket weaving
Tlingit, **1:**351
Tsimshian, **1:**355
Chimes
Bavarians, **4:**35
Chimiding (religious belief)
Pemon, **7:**273
Chinatowns
East Asians of Canada, **1:**95
East Asians of the United States, **1:**99, 100,
    101
Chivalry
Dalmatians, **4:**87
Chochiman (religious belief)
Pemon, **7:**273
Chocolate manufacture
Flemish, **4:**106
Walloons, **4:**276
Cholera
Cheyenne, **1:**65

Ch'ondogyo
    Korean, 5:148
Chong Yang (holiday)
    Hakka, 6:439
Choral singing
    choral groups
        Kipsigis, 9:165
        Ndembu, 9:241
        Tswana, 9:364
    Icelanders, 4:148
    Sherpa, 3:259
    Sorbs, 4:253-254
    Vlach Gypsies of Hungary, 4:272
Chosen people
    Thadou, 3:288
Christian Community of Universal Brother-
        hood (Doukhobors), 1:90, 91, 92
Christian influences
    on Pomaks, 4:205
Christianity (undifferentiated)
    Ache, 7:6
    African Americans, 1:13
    Akan, 9:12
    Alorese, 5:14, 15
    Arab Americans, 1:24, 25
    Bagobo, 5:29
    Bahamians, 8:20
    Bakairi, 7:75
    Balantak, 5:35
    Banggai, 5:38
    Baniwa-Curripaco-Wakuenai, 7:79
    Barama River Carib, 7:82
    Barbadians, 8:23
    Batak, 5:39
    Baul songs, 3:26
    Bedouin, 9:45
    Bisaya, 5:42
    Blang, 6:422
    Boazi, 2:30
    Bugle, 8:33
    Bunun, 5:56, 57, 58
    Burakumin, 5:63
    Burmese, 5:65
    Candoshi, 7:94
    Central Thai, 5:71
    Chayahuita, 7:111
    Cherokee pastors, 1:62
    Chimbu, 2:37
    Chin, 5:65
    Chinese in Southeast Asia, 5:77
    Chipaya, 7:116
    Chiriguano, 7:121
    Circassians, 6:90;9:67
    Cook Islands, 2:42
    Cotabato Manobo, 5:79
    Culina, 7:148
    Curaçao, 8:98
    Dani, 2:45
    Dobu, 2:50, 51
    Dogon, 9:73
    Dusun, 5:83
    East Asians of Canada, 1:97-98
    East Asians of the United States, 1:103
    Edo, 9:82
    Eipo, 2:58
    Emberá, 7:157
    Europeans in South Asia, 3:79
    Ewe and Fon, 9:87-88

    Fali, 9:96, 97
    Foi, 2:60
    Fore, 2:62, 64
    French of India, 3:80
    Ganda, 9:105
    Garo converts, 3:82, 84
    Gayo, 5:89
    Gogodala, 2:84
    Hakka, 6:438, 439
    Herero, 9:118
    Hmong, 5:94
    Huichol, 8:127
    Hupa, 1:152
    Hutterites, 1:154
    Ibaloi, 5:95
    Igbo, 9:123
    Indian Christians, 3:103
    Indonesian, 5:103
    Iraqw, 9:126
    Itonama, 7:179
    Japanese, 5:104, 105, 109
    Jingpo, 6:455-456, 458
    Kachin, 5:65
    Kapingamarangi, 2:110
    Karen, 5:65, 126, 128-129
    Kashubians, 4:159
    Kenyah-Kayan-Kajang, 5:134
    Khasi converts, 3:125
    Kickapoo, 1:185
    Kikuyu, 9:162
    Kipsigis, 9:165
    Kolisuch'ok, 5:144
    Kosrae, 2:128, 129
    Koya converts, 3:139
    Kubachins, 6:219
    Kumyks, 6:223
    Kwoma, 2:134, 136
    Kyrgyz, 6:228
    Ladinos, 8:152
    Lak, 2:139
    Lakalai, 2:142
    Laks, 6:233
    Lango, 9:181
    Lao, 5:159
    Laz, 6:239, 240
    Luyia, 9:205
    Madurese, 5:168
    Mae Enga, 2:150
    Mafulu, 2:153
    Maká, 7:217
    Makushi, 7:219
    Malayali converts, 3:166
    Manihiki, 2:172
    Maonan, 6:468
    Marshall Islands, 2:194
    Mataco, 7:229
    Mehinaku, 7:238
    Melanau, 5:178, 180
    Melpa, 2:202
    Mende, 9:223
    Mentaweian, 5:181
    Miao, 6:472
    Mimika, 2:208
    Minahasans, 5:181
    Miyanmin, 2:211
    Mizo converts, 3:179
    Mohave, 1:241
    Mossi, 9:229

    Motu, 2:215
    Murik, 2:222
    Murngin, 2:224, 226
    Ndembu, 9:240
    Niue, 2:252
    Nivaclé, 7:250
    North Alaskan Eskimos, 1:261
    Okiek, 9:261
    Ontong Java, 2:254
    Orochi, 6:295
    Orok, 6:297
    Ossetes, 6:301
    Palestinians, 9:265
    Penan, 5:210
    Pende, 9:274
    Pima-Pago, 1:290
    Pokot, 9:283
    Polynesians, 1:292
    Rennell Island, 2:277
    Rotinese, 5:214
    Saluan, 5:217
    Sangir, 5:224
    Santa Cruz, 2:292
    Selepet, 2:295
    Selung/Moken, 5:232
    Senoi, 5:238
    Shipibo, 7:306
    Shona, 9:314
    Shors, 6:331
    Singaporean, 5:242
    South Asians in Southeast Asia, 5:243
    Swazi, 9:332
    Syrian Christians of Kerala, 3:271-275
    Tabasarans, 6:350
    Tahiti, 2:307
    Tairora, 2:309
    Tanna, 2:315
    Telefolmin, 2:321
    Tikopia, 2:326
    Toba, 7:333
    Toda, 3:295, 297
    Tofalar, 6:363
    Tojolab'al, 8:263
    Tokelau, 2:330
    Tolai, 2:335
    Tonga, 2:336-337, 338;9:355
    Toraja, 5:283
    Torres Strait Islanders, 2:346
    Trio, 7:336, 337
    Tsimihety, 9:359
    Turks, 9:376
    Usino, 2:361
    Wáiwai, 7:347, 348
    Wamira, 2:367
    Wantoat, 2:369
    Waorani, 7:353
    Wape, 2:372
    Wik Mungkan, 2:379
    Woleai, 2:383
    Yap, 2:391
    Yoruba, 9:393
    Yukagir, 6:413
    Zoroastrians, 9:409
    Zulu, 9:412
    see also Orthodox Christianity; Protes-
        tantism; Roman Catholicism; Syn-
        cretism; specific denominations and
        sects

Christmas (holiday)
  Aleuts, **6:**18
  Ambae, **2:**12
  Anuta, **2:**15
  Armenians, **6:**31
  Belarussians, **6:**61
  Carpatho-Rusyns, **6:**71
  Dolgan, **6:**102
  Futuna, **2:**67
  Gahuku-Gama, **2:**70
  Georgians, **6:**135
  Gypsies, **6:**148
  Khevsur, **6:**196
  Kiribati, **2:**123
  Kosrae, **2:**130
  Lahu, **5:**154
  Manx, **4:**171
  Moldovans, **6:**269
  Old Believers, **1:**274;**6:**294
  Orcadians, **4:**188
  Peloponnesians, **4:**194
  Poles, **6:**309
  Pukapuka, **2:**272
  Romanians, **4:**214
  Siberiaki, **6:**334
  Siberian Germans, **6:**339
  Slav Macedonians, **4:**241
  Tagalog, **5:**251
  Telefolmin, **2:**323
  Torres Strait Islanders, **2:**347
  Ukrainian peasants, **6:**387
  Ukrainians, **6:**394
  Ukrainians of Canada, **1:**359
  Vietnamese, **5:**287
Chromium mining
  Slav Macedonians, **4:**240
Church of Christ
  Ambae, **2:**10
  Pentecost, **2:**261, 262, 263
  Tagalog, **5:**250
Church of England. *See* Anglicanism
Church of God
  Kittsians and Nevisians, **8:**145
  Turks and Caicos Islanders, **8:**273
Church of Melanesia
  Ontong Java, **2:**255
  Tikopia, **2:**325, 326
Church of Scotland
  Highland Scots, **4:**141
  Lowland Scots, **4:**163
  Orcadians, **4:**187
Church of South India
  Syrian Christian of Kerala, **3:**274
  Toda, **3:**297
  see also Anglicanism
Church of the Nazarene
  Cape Verdeans, **4:**56
  Wovan, **2:**385
Church-state separation
  Baluchi, **3:**24
  Mennonites, **1:**219
Cicumcision
  Chagga, **9:**62
Cinema. *See* Film industry
Circassians, **6:**89
Circle Dance
  Southern Paiute (and Chemehuevi),
    1:332

Circumcision
  Ajarians, **6:**14
  Anuta, **2:**15
  Arabs, **9:**24
  Aranda, **2:**18
  Ata Sikka, **5:**20, 22
  Ata Tana 'Ai, **5:**26
  Baggara, **9:**31
  Bajau, **5:**33
  Bamiléké, **9:**39
  Bedouin, **9:**45
  Bene Israel, **3:**28
  Berbers of Morocco, **9:**52
  Bohra, **3:**48
  Bukharan Jews, **6:**65
  Crimean Tatars, **6:**94
  Dungans, **6:**110
  Edo, **9:**81
  Falasha, **9:**92
  Gayo, **5:**90
  Gusii, **9:**110
  Huarayo, **7:**178
  Hui, **6:**453
  Iraqw, **9:**125
  Javanese, **5:**112
  Jews, Arabic-speaking, **9:**136
  Kamilaroi, **2:**104
  Karaites, **6:**165;**9:**155
  Kikuyu, **9:**162
  Kilenge, **2:**119
  Kipsigis, **9:**165
  Kpelle, **9:**173
  Kyrgyz, **6:**231
  Lesu, **2:**146, 147
  Lithuanian Jews, **6:**246
  Luba of Shaba, **9:**192
  Lunda, **9:**197, 199
  Luyia, **9:**205, 206
  Makassar, **5:**174
  Mbeere, **9:**222
  Meo, **3:**174
  Mijikenda, **9:**224
  Mountain Jews, **6:**273
  Nubians, **9:**248
  Ogan-Besemah, **5:**198
  Pamir peoples, **6:**306
  Pathan, **3:**232
  Pedi, **9:**270
  Pende, **9:**274
  Pentecost, **2:**264
  peripatetics of Iraq, Syria, Lebanon, Jordan,
    Israel, Egypt, Sudan, and Yemen,
    9:277
  peripatetics of the Maghreb, **9:**278
  Pintupi, **2:**266
  Pokot, **9:**282, 283
  Qashqa'i, **9:**287
  Rukuba, **9:**290
  Sakalava, **9:**296
  Samal, **5:**220
  San-speaking peoples, **9:**303
  Selepet, **2:**294
  Selkup, **6:**327
  Shahsevan, **9:**310
  Suku, **9:**322
  Swahili, **9:**328
  Tajiks, **6:**354
  Tangu, **2:**312

  Tanna, **2:**314
  Tausug, **5:**263
  Ternatan/Tidorese, **5:**276
  tropical-forest foragers, **9:**357
  Tuareg, **9:**369
  Warlpiri, **2:**374
  Wolof, **9:**379, 380
  Yemenis, **9:**390
  Yezidis, **6:**410
  Yörük, **9:**396
  Zande, **9:**398, 399
  Zaramo, **9:**402
  Zarma, **9:**405
Circumcision (female). *See* Clitoridectomy
Circumcision (royal)
  Sakalava, **9:**294, 296, 298
"Circumcision queen"
  Mande, **9:**216
Circus managers
  Piemontese Sinti, **4:**200
  Spanish Rom, **4:**254, 255
Citrus fruit growing
  Catalans, **4:**62
  Cretans, **4:**70
  Cypriots, **4:**80
  Peloponnesians, **4:**193
  Sicilians, **4:**236
  Sipakapense, **8:**235
  Yörük, **9:**394
City life. *See* Urban areas
Civil disobedience
  Dutch, **4:**94
Civil rights. *See* Ethnic groups, rights
    movements
Civil service. *See* Government employment
Civil war
  Basques, **4:**30
  Bengali, **3:**30
  Castilians, **4:**58
  Catalans, **4:**62
  Cherokee, **1:**62
  Croats, **4:**74
  Kashmiri, **3:**122
  Tamil of Sri Lanka, **3:**284
  Tanaina, **1:**336
  see also Political violence
Clan
  Abor, **3:**4
  Albanian-Americans, **1:**107
  Albanians, **4:**5, 6
  Andamanese, **3:**9
  Apache, **1:**372
  Appalachians, **1:**22
  Badaga, **3:**16
  Baluchi, **3:**23
  Bau, **2:**23
  Bhil, **3:**39
  Bhuiya, **3:**43
  Brahmans of Nepal, **3:**52
  Burusho, **3:**55
  Chácobo, **7:**106
  Chamacoco, **7:**109
  Chenchu, **3:**61
  Cherokee, **1:**61
  Chhetri of Nepal, **3:**52
  Chickasaw, **1:**66
  Chin, **3:**65
  Chitpavan Brahman, **3:**70

Clan (cont'd)
  Choctaw, 1:72
  Cocopa, 1:74
  Corsicans, 4:68
  Crow, 1:83
  Cubeo, 7:140
  Delaware, 1:86
  Desana, 7:152
  East Asians of Canada, 1:97
  Fox, 1:128, 129, 130
  Garo, 3:82, 83
  Gond, 3:85
  Guajiro, 7:168
  Gujar, 3:89
  Gurung, 3:94
  Hidatsa, 1:147
  Highland Scots, 4:141
  Hopi, 1:149-150
  Hopi-Tewa, 1:151
  Huron, 1:152
  Hutterites, 1:154
  Inughuit, 1:161
  Irish, 4:153
  Irula, 3:106
  Jat, 3:112
  Ka'wiari, 7:198-199
  Keres Pueblo Indians, 1:180
  Khasi, 3:124, 125
  Kickapoo, 1:185, 186
  Klingit, 1:352, 353
  Kond, 3:133
  Kota, 3:136, 137
  Kutchin, 1:196
  Lakher, 3:146
  Lepcha, 3:149
  Lillooet, 1:206
  Limbu, 3:150
  Macuna, 7:213
  Magar, 3:154, 156-157
  Mandan, 1:214, 215
  Maricopa, 1:216
  Mauritian, 3:172
  Menominee, 1:221
  Meo, 3:174
  Miami, 1:231
  Montenegrins, 4:173
  Munda, 3:182, 183
  Nagas, 3:189, 190
  Navajo, 1:252
  Nepali, 3:202, 203
  Nyinba, 3:211
  Ojibwa, 1:270
  Omaha, 1:275
  Osage, 1:278, 279
  Pahari, 3:221
  Palikur, 7:262
  Pathan, 3:231, 232
  Piapoco, 7:274
  Piro, 7:280
  Ponca, 1:296
  Potawatomi, 1:297
  Punjabi, 3:239
  Quechan, 1:301
  Rajput, 3:249
  Reddi, 3:249-250
  Sadhu, 3:252
  Santal, 3:253, 254
  Selepet, 2:294

  Seminole, 1:313
  Seminole of Oklahoma, 1:314
  Shawnee, 1:317
  Sherpa, 3:258
  Slav Macedonians, 4:240-241
  Suruí, 7:312, 313
  Tamang, 3:275
  Tanaina, 1:336
  Telugu, 3:286
  Thadou, 3:288
  Thakali, 3:291
  Ticuna, 7:329
  Tlingit, 1:351, 352, 353
  Tonkowa, 1:354
  Tsimshian, 1:355
  Tunebo, 7:338
  Ute, 1:361
  Winnebago, 1:381-382
  Yagua, 7:372
  Yankton, 1:386
  Yuit, 1:391, 392
  Zuni, 1:398, 399
  see also Endogamy; Exogamy; Fictive clan;
    Patriclan; Phratries; Tiyospayes
Clan deities
  Thakali, 3:291
Clan grave
  Thakali, 3:291
Clann
  Gaels (irish), 4:116
  Tory Islanders, 4:265
Class division. See under Status, basis of
Classificatory kinship terminology. See under
    Kinship terminology
Class immobility
  Madeirans, 4:165
  see also Castes
Class mobility
  Bhuiya, 3:43
  Chin, 3:66
  Croats, 4:74
  German Swiss, 4:126
  Greeks, 4:133
  Javanese, 5:112-113
  Jews, 1:169
  Khmer, 5:137
  Lingayat, 3:153
  Mauritian, 3:172
  Melanau, 5:179
  Nias, 5:196
  Samal Moro, 5:223
  see also Hypergamy; Sanskritization
Clay dolls
  Quechan, 1:301
Clay figurines
  Kanja, 3:120
Clay painting
  Andamanese, 3:11
Clay pipes
  Iroquois, 1:165
Clay work
  Afro-Hispanic Pacific Lowlanders, 7:23
  Toba, 7:332
  Yukpa, 7:383
  see also Pottery
Cleanliness (social emphasis on)
  Santal, 3:254
  see also Purity and pollution codes

Clitoridectomy
  Arabs, 9:24
  Baggara, 9:31
  Bajau, 5:33
  Bedouin, 9:45
  Chagga, 9:62
  Edo, 9:81
  Kikuyu, 9:162
  Mande, 9:216
  Samal, 5:220
  Yakö, 9:385
Clitoridectomy (before first menses)
  Mbeere, 9:222
Clitoridectomy (initiation)
  Gusii, 9:110
  Kipsigis, 9:165
  Kpelle, 9:173-174
  Pokot, 9:283
Clocks and watches
  clock stopped at death
    Kashubians, 4:159
  making
    Frisians, 4:111
    German Swiss, 4:125
Closed community
  Amish, 1:18
  Bulgarian Gypsies, 4:40, 43
  Hasidim, 1:142-145
  Highland Scots, 4:141
  Hutterites, 1:153
  Irish Travelers, 1:164
  Irish Travellers, 4:155
  Mennonites, 1:218-219
  Ozarks, 1:280-282
  Parsi, 3:228
  Qalandar, 3:246
  Rom of Czechoslovakia, 4:219
  Rominche, 4:216, 217
  Slovensko Roma, 4:250
  Spanish Rom, 4:255
  Vlach Gypsies of Hungary, 4:270-273
Cloth. See under Money and wealth; Textiles
Clothing
  animal skins
    Northern Shoshone Bannock, 1:266
    Ojibwa, 271;1:269
    Yuit, 1:390
  bark-cloth and cotton
    Pauserna, 7:270
  bark-cloth tunic shirts
    Itonama, 7:179
    Mataco, 7:227
    Moré, 7:243
    Yuracaré, 7:396
  black robes
    Mount Athos, 4:177
  ceremonial
    Asurini, 7:62
    Copper Eskimo, 1:79
    Hutterites, 1:154
    Ka'wiari, 7:200
    Kilenge, 2:119
    Kwakiutl, 1:200
    Macuna, 7:214
    Ndebele, 9:238
    Paï-Tavytera, 7:259
    Pomo, 1:294
  colorful traditional costumes

Slav Macedonians, **4:**241
conical hat
    Nootka, **1:**257
dirndl
    Barvarians, **4:**35
discount selling
    Gitanos, **4:**129
distinctive
    Amish, **1:**18
    Baul, **3:**26
    Bavarians, **4:**35
    Bengali Shakta, **3:**35
    Hasidim, **1:**142
    Khasi, **3:**125
    Parsi, **3:**229
    peripatetics, **3:**236
    Romanian subregions, **4:**213
    Sadhu, **3:**251
    Saraguro, **7:**295
    Seminole, **1:**313
    Sorbs, **4:**253, 254
    Thakur, **3:**293
    see also Head covering; Purdah; Veiling
        of women
elaborate decoration
    Dolgan, **6:**102
    Hare, **1:**140
    Hidatsa, **1:**146
    Ingalik, **1:**158
    Karachays, **6:**161
    Kazakhs, **6:**182
    Tanaina, **1:**337
feathered headdress
    Washoe, **1:**370
feathered headdress and aprons
    Paresí, **7:**269
feathered headdress and ornaments
    Chácobo, **7:**106
felt
    Vlachs, **4:**274
fur caps and boots
    Tanana, **1:**339
fur robe
    Western Shoshone, **1:**375
gazelle-skin shirt/dress
    Sleb, **9:**315
huipil (dresses)
    Triqui, **8:**271, 272
    Yukateko, **8:**310
indicating initiate level
    Akha, **5:**12
for initiation
    Zoroastrians, **9:**409
kente cloth
    Ewe and Fon, **9:**88
leather garments
    Metis of Western Canada, **1:**228
    Montagnais-Naskapi, **1:**246
leaves for women
    Lobi-Dagarti peoples, **9:**186
lederhosen
    Bavarians, **4:**35
long dress
    Paraujano, **7:**268
manufacture
    Dyula, **9:**76, 77-78
    East Asians of Canada, **1:**96
    East Asians of the United States, **1:**100

Romanians, **4:**213
mola (multilayered cloth)
    Kuna, **8:**147
mourning. *See* Mourning
painted decorations
    Miami, **1:**232
    Montagnais-Naskapi, **1:**246
penis shields. *See under* Nudity
poncho
    Tunebo, **7:**338
red color
    Tzotzil of Zinacantan, **8:**292
sealskin
    West Greenland Inuit, **1:**377
shredded cedar bark
    Nootka, **1:**256
string skirts
    Ayoreo, **7:**70
traditional
    Old Believers, **1:**274
    Vlachs, **4:**274
traditional costume manufacture
    German Swiss, **4:**127
    Norwegians, **4:**181, 182
    Seminole, **1:**313
    Slovaks, **4:**243, 245
wedding
    Altaians, **6:**22
    Karen, **5:**127
    Nicobarese, **3:**209
women's kilts
    Noanamá, **7:**252
    see also Body painting and ornamentation;
        Footwear; Nudity; Tailoring; Tattooing
Cloth weaving. *See* Textiles; Weaving; *specific*
        types of cloth
Cloud spirits
    Taos, **1:**343
Clove production
    Moluccans—North, **5:**188
    Ternatan/Tidorese, **5:**274
Clowns
    Hopi, **1:**149, 150
    Tewa Pueblos, **1:**349
    Zuni, **1:**399
Cnflict sources
    political
        Itza', **8:**135
Coal mining
    Appalachians, **1:**22
    Lowland Scots, **4:**163
    Poles, **4:**203
    Silesians, **4:**238
    Sorgs, **4:**253
    Walloons, **4:**277
    Welsh, **4:**279
Cocaine production
    Chimane, **7:**112
Coca leaf growing
    Afro-Bolivians, **7:**8
    Desana, **7:**152
    Páez, **7:**257
    Tanimuka, **7:**318
    Tatuyo, **7:**323
    Tunebo, **7:**337
    Witoto, **7:**364
Cochineal insect (dye)
    Paya, **8:**209

Cocoa growing
    Afro-Bolivians, **7:**8
    Afro-Colombians, **7:**16
    Afro-Venezuelans, **7:**26
    Araweté, **7:**56
    Barí, **7:**84
    Blacks of Costa Rica, **8:**25
    Bribri, Cabécar, **8:**27
    Chiquitano, **7:**118
    Chocó, **7:**122
    Ch'ol, **8:**64
    Chontal of Tabasco, **8:**68
    Colorado, **7:**131
    Cuna, **7:**149
    Dominicans, **8:**101
    Emberá, **7:**155
    Mandak, **2:**170
    Mayoruna, **7:**234
    Nasioi, **2:**233
    Samoa, **2:**287
    Sio, **2:**299
    Siwai, **2:**302
    Tolai, **2:**334
    Tunebo, **7:**337
    Witoto, **7:**364
    Zoque, **8:**315
    see also Chocolate manufacture
Coconuts and coconut products
    Andamanese, **3:**9
    Anuta, **2:**14
    Cape Verdeans, **4:**55
    Kapingamarangi, **2:**108
    Keraki, **2:**112
    Kiribati, **2:**121
    Kosrae, **2:**128
    Kuna, **8:**147, 149
    Kurtatchi, **2:**131
    Li, **6:**464
    Mangareva, **2:**172
    Manihiki, **2:**172
    Manus, **2:**174
    Marind-anim, **2:**183
    Marshall Islands, **2:**192
    Mekeo, **2:**198
    Mijikenda, **9:**224
    Motu, **2:**213
    Mundugumor, **2:**218
    Nasioi, **2:**233
    Nayar, **3:**198
    Nicobarese, **3:**209
    Niue, **2:**251
    Nomoi, **2:**252
    Ontong Java, **2:**254, 255
    Pukapuka, **2:**271
    Rennell Island, **2:**277
    Sakalava, **9:**294
    Samal Moro, **5:**222
    San Cristobal, **2:**289
    Sinhalese, **3:**265
    Syrian Christian of Kerala, **3:**273
    Tokelau, **2:**331
    Tonga, **2:**337
    Tongareva, **2:**340
    Tuvalu, **2:**355
    Ulithi, **2:**358
    Waropen, **2:**376
    Wogeo, **2:**380
    Yakan, **5:**288

Coconuts and coconut products (cont'd)
    Zaramo, 9:401
Cod fishing
    Basques, 1:32, 33;4:30
    East Greenland Inuit, 1:106
    Klallam, 1:190
    Nootka, 1:256
    Shetlanders, 4:233
    West Greenland Inuit, 1:377
Coffee
    extensive drinking of
        Walloons, 4:276
    as male property
        Chagga, 9:61
Coffee grounds, fortune-telling from
    Dalmatians, 4:87
Coffee growing
    Afro-Bolivians, 7:8
    Afro-Colombians, 7:16
    Alur, 9:13
    Amuesha, 7:38
    Ashaninca, 7:91
    Awakateko, 8:15
    Bamiléké, 9:38
    Batak, 5:39
    Betsileo, 9:54
    Bukidnon, 5:53
    Campa del Alto Perené, 7:91
    Cashibo, 7:104
    Chagga, 9:61, 62
    Chatino, 8:51
    Chimbu, 2:35, 36
    Ch'ol, 8:64
    Chuj, 8:71
    Dominicans, 8:101
    Emberá, 7:155
    Gainj, 2:71
    Gayo, 5:88
    Gururumba, 2:92
    Gusii, 9:108
    Kewa, 2:115
    Konso, 9:169
    Kwoma, 2:134
    Mae Enga, 2:149
    Mazatec, 8:168
    Melpa, 2:201
    Mende, 9:223
    Mixe, 8:174
    Mixtec, 8:177
    Nahua of the Huasteca, 8:185
    Nahuat of the Sierra de Puebla, 8:192
    Nomatsiguenga, 7:91
    Nyakyusa and Ngonde, 9:253
    Ogan-Besemah, 5:198
    Páez, 7:257
    Palikur, 7:262
    Puerto Ricans, 8:221
    Q'eqchi', 8:226
    Rapa, 2:274
    Sambia, 2:284
    Selepet, 2:293
    Suruí, 7:312
    Syrian Christian of Kerala, 3:273
    Tanna, 2:314
    Totonac, 8:264
    Triqui, 8:270
    Tzotzil and Tzeltal of Pantelhó, 8:276
    Tz'utujil, 8:297

Wantoat, 2:368
Wasteko, 8:302
Xikrin, 7:367
Yukpa, 7:383
Zande, 9:398
Zapotec, 8:312
Zoque, 8:315
Cofradia (fraternal order)
    Andalusians, 4:12
    Castilians, 4:60
Cofradía system
    Tz'utujil, 8:298
    Zoque, 8:316
Cognatic kin. See Kinship, cognatic
Cohabiting couple. See Living together
Coins, death-related practices
    Albanians, 4:8
Cold hell belief
    Bretons, 4:40
Collateral joint family. See Family, joint sys-
        tem
Collective farms. See Agriculture, collective;
        Landholding, collective
Colony
    Hutterites, 1:153, 154
Color (racial). See Skin color
Colors. See Dyes; Mourning; Symbolism;
        Taboos
Comb making
    Bulgarian Gypsies, 4:41
Coming of age
    boy's entrance into a age-graded society
        Gros Venture, 1:134
    boy's forearm branded at age eight or ten
        Santal, 3:254
    boy's killing first game
        Cree, 1:81
    boy's thirteenth birthday
        Ashkenazim, 6:36
        Bene Israel, 3:28
        Karaites, 9:155
    boy's vision quest. See Vision quest
    debutante presentation
        Azoreans, 4:28
    fiesta for girls
        Seri, 8:235
    girl puts on sari
        Tamil, 3:278
    girl's fifteenth birthday
        Costa Ricans, 8:80-81
        Italian Mexicans, 8:131-132
        Mazahua, 8:166
        Nahua of the State of Mexico, 8:189
    girl's seclusion and taboos
        Haida, 1:136
        see also Menstruation
    girl's tattooing at age fourteen
        Santal, 3:254
    head shaving of boys and girls at age 16
        Kota, 3:137
    see also Initiation rites
Commercial centers. See Markets and fairs;
        Shopping centers
Common ancestry. See Apical ancestry
Common-interest associations. See Associa-
        tions, clubs, and societies
Common-law marriage
    Afro-Hispanic Pacific Lowlanders, 7:21

Antigua and Barbuda, 8:9
Barbadians, 8:22
cattle ranchers of Huasteca, 8:43
Chatino, 8:51
Chinese in Caribbean, 8:57
Chontal of Tabasco, 8:68
Cook Islands, 2:41
Costa Ricans, 8:80
Creoles of Nicaragua, 8:85
Cubans, 8:88
Cuicatec, 8:92
Dominicans, 8:102
Flemish, 4:107
Jamaicans, 8:138
Kuna, 8:148
Saint Lucians, 8:231
Swedes, 4:257
Tzotzil of San Bartolomé de los Llanos,
        8:289
Yaqui, 8:306
Zapotec, 8:312
see also Living together
Communal household. See Household,
        communal
Communality, strong sense of
    Taos, 1:342
Communal labor allocation. See Labor,
        communal allocation
Communal living. See Houses and housing,
        communal
Communal practices
    Acadians, 1:8
    Baffinland Inuit, 1:31
    Burusho, 3:55, 56
    Cherokee, 1:61
    Copper Eskimo, 1:78
    Danes, 4:89, 90
    Delaware, 1:86
    Dogrib, 1:88
    Doukhobors, 1:90, 91, 92
    Eastern Shoshone, 1:105
    Finns, 4:103, 104
    Frisians, 4:111
    Greek-speaking Jews of Greece, 4:135
    Hungarians, 4:144
    Hutterites, 1:153, 154
    Japanese of Canada, 1:95, 97
    Japanese in the United States, 1:102
    Jews of Israel, 9:150
    Jews of Yemen, 9:150
    Leonese, 4:161
    Madeirans, 4:165
    Maricopa, 1:216
    Mennonites, 1:219
    Metis of Western Canada, 1:227
    Mormons, 1:246, 248
    Mount Athos, 4:175-176
    Piemontese Sinti, 4:201
    Pomaks, 4:205
    Romanians, 4:214
    Selepet, 2:294
    Shakers, 1:316
    Shetlanders, 4:233
    Slavey, 1:320
    Slovenes, 4:247
    Swedes, 4:258
    Taos, 1:342
    Tiroleans, 4:263-264

Tory Islanders, 4:266
Vlachs, 4:274
Yavapai, 1:386
Yokuts, 1:388
Yuit, 1:391
  see also Communitarianism; _under_ specific
    subjects, e.g., Landholding
Commune (local governing unit)
  Piemontese, 4:199
  Provencal, 4:211
  Romanians, 4:214
  Sardinians, 4:227
  Sicilians, 4:236
  Slovenes, 4:248
Communications industry
  Jews, 1:169
Communidad (neighboring villages)
  Castilians, 4:59-60
Communitarianism
  Lingayat, 3:151, 153
  Shakers, 1:316
  Sinhalese, 3:265
  see also Egalitarianism
Community pressures. _See_ Public opinion
Compadrazgo (fictive kin)
  Amuzgo, 8:5
  Chinantec, 8:54
  Chontal of Tabasco, 8:68
  Guarijío, 8:118
  Itza', 8:134
  K'iche', 8:142
  Ladinos, 8:152
  Latinos, 1:205
  Mam, 8:158
  Mazahua, 8:165, 166
  Mixtec, 8:177
  Nahua of the State of Mexico, 8:189
  Otomí of the Sierra, 8:202
  Otomí of the Valley of Mezquital,
    8:205
  Pame, 8:208
  Pima Bajo, 8:212
  Poqomam, 8:218, 219
  Puerto Ricans, 8:222
  Q'anjob'al, 8:225
  Totonac, 8:265
  Tzotzil and Tzeltal of Pantelhó, 8:276
  Tzotzil of Chamula, 8:280
  Tzotzil of San Bartolomé de los Llanos,
    8:288
  Tz'utujil, 8:297
  Wasteko, 8:303
  Zapotec, 8:312
  Zoque, 8:316
Compadrio (fictive kin)
  Cape Verdeans, 4:55
Compassionate deity
  Lingayat, 3:151
Competitiveness
  as conflict source
    Kwakiutl, 1:199
    Maltese, 4:168, 169
  as marked social trait
    Khoja, 3:128
Competitive singing. _See_ Song duels
Compound
  Kanbi, 3:118
  Pathan, 3:231, 232

Tamil of Sri Lanka, 3:281
Washoe, 1:368
Con Cabur (feast)
  Cham, 5:73
Concubinage
  Arubans, 8:12
  Desana, 7:153
  Han, 6:444, 445
  Herero, 9:117-118
  Kanuri, 9:152
  Kol, 3:130
  Mazatec, 8:168
  Nayar, 3:199
  Tahiti, 2:306
  Tetum, 5:276
  Tswana, 9:362
Condolence ceremonies
  Iroquois, 1:167
Confederacy
  Cayuga, 1:55
  Iroquois, 1:164
  Mohawk, 1:242
  Nootka, 1:257
  Oneida, 1:275
  Onondaga, 1:276
  Pennacock, 1:286
  Powhatan, 1:297
  Senaca, 1:315
Confessional groups
  Doukhobors, 1:90
Confinement (as social control). _See_
    Imprisonment
Conflict avoidance. _See_ Avoidance;
    Withdrawal
Conflict causes
  adultery
    Gebusi, 2:78
    Guadalcanal, 1:91
    Malekula, 2:166
    Manurese, 5:167
    Sambia, 2:285
    Trobriand Islands, 2:350
    Truk, 2:352
    Wanano, 7:350
    Yurok, 1:395
  alcohol
    Catawba, 1:54
    Culina, 7:147
    Mescalero Apache, 1:225
    Micmac, 1:235
    Micronesians, 1:238
    Ojibwa, 1:270
    Pume, 7:284
    Shetlanders, 4:234
    Tonga, 9:355
    West Greenland Inuit, 1:378
  assaults
    Tlingit, 1:352
  borders and boundaries
    Alsatians, 4:8-9
    Canarians, 4:52
    Luiseño, 1:208
    Mohave, 1:241
    Poles, 4:204
    Romanians, 4:214
    Saami, 4:222
    Slovenes, 4:249
    Western Apache, 1:373

Yurok, 1:395
cultural and ethnic
  Chakma, 3:60
  Cherokee, 1:62
  Choctaw, 1:72
  Cora, 8:77
  Creoles of Nicaragua, 8:85
  Luyia, 9:205
  Palestinians, 9:266
  Swiss, Italian, 4:262
  Tlingit, 1:352-353
  Ute, 1:362
  see also Political violence
domestic violence. _See_ Domestic violence
drugs
  Bahamians, 8:20
  Madeirans, 4:166
factionalism
  Boruca, Bribri, Cabécar, 8:29
  Taos, 1:343
  Teton, 1:346
  Zuni, 1:399
family relations
  Calandar, 3:248
  Creoles of Nicaragua, 8:85
  Greeks, 4:133
  Mataco, 7:229
  North Alaskan Eskimos, 1:260
  Pasiegos, 4:191
  peripatetics, 3:236
  Piemontese, 4:198
  Rom, 1:305
feuds between kin groups. _See_ Blood feud
financial transactions
  Bulgarians, 4:45
  Slovensko Roma, 4:251
  Vlach Gypsies of Hungary, 4:272
fishing rights
  Yurok, 1:395
grudges
  Tamil of Sri Lanka, 1:283
honor
  Ionians, 4:150
  Pathan, 3:233
  Yörük, 9:396
horse taking
  Blackfoot, 1:41
hunting and trapping encroachments
  Montagnais-Naskapi, 1:246
  Ojibwa, 1:270
  Slavey, 1:320
inheritance
  Bulgarians, 4:45
  Castilians, 4:60
  Poles, 4:203
  Portuguese, 4:207
  Romanians, 4:214
  Slovaks, 4:244, 245
  Slovenes, 4:249
  Tory Islanders, 4:266
intergenerational value conflicts
  South and Southeast Asians of Canada,
    1:323
lack of "respect"
  Vlach Gypsies of Hungary, 4:272
land and water use
  Western Apache, 1:373
land rights

Conflict causes (cont'd)
  Bengali, 3:33
  Cheyenne, 1:65
  Chin, 3:66
  Cora, 8:77
  Northern Paiute, 1:264
  Tzotzil and Tzeltal of Pantelhó, 8:277
  Ute, 1:362
  Vlachs, 4:275
  leadership rivalries
    Teton, 1:346
  linguistic rights
    Walloons, 4:276
  love rivalry
    Micmac, 1:235
  marriage collapse
    Vlach Gypsies of Hungary, 4:272
  marriage partner choice
    Slovensko Roma, 4:251
  methods of dealing with Whites
    Cherokee, 1:62
    Choctaw, 1:72
    Quechan, 1:302
  Norse cultural identity
    Shetlanders, 4:234
  patron saint rivalry
    Maltese, 4:168, 169
  personal affronts
    Albanians, 4:6-7
    Cretans, 4:71
    Romanians, 4:214
    Wiyot, 1:385
  poaching
    Wiyot, 1:385
  political
    Yuit, 1:392
    see also Political violence
  political corruption
    Chuj, 8:73
  political parties
    Amuzgo, 8:5
    Maltese, 4:168
    Vedda, 3:302
  property
    Canarians, 4:52
    Castilians, 4:60
    Chin, 3:66
    Highland Scots, 4:141
    Northern Paiute, 1:264
    Punjabi, 3:241
    Romanians, 4:214
    Slovaks, 4:245
    Slovenes, 4:249
  revenge
    Aleut, 1:16
    Blackfoot, 1:41
    Klamath, 1:192
  rivalry
    Amuzgo, 8:5
    Micmac, 1:235
    Pathan, 3:233
  sectarianism
    Northern Irish, 4:180
  slave taking
    Aleut, 1:16
    Klamath, 1:192
  sorcery suspicions
    Ojibwa, 1:270

status competition
  Tamil of Sri Lanka, 3:283
surprise and staged battles
  Wiyot, 1:385
suspiciousness of "enemies"
  Santal, 3:254
  Sinhales, 3:267
  Tamil, 3:278
  Tamil of Sri Lanka, 3:283
trade
  Cheyenne, 1:65
  Quechan, 1:301
  Thakali, 3:291
tribute demands
  Yurok, 1:394
women as
  Chin, 3:66
  Madeirans, 4:166
  Slavey, 1:320
  see also Blood feud; Feuding; Nationalist
    movements
Conflict resolution
  acquiescence
    Kmhmu, 5:141
  adjudication
    Abor, 3:5
    Ata Tana 'Ai, 5:25
    Dai, 6:426
    Dargins, 6:98
    Iban, 5:98
    Kipsigis, 9:165
    Kubachins, 6:219
    Kuna, 8:149
    Lisu, 5:166
    Mountain Jews, 6:273
    Palu'e, 5:207
    Qalandar, 3:248
    Sasak, 5:227
    Tewa Pueblos, 1:349
    Toda, 3:297
    Xoraxané Romá, 4:283
    Yuit, 1:391
    see also Court system
  adjudication by entire village
    Ewe and Fon, 9:87
  antiwitchcraft rituals
    Ndembu, 9:240
  arbitration
    Aymara, 7:67
    Ngawbe, 8:197
    Nyakyusa and Ngonde, 9:254
    Vlach Gypsies of Hungary, 4:272
  avoidance. *See* Avoidance
  blood vengeance
    Amahuaca, 7:36
    Amuzgo, 8:5
    Araucanians, 7:54
    Araweté, 7:57
    Catawba, 1:54
    Central Yup'ik Eskimos, 1:58
    Cherokee, 1:62
    Copper Eskimo, 1:78
    Emberá, 7:157
    Ingalik, 1:158
    Klamath, 1:192
    Konso, 9:171
    Kwakiutl, 1:199
    Lango, 9:179-180

Mataco, 7:229
Montenegrins, 4:173
Nivaclé, 7:250
North Alaskan Eskimos, 1:260
Sara, 9:306
Slavey, 1:320
Tanaina, 1:336
Ticuna, 7:329
Triqui, 8:272
Truk, 2:353
Ute, 1:362
West Greenland Inuit, 1:378
Xikrin, 7:369
Yokuts, 1:388
Yörük, 9:396
blood-wealth payments
  Iraqw, 9:126
brotherhood meetings
  Mennonites, 1:219
ceremonial reconciliation
  Konso, 9:171
by close kin
  Kashinawa, 7:196-197
community assembles until crime is
    confessed
  Tigray, 9:348
compensation payment. *See under*
    Punishment
compromise
  Danes, 4:90
  Kmhmu, 5:141
consensus
  African Americans, 1:13
council meetings
  Saramaka, 7:297
debate
  Chambri, 2:32
  Gahuku-Gama, 2:70
  Nias, 5:196
  Semang, 5:235
  Tahiti, 2:306
  Tangu, 2:310
  Trobriand Islands, 2:350
discussion
  Tsimihety, 9:359
dispersal
  San-speaking peoples, 9:303
divination
  San-speaking peoples, 9:303
  Saramaka, 7:297
dueling
  Yanomamö, 7:376
  Yuracaré, 7:396
dues
  Thadou, 3:289
by elders
  Baniwa-Curripaco-Wakuenai, 7:79
  Circassians, 9:67
  Cuicatec, 8:93
  Dyula, 9:77
  Falasha, 9:92
  Gurung, 3:95
  Karajá, 7:190
  Karamojong, 9:157
  Kongo, 9:168
  Maasai, 9:209
  Maká, 7:217
  Mijikenda, 9:225

Nambudiri Brahman, 3:193
Ndembu, 9:240
North Alaskan Eskimos, 1:260
Nubians, 9:247-248
Otomí of the Sierra, 8:202
Somalis, 9:318
Terena, 7:326
Tiv, 9:351
Tory Islanders, 4:266
Tuareg, 9:368
emergency powers
Northern Irish, 4:180
fighting
Irish Travellers, 4:156
Mataco, 7:229
Micmac, 1:235
Mohave, 1:241
Yanomamö, 7:376
fighting with knives
Pashai, 9:267
flight. _See subhead_ withdrawal _below_
gift exchange
Malekula, 2:166
Tor, 2:344
governmental
Afar, 9:8
group discussion
Montagnais-Naskapi, 1:245
homicide
Copper Eskimo, 1:78
killing by witchcraft
Seri, 8:234
leader's intervention
Bamiléké, 9:39
Carib of Dominica, 8:40
Salasaca, 7:291
mediation
Abelam, 2:5
Andis, 6:26
Armenians, 6:31
Berbers of Morocco, 9:52
Bugis, 5:51
Bukidnon, 5:54
Chimbu, 2:37
Don Cossacks, 6:106
Futuna, 2:67
Garo, 3:83-84
Gayo, 5:89
Georgians, 6:135
Guadalcanal, 2:91
Hawaiians, 2:97
Hill Pandaram, 3:100
Japanese, 5:109
Jews of Iran, 9:141
Jingpo, 6:458
Korean, 5:148
Kubachins, 6:219
Kwoma, 2:135-136
Lahu, 5:153
Lao, 5:159
Maguindanao, 5:170
Malekula, 2:166
Marquesas Islands, 2:190
Muong, 5:191
Nissan, 2:250
Nogays, 6:289
Nuer, 9:250
Nuristanis, 9:251

Ojibwa, 1:270
Orokolo, 2:260
Pintupi, 2:266
She, 6:490
Sherpa, 3:259
Slovensko Roma, 4:251
Svans, 6:345
T'in, 5:279
Toraja, 5:282
Torres Strait Islanders, 2:347
Yap, 2:393
meetings
Okiek, 9:261
moots
Garia, 2:75
Gayo, 5:89
Gogodala, 2:84
Gururumba, 2:94
Kalingas, 5:123
Pentecost, 2:263
Sambia, 2:285
Tairora, 2:309
Tangu, 2:312
Tanna, 2:314
Temiar, 5:270
Usino, 2:362
Wovan, 2:387
Yangoru Boiken, 2:390
by mother's brother
Seminole, 1:313
mutual absolution
Usino, 2:362
negotiation
Circassians, 9:67
Pomo, 1:295
Puerto Ricans, 8:223
oath taking
Nagas, 3:190
oracles
Bamiléké, 9:39
by ordeal
Ilongot, 5:102
Palaung, 5:203
Palu'e, 5:208
ostracism
Micmac, 1:235
Rom, 1:305
payback
Kapauku, 2:107
Kewa, 2:117
Mafulu, 2:153
Maring, 2:187
Melpa, 2:202
Murngin, 2:226
Muyu, 2:229
Nasioi, 2:235
Sengseng, 2:297
Tauade, 2:319
Wape, 2:372
peace lodge
Winnebago, 1:382
physical intervention
Maká, 7:217
potlatch
Alorese, 5:15
property settlements
Nootka, 1:257
public opinion

German Swiss, 4:127
Montserratians, 8:181
Rom, 1:305
Sumu, 8:238
Wasteko, 8:303
quarreling heatedly
Afro-Hispanic Pacific Lowlanders, 7:22
Seri, 8:234
religious court system
Sea Islanders, 1:310
by religious figures
Pathan, 3:233
relocation
Apalai, 7:47
Barí, 7:85
Canelos Quichua, 7:101
Cuiva, 7:144
Panare, 7:266
Piaroa, 7:277
Piro, 7:280
Trio, 7:336
Tzotzil of Chamula, 8:281
Waimiri-Atroari, 7:344
Wanano, 7:350
Wapisiana, 7:356
Yekuana, 7:381
reparations. _See subhead_ compensation payments _above_
retaliation
Ute, 1:362
revenge
Amuzgo, 8:5
Easter Island, 2:55
Foi, 2:61
Kiwai, 2:126
Micmac, 1:234, 235
Nootka, 1:257
Ute, 1:362
ritual purification
Lahu, 5:153
Tor, 2:344
ritual tests of innocence
Lahu, 5:153
separation
Akawaio, 7:32
Chamacoco, 7:109
Yekuana, 7:381
shaman murder
Maká, 7:217
song duels
Asiatic Eskimos, 6:42
Nivaclé, 7:250
West Greenland Inuit, 1:378
Yuit, 1:392
sports
Garia, 2:75
Mataco, 7:229
Micmac, 1:235
Pukapuka, 2:272
Tokelau, 2:332
Yuit, 1:392
suppression of individual will
Mount Athos, 4:176
tribal law
Circassians, 9:67
withdrawal
Agta, 5:6
Andamanese, 3:10

Conflict resolution (cont'd)
  Bajau, **5**:34
  Central Thai, **5**:71
  Cree, **1**:82
  Delaware, **1**:86
  Hare, **1**:141
  Irish Travellers, **4**:156
  Kmhmu, **5**:141
  Mandan, **1**:215
  Qiang, **6**:487
  Sakalava, **9**:297
  Semang, **5**:235
  Sherpa, **3**:259
  Temiar, **5**:270
  Tewa Pueblos, **1**:349
  West Greenland Inuit, **1**:378
  Wik Mungkan, **2**:378-379
  Winnebago, **1**:382
  Wogeo, **2**:381
  Yangoru Boiken, **2**:390
  by women's informal negotiation
    Andamanese, **3**:10
  by women's negotiation
    Gusii, **9**:110
  see also Court system; Law; Punishment;
    Social control measures; Warfare
Conflict sources
  women
    Ingalik, **1**:158
Conformity (as social virtue)
  Amish, **1**:18
  hijra, **3**:97
  Hungarians, **4**:144
  Madeirans, **4**:165
  Newar, **3**:207
  Norwegians, **4**:182
  Tamil, **3**:278
Confrontation avoidance. *See* Avoidance
Confucianism
  Central Thai, **5**:71
  Chinese in Southeast Asia, **5**:77
  Gayo, **5**:89
  Hakka, **6**:438
  Han, **6**:443, 446
  Japanese, **5**:108, 109
  Jingpo, **6**:458
  Kolisuch'ok, **5**:143
  Korean, **5**:145, 146, 147, 148
  Koreans, **6**:206
  Singaporean, **5**:242
  Vietnamese, **5**:286
Congregationalism
  Cape Coloureds, **9**:60
  Hawaiians, **2**:95, 97
  Mandan, **1**:215
  Pohnpei, **2**:269
  Pukapuka, **2**:272
  Welsh, **4**:280
  see also Calvinism
Conscientious objection. *See* Nonviolence
Conscription. *See* Military service, compulsory
Consensual unions. *See* Living together
Consensus-seekers
  Dogrib, **1**:89
Conservatism
  Ozarks, **1**:281
Conservativism
  Aveyronnais, **4**:24

Construction industry
  Jews of Kurdistan, **9**:146
Contraception. *See* Birth control
Contract labor. *See* Labor, contract
Contract marriage. *See* Marriage, arranged
Conversion
  Awakateko, **8**:16
  Bukharan Jews, **6**:63
  Karaites, **9**:154
  Mamprusi, **9**:214
  Mazahua, **8**:166
  Mormons, **1**:247
  Muslim, **3**:185
  Neo-Buddhist, **3**:200
  Sephardic Jews, **4**:228, 229
  Shakers, **1**:316
  Untouchables, **3**:298
  Zoroastrians, **9**:408
  see also Christianity; Hindu influences;
    Islam; Missions; Sycretism
Cooking
  gender-shared
    Abor, **3**:4
    Baiga, **3**:19
  rotation of bread-baking for weekly mass
    Leonese, **4**:162
  traditional foods by men
    Tanana, **1**:339
Cooneyites
  Northern Irish, **4**:180
Cooperation (as social virtue)
  Danes, **4**:89
  Frisians, **4**:111
  Montagnais-Naskapi, **1**:245
  Mundurucu, **7**:245
Cooperative arrangements. *See* Communal
    practices
Cooperatives. *See* Agriculture, cooperatives;
    Labor exchange; Villages, cooperative
Copper mining
  Cornish, **4**:65
  Cypriots, **4**:80
Coppersmithing
  Bulgarian Gypsies, **4**:41
  Gypsies and caravan dwellers in the
    Netherlands, **4**:137
  Newar, **3**:206, 207
  peripatetics, **1**:287
  Rom, **1**:304
  Untouchable service caste, **3**:159
  Vlachs, **4**:274
  Xoraxané Romá, **4**:281
Copper tools
  Copper Eskimo, **1**:76, 77
Copra production
  Ambae, **2**:11
  Bikini, **2**:27
  Dobu, **2**:50
  Kapingamarangi, **2**:108
  Kiribati, **2**:121
  Kosrae, **2**:128
  Malekula, **2**:164
  Manam, **2**:167
  Mandak, **2**:170
  Marquesas Islands, **2**:189
  Marshall Islands, **2**:192
  Nasioi, **2**:233
  Nguna, **2**:242

  Ontong Java, **2**:254
  Pentecost, **2**:262
  Pukapuka, **2**:271, 272
  Rotuma, **2**:281
  Samal, **5**:219
  Samoa, **2**:287
  Santa Cruz, **2**:290
  Selepet, **2**:293
  Siwai, **2**:302
  Tanna, **2**:314
  Toala, **5**:280
  Tokelau, **2**:331
  Tolai, **2**:333, 334
  Truk, **2**:352
  Tuvalu, **2**:355
  Ulithi, **2**:358
  Woleai, **2**:383
  Yakan, **5**:289
  Yap, **2**:391, 392
Coptic church
  Arab Americans, **1**:25
  Copts, **9**:68-69
Cordophones
  Croats, **4**:75
Corn. *See* Maize
Corporal punishment. *See under* Child disci-
    pline; *under* Punishment
Corporate landholding. *See* Landholding,
    corporate
Corpse. *See* Dead, the; Mortuary practices
Corsicans, **4**:65, 66, 67
Cosmology
  Abor, **3**:5
  Albanians, **4**:7
  Andamanese, **3**:11
  Bella Coola, **1**:36
  Betsileo, **9**:57
  Bondo, **3**:50
  Catawba, **1**:55
  Central Yup'ik Eskimos, **1**:58-59
  Chagga, **9**:62
  Chatino, **8**:52
  Cherokee, **1**:62
  Cheyenne, **1**:65-66
  Chickasaw, **1**:66
  Chin, **3**:67
  Cuicatec, **8**:93
  Delaware, **1**:86
  Flathead, **1**:128
  Fox, **1**:130
  Gujarati, **3**:92
  Hidsata, **1**:147-148
  Hutterites, **1**:154
  Kwakiutl, **1**:200
  Mam, **8**:160
  Mataco, **7**:227
  Menominee, **1**:222
  Mescalero Apache, **1**:225
  Mixtec, **8**:178
  Navajos, **1**:253
  Nyakyusa and Ngonde, **9**:254
  Pame, **8**:208
  Pende, **9**:273-274
  Pokot, **9**:283
  Purum, **3**:244
  Q'anjob'al, **8**:225
  Q'eqchi', **8**:227
  Thadou, **3**:289

Tlingit, **1**:353
Toda, **3**:297, 298
Tojolab'al, **8**:262
Tzotzil of Zinacantan, **8**:293-294
Vlach Gypsies of Hungary, **4**:272
Wasteko, **8**:303
Winnebago, **1**:382
Yekuana, **7**:381
Yurok, **1**:395
see also Afterlife; Creation stories; World
  concept
Costume. _See_ Clothing
Cottage industry
  Azoreans, **4**:27
  Bulgarians, **4**:43
  Cretans, **4**:70
  German Swiss, **4**:127
  Greek-speaking Jews of Greece, **4**:135
  Highland Scots, **4**:140
  Ionians, **4**:149
  Leonese, **4**:161
  Madeirans, **4**:165
  Oriya, **3**:216
  Portuguese, **4**:206
  Shakers, **1**:316
  Swiss, Italian, **4**:260
  Zuni, **1**:397-398
Cottages. _See under_ Houses and housing
Cotton growing
  Abor, **3**:4
  Aguaruna, **7**:29
  Akawaio, **7**:31
  Alur, **9**:13
  Amahuaca, **7**:34
  Anavil Brahman, **3**:7
  Angaité, **7**:43
  Asurini, **7**:61
  Bororo, **7**:86
  Cajuns, **1**:49
  Cashibo, **7**:104
  Cham, **5**:72
  Chimane, **7**:112
  Chin, **3**:61
  Cocama, **7**:130
  Dai, **6**:424
  Emerillon, **7**:159
  Fali, **9**:94, 95
  Fulniô, **7**:161
  Ganda, **9**:104
  Garifuna, **8**:113
  Guajajára, **7**:166
  Guarayu, **7**:174
  Han, **6**:442
  Hopi, **1**:149
  Hoti, **7**:175
  Ifugao, **5**:99
  Iteso, **9**:128
  Jebero, **7**:181
  Jino, **6**:460
  Jivaro, **7**:182
  Karakalpaks, **6**:167
  Kédang, **5**:131
  Kittsians and Nevisians, **8**:146
  Konso, **9**:169
  Koreans, **6**:206
  Krikati/Pukobye, **7**:204
  Kyrgyz, **6**:229
  Lengua, **7**:210

  Maricopa, **1**:216
  Maxakali, **7**:233
  Mayoruna, **7**:234
  Mbeere, **9**:221
  Mikir, **3**:175
  Mocoví, **7**:240
  Mojo, **7**:242
  Montserratians, **8**:180
  Moré, **7**:242
  Muong, **5**:190
  Nambicuara, **7**:247
  Nyamwezi and Sukuma, **9**:256
  Opata, **8**:199
  Paï-Tavytera, **7**:259
  Palikur, **7**:262
  Panare, **7**:265
  Paresí, **7**:269
  Pemon, **7**:271
  Punjabi, **3**:238
  Rikbaktsa, **7**:287
  Saliva, **7**:292
  Santal, **3**:253
  Sara, **9**:305
  Sherente, **7**:302
  Shona, **9**:312
  Sirionó, **7**:310
  Suruí, **7**:312
  Suya, **7**:315
  Tajik, **6**:352
  Tapirapé, **7**:320
  Telugu, **3**:285
  Toba, **7**:331
  Tupari, **7**:339
  Turkmens, **6**:369
  Uighur, **6**:382, 499, 500
  Uzbeks, **6**:396, 398
  Wáiwai, **7**:346
  Wapisiana, **7**:355
  Waurá, **7**:360
  Xibe, **6**:504
  Xikrin, **7**:367
  Yekuana, **7**:381
  YörÜk, **9**:394
  Yuracaré, **7**:395
  Zande, **9**:398
Cotton sashes
  Navajo, **1**:251
Cotton thread
  Boruca, Bribri, Cabécar, **8**:27-28
  Tzotzil of Zinacantan, **8**:292
Cotton weaving
  Cape Verdeans, **4**:55
  Dai, **6**:424
  Hani, **6**:450
  Mingrelians, **6**:263
  Mossi, **9**:231
  Pamir peoples, **6**:305
  Pima-Papago, **1**:288
  Tewa Pueblos, **1**:348
  Tiv, **9**:350
  see also Weaving
Council
  Abor, **3**:5
  Arikara, **1**:26
  Badaga, **3**:17
  Bavarians, **4**:34
  Bengali, **3**:33
  Bhil, **3**:40

  Bhuiya, **3**:44
  Brahman of Nepal, **3**:53
  Cayuga, **1**:55
  Cheyenne, **1**:65
  Chhetri of Nepal, **3**:53
  Chin, **3**:66
  Choctaw, **1**:72
  Cocopa, **1**:74
  Coorg, **3**:73
  Finns, **4**:103
  Flathead, **1**:128
  Fox, **1**:129
  Gond, **3**:86
  Guambiano, **7**:173
  Gujarati, **3**:91-92
  Hidsata, **1**:147
  Highland Scots, **4**:141
  Hopi, **1**:149-150
  Huron, **1**:152
  Hutterite, **1**:154
  Iroquois, **1**:166
  Irula, **3**:107
  Jat, **3**:112
  Jatav, **3**:115
  Keres Pueblo Indians, **1**:181
  Kickapoo, **1**:185
  Klamath, **1**:192
  Kol, **3**:130
  Kond, **3**:133
  Koya, **3**:141
  Kutenai, **1**:197
  Lakher, **3**:147
  Leonese, **4**:161, 162
  Mandan, **1**:215
  Maricopa, **1**:216
  Mataco, **7**:229
  Menominee, **1**:221
  Mescalero Apache, **1**:225
  Mikir, **3**:176
  Mizo, **3**:178-179
  Mohawk, **1**:242
  Montenegrins, **4**:173
  Mount Athos, **4**:176
  Munda, **3**:184
  Nagas, **3**:190
  Navajo, **1**:252, 253
  Nayar, **3**:199, 207
  Nepali, **3**:204
  Nicobarese, **3**:210
  Northern Paiute, **1**:264
  Okanagon, **1**:272
  Omaha, **1**:275
  Oriya, **3**:217
  Parsi, **3**:229
  Pathan, **3**:232, 233
  peripatetics, **3**:234, 236
  Piemontese, **4**:199
  Pima-Papago, **1**:289
  Provencal, **4**:211
  Punjabi, **3**:241
  Quechan, **1**:302
  Romanians, **4**:214
  Salasaca, **7**:290
  Sardinians, **4**:227
  Seminole of Oklahoma, **1**:314
  Shawnee, **1**:317
  Slovenes, **4**:248
  Sora, **3**:270

Council (cont'd)
  Syrian Christian of Kerala, **3:**274
  Tamil, **3:**278
  Taos, **1:**342
  Tewa Pueblos, **1:**349
  Tharu, **3:**293
  Thompson, **1:**350
  Toda, **3:**297
  Ute, **1:**362
  Vellala, **3:**305
  Western Apache, **1:**373
  Western Shoshone, **1:**374
  Yankton, **1:**386
  Zuni, **1:**398-399
  see also under Elders council
Country-western music
  Cajuns, **1:**51
Courtship
  competitive
    Mekeo, **2:**199
  couple spend day and night together
    Lakher, **3:**146
  dating not permitted
    East Indians in Trinidad, **8:**106
    South and Southeast Asians of Canada,
      1:323
  doll as engagement gift
    Fali, **9:**95
  engagement gift to woman
    Swiss, Italian, **4:**261
  engagement permits premarital sex
    Norwegians, **4:**181
    Pasiegos, **4:**190
  female dormitory locale
    Bondo, **3:**49
  at fiestas
    Castilians, **4:**60
  gift exchange
    Metis of Western Canada, **1:**228
  gift by male suitor to girl's father
    Walapai, **1:**365
  girl's shyness
    Western Apache, **1:**372
  in kitchen
    Pasiegos, **4:**190
  late fall and winter
    Shetlanders, **4:**233
  lengthy
    Calabrese, **4:**49
    Shahsevan, **9:**309
    Tiroleans, **4:**263
    Welsh, **4:**280
  long engagement
    Cypriots, **4:**80
    Gahuku-Gama, **2:**69
    Maltese, **4:**168
  monitored by family and community
    Calabrese, **4:**49
  playing wooden flute outside woman's
    shelter at night
    Quechan, **1:**301
  ritualized with prior parental approval
    Mizo, **3:**178
  ritualized stages
    Sherpa, **3:**258
  sanctioned premarital sex. *See* Premarital
    sex, sanctioned
  village work bees

Bulgarians, **4:**44
whistle language
  Kickapoo, **1:**184
woman's flirting initiating
  Andalusians, **4:**11
  Castilians, **4:**60
young men's associations
  Romanians, **4:**214
see also Marriage
Court system
  Bavarians, **4:**34-35
  Canela, **7:**96-97
  Chipaya, **7:**116
  Costa Ricans, **8:**81
  English, **4:**97
  Faroe Islanders, **4:**100
  Flemish, **4:**108
  Hungarians, **4:**144
  Ionians, **4:**150
  Kanjar, **3:**121
  Lakher, **3:**147
  Mandan, **1:**215
  Manx, **4:**171
  Mescalero Apache, **1:**225
  Nambudiri Brahman, **3:**193
  Norwegians, **4:**182
  Nyamwezi and Sukuma, **9:**257
  Peloponnesians, **4:**194
  Poles, **4:**204
  Qalandar, **3:**248
  Santal, **3:**254
  Sea Islanders, **1:**310
  Serbs, **4:**232
  Shetlanders, **4:**234
  Syrian Christian of Kerala, **3:**274
  Tamil, **3:**278
  Thadou, **3:**289
  Welsh, **4:**280
Cousin marriage
  cross-cousin arranged
    Andamanese, **3:**10
  cross-cousin asymmetrical preferred
    De'ang, **6:**430
  cross-cousin bilateral permitted
    Haida, **1:**136
  cross-cousin bilateral preferred
    Araweté, **7:**57
    Guahibo-Sikuani, **7:**165
    Huichol, **8:**126
    Kashinawa, **7:**196
    Ka'wiari, **7:**199
    Koya, **3:**141
    Montagais-Naskapi, **1:**245
    Nasioi, **2:**234
    Nomoi, **2:**252
    San-speaking peoples, **9:**303
    Tanimuka, **7:**319
    Tanna, **2:**314
    Waimiri-Atroari, **7:**343
  cross-cousin bilateral prescribed
    Mardudjara, **2:**180
    Trio, **7:**336
    Waorani, **7:**352
  cross-cousin bilateral prohibited
    Cuicatec, **8:**92
  cross-cousin classificatory preferred
    Wik Mungkan, **2:**378
  cross-cousin encouraged

Cochin Jew, **3:**72
Nu, **6:**481
cross-cousin for later-born daughters
  Swahili, **9:**328
cross-cousin infant betrothal
  Fore, **2:**63
cross-cousin matrilateral asymmetrical pre-
    ferred
  Jingpo, **6:**457
cross-cousin matrilateral practiced
  Yukuna, **7:**387
cross-cousin matrilateral preferred
  Chambri, **2:**32
  Daur, **6:**429
  Evenki (Northern Tungus), **6:**121
  Garo, **3:**83
  Lakher, **3:**146
  Magar, **3:**157
  Mamprusi, **9:**212
  Mizo, **3:**178
  Mulam, **6:**476
  Muyu, **2:**228
  Ningerum, **2:**247
  Nivkh, **6:**284
  Rotinese, **5:**214
  Suya, **7:**316
  Yao, **6:**505
cross-cousin matrilateral preferred but not
    prestigious
  Endenese, **5:**85
cross-cousin matrilateral prescribed
  Kmhmu, **5:**140
  Palu'e, **5:**206
cross-cousin no longer practiced
  Ewenki, **6:**434
cross-cousin obligated
  Panare, **7:**266
cross-cousin patrilateral distant the ideal
  Western Apache, **1:**372
cross-cousin patrilateral preferred
  Minangkabau, **5:**183
  Naxi, **6:**479
  Wanano, **7:**350
cross-cousin patrilateral prohibited
  Fore, **2:**63
cross-cousin permitted
  Bakairi, **7:**74
  Culina, **7:**147
  Jivaro, **7:**183
  Maratha, **3:**169
  Maxakali, **7:**233
  Nicobarese, **3:**209
  Parsi, **3:**228
  Pauserna, **7:**270
  Rom, **1:**305
  Saami, **4:**221
  Saraguro, **7:**294
  Suruí, **7:**313
  Winnebago, **1:**381
cross-cousin preferred
  Afar, **9:**8
  Amuesha, **7:**38
  Apiaká, **7:**49
  Araucanians, **7:**53
  Asurini, **7:**61
  Badaga, **3:**16
  Bagirmi, **9:**34
  Baniwa-Curripaco-Wakuenai, **7:**78

Barama River Carib, 7:81
Barí, 7:84
Bau, 2:23
Bene Israel, 3:28
Bhil, 3:39
Chácobo, 7:106
Chimane, 7:112
Chipewyan, 1:68
Cubeo, 7:140-141
Desana, 7:153
Emerillon, 7:159
Ewe and Fon, 9:85
Fali, 9:95
Garifuna, 8:114
Gond, 3:85
Gurung, 3:94
Hare, 1:141
Hausa, 9:113
Kazakhs, 6:180
Kongo, 9:167
Kota, 3:136
Kumeyaay, 1:194
Kurds, 9:176
Labbai, 3:144
Lahu, 5:152
Lau, 2:144
Lesu, 2:146
Lisu, 5:165
Lunda, 9:197
Makushi, 7:219
Manus, 2:174
Marubo, 7:222
Mashco, 7:226
Mayoruna, 7:234
Moor of Sri Lanka, 3:181
Nambicuara, 7:247
Nayaka, 3:195
Ngatatjara, 2:240
Nguna, 2:243
Nubians, 9:247
Nyinba, 3:212
Okkaliga, 3:214
Puinave, 7:281
Pume, 7:284
Pumi, 6:484
Rikbaktsa, 7:287
Samal Moro, 5:223
Sinhalese, 3:265, 266
Siwai, 2:303
Suku, 9:321
Swahili, 9:328
Tamil, 3:277
Tanaina, 1:336
Tangu, 2:311
Tlingit, 1:352
Tonga, 9:353-354
Tujia, 6:498
Tunebo, 7:338
Vedda, 3:302
Vellala, 3:305
Wa, 6:502
Wáiwai, 7:347
Wapisiana, 7:355
Wayapi, 7:362
Wolof, 9:379
Yagua, 7:372
Yekuana, 7:381
Yi, 6:507

Yörük, 9:395
Zande, 9:402
Zaramo, 9:402
cross-cousin prescribed
    Kariera, 2:111
    Kédang, 5:132
    Munda, 3:183
    Yanomamö, 7:375
    Yukpa, 7:384
cross-cousin prohibited
    Cree, 1:81
    Dieri, 2:49
    Konso, 9:170
    Mbeere, 9:221
    Newar, 3:207
    Nyakyusa and Ngonde, 9:253
    San-speaking peoples, 9:303
    Seri, 8:234
cross-cousin prohibited but practiced
    Pemon, 7:272
cross-cousin the ideal
    Matsigenka, 7:231
    Mehinaku, 7:237
    Piaroa, 7:277
cross-cousin the norm
    Ajië, 2:8
    Akawaio, 7:32
    Amahuaca, 7:35
    Bohra, 3:47
    Hill Pandaram, 3:100
    Karihona, 7:192
    Macuna, 7:213
    Mahar, 3:164
    Muslim, 3:185
first-cousin avoided
    Yukateko, 8:309
first-cousin believed risky
    Betsileo, 9:56
first-cousin permitted
    Agaria, 3:6
    Basques, 4:31
    Cape Verdeans, 4:55
    Castilians, 4:60
    Dogon, 9:72
    Gitanos, 4:129
    Greek-speaking Jews of Greece, 4:135
    Jews, Arabic-speaking, 9:135
    Piemontese Sinti, 4:200
    Santa Cruz, 2:291
first-cousin practiced
    Vlach Gypsies, 4:272
    Yörük, 9:395
first-cousin practiced although prohibited
    Portuguese, 4:207
first cousin preferred
    Hazara, 9:115
first-cousin prohibited
    Ahir, 3:7
    Canarians, 4:52
    Catawba, 1:54
    Friuli, 4:113
    German Swiss, 4:126
    Greeks, 4:132
    North Alaskan Eskimos, 1:260
    Pawnee, 1:284
    Romanians, 4:213
    Shetlanders, 4:234
    Tanana, 1:339

Xoraxané Romá, 4:282
as immoral
    Bugle, 8:32
lower bride-price for
    Kanuri, 9:152
not practiced
    Brahman and Chhetri of Nepal, 3:52
parallel-cousin considered incestuous
    Apalai, 7:46
    Chácobo, 7:106
    Maxakali, 7:233
parallel-cousin for firstborn daughter
    Swahili, 9:328
parallel-cousin for nobility
    Songhay, 9:319
parallel-cousin permitted
    Nicobarese, 3:209
    Parsi, 3:228
parallel-cousin practiced
    Berbers of Morocco, 9:50
    Dyula, 9:77
    East Indians in Trinidad, 8:106
    Qashqa'i, 9:286
    Tandroy, 9:337
    Tswana, 9:362
parallel-cousin preferred
    Bedouin, 9:44
    Fulani, 9:102
    Ghorbat, 9:107
    Pathan, 3:232
    peripatetics of Afghanistan, Iran, and
        Turkey, 9:275
    Qalandar, 3:247
    Swahili, 9:328
parallel-cousin prohibited
    Cree, 1:81
    Cuiva, 7:144
    Konso, 9:170
    Kota, 3:136
    Moor of Sri Lanka, 3:181
    Puinave, 7:281
    Seri, 8:234
    Wapisina, 7:355
    Winnebago, 1:381
    Yi, 6:507
parallel-cousin widespread
    Muslim, 3:185
permitted
    Bai, 6:420
    Divehi, 3:77-78
    Q'eqchi', 8:226
    Tswana, 9:362
practiced
    Arab Americans, 1:24
preferred
    Baggara, 9:30
    Jews of Kurdistan, 9:146
    Kapingamarangi, 2:109
    Khinalughs, 6:200
    Pedi, 9:270
    Persians, 9:279
    Tats, 6:359
    Tuareg, 9:368
    Zoroastrians, 9:408
preferred but rare
    Circassians, 9:67
prohibited
    Grasia, 3:88

Cousin marriage (cont'd)
    Inughuit, **1:**160
    Mazahua, **8:**165
    Triqui, **8:**271
    Tzotzil of San Bartolomé de los Llanos,
        8:288
    prohibited strongly
      Kol, **3:**130
      Kond, **3:**133
      Meo, **3:**174
      Nambudiri Brahman, **3:**193
      Rom of Czechoslovakia, **4:**218-219
    prohibited through second cousin
      Cypriots, **4:**80
      Eastern Shoshone, **1:**105
      Mazatec, **8:**169
      Ngawbe, **8:**196
      Pima-Papago, **1:**289
      Rominche, **4:**216
      Ute, **1:**361
    prohibited through third cousin
      Cretans, **4:**70
      Lozi, **9:**188
      Tewa Pueblos, **1:**348
      Triqui, **8:**271
    second-cousin permitted
      Piemontese Sinti, **4:**200
      Romanians, **4:**213
Cousin rivalry
    Pathan, **3:**232, 233
Cousin terminology. *See* Kinship terminology
Couvade. *See under* Childbirth
Cow, sacred
    Gujarati, **3:**92
Cowrie shells
    Divehi, **3:**76
Cows. *See* Cattle
Coyote
    creator
      Pomo, **1:**295
    culture hero
      Kiowa, **1:**188
      Northern Shoshone and Bannock,
        1:267, 268
      Shuswap, **1:**318
    mythological importance
      Nez Percé, **1:**254
      Ute, **1:**362
    symbolism
      Jicarilla, **1:**174
      Karok, **1:**177
Crab fishing
    Orcadians, **4:**186-187
Cradle board manufacture
    Western Apache, **1:**372
Cradles, woven
    Washoe, **1:**370
Craft guilds
    Edo, **9:**80
Crafts. *See* Decorative arts; *specific types, e.g.,*
    Pottery
Creation stories
    Abor, **3:**5
    Ambae, **2:**12
    Aranda, **2:**18
    Asurini, **7:**62
    Ata Tana 'Ai, **5:**25
    Bhuiya, **3:**42-43

Chin, **3:**67
Chitpavan Brahman, **3:**68
Ch'ol, **8:**66
Cinta Larga, **7:**129
Cubeo, **7:**141
Dusun, **5:**83
Fore, **2:**64
Garia, **2:**74, 76
Goodenough Island, **2:**85, 86
Guadalcanal, **2:**91
Guajiro, **7:**169
Iatmul, **2:**98, 100
Iban, **5:**98
Igbo, **9:**123
Kachin, **5:**119
Kalimantan Dayaks, **5:**120
Kapauku, **2:**107
Karen, **5:**129
Kashubians, **4:**159
Ka'wiari, **7:**199
Kogi, **7:**202
Kuna, **8:**150
Kurumbas, **3:**142-143
Kwoma, **2:**134
Lahu, **5:**153
Lak, **2:**139
Lakher, **3:**147
Macuna, **7:**214
Mae Enga, **2:**150
Mafulu, **2:**153
Mailu, **2:**156
Maisin, **2:**157
Makassar, **5:**173
Mandan, **1:**215
Marind-anim, **2:**184
Maring, **2:**187
Marubo, **7:**223
Matsigenka, **7:**232
Mejbrat, **2:**195, 197
Melanau, **5:**180
Mescalero Apache, **1:**225
Minangkabau, **5:**181, 182
Miyanmin, **2:**209
Muong, **5:**192
Nagas, **3:**189
Nahuat of the Sierra de Puebla, **8:**193
Navajo, **1:**253
Nguna, **2:**244
Nias, **5:**194
Ningerum, **2:**246
Nivkh, **6:**285
Northern Shoshone and Bannock, **1:**267
Orok, **6:**296
Palu'e, **5:**208
Panare, **7:**266-267
Paraujano, **7:**268
Paresí, **7:**269-270
Pawnee, **1:**285
Piaroa, **7:**278
Pintupi, **2:**266
Poqomam, **8:**219
Puinave, **7:**281-282
Purum, **3:**244
Qiang, **6:**487
Samoa, **2:**288
Semang, **5:**235
Sio, **2:**301
Siwai, **2:**304

Tauade, **2:**320
Teton, **1:**346
Tewa Pueblos, **1:**349
Tokelau, **2:**330
Tonga, **2:**338
Tongareva, **2:**341
Torres Strait Islanders, **2:**347
tropical-forest foragers, **9:**357
Tuvalu, **2:**355
Vellala, **3:**304
Walapai, **1:**364
Wantoat, **2:**369
Wasteko, **8:**303
Wayapi, **7:**363
Western Apache, **1:**373
Wik Mungkan, **2:**379
Witoto, **7:**365
Wogeo, **2:**381
Yezidis, **6:**410
Yokuts, **1:**388
Yukpa, **7:**384
Yurok, **1:**395
see also Cosmology
Creator
    Abor, **3:**5
    Baiga, **3:**21
    Bondo, **3:**50, 51
    Cheyenne, **1:**65, 66
    Chin, **3:**67
    Comanche, **1:**75
    Gond, **3:**86
    Hidsata, **1:**147
    Iroquois, **1:**166-167
    Jicarilla, **1:**173
    Khasi, **3:**125
    Lakher, **3:**147
    Lingayat, **3:**151
    Micmac, **1:**235
    Mohave, **1:**241
    Muslim, **3:**186
    Nuer, **9:**250
    Omaha, **1:**275
    Osage, **1:**278
    Ottawa, **1:**280
    Parsi, **3:**229
    Pawnee, **1:**285
    Pima-Papago, **1:**290
    Pomo, **1:**295
    Ponca, **1:**296
    Quechan, **1:**302
    Santee, **1:**307
    Shuswap, **1:**318
    Sora, **3:**270
    Telugu, **3:**287
    Thadou, **3:**289
    Tlingit, **1:**353
    Ute, **1:**362
    Walapai, **1:**364
    Wichita, **1:**379
    Winnebago, **1:**382
    Wiyot, **1:**385
    Yurok, **1:**395
    see also Supreme being
Creator (androgenous)
    Mescalero Apache, **1:**225
Creator (female)
    Khasi, **3:**125
Credit. *See* Financial services

Cremation
  Amahuaca, 7:36
  Bai, 6:421
  Balinese, 5:37
  Bania, 3:25
  Bengali, 3:34
  Bhil, 3:42
  Brahman and Chhetri of Nepal, 3:53
  Cashibo, 7:104
  Chakma, 3:61
  Cham, 5:74
  Chitpavan Brahman, 3:70
  Choiseul Island, 2:39
  Cocopa, 1:74
  Cuiva, 7:145
  Dai, 6:428
  Dani, 2:45
  De'ang, 6:431
  Dutch, 4:94
  Gond, 3:87
  Gujarati, 3:92
  Jatav, 3:115
  Kalimantan Dayaks, 5:120
  Kapauku, 2:107
  Khmer, 5:138
  Klamath, 1:192
  Kol, 3:131
  Koryaks and Kerek, 6:210
  Kota, 3:138
  Kumeyaay, 1:195
  Lahu, 5:154;6:463
  Lao, 5:160
  Lao Isan, 5:163
  Maricopa, 1:216
  Marubo, 7:223
  Mocoví, 7:241
  Mohave, 1:242
  Moinba, 6:473
  Nasioi, 2:235
  Naxi, 6:480
  Nayar, 3:200
  Nepali, 3:205
  Nivkh, 6:285
  Oriya, 3:218
  Pahari, 3:223
  Pomo, 1:294
  Qiang, 6:487
  Quechan, 1:302
  Santal, 3:255
  She, 6:491
  Sherpa, 3:260
  Sinhalese, 3:267
  Tai Lue, 5:256
  Tamil, 3:279
  Tamil of Sri Lanka, 3:284
  Tanaina, 1:337
  Tasmanians, 2:317
  Telugu, 3:287
  Toda, 3:298
  Tu, 6:497
  Tujia, 6:499
  Waimiri-Atroari, 7:344
  Wáiwai, 7:348
  Walapai, 1:366
  Washoe, 1:370
  Western Shoshone, 1:375
  Wik Mungkan, 2:379
  Xibe, 6:504

  Xokléng, 7:371
  Yanomamö, 7:377
  Yao of Thailand, 5:293
  Yokuts, 1:389
Creoles
  Aleuts, 6:17
  Chinese in Caribbean, 8:55, 57
  Chuvans, 6:80
  Itelmen, 6:152
  Mauritian, 3:171, 172
  Moluccans—North, 5:188
  Sea Islanders, 1:308, 309
Crests
  Haida, 1:136
  Tsimshian, 1:355
Crime
  high rate
    Jamaicans, 8:139
    Puerto Ricans, 8:223
  low rate
    Antigua and Barbuda, 8:10
    Gaels (Irish), 4:117
    Japanese, 5:109
  organized
    Sicilians, 4:237
    Thug, 3:294
  petty
    Dutch, 4:94
  rarity
    Lepcha, 3:149
  rising rate
    Arubans, 8:13
  see also Blood feud; Conflict causes; Murder; Political violence; Punishment; Social control measures
Crocheting
  Guajiro, 7:168
Crofting
  Highland Scots, 4:139-140, 141
  Orcadians, 4:186, 187
  Shetlanders, 4:233, 234
  Tory Islanders, 4:265
Cross-cousin marriage. *See under* Cousin marriage
Cross symbol
  Q'anjob'al, 8:225
  Tigray, 9:348
Crow-type kinship terminology. *See under* Kinship terminology
"Cry" ceremony. *See* Mourning Ceremony
Crystal. *See* Glassmaking
Cuisine. *See* Food
Cult houses
  Chimane, 7:113
Cults
  ancestor
    Kazakhs, 6:181
    Kurds, 6:227
    Kurumbas, 3:143
    Orochi, 6:295
    Udis, 6:378
  animals and birds
    Itelman, 6:153
    Koryaks and Kerek, 6:209
    Kubachins, 6:219
    Siberian Tatars, 6:342
    Yukagir, 6:413
  bear

  Orochi, 6:295
  bullroarer
    Orokolo, 2:260
  dairy
    Toda, 3:296-297, 298
  of the dead
    Abkhazians, 6:9
    Karelians, 6:171, 172
    Khevsur, 6:197
    Portuguese, 4:208
    Tagbanuwa, 5:251
  dead twins
    Nivkh, 6:285
  of exchange
    Yukagir, 6:413
  fertility
    Mendi, 2:205
    Orokaiva, 2:258
    Rutuls, 6:321
  fire
    Azerbaijani Turks, 6:50
    Kazakhs, 6:181
    Kurds, 6:226-227
    Siberian Tatars, 6:342
    Tabasarans, 6:350
  heroes
    Kriashen Tatars, 6:212
  hunting
    Rutuls, 6:321
  initiation
    Mountain Arapesh, 2:217
  men's
    Boazi, 2:29
    Ningerum, 2:246, 247, 248
    Selepet, 2:294
    Tolai, 2:335
    Tor, 2:344
    Usino, 2:363
    Wantoat, 2:369
  millennarian. *See* Cargo cults; Ghost Dance; Millenarianism
  raven
    Itelmen, 6:153
    Koryaks and Kerek, 6:209
    Yukagir, 6:413
  rocks
    Azerbaijani Turks, 6:50
    Karachays, 6:161
  secret
    Telefolmin, 2:323
  sky
    Kazakhs, 6:181
    Tabasarans, 6:350
  sun and moon
    Udis, 6:378
  Taro
    Orokaiva, 2:257
  tiger
    Orochi, 6:295
  totemic
    Torres Strait Islanders, 2:347
    Wik Mungkan, 2:378
  trees
    Siberian Tatars, 6:342
  trees, stones, and water
    Kurds, 6:226-227
    Tabasarans, 6:350
  yam

Cults (cont'd)
    Yangoru Boiken, 2:390
    Zion Revival
        Jamaicans, 8:139
Cultural diversity
    Malayali, 3:165
Cultural revivals
    Maliseet, 1:213
Cultural secretness
    Taos, 1:342, 343
    Tewa Pueblos, 1:349
Culture-contact effects
    Kowa, 1:186
    Pahari, 3:221
    Purum, 3:242
    see also Assimilation; Christianity; Hindu
        influences
Culture hero
    Amahuaca, 7:36
    Apalai, 7:47
    Asurini, 7:62
    Barí, 7:85
    Canela, 7:97
    Chácobo, 7:106-107
    Chimane, 7:113
    Cinta Larga, 7:129
    Craho, 7:138
    Cubeo, 7:141
    Culina, 7:148
    Cuna, 7:151
    Guahibo-Sikuani, 7:165-166
    Guajiro, 7:169
    Hidatsa, 1:147
    Huarayo, 7:178
    Kagwahiv, 7:185
    Karihona, 7:193
    Kickapoo, 1:185
    Kiowa, 1:188
    Klamath, 1:192
    Kuikuru, 7:209
    Maliseet, 1:212
    Micmac, 1:235
    Navajo, 1:253
    Nivaclé, 7:250
    Northern Shoshone and Bannock,
        1:267
    Panare, 7:266-267
    Paraujano, 7:268
    Piaroa, 7:278
    Pima-Papago, 1:290
    Pume, 7:284
    Siona-Secoya, 7:309
    Sirionó, 7:311
    Tanimuka, 7:319
    Tapirapé, 7:321
    Tatuyo, 7:324
    Terena, 7:327
    Ticuna, 7:330
    Tlingit, 1:353
    Yukagir, 6:413
    see also Trickster culture hero
Culture hero (female)
    Mescalero Apache, 1:225
Culture-specific disorders
    Hutterites, 1:155
Curanderos (folk healers)
    Galicians, 4:120
    Latinos, 1:206

Curare
    Canelos Quichua, 7:101
    Karihona, 7:192
    Panare, 7:265
    Piaroa, 7:276
    Puinave, 7:281
    Tatuyo, 7:323
    Yagua, 7:372
Curers. See Healers
Curing societies
    Zuni, 1:399, 400
Currency. See Barter; Money and wealth
Cursing
    disease caused by
        Mbeere, 9:223
    infertility caused by
        Mbeere, 9:223
    as social control
        Atoni, 5:28
        Khasi, 3:125
        Kipsigis, 9:165
        Maasai, 9:209
        Mbeere, 9:222
        Pokot, 9:283
        Yoruba, 9:393
Cushitic religion
    Afar, 9:8
Cutlery making
    Auvergnats, 4:22

Dairy cult
    Toda, 3:296-297, 298
Dairy products
    Acadians, 1:7
    Aveyronnais, 4:25
    Baggara, 9:30
    Bavarians, 4:33
    Bretons, 4:38
    Cornish, 4:65
    Cyclades, 4:77
    Danes, 4:89
    English, 4:96
    Finns, 4:102
    Frisians, 4:110, 111
    German Swiss, 4:125
    Italian Mexicans, 8:131
    Jews of Iran, 9:140
    Kipsigis, 9:164
    Lur, 9:202
    Manx, 4:170
    Mennonites, 1:217;7:239
    Nandi and other Kalenjin peoples, 9:232
    Northern Irish, 4:178
    Nuristanis, 9:250
    Pasiegos, 4:189, 190
    Portuguese, 4:206
    Qashqa'i, 9:285
    Saraguro, 7:294
    Sardinians, 4:226
    Sherpa, 3:258
    Swedes, 4:257
    Syrian Christian of Kerala, 3:274
    Tiroleans, 4:263
    Toda, 3:296-297
    Vlach, 4:274
    Walloons, 4:276
    Welsh, 4:279
    see also Cheese making; Milk

Dakota-type kinship terminology. See under
    Kinship terminology
Dalmatians, 4:86
Dan (ceremony)
    Dai, 6:427
Dance
    amateur groups
        Jews of Yemen, 9:150
    animal and bird names
        Wasteko, 8:303
    animal ballets
        Guadalcanal, 2:91
    animistic
        Chukchee, 6:78-79
    as art form
        Abor, 3:5
        Andalusians, 4:12
        Anuta, 2:15
        Bau, 2:24
        Belau, 2:27
        Burakumin, 5:63
        Central Thai, 5:71
        Chechen-Ingush, 6:75
        Chinese in Southeast Asia, 5:77
        Cook Islands, 2:42
        Cotopaxi Quichua, 7:135
        Cuiva, 7:145
        Desana, 7:154
        Gond, 3:87
        Goodenough Island, 2:88
        Greeks, 6:144
        Gujarati, 3:92
        Gypsies, 6:146, 148
        Irula, 3:108
        Javanese, 5:113
        Kaluli, 2:103
        Khanty, 6:192
        Khmer, 5:138
        Kumyks, 6:223
        Kwakiutl, 1:200
        Lahu, 5:154;6:463
        Lao, 5:159
        Malaita, 2:163
        Mansi, 6:255
        Modang, 5:187
        Motu, 2:215
        Nasioi, 2:235
        Naxi, 6:480
        Nissan, 2:251
        Ontong Java, 2:255
        Oriya, 3:218
        Pukapuka, 2:272
        Rotuma, 2:283
        Samal Moro, 5:224
        Samoa, 2:289
        Santa Cruz, 2:292
        Sara, 9:307
        Saramaka, 7:298
        Sasak, 5:227
        Sherpa, 3:259
        Shipibo, 7:306
        Tajiks, 6:354
        Tamil, 3:279
        Terena, 7:327
        Tikopia, 2:326
        Tlingit, 1:351
        Toda, 3:297
        Truk, 2:353

Ulithi, **2:**360
Usino, **2:**363
Warlpiri, **2:**375
Zhuang, **6:**511
ceremonial
Abenaki, **1:**5
Alur, **9:**15
Andamanese, **3:**11
Apiaká, **7:**50
Awakateko, **8:**17
Aymara, **7:**68
Baiga, **3:**21
Bakairi, **7:**75
Balinese, **5:**37
Bhuiya, **3:**44
Bhutanese, **3:**46
Boazi, **2:**30-31
Bondo, **3:**50
Bonerate, **5:**46
Bugis, **5:**51
Burusho, **3:**56
Cahita, **8:**36
Cape Verdeans, **4:**56
Central Yup'ik Eskimos, **1:**59
Chimila, **7:**114
Cree, **1:**82
Dobu, **2:**52
Dogrib, **1:**89
Eastern Shoshone, **1:**106
Ewe and Fon, **9:**86
Fulniô, **7:**161
Gainj, **2:**73
Greeks, **4:**134
Guajiro, **7:**169
Haida, **1:**136
Hare, **1:**142
Havasupai, **1:**145
Hopi, **1:**150
Hupa, **1:**152
Ingalik, **1:**158
Jews of Iran, **9:**141
Kalingas, **5:**123
Kapingamarangi, **2:**110
Karajá, **7:**191
Karihona, **7:**193
Khasi, **3:**126
Kickapoo, **1:**186
Kilenge, **2:**120
Kiowa, **1:**187, 188
Klamath, **1:**192
Kogi, **7:**202
Kubachins, **6:**219
Kumeyaay, **1:**195
Kurtatchi, **2:**133
Kwakiutl, **1:**100
Lakher, **3:**147
Lau, **2:**145
Lozi, **9:**189
Maguindanao, **5:**171
Maká, **7:**218
Malekula, **2:**166
Maliseet, **1:**212, 213
Manus, **2:**175
Maring, **2:**188
Mazahua, **8:**166
Mbeere, **9:**222
Mehinaku, **7:**239
Miami, **1:**232

Mocoví, **7:**241
Nagas, **3:**191
Nayaka, **3:**196
Ngatatjara, **2:**241
Ngawbe, **8:**198
Nicobarese, **3:**210
Nivaclé, **7:**251
Nootka, **1:**257
Northern Paiute, **1:**265
Northern Shoshone and Bannock, **1:**267
Ojibwa, **1:**270
Okanagon, **1:**272
Orokaiva, **2:**257
Otomí of the Sierra, **8:**202
Palikur, **7:**263
Panare, **7:**267
Pawnee, **1:**285
Pemon, **7:**273
Piaroa, **7:**278
Pomo, **1:**295
Purum, **3:**244
Salasaca, **7:**291
San-speaking peoples, **9:**303
Santal, **3:**255
Sarsi, **1:**308
Seminole of Oklahoma, **1:**314
Shakers, **1:**316
Shawnee, **1:**317
Sidi, **3:**260-261
Sirionó, **7:**311
Siwai, **2:**304
Slav Macedonians, **4:**241
Sora, **3:**270
Southern Paiute (and Chemehuevi),
    1:332
Tarahumara, **8:**242
Tatuyo, **7:**324
Temiar, **5:**271, 272, 273
Teton, **1:**346
Tiwi, **2:**329
Toba, **7:**333
Tolai, **2:**335
Toraja, **5:**283
Tz'utujil, **8:**298
Ute, **1:**362
Vedda, **3:**303
Wa, **6:**503
Wáiwai, **7:**348
Wape, **2:**372
Waurá, **7:**360
Witoto, **7:**365
Wiyot, **1:**385
Yaqui, **8:**307
Yukpa, **7:**384
Yurok, **1:**395
Zarma, **9:**406
Zoque, **8:**317
Zuni, **1:**399, 400
see also Folk dancing
ceremonial dance grounds
Kewa, **2:**115
ceremonial seven-year
Dogon, **9:**73
children
Cahita, **8:**36
circle
Georgians, **6:**136
Qiang, **6:**487

Wa, **6:**503
competitive feasts
Siane, **2:**298
costumed
Tolai, **2:**335
couples
Awá Kwaiker, **7:**65
Ionians, **4:**150
eremonial
Sio, **2:**301
feather ornament use
Tauade, **2:**320
festival
Amuzgo, **8:**6
Guarijío, **8:**119
Gururumba, **2:**94
Jamaicans, **8:**139
Lithuanians, **6:**251
Mae Enga, **2:**151
Marshall Islands, **2:**194
Miao, **6:**471
Tujia, **6:**499
Yakut, **6:**407
flamenco
Gitanos, **4:**131
folk
Abkhazians, **6:**9
Andis, **6:**27
Auvergnats, **4:**23
Azoreans, **4:**29
Bashkirs, **6:**56
Basques, **1:**34;**4:**32
Bavarians, **4:**35
Bulgarians, **4:**45
Catalans, **4:**64
Circassians, **9:**67-68
Croats, **4:**75
Cubans, **8:**90
Dai, **6:**428
Faroe Islanders, **4:**100
Galicians, **4:**120
Greeks, **4:**134
Hmong, **5:**94
Hungarians, **4:**145
Koryaks and Kerek, **6:**210
Latvians, **6:**238
Madeirans, **4:**166
Moldovans, **6:**268, 269
Orochi, **6:**295
Ossetes, **6:**301
Peloponnesians, **4:**194
Punjabi, **3:**242
Rom of Czechoslovakia, **4:**219
Shetlanders, **4:**234
Slav Macedonians, **4:**241
Slovaks, **4:**245
Syrian Christian of Kerala, **3:**274
Tory Islanders, **4:**266
Turks, **9:**376
Ukrainians, **6:**394
Vlach Gypsies of Hungary, **4:**272
fondness for
Guarayu, **7:**174
funerary
Alur, **9:**15
Ewe and Fon, **9:**88
Lak, **2:**139
Lesu, **2:**147

Dance (cont'd)
　　Lugbara, **9:**195
　　Ndembu, **9:**241
　　tropical-forest foragers, **9:**357
　　Yezidis, **6:**411
　girls taught as toddlers
　　Fulani, **9:**102
　hand-clapping
　　Tanna, **2:**315
　huapango
　　cattle ranchers of Huasteca, **8:**44
　hula
　　Hawaiians, **2:**97
　"John Canoe"
　　Garifuna, **8:**115
　　Jamaicans, **8:**139
　Jombee
　　Montserratians, **8:**181
　male competitive
　　Torres Strait Islanders, **2:**347
　male courting
　　Lakalai, **2:**142
　male-only
　　Yurok, **1:**395
　male teams
　　Nyamwezi and Sukuma, **9:**258
　matrilineage-owned
　　Trobriand Islands, **2:**351
　mimicry and pantomime
　　Emberá and Wounaan, **8:**111
　　Mailu, **2:**156
　oracle
　　Afar, **9:**8
　as pagan vs. Christian division
　　Motu, **2:**215
　pascola
　　Cahita, **8:**37
　　Guarijío, **8:**119
　　Opata
　　　Ngawbe, **8:**200
　　Pima Bajo, **8:**213
　　Seri, **8:**235
　performance. *See* subhead as art form *above*
　pig feast
　　Kapauku, **2:**107
　　Manam, **2:**169
　popular
　　Kongo, **9:**168
　public contests
　　Lango, **9:**181
　religious
　　Bai, **6:**421
　　Even, **6:**119
　　Manchu, **6:**468
　　Païˇ-Tavytera, **7:**260
　　Xikrin, **7:**369
　ring shout
　　Sea Islanders, **1:**310
　ritual. *See* subhead ceremonial *above*
　round
　　Miskito, **8:**172
　　Northern Shoshone and Bannock, **1:**267
　　Slav Macedonians, **4:**241
　　Ukrainians, **6:**394
　royal ceremonies
　　Sakalava, **9:**296
　separate female and male
　　Afro-Bolivians, **7:**10

　Araucanians, **7:**55
　Bau, **5:**24
　Guadalcanal, **2:**91
　Laz, **6:**240
　Matsigenka, **7:**232
　Santal, **3:**255
　Siwai, **2:**304
　Tupari, **7:**341
　Waimiri-Atroari, **7:**345
　Woleai, **2:**384
　sitting and standing
　　Kiribati, **2:**123
　　Pohnpei, **2:**269
　　Woleai, **2:**384
　social
　　Cajuns, **1:**50
　　Choctaw, **1:**73
　　Circassians, **6:**89
　　Khmer, **5:**138
　　Kongo, **9:**168
　　Kumeyaay, **1:**195
　　Limbu, **3:**151
　　Lisu, **5:**166;**6:**466
　　Nguna, **2:**244
　　Ozarks, **1:**282
　　Waorani, **7:**353
　social communal
　　Faroe Islanders, **4:**100
　spirit possession
　　Acholi, **9:**6
　　Tonga, **9:**355
　tambu/tumba
　　Curaçao, **8:**98
　traditional
　　Afro-Bolivians, **7:**9
　　Ambonese, **5:**19
　　Bajau, **5:**35
　　Cahita, **8:**37
　　Chuvans, **6:**83
　　Endenese, **5:**86
　　Hawaiians, **2:**97
　　Kalmyks, **6:**157
　　Malisetts, **4:**212
　　Samal, **5:**221
　trance
　　Khoi, **9:**160
　　San-speaking peoples, **9:**304
　tribal
　　Shahsevan, **9:**310
　Tuburi and Tugurada
　　Guarijío, **8:**119
　Volador
　　Totonac, **8:**266
　war
　　Yakan, **5:**290
　wedding
　　Avars, **6:**45
　　Baggara, **9:**31
　　Circassians, **9:**67
　　Meskhetians, **6:**261
　　Moldovans, **6:**268
　　Mountain Jews, **6:**272
　　Qashqa'i, **9:**287
　　Tabasarans, **6:**349
　　Tats, **6:**360
　　Uighur, **6:**383
　　Wa, **6:**503
　women-only

　Emberá and Wounaan, **8:**111
　Wolof, **9:**380
　women select mates
　　Fulani, **9:**102
　women's fertility
　　Maasai, **9:**209
　　Yap, **2:**394
Dance lodge
　Nez Percé, **1:**254
Dancing Society
　Nootka, **1:**257
Daoism
　Bai, **6:**421
　Chinese in Southeast Asia, **5:**77
　Chinese in the United States, **1:**103
　Hakka, **6:**438
　Han, **6:**447
　Japanese, **5:**109
　Jing, **6:**454
　Manchu, **6:**468
　Maonan, **6:**468, 469
　Miao, **6:**472
　Mulam, **6:**477
　Muong, **5:**192
　Naxi, **6:**479
　Qiang, **6:**487
　Singaporean, **5:**242
　Tu, **6:**497
　Tujia, **6:**499
　Vietnamese, **5:**286
　Yao, **6:**505
　Yi, **6:**507
　Zhuang, **6:**511, 512
Dates (palm)
　growing
　　Nubians, **9:**246, 247
　　Teda, **9:**340
　offered at tomb for benediction
　　Tuareg, **9:**369
　see also Palm fruits
Dating. *See* Courtship
Daughter-son marriage exchange. *See* Marriage, son-daughter exchange
Daughters. *See* Family; Mother; *specific issues*
Day care (governmental). *See under* Child care
Day of Souls
　Georgians, **6:**135
Day of Spring
　Kubachins, **6:**219
Day of the Cross
　Itza', **8:**135
Day of the Dead
　cattle ranchers of Huasteca, **8:**44
　Cuicatec, **8:**93
　Latinos, **1:**206
　Mazahua, **8:**166
　Nahua of the Huasteca, **8:**187
　Otomí of the Sierra, **8:**203
　Otomí of the Valley of Mezquital, **8:**206
　Poqomam, **8:**219
　Q'eqchi', **8:**227
　Tepehua, **8:**249
　Totonac, **8:**266
　Tzotzil and Tzeltal of Pantelhó, **8:**278
　Zoque, **8:**317
Deacons
　Shakers, **1:**316

Dead, the
  burial of. _See_ Cemeteries; Mortuary
      practices
  communication with living
      Shakers, **1:**316
  communication with living at gravesites
      Suku, **9:**323
  corpse exposure
      Parsi, **3:**230
  cult headtaking
      Thadou, **3:**289
  debate before
      Sora, **3:**270
  dreaming as communication with
      Zoroastrians, **9:**410
  effort to cause kin's early death to achieve
      reunion
      San-speaking peoples, **9:**304
  food for
      Bhil, **3:**42
      Brahman and Chhetri of Nepal, **3:**54
      Menominee, **1:**222
      Nicobarese, **3:**210
      Phil, **3:**42
      Romanians, **4:**215
      Tory Islanders, **4:**266
  funeral and memorial services. _See_ Mortu-
      ary practices
  gradual separation from the living
      Vlach Gypsies of Hungary, **4:**272-273
  male-body display
      Albanians, **4:**8
  malevolent deeds by
      Piemontese Sinti, **4:**201
  memorial posts and stones. _See_ Memorial
      posts and stones
  naming for. _See_ Names
  petitioned by living
      Chontal of Tabasco, **8:**69
  prohibition on exhibiting photo of
      Slovensko Roma, **4:**252
  prohibitions on mentioning name of
      Mohave, **1:**242
      Slovensko Roma, **4:**250
  relations with living
      Slav Macedonians, **4:**241
      Sora, **3:**270
      Spanish Rom, **4:**255
      Vedda, **3:**303
  respect system for
      Slovensko Roma, **4:**251
      Spanish Rom, **4:**255
  return of. _See_ Ghosts; Vampires
Death
  acceptance as end of allotted life span
      Western Apache, **1:**373
  acceptance of inevitability
      Frisians, **4:**112
      Mandan, **1:**215
      Osage, **1:**279
      Portuguese, **4:**208
      Tanana, **1:**340
  accidental
      Hill Pandaram, **3:**100
      Irish Travellers, **4:**154
  annual celebration
      Maltese, **4:**169
      see also All Souls' Day

associated with night
    Osage, **1:**279
body given to church while soul remains in
    relatives' care
    Vlach Gypsies of Hungary, **4:**273
body separated from soul
    Dogon, **9:**74
    Lango, **9:**182
    Sara, **9:**307
body separated from spirit
    Iteso, **9:**130
causes of. _See heading_ Death, causes of _below_
confession before
    Amhara, **9:**21
cults. _See under_ Cults; Mediums
dreams foretelling
    Konso, **9:**171
    Miskito, **8:**172
by exposure
    Itelmen, **6:**154
fear of
    Agta, **5:**6
    Maliseet, **1:**213
    Maltese, **4:**169
    Navajo, **1:**253
    Nootka, **1:**257
    Palaung, **5:**203
fear of others' deaths
    Pima-Papgo, **1:**290
fear of premature
    Osage, **1:**279
fear of spirits of
    Washoe, **1:**370
finality of
    Tiwi, **2:**329-230
ghosts and souls believed audible and
    visible
    Wiyot, **1:**385
ghosts as omen of
    Tory Islanders, **4:**266
good/bad
    Albanians, **4:**8
    Bunun, **5:**58
    Dai, **6:**428
    De'ang, **6:**431
    Jingpo, **6:**459
    Koryaks and Kerek, **6:**210
    Lahu, **5:**154
    Lisu, **5:**166
    Miao, **6:**472
    Modang, **5:**187
    Naxi, **6:**480
    Palaung, **5:**203
    Palu'e, **5:**209
    Qiang, **6:**487
    Rotinese, **5:**214
    Russian peasants, **6:**313
    Tai Lue, **5:**256
    T'in, **5:**280
    Ukrainian peasants, **6:**388
    Vietnamese, **5:**286
    Zhuang, **6:**512
imagery
    Austrians, **4:**21
involvement with recently dead kin
    Gitanos, **4:**130
legendary figure
    Bretons, **4:**40

of little importance
    Marind-anim, **2:**184
living life of symbolic
    Mount Athos, **4:**177
as loss of shadow
    Slavey, **1:**320
naming taboos. _See_ Taboos, names
necromancy
    Creoles of Nicaragua, **8:**86
    Khasi, **3:**126
not feared
    Romanians, **4:**214
not seen as tragedy
    Ukrainians, **6:**394
only two ideal kinds of
    Winnebago, **1:**382
ordinary vs. violent
    Zapotec, **8:**314
as personal defeat
    Acholi, **9:**6
personified forms
    Kashubians, **4:**159
as polluting
    Ingalik, **1:**157
    Jicarilla, **1:**174
    Rom, **1:**306
portents of
    Micmac, **1:**235
predetermined by person's "invisible
    road"
    Zuni, **1:**400
as punishment. _See_ Punishment, capital
relatives move away after
    Irish Travellers, **4:**156
renders house unclean
    Khevsur, **6:**197
as skeleton with scythe
    Bretons, **4:**40
soul lingering after
    Kashubians, **4:**159
    Mohave, **1:**242
    Ute, **1:**362
    Vlach Gypsies of Hungary, **4:**272-273
soul's gradual separation from body
    Vlach Gypsies of Hungary, **4:**272-273
spirit lingering after
    Bretons, **4:**40
    Tewa Pueblos, **1:**350
    Zuni, **1:**400
spirit pacification
    Washoe, **1:**370
spirit returns if religious arrangements not
    carried out
    Maltese, **4:**169
taboos. _See_ Taboos, mortuary
three elements of body break up
    Zarma, **9:**406
as transitory period
    Awá Kwaiker, **7:**65
    Chuj, **8:**74
    Dalmatians, **4:**87
voluntary
    Asiatic Eskimos, **6:**42
in warfare as ideal
    Winnebago, **1:**382
see also Afterlife; Cemeteries; Homicide; In-
    fanticide; Mortuary practices; Mourn-
    ing; Murder; Suicide

Death, causes of
  anger and aggression
    Mixe, **8:**175
    Pawnee, **1:**286
  Bad Dead
    Yakö, **9:**387
  curses
    Akawaio, **7:**33
  demons
    Mashco, **7:**227
  devils
    Bagirmi, **9:**35
  Disease Giver
    Winnebago, **1:**382
  divine retribution
    Tahiti, **2:**307
  dreams
    Zuni, **1:**400
  evil eye
    Ionians, **4:**150
  evil spirits
    Sumu, **8:**239
    Washoe, **1:**370
  ghosts
    Itonama, **7:**179
    Khoi, **9:**160
  kachina dances
    Zuni, **1:**400
  magic
    Zande, **9:**400
  no natural cause
    Daribi, **2:**48
    Marshall Islands, **2:**194
    Mekeo, **2:**200
    Mendi, **2:**205
    Mocoví, **7:**241
    Murngin, **2:**226
    Ngatatjara, **2:**241
  not following religious rules
    Zuni, **1:**400
  not following ritual avoidances
    Khoi, **9:**160
  not following ritual restrictions
    Baniwa-Curripaco-Wakuenai,
      7:80
  not following tribal customs
    Mandan, **1:**215
  shamans
    Apalai, **7:**47
    Chácobo, **7:**107
    Chorote, **7:**126
    Karihona, **7:**193
    Lengua, **7:**211
    Mundurucu, **7:**245
    Tapirapé, **7:**321-322
    Wapisiana, **7:**356
    Witoto, **7:**365
    Yanomamö, **7:**377
    Yukuna, **7:**390
  social
    Murik, **2:**223
  sorcery and witchcraft
    Abelam, **2:**4, 6
    Akawaio, **7:**33
    Bagirmi, **9:**35
    Bamiléké, **9:**40
    Baniwa-Curripaco-Wakuenai, **7:**80
    Betsileo, **9:**57

    Chiriguano, **7:**122
    Dyula, **9:**78
    Fipa, **9:**100
    Gahuku-Gama, **2:**70
    Gebusi, **2:**79
    Kaluli, **2:**103
    Kapauku, **2:**107
    Karajá, **7:**191
    Kewa, **2:**117
    Kurtatchi, **2:**133
    Lakalai, **2:**142
    Lengua, **7:**211
    Lunda, **9:**199
    Luyia, **9:**206
    Mafulu, **2:**153
    Mailu, **2:**156
    Maliseet, **1:**213
    Marquesas Islands, **2:**191
    Mekeo, **2:**199
    Mocoví, **7:**241
    Mundurucu, **7:**245
    Murik, **2:**223
    Nasioi, **2:**235
    Ningerum, **2:**248
    Pawnee, **1:**286
    Seri, **8:**234
    Shawnee, **1:**286
    Siona-Secoya, **7:**309
    Sumu, **8:**239
    Suya, **7:**316, 317
    Temne, **9:**345
    Tonga, **9:**355
    Tubatulabal, **1:**355
    Ulithi, **2:**360
    Wáiwai, **7:**348
    Winnebago, **1:**382
    Wogeo, **2:**382
    Yagua, **7:**374
    Yangoru Boiken, **2:**390
    Zande, **9:**400
    Zuni, **1:**400
  soul abandons body
    Tarahumara, **8:**242
  soul abduction
    Chinantec, **8:**55
    Kaingáng, **7:**186
    Xokléng, **7:**371
  soul loss
    Han, **6:**447
    Jingpo, **6:**459
    Kachin, **5:**119
    Nivaclé, **7:**251
    Taiwan aboriginal peoples, **5:**257
    Tzotzil of Chamula, **8:**281
    Wáiwai, **7:**348
  spirits
    Agta, **5:**6
    Anuak, **9:**22
    Apalai, **7:**47
    Baniwa-Curripaco-Wakuenai, **7:**80
    Candoshi, **7:**94
    Chácobo, **7:**107
    Chiriguano, **7:**122
    Cinta Larga, **7:**129
    Dani, **2:**45
    Dyula, **9:**78
    Gainj, **2:**73
    Karen, **5:**129

    Khoi, **9:**160
    Kurtatchi, **2:**133
    Lau, **2:**145
    Lengua, **7:**211
    Mae Enga, **2:**151
    Maliseet, **1:**213
    Mansi, **6:**255
    Manus, **2:**176
    Maring, **2:**188
    Matsigenka, **7:**232
    Murik, **2:**222
    Muyu, **2:**229
    Nasioi, **2:**235
    Ndebele, **9:**237
    Nivaclé, **7:**251
    Ontong Java, **2:**255
    Pemon, **7:**273
    Pentecost, **2:**264
    Romanians, **4:**214
    Sakalava, **9:**299
    Selung/Moken, **5:**232
    Shahsevan, **9:**310
    Sio, **2:**301
    Trio, **7:**336
    Ulithi, **2:**360
    Wáiwai, **7:**348
    Wamira, **2:**367
    Wapisiana, **7:**356
    Wovan, **2:**387
    Yuqui, **7:**394
  supernatural
    Apalai, **7:**47
    Berbers of Morocco, **9:**52
    Lunda, **9:**199
    Luyia, **9:**206
    Ndebele, **9:**238
    Tswana, **9:**364
  taboo violation
    Kalingas, **5:**123
    Maring, **2:**188
    Ulithi, **2:**360
    Wáiwai, **7:**348
    Winnebago, **1:**382
    Wogeo, **2:**382
    Yagua, **7:**374
  theft of person's mind
    Yukuna, **7:**390
Death penalty. *See* Punishment, capital
Death rate
  high
    Asiatic Eskimos, **6:**38
    Irish Travellers, **4:**154
    Philippine Negritos, **5:**211
  high for violent deaths
    West Greenland Inuit, **1:**378
  see also Infant and child mortality rates
Death squads
    Sinhalese, **3:**267
Debate format
    Sora, **3:**270
Debt assumption
    Lakher, **3:**146
Debt servitude. *See* Labor, bonded; Labor, debt
      peonage
Debutantes
    Azoreans, **4:**28
Deceased. *See* Afterlife; Dead, the; Death;
      Mortuary practices

Decorated graves. *See* Cemeteries, grave
  decoration
Decorative arts
  Azoreans, **4:**27
  Bondo, **3:**51
  Bulgarians, **4:**43
  Canarians, **4:**52
  Cape Verdeans, **4:**55
  Chin, **3:**67
  Croats, **4:**75
  Danes, **4:**90
  Finns, **4:**102, 104
  Frisians, **4:**110, 111, 112
  Greeks, **4:**134
  Gujarati, **3:**92
  Highland Scots, **4:**140
  Hungarians, **4:**144, 145
  Irish Travellers, **4:**156
  Khasi, **3:**126
  Kiowa, **1:**187, 189
  Kiribati, **2:**121
  Klamath, **1:**192
  Kwakiutl, **1:**198, 200
  Madeirans, **4:**165
  Maltese, **4:**169
  Menominee, **1:**222
  Micmac, **1:**235
  Mohave, **1:**242
  Navajo, **1:**251
  Newar, **3:**208
  Nootka, **1:**256, 257
  North Alaskan Eskimos, **1:**259, 261
  Old Believers, **1:**274
  Orcadians, **4:**187
  Oriya, **3:**218
  Pahari, **3:**223
  Pandit of Kashmir, **3:**226
  Pathan, **3:**233
  Poles, **4:**203
  Pomo, **1:**295
  Portuguese, **4:**208
  Romanians, **4:**214
  Saami, **4:**221, 222
  Sarakatsani, **4:**224-225
  Shakers, **1:**316
  Slav Macedonians, **4:**241
  Slovaks, **4:**245
  Slovenes, **4:**249
  Sorbs, **4:**253
  Swedes, **4:**258
  Tanaina, **1:**337
  Taos, **1:**342
  Tasmanians, **2:**317
  Teton, **1:**345
  Tewa Pueblos, **1:**349
  Tlingit, **1:**351
  Yokuts, **1:**389
  Zuni, **1:**397-398
  see also Body painting and ornamentation;
    Carved objects; Visual arts; *specific art
    forms and mediums*
Deer hunting
  Arikara, **1:**26
  Chiricahua, **1:**70
  Delaware, **1:**85
  Kalapuya, **1:**175
  Karok, **1:**176
  Kickapoo, **1:**183

Micmac, **1:**233
Ojibwa, **1:**269
Osage, **1:**277
Potawztomi, **1:**297
Western Shoshone, **1:**374
Wintun, **1:**383
Yavapai, **1:**386
Yokuts, **1:**387
Yurok, **1:**394
Deer hunting (sport)
  Highland Scots, **4:**140
Deerskin trade
  Catawba, **1:**53
  Choctaw, **1:**71
  Maliseet, **1:**211
Defloration ritual. *See* Virginity
Deformities. *See* Disabled
Deities. *See* Creator; Spirits; Supreme being;
    Polytheism; Women deities
Democratic political organization
  Aquitaine, **4:**15
  Armenians, **6:**31
  Arubans, **8:**13
  Austrians, **4:**20
  Balinese, **5:**37
  Bulgarians, **4:**45
  Burgundians, **4:**47
  Cape Verdeans, **4:**56
  Cham, **5:**73
  Danes, **4:**89, 90
  Dutch, **4:**93
  Faroe Islanders, **4:**99
  Gaels (Irish), **4:**117
  Germans, **4:**123
  German Swiss, **4:**126
  Gond, **3:**86
  Gujarati, **3:**91
  Hungarians, **4:**143, 144
  Icelanders, **4:**147
  Irish, **4:**153
  Kiribati, **2:**123
  Kubachins, **6:**219
  Mauritian, **3:**172-173
  Nauru, **2:**237
  Navajo, **1:**252
  Oroquen, **6:**482
  Peloponnesians, **4:**194
  Pukapuka, **2:**272
  Punjabi, **3:**241
  Sardinians, **4:**227
  Sinhalese, **3:**266
  Swiss, Italian, **4:**262
  Syrian Christian of Kerala, **3:**274
  Tabasarans, **6:**350
  Tamil of Sri Lanka, **3:**282
  Telugu, **3:**286
  Walloons, **4:**275
Demons. *See* Devil and demons; Evil spirits
Demonstrations and strikes
  Auvergnats, **4:**23
  Bretons, **4:**39
  Jatav, **3:**115
  Mauritian, **3:**173
  see also Political violence
Dentalium shell. *See* Shell
Deportation. *See* Punishment, banishment
Derision singing
  Copper Eskimo, **1:**78

Dervishes
  Albanians, **4:**7
Descent
  adelphic
    Shona, **9:**313
  agnatic
    Albanians, **4:**5, 6
    Basseri, **9:**42
    Chin, **3:**65
    Coorg, **3:**74
    Cretans, **4:**70
    Faroe Islanders, **4:**99
    Gujarati, **3:**91
    Gurung, **3:**94
    Nuristanis, **9:**251
    Nyakyusa and Ngonde, **9:**253
    Okkaliga, **3:**214
    Pedi, **9:**270
    Serbs, **4:**231
    Slav Macedonians, **4:**240
    Tswana, **9:**362
    Vlachs, **4:**274
  agnatic extended
    Ewe and Fon, **9:**86
  ambilateral
    Cuicatec, **8:**92
  ambilineal
    Aranda, **2:**17
    Betsileo, **9:**55
    Kiribati, **2:**122
    Lau, **2:**144
    Marshall Islands, **2:**193
    Nootka, **1:**256, 257
    Zapotec, **8:**312
  apical
    Albanians, **4:**5
    Bhuiya, **3:**43
    Coorg, **3:**74
    Magar, **3:**157
    peripatetics, **3:**235
    Qalandar, **3:**247
    Sayyid, **3:**256
    Vellala, **3:**304, 305
  bilateral, **8:**245
    Abenaki, **1:**5
    Acehnese, **5:**3
    Achumawi, **1:**10
    Afro-Hispanic Pacific Lowlanders, **7:**21
    Afro-Venezuelans, **7:**26
    Agta, **5:**5
    Aguaruna, **7:**30
    Alorese, **5:**15
    Ambonese, **5:**18
    Andalusians, **4:**11
    Andamanese, **3:**10
    Andis, **6:**25
    Antigua and Barbuda, **8:**9
    Appalachians, **1:**22
    Aranda, **2:**17
    Arapaho, **1:**26
    Araweté, **7:**56
    Arubans, **8:**12
    Austrians, **4:**20
    Auvergnats, **4:**22
    Avars, **6:**45
    Aymara, **7:**67
    Azoreans, **4:**28
    Baffinland Inuit, **1:**30

Descent (cont'd)
Bagobo, **5**:29
Bajau, **5**:33
Bakairi, **7**:74
Balantak, **5**:35
Banggai, **5**:38
Basques, **1**:33;**4**:31
Bemba, **9**:46
Bilaan, **5**:42
Bisaya, **5**:42-43, 43
Boazi, **2**:29
Bolaang Mongondow, **5**:43
Bonerate, **5**:45
Bretons, **4**:39
Bugis, **5**:50
Bukidnon, **5**:53
Bulgarian Gypsies, **4**:41
Bulgarians, **4**:44
Burgundians, **4**:47
Burmese, **5**:65
Cahita, **8**:36
Callahuaya, **7**:89
Canarians, **4**:52
Candoshi, **7**:93
Canela, **7**:96
Canelos Quichua, **7**:99-100
Cape Verdeans, **4**:55
Carib of Dominica, **8**:39
Castilians, **4**:60
Catalans, **4**:63
Catawba, **1**:54
Central Thai, **5**:70
Chatino, **8**:51, 50
Cheyenne, **1**:64
Chinantec, **8**:54
Chipewyan, **1**:68
Chocó, **7**:123
Chontal of Tabasco, **8**:68
Chorote, **7**:125
Chuj, **8**:72
Comanche, **1**:75
Copper Eskimo, **1**:77-78
Costa Ricans, **8**:80
Cotopaxi Quichua, **7**:133
Cree, **1**:81
Creoles of Nicaragua, **8**:85
Culina, **7**:147
Cuna, **7**:150
Cyclades, **4**:77
Cypriots, **4**:80
Czechs, **4**:83
Dalmatians, **4**:86
Dinka, **9**:70
Divehi, **3**:77
Dogrib, **1**:88
Dusun, **5**:81
Dutch, **4**:93
East Indians in Trinidad, **8**:105
English, **4**:94
Faroe Islanders, **4**:99
Finns, **4**:103
Fipa, **9**:99
Flemish, **4**:107
French Canadians, **1**:132
Frisians, **4**:111
Friuli, **4**:113
Gaels (Irish), **4**:116
Gainj, **2**:72

Germans, **4**:122
German Swiss, **4**:126
Gorotire, **7**:162
Greek Cypriots, **4**:80
Greeks, **4**:132
Gypsies, **6**:146
Hanunóo, **5**:91
Hausa, **9**:112
Hawaiians, **2**:96
Hidatsa, **1**:147
Hutterites, **1**:154
Ibaloi, **5**:95
Iban, **5**:97
Ifugao, **5**:99
Ingalik, **1**:156, 157
Inughuit, **1**:160
Irish Travelers, **1**:163
Irish Travellers, **4**:156
Itza', **8**:134
Jamaicans, **8**:138
Javanese, **5**:112
Jews, **1**:169
Jews of Israel, **9**:143
Jicarilla, **1**:173
Kalapalo, **7**:187
Kalimantan Dayaks, **5**:120
Kalingas, **5**:122
Kanjar, **3**:120
Kapauku, **2**:106
Karachays, **6**:160
Karajá, **7**:189
Karen, **5**:127
Kazakhs, **6**:179
Kenyah-Kayan-Kajang, **5**:134
Khmer, **5**:136, 137
K'iche', **8**:141
Kiowa, **1**:187
Kmhmu, **5**:140
Korean, **5**:147
Kosrae, **2**:129
Krikati/Pukobye, **7**:204
Krymchaks, **6**:215
Kuikuru, **7**:207
Kuna, **8**:148, 149
Lahu, **5**:152;**6**:463
Laki, **5**:154
Lao, **5**:158
Lao Isan, **5**:161
Latinos, **1**:205
Latvians, **6**:237
Lengua, **7**:211
Leonese, **4**:161
Lithuanian Jews, **6**:246
Lithuanians, **6**:250
Lozi, **9**:188
Madeirans, **4**:165
Madurese, **5**:167
Maguindanao, **5**:169
Maká, **7**:216
Makassar, **5**:172
Makushi, **7**:219
Malaita, **2**:161, 162
Malay, **5**:175
Maltese, **4**:168
Mam, **8**:159
Manam, **2**:168
Mansi, **6**:253
Manx, **4**:170

Maori, **2**:177
Maranao, **5**:177
Mardudjara, **2**:180
Martiniquais, **8**:162
Matsigenka, **7**:231
Mazahua, **8**:165
Mehinaku, **7**:237
Melanau, **5**:179
Mennonites, **1**:218
Menominee, **1**:221
Miao, **6**:471
Mingrelians, **6**:264
Mixe, **8**:174
Mixtec, **8**:177
Miyanmin, **2**:211
Mocoví, **7**:241
Modang, **5**:186
Moldovans, **6**:267
Montserratians, **8**:180
Mundugumor, **2**:219
Murik, **2**:222
Nahua of the Huasteca, **8**:186
Nahuat of the Sierra de Puebla, **8**:192
Nauru, **2**:237
Nayaka, **3**:195
Nez Percé, **1**:254
Nguna, **2**:243
Ningerum, **2**:247
Niue, **2**:251
Nivaclé, **7**:249
Northern Irish, **4**:179
Northern Paiute, **1**:264
Northern Shoshone and Bannock, **1**:267
Occitans, **4**:185
Ontong Java, **2**:254
Otavalo, **7**:254
Ozarks, **1**:281
Páez, **7**:257
Pame, **8**:208
Panare, **7**:266
Paraujano, **7**:268
Pasiegos, **4**:190
Peloponnesians, **4**:193
Pemon, **7**:272
Penan, **5**:210
Piemontese, **4**:198
Piemontese Sinti, **4**:200
Pima Bajo, **8**:211
Pima-Papago, **1**:289
Poles, **6**:307
Pomo, **1**:294
Popoluca, **8**:217
Poqomam, **8**:218
Portuguese, **4**:207
Pukapuka, **2**:271, 272
Qalandar, **3**:247
Qashqa'i, **9**:285
Q'eqchi', **8**:226
Rapa, **2**:274, 275
Raroia, **2**:276
Romanians, **4**:213, 214
Rotuma, **2**:282
Russians, **6**:316
Rutuls, **6**:320
Saami, **4**:221
Sagada Igorot, **5**:216
Saint Lucians, **8**:231
Salasaca, **7**:290

Saluan, 5:217
Samal, 5:219, 220
Samal Moro, 5:223
San Cristobal, 2:289
San-speaking peoples, 9:303
Saraguro, 7:294
Sardinians, 4:226
Sasak, 5:226
Selung/Moken, 5:232
Seri, 8:234
Shan, 5:240
Shetlanders, 4:233
Siberiaki, 6:333
Sinhalese, 3:265, 266
Slavey, 1:319, 320
Slovaks, 4:244
Slovenes, 4:248
Southern Paiute (and Chemehuevi),
    1:331
Subanun, 5:245
Sulod, 5:246
Sundanese, 5:247
Suruí, 7:312
Swedes, 4:257
Tabasarans, 6:349
Tagalog, 5:249
Tahiti, 2:306
Taiwan aboriginal peoples, 5:257
Tamil of Sri Lanka, 3:282
Tangu, 2:312
Taos, 1:342
Tats, 6:359
Tausug, 5:263
Telefolmin, 2:322
Temiar, 5:268
Tepehuan of Chihuahua, 8:252, 253
Ternatan/Tidorese, 5:275
Tewa Pueblos, 1:348
Tigray, 9:347
T'in, 5:278
Toba, 7:332
Tor, 2:343
Toraja, 5:282
Torres Strait Islanders, 2:346
Tory Islanders, 4:265
Trinidadians and Tobagonians, 8:268
Triqui, 8:271
Truk, 2:352
Tsakhurs, 6:366
Tuareg, 9:367
Tupari, 7:340
Tzeltal, 8:274
Tzotzil and Tzeltal of Pantelhó, 8:277
Tzotzil of San Bartolomé de los Llanos,
    8:288
Tz'utujil, 8:297, 298
Vedda, 3:302
Vietnamese, 5:285
Wáiwai, 7:347
Wamira, 2:366
Waorani, 7:352
Warao, 7:358
Wasteko, 8:302
Wayapi, 7:362
Western Shoshone, 1:375
West Greenland Inuit, 1:377
Wik Mungkan, 2:378
Wogeo, 2:381

Xikrin, 7:368
Xoraxané Romá, 4:282
Yakan, 5:289
Yap, 2:392
Yaqui, 8:306
Yekuana, 7:381
Yoruba, 9:392
Yukpa, 7:383, 384
Zapotec, 8:312
Zoque, 8:316
bilateral ascent
    Triqui, 8:271
bilineal
    Huichol, 8:126
    Sakalava, 9:295
double
    Igbo, 9:122
    Nubians, 9:247
double-unilineal
    Toda, 3:296
double unilineal
    Yakö, 9:385
matrilineal
    Akan, 9:11
    Aleut, 1:15
    Ambae, 2:12
    Andamanhese, 3:10
    Ata Tana 'Ai, 5:24
    Belau, 2:26
    Catawba, 1:54
    Cham, 5:73
    Cherokee, 1:61
    Choctaw, 1:72
    Chukchee, 6:77
    Creoles of Nicaragua, 8:85
    Crow, 1:83
    Curaçao, 8:97
    Delaware, 1:86
    Divehi, 3:76-77
    Dobu, 2:50, 51
    Dominicans, 8:102
    Ewe and Fon, 9:86
    Garifuna, 8:114
    Garo, 3:81-82, 83
    Guahibo-Sakuani, 7:165
    Guajiro, 7:168
    Haida, 1:136
    Hidatsa, 1:147
    Hopi, 1:149
    Hopi-Tewa, 1:151
    Huron, 1:152
    Igbo, 9:122
    Ingalik, 1:156
    Iroquois, 1:166
    Jews, 1:169
    Jino, 6:460
    Kapingamarangi, 2:109
    Keres Pueblo Indians, 1:180
    Kerintji, 5:134
    Khasi, 3:124-125
    Kickapoo, 1:185
    Komi, 6:204
    Kosrae, 2:128, 129
    Kurtatchi, 2:132
    Kutchin, 1:196
    Lak, 2:138
    Lamaholot, 5:155
    Lao Isan, 5:162

Lesu, 2:146, 147
Lipan Apache, 1:208
Lunda, 9:197
Mandak, 2:171
Mandon, 1:214
Mappila, 3:167, 185
Maring, 2:185
Marshall Islands, 2:193
Mejbrat, 2:196
Mescalero Apache, 1:224, 225
Micronesians, 1:237
Minangkabau, 5:181, 182, 183
Nambicuara, 7:247
Nasioi, 2:234
Navajo, 1:252
Naxi, 6:478
Nayar, 3:198, 199
Ndembu, 9:239
Nguna, 2:243
Nissan, 2:250
Nomoi, 2:252
Ogan-Besemah, 5:198
Pawnee, 1:284, 285
Pende, 9:272
Pohnpei, 2:268
Qiang, 6:485, 486
Rhadé, 5:212
Rossel Island, 2:279
Saramaka, 7:297
Seminole, 1:313
Seminole of Oklahoma, 1:314
Siwai, 2:302, 303
Suku, 9:321
Taiwan aboriginal peoples, 5:257
Tamil, 3:277
Tanaina, 1:336
Tanana, 1:339
Tetum, 5:276
Tiwi, 2:328, 329
Tlingit, 1:352
Toda, 3:297
Tolai, 2:335
Tonga, 9:353, 354
Tonkawa, 1:354
Trobriand Islands, 2:348, 349
Tsimshian, 1:354-355
Ulithi, 2:359
Vellala, 3:304
Wamira, 2:366
Western Apache, 1:372
Winnebago, 1:381
Woleai, 2:383
Zande, 9:401
Zaramo, 9:401
Zuni, 1:398
matrilineal/patrilineal
    Bamiléké, 9:39
    Betsileo, 9:56
    Lobi-Dagarti peoples, 9:184
    Sara, 9:306
    Yakö, 9:385
multilineal
    Blackfoot, 1:41
nonunilineal
    Kwakiutl, 1:198, 199
patrilineal, 1:270;2:198-199;6:278-279
    Abelam, 2:5
    Abkhazians, 6:7

Descent (cont'd)
Abor, 3:4
Achang, 6:418
Acholi, 9:4-5, 5
Agaria, 3:6
Aguaruna, 7:30
Ainu, 5:8
Ajië, 2:8
Akha, 5:12
Albanians, 4:5, 6
Aleuts, 6:18
Alorese, 5:15
Altaians, 6:22
Alur, 9:13
Amahuaca, 7:35
Ambae, 2:12
Ambonese, 5:18
Amhara, 9:19
Amuesha, 7:38
Anuak, 9:22
Anuta, 2:14
Apalai, 7:46
Appalachians, 1:22
Arab Americans, 1:24
Arabs, 9:24
Araucanians, 7:53
Armenians, 6:29
Asiatic Eskimos, 6:40, 41
Asmat, 2:20
Asurini, 7:61
Ata Sikka, 5:21
Atoni, 5:27
Avars, 6:46
Aveyronnais, 4:25
Awakateko, 8:16
Azerbaijani Turks, 6:49
Baggara, 9:30, 31
Bagirmi, 9:34
Bai, 6:420
Baiga, 3:20
Balinese, 5:36, 37
Balkars, 6:53
Baluchi, 3:23
Bamiléké, 9:39
Baniwa-Curripaco-Wakuenai, 7:78
Bashkirs, 6:56
Basseri, 9:42
Batak, 5:39, 40
Bavarians, 4:34
Bedouin, 9:44
Belarussians, 6:61
Berbers of Morocco, 9:50, 51
Betsileo, 9:55
Bhil, 3:39
Bhuiya, 3:43
Bohra, 3:47
Bosnian Muslims, 4:36
Brahman of Nepal, 3:52
Brahui, 3:54
Bukharan Jews, 6:64
Bunun, 5:57
Buriats, 6:67
Burusho, 3:55
Callahuaya, 7:89
Cape Verdians, 4:55
Chagga, 9:61
Chakma, 3:59
Chambri, 2:32

Chechen-Ingush, 6:74
Chenchu, 3:61
Chhetri of Nepal, 3:52
Chimbu, 2:36
Chinese in Southeast Asia, 5:76
Chipaya, 7:116
Chiriguano, 7:120
Choctaw, 1:72
Ch'ol, 8:65, 64
Chuvans, 6:81, 82
Cinta Larga, 7:128
Circassians, 6:88, 89
Cocopa, 1:74
Comox, 1:76
Coorg, 3:74
Cowichan, 1:79
Croats, 4:73
Cubans, 8:88
Dai, 6:425, 426
Danes, 4:89
Dani, 2:44
Dargins, 6:98
Daribi, 2:47
Daur, 6:429
De'ang, 6:430
Desana, 7:153
Dieri, 2:49
Dogon, 9:72
Dominicans, 8:102
Don Cossacks, 6:105, 106
Dong, 6:431
Drung, 6:432
Dutch, 4:93
Edo, 9:80
Eipo, 2:57
Emberá and Wounaan, 8:110
Endenese, 5:85
Even, 6:118
Evenki (Northern Tungus), 6:121, 122
Ewe and Fon, 9:85, 86
Ewenki, 6:434
Fali, 9:96, 95
Fore, 2:64
Fox, 1:129
French Canadians, 1:132
Fulani, 9:101-102
Galicians, 4:120
Garia, 2:75;3:81
Gebusi, 2:77, 78
Georgians, 6:133
Ghorbat, 9:106
Gnau, 2:81
Gogodala, 2:84
Gond, 3:85, 86
Goodenough Island, 2:86, 87
Greeks, 6:143
Greek-speaking Jews of Greece, 4:135
Guahibo-Sikuani, 7:165
Gujar, 3:89
Gujarati, 3:91
Gusii, 9:109
Hakka, 6:437, 438
Han, 6:443-444, 445
Hani, 6:450
Havasupai, 1:145
Hawaiians, 2:96
Hazara, 9:115
Hidatsa, 1:147

Highland Scots, 4:140
Hindu, 3:102
Hmong, 5:93, 94
Huichol, 8:126
Iatmul, 2:99
Igbo, 9:122
Ingilos, 6:151
Iraqw, 9:125
Iteso, 9:129
Japanese, 5:107
Jatav, 3:114
Jews of Algeria, 9:138
Jews, Arabic-speaking, 9:135
Jews of Iran, 9:140
Jews of Kurdistan, 9:146
Jingpo, 6:457
Jino, 6:460
Jivaro, 7:182
Kachin, 5:116
Kalmyks, 6:156
Kaluli, 2:102
Kanbi, 3:118
Kapauku, 2:105, 106
Karaites, 9:154
Karakalpaks, 6:167
Karelians, 6:170, 171
Karihona, 7:192
Karok, 1:176
Ka'wiari, 7:198-199
Kédang, 5:132
Keraki, 2:113
Ket, 6:184
Kewa, 2:116
Khakas, 6:188
Khanty, 6:191
Khevsur, 6:196
Khoi, 9:159
Kickapoo, 1:184
Kikapu, 8:144
Kipsigis, 9:164
Kirgiz, 6:461
Kiwai, 2:125, 126
Kmhmu, 5:140
Komi, 6:204
Kond, 3:133
Konso, 9:170
Korean, 5:147
Korku, 3:134
Koryaks and Kerek, 6:208, 209
Kota, 3:136
Koya, 3:140, 141
Kpelle, 9:173
Krymchaks, 6:215
Kubachins, 6:218
Kumeyaay, 1:194
Kumyks, 6:222
Kurds, 9:175, 176
Kwakiutl, 1:199
Kwoma, 2:134, 135
Kyrgyz, 6:228, 230
Lahu, 5:152
Lakandon, 8:154
Lakher, 3:146
Laks, 6:234
Lamaholot, 5:155, 156
Lango, 9:179
Lau, 2:144
Leonese, 4:161

Lepcha, 3:149
Lezgins, 6:243
Lhoba, 6:464
Limbu, 3:150
Lingayat, 3:152
Lisu, 5:165;6:465;5:165
Luba of Shaba, 9:191
Lugbara, 9:194
Luyia, 9:204
Maasai, 9:208
Mae Enga, 2:150, 149
Mafulu, 2:152
Magar, 3:154, 156, 157
Mahar, 3:164
Mailu, 2:155, 155
Maisin, 2:159, 158
Malekula, 2:165, 165
Maliseet, 1:211
Mam, 8:158
Mamprusi, 9:212
Manam, 2:168
Manchu, 6:467
Mande, 9:215
Mansi, 6:254
Manus, 2:175, 174
Manx, 4:170
Maonan, 6:468
Maratha, 3:169
Maricopa, 1:216
Marind-anim, 2:183, 183
Maring, 2:186, 186
Mashco, 7:226
Mbeere, 9:221, 221
Mekeo, 2:199
Melpa, 2:201, 201
Menominee, 1:221
Mentaweian, 5:181
Miami, 1:231
Mijikenda, 9:224
Mikir, 3:175
Mingrelians, 6:264, 263-264
Miwok, 1:240
Mizo, 3:178
Mohave, 1:241
Mongols, 6:475
Montagnais-Naskapi, 1:245
Montenegrins, 4:173
Mossi, 9:228
Motu, 2:214
Mountain Arapesh, 2:216
Mulam, 6:476, 476-477
Munda, 3:182, 183
Mundugumor, 2:219
Mundurucu, 7:245
Muong, 5:191
Murngin, 2:225
Muslim, 3:185
Muyu, 2:228, 229
Nagas, 3:189, 190
Nahuat of the Sierra de Puebla, 8:192
Namau, 2:231
Nambudiri Brahman, 3:193
Nandi and other Kalenjin peoples, 9:233
Naxi, 6:478, 479
Ndebele, 9:236
Nepali, 3:203, 204
Newar, 3:207
Nganasan, 6:281

Ngatatjara, 2:240
Nias, 5:195, 196
Ningerum, 2:246
Nissan, 2:249, 250
Nivkh, 6:284
Nogays, 6:288
Northern Irish, 4:179
Nuer, 9:249
Nyinba, 3:211
Ogan-Besemah, 5:198
Okiek, 9:261
Old Believers, 6:292, 293
Omaha, 1:275
Ontong Java, 2:254
Oriya, 3:217
Orokaiva, 2:257, 257
Orokolo, 2:259, 259, 260
Osage, 1:278
Ossetes, 6:300
Otomí of the Valley of Mezquital, 8:205
Ozarks, 1:280
Pahari, 3:221
Palestinians, 9:265
Palu'e, 5:207, 206
Pamir peoples, 6:303, 305
Pandit of Kashmir, 3:225
Parsi, 3:228
Pashai, 9:267
Pathan, 3:232
Pentecost, 2:262, 263, 263
peripatetics, 3:235
Pintupi, 2:266
Pohnpei, 2:269
Pokot, 9:282
Pomaks, 4:205
Popoloca, 8:216
Purum, 3:243
Q'anjob'al, 8:225
Qashqa'i, 9:285
Rikbaktsa, 7:287
Rom, 1:304, 305
Rotinese, 5:214, 213
Rukuba, 9:290, 289
Russian peasants, 6:312
Sambia, 2:285, 285
Samoa, 2:288
Santa Cruz, 2:291
Santal, 3:253
Sarakatsani, 4:224
Sasak, 5:226
Selepet, 2:293
Selkup, 6:326
Sengseng, 2:297
Serbs, 4:231
Shahsevan, 9:308
Sharanahua, 7:299
Shawnee, 1:317
She, 6:490, 490
Sherpa, 3:258
Shilluk, 9:311
Shona, 9:313
Shors, 6:330
Siane, 2:298-299
Siberiaki, 6:333
Sio, 2:300, 300
Siona-Secoya, 7:308
Slav Macedonians, 4:240
Slovaks, 4:244

Somalis, 9:317
Songhay, 9:319
Sora, 3:269
South and Southeast Asians of Canada, 1:323
Sunwar, 3:271
Suri, 9:325
Suruí, 7:312
Svans, 6:345, 344
Swahili, 9:328
Swazi, 9:330-331
Syrian Christian of Kerala, 3:273
Tabasarans, 6:350
Tacana, 7:318
Tairora, 2:308, 309
Taiwan aboriginal peoples, 5:258, 257, 258
Tajik, 6:492
Tajiks, 6:353
Talysh, 6:356
Tamang, 3:275
Tamil, 3:277
Tandroy, 9:337
Tanimuka, 7:319
Tatuyo, 7:323
Tauade, 2:319, 319
Tausug, 5:263
Teda, 9:340
Telugu, 3:285, 286
Temne, 9:344, 343
Tetum, 5:276
Thadou, 3:288
Thakali, 3:291
Tibetans, 6:495
Tikopia, 2:325, 325
Tiv, 9:350
Tofalar, 6:363
Tonga, 2:337
Tongareva, 2:340
Torres Strait Islanders, 2:346
Totonac, 8:265
Triqui, 8:271
tropical-forest foragers, 9:357
Tuareg, 9:368
Tujia, 6:498
Turkana, 9:372
Turkish Cypriots, 4:80
Turkmens, 6:370
Tzeltal, 8:274, 274
Tzotzil and Tzeltal of Pantelhó, 8:276
Tzotzil of Chamula, 8:280
Tzotzil of San Bartolomé de los Llanos, 8:288
Tzotzil of Zinacantan, 8:293
Udis, 6:377, 377
Uighur, 6:383, 383
Ukrainian peasants, 6:387
Usino, 2:362, 362
Uvea, 2:364
Uzbeks, 6:398, 397
Vellala, 3:304, 305
Volga Tatars, 6:401
Wa, 6:503, 502
Walapai, 1:365
Wamira, 2:366
Wanano, 7:349
Wantoat, 2:369, 368
Wape, 2:371, 371

Descent (cont'd)
  Waropen, 2:376
  Wayapi, 7:362
  Wik Mungkan, 2:378
  Winnebago, 1:381
  Wiyot, 1:384
  Wogeo, 2:381
  Wolof, 9:379
  Wovan, 2:386, 386
  Xibe, 6:504
  Xoraxané Romá, 4:282
  Yagua, 7:372
  Yakut, 6:406, 405
  Yangoru Boiken, 2:389
  Yanomamö, 7:375
  Yao, 6:505, 505
  Yao of Thailand, 5:292
  Yemenis, 9:389
  Yezidis, 6:409
  Yi, 6:506
  Yir Yoront, 2:395
  Yokuts, 1:388
  Yörük, 9:395
  Yukagir, 6:413
  Yukuna, 7:387
  Yuqui, 7:393
  Zamindar, 3:307
  Zande, 9:398, 398, 401
  Zarma, 9:405
  Zhuang, 6:510
  Zulu, 9:411
  see also Surnames
  patrilineal/matrilineal
    Bamiléké, 9:38
    East Indians in Trinidad, 8:106
    Herero, 9:117
    Lobi-Dagarti peoples, 9:184
    Okiek, 9:260
    Tandroy, 9:337
    Wolof, 9:378
    Zaramo, 9:401
Descriptive kinship terminology. *See* Kinship
      terminology, bifurcate-collateral
Design
  modern
    Danes, 4:90
    Finns, 4:104
    Swedes, 4:258
  motifs
    Chin, 3:67
    Hungarians, 4:145
    Mekeo, 2:200
    Menominee, 1:222
    Micmac, 1:234
    Montagnais-Naskapi, 1:246
    Ojibwa, 1:271
    Woleai, 2:384
  woven into baskets
    Yokuts, 1:389
  see also Beadwork; Decorative arts; Needle-
      work; Symbolism
Detention camps. *See* Internment camps
Devaks (emblems)
  Maratha, 3:169
Devi (female deity)
  Maratha, 3:170
  see also Jogeshvari; Shaktism
Devils and demons

Bagirmi, 9:35
Bugle, 8:33
Gaels (Irish), 4:117
Kashubians, 4:159
Mashco, 7:226-227
Matsigenka, 7:232
Micmac, 1:235
Nambicuara, 7:247
Piro, 7:280
Saraguro, 7:295
Tarahumara, 8:242
Telefolmin, 2:323
Walloons, 4:278
Yanomamö, 7:377
Zapotec, 8:313
see also Evil spirits; Exorcism
Devotionalism
  Tamil, 3:279
Dharma (moral code)
  Brahman and Chhetri of Nepal, 3:53
  castes, Hindu, 3:57
  Pahari, 3:222, 223
  Pandit of Kashmir, 3:226
  see also Karma
Dhom (animistic belief)
  Thakali, 3:291, 292
Diamond industry
  Hasidim, 1:143
Diamond mining
  Tswana, 9:361
Diaspora
  Cajuns, 1:48
  French Canadians, 1:130, 131
Dichotomic settlements
  Newar, 3:206
Diet. *See* Food; *specific crops*
Dietary laws and restrictions. *See under*
      Food
Diformities
  killing of children with
    Cocama, 7:130
Dikes
  Dutch, 4:93
  Frisians, 4:110
Diplomacy
  Nambudiri Brahman, 3:192
  peripatetics, 3:234
Direct address avoidance
  Limbu, 3:150
Disabled
  abandonment of
    Comanche, 1:75
    Kiowa, 1:189
    Qalandar, 3:248
  fear of deformities
    Bhil, 3:41
  killing of children, 6:451
Disciples
  Sadhu, 3:251
Discipline. *See* Child discipline; Social
      control measures
Disease, causes of. *See* Illness, causes of
Disease decimation. *See* Epidemics; *specific
      diseases*
Disease Giver (deity)
  Winnebago, 1:382
Diskonter (healer)
  Bretons, 4:40

Disputes (as group interaction)
  Gitanos, 4:130
Dispute settlement. *See* Conflict resolution;
      Court system
Dissari (shaman)
  Bondo, 3:50, 51
Dissimulation (as social trait)
  Tamil, 3:278
Dissolution of marriage. *See* Annulment;
      Divorce
Distinctive appearance. *See* Appearance,
      distinctive; Clothing, distinctive
Divination
  Abor, 3:5
  Acholi, 9:6
  Alur, 9:15
  Balkars, 6:54
  Bamiléké, 9:39, 40
  Betsileo, 9:57
  Bhil, 3:41
  Callahuaya, 7:90
  Chagga, 9:62
  Chin, 3:67
  Dogon, 9:73
  Edo, 9:82
  Ewe and Fon, 9:88
  Fali, 9:96, 97
  Finns, 4:104
  Gond, 3:86
  Greeks, 4:134
  Guajiro, 7:169
  Gurung, 3:95
  Gusii, 9:110
  Iban, 5:98
  Igbo, 9:123
  Iglulik Inuit, 1:155
  Iraqw, 9:126
  Iteso, 9:130
  Karen, 5:129
  Khanty, 6:192
  Khasi, 3:126
  Kongo, 9:168
  Koya, 3:141
  Kriashen Tatars, 6:212
  Kurumbas, 3:143
  Lisu, 5:166
  Lozi, 9:189
  Luba of Shaba, 9:193
  Lunda, 9:198-199
  Maasai, 9:209
  Mbeere, 9:222
  Menominee, 1:222
  Miao, 6:472
  Mikir, 3:176
  Miwok, 1:240
  Montagnais-Naskapi, 1:246
  Mulam, 6:477
  Munda, 3:184
  Nandi and other Kalenjin peoples, 9:234
  Nayaka, 3:196
  Noanamá, 7:251
  North Alaskan Eskimos, 1:261
  Nyakyusa and Ngonde, 9:254
  Nyamwezi and Sukuma, 9:257
  Okiek, 9:261, 262
  Pacific Eskimo, 1:283
  Pahari, 3:223
  Pedi, 9:270

Pima-Papago, **1:**290
Potawatomi, **1:**297
Rukuba, **9:**291
Sakalava, **9:**298
San-speaking peoples, **9:**302, 303, 304
Santal, **3:**255
Sara, **9:**306
Saramaka, **7:**297, 298
Slovaks, **4:**245
Suri, **9:**326
Swazi, **9:**332
Tandroy, **9:**338
Temne, **9:**345
Tigray, **9:**349
Tiv, **9:**351
Tswana, **9:**364
Turkana, **9:**372
Vietnamese, **5:**286
Yakö, **9:**387
Yao of Thailand, **5:**293
Yuit, **1:**392
Zande, **9:**399
Zaramo, **9:**402
Zhuang, **6:**511
Zulu, **9:**412
see also Shamanism
Divine Couple (deities)
  Baul, **3:**26
Divorce
  by abduction
    Mountain Arapesh, **2:**216
  bride-wealth kept (if husband initiates
      without cause)
    Gurung, **3:**94
  bride-wealth never returned
    Kol, **3:**130
  bride-wealth returned
    Alur, **9:**14
    Irula, **3:**107
    Kurds, **9:**176
    Luba of Shaba, **9:**192
    Qalandar, **3:**247
    Yurok, **1:**395
  bride-wealth returned (if wife initiates)
    Temne, **9:**344
  bride-wealth returned (if wife initiates or at
      fault)
    Gurung, **3:**94
  bride-wealth returned (if woman at fault)
    Chin, **3:**65
  bride-wealth returned (pro-rated)
    Karok, **1:**176
    Rom, **1:**305
    Suku, **9:**321
  business reasons not to
    Flemish, **4:**107
  common
    Acholi, **9:**5
    Akha, **5:**12
    Alorese, **5:**15
    Aranda, **2:**17
    Ashkenazim, **6:**35
    Bajau, **5:**33
    Bedouin, **9:**44
    Belau, **2:**26
    Bugis, **5:**50
    Central Thai, **5:**71
    Chechen-Ingush, **6:**74

Chimbu, **2:**36
Circassians, **6:**88
Cook Islands, **2:**41
Czechs, **4:**83
Danes, **4:**90
Dobu, **2:**51
Dogon, **9:**72
Don Cossacks, **6:**106
Eipo, **2:**57
Falasha, **9:**91
Fore, **2:**64
Goodenough Island, **2:**87
Hausa, **9:**113
Hungarians, **4:**144
Javanese, **5:**112
Kapingamarangi, **2:**109
Kédang, **5:**132
Kewa, **2:**116
Kiwai, **2:**126
Koya, **3:**141
Kurtatchi, **2:**132
Lahu, **5:**153
Latvians, **6:**237
Lesu, **2:**146
Lithuanians, **6:**251
Lozi, **9:**188
Maisin, **2:**159
Malay, **5:**175
Manx, **4:**171
Miami, **1:**231
Nagas, **3:**189
Navajo, **1:**252
North Alaskan Eskimos, **1:**260
Northern Shoshone and Bannock, **1:**267
Nyamwezi and Sukuma, **9:**257
peripatetics of Iraq, Syria, Lebanon,
    Jordan, Israel, Egypt, Sudan, and
    Yemen, **9:**277
Piro, **7:**280
Samoa, **2:**288
Sasak, **5:**226
Senoi, **5:**238
Serbs, **4:**231
Shona, **9:**313
Siwai, **2:**303
Slovaks, **4:**244
Subanun, **5:**245
Swahili, **9:**328
Taiwan aboriginal peoples, **5:**257
Tandroy, **9:**337
Ternatan/Tidorese, **5:**275
T'in, **5:**278
Tongareva, **2:**340
Toraja, **5:**282
Truk, **2:**352
Tuvans, **6:**374
Tzotzil of Chamula, **8:**280
Tzotzil of San Bartolomé de los Llanos,
    8:288
Ulithi, **2:**359
Ute, **1:**361
Vlach Gypsies of Hungary, **4:**272
Walapai, **1:**365
Western Shoshone, **1:**375
Wogeo, **2:**381
Woleai, **2:**383
Wolof, **9:**379
Yap, **2:**39

Yoruba, **9:**392
common before children are born
  Pokot, **9:**282
  San-speaking peoples, **9:**303
conflict-ridden
  Slovensko Roma, **4:**251
consent of both parties needed
  Khoja, **3:**127-128
de factor immediately after marriage
  Punjabi, **3:**240
difficult
  Chinese in Southeast Asia, **5:**76
  Santa Cruz, **2:**291
  Tangu, **2:**311
  see also Divorce, rare
difficult for wives
  Swahili, **9:**328
discouraged
  Alur, **9:**14
  Batak, **5:**40
  Chambri, **2:**32
  Danes, **4:**87
  Huichol, **8:**126
  Ionians, **4:**150
  Italian Mexicans, **8:**131
  Kashubians, **4:**159
  Kwoma, **2:**135
  Lao, **5:**158
  Mormons, **1:**248-249
  Ndembu, **9:**240
  Nubians, **9:**247
  Occitans, **4:**185
  Poles, **6:**308
  Selung/Moken, **5:**232
  Shona, **9:**313
  Swazi, **9:**331
  Torres Strait Islanders, **2:**346
  Zhuang, **6:**511
easy
  Abelam, **2:**5
  Abor, **3:**4
  Akan, **9:**11
  Badaga, **3:**16
  Bagirmi, **9:**34
  Bau, **2:**23
  Burmese, **5:**65
  Catawba, **1:**54
  Central Yup'ik Eskimos, **1:**57-58
  Cherokee, **1:**61
  Cree, **1:**81
  Culina, **7:**147
  Dai, **6:**425
  Dani, **2:**44
  Daribi, **2:**47
  Delaware, **1:**86
  Divehi, **3:**77
  Don Cossacks, **6:**105
  Dyula, **9:**77
  Easter Island, **2:**54
  Edo, **9:**80
  Gond, **3:**85
  Grasia, **3:**88
  Gros Ventre, **1:**134
  Hani, **6:**450
  Herero, **9:**118
  Huarayo, **7:**178
  Iban, **5:**97
  Iroquois, **1:**166

Divorce (cont'd)
  Jicarilla, 1:173
  Kachin, 5:117
  Khasi, 3:124
  Kickapoo, 1:184
  Kiowa, 1:187
  Kiribati, 2:122
  Klamath, 1:192
  Kota, 3:137
  Koya, 3:141
  Kuikuru, 7:208
  Kwakiutl, 1:198
  Lahu, 6:463
  Lamaholot, 5:156
  Mahar, 3:164
  Manam, 2:168
  Maori, 2:177
  Maring, 2:186
  Mizo, 3:178
  Mohave, 1:241
  Mundurucu, 7:245
  Nagas, 3:189
  Nasioi, 2:234
  Ngatatjara, 2:240
  Northern Shoshone and Bannock, 1:267
  Ojibwa, 1:270
  Pahari, 3:221
  Parsi, 3:228
  Penan, 5:210
  Pomo, 1:294
  Quechan, 1:301
  Rominche, 4:216
  Rotinese, 5:214
  Santal, 3:253
  Seminole, 1:313
  Shan, 5:240
  Sherpa, 3:258
  Sinhalese, 3:266
  Slavey, 1:319
  Sora, 3:269
  Tahiti, 2:306
  Tai Lue, 5:254
  Telefolmin, 2:322
  Thadou, 3:288
  Tolai, 2:335
  Trobriand Islands, 2:350
  Usino, 2:362
  Vedda, 3:302
  Wamira, 2:366
  Western Apache, 1:372
  Yokuts, 1:388
  Zuni, 1:398
  easy for husbands
    Swahili, 9:328
  forbidden
    Ambae, 2:12
    Amhara, 9:19
    Anuta, 2:14
    Chinantec, 8:54
    Cypriots, 4:80
    Friuli, 4:113
    Irish, 4:153
    Karaites, 6:165
    Malekula, 2:165
    Maltese, 4:168
    Sengseng, 2:297
    Tagalog, 5:250
    Tory Islanders, 4:265

  Wovan, 2:386
  Zapotec, 8:312
  grounds. *See* Divorce grounds *heading below*
  husband finds wife new husband
    Lakandon, 8:154
  husband receives compensation from "other
      man," 3:6
    Gujar, 3:89
    Koli, 3:132
  husband renounces wife three times
    Kurds, 9:176
  husband seldom initiates
    Yakö, 9:385
  husband "throws wife away" at public
      gathering
    Cheyenne, 1:65
  impossible after child is born
    Punjabi, 3:240
  informal
    Asiatic Eskimos, 6:41
    Miskito, 8:171
    Mixe, 8:174
    Piro, 7:280
    Shipibo, 7:305
    Sumu, 8:238
    Tsimihety, 9:358
    Waorani, 7:352
    Yuqui, 7:393
  initiated by either spouse
    Cuna, 7:150
    Gurung, 3:94
    Krikati/Pukobye, 7:205
    Pawnee, 1:285
    Purum, 3:243
    Qalandar, 3:247
    Siona-Secoya, 7:308
    Washoe, 1:369
    Western Apache, 1:372
    Wiyot, 1:384
    Yokuts, 1:388
    Yurok, 1:395
  initiated by husband
    Berbers of Morocco, 9:50-51
    peripatetics of Iraq, Syria, Lebanon,
        Jordan, Israel, Egypt, Sudan, and
        Yemen, 9:277
    Yemenis, 9:389
    Yörük, 9:395
  initiated by husband for any reason
    Mizo, 3:178
  initiated by wife
    Andalusians, 4:11
    Nivaclé, 7:249
    Tiv, 9:351
    Yakö, 9:385
  initiated by wife's family
    Ewe and Fon, 9:86
  initiating spouse pays compensation, 3:141
  insurance paid to wife
    Basseri, 9:42
  migration following
    Afro-Bolivians, 7:9
  by mutual consent
    Greeks, 4:132
    Mescalero Apache, 1:224
  negotiated
    Amhara, 9:19
  nonstigmatized

  Northern Paiute, 1:264
  permitted
    Andis, 6:26
    Ata Tana 'Ai, 5:24
    Avars, 6:45
    Aymara, 7:67
    Bai, 6:420
    Balinese, 5:37
    Bukharan Jews, 6:64
    Carpatho-Rusyns, 6:70
    Cham, 5:73
    Chuvash, 6:85
    Dargins, 6:97, 98
    De'ang, 6:430
    Dusun, 5:82
    English, 4:97
    Evenki (Northern Tungus), 6:122
    Gayo, 5:89
    Gujar, 3:89
    Han, 6:444, 445
    Itelmen, 6:153
    Kalmyks, 6:156
    Kapauku, 2:106, 107
    Khmer, 5:136
    Kmhmu, 5:140
    Kriashen Tatars, 6:212
    Krymchaks, 6:215
    Kubachins, 6:218
    Kumyks, 6:222, 223
    Lak, 2:138
    Lithuanian Jews, 6:246
    Madurese, 5:167
    Maguindanao, 5:170
    Makassar, 5:174
    Mandak, 2:171
    Maonan, 6:468
    Maroni Carib, 7:220
    Mashco, 7:226
    Mataco, 7:229
    Melanau, 5:179
    Melpa, 2:201
    Mendi, 2:204
    Miao, 6:471
    Minangkabau, 5:183
    Mountain Jews, 6:272
    Mulam, 6:476, 477
    Murik, 2:222
    Murngin, 2:225
    Ogan-Besemah, 5:198
    Orokaiva, 2:257
    Ossetes, 6:301
    Palikur, 7:262
    Pemon, 7:272
    Piaroa, 7:277
    Pume, 7:280
    Rennell Island, 2:277
    Rikbaktsa, 7:287
    Sagada Igorot, 5:216
    Salar, 6:488
    Salasaca, 7:290
    Saliva, 7:292
    Samal, 5:220
    Sara, 9:306
    Saraguro, 7:294
    Semang, 5:235
    Shui, 6:491
    Siberiaki, 6:333
    Tacana, 7:318

Tasmanians, 2:316
Tats, 6:360
Tausug, 5:263
Temiar, 5:269
Ticuna, 7:329
Trio, 7:336
Tupari, 7:340
Wapisiana, 7:355
Xoraxané Romá, 4:282
Yakan, 5:289
Yanomamö, 7:375
Yao, 6:505
Yezidis, 6:409
Yukuna, 7:387
prior to legal marriage
  Canelos Quichua, 7:100
rare
  Abkhazians, 6:8
  Agta, 5:5-6
  Ambonese, 5:18
  Andalusians, 4:11
  Andamanese, 3:10
  Asmat, 2:20
  Atoni, 5:28
  Aveyronnais, 4:25
  Azerbaijani Turks, 6:49
  Azoreans, 4:28
  Balkars, 6:54
  Bene Israel, 3:28
  Bengali, 3:32
  Betsileo, 9:56
  Bonerate, 5:45
  Bukidnon, 5:54
  Bulgarians, 4:44
  Burusho, 3:55-56
  Calabrese, 4:49
  Castilians, 4:60
  Chipewyan, 1:69
  Circassians, 9:67
  Cretans, 4:70
  Druze, 9:74
  Dungans, 6:109
  Ewenki, 6:434
  Faroe Islanders, 4:99
  Fipa, 9:99
  Foi, 2:60
  Gebusi, 2:78
  Georgians, 6:133
  Ghorbat, 9:107
  Gururumba, 2:93
  Gusii, 9:109
  Hmong, 5:93
  Ingalik, 1:157
  Iteso, 9:129
  Jamaicans, 8:138
  Japanese, 5:107
  Jews of Iran, 9:140
  Jingpo, 6:457
  Karakalpaks, 6:167
  Karen, 5:128
  Kilenge, 2:119
  Kipsigis, 9:164
  Konso, 9:170
  Korean, 5:147
  Kosrae, 2:129
  Lakalai, 2:141
  Lakher, 3:146
  Lingayat, 3:152

Lisu, 5:165
Lugbara, 9:194
Madeirans, 4:165
Mae Enga, 2:150
Mailu, 2:155
Makassar, 5:173
Malaita, 2:162
Maliseet, 1:211
Mardudjara, 2:180
Marshall Islands, 2:193
Mbeere, 9:221
Mekeo, 2:199
Mingrelians, 6:264
Mixe, 8:174
Miyanmin, 2:211
Mongols, 6:475
Motu, 2:214
Muong, 5:191
Muyu, 2:229
Namau, 2:231
Nandi and other Kalenjin peoples, 9:233
Nauru, 2:237
Naxi, 6:479
Nias, 5:196
Nicobarese, 3:209
Ningerum, 2:247
Nissan, 2:250
Nyinba, 3:212
Oroquen, 6:483
Palu'e, 5:206
Pandit of Kashmir, 3:225
Pathan, 3:232
Pentecost, 2:263
Piemontese Sinti, 4:200
Pohnpei, 2:268
Punjabi, 3:240
Rapa, 2:274
Rossel Island, 2:279
Russian peasants, 6:312
Saami, 4:221
Samal Moro, 5:223
Sambia, 2:285
Sardinians, 4:226
Seri, 8:234
Shetlanders, 4:234
Sicilians, 4:236
Sio, 2:300
Slav Macedonians, 4:240
Slovenes, 4:248
South and Southeast Asians of Canada,
  1:323
Suri, 9:325
Svans, 6:345
Syrian Christian of Kerala, 3:273
Tajiks, 6:353
Tamil, 3:277
Tamil of Sri Lanka, 3:282
Tanana, 1:339
Tanna, 2:314
Tikopia, 2:325
Tlingit, 1:352
Tujia, 6:498
Tuvalu, 2:356
Vellala, 3:305
Wa, 6:503
Wantoat, 2:369
Waorani, 7:352
Wape, 2:371

Warlpiri, 2:374
Waropen, 2:376
Yangoru Boiken, 2:389
Yukateko, 8:309
rare after birth of child
  Maká, 7:217
  Pokot, 9:282
  San-speaking peoples, 9:303
rare for firstborn daughters
  Swahili, 9:328
reconciliation attempts
  Irula, 3:106-107
  Kanjar, 3:121
  Lingayat, 3:152
  Tigray, 9:348
regulations equal for either spouse
  Karaites, 9:155
regulations favor woman
  Lakher, 3:146
religious court
  Karaites, 9:155
remarriage following. _See under_ Remarriage
stigma
  Nepali, 3:204
stigma for woman
  Poles, 4:203
after three reconciliation attempts
  Irula, 3:107
unknown
  Sarakatsani, 4:224
  Shahsevan, 9:309
wife ejects husband from tent
  Tuareg, 9:367
wife gets no compensation
  Kol, 3:130
wife gets one-third of joint property
  Nagas, 3:189
wife keeps house and garden
  Kashinawa, 7:195
wife looked after by brother or older son
  Baggara, 9:31
wife moves out of house
  Yuit, 1:391
wife removes husband's belongings from her
    house
  Mescalero Apache, 1:224
wife returns to natal home
  Luyia, 9:20
  Ndebele, 9:236
  Palestinians, 9:265
  Tswana, 9:362
  Yagua, 7:372-373
wife returns to natal home and takes new
    man
  Tatuyo, 7:323
see also Annulment; Child custody
Divorce grounds
  adultery
    Agaria, 3:6
    Amahuaca, 7:35
    Apiaká, 7:49
    Araucanians, 7:53
    Bakairi, 7:74
    Baniwa-Curripaco-Wakuenai, 7:78
    Burusho, 3:55
    Cheyenne, 1:65
    Cubeo, 7:140, 141
    Guadalcanal, 2:90

Divorce grounds (cont'd)
  Irula, 3:106
  Karok, 1:176
  Ka'wiari, 7:199
  Kol, 3:130
  Koli, 3:132
  Kpelle, 9:173
  Lakher, 3:146
  Lugbara, 9:194
  Maguindano, 5:170
  Miami, 1:231
  Ontong Java, 2:254
  Pima-Papago, 1:289
  Swazi, 9:331
  Tauade, 2:319
  Ute, 1:361
  Walapai, 1:365
  Washoe, 1:369
  Wiyot, 1:384
  Wogeo, 2:381
alcoholism
  Norwegians, 4:181
bad omens
  Ifugao, 5:100
bad temper
  Bhuiya, 3:44
  Gond, 3:85
  Pima-Papago, 1:289
childlessness
  Albanians, 4:5
  Araucanians, 7:53
  Araweté, 7:57
  Berbers of Morocco, 9:51
  Cubeo, 7:141
  Cuiva, 7:144
  Ifugao, 5:100
  Inughuit, 1:160
  Ka'wiari, 7:199
  Kol, 3:130
  Kpelle, 9:173
  Kurds, 9:176
  Lugbara, 9:194
  Maguindanao, 5:170
  Montenegrins, 4:173
  Punjabi, 3:240
  Swazi, 9:331
  Ute, 1:361
  Wayapi, 7:362
  Yawalapití, 7:379
  Yurok, 1:395
child's death
  Amuesha, 7:38
cruelty
  Guadalcanal, 2:90
  Ifugao, 5:100
desertion
  Araucanians, 7:53
  Ifugao, 5:100
extravagance
  Agaria, 3:6
failure to bear male offspring
  Montenegrins, 4:173
failure to do housework
  Bakairi, 7:74
  Bhuiya, 3:44
  Gond, 3:85
failure to pay bride-wealth
  Maguindanao, 5:170

failure to provide
  Gond, 3:85
  Irula, 3:106
  Kpelle, 9:173
  Yuracaré, 7:396
failure to work
  Amahuaca, 7:35
  Bakairi, 7:74
  Ontong Java, 2:254
husband's failure to give funeral contribution
  Mamprusi, 9:213
impotence
  Lakher, 3:146
improvidence
  Washoe, 1:369
incompatibility
  Guadalcanal, 2:90
  Karok, 1:176
  Kol, 3:130
  Maguindano, 5:170
  Ontong Java, 2:254
  Ute, 1:361
  Walapai, 1:365
  Washoe, 1:369
  Winnebago, 1:381
jealousy
  Walapai, 1:365
madness
  Lakher, 3:146
mistreatment
  Agraria, 3:6
  Araucanians, 7:53
  Bakairi, 7:74
  Baniwa-Curripaco-Wakuenai, 7:78
  Cheyenne, 1:65
  Gond, 3:85
  Ontong Java, 2:254
personal friction
  Norwegians, 4:181
wife beating
  Gond, 3:85
Divorce rate
  decline
    Walapai, 1:365
  high
    Lunda, 9:197
    Somalis, 9:317
  low
    Berbers of Morocco, 9:50
    Greeks, 4:132
    Norwegians, 4:181
    Orcadians, 4:187
  rising
    Bavarians, 4:34
    Croats, 4:73
    Germans, 4:122
    Old Believers, 1:274
    Selepet, 2:294
    Walloons, 4:277
Diyin (shaman)
  Western Apache, 1:373
Dogs
  breeding
    Emerillon, 7:159
  domesticated
    Andamanese, 3:9
    Copper Eskimo, 1:77
    Cree, 1:81

  Hill Pandaram, 3:99
  Inughuit, 1:160
  Miami, 1:231
  Nayaka, 3:195
  North Alaskan Eskimos, 1:259
  Pima-Papago, 1:288
  Saami, 4:221
  Tanaina, 1:335
  West Greenland Inuit, 1:377
  Wiyot, 1:384
  hunting
    Amahuaca, 7:34
    Angaité, 7:43
    Chocó, 7:123
    Jivaro, 7:182
    Krikati/Pukobye, 7:204
    Lengua, 7:210
    Marubo, 7:222
    Mocoví, 7:240
    Mojo, 7:242
    Paresí, 7:269
    Piapoco, 7:274
    Sardinians, 4:226
    Tacana, 7:318
    Trio, 7:335
    Wáiwai, 7:346
    Wiyot, 1:384
    Xokléng, 7:370
    Yuracaré, 7:395
    Yurok, 1:394
  raising
    Ainu, 5:8
    Bilaan, 5:42
    Bontok, 5:46
    Cham, 5:72
    Chuvans, 6:81
    Ewenki, 6:434
    Ilongot, 5:101
    Kalimantan Dayaks, 5:120
    Kenyah-Kayan-Kajang, 5:133
    Koryaks and Kerek, 6:208
    Murut, 5:193
    Ndaonese, 5:194
    Nivkh, 6:284
    Orochi, 6:295
    Orok, 6:296
    Oroquen, 6:482
    Palu'e, 5:205
    Saami, 6:323
    Sagada Igorot, 5:216
    Saluan, 5:217
    Selung/Moken, 5:231
    Senoi, 5:237
    Taiwan aboriginal peoples, 5:257
    Yakut, 6:405
    Yukagir, 6:412
Dogsled use
  Asiatic Eskimos, 6:40
  Copper Eskimo, 1:77
  Inughuit, 1:160
  Labrador Inuit, 1:201
  North Alaskan Eskimos, 1:259
  Tamaoma, 1:335
  Tanana, 1:339
  West Greenland Inuit, 1:377
Dokhma. *See* Towers of Silence
Doll making
  Hopi, 1:150

Nagas, 3:191
Seminole, 1:313
Walapai, 1:364
Western Apache, 1:372
Zuni, 1:399
Domesticated animals. *See specific animals*
Domestic roles. *See* Gender roles
Domestic service
Akan, 9:11
Black West Indians in the United States,
1:45
East Asians of the United States, 1:100
Pahari, 3:220
Domestic violence
Ache, 7:6
Amahuaca, 7:35
Asmat, 2:20
Bakairi, 7:74
Baniwa-Curripaco-Wakuenai, 7:78
Barbadians, 8:23, 24
Cotopaxi Quichua, 7:134
Emberá, 7:157
Flemish, 4:108
Gebusi, 2:78
Manx, 4:171
Namau, 2:231, 232
Palikur, 7:263
Piro, 7:280
Rom of Czechoslovakia, 4:218
Russians, 6:316
Shipibo, 7:305
Tairora, 2:309
Yawalapití, 7:379
Domowina groups
Sorbs, 4:253
Donkey use
Sardinians, 4:226
Turkana, 9:371
Doppelgänger
Andis, 6:27
Dormitories (single male or female)
Abor, 3:3, 4, 5
Bhuiya, 3:44
Boazi, 2:29, 30
Bondo, 3:48, 49
Bontok, 5:46
Chin, 3:66
Gainj, 2:72
Garia, 2:74
Garo, 3:82, 83
Gayo, 5:89
Ifugao, 5:99
Kenyah-Kayan-Kajang, 5:133
Keraki, 2:113
Kiribati, 2:122
Kiwai, 2:124, 126
Kmhmu, 5:140
Lak, 2:137
Lunda, 9:197
Luyia, 9:203
Mandak, 2:171
Mekeo, 2:198
Mikir, 3:176
Miyanmin, 2:209
Modang, 5:185, 187
Nagas, 3:188, 190
Nasioi, 2:234
Ndebele, 9:235

Nissan, 2:249
Okiek, 9:261
Oriya, 3:215
Orokaiva, 2:256
Pintupi, 2:265
Sagada Igorot, 5:216
Santa Cruz, 2:291
Sea Nomads of the Andaman, 5:229
Semang, 5:235
Siwai, 2:303
Tairora, 2:309
Taiwan aboriginal peoples, 5:257
Tokelau, 2:331
Tor, 2:344
Trobriand Islands, 2:349
Truk, 2:352
Ulithi, 2:358
Wape, 2:371
Warlpiri, 2:374
Waropen, 2:376
Wik Mungkan, 2:378
Woleai, 2:383
see also Gender-specific housing
Dorset culture
Baffinland Inuit, 1:28
Double-unilineal descent
Toda, 3:296
Dowry
Achang, 6:418
Albanians, 4:5
Anavil Brahman, 3:8
Andis, 6:26
Ashkenazic Jews, 4:16
Avars, 6:45
Aveyronnais, 4:25
Bai, 6:420
Basques, 4:31
Bene Israel, 3:28
Bukharan Jews, 6:64
Bulgarians, 4:44
Chuvash, 6:84
Corsicans, 4:67
Cretans, 4:70
Croats, 4:73
Cyclades, 4:77, 78
Cypriots, 4:80
Dolgan, 6:101
Don Cossacks, 6:105
Even, 6:119
Evenki (Northern Tungus), 6:122
Gaels (Irish), 4:116
Greeks, 4:133;6:143
Greek-speaking Jews of Greece, 4:135
Guarijío, 8:118
Hani, 6:450
Hausa, 9:113
Hungarians, 4:144
Ingilos, 6:150
Ionians, 4:149, 150
Irish Travelers, 1:163
Jatav, 3:114
Jews of Iran, 9:140
Jicarilla, 1:173
Kachin, 5:117
Karachays, 6:160
Karaites, 6:165
Karakalpaks, 6:167
Kashubians, 4:159

Kazakhs, 6:180
Khanty, 6:191
Khevsur, 6:195
Khinalughs, 6:200
Kol, 3:130
Krymchaks, 6:215
Kumyks, 6:222, 223
Lisu, 5:165;6:466
Lithuanian Jews, 6:246
Malay, 5:175
Maltese, 4:168
Manchu, 6:467
Mansi, 6:253
Maori, 2:177
Maris, 6:257
Moldovans, 6:267
Moor of Sri Lanka, 3:181
Nambudiri Brahman, 3:193
Naxi, 6:479
Nepali, 3:203, 204
Nubians, 9:247
Nyinba, 3:212
Old Believers, 1:273, 274
Oriya, 3:217
Orok, 6:296
Oroquen, 6:483
Ossetes, 6:300
Palaung, 5:202
Palu'e, 5:206
Pandit of Kashmir, 3:225
Pathan, 3:232
Peloponnesians, 4:193, 194
peripatetics of Iraq, Syria, Lebanon, Jordan,
Israel, Egypt, Sudan, and Yemen, 9:277
Pomaks, 4:205
Punjabi, 3:240
Russians, 6:316
Santal, 3:254
Sarakatsani, 4:224
She, 6:490
Sherpa, 3:258, 259
Sicilians, 4:236
Slav Macedonians, 4:240
Slovaks, 4:244
Slovenes, 4:248
Swahili, 9:328
Swedes, 4:257
Tamil, 3:277
Tamil of Sri Lanka, 3:282
Tats, 6:359
Temne, 9:343
Tigray, 9:348
Tiroleans, 4:263
Toda, 3:296
Tsimihety, 9:358
Tuareg, 9:367
Tujia, 6:498
Vellala, 3:305
Volga Tatars, 6:401
Yakut, 6:406
Yao, 6:505
Yi, 6:507
Zamindar, 3:307
Zhuang, 6:511
see also Trousseau
Dragon Boat Festival
Hakka, 6:439
Miao, 6:472

Drama
  Altaians, **6**:23
  Azerbaijani Turks, **6**:50
  Bai, **6**:421
  Balinese, **5**:37
  Burakumin, **5**:63
  Burusho, **3**:56
  Canela, **7**:97
  Chechen-Ingush, **6**:75
  Chimbu, **2**:37
  Chinese in Southeast Asia, **5**:77
  English, **4**:97
  Georgian Jews, **6**:128
  Greeks, **6**:143
  Gujarati, **3**:92
  hijra, **3**:98
  Japanese, **5**:110
  Javanese, **5**:113
  Karakalpaks, **6**:168
  Kazakhs, **6**:182
  Khmer, **5**:138
  Komi, **6**:204
  Koreans, **6**:206
  Kwakiutl, **1**:200
  Latinos, **1**:206
  Lithuanians, **6**:251
  Mahar, **3**:165
  Maká, **7**:218
  Oriya, **3**:218
  Ossetes, **6**:301
  Poles, **6**:309
  Rajput, **3**:249
  Santa Cruz, **2**:292
  Santal, **3**:255
  Tagalog, **5**:251
  Tai Lue, **5**:256
  Tajiks, **6**:354
  Tamil, **3**:279
  Tuvalu, **2**:357
  Tuvans, **6**:374
  Udmurt, **6**:381
  Ukrainians, **6**:394
  Yakut, **6**:407
  see also Entertainers; Opera; Shadow play
Dravidian kinship system. See Cousin marriage, cross-cousing *headings ; under* Kinship terminology
Drawing (art)
  Futuna, **2**:67
Dreadlock hairstyle
  Black West Indians in the United States, **1**:46
Dream quest. See Vision quest
Dreams
  as cause of death
    Zuni, **1**:400
  dead communicate through
    Moldovans, **6**:269
    Sakalava, **9**:299
    Zoroastrians, **9**:410
  foretelling death
    Konso, **9**:171
    Miskito, **8**:172
  interpretation
    Mohave, **1**:241
    Montagnais-Naskapi, **1**:246
    Rom of Czechoslovakia, **4**:219
    Sadhu, **3**:251

  Sakalava, **9**:298
  in medical diagnosis
    Desana, **7**:154
    Mohave, **1**:242
  as omens
    Mohave, **1**:241
    Moldovans, **6**:269
  as power source
    Chipewyan, **1**:69
    Cree, **1**:82
    Flathead, **1**:128
    Hare, **1**:142
    Havasupai, **1**:145
    Huron, **1**:152
    Ingalik, **1**:158
    Iroquois, **1**:167
    Mohave, **1**:241
    Northern Shoshone and Bannock, **1**:267
    Nyakyusa and Ngonde, **9**:254
    Ojibwa, **1**:270
    Quechan, **1**:302
    Sarsi, **1**:308
    Ute, **1**:362
    Western Shoshone, **1**:375
    see also Guardian spirits
  prophetic
    Winnebago, **1**:381
  in religious beliefs
    Araucanians, **7**:54
    Karihona, **7**:193
    Mashco, **7**:226, 227
    Miami, **1**:232
    Omaha, **1**:275
    Saramaka, **7**:28
    Spokane, **1**:333
    see also Dreamtime
  revelatory
    Luba of Shaba, **9**:192
    Menominee, **1**:222
    Ottawa, **1**:280
  Senoi dream therapy
    Temiar, **5**:271-272
  as source of shaman power
    Angaité, **7**:44
    Asurini, **7**:62
    Kagwahiv, **7**:185
    Miwok, **1**:240
    Mohave, **1**:241, 242
    Northern Paiute, **1**:265
    Ojibwa, **1**:271
    Pomo, **1**:295
    Slavey, **1**:320
    Tanaina, **1**:337
    Ute, **1**:362
    Walapai, **1**:366
    Yukpa, **7**:384
  as source of skill and knowledge
    Mohave, **1**:241
  as source of songs
    Mohave, **1**:241
    Shavante, **7**:301
    Southern Paiute (and Chemehuevi), **1**:332
Dream therapy
  Temiar, **5**:271-272
Dreamtime
  Mardudjara, **2**:181

  Murngin, **2**:226
  Ngatatjara, **2**:240, 241
  Pintupi, **2**:265, 266
  Tiwi, **2**:328, 329
  Warlpiri, **2**:374
Dress. See Clothing
Drought
  Cape Verdeans, **4**:54, 55
Drugs
  addiction
    Kikapu, **8**:145
  manufacture
    Chimane, **7**:112
    Dutch, **4**:94
    German Swiss, **4**:125
    Nayar, **3**:198
  pharmacopoeia
    Pima Bajo, **8**:211
    Santal, **3**:253, 255
  trade
    Jamaicans, **8**:139
  see also Coca leaf growing; Hallucinogen use; Marijuana growing; Opium; Peyote ritual
Drum dance
  Dogrib, **1**:89
  Hare, **1**:142
Drumming contests
  Yuit, **1**:391
Drums and drumming
  Alorese, **5**:14, 15
  Aymara, **7**:68
  Basques, **4**:32
  Bulgarian Gypsies, **4**:41
  Chipewyan, **1**:69
  Chiriguano, **7**:122
  Chocó, **7**:123
  Ewe and Fon, **9**:86, 88
  Greeks, **4**:134
  Huarayo, **7**:178
  Lozi, **9**:189
  Matsigenka, **7**:232
  Mohave, **1**:241
  Montagnais-Naskapi, **1**:246
  Mossi, **9**:228
  Ndembu, **9**:241
  Nyamwezi and Sukuma, **9**:258
  Ojibwa, **1**:271
  Pedi, **9**:270, 271
  Qashqa'i, **9**:287
  Sakalava, **9**:298
  Saraguro, **7**:295
  Shipibo, **7**:306
  Shona, **9**:314
  Sidi, **3**:260
  Siona-Secoya, **7**:309
  Suku, **9**:323
  Swazi, **9**:333
  Taos, **1**:342
  Temne, **9**:345
  Thompson, **1**:350
  Toba, **7**:333
  Tonga, **9**:355
  Trinidadians and Tobagonians, **8**:269
  Tuareg, **9**:369
  Wolof, **9**:380
  Yuit, **1**:392
  Zhuang, **6**:511

Drum Society festivals
  Miao, **6:**472
Drunkenness. *See* Alcohol
Druze religion
  Arab Americans, **1:**24
  Druze, **9:**74-75
  Palestinians, **9:**266
Dry cultivation. *See under* Agriculture
Dry funeral
  Kota, **3:**138
Dry-paintings
  Navajo, **1:**253
Dual worlds (cosmology)
  Albanians, **4:**7
  Mataco, **7:**226-227
  Menominee, **1:**222
  Toda, **3:**297, 298
  see also Afterlife
Duan Wu (festival)
  Hani, **6:**451
Duck raising
  Batak, **5:**39
  Bugis, **5:**49
  Central Thai, **5:**70
  Cham, **5:**72
  Dusun, **5:**81
  Kashubians, **4:**158
  Mojo, **7:**242
  Samal Moro, **5:**222
  Tausug, **5:**262
  Ternatan/Tidorese, **5:**275
  Vietnamese, **5:**285
  Wapisiana, **7:**355
Dueling
  Nivkh, **6:**285
  Tasmanians, **2:**317
  Warlpiri, **2:**374
Dues (as social control)
  Thadou, **3:**289
Dugout canoes. *See* Canoe building
Dukhobors
  Siberiaki, **6:**334
Dulha Deo (deity)
  Agaria, **3:**6
Durga (goddess)
  Bengali, **3:**34
  Brahman and Chhetri of Nepal, **3:**53
Durwaza (gateway)
  Punjabi, **3:**237
Dutch Reformed Church
  Afrikaners, **9:**9
  Cape Coloureds, **9:**59
  Dutch-Americans, **1:**110
  Frisians, **4:**111
Dwarfs
  anthropomorphic
    Southern Paiute (and Chemehuevi),
      1:332
  blamed for misfortune
    Kashubians, **4:**159
  dwarfism
    Amish, **1:**19
  in religious beliefs
    Yukpa, **7:**384
Dyes
  Bukharan Jews, **6:**64
  Cape Verdeans, **4:**55
  Mountain Jews, **6:**272

Paya, **8:**209
Tetum, **5:**276

Eagle (creator)
  Yokuts, **1:**388
Eagle Dance
  Comanche, **1:**75
Eagle moiety
  Haida, **1:**136
Eagle reverance
  Kaumeyaay, **1:**195
  Kiowa, **1:**188
  Kumeyaay, **1:**195
Ear cutting
  Swazi, **9:**331
Earpieces
  Nootka, **1:**257
Ear piercing. *See under* Body piercing; Earrings
Earrings
  Irula, **3:**108
  Kond, **3:**133
  Kota, **3:**137
  Nagas, **3:**190
  Nootka, **1:**257
  Purum, **3:**244
  Toda, **3:**297
Earth deity
  Comanche, **1:**75
Earth Lodge Cult
  Pomo, **1:**295
Earth Maker (creator)
  Winnebago, **1:**382
Earth Mother (deity)
  Zuni, **1:**399
Earthquakes
  Ionians, **4:**149
  Japanese, **5:**106
  Pacific Eskimo, **1:**282, 283
Earth Surface People (supernaturals)
  Navajo, **1:**253
Earth world. *See* Cosmology
Earth worship
  Lobi-Dagarti peoples, **9:**185
Easter
  Aleuts, **6:**18
Easter (holiday)
  Ambae, **2:**12
  Amhara, **9:**20
  Anuta, **2:**15
  Armenians, **6:**31
  Belarussians, **6:**61
  Carpatho-Rusyns, **6:**71
  Cora, **8:**77
  Cyclades, **4:**78
  Cypriots, **4:**81
  Dolgan, **6:**102
  Frisians, **4:**112
  Futuna, **2:**67
  Georgians, **6:**135
  Greeks, **4:**133
  Gypsies, **6:**148
  Ingilos, **6:**151
  Khevsur, **6:**196
  Kiribati, **2:**123
  Kriashen Tatars, **6:**212
  Manx, **4:**171
  Moldovans, **6:**269
  Montenegrins, **4:**173

Mount Athos, **4:**176
Old Believers, **1:**274
Orcadians, **4:**188
Peloponnesians, **4:**194
Pima Bajo, **8:**213
Poles, **6:**309
Russians, **6:**317
Sarakatsani, **4:**224
Siberiaki, **6:**334
Siberian Germans, **6:**339
Slav Macedonians, **4:**241
Syrian Christian of Kerala, **3:**274
Tagalog, **5:**251
Tarahumara, **8:**242
Ukrainian peasants, **6:**387
Ukrainians, **6:**394
Ukrainians of Canada, **1:**359
Vietnamese, **5:**287
Eastern Catholicism. *See* Uniate Catholicism
Eastern Orthodoxy. *See* Orthodox
    Christianity
Easter Ride (ceremony)
  Sorbs, **4:**253
Eating. *See* Food
Eclectic folk religion. *See* Syncretism
Ecstasy (religious)
  Baul, **3:**27
  Bengali Vaishnava, **3:**36-37
  Shakers, **1:**316
Ecumenism
  San-speaking peoples, **9:**303
Education
  acculturation by
    South and Southeast Asians of Canada,
      1:323
  belief in limits on
    Mennonites, **1:**219
  boys given preference
    Vietnamese, **5:**285
  compulsory
    Batak, **5:**40
    Cypriots, **4:**81
    German Swiss, **4:**126
    Greeks, **4:**133
    Japanese, **5:**108
    Korean, **5:**147
    Madeirans, **4:**165
    Slovaks, **4:**244
    Tanana, **1:**339
    Tiroleans, **4:**263
    Walloons, **4:**277
  county library and museum as center
    Shetlanders, **4:**234
  culture preservation
    Walapai, **1:**365
  distrust of public schools
    African Americans, **1:**12
  dropping out to marry
    Old Believers, **1:**274
  as economic advancement means
    Japanese, **5:**107
    Sicilians, **4:**236
  equal access
    Lowland Scots, **4:**163
  esteemed
    Armenians, **6:**31
    Ashkenazim, **6:**34-35
    Bene Israel, **3:**28

Education (cont'd)
  Catawba, **1:**54
  Croats, **4:**73
  Czechs, **4:**84
  East Asians in the United States, **1:**101
  Ionians, **4:**150
  Krymchaks, **6:**215
  Lithuanian Jews, **6:**245, 246
  Lithuanians, **6:**249
  Lowland Scots, **4:**163
  Mormons, **1:**248
  Palestinians, **9:**266
  Pende, **9:**273
  Tewa Pueblos, **1:**349
  Tlingit, **1:**351
  Tonga, **9:**354
  Zuni, **1:**398
  ethnic culture
    African Americans, **1:**12
    Ukrainians of Canada, **1:**358
  folk high schools
    Dane, **4:**89
  formal crafts and technical training
    Navajo, **1:**252
  "hedge schools"
    Gales (Irish), **4:**115
  low attainment levels
    Ute, **1:**361
  myth recitation
    Navajo, **1:**252
  not highly valued
    Micmac, **1:**234
  preschools
    Slovaks, **4:**244
    Swedes, **4:**258
    Walloons, **4:**277
  private Catholic schools
    Flemish, **4:**107
  rejection of formal
    Rominche, **4:**217
    Slovensko Roma, **4:**250
  religious schools
    Mennonites, **1:**218-219
    Northern Irish, **4:**179
  resistance to public schools
    Amish, **1:**20
    Doukhobor, **1:**92
    Ozarks, **1:**281
  restrictions
    East Asians of Canada, **1:**96
    Hasidim, **1:**144
  Rotinese, **5:**212
  scholars and teachers
    Chitpavan Brahman, **3:**69
    Nambudiri Brahman, **3:**193
  sexual
    Kiwai, **2:**127
  as status marker
    Chakma, **3:**60
    Croats, **4:**74
    Maliseet, **1:**212
  track system
    Germans, **4:**123
  universal
    Ogan-Besemah, **5:**198
  of women
    Parsi, **3:**228
    Teton, **1:**345

  see also Literacy
Eel fishing
  Betsileo, **9:**54
Efficiency (as social virtue)
  Shakers, **1:**316
Effigies
  Toraja, **5:**283
Egalitarian
  peripatetics of Afghanistan, Iran, and
    Turkey, **9:**276
Egalitarianism
  Akha, **5:**12
  Amuesha, **7:**38
  Apiaká, **7:**50
  Aranda, **2:**18
  Asmat, **2:**20
  Aymara, **7:**67
  Bajau, **5:**33
  Bakairi, **7:**75
  Barí, **7:**85
  Basques, **4:**31
  Bhil, **3:**38
  Boazi, **2:**30
  Bondo, **3:**50
  Candoshi, **7:**93
  Canelos Quichua, **7:**100
  Central Yup'ik Eskimos, **1:**58
  Chambri, **2:**32
  Chechen-Ingush, **6:**74
  Chimane, **7:**112
  Cook Islands, **2:**42
  Craho, **7:**138
  Cree, **1:**82
  Czechs, **4:**84
  Danes, **4:**90
  Daur, **6:**429
  Delaware, **1:**86
  Dobu, **2:**51
  Dogrib, **1:**89
  egalitarian
    Tandroy, **9:**338
  Faroe Islanders, **4:**99
  Finns, **4:**103
  Fore, **2:**64
  Gayo, **5:**89
  Gebusi, **2:**78
  Gitanos, **4:**130
  Gogodala, **2:**84
  Goodenough Island, **2:**87
  Guahibo-Sikuani, **7:**165
  Hawaiians, **2:**97
  Hezhen, **6:**452
  Highland Scots, **4:**141
  Hill Pandaram, **3:**100
  Hmong, **5:**94
  Huarayo, **7:**178
  Iban, **5:**98
  Javanese, **5:**112
  Kalimantan Dayaks, **5:**120
  Kaluli, **2:**103
  Kashinawa, **7:**196
  Kickapoo, **1:**185
  Kiwai, **2:**126
  Koya, **3:**141
  Kurtatchi, **2:**132
  Lahu, **5:**153
  Lao, **5:**159
  Lingayat, **3:**151

  Mae Enga, **2:**150
  Maisin, **2:**159
  Malaita, **2:**162
  Mardudjara, **2:**181
  Marubo, **7:**223
  Mataco, **7:**229
  Mejbrat, **2:**196
  Miao, **6:**469
  Mundugumor, **2:**219
  Muyu, **2:**229
  Nasioi, **2:**235
  Nayaka, **3:**196
  Ngatatjara, **2:**241
  Nissan, **2:**250
  Northern Paiute, **1:**264
  Orcadians, **4:**187
  Orokolo, **2:**260
  Panare, **7:**266
  Peloponnesians, **4:**194
  Pemon, **7:**272
  Pintupi, **2:**266
  Piro, **7:**280
  Pukapuka, **2:**272
  Qiang, **6:**487
  Saami, **4:**222
  Samal, **5:**220
  Santal, **3:**254
  Saramaka, **7:**297
  Sea Nomads of the Andaman, **5:**228
  Selepet, **2:**294
  Semang, **5:**235
  Sherpa, **3:**259
  Shetlanders, **4:**234
  Shipibo, **7:**305
  Siona-Secoya, **7:**308
  Slavey, **1:**320
  Tairora, **2:**309
  Telefolmin, **2:**323
  Temiar, **5:**270
  Tewa Pueblos, **1:**349
  Thakli, **3:**291
  Tokelau, **2:**332
  Tor, **2:**343
  Torres Strait Islanders, **2:**347
  Tory Islanders, **4:**266
  Trio, **7:**336
  Turkmens, **6:**371
  Tuvalu, **2:**356
  Vedda, **3:**302
  Vlach Gypsies of Hungary, **4:**272
  Walloons, **4:**277
  Wantoat, **2:**369
  Waorani, **7:**353
  Washoe, **1:**369
  Welsh, **4:**280
  Wovan, **2:**387
  Yagua, **7:**373
  Yawalapití, **7:**379
  see also Communitarianism; Gender
    equality
Eggs
  decoration
    Croats, **4:**75
    Slav Macedonians, **4:**241
    Slovaks, **4:**245
    Sorbs, **4:**253
    Ukrainians of Canada, **1:**359
  production

Orcadians, **4**:187
  Syrian Christian of Kerala, **3**:273
as women's personal source of income
  Sarakatsani, **4**:224
see also Turtle egg collection
Eid-e Fitr (holiday)
  Tajiks, **6**:354
Eid-e Qorban (holiday)
  Tajiks, **6**:354
Elderly
  abandonment of
    Kiowa, **1**:189
    Western Shoshone, **1**:375
  care by married child who inherits farm,
    4:158-159
  care by married daughter, **4**:161
    Welsh, **4**:280
  care by unmarried daughter
    Azoreans, **4**:28
  care by unmarried son
    Gaels (Irish), **4**:116
  economic roles
    Quechan, **1**:301
  government services
    Highland Scots, **4**:142
  high percentage of
    Ionians, **4**:148, 149-150
  no efforts to prolong lives
    Awá Kwaiker, **7**:65
  old-age homes
    Flemish, **4**:107
  remain in own homes
    Galicians, **4**:120
    Walloons, **4**:277
  role in educating young people
    Tlingit, **1**:352
  subsistence contribution by
    Yuit, **1**:391
  suicide by
    Ayoreo, **7**:71
  terms of address
    Saami, **4**:221
  see also Household, three-generational
    stem; Retirees; Widowers; Widows
Elder respect
  Azoreans, **4**:28
  Black Creoles of Louisiana, **1**:39
  Canarians, **4**:52
  Catawba, **1**:54
  Chakma, **3**:60
  Cherokee, **1**:62
  Choctaw, **1**:72
  Delaware, **1**:86
  East Asians in Canada, **1**:96, 97
  Irish Travellers, **4**:156
  Latinos, **1**:205
  Madeirans, **4**:165
  Maliseet, **1**:212
  Maltese, **4**:168
  Mescalero Apache, **1**:225
  Mormons, **1**:248
  Northern Paiute, **1**:264
  Oriya, **3**:217
  Pahari, **3**:221
  Quechan, **1**:302
  Romanians, **4**:214
  Tlingit, **1**:352
  Ute, **1**:361

Yuit, **1**:391
  see also Ancestor worship; Conflict resolu-
    tion, by elders; Leadership, elder
Elders council
  Bulgarian Gypsies, **4**:41
  Canela, **7**:96
  Nagas, **3**:190
  Nambudiri Brahman, **3**:193
  Newar, **3**:207
  peripatetics, **3**:236
  Purum, **3**:244
  Romanians, **4**:214
  Yekuana, **7**:381
  see also Leadership, elders
Eldest son inheritance. _See_ Primogeniture
Electric power
  Slav Macedonians, **4**:240
  Slovaks, **4**:243
  Slovenes, **4**:247
  Swedes, **4**:257
Electronic industry
  Bulgarians, **4**:43
  Germans, **4**:122
  German Swiss, **4**:125
  Welsh, **4**:279
Elephants
  Dai, **6**:424
Elk hunting
  Kalapuya, **1**:175
Elopement. _See under_ Marriage
Elves, belief in
  Gaels (Irish), **4**:117
Emakame (ceremony)
  Mimika, **2**:208
Emasculation ritual
  hijra, **3**:96, 97-98
Emblems. _See_ Totems
Embroidery
  Ainu, **5**:10
  Asiatic Eskimos, **6**:42
  Azoreans, **4**:27
  Bashkirs, **6**:56
  Belarussians, **6**:61
  Bouyei, **6**:422
  Burusho, **3**:56
  Canarians, **4**:51
  Chukchee, **6**:78
  Chuvans, **6**:82
  Chuvash, **6**:85
  Dogrib, **1**:88
  Doukhobor, **1**:93
  Dyula, **9**:76, 77-78
  Ewenki, **6**:434
  Frisians, **4**:112
  Gayo, **5**:90
  German Swiss, **4**:127
  Greeks, **4**:134
  Hare, **1**:140
  Hezhen, **6**:452
  Hmong, **5**:94
  Jat, **3**:113
  Jingpo, **6**:459
  Karelians, **6**:170
  Karen, **5**:129
  Kriashen Tatars, **6**:212
  Kubachins, **6**:217
  Lahu, **5**:154
  Lithuanians, **6**:251

Madeirans, **4**:165
Maliseet, **1**:211
Mandan, **1**:214
Maris, **6**:257
Miao, **6**:471, 472
Muong, **5**:192
Nyinba, **3**:213
Ogan-Besemah, **5**:198
Old Believers, **1**:274
Orochi, **6**:295
Oroquen, **6**:482
Palaung, **5**:203
Pathan, **3**:233
Portuguese, **4**:208
Qiang, **6**:487
Romanians, **4**:213, 214
Russian peasants, **6**:311, 313
Sarakatsani, **4**:224-225
She, **6**:490
Siberian Germans, **6**:339
Siberian Tatars, **6**:342
Sicilians, **4**:237
Sindhi, **3**:261, 263
Slav Macedonians, **4**:241
Slovaks, **4**:243, 245
Tabasarans, **6**:349
Tajiks, **6**:354
Tanaina, **1**:337
Toda, **3**:296, 297-298
Tu, **6**:496
Tujia, **6**:498
Ukrainian peasants, **6**:386, 388
Ukrainians, **6**:392
Ukrainians of Canada, **1**:359
Uzbeks, **6**:397, 500
Yao, **6**:505
Yao of Thailand, **5**:291
Zhuang, **6**:510
see also Beadwork; Quill work
Emotional religious expression. _See_ Ecstasy
  (religious)
Emotional restraint
  Hare, **1**:141
  Highland Scots, **4**:141
  Kapingamarangi, **6**:110-111
  Norwegians, **4**:182
  Slavey, **1**:320
Employment. _See_ Labor; Occupational
  specialization
Encampments, temporary
  Rominche, **4**:216
Endogamy
  Andamanese, **3**:10
  Appalachians, **1**:22
  Arab Americans, **1**:24
  Arabs, **9**:24
  Azoreans, **4**:28
  Baggara, **9**:30
  Baiga, **3**:19-20
  Baluchi, **3**:23
  Bania, **3**:24, 25
  Basques, **1**:33;**4**:31
  Bene Israel, **3**:27
  Bhil, **3**:39
  Bhuiya, **3**:43
  Black West Indians in the United States,
    1:46
  Bosnian Muslims, **4**:36

Endogamy (cont'd)
  Bulgarians, **4**:44
  Cajuns, **1**:49
  castes, Hindu, **3**:57, 91
  Central Yup'ik Eskimos, **1**:57
  Circassians, **9**:67
  Cochin Jew, **3**:72
  Comanche, **1**:75
  Corsicans, **4**:67, 68
  Cypriots, **4**:80
  Dogon, **9**:72
  Dutch, **4**:93
  Falasha, **9**:91
  Finns, **4**:103
  Fulani, **9**:102
  German Swiss, **4**:126
  Ghorbat, **9**:107
  Gypsies and caravan dwellers in the
      Netherlands, **4**:138
  Ingalik, **1**:157
  Irish Travelers, **1**:163
  Irula, **3**:106
  Italian Mexicans, **8**:131
  Jatav, **3**:113, 114
  Karaites, **9**:154
  Kol, **3**:129-130
  Kurds, **9**:176
  Madeirans, **4**:165
  Martiniquais, **8**:162
  Mazahua, **8**:165
  Mixe, **8**:174
  Nahua of the State of Mexico, **8**:189
  Nahuat of the Sierra de Puebla, **8**:192
  Newar, **3**:207
  Nubians, **9**:247
  Occitans, **4**:185
  Old Believers, **1**:274
  Orcadians, **4**:187
  Parsi, **3**:228
  Pathan, **3**:232
  Pawnee, **1**:284
  peripatetics of Iraq, Syria, Lebanon, Jordan,
      Israel, Egypt, Sudan, and Yemen,
      9:277
  Pima Bajo, **8**:211
  Portuguese, **4**:207
  Qalandar, **3**:247
  Qashqa'i, **9**:285, 286
  Romanians, **4**:213
  Samaritans, **9**:300
  Santal, **3**:253
  Shetlanders, **4**:233
  Sicilians, **4**:236
  Sinhalese, **3**:266
  Slovaks, **4**:244
  Slovenes, **4**:248
  Somalis, **9**:317
  Swiss, Italian, **4**:261
  Syrian Christian of Kerala, **3**:273
  Tamang, **3**:275
  Thakali, **3**:291
  Tharu, **3**:293
  Tiroleans, **4**:263
  Tuareg, **9**:368
  Tz'utujil, **8**:297
  Vellala, **3**:303, 305
  Welsh, **4**:280
  Wolof, **9**:378
  Yakö, **9**:385
  Yörük, **9**:395
  Zapotec, **8**:312
  Zoque, **8**:316
  see also Cousin marriage; Inbreeding
Engagement. *See* Courtship
Engineering
  Bau, **2**:22
  Belau, **2**:25
  German Swiss, **4**:125
  Hawaiians, **2**:96
  Kosrae, **2**:128
  Wamira, **2**:365
Engraving
  Tetum, **5**:276
Enslavement. *See* Slavery
Entertainers
  Bulgarian Gypsies, **4**:41
  Gitanos, **4**:129
  Gypsies and caravan dwellers in the
      Netherlands, **4**:137
  Jews of Yemen, **9**:150
  Kanjar, **3**:118-119, 121
  Kyrgyz, **6**:231
  Laks, **6**:234
  peripatetics, **1**:287;**3**:234, 235, 236
  peripatetics of Afghanistan, Iran, and
      Turkey, **9**:275
  peripatetics of Iraq, Syria, Lebanon, Jordan,
      Israel, Egypt, Sudan, and Yemen,
      9:277
  Piemontese Sinti, **4**:200
  Qalander, **3**:245-248
  Tamil, **3**:279
  Tandroy, **9**:338
  Vlach Gypsies of Hungary, **4**:271
  Yagua, **7**:373
  see also Drama; Music and song; Puppetry
Entertainment industry
  Jews, **1**:169
Entrepreneurs
  Latinos, **1**:204
  Parsi, **3**:228
  South and Southeast Asians of Canada,
      1:322
  Syrian Christian of Kerala, **3**:273
  Tamil, **3**:277
  Tetons, **1**:345
  see also Self-employed; Shopkeeping; Small
      businesses; *other specific types*
Environmental degradation
  Basques, **4**:31
  Dongxiang, **6**:432
  Filipino, **5**:87
  Kazakhs, **6**:175
  Philippine Negritos, **5**:211
  Swiss, Italian, **4**:259
  Uzbeks, **6**:397
Environmentalism
  Germans, **4**:123
Envy. *See* Evil eye
Epic
  Albanians, **4**:7
  Baluchi, **3**:24
  Bengali, **3**:34
  Croats, **4**:75
  Dalmatians, **4**:87
  Finns, **4**:104
  Gaels (Irish), **4**:115, 117
  Gond, **3**:87
  Icelander-Canadians, **1**:123
  Montenegrins, **4**:174
  Serbs, **4**:232
  Tamil, **3**:279
  Vlachs, **4**:275
  see also Bards; Narrative poetry
Epidemics
  Ache, **7**:3, 4
  Aleuts, **6**:17
  Andamanese, **3**:8
  Arikara, **1**:26
  Asiatic Eskimos, **6**:38
  Asmat, **2**:19
  Bau, **2**:22
  Blackfoot, **1**:41
  Cahuilla, **1**:47
  Central Yup'ik Eskimos, **1**:56, 58
  Cheyenne, **1**:65
  Chinook, **1**:67
  Cree, **1**:809
  Dai, **6**:428
  Dobu, **2**:50, 52
  Easter Island, **2**:53
  Eastern Shoshone, **1**:104, 105
  Emerillon, **7**:158
  Ewenki, **6**:433
  Gebusi, **2**:77
  Guajajára, **7**:166
  Hawaiians, **2**:95
  Huron, **1**:152
  Ingalik, **1**:156
  Itelmen, **6**:152, 153
  Kalapuya, **1**:175
  Kalingas, **5**:123
  Kaluli, **2**:101
  Kazakhs, **6**:174
  Kilenge, **2**:118
  Koryaks and Kerek, **6**:209
  Kutenai, **1**:197
  Lahu, **6**:463
  Lak, **2**:137
  Lesu, **2**:145
  Mandan, **1**:213
  Maring, **2**:185
  Marquesas Islands, **2**:189
  Mekeo, **2**:198
  Menominee, **1**:220
  Miyanmin, **2**:209
  Montagnais-Naskapi, **1**:244
  Nanai, **6**:276
  Ngatatjara, **2**:239
  Nias, **5**:197
  Ningerum, **2**:245
  North Alaskan Eskimos, **1**:258
  Okanagon, **1**:271
  Omaha, **1**:275
  Ossetes, **6**:302
  Pacific Eskimo, **1**:282
  Pawnee, **1**:284
  Piapoco, **7**:274
  Piaroa, **7**:275
  Pohnpei, **2**:267
  Pomo, **1**:293
  Puinave, **7**:282
  Pukapuka, **2**:270
  Rapa, **2**:273

Rotuma, 2:280
Saliva, 7:292
Santa Cruz, 2:290
Sea Nomads of the Andaman, 5:229
Selung/Moken, 5:232
Sharanahua, 7:299
Shavante, 7:300
Shuswap, 1:317
Tahiti, 2:305
Tanaina, 1:334
Tapirapé, 7:320
Thompson, 1:350
Tofalar, 6:363
Tokelau, 2:330
Tolowa, 1:353
Tongareva, 2:339
Waimiri-Atroari, 7:344
Walapai, 1:363, 364
Wintun, 1:383
Wogeo, 2:380
Yangoru Boiken, 2:390
Yap, 2:391
Yokuts, 1:387
Yuit, 1:390
Yukagir, 6:412
Epiphany. *See* Twelfth Night
Episcopalians. *See* Anglicanism
Equally shared inheritance. *See under*
        Inheritance
Equal rights. *See* Civil rights; Egalitarianism;
        Gender equality
Er (holiday)
    Rutuls, 6:321
Eskimo-type kinship terminology. *See under*
        Kinship terminology
Estate farms. *See under* Agriculture
Eternal being. *See* Supreme being
Ethnic groups
    boundaries
        Arubans, 8:13
    class divisions by
        Manx, 4:171
    cultural revival
        Metis of Western Canada, 1:227
        Ojibwa, 1:269
        Seminole of Oklahoma, 1:315
        Welsh, 4:280
    divisions
        Jews of Israel, 9:143
        Jews of the Middle East, 9:148
        Nuristanis, 9:251
        Transylvanian, 4:266-269
        Yoruba, 9:393
    labor divisions by
        Romanians, 4:213
    multiethnic society
        Dutch, 4:93
        Nyinba, 3:211
    numerically significant minorities
        Romanians, 4:212, 213
    recent formation
        Danes, 4:90
        Dolgan, 6:99
        English, 4:96
        Even, 6:116
        Swedes, 4:257
    retention of identity
        Molokans, 1:243

    peripatetics, 1:287
rights movements
    African Americans, 1:11, 12
    Bulgarian Gypsies, 4:41
    East Asians of Canada, 1:96, 97
    East Asians of the United States, 1:100,
        102
    Lumbee, 1:209
    Rom of Czechoslovakia, 4:218
separatism
    Cypriotes, 4:81, 97
    Finland, 4:102
tensions
    Afro-Bolivians, 7:8, 9
    Afro-Brazilians, 7:12, 13
    Czechs, 4:83, 84
    English, 4:96, 97
    Hungarians, 4:145
    Irish, 4:151
    Mam, 8:159
    Manx, 4:170, 171
    Martiniquais, 8:163
    Mount Athos, 4:176
    Provencal, 4:210
    Slav Macedonians, 4:239
    Slovenes, 4:249
    Swiss, Italian, 4:262
    Transylanian ethnic groups,
        4:269
tradition of tolerance
    Dutch, 93
urban communities. *See* Urban areas,
        ethnic communities
see also Assimilation; Political violence
Eulachon fishing
    Kwakiutl, 1:198
Eunuch
    hijra, 3:96
Evangelicalism
    Amuesha, 7:39
    Appalachians, 1:22-23
    Baniwa-Curripaco-Wakuenai, 7:77, 80
    Bavarians, 4:35
    Chipaya, 7:116
    Cotopaxi Quichua, 7:134
    Highland Scots, 4:141
    Latinos, 1:206
    Maká, 7:217, 218
    Ningerum, 2:247
    Northern Irish, 4:180
    Otavalo, 7:255
    Páez, 7:258
    Piaroa, 7:277-278
    Piemontese Sinti, 4:201
    Puinave, 7:282
    Rom, 1:305
    Rukuba, 9:291
    Salasaca, 7:291
    Saramaka, 7:298
    Siberian Germans, 6:339
    Sirionó, 7:311
    Syrian Christian of Keral, 3:274
    Warao, 7:359
    Winnebago, 1:380
    see also Lutheranism; Methodism; Pente-
        costalism
Evening Star (spirit power)
    Pawnee, 1:285

Evergreen wreath
    Austrians, 4:21
Evil eye
    Albanians, 4:6, 7
    Armenians, 6:31
    Azerbaijani Turks, 6:50
    Azoreans, 4:28
    Balkars, 6:54
    Basques, 4:32
    Bulgarians, 4:45
    Calabrese, 4:50
    Canarians, 4:53
    Chin, 3:64
    Cretans, 4:71
    Croats, 4:74
    Cyclades, 4:78
    Divehi, 3:78
    Don Cossacks, 6:107
    Galicians, 4:120
    Gond, 3:87
    Greeks, 4:134
    Ionians, 4:150
    Jatav, 3:115
    Kashubians, 4:159
    Konso, 9:171
    Kubachins, 6:219
    Nubians, 9:248
    Nyinba, 3:213
    Portuguese, 4:208
    Qalandar, 3:248
    Sarakatsani, 4:224
    Shahsevan, 9:310
    Slav Macedonians, 4:241
    Slovaks, 4:245
    Turks, 9:376
    Volga Tatars, 6:402
    Yörük, 9:396
    see also Amulets
Evil spirits
    Abor, 3:5
    Acadians, 1:9
    Andamanese, 3:11
    Baiga, 3:21
    Bhil, 3:41, 42
    Blackfoot, 1:42
    Bondo, 3:50
    Brahman and Chhetri of Neapl, 3:54
    Catawba, 1:55
    Central Yup'ik Eskimos, 1:59
    Chakma, 3:60
    Cherokee, 1:62
    Cheyenne, 1:66
    Chickaasaw, 1:66
    Choctaw, 1:73
    Comanche, 1:75
    Dai, 6:428
    Delaware, 1:86
    Flathead, 1:128
    Fox, 1:130
    Frisians, 4:112
    Gaels (Irish), 4:117
    Gond, 3:86
    Hill Pandaram, 3:100
    Iroquois, 1:167
    Irula, 3:108
    Jing, 6:454
    Kashubians, 4:159
    Kol, 3:130

Evil spirits (cont'd)
Lakher, 3:147
Lepcha, 3:149
Menominee, 2:222
Miao, 6:472
Montagnais-Naskapi, 1:246
Munda, 3:184
Nagas, 3:190
Newar, 3:208
Nicobarese, 3:210
Nu, 6:481
Ojibwa, 1:270
Oriya, 3:218
Purum, 3:244
Romanians, 4:214
Rutuls, 6:321
Santal, 3:255
Siberian Tatars, 6:342
Tajik, 6:492
Tajiks, 6:354
Talysh, 6:357
Tanana, 1:340
Telegu, 3:287
Tujia, 6:499
Yuit, 1:392
Zhuang, 6:512
see also Devils and demons; Exorcism; under
Illness, causes of
Evil spirits (female)
Gaels (Irish), 4:117
Kashubians, 4:159
Exchange
ceremonial
Abelam, 2:4
Ajië, 2:7, 8, 9
Ata Sikka, 5:21
Baniwa-Curripaco-Wakuenai, 7:79
Chimbu, 2:35
Dani, 2:43
Desana, 7:154
Foi, 2:61
Gururumba, 2:92, 93
Kaluli, 2:101, 102, 103
Keraki, 2:114
Kewa, 2:117
Kiwai, 2:125
Lak, 2:138
Lau, 2:145
Lesu, 2:147
Macuna, 7:214
Maisin, 2:159
Manam, 2:169
Manus, 2:174, 175
Mardudjara, 2:180, 181
Mejbrat, 2:195
Mendi, 2:203, 205
Mountain Arapesh, 2:216
Ngatatjara, 2:240
Selepet, 2:294
Suruí, 7:313
Tairora, 2:308
Tangu, 2:312
Tanna, 2:315
Tatuyo, 7:324
Tikopia, 2:325, 326
Trobriand Islands, 2:351
Wanano, 7:350
Yokuts, 1:388

competitive
Iatmul, 2:99
Kosrae, 2:130
Mountain Arapesh, 2:217
Santa Cruz, 2:292
Trobriand Islands, 2:350
Yangoru Boiken, 2:389
cult
Yukagir, 6:413
fictive brothers
Yuit, 1:391
food preparation
Kalapalo, 7:187
gift. See Gift exchange
gift for work
Winnebago, 1:381
hiri system
Motu, 2:213
Namau, 2:231
Orokolo, 2:259
kula
Dobu, 2:50, 51, 52
Goodenough Island, 2:86
Rossel Island, 2:278
Trobriand Islands, 2:349, 350, 351
labor
Araucanians, 7:53
Bulgarians, 4:43, 44
Cape Verdeans, 4:56
Chiquitano, 7:118
Kalapalo, 7:187, 187
Magar, 3:156
Mehinaku, 7:236, 236
Murut, 5:193, 193
Newar, 3:206, 207
Páez, 7:257, 257
Rikbaktsa, 7:288, 288
Romanians, 4:213
Shetlanders, 4:233, 233
Sora, 3:269
Sumu, 8:238, 238
Welsh, 4:279, 279
marriage. See Marriage, prestations
networks
Russians, 6:316
obligations
Chechen-Ingush, 6:73
Even, 6:118
Evenki (Northern Tungus), 6:121, 123
Nanai, 6:276
Orochi, 6:295
Pamir Peoples, 6:306
Selkup, 6:327
Wape, 2:372
Woleai, 2:383
Yukagir, 6:413
partners
Mendi, 2:204, 205
Yangoru Boiken, 2:389
partners, hereditary
Manam, 2:168
Mekeo, 2:198
Murik, 2:221
pig
Garia, 2:75, 76
Siwai, 2:304
Tairora, 2:308
Tanna, 2:315

Tauade, 2:319
Wamira, 2:366
Yangoru Boiken, 2:390
prescribed kinship
Winnebago, 1:381
relationships
Agta, 5:5
salt
Nyakyusa and Ngonde, 9:253
social
Awá Kwaiker, 7:64
Aymara, 7:68
Belau, 2:25
Cotopaxi Quichua, 7:133
Craho, 7:137
Macuna, 7:214
Mataco, 7:229
Mehinaku, 7:236
Otavalo, 7:254
Panare, 7:266
Pemon, 7:272
Rikbaktsa, 7:288
Waorani, 7:352
Warao, 7:357
as social survival mechanism
Yuit, 1:392
spouse
Copper Eskimo, 1:78
suki relationships
Tagalog, 5:249
trade
Mashco, 7:225-226
Motu, 2:213
see also Barter; Gift exchange
Exchange marriage. See Marriage, son-
daughter exchange
Exchange mechanisms. See Barter; Money and
wealth
Excommunication. See under Punishment
Execution. See Punishment, capital
Exile. See Punishment, banishment
Exogamy
Abenaki, 1:5
Abor, 3:4
Achumawi, 1:10
Akan, 9:11
Albanians, 4:5
Aleut, 1:15
Anambé, 7:42
Arapaho, 1:26
Badaga, 3:16
Bamiléké, 9:38
Bengali, 3:31-32
Berbers of Morocco, 9:50
Bhil, 3:39
Bhuiya, 3:43-44
Bondo, 3:49
Brahman of Nepal, 3:52
Callahuaya, 7:89
Chakma, 3:59
Chenchu, 3:61
Cherokee, 1:61
Chhetri of Nepal, 3:52
Chitpavan Brahman, 3:70
Choctaw, 1:72
Chorote, 7:125
Cocopa, 1:74
Crow, 1:83

Dalmatians, 4:86
Delaware, 1:86
Desana, 7:152-153
East Asians in the United States, 1:101
Fali, 9:95
Fox, 1:129
Garo, 3:83
Gond, 3:85
Hidatsa, 1:147
Highland Scots, 4:140
Hopi, 1:149
Hopi-Tewa, 1:151
Iraqw, 9:125
Irula, 3:106
Iteso, 9:129
Jat, 3:112
Jativ, 3:114
Karihona, 7:192
Keres Pueblo Indians, 1:180
Khasi, 3:124
Khoi, 9:159
Kiowa, 1:187
Kond, 3:133
Kota, 3:136
Koya, 3:140, 141
Limbu, 3:150
Maratha, 3:169
Maricopa, 1:216
Mashco, 7:226
Mazahua, 8:165
Miami, 1:231
Mocoví, 7:241
Mossi, 9:229
Mundurucu, 7:245
Nagas, 3:189-190, 190
Navajo, 1:252
Nepali, 3:203
Netsilik Inuit, 1:254
Nyinba, 3:211
Ojibwa, 1:270
Osage, 1:278
Pandit of Kashmir, 3:225
Punjabi, 3:239
Quechan, 1:33301
Rukuba, 9:290
Selkup, 6:326
Seminole, 1:313
Seminole of Oklahoma, 1:314
Serbs, 4:231
Shavante, 7:301
Sherente, 7:302
Somalis, 9:317
Sora, 3:269
Tanaina, 1:336
Tanana, 1:339
Teda, 9:340
Ticuna, 7:329
Tsimshian, 1:355
Tunebo, 7:338
Ute, 1:361
Vellala, 3:304-305
Vlachs, 4:274
Wanano, 7:349
Western Apache, 1:372
Winnebago, 1:381
Xoraxané Romá, 4:282
Yagua, 7:372
Yawalapití, 7:379

Yokuts, 1:388
Yuit, 1:391
Zaramo, 9:402
Zuni, 1:398
Exorcism
    Acadians, 1:9
    Bhil, 3:41
    Bhutanese, 3:46
    Bulgarians, 4:45
    Chakma, 3:60
    Gurung, 3:95
    Hill Pandaram, 3:100
    Kol, 3:130
    Kota, 3:137
    Kurumbas, 3:143
    Lozi, 9:189
    Magar, 3:162
    Maliseet, 1:213
    Nayaka, 3:196
    Newar, 3:208
    Oriya, 3:218
    Pahari, 3:223
    Sadhu, 3:251
    Santal, 3:255
    Sherpa, 3:259, 260
    Sidi, 3:260
    Tandroy, 9:338
    Toda, 3:207
    Tuareg, 9:369
    Vedda, 3:303
    Yao of Thailand, 5:293
Exports. _See_ Traders; _specific commodities_
Extended family. _See under_ Family
Extramarital liasons. _See_ Adultery

Face blackening
    Fox, 1:130
Face painting
    Bugle, 8:34
    Cree, 1:82
    Cuna, 7:151
    Emberá, 7:158
    Haida, 1:136
    Huarayo, 7:178
    Ingalik, 1:158
    Kalapuya, 1:175
    Matsigenka, 7:232
    Mayoruna, 7:235
    Miami, 1:231
    Mohave, 1:242
    Ngawbe, 8:198
    Nootka, 1:257
    Païa-Tavytera, 7:259
    Paraujano, 7:268
    Pume, 7:284
    Siona-Secoya, 7:309
    Tanna, 2:315
    Walapai, 1:366
    see also Body painting and ornamentation
Face scarification
    Lugbara, 9:194
    Mossi, 9:231
    Tigray, 9:348
Face tattooing
    Bedouin, 9:45
    Kond, 3:133
Factional systems
    Punjabi, 3:241

Factories. _See_ Industrialization
Fairies, belief in
    Gaels (Irish), 4:117
Fairs. _See_ Markets and fairs
Fairy tales
    Albanians, 4:7
Fais do-do (dance)
    Cajuns, 1:51
Faith healing
    Appalachians, 1:23
False Face Mask
    Iroquois, 1:167
Family
    affinial relations
        Brahman and Chhetri of Nepal, 3:53
        Bulgarians, 4:44
        Canarians, 4:52
        Cyclades, 4:77
        Easter Island, 2:54
        Jivaro, 7:182
        Limbu, 3:150
        Pokot, 9:282
        Romanians, 4:213
        Rom of Czechoslovakia, 4:219
        Teton, 1:345
        Welsh, 4:279
        Xoraxané Romá, 4:282
    affinial taboos. _See_ Mother-in-law
            avoidance; Taboos, in-law
    augmented
        Bene Israel, 3:28
    avoidance relations
        Boruca, Bribri, Cabécar, 8:29
        Chuvans, 6:82
        Garia, 3:81
        Khoi, 9:159
        Murngin, 2:226
        Santak, 3:253
        Winnebago, 1:381
        see also Marriage, avoidance relationships
    bilateral group
        Northern Shoshone and Bannock, 1:267
    blood brotherhood. _See_ Blood brotherhood
    both sides equal
        Orcadians, 4:187
    boundaries
        Highland Scots, 4:141
    businesses
        Flemish, 4:106-107
    business-owner wives
        Flemish, 4:106-107
    as center of religious life
        Sarakatsani, 4:224
    compounds
        Kanbi, 3:118
        Pathan, 3:232
        Tamil of Sri Lanka, 3:281
        Washoe, 1:369
    conflict as norm
        Pasiegos, 4:191
        Piemontese, 4:198
        see also Blood feud; _under_ Conflict causes
    conjugal
        Nayaka, 3:195, 196
    cooking and eating together defining
        Dalmatians, 4:86
        Sea Islanders, 1:310
    corporate unit

Family (cont'd)
  Bulgarians, 4:44
  Croats, 4:73
  Dalmatians, 4:86
  Slav Macedonians, 4:240-241
  Slovenes, 4:248
courtesy relatives. *See* Fictive kin
cousin rivalry
  Pathan, 3:232, 233
deities
  Magar, 3:161
  see also Ancestor worship
as economic unit. *See* Household, as
    economic unit
eldest children
  Truk, 2:352-353
eldest son-mother ties
  Ayeronnais, 4:25
  Rom of Czechoslovakia, 4:219
extended
  Acadians, 1:8
  Afro-Venezuelans, 7:27
  Aimaq, 9:10
  Akawaio, 7:32
  Albanians, 4:4, 5, 6
  Antigua and Barbuda, 8:9
  Appalachians, 1:22
  Arab Americans, 1:24
  Araucanians, 7:53
  Araweté, 7:57
  Arubans, 8:12
  Assyrians, 9:27
  Austrians, 4:20
  Auvergnats, 4:22
  Awakateko, 8:16
  Azoreans, 4:27-28
  Baffinland Inuit, 1:30
  Bagirmi, 9:34
  Basques, 1:33
  Bavarians, 4:34
  Bedouin, 9:44
  Bengali, 3:31, 32
  Betsileo, 9:56
  Blackfoot, 1:42
  Boruca, Bribri, Cabécar, 8:28
  Bretons, 4:39
  Bugle, 8:33
  Bulgarian Gypsies, 4:41
  Bulgarians, 4:44
  Burusho, 3:56
  Cahita, 8:36
  Cajuns, 1:49-50
  Callahuaya, 7:89
  Caribou Inuit, 1:51
  Carrier, 1:52
  Cashibo, 7:104
  Catawba, 1:54
  cattle ranchers of Huasteca, 8:43
  Central Yup'ik Eskimpos, 1:56, 57
  Chamacoco, 7:109
  Chatino, 8:51
  Cherokee, 1:61
  Cheyenne, 1:65
  Chiricahua, 1:70
  Chiriguano, 7:120, 121
  Choctaw, 1:72
  Ch'ol, 8:65
  Chorote, 7:125

  Comox, 1:76
  Corsicans, 4:67
  Costa Ricans, 8:80
  Cotopaxi Quichua, 7:133
  Cowichan, 1:79
  Cree, 1:80
  Creoles of Nicaragua, 8:85
  Croat-Canadians, 1:120
  Cubans, 8:88
  Cuicatec, 8:92
  Cuiva, 7:144
  Culina, 7:147
  Dogon, 9:72
  Eastern Shoshone, 1:105
  East Greenland Inuit, 1:106
  Edo, 9:80
  English, 4:96-97
  Fali, 9:96
  Fox, 1:129
  Gorotire, 7:162
  Greek-speaking Jews of Greece, 4:135
  Guajajára, 7:167
  Gurung, 3:94
  Hausa, 9:113
  Hidatsa, 1:147
  Huichol, 8:126
  Hungarians, 4:144
  Iroquois, 1:166
  Irula, 3:107
  Italian-Americans, 1:113
  Italian Mexicans, 8:131
  Jatav, 3:114
  Jews, Arabic-speaking, 9:135
  Jews of Iran, 9:140
  Jicarilla, 1:173
  Kanbi, 3:118
  Kanuri, 9:152
  Karajá, 7:189
  Karok, 1:176
  Khasi, 3:124
  Kickapoo, 1:184
  Kipsigis, 9:165
  Koya, 3:141
  Kpelle, 9:173
  Kumeyaay, 1:194
  Ladinos, 8:152
  Latinos, 1:204-205
  Lengua, 7:210
  Lepcha, 3:149
  Lingayat, 3:152
  Luyia, 9:205
  Madeirans, 4:165
  Maká, 7:217
  Maliseet, 1:211-212
  Mam, 8:158, 159
  Mandan, 1:215
  Maratha, 3:169
  Mataco, 7:229
  Mauritian, 3:172
  Mazahua, 8:165
  Mbeere, 9:221
  Mende, 9:223
  Mennonites, 1:218
  Menominee, 1:221
  Mescalero Apache, 1:225
  Mixe, 8:174
  Mocoví, 7:241
  Montenegrins, 4:173

  Mossi, 9:228, 229
  Nahua of the Huasteca, 8:185
  Nandi and other Kalenjin peoples, 9:232
  Navajo, 1:251, 252
  Nayar, 3:198, 199
  Ndebele, 9:237
  Nepali, 3:204
  Netsilik Inuit, 1:254
  Newar, 3:207
  Nez Percé, 1:254
  Ngawbe, 8:196
  Nivaclé, 7:249
  Nomatsiguenga, 7:91
  North Alaskan Eskimos, 1:260
  Nubians, 9:247
  Nyamwezi and Sukuma, 9:257
  Occitans, 4:185
  Old Believers, 1:273, 274
  Oraon, 3:214
  Oriya, 3:217
  Otomí of the Sierra, 8:201
  Pahari, 3:220, 221
  Païˉ-Tavytera, 7:259
  Palestinians, 9:265
  Pandit of Kashmir, 3:225
  Parsi, 3:228
  peripatetics, 3:235
  peripatetics of Iraq, Syria, Lebanon,
      Jordan, Israel, Egypt, Sudan, and
      Yemen, 9:277
  Persians, 9:279
  Piemontese, 4:198
  Pima-Papago, 1:289
  Piro, 7:280
  Poles, 4:203
  Polish-Americans, 1:115
  Polynesians, 1:291-292
  Pomaks, 4:205
  Poqomam, 8:218
  Portuguese-Canadians, 1:125
  Potawatomi, 1:297
  Qashqa'i, 9:286
  Q'eqchi', 8:226
  Quechan, 1:301
  Rikbaktsa, 7:287
  Rom, 1:305
  Rom of Czechoslovakia, 4:219
  Saint Lucians, 8:231
  Sakalava, 9:296
  San-speaking peoples, 9:303
  Santal, 3:254
  Sara, 9:306
  Saraguro, 7:294
  Sarakatsani, 4:224
  Serbs, 4:213, 231
  Shahsevan, 9:309
  Shipibo, 7:305
  Siona-Secoya, 7:308
  Slav Macedonians, 4:240, 241
  Slovaks, 4:244
  Slovenes, 4:248
  Somalis, 9:317
  Spanish Rom, 4:255
  Swazi, 9:330
  Syrian Christian of Kerala, 3:273
  Tamil, 3:278
  Tanana, 1:339
  Taos, 1:342

Tapirapé, 7:321
Tarascans, 8:245
Terena, 7:325
Teton, 1:345
Toba, 7:332
Tojolab'al, 8:261
Totonac, 8:265
Triqui, 8:271
Turks, 9:375
Tz'utujil, 8:298
Vellala, 3:305
Vlachs, 4:274
Waorani, 7:352
Washoe, 1:369
Wasteko, 8:302, 303
Western Apache, 1:371, 373
Winnebago, 1:381
Xhosa, 9:381
Xikrin, 7:368
Yawalapití, 7:379
Yokuts, 1:388
Yoruba, 9:392
Yuit, 1:391
Yukuna, 7:387
Zapotec, 8:312
  see also Household, communal
extended headed by son-in-law
  Osage, 1:278
extended patrilateral
  Jews of Iran, 9:140
extended patrilineal
  Circassians, 9:66, 67
  Ewe and Fon, 9:86
  Haitians, 8:122
  Mazatec, 8:168
  Nahuat of the Sierra de Puebla, 8:192
  Tepehuan of Durango, 8:256
  Tzotzil of Zinacantan, 8:293
extended patrilocal
  Amhara, 9:19
  Chocho, 8:63
  Huave, 8:123
  K'iche', 8:142
  Nahua of the Huasteca, 8:186
  Pame, 8:208
  Q'anjob'al, 8:225
  Tojolab'al, 8:261
familija/fajta
  Rom of Czechoslovakia, 4:219
father responsible for religious life, 4:224
father. _See_ Father
firstborn-parental avoidance in early years
  Zarma, 9:405
grandparents. _See_ Grandparent
"great"
  Xoraxané Romá, 4:282
honor. _See_ Honor code
importance of
  Corsicans, 4:67
  Cypriots, 4:80
  Mormons, 1:248
in-law relations. _See_ subhead affinial
    relations _above_
intergenerational value conflicts
  South and Southeast Asians of Canada,
    1:323
joint-family system
  Bene Israel, 3:28

Coorg, 3:74
Finns, 4:103
Grasia, 3:88
Gujarati, 3:91
Hungarians, 4:144
Jat, 3:112
Kanbi, 3:118
Kanjar, 3:120
Korku, 3:134
Nicobarese, 3:209, 210
Okkaliga, 3:214
Oriya, 3:217
Pahari, 3:220, 221
Pathan, 3:232
Slovenes, 4:248
  see also subhead corporate unit _above_
lifelong obligations to
  Navajo, 1:252
limited to closest relatives
  Czechs, 4:83
male authority figures remain at home
  Tuareg, 9:368
maternal kin high status
  Easter island, 2:54
maternal kin low status
  Mongo, 9:226
maternal uncle. _See_ Uncle, maternal
matriarchal
  Sakalava, 9:296
matrifocal
  Arubans, 8:12
  Azoreans, 4:28
  Calabrese, 4:49
  Cape Verdeans, 4:55
  Garifuna, 8:114
  Jamaicans, 8:138
  Ndebele, 9:237
  Saint Lucians, 8:231
  see also Descent, matrilineal; Mother
matrifocal extended
  Lenca, 8:156
mothers. _See_ Mother
nuclear
  Abor, 3:4, 5
  Ache, 7:5
  Acholi, 9:5
  Amahuaca, 7:35
  Anambé, 7:42
  Andamanese, 3:10
  Apalai, 7:46
  Aquitaine, 4:14
  Arubans, 8:12
  Auvergnats, 4:22
  Awakateko, 8:16
  Aymara, 7:67
  Bagirmi, 9:34
  Bahamians, 8:19
  Bakairi, 7:74
  Baniwa-Curripaco-Wakuenai, 7:78
  Basque, 4:31
  Basseri, 9:41
  Bedouin, 9:44
  Bene Israel, 3:28
  Berbers of Morocco, 9:51
  Betsileo, 9:56
  Bhil, 3:40
  Bhuiya, 3:44
  Boruca, Bribri, Cabécar, 8:28

Bretons, 4:39
Bugle, 8:32
Bulgarians, 4:44
Cahita, 8:36
Calabrese, 4:49
Canarians, 4:52
Castilians, 4:60
Cayman Islanders, 8:47
Chácobo, 7:106
Chinantec, 8:54
Chinese in Caribbean, 8:57
Chipaya, 7:116
Ch'ol, 8:65
Chontal of Tabasco, 8:68
Chuj, 8:72
Cora, 8:76
Costa Ricans, 8:80
Creoles of Nicaragua, 8:85
Cretans, 4:70
Cubans, 8:88
Cubeo, 7:141
Cuicatec, 8:92
Curaçao, 8:97
Danes, 4:89
Delaware, 1:86
Dogon, 9:72
Dutch, 4:93
East Indians in Trinidad, 8:106
Edo, 9:80
Emberá, 7:157
English, 4:97
Ewe and Fon, 9:86
Falasha, 9:91, 92
Faroe Islanders, 4:99
Fipa, 9:98, 99
Flemish, 4:107
Frisians, 4:111
Galicians, 4:120
Germans, 4:122
Ghorbat, 9:106
Gitanos, 4:129
Greeks, 4:133
Greek-speaking Jews of Greece, 4:135
Guahibo-Sikuani, 7:165
Guambiano, 7:172
Guarijío, 8:118
Gusii, 9:109
Haitians, 8:122
Hare, 1:141
Herero, 9:118
Huichol, 8:126
Hungarians, 4:144
Iglulik Inuit, 1:155
Ionians, 4:149, 150
Irish Travellers, 4:156
Jamaicans, 8:138
Jews, 1:169
Jews, Arabic-speaking, 9:135
Jews of Iran, 9:140
Jews of Israel, 9:143
Kalapalo, 7:187
Kanuri, 9:153
Karaites, 9:155
Kashinawa, 7:196
Ka'wiari, 7:199
Keres Pueblo Indians, 1:180
K'iche', 8:142
Kickapoo, 1:184

Family (cont'd)
    Kikapu, 8:144
    Kikuyu, 9:161
    Kogi, 7:202
    Kpelle, 9:173
    Kuikuru, 7:207, 208
    Kutchin, 1:196
    Kwakiutl, 1:199
    Ladinos, 8:152
    Lenca, 8:156
    Lozi, 9:188
    Macuna, 7:213
    Maltese, 4:168
    Mam, 8:159
    Manx, 4:170
    Mashco, 7:226
    Matsigenka, 7:231
    Mauritian, 3:172
    Mazahua, 8:165
    Mazatec, 8:168, 169
    Mbeere, 9:221
    Miami, 1:231
    Micmacs, 1:234
    Mikir, 3:175
    Miskito, 8:171, 172
    Mixe, 8:174
    Nagas, 3:190
    Nahua of the Huasteca, 8:185, 186
    Nahua of the State of Mexico, 8:189
    Nandi and other Kalenjin peoples, 9:232
    Navajo, 1:252
    Nayaka, 3:194
    Ndebele, 9:236
    Ngawbe, 8:196
    Nicobarese, 3:209
    Northern Irish, 4:179
    Northern Paiute, 1:264
    Northern Shoshone and Bannock, 1:267
    Norwegians, 4:181
    Nyakyusa and Ngonde, 9:253
    Occitans, 4:185
    Okiek, 9:260-261
    Opata, 8:200
    Orcadians, 4:187
    Oriya, 3:217
    Otomí of the Sierra, 8:201
    Otomí of the Valley of Mezquital, 8:205
    Páez, 7:257
    Pame, 8:208
    Panare, 7:266
    Paraujano, 7:268
    Parsi, 3:228
    Pasiegos, 4:190
    Pathan, 3:232
    Peloponnesians, 4:193
    Pemon, 7:272
    peripatetics of Afghanistan, Iran, and
        Turkey, 9:275
    Persians, 9:279
    Piaroa, 7:277
    Piemontese, 4:198
    Piemontese Sinti, 4:201
    Pima Bajo, 8:211, 212
    Popoluca, 8:217
    Poqomam, 8:218
    Provencal, 4:211
    Pume, 7:284
    Purum, 3:243

    Qalandar, 3:247
    Q'anjob'al, 8:225
    Q'eqchi', 8:226
    Saami, 4:222
    Sakalava, 9:296
    Salasaca, 7:290
    Samaritans
        Sakalava, 9:300
    Seri, 8:234
    Sherpa, 3:258
    Shetlanders, 4:234
    Shona, 9:313
    Sicilians, 4:236
    Slavey, 1:319
    Slovaks, 4:244
    Slovensko Roma, 4:251
    Sorbs, 4:253
    South and Southeast Asians of canada,
        1:323
    Southern Paiute (and Chemehuevi),
        1:331
    Suya, 7:316
    Swazi, 9:331
    Swedes, 4:257
    Swiss, italian, 4:261
    Syrian Christian of Kerala, 3:273
    Tanana, 1:339
    Tatuyo, 7:323
    Teda, 9:340
    Telugu, 3:286
    Tepehuan of Chihuahua, 8:253
    Tepehuan of Durango, 8:256
    Thakali, 3:291
    Ticuna, 7:329
    Tigray, 9:348
    Tojolab'al, 8:261
    Tonga, 9:353
    Tory Islanders, 4:265
    Totonac, 8:265
    Triqui, 8:271
    Tsimihety, 9:359
    Tswana, 9:363
    Tuareg, 9:367
    Tubatulabal, 1:355
    Tupari, 7:340
    Tzeltal, 8:274
    Tzotzil and Tzeltal of Pantelhó, 8:276
    Tzotzil of Zinacantan, 8:293
    Tz'utujil, 8:298
    Walloons, 4:277
    Wapisiana, 7:355
    Wasteko, 8:303
    Wayapi, 7:362
    Welsh, 4:280
    Western Shoshone, 1:375
    Yakö, 9:385
    Yanomamö, 7:376
    Yokuts, 1:388
    Yukateko, 8:309
    Yuracaré, 7:396
    Zapotec, 8:312
    Zoque, 8:316
paribar (parivar) unit
    Bengali, 3:32
    Punjabi, 3:238, 239
paternal aunt. See Aunt, paternal
patriarchy. See Patriarchal family structure
single-parent. See under Household

    as social unit. See Clan
    state nonintervention policy
        Flemish, 4:108
    stem. See Household, three-generational
        stem
    uncle. See Uncle headings
    vendettas. See Blood feud
    violence. See under Conflict causes
    see also Band; Child headings; Children;
        Descent; Household; Inheritance;
        Kinship; Kinship terminology; Siblings
Family as social unit. See Clan
Family histories
    Chitpavan Brahman, 3:70
Family planning. See Birth control
Family size
    decreased
        German Swiss, 4:126
    large
        African Americans, 1:12
        Appalachians, 1:22
        Bavarians, 4:34
        Cochin Jew, 3:72
        Hutterites, 1:153, 154
        Irish Travellers, 4:154, 156
        Lakher, 3:146
        Mizo, 3:178
        Pasiegos, 4:190
        Vlach Gypsies of Hungary, 4:272
    limited to three children
        Tapirapé, 7:321
    one to three children
        Welsh, 4:280
    small
        Dutch, 4:93
        Finns, 4:103
        Piemontese, 4:198
    two-child
        Czechs, 4:80
Famine
    Cape Verdeans, 4:54
    Irish, 4:152, 163
    Montagnais-Naskapi, 1:244
    North Alaskan Eskimos, 1:258
    Tandroy, 9:337
    Tikopia, 2:324
    Tongareva, 2:340
    Yuit, 1:390
    Yukagir, 6:412
Fandita ritual
    Divehi, 3:78
Farming. See Agriculture; specific crops
Fascism
    Bavarians, 4:33
    Castilians, 4:58
Fasting
    by children
        Fox, 1:129
        Old Believers, 6:293
    funerary
        Catawba, 1:55
    as personal discipline
        Hidsata, 1:147
    as puberty rite
        Miami, 1:231
        Ojibwa, 1:270
    religious
        Flathead, 1:128

Fox, **1:**130
Gujarati, **3:**92
Hidsata, **1:**147
Menominee, **1:**222
Miami, **1:**232
Old Believers, **1:**274;**6:**293
Pathan, **3:**233
Svans, **6:**346
ritual
Kanuri, **9:**153
as shaman initiation
Wintun, **1:**383
see also Ramadan
Fate, strong belief in
Persians, **9:**280
Vlachs, **4:**275
Father
absences
Sherpa, **3:**259
childbirth couvade
Asurini, **7:**62
Barama River Carib, **7:**81
Chayahuita, **7:**111
Chiquitano, **7:**118
Emerillon, **7:**159
Guarayu, **7:**174
Krikati/Pukobye, **7:**205
Pauserna, **7:**270
Saliva, **7:**292
Tacana, **7:**318
Trio, **7:**336
Wayapi, **7:**362
child respect for
Maltese, **4:**168
emotional remoteness
Andalusians, **4:**11
Castilians, **4:**60
multiple paternity
Araweté, **7:**56
Asurini, **7:**61-62
Krikati/Pukobye, **7:**205
Tapirapé, **7:**321
paternity ritual
Toda, **3:**297
postbirth role
Nagas, **3:**190
superior-subordinate relationship with son
Kanuri, **9:**152
see also Child _headings_; Descent, patrilineal;
Patriarchal family structure
Father Dance
Eastern Shoshone, **1:**106
Father-in-law
authority over son-in-law
Easter Island, **2:**54
Father ritual
Toda, **3:**297
Father Sun
Taos, **1:**343
Father's Way religion
Kuna, **8:**150
Fear. _See under_ Social control measures
Feasting
ceremonial
Araweté, **7:**57
Goodenough Island, **2:**88
Guadalcanal, **2:**91
Lesu, **2:**147

Mafulu, **2:**153
Mailu, **2:**155
Maliseet, **4:**212
Marquesas Islands, **2:**189
Montenegrins, **4:**174
Pohnpei, **2:**268
Rom, **1:**306
Spanish Rom, **4:**255
competitive
Alorese, **5:**15
Belau, **2:**27
Goodenough Island, **2:**87
Kosrae, **2:**130
Lak, **2:**138
Marquesas Islands, **2:**190
Mekeo, **2:**199
Nguna, **2:**242
Sagada Igorot, **5:**217
Siane, **2:**298, 299
to contact guardian spirit
Miami, **1:**232
funerary
Abkhazians, **6:**9
Acholi, **9:**6
Alorese, **5:**15, 16
Ambae, **2:**11, 13
Asiatic Eskimos, **6:**42
Balkars, **6:**54
Belarussians, **6:**61-62
Berbers of Morocco, **9:**52
Carpatho-Rusyns, **6:**71
Chechen-Ingush, **6:**75
Circassians, **6:**91
Dargins, **6:**98
Daribi, **2:**48
Don Cossacks, **6:**107
Easter Island, **2:**55
Futuna, **2:**67
Goodenough Island, **2:**88
Guadalcanal, **2:**91
Itelmen, **6:**154
Javanese, **5:**113
Karachays, **6:**162
Kashubians, **4:**159
Kazakhs, **6:**182
Khevsur, **6:**197
Khinalughs, **6:**202
Kriashen Tatars, **6:**212
Lak, **2:**137, 139
Lenca, **8:**156
Lesu, **2:**147
Mae Enga, **2:**150, 151
Malaita, **2:**161
Manam, **2:**169
Mandak, **2:**172
Mansi, **6:**255
Maris, **6:**258
Marquesas Islands, **2:**191
Mejbrat, **2:**197
Mekeo, **2:**200
Melpa, **2:**202
Mendi, **2:**205
Mingrelians, **6:**265
Mixe, **8:**175
Mixtec, **8:**178
Muong, **5:**192
Murut, **5:**193
Namau, **2:**232

Nissan, **2:**251
Ogan-Besemah, **5:**199
Orokolo, **2:**260
Ossetes, **6:**302
Pentecost, **2:**264
Pima Bajo, **8:**214
Pohnpei, **2:**270
Poqomam, **8:**219
Rom, **1:**306
Rotinese, **5:**214
Rutuls, **6:**321
Siberian Estonians, **6:**337
Slovenes, **4:**249
Talysh, **6:**357
Tanaina, **1:**337
Tanana, **1:**349
Tats, **6:**360
Tauade, **2:**319
Tausug, **5:**264
Tokelau, **2:**333
Turkmens, **6:**371
Tuvans, **6:**374
Udis, **6:**378
Ukrainians, **6:**394
Vlachs, **4:**275
Welsh, **4:**280
Yap, **2:**394
hunting ritual
Montagnais-Naskapi, **1:**246
intersocietal
North Alaskan Eskimos, **1:**259
memorial
Amhara, **9:**21
Baggara, **9:**32
Berbers of Morocco, **9:**52
Jatav, **3:**115, 115
Jews of Iran, **9:**141
Rom, **1:**306, 306
Shahsevan, **9:**310
Tamil, **3:**279, 279
Tamil of Sri Lanka, **3:**284, 284
Tanana, **1:**340
Vlachs, **4:**275
merit
Chin, **3:**64, 66
Nias, **5:**195, 196, 197
for pilgrimage to Mecca
Nubians, **9:**248
provision (as penalty)
Munda, **3:**184
religious celebrations
Andalusians, **4:**12
Castilians, **4:**61
as resource redistribution
Bisaya, **5:**43
of saints. _See specific saints_
wedding
Abkhazians, **6:**8
Amuzgo, **8:**5
Baggara, **9:**31
Bukharan Jews, **6:**64
Buriats, **6:**68
Circassians, **6:**88;**9:**67
Dai, **6:**425
Dolgan, **6:**101
Georgians, **6:**133
Guadalcanal, **2:**91
Han, **6:**445

Feasting (cont'd)
    Iraqw, **9:**125
    Karen, **5:**127
    Lahu, **5:**152
    Malay, **5:**175
    Meskhetians, **6:**260
    Mountain Jews, **6:**272
    Murut, **5:**193
    Nandi and other Kalenjin peoples, **9:**233
    Palaung, **5:**202
    Pamir peoples, **6:**306
    Piemontese Sinti, **4:**200
    Romanians, **4:**213-214
    Rotinese, **5:**213
    Semang, **5:**235
    She, **6:**491
    Shilluk, **9:**311
    Shors, **6:**331
    T'in, **5:**278
    Tofalar, **6:**363
    Torres Strait Islanders, **2:**346
    Uighur, **6:**383
    Ukrainians, **6:**393
    Uzbeks, **6:**397
    Wa, **6:**502
    Yakut, **6:**406
    Yokuts, **1:**388
    Yugur, **6:**508
    see also Potlatch
Feast of Sacrifice
    Qashqa'i, **9:**286
    Samal Moro, **5:**224
    Shahsevan, **9:**309
Feast of Sowing
    Dogon, **9:**73
Feast of the Assumption of the Virgin
    Peloponnesians, **4:**194
Feast of the Dead
    Kuikuru, **7:**209
    Sherente, **7:**303
Feather Dance
    Kiowa, **1:**188
Feathered headdress. *See under* Clothing
Feathered Pipe rite
    Gros Ventre, **1:**134
Feathers
    ritual use of
        Taos, **1:**341, 342
    as wealth
        Santa Cruz, **2:**291
        Tauade, **2:**318
Feather work
    Apiaká, **7:**48
    Araweté, **7:**56
    Asurini, **7:**61
    Chácobo, **7:**106
    Chamacoco, **7:**108, 110
    Chayahuita, **7:**111
    Cinta Larga, **7:**127
    Culina, **7:**148
    Desana, **7:**152
    Guarayu, **7:**174
    Huarayo, **7:**178
    Karajá, **7:**188, 189
    Kashinawa, **7:**195
    Krikati/Pukobye, **7:**204
    Mashco, **7:**227
    Mehinaku, **7:**236

    Nivaclé, **7:**251
    Northern Paiute, **1:**263
    Paresí, **7:**269
    Rikbaktsa, **7:**287, 288
    Sherente, **7:**303
    Siona-Secoya, **7:**307
    Suya, **7:**315
    Tatuyo, **7:**323, 324
    Terena, **7:**327
    Ticuna, **7:**328-329
    Trio, **7:**336
    Wáiwai, **7:**348
    Waorani, **7:**353
    Xikrin, **7:**369
Federalist political organization
    Kumeyaay, **1:**195
    Swiss, Italian, **4:**262
Federation government
    Kumeyaay, **1:**195
    Swiss, Italian, **4:**262
"Feed the ghosts" practice
    Kickapoo, **1:**186
Felt
    Andis, **6:**25
    Balkars, **6:**53
    Chechen-Ingush, **6:**75
    Kazakhs, **6:**177
    Khinalughs, **6:**198
    Kubachins, **6:**217
    Mingrelians, **6:**263
    Talysh, **6:**356
    Tsakhurs, **6:**366
    Vlachs, **4:**274
Females. *See* Gender *headings;* Women
    headings; related topics
Female deities. *See* Women deities
Female-headed households. *See* Household,
    women as head
Female infanticide. *See* Infanticide
Feminist movement
    Afro-Brazilians, **7:**12
    French Canadians, **1:**132
"Feminization" of population. *See* Men,
    emigration; Family, matrifocal
Ferrymen
    Untouchable service caste, **3:**160
Fertility goddess
    Oraon, **3:**215
Fertility rate. *See* Birthrate
Fertility rites. *See* Ceremonies, fertility
Festival of Eating the New Rice
    Lahu, **5:**154
Festival of Lights
    Central Thai, **5:**71
Festival of Mohammed's Night Journey
    Samal Moro, **5:**224
Festivals. *See* Ceremonies; *under* Dance;
    Feasting; *specific festivals*
Festival of the Dead
    Iban, **5:**99
    Tzotzil of Chamula, **8:**281
Festival of the Plow
    Volga Tatars, **6:**402
Feud. *See* Blood feud; Feuding
Feudalism
    Achang, **6:**418
    Calabrese, **4:**48
    Dai, **6:**425

feudal
    Dai, **6:**426
    Germans, **4:**122
    Jatav, **3:**114
    Kurds, **9:**176
    Lahu, **6:**463
    Lingayat rejection of, **3:**151
    Moinba, **6:**473
    Nayar, **3:**198, 199
    Orcadians, **4:**187, 187
    Qiang, **6:**486
    Romanians, **4:**213, 213
    Slovaks, **4:**244, 244
    Tabasarans, **6:**349
    Tats, **6:**359
    Tsakhurs, **6:**366
    Zhuang, **6:**510
    see also Patron-client system
Feuding
    Abkhazians, **6:**7, 8
    Andis, **6:**27
    Aranda, **2:**18
    Armenians, **6:**29
    Avars, **6:**26
    Batak, **5:**41
    Bisaya, **5:**43
    Chechen-Ingush, **6:**74
    Chin, **3:**66
    Circassians, **6:**89-90
    Ewenki, **6:**434
    Georgians, **6:**135
    Hakka, **6:**438
    Ifugao, **5:**100
    Ilongot, **5:**102
    Itelmen, **6:**153
    Khevsur, **6:**194, 196
    Laks, **6:**234
    Laz, **6:**240
    Lisu, **5:**165
    Madurese, **5:**167
    Maguindanao, **5:**170
    Malaita, **2:**162
    Mansi, **6:**254
    Montenegrins, **4:**173
    Nguna, **2:**242
    Ontong Java, **2:**254
    Orokaiva, **2:**257
    Ossetes, **6:**300
    Qiang, **6:**487
    Rotinese, **5:**214
    Samal, **5:**220
    Santa Cruz, **2:**292
    Sardinians, **4:**227
    Siwai, **2:**304
    Svans, **6:**346
    Taiwan aboriginal peoples, **5:**257
    Tangu, **2:**312
    Tausug, **5:**262, 264
    Wape, **2:**372
    Yezidis, **6:**410
    Yi, **6:**506, 507, 508
    see also Blood feud
Fictive brothers
    Yuit, **1:**391
Fictive clan
    East Asians of Canada, **1:**97
    East Asians of the United States,
        1:101

Fictive kin
  Ache, **7**:6
  Afro-Bolivians, **7**:9
  Afro-Colombians, **7**:17
  Afro-Hispanic Pacific Lowlanders, **7**:21
  Afro-Venezuelans, **7**:26
  Albanians, **4**:6
  Amhara, **9**:19
  Amuzgo, **8**:5
  Andalusians, **4**:11, 12
  Apiaká, **7**:49
  Arubans, **8**:12
  Azoreans, **4**:28
  Baffinland Inuit, **1**:30
  Bamiléké, **9**:38
  Barí, **7**:84
  Bedouin, **9**:45
  Betsileo, **9**:55
  Black Creoles of Louisiana, **1**:38
  Bosnian Muslims, **4**:36
  Bretons, **4**:39
  Bulgarians, **4**:44
  Burgundians, **4**:47
  Cahita, **8**:36
  Callahuaya, **7**:89
  Canarians, **4**:52
  Cape Verdeans, **4**:55
  Carib of Dominica, **8**:39
  Carpatho-Rusyns, **6**:70
  Castilians, **4**:60
  cattle ranchers of Huasteca, **8**:43
  Chocho, **8**:63
  Chontal of Tabasco, **8**:68
  Circassians, **6**:89, 90
  Cubans, **8**:88
  Cyclades, **4**:77
  Cypriots, **4**:80
  Dalmatians, **4**:86
  Don Cossacks, **6**:105
  Easter Island, **2**:54
  Filipino, **5**:87
  Georgians, **6**:133
  German Swiss, **4**:126
  Gorotire, **7**:162
  Greeks, **4**:132;**6**:143
  Guambiano, **7**:172
  Hakka, **6**:437
  Huave, **8**:123
  Hungarians, **4**:144
  Japanese, **5**:108
  Jatav, **3**:114
  Jews of Iran, **9**:140
  Kajar, **3**:120
  Kyrgyz, **6**:230
  Latinos, **1**:205
  Luba of Shaba, **9**:192
  Madeirans, **4**:165
  Maltese, **4**:168
  Meskhetians, **6**:260
  Micronesians, **1**:237
  Mingrelians, **6**:263-264
  Mixe, **8**:174
  Moldovans, **6**:268
  Montenegrins, **4**:173, 173-174
  Murik, **2**:222
  Nahua of the Huasteca, **8**:186
  Nahuat of the Sierra de Puebla, **8**:192
  Nogays, **6**:288

  Nuristanis, **9**:251
  Old Believers, **1**:273;**6**:292, 293
  Oriya, **3**:217
  Orokolo, **2**:260
  Otavalo, **7**:254
  Pacific Eskimo, **1**:283
  Peloponnesians, **4**:193
  Pende, **9**:272-273
  Poqomam, **8**:218, 219
  Portuguese, **4**:207
  Romanians, **4**:213-214
  Russians, **6**:316
  Saint Lucians, **8**:231
  Salasaca, **7**:290
  Serbs, **4**:231
  Sicilians, **4**:236
  Slavey, **1**:319
  Slav Macedonians, **4**:240
  Somalis, **9**:318
  Swiss, Italian, **4**:261
  Tarascans, **8**:245, 246
  Tonga, **2**:338;**9**:354
  Totonac, **8**:266
  Tuareg, **9**:368
  Ukrainian peasants, **6**:387
  Ukranians of Canada, **1**:358
  Vlachs, **4**:274
  Warao, **7**:358
  Wasteko, **8**:303
  Yagua, **7**:373
  Yaqui, **8**:307
  Yuit, **1**:391
  Yukuna, **7**:388
  see also Blood brotherhood; Compadrazgo
Fictive uncles
  Black Creoles of Louisiana, **1**:38
Field labor. *See* Labor, field
Fiestas
  Andalusians, **4**:12
  Castilians, **4**:61
Fiesta of the Cross
  Otomí of the Sierra, **8**:203
Fig growing
  Montenegrins, **4**:172
Fighting. *See* Aggressiveness; Warfare
Figurines
  Keres Pueblo Indians, **1**:179
Film industry
  Ashkenazim, **6**:36
  Bengali, **3**:34
  Europeans in South Asia, **3**:80
  Germans, **4**:123
  Punjabi, **3**:242
  Sinhalese, **3**:267
  Tagalog, **5**:251
  Yakut, **6**:407
Final Judgment. *See* Judgment Day
Financial services
  accounting
    Chitpavan Brahman, **3**:69
  banking
    Bahamians, **8**:18
    German Swiss, **4**:125
    Swiss, **4**:259
    Swiss, Italian, **4**:260-261
    Vlachs, **4**:274
  loans
    Bania, **3**:24-25

  Kapauku, **2**:105, 106-107
  Magar, **3**:156
  Pasiegos, **4**:190
  Tamil, **3**:277
  Vaisya, **3**:300
  rapid counting
    Divehi, **3**:76
  see also Moneylending; Tax collectors
Fines. *See under* Punishment
Finger weaving
  Osage, **1**:277
Fire
  sacralization
    Even, **6**:119
    Ket, **6**:185
    Kurds, **6**:226
    Nivkh, **6**:284
    Osage, **1**:279
    Parsi, **3**:229
    Sadhu, **3**:251-252
    Sengseng, **2**:298
    Ukrainian peasants, **6**:387
    Ukrainians, **6**:394
  symbol
    Parsi, **3**:229
  widow immolation
    Chitpavan Brahman, **3**:70
Firearms. *See* Gun manufacture
Firewalking
  Bonerate, **5**:46
  Chinese in Southeast Asia, **5**:77
  Japanese, **5**:109
  Mauritian, **3**:173
Fireworks
  Ahir, **3**:7
  Maltese, **4**:169
First communion
  Italian Mexicans, **8**:131
First-cousin marriage. *See under* Cousin
  marriage
First Creator (culture hero)
  Hidatsa, **1**:147
  Mandan, **1**:215
First Fruit Festival
  Okanagon, **1**:272
Fish curing
  Tory Islanders, **4**:265
Fish farming
  Lunda, **9**:197
Fishing
  Acehnese, **5**:3
  Afar, **9**:7
  Afro-Hispanic Pacific Lowlanders, **7**:20
  Afro-Venezuelans, **7**:26
  Ainu, **5**:7, 8
  Akawaio, **7**:31
  Akha, **5**:11
  Aleuts, **6**:18
  Altaians, **6**:21
  Alur, **9**:13
  Amahuaca, **7**:34
  Ambonese, **5**:18
  Amhara, **9**:18
  Amuesha, **7**:37
  Anambé, **7**:41
  Angaité, **7**:43
  Anuta, **2**:14
  Apalai, **7**:45

Fishing (cont'd)
Apiaká, 7:48
Araucanians, 7:52
Araweté, 7:56
Asiatic Eskimos, 6:39
Asmat, 2:19
Asurini, 7:61
Ata Sikka, 5:20
Ayoreo, 7:70
Bagirmi, 9:33
Bagobo, 5:29
Bajau, 5:31, 32
Bakairi, 7:74
Baniwa-Curripaco-Wakuenai, 7:77
Barama River Carib, 7:80
Barí, 7:83, 84
Bau, 2:22, 23
Baweanese, 5:41
Belau, 2:25
Boazi, 2:29
Bonerate, 5:44
Bontok, 5:46
Bororo, 7:86
Butonese, 5:67
Canelos Quichua, 7:99
Caquinte, 7:91
Cashibo, 7:104
Central Thai, 5:70
Chácobo, 7:105
Cham, 5:72
Chamacoco, 7:108
Chambri, 2:31
Chamorros, 2:34
Chayahuita, 7:111
Chimane, 7:112
Chipaya, 7:115
Chiquitano, 7:118
Chiriguano, 7:120
Chocó, 7:123
Chorote, 7:124
Chukchee, 6:77
Chuvans, 6:80, 81
Cinta Larga, 7:127
Cocama, 7:130
Colorado, 7:131
Cora, 8:76
Costa Ricans, 8:79
Cotabato Manobo, 5:79
Creoles of Nicaragua, 8:84
Cubeo, 7:140
Culina, 7:146
Cuna, 7:149
Dai, 6:424
Desana, 7:152
Dinka, 9:70
Dobu, 2:50
Dolgan, 6:100
Don Cossacks, 6:104
Drung, 6:432
East Indians in Trinidad, 8:105
Emberá, 7:155
Emberá and Wounaan, 8:109, 110
Emerillon, 7:159
Estonian, 6:113
Even, 6:117, 118
Evenki (Northern Tungus), 6:120, 121
Ewe and Fon, 9:84, 86
Ewenki, 6:433

Garifuna, 8:113
Gayo, 5:88
Gebusi, 2:77
Gnau, 2:80
Gogodala, 2:83
Goodenough Island, 2:86
Gorontalese, 5:90
Gorotire, 7:162
Guadalcanal, 2:89
Guahibo-Sikuani, 7:164-165
Guajajára, 7:166-167
Guarayu, 7:174
Hanunóo, 5:91
Hawaiians, 2:96
Hezhen, 6:452
Hoti, 7:175
Huarayo, 7:177
Huave, 8:123
Huichol, 8:125
Iatmul, 2:98
Iban, 5:97
Ilongot, 5:101
Itelmen, 6:152
Jamináwa, 7:180
Japanese, 5:105
Javanese, 5:111
Jebero, 7:181
Jing, 6:454
Jivaro, 7:182
Kagwahiv, 7:184, 185
Kalagan, 5:119
Kalapalo, 7:187
Kalimantan Dayaks, 5:120
Kanuri, 9:151
Kapingamarangi, 2:109
Karajá, 7:188
Karelians, 6:170
Karen, 5:126
Karihona, 7:192
Kashinawa, 7:195
Kashubians, 4:158
Ka'wiari, 7:198
Kenyah-Kayan-Kajang, 5:133
Keraki, 2:113
Kerintji, 5:134
Ket, 6:184
Khakas, 6:188
Khanty, 6:190
Kiribati, 2:121
Kiwai, 2:125
Komi, 6:204
Korean, 5:146
Koreans, 6:206
Koryaks and Kerek, 6:207, 208
Kpelle, 9:173
Kriashen Tatars, 6:211
Krikati/Pukobye, 7:204
Kuikuru, 7:207
Kurtatchi, 2:131
Kwoma, 2:134
Lak, 2:137
Lakandon, 8:154
Lamaholot, 5:155
Lamet, 5:157
Lango, 9:179
Lau, 2:143
Lenca, 8:155
Lengua, 7:210

Lozi, 9:187
Luba of Shaba, 9:191
Lunda, 9:196
Macuna, 7:212
Madurese, 5:167
Maguindanao, 5:169
Mailu, 2:154
Makassar, 5:172
Malaita, 2:161
Malay, 5:175
Manam, 2:167
Mandak, 2:170
Mangareva
   Mandak, 2:171
Mansi, 6:252
Manus, 2:173
Maori, 2:177
Maranao, 5:177
Marinahua, 7:220
Maring, 2:185
Maroni Carib, 7:220
Marquesas Islands, 2:189
Marshall Islands, 2:192
Marubo, 7:222
Mataco, 7:228
Matsigenka, 7:231
Mayoruna, 7:234
Mehinaku, 7:236
Mejbrat, 2:195
Mekeo, 2:198
Melanau, 5:178
Mentaweian, 5:181
Miao, 6:470
Micmac, 1:233
Mimika, 2:206
Minangkabau, 5:182
Miskito, 8:171
Mnong, 5:184
Mocoví, 7:240
Modang, 5:186
Mohave, 1:241
Mojo, 7:242
Moluccans—North, 5:188
Moluccans—South, 5:188
Mon, 5:189
Montagnais-Naskapi, 1:244
Motu, 2:213
Movima, 7:243
Mundugumor, 2:218
Mundurucu, 7:244
Muong, 5:190
Murik, 2:221
Murut, 5:193
Namau, 2:231
Nambicuara, 7:247
Nanai, 6:275, 279
Nauru, 2:237
Nez Percé, 1:254
Ngawbe, 8:195
Nias, 5:195
Ningerum, 2:246
Niue, 2:251
Nivaclé, 7:249
Nivkh, 6:283, 284
Noanamá, 7:251
Nomatsiguenga, 7:91
Nomoi, 2:252
Nootka, 1:256

North Alaskan Eskimos, 1:258, 259
Northern Metis, 1:262
Northern Paiute, 1:263
Northern Shoshone and Bannock, 1:266, 267
Ontong Java, 2:254, 255
Orochi, 6:295
Orok, 6:296
Orokaiva, 2:256
Orokolo, 2:259
Oroquen, 6:482
Ottawa, 1:279
Ozarks, 1:281
Pacific Eskimo, 1:282
Pajonalino, 7:91
Palaung, 5:201
Palikur, 7:262
Palu'e, 5:205
Pame, 8:207
Panare, 7:265
Paraujano, 7:267
Paya, 8:209
Pemon, 7:271
Penan, 5:210
Pentecost, 2:262
Piapoco, 7:274
Piaroa, 7:276
Pima Bajo, 8:211
Piro, 7:279
Pohnpei, 2:268
Pomo, 1:293
ponds
    Tai Lue, 5:253
Popoluca, 8:216
Puerto Ricans, 8:221
Puinave, 7:281
Pukapuka, 2:270, 271
Pume, 7:283
Q'eqchi', 8:226
Rapa, 2:274
Rennell Island, 2:277
Rikbaktsa, 7:287
Rotinese, 5:213
Rotuma, 2:281
Saami, 4:221;6:323
Saliva, 7:292
Samal, 5:219
Samal Moro, 5:222
Samoa, 2:287
San Cristobal, 2:289
San-speaking peoples, 9:302
Santa Cruz, 2:290
Santee, 1:307
Sara, 9:305
Saramaka, 7:296
Sea Nomads of the Andaman, 5:229
Selkup, 6:325, 326
Selung/Moken, 5:231
Senoi, 5:237
Seri, 8:233
Sharanahua, 7:299
Shavante, 7:300-301
Sherente, 7:302
Shilluk, 9:311
Shui, 6:491
Siberiaki, 6:333
Siberian Estonians, 6:336
Siberian Tatars, 6:341

Sio, 2:300
Siona-Secoya, 7:307
Sirionó, 7:310
Siwai, 2:302
Slavey, 1:319
Somalis, 9:316
Stieng, 5:243
Subanun, 5:244
Suku, 9:321
Sulod, 5:246
Sumu, 8:237
Sundanese, 5:247
Suri, 9:327
Suruí, 7:312
Suya, 7:315
Tacana, 7:318
Tagalog, 5:249
Tagbanuwa, 5:251
Tahiti, 2:305
Taiwan aboriginal peoples, 5:257, 258
Tanana, 1:338
Tanimuka, 7:318, 319
Tanna, 2:313
Tapirapé, 7:320-321
Tatuyo, 7:322-323
Tausug, 5:262
Temiar, 5:266, 267
Ternatan/Tidorese, 5:274
Ticuna, 7:328
Tikopia, 2:325
Tiwi, 2:327
Tlingit, 1:351
Tobelorese, 5:280
Tofalar, 6:362
Tokelau, 2:331
Tolai, 2:334
Tolowa, 1:353
Tonga, 2:337;9:353
Tongareva, 2:340
Tor, 2:342
Trio, 7:335
Trobriand Islands, 2:349
Truk, 2:352
Tubatulabal, 1:355
Tujia, 6:498
Tunebo, 7:338
Tupari, 7:339-340
Turkana, 9:371
Tuscarora, 1:356
Tuvalu, 2:355, 356
Udmurt, 6:379, 380
Ukrainian peasants, 6:386
Ukrainians, 6:392
Ulithi, 2:358
Uvea, 2:364
Volga Tatars, 6:401
Wáiwai, 7:346
Wamira, 2:365
Wanano, 7:349
Waorani, 7:352
Wapisiana, 7:355
Warao, 7:357
Waropen, 2:376
Washoe, 1:368
Waurá, 7:360
Wayapi, 7:361
West Greenland Inuit, 1:377
Wik Mungkan, 2:377

Winnebago, 1:381
Wintun, 1:383
Witoto, 7:365
Wogeo, 2:380
Woleai, 2:383
Xikrin, 7:367
Yagua, 7:372
Yakut, 6:405
Yanomamö, 7:375
Yaqui, 8:306
Yawalapití, 7:378
Yekuana, 7:381
Yir Yoront, 2:395
Yokuts, 1:387
Yukagir, 6:412, 413
Yukpa, 7:383
Yukuna, 7:386
Yuqui, 7:391, 392
Yuracaré, 7:395
Yurok, 1:394
Zhuang, 6:510
    see also Ceremonies, fishing; *specific fish,*
        e.g., Salmon fishing
Fishing (by women)
    Zande, 9:398
Fishing chief
    Ute, 1:362
Fishing industry
    Andamanese, 3:9
    Basques, 4:31
    Bretons, 4:38
    Dalmatians, 4:86
    Danes, 4:89
    Divehi, 3:76
    East Asians of the United States, 1:100
    Faroe Islanders, 4:98, 99
    Finns, 4:106
    Galicians, 4:119
    Highland Scots, 4:139-140
    Icelanders, 4:146-147
    Ingalik, 1:156, 157
    Japanese of Canada, 1:95-96
    Klallam, 1:190
    Klamath, 1:191
    Kwakiutl, 1:197-198
    Manx, 4:170
    Norwegians, 4:181
    Orcadians, 4:186-187
    Peloponnesians, 4:193
    Portuguese, 4:206, 207
    Sea Islanders, 1:310
    Shetlanders, 4:233, 234
    Telugu, 3:285
    Tory Islanders, 4:265
    Vedda, 3:301
    West Greenland Inuit, 1:377
    see also specific kinds of fish
Fishing (sea cucumbers)
    Sakalava, 9:293
Fishing (sport)
    Highland Scots, 4:140
Flamenco
    Andalusians, 4:12
Flat Pipe rite
    Gros Ventre, 1:134
Flax
    growing
        Latvians, 6:236

Flax (cont'd)
    Lithuanians, **6:**250
    Pomaks, **4:**205
    processing
        Leonese, **4:**161
        Swedes, **4:**258
Flint objects
    North Alaskan Eskimos, **1:**259
Flirting
    Andalusians, **4:**11
Flogging. *See* Punishment
    corporal
Flotsam and jetsam harvesting
    Tory Islanders, **4:**265
Flounder fishing
    Klallam, **1:**190
Flower
    fertility symbol
        Santal, **3:**255
    motifs
        Hungarians, **4:**145
Flower ceremony
    Otomí of the Sierra, **8:**202
    Saint Lucians, **8:**232
    Santal, **3:**255
Flower industry
    Canarians, **4:**51
    Guadeloupians, **8:**116
Flute
    Basques, **4:**32
    Chakma, **3:**58, 61
    Daribi, **2:**48
    Garo, **3:**84
    Ojibwa, **1:**271
    see also Musical instruments, wind/woodwind
Föhn, madness associated with
    German Swiss, **4:**127
Folk arts
    Albanians, **4:**7
    Auvergnats, **4:**23
    Basques, **4:**32
    Bavarians, **4:**34, 35
    Bulgarian Gypsies, **4:**41
    Bulgarians, **4:**45
    Burgundians, **4:**47
    Croats, **4:**75
    Danes, **4:**90
    Flemish, **4:**108
    German Swiss, **4:**127
    Greeks, **4:**134
    Hungarians, **4:**145
    Latinos, **1:**206
    Madeirans, **4:**165
    Oriya, **3:**218
    Santal, **3:**255
    Sarakatsani, **4:**224-225
    Slovenes, **4:**249
    Sorbs, **4:**253
    South and Southeast Asians of Canada, **1:**324
    Ukrainians, **6:**394
    Ukrainians of Canada, **1:**359
    see also Dance, folk; Decorative arts; *specific genres*
Folk beliefs. *See* Supernatural beliefs
Folk dancing. *See* Dance, folk
Folk healers. *See* Curanderos; Healers;
    Shamanism

Folk high schools
    Danes, **4:**89
Folk law. *See under* Law
Folklore. *See* Folk arts; Oral tradition;
    Storytelling
Folk musicians. *See* Dance, folk; Music and
    song; *specific instruments*
Folk opera
    Flemish, **4:**108
    Oriya, **3:**218
Folk paintings
    Cotopaxi Quichua, **7:**135
Folk processions
    Flemish, **4:**108
Folk remedies. *See* Herbal, plant, and root
    medicine; *under* Medical practices and
    treatments
Folk songs
    Latvian-Canadian, **1:**124
Folktales. *See* Oral tradition; Storytelling
Folk theater
    Santal, **3:**255
    see also Shadow play
Food
    appetite suppression
        Goodenough Island, **2:**88
    caste-specific diet
        Telugu, **3:**286
    cheese specialty
        Galicians, **4:**121
    childbirth dietary restrictions
        Nootka, **1:**256
    children's diet
        Brahman and Chhetri of Nepal, **3:**53
        Tamil, **3:**278
        Tamil of Sri Lanka, **3:**282
        see also Breast-feeding
    communal sharing
        Yuit, **1:**391
    cooking. *See* Cooking
    cooking and eating together as family
        definition
        Dalmations, **4:**86
        Sea Islanders, **1:**310
    dairy product emphasis
        Finns, **4:**102
        Vlachs, **4:**274
    dietary laws and restrictions
        Bene Israel, **3:**28
        Bohra, **3:**47
        Eastern Shoshone, **1:**104, 105
        Falasha, **9:**92
        Fulani, **9:**103
        Greek-speaking Jews of Greece, **4:**136
        Haida, **1:**136
        Jews of Algeria, **9:**138
        Jews of Iran, **9:**140, 141
        Jews of Yemen, **9:**149
        Kanuri, **9:**152, 153
        Karaites, **9:**155
        Karamojong, **9:**157
        Kikuyu, **9:**161
        Konso, **9:**169
        Lobi-Dagarti peoples, **9:**184
        Lunda, **9:**199
        Maasai, **9:**208
        Maratha, **3:**169
        Mossi, **9:**229

Mount Athos, **4:**176
Okiek, **9:**262
Old Believers, **1:**274
Rastafarians, **8:**229
relatives of deceased
    Ngawbe, **8:**198
Rom of Czechoslovakia, **4:**219
Telugu, **3:**286
Tsimihety, **9:**358
"hot" and "cold" categories
    Tamil, **3:**279
as illness cause
    Macuna, **7:**215
importance of
    Tamil, **3:**278
insects. *See* Insects, edible
malnourishment
    Gebusi, **2:**77
meat emphasis
    Kashinawa, **7:**195
in medical treatment
    Apalai, **7:**47
    Apiaká, **7:**50
    Baniwa-Curripaco-Wakuenai, **7:**80
    Desana, **7:**154
    Krikati/Pukobye, **7:**206
    Pemon, **7:**273
mortuary prohibitions
    Limbu, **3:**150
pastries and sweets
    Sicilians, **4:**237
preparation. *See* Cooking
as preventive medicine
    Flemish, **4:**109
reciprocity
    Kalapalo, **7:**187
restauranteurs
    Arab Americans, **1:**24
    Aveyronnais, **4:**24
    East Asians of Canada, **1:**96
    East Asians of the United States, **1:**100
    Galicians, **4:**121
    Greek-Americans, **1:**112
as sacrifice
    Miami, **1:**232
    Miao, **6:**472
sexually segregated eating
    Hawaiians, **2:**96
    Marquesas Islands, **2:**190
    Pentecost, **2:**263
    Tahiti, **2:**306
shellfish emphasis
    Galicians, **4:**121
shortages
    Cubans, **8:**88
specialties
    Aveyronnais, **4:**25
    Bavarians, **4:**33
    Bohra, **3:**47
    Walloons, **4:**276
for the dead. *See* Dead, the, food for
traditional bread
    Vlach Gypsies of Hungary, **4:**271
traditional cuisine
    Cajuns, **1:**50, 51
    Italian-Americans, **1:**113
    Latino, **1:**204
    Maltese, **4:**167-168

Norwegians, **4**:181
Pomaks, **4**:205
Serbs, **4**:230
Sicilians, **4**:236
Walloons, **4**:276
vegetarianism
  Araucanians, **7**:52
  Bania, **3**:24, 25
  Doukhobors, **1**:90, 92
  Grasia, **3**:88
  Jain, **3**:109
  Mount Athos, **4**:176
  Nayar, **3**:197
  Rajput, **3**:249
  Tamil, **3**:279
  Toba, **7**:333
  Toda, **3**:295
  see also Famine; Fasting; Feasting; _under_
    Taboos
Food debts
  Goodenough Island, **2**:87
Food gathering. _See_ Hunting and gathering
Food preservation
  Aymara, **7**:66
  Chamacoco, **7**:108
  Chimane, **7**:112
  Mayoruna, **7**:234
  Noanamá, **7**:251
  Shavante, **7**:300, 301
Food processing industry
  Bulgarians, **4**:43
  see also Canneries; _specific foods_
Food sharing
  with in-laws
    Sharanahua, **7**:299
  as social virtue
    Ache, **7**:4
    Kashinawa, **7**:196
    Matsigenka, **7**:232
    Mehinaku, **7**:236
    Piro, **7**:279
    Shavante, **7**:300
    Shipibo, **7**:304
    Suya, **7**:316
    Tapirapé, **7**:320
    Wanano, **7**:349
    Yuit, **1**:391, 392
  by widowers
    Pume, **7**:284
Football. _See under_ Sports
Foot binding
  Han, **6**:443
Foot washing, ceremonial
  Amish, **1**:18
  Mennonites, **1**:219
Footwear
  moccasins
    Kiowa, **1**:187
    Taos, **1**:3432
    Western Shoshone, **1**:375
    Wiyot, **1**:384
    Zuni, **1**:399
  sandal making
    Pume, **7**:283
  shoemaking
    Bulgarian Gypsies, **4**:41
    Jatav, **3**:114
    Krymchaks, **6**:214

Laks, **6**:234
Rutuls, **6**:319, 321
Talysh, **6**:356
Vlachs, **4**:274
tapir sandals
  Ayoreo, **7**:70
wooden shoes
  Burgundians, **4**:47
  Pasiegos, **4**:190
Foragers. _See_ Hunting and gathering
Forced labor. _See_ Blackbirding; _under_ Labor;
  Slavery
Foreign trade. _See_ Traders
Forest products
  Akan, **9**:11
  Burgundians, **4**:46
  Castilians, **4**:59
  Chakma, **3**:59
  Finns, **4**:202
  Kol, **3**:129
  Kond, **3**:132
  Konso, **9**:169
  Magar, **3**:156
  Navajo, **1**:251
  Nayaka, **3**:194, 195
  Sikkimese, **3**:262
  see also specific products
Forestry
  Acadians, **1**:7
  Afro-Colombians, **7**:16
  Afro-Hispanic Pacific Lowlanders, **7**:20
  Appalachians, **1**:22
  Asháninca, **7**:91
  Bonan, **6**:422
  Bouyei, **6**:422
  Burmese, **5**:64-65
  Campa del Pichis, **7**:91
  Candoshi, **7**:93
  Canelos Quichua, **7**:99
  Carrier, **1**:52
  Cashibo, **7**:104
  Choctaw, **1**:71
  Cocama, **7**:130
  Daur, **6**:429
  Dong, **6**:431
  East Asians of the United States, **1**:100
  Estonian, **6**:113
  Finns, **4**:102
  Hani, **6**:450
  Hupa, **1**:152
  Iban, **5**:97
  Itza', **8**:134
  Kalimantan Dayaks, **5**:120
  Karelians, **6**:170
  Klamath, **1**:191
  Komi, **6**:204
  Kutenai, **1**:197
  Kwakiutl, **1**:198
  Kyrgyz, **6**:229
  Laz, **6**:240
  Lithuanian Jews, **6**:246
  Mandan, **1**:214
  Mataco, **7**:228
  Mayoruna, **7**:235
  Menominee, **1**:221
  Moluccans—North, **5**:188
  Mount Athos, **4**:175
  Norwegians, **4**:181

Ozarks, **1**:281
Pima Bajo, **8**:211
Piro, **7**:279
Romanians, **4**:213
Russian peasants, **6**:311
Shui, **6**:491
Slovenes, **4**:247, 248
Suruí, **7**:312
Swedes, **4**:257
Talysh, **6**:355
Warao, **7**:357
Yao, **6**:505
Forests
  camps
    Hill Pandaram, **3**:98, 99
  reforestation projects
    Highland Scots, **4**:140
  spirits
    Santal, **3**:254, 255
  timber scarcity
    Gales (Irish), **4**:115
Forgiveness rituals
  Creek, **1**:83
Formulist (religious reciter)
  Yurok, **1**:395
Fortification. _See_ Villages, fortified
Fortune-telling
  Bulgarian Gypsies, **4**:41
  Burusho, **3**:56
  Dalmatians, **4**:87
  Georgians, **6**:136
  Gypsies, **6**:146
  Ingilos, **6**:151
  Irish Travellers, **4**:155
  Jews of Iran, **9**:141
  Karaites, **9**:155
  Khasi, **3**:126
  Magar, **3**:162
  Meskhetians, **6**:261
  peripatetics, **1**:287;**3**:234, 235, 236
  peripatetics of Iraq, Syria, Lebanon, Jordan,
    Israel, Egypt, Sudan, and Yemen,
    9:277
  peripatetics of the Maghreb, **9**:278
  Piemontese Sinti, **4**:200, 201
  Rom, **1**:303, 304
  Rominche, **4**:216
  Sadhu, **3**:251
  Selkup, **6**:327
  Sleb, **9**:315
  Tajiks, **6**:354
  Talysh, **6**:357
  Tamil, **3**:279
  Ukrainian peasants, **6**:387
  Vietnamese, **5**:286
  Vlachs, **4**:275
  Yakan, **5**:290
  see also Mediums; Omens, importance of
Forty-three Group (painting school)
  Sinhalese, **3**:267
Fosterage, **9**:55
  Abelam, **2**:5
  Ajië, **2**:9
  Amahuaca, **7**:35
  Bamiléké, **9**:37
  Betsileo, **9**:56
  Circassians, **6**:89
  Goodenough Island, **2**:87

Fosterage (cont'd)
Mescalero Apache, 1:225
Montserratians, 8:181
Nias, 5:195
Nogays, 6:288
Pukapuka, 2:272
Rapa, 2:275
Sakalava, 9:295, 296
Sea Islanders, 1:310
Seminole, 1:313
Tabasarans, 6:349
Temne, 9:344
Tongareva, 2:340
Warao, 7:358
see also Adoption practices
Fraternal order. See Brotherhood societies
Fraternal polyandry. See Polyandry, fraternal
Fraternal polyandry. See Polyandry (fraternal)
Free Church of Scotland
Highland Scots, 4:11
Lowland Scots, 4:163
Orcadians, 4:187
Free Estonian Church
Estonian, 6:115
Freemasonry
Flemish, 4:108
Jatav, 3:114
Mahar, 3:164
Free port system
Canarians, 4:51
Frescoes
Zhuang, 6:511
Friendliness (as social virtue)
Nayaka, 3:195
see also Neighborliness
Friendship
dyadic
Carib of Dominica, 8:39
formalized
Copper Eskimo, 1:78
Pomo, 1:294
importance of
Cuna, 7:150
Norwegians, 4:181
Xikrin, 7:368
more important than kinship
Portuguese, 4:207
mutual assistance networks
Sardinians, 4:227
Fruit festival
Sherpa, 3:259
Fruit growing
Bulgarians, 4:43
Ch'ol, 8:64
Cretans, 4:70
Dalmatians, 4:86
East Asians of the United States, 1:99
German Swiss, 4:125
Kikuyu, 9:161
Mijikenda, 9:224
Mingrelians, 6:263
Moldovans, 6:266, 267
Mon, 5:189
Naxi, 6:478
Old Believers, 1:273
Pathan, 3:231
Peloponnesians, 4:193
Provencal, 4:210

Salar, 6:488
Tajiks, 6:352
Talysh, 6:355
Tuscans, 4:269
Udis, 6:376
Uighur, 6:499
Vlachs, 4:274
Yezidis, 6:409
Zhuang, 6:510
Zuni, 1:397
see also specific fruits
Fruit trees
matrilineal inheritance
Kongo, 9:167
Fundamentalism, Christian
Appalachians, 1:22-23
Blacks in Canada, 1:44
Carib of Dominica, 8:40
Ch'ol, 8:65
Dominicans, 8:103
Itza', 8:135
Ladinos, 8:153
Lunda, 9:198
Martiniquais, 8:163
Miskito, 8:172
Molokans, 1:243
Nahua of the Huasteca, 8:187
Nahuat of the Sierra de Puebla, 8:193
Ozarks, 1:281
Seri, 8:235
Shakers, 1:316
Furniture
bed-cupboard
Frisians, 4:110
built-in
Sherpa, 3:258
design and manufacture
Danes, 4:89
Shakers, 1:316
Swedes, 4:258
factories
Slovenes, 4:247
manufacture of rustic
peripatetics, 1:287
straw-backed chair-making
Orcadians, 4:187
Fur trade
Abenaki, 1:4
Ahtna, 1:14
Aleut, 1:15
Baffinland Inuit, 1:28, 29-30
Carrier, 1:52
Central Yup'ik Eskimos, 1:56, 57
Cherokee, 1:61
Copper Eskimo, 1:77
Cree, 1:80, 80-81
Dargins, 6:98
Daur, 6:429
Delaware, 1:85
Dogrib, 1:88
Dolgan, 6:100, 101
Eastern Shoshone, 1:105
East Greenland Inuit, 1:106
Even, 6:117
Evenki (Northern Tungus), 6:121
Finns, 4:102
Flathead, 1:128
Fox, 1:129

Frisians, 4:111
Hare, 1:139-140
Hidatsa, 1:146
Itelmen, 6:152
Karelians, 6:170
Khanty, 6:190
Koryaks and Kerek, 6:207
Kwakiutl, 1:198
Labrador Inuit, 1:201
Macuna, 7:213
Maliseet, 1:211
Mandan, 1:214
Mansi, 6:252-253
Menominee, 1:220, 221
Metis of Western Canada, 1:226, 227, 228, 229
Miami, 1:231
Micmac, 1:233
Montagnais-Naskapi, 1:244, 245, 246
Nanai, 6:275
Netsilik Inuit, 1:254
Nganasan, 6:281
Nivaclé, 7:249
Nootka, 1:256
North Alaskan Eskimos, 1:258
Northern Shoshone and Bannock, 1:267
Ojibwa, 1:268, 269
Orok, 6:296
Osage, 1:277
Pacific Eskimo, 1:282, 283
Russian-Americans, 1:116
Saami, 6:323
Selkup, 6:326
Sharanahua, 7:299
Shors, 6:329, 330
Siberiaki, 6:332
Slavey, 1:319, 320
Tanaina, 1:335, 336
Tofalar, 6:362
Tsimshian, 1:354
Tuvans, 6:373
Ute, 1:361
Volga Tatars, 6:401
West Greenland Inuit, 1:377
Winnebago, 1:381
Yakut, 6:404, 405
Yukagir, 6:412, 413
Fur tree
Shawnee, 1:317

Gabé (ceremony)
Mafulu, 2:153
Gadu:gi (Cherokee mutual aid society), 1:61
Gadzosi seed burial
Nagas, 3:191
Gait Kurban
Volga Tatars, 6:402
Gambling
Hare, 1:142
Mardudjara, 2:180
Pomo, 1:295
Tiwi, 2:328
Games
Basques, 1:32, 33
Choctaw, 1:73
Dogrib, 1:89
Hare, 1:142
Jicarilla, 1:174

Kota, **3:**137
Paresí, **7:**269
Pomo, **1:**295
Salasaca, **7:**290
Tacana, **7:**318
Toba, **7:**333
Yawalapití, **7:**379
Yokuts, **1:**388
see also Sports
Ganapati (deity)
    Bania, **3:**25
Ganesh (deity)
    Chitpavan Brahman, **3:**70
Gangs
    African American, **1:**12
    Yap, **2:**393
Ganja use
    Baiga, **3:**19
Gaonbura (village officials)
    Nagas, **3:**190
Gardeners
    Basques, **1:**33
    Doukhobors, **1:**91
    East Asians of the United States, **1:**100
Gardening
    Irula, **3:**104-105
    Mauritian, **3:**171
    Thakali, **3:**290
    Winnebago, **1:**380, 381
Garlic, medicinal use of
    Bulgarians, **4:**45
    Romanians, **4:**214
Garment industry. _See_ Clothing, manufacture
Gasoline stations
    Arab Americans, **1:**24
    East Asians of Canada, **1:**96
Gathering
    Agta, **5:**4, 5
    Ainu, **5:**7, 8
    Aranda, **2:**16
    Asmat, **2:**19
    Ata Tana 'Ai, **5:**23
    Bagobo, **5:**29
    Dogon, **9:**72
    Fali, **9:**94
    Gnau, **2:**80
    Gururumba, **2:**92
    Huichol, **8:**125
    Iatmul, **2:**98
    Itelmen, **6:**152
    Iteso, **9:**128
    Jino, **6:**460
    Kamilaroi, **2:**104
    Karadjeri, **2:**111
    Karen, **5:**126
    Kariera, **2:**111
    Ket, **6:**183
    Khoi, **9:**159
    Kpelle, **9:**173
    Kriashen Tatars, **6:**211
    Kubu, **5:**150
    Lahu, **5:**151
    Lamet, **5:**157
    Lisu, **6:**465
    Lozi, **9:**187
    Manchu, **6:**467
    Mansi, **6:**252
    Mardudjara, **2:**179

Maring, **2:**185
Melanau, **5:**178
Miao, **6:**470, 471
Modang, **5:**186
Mongo, **9:**226
Muong, **5:**190
Murngin, **2:**224
Nenets, **6:**278
Ngatatjara, **2:**239
Oroquen, **6:**482
Philippine Negritos, **5:**211
Pintupi, **2:**264, 265
Qiang, **6:**485
San-speaking peoples, **9:**302
Sea Nomads of the Andaman, **5:**227, 228
Semang, **5:**233, 234
Seri, **8:**233
She, **6:**489
Siberian Estonians, **6:**336
Suri, **9:**325
Tasaday, **5:**259-261
Tasmanians, **2:**316
Tepehuan of Chihuahua, **8:**253
Tepehuan of Durango, **8:**256
Tiwi, **2:**327
Tofalar, **6:**362
Tonga, **9:**353
tropical-forest foragers, **9:**356
Tsimihety, **9:**358
Ukrainian peasants, **6:**386
Warlpiri, **2:**373
Wik Mungkan, **2:**377
Yao, **6:**505
Yir Yoront, **2:**395
Yukagir, **6:**413
Yumbri, **5:**294
see also Hunting and gathering
Gayal (bovid)
    Chin, **3:**63-64
Gazelle hunting
    Sleb, **9:**315
Geese raising
    Kashubians, **4:**158
    Volga Tatars, **6:**401
Gelygpa Buddhism
    Buriats, **6:**68
Gemeinde (commune)
    German Swiss, **4:**126
Gem traders
    Moor of Sri Lanka, **3:**180
Gender equality
    Assyrians, **9:**27
    Baha'is, **9:**35
    Basques, **4:**31
    Bonerate, **5:**45
    Catawba, **1:**54
    Central Yup'ik Eskimos, **1:**58
    Chenchu, **3:**62
    Costa Ricans, **8:**80
    Danes, **4:**90
    Germans, **4:**122
    Grasia, **3:**88
    Han, **6:**443
    Hopi, **1:**149, 150
    Inughuit, **1:**160
    Leonese, **4:**161
    Mormons, **1:**248
    Nicobarese, **3:**209, 210

Northern Paiute, **1:**264
Pamir peoples, **6:**305-306
Parsi, **3:**228
Pomo, **1:**294
Shakers, **1:**316
Southern Paiute (and Chemehuevi), **1:**331
Tanaina, **1:**336
Tanana, **1:**339
Tepehuan of Chihuahua, **8:**252
Teton, **1:**345
see also Gender roles; Inheritance, equally
    shared; Women _headings_
Gender identity
    Chukchee, **6:**78
    Kiribati, **2:**122
    Yukuna, **7:**387
    see also Berdache; Transsexuality;
        Transvestite
Gender roles
    ceremony management
        Culina, **7:**148
        Mandan, **1:**214
    complementary
        Norwegians, **4:**181
        Tewa Pueblos, **1:**349
    distinct
        Mbeere, **9:**221
        Mennonites, **1:**218
        Miami, **1:**231
        North Alaskan Eskimos, **1:**259
        Ozarks, **1:**281
        Slovenes, **4:**248
    flexible
        Galicians, **4:**119
        Hill Pandaram, **3:**99
        Koya, **3:**140
        Lepcha, **3:**149
        Magar, **3:**158
        Mizo, **3:**178
        Nayaka, **3:**195
        Pasiegos, **4:**190
        Romanians, **4:**213
        Sora, **3:**269
    girls' shyness with boys
        Western Apache, **1:**372
    male domestic proscriptions
        Castilians, **4:**59
    male honor code. _See_ Virginity, valuation
    male nonperformance of domestic tasks
        Andalusians, **4:**11
        Provencal, **4:**210
        Swiss, Italian, **4:**261
    pronounced differentiation
        Ionians, **4:**149, 150
        Rominche, **4:**216
    pronounced inequality
        Italian Mexicans, **8:**131
    reversed
        Kanjar, **3:**120, 121
        see also Transsexuality
    separate activity domains
        Highland Scots, **4:**140
        Serbs, **4:**131
    separate designated socializing areas in
        community
        Sardinians, **4:**226
    separate social activities
        Ozarks, **1:**281

Gender roles (cont'd)
  Slovaks, **4**:245
  shared tasks
    Abor, **3**:4
    Baiga, **3**:19
    Menominee, **1**:221
    Seminole, **1**:313
  socialization to meet established expectations
    Sardinians, **4**:227
  stereotyping of
    Kwakiutl, **1**:199
  well defined conceptions of ideal
    Rom of Czechoslovakia, **4**:219
  women forbidden from rituals
    Ainu, **5**:8
  women's higher value
    Hopi, **1**:149, 150
  women's public deference vs. private
      domestic power
    Persians, **9**:279
  see also Women, high status
Gender separation
  Ashkenazic Jews, **4**:16
  Chipewyan, **1**:69
  Coorg, **3**:74
  Cyclades, **4**:77-78
  Don Cossacks, **6**:106
  Garia, **2**:75
  Gururumba, **2**:94
  Gypsies, **6**:147
  Hasidim, **1**:144
  Hawaiians, **2**:96
  Kanuri, **9**:152
  Makassar, **5**:172, 173
  Mimika, **2**:208
  Nagas, **3**:190
  Pawnee, **1**:285
  Persians, **9**:279
  Pintupi, **2**:265
  Qiang, **6**:486
  Shakers, **1**:316
  Sindhi, **3**:263
  Sinhalese, **3**:265
  Taiwan aboriginal peoples, **5**:258
  Tajiks, **6**:353
  Tausug, **5**:263
  Western Apache, **1**:372
  see also Dormitories; Food, sexually segre-
      gated eathing; Menstruation; Purdah;
      Women's activity curtailment
Gender-specific housing
  Abelam, **2**:5
  Ajië, **2**:7
  Akha, **5**:11
  Ambae, **2**:11
  Asmat, **2**:20
  Balkars, **6**:52
  Central Yup'ik Eskimos, **1**:57, 58
  Chácobo, **7**:105
  Chimbu, **2**:35, 36
  Dani, **2**:43
  Dariba, **2**:46
  Foi, **2**:60, 61
  Fore, **2**:62, 64
  Gahuku-Gama, **2**:69-70
  Garia, **2**:74, 75
  Gebusi, **2**:77, 78

Gnau, **2**:80, 81
Gogodala, **2**:83, 84
Gururumba, **2**:92
Hani, **6**:450
Hawaiians, **2**:96
Highland Scots, **4**:140
Iatmul, **2**:98
Kaluli, **2**:101
Kapauku, **2**:105
Kapingamarangi, **2**:109
Karachays, **6**:159
Lak, **2**:137
Lakalai, **2**:141
Lesu, **2**:146
Mae Enga, **2**:149, 150
Mafulu, **2**:152
Malekula, **2**:164
Manus, **2**:173, 174
Marind-anim, **2**:183
Maring, **2**:185, 186
Melpa, **2**:201
Mendi, **2**:203
Miyanmin, **2**:209, 211
Muong, **5**:190
Namau, **2**:231
Ningerum, **2**:245
Pentecost, **2**:262
Rotinese, **5**:213
Sambia, **2**:284
Selepet, **2**:293, 294
Selkup, **6**:326
Sengseng, **2**:296, 297
Siane, **2**:299
Svans, **6**:345
Tairora, **2**:309
Tauade, **2**:318
Torres Strait Islanders, **2**:345
Tzotzil of Zinacantan, **8**:292
Usino, **2**:361
Wantoat, **2**:369
Wogeo, **2**:381
Wovan, **2**:385
Yangoru Boiken, **2**:389
see also Dormitories (single male or female);
    Men's houses
Geneologies
  Gnau, **2**:81
  Kachin, **5**:116
  Ozarks, **1**:281
Generation gaps
  East Asians in the United States, **1**:101
Generosity, as social virtue
  Ache, **7**:5
  Amuesha, **7**:38
  Blackfoot, **1**:42
  Hidsata, **1**:147
  Kashinawa, **7**:196
  Kiowa, **1**:188
  Montagnais-Naskapi, **1**:245
  Northern Paiute, **1**:264
  Slavey, **1**:320
  Tanana, **1**:339
  Tapirapé, **7**:321
  Winnebago, **1**:382
  Yukuna, **7**:388
  see also under Leadership qualities
Genetic diseases
  Amish, **1**:19

Genna (magicoreligious rite)
  Nagas, **3**:191
  Purum, **3**:244
Geomancy
  Hakka, **6**:438
  Han, **6**:447
  Hani, **6**:451
Geometric motif
  Mekeo, **2**:200
  Menominee, **1**:222
Georgian Orthodox. *See* Orthodox
    Christianity
Gerontogamy
  Badaga, **3**:16
  Baiga, **3**:20
  Bondo, **3**:49
  Parsi, **3**:228
Ghettos
  East Asians of Canada, **1**:95
  Vlach Gypsies of Hungary, **4**:217
Ghost Dance
  Eastern Shoshone, **1**:106
  Pawnee, **1**:285
  Pomo, **1**:295
  Southern Paiute (and Chemehuevi), **1**:332
  Teton, **1**:346
  ute, **1**:362
  Walapai, **1**:364
  Whichita, **1**:379
  Yokuts, **1**:387
Ghost-Keeping Ceremony
  Teton, **1**:346
Ghost ritual
  Bhil, **3**:41
  Bondo, **3**:51
Ghosts, beliefs about
  Agta, **5**:6
  Anuta, **2**:15
  Ata Tana 'Ai, **5**:26
  Atoni, **5**:28
  Bahnar, **5**:30
  Bhil, **3**:41
  Bisaya, **5**:43
  Boazi, **2**:30
  Bondo, **3**:51
  Bontok, **5**:46
  Burmese, **5**:65
  Butonese, **5**:68
  Canela, **7**:97-98
  Chimbu, **2**:37
  Chin, **3**:67
  Chinese in Southeast Asia, **5**:77
  Choiseul Island, **2**:39
  Circassians, **6**:90
  Copper Eskimo, **1**:78, 79
  Dani, **2**:45
  Daribi, **2**:48
  Eastern Shoshone, **1**:106
  Eipo, **2**:58
  Foi, **2**:61
  Fore, **2**:64, 65
  Frisians, **4**:112
  Gaels (Irish), **4**:117
  Garo, **3**:84
  Grasia, **3**:88
  Guadalcanal, **2**:91
  Guajiro, **7**:169, 170
  Gururumba, **2**:94

Hakka, **6:**439
Han, **6:**447
Hanunóo, **5:**91
Hare, **1:**142
Iatmul, **2:**100
Iglulik Inuit, **1:**155
Itonama, **7:**179
Jatav, **3:**115
Javanese, **5:**114
Jicarilla, **1:**174
Kaluli, **2:**103
Kapingamarangi, **2:**110
Karen, **5:**129
Khmer, **5:**137
Khoi, **9:**160
Kickapoo, **1:**186
Kiwai, **2:**127
Konso, **9:**171
Kurtatchi, **2:**133
Lahu, **5:**153
Lak, **2:**139
Lakalai, **2:**142
Lao, **5:**159
Lesu, **2:**147
Lugbara, **9:**195
Mae Enga, **2:**151
Mafulu, **2:**153
Maisin, **2:**159
Malay, **5:**176
Malekula, **2:**166
Maratha, **3:**170
Marquesas Islands, **2:**190
Mejbrat, **2:**197
Melpa, **2:**202
Mendi, **2:**205
Menominee, **1:**222
Miao, **6:**472
Mimika, **2:**208
Modang, **5:**187
Mulam, **6:**477
Mundugumor, **2:**220
Namau, **2:**232
Nasioi, **2:**235
Naxi, **6:**480
Ndembu, **9:**241
Nepali, **3:**205
Newar, **3:**208
Ngatatjara, **2:**241
Ningerum, **2:**247, 248
Nissan, **2:**251
Northern Paiute, **1:**264-265
Nu, **6:**481
Ojibwa, **1:**270
Orcadians, **4:**188
Orokaiva, **2:**257
Orokolo, **2:**258-259, 260
Pahari, **3:**223
Palaung, **5:**203
Pintupi, **2:**267
Piro, **7:**280
Pukapuka, **2:**272, 273
Rapa, **2:**275
Raroia, **2:**276
Rominche, **4:**217
Rossel Island, **2:**280
Samal Moro, **5:**224
San Cristobal, **2:**289
Sedang, **5:**230

Sengseng, **2:**297, 298
Senoi, **5:**239
She, **6:**490
Siane, **2:**299
Sio, **2:**301
Sorbs, **4:**253
Southern Paiute (and Chemehuevi), **1:**332
Subanun, **5:**245, 246
Tagalog, **5:**251
Tairora, **2:**309, 310
Tasmanians, **2:**317
Tatuyo, **7:**323, 324
Tauade, **2:**320
Telugu, **3:**287
Teton, **1:**346
Tikopia, **2:**326
T'in, **5:**280
Tokelau, **2:**333
Tongareva, **2:**341
Tor, **2:**344
Tory Islanders, **4:**266
Tujia, **6:**499
Usino, **2:**363
Ute, **1:**362
Wamira, **2:**367
Wape, **2:**372
Wik Mungkan, **2:**379
Woleai, **2:**384
Wovan, **2:**387
Yakö, **9:**387
Yap, **2:**394
Yi, **6:**508
Zande, **9:**399, 400
Zarma, **9:**406
see also Ancestral spirits
Giants, belief in
Kashubians, **4:**159
Gift exchange
Abenaki, **1:**5
Achumawi, **1:**10
Barí, **7:**84
Fox, **1:**129, 130
Gujarati, **3:**92
Hausa, **9:**112
Kickapoo, **1:**184
Klamath, **1:**191
Kwakiutl, **1:**200
Limbu, **3:**150
Magar, **3:**158
Malay, **5:**175
Maori, **2:**177
Maratha, **3:**169
Nootka, **1:**257
peripatetics of Iraq, Syria, Lebanon, Jordan, Israel, Egypt, Sudan, and Yemen, **9:**277
Pomo, **1:**294
San-speaking peoples, **9:**303
Sherpa, **3:**258, 259
Tamil, **3:**278
Tandroy, **9:**338
Warlpiri, **2:**374
Western Apache, **1:**373
Winnebago, **1:**381
see also Potlatch; _under_ Marriage
Gill-net fishing
Dogrib, **1:**88
Ginger growing
Anavil Brahman, **3:**7

Gin. _See under_ Alcohol
Girls' houses. _See_ Dormitories
Gisaro (ceremony)
Kaluli, **2:**103
Glass beads
Northern Paiute, **1:**263
Ojibwa, **1:**270
Zuni, **1:**398
Glass design
Swedes, **4:**258
Glassmaking
Czechs, **4:**83
Sorbs, **4:**253
Ukrainians, **6:**392
Walloons, **4:**277
Glass painting
Croats, **4:**75
Glass pictures
Rom of Czechoslovakia, **4:**219
Glooscap (culture hero)
Micmac, **1:**235
Gnabag (celebration)
Temiar, **5:**272
Gnosticism
Yezidis, **6:**410
Yugur, **6:**509
Goadherding
Teda, **9:**340
Goatherding
Cretans, **4:**70
Kalasha, **3:**116
Maasai, **9:**207
Montenegrins, **4:**172
Nuer, **9:**249
Pashai, **9:**267
Peloponnesians, **4:**193
Qashqa'i, **9:**285
San-speaking peoples, **9:**302
Sarakatsani, **4:**223-224
Shahsevan, **9:**308
Somalis, **9:**316
Suri, **9:**324
Turkana, **9:**371
Goat raising
Azerbaijani Turks, **6:**49
Balkars, **6:**53
Buriats, **6:**66
Cham, **5:**72
Don Cossacks, **6:**104
Ewenki, **6:**433
Gayo, **5:**88
Guajiro, **7:**168
Karachays, **6:**159
Karakalpaks, **6:**167
Karelians, **6:**170
Kédang, **5:**131
Kenyah-Kayan-Kajang, **5:**133
Kirgiz, **6:**461
Kmhmu, **5:**139
Kurds, **6:**226
Kyrgyz, **6:**229
Laks, **6:**234
Lamaholot, **5:**155
Laz, **6:**240
Lezgins, **6:**242
Madurese, **5:**167
Maguindanao, **5:**169
Makassar, **5:**172

Goat raising (cont'd)
　Miao, **6:**470
　Minahasans, **5:**181
　Mocoví, **7:**240
　Navajo, **1:**251
　Naxi, **6:**478
　Ndebele, **9:**236
　Nogays, **6:**287
　Palu'e, **5:**205
　Pamir peoples, **6:**304
　Saluan, **5:**217
　Svans, **6:**344
　Ternatan/Tidorese, **5:**275
　Tswana, **9:**361
　Tu, **6:**496
　Yakan, **5:**289
　Yi, **6:**506
　Yörük, **9:**394
　Yugur, **6:**508
　Zande, **9:**398
Goat sacrifice. *See* Sacrifice, livestock
Goblins, belief in
　Kashubians, **4:**159
God
　male-female elements
　　Shakers, **1:**316
　as paternalistic
　　Sarakatsani, **4:**224
　within
　　Doukhobors, **1:**90, 92
　see also Creator; Monotheism; Supreme
　　being
Goddess worship. *See* Women deities
God men (religious specialist)
　Toda, **3:**297
Godparenthood. *See* Fictive kin
Gods. *See* Spirits; Polytheism
Going to the Waters to Avoid the Evil Eye
　　(festival)
　Kubachins, **6:**219
Gold
　as primal symbol
　　Cuna, **7:**151
Gold mining
　Akan, **9:**11
　Carrier, **1:**52
　East Asians of Canada, **1:**94
　Lobi-Dagarti peoples, **9:**183
　Suri, **9:**325
Gold panning
　Vlachs, **4:**274
Goldsmithing
　Chuvash, **6:**85
　Hani, **6:**450
　Kubachins, **6:**217
　Mongols, **6:**474
　Ndaonese, **5:**194
　Ogan-Besemah, **5:**198
　Pahari, **3:**223
　Sora, **3:**270
　Tamil, **3:**277
　Untouchable service caste, **3:**159-
　　160
　Vlachs, **4:**274
Gong making
　Khasi, **3:**126
Good and evil, duality of. *See* Afterlife; Dual
　　worlds

Good Friday importance
　Tagalog, **5:**251
Gossip (as social control). *See under* Social
　　sanctions
Got. *See* Clan
Gothic architecture
　Bretons, **4:**40
Gotra. *See* Castes
Government employment
　Aveyronnais, **4:**24
　Bosnian Muslims, **4:**36
　Maltese, **4:**167
　Mandan, **1:**214
　Mauritian, **3:**171, 172
　Parsi, **3:**228-229
　Piemontese, **4:**199
　Tetons, **1:**345
　Ute, **1:**361
　West Greenland Inuit, **1:**377
Government welfare assistance
　Central Yup'ik Eskimos, **1:**57
　Cherokee, **1:**61
　Choctaw, **1:**71
　Gaels (Irish), **4:**115
　Gypsies and caravan dwellers in the
　　Netherlands, **4:**137-138
　Highland Scots, **4:**142
　Irish, **4:**153
　Irish Travellers, **4:**155
　Mandan, **1:**214
　Mardudjara, **2:**180
　Metis of Western Canada, **1:**228
　North Alaskan Eskimos, **1:**258, 259
　Northern Irish, **4:**178
　Ozarks, **1:**281
　Pima-Papago, **1:**288
　Pintupi, **2:**265
　Tetons, **1:**345
　Tewa Pueblos, **1:**348
　Ulithi, **2:**358
　see also Welfare state
Govi Maduna (ceremony)
　Mailu, **2:**155, 156, 157
Grain farming. *See* Cereal farming; *specific
　　grains*
Grandparent
　as child caregivers. *See* Child care, by
　　grandparents
　deities
　　Magar, **3:**161
　　Yuit, **1:**392
　grandchild relations
　　Hawaiians, **2:**96
　　Khoi, **9:**159
　　Lau, **2:**144
　　Lunda, **9:**198
　　Luyia, **9:**205
　　Maori, **2:**177
　　Mardudjara, **2:**181
　marriage with grandchild
　　Baiga, **3:**20
　preteens live with
　　Lunda, **9:**197
　see also Elderly; Elder respect; Family types,
　　three-generational stem
Grape growing
　Ajarians, **6:**14
　Azerbaijani Turks, **6:**49

　Basques, **4:**31
　Calabrese, **4:**49
　Castilians, **4:**59
　Catalans, **4:**62
　Cretans, **4:**71
　Crimean Tatars, **6:**93
　Cyclades, **4:**77
　Dalmations, **4:**86
　Gagauz, **6:**125
　Germans, **6:**139
　Ingilos, **6:**150
　Ionians, **4:**149
　Ladin, **4:**160
　Moldovans, **6:**267
　Montenegrins, **4:**172
　Mountain Jews, **6:**272
　Occitans, **4:**183, 184
　Peloponnesians, **4:**193
　Portuguese, **4:**206
　Provencal, **4:**210
　Sicilians, **4:**236
　Slovaks, **4:**243
　Tabasarans, **6:**348
　Tajiks, **6:**352
　Tuscans, **4:**269
　Udis, **6:**376
　Vlachs, **4:**274
　see also Wine making and trade
Grapic arts. *See* Visual arts
Grass basketry
　Aleut, **1:**15, 16
　Central Yup'ik Eskimos, **1:**57
Grass Dance
　Assiniboin, **1:**27
Grave decoration. *See under* Cemeteries
Grave markers
　crosses, icons, and other decorations
　　Dolgan, **6:**102
　gabled grave house
　　Ojibwa, **1:**271
　headstone laying
　　Cook Islands, **2:**42
　headstone unveiling
　　Torres Strait Islanders, **2:**347
　posts and stones
　　Albanians, **4:**8
　　Chin, **3:**64, 67
　　Fox, **1:**130
　　Gond, **3:**87
　　Khasi, **3:**126
　　Menominee, **1:**222
　　Mizo, **3:**179
　　Sora, **3:**270
　rocks
　　Ute, **1:**363
　small house
　　Tanaina, **1:**337
　small stones
　　Albanians, **4:**8
　　Chin, **3:**67
　stones mark head and feet
　　Kurds, **9:**177
　stone tomb
　　Cornish, **4:**64
　stone tombs
　　Cornish, **4:**64
　tomb
　　Tandroy, **9:**338

totem painted on grave stick
    Menominee, 1:222
unmarked graves
    Qalandar, 3:248
Grave Sweeping (festival)
    She, 6:491
Graveyards. *See* Cemeteries
Great Hare (creator spirit)
    Ottawa, 1:280
Great Horned Snake (supernatural)
    Seminole of Oklahoma, 1:315
Great Spirit
    Ojibwa, 1:270
    Walapai, 1:364
    Yankton, 1:386
Greek Catholicism
    Carpatho-Rusyns, 6:71
Greek Orthodox Church. *See* Orthodox
        Christianity (Greek Orthodox)
Greek system of kinship terminology. *See*
        under Kinship terminology
Green Corn Ceremony
    Cherokee, 1:62
    Choctaw, 1:73
    Creek, 1:83
    Seminole, 1:314
    Seminole of Oklahoma, 1:314
Green funeral
    Kota, 3:138
Green revolution. *See under* Agriculture
Green Thursday (holiday)
    Carpatho-Rusyns, 6:71
Gren mahé (ceremony)
    Ata Tana 'Ai, 5:26
Grocery trade
    Arab Americans, 1:24
    East Asians of Canada, 1:96
    East Asians of the United States, 1:101
Groom-price
    Kanbi, 3:118
    Santal, 3:253
Groom-service
    Hopi, 1:149
    Tuareg, 9:368
    Tubatulabal, 1:355
    Western Apache, 1:372
    Winnebago, 1:381
    Yuit, 1:391
Grossefamilie (lineal relationships)
    Austrians, 4:20
Ground drawings
    Jicarilla, 1:174
Groundnut growing
    Santal, 3:253
    Shona, 9:312
    Tandroy, 9:336
Grub collection
    Krikati/Pukobye, 7:204
    Tupari, 7:340
Guanyin Festival
    Bai, 6:421
Guardian spirit
    Achumawi, 1:10
    Bai, 6:421
    Bhil Muslims, 3:41
    Bukidnon, 5:55
    Butonese, 5:68
    Central Thai, 5:71

Chakma, 3:60
Chinook, 1:67
Chumash, 1:73
Comox, 1:76
Dusun, 5:83
Even, 6:119
Evenki (Northern Tungus), 6:123
Flathead, 1:128
Gaels (Irish), 4:117
Gayo, 5:89
Hani, 6:451
Kachin, 5:118
Kalapuya, 1:175
Karachays, 6:161
Karelians, 6:171, 172
Kédang, 5:133
Khmer, 5:137
Komi, 6:204
Koryaks and Kerek, 6:209
Labrador Inuit, 1:202
Lahu, 5:153
Lakher, 3:147
Lao Isan, 5:162
Lillooets, 1:207
Mansi, 6:254, 255
Maonan, 6:468
Menominee, 1:222
Miami, 1:231, 232
Miao, 6:472
Murut, 5:193
Nez Percé, 1:254
Nootka, 1:257
Northern Shoshone and Bannock,
    1:267
Okanagon, 1:272
Ottawa, 1:280
Palaung, 5:203
Quechan, 1:302
Sagada Igorot, 5:216
Shan, 5:241
Shuswap, 1:318
Siberiaki, 6:333, 334
Siberian Estonians, 6:337
Siberian Tatars, 6:342
Spokane, 1:333
Tabasarans, 6:350
Tai Lue, 5:253, 255
Ternatan/Tidorese, 5:276
Teton, 1:346
Thompson, 1:350
T'in, 5:278, 279
Tlingit, 1:353
Ukrainian peasants, 6:388
Vietnamese, 5:285, 286
Wiyot, 1:385
Yao of Thailand, 5:293
see also Personal god
Guerrilla activity. *See* Raiders; Terrorist
    movements
Guest workers
    Austrian discrimination against, 4:21
    Calabrese as, 4:49
    Serbs as, 4:230
Guides
    Seminole, 1:312
    Sherpa, 3:257-258
Guilds
    Samoa, 2:287

Gun control
    Jamaicans, 8:139
Gun manufacture
    Balkars, 6:53
    Pathan, 3:231, 233
    Walloons, 4:277
Gurus
    Baul, 3:26
    hijra, 3:97
    Sikh, 3:261
Guthi (ritual group)
    Newar, 3:207

Haddock fishing
    Shetlanders, 4:233
Haggling
    Piemontese Sinti, 4:200
Hair
    dreadlocks
        Black West Indians in the United States,
            1:46
    male stiffened scalp lock
        Pawnee, 1:283
    male styles
        Nootka, 1:257
    married women's
        Brahman and Chhetri of Nepal, 3:53
    ornaments
        Swedes, 4:258
    plucking
        Yuqui, 7:394
    puberty customs
        Sora, 3:270
    religious customs
        Old Believers, 1:274
        Sadhu, 3:251
        Sikh, 3:261
        see also Head shaving
    removal of all body and facial
        Yuracaré, 7:396
    styling
        Pokot, 9:283
    women's elaborate hairdos
        Betsileo, 9:57
    see also Head covering; Head shaving;
        Veiling of women
Hair cutting
    of adulterous woman
        Rom of Czechoslovakia, 4:219
    female puberty rite
        Kuna, 8:150, 150
    gender designation
        Cotopaxi Quichua, 7:134
    initiation
        Paï-Tavytera, 7:260
        Ticuna, 7:330
        Yanomamö, 7:376
        Yawalapití, 7:380
        Yekuana, 7:381
    mourning
        Chamacoco, 7:110
        Krikati/Pukobye, 7:206
        Lengua, 7:211
        Ute, 1:362
    ritual
        Albanians, 4:6, 7
        Bajau, 5:33
        Bonerate, 5:46

Hair cutting (cont'd)
  Bosnian Muslims, 4:36
  Callahuaya, 7:89
  Cocama, 7:130
  Cook Islands, 2:42
  Cuna, 7:151
  Samal, 5:220
  Tausug, 5:263
  taboos
    Mojo, 7:242
Hairy Man (quasi-spirit)
  Tanaina, 1:336
Hake fishing
  Basques, 4:31
Halibut fishing
  Klallam, 1:190
  Kwakiutl, 1:198
  Nootka, 1:256
  Tlingit, 1:351
  West Greenland Inuit, 1:377
Hallelujah (religious belief)
  Akawaio, 7:32-33
  Pemon, 7:272, 273
Halloween
  Northern Ireland, 4:178
  Orcadians, 4:188
Hallucinogen use
  Amahuaca, 7:36
  Cocama, 7:130
  Desana, 7:153-154
  Guahibo-Sikuani, 7:166
  Huarayo, 7:178
  Karihona, 7:193, 194
  Kashinawa, 7:197
  Matsigenka, 7:232
  Piapoco, 7:274
  Piaroa, 7:278
  Piro, 7:280
  Puinave, 7:282
  Saliva, 7:292
  Shipibo, 7:306
  Siona-Secoya, 7:309
  Tatuyo, 7:324
  Waorani, 7:353
  Wayapi, 7:363
  Yagua, 7:373
  Yanomamö, 7:377
  see also Opium use; Opium use
Hamlets. See Villages
Hammocks
  Asurini, 7:42
  Kagwahiv, 7:185
  Karihona, 7:192
  Kuna, 8:147
Hanafi law
  Bengali, 3:33
Hand game
  Dogrib, 1:89
Handicapped. See Disabled
Handicrafts. See Decorative arts; specific
    kinds
Handsome Lake religion
  Iroquois, 1:167
Hansik (holiday)
  Korean, 5:148
  Koreans, 6:206
Hanukkah (holiday)
  Mountain Jews, 6:273

Haowasa (ceremony)
  Dai, 6:427
Hare (deity)
  Winnebago, 1:382
Hare hunting. See Rabbit hunting
Hare Krishna
  Bengali Vaishnava, 3:37
  Edo, 9:82
Hari Raya Hadji (feast)
  Bajau, 5:34
  Samal, 5:221
  Tausug, 5:264
Hari Raya Puasa (feast)
  Bajau, 5:34
  Samal, 5:221
  Samal Moro, 5:224
  Tausug, 5:264
Harmony
  in nature
    Choctaw, 1:72
  as social virtue
    Montagnais-Naskapi, 1:245
    Yuit, 1:392
    Zuni, 1:399
  with supernatural powers
    Navajo, 1:253
Harp playing
  Bavarians, 4:35
  Bretons, 4:40
Harvest ceremonies. See under Ceremonies
Harvest Home (holiday)
  Orcadians, 4:188
Hashish growing. See Opium growing
Hasidim
  Ashkenazim, 6:36
Hat
  wearing as initiation
    Kurtatchi, 2:132
  woven
    Wiyot, 1:384
  woven conical
    Nootka, 1:257
  see also Head covering
Hawaiian-type kinship terminology. See under
    Kinship terminology
Hayduks (guerrilla bands)
  Slav Macedonians, 4:241
Haying
  Gaels (Irish), 4:115, 116
  Irish, 4:152
  Tory Islanders, 4:265
Head covering
  Hasidim, 1:142
  Jatav, 3:114
  Khasi, 3:125
  Old Believers, 1:274
  see also Veiling of women
Head-hunting
  Alorese, 5:15
  Ambonese, 5:17
  Asmat, 2:20
  Ata Sikka, 5:22
  Atoni, 5:28
  Belau, 2:27
  Boazi, 2:29, 30
  Bontok, 5:46
  Chambri, 2:32
  Chin, 3:66-67

  Dusun, 5:83
  Garo, 3:82
  Gogodala, 2:84
  Iatmul, 2:98
  Iban, 5:96, 99
  Ifugao, 5:100
  Ilongot, 5:102
  Jebero, 7:181
  Kachin, 5:118
  Kalimantan Dayaks, 5:120
  Kalingas, 5:121, 122, 123
  Kenyah-Kayan-Kajang, 5:133, 134
  Keraki, 2:113, 114
  Khasi, 3:125
  Kiwai, 2:126
  Mailu, 2:154, 155, 156
  Marind-anim, 2:182, 184
  Modang, 5:185, 187
  Moluccans—South, 5:188
  Murik, 2:221, 222
  Murut, 5:193
  Nagas, 3:190
  Namau, 2:230, 232
  Nasioi, 2:233
  Nias, 5:196
  Rotinese, 5:214
  Taiwan aboriginal peoples, 5:257, 258
  Thadou, 3:289
  Toradja, 5:281
  Toraja, 5:282
  Torres Strait Islanders, 2:347
  Wa, 6:503
Head imagery
  Nagas, 3:191
Headmen
  Anuak, 9:22
  Barama River Carib, 7:82
  Basseri, 9:42
  Blackfoot, 1:41, 42
  Bororo, 7:87
  Craho, 7:138
  Dogon, 9:73
  Emerillon, 7:159
  Jivaro, 7:182
  Khoi, 9:160
  Kongo, 9:168
  Konso, 9:171
  Lengua, 7:210-211
  Luyia, 9:205
  Macuna, 7:214
  Mundurucu, 7:245
  Ndebele, 9:237
  Northern Paiute, 1:264
  Paraujano, 7:268
  Pima-Papago, 1:289
  Pume, 7:284
  Qashqa'i, 9:286
  Quechan, 1:302
  Saliva, 7:292
  Saramaka, 7:297
  Siona-Secoya, 7:308
  Southern Paiute (and Chemehuevi), 1:332
  Suruí, 7:313
  Warao, 7:358
  Washoe, 1:369
  Wayapi, 7:361
  Witoto, 7:365
  Yanomamö, 7:376

Yekuana, 7:381
Yokuts, 1:388
Yukpa, 7:384
Yukuna, 7:386, 388
see also Chiefdom
Headress
　feathered
　　Washoe, 1:370
Head shaving
　Ashkenazic Jews, 4:16
　Bhil, 3:40
　Brahman and Chhetri of Nepal, 3:53, 54
　Irula, 3:108
　Kota, 3:137
　Nicobarese, 3:209
　Okiek, 9:261
Headstone. *See* Grave markers
Healers
　Abenaki, 1:6
　Abor, 3:5
　Afro-Hispanic Pacific Lowlanders, 7:23
　Andamanese, 3:11
　Auvergnats, 4:23
　Aveyronnais, 4:26
　Azoreans, 4:28, 29
　Bamiléké, 9:39
　Berbers of Morocco, 9:52
　Betsileo, 9:57
　Bhil, 3:41
　Black Creoles of Louisiana, 1:39
　Bondo, 3:50, 51
　Bretons, 4:40
　Canarians, 4:53
　cattle ranchers of Huasteca, 8:44
　Chakma, 3:60, 61
　Chatino, 8:52
　Cheyenne, 1:66
　Chontal of Tabasco, 8:69
　Cora, 8:77
　Cretans, 4:71
　Dogon, 9:73
　Doukhobors, 1:93
　Edo, 9:82
　Falasha, 9:92
　Greeks, 4:134
　Gusii, 9:110
　Haida, 1:126
　Iteso, 9:130
　Khoi, 9:160
　K'iche,' 8:142
　Kongo, 9:168
　Krikati/Pukobye, 7:205
　Kumeyaay, 1:195
　Kwakiutl, 1:200
　Ladinos, 8:153
　Lango, 9:181
　Latinos, 1:206
　Luyia, 9:206
　Madeirans, 4:166
　Maliseet, 1:212
　Mazahua, 8:166
　Mbeere, 9:222
　Micmac, 1:235
　Mixe, 8:175
　Mossi, 9:231
　Navajo, 1:253
　Ndebele, 9:237
　Ndembu, 9:240, 241

Newar, 3:208
Ngawbe, 8:198
Ojibwa, 1:271
Okiek, 9:261, 262
Otavalo, 7:255
Pahari, 3:223
Paï-Tavytera, 7:260
Pame, 8:208
Pima Bajo, 8:214
Pokot, 9:283
Popoloca, 8:216
Portuguese, 4:208
Puerto Ricans, 8:223
Purum, 3:244
Q'eqchi,' 8:227
Rom of Czechoslovakia, 4:219
Saami, 4:222
Sakalava, 9:298
Salasaca, 7:291
San-speaking peoples, 9:302, 303-304
Shona, 9:314
Slovaks, 4:245
Songhay, 9:320
Southern Paiute (and Chemehuevi), 1:332
Swazi, 9:333
Swedes, 4:258
Tandroy, 9:338
Tarahumara, 8:242
Tepehuan of Durango, 8:258
Thadou, 3:289
Thompson, 1:350
Tojolab'al, 8:263
Totonac, 8:266
tropical-forest foragers, 9:357
Tswana, 9:364
Vlach Gypsies of Hungary, 4:272
Washoe, 1:370
Wasteko, 8:303, 304
Winnebago, 1:382
Wiyot, 1:385
Yaqui, 8:307
Yemenis, 9:390
Zapotec, 8:313
Zarma, 9:406
Zoque, 8:317
see also Shamanism; Witch doctor
Hearth
　as domestic grouping
　　Barí, 7:84-85
　　Canela, 7:96
　　Makushi, 7:219
　importance
　　Castilians, 4:59
　　Munda, 3:182
　tiled
　　Frisians, 4:110
Heart-stealing belief
　Hopi, 1:150
Heaven. *See* Afterlife
Heiress marriage
　Khasi, 3:124
Hell. *See* Afterlife
Hellenic Orthodox church. *See* Orthodox
　　Christianity
Hemophilia
　Amish, 1:19
Hemp growing
　Ozarks, 1:281

Páez, 7:257
Pomaks, 4:205
Shors, 6:329
Henna ceremony
　Jews of Algeria, 9:138
Heraldic emblem
　Kiowa, 1:189
Heraldry
　Kwakiutl, 1:200
Herbal, plant, and root medicine
　Acadian, 1:9
　Acholi, 9:6
　Afro-Venezuelans, 7:28
　Agta, 5:6
　Akha, 5:13
　Alur, 9:15
　Amahuaca, 7:33
　Ambae, 2:13
　Amuesha, 7:39
　Anambé, 7:43
　Angaité, 7:44
　Apiaká, 7:50
　Araucanians, 7:55
　Asmat, 2:21
　Asurini, 7:62
　Atoni, 5:28
　Aveyronnais, 4:26
　Aymara, 7:68
　Azerbaijani Turks, 6:50
　Azoreans, 4:28, 29
　Badaga, 3:18
　Bai, 6:421
　Bamiléké, 9:40
　Baniwa-Curripaco-Wakuenai, 7:80
　Basques, 4:32
　Bavarians, 4:35
　Bedouin, 9:46
　Belarussians, 6:61
　Belau, 2:27
　Boruca, Bribri, Cabécar, 8:27, 30
　Bretons, 4:40
　Bugis, 5:51
　Bugle, 8:34
　Bukidnon, 5:55
　Bulgarians, 4:45
　Burusho, 3:56
　Butonese, 5:69
　Cahita, 8:37
　Callahuaya, 7:90
　Canarians, 4:53
　Candoshi, 7:94
　Canela, 7:97
　Carib of Dominica, 8:40
　Central Yup'ik Eskimos, 1:59
　Chácobo, 7:107
　Chatino, 8:52
　Cherokee, 1:62
　Cheyenne, 1:66
　Chimane, 7:113
　Chin, 3:67
　Chinantec, 8:55
　Chinese in Caribbean, 8:58
　Chinese in Southeast Asia, 5:77
　Chipaya, 7:117
　Chiquitano, 7:118
　Chiriguano, 7:122
　Choctaw, 1:73
　Ch'ol, 8:66

Herbal, plant, and root medicine (cont'd)
  Chuj, 8:74
  Chumash, 1:73
  Chuvash, 6:85
  Cinta Larga, 7:129
  Circassians, 9:68
  Cook Islands, 2:42
  Craho, 7:138
  Cree, 1:81, 82
  Creoles of Nicaragua, 8:86
  Croats, 4:75
  Cubans, 8:90
  Culina, 7:148
  Czechs, 4:84
  Dai, 6:428
  Daribi, 2:48
  Delaware, 1:86
  Desana, 7:154
  Dogon, 9:73
  Dyula, 9:78
  Edo, 9:82
  Emberá, 7:158
  Endenese, 5:86
  Even, 6:119
  Evenki (Northern Tungus), 6:124
  Ewe and Fon, 9:88
  Ewenki, 6:434
  Falasha, 9:92
  Flemish, 4:109
  Gaels (Irish), 4:117
  Garo, 3:84
  Gayo, 5:90
  Gond, 3:87
  Greeks, 4:134
  Guajiro, 7:170
  Guarijío, 8:119
  Gusii, 9:110
  Haitians, 8:123
  Hakka, 6:439
  Hanunóo, 5:91
  Hare, 1:142
  Hill Pandaram, 3:100
  Hmong, 5:95
  Hoti, 7:176
  Huarayo, 7:179
  Hungarians, 4:145
  Irula, 3:108
  Iteso, 9:130
  Itza,' 8:135
  Jamaicans, 8:139
  Japanese, 5:110
  Jatav, 3:115
  Javanese, 5:113
  Jews of Iran, 9:141
  Jews of Kurdistan, 9:146
  Jingpo, 6:459
  Kaluli, 2:103
  Kapingamarangi, 2:108, 110
  Karachays, 6:162
  Karajá, 7:190, 191
  Karihona, 7:193
  Karok, 1:177
  Kashinawa, 7:197
  Kewa, 2:117
  Khevsur, 6:196
  Khinalughs, 6:201
  Khoi, 9:160
  Kickapoo, 1:185-186

  Kikapu, 8:145
  Kiribati, 2:123
  Klingit, 1:353
  Kmhmu, 5:141
  Kogi, 7:203
  Korean, 5:148
  Kota, 3:138
  Krikati/Pukobye, 7:206
  Kubachins, 6:219
  Kuikuru, 7:209
  Kumeyaay, 1:195
  Kuna, 8:150
  Kwakiutl, 1:200
  Ladinos, 8:153
  Lahu, 5:154;6:462, 463
  Lakalai, 2:142
  Lango, 9:181
  Lao Isan, 5:163
  Latinos, 1:206
  Lenca, 8:156
  Lezgins, 6:243
  Li, 6:464
  Lingayat, 3:153
  Lisu, 5:166;6:465
  Lunda, 9:199
  Maasai, 9:209
  Mafulu, 2:153
  Malay, 5:176
  Maliseet, 1:212
  Mam, 8:160
  Manchu, 6:467
  Mansi, 6:255
  Manus, 2:176
  Maori, 2:178
  Maris, 6:258
  Marshall Islands, 2:194
  Martiniquais, 8:164
  Marubo, 7:223
  Mataco, 7:229
  Matsigenka, 7:232
  Mazahua, 8:166
  Mazatec, 8:169
  Mehinaku, 7:239
  Melanau, 5:180
  Melpa, 2:202
  Miami, 1:232
  Miao, 6:472
  Micmac, 1:235
  Minangkabau, 5:184
  Mingrelians, 6:265
  Miskito, 8:172
  Mixe, 8:175
  Mixtec, 8:178
  Miyanmin, 2:212
  Mongo, 9:226
  Montserratians, 8:181
  Murik, 2:223
  Murngin, 2:227
  Nagas, 3:191
  Nahua of the Huasteca, 8:187
  Nahua of the State of Mexico, 8:188
  Nahuat of the Sierra de Puebla, 8:193
  Nambicuara, 7:247
  Nandi and other Kalenjin peoples, 9:234
  Nasioi, 2:235
  Naxi, 6:480
  Nayaka, 3:195, 196
  Ndembu, 9:240, 241

  Newar, 3:208
  Ngawbe, 8:198
  Nguna, 2:244
  Nias, 5:197
  Nivkh, 6:285
  Noanamá, 7:252
  Northern Paiute, 1:265
  Northern Shoshone and Bannock, 1:267
  Nyamwezi and Sukuma, 9:258
  Nyinba, 3:213
  Ogan-Besemah, 5:199
  Okiek, 9:262
  Old Believers, 1:274;6:294
  Oriya, 3:218
  Orochi, 6:295
  osage, 1:279
  Ossetes, 6:302
  Otavalo, 7:255
  Otomí of the Sierra, 8:203
  Otomí of the Valley of Mezquital, 8:206
  Ozarks, 1:282
  Pahari, 3:223
  Paï-Tavytera, 7:260
  Palu'e, 5:209
  Pandit of Kashmir, 3:226
  Paresí, 7:269
  Pemon, 7:273
  Pentecost, 2:264
  Piapoco, 7:274
  Piaroa, 7:278
  Piemontese Sinti, 4:201
  Pima Bajo, 8:214
  Pintupi, 2:267
  Piro, 7:280
  Pokot, 9:283
  Pomo, 1:296
  Popoloca, 8:216
  Provencal, 4:210-211
  Puerto Ricans, 8:223
  Qashqa'i, 9:287
  Q'eqchi,' 8:227
  Qiang, 6:485
  Rapa, 2:276
  Rikbaktsa, 7:288
  Romanians, 4:214
  Rukuba, 9:291
  Russian peasants, 6:313
  Rutuls, 6:321
  Saint Lucians, 8:232
  Sakalava, 9:298
  Salasaca, 7:291
  Saliva, 7:292
  Sambia, 2:286
  Samoa, 2:289
  Santal, 3:255
  Saraguro, 7:295
  Sarakatsani, 4:225
  Sea Islanders, 1:310-311
  Semang, 5:236
  Seminole of Oklahoma, 1:315
  Shahsevan, 9:310
  Sherpa, 3:260
  Shipibo, 7:306
  Shona, 9:314
  Siberiaki, 6:334
  Siberian Estonians, 6:337
  Sinhalese, 3:267
  Siona-Secoya, 7:308, 309

Siwai, 2:304
Slavey, 1:320
Slovaks, 4:245
Southern Paiute (and Chemehuevi), 1:332
Subanun, 5:246
Suku, 9:323
Sumu, 8:239
Suri, 9:326
Suya, 7:317
Svans, 6:346
Swahili, 9:329
Swazi, 9:332
Swedes, 4:258
Tabasarans, 6:350
Tagalog, 5:251
Tahiti, 2:307
Tai Lue, 5:256
Tairora, 2:310
Tajiks, 6:354
Tamil, 3:279
Tanaina, 1:337
Tandroy, 9:338
Tanna, 2:315
Tarahumara, 8:242
Tasmanians, 2:317
Tats, 6:360
Tauade, 2:320
Tausug, 5:264
Temiar, 5:272, 273
Terena, 7:327
Teton, 1:346
Tewa Pueblos, 1:349
Thakali, 3:292
Tibetans, 6:496
Ticuna, 7:330
Tikopia, 2:326
Tiv, 9:351
Tofalar, 6:364
Tojolab'al, 8:263
Tokelau, 2:333
Tolai, 2:335
Tonga, 9:355
Torres Strait Islanders, 2:347
Tory Islanders, 4:266
Totonac, 8:266
Trio, 7:336
Trobriand Islands, 2:351
Tsakhurs, 6:368
Tsimihety, 9:359
Tswana, 9:364
Tuareg, 9:369
Tubatulabal, 1:355
Tujia, 6:499
Turkana, 9:373
Tuvalu, 2:357
Tuvans, 6:374
Tzotzil and Tzeltal of Pantelhó, 8:278
Tz'utujil, 8:298
Ukrainian peasants, 6:388
Ukrainians, 6:393
Ute, 1:362
Vedda, 3:303
Vlachs, 4:275
Wa, 6:504
Wamira, 2:367
Wanano, 7:350
Waorani, 7:353
Wape, 2:372

Wapisiana, 7:356
Warao, 7:359
Warlpiri, 2:374
Washoe, 1:370
Wasteko, 8:304
Wayapi, 7:363-364
Western Shoshone, 1:375
Wik Mungkan, 2:379
Wiyot, 1:385
Wovan, 2:387
Xikrin, 7:369
Yagua, 7:374
Yakut, 6:407
Yanomamö, 7:377
Yao of Thailand, 5:293
Yap, 2:394
Yaqui, 8:307
Yawalapití, 7:380
Yi, 6:508
Yuit, 1:393
Yukateko, 8:310
Yukpa, 7:385
Yuqui, 7:394-395
Zande, 9:400
Zhuang, 6:511
Zoque, 8:317
Zuni, 1:400
Herd boy
    Tigray, 9:347
Herding
    Afar, 9:7
    Andalusians, 4:10
    Aveyronnais, 4:25
    Baggara, 9:29-30
    Basseri, 9:41
    Bedouin, 9:43
    Bosnian Muslims, 4:36
    Callahuaya, 7:88
    Castilians, 4:59
    Cornish, 4:65
    Cretans, 4:70, 71
    Dinka, 9:70
    Fulani, 9:101
    Kalasha, 3:116
    Kanuri, 9:151
    Karamojong, 9:157
    Khoi, 9:158
    Koya, 3:140
    Kurds, 9:175
    Lango, 9:179
    Leonese, 4:161
    Lur, 9:201-202
    Maasai, 9:207
    Montenegrins, 4:172
    Nandi and other Kalenjin peoples, 9:232
    Nepali, 3:202
    Nuer, 9:249
    Nyinba, 3:211
    Okiek, 9:259
    Ozarks, 1:281
    Pashai, 9:267
    Pasiegos, 4:188, 189, 190
    Peloponnesians, 4:193
    peripatetics of Afghanistan, Iran, and
        Turkey, 9:275
    peripatetics of the Maghreb, 9:278
    Qashqa'i, 9:285
    San-speaking peoples, 9:302

Sarakatsani, 4:223-224
Sardinians, 4:226, 227
Shahsevan, 9:308
Sherpa, 3:258
Sicilians, 4:236
Somalis, 9:316
Suri, 9:324
Swiss, Italian, 4:260
Tandroy, 9:336
Teda, 9:340
Tsakonians, 4:269
Tswana, 9:361
Tuareg, 9:367
Turkana, 9:371
Vlachs, 4:274-275
Yörük, 9:394
    see also Seminomads
Hereditary land ownership. See Inheritance;
        Landholding, hereditary
Hereditary leadership. See Leadership,
        hereditary
Hereditary priesthood. see Priests, hereditary
Hereditary servants
    Pahari, 3:220
    see also Slavery
Hereditary social position. See Castes;
        Nobility, Royalty; under Status, basis of
Heresy
    Occitans, 4:185
    Piemontes, 4:199
    Slav Macedonians, 4:241
    Yezdis, 6:408
Hermits
    Mount Athos, 4:175, 176
    Occitans, 4:185
Herring fishing
    Central Yup'ik Eskimos, 1:57
    Highland Scots, 4:139-140
    Kawkiutl, 1:198
    Klallam, 1:190
    Manx, 4:170
    Nootka, 1:256
    Shetlanders, 4:233
    Tlingit, 1:351
    Tory Islanders, 4:265
Hestanov (Cheyenne universe), 1:65
Hevehe (ceremony)
    Orokolo, 2:260
Hide
    clothing and furnishings
        North Alaskan Eskimos, 1:259
        Northern Piute, 1:263
        Northern Shoshone and Bannock, 1:266
        Pawnee, 1:284
        Tanaina, 1:335
        Taos, 1:342
        Thompson, 1:350
        Western Shoshone, 1:375
        Yuit, 1:390
    embroidery
        Mandan, 1:214
    manufacture
        Khoi, 9:159
    pictographic painting/ornamentation
        Teton, 1:345
    tanning
        Western Apache, 1:372
    trade

Hide (cont'd)
    Frisians, **4**:111
    Mandan, **1**:214
    Metis of Western Canada, **1**:227
    Montagnais-Naskapi, **1**:246
    Osage, **1**:277
    Seminole, **1**:312
    Yuit, **1**:390
    see also Fur trade; Leather work
    see also Deerskin trade; Leather work
Hierarchical deities
    Vedda, **3**:302, 303
Hierarchical society
    Abkhazians, **6**:8
    Afrikaners, **9**:9
    Amuzgo, **8**:5
    Andis, **6**:26
    Anuta, **2**:15
    Ata Sikka, **5**:21-22
    Atoni, **5**:28
    Austrians, **4**:20
    Avars, **6**:46
    Aveyronnais, **4**:26
    Azoreans, **4**:28
    Bahnar, **5**:30
    Bajau, **5**:33-34
    Balkars, **6**:54
    Barbadians, **8**:23
    Batak, **5**:40
    Belau, **2**:26
    Berbers of Morocco, **9**:51
    Bolaang Mongondow, **5**:43
    Bonerate, **5**:44, 45
    Bretons, **4**:39
    Bugis, **5**:50
    Burakumin, **5**:62
    Butonese, **5**:67, 68
    Castilians, **4**:60
    Catalans, **4**:63
    Central Thai, **5**:71
    Chakma, **3**:60
    Chamorros, **2**:34
    Chin, **3**:66
    Circassians, **6**:88
    Corsicans, **4**:67
    Crimean Tatars, **6**:93
    Dai, **6**:426
    East Indians in Trinidad, **8**:105
    Edo, **9**:81
    Futuna, **2**:67
    Garia, **3**:81
    Georgians, **6**:135
    Greeks, **4**:133
    Han, **6**:443-444
    Hawaiians, **2**:95, 96
    Hindu castes, **3**:57, 113
    Jamaicans, **8**:138
    Japanese, **5**:108
    Jat, **3**:112
    Javanese, **5**:112
    Jingpo, **6**:457-458
    Kachin, **5**:116, 118
    Kapingamarangi, **2**:110
    Karamojong, **9**:157
    Kenyah-Kayan-Kajang, **5**:134
    Khmer, **5**:137
    Kiribati, **2**:122
    Kolisuch'ok, **5**:141

Kosrae, **2**:128
Kpelle, **9**:174
Kshatriya, **3**:142
Kumeyaay, **1**:195
Kumyks, **6**:223
Kwakiutl, **1**:199
Lakher, **3**:146
Laki, **5**:154
Laks, **6**:233, 234
Lao Isan, **5**:162
Lau, **2**:144
Lhoba, **6**:464
Lisu, **5**:166
Luba of Shaba, **9**:192
Maguindanao, **5**:169
Maha Sabha as head
    East Indians in Trinidad, **8**:106
Makassar, **5**:173
Maltese, **4**:168
Manam, **2**:168
Mande, **9**:215
Manggarai, **5**:176
Maori, **2**:178
Marquesas Islands, **2**:189
Melanau, **5**:179
Mizo, **3**:178
Modang, **5**:186
Muong, **5**:191
Murut, **5**:193
Nayar, **3**:198, 199, 204
Newar, **3**:207
Nguna, **2**:244
Nias, **5**:196
Niue, **2**:251
Nomoi, **2**:252
Nootka, **1**:256, 257
Nuristanis, **9**:251
Nyinba, **3**:212
Oriya, **3**:217
Osage, **1**:278
Pacific Eskimo, **1**:283
Pahari, **3**:220-221, 222
Palu'e, **5**:207
Pende, **9**:273
Pentecost, **2**:263
peripatetics, **3**:234
Pohnpei, **2**:269
Portuguese, **4**:207-208
Pumi, **6**:483-484
Punjabi, **3**:239
Purum, **3**:244
Rajput, **3**:249
Samal, **5**:220
Sambia, **2**:285
Santal, **3**:253, 254
Sasak, **5**:226
Scheduled Castes and Scheduled Tribes, **3**:256-257
Selkup, **6**:327
Shan, **5**:240
Shuswap, **1**:317
Sidi, **3**:260
Slovenes, **4**:248
Spanish-type, **8**:242
Svans, **6**:343
Tagalog, **5**:248, 250
Tahiti, **2**:306
Tai Lue, **5**:254-255

Taiwan aboriginal peoples, **5**:257
Talysh, **6**:356
Tamil, **3**:278
Tausug, **5**:263-264
Teda, **9**:340
Telugu, **3**:286
Tetum, **5**:276
Tewa Pueblos, **1**:349
Tibetans, **6**:494
Tlingit, **1**:352
Toda, **3**:296-297
Tonga, **2**:338
Toraja, **5**:282
Trobriand Islands, **2**:350
Tsimshian, **1**:354
Untouchables, **3**:299
Vaisya, **3**:300
Vellala, **3**:303, 304, 305
Wa, **6**:501
Woleai, **2**:383-384
Wolof, **9**:379
Yakut, **6**:406
Yaqui, **8**:307
Yemenis, **9**:389
Yezidis, **6**:409
Yi, **6**:507
Yurok, **1**:395
see also Cargo system; Castes; Class mobility; Egalitarianism; Feudalism; Nobility; Patron-client system; Royalty; Sanskritization; Status, basis of
High-altitude agriculture. *See* Agriculture, high-altitude
Higher education. *See* Education
High god. *See* Creator
Highwaymen. *See* Brigandage
Hilap Inui (air deity)
    Copper Eskimo, **1**:79
Hillside farming. *See* Agriculture, terraced
Hill spirits
    Hill Pandaram, **3**:100
Hinayana Buddhism
    Dai, **6**:247
Hindu influences
    on Bene Israel, **3**:28
    on Bhil, **3**:42
    on Bhuiya, **3**:44
    on Bohra, **3**:48
    on Bondo, **3**:50, 51
    on Cochin Jews, **3**:73
    on Garia, **3**:81
    on Grasia, **3**:88
    on Gujar, **3**:88, 89
    on Gujar Muslims, **3**:88, 89
    on Gurung, **3**:95
    on Irula, **3**:108
    on Jain, **3**:109
    on Jat, **3**:113
    on Jatav, **3**:115
    on Khoja, **3**:127
    on Koya, **3**:139
    on Kurumbas, **3**:143
    on Limbu, **3**:150
    on Meo, **3**:174
    on Munda, **3**:184
    on Muslim, **3**:185
    on Nayaka, **3**:196
    on Nyinba, **3**:213

on Oraon, **3:**215
on Purum, **3:**244
on Rom of Czechoslovakia, **4:**219
on Santal, **3:**255
on Thakali, **3:**291-292
on Tharu, **3:**293
on Toda, **3:**297
on Vedda, **3:**302, 303
Hinduism
Ahir, **3:**7
Assamese, **3:**14
Badaga, **3:**15, 16, 17
Balinese, **5:**35, 37
Bania, **3:**24, 25
Barbadians, **8:**23
Bengali; **3:**29, 30, 31-32, 33, 34
Bengali Shakta, **3:**35-36
Bengali Vaishnava, **3:**36-37
Bhil, **3:**38, 40, 41
Bihari, **3:**46
Brahman, **3:**51
Brahman of Nepal, **3:**51, 53
Bugis, **5:**51
Butonese, **5:**66, 68
Central Thai, **5:**71
Cham, **5:**73
Chhetri of Nepal, **3:**51, 53
Chitpavan Brahman, **3:**70
Coorg, **3:**73
Dusun, **5:**80
East Indians in Trinidad, **8:**106
Gond, **3:**84, 85, 86
Guadeloupians, **8:**116
Gujar, **3:**89
Gujarati, **3:**91, 92
hijra, **3:**96, 97-98
Hindu, **3:**102
Indonesian, **5:**103
Jat, **3:**111, 112
Javanese, **5:**113
Kalasha, **3:**116
Kanarese, **3:**117
Kanbi, **3:**118
Khmer, **5:**137
Khoja converts, **3:**127
Kol, **3:**130, 131
Korku, **3:**133
Kota, **3:**137-138
Kshatriya, **3:**142
Lamaholot, **5:**155
Lao, **5:**159
Lingayat rejection of, **3:**151, 153
Mager, **3:**154-162
Mahar, **3:**165
Malay, **5:**176
Maratha, **3:**170
Mauritian, **3:**171, 172, 173
Nambudiri Braham, **3:**193-194
Nayar, **3:**199-200
Nepali, **3:**204-205
Newar, **3:**206, 207, 208
Oriya, **3:**217-218
Pahari, **3:**222-223
Pandit of Kashmir, **3:**224, 226
peripatetics, **3:**234-235, 236
Punjabi, **3:**241
Rajput, **3:**249
Sadhu, **3:**251-252

Sasak, **5:**225
Singaporean, **5:**242
Sinhalese, **3:**267
Sora, **3:**268, 270
South and Southeast Asians of Canada,
    1:324
South Asians in Southeast Asia, **5:**243
Sunwar, **3:**271
Tai Lue, **5:**255
Tamil, **3:**278, 279
Tamil of Sri Lanka, **3:**280-281, 283, 284
Telugu, **3:**286-287
Thakur, **3:**293
Trinidadians and Tobagonians, **8:**269
Untouchables, **3:**299
Vellala, **3:**303, 305-306
see also Brahman; Castes; Lingayatism;
    specific deities
Hinduism (Vaishnava)
Bania, **3:**25
Baul, **3:**26
Bengali, **3:**33, 36-37
Bondo, **3:**50
Hindu, **3:**102
Irula, **3:**108
Nayar, **3:**200
Nepali, **3:**204
Oriya, **3:**217-218
Telugu, **3:**287
Vellala, **3:**305
Hired labor. _See_ Wage labor
Hoa Hao (religion)
Vietnamese, **5:**286
Hobgoblins
Menominee, **1:**222
Hoe use. _See under_ Agriculture
Hogs. _See_ Pig _headings_
Holiday of the Flowers
Kubachins, **6:**219
Hololo (holiday)
Itelmen, **6:**154
Koryaks and Kerek, **6:**209
Holy Ground cult
Western Apache, **1:**373
Holy men
Maratha, **3:**170
see also Priesthood
Holy People (supernaturals)
Navajo, **1:**253
Holy Week
Cahita, **8:**37
Cora, **8:**76
Greeks, **4:**133
Maltese, **4:**169
Pima Bajo, **8:**213-214
Provencal, **4:**211
see also Easter
Holy well cults
Irish, **4:**153
Home industry. _See_ Cottage industry
Homeopathic medicine. _See under_ Medical
    practices and treatments
Home-repair trades
peripatetics, **1:**287
Homicide. _See_ Infanticide; Murder
"Homing." _See_ Living together
Homosexuality
Foi, **2:**60

Gebusi, **2:**77, 79
Kaluli, **2:**102
Keraki, **2:**114
Kiwai, **2:**126
Marind-anim, **2:**183, 184
Sambia, **2:**285
Honesty (as social virtue)
hijra, **3:**97
Honey
for beer
Kikuyu, **9:**161
Mbeere, **9:**221
for mead
Sakalava, **9:**298
medicinal use
Sarakatsani, **4:**225
symbolizing life
tropical-forest foragers, **9:**357
valued
Mbeere, **9:**221
for wine
Okiek, **9:**260
Honey collection
Ache, **7:**4
Araweté, **7:**56
Ayoreo, **7:**70
Chamacoco, **7:**108
Chiquitano, **7:**118
Chorote, **7:**124
Cinta Larga, **7:**127
Emerillon, **7:**159
Gorotire, **7:**162
Hoti, **7:**175
Irula, **3:**105
Kagwahiv, **7:**185
Kaingáng, **7:**186
Karajá, **7:**188
Konso, **9:**169
Kuikuru, **7:**207
Lengua, **7:**210
Mataco, **7:**228
Mocoví, **7:**240
Nayaka, **3:**194, 195
Okiek, **9:**259
Old Believers, **1:**273
Paï-Tavytera, **7:**259
Panare, **7:**265
Paresí, **7:**269
Piapoco, **7:**274
Piaroa, **7:**276
Rikbaktsa, **7:**287
Sakalava, **9:**293
Sirionó, **7:**310
Suruí, **7:**312
Tacana, **7:**318
Toba, **7:**331
Trio, **7:**335
Tunebo, **7:**338
Vedda, **3:**301
Xikrin, **7:**367
Xokléng, **7:**370
Yagua, **7:**372
Yawalapití, **7:**379
Yuqui, **7:**392
Honor code
Albanians, **4:**6
Andalusians, **4:**11

Honor code (cont'd)
  Baluchi, 3:23
  Calabrese, 4:50
  Castilians, 4:60
  Chechen-Ingush, 6:74-75
  Corsicans, 4:67, 68
  Cypriots, 4:80-81
  Dalmatians, 4:87
  Falasha, 9:92
  Ionians, 4:150
  Klingit, 1:352
  Latinos, 1:205
  Montenegrins, 4:173
  Pathan, 3:232-233
  Sarakatsani, 4:224
  Sardinians, 4:227
  Sicilians, 4:236
  Yemenis, 9:390
  see also Blood feud
Hóriómu (ceremony)
  Kiwai, 2:126
Horn work
  Oriya, 3:218
  Saami, 4:221, 258
Horse
  for bison hunting
    Northern Shoshone and Bannock,
      1:266
    Pawnee, 1:284
  as groom's gift to in-laws
    Teton, 1:345
  importance
    Assiniboin, 1:27
    Kiowa, 1:186, 187, 188
    Klamath, 1:192
    Taos, 1:342
    Teton, 1:346
  as pleasure animal
    Northern Paiute, 1:263
  as prestige symbol
    Kanuri, 9:151
    Winnebago, 1:381
  women proscribed from working with
    Lowland Scots, 4:163
Horse Dance
  Teton, 1:346
Horse racing
  Circassians, 6:88
  Ewenki, 6:434
  Kalmyks, 6:157
  Khevsur, 6:197
  Khinalughs, 6:201
  Tabasarans, 6:349
  Yakut, 6:407
Horse raising
  Altaians, 6:21
  Belarussians, 6:60
  Buriats, 6:66
  Circassians, 6:88
  Daur, 6:429
  Don Cossacks, 6:104
  Evenki (Northern Tungus), 6:121
  Ewenki, 6:433
  Gypsies, 6:146
  Kalmyks, 6:155, 156
  Kazak, 6:460
  Kazakhs, 6:176-177
  Ket, 6:183

Khanty, 6:190
Kiowa, 1:187
Kirgiz, 6:461
Kumyks, 6:221
Kyrgyz, 6:229
Laks, 6:234
Lezgins, 6:242
Lisu, 5:164
Mansi, 6:253
Maris, 6:257
Mocoví, 7:240
Mulam, 6:476
Nu, 6:481
Otavalo, 7:253
Rotinese, 5:213
Sasak, 5:226
Siberiaki, 6:333
Siberian Tatars, 6:341
Tacana, 7:318
Tagalog, 5:249
Terena, 7:325
Toba, 7:331
Tsakhurs, 6:365
Uzbeks, 6:396
Yakut, 6:405, 406
Yao of Thailand, 5:291
Horse smuggling
  Slovenes, 4:247
Horse trading
  Bulgarian Gypsies, 4:41
  Gypsies and caravan dwellers in the
    Netherlands, 4:137
  Hidatsa, 1:146
  Kickapoo, 1:184
  Kiowa, 1:187
  Osage, 1:277
  peripatetics, 1:287
  Piemontese Sinti, 4:200
  Rom, 1:304
  Rominche, 4:216
  Slovensko Roma, 4:250
  Vlach Gypsies of Hungary, 4:271
Horticulture. See Agriculture; Flower industry;
    Gardening; specific crops
Hospitality (as social virtue)
  Abkhazians, 6:8
  Andis, 6:24
  Armenians, 6:29, 30
  Balkars, 6:53
  Chechen-Ingush, 6:73, 74
  Circassians, 6:89
  Don Cossacks, 6:106
  Dungans, 6:110
  Evenki (Northern Tungus), 6:122
  Georgians, 6:134
  Gypsies, 6:147
  Ingilos, 6:150
  Karachays, 6:161
  Khinalughs, 6:198
  Kumyks, 6:221
  Mountain Jews, 6:273
  Nayaka, 3:195
  Nogays, 6:289
  Pamir peoples, 6:304
  Tamil, 3:278
  Turkmens, 6:371
  Volga Tatars, 6:400
  Yukagir, 6:413

Hostage-taking
  Balkars, 6:52
Hostility. See Aggressiveness; Warfare
Hosts of the Lord
  Romanians, 4:214
Hotels
  Basque, 1:33, 34
  Vlachs, 4:274
Household
  adult siblings' rights
    Highland Scots, 4:141
  adult siblings
    Northern Irish, 4:179
  ambilocal extended family
    Quechan, 1:301
  as autonomous religious community
    Sarakatsani, 4:224
  communal
    Albanians, 4:5, 6
    Andalusians, 4:11
    Bengali, 3:32
    Chakma, 3:59
    Cypriots, 4:80
    hijra, 3:97
    Jatav, 3:114
    Kanjar, 3:121
    Leonese, 4:161
    Mandan, 1:214
    Mescalero Apache, 1:225
    Montagnais-Naskapi, 1:245
    Nicobarese, 3:209
    Oriya, 3:217
    Punjabi, 3:239
    Rom, 1:305
    Walapai, 1:365
    see also Family, extended
  co-resident
    Tzotzil of San Bartolomé de los Llanos,
      8:289
  council representation
    Leonese, 4:161
  co-wives in separate locations
    Nuer, 9:250
  dominant male head
    Highland Scots, 4:141
    Portuguese, 4:207
  as economic unit
    Auvergnats, 4:22
    Aveyronnais, 4:25
    Azoreans, 4:28
    Bosnian Muslims, 4:36
    Bulgarians, 4:44
    Catalans, 4:62
    Croats, 4:73
    Flemish, 4:106-107
    Garo, 3:82, 83
    Highland Scots, 4:140, 141
    Kashubians, 4:158-159
    Kwakiutl, 1:199
    Mizo, 3:178
    Nambudiri Brahman, 3:193
    Navajo, 1:252
    North Alaskan Eskimos, 1:260
    Nyinba, 3:212
    Old Believers, 1:274
    Ozarks, 1:281
    Pandit of Kashmir, 3:225
    Pathan, 3:232

peripatetics, 3:235
Piemontese Sinti, 4:200
Polynesians, 1:292
Rom of Czechoslovakia, 4:219
Serbs, 4:231
extended family. _See_ Family, extended
flexible
Irish Travellers, 4:156
Sakalava, 9:296
frequent residency shifts
Washoe, 1:369
groups
Montagnais-Naskapi, 1:245
Piemontese Sinti, 4:200
hearth group
Barí, 7:84-85
Canela, 7:96
Makushi, 7:219
lodgers
Northern Irish, 4:179
Pasiegos, 4:190
male and female head
Sardinians, 4:226
male authority. _See_ Patriarchal family
structure
married couple joint headship
Portuguese, 4:207
maternal lineage
Zuni, 1:398
matrilineally related women of several
generations
Western Apache, 1:372
ménage definitions
Provencal, 4:211
as most important social institution
Sardinians, 4:226, 227
multifamily
Tswana, 9:363
multigenerational
Micronesians, 1:237
nuclear family. _See_ Family, nuclear
as political unit
Matsigenka, 7:232
self-sufficient
Kashubians, 4:159
single-parent
Burakumin, 5:61
Evenki (Northern Tungus), 6:122
Japanese, 5:107-108
Khmer, 5:137
Latvians, 6:237
Poles, 4:203
Russians, 6:316
Sea Islanders, 1:310
single-person
Japanese, 5:107
Swiss, Italian, 4:261
single woman as head
Tonga, 9:354
Tswana, 9:363
strong relationships to paternal
Rom, 1:304
three-generational stem
Aveyronnais, 4:25
Basques, 4:31
Bulgarians, 4:44
Canarians, 4:52
Cape Verdeans, 4:55

Catalans, 4:62, 63
Croats, 4:73
Cypriot, 4:80
Cypriots, 4:80
Dalmatians, 4:86, 86-87
Danes, 4:89, 90
Greeks, 4:133
Kashubians, 4:159
Mixe, 8:174
Ndebele, 9:236-237
North Alaskan Eskimos, 1:260
Northern Irish, 4:179
Norwegians, 4:181
Poles, 4:203
Portuguese, 4:207
Romanians, 4:214
Slovenes, 4:248
Tewa Pueblos, 1:348
Tuscans, 4:270
Ute, 1:361
three-to-four generations
Pomo, 1:294
Potawatomi, 1:297
two-generation
Vlach Gypsies of Hungary, 4:272
variable
Chagga, 9:62
visiting relatives
Seminole, 1:313
women as head
Antigua and Barbuda, 8:9
Awakateko, 8:16
Latinos, 1:205
Martiniquais, 8:163
Sea Islanders, 1:310
Tojolab'al, 8:261
Tonga, 9:354
Tswana, 9:363
see also Family; Residence (newly married)
Household gods
Baiga, 3:21
Brahman and Chhetri of Nepal, 3:53
Chitpavan Brahman, 3:70
Limbu, 3:151
Mikir, 3:176
Munda, 3:184
Pahari, 3:222
House religion
Bemba, 9:47
Houses and housing
adjacent connected
North Alaskan Eskimos, 1:260
adobe
Fali, 9:94
Kongo, 9:167
Lenca, 8:155
Luba of Shaba, 9:191
Mam, 8:158
Mixe, 8:174
Mixtec, 8:176
Mossi, 9:228, 229
Pima Bajo, 8:210
Poqomam, 8:218
Pueblo Indians, 1:298
Taos, 1:341
Temne, 9:342
Tepehuan of Durango, 8:256
Tewa Pueblos, 1:347

Tuareg, 9:367
Zoque, 8:315
Zuni, 1:397
alignment
Irula, 3:104
arranged according to married sons' birth
order
Luyia, 9:203
arranged in circle
Bororo, 7:87
Chamacoco, 7:108
Craho, 7:136
Gorotire, 7:162
Krikati/Pukobye, 7:203-204
Kuikuru, 7:207
Mehinaku, 7:236
Saami, 4:220
Suya, 7:315
Tapirapé, 7:321
Yawalapití, 7:378
arrangement denoting status
Maltese, 4:167
bachelor
Chiquitano, 7:118
Kipsigis, 9:164
Luyia, 9:203
Shavante, 7:301
Sherente, 7:302
Tonga, 9:354
see also Dormitories
bamboo
Chakma, 3:58
Chenchu, 3:61
Grasia, 3:88
Hill Pandaram, 3:99
Kuna, 8:147
banana husk roof
Mixtec, 8:176
bark-covered
Shawnee, 1:317
Winnebago, 1:380
below-ground tunnel entrance
Yuit, 1:390
boat
Bajau, 5:30-35
brick
Shona, 9:312
Turks, 9:375
Vlachs, 4:274
Walloons, 4:276
brick and stucco
Serbs, 4:230
brick and stucco
Black Creoles of California, 1:38
burned brick
Kongo, 9:167
cane
Poqomam, 8:218
caravan
Gypsies and caravan dwellers in the
Netherlands, 4:136-138
Irish Travellers, 4:155
Ozarks, 1:281
peripatetics, 1:287
Piemontese Sinti, 4:200
Rominche, 4:216
Slovensko Roma, 4:250
Xoraxané Romá, 4:281

Houses and housing (cont'd)
  cave-dwelling
    Mount Athos, 4:175, 176
    Tasaday, 5:259-261
    Western Shoshone, 1:374
  ceilidhe
    Northern Ireland, 4:178
  cement
    Tandroy, 9:336
    Temne, 9:342
    Tzotzil of Chamula, 8:279
  ceremonial hut
    Paresí, 7:269
  around church
    Maltese, 4:167
    Nahua of the State of Mexico, 8:188
  circular
    Luyia, 9:203
    Mbeere, 9:220
    Mossi, 9:228
    Pawnee, 1:284
    Swazi, 9:330
  circular brush
    Walapai, 1:364
    Western Shoshone, 1:374
  circular domed brush- and mud-covered
    Tubatulabal, 1:355
  clay
    Kurds, 9:175
  clay-brick
    Suku, 9:321
  cliff dwellings
    Pueblo Indians, 1:298
  close together
    Highland Scots, 4:139
  clustered, 1:263
  coconut-palm roof
    Zaramo, 9:401
  communal
    Hutterites, 1:153
    Yokuts, 1:388
  compound around parental yard
    Sea Islanders, 1:310
  concentric
    Maltese, 4:167
  concrete
    Tswana, 9:361
    Yoruba, 9:391
  concrete block
    Tory Islanders, 4:265
  conical
    Ojibwa, 1:269
    Okanagon, 1:272
    Washoe, 1:368
    Western Shoshone, 1:374
  cooking porch
    Pima Bajo, 8:210
  coral block
    Swahili, 9:327
  cottages
    Black Creoles of California, 1:38
    Cajun, 1:49
    Cape Coloureds, 9:59
  croft
    Highland Scots, 4:139
  domed
    Northern Paiute, 1:263
    Sarakatsani, 4:223

    Washoe, 1:368
  as dowry provision
    Ionians, 4:149, 150
    Peloponnesians, 4:193
    Sicilians, 4:236
  earth-covered
    Pima-Papago, 1:288
  earth-covered log
    Navajo, 1:252
  earthlodge settlements
    Arikara, 1:26
    Hidatsa, 1:146
    Klamath, 1:192
    Lillooet, 1:206
    Luiseño, 1:208
    Mandan, 1:213
    Omaha, 1:275
    Pawnee, 1:284
    Shuswap, 1:318
    see also subhead semisubterranean
  earthquake-resistant
    Tz'utujil, 8:297
  east-facing entrance
    Chipaya, 7:115
    Washoe, 1:368
    Xhosa, 9:381
  east-to-west orientation
    Tunebo, 7:337
  elevated
    Sakalava, 9:293
  expensive
    Japanese, 5:107
  extended porches
    Awakateko, 8:15
  flat roof
    Jews of Iran, 9:140
    Kurds, 9:175
    Maltese, 4:167
    Turks, 9:375
  frame
    Central Yup'ik Eskimos, 1:56
    Ojibwa, 1:269
  German village-style
    Mennonites, 7:239
  government projects
    Irish Travellers, 4:155
  grandparent quarters
    Northern Irish, 4:179
    Norwegians, 4:181
  grass
    Kanuri, 9:152
    San-speaking peoples, 9:302
    Suku, 9:321
    Tuareg, 9:367
  grass roof
    Popoluca, 8:216
    Tepehuan of Durango, 8:256
  hardpan blocks
    Popoloca, 8:216
  hearth importance
    Castilians, 4:59
    Munda, 3:182
    Sarakatsani, 4:223
  hillside
    Kurds, 9:175
    Occitan, 4:184
  hilltop
    Marubo, 7:221-222

hip roof
  Ngawbe, 8:195
house naming
  Nayar, 3:197
iron roof
  Alur, 9:13
  Edo, 9:79
  Ewe and Fon, 9:84
  Gusii, 9:108
  Kongo, 9:167
  Tandroy, 9:336
  Temne, 9:342
  Zande, 9:397
jungle
  Sora, 3:268, 269
kitchen of primary importance
  Afro-Venezuelans, 7:26
  Guambiano, 7:171
kitchen separate
  Afro-Bolivians, 7:8
  Akawaio, 7:31
  Callahuaya, 7:88
  Cariña, 7:102
  Cotopaxi Quichua, 7:132
  Guajiro, 7:168
  Nahua of the Huasteca, 8:185
  Paraujano, 7:268
  Sharanahua, 7:299
  Shipibo, 7:304
kitchen for women and children
  Kipsigis, 9:164
leaf shelters
  Hill Pandram, 3:99
limestone
  Palestinians, 9:265
limestone blocks
  Maltese, 4:167
log cabins
  Central Yup'ik Eskimos, 1:56
  Cree, 1:80
  Dogrib, 1:88
  Kutchin, 1:196
  Mixtec, 8:176
  Ojibwa, 1:269
  Shuswap, 1:318
  Tanaina, 1:335
  Tanana, 1:338
  Triqui, 8:270
  Vlachs, 4:274
longhouse
  Achumawi, 1:9
  Algonkin, 1:17
  East Greenland Inuit, 1:106
  Iroquois, 1:165, 166
  Kwakiutl, 1:198
  Lillooet, 1:206
  Nootka, 1:255, 257
  Shawnee, 1:317
  Tlingit, 1:351, 352
  West Greenland Inuit, 1:376
  Wichita, 1:379
married children's quarters
  Sicilians, 4:236
  Slovaks, 4:244
mat
  Cape Coloureds, 9:59
  Khoi, 9:158, 159
metal roof

Iraqw, 9:124
Lango, 9:178
Luba of Shaba, 9:191
Mossi, 9:228
Zande, 9:397
millet stalks
    Wolof, 9:378
mud
    Arabs, 9:24
    Baggara, 9:29
    Bamiléké, 9:37
    Dinka, 9:70
    Edo, 9:79
    Ewe and Fon, 9:84
    Igbo, 9:122
    Iraqw, 9:124
    Jews of Iran, 9:140
    Kanuri, 9:152
    Lugbara, 9:194
    Luyia, 9:204
    Mbeere, 9:220
    Ndebele, 9:236
    Ndembu, 9:239
    Palestinians, 9:265
    Rukuba, 9:290
    Shilluk, 9:310
    Somalis, 9:316
    Tswana, 9:361
    Yoruba, 9:391
    Zarma, 9:404
mud-brick
    Bulgarians, 4:43
mud-cornstalk
    Tzotzil and Tzeltal of Pantelhó, 8:276
mud-mule dung
    Sarakatsani, 4:223
mud-reed-mesquite
    Yaqui, 8:306
mud-thatch
    tropical-forest foragers, 9:356
multifamily
    Apiaká, 7:48
    Asurini, 7:61
    Avars, 6:44
    Bajau, 5:33
    Baniwa-Curripaco-Wakuenai, 7:77
    Barí, 7:83
    Batak, 5:39
    Bukharan Jews, 6:64
    Bukidnon, 5:53
    Canelos Quichua, 7:100
    Cariña, 7:102
    Cashibo, 7:104
    Chambri, 2:32
    Chiriguano, 7:120
    Cubeo, 7:140
    Culina, 7:146
    Dariba, 2:46
    De'ang, 6:430
    Desana, 7:152, 153
    Drung, 6:432
    Dusun, 5:80
    Gayo, 5:88
    Gebusi, 2:77
    Gogodala, 2:83, 84
    Huarayo, 7:177, 178
    Iban, 5:96
    Ilongot, 5:101

Jivaro, 7:182
Kachin, 5:115
Kalimantan Dayaks, 5:120
Karen, 5:126
Karihona, 7:192
Kashinawa, 7:195
Ka'wiari, 7:198, 199
Kenyah-Kayan-Kajang, 5:133
Kerintji, 5:134
Kiwai, 2:124
Koryaks and Kerek, 6:209
Kyrgyz, 6:230
Lahu, 6:462
Lengua, 7:210
Macuna, 7:212
Maguindanao, 5:170
Maranao, 5:177
Mashco, 7:225
Mayoruna, 7:234
Melanau, 5:178
Mendi, 2:205
Mimika, 2:207
Minangkabau, 5:183
Montagnais-Naskapi, 1:245
Moré, 7:243
Murut, 5:193
Ngeh, 5:194
Nootka, 1:255
Pacific Eskimo, 1:283
Palaung, 5:201
Panare, 7:265
Paresí, 7:269
Pawnee, 1:284, 285
Piaroa, 7:276
Rhadé, 5:211
Romanians, 4:213
Sedang, 5:230
Senoi, 5:237
Sirionó, 7:310
Tanaina, 1:335
Tanimuka, 7:319
Taos, 1:341
Tatuyo, 7:322, 323
Ticuna, 7:328
Tlingit, 1:351
Tupari, 7:339
Volga Tatars, 6:401
Waimiri-Atroari, 7:342
Wáiwai, 7:346
Wanano, 7:350
Waorani, 7:351-352
Waropen, 2:376
Waurá, 7:360
Winnebago, 1:381
Witoto, 7:365
Xikrin, 7:367
Yagua, 7:372
Yanomamö, 7:375
Yawalapití, 7:378
Yekuana, 7:381
Yukuna, 7:386
multiple house ownership
    Aymara, 7:66
    Kogi, 7:201
multistoried
    Taos, 1:341
open central space
    Leonese, 4:160

open pole-framed
    Mohave, 1:240
outside living
    Nayaka, 3:195
oval-shaped
    Yokuts, 1:387
palm-frond
    Ewe and Fon, 9:84
    Sakalava, 9:293
    Yakö, 9:383
palm roof
    Q'eqchi,' 8:226
    Zoque, 8:315
patio
    Mossi, 9:229
pay-as-you-go building of
    Serbs, 4:230
on pilings
    Miskito, 8:171
plank
    Comox, 1:76
    Cowichan, 1:79
    Tsimshian, 1:355
pole
    Mbeere, 9:220
    Ngawbe, 8:195
    Seminole, 1:312, 313
    Zaramo, 9:401
pole walls
    Pame, 8:207
    Q'anjob'al, 8:225
    Q'eqchi,' 8:226
portable huts
    Somalis, 9:316
proximal
    Bene Israel, 3:28
public housing
    Puerto Ricans, 8:221
pueblo. See subhead adobe above
quadrangular
    Mazatec, 8:168
raised
    Afro-Colombians, 7:16
    Emberá, 7:155
    Emerillon, 7:159
    Huarayo, 7:177
    Paraujano, 7:268
    Seminole, 1:312, 313
    Sharanahua, 7:299
    Warao, 7:357
    Yagua, 7:372
    Yukuna, 7:386
reception huts
    Tiv, 9:350
red-tile roofs
    Occitans, 4:184
    Provencals, 4:210
redwood rectangular
    Wiyot, 1:384
reed
    Khoi, 9:158, 159
religious/ceremonial function
    Païa-Tavytera, 7:259
representing world
    Tanimuka, 7:319
    Tzotzil of San Andrés Larraínzar, 8:284
roofing as status indicator
    Nagas, 3:190

Houses and housing (cont'd)
  rope-tied decorations
    Yap, 2:394
  round
    Fali, 9:94
    Iraqw, 9:124
    Khoi, 9:158
    Lozi, 9:187
    Lugbara, 9:194
    Mossi, 9:229
    Nandi and other Kalenjin peoples, 9:232
    Ngawbe, 8:195
    San-speaking peoples, 9:302
  round windowless
    Gusii, 9:108
  in row
    Guajajára, 7:167
    Walloons, 4:276
    Welsh, 4:279
  sapling frame
    Khoi, 9:158
  scattered
    Yakan, 5:288
  seasonal
    Andamanese, 3:9
    Ayoreo, 7:69
    Chuvans, 6:81
    Cuiva, 7:143
    Hidsata, 1:146
    Itelmen, 6:152
    Kikapu, 8:143-144
    Kwakiutl, 1:198
    Metis of Western Canada, 1:226, 227
    Miami, 1:230
    Mohave, 1:240
    Montenegrins, 4:172
    Navajo, 1:251
    Nootka, 1:255, 257
    North Alaskan Eskimos, 1:259
    Ojibwa, 1:269
    Okanagon, 1:272
    Ottawa, 1:279
    Pacific Eskimo, 1:283
    Pawnee, 1:284
    Potawatomi, 1:297
    Santee, 1:307
    Sarakatsani, 4:223
    Swiss, Italian, 4:260
    Tanaina, 1:335
    Tanana, 1:338
    Teton, 1:344
    Toda, 3:295
    Tubatulabal, 1:355
    Ute, 1:360
    Vlachs, 4:274
    Western Shoshone, 1:374
    West Greenland Inuit, 1:376
    Wichita, 1:379
    Yuqui, 7:391
  second or summer houses
    Highland Scots, 4:139
    Lillooet, 1:206
    Pahari, 3:220
    Swiss, Italian, 4:261
    Yuit, 1:390
  semisubterranean
    Achumawi, 1:9
    Ahtna, 1:14

    Aleut, 1:15
    Central Yup'ik Eskimos, 1:56
    Frisians, 4:110
    Ingalik, 1:156
    Karok, 1:176
    Klamath, 1:191
    Kutchin, 1:196
    Labrador Inuit, 1:201
    Luiseño, 1:208
    North Alaskan Eskimos, 1:259
    Okanagon, 1:272
    Pacific Eskimo, 1:283
    Shuswap, 1:318
    Tanaina, 1:335
    Thompson, 1:350
    Yuit, 1:390
  sexually segregated. See Dormitories;
      Gender-specific housing
  single-room
    Bamiléké, 9:37
    Nahua of the Huasteca, 8:185
    Nahuat of the Sierra de Puebla, 8:191
    Pame, 8:207
    Q'eqchi,' 8:226
    San-speaking peoples, 9:302
    Tzotzil of Zinacantan, 8:292
    Zoque, 8:315
  slate roof
    Tory Islanders, 4:265
  sleeping
    Kuna, 8:147
    Lango, 9:178
    Nahua of the Huasteca, 8:185
  small windows
    Montenegrins, 4:172
  snow
    Caribou Inuit, 1:51
    Copper Eskimo, 1:76-77
  sod
    Aleu, 1:15
    Central Yup'ik Eskimos, 1:56
    see also subhead earthlodge settlements
      above
  steam bath
    Mazatec, 8:168
  stick walls
    Popoluca, 8:216
  stone
    Albanians, 4:4
    Azoreans, 4:27
    Basques, 4:30
    Bedouin, 9:43
    Galicians, 4:119
    Kurds, 9:175
    Montenegrins, 4:172
    Palestinians, 9:265
    Provencal, 4:210
    Tory Islanders, 4:265
    Turks, 9:375
  stone and peat
    West Greenland Inuit, 1:376
  stone cabaña
    Pasiegos, 4:190, 191
  straw roof
    Zarma, 9:404
  subterranean
    Aleuts, 6:18
    Armenians, 6:29

    Asiatic Eskimos, 6:39
    Balkars, 6:52
    Chukchee, 6:77
    Even, 6:117
    Iraqw, 9:124
    Itelmen, 6:152
    Ket, 6:184
    Khanty, 6:190
    Koryaks and Kerek, 6:208, 209
    Kurds, 6:226
    Nivkh, 6:283
    Siberian Tatars, 6:341
    Taiwan aboriginal peoples, 5:257, 258
  temporary
    Western Shoshone, 1:374
  tents
    Altaians, 6:21, 22
    Balkars, 6:52
    Basseri, 9:41
    Bedouin, 9:43
    Buriats, 6:66
    Chukchee, 6:77
    Dolgan, 6:100
    Even, 6:117
    Evenki (Northern Tungus), 6:121
    Ewenki, 6:433
    Ghorbat, 9:106
    Irish Travellers, 4:155
    Kalmyks, 6:157
    Kanjar, 3:119-120, 121
    Kazak, 6:460
    Kazakhs, 6:176
    Ket, 6:183
    Khakas, 6:187
    Khanty, 6:190
    Kirgiz, 6:461
    Koryaks and Kerek, 6:208
    Kurds, 6:226;9:175
    Lur, 9:202
    Mongols, 6:474
    Nenets, 6:278
    Nganasan, 6:280-281
    Nivkh, 6:283-284
    Nogays, 6:287
    Orok, 6:296
    Oroquen, 6:482
    Pathan, 3:231
    Qalandar, 3:246, 247
    Qashqa'i, 9:285
    Saami, 4:220;6:323
    Shors, 6:329
    Sleb, 9:315
    Tajik, 6:492
    Tatars, 6:492
    Tofalar, 6:362
    Tuareg, 9:367
    Turkmens, 6:369
    Tuvans, 6:373
    Xoraxané Romá, 4:281
    Yukagir, 6:413
  tents (black felt)
    Vlachs, 4:274
  tents (canvas)
    Copper Eskimo, 1:77
    Dogrib, 1:88
    Kutchin, 1:196
    Labrador Inuit, 1:201
    Shuswap, 1:318

Tanaina, **1:**335
Tanana, **1:**338
tent (sealskin)
West Greenland Inuit, **1:**376
tents (skin)
Tanana, **1:**338
tents (temporary)
Kyrgyz, **6:**229
terraced
Iroquois, **1:**165
Nahua of the State of Mexico, **8:**188
terra-cotta
Bengali, **3:**34
thatched
Mbeere, **9:**220
Tswana, **9:**361
Yoruba, **9:**391
Zande, **9:**397
Zarma, **9:**404
thatched roof
Andamanese, **3:**9
Baggara, **9:**29
Bamiléké, **9:**37
Chenchu, **3:**61
Dinka, **9:**70
Ewe and Fon, **9:**84
Fali, **9:**94
Gaels (Irish), **4:**115
Gusii, **9:**108
Hill Pandaram, **3:**99
Igbo, **9:**122
Iraqw, **9:**124
Kanuri, **9:**152
Kashubians, **4:**158
Kongo, **9:**167
Kota, **3:**135
Kpelle, **9:**172
Kuna, **8:**147
Lango, **9:**178
Lenca, **8:**155
Lozi, **9:**187
Luyia, **9:**203
Magar, **3:**155
Mossi, **9:**228, 229
Nahua of the Huasteca, **8:**185
Nandi and other Kalenjin peoples, **9:**232
Nayaka, **3:**195
Ndebele, **9:**236
Ndembu, **9:**239
Nicobarese, **3:**209
Paniyan, **3:**227
Popoloca, **8:**216
Poqomam, **8:**218
Q'anjob'al, **8:**225
San-speaking peoples, **9:**302
Sarakatsani, **4:**223
Seminole, **1:**312
Shilluk, **9:**310
Sinhalese, **3:**265
Somalis, **9:**316
Sora, **3:**268
Sorbs, **4:**252
Tandroy, **9:**336
Tory Islanders, **4:**265
Tzotzil and Tzeltal of Pantelhó, **8:**276
Wolof, **9:**378
Zaramo, **9:**401
tile roof

Popoloca, **8:**216
Serbs, **4:**230
Slovenes, **4:**247
Temne, **9:**342
Tzotzil of Chamula, **8:**279
tin
Sakalava, **9:**293
tin roof
Bamiléké, **9:**37
Pedi, **9:**269
Somalis, **9:**316
Suku, **9:**321
Tswana, **9:**361
Yoruba, **9:**391
tipis
Arapaho, **1:**26
Assiniboin, **1:**27
Comanche, **1:**75
Copper Eskimo, **1:**77
Crow, **1:**83
Dogrib, **1:**88
Eastern Shoshone, **1:**104, 105
Kiowa, **1:**189
Naskapi, **1:**244
Northern Shoshone and Bannock, **1:**266
Omaha, **1:**275
Pawnee, **1:**284
Sarsi, **1:**308
Teton, **1:**344, 345
Thompson, **1:**350
Tonkawa, **1:**354
Wichita, **1:**379
trailers. _See subhead_ caravan _above_
two-level
Konso, **9:**169
two-room
Kongo, **9:**167
Nandi and other Kalenjin peoples, **9:**232
Ndembu, **9:**239
Suku, **9:**321
Tepehuan of Durango, **8:**256
walled
Aymara, **7:**66
Ionians, **4:**149
without walls
Seminole, **1:**312
walrus-hide covered
Yuit, **1:**390
wattle and daub
Betsileo, **9:**54
Kongo, **9:**167
Kpelle, **9:**172
Lozi, **9:**187
Nandi and other Kalenjin peoples, **9:**232
San-speaking peoples, **9:**302
Seri, **8:**233
Suku, **9:**321
Tigray, **9:**347
Yakö, **9:**383
wattle and thatch
Lugbara, **9:**194
wedding
Baggara, **9:**30
as wedding gift
Sherpa, **3:**259
on wheels
Nogays, **6:**287
wickiup

Western Apache, **1:**371
Western Shoshone, **1:**374
wigwam
Delaware, **1:**85
Maliseet, **1:**210
Montagnais, **1:**244
Ojibwa, **1:**269
Osage, **1:**277
Winnebago, **1:**380, 381
windowless
Araweté, **7:**56
windows of seal intestines
West Greenland Inuit, **1:**376
wood-beamed
Sarakatsani, **4:**223
wooden
Popoloca, **8:**216
Seri, **8:**233
Yakö, **9:**383
wood plank
Tandroy, **9:**336
Yurok, **1:**394
woodwork carved and painted
Sorbs, **4:**252
zinc roof
Kpelle, **9:**172
Shona, **9:**312
Tigray, **9:**347
Yoruba, **9:**391
see also Dormitories; Gender-specific
housing; Men's houses
Hukdar (lineage tracer)
Magar, **3:**157
Human body. _See_ Body _headings_
Human figure representation
Nagas, **3:**191
Human sacrifice. _See_ Sacrifice, human
Humility (as social virtue)
Old Believers, **1:**274
Shakers, **1:**316
Tanana, **1:**339
Tewa Pueblos, **1:**349
Humor
aggressive
Mimika, **2:**207
Murik, **2:**222
as art form
Andis, **6:**27
Bau, **2:**24
Tokelau, **2:**331, 332
see also Joking
Hungry Ghosts (festival)
Chinese in Southeast Asia, **5:**77
Hunters
booty sharing
West Greenland Inuit, **1:**378
as castelike group
Teda, **9:**340
supernatural abilities
tropical-forest foragers, **9:**357
see also under Leadership qualities
Hunting
Agta, **5:**4, 5
Ainu, **5:**7, 8
Akha, **5:**11
Aleuts, **6:**18
Altaians, **6:**21
Alur, **9:**13

Hunting (cont'd)
  Anuak, **9:**22
  Aranda, **2:**16
  Asiatic Eskimos, **6:**39
  Asmat, **2:**19
  Ata Tana 'Ai, **5:**23
  Bagobo, **5:**29
  Bamiléké, **9:**38
  Bisaya, **5:**42
  Boazi, **2:**29
  Bontok, **5:**46
  Buriats, **6:**66
  Cham, **5:**72
  Chukchee, **6:**76
  Chuvans, **6:**80, 81
  Circassians, **6:**88
  Cotabato Manobo, **5:**79
  Daur, **6:**429
  Dinka, **9:**70
  Dolgan, **6:**100
  Don Cossacks, **6:**104
  Eipo, **2:**56
  Emberá and Wounaan, **8:**110
  Even, **6:**117, 118
  Evenki (Northern Tungus), **6:**120, 121
  Ewenki, **6:**433, 434
  Fali, **9:**94, 95
  Garifuna, **8:**113
  Gnau, **2:**80
  Gogodala, **2:**83
  Goodenough Island, **2:**86
  Gururumba, **2:**92
  Hanunóo, **5:**91
  Hezhen, **6:**452
  Hidatsa, **1:**146
  Huichol, **8:**125
  Iatmul, **2:**98
  Iban, **5:**97
  Ilongot, **5:**101
  Ingalik, **1:**156
  Itelmen, **6:**152
  Jingpo, **6:**456
  Jino, **6:**460
  Kachin, **5:**116
  Kalmyks, **6:**155
  Kamilaroi, **2:**104
  Karadjeri, **2:**111
  Karelians, **6:**170
  Karen, **5:**126
  Kariera, **2:**111
  Keraki, **2:**113
  Ket, **6:**183, 184
  Khakas, **6:**188
  Khanty, **6:**190
  Kiowa, **1:**187
  Kiwai, **2:**125
  Komi, **6:**204
  Koryaks and Kerek, **6:**207
  Kpelle, **9:**173
  Kubu, **5:**150
  Lahu, **5:**151, 152;**6:**462
  Lak, **2:**138
  Lakandon, **8:**154
  Laki, **5:**154
  Lamet, **5:**157
  Laz, **6:**240
  Lenca, **8:**155
  Lhoba, **6:**464

  Lisu, **5:**165;**6:**465
  Lozi, **9:**187
  Luba of Shaba, **9:**191
  Lunda, **9:**196
  Mailu, **2:**154
  Maisin, **2:**158
  Manchu, **6:**467
  Mansi, **6:**252-253
  Mardudjara, **2:**179
  Maring, **2:**185
  Maris, **6:**257
  Mekeo, **2:**198, 200
  Melanau, **5:**178
  Mentaweian, **5:**181
  Miao, **6:**470, 471
  Miskito, **8:**171
  Miyanmin, **2:**210
  Mnong, **5:**184
  Modang, **5:**186
  Moinba, **6:**473
  Mongo, **9:**226
  Mongols, **6:**474
  Montagnais-Naskapi, **1:**244, 245, 246
  Mundugumor, **2:**218
  Muong, **5:**190
  Murngin, **2:**224
  Namau, **2:**231
  Nanai, **6:**275, 278, 279
  Ndembu, **9:**239
  Netsilik Inuit, **1:**254
  Nez Percé, **1:**254
  Nganasan, **6:**280, 281, 282
  Ngatatjara, **2:**239
  Ngawbe, **8:**195
  Ningerum, **2:**245
  Nivkh, **6:**284
  North Alaskan Eskimos, **1:**258, 259, 261
  Northern Metis, **1:**262
  Ojibwa, **1:**269
  Okiek, **9:**259
  Orochi, **6:**295
  Orok, **6:**296
  Orokolo, **2:**259
  Oroquen, **6:**482, 483
  Ozarks, **1:**281
  Penan, **5:**210
  Philippine Negritos, **5:**211
  Pima Bajo, **8:**211
  Pintupi, **2:**264, 265
  Popoluca, **8:**216
  Qiang, **6:**485
  ritual
    Cora, **8:**76
  Rukuba, **9:**289
  Saami, **6:**323
  Sakalava, **9:**293
  Sambia, **2:**284
  San-speaking peoples, **9:**302
  Sea Nomads of the Andaman, **5:**227, 228
  Selepet, **2:**293
  Selkup, **6:**325
  Selung/Moken, **5:**231
  Semang, **5:**233, 234
  Senoi, **5:**237
  Seri, **8:**233
  She, **6:**489
  Shilluk, **9:**311
  Shors, **6:**329

  Siberiaki, **6:**333
  Siberian Estonians, **6:**336
  Siberian Tatars, **6:**341
  Sleb, **9:**315
  Stieng, **5:**243
  Suku, **9:**321
  Sulod, **5:**246
  Sumu, **8:**237
  Suri, **9:**325
  Svans, **6:**344
  Tagbanuwa, **5:**251
  Taiwan aboriginal peoples, **5:**257
  Tangu, **2:**311
  Taos, **1:**341
  Tasaday, **5:**259-261
  Tasmanians, **2:**316
  Telefolmin, **2:**321, 322
  Temiar, **5:**266, 267, 268
  Tepehuan of Chihuahua, **8:**253
  T'in, **5:**278
  Tiwi, **2:**327
  Tofalar, **6:**362
  Tonga, **9:**353
  Tujia, **6:**498
  Tuvans, **6:**373
  Udmurt, **6:**379, 380
  Ukrainian peasants, **6:**386
  Ukrainians, **6:**392
  Volga Tatars, **6:**401
  Wape, **2:**371
  Warlpiri, **2:**373
  Wik Mungkan, **2:**377
  Wogeo, **2:**380
  Wovan, **2:**386
  Xibe, **6:**504
  Yakut, **6:**405
  Yao, **6:**505
  Yir Yoront, **2:**395
  Yukagir, **6:**412-413
  Yumbri, **5:**294
  Zande, **9:**398
  see also Bison hunting; Fur trade; Hunting
    and gathering; Marine animal hunting;
    Taboos, hunting; *other types of animals*
Hunting (sport)
  Highland Scots, **4:**140
Hunting and gathering
  Ache, **7:**4
  Akawaio, **7:**31
  Amahuaca, **7:**34
  Amuesha, **7:**37
  Anambé, **7:**41
  Angaité, **7:**43
  Apalai, **7:**45
  Apiaká, **7:**48
  Araucanians, **7:**52
  Araweté, **7:**56
  Arikara, **1:**26
  Ashaninca, **7:**91
  Asurini, **7:**61
  Ayoreo, **7:**69, 70
  Bakairi, **7:**74
  Baniwa-Curripaco-Wakuenai, **7:**77
  Barama River Carib, **7:**80
  Barí, **7:**83, 84
  Baure, **7:**86
  Bororo, **7:**86
  Canelos Quichua, **7:**99

Caquinte, **7**:91
Cariña, **7**:102
Cashibo, **7**:104
Chácobo, **7**:105
Chayahuita, **7**:111
Chenchu, **3**:61
Chimane, **7**:112
Chipaya, **7**:115-116
Chiquitano, **7**:118
Chiriguano, **7**:120
Chocó, **7**:123
Chorote, **7**:124
Cinta Larga, **7**:127
Colorado, **7**:131
Cubeo, **7**:140
Cuiva, **7**:143
Culina, **7**:146
Cuna, **7**:149
Desana, **7**:152
Emberá, **7**:155
Gorotire, **7**:162
Guahibo-Sikuani, **7**:164-165, 166
Guajajára, **7**:166, 167
Havasupai, **1**:145
Hill Pandaram, **3**:99
Hopi, **1**:149
Hopi-Tewa, **1**:151
Hoti, **7**:175
Huarayo, **7**:177
Huron, **1**:152
Iroquois, **1**:165
Irula, **3**:105
Jamináwa, **7**:180
Jebero, **7**:181
Jicarilla, **1**:72
Jivaro, **7**:182
Kadiwéu, **7**:183
Kagwahiv, **7**:184, 185
Kaingáng, **7**:186
Kalapalo, **7**:187
Kalapuya, **1**:175
Karihona, **7**:192
Karok, **1**:176
Kashinawa, **7**:195
Ka'wiari, **7**:198
Kickapoo, **1**:183, 184
Kiowa, **1**:187
Klamath, **1**:191
Koya, **3**:140
Krikati/Pukobye, **7**:204
Kurumbas, **3**:143
Kutchin, **1**:196
Kwakiutl, **1**:198
Labrador Inuit, **1**:201
Lengua, **7**:210
Lillooet, **1**:206
Lipan Apache, **1**:207
Luiseño, **1**:164
Macuna, **7**:212-213
Maká, **7**:216
Maliseet, **1**:211
Maricopa, **1**:216
Marinahua, **7**:220
Maroni Carib, **7**:220
Marubo, **7**:222
Mashco, **7**:225
Mataco, **7**:228
Matsigenka, **7**:231

Maxakali, **7**:233
Mayoruna, **7**:234
Menominee, **1**:220
Mescalero Apache, **1**:224
Miami, **1**:231
Micmac, **1**:233
Miwok, **1**:239-240
Mocoví, **7**:240
Mojo, **7**:242
Montagnais-Naskapi, **1**:244
Moré, **7**:243
Movima, **7**:243
Munda, **3**:182
Mundurucu, **7**:244
Nambicuara, **7**:247
Nayaka, **3**:195
Nez Percé, **1**:254
Nivaclé, **7**:249
Nomatsiguenga, **7**:91
Northern Paiute, **1**:263
Northern Shoshone and Bannock, **1**:266, 267
Osage, **1**:277
Ottawa, **1**:279
Pacific Eskimo, **1**:283
Paï-Tavytera, **7**:259
Palikur, **7**:262
Panare, **7**:265
Paresí, **7**:269
Pemon, **7**:271
Piapoco, **7**:274
Piaroa, **7**:276
Piro, **7**:279
Pomo, **1**:293-294
Potawatomi, **1**:297
Puinave, **7**:281
Rikbaktsa, **7**:287
Saliva, **7**:292
San-speaking peoples, **9**:302
Santal, **3**:253, 255
Santee, **1**:307
Saramaka, **7**:296
Sharanahua, **7**:299
Shavante, **7**:300
Shawnee, **1**:317
Sherente, **7**:302
Siona-Secoya, **7**:307
Sirionó, **7**:310
Slavey, **1**:319
Southern Paiute (and Chemehuevi), **1**:330-331
Spokane, **1**:333
Suruí, **7**:312
Suya, **7**:315
Tacana, **7**:318
Tanaina, **1**:335
Tanana, **1**:338
Tanimuka, **7**:318, 319
Taos, **1**:341
Tapirapé, **7**:320
Tatuyo, **7**:323
Teton, **1**:344-345
Tewa Pueblos, **1**:348
Thompson, **1**:350
Ticuna, **7**:328
Tlingit, **1**:351
Toba, **7**:331
Tonkawa, **1**:354

Trio, **7**:335
tropical-forest foragers, **9**:356
Tubatulabal, **1**:355
Tunebo, **7**:338
Tupari, **7**:339
Tuscarora, **1**:356
Ute, **1**:360
Vedda, **3**:300-301, 302
Walapai, **1**:364, 365
Waorani, **7**:352
Wapisiana, **7**:355
Warao, **7**:357
Washoe, **1**:367, 368
Waurá, **7**:360
Wayapi, **7**:361
Western Apache, **1**:371
Western Shoshone, **1**:374
Winnebago, **1**:380-381
Witoto, **7**:365
Wiyot, **1**:384
Xikrin, **7**:367, 368
Xokléng, **7**:370
Yagua, **7**:372
Yanomamö, **7**:375
Yavapai, **1**:386
Yekuana, **7**:381
Yokuts, **1**:387
Yuit, **1**:390-391
Yukpa, **7**:383
Yukuna, **7**:386
Yuqui, **7**:391-392
Yuracaré, **7**:395
Yurok, **1**:394
see also Fishing; Seminomads
Hunting chief
    Ute, **1**:361-362
Hunting group
    Chipewyan, **1**:69
    Cree, **1**:81, 82
Hunting magic
    Tanaina, **1**:336, 337
Hunting rites
    Koya, **3**:140
    Munda, **3**:184
    Oraon, **3**:215
    tropical-forest foragers, **9**:357
    Ute, **1**:361
    Yuit, **1**:392
Hunting songs
    Tanana, **1**:340
Hunt Society
    Tewa Pueblos, **1**:349
Husband
    considered guest in wife's house
        Minangkabau, **5**:183
    worship
        Magar, **3**:158
    see also Gender roles; Marriage; Patriarchal family structure
Hus (feast)
    Rotinese, **5**:214
Hwan-Gap
    Koreans, **6**:206
Hydroelectric power
    Slav Macedonians, **4**:240
    Swedes, **4**:257
Hymn tradition
    Doukhobors, **1**:93

Hymn tradition (cont'd)
  Hutterites, 1:155
  Welsh-Canadians, 1:127
Hypergamy
  Anavil Brahman, 3:8
  Aveyronnais, 4:25
  Badaga, 3:16
  Bengali, 3:31
  Canarians, 4:52
  Cape Verdeans, 4:55
  Chin, 3:66
  Flemish, 4:107
  Gujarati, 3:91
  Kanbi, 3:118
  Muslim, 3:185
  Nepali, 3:203
  Santal, 3:253
Hypogamy
  Badaga, 3:16

Iconography
  Karajá, 7:191
  Koya, 3:141
  Old Believers, 1:274
  Sherpa, 3:259
  Slav Macedonians, 4:241
  see also Symbolism; Totems
Icon painting
  Romanians, 4:214
  Slav Macedonians, 4:241
Icon worship
  Cypriots, 4:81
  Mount Athos, 4:176
  Sarakatsani, 4:224
Id al-fitr (holiday)
  Madurese, 5:168
Idiorhythmic monasteries
  Mount Athos, 4:175-176
Idol worship
  Gujarati, 3:92
Ilegitimacy
  Bavarians, 4:34
  Cape Verdeans, 4:55
  Chin, 3:64
Illegitimacy
  Antigua and Barbuda, 8:9
  Baffinland Inuit, 1:30
  Bahamians, 8:19
  Bhuiya, 3:44
  Carib of Dominica, 8:39
  Chuvans, 6:82
  Costa Ricans, 8:80
  Danes, 4:89
  Garifuna, 8:114
  Germans, 4:122
  Gorotire, 7:163
  Manus, 2:174
  Nicobarese, 3:209
  Otavalo, 7:254
  Tory Islanders, 4:266
  Ute, 1:361
Illegitimacy rate
  high
    Cherokee, 1:61
    Portuguese, 4:207
    Western Apache, 1:373
  increasing
    Micmac, 1:234

low
  Northern Irish, 4:179
Illigitimacy
  Kongo, 9:167
Illiteracy. See Literacy
Illness, causes of
  alien objects
    Mohave, 1:242
    Washoe, 1:370
  ancestors
    Kogi, 7:203
    Lunda, 9:198
    Mbeere, 9:223
    Okiek, 9:261, 262
    Saramaka, 7:298
    Yakö, 9:387
  anger and hostility
    Mixe, 8:175
    Pawnee, 1:285
    Tepehua, 8:249
  antisocial behavior
    Wasteko, 8:303
    Zoque, 8:317
  bad feelings
    Washoe, 1:370
  bad fortune
    Dusun, 5:83
  contact with non-Indians
    Bakairi, 7:75
    Karajá, 7:191
  contamination
    Guajiro, 7:170
    Guambiano, 7:173
  cosmic imbalance
    Asmat, 2:21
  cursing
    Mbeere, 9:223
  the dead
    Mazahua, 8:166
  deities
    Mazatec, 8:169
  depletion of power
    Chambri, 2:32
  dietary changes
    Portuguese, 4:208
  disobedience
    Anuta, 2:15
    Fore, 2:65
  disresepect for game
    Maliseet, 2:213
  divine punishment
    Abkhazians, 6:9
    Don Cossacks, 6:107
    Kiribati, 2:123
    Mongols, 6:476
    Nias, 5:197
    Paï-Tavytera, 7:260
    Pukapuka, 2:272
    Svans, 6:346
    Tahiti, 2:307
    Wantoat, 2:370
    Yukateko, 8:310
  drafts
    Hungarians, 4:145
  dreams
    Mohave, 1:242
  emotional distress
    Khmer, 5:138

emotions
  Greeks, 4:134
  Somalis, 9:318
  Vietnamese, 5:287
enemies
  Cuiva, 7:145
envy
  Tzotzil of San Bartolomé de los Llanos,
    8:291
evil eye
  Ionians, 4:150
  Slovaks, 4:245
evil spirits
  Cuiva, 7:145
  Micmac, 1:235
  Montagnais-Naskapi, 1:246
  Romanians, 4:214
  Yawalapití, 7:380
evil wind
  Otavalo, 7:255
extraterrestrial beings
  Chamacoco, 7:110
food
  Macuna, 7:215
foreign objects
  Otavalo, 7:255
fright
  Central Thai, 5:71
  Otavalo, 7:255
  Yemenis, 9:390
funerary custom neglect
  Nyakyusa and Ngonde, 9:254
genetic
  Amish, 1:19
  Portuguese, 4:208
ghosts, 1:242
  Guajiro, 7:170
  Konso, 9:171
  Yakö, 9:387
  Zarma, 9:406
guilt
  Awá Kwaiker, 7:65
hardship
  Vietnamese, 5:287
heartbreak
  Vietnamese, 5:287
human error
  Yakö, 9:387
ill-willed person
  Swazi, 9:333
  Tzotzil of Chamula, 8:281
imbalance of body elements
  Balinese, 5:37
  Bonerate, 5:46
  Burmese, 5:65
  Central Thai, 5:71
  Tanna, 2:315
  Vietnamese, 5:287
imbalance of body's spirits
  Lao, 5:159
imbalance of hot and cold
  Dalmations, 4:87
  Mejbrat, 2:197
  Melanau, 5:180
  Rapa, 2:276
imbalance of humors
  Austrians, 4:21
  Han, 6:448

Nepali, **3**:205
inappropriate behaviors toward spirits
  Montagnais-Naskapi, **1**:246
inbreeding
  Zoroastrians, **9**:408
invisible forces
  Araweté, **7**:57
  Emberá, **7**:157
  Toba, **7**:333
life events
  Cubeo, **7**:142
  Ka'wiari, **7**:200
life force weakening
  Dogon, **9**:73
magic
  Suku, **9**:323
magical instrusion of objects
  Tanaina, **1**:337
menstrual pollution
  Boazi, **2**:31
  Kiwai, **2**:127
  Mountain Arapesh, **2**:217
  Sengseng, **2**:298
  Yangoru Boiken, **2**:390
moral failings
  Greeks, **4**:134
  Mixtec, **8**:178
moral imbalance
  Manam, **2**:169
  Pukapuka, **2**:272
nahualism
  Amuzgo, **8**:6
  Pame, **8**:208
natural
  Ambonese, **5**:19
  Lesu, **2**:147
  Mohave, **1**:242
  Nissan, **2**:251
natural forces
  Chiriguano, **7**:122
  Kiwai, **2**:127
  Sirionó, **7**:311
negativity
  Tepehua, **8**:249
personified forms
  Kashubians, **4**:159
poison
  Pomo, **1**:295
  Quechan, **1**:302
  Rikbaktsa, **7**:288
  Wiyot, **1**:385
possession
  Ayoreo, **7**:72
  Pume, **7**:285
profiteering
  Nias, **5**:197
retribution
  Okanagon, **1**:271
ritual pollution
  Baniwa-Curripaco-Wakuenai, **7**:80
  Japanese, **5**:110
  Yanomamö, **7**:377
seasonal changes
  Cubeo, **7**:142
  Ka'wiari, **7**:200
semen loss
  Gururumba, **2**:94
shamans

Apalai, **7**:47
Chorote, **7**:126
Huarayo, **7**:179
Karihona, **7**:193
Lengua, **7**:211
Maká, **7**:218
Mundurucu, **7**:245
Ticuna, **7**:330
Toba, **7**:333
Warao, **7**:359
Yanomamö, **7**:377
  see also subhead sorcery and witchcraft
    below
social dysfunction
  Greeks, **4**:134
  Kogi, **7**:203
social imbalance
  Ata Tana 'Ai, **5**:26
  Hawaiians, **2**:97
  Murik, **2**:223
  Palu'e, **5**:209
  Semang, **5**:235
  Usino, **2**:363
  Wasteko, **8**:304
sorcery and witchcraft
  Abelam, **2**:4, 6
  Aguaruna, **7**:30
  Ambae, **2**:11
  Ambonese, **5**:19
  Amuesha, **7**:39
  Ata Sikka, **5**:22
  Bagirmi, **9**:35
  Bakairi, **7**:75
  Balinese, **5**:37
  Baniwa-Curripaco-Wakuenai, **7**:80
  Betsileo, **9**:57
  Chimane, **7**:113
  Chimbu, **2**:37
  Chipewyan, **1**:69
  Chiquitano, **7**:118
  Chiriguano, **7**:122
  Chuj, **8**:74
  Cora, **8**:77
  Cubeo, **7**:142
  Cuicatec, **8**:93
  Culina, **7**:148
  Dobu, **2**:52
  Dogon, **9**:73
  Dusun, **5**:83
  Dyula, **9**:78
  Edo, **9**:82
  Emberá, **7**:158
  Endenese, **5**:86
  Fipa, **9**:100
  Foi, **2**:61
  Fore, **2**:65
  Garia, **2**:76
  Gebusi, **2**:79
  Gogodala, **2**:84
  Goodenough Island, **2**:88
  Guadalcanal, **2**:91
  Guarijío, **8**:119
  Gururumba, **2**:94
  Jebero, **7**:181
  Kapauku, **2**:107
  Karajá, **7**:191
  Ka'wiari, **7**:200
  Kiribati, **2**:123

Kiwai, **2**:127
Krikati/Pukobye, **7**:205
Kuikuru, **7**:209
Kurtatchi, **2**:133
Kwoma, **2**:136
Lesu, **2**:147
Lozi, **9**:189
Mafulu, **2**:153
Mailu, **2**:156
Maisin, **2**:160
Makassar, **5**:174
Maori, **2**:178
Marquesas Islands, **2**:191
Mazahua, **8**:166
Mbeere, **9**:222
Mehinaku, **7**:239
Mejbrat, **2**:197
Menominee, **1**:222
Mohave, **1**:242
Mongo, **9**:227, 227
Mundugumor, **2**:220
Mundurucu, **7**:245
Nahuat of the Sierra de Puebla, **8**:193
Namau, **2**:232
Nasioi, **2**:235
Navajo, **1**:253
Ngatatjara, **2**:241
Ningerum, **2**:248
Nissan, **2**:251
Ojibwa, **1**:272
Orokolo, **2**:260
Païˉ-Tavytera, **7**:260
Palu'e, **5**:209
Paresí, **7**:269
Pawnee, **1**:285
Piaroa, **7**:278
Pohnpei, **2**:269
Quechan, **1**:302
Rikbaktsa, **7**:288
Rossel Island, **2**:280
Samal Moro, **5**:224
Sambia, **2**:286
Saramaka, **7**:298
Sasak, **5**:227
Selepet, **2**:295
Seminole of Oklahoma, **1**:315
Sengseng, **2**:298
Siona-Secoya, **7**:309
Suku, **9**:323
Tangu, **2**:312
Tanna, **2**:315
Taro, **2**:307
Telefolmin, **2**:323
Temne, **9**:345
Tepehuan of Chihuahua, **8**:254
Tigray, **9**:349
Tonga, **9**:355
Toraja, **5**:283
Tupari, **7**:341
Usino, **2**:363
Vietnamese, **5**:287
Waimiri-Atroari, **7**:344, 345
Wanano, **7**:350
Wantoat, **2**:370
Washoe, **1**:370
West Greenland Inuit, **1**:378
Wik Mungkan, **2**:379
Wogeo, **2**:381

Illness, causes of (cont'd)
   Wovan, **2:**387
   Yagua, **7:**373
   Yakö, **9:**387
   Yangoru Boiken, **2:**390
   Zande, **9:**399-400
   Zapotec, **8:**313
   Zoque, **8:**317
   Zuni, **1:**400
  soul loss
   Akha, **5:**13
   Angaité, **7:**44
   Asiatic Eskimos, **6:**42
   Bisaya, **5:**43
   Bonerate, **5:**46
   Bugis, **5:**51
   Chamacoco, **7:**110
   Craho, **7:**138
   Cuicatec, **8:**217
   Evenki (Northern Tungus), **6:**124
   Han, **6:**447
   Ifugao, **5:**100
   Jingpo, **6:**459
   Karen, **5:**129
   Ket, **6:**185
   Khanty, **6:**192
   Maká, **7:**218
   Marquesas Islands, **2:**191
   Mehinaku, **7:**239
   Menominee, **1:**222
   Mohave, **1:**242
   Mundugumor, **2:**220
   Mundurucu, **7:**245-246
   Nivaclé, **7:**251
   Popoluca, **8:**217
   Quechan, **1:**302
   Rotuma, **2:**283
   Sengseng, **2:**298
   Taiwan aboriginal peoples, **5:**257
   Tanaina, **1:**337
   Temiar, **5:**272
   Trio, **7:**336
   Truk, **2:**353
   Tzotzil of San Andrés Larraínzar, **8:**285
   Waropen, **2:**376
   Wiyot, **1:**385
   Yekuana, **7:**381
   Zapotec, **8:**313
  souls of the dead
   Paraujano, **7:**268
  spirits
   Agta, **5:**6
   Ainu, **5:**9
   Akha, **5:**13
   Albanians, **4:**7
   Ambonese, **5:**19
   Amhara, **9:**21
   Amuesha, **7:**39
   Andis, **6:**27
   Anuak, **9:**22
   Anuta, **2:**15
   Apalai, **7:**47
   Araweté, **7:**57
   Asiatic Eskimos, **6:**42
   Asmat, **2:**21
   Ata Sikka, **5:**22
   Bai, **6:**421
   Balinese, **5:**37

Balkars, **6:**54
Baniwa-Curripaco-Wakuenai, **7:**80
Batak, **5:**41
Bau, **2:**24
Bedouin, **9:**46
Bhil, **3:**41
Boazi, **2:**30
Bondo, **3:**51
Burusho, **3:**56
Butonese, **5:**68, 69
Candoshi, **7:**94
Central Thai, **5:**71
Chagga, **9:**62
Chakma, **3:**60, 61
Chin, **3:**67
Chipaya, **7:**117
Chukchee, **6:**77
Cuna, **7:**151
Dani, **2:**45
Daribi, **2:**48
Dogon, **9:**73
Dusun, **5:**83
Dyula, **9:**78
Foi, **2:**61
Fore, **2:**65
Gainj, **2:**73
Garia, **2:**76
Gayo, **5:**89, 90
Gogodala, **2:**84
Gond, **3:**86-87
Goodenough Island, **2:**88
Guadalcanal, **2:**91
Gujarati, **3:**92
Hani, **6:**451
Hanunóo, **5:**91
Hawaiians, **2:**97
Huarayo, **7:**179
Ilongot, **5:**102
Iteso, **9:**130
Japanese, **5:**110
Jicarilla, **1:**174
Jingpo, **6:**458, 459
Karen, **5:**129
Karok, **1:**177
Kashinawa, **7:**197
Khasi, **3:**126
Khmer, **5:**137, 138
Kiowa, **1:**189
Kiribati, **2:**123
Kiwai, **2:**127
Kmhmu, **5:**141
Kogi, **7:**203
Kol, **3:**130
Koya, **3:**141-142
Kriashen Tatars, **6:**212
Kumeyaay, **1:**195
Kurtatchi, **2:**133
Lahu, **5:**154;**6:**463
Lakher, **3:**147, 148
Lango, **9:**181
Lao, **5:**159
Lau, **2:**145
Lepcha, **3:**149
Lisu, **5:**166
Luba of Shaba, **9:**193
Lunda, **9:**199
Mae Enga, **2:**151
Maisin, **2:**160

Makassar, **5:**174
Malaita, **2:**163
Manus, **2:**175, 176
Maonan, **6:**468
Maring, **2:**188
Marquesas Islands, **2:**191
Mehinaku, **7:**238, 239
Melanau, **5:**180
Mikir, **3:**176
Modang, **5:**186
Mongols, **6:**476
Munda, **3:**184
Murik, **2:**222
Muyu, **2:**229
Namau, **2:**232
Nambicuara, **7:**247
Naxi, **6:**480
Nayaka, **3:**196
Ndebele, **9:**237
Nepali, **3:**205
Newar, **3:**208
Ningerum, **2:**248
Nissan, **2:**251
Nivaclé, **7:**251
Nyinba, **3:**213
Ontong Java, **2:**255
Oriya, **3:**218
Orokaiva, **2:**258
Otavalo, **7:**255
Paï-Tavytera, **7:**260
Palaung, **5:**203
Panare, **7:**267
Pandit of Kashmir, **3:**226
Pathan, **3:**233
Penan, **5:**210
Pentecost, **2:**264
Piaroa, **7:**278
Pukapuka, **2:**272
Pume, **7:**285
Purum, **3:**244
Qiang, **6:**487
Rapa, **2:**275, 276
Sakalava, **9:**299
Salasaca, **7:**291
Samal Moro, **5:**224
Sambia, **2:**286
Samoa, **2:**289
Sasak, **5:**227
Selepet, **2:**295
Selung/Moken, **5:**232
Shahsevan, **9:**310
Shipibo, **7:**306
Shui, **6:**491
Siwai, **2:**304
Slav Macedonians, **4:**241
Sora, **3:**270
Suruí, **7:**314
Swazi, **9:**333
Swedes, **4:**258
Tanna, **2:**315
Telefolmin, **2:**323
Temiar, **5:**272
Tepehuan of Chihuahua, **8:**254
Tikopia, **2:**326
T'in, **5:**279
Toba, **7:**333
Toda, **3:**298
Tonga, **9:**355

Trio, 7:336
Trobriand Islands, 2:350
Truk, 2:353
Ulithi, 2:360
Usino, 2:363
Vedda, 3:303
Vietnamese, 5:287
Waimiri-Atroari, 7:345
Wantoat, 2:370
Waorani, 7:353
Wape, 2:372
Woleai, 2:384
Yakö, 9:387
Yangoru Boiken, 2:390
Yao of Thailand, 5:293
Yekuana, 7:381
Yemenis, 9:390
Yuqui, 7:394
supernatural
    Apalai, 7:47
    Araucanians, 7:54
    Araweté, 7:57
    Asurini, 7:62
    Aymara, 7:68
    Cahita, 8:77
    Chiriguano, 7:122
    Dogon, 9:73
    Fali, 9:97
    Fipa, 9:99, 100
    Guajiro, 7:170
    Guambiano, 7:173
    Jebero, 7:181
    Mandan, 1:215
    Mbeere, 9:222-223
    Palikur, 7:263-264
    Pame, 8:208
    Pomo, 1:295
    Popoluca, 8:217
    Poqomam, 8:219
    Southern Paiute (and Chemehuevi),
        1:332
    Tzotzil of San Bartolomé de los Llanos,
        8:291
    Warao, 7:359
    Washoe, 1:370
taboo violation
    Anuta, 2:15
    Asiatic Eskimos, 6:42
    Awá Kwaiker, 7:65
    Boazi, 2:31
    Chamacoco, 7:110
    Chimane, 7:113
    Chorote, 7:126
    Cubeo, 7:142
    Dobu, 2:52
    Garia, 2:76
    Gnau, 2:82
    Goodenough Island, 2:88
    Guadalcanal, 2:91
    Kalingas, 5:123
    Ka'wiari, 7:200
    Kewa, 2:117
    Krikati/Pukobye, 7:205
    Lau, 2:145
    Maori, 2:178
    Maring, 2:188
    Mejbrat, 2:197
    Mountain Arapesh, 2:217

Mundugumor, 2:220
Nivkh, 6:285
Piaroa, 7:278
Pima-Papago, 1:289, 290
Pohnpei, 2:269
Pomo, 1:295
Quechan, 1:302
Rikbaktsa, 7:288
Rossel Island, 2:280
Saramaka, 7:298
Semang, 5:236
Sengseng, 2:298
Siona-Secoya, 7:309
Sirionó, 7:311
Siwai, 2:304
Telefolmin, 2:323
Toba, 7:333
West Greenland Inuit, 1:378
Wiyot, 1:385
Xikrin, 7:369
Yagua, 7:373
Yangoru Boiken, 2:390
Yanomamö, 7:377
Yurok, 1:395
Zuni, 1:400
thorns
    Huarayo, 7:179
totemic association
    Ajië, 2:9-10
unfulfilled vow
    Makassar, 5:174
weather change
    Lao, 5:159
winds in body
    Toraja, 5:283
wrongdoings
    Yurok, 1:395-396
see also Medical practices and treatments
Ilols (seers)
    Tzotzil of Chamula, 8:281
Image casting
    Newar, 3:206
Imagery. See Iconography; Symbolism
Imitation (socialization by). See Child-rearing
        philosophy, adult role models
Immortality. See Afterlife; Reincarnation
        beliefs
Impartible inheritance. See Primogeniture
Impotence
    caused by evil eye
        Ionians, 4:150
    as divorce ground
        Lakher, 3:146
Impressment. See Blackbirding
Imprisonment. See Punishment, incarceration
"In bass" singing
    Croats, 4:75
Inbreeding
    Amish, 1:19-20
    Appalachians, 1:22
    Madeirans, 4:165
Incarceration. See under Punishment
Incest prohibitions
    Abkhazians, 6:8
    Ache, 7:5
    Apalai, 7:46
    Araweté, 7:56
    Armenians, 6:29

Arubans, 8:12
Asmat, 2:20
Bamiléké, 9:38
Barí, 7:84
Boruca, Bribri, Cabécar, 8:29
Buriats, 6:67
Canarians, 4:52
Candoshi, 7:93
Chácobo, 7:106
Cora, 8:76
Craho, 7:137
Cretans, 4:70
Cypriots, 4:80
Edo, 9:82
Emberá, 7:156
Emberá and Wounaan, 8:110
Evenki (Northern Tungus), 6:121
Hare, 1:141
Iban, 5:97
Ifugao, 5:100
Iteso, 9:130
Jews, Arabic-speaking, 9:135
Kapingamarangi, 2:109
Karajá, 7:189
Karihona, 7:193
Kashinawa, 7:196
Ka'wiari, 7:199
Kazakhs, 6:179
K'iche,' 8:142
Koryaks and Kerek, 6:209
Lepcha, 3:149
Lesu, 2:147
Luba of Shaba, 9:192
Lugbara, 9:194
Macuna, 7:213
Magar, 3:156, 157
Maguindanao, 5:170
Maká, 7:216
Maxakali, 7:233
Mazahua, 8:165
Meskhetians, 6:260
Modang, 5:186
Moldovans, 6:267
Mountain Jews, 6:272
Nandi and other Kalenjin peoples, 9:234
Nomoi, 2:252
North Alaskan Eskimos, 1:260
Nyamwezi and Sukuma, 9:256
Old Believers, 1:273;6:293
Ontong Java, 2:254-255
Otavalo, 7:254
Palikur, 7:262
Pende, 9:273
Piro, 7:280
Puinave, 7:281
Qiang, 6:486
Semang, 5:235
Sengseng, 2:296
Shipibo, 7:305
Shona, 9:313
Siona-Secoya, 7:308
Suruí, 7:313, 314
Swazi, 9:331
Taiwan aboriginal peoples, 5:258
Tandroy, 9:338
Tapirapé, 7:321
Telefolmin, 2:322
Terena, 7:326

Incest prohibitions (cont'd)
  Ticuna, 7:329, 329
  Tlingit, 1:352
  Tolai, 2:334
  Trobriand Islands, 2:350
  Ukrainian peasants, 6:387
  uncle/niece forbidden
    Karaites, 9:154
  Wanano, 7:349
  Wapisiana, 7:355
  Washoe, 1:369
  Wiyot, 1:384
  Wogeo, 2:381
  Xoraxané Romá, 4:282
  Yaqui, 8:306
  Yoruba, 9:392
  Yukpa, 7:383
  Yuqui, 7:393
  Yuracaré, 7:396
  see also Cousin marriage; Marriage,
    avodiance relationships
Incision (as initiation rite)
  Gayo, 5:90
Indemnity payments
  Lakher, 3:146, 147
Indentured children
  Badaga, 3:16
Indigo dyes
  Cape Verdeans, 4:55
Individual autonomy (as valued trait)
  Calabrese, 4:49-50
  Cretans, 4:70
  Czechs, 4:84
  Finns, 4:103
  Hill Pandaram, 3:100
  Nayaka, 3:195, 196
  Sherpa, 3:259
  Slavey, 1:320
  Vlach Gypsies of Hungary, 4:272
  Washoe, 1:369
  Western Apache, 1:372, 373
Industrialization
  Basques, 4:31
  Bavarians, 4:33
  Bretons, 4:38
  Bulgarians, 4:43
  Burgundians, 4:46, 47
  Danes, 4:89
  English, 4:96
  Flemish, 4:106
  Fruili, 4:113
  Germans, 4:122
  German Swiss, 4:125
  Greeks, 4:132
  Irish, 4:152, 153
  Lowland Scots, 4:162-163
  Maltese, 4:167
  Mauritian, 3:171
  Northern Irish, 4:178
  Piemontese, 4:198
  Poles, 4:202, 203
  Portuguese, 4:206, 207
  Provencal, 4:210
  Punjabi, 3:238
  Romanians, 4:213
  Silesian, 4:238
  Slav Macedonians, 4:240
  Slovaks, 4:243

  Slovenes, 4:247
  Swedes, 4:257
  Swiss, Italian, 4:260-261
  Syrian Christian of Kerula, 3:273
  Tuscans, 4:269
  Walloons, 4:277
  Welsh, 4:278, 279
  see also specific industries and products
Infant and child mortality rates
  Buriats, 6:68
  Calabrese, 4:48, 49
  Choiseul Island, 2:38
  De'ang, 6:429
  Jews of Kurdistan, 9:146
  Kalmyks, 6:157
  Karakalpaks, 6:168
  Lango, 9:180
  Maltese, 4:167
  Ossetes, 6:302
  Pahari, 3:223
  Peloponnesians, 4:194
  Qalandar, 3:248
  Sinhalese, 3:266
  Turkmens, 6:371
  Uzbeks, 6:397
  Wasteko, 8:304
Infanticide
  Ache, 7:6
  Amahuaca, 7:35
  Asiatic Eskimos, 6:42
  Asmat, 2:19
  Ayoreo, 7:71
  Bhil, 3:41
  Cocama, 7:130
  Comanche, 1:75
  Copper Eskimo, 1:78
  Eipo, 2:57
  Han, 6:445
  Hani, 6:451
  Jat, 3:112
  Mailu, 2:155-156
  Maori, 2:177
  Mojo, 7:242
  Suruí, 7:313
  Tapirapé, 7:321
  Tasmanians, 2:316
  Toga, 3:296
  Warao, 7:359
  Yawalapití, 7:379
  Yuracaré, 7:396
Infant mortality rate
  Evenki (Northern Tungus), 6:122
Infants
  betrothal of
    Amahuaca, 7:35
    Mayoruna, 7:234
  carried on back
    Ewe and Fon, 9:86
    Hausa, 9:113
    Tzotzil and Tzeltal of Pantelhó, 8:277
    Tzotzil of Zinacantan, 8:293
    Vlachs, 4:274
    Wolof, 9:379
  close care by mother
    Piemontese Sinti, 4:201
    Slovas, 4:244
  cradle boards, 1:231
    Menominee, 1:221

    Miami, 1:231
    Nootka, 1:256
    Zuni, 1:398
  feet binding
    Itonama, 7:179
  forehead flattening
    Nootka, 1:256
  head flattening
    Cashibo, 7:104
  illness believed caused by reincarnating
    ancestor
    Yakö, 9:387
  lack of paternal contact
    Kogi, 7:202
  lips steeped in haoma drink at birth
    Zoroastrians, 9:409
  not mourned after death
    Lobi-Dagarti peoples, 9:186
  painted black after birth
    Chocó, 7:123
  secluded with mother for first three months
    Konso, 9:172
  swaddling
    Abkhazians, 6:8
    Armenians, 6:30
    Kashubians, 4:159
    Slovenes, 4:248
    Tarascans, 8:246
    Ukrainian peasants, 6:388
  see also Breast-feeding; Child-rearing phi-
    losophy
Infertility
  ancestors as cause
    Lunda, 9:198
  evil eye as cause, 4:150
  as grounds for divorce. *See* Divorce grounds,
    childlessness
  as reason for body to be left for scavengers
    Nandi and other Kalenjin peoples, 9:234
  as serious misfortune
    Acholi, 9:5
  as sign of curse
    Maasai, 9:210
  as social control threat
    Mbeere, 9:222
  sorcery/witchcraft as cause
    Mongo, 9:227
  substitute wife used
    Ndebele, 9:236
  woman blamed
    Luyia, 9:205
  woman may bear child for sister
    Sakalava, 9:296
Infidelity. *See* Adultery
Influenza
  Chipewyan, 1:67
  Cree, 1:80
Informal economy
  Gitanos, 4:129
  Irish Travellers, 4:155
  Piemontese Sinti, 4:200
  Romanians, 4:213
  Rominche, 4:216
  Slovaks, 4:243
  Slovensko Roma, 4:250
  Vlach Gypsies of Hungary, 4:272
Inheritance
  absence of rules

Western Shoshone, 1:375
according to father's choice
  Poles, 4:203
according to need
  Melpa, 2:201
  Mixe, 8:174
  Otomí of the Sierra, 8:201
  Senoi, 5:238
  Yap, 2:393
according to need or appropriateness
  Slavey, 1:320
according to past contribution to family
  Bunun, 5:57
according to wishes of deceased
  Micmacs, 1:234
  Taos, 1:342
  Tongareva, 2:340
of acquired items
  Apíaká, 7:49
by adult unmarried children
  Tairora, 2:309
of ancestor's bones
  Sirionó, 7:310
of animals
  Craho, 7:137
  Guajiro, 7:169
  Nivaclé, 7:249
anticipatory. *See subhead* distribution before
    death *below*
based on co-residence
  Georgians, 6:132
at birth
  Tahiti, 2:306
by brothers
  Candoshi, 7:93
  Lobi-Dagarti peoples, 9:184
  Luba of Shaba, 9:192
  Nandi and other Kalenjin peoples, 9:233
  Ndembu, 9:240
  Palikur, 7:263
  Suri, 9:325
of business property
  Flemish, 4:107
after ceremonial adoption
  Miami, 1:231
of ceremonial knowledge
  Karajá, 7:189
  Kuikuru, 7:208
  Navajo, 1:252
  Palu'e, 5:207
  Suya, 7:316
by child at marriage
  Welsh, 4:280
by child who cares for parents
  Poqomam, 8:218
  Q'eqchi,' 8:227
  Tarascans, 8:245
  Tigray, 9:348
clan
  Gururumba, 2:93
  Lahu, 5:153
  Tokelau, 2:331
by co-wives' sons
  Nandi and other Kalenjin peoples, 9:233
croft system
  Highland Scots, 4:141
  Shetlanders, 4:233, 234
by daughters-in-law from woman

Tiv, 9:351
by daughters of mother's house
  Tewa Pueblos, 1:348
daughters receive one-fourth
  Bedouin, 9:44
daughters receive one-third
  Tuareg, 9:368
of debt
  Ifugao, 5:100
decided on deathbed
  Yuracaré, 7:396
distribution before death
  Andis, 6:26
  Garifuna, 8:114
  Huichol, 8:126
  Karen, 5:127
  Lao, 5:159
  Madurese, 5:167
  Qashqa'i, 9:286
  Sagada Igorot, 5:216
  San-speaking peoples, 9:303
  Sardinians, 4:227
  Tory Islanders, 4:266
  Turkmens, 6:370
  Western Apache, 1:372
  Yörük, 9:395
  Zoque, 8:316
during lifetime in exchange for support
  Pasiegos, 4:190
each spouse's property passes separately
  Pasiegos, 4:190
educational provisions as form of
  Sicilians, 4:236
by eldest son. *See* Primogeniture
by eldest child at marriage
  Kashubians, 4:158-159
by eldest married child
  Ngawbe, 8:196
eldest responsible son gets rifle
  Suri, 9:325
by eldest son of first wife
  Alur, 9:13
  Swazi, 9:331
equal distribution
  Armenians, 6:30
  Bavarians, 4:34
  Bretons, 4:38, 39
  Bulgarians, 4:44
  Butonese, 5:67
  Central Thai, 5:71
  Chinese in Southeast Asia, 5:76
  Costa Ricans, 8:80
  Cretans, 4:70
  Cypriots, 4:80
  Dusun, 5:82
  Faroe Islanders, 4:99
  Flemish, 4:107
  Galicians, 4:120
  Georgians, 6:134
  German Swiss, 4:126
  Greeks, 4:132, 133
  Haitians, 8:122
  Hungarians, 4:144
  Iban, 5:98
  Ionians, 4:149, 150
  Itza,' 8:134
  Jamaicans, 8:138
  Javanese, 5:112

Kalingas, 5:122
Karelians, 6:171
Korean, 5:147
Ladinos, 8:153
Lahu, 6:463
Madeirans, 4:165
Madurese, 5:167
Maguindanao, 5:170
Makassar, 5:173
Malay, 5:175
Maltese, 4:168
Manx, 4:171
Maori, 2:178
Melanau, 5:179
Mendi, 2:204
Peloponnesians, 4:194
Pima Bajo, 8:212
Pohnpei, 2:269
Qiang, 6:486
Romanians, 4:214
Rotuma, 2:282
Saint Lucians, 8:231
Samal Moro, 5:223
Sardinians, 4:227
Sea islanders, 1:310
Sicilians, 4:236
Slovaks, 4:244
Subanun, 5:245
Sundanese, 5:247
Tagalog, 5:250
Ternatan/Tidorese, 5:275
Tewa Pueblos, 1:348
Toraja, 5:282
Tuvans, 6:374
Tzotzil of Chamula, 8:280
Ukrainians, 6:393
Vietnamese, 5:285
Welsh, 4:280
Yakan, 5:289
Yao of Thailand, 5:292
see also Dowry
equal in kind and quality
  Leonese, 4:161
equally divided among sons
  Montenegrins, 4:173
  Serbs, 4:231
equally divided among sons and daughters
  Andalusians, 4:11
  Azoreans, 4:28
  Burgundians, 4:47
  Canarians, 4:52
  Castilians, 4:60
  Cretans, 4:70
  Cyclades, 4:78
  Dyula, 9:77
  Nubians, 9:247
  Palestinians, 9:265
  Pasiegos, 4:190
  Provencal, 4:211
  Sinhalese, 3:266
  Somalis, 9:317
  Tamil of Sri Lanka, 3:282
  Vedda, 3:302
  Zoroastrians, 9:409
equally divided among sons, daughters, and
    spouse
  Sardinians, 4:227
equally divided among sons only

Inheritance (cont'd)
  Bulgarians, 4:44
  Croats, 4:73
  Nepali, 3:204
  Newar, 3:207
  Nyinba, 3:212
  Pathan, 3:232
  Pundit of Kashmir, 3:225
  Punjabi, 3:240
  Santal, 3:254
  Sherpa, 3:259
  Sora, 3:266
  Telugu, 3:285, 286
  Toda, 3:296
  equal with bias toward sons
    Sorbs, 4:253
  by family group
    North Alaskan Eskimos, 1:260
  father names only one son as heir
    Irish, 4:153
  father to son
    Candoshi, 7:93
    Canela, 7:96
    Chimane, 7:113
    Cubeo, 7:141
    Desana, 7:153
    Guahibo-Sikuani, 7:165
    Ka'wiari, 7:199
    Kogi, 7:202
    Macuna, 7:213
    Mandan, 1:215
    Matsigenka, 7:232
    Saramaka, 7:297
    Tatuyo, 7:323
    Ticuna, 7:329
    Yukuna, 7:387
  of feather ornaments
    Apalai, 7:46
  female
    Hawaiians, 2:96
    Javanese, 5:112
  female dowry as. See Dowry
  firstborn son primacy. See Primogeniture
  flexible forms of property division
    Provencal, 4:211
  of fruit trees
    Kuikuru, 7:208
  by game playing
    Salasaca, 7:290
  gender-specific
    Kenyah-Kayan-Kajang, 5:134
    Marind-anim, 2:183
    Minangkabau, 5:183
    Namau, 2:231
    Ontong Java, 2:254
    Rossel Island, 2:279
    Santa Cruz, 2:291
    Yangoru Boiken, 2:389
  by gravedigger
    Chamacoco, 7:109
  of harvest rights
    Krikati/Pukobye, 7:205
  heir becomes parent to children of deceased
    Tonga, 9:354
  heirs divide personal property
    Cypriots, 4:80
  by household group
    Navajo, 1:252

of houses
  Karajá, 7:189
  Otavalo, 7:254
  Palikur, 7:263
  Piro, 7:280
houses may never by sold
  Dogon, 9:72
houses passed along female line
  Cyclades, 4:77
by immediate family
  Atoni, 5:28
  Japanese, 5:108
impartible. See Primogeniture
Islamic law
  Bagirmi, 9:34
  Circassians, 9:66, 67
  Fulani, 9:102
  Ghorbat, 9:107
  Hausa, 9:113
  Teda, 9:341
of land. See Landholding, hereditary
of land-use rights
  Guambiano, 7:172-173
  Páez, 7:257
last-born child preference. See Ultimo-
    geniture
as lifelong process
  Cotopaxi Quichua, 7:134
limited to small keepsakes
  Slovensko Roma, 4:251
male-controlled
  Cuicatec, 8:92
male heir importance
  Montenegrins, 4:173
  Serbs, 4:231
male line
  Alur, 9:13
  Chagga, 9:62
  Emberá and Wounaan, 8:110
  Vlachs, 4:274
males only. See Women's inheritance
    proscriptions
marriage portion in advance of
  Leonese, 4:161
by married children only
  Yukateko, 8:309
material objects to appropriate users
  Yuit, 1:391
from maternal uncle after specified gift is
    given
  Tswana, 9:363
matriclan uncle to nephew
  Tlingit, 1:352
matrilineal elders control
  Ndembu, 9:240
  Suku, 9:322
of medical knowledge
  Swedes, 4:258
mother to children
  Edo, 9:80
  Suri, 9:326
mother to daughter
  Bakairi, 7:74
  Candoshi, 7:93
  Canela, 7:96
  Cubeo, 7:141
  Guahibo-Sikuani, 7:165
  Karajá, 7:189

  Kogi, 7:202
  Mandan, 1:215
  Matsigenka, 7:232
  Navajo, 1:252
  Saraguro, 7:294
  Tatuyo, 7:323
  Ticuna, 7:329
  Yukuna, 7:387
mother to daughters
  Temne, 9:344
mother to son
  Nandi and other Kalenjin peoples, 9:233
mother to sons
  Iraqw, 9:125
mother to youngest son
  Maasai, 9:208
of names
  Kashinawa, 7:196
  Mayoruna, 7:234
  Ndembu, 9:240
  Suya, 7:316
negligible
  Tsimihety, 9:359
no concept of
  Northern Shoshone and Bannock, 1:267
  Quechan, 1:301
  Tubatulabal, 1:355
  Washoe, 1:369
noninheriting son
  Chin, 3:65
of official positions
  Tatuyo, 7:323
oldest adult in family decides
  Yaqui, 8:306
oldest child bias
  Osage, 1:278
oldest son. See Primogeniture
by one chosen child
  Orcadians, 4:187
by one son only
  Bamiléké, 9:38
at owner's discretion
  Frisians, 4:111
parental right to dispose of third share
    (terço)
  Portuguese, 4:207
partible. See subhead equal distribution
    above
partilas
  Portuguese, 4:207
rabbinic law
  Jews of Israel, 9:143
of rceremonial knowledge
  Macuna, 7:213
of religious objects
  Chipaya, 7:116
  Suruí, 7:313
by resident children
  Ogan-Besemah, 5:198
of rights and privileges
  Nootka, 1:257
of shaman role
  Nivaclé, 7:249
  Paraujano, 7:268
  Suruí, 7:313
  Trio, 7:336
  Yukuna, 7:387
sibling

Ossetes, **6:**301
by sister's children
    Montagnais-Naskapi, **1:**245
    Navajo, **1:**252
by sister's son
    Guadalcanal, **2:**90
    Trobriand Islands, **2:**350
of skills
    Kolisuch'ok, **5:**144
by son at time of marriage
    Gaels (Irish), **4:**116
by son (chosen by father)
    Guarijío, **8:**118
of songs or other nonmaterial property
    Yuit, **1:**391
by son-in-law at time of marriage
    Osage, **1:**278
by sons
    East Indians in Trinidad, **8:**106
    Fali, **9:**95
    Italian Mexicans, **8:**131
    Iteso, **9:**129
    Jews, Arabic-speaking, **9:**135
    K'iche,' **8:**142
    Kikapu, **8:**144
    Kipsigis, **9:**165
    Kurds, **9:**176
    Mazahua, **8:**165
    Mixtec, **8:**177
    Otomí of the Valley of Mezquital, **8:**205
    Sarakatsani, **4:**224
    Suri, **9:**325
    Totonac, **8:**265
    Tzotzil and Tzeltal of Pantelhó, **8:**277
    YörÜk, **9:**395
by sons and male relatives primarily
    Yurok, **1:**395
by sons of bride-wealth marriage
    Nyamwezi and Sukuma, **9:**257
by sons for hunting equipment
    Suku, **9:**322
sons receive cattle from mother
    Maasai, **9:**208
by spouse
    Afro-Colombians, **7:**17
    Araweté, **7:**57
    Ayoreo, **7:**71
    Canelos Quichua, **7:**100
    Chamacoco, **7:**109
    Galicians, **4:**120
    Krikati/Pukobye, **7:**205
    Miskito, **8:**172
    Palikur, **7:**263
    Puerto Ricans, **8:**222
    Semang, **5:**235
    Senoi, **5:**238
of trapping lines
    Slavey, **1:**320
of valued items
    Amahuaca, **7:**35
    Chácobo, **7:**106
    Pemon, **7:**272
    Trio, **7:**336
verbal will
    Blackfoot, **1:**42
woman to brothers
    Circassians, **9:**67
    Nuristanis, **9:**251

Shahsevan, **9:**309
by youngest married son
    Pedi, **9:**270
youngest son gets last portion
    Qashqa'i, **9:**286
youngest son. _See_ Ultimogeniture
see also Descent; Kinship
Inherited land. _See_ Landholding, hereditary
Inherited occupations. _See_ Occupations,
    hereditary
Inherited priesthood. _See_ Priests, hereditary
Initiation rites
    Abelam, **2:**4, 5, 6
    Ache, **7:**7
    Afar, **9:**8
    Ajië, **2:**9
    Akawaio, **7:**33
    Akha, **5:**12, 13
    Amuesha, **7:**39
    Andamanese, **3:**11
    Anuta, **2:**15
    Apalai, **7:**46, 47
    Aranda, **2:**18
    Asmat, **2:**21
    Asurini, **7:**62
    Ata Sikka, **5:**22
    Ata Tana 'Ai, **5:**26
    Azoreans, **4:**28
    Bamiléké, **9:**39
    Baniwa-Curripaco-Wakuenai, **7:**78
    Boazi, **2:**30
    Bonerate, **5:**45
    Bugle, **8:**34
    Bukharan Jews, **6:**65
    Canela, **7:**97
    Cashibo, **7:**104
    Chácobo, **7:**107
    Chambri, **2:**32
    Chayahuita, **7:**111
    Chimbu, **2:**36
    Chocó, **7:**123
    Chorote, **7:**126
    Cocama, **7:**130
    Cook Islands, **2:**42
    Cora, **8:**76
    Cuiva, **7:**145
    Cuna, **7:**151
    Dani, **2:**44
    Dargins, **6:**98
    Daribi, **2:**48
    Desana, **7:**154
    Dieri, **2:**49
    Easter Island, **2:**54
    Eipo, **2:**58
    Emberá, **7:**158
    Emerillon, **7:**159
    Fali, **9:**96
    Fore, **2:**64, 65
    Fulani, **9:**103
    Fulniô, **7:**161
    Gahuku-Gama, **2:**69, 70
    Gainj, **2:**72
    Garia, **2:**75, 76
    Gebusi, **2:**77, 78
    Gnau, **2:**81, 82
    Gogodala, **2:**84
    Gorotire, **7:**163
    Guadalcanal, **2:**90

Guajajára, **7:**167
Guajiro, **7:**169
Guarayu, **7:**174
Gururumba, **2:**94
Gusii, **9:**110
Huarayo, **7:**178
Iatmul, **2:**99, 100
Iraqw, **9:**125
Jebero, **7:**181
Jivaro, **7:**183
Kagwahiv, **7:**185
Kamilaroi, **2:**104
Karajá, **7:**190, 191
Kariera, **2:**111
Karihona, **7:**193
Kashinawa, **7:**197
Ka'wiari, **7:**200
Keraki, **2:**113, 114
Khanty, **6:**191, 192
Kilenge, **2:**119
Kipsigis, **9:**165
Kiwai, **2:**126, 127
Kpelle, **9:**173, 173-174, 174
Krikati/Pukobye, **7:**205
Kuna, **8:**150
Kurtatchi, **2:**131, 132
Kwoma, **2:**135
Lakalai, **2:**142
Lesu, **2:**146
Luba of Shaba, **9:**192
Lugbara, **9:**194
Luiseño, **1:**208
Lunda, **9:**199
Macuna, **7:**214
Mafulu, **2:**153
Mailu, **2:**154, 155
Maisin, **2:**159
Maká, **7:**217-218
Mardudjara, **2:**180, 181
Marind-anim, **2:**183, 184
Maroni Carib, **7:**220
Mashco, **7:**226, 227
Mataco, **7:**229
Maxakali, **7:**233
Mehinaku, **7:**237-238
Mejbrat, **2:**196, 197
Mescalero Apache, **1:**225
Miami, **1:**231
Miyanmin, **2:**211, 212
Mountain Arapesh, **2:**217
Mundugumor, **2:**220
Murik, **2:**223
Muyu, **2:**230
Namau, **2:**231, 232
Nambicuara, **7:**247
Nandi and other Kalenjin peoples, **9:**233
Ndebele, **9:**237
Ndembu, **9:**240
Ngatatjara, **2:**241
Ngawbe, **8:**196
Ningerum, **2:**248
Nivaclé, **7:**250, 251
Noanamá, **7:**252
Ojibwa, **1:**270
Okiek, **9:**261
Orokolo, **2:**260
Páez, **7:**257
Paï-Tavytera, **7:**259-260

Initiation rites (cont'd)
  Palaung, **5:**202
  Panare, **7:**266, 267
  Parsi, **3:**229
  Pedi, **9:**270
  Pende, **9:**274
  Pima-Papago, **1:**290
  Pintupi, **2:**266
  Pokot, **9:**283
  Puinave, **7:**282
  Quechan, **1:**301
  Rikbaktsa, **7:**287-288, 288
  Rukuba, **9:**290
  Sambia, **2:**285
  San-speaking peoples, **9:**303
  Santal, **3:**254
  Sara, **9:**307
  Selepet, **2:**294
  Seminole of Oklahoma, **1:**314
  Shavante, **7:**301
  Shipibo, **7:**305
  Sio, **2:**300, 301
  Sirionó, **7:**310, 311
  Slavey, **1:**320
  Suruí, **7:**313
  Suya, **7:**317
  Swahili, **9:**328
  Tairora, **2:**310
  Tangu, **2:**312
  Taos, **1:**343
  Tapirapé, **7:**321
  Tasmanians, **2:**316-317, 317
  Tatuyo, **7:**324
  Tauade, **2:**320
  Tausug, **5:**263
  Telefolmin, **2:**322, 323
  Temne, **9:**344, 345
  Thakali, **3:**291
  Ticuna, **7:**330
  Tiwi, **2:**329
  Toba, **7:**333
  Tongareva, **2:**341
  Tor, **2:**344
  Torres Strait Islanders, **2:**346
  Trio, **7:**336
  Tuareg, **9:**369
  Tupari, **7:**340
  Ulithi, **2:**360
  Usino, **2:**363
  Ute, **1:**361
  Waimiri-Atroari, **7:**345
  Wáiwai, **7:**347
  Wanano, **7:**350
  Wapisiana, **7:**355
  Warlpiri, **2:**374
  Waropen, **2:**376
  Wayapi, **7:**362, 363
  Western Apache, **1:**373
  Western Shoshone, **1:**375
  Wik Mungkan, **2:**378, 379
  Wintun, **1:**383
  Wogeo, **2:**381
  Wovan, **2:**387
  Xikrin, **7:**369
  Yagua, **7:**373
  Yangoru Boiken, **2:**388, 389, 390
  Yanomamö, **7:**376
  Yao of Thailand, **5:**293

  Yawalapití, **7:**380
  Yekuana, **7:**381
  Yi, **6:**507
  Yukuna, **7:**388, 389
  Zande, **9:**398, 399
  Zaramo, **9:**402, 402-403, 403
  Zoroastrians, **9:**409
  see also Coming of age; Menstruation; Rites
    of passage; Seclusion
Inkgura (festival)
  Aranda, **2:**18
In-laws. *See* Family, affinial relations; Mother-
    in-law
In-law taboos. *See under* Taboos
Innkeeping
  Vlachs, **4:**274
Insanity. *See* Madness
Insects, edible
  ants
    Alur, **9:**13
    Iteso, **9:**128
  grasshoppers
    Alur, **9:**13
    Mongo, **9:**226
    Sakalava, **9:**293
  termites
    Zande, **9:**398
Instruments. *See* Musical instruments; *specific*
    instruments
Insularity. *See* Closed community
Insults (song duels)
  West Greenland Inuit, **1:**378
Insurance industry
  German Swiss, **4:**125
Insurgency. *See* Civil war; Nationalist
    movements; Raiders
Intercaste marriage
  Punjabi, **3:**240
  see also Hypergamy
Intercession, religious beliefs in. *See* Madonna
    worship; Patron saint
Intergenerational marriage. *See* Marriage,
    intergenerational
Intermarriage
  Abkhazians, **6:**8
  Afro-Bolivians, **7:**9
  Armenian-Americans, **1:**108
  Ashkenazim, **6:**35
  Azerbaijani Turks, **6:**49
  Bhil, **3:**39
  Bouyei, **6:**423
  Brahui, **3:**54
  Carpatho-Rusyns, **6:**70
  Cherokee, **1:**62
  Chinese in Caribbean, **8:**57
  Chinese of Costa Rica, **8:**61
  Chukchee, **6:**77
  Circassians, **9:**67
  Cree, **1:**80, 82
  Creoles of Nicaragua, **8:**85
  cross-ethnic
    Lobi-Dagarti peoples, **9:**184
  Dolgan, **6:**101
  Dungans, **6:**109
  East Asians of the United States, **1:**101,
    102
  Eastern Shoshone, **1:**105
  East Indians in Trinidad, **8:**106

  Emberá and Wounaan, **8:**110
  Evenki (Northern Tungus), **6:**122
  Germans, **6:**139
  Greek-speaking Jews of Greece, **4:**135
  Hezhen, **6:**452
  Hui, **6:**453
  Ingalik, **1:**156, 157
  Italian Mexicans, **8:**131
  Itelmen, **6:**153
  Japanese, **7:**59
  Japanese in Canada, **1:**96
  Jews, **1:**169
  Jews of Algeria, **9:**138
  Kalibugan, **5:**120
  Kalingas, **5:**121
  Karakalpaks, **6:**166
  Kazakhs, **6:**179
  Koreans, **6:**206
  Koreans in Japan, **5:**149
  Koryaks and Kerek, **6:**209
  Kriashen Tatars, **6:**211
  Krymchaks, **6:**214
  Kui, **5:**150
  Kyrgyz, **6:**230
  Ladinos, **8:**152
  Latinos, **1:**205
  Lunda, **9:**197
  Maliseet, **1:**210
  Mamprusi, **9:**214
  Manchu, **6:**467
  Mansi, **6:**253
  Maris, **6:**257
  Menominee, **1:**220
  Metis of Western Canada, **1:**226, 228
  Micronesians, **1:**237
  Mocoví, **7:**241
  Moinba, **6:**473
  Moldovans, **6:**267
  Mossi, **9:**229
  Nahua of the Huasteca, **8:**186
  Nganasan, **6:**281
  Nuristanis, **9:**251
  Old Believers, **6:**293
  Opata, **8:**200
  Orochi, **6:**294
  Orok, **6:**296
  Osage, **1:**276
  Otomí of the Valley of Mezquital, **8:**205
  Pamir peoples, **6:**306
  Poles, **6:**307, 308
  Qashqa'i, **9:**285
  Rominche, **4:**216
  Sakalava, **9:**300
  Seminole, **1:**313
  Seri, **8:**234
  Siberiaki, **6:**331, 333
  Siberian Estonians, **6:**336
  Siberian Germans, **6:**339
  Sumu, **8:**238
  Tajiks, **6:**353
  Terena, **7:**326
  Toba, **7:**332
  Toda, **3:**297
  Tofalar, **6:**363
  tropical-forest foragers, **9:**357
  Tupari, **7:**340
  Turkmens, **6:**370
  Ucayalino, **7:**91

Uighur, **6:**383
Uzbeks, **6:**500
Volga Tatars, **6:**401
West Greenland Inuit, **1:**378
Yao of Thailand, **5:**291
see also Inbreeding; Mixed-race ancestry
Intermarriage proscriptions
Afrikaners, **9:**9
Assyrians, **9:**27
Konso, **9:**169
Kuna, **8:**148
Lakandon, **8:**154
Parsi, **3:**228
Santal, **3:**253
Somalis, **9:**318
Internal migration. _See_ Migration' Nomads;
Seminomads
Internal voice
Doukhobors, **1:**90, 92
International Society for Krishna Consciousness. _See_ Hare Krishna
Internment camps
Haitians, **1:**137
Japanese in Canada, **1:**95, 97, 98
Japanese in the United States, **1:**99-100
Intoxicating beverages. _See_ Alcohol
Intracaste or class marriage. _See_ Hypergamy;
Hypogamy
Introcision (as initiation rite)
Aranda, **2:**18
Inventions and innovations
Shakers, **1:**316
Invisible Church
Kiowa, **1:**188
Invisible forces (religious belief)
Emberá, **7:**157-158
Ipecac collection
Pauserna, **7:**270
Iron and steel production
Slovenes, **4:**247
Sorbs, **4:**253
Swedes, **4:**257
Walloons, **4:**277
Welsh, **4:**279
Iron exchange
Nyakyusa and Ngonde, **9:**253
Iron mining
Cypriots, **4:**80
Slav Macedonians, **4:**240
Iron smelting
Agaria, **3:**6
Iron working
Acholi, **9:**4
Burgundians, **4:**46
Estonian, **6:**112
Igbo, **9:**121
Iroquois kinship terminology. _See under_
Kinship terminology
Irrigation. _See under_ Agriculture
Irsin (ceremony)
Taiwan aboriginal peoples, **5:**257
Islam
African Americans, **1:**12, 13
Ajarians, **6:**14
Akan, **9:**12
Albanians, **4:**7
Alorese, **5:**14, 15
Ambonese, **5:**16, 17, 19

Andalusians, **4:**10
Arab Americans, **1:**23, 24, 25
Arabs, **9:**22, 25
Baggara, **9:**31
Bagirmi, **9:**34
Balantak, **5:**35
Banggai, **5:**38
Barbadians, **8:**23
Batak, **5:**41
Bengali, **3:**29, 30, 31, 32-33, 34
Bhil, **3:**38, 41
Bihari, **3:**46
Bisaya, **5:**42
Bohra, **3:**47
Bolaang Mongondow, **5:**43
Bonerate, **5:**45-46
Bosnian Muslims, **4:**36
Brahui, **3:**54
Bukharan Jews, **6:**62-63
Bulgarian Gypsies, **4:**41, 42
Bulgarians, **4:**45
Burusho, **3:**56
Butonese, **5:**66, 68, 69
Central Thai, **5:**69, 71
Chinese in Southeast Asia, **5:**74-75, 76
Chuvash, **6:**85
Divehi, **3:**75, 77, 78
Don Cossacks, **6:**107
Dusun, **5:**80, 83
Dyula, **9:**77
Endenese, **5:**84
Fali, **9:**96, 97
Filipino, **5:**86
Fipa, **9:**99
Ganda, **9:**105
Garia, **3:**81
Gayo, **5:**89
Gujar, **3:**88, 89
Hausa, **9:**114
hijra, **3:**96
Jat, **3:**111, 112
Javanese, **5:**112, 113
Kalagan, **5:**119
Kalibugan, **5:**120
Kanuri, **9:**152-153
Kashmiri, **3:**122
Kédang, **5:**131, 132
Kerintji, **5:**134
Khevsur, **6:**196
Khmer, **5:**137
Khoja converts, **3:**127-128
Kohistani, **3:**128
Kpelle, **9:**174
Kriashen Tatars, **6:**210-211
Kubu, **5:**150
Kurds, **6:**226
Labbai, **3:**144
Laki, **5:**154
Lamaholot, **5:**154, 155, 156
Lobi-Dagarti peoples, **9:**185
Luyia, **9:**205
Maguindanao, **5:**168, 170, 171
Makassar, **5:**171, 173, 174
Mamprusi, **9:**214
Manggarai, **5:**176
Mappila, **3:**166, 167
Maris, **6:**258
Martiniquais, **8:**163

Mauritian, **3:**171, 172, 173
Mende, **9:**223
Meo, **3:**174
Meskhetians, **6:**260
Mogul, **3:**179-180
Moluccans—North, **5:**188
Moluccans—South, **5:**188
Mongols, **6:**476
Montenegrins, **4:**173
Moor of Sri Lanka, **3:**180-181
Mossi, **9:**228
Mountain Jews, **6:**271
Muna, **5:**189
Muslim, **3:**184-186
Nepali, **3:**204
Nias, **5:**195, 196
Ossetes, **6:**300, 301
Pak Thai, **5:**200
Palawan, **5:**204
Pathan, **3:**230, 233
peripatetics of Iraq, Syria, Lebanon, Jordan,
Israel, Egypt, Sudan, and Yemen,
9:277
peripatetics of the Maghreb, **9:**278
Pomaks, **4:**204, 205
Provencal, **4:**211
Punjabi, **3:**241
Rajput, **3:**249
Sakalava, **9:**298
Saluan, **5:**217
Sangir, **5:**224
Sasak, **5:**225, 227
Sayyid, **3:**256
Sea Nomads of the Andaman, **5:**228, 229
Selung/Moken, **5:**232
Semang, **5:**234
Senoi, **5:**237, 238
separatism from
Zoroastrians, **9:**409
Sheik, **3:**257
Siberian Tatars, **6:**340-341, 342
Sidi, **3:**260, 261
Sindhi, **3:**263
Singaporean, **5:**242
Sleb, **9:**315
South and Southeast Asians of Canada,
1:324
South Asians in Southeast Asia, **5:**243
Subanun, **5:**245
Sundanese, **5:**246, 247
Tatars, **6:**492
Teda, **9:**340
Temiar, **5:**266, 267, 272, 273
Ternatan/Tidorese, **5:**276
Tidong, **5:**277
Toala, **5:**280
Toraja, **5:**283
Trinidadians and Tobagonians, **8:**269
Udmurt, **6:**380
Xoraxané Romá, **4:**283
Yakan, **5:**288, 290
Yoruba, **9:**393
Zamindar, **3:**306, 307
Zaramo, **9:**403
Zarma, **9:**406
see also Sufism
Islam (Alawites)
Kurds, **9:**176

Islam (Druze)
　Arab Americans, 1:24
　Druze, 9:74-75
　Palestinians, 9:266
Islam (Hanafi)
　Salar, 6:488
Islam (Ismaili)
　Burusho, 3:56
　Kirgiz, 6:461
　Pamir peoples, 6:303, 304, 306
　South and Southeast Asians of Canada,
　　1:324
　Tajiks, 6:353, 492
Islam (Ithna Ash'ari)
　Tajiks, 6:353
Islam (Shia)
　Albanians, 4:7
　Arab Americans, 1:25
　Azerbaijani Turks, 6:49, 50
　Basseri, 9:42
　Bohra, 3:47-48
　Bonan, 6:422
　Cham, 5:73
　Dongxiang, 6:432
　Ghorbat, 9:107
　Jat, 3:112
　Khoja, 3:127
　Kirgiz, 6:461
　Kurds, 9:176
　Lezgins, 6:243
　Lur, 9:202
　peripatetics of Afghanistan, Iran, and
　　Turkey, 9:276
　Persians, 9:280
　Qashqa'i, 9:286
　Qizilbash, 9:288
　Sayyid, 3:256
　Shahsevan, 9:309
　South and Southeast Asians of Canada,
　　1:324
　Tajik, 6:492
　Talysh, 6:357
　Tats, 6:360
　Turks, 9:376
　Yemenis, 9:390
Islam (Sunni)
　Abkhazians, 6:6, 9
　Acehnese, 5:3, 4
　Aghuls, 6:11
　Aimaq, 9:10
　Andis, 6:24, 26
　Arab Americans, 1:25
　Avars, 6:43, 44, 46, 47
　Bajau, 5:31, 34
　Balkars, 6:53, 54
　Baluchi, 3:22, 24
　Bashkirs, 6:55, 56
　Baweanese, 5:42
　Bedouin, 9:45
　Bengali, 3:33, 34
　Berbers of Morocco, 9:52
　Bohra, 3:47, 48
　Bonan, 6:422
　Bonerate, 5:43
　Brahui, 3:54
　Bugis, 5:51
　Chechen-Ingush, 6:75
　Circassians, 6:90;9:67

Crimean Tatars, 6:94
Dargins, 6:98
Divehi, 3:78
Dongxiang, 6:432
Druze, 9:75
Dungans, 6:107, 108, 110
Fulani, 9:101, 103
Garia, 3:81
Gayo, 5:88
Georgians, 6:129, 131, 135
Ghorbat, 9:107
Gorontalese, 5:90
Greeks, 6:141
Gujar, 3:89
Gypsies, 6:148
Hui, 6:452, 453
Indonesian, 5:102-103
Ingilos, 6:150, 151
Jat, 3:112
Karachays, 6:160, 161
Karakalpaks, 6:165, 166, 168
Kazakhs, 6:179, 180, 181
Khinalughs, 6:201
Khoja, 3:127
Kubachins, 6:219
Kumyks, 6:223
Kurds, 9:176
Kyrgyz, 6:228, 229, 231
Laks, 6:233, 234
Laz, 6:239, 240
Lezgins, 6:242, 243
Madurese, 5:167
Malay, 5:174, 176
Mappila, 3:167
Mauritian, 3:173
Melanau, 5:178, 180
Minangkabau, 5:184
Muslim, 3:185, 186
Nogays, 6:289
Nubians, 9:248
Palestinians, 9:266
Pamir peoples, 6:306
Pathan, 3:230, 233
peripatetics of Afghanistan, Iran, and
　Turkey, 9:276
Qizilbash, 9:288
Rutuls, 6:321
Samal, 5:220
Samal Moro, 5:221, 222, 224
Sayyid, 3:256
Sheikh, 3:257
Sindhi, 3:263
Somalis, 9:318
South and Southeast Asians of Canada,
　1:324
Swahili, 9:328
Tabasarans, 6:347, 350
Tajiks, 6:351, 352, 353
Talysh, 6:357
Tats, 6:360
Tausug, 5:262, 264
Tomini, 5:280
Tsakhurs, 6:365, 367, 368
Turkish Cypriots, 4:81
Turkmens, 6:369, 370, 371
Turks, 9:376
Uighur, 6:381, 383, 384, 499, 500
Uzbeks, 6:396, 398, 500

Volga Tatars, 6:402
Yemenis, 9:390
Yörük, 9:396
Islam (Wahhabiyaa)
　Dongxiang, 6:432
Ismaili Muslims. *See* Islam (Ismaili)
Isolated communities
　American Isolates, 1:17-18
　Appalachians, 1:21-23
　Cajuns, 1:48, 49
　Cherokee, 1:60
　Fox, 1:129
Isolation practices. *See* Seclusion
Istalinga (symbol of Shiva)
　Lingayat, 3:151, 153
Itinerants
　Gitanos, 4:129
　Gypsies and caravan dwellers in the
　　Netherlands, 4:137-138
　Irish Travelers, 1:162-164
　Irish Travellers, 4:154-157
　Itinerants of the Maghreb, 9:278
　Micmac, 1:233
　peripatetics, 1:286-287;3:233-236;4:195-
　　197
　peripatetics of Afghanistan, Iran, and
　　Turkey, 9:275
　peripatetics of Iraq, Syria, Lebanon, Jordan,
　　Israel, Egypt, Sudan, and Yemen,
　　9:276-278
　peripatetics of Maghreb, 9:278
　Piemontese Sinti, 4:199-201
　Qalandar, 3:245-248
　Rom, 1:303-306
　Rominche, 4:216-217
　Scandinavian Itinerants, 4:228
　Sleb, 9:315
　Slovensko Roma, 4:249-251
　Spanish Rom, 4:254-255
　Vlach Gypsies of Hungary, 4:270-273
　Xoraxané Romá, 4:281-283
　see also Nomads; Seminomads
Itinerant tradesmen. *See* Peddlers
Ivory carving. *See under* Carved objects
Ivory sculpture
　Edo, 9:82

Jacobite Syrian Church
　Jacobites, 9:131-133
　Syrian Christian of Kerala, 3:274
Jaguars (religious symbol)
　Asurini, 7:62
　Baure, 7:86
　Chimane, 7:113
　Culina, 7:148
　Maká, 7:217
　Maxakali, 7:233
　Mojo, 7:242
　Piaroa, 7:278
　Piro, 7:280
　Sirionó, 7:311
　Tatuyo, 7:324
　Waorani, 7:353
　Warao, 7:359
Jahkreini (visible deities)
　Magar, 3:161
Jai alai (game)
　Basques, 1:32, 33

Jail. *See* Punishment, incarceration
Jainism
  Bania, 3:24, 25
  Gujarati, 3:92
  Jain, 3:109-110
  Kanarese, 3:117
Jamaa movement
  Luba of Shaba, 9:192
Jansenism
  Basques, 1:34;4:32
Jati. *See* Castes
Jazz
  Black Creoles of Louisiana, 1:39-40
Jealousy
  Blackfoot, 1:42
  Ndembu, 9:240
Jehovah's Witnesses
  Bamiléké, 9:39
  Flemish, 4:108
  Galicians, 4:120
  Haitians, 1:138
  Martiniquais, 8:163
  Micronesians, 1:238
  Nyakyusa and Ngonde, 9:254
  Transylvanian ethnic groups, 4:268
Jenmom system (land ownership)
  Syrian Christian of Kerala, 3:273
Jesus Christ
  pagan synthesis
    Pima-Papago, 1:290
  Peyote spirit equated with
    Winnebago, 1:382
Jet carving
  Pume, 7:284-285
Jewelry making
  Afro-Hispanic Pacific Lowlanders, 7:23
  Asurini, 7:61
  Bakairi, 7:74
  Bondo, 3:51
  Callahuaya, 7:88, 90
  Cinta Larga, 7:127
  Kalapalo, 7:187
  Karen, 5:129
  Kashinawa, 7:195
  Keres Pueblo Indians, 1:179, 180
  Kiowa, 1:189
  Kubachins, 6:216, 217, 219
  Kumeyaay, 1:194
  Kyrgyz, 6:231
  Laks, 6:234
  Lisu, 5:165, 166;6:465
  Miao, 6:472
  Minangkabau, 5:182
  Mundurucu, 7:244, 245
  Navajo, 1:251
  Ndaonese, 5:194
  Nubians, 9:248
  Orcadians, 4:187, 188
  Pahari, 3:223
  Pamir peoples, 6:305
  Santal, 3:255
  Shetlanders, 4:234
  Sinhalese, 3:267
  Sora, 3:270
  Swedes, 4:258
  Talysh, 6:356
  Tewa Pueblos, 1:349
  Tlingit, 1:351

Tujia, 6:499
Volga Tatars, 6:401
Waimiri-Atroari, 7:343
Walapai, 1:366
Washoe, 1:370
Yakut, 6:407
Yekuana, 7:381
Zuni, 1:397-398, 399
see also Beadwork; Goldsmithing;
  Silversmithing
Jewelry wearing. *See* Body painting and
  ornamentation; Body piercing;
  Earrings; Toe rings
Jhankris (visible deities)
  Magar, 3:161
Jharkhand tribalist movement
  Santal, 3:252, 254
Jhum agriculture. *See* Agriculture, slash-and-
  burn
Jihad (holy struggle)
  Pathan, 3:232
Jimsonweed use
  Tubatulabal, 1:355
Jirga (council)
  Pathan, 3:232, 233
Jogeshvari (female deity)
  Chitpavan Brahman, 3:70
Joint-family system. *See under* Family
Jojoba nut industry
  Western Apache, 1:372
Joking
  among household members, 4:141
  as art form
    Bau, 5:24
  kinship relationship
    Lobi-Dagarti peoples, 9:184
    Luba of Shaba, 9:192
    Nyamwezi and Sukuma, 9:256
    Tonga, 9:353
    Tuareg, 9:368
    West Greenland Inuit, 1:378
    Winnebago, 1:381
    Wolof, 9:378
    Yuit, 1:391
  kinship restrictions
    Munda, 3:183
    Santal, 3:253
  partnerships
    Copper Eskimo, 1:78
    Ingalik, 1:158
  ritualistic
    Sikh, 3:261
  as social control measure
    Frisians, 4:112
  see also Humor
Journey (as initiation)
  Iban, 5:98
  Kariera, 2:111
Judaism
  Andalusians, 4:9, 10
  Ashkenazic Jews, 4:15-17
  Ashkenazim, 6:31-37
  Austrian-Americans, 1:108
  Austrian-Canadians, 1:119
  Barbadians, 8:23
  Bene Israel, 3:27, 28
  Bukharan Jews, 6:62-65
  Bulgarians, 4:45

Catalans, 4:63
Circassians, 6:90
Cochin Jew, 3:71-73
Don Cossacks, 6:107
Flemish, 4:108
Georgian Jews, 6:126-128
Georgians, 6:131
Germans, 4:123
Greek-speaking Jews of Greece,
  4:134-136
Han, 6:448
Hasidim, 1:142, 143-144
Jews, 1:168-171
Jews, Arabic-speaking, 9:134-136
Jews of Algeria, 9:137-138
Jews of Iran, 9:138-141
Jews of Kurdistan, 9:144-147
Jews of the Middle East, 9:147-148
Jews of Yemen, 9:149-150
Karaites, 6:162, 165
Krymchaks, 6:213, 214, 215
Kumyks, 6:223
Lithuanian Jews, 6:243, 246
Mountain Jews, 6:270, 271, 273, 274
Romanian-Americans, 1:115
Russian-Canadians, 1:125
Sephardic Jews, 4:229
Tats, 6:360
Turks, 9:376
Yemenis, 9:390
Yezidis, 6:410
Judaism (non-Talmudic)
  Falasha, 9:89-92
  Karaites, 9:153-156
Judaism (separatism from)
  Zoroastrians, 9:409
Judgment Day. *See under* Afterlife
Judicial system. *See* Court system; Law
Jugglers. *See* Entertainers
Jumbie religion
  Montserratians, 8:181
Jumping Dance
  Wiyot, 1:385
  Yurok, 1:395
Junkanoo ceremony
  Bahamians, 8:20
Jural system. *See* Court system; Law
Justice. *See* Conflict resolution; Court system;
  Punishment
Juwo (ceremony)
  Kapauku, 2:107

Kaamulan (celebration)
  Bukidnon, 5:55
Kachina dolls
  Hopi, 1:150
  Zuni, 1:399
Kachinas
  Hopi, 1:148, 150
  Keres Pueblo Indians, 1:182
  Zuni, 1:398, 399, 400
Kad Bhagavadi (female deity)
  Paniyan, 3:227
Kaddish (prayer)
  Ashkenazim, 6:36
  Bukharan Jews, 6:65
Kaiko (ceremony)
  Maring, 2:187

Kale growing
  Orcadians, **4:**186
  Shetlanders, **4:**233
Kali (goddess)
  Bengali, **3:**34
  Bengali Shakta, **3:**35
  Brahman and Chhetri of Nepal,
    3:53
  Thug, **3:**294
  see also Shiva
Kalika (female deity)
  Bhil, **3:**41
Kamal (religious practictiner)
  Garo, **3:**84
Kanun (traditional law)
  Albanians, **4:**6
Karma
  Bengali, **3:**34
  Brahman and Chhetri of Nepal, **3:**53
  castes, Hindu, **3:**57
  Jain, **3:**109
  Pahari, **3:**222, 223
  Pandit of Kashmir, **3:**226
  Rom of Czechoslovakia, **4:**219
  Sherpa, **3:**260
  Sinhalese, **3:**267
  Untouchables, **3:**299
  see also Dharma; Reincarnation
    beliefs
Kashmir Shaivism
  Pandit of Kashmir, **3:**226
Kasti. *See* Sacred thread
Kataragama (deity)
  Vedda, **3:**303
Kathin (festival)
  Lao Isan, **5:**163
Katun (festival)
  Khmer, **5:**137
Kaul (ceremony)
  Melanau, **5:**180
Kavacha (talisman)
  Sadhu, **3:**251
Kava drinking
  Ambae, **2:**11, 12
  Anuta, **2:**15
  Bau, **2:**24
  Futuna, **2:**67
  Gebusi, **2:**79
  Gogodala, **2:**83, 84
  Kosrae, **2:**128
  Lau, **2:**145
  Marind-anim, **2:**183
  Nguna, **2:**242
  Pentecost, **2:**262
  Pohnpei, **2:**268
  Rotuma, **2:**283
  Samoa, **2:**289
  Tanna, **2:**313, 314, 315
  Tikopia, **2:**326
  Tonga, **2:**337, 339
  Usino, **2:**363
Kaware (ceremony)
  Mimika, **2:**208
Kayak use
  Iglulik Inuit, **1:**155
  Inughuit, **1:**159
  Labrador Inuit, **1:**201
  West Greenland Inuit, **1:**377

Keening
  Cretans, **4:**71
  Croats, **4:**75
Keepers of the faith
  Iroquois, **1:**167
Keepers of the Smoke
  Pima-Papago, **1:**289
Kelp gathering
  Miwok, **1:**240
  Tory Islanders, **4:**265
Kemovo (religious practitioner)
  Nagas, **3:**190
Kemukemps (trickster culture hero)
  Klamath, **1:**192
Kenaf growing
  Lao Isan, **5:**161
Kente cloth
  Ewe and Fon, **9:**88
Khao phansa (festival)
  Lao Isan, **5:**163
Kharsk Deo (deity)
  Ahir, **3:**7
Khazangpa. *See* Mediums
Khels (village division)
  Nagas, **3:**188
Khenduri (feast)
  Minangkabau, **5:**184
Khimintu (creator)
  Micmac, **1:**235
Khoti system
  Chitpavan Brahman, **3:**69
Khung Mua (ceremony)
  Muong, **5:**192
Khysty (religion)
  Siberiaki, **6:**334
Kibbutz
  Jews of Israel, **9:**142
Kiccimanito (Great Spirit)
  Ojibwa, **1:**270
Kidnapping
  Desana, **7:**153
  Mayoruna, **7:**234
Kihupfuma (religious practioner)
  Nagas, **3:**190
Killer of Enemies (culture hero)
  Mescalero Apache, **1:**225
Kin, fictive. *See* Fictive kin
Kinnikasus (creator)
  Wichita, **1:**379
Kinship
  between living and dead
    Finns, **4:**104
  based on ancestor patriclans
    Sara, **9:**305
  based on men's clubs
    Santa Cruz, **2:**291
  based on proximity
    Ayoreo, **7:**70
    Highland Scots, **4:**141
  based on river of residence
    Huarayo, **7:**177
  camps
    Walapai, **1:**365
  ceremonial. *See* Fictive kin
  Cherkess-Trobriand system
    Circassians, **6:**88
  clann
    Gaels (Irish), **4:**116

  Tory Islanders, **4:**265
class/status/color
  Cape Coloureds, **9:**59
closest relatives
  Czechs, **4:**83
cognatic
  Akawaio, **7:**31-32
  Amahuaca, **7:**35
  Ambae, **2:**11
  Amuesha, **7:**38
  Bugle, **8:**32
  Cariña, **7:**103
  Chatino, **8:**50
  Choiseul Island, **2:**38-39
  Emberá, **7:**156
  Fipa, **9:**99
  Garia, **2:**75
  Guahibo-Sikuani, **7:**165
  Irish Travellers, **4:**156
  Miyanmin, **2:**210
  Montserratians, **8:**180
  Nahuat of the Sierra de Puebla, **8:**192
  Ngawbe, **8:**196
  Norwegians, **4:**181
  Orcadians, **4:**187
  Piaroa, **7:**277
  Samoa, **2:**288
  Sea Islanders, **1:**310
  Sengseng, **2:**296
  Shetlanders, **4:**233
  Swedes, **4:**257
  Swiss, Italian, **4:**261
  Telefolmin, **2:**322
  Tokelau, **2:**331
  Tory Islanders, **4:**265
  Trio, **7:**335
  Tuvalu, **2:**356
  Yoruba, **9:**392
  Zande, **9:**398
consanguineal
  Bahamians, **8:**19
  Jamaicans, **8:**138
  Otomí of the Valley of Mezquital, **8:**205
  Piemontese Sinti, **4:**200
  Saami, **4:**221
defined by coresidence
  Mendi, **2:**204
  Miyanmin, **2:**210
  Ningerum, **2:**246-247
defined by cutting with same circumcision
    knife
  Pokot, **9:**282
defined by proximity and stage of life
  English, **4:**94-95
defined by shared activity
  Vlach Gypsies of Hungary, **4:**271
Dravidian. *See* Dravidan kinship system
entenado (semiadoption)
  Ladinos, **8:**152
European family-type
  Kongo, **9:**167
extensive links
  Cayman Islanders, **8:**47
female networks
  Curaçao, **8:**97
feuds. *See* Blood feud
group-based
  Mataco, **7:**228

horizontal
  Mejbrat, 2:196
  Mimika, 2:207
  Tangu, 2:311
importance of
  Pomo, 1:294, 295
  Welsh, 4:279
intermarriage ties
  Nuristanis, 9:251
joking relationship. _See under_ Joking
kumstvo
  Slav Macedonians, 4:240
lack of formalized groups
  Gitanos, 4:129
  Northern Shoshone and Bannock, 1:267
  Vlach Gypsies of Hungary, 4:271
local solidarity
  Shetlanders, 4:233
multiple paternity concept
  Araweté, 7:56
mutual obligation
  Madeirans, 4:165
  Rominche, 4:216
  Southern Paiute (and Chemehuevi),
    1:331
  Winnebago, 1:381
name-sets
  Pokot, 9:282
  Tanna, 2:314
nonunilineal associations
  Garifuna, 8:114
parallel
  Kogi, 7:201
by patronym
  Dyula, 9:76
section-based
  Marubo, 7:222
sibling sets
  Ache, 7:5
as social network basis
  Sardinians, 4:226
stani
  Sarakatsani, 4:224
by stock partnerships
  Pokot, 9:282
strong ties
  Manx, 4:170
  Ozarks, 1:281
  Rom, 1:305
teasing relationship
  Winnebago, 1:381
three-genertional ties
  Old Believers, 1:273
weak ties
  Swedes, 4:257
zadruga
  Slav Macedonians, 4:240-241
see also Clan; Cousin marriage; Descent;
    Family; Fictive kin; Incest prohibi-
    tions; Lineages; Moieties; Siblings
Kinship terminology
  according to gender of speaker
    Russian peasants, 6:312
  affines having special terms
    Old Believers, 1:273
    Saami, 4:221
    Serbs, 4:231
    Welsh, 4:279-280

Xoraxané Romá, 4:282
age and sex reflected in
  Taos, 1:342
age-based
  Betsileo, 9:55
  Dyula, 9:77
  Pokot, 9:282
  Sakalava, 9:295
  Shona, 9:313
  Tswana, 9:362
  Tzotzil of Zinacantan, 8:293
alternate generations merged
  Tonga, 9:353
ambiguous
  Fulani, 9:102
analytical
  Circassians, 6:88
Andean-type
  Cotopaxi Quichua, 7:133
antidescent ideology
  Vlach Gypsies of Hungary, 4:271
Arabic-type
  Circassians, 9:66
  Dargins, 6:97
  Nubians, 9:247
Bengali-type
  Sora, 3:269
bifurcate
  Iteso, 9:129
  Ukrainians of Canada, 1:358
bifurcate-collateral
  Albanians, 4:5
  Arab Americans, 1:24
  Bengali, 3:31
  Bhil, 3:39
  Chácobo, 7:106
  Cree, 1:81
  Danes, 4:89
  Ewenki, 6:434
  Faroe Islanders, 4:99
  Finns, 4:103
  Gales (Irish), 4:116
  Guahibo-Sikuani, 7:165
  Hakka, 6:437
  Hungarians, 4:144
  Jatav, 3:114
  Jews, Arabic-speaking, 9:135
  Jews of Iran, 9:140
  Kalmyks, 6:156
  Kewa, 2:116
  Kiowa, 1:187
  Miskito, 8:171
  Qalandar, 3:247
  Serbs, 4:231
  Seri, 8:234
  Slovaks, 4:244
  Slovensko Roma, 4:250
  Somalis, 9:317
  Tewa Pueblos, 1:348
  Tibetans, 6:495
  Tsakhurs, 6:366
  Ute, 1:361
  Vlachs, 4:274
  Warao, 7:358
  Washoe, 1:369
  Western Apache, 1:372
bifurcate-collateral avuncular
  East Indians in Trinidad, 8:106

Quechan, 1:301
bifurcate-collateral for males
  Montenegrins, 4:173
bifurcate-generational
  Ayoreo, 7:70
  Saami, 4:221
bifurcate-merging
  Amahuaca, 7:35
  Canelos Quichua, 7:100
  Chimbu, 2:36
  Chin, 3:65
  Dyula, 9:77
  Herero, 9:117
  Kachin, 5:117
  Kpelle, 9:173
  Krikati/Pukobye, 7:204
  Luba of Shaba, 9:192
  Makushi, 7:219
  Mardudjara, 2:180
  Maring, 2:186
  Mbeere, 9:221
  Mehinaku, 7:237
  Mejbrat, 2:196
  Mizo, 3:178
  Mundurucu, 7:245
  Nambicuara, 7:247
  Ngawbe, 8:196
  Orcadians, 4:187
  Otavalo, 7:254
  Palikur, 7:262
  Panare, 7:266
  Pedi, 9:270
  Rukuba, 9:289
  San-speaking peoples, 9:303
  Saramaka, 7:297
  Selepet, 2:294
  Shetlanders, 4:233
  Songhay, 9:319
  Wáiwai, 7:347
  Wantoat, 2:368
  Warlpiri, 2:374
  Welsh, 4:279
  Wolof, 9:378
  Zarma, 9:405
bilateral
  Awakateko, 8:16
  Balkars, 6:53
  Chuj, 8:72
  Huave, 8:123
  Mam, 8:158
  Melanau, 5:179
  Otomí of the Sierra, 8:201
  Sagada Igorot, 5:216
  Semang, 5:235
  Temiar, 5:269
  Tigray, 9:348
  Tzotzil and Tzeltal of Pantelhó, 8:278
Cherkess-Trobriand
  Circassians, 6:88
classificatory
  Bhil, 3:39
  Bhuiya, 3:43
  Callahuaya, 7:89
  Chechen-Ingush, 6:74
  Ewenki, 6:434
  Georgians, 6:133
  Gusii, 9:109
  Luyia, 9:204

Kinship terminology (cont'd)
  Mamprusi, **9:**212
  Menominee, **1:**221
  Ndebele, **9:**236
  Ndembu, **9:**240
  Nganasan, **6:**281
  Pedi, **9:**270
  Rutuls, **6:**320
  Saami, **4:**221
  Sakalava, **9:**295
  Tswana, **9:**362
  Tuareg, **9:**367
  Turkana, **9:**372
  Yoruba, **9:**392
  cognatic
    Gypsies, **6:**146
    Micmacs, **1:**234
  consanguineal
    Montenegrins, **4:**173
    Tojolab'al, **8:**261
    Welsh, **4:**279-280
    Xoraxané Romá, **4:**282
  cousin-based
    Awá Kwaiker, **7:**64
  cousin numbering
    Swedes, **4:**257
  cousins not distinguished
    Kuna, **8:**148
  cousins as siblings
    Bamiléké, **9:**38
  Crow-Omaha type
    Fali, **9:**95
  Crow-type
    Ambae, **2:**11
    Belau, **2:**26
    Bororo, **7:**87
    Canela, **7:**96
    Choctaw, **1:**72
    Craho, **7:**137
    Dobu, **2:**50
    Guajiro, **7:**168
    Hidatsa, **1:**147
    Hopi, **1:**149
    Klingit, **1:**352
    Kongo, **9:**167
    Krikati/Pukobye, **7:**205
    Lobi-Dagarti peoples, **9:**184
    Malekula, **2:**165
    Mandan, **1:**214
    Manus, **2:**174
    Nyamwezi and Sukuma, **9:**256
    Pawnee, **1:**284
    Pentecost, **2:**263
    Pohnpei, **2:**268
    Pomo, **1:**294
    Rossel Island, **2:**279
    Sirionó, **7:**310
    Suku, **9:**321
    Tonga, **9:**353
    Trobriand Islands, **2:**349
    Truk, **2:**352
    Ulithi, **2:**359
    Wapisiana, **7:**355
    Yap, **2:**393
    Zuni, **1:**398
  Dakota-type
    Badaga, **3:**16
    Marind-anim, **2:**183

  Northern Shoshone and Bannock, **1:**267
  Ticuna, **7:**329
denotes gender of both parties
  Svans, **6:**345
denoting consanguineal/affinial kin
  Chuvans, **6:**81
  Hakka, **6:**437
  Hmong, **5:**93
  Kmhmu, **5:**140
  Lao, **5:**158
  Tofalar, **6:**363
  Ukrainians, **6:**393
denoting matrilineal/patrilineal tie
  Asiatic Eskimos, **6:**41
  Ata Tana 'Ai, **5:**24
  Chinese in Southeast Asia, **5:**76
  Evenki (Northern Tungus), **6:**122
  Han, **6:**444
  Iatmul, **2:**99
  Kriashen Tatars, **6:**211
  Mansi, **6:**253
  Nogays, **6:**288
  Poles, **6:**308
  Rotinese, **5:**213
  Turkmens, **6:**370
  Uzbeks, **6:**397
  Volga Tatars, **6:**401
denoting relative age
  Ambonese, **5:**18
  Bajau, **5:**33
  Boazi, **2:**29-30
  Bonerate, **5:**45
  Chimbu, **2:**36
  Chinese in Southeast Asia, **5:**76
  Dusun, **5:**81
  Ewenki, **6:**434
  Gahuku-Gama, **2:**69
  Gnau, **2:**81
  Hakka, **6:**437
  Han, **6:**444
  Hmong, **5:**93
  Japanese, **5:**107
  Javanese, **5:**112
  Karen, **5:**127
  Kilenge, **2:**119
  Kmhmu, **5:**140
  Lahu, **6:**463
  Lao, **5:**158
  Lao Isan, **5:**161
  Mansi, **6:**253
  Marind-anim, **2:**183
  Miyanmin, **2:**210
  Naxi, **6:**479
  Nenets, **6:**279
  Nias, **5:**195
  Rotinese, **5:**213
  Samal, **5:**220
  Sasak, **5:**226
  Selkup, **6:**326
  Semang, **5:**235
  Shan, **5:**240
  Subanun, **5:**245
  Tajiks, **6:**353
  Tausug, **5:**263
  T'in, **5:**278
  Tiwi, **2:**328
  Tofalar, **6:**363
  Turkmens, **6:**370

  Uighur, **6:**383
  Uzbeks, **6:**397
  Volga Tatars, **6:**401
  Yakan, **5:**289
  Yakut, **6:**405
  Yao of Thailand, **5:**292
descriptive. *See subhead* bifurcate-collateral *above*
Dravidian-type
  Amuesha, **7:**38
  Apalai, **7:**46
  Araweté, **7:**56
  Atoni, **5:**27
  Baniwa-Curripaco-Wakuenai, **7:**78
  Cariña, **7:**103
  Cubeo, **7:**140
  Cuiva, **7:**143
  Desana, **7:**152
  Divehi, **3:**76-77
  Hill Pandaram, **3:**99-100
  Irula, **3:**106
  Kashinawa, **7:**195-196
  Ka'wiari, **7:**199
  Kota, **3:**136
  Koya, **3:**141
  Macuna, **7:**213
  Matsigenka, **7:**231
  Nambudiri Brahman, **3:**193
  Nayar, **3:**198
  Nivaclé, **7:**249
  Páez, **7:**257
  Panare, **7:**266
  Piaroa, **7:**277
  Pume, **7:**284
  Sinhalese, **3:**265
  Siwai, **2:**303
  Tamil, **3:**277, 278
  Tamil of Sri Lanka, **3:**282
  Tanna, **2:**314
  Tatuyo, **7:**323
  Telugu, **3:**286
  Toda, **3:**296
  Trio, **7:**335
  Tunebo, **7:**338
  Vedda, **3:**302
  Vellala, **3:**305
  Waimiri-Atroari, **7:**343
  Wanano, **7:**349
  Waorani, **7:**352
  Wayapi, **7:**362
  Wik Mungkan, **2:**378
  Yagua, **7:**372
  Yukuna, **7:**387
  Yuqui, **7:**393
elaborate
  Pomo, **1:**294
English
  Chinese in Caribbean, **8:**57
  Manx, **4:**170
  Northern Irish, **4:**179
  Shetlanders, **4:**233
  Spanish Rom, **4:**255
  Trinidadians and Tobagonians, **8:**268
  Welsh, **4:**279
Eskimo-type
  Achang, **6:**418
  Agta, **5:**5
  Azoreans, **4:**28

Bahamians, **8**:19
Bajau, **5**:33
Barbadians, **8**:22
Basques, **4**:31
Bisaya, **5**:43
Bugis, **5**:50
Bulgarians, **4**:44
Cahita, **8**:36
Canarians, **4**:52
cattle ranchers of Huasteca, **8**:43
Chatino, **8**:50
Chipewyan, **1**:68
Chocó, **7**:123
Copper Eskimo, **1**:78
Costa Ricans, **8**:80
Creoles of Nicaragua, **8**:85
Cyclades, **4**:77
Czechs, **4**:83
Dai, **6**:425
Dusun, **5**:81
Dutch, **4**:93
Emberá, **7**:156
Falasha, **9**:91
Faroe Islanders, **4**:99
Finns, **4**:103
Frisians, **4**:111
Garifuna, **8**:114
Gayo, **5**:89
Germans, **4**:122
Greeks, **4**:132
Guambiano, **7**:172
Iban, **5**:97
Ingalik, **1**:157
Ionians, **4**:150
Irish Travellers, **4**:156
Jamaicans, **8**:138
Jews, **1**:169
Kalingas, **5**:122
Kenyah-Kayan-Kajang, **5**:134
Khmer, **5**:136
K'iche,' **8**:142
Latvians, **6**:237
Madeirans, **4**:165
Makassar, **5**:173
Nahua of the Huasteca, **8**:186
Nahuat of the Sierra de Puebla, **8**:192
North Alaskan Eskimos, **1**:260
Northern Paiute, **1**:264
Pathan, **3**:232
Peloponnesias, **4**:193
Piemontese Sinti, **4**:200
Poles, **4**:203
Poqomam, **8**:218
Puerto Ricans, **8**:222
Pukapuka, **2**:271
Rom, **1**:304
Romanians, **4**:213
Salasaca, **7**:290
Samal, **5**:220
Samal Moro, **5**:223
San-speaking peoples, **9**:303
Saraguro, **7**:294
Sasak, **5**:226
Sicilians, **4**:236
Slovaks, **4**:244
Southern Paiute (and Chemehuevi), **1**:331
Swedes, **4**:257

Swiss, Italian, **4**:261
Tagalog, **5**:249
Tausug, **5**:263
Temne, **9**:343
Tongareva, **2**:340
Toraja, **5**:282
Ukrainians of Canada, **1**:358
Vlach Gypsies of Hungary, **4**:271
West Greenland Inuit, **1**:377
Farsi
    Zoroastrians, **9**:408
fictive for business
    Jews of Iran, **9**:140
formal and informal
    Poles, **6**:307
gender-based
    Bedouin, **9**:44
    Chinese of Costa Rica, **8**:61
    Pokot, **9**:282
    Sakalava, **9**:295
    Shona, **9**:313
    Tzotzil of Zinacantan, **8**:293
gender distinctions ignored
    Itelmen, **6**:153
    Nenets, **6**:279
generational
    Acehnese, **5**:3
    Alorese, **5**:15
    Bajau, **5**:33
    Bonerate, **5**:45
    Chinese in Southeast Asia, **5**:76
    Evenki (Northern Tungus), **6**:122
    Hmong, **5**:93
    Javanese, **5**:112
    Kaluli, **2**:102
    Karen, **5**:127
    Kenyah-Kayan-Kajang, **5**:134
    Kiwai, **2**:125
    Lahu, **5**:152
    Lao, **5**:158
    Mailu, **2**:155
    Malay, **5**:175
    Mansi, **6**:253
    Mardudjara, **2**:180
    Melanau, **5**:179
    Minangkabau, **5**:183
    Nissan, **2**:250
    Qiang, **6**:486
    Sagada Igorot, **5**:216
    Samal, **5**:220
    Senoi, **5**:238
    Subanun, **5**:245
    Sundanese, **5**:247
    Tabasarans, **6**:349
    Tai Lue, **5**:254
    Tausug, **5**:263
    Temiar, **5**:269
    Tikopia, **2**:325
    Tiwi, **2**:328
    Tor, **2**:343
    Washoe, **1**:369
    Woleai, **2**:383
Greek-type
    Cretans, **4**:70
    Xoraxané Romá, **4**:282
Hawaiian-type
    Acehnese, **5**:3
    Agta, **5**:5

Alorese, **5**:15
Ambonese, **5**:18
Anuta, **2**:14
Balinese, **5**:37
Belau, **2**:26
Betsileo, **9**:55
Blackfoot, **1**:42
Burusho, **3**:55
Central Thai, **5**:70
Cham, **5**:73
Cheyenne, **1**:64
Chimane, **7**:112
Chinantec, **8**:54
Chiriguano, **7**:120
Chocó, **7**:123
Choiseul Island, **2**:39
Chorote, **7**:125
Comanche, **1**:75
Cook Islands, **2**:41
Cora, **8**:76
Daribi, **2**:47
Delaware, **1**:86
Easter Island, **2**:54
Eastern Shoshone, **1**:105
East Indians in Trinidad, **8**:106
Edo, **9**:80
Emberá, **7**:156
Futuna, **2**:67
Gainj, **2**:72
Garifuna, **8**:114
Gogodala, **2**:83
Goodenough Island, **2**:86
Guadalcanal, **2**:90
Hawaiians, **2**:96
Huichol, **8**:126
Iban, **5**:97
Ilongot, **5**:102
Iteso, **9**:129
Jatav, **3**:114
Kapingamarangi, **2**:109
Karajá, **7**:189
Khmer, **5**:136
Kilenge, **2**:119
Kiowa, **1**:187
Kiribati, **2**:122
Kiwai, **2**:125
Klamath, **1**:191
Kogi, **7**:201
Kol, **3**:130
Kongo, **9**:167
Korean, **5**:147
Kosrae, **2**:129
Kuikuru, **7**:207
Kurtatchi, **2**:132
Kwakiutl, **1**:198
Lao Isan, **5**:161
Lengua, **7**:211
Lisu, **5**:165
Luba of Shaba, **9**:192
Maká, **7**:216
Malaita, **2**:162
Manam, **2**:168
Maori, **2**:177
Marquesas Islands, **2**:190
Marshall Islands, **2**:193
Mataco, **7**:228-229
Mejbrat, **2**:196
Mekeo, **2**:199

Kinship terminology (cont'd)
  Mimika, 2:207
  Minangkabau, 5:183
  Miskito, 8:171
  Mixe, 8:174
  Mixtec, 8:177
  Miyanmin, 2:210
  Mocoví, 7:241
  Mohave, 1:241
  Motu, 2:214
  Mundugumor, 2:219
  Murik, 2:222
  Nahua of the Huasteca, 8:186
  Nahuat of the Sierra de Puebla, 8:192
  Namau, 2:231
  Nauru, 2:237
  Newar, 3:207
  Ngawbe, 8:196
  Nissan, 2:250
  Nivaclé, 7:249
  Northern Shoshone and Bannock, 1:267
  Ontong Java, 2:254
  Oriya, 3:217
  Pahari, 3:221
  Paraujano, 7:268
  Pomo, 1:294
  Pukapuka, 2:271
  Rapa, 2:274
  Raroia, 2:276
  Rotuma, 2:282
  Rukuba, 9:289
  Samal, 5:220
  Samoa, 2:288
  Santa Cruz, 2:291
  Sara, 9:306
  Sasak, 5:226
  Sengseng, 2:296-297
  Shipibo, 7:304, 305
  Sio, 2:300
  Slovaks, 4:244
  Somalis, 9:317
  Subanun, 5:245
  Tagalog, 5:249
  Tahiti, 2:306
  Tapirapé, 7:321
  Temiar, 5:269
  Terena, 7:326
  Ternatan/Tidorese, 5:275
  Tibetans, 6:495
  Tikopia, 2:325
  Toba, 7:332
  Tokelau, 2:331
  Tonga, 2:337
  Tongareva, 2:340
  Tor, 2:343
  Toraja, 5:282
  Triqui, 8:271
  tropical-forest foragers, 9:357
  Tuvalu, 2:356
  Warao, 7:358
  Western Shoshone, 1:375
  Woleai, 2:383
  Yap, 2:393
  Yekuana, 7:381
  Yokuts, 1:388
  Zapotec, 8:312
  Indo-European pattern
    Dalmatians, 4:86

Iranian-type
  Ossetes, 6:300
Iroquois-type
  Abelam, 2:5
  Acholi, 9:5
  Akawaio, 7:32
  Anuta, 2:14
  Bagirmi, 9:34
  Baiga, 3:20
  Bakairi, 7:74
  Bau, 2:23
  Bondo, 3:49
  Chácobo, 7:106
  Cree, 1:81
  Daribi, 2:47
  Dobu, 2:50
  Dyula, 9:77
  Ewe and Fon, 9:86
  Fipa, 9:99
  Fore, 2:63
  Gainj, 2:72
  Garia, 2:75
  Gayo, 5:89
  Guahibo-Sikuani, 7:165
  Hare, 1:141
  Herero, 9:117
  Huarayo, 7:177
  Iroquois, 1:166
  Jicarilla, 1:173
  Kapauku, 2:106
  Keraki, 2:113
  Kewa, 2:116
  Khasi, 3:124
  Kpelle, 9:173
  Kuikuru, 7:207-208
  Lak, 2:138
  Lakalai, 2:141
  Lengua, 7:211
  Lisu, 6:465
  Lunda, 9:197
  Luyia, 9:204
  Mae Enga, 2:149
  Maisin, 2:158
  Makushi, 7:219
  Malaita, 2:162
  Maliseet, 1:211
  Mam, 8:158
  Mandak, 2:171
  Maring, 2:186
  Mbeere, 9:221
  Mejbrat, 2:196
  Melpa, 2:201
  Montagnais-Naskapi, 1:245
  Mundugumor, 2:219
  Muyu, 2:228
  Nasioi, 2:234
  Navajo, 1:252
  Nivkh, 6:284
  Nyakyusa and Ngonde, 9:253
  Nyamwezi and Sukuma, 9:256
  Ogan-Besemah, 5:198
  Ojibwa, 1:270
  Orokaiva, 2:257
  Orokolo, 2:259
  Palikur, 7:262
  Panare, 7:266
  Pemon, 7:272
  Pukapuka, 2:271

Quechan, 1:301
Rikbaktsa, 7:287
San-speaking peoples, 9:303
Santa Cruz, 2:291
Selepet, 2:294
Sio, 2:300
Songhay, 9:319
Suku, 9:321
Suruí, 7:312
Tairora, 2:309
Tanana, 1:339
Tangu, 2:311
Tauade, 2:319
Telefolmin, 2:322
Teton, 1:345
Tolai, 2:335
Tonga, 9:353
Tor, 2:343
Wamira, 2:366
Wantoat, 2:368
Western Apache, 1:372
Wogeo, 2:381
Wovan, 2:386
Yanomamö, 7:375
Yawalapití, 7:379
Yekuana, 7:381
Yuit, 1:391
Yukpa, 7:383
Zarma, 9:405
Islamic
  Gayo, 5:89
Latin roots
  Portuguese, 4:207
lineal
  Cahita, 8:36
  cattle ranchers of Huasteca, 8:43
  Finns, 4:103
  Maká, 7:216
  Mixe, 8:174
  Pima Bajo, 8:212
  Salasaca, 7:290
  Serbs, 4:231
  Toba, 7:332
lineal for females
  Montenegrins, 4:173
maternal relatives distinguished from
    paternal
  Mescalero Apache, 1:224
Maya
  Itza,' 8:134
Mexican
  Cahita, 8:36
nonbifurcate-collateral
  Afro-Hispanic Pacific Lowlanders, 7:21
not classified
  Hausa, 9:113
Omaha-type
  Araucanians, 7:53
  Aymara, 7:67
  Berbers of Morocco, 9:50
  Bunun, 5:57
  Chambri, 2:32
  Chin, 3:65
  Ch'ol, 8:64
  Craho, 7:137
  Dani, 2:44
  Eipo, 2:57
  Fox, 1:129

Gebusi, 2:78
Gururumba, 2:93
Han, 6:444
Jingpo, 6:457
Kachin, 5:117
Kickapoo, 1:184
Kikapu, 8:144
Kipsigis, 9:164
Konso, 9:170
Kumeyaay, 1:194
Kwoma, 2:134
Lakher, 3:146
Lango, 9:180
Lobi-Dagarti peoples, 9:184
Maasai, 9:208
Malaita, 2:162
Mendi, 2:204
Menominee, 1:221
Miami, 1:231
Mikir, 3:175
Mizo, 3:178
Mountain Arapesh, 2:216
Nagas, 3:189
Nandi and other Kalenjin peoples, 9:233
Naxi, 6:479
Ningerum, 2:247
Nyinba, 3:212
Okiek, 9:260
Omaha, 1:275
Osage, 1:278
Pomo, 1:294
Sambia, 2:285
Sherpa, 3:258
Siona-Secoya, 7:308
Suri, 9:325
Suya, 7:316
Tairora, 2:309
Thadou, 3:288
Tupari, 7:340
Tzeltal, 8:274
Wape, 2:371
Winnebago, 1:381
Xikrin, 7:368
Yangoru Boiken, 2:389
Yokuts, 1:388
Zoque, 8:316
personal names
Tuareg, 9:367
Portuguese (Brazilian)-type
Apiaká, 7:49
proper name use avoided
Piro, 7:280
reciprocal
Mam, 8:159
replace personal names
Kuna, 8:148
Russian-type
Chuvans, 6:81
self-reciprocity
Somalis, 9:317
Spanish-type
Itza,' 8:134
Ladinos, 8:152
Mazahua, 8:165
Tz'utujil, 8:297
Sudanese-type
Asurini, 7:61
Bengali, 3:31

Berbers of Morocco, 9:50
Jews, Arabic-speaking, 9:135
Jews of Iran, 9:140
Palestinians, 9:265
Purum, 3:243
Shahsevan, 9:308
Shipibo, 7:304
Slovensko Roma, 4:250
Somalis, 9:317
Vietnamese, 5:285
Xoraxané Romá, 4:282
Yörük, 9:395
Turkic-type
Karachays, 6:160
Kazakhs, 6:179
Turkish
Circassians, 9:66
vocatives
Dogon, 9:72
Western system
Jews of Israel, 9:143
wife giver/taker distinction
Akha, 5:12
Nias, 5:195
Yankee-type
Tagalog, 5:249
Yuman-type
North Alaskan Eskimos, 1:260
Yaqui, 8:306
"Kiowa Five" (artists), 1:189
Kipat land system
Limbu, 3:150
Nepali, 3:203
Kiribati Protestant Church
Kiribati, 2:123
Kisiihiat (Kickapoo supreme deity), 1:185
Kiva groups
Keres Pueblo Indians, 1:180
Pueblo Indians, 1:298
Taos, 1:342, 343
Tewa Pueblos, 1:347, 349
Zuni, 1:399
Kïzgalin (festival)
Meskhetians, 6:261
Knitting
Acadians, 1:8
Bulgarians, 4:43
Georgians, 6:136
Highland Scots, 4:140
Karachays, 6:160
Khinalughs, 6:199
Kubachins, 6:217
Maltese, 4:168
Naxi, 6:478
Orcadians, 4:187, 188
Rutuls, 6:319
Saami, 6:323
Shetlanders, 4:234
Siberian Estonians, 6:336
Tats, 6:359
Tory Islanders, 4:265
Tsakhurs, 6:366, 367
Knives
making
Fruili, 4:113
reindeer horn
Saami, 4:221, 258
sharpening

Piemontese Sinti, 4:200
Rominche, 4:216
stone-blade
West Greenland Inuit, 1:377
Koolex. *See* Potlatch
Kosher diet. *See* Food, dietary laws and
restrictions
Koumbari relationship
Cypriots, 4:80
Kovave (ceremony)
Orokolo, 2:260
Krishna (deity)
Bengali Vaishnava, 3:36-37
Brahman and Chhetri of Nepal, 3:53
Irula, 3:108
Kubam-bairam (holiday)
Kubachins, 6:219
Kukumat (creator)
Quechan, 1:302
Kula exchange
Dobu, 2:50, 51, 52
Goodenough Island, 2:86
Rossel Island, 2:278
Trobriand Islands, 2:349, 350, 351
Kulama (ceremony)
Tiwi, 2:329
Kuloskap (Koluskap) (culture hero)
Maliseet, 1:212
Kuls (totemic groups)
Maratha, 3:169
Kumara
Maori, 2:177
Kumina (ancestor cult)
Jamaicans, 8:139
Kundalini (female deity)
Bengali Shakta, 3:35
Kurban Bairam [Bayram] (holiday)
Karakalpaks, 6:168
Siberian Tatars, 6:342
Tabasarans, 6:351
Talysh, 6:357
Turkmens, 6:371
Kurijmoj (ceremony)
Marshall Islands, 2:194
Kurmukhoba (holiday)
Ingilos, 6:151
Kuru (disease)
Fore, 2:62
Kwanza (holiday)
African Americans, 1:13
Kwulacan (Delaware term for stress), 1:86

Labor
age-based
Betsileo, 9:55
Cahita, 8:35
Fulani, 9:101
Iraqw, 9:125
Lango, 9:179
Mixtec, 8:177
Nandi and other Kalenjin peoples, 9:233
Okiek, 9:260
San-speaking peoples, 9:302
Suri, 9:325
Swazi, 9:330
Tandroy, 9:337
Tigray, 9:347
Yoruba, 9:392

Labor (cont'd)
  age equality
    Tepehuan of Chihuahua, 8:252
  age specialization
    Cotopaxi Quichua, 7:133
  belief in spiritual value of
    Lingayat, 3:153
  birthplace as factor
    Chinese in Caribbean, 8:57
  bonded
    Badaga, 3:16
    Bavarians, 4:34
    Cape Verdeans, 4:55
    Pahari, 3:211
    Paniyan, 3:227
    Tamil of Sri Lanka, 3:281
    Yurok, 1:395
  child
    Hmong, 5:93
    see also Child tasks
  class divisions
    Chamorros, 2:34
    Dominicans, 8:101
    English, 4:96
    Korean, 5:146
    Kurds, 9:175
    Tuareg, 9:367
    Wolof, 9:378
  collective
    Guambiano, 7:171
    Kagwahiv, 7:185
    Nivaclé, 7:249
  communal
    Bhil, 3:39
    Emberá and Wounaan, 8:109, 110
    Gorotire, 7:163
    Guahibo-Sikuani, 7:165
    Karajá, 7:189
    Salasaca, 7:290
    Saraguro, 7:295
    Xikrin, 7:368
  community work
    Tojolab'al, 8:262
  contract
    Japanese, 7:60
    Manam, 2:167
    Miyanmin, 2:210
    Tangu, 2:312
    Usino, 2:361
  cooperative
    Mossi, 9:228, 230
    Saint Lucians, 8:231
    Shetlanders, 4:233
    Suruí, 7:313
    Swedes, 4:258
    Temne, 9:343
    Welsh, 4:279
  corvée
    Javanese, 5:112
    Jingpo, 6:458
    Muong, 5:190
    Sasak, 5:225
    Tibetans, 6:494
    Yao, 6:505
    Yuan, 5:294
  debt peonage
    Amahuaca, 7:34
    Chimila, 7:114

    Kashinawa, 7:195
    Yagua, 7:372, 373
    Yukuna, 7:386-387
  equal
    Sara, 9:305
    Swahili, 9:327
  ethnic divisions
    Amhara, 9:18
    Arubans, 8:12
    Dominicans, 8:101
    Flemish, 4:106
    Romanians, 4:213
  exchange. See Exchange, labor
  as export
    Otomí of the Valley of Mezquital, 8:204,
      205
    Puerto Ricans, 8:221
    Yemenis, 9:388
  field
    Magar, 3:156
    Mahar, 3:164
    Mauritian, 3:171
  forced
    Ajië, 2:7
    Guadalcanal, 2:89
    Khasi, 3:125
    Lak, 2:137
    Lakalai, 2:140
    Magar, 3:160
    Malaita, 2:160
    Mekeo, 2:198
    Pomo, 1:293
    Thadou, 3:289
    Torres Strait Islanders, 2:345
    see also Blackbirding; Slavery
  gender segregation
    Druze, 9:74
  guest workers
    Austria, 4:21
    Calabrese, 4:49
    Malayali, 3:166
    Mappila, 3:167
    Pathan, 3:231
  hired. See Wage labor
  imported
    Kittsians and Nevisians, 8:146
  impressment. See Blackbirding
  indentured
    Wape, 2:371
  joblessness. See Unemployment
  kin group specialization
    Dyula, 9:76
  landless day laborers
    Portuguese, 4:207
  manual despised
    Ambonese, 5:18
  migrant. See Migrant workers
  mixed
    Lobi-Dagarti peoples, 9:184
    Sakalava, 9:294
    San-speaking peoples, 9:302
    Tswana, 9:362
    Yakö, 9:384
  multiple jobs
    Antigua and Barbuda, 8:8
    Puerto Ricans, 8:221
  no division by sex
    Central Thai, 5:70

    Frisians, 4:111
    Galicians, 4:119
  pedigree
    Swazi, 9:330
  plantation
    Irula, 3:104, 105
    Nasioi, 2:233
    Telefolmin, 2:321
  protection
    Japanese, 5:106
  reciprocal. See Exchange, labor
  recruitment
    Gainj, 2:71
    Gnau, 2:80
    Kapingamarangi, 2:108
    Kilenge, 2:118
    Kiribati, 2:123
    Lesu, 2:145, 146
    Maisin, 2:157
    Malaita, 2:161
    Mardudjara, 2:179
    Pentecost, 2:262
    Rotuma, 2:281
    Tanna, 2:313
    Telefolmin, 2:323
    Wape, 2:370
    Wogeo, 2:380
  riots
    Curaçao, 8:97
  shared
    Akan, 9:11
    Antigua and Barbuda, 8:8
    Lugbara, 9:194
    Mamprusi, 9:211
    Mixe, 8:174
    Qashqa'i, 9:285
    Zarma, 9:405
  skill ownership rights
    Mandan, 1:214
  specialized functions in polygynous
      families
    Somalis, 9:317
  strikes
    Provencal, 4:211
  tenant
    Pedi, 9:270
  traded for goods
    Kashinawa, 7:195
    Matsigenka, 7:231
    Mayoruna, 7:235
    Yukuna, 7:386-387
  traditional women's occupations
    German Swiss, 4:125
  worker self-management
    Serbs, 4:230
  work ethic
    Flemish, 4:107
  work parties
    Shona, 9:313
    Swazi, 9:330
    Temne, 9:343
    see also Slavery; Unemployment
Labor exchange. See Exchange, labor
Labor unions
    Germans, 4:122
    Icelanders, 4:147, 148
    Japanese, 5:107
    Walloons, 4:277

Lace work
  Auvergnats, **4:**22
  Finns, **4:**102
  Flemish, **4:**106, 108-109
  Provencal, **4:**210
  Sicilians, **4:**237
  Slovaks, **4:**243
  Walloons, **4:**277
Lacquerware
  Sindhi, **3:**263
Laestadianism
  Finns, **4:**104
  Saami, **4:**222
  Swedes, **4:**258
Lakshmi (female deity)
  Bengali, **3:**34
Lamaism. _See_ Buddhism (Tibetan)
Laments for the dead. _See_ Keening
Lammas (holiday)
  Orcadians, **4:**188
Landholding
  absentee landlords
    Portuguese, **4:**207
    Provencal, **4:**210
    Sicilians, **4:**235, 236, 237
    Tuscans, **4:**270
    see also Leaseholds; Sharecropping;
      Tenant farming
  by age village
    Nyakyusa and Ngonde, **9:**253
  agrarian reforms
    Canarians, **4:**52
    Finns, **4:**103
    Germans, **4:**122
    Greeks, **4:**132
    Hungarians, **4:**144
    Ionians, **4:**149
    Irish, **4:**153
    Portuguese, **4:**207
    Romanians, **4:**123
    Sicilians, **4:**236
    Slovaks, **4:**244
    Slovenes, **4:**247
  for all to use
    Northern Paiute, **1:**263
  "Alp rights"
    German Swiss, **4:**125
  ancestral claims
    Canelos Quchua, **7:**99
    Canelos Quichua, **7:**99
    Kanbi, **3:**118
    Ka'wiari, **7:**198
    Khasi, **3:**124
    Maltese, **4:**168
    Mamprusi, **9:**212
    Mossi, **9:**228
    Pende, **9:**272
    Tsimihety, **9:**358
    Tzotzil of Zinacantan, **8:**293
    Yukuna, **7:**387
  as aristocracy basis
    English, **4:**97
  by band
    Tanana, **1:**339
  based on communication of intent
    Apiaká, **7:**49
    Matsigenka, **7:**231
  based on creation myth

  Tatuyo, **7:**323
based on pasturage rights
  Guajiro, **7:**168
based on territorial dominions
  Karajá, **7:**189
as basis of wealth
  Pasiegos, **4:**190
bilateral
  San-speaking peoples, **9:**302
bilineal
  Sakalava, **9:**295
caretaking
  Hawaiians, **2:**96
caste
  Okkaliga, **3:**214
  Pahari, **3:**220
  Tamil, **3:**277
by chief
  Amahuaca, **7:**35
  Guajajára, **7:**166
  Kosrae, **2:**129
  Pohnpei, **2:**268
  Temne, **9:**343
  Wáiwai, **7:**346
church
  Mormons, **1:**248
  Romanians, **4:**214
clan
  Abelam, **2:**4
  Ajarians, **6:**14
  Atoni, **5:**27
  Avars, **6:**45
  Balkars, **6:**53
  Bau, **2:**23
  Belau, **2:**26
  Boazi, **2:**29
  Choiseul Island, **2:**38
  Chuvans, **6:**81
  Cook Islands, **2:**41
  Daribi, **2:**47
  Easter Island, **2:**54
  Even, **6:**118
  Foi, **2:**60
  Georgians, **6:**132, 134
  Gnau, **2:**80
  Gogodala, **2:**83
  Gururumba, **2:**93
  Iatmul, **2:**99
  Kapingamarangi, **2:**109
  Kazakhs, **6:**177
  Kewa, **2:**116
  Kilenge, **2:**119
  Kubachins, **6:**218
  Kwoma, **2:**135
  Lak, **2:**138
  Lakalai, **2:**141
  Laks, **6:**234
  Lamaholot, **5:**155
  Lau, **2:**144
  Lesu, **2:**146
  Mae Enga, **2:**149
  Mafulu, **2:**152
  Mailu, **2:**155
  Manam, **2:**168
  Mandak, **2:**170
  Mandan, **1:**215
  Mansi, **6:**253
  Manus, **2:**174

Maori, **2:**177
Mardudjara, **2:**180
Maring, **2:**186
Marshall Islands, **2:**193
Mekeo, **2:**198
Mimika, **2:**207
Miyanmin, **2:**210
Motu, **2:**213-214
Mountain Arapesh, **2:**216
Mundugumor, **2:**219
Murngin, **2:**225
Namau, **2:**231
Nasioi, **2:**234
Ngatatjara, **2:**240
Nguna, **2:**243
Ningerum, **2:**246
Niue, **2:**251
Ontong Java, **2:**254
Orokolo, **2:**259
Pamir Peoples, **6:**305
Pintupi, **2:**265
Pukapuka, **2:**271
Rapa, **2:**274
Raroia, **2:**276
Rotuma, **2:**281
Selepet, **2:**293
Selkup, **6:**327
Seminole, **1:**313
Shors, **6:**330
Sio, **2:**300
Siwai, **2:**303
Tairora, **2:**308
Talysh, **6:**356
Tanaina, **1:**335
Tauade, **2:**318
Tikopia, **2:**325
Tiwi, **2:**328
Tokelau, **2:**331
Tolai, **2:**334
Trobriand Islands, **2:**349
Truk, **2:**352
Ulithi, **2:**359, 360
Wantoat, **2:**368, 369
Wape, **2:**371
Wik Mungkan, **2:**377
Woleai, **2:**383
Wovan, **2:**386
Yangoru Boiken, **2:**389
Yap, **2:**392
collective, **4:**274
  Ainu, **5:**8
  Ajië, **2:**9
  Ambonese, **5:**18
  Anuta, **2:**14
  Asiatic Eskimos, **6:**40
  Asmat, **2:**19
  Ata Tana 'Ai, **5:**24
  Avars, **6:**45
  Belau, **2:**26
  Blang, **6:**421
  Bonerate, **5:**45
  Buriats, **6:**67
  Butonese, **5:**67
  Carib of Dominica, **8:**39
  Cham, **5:**73
  Chechen-Ingush, **6:**73
  Crimean Tatars, **6:**93
  Czechs, **4:**83

Landholding (cont'd)
  Dargins, 6:98
  De'ang, 6:430
  Dinka, 9:70
  Don Cossacks, 6:105
  Endenese, 5:85
  Falasha, 9:91
  Fore, 2:63
  Futuna, 2:66
  Gainj, 2:72
  Garia, 2:74
  Han, 6:444
  Hani, 6:450
  Hungarians, 4:144
  Javanese, 5:112
  Jingpo, 6:456
  Jino, 6:460
  Kachin, 5:116
  Kalingas, 5:122
  Kalmyks, 6:156
  Karachays, 6:160
  Kédang, 5:132
  Khinalughs, 6:200
  Kiwai, 2:125
  Kmhmu, 5:140
  Kriashen Tatars, 6:211
  Kubachins, 6:218
  Kuna, 8:148
  Kurds, 9:176
  Kurtatchi, 2:132
  Lezgins, 6:242
  Madurese, 5:167
  Maguindanao, 5:169
  Melanau, 5:179
  Muong, 5:190
  Ngawbe, 8:196
  Nias, 5:195
  North Alaskan Eskimos, 1:259
  Pima-Papago, 1:289
  Pokot, 9:282
  Pukapuka, 2:271
  Russian peasants, 6:311
  Rutuls, 6:320
  Samoa, 2:287
  Senoi, 5:237
  Slav Macedonians, 4:240
  Slovaks, 4:244
  Slovenes, 4:247
  Subanun, 5:244
  Sundanese, 5:247
  Svans, 6:344
  Tai Lue, 5:254
  Taiwan aboriginal peoples, 5:257
  Tasmanians, 2:316
  Tats, 6:359
  Temiar, 5:268
  Tofalar, 6:362
  Tor, 2:343
  Tsakhurs, 6:366
  Turkmens, 6:370
  Tuvalu, 2:356
  Udis, 6:377
  Vietnamese, 5:285
  Wa, 6:502
  Warlpiri, 2:374
  Wogeo, 2:380
  Yao of Thailand, 5:292
  Yokuts, 1:388
Comarca law
  Emberá and Wounaan, 8:110
communal
  Afro-Colombians, 7:16, 17
  Akawaio, 7:31
  Albanians, 4:4, 5, 6
  Amuesha, 7:38
  Amuzgo, 8:5
  Araucanians, 7:53
  Asháninca, 7:91
  Austrian, 4:19-20
  Awá Kwaiker, 7:63
  Aymara, 7:67
  Azoreans, 4:27
  Bakairi, 7:74
  Baluchi, 3:23
  Baniwa-Curripaco-Wakuenai, 7:77-78
  Basques, 4:30
  Bulgarians, 4:43, 44
  Castilians, 4:59-60
  Chácobo, 7:106
  Chakma, 3:59
  Chatino, 8:50
  Chimane, 7:112
  Chinantec, 8:53
  Chipaya, 7:115
  Chuj, 8:71
  Cinta Larga, 7:127
  Corsicans, 4:67, 68
  Cotopaxi Quichua, 7:133
  Craho, 7:137
  Cuicatec, 8:92
  Danes, 4:87, 89
  Divehi, 3:76
  Emberá, 7:156
  Finns, 4:102
  Garo, 3:83
  Guambiano, 7:172
  Hidatsa, 1:146
  Hill Pandaram, 3:99
  Huichol, 8:126
  Hutterites, 1:153
  Inughuit, 1:160
  Karok, 1:176
  Khoi, 9:159
  Kikapu, 8:144
  Kogi, 7:201
  Kuikuru, 7:207
  Kumeyaay, 1:194
  Kurds, 9:176
  Ladinos, 8:152
  Lenca, 8:155, 156
  Leonese, 4:161
  Macuna, 7:213
  Makushi, 7:218
  Mamprusi, 9:212
  Marubo, 7:222
  Mashco, 7:226
  Mazatec, 8:168
  Mixe, 8:174
  Mixtec, 8:177
  Mizo, 3:178
  Navajo, 1:252
  Nayaga, 3:195
  Ndebele, 9:236
  Otomí of the Sierra, 8:201
  Páez, 7:257
  Pawnee, 1:284
  Pedi, 9:270
  Pomo, 1:294
  Portuguese, 4:207
  Puinave, 7:281
  Purum, 3:243
  Rikbaktsa, 7:287
  Salasaca, 7:290
  Saraguro, 7:294
  Saramaka, 7:297
  Sardinians, 4:226
  Seminole, 1:313
  Shakers, 1:316
  Sirionó, 7:310
  Sumu, 8:238
  Suruí, 7:312
  Swazi, 9:330
  Swiss, Italian, 4:261
  Tamang, 3:275
  Taos, 1:342
  Tepehuan of Durango, 8:256
  Tigray, 9:347
  Toba, 7:331, 332
  Toda, 3:296
  Tory Islanders, 4:265
  Triqui, 8:271
  Tswana, 9:362
  Turkana, 9:371
  Tzotzil of San Bartolomé de los Llanos,
    8:288
  Veddas, 3:301
  Walapai, 1:365
  Wanano, 7:349
  Washoe, 1:368
  West Greenland Inuit, 1:377
  Yagua, 7:372
  Yaqui, 8:306
  Yukpa, 7:383
  Yukuna, 7:387
  Yurok, 1:394
  Zapotec, 8:312
cooperative
  Pima Bajo, 8:212
  Totonac, 8:265
corporate family unit
  Alur, 9:13
  Austrians, 4:19-20
  Bulgarians, 4:44
  Dalmatians, 4:86
corporate groups
  cattle ranchers of Huasteca, 8:43
  Flemish, 4:107
  North Alaskan Eskimos, 1:258, 259
  Pacific Eskimo, 1:283
  Romanians, 4:213
  Swedes, 4:257
  Tlingit, 1:352
crofting
  Highland Scots, 4:139, 141
  Orcadians, 4:187
  Shetlanders, 4:233, 234
  Tory Islanders, 4:265
"customary range" system
  Walapai, 1:365
direct
  Andalusians, 4:11
  Auvergnats, 4:22
  Bavarians, 4:34
  Bretons, 4:38

Canarians, **4:**52
Catalans, **4:**62
disputes
   Canarians, **4:**52
   Castilians, **4:**60
domaine congéable
   Bretons, **4:**38
ejido system
   Cahita, **8:**36
   Ch'ol, **8:**64
   Cuicatec, **8:**92
   Lenca, **8:**155
   Mazahua, **8:**165
   Mazatec, **8:**168
   Nahua of the Huasteca, **8:**185
   Nahua of the State of Mexico, **8:**188, 189
   Nahuat of the Sierra de Puebla, **8:**192
   Opata, **8:**199
   Otomí of the Sierra, **8:**201
   Otomí of the Valley of Mezquital, **8:**204, 205
   Tarascans, **8:**245
   Tepehuan of Chihuahua, **8:**252
   Tzotzil and Tzeltal of Pantelhó, **8:**276
   Tzotzil of Chamula, **8:**280
   Tzotzil of San Bartolomé de los Llanos, **8:**288
   Yukateko, **8:**309
   Zapotec, **8:**312
   Zoque, **8:**316
by eldest clan member
   Murik, **2:**221
enclosures
   Swedes, **4:**257
exclusive use rights
   Lobi-Dagarti peoples, **9:**184
family
   Bakhtiari, **9:**36
   Creoles of Nicaragua, **8:**84-85
   Dutch, **4:**92-93
   Fipa, **9:**99
   Huichol, **8:**126
   Jamaicans, **8:**138
   Miskito, **8:**171
   Nandi and other Kalenjin peoples, **9:**233
   Pomo, **1:**294
   Swiss, Italian, **4:**261
   Tory Islanders, **4:**265
   Triqui, **8:**271
fee simple
   Nahuat of the Sierra de Puebla, **8:**192
feudal. *See* Feudalism
first settlers
   Garifuna, **8:**114
   Luba of Shaba, **9:**191
   Ndembu, **9:**239
fluid rights
   Montagnais-Naskapi, **1:**245
by force
   Iceland, **4:**147
foreign ownership restrictions
   German Swiss, **4:**125
fragmented
   Bretons, **4:**18
   Ionians, **4:**149
   Orcadians, **4:**186
   Peloponnesians, **4:**193

Portuguese, **4:**207
Provencals, **4:**211
Serbs, **4:**231
Slovaks, **4:**244
free building land availability
   West Greenland Inuit, **1:**377
freehold
   Creoles of Nicaragua, **8:**84
   Faroe Islanders, **4:**99
   Montserratians, **8:**180
generation property
   Bahamians, **8:**19
government
   Afro-Venezuelans, **7:**26
   Bavarians, **4:**34
   Candoshi, **7:**93
   Chiriguano, **7:**120
   Chorote, **7:**125
   Cook Islands, **2:**41
   Cubans, **8:**88
   Easter Island, **2:**54
   Futuna, **2:**66
   Herero, **9:**117
   Jews of Israel, **9:**143
   Kongo, **9:**167
   Korean, **5:**146
   Lao, **5:**158
   Metis of Western Canada, **1:**228
   Miwok, **1:**239
   Newar, **3:**207
   Nivaclé, **7:**249
   North Alaskan Eskimos, **1:**260
   Nyinba, **3:**212
   Piaroa, **7:**277
   Piro, **7:**280
   Shahsevan, **9:**308
   Suri, **9:**325
   Tandroy, **9:**337
   Tausug, **5:**263
   Ticuna, **7:**329
   Tonga, **2:**337
   Wolof, **9:**378
   Yoruba, **9:**392
government trust
   Western Apache, **1:**372
grants
   Cape Verdeans, **4:**43, 55
grazing rights
   Shahsevan, **9:**308
grazing vs. farming rights
   Montenegrins, **4:**172
growth-management plan
   Manx, **4:**170
"hay privilege"
   Metis of Western Canada, **1:**228
hereditary
   Afro-Bolivians, **7:**8-9
   Araucanians, **7:**53
   Austrians, **4:**20
   Auvergnats, **4:**22
   Aveyronnais, **4:**25, 26
   Basques, **4:**31
   Bavarians, **4:**34
   Burgundians, **4:**47
   Canelos Quichua, **7:**100
   Cape Verdeans, **4:**55
   Cashibo, **7:**104
   Corsicans, **4:**67

Cretans, **4:**70
Cuna, **7:**149, 150
Desana, **7:**153
Emberá, **7:**157
Gaels (Irish), **4:**116
German Swiss, **4:**125, 126
Ka'wiari, **7:**199
Lakher, **3:**145-146
Magar, **3:**157
Manx, **4:**171
Munda, **3:**183
Nambudiri Brahman, **3:**193
Nivaclé, **7:**249
Nootka, **1:**256
Old Believers, **1:**274
Orcadians, **4:**187
Pahari, **3:**220, 221
Pandit of Kashmir, **3:**225
Rajput, **3:**249
Salasaca, **7:**290
Sora, **3:**269
Swedes, **4:**258
Tigray, **9:**347
Tiroleans, **4:**263
Toba, **7:**332
Vellala, **3:**305
Yukuna, **7:**387
Zamindar, **3:**306, 307
see also Feudalism; *subhead* ancestral
   claims *above*
homesteads
   Winnebago, **1:**380
household
   Quechan, **1:**301
   Telugu, **3:**285
individual
   Achang, **6:**418
   Acholi, **9:**4
   Ajië, **2:**8
   Akha, **5:**12
   Alorese, **5:**15
   Ambae, **2:**11
   Andis, **6:**25
   Bagirmi, **9:**34
   Bajau, **5:**33
   Balinese, **5:**36
   Balkars, **6:**53
   Boruca, Bribri, Cabécar, **8:**28
   Buriats, **6:**67
   Carpatho-Rusyns, **6:**70
   Cham, **5:**73
   Chambri, **2:**32
   Chatino, **8:**50
   Circassians, **6:**88;**9:**66
   Costa Ricans, **8:**80
   Cotopaxi Quichua, **7:**133
   Crimean Tatars, **6:**93
   Cuicatec, **8:**92
   Desana, **7:**152
   Dobu, **2:**50
   Dogon, **9:**72
   Dyula, **9:**76
   East Indians in Trinidad, **8:**105
   Eipo, **2:**57
   Emberá and Wounaan, **8:**110
   Endenese, **5:**85
   Estonian, **6:**113
   Filipino, **5:**87

Landholding (cont'd)
 Flemish, **4**:107
 Frisians, **4**:111
 Gayo, **5**:89
 Gusii, **9**:109
 Haitians, **8**:121
 Han, **6**:443
 Iraqw, **9**:125
 Jews of Iran, **9**:140
 Jews of Yemen, **9**:149
 Jingpo, **6**:456
 Kalimantan Dayaks, **5**:120
 Kaluli, **2**:102
 Kapauku, **2**:105
 Kapingamarangi, **2**:109
 Karachays, **6**:160
 Kédang, **5**:132
 Kenyah-Kayan-Kajang, **5**:134
 Keraki, **2**:113
 Khinalughs, **6**:200
 Khmer, **5**:136
 Kipsigis, **9**:164
 Kogi, **7**:201
 Konso, **9**:170
 Kuikuru, **7**:207
 Kuna, **8**:148
 Kyrgyz, **6**:230
 Ladinos, **8**:152
 Lahu, **5**:152;**6**:462
 Lamaholot, **5**:155
 Latvians, **6**:237
 Lisu, **6**:465
 Luyia, **9**:204
 Madurese, **5**:167
 Maisin, **2**:158
 Makassar, **5**:172
 Malekula, **2**:165
 Manx, **4**:170
 Marind-anim, **2**:183
 Mazatec, **8**:168
 Melanau, **5**:179
 Melpa, **2**:201
 Mennonites, **1**:218
 Mixtec, **8**:177
 Muyu, **2**:228
 Nahua of the Huasteca, **8**:185
 Nandi and other Kalenjin peoples, **9**:233
 Nauru, **2**:237
 Naxi, **6**:478
 Nepali, **3**:203
 Nias, **5**:195
 Nissan, **2**:249
 Nomoi, **2**:252
 Nubians, **9**:247
 Nyakyusa and Ngonde, **9**:253
 Ogan-Besemah, **5**:198
 Okiek, **9**:260
 Opata, **8**:199
 Otavalo, **7**:254
 Otomí of the Sierra, **8**:201
 Palu'e, **5**:206
 Pawnee, **1**:284
 Peloponnesians, **4**:193
 Pentecost, **2**:262
 Poles, **4**:203
 Provencal, **1**:210
 Puerto Ricans, **8**:222
 Qashqa'i, **9**:285

 Raroia, **2**:277
 Rennell Island, **2**:277
 Rutuls, **6**:31, 320
 Samal, **5**:219
 Sambia, **2**:285
 Santa Cruz, **2**:291
 Saraguro, **7**:294
 Sardinians, **4**:226
 Serbs, **4**:231
 Sundanese, **5**:247
 Svans, **6**:344
 Swedes, **4**:257
 Syrian Christian of Kerala, **3**:273
 Taiwan aboriginal peoples, **5**:257
 Tapirapé, **7**:320
 Tats, **6**:359
 Telefolmin, **2**:322
 Tequistlatec, **8**:259
 Teton, **1**:344
 Tibetans, **6**:494
 Tongareva, **2**:340
 Totonac, **8**:265
 Triqui, **8**:271
 Truk, **2**:352
 Tsakhurs, **6**:366
 Turkmens, **6**:370
 Tzotzil and Tzeltal of Pantelhó, **8**:276
 Tzotzil of Chamula, **8**:280
 Tzotzil of San Bartolomé de los Llanos, **8**:288
 Udis, **6**:377
 Volga Tatars, **6**:401
 Wa, **6**:502
 Wamira, **2**:366
 Yakan, **5**:289
 Yemenis, **9**:389
 Yörük, **9**:395
 Zamindar, **3**:306-307
 Zapotec, **8**:312
 Zuni, **1**:398
individual women
 Yokuts, **1**:388
infield/outfield division
 Faroe Islanders, **4**:99
informal
 Miami, **1**:231
inherited at birth
 San-speaking peoples, **9**:303
kin-based clusters
 Sea Islanders, **1**:309-310
by king
 Bamiléké, **9**:38
 Edo, **9**:80
 Ewe and Fon, **9**:85
 Lozi, **9**:188
king allots to chiefs
 Swazi, **9**:330
kin groups
 Bugle, **8**:32
 Igbo, **9**:122
 Suku, **9**:321
lack of concept
 Northern Shoshone and Bannock, **1**:267
 Slavey, **1**:319
land cannot be bought or sold
 Shona, **9**:313
land use rights
 Nicobarese, **3**:209

 legal claims for aboriginal
  Oneida, **1**:276
lending
 Iraqw, **9**:125
 Western Apache, **1**:372
lineage
 Nepali, **3**:203
lodge group
 Mandan, **1**:215
by male head of household
 Kashubians, **4**:158-159
matrilineal
 Kongo, **9**:167
 Micronesians, **1**:237
 Pende, **9**:273
 Yakö, **9**:384-385
meadowland
 Pasiegos, **4**:189, 190
by men
 Kipsigis, **9**:164
by men's clubs
 Kilenge, **2**:119
not inheritable
 Lunda, **9**:197
open field system
 Danes, **4**:89
original settlers
 Betsileo, **9**:55
owner permission required
 Shipibo, **7**:304
 Wayapi, **7**:361
ownership not fixed
 Lango, **9**:179
patrilateral
 Yoruba, **9**:392
patrilineal
 Acholi, **9**:4
 Berbers of Morocco, **9**:50
 Chagga, **9**:61
 Dinka, **9**:70
 Ewe and Fon, **9**:85
 Fulani, **9**:101
 Ganda, **9**:105
 Ibibio, **9**:119
 Lobi-Dagarti peoples, **9**:184
 Luyia, **9**:205
 Mossi, **9**:228
 Rukuba, **9**:289
 Sakalava, **9**:295
 Tswana, **9**:362
 Wolof, **9**:378
 Yakö, **9**:384
personal names based on
 Tanna, **2**:314
personal relationship with property
 Kashubians, **4**:159
political fee for use
 Ndebele, **9**:236
praderas (meadows)
 Pasiegos, **4**:189
privatized
 Tz'utujil, **8**:297
raikar system
 Nepali, **3**:203
rancho
 Pima Bajo, **8**:211, 212
reervation, **1**:240, 241
rentals. *See* Leaseholds

reservation
  Boruca, Bribri, Cabécar, 8:28
  Mandan, 1:214, 215
  Menominee, 1:220, 221
  Mescalero Apache, 1:223, 224
  Micmac, 1:234
  Mohawk, 1:242
  Navajo, 1:250, 251
  Nez Percé, 1:254
  Northern Paiute, 1:264
  Northern Shoshone and Bannock, 1:266
  Ojibwa, 1:269
  Okanagon, 1:271
  Omaha, 1:275
  Onondaga, 1:276
  Osage, 1:277
  Pawnee, 1:284
  Pima-Papago, 1:288
  Pomo, 1:294
  Potawatomi, 1:296-297
  Pueblo Indians, 1:298, 299
  Quechan, 1:300-301
  Santee, 1:307
  Sauk, 1:308
  Seminole, 1:312, 313
  Seneca, 1:315
  Shuswap, 1:317
  Spokane, 1:333
  Taos, 1:342
  Teton, 1:344, 345
  Tuscarora, 1:356
  Ute, 1:361
  Walapai, 1:364, 365
  Western Apache, 1:371, 372
  Western Shoshone, 1:374
  Winnebago, 1:380
  Yankton, 1:386
  Yavapai, 1:386
  Zuni, 1:396, 397
restrictions
  Chin, 3:65
  see also Women's inheritance proscriptions
rights passed at puberty
  Afro-Colombians, 7:17
rising property values
  Dalmatians, 4:86
rundale system
  Tory Islanders, 4:265
sale limitation
  Swiss, Italian, 4:261
scattered
  Irish, 4:153
  Occitans, 4:185
seasonal letting
  Northern Irish, 4:179
shamanic ancestor
  Canelos Quichua, 7:99
shareholders
  Yemenis, 9:389
sharing
  Swiss, Italian, 4:261
size based on need
  Callahuaya, 7:88
speculation and rising values
  Manx, 4:170
squattage
  Metis of Western Canada, 1:228

Montserratians, 8:180
  Puerto Ricans, 8:222
state trust
  Seminole, 1:312
temporary use rights
  Saramaka, 7:297
tenancy. _See_ Leaseholds
tenure
  Nambudiri Brahman, 3:193
totemic groups
  Boazi, 2:29
transfer rights
  Iraqw, 9:125
tribal
  Hidatsa, 1:146-147
  Ndebele, 9:236
  Pedi, 9:270
  Tewa Pueblos, 1:348
  Winnebago, 1:381
tribal lands privatized
  Q'eqchi,' 8:226
Udal system
  Orcadians, 4:187
"use-basis"
  Afro-Hispanic Pacific Lowlanders, 7:21
  Amahuaca, 7:35
  Apalai, 7:46
  Araweté, 7:56
  Asháninca, 7:91
  Ayoreo, 7:70
  Barí, 7:84
  Canela, 7:96
  Cubeo, 7:140
  Culina, 7:147
  Finns, 4:102
  Kaingáng, 7:186
  Kashinawa, 7:195
  Krikati/Pukobye, 7:204
  Kuikuru, 7:207
  Macuna, 7:213
  Mataco, 7:228
  Mayoruna, 7:235
  Mehinaku, 7:237
  Mohave, 1:241
  Mundurucu, 7:244
  Navajo, 1:252
  Nyamwezi and Sukuma, 9:256
  Osage, 1:277
  Panare, 7:265
  Pemon, 7:272
  Piaroa, 7:277
  Pume, 7:283
  Sara, 9:305
  Siona-Secoya, 7:308
  Somalis, 9:317
  Suya, 7:316
  Ticuna, 7:329
  Tonga, 9:353
  Trio, 7:335
  Waimiri-Atroari, 7:343
  Waorani, 7:352
  Xokléng, 7:370
  Yanomamö, 7:375
  Yuit, 1:391
usufruct rights
  Akha, 5:12
  Ambae, 2:11
  Ambonese, 5:18

Azerbaijani Turks, 6:49
  Bamiléké, 9:38
  Bedouin, 9:44
  Bukidnon, 5:53
  Don Cossacks, 6:105
  Emberá and Wounaan, 8:110
  Evenki (Northern Tungus), 6:121
  Garia, 2:74
  Gebusi, 2:78
  Germans, 6:140
  Hanunóo, 5:91
  Iban, 5:97
  Itza,' 8:134
  Javanese, 5:112
  Kalimantan Dayaks, 5:120
  Kapauku, 2:105
  Karen, 5:127
  Kazakhs, 6:174
  Khanty, 6:191
  Kiwai, 2:125
  Kmhmu, 5:140
  Kubachins, 6:218
  Kuna, 8:149
  Kwoma, 2:135
  Ladinos, 8:152
  Lahu, 5:152
  Lango, 9:179
  Leonese, 4:161
  Lisu, 5:165
  Mafulu, 2:152
  Malekula, 2:165
  Mam, 8:158
  Mamprusi, 9:212
  Mixe, 8:174
  Ningerum, 2:246
  Nissan, 2:250
  Northern Paiute, 1:263, 264
  Peloponnesians, 4:194
  Rotuma, 2:281
  Saami, 4:221
  Senoi, 5:237
  Shan, 5:240
  Suku, 9:321
  Sumu, 8:238
  Sundanese, 5:247
  Tagalog, 5:249
  Tairora, 2:308
  Taiwan aboriginal peoples, 5:257
  Tanana, 1:339
  Tausug, 5:263
  T'in, 5:278
  Tory Islanders, 4:265
  Tsimihety, 9:358
  Tswana, 9:363
  Usino, 2:361
  Ute, 1:361
  Zarma, 9:405
village
  Edo, 9:80
  Tequistlatec, 8:259
water rights
  Nootka, 1:256
  see also Agriculture; Feudalism; Patron-client system; Women's property rights
Land leasing. _See_ Leasehold
Landlessness
  Bugis, 5:50
  Central Thai, 5:70

Landlessness (cont'd)
  Dusun, 5:81
  Finns, 4:103
  Sasak, 5:226
  Siberian Estonians, 6:335
  Siberian Germans, 6:338
  Toraja, 5:282
  see also Sharecropping; Tenant farming
Land of the Dead. See under Afterlife
Landowning. See Landholding
Land reclamation
  Dutch, 4:93
  Flemish, 4:106
  Frisians, 4:111
  Piemontese, 4:198
Land rights, indigenous
  Aleut, 1:15
  Central Yup'ik Eskimos, 1:57
  Cherokee, 1:61
  Choctaw, 1:71, 71-72
  Cree, 1:80
  Delaware, 1:85
  Kwakiutl, 1:198
  see also Landholding, reservation
Language
  aphorisms
    Bretons, 4:39
  archaic
    Mount Athos, 4:174
    Pontic, 4:205
  aristocratic
    Yurok, 1:395
  bilinguality
    Alsatians, 4:8
    Auvergnats, 4:21
    Aveyronnais, 4:24
    Bulgarian Gypsies, 4:41
    Doukhobors, 1:90, 92
    East Asians of Canada, 1:94
    German Swiss, 4:125
    Latinos, 1:203
    Maltese, 4:167
    Manx, 4:169
    Polynesians, 1:291
    Rom of Czechoslovakia, 4:218
    Sicilians, 4:235
    Vlachs, 4:273
    Walapai, 1:365
    Welsh, 4:278, 280
    Xoraxané Romá, 4:281
  ceremonial
    Batak, 5:38-39
  complex
    Javanese, 5:111
  cultural
    Greek-speaking Jews of Greece, 4:136
  distinctive
    Sea Islanders, 1:308, 309
  as division of labor distinction
    Highland Scots, 4:140
  enforcing rank
    Aleuts, 6:18
    Sasak, 5:225
  gender differences
    Andis, 6:23
  hunting
    Circassians, 6:86
  literary

  Dargins, 6:96
  Gaels (Irish), 4:115
  Georgians, 6:130
  Icelanders, 4:148
  Irish, 4:151
  Komi, 6:203
  Koreans, 6:206
  Kubachins, 6:216
  Lithuanians, 6:249
  Nogays, 6:286-287
  Ossetes, 6:298
  Romansch, 4:215-216
  Selkup, 6:325
  Sephardic Jews, 4:228
  Siberian Germans, 6:338
  Siberian Tatars, 6:341
  Sorbs, 4:252
  Turkmens, 6:368-369
  Ukrainians, 6:389
  Uzbeks, 6:395-396
  Volga Tatars, 6:399
minority maintenance of own
  Ladin, 4:160
outlawing of
  Gaels (Irish), 4:115
patois
  Occitans, 4:183
  Provencal, 4:211
punning
  Auvergnats, 4:23
revival
  Manx, 4:169
ritual
  Ata Tana 'Ai, 5:26
  Palu'e, 5:207
sign
  Warlpiri, 2:373
special vocabulary for royalty
  Khmer, 5:135
trilinguality
  Metis of Western Canada, 1:226
women's
  Circassians, 6:86
Lantern Festival
  Hakka, 6:439
Large families. See under Family size
Last Judgment. See Afterlife
Latex extraction
  Suruí, 7:312
Latifundia. See Agriculture, estate farms;
    Agriculture, plantation
Latter Day Saints, Church of Jesus Christ of.
    See Mormons
Laundries
  East Asians of Canada, 1:96
  East Asians of the United States, 1:100
Law
  codified
    Dargins, 6:98
    Han, 6:447
    Kalmyks, 6:157
    Mongols, 6:475
  common law
    Cora, 8:77
    Danes, 4:90
    English, 4:97
  emphasis on
    Germans, 4:123

  folk
    Frisian, 4:111, 112
  Hanafi
    Bengali, 3:33
  Kanun
    Albanians, 4:6
  liability
    Yurok, 1:395
  Napoleonic Code
    Aquitaine, 4:14
    Austrians, 4:20-21
    Provencal, 4:211
  oral
    Albanians, 4:6
    Qalandar, 3:248
  right of appeal
    Tahiti, 2:306
  Roman civil
    Greeks, 4:133
    Swiss, Italian, 4:261
  Sharia
    Divehi, 3:78
  see also Conflict resolution; Court system
Lawlessness
  Siberiaki, 6:334
Lay associations. See Cofradia
Lay clergy
  Mennonites, 1:219
  Montenegrins, 4:173
  Old Believers, 1:274
Layered universe belief
  Winnebago, 1:382
Leadership
  absolute power
    Burusho, 3:56
    Tikopia, 2:326
  by active older male
    Metis of Western Canada, 1:229
  by advice rather than commands
    Rominche, 4:217
  advisers
    Northern Paiute, 1:264
  by alcaldes
    Salasaca, 7:290
  alternating
    Futuna, 2:67
  authoritarian
    Madeirans, 4:166
    Sinhalese, 3:266
    Tamil of Sri Lanka, 3:83, 282
  authority over power
    Tanaina, 1:336
  autocratic
    Lau, 2:144
  based on birth order
    Ka'wiari, 7:199
  based on number of relatives
    Rikbaktsa, 7:288
  based on ranking
    Tanaina, 1:336
  collective
    Balkars, 6:54
    Gebusi, 2:78
    Hmong, 5:94
    Kiwai, 2:126
    Maring, 2:187
    Russian peasants, 6:312
    Rutuls, 6:320

Siberiaki, **6:**334
Svans, **6:**345
Tsakhurs, **6:**367
Udmurt, **6:**380
conferences
Mennonites, **1:**219
consensus
Aymara, **7:**67
Baniwa-Curripaco-Wakuenai, **7:**79
Candoshi, **7:**93
Chimane, **7:**113
Cubeo, **7:**141
Dani, **2:**45
Gururumba, **2:**93
Mafulu, **2:**153
Mescalero Apache, **1:**225
Motu, **2:**215
Northern Paiute, **1:**264
Orokolo, **2:**260
Paï-Tavytera, **7:**259
Pima-Papago, **1:**289
Toba, **7:**332
Yanomamö, **7:**376
Yuqui, **7:**394
continual validation of
Tanana, **1:**339
despotic
Burusho, **3:**56
by divine right
Hawaiians, **2:**97
Makassar, **5:**173
by dream-derived powers
Quechan, **1:**302
by elders
Apalai, **7:**47
Bulgarian Gypsies, **4:**41
Luo, **9:**200
Mbeere, **9:**222
Mennonites, **1:**219
Nagas, **3:**190
Nambudiri Brahman, **3:**193
Newar, **3:**207
peripatetics, **3:**236
Piemontese Sinti, **4:**201
Purum, **3:**244
Rom, **1:**305
Shakers, **1:**316
Suku, **9:**322
Temne, **9:**344
Tsimihety, **9:**359
Yuit, **1:**391
by eldest brother
Baniwa-Curripaco-Wakuenai, **7:**79
by eldest man
Marubo, **7:**223
elected
Mescalero Apache, **1:**225
Metis of Western Canada, **1:**227, 229
Nez Percé, **1:**254
Slav Macedonians, **4:**241
Teton, **1:**346
Tubatulabal, **1:**355
see also Democratic political organization
elected elder
Mennonites, **1:**219
elected by elder males
Mandan, **1:**215
ephemeral

Montagnais-Naskapi, **1:**245
by family head
Ashaninca, **7:**91
North Alaskan Eskimos, **1:**260
Ticuna, **7:**329
Tiroleans, **4:**264
Yuracaré, **7:**396
feudal. _See_ Feudalism
first among equals
Swedes, **4:**258
by founding couple
Araweté, **7:**57
by head shepherd
Vlachs, **4:**275
hereditary
Akha, **5:**12
Ambonese, **5:**18-19
Anuta, **2:**15
Asiatic Eskimos, **6:**41
Atoni, **5:**28
Badaga, **3:**16, 17
Baluchi, **3:**23
Bau, **2:**24
Bhil, **3:**40
Bhuiya, **3:**44
Bondo, **3:**50
Cayuga, **1:**55
Chakma, **3:**60
Cham, **5:**73
Chamorros, **2:**34
Chickasaw, **1:**66
Chin, **3:**66
Coorg, **3:**73
De'ang, **6:**430-431
Easter Island, **2:**54
Haida, **1:**136
Hasidim, **1:**143, 144
Havasupai, **1:**145
Highland Scots, **4:**141
Jat, **3:**112
Jatav, **3:**114
Kalingas, **5:**122
Karen, **5:**128
Keraki, **2:**114
Khasi, **3:**125
Kickapoo, **1:**185
Kilenge, **2:**119
Kiowa, **1:**188
Klallam, **1:**190
Kond, **3:**133
Kosrae, **2:**129
Kumeyaay, **1:**195
Kurtatchi, **2:**132
Kurumbas, **3:**143
Luiseño, **1:**208
Mafulu, **2:**153
Magar, **3:**160
Mansi, **6:**254
Manus, **2:**175
Maori, **2:**178
Maricopa, **1:**216
Marshall Islands, **2:**194
Mekeo, **2:**199
Miami, **1:**231
Micmac, **1:**234
Miwok, **1:**240
Modang, **5:**186
Mohawk, **1:**242

Nguna, **2:**244
Nicobarese, **3:**210
Nissan, **2:**250
Nivkh, **6:**284
Nootka, **1:**256
Ojibwa, **1:**270
Oneida, **1:**276
Onondaga, **1:**276
Osage, **1:**278
Pacific Eskimo, **1:**283
Pahari, **3:**221
Palu'e, **5:**207
Paresí, **7:**269, 269
Pawnee, **1:**285
Penan, **5:**210
Rennell Island, **2:**277
Senaca, **1:**315
Sherente, **7:**303, 303
Sora, **3:**269, 270
Tacana, **7:**318, 318
Tai Lue, **5:**254
Taiwan aboriginal peoples, **5:**257
Tauade, **2:**319
Temiar, **5:**266
Toala, **5:**280
Tongareva, **2:**341
Trobriand Islands, **2:**350
Ulithi, **2:**359
Uvea, **2:**364
Wa, **6:**502, 503
Walapai, **1:**365
Wamira, **2:**366
Wapisiana, **7:**355, 355
Wintun, **1:**383
Witoto, **7:**365, 365
Wogeo, **2:**381
Yangoru Boiken, **2:**389
Yankton, **1:**386
Yokuts, **1:**388
Yugur, **6:**508
Yuqui, **7:**394, 394
see also Monarchy
by house construction director
Barí, **7:**85
of household group
Kalapalo, **7:**187
Mundurucu, **7:**243
humiliation rite
Pende, **9:**274
kinship-based
Apiaká, **7:**50
Araucanians, **7:**54
Bakairi, **7:**75
Ojibwa, **1:**270
lack of formal
Chipewyan, **1:**69
Northern Shoshone and Bannock, **1:**267
Rominche, **4:**216
Spanish Rom, **4:**255
Western Apache, **1:**372
Xoraxané Romá, **4:**282
"little old men"
Osage, **1:**278, 279
male only
Osage, **1:**277
by matrilineage head
Guajiro, **7:**169
matrilineal

Leadership (cont'd)
    Western Apache, 1:372
  by mayor
    Chipaya, 7:116
  meritocracy
    Albanians, 4:6
    Bulgarian Gypsies, 4:41
    Eipo, 2:58
    Mountain Arapesh, 2:217
  military democracy
    Don Cossacks, 6:106
  by oldest active male
    Hoti, 7:175-176
    Pemon, 7:272
  by oldest member of lineage
    Cinta Larga, 7:128
  religious
    Acehnese, 5:3
    Avars, 6:46
    Kapingamarangi, 2:110
    Malaita, 2:162
    Marind-anim, 2:184
    Tahiti, 2:306
    Yakan, 5:289
  religious elite
    Winnebago, 1:382
  resistance to offical
    Vlach Gypsies of Hungary, 4:272
  rotating
    Malekula, 2:165
  by saila
    Cuna, 7:150
  by seniority
    Afro-Colombians, 7:17
  by shaman
    Piaroa, 7:277
    Tunebo, 7:338
  split
    Ata Tana 'Ai, 5:25
    Atoni, 5:28
    Bunun, 5:57
    Lamaholot, 5:156
    Manihiki, 2:172-173
    Pohnpei, 2:269
    Rotuma, 2:282
    Truk, 2:353
    Yap, 2:393
  by women. See Women political leaders
  women's influence. See Women, political
      power
  see also Chiefdom; Council; Headmen;
      Political organization; Priesthood;
      Shamanism
Leadership qualities
  ability
    North Alaskan Eskimos, 1:260
    Nu, 6:481
    T'in, 5:279
    Washoe, 1:369
  achievement
    Tanana, 1:339
  age
    Aghuls, 6:11
    Ainu, 5:8
    Aleuts, 6:18
    Aranda, 2:18
    Armenians, 6:31
    Bai, 6:420

    Belarussians, 6:61
    Bisaya, 5:43
    Chechen-Ingush, 6:74
    Dargins, 6:98
    Evenki (Northern Tungus), 6:122
    Georgians, 6:134
    Gnau, 2:81
    Greeks, 6:143
    Gypsies, 6:147
    Jino, 6:460
    Karachays, 6:161
    Khevsur, 6:196
    Koryaks and Kerek, 6:209
    Kriashen Tatars, 6:212
    Lesu, 2:147
    Lisu, 5:166
    Malaita, 2:162
    Mandak, 2:171
    Mardudjara, 2:181
    Melanau, 5:179
    Mimika, 2:208
    Motu, 2:214
    Murik, 2:222
    Murngin, 2:225-226
    Ngatatjara, 2:241
    Ningerum, 2:247
    Palaung, 5:203
    Pintupi, 2:266
    Rennell Island, 2:277
    Rossel Island, 2:279
    Sagada Igorot, 5:216
    Sulod, 5:246
    Tanna, 2:314
    T'in, 5:279
    Tokelau, 2:332
    Truk, 2:353
    Warlpiri, 2:375
    Waropen, 2:376
    Yakan, 5:289
    Yangoru Boiken, 2:389
    Yao of Thailand, 5:292
    Yap, 2:393
  age/experience
    Apiaká, 7:50
    Chimane, 7:113
    Wapisiana, 7:355
  agricultural success
    Sio, 2:301
  artistic
    Kwoma, 2:135
  battle prowess
    Boazi, 2:30
    Choiseul Island, 2:39
    Foi, 2:61
    Gahuku-Gama, 2:70
    Gainj, 2:72
    Goodenough Island, 2:87
    Kewa, 2:117
    Kwoma, 2:135
    Maká, 7:217
    Malaita, 2:162
    Mashco, 7:226
    Mimika, 2:208
    Miyanmin, 2:211
    Mundugumor, 2:219
    Namau, 2:232
    Nivaclé, 7:250
    Ojibwa, 1:270

    Osage, 1:278
    Sengseng, 2:297
    Sio, 2:301
    Sirionó, 7:310
    Tairora, 2:309
    Terena, 7:326
    Wantoat, 2:369
    Wik Mungkan, 2:378
    Yavapai, 1:386
  bravery
    Ewenki, 6:434
    Kyrgyz, 6:231
    Toraja, 5:282
    Walapai, 1:365
  candidness
    Ewenki, 6:434
  character
    Afro-Colombians, 7:17
  charisma, 2:20
    Abenaki, 1:5
    Macuna, 7:214
    Ojibwa, 1:270
    Pume, 7:284
    Rom, 1:305
    Rominche, 4:217
    Santal, 3:254
    Tacana, 7:318
    Toraja, 5:282
    Western Apache, 1:372
  cleverness
    Tor, 2:344
  commercial success
    Menominee, 1:221
    Slavey, 1:320
  competency
    Seminole, 1:313
  consensus building
    Ilongot, 5:102
  craftsmanship
    Yawalapití, 7:379
  decision-making ability
    Ute, 1:361
  devoutness
    Kyrgyz, 6:231
  diligence
    Tupari, 7:340
  equitable distribution of land
    Gururumba, 2:93
  experience
    Afro-Colombians, 7:17
  fishing prowess
    Yawalapití, 7:379
  generosity
    Nasioi, 2:235
    Nissan, 2:250
    Orokaiva, 2:257
    Pima-Papago, 1:289
    Slavey, 1:320
    Tanana, 1:339
    Tauade, 2:319
    Torres Strait Islanders, 2:347
    Tupari, 7:340
    Wamira, 2:366
    Washoe, 1:369
    Yangoru Boiken, 2:390
  humor
    Pima-Papago, 1:289
  hunting prowess

Ewenki, **6**:434
Nambicuara, **7**:247
Ojibwa, **1**:270
Sirionó, **7**:310
Slavey, **1**:320
Tanana, **1**:339
Ute, **1**:361
intelligence
Nu, **6**:481
Toraja, **5**:282
Tupari, **7**:340
kinship
Aguaruna, **7**:30
Gnau, **2**:81
Mardudjara, **2**:181
Tacana, **7**:318
knowledge
Montagnais-Naskapi, **1**:245
Tanna, **2**:314
landownership
Bikini, **2**:27
language skills
Quechan, **1**:302
Yawalapití, **7**:379
longest beard
Ewenki, **6**:434
marriage arranging
Garia, **2**:75
Lakalai, **2**:142
Tiwi, **2**:329
modesty
Washoe, **1**:369
moral standing
Nu, **6**:481
negotiating skill
Foi, **2**:61
Fore, **2**:64
Gahuku-Gama, **2**:70
Melpa, **2**:202
Mundugumor, **2**:219
Nissan, **2**:250
Pintupi, **2**:266
Sio, **2**:301
Tairora, **2**:309
oratorical skill
Foi, **2**:61
Garia, **2**:75
Iatmul, **2**:99
Ilongot, **5**:102
Kalingas, **5**:122
Kwoma, **2**:135
Kyrgyz, **6**:231
Maká, **7**:217
Mataco, **7**:229
Mehinaku, **7**:238
Melpa, **2**:202
Mendi, **2**:205
Menominee, **1**:221
Miami, **1**:231
Mimika, **2**:208
Suya, **7**:316
Tangu, **2**:312
Tauade, **2**:319
Tupari, **7**:340
Walapai, **1**:365
Wapisiana, **7**:355
Wik Mungkan, **2**:378
Yangoru Boiken, **2**:390

organization
Chimbu, **2**:37
Fore, **2**:64
Sengseng, **2**:297
Tauade, **2**:319
Wamira, **2**:366
Wik Mungkan, **2**:378
personal power
Culina, **7**:147
persuasiveness
Senoi, **5**:238
political skill
Macuna, **7**:214
prestige
Chamacoco, **7**:108
Mejbrat, **2**:196
Motu, **2**:214
Sarsi, **1**:308
Siwai, **2**:303
sacred knowledge
Macuna, **7**:214
Ngatatjara, **2**:241
Ojibwa, **1**:270
sacred power
Hawaiians, **2**:97
Pentecost, **2**:263
Selepet, **2**:294
sensitivity to group wishes
Montagnais-Naskapi, **1**:245
soft-spokenness
Pima-Papago, **1**:289
special prowess
Menominee, **1**:221
storytelling skills
Huarago, **7**:17
strength
Ache, **7**:6
Namau, **2**:232
supernatural powers
Banaro, **2**:21
Dani, **2**:45
Dobu, **2**:51, 52
Futuna, **2**:67
Garia, **2**:75
Iatmul, **2**:99
Rennell Island, **2**:277
Tauade, **2**:320
Toba, **7**:332
Wogeo, **2**:381
toughness
Waropen, **2**:376
vigor
Tupari, **7**:340
wealth
Chambri, **2**:32
Garia, **2**:75
Guadalcanal, **2**:90
Kapauku, **2**:106
Kewa, **2**:117
Kyrgyz, **6**:231
Lak, **2**:139
Mejbrat, **2**:196
Melpa, **2**:202
Mendi, **2**:205
Motu, **2**:214
Orokaiva, **2**:257
Rossel Island, **2**:279
San Cristobal, **2**:289

Sengseng, **2**:297
Siwai, **2**:303
Tanana, **1**:339
Tolai, **2**:335
Tolowa, **1**:353
Tor, **2**:344
Usino, **2**:362
Western Apache, **1**:372
Yakan, **5**:289
wisdom
Miami, **1**:231
Nasioi, **2**:234
Orokaiva, **2**:257
Quechan, **1**:302
Sio, **2**:301
Tanana, **1**:339
Tokelau, **2**:332
Ute, **1**:361
Walapai, **1**:365
Wamira, **2**:366
Washoe, **1**:369
work initiative
Wapisiana, **7**:355
Leaf shelters
Hill Pandaram, **3**:99
Leaf work
Baiga, **3**:19
Santal, **3**:253
League
Iroquois, **1**:164, 166
Leaseholds
Andalusians, **4**:11
Austrians, **4**:19
Azoreans, **4**:27
Bugis, **5**:50
Calabrese, **4**:49
Cape Verdeans, **4**:54, 55
Faroe Islanders, **4**:99
Germans, **6**:139
Han, **6**:443
Herero, **9**:117
Ifugao, **5**:100
Ionians, **4**:149
Irula, **3**:106
Jews of Iran, **9**:140
Jews of Yemen, **9**:149
Korean, **5**:146
Maltese, **4**:168
Miao, **6**:471
Montserratians, **8**:180
Mount Athos, **4**:175
Mulam, **6**:476
Occitans, **4**:184-185
Orcadians, **4**:187
Otomí of the Valley of Mezquital, **8**:204
Portuguese, **4**:207
Provencal, **4**:210
Sarakatsani, **4**:223, 224
Sardinians, **4**:226
Tagalog, **5**:249
Tujia, **6**:498
Yi, **6**:506
see also Tenant farming
Leather work
Abkhazians, **6**:7
Altaians, **6**:21
Avars, **6**:45
Belarussians, **6**:60

Leather work (cont'd)
  Burakumin, **5:**61
  Buriats, **6:**68
  Catalans, **4:**62
  Chamacoco, **7:**108
  Chechen-Ingush, **6:**75
  Dargins, **6:**97, 98
  Delaware, **1:**85
  Dogrib, **1:**88
  Eastern Shoshone, **1:**105
  Hidatsa, **1:**146
  Jatav, **3:**113, 114, 115
  Kazakhs, **6:**182
  Kiowa, **1:**187
  Kota, **3:**135
  Kriashen Tatars, **6:**211
  Kumyks, **6:**221
  Kyrgyz, **6:**229, 231
  Laks, **6:**234
  Mongols, **6:**474
  Mountain Jews, **6:**272
  Northern Shoshone and Bannock, **1:**266,
    267
  Oroquen, **6:**482
  Osage, **1:**277
  Romanians, **4:**213
  Siberian Tatars, **6:**341
  Tamil, **3:**277
  Tsakhurs, **6:**366
  Ukrainian peasants, **6:**386
  Ukrainians, **6:**392
  Untouchable service caste, **3:**160, 161, 299
  Ute, **1:**361
  Volga Tatars, **6:**401
  Western Apache, **1:**372
  see also Hide
Lederhosen (leather shorts)
  Bavarians, **4:**35
Legal system. See Court system; Law
Legends. See Oral tradition
Legume growing
  Kond, **3:**132
  Koya, **3:**140
  Lugbara, **9:**194
  Persians, **9:**279
  Santal, **3:**253
  Telugu, **3:**285
  see also Bean growing
Leipreachán
  Gaels (Irish), **4:**117
Lent (holiday)
  Cahita, **8:**37
  Carpatho-Rusyns, **6:**71
  Central Thai, **5:**71
  Lao, **5:**159
  Syrian Christian of Kerala, **3:**274
  Torres Strait Islanders, **2:**347
  Yaqui, **8:**307
Lentil growing
  Kurds, **9:**175
  Tsakhurs, **6:**365
Leopards (sacred)
  Mangbetu, **9:**217
Leuts
  Hutterites, **1:**154
Levirate marriage
  Achang, **6:**418
  Agaria, **3:**6

Albanians, **4:**5
Amahuaca, **7:**35
Andamanese, **3:**10
Araucanians, **7:**53
Araweté, **7:**57
Aveyronnais, **4:**25
Bretons, **4:**39
Bukharan Jews, **6:**64
Buriats, **6:**67
Cree, **1:**81
Dinka, **9:**70
Drung, **6:**432
Ewenki, **6:**434
Fali, **9:**97
Fox, **1:**129
Gros Ventre, **1:**134
Gusii, **9:**109
Hmong, **5:**93
Huarayo, **7:**178
Ilongot, **5:**102
Iraqw, **9:**125
Jews, Arabic-speaking, **9:**135
Jingpo, **6:**457
Jivaro, **7:**183
Kachin, **5:**117
Kalmyks, **6:**156
Karachays, **6:**160
Karaites, **6:**165
Karajá, **7:**189
Karakalpaks, **6:**168
Karok, **1:**176
Kazakhs, **6:**180
Keraki, **2:**113
Khasi, **3:**124
Kiowa, **1:**187
Klamath, **1:**191
Konso, **9:**170
Kpelle, **9:**173
Kumeyaay, **1:**194
Kwoma, **2:**135
Lakalai, **2:**141
Luba of Shaba, **9:**192
Luyia, **9:**205
Mae Enga, **2:**149
Maká, **7:**216
Mamprusi, **9:**213
Mansi, **6:**253
Maonan, **6:**468
Mbeere, **9:**221
Miyanmin, **2:**211
Montagnais-Naskapi, **1:**245
Mossi, **9:**229
Mountain Arapesh, **2:**216
Mountain Jews, **6:**272
Munda, **3:**183
Muong, **5:**191
Nenets, **6:**279
Nomoi, **2:**252
Nu, **6:**481
Orochi, **6:**295
Osage, **1:**278
Ossetes, **6:**300
Pahari, **3:**221
Pima-papago, **1:**289
Pomo, **1:**294
Qiang, **6:**486
Rapa, **2:**274
Rutuls, **6:**320

Santal, **3:**254
Sarsi, **1:**308
Shipibo, **7:**305
Southern Paiute (and Chemehuevi), **1:**331
Swazi, **9:**333
Tabasarans, **6:**349
Tajiks, **6:**353
Tats, **6:**359
Terena, **7:**326
Tiwi, **2:**328
Toba, **7:**332
Truk, **2:**352
Tsakhurs, **6:**367
Tsimihety, **9:**358
Tunebo, **7:**338
Ute, **1:**361
Waimiri-Atroari, **7:**344
Washoe, **1:**369
Wayapi, **7:**362
Western Apache, **1:**372
Western Shoshone, **1:**375
Winnebago, **1:**381
Wolof, **9:**379
Yagua, **7:**372
Yanomamö, **7:**375
Lidepfu (religious practitioner)
  Nagas, **3:**190
Life-cycle rituals
  Abor, **3:**5
  Acholi, **9:**6
  Albanians, **4:**6, 7
  Andalusians, **4:**12
  Baggara, **9:**31
  Bania, **3:**25
  Basseri, **9:**42
  Berbers of Morocco, **9:**52
  Bretons, **4:**39-40
  Burgundians, **4:**47
  Chagga, **9:**62
  Cherokee, **1:**62
  Chuj, **8:**73
  Croats, **4:**75
  Cyclades, **4:**78
  East Indians in Trinidad, **8:**107
  Edo, **9:**82
  Fipa, **9:**99
  Fulani, **9:**103
  Hausa, **9:**112, 114
  Herero, **9:**118
  hijra participation, **3:**96
  Hindu, **3:**102
  Iteso, **9:**130
  Jatav, **3:**115
  Jews of Algeria, **9:**138
  Jews, Arabic-speaking, **9:**136
  Jews of Yemen, **9:**149, 150
  Karaites, **9:**156
  Khoi, **9:**160
  Kikuyu, **9:**162
  Kumeyaay, **1:**195
  Kwakiutl, **1:**200
  Luba of Shaba, **9:**193
  Luiseño, **1:**208
  Maliseet, **1:**212
  Maratha, **3:**170
  Munda, **3:**184
  Nagas, **3:**190, 191
  Nandi and other Kalenjin peoples, **9:**234

Newar, 3:208
Nyinba, 3:213
Okiek, 9:261
Otomí of the Sierra, 8:203
Parsi, 3:229
Pedi, 9:270
Punjabi, 3:241
Purum, 3:244
Sadhu, 3:251
Santal, 3:255
Shahsevan, 9:310
Tewa Pueblos, 1:348, 349
Tswana, 9:364
Vlach Gypsies of Hungary, 4:272
Wolof, 9:380
Yakö, 9:387
see also Childbirth; Initiation; Marriage;
    Mortuary practices
Life essence (religious belief)
Karihona, 7:193
Life Giver (deity)
Western Apache, 1:373
Life-giving force. *See* Creator
Light festivals
Ahir, 3:7
Brahman and Chhetri of Nepal, 3:53
Mountain Jews, 6:273
see also Fire
Light industry
Bretons, 4:38
Hungary, 4:143-144
Slovaks, 4:243
Welsh, 4:279
Lightning. *See* Thunder and lightning
    significance
Limestone
Dalmatians, 4:86
Flemish, 4:106
Lineages
Haida, 1:136
Koya, 3:140, 141
Limbu, 3:150
Rajput, 3:249
Rom, 1:305
Serbs, 4:231
Sherpa, 3:258
Shetlanders, 4:233
Songhay, 9:319
Sora, 3:270
Tamang, 3:275
Tanaina, 1:336
Vlachs, 4:274, 275
Yokuts, 1:388
Lineal joint family. *See* Family, joint-family
    system
Lingayatism
Kanarese, 3:117
Lingayat, 3:151, 153
Linoleum peddlers
Irish Travelers, 1:163
peripatetics, 1:287
Lip piercing. *See under* Body piercing
Lip plugs
Ingalik, 1:158
Liquor. *See* Alcohol
Literacy
Malayalis, 3:166
Nayar, 3:199

Parsi, 3:228
Punjabi, 3:240
Rom of Czechoslovakia, 4:218
Sherpa, 3:257
Slovensko Roma, 4:250
Syrian Christian of Kerala, 3:272
Tamil, 3:276, 278
Xoraxané Romá, 4:281
see also Education
Literati
Arab Americans, 1:24
Literature
Abkhazians, 6:9
Altaians, 6:23
Armenians, 6:31
Ashkenazim, 6:36-37
Azerbaijani Turks, 6:47
Balkars, 6:54
Basques, 4:32
Bavarians, 4:35
Bengali, 3:34
Bretons, 4:40
Bukharan Jews, 6:65
Buriats, 6:68
Castilians, 4:61
Catalans, 4:63-64
Chechen-Ingush, 6:73, 75
Chinese in Southeast Asia, 5:77
Chukchee, 6:78
Circassians, 6:90
Cornish, 4:64
Crimean Tatars, 6:94
English, 4:97
Estonian, 6:115
Europeans in South Asia, 3:80
Evenki (Northern Tungus), 6:124
Flemish, 4:108
folklore
    Lur, 9:202
Friuli, 4:113-114
Galician, 4:120-212
Georgian Jews, 6:128
Georgians, 6:136
Greeks, 4:134;6:143
Gypsies, 6:148
Han, 6:448
Hui, 6:453
Icelander-Canadians, 1:123
Icelanders, 4:148
Ingilos, 6:149
Irish, 4:153
Japanese, 5:110
Javanese, 5:113
Karaites, 6:164
Kazakhs, 6:174, 182
Khasi, 3:126
Khmer, 5:138
Kiowa, 1:189
Komi, 6:204
Koreans, 6:207
Kumyks, 6:224
Kurds, 6:227
Laks, 6:233
Lao, 5:159
Lingayat, 3:151, 153
Lithuanians, 6:251
Lowland Scots, 4:163
Mahar, 3:163, 165

Mauritian, 3:173
Moldovans, 6:269
Mountain Jews, 6:272
Nanai, 6:275
Occitans, 4:185, 211
Orcadians, 4:188
Parsi, 3:229
Poles, 6:309
Puerto Ricans, 8:223
Punjabi, 3:242
Rajput, 3:249
Rotinese, 5:214
Russian peasants, 6:313
Santal, 3:255
Sephardic Jews, 4:228, 229
short stories published in Persian
    Qashqa'i, 9:287
Sicilians, 4:237
Sinhalese, 3:267
Syrian Christians of Kerala, 3:272
Tagalog, 5:251
Tajiks, 6:354
Tamil, 3:276
Tibetans, 6:496
Trinidadians and Tobagonians, 8:269
Udmurt, 6:379, 380
Uighur, 6:384-385
Uzbeks, 6:398
Vietnamese, 5:287
Volga Tatars, 6:400, 403
West Greenland Inuit, 1:378
Yukagir, 6:413
Zoque, 8:317
see also Epic; Mythology; Oral tradition;
    Poetry; Storytelling
Litigants. *See* Court system
"Little people" (supernatural)
Gaels (Irish), 4:117
Seminole of Oklahoma, 1:315
Yavapai, 1:386
Livestock
inheritance
    Guajiro, 7:169
    Nivaclé, 7:249
small breeds
    Shetlanders, 4:233
trades
    Gitanos, 4:129
    Irish, 4:152
see also Herding; Seminomads; *specific kinds*
Livestock raising
Afar, 9:7
Amhara, 9:18
Bagirmi, 9:33
Bedouin, 9:43
Khoi, 9:160
Lugbara, 9:194
Mamprusi, 9:211
Mbeere, 9:221
Sleb, 9:315
Somalis, 9:316
Livestock sacrifice. *See* Sacrifice, livestock
Living together
Andalusian, 4:11
Austrians, 4:20
Cretans, 4:70
Danes, 4:89-90
Finns, 4:103

Living together (cont'd)
Frisians, 4:111
Grasia, 3:88
Hill Pandaram, 3:100
Inughuit, 1:160
Nandi and other Kalenjin peoples, 9:233
Nayaka, 3:195
Norwegians, 4:181
Pasiegos, 4:190
Portuguese, 4:207
Sora, 3:269
Swedes, 4:257
Swiss, Italian, 4:261
Thadou, 3:288
Zapotec, 8:312
see also Common-law marriage
"Living widows"
Azoreans, 4:28
Llama herding
Araucanians, 7:52
Aymara, 7:66
Callahuaya, 7:88
Chipaya, 7:115
Cotopaxi Quichua, 7:133
Nivaclé, 7:249
Loanmaking. *See* Financial services, loans
Lobster industry
Acadians, 1:7
Orcadians, 4:186-187
Shetlanders, 4:233
Tory Islanders, 4:265
Lodges. *See* Associations, clubs, and societies
Lofty Wanderer (supernatural)
Yavapai, 1:386
Log cabins. *See under* Houses and housing
Logging. *See* Forestry
Lone Man (culture hero)
Mandan, 1:215
Longanis (sorcerer)
Mauritian, 3:173
Long Ears (supernatural)
Seminole of Oklahoma, 1:315
Longevity
Galicians, 4:120
Longhouses. *See under* Houses and housing
Long-life ceremonies
Jicarilla, 1:174
Lontar palm
Rotinese, 5:213
Lost tribes
Bene Israel, 3:27
Love magic packets
Toba, 7:332
Low-ranking castes
Mahar, 3:163-165
Schedules Castes and Scheduled Tribes,
3:256-257
Sudra, 3:271
Tamang, 3:275
Tharu, 3:293
Untouchables, 3:299
Luck, belief in
Tanaina, 1:336
Lumbering. *See* Forestry
Lunar New Year (festival)
Lahu, 5:154
Lutheranism
Bavarians, 4:35

Chimbu, 2:35
Estonians, 6:111, 114
Faroe Islanders, 4:100
Finns, 4:104
Gahuku-Gama, 2:68, 70
Germans, 4:121;6:140
Gusii, 9:110
Gypsies, 6:148
Icelanders, 4:146, 148
Karelians, 6:169, 171
Kewa, 2:117
Kpelle, 9:174
Latvian-Canadians, 1:124
Latvians, 6:236, 238
Lithuanians, 6:251
Manus, 2:173
Melpa, 2:202
Norwegian-Canadians, 1:124
Norwegians, 4:182
Nyakyusa and Ngonde, 9:254
Palestinians, 9:266
Poles, 4:204
Saami, 4:222
Selepet, 2:293, 295
Siberian Estonians, 6:335, 337
Siberian Germans, 6:339
Sio, 2:1299
Slovaks, 4:245
Sorbs, 4:253
Swedes, 4:258
Transylvanian ethnic groups, 4:268
Usino, 2:361, 363
Wantoat, 2:368
Western Apache, 1:373
West Greenland Inuit, 1:378
Zaramo, 9:403

Macaques. *See* Monkey trainers
Macedonian Orthodox Church
Slav Macedonians, 4:241
Machado-Joseph disease
Portuguese, 4:208
Machete use
Lakher, 3:145
Machine building and tools
Bulgarians, 4:43
Machinery manufacturing
Poles, 4:203
Machismo (manliness)
Cape Verdeans, 4:55, 56
Llatinos, 1:205
Machong (matrilineal descent group)
Garo, 3:82, 83
Mackerel fishing
Manx, 4:170
Macumba (religion)
Afro-Brazilians, 7:13
Madness. *See* Mental illness
Madonna worship
Andalusians, 4:12
Azoreans, 4:28
Basques, 4:32
Calabrese, 4:50
Canarians, 4:52
Latinos, 1:205
Sicilians, 4:237
Mafia
Sicilians, 4:237

Mage (ceremony)
Lakalai, 2:142
Magic. *See* Magicians; Spellcasting; Sorcery
and witchcraft; Supernatural beliefs
Magical charms. *See* Amulets
Magical words. *See* Mantras
Magicians
Aymara, 7:68
Chamacoco, 7:110
Gond, 3:86
Nicobarese, 3:209
Oriya, 3:218
Qalandar, 3:246
Tamil, 3:279
Thadou, 3:289
see also Sorcery
Magicoreligious practices. *See* Shamanism;
Supernatural beliefs
Magnesite beads
Pomo, 1:294
Magpies (as omen)
Irish Travellers, 4:156
Maguey growing
Zapotec, 8:312
Mahaprabhu (supreme being)
Bondo, 3:50, 51
Mahaveda. *See* Bhagwan
Mahayana Buddhism. *See* Buddhism
(Mahayana)
Ma'heo'o (creator)
Cheyenne, 1:65, 66
Mahotsavas (festivals)
Baul, 3:26
Maiheyuno (personal spirit)
Cheyenne, 1:65
Maipa (medicine man)
Purum, 3:244
Maize
beer
Lugbara, 9:194
ceremonies. *See* Green Corn Ceremony
cultivated by women
Nuer, 9:249
divination
Mixe, 8:175
goddess
Bugle, 8:33
healing ritual
Mazatec, 8:169
as resurrection symbol
Cuicatec, 8:93
sacred
Cora, 8:77
Maize growing
Abkhazians, 6:7
Ache, 7:4
Afro-Colombians, 7:16
Afro-Venezuelans, 7:26
Aguaruna, 7:29
Algonkin, 1:17
Alorese, 5:14
Amahuaca, 7:34
Amuesha, 7:37
Amuzgo, 8:4
Anambé, 7:41
Angaité, 7:43
Anuak, 9:21

Apiaká, 7:48
Araucanians, 7:52
Araweté, 7:56
Arikara, 1:26
Asháninca, 7:91
Asurini, 7:61
Ata Sikka, 5:20
Ata Tana 'Ai, 5:23
Atoni, 5:27
Awakateko, 8:15
Awá Kwaiker, 7:63
Ayoreo, 7:70
Bagobo, 5:29
Bahamians, 8:18
Bai, 6:419
Bajau, 5:32
Bakairi, 7:74
Bamiléké, 9:38
Banggai, 5:38
Baweanese, 5:41
Bilaan, 5:42
Blang, 6:421
Bonerate, 5:44
Bororo, 7:86
Boruca, 8:27, 28
Bouyei, 6:422
Bugle, 8:32
Bukidnon, 5:53
Bunun, 5:56
Butonese, 5:67
Cajuns, 1:49
Campa del Pichis, 7:91
Candoshi, 7:93
Canela, 7:95
Canelos Quichua, 7:99
Cape Verdeans, 4:55
Cashibo, 7:104
cattle ranchers of Huasteca, 8:42
Central Thai, 5:70
Chácobo, 7:105
Cham, 5:72
Chayahuita, 7:111
Chechen-Ingush, 6:73
Chimane, 7:112
Chimila, 7:114
Chiquitano, 7:118
Chiriguano, 7:120
Chocó, 7:122
Choctaw, 1:71
Ch'ol, 8:64
Chorote, 7:124
Chuj, 8:71
Cinta Larga, 7:127
Circassians, 6:88
Cocama, 7:130
Cocopa, 1:74
Colorado, 7:131
Cora, 8:76
Cotabato Manobo, 5:79
Creek, 1:83
Cuna, 7:149
De'ang, 6:430
Delaware, 1:84
Dongxiang, 6:432
Drung, 6:432
Easter Island, 2:54
Emberá, 7:155
Emerillon, 7:159

Endenese, 5:85
Ewe and Fon, 9:85
Falasha, 9:91
Filipino, 5:87
Fipa, 9:98
Gelao, 6:435
Georgians, 6:132
Gorontalese, 5:90
Gorotire, 7:162
Grasia, 3:88
Guahibo-Sikuani, 7:164
Guajajára, 7:166
Guambiano, 7:171
Guarayu, 7:174
Guarijío, 8:117
Gusii, 9:108
Hani, 6:450
Hanunóo, 5:91
Hausa, 9:112
Hidatsa, 1:146
Hmong, 5:93
Hopi, 1:149
Hopi-Tewa, 1:151
Hoti, 7:175
Huarayo, 7:177
Huave, 8:123
Ilanon, 5:101
Ilongot, 5:101
Iraqw, 9:125
Iroquois, 1:165
Iteso, 9:128
Itonama, 7:179
Ixil, 8:136
Jebero, 7:181
Jingpo, 6:456
Jino, 6:460
Jivaro, 7:182
Kachin, 5:116
Kagwahiv, 7:184
Kaingáng, 7:186
Kalagan, 5:119
Kalapalo, 7:187
Kalasha, 3:116
Kalmyks, 6:156
Karachays, 6:159
Karajá, 7:188
Karen, 5:126
Karihona, 7:192
Kédang, 5:131
Kenyah-Kayan-Kajang, 5:133
Khevsur, 6:194
K'iche,' 8:141
Kikuyu, 9:161
Kipsigis, 9:164
Kmhmu, 5:139
Kogi, 7:201
Kond, 3:132
Konso, 9:169
Koreans, 6:206
Krikati/Pukobye, 7:204
Kuikuru, 7:207
Kyrgyz, 6:229
Lahu, 5:152;6:462
Lakandon, 8:154
Lamaholot, 5:155
Lao Isan, 5:161
Lenca, 8:155
Lengua, 7:210

Lepcha, 3:148
Li, 6:464
Limbu, 3:150
Lipan Apache, 1:207
Lisu, 5:164;6:465
Loven, 5:166
Luba of Shaba, 9:191
Lugbara, 9:194
Luyia, 9:204
Magar, 3:155
Maguindanao, 5:169
Makassar, 5:172
Mam, 8:158
Mamprusi, 9:211
Manchu, 6:467
Mandan, 1:214
Manggarai, 5:176
Maonan, 6:468
Maranao, 5:177
Maricopa, 1:216
Marinahua, 7:220
Maroni Carib, 7:220
Marubo, 7:222
Mataco, 7:228
Matsigenka, 7:231
Maxakali, 7:233
Mayoruna, 7:234
Mazahua, 8:165
Mazatec, 8:168
Mbeere, 9:220
Mehinaku, 7:236
Miami, 1:23
Miao, 6:470
Mijikenda, 9:224
Minahasans, 5:181
Mingrelians, 6:263
Miskito, 8:171
Mixe, 8:173
Mnong, 5:184
Mocoví, 7:240
Mohave, 1:240
Moinba, 6:473
Mojo, 7:242
Moldovans, 6:266, 267
Mongo, 9:226
Moré, 7:242
Mulam, 6:476
Muna, 5:189
Muong, 5:190
Murut, 5:193
Nahua of the Huasteca, 8:185
Nahuat of the Sierra de Puebla, 8:191
Nambicuara, 7:247
Nandi and other Kalenjin peoples, 9:232
Navajo, 1:251
Naxi, 6:478
Ndebele, 9:236
Nepali, 3:202
Newar, 3:206
Nicobarese, 3:209
Nivaclé, 7:249
Noanamá, 7:251
Nu, 6:480
Nyamwezi and Sukuma, 9:256
Ojibwa, 1:269
Okiek, 9:259
Omaha, 1:275
Opata, 8:199

Maize growing (cont'd)
  Osage, 1:277
  Otavalo, 7:253
  Otomí of the Sierra, 8:201
  Otomí of the Valley of Mezquital, 8:204
  Ottawa, 1:279
  Ozarks, 1:281
  Páez, 7:257
  Paï-Tavytera, 7:259
  Pajonalino, 7:91
  Palu'e, 5:205
  Pame, 8:207
  Panare, 7:265
  Pandit of Kashmir, 3:224
  Paresí, 7:269
  Pashai, 9:267
  Pathan, 3:231
  Pauserna, 7:270
  Pawnee, 1:384
  Paya, 8:209
  Pedi, 9:269
  Pemon, 7:271
  Philippine Negritos, 5:211
  Piapoco, 7:274
  Piaroa, 7:276
  Pima Bajo, 8:211
  Pomaks, 4:205
  Popoluca, 8:216
  Poqomam, 8:218
  Portuguese, 4:206
  Potawatomi, 1:297
  Powhatan, 1:297
  Pume, 7:283
  Pumi, 6:483
  P'u Noi, 5:211
  Q'anjob'al, 8:225
  Q'eqchi,' 8:226
  Quechan, 1:301
  Rhadé, 5:212
  Rikbaktsa, 7:287
  Romanians, 4:213
  Rotinese, 5:213
  Salasaca, 7:289
  Saliva, 7:292
  Saluan, 5:217
  Samal, 5:219
  San-speaking peoples, 9:302
  Santee, 1:307
  Saraguro, 7:294
  Saramaka, 7:296
  Semang, 5:234
  Senoi, 5:237
  Serbs, 4:230
  Sharanahua, 7:299
  Shavante, 7:300
  Shawnee, 1:317
  Sherente, 7:302
  Shilluk, 9:311
  Shipibo, 7:304
  Shona, 9:312
  Siona-Secoya, 7:307
  Sirionó, 7:310
  Slovaks, 4:243
  Somalis, 9:316
  Sulod, 5:246
  Sumu, 8:237
  Sunwar, 3:271
  Suri, 9:325

  Suruí, 7:312
  Suya, 7:315
  Swazi, 9:330
  Tagbanuwa, 5:251
  Tandroy, 9:336
  Tanimuka, 7:318
  Taos, 1:341
  Tapirapé, 7:320
  Tarahumara, 8:242
  Tats, 6:358
  Tausug, 5:262
  Tay, 5:265
  Tepehuan of Chihuahua, 8:252
  Tepehuan of Durango, 8:256
  Tequistlatec, 8:259
  Terena, 7:325
  Ternatan/Tidorese, 5:274
  Tetum, 5:276
  Tewa Pueblos, 1:348
  Ticuna, 7:328
  T'in, 5:278
  Tlapanec, 8:259
  Toala, 5:280
  Tobelorese, 5:280
  Tomini, 5:280
  Toraja, 5:281
  Totonac, 8:264
  Trio, 7:335
  Triqui, 8:270
  Tsakhurs, 6:365
  Tujia, 6:498
  Tunebo, 7:337
  Tupari, 7:339
  Tzotzil and Tzeltal of Pantelhó, 8:276
  Tzotzil of Chamula, 8:279
  Tzotzil of San Andrés Larraínzar, 8:284
  Tzotzil of San Bartolomé de los Llanos, 8:287
  Tzotzil of Zinacantan, 8:292
  Tz'utujil, 8:297
  Vedda, 3:301
  Vietnamese, 5:285
  Visayan, 5:287
  Walapai, 1:364
  Waorani, 7:352
  Wapisiana, 7:355
  Warao, 7:357
  Wasteko, 8:302
  Waurá, 7:360
  Wichita, 1:379
  Winnebago, 1:380
  Witoto, 7:364
  Xhosa, 9:381
  Xikrin, 7:367
  Xokléng, 7:370
  Yagua, 7:372
  Yao of Thailand, 5:291
  Yekuana, 7:381
  Yi, 6:506
  Yukateko, 8:309
  Yukpa, 7:383
  Yuqui, 7:392
  Yuracaré, 7:395
  Zapotec, 8:312
  Zhuang, 6:510
  Zoque, 8:315
  Zuni, 1:397
Makarrata (ceremony)
  Murngin, 2:226

Making of Relatives (ceremony)
  Teton, 1:346
Malagan (ceremony)
  Mandak, 2:172
Malanggan (ceremony)
  Lesu, 2:146, 147
Malanka (holiday)
  Ukrainian peasants, 6:387, 388
Malaria
  Calabrese, 4:50
  Corsicans, 4:66
  Lobi-Dagarti peoples, 9:186
  Qalandar, 3:248
  Sardinians, 4:226
  Somalis, 9:318
  Tor, 2:344
  Wamira, 2:367
Male status. *See* Men, status of
Malevolent spirits. *See* Evil spirits
Malnourishment
  Gebusi, 2:77
Mama Chi religion
  Ngawbe, 8:197
Mama Tchamba relgion
  Ewe and Fon, 9:87
Mana
  Futuna, 2:67
  Maori, 2:177, 178
  Namau, 2:232
  Niue, 2:252
  Orokolo, 2:260
  San Cristobal, 2:289
  Truk, 2:353
Mandaean Gnosticism
  Yezidis, 6:410
Mandale (deity)
  Magar, 3:161
Mandira. *See* Monasticism
Man-gods
  Pima-Papago, 1:290
Manhao (sacred band)
  Cheyenne, 1:65
Manhastoz (bunch)
  Cheyenne, 1:65
Manicheanism
  Slav Macedonians, 4:241
  Uighur, 6:382, 384, 499
  Yezidis, 6:410
Manioc growing
  Ache, 7:4
  Afro-Venezuelans, 7:26
  Aguaruna, 7:29
  Amahuaca, 7:34
  Amuesha, 7:37
  Anambé, 7:41
  Angaité, 7:43
  Anuta, 2:14
  Apalai, 7:45
  Apiaká, 7:48
  Asurini, 7:61
  Bakairi, 7:74
  Baniwa-Curripaco-Wakuenai, 7:77
  Barí, 7:83
  Bororo, 7:86
  Campa del Pichis, 7:91
  Canela, 7:95, 96
  Canelos Quichua, 7:99
  Cariña, 7:102

Cashibo, **7**:104
Chácobo, **7**:105
Chayahuita, **7**:111
Chimane, **7**:112
Chimila, **7**:114
Chiquitano, **7**:118
Chiriguano, **7**:120
Chocó, **7**:122
Chorote, **7**:124
Cinta Larga, **7**:127
Colorado, **7**:131
Craho, **7**:136
Cubeo, **7**:140
Culina, **7**:146
Cuna, **7**:149
Desana, **7**:152
Dusun, **5**:81
Emerillon, **7**:159
Ewe and Fon, **9**:85
Garifuna, **8**:113
Gorotire, **7**:162
Guahibo-Sikuani, **7**:164
Guajajára, **7**:166
Guarayu, **7**:174
Hoti, **7**:175
Huarayo, **7**:177
Ilongot, **5**:101
Itonama, **7**:179
Jebero, **7**:181
Jivaro, **7**:182
Kagwahiv, **7**:184
Kalapalo, **7**:187
Karajá, **7**:188
Karihona, **7**:192
Ka'wiari, **7**:198
Kongo, **9**:167
Kpelle, **9**:173
Krikati/Pukobye, **7**:204
Kuikuru, **7**:207
Lak, **2**:137
Lakalai, **2**:140
Lau, **2**:143
Lengua, **7**:210
Macuna, **7**:212
Makushi, **7**:218
Marinahua, **7**:220
Maring, **2**:185
Maroni Carib, **7**:220
Marubo, **7**:222
Mashco, **7**:225
Matsigenka, **7**:231
Maxakali, **7**:233
Mayoruna, **7**:234
Mehinaku, **7**:236
Miskito, **8**:171
Mocoví, **7**:240
Mojo, **7**:242
Moré, **7**:242
Mundurucu, **7**:244
Nguna, **2**:242
Nivaclé, **7**:249
Noanamá, **7**:251
Páez, **7**:257
Paï-Tavytera, **7**:259
Pajonalino, **7**:91
Palikur, **7**:262
Panare, **7**:265
Paresí, **7**:269

Pauserna, **7**:270
Pemon, **7**:271
Pende, **9**:272
Piapoco, **7**:274
Piaroa, **7**:276
Piro, **7**:279
Puinave, **7**:281
Pume, **7**:283
Rikbaktsa, **7**:287
Sakalava, **9**:293-294
Saliva, **7**:292
Sara, **9**:305
Sengseng, **2**:296
Senoi, **5**:237
Sharanahua, **7**:299
Shavante, **7**:300
Sherente, **7**:302
Shipibo, **7**:304
Sinhalese, **3**:265
Siona-Secoya, **7**:307
Sirionó, **7**:310
Suku, **9**:321
Suya, **7**:315
Tamil of Sri Lanka, **3**:281
Tandroy, **9**:336
Tanimuka, **7**:318-319
Tapirapé, **7**:320
Tatuyo, **7**:322
Ticuna, **7**:328
Tikopia, **2**:325
Toba, **7**:331
Tunebo, **7**:337
Tupari, **7**:339
Vedda, **3**:301
Waimiri-Atroari, **7**:343
Wáiwai, **7**:346
Wanano, **7**:349
Waorani, **7**:352
Warao, **7**:357
Waurá, **7**:360
Witoto, **7**:364-365
Wolof, **9**:378
Xikrin, **7**:367
Yagua, **7**:372
Yawalapití, **7**:378
Yekuana, **7**:381
Yukuna, **7**:386
Yuqui, **7**:392
Yuracaré, **7**:395
Zarma, **9**:404
Manitou (spirit)
    Delaware, **1**:86
    Fox, **1**:130
    Miami, **1**:232
Mantras (magical words)
    Bengali, **3**:34
    Bengali Shakta, **3**:35
    Newar, **3**:208
    Santal, **3**:255
    Tamil, **3**:279
Manu, laws of
    Anavil Brahman, **3**:8
Manufacturing. _See_ Industrialization; _specific
        products_
Maple syrup production
    Ojibwa, **1**:269
Marble
    Cyclades, **4**:77

Friuli, **4**:113
Mardi Gras (festival)
    Black Creoles of Louisiana, **1**:39-40
    Cajuns, **1**:50
    Germans, **4**:123
Marginality
    Gitanos, **4**:130
    Gypsies and caravan dwellers in the
        Netherlands, **4**:138
    Irish Travellers, **4**:154-156
    Pasiegos, **4**:189
    Untouchables (India), **3**:299
    Vedda, **3**:301
    Vlach Gypsies of Hungary, **4**:270-273
    Wiyot, **1**:384
    Xoraxané Romá, **4**:281
Mari (deity class)
    Magar, **3**:161, 162
Mariai (female deity)
    Mahar, **3**:165
Marijuana growing
    Chatino, **8**:49
    Jamaicans, **8**:137
    Krikati/Pukobye, **7**:204
Marine animal hunting
    Aleut, **1**:15
    Baffinland Inuit, **1**:28, 29
    Kwakiutl, **1**:198
    Labroador Inuit, **1**:201
    Nootka, **1**:256
    Pacific Eskimo, **1**:282, 283
    Tolowa, **1**:353
    West Greenland Inuit, **1**:377, 378, 379
    Yuit, **1**:390, 392
    see also specific animals
Mariners
    Basques, **4**:30, 31
    Cornish, **4**:65
    Cyclades, **4**:77
    Danes, **4**:89
    Dutch, **4**:92
    Estonian, **6**:113
    Frisians, **4**:111
    Ionians, **4**:148, 149
    Occitans, **4**:184
    Peloponnesians, **4**:193
    see also Boat nomads; Fishing industry
Marist devotion. _See_ Madonna worship
Market activities. _See_ Traders
Markets and fairs
    Auvergnats, **4**:22
    Bajau, **5**:32
    Balinese, **5**:36
    Bonerate, **5**:45
    Central Thai, **5**:70
    Chechen-Ingush, **6**:73
    Dalmatians, **4**:86
    Dusun, **5**:81
    English, **4**:96
    Finns, **4**:102
    Frisians, **4**:111
    Galicians, **4**:119
    Gitanos, **4**:129
    Greeks, **4**:132
    Hungarians, **4**:144
    Lisu, **5**:165
    Madeirans, **4**:165
    Makassar, **5**:172

Markets and fairs (cont'd)
  Malay, **5:**175
  Maltese, **4:**168
  Manx, **4:**170
  Mingrelians, **6:**263
  Nias, **5:**195
  North Alaska Eskimos, **1:**259
  Norwegians, **4:**181
  Occitans, **4:**184
  Old Believers, **6:**292
  Pasiegos, **4:**189
  Peloponnesians, **4:**193
  Poles, **4:**203
  Provencal, **4:**210
  Serbs, **4:**230
  Sicilians, **4:**236, 237
  Slovenes, **4:**248
  Swiss, Italian, **4:**261
  Tai Lue, **5:**253
  Tanaina, **1:**335
  Tanana, **1:**339
  Teton, **1:**345
  Tetum, **5:**276
  Tewa Pueblos, **1:**348
  Tibetans, **6:**494
  Toraja, **5:**282
  Welsh, **4:**279
  Zhuang, **6:**510
Marking stake
  Nagas, **3:**188
Maronites
  Arab Americans, **1:**24, 25
  Cypriots, **4:**81
Marriage
  by abduction
    Achang, **6:**418
    Albanians, **4:**5-6
    Altaians, **6:**22
    Andis, **6:**26
    Avars, **6:**45
    Bhil, **3:**39
    Bhuiya, **3:**44
    Buriats, **6:**67
    Chechen-Ingush, **6:**74
    Chuj, **8:**72
    Chuvash, **6:**84
    Circassians, **6:**88
    Corsicans, **4:**67
    Cretans, **4:**70, 71
    Dai, **6:**425
    Dalmatians, **4:**86
    Don Cossacks, **6:**105
    Evenki (Northern Tungus), **6:**122
    Georgians, **6:**133
    Guarijío, **8:**118
    Gypsies, **6:**147
    Jingpo, **6:**457
    Karachays, **6:**160
    Kazakhs, **6:**180
    Khanty, **6:**191
    Khevsur, **6:**195
    Khinalughs, **6:**200
    Kriashen Tatars, **6:**212
    Ladinos, **8:**152
    Lobi-Dagarti peoples, **9:**184
    Macuna, **7:**213, 214
    Magar, **3:**158
    Mashco, **7:**226

  Mayoruna, **7:**234
  Mingrelians, **6:**264
  Nepali, **3:**203
  Orokaiva, **2:**257
  Qiang, **6:**486
  Rutuls, **6:**320
  Samal, **5:**220
  Santal, **3:**253
  Siberian Tatars, **6:**342
  Tabasarans, **6:**349
  Talysh, **6:**356
  Tasmanians, **2:**316
  Tats, **6:**359
  Tausug, **5:**263
  Tepehuan of Chihuahua, **8:**253
  Thakali, **3:**291
  Toda, **3:**296
  Tojolab'al, **8:**261
  Wogeo, **2:**381
  Yakut, **6:**406
  Yi, **6:**507
  Yörük, **9:**395
  see also Elopment
absence of ceremony
  Asiatic Eskimos, **6:**41
  Ata Tana 'Ai, **5:**24
  Bugle, **8:**32
  Haitians, **8:**122
  Karelians, **6:**171
  Kédang, **5:**132
  Ngawbe, **8:**196
  Penan, **5:**210
  Pima Bajo, **8:**212
  Poqomam, **8:**218
  Selung/Moken, **5:**232
  Senoi, **5:**238
  Southern Paiute (and Chemehuevi),
    1:331
  Walapai, **1:**365, 366
  West Greenland Inuit, **1:**377
  Yuit, **1:**391
  Yukuna, **7:**387
as achieving adulthood status. *See*
  Adulthood
age differences
  Baiga, **3:**20
  Berbers of Morocco, **9:**50
  Copper Eskimo, **1:**78
  Gros Ventre, **1:**134
  Nyakyusa and Ngonde, **9:**253
  Parsi, **3:**228
  see also older-younger *subheadings below*
age mates of parents
  Yakö, **9:**385
arranged
  Abkhazians, **6:**8
  Achang, **6:**418
  Agaria, **3:**6
  Ajië, **2:**8
  Albanians, **4:**5
  Ambonese, **5:**18
  Andamanes, **3:**10
  Arabs, **9:**24
  Aranda, **2:**17
  Armenians, **6:**29
  Ashkenazim, **6:**34
  Atoni, **5:**27
  Azoreans, **4:**28

  Baffinland Inuit, **1:**30
  Bai, **6:**420
  Bajau, **5:**33
  Baluchi, **3:**23
  Basseri, **9:**42
  Bengali, **3:**31-32
  Bhil, **3:**39
  Bhuiya, **3:**44
  Bisaya, **5:**43
  Bonerate, **5:**45
  Bouyei, **6:**423
  Brahman of Nepal, **3:**52
  Bugis, **5:**50
  Bukidnon, **5:**54
  Bulgarian Gypsies, **4:**41
  Bunun, **5:**56
  Buriats, **6:**67
  Burmese, **5:**65
  Butonese, **5:**67
  Carpatho-Rusyns, **6:**70
  castes, Hindu, **3:**57
  Central Thai, **5:**70
  Chakma, **3:**59
  Chechen-Ingush, **6:**74
  Cheyenne, **1:**65
  Chhetri of Nepal, **3:**52
  Chinantec, **8:**54
  Chinese in Caribbean, **8:**57
  Chinese of South Asia, **3:**68
  Chipewyan, **1:**68
  Chocho, **8:**63
  Chontal of Tabasco, **8:**68
  Chuvans, **6:**82
  Coorg, **3:**74
  Copper Eskimo, **1:**78
  Corsicans, **4:**67
  Cree, **1:**81
  Croats, **4:**73
  Cyclades, **4:**77
  Cypriots, **4:**80
  Dai, **6:**425
  Dani, **2:**44
  Daur, **6:**429
  Dolgan, **6:**101
  Doukhobor, **1:**91
  Drung, **6:**432
  Dungans, **6:**111
  East Asians in Canada, **1:**96
  East Asians in the United States, **1:**99
  Easter Island, **2:**54
  Eastern Shoshone, **1:**105
  Evenki (Northern Tungus), **6:**122
  Ewe and Fon, **9:**86
  Ewenki, **6:**434
  Fali, **9:**95
  Fipa, **9:**99
  Gaels (irish), **4:**116
  Gahuku-Gama, **2:**69
  Gelao, **6:**435
  Gitanos, **4:**129
  Gond, **3:**85
  Greeks, **6:**143
  Gros Ventre, **1:**134
  Guadalcanal, **2:**90
  Gujar, **3:**89
  Gujarati, **3:**91
  Gurung, **3:**94
  Gypsies, **6:**147

Haida, 1:136
Han, 6:444, 445
Hani, 6:450
Hasidim, 1:144
Hidatsa, 1:147
Iban, 5:97
Ifugao, 5:100
Igbo, 9:122
Iraqw, 9:125
Irish Travelers, 1:163
Iroquois, 1:166
Irula, 3:106
Japanese, 5:107
Jatav, 3:114
Jingpo, 6:457
Kachin, 5:117
Kalmyks, 6:156
Kaluli, 2:102
Kanjar, 3:120-121
Kapauku, 2:106
Kapingamarangi, 2:109
Kazak, 6:460
Kazakhs, 6:180
Keraki, 2:113
Khmer, 5:136
K'iche,' 8:142
Kirgiz, 6:461
Kiribati, 2:122
Kiwai, 2:125
Kmhmu, 5:140
Konso, 9:170
Korean, 5:147
Kriashen Tatars, 6:212
Krymchaks, 6:215
Kumeyaay, 1:194
Kurds, 9:176
Kwoma, 2:135
Kyrgyz, 6:230
Lakalai, 2:141
Lakher, 3:146
Laks, 6:234
Lao Isan, 5:161
Lenca, 8:156
Lezgins, 6:243
Li, 6:464
Limbu, 3:150
Lingayat, 3:152
Lisu, 6:465
Lithuanians, 6:251
Mailu, 2:155
Makassar, 5:173
Malay, 5:175
Manam, 2:168
Manihiki, 2:172
Maonan, 6:468
Maris, 6:257
Mazahua, 8:165
Mazatec, 8:169
Mekeo, 2:199
Melanau, 5:179
Mingrelians, 6:264
Mixtec, 8:177
Moldovans, 6:267
Mongols, 6:475
Moor of Sri Lanka, 3:181
Motu, 2:214
Mulam, 6:476
Muong, 5:191

Nagas, 3:189
Namau, 2:231
Naxi, 6:479
Ndebele, 9:237
Nepali, 3:203
Newar, 3:207
Ngawbe, 8:196
Nguna, 2:243
Nissan, 2:250
Niue, 2:251
Nogays, 6:288
Nomoi, 2:252
Nu, 6:481
Ontong Java, 2:254
Oriya, 3:217
Orokaiva, 2:257
Oroquen, 6:483
Pamir peoples, 6:305
Pandit of Kashmir, 3:225
Paniyan, 3:227
Pathan, 3:232
Pentecost, 2:263
peripatetics, 3:235
Persians, 9:279
Pintupi, 2:266
Poqomam, 8:218
Pumi, 6:484
Punjabi, 3:240
Qalandar, 3:247
Reddi, 3:250
Rossel Island, 2:279
Rotuma, 2:282
Rutuls, 6:320
Saami, 6:324
Salar, 6:488
Samal, 5:220
San-speaking peoples, 9:303
Sasak, 5:226
Selepet, 2:294
Seri, 8:234
Sherpa, 3:258
Siberiaki, 6:333
Siberian Tatars, 6:342
Svans, 6:345
Syrian Christian of Kerala, 3:273
Tabasarans, 6:349
Tajik, 6:492
Tajiks, 6:353
Tamil, 3:277
Tamil of Sri Lanka, 3:281, 282
Tangu, 2:311
Tasmanians, 2:316
Tauade, 2:319
Tausug, 5:263
Telugu, 3:286
Tepehuan of Durango, 8:256
Ternatan/Tidorese, 5:275
Thadou, 3:288
Thakali, 3:291
Tiwi, 2:328
Toda, 3:296
Toraja, 5:282
Totonac, 8:265
Tu, 6:497
Turks, 9:375
Tuvans, 6:374
Vellala, 3:305
Vietnamese, 5:285

Wantoat, 2:368
Warlpiri, 2:374
Wasteko, 8:303
Wogeo, 2:381
Xibe, 6:504
Yakan, 5:289
Yakut, 6:406
Yemenis, 9:389
Yugur, 6:508
see also Bride-price; Dowry
arranged after rainy-season contests
Suri, 9:325
arranged but bride may reject groom
Aimaq, 9:10
Bedouin, 9:44
arranged by chief
Sirionó, 7:310
arranged by couple
Pomo, 1:294
arranged by elders
Luyia, 9:205
Maasai, 9:208
Nootka, 1:256
Yoruba, 9:392
Yuit, 1:391
arranged by extended family without
   couple's knowledge
Osage, 1:278
arranged by family
Amhara, 9:19
Bakairi, 7:74
Baniwa-Curripaco-Wakuenai, 7:78
Canela, 7:96
Canelos Quichua, 7:100
Chipaya, 7:116
Cuna, 7:150
Ionians, 4:150
Irish Travellers, 4:156
Itonama, 7:179
Kadiwéu, 7:183
Kagwahiv, 7:185
Macuna, 7:213
Maká, 7:216
Makushi, 7:219
Matsigenka, 7:231
Mehinaku, 7:237
Micmacs, 1:234
Montenegrins, 4:173
Navajo, 1:252
Northern Paiute, 1:264
Ojibwa, 1:270
Otavalo, 7:254
Paresí, 7:269
Pomaks, 4:205
Pomo, 1:294
Rom of Czechoslovakia, 4:218
Shipibo, 7:305
Siona-Secoya, 7:308
Slovenes, 4:248
South and Southeast Asians of Canada,
   1:323
Tupari, 7:340
Ute, 1:361
Vlachs, 4:274
Waorani, 7:352
Washoe, 1:369
Wayapi, 7:362
Yawalapití, 7:379

Marriage (cont'd)
Yokuts, **1:**388
Yörük, **9:**395
arranged by family of groom
Rom, **1:**304-305
Sarakatsani, **4:**224
Spanish Rom, **4:**255
arranged by groom's father's sister
Ewe and Fon, **9:**86
arranged by intermediary
Ionians, **4:**150
arranged by kin groups
Menominee, **1:**221
arranged by lineages
Mossi, **9:**229
Okiek, **9:**260
arranged by male clan member
Chamacoco, **7:**109
arranged by matchmaker
Greek-speaking Jews of Greece, **4:**135
Kashubians, **4:**159
Mennonites, **1:**218
arranged by maternal uncle
Pawnee, **1:**284
arranged by older woman relative
Slav Macedonians, **4:**240
arranged by older women
Betsileo, **9:**56
asymmetrical
Akha, **5:**12
Batak, **5:**39-40
Bonerate, **5:**45
Chin, **3:**65
Endenese, **5:**85
Kachin, **5:**117, 119
Kédang, **5:**132
Kmhmu, **5:**140
Lamaholot, **5:**155
avoidance relationships
Abkhazians, **6:**8
Chechen-Ingush, **6:**74
Chuvans, **6:**82
Dargins, **6:**98
Georgian Jews, **6:**127
Greeks, **6:**143
Ingilos, **6:**150
Jews, Arabic-speaking, **9:**135
Karachays, **6:**161
Karaites, **9:**154
Kazakhs, **6:**180
Khanty, **6:**191
Khinalughs, **6:**201
Mailu, **2:**155
Mingrelians, **6:**264
Ndebele, **9:**236
Ngatatjara, **2:**240
Nyakyusa and Ngonde, **9:**252
Selepet, **2:**294
Selkup, **6:**327
Shors, **6:**331
Tangu, **2:**311
Tats, **6:**360
Temiar, **5:**269
Udis, **6:**377
avuncular
Araweté, **7:**57
Cocama, **7:**130
Karajá, **7:**189

Nambicuara, **7:**247
Shahsevan, **9:**308
Suruí, **7:**313
Ticuna, **7:**329
Vellala, **3:**305
Yukpa, **7:**384
bathing ritual
Bukharan Jews, **6:**64
birth of two or three children makes final
Nuer, **9:**250
bride-capture. See subhead by abduction
above
bride does not participate
Karachays, **6:**161
bride given two best men for protection
Amhara, **9:**19
bride lives with groom's family before
marriage
Mam, **8:**159
bride moves in with husband
Mandan, **1:**214
bride must prove virginity. See Virginity
bride-price. See Bride-price
bride's brothers may veto
Jews of Iran, **9:**140
bride-service. See Bride-service
bride-theft. See subhead by abduction above
bride-wealth. See Bride-price
to brother of husband. See Levirate mar-
riage
caste or status differences. See Hypergamy;
Hypogamy
ceremonies
Amhara, **9:**19
Amuesha, **7:**38
Araucanians, **7:**53
Aymara, **7:**67
Baiga, **3:**20
Bania, **3:**25
Brahman and Chhetri of Nepal, **3:**52-53
Bretons, **4:**39
Bulgarian Gypsies' participation, **4:**41,
42
Bulgarians, **4:**44
Canarians, **4:**52
Candoshi, **7:**93
Canelos Quichua, **7:**100
Cariña, **7:**103
Castilians, **4:**60
Chatino, **8:**51
Cinta Larga, **7:**128
Cochin Jews, **3:**73
Croats, **4:**75
Divehi, **3:**77
Faroe Islanders, **4:**100
Garia, **3:**81
Gond, **3:**85
Guambiano, **7:**172
Irula, **3:**106
Jatav, **3:**115
Khasi, **3:**124
Khoja, **3:**127
Koli, **3:**131-132
Kota, **3:**136
Kuikuru, **7:**208
Lakher, **3:**146
Lepcha, **3:**149
Magar, **3:**157-158

Mappila, **3:**167
Maroni Carib, **7:**220
Mehinaku, **7:**237
Montenegrins, **4:**173
Moor of Sri Lanka, **3:**181
Mundurucu, **7:**245
Nagas, **3:**189
Nayar, **3:**198-199
Otavalo, **7:**254
Otomí of the Sierra, **8:**201
Pame, **8:**208
Parsi, **3:**229
Rajput, **3:**249
Rikbaktsa, **7:**287
Salasaca, **7:**290
Shavante, **7:**301
Siona-Secoya, **7:**308
Siwai, **2:**304
Slovaks, **4:**244
Tamil, **3:**277
Tamil of Sri Lanka, **3:**282
Telegu, **3:**287
Thadou, **3:**288
Toba, **7:**332
Tzotzil of Zinacantan, **8:**293
Yukateko, **8:**309
Yuqui, **7:**393
chaperoned and unconsumated during first
few days
Western Apache, **1:**372
circumcision before
Chagga, **9:**62
clan system regulations
Kikapu, **8:**144
Mbeere, **9:**221
Suri, **9:**325
clitoridectomy before
Nandi and other Kalenjin peoples, **9:**233
clothing
Altaians, **6:**22
Karen, **5:**127
Nicobarese, **3:**209
consumation delayed
Montenegrins, **4:**173
contract
Apalai, **7:**46
Gaels (Irish), **4:**116
Karaites, **9:**155
Lithuanian Jews, **6:**246
Oroquen, **6:**483
Rom, **1:**305
Tats, **6:**359
Tigray, **9:**348
see also Bride-price; Bride-service; Dowry
couple do not attend ceremony
Fulani, **9:**102
cousin. See Cousin marriage
with a defined relative
Aranda, **2:**17
Chambri, **2:**32
Dieri, **2:**49
Iatmul, **2:**99
Kachin, **5:**116
Kamilaroi, **2:**104
Madurese, **5:**167
Makassar, **5:**173
Minangkabau, **5:**183
Rennell Island, **2:**277

Waropen, **2**:376
Wovan, **2**:386
Yangoru Boiken, **2**:389
delayed
  Falasha, **9**:91
  Germans, **4**:122
  Highland Scots, **4**:140
  Okiek, **9**:260
  Orcadians, **4**:187
  Piemontese, **4**:200
  Qashqa'i, **9**:286
  see also subhead later in life _below_
delayed by economic/career considerations
  Czechs, **4**:83
  Dutch, **4**:93
  English, **4**:97
  Tiroleans, **4**:268
delayed by education/career considerations
  Jews of Algeria, **9**:138
delayed for military service
  Jews of Israel, **9**:143
delayed transfer of wife
  Dong, **6**:431
  Han, **6**:444
  Jingpo, **6**:457
  Li, **6**:464
  Maonan, **6**:468
  Miao, **6**:471
  Mulam, **6**:476
  Shui, **6**:491
  Yi, **6**:507
  Zhuang, **6**:511
descent group-based
  Kogi, **7**:202
disruptions common
  Iteso, **9**:129
divorcée as first wife
  Kanuri, **9**:152
double standard
  Bahamians, **8**:19
dowry. _See_ Dowry
dual
  Trinidadians and Tobagonians, **8**:268
early
  Afar, **9**:8
  Ambae, **2**:12
  Amhara, **9**:18
  Arabs, **9**:24
  Fulani, **9**:102
  Goodenough Island, **2**:86
  Jews of Israel, **9**:143
  Kanuri, **9**:152
  Martiniquais, **8**:162
  Mongols, **6**:475
  Pame, **8**:208
  peripatetics of Afghanistan, Iran, and
    Turkey, **9**:275
  peripatetics of Iraq, Syria, Lebanon,
    Jordan, Israel, Egypt, Sudan, and
    Yemen, **9**:277
  Popoloca, **8**:216
  Puerto Ricans, **8**:222
  Q'eqchi,' **8**:226
  Sumu, **8**:238
  Ternatan/Tidorese, **5**:275
  Turkmens, **6**:370
  Turks, **9**:375
  Yezidis, **6**:409

early betrothal. _See_ Child betrothal
as economic agreement
  Belau, **2**:26
  Cotopaxi Quichua, **7**:133
  Navajo, **1**:252
  Swedes, **4**:257
as economic necessity
  Western Shoshone, **1**:375
as economic partnership
  Flemish, **4**:107
  Ozarks, **1**:281
elders' approval needed
  Acholi, **9**:5
elder siblings first
  Armenians, **6**:30
  Azerbaijani Turks, **6**:49
  Karachays, **6**:160
  Mingrelians, **6**:264
by eldest son only
  Nambudiri Brahman, **3**:193
by elopement
  Acholi, **9**:5
  Ambonese, **5**:18
  Andis, **6**:26
  Avars, **6**:45
  Awakateko, **8**:16
  Bai, **6**:420
  Bajau, **5**:33
  Bamiléké, **9**:38
  Bhil, **3**:39, 40
  Bhuiya, **3**:44
  Bugis, **5**:51
  Bulgarian Gypsies, **4**:41
  Cahita, **8**:36
  Chechen-Ingush, **6**:74
  Chinantec, **8**:54
  Chontal of Tabasco, **8**:68
  Circassians, **9**:67
  Corsicans, **4**:67
  Cretans, **4**:70
  Dai, **6**:425
  Ewenki, **6**:434
  Garia, **2**:75
  Gitanos, **4**:129
  Gond, **3**:85
  Greeks, **6**:143
  Gusii, **9**:109
  Hanunóo, **5**:91
  Hidsata, **1**:147
  Itza,' **8**:134
  Kalasha, **3**:116
  Kapauku, **2**:106
  Karachays, **6**:160
  Kiowa, **1**:187
  Kiribati, **2**:122
  Kol, **3**:130
  Kriashen Tatars, **6**:212
  Lahu, **6**:463
  Lakalai, **2**:141
  Limbu, **3**:150
  Lisu, **6**:465
  Lobi-Dagarti peoples, **9**:184
  Luyia, **9**:205
  Mafulu, **2**:152
  Magar, **3**:158
  Makassar, **5**:173
  Mazahua, **8**:165
  Mekeo, **2**:199

Miao, **6**:471
Miyanmin, **2**:210
Muong, **5**:191
Nahua of the Huasteca, **8**:186
Nepali, **3**:203-204
Newar, **3**:207
Nu, **6**:481
Okiek, **9**:260
Palaung, **5**:202
Pentecost, **2**:263
Piemontese Sinti, **4**:200
Rom, **1**:305
Santal, **3**:253
Sasak, **5**:226
Shan, **5**:240
Shui, **6**:491
Slovensko Roma, **4**:251
Swazi, **9**:331
Tats, **6**:359
Tausug, **5**:263
Thadou, **3**:288
Tikopia, **2**:325
Tojolab'al, **8**:261
Tonga, **9**:354
Tor, **2**:343
Totonac, **8**:265
Tzotzil and Tzeltal of Pantelhó, **8**:277
Tzotzil of Zinacantan, **8**:293
Wogeo, **2**:381
Wovan, **2**:386
Xoraxané Romá, **4**:282
Yezidis, **6**:409
YörÜk, **9**:395
Zhuang, **6**:511
Zoque, **8**:316
endogamous. _See_ Endogamy
exchange of goods
  Chamacoco, **7**:109
  Wayapi, **7**:362
exchange of siblings
  Amahuaca, **7**:35
exogamous. _See_ Exogamy
expected
  Yukateko, **8**:309
fake
  Arubans, **8**:12
family approval needed
  Itza,' **8**:134
  Miami, **1**:231
father or brother consent needed
  Guarayu, **7**:174
  Pauserna, **7**:270
with father's sister
  Akawaio, **7**:32
  Araweté, **7**:57
  Yukpa, **7**:384
feast. _See_ Feasting, wedding
female exchange
  Banaro, **2**:21
  Boazi, **2**:29, 30
  Buriats, **6**:67
  Even, **6**:119
  Kiwai, **2**:125
  Tabasarans, **6**:349
female-initiated proposal
  Maká, **7**:216
fights during festivities
  Rominche, **4**:217

Marriage (cont'd)
after four nights of platonic sleeping together
Quechan, 1:301
forced
Guadalcanal, 2:90
formal announcements and family visits
Shetlanders, 4:233-234
free choice
Abkhazians, 6:8
Ache, 7:5
Akha, 5:12
Alorese, 5:15
Atoni, 5:27
Aymara, 7:67
Bukidnon, 5:54
Bulgarians, 4:44
Butonese, 5:67
Cariña, 7:103
Cham, 5:73
Chin, 3:65
Circassians, 6:88
Czechs, 4:83
Dani, 2:44
Dusun, 5:82
Easter Island, 2:54
Ewenki, 6:434
Gebusi, 2:78
Georgians, 6:133
Goodenough Island, 2:86
Guambiano, 7:172
Han, 6:445
Hmong, 5:93
Japanese, 5:107
Javanese, 5:112
Khasi, 3:124
Kilenge, 2:119
Kmhmu, 5:140
Korean, 5:147
Krymchaks, 6:215
Lahu, 6:463
Lao Isan, 5:161
Leonese, 4:161
Lingayat, 3:152
Lithuanians, 6:251
Maisin, 2:158
Makushi, 7:219
Manx, 4:171
Maring, 2:186
Mendi, 2:204
Miao, 6:471
Miyanmin, 2:210
Motu, 2:214
Muyu, 2:228
Nguna, 2:243
Nogays, 6:289
Shahsevan, 9:309
Shan, 5:240
Shui, 6:491
Sundanese, 5:247
Syrian Christian of Kerala, 3:273
Tajiks, 6:353
Tamil of Sri Lanka, 3:282
Taos, 1:342
Tepehuan of Chihuahua, 8:253
Tor, 2:343
Toraja, 5:282
Tujia, 6:498

Usino, 2:362
Vietnamese, 5:285
Wa, 6:503
Walloons, 4:277
Yangoru Boiken, 2:389
Yao of Thailand, 5:292
Yezidis, 6:409
Yoruba, 9:392
Yurok, 1:395
of generation members
Panare, 7:266
Ticuna, 7:329
ghost
Dinka, 9:70
Iraqw, 9:125
gift exchange
Batak, 5:40
Kickapoo, 1:184
Mandan, 1:214
Mixe, 8:174
Osage, 1:278
Pacific Eskimo, 1:283
Pomo, 1:294
Poqomam, 8:218
Sarsi, 1:308
Swedes, 4:257
Tandroy, 9:337
Teton, 1:345
Tojolab'al, 8:261
Tubatulabal, 1:355
Tuvalu, 2:356
Waropen, 2:376
Yaqui, 8:306
Zuni, 1:398
gift giving
Betsileo, 9:56
Bulgarians, 4:44
Canarians, 4:52
Ewe and Fon, 9:86
Greeks, 6:143
Highland Scots, 4:141
Javanese, 5:112
Khanty, 6:191
Mam, 8:159
Mountain Jews, 6:272
Nu, 6:481
Pokot, 9:282
Talysh, 6:356
Temiar, 5:269
Tzotzil of Zinacantan, 8:293
Yokuts, 1:388
Yuit, 1:391
gifts by male suitor to woman's father
Walapai, 1:365
gifts to bride from groom
Ewe and Fon, 9:86
Okiek, 9:260
Tzotzil and Tzeltal of Pantelhó, 8:277
groom-price
Kanbi, 3:118
Santal, 3:253
groom probation
Micmac, 1:234
see also Bride-service
groom-service. See Groom-service
groom's hands tied during ceremony
Tepehuan of Durango, 8:256

groom slings his hammock in father-in-law's house
Pemon, 7:272
groom spends night with bride and is discovered by parents
Kickapoo, 1:184
groom ties necklace around bride's neck
Irula, 3:106
group
Nivkh, 6:284
guardian selected in case of divorce
Tigray, 9:348
guests defray wedding costs
Rom, 1:305
"half-marriage" (lacking bride-price)
Wiyot, 1:384
Yurok, 1:395
heiress
Khasi, 3:124
hijra participation in wedding ceremony, 3:96
to husband's brother. See Levirate marriage
husband's legal authority
German Swiss, 4:126
husbands may beat wives
Nandi and other Kalenjin peoples, 9:233
husbands' unlimited authority
Don Cossacks, 6:105
husband worship
Magar, 3:158
importance of
Peloponnesians, 4:193, 194
infant betrothal. See Child betrothal
informal
Burakumin, 5:61
Hawaiians, 2:96
Mohave, 1:241
Naxi, 6:479
Pumi, 6:484
Qiang, 6:486
Tu, 6:497
Yugur, 6:509
see also Living together
initiated by groom's parents
Nootka, 1:256
initiated by man asking woman's mother to make him hammock
Yuqui, 1:393
interethnic and interracial. See Intermarriage
intergenerational. See subhead age differences above
intersectional
Berbers of Morocco, 9:50
intertribal
Herero, 9:117
"in the hammock"
Kuna, 8:148
intimate touching during ceremony
Itelmen, 6:153
Koryaks and Kerek, 6:209
irregular forms of
Gond, 3:85
Santal, 3:253
Thadou, 3:288
see also Living together
Islamic practice
Bajau, 5:35

landholding as important factor
  Awá Kwaiker, 7:64
  Provencal, 4:211
  Romanians, 4:214
  Tiroleans, 4:263
later in life
  Abkhazians, 6:8
  Antigua and Barbuda, 8:9
  Circassians, 6:88
  Fali, 9:95
  Northern Irish, 4:179
  Piemontese, 4:198
  Sardinians, 4:226
  Tory Islanders, 4:265
  Welsh, 4:280
later for wealthy women
  Ndebele, 9:236
lavish celebration
  Highland Scots, 4:141
  Hungarians, 4:144
  Maltese, 4:168
lengthy celebration
  Armenians, 6:30
  Dungans, 6:111
  Gypsies, 6:147
  Jews of Yemen, 9:150
  Karachays, 6:161
  Karelians, 6:171
  Kashubians, 4:159
  Khinalughs, 6:200
  Krymchaks, 6:215
  Kubachins, 6:218
  Old Believers, 1:274
  Qashqa'i, 9:287
  Rom, 1:305
  Slovenes, 4:248
  Tabasarans, 6:349
  Tofalar, 6:363
  Tsakhurs, 6:367
  Ukrainian peasants, 6:387
  Yörük, 9:396
levirate. See Levirate marriage
living together prior to
  Nandi and other Kalenjin peoples, 9:233
  Zapotec, 8:312
long engagement. See under Courtship
love match
  Bulgarians, 4:44
  Chin, 3:65
  Dutch, 4:93
  German, 4:122
  Ionians, 4:150
  Khasi, 3:124
  Lingayat, 3:152
  Syrian Christian of Kerala, 3:273
  Tamil of Sri Lanka, 3:282
lucky day for wedding
  Orcadians, 4:187
mail-order brides
  Basques, 1:34
male inheritance at time of
  Gaels (Irish), 4:116
as means to elevate rank. See Hypergamy;
  Hypogamy
mediated
  Altaians, 6:22
  Andis, 6:26
  Armenians, 6:29

  Ashkenazim, 6:34
  Balkars, 6:53
  Bukharan Jews, 6:64
  Chuvans, 6:82
  Dai, 6:425
  Dargins, 6:97
  Daur, 6:429
  Dolgan, 6:101
  Don Cossacks, 6:105
  Dungans, 6:111
  Greeks, 6:143
  Gypsies, 6:147
  Japanese, 5:107
  Kachin, 5:117
  Karachays, 6:160
  Karaites, 6:165
  Karen, 5:127
  Kazakhs, 6:179, 180
  Ket, 6:184
  Khinalughs, 6:200
  Khmer, 5:136
  Korean, 5:147
  Kumyks, 6:222
  Lahu, 5:152
  Lithuanian Jews, 6:246
  Lithuanians, 6:251
  Mansi, 6:253
  Mountain Jews, 6:272
  Palaung, 5:202
  Rutuls, 6:320
  Salar, 6:488
  Samal, 5:220
  Selkup, 6:327
  Selung/Moken, 5:232
  Taiwan aboriginal peoples, 5:258
  Tats, 6:360
  Tsakhurs, 6:367
  Uzbeks, 6:397
  Vietnamese, 5:285
  Yakut, 6:406
  Zhuang, 6:511
minors
  Han, 6:444, 445
  Maonan, 6:468
mixed. See Intermarriage
mock battle between couple's families
  Shilluk, 9:311
monogamous. See Monogamy
as most important life-cycle ceremony
  Ukrainians of Canada, 1:358
with mother and daughter
  Apalai, 7:46
  Emberá, 7:156
  Mojo, 7:242
multiple husbands. See Polygyny
multiple spouses. See Polygamy
multiple wedding ceremonies
  Bretons, 4:39
  Burusho, 3:55, 56
multiple wives. See Polyandry
newlyweds remain in parents homes
  Leonese, 4:161
older man–young woman
  Badaga, 3:16
  Baiga, 3:20
  Bondo, 3:49
  Parsi, 3:228
older woman–young man

  Bondo, 3:49
oldest son
  Nambudiri Brahman, 3:193
old widows as first wives
  Lakandon, 8:154
palm wine given to bride's father
  Pende, 9:273
parental resistance to
  Tory Islanders, 4:265
patrilateral encouraged
  Tlingit, 1:352
payments in livestock
  San-speaking peoples, 9:303
petition
  Tzotzil of Chamula, 8:280
  Tzotzil of Zinacantan, 8:293
preference for young girls
  Wapisiana, 7:355
pregnancy-motivated
  Bavarians, 4:34
  Norwegians, 4:181
  Zapotec, 8:312
preliminary agreement between families
  Xoraxané Romá, 4:282
prepuberty. See subhead youth below
prestations
  Alorese, 5:15
  Asiatic Eskimos, 6:41
  Ata Sikka, 5:21
  Chambri, 2:32
  Chuvans, 6:82
  Dani, 2:44
  Dobu, 2:51
  Eipo, 2:57
  Fore, 2:63
  Gayo, 5:89
  Iatmul, 2:99
  Karachays, 6:160
  Kédang, 5:132, 133
  Kewa, 2:116
  Khinalughs, 6:200
  Kiwai, 2:125
  Kumyks, 6:222
  Kurtatchi, 2:132
  Kwoma, 2:134-135
  Lahu, 6:463
  Lak, 2:138
  Lamaholot, 5:155
  Mae Enga, 2:150
  Mailu, 2:155
  Maisin, 2:158
  Manchu, 6:467
  Mejbrat, 2:196
  Mekeo, 2:199
  Melpa, 2:201
  Mendi, 2:204
  Motu, 2:214
  Nasioi, 2:234
  Nganasan, 6:281
  Nias, 5:196
  Nogays, 6:288
  Nu, 6:481
  Oroquen, 6:483
  Ossetes, 6:300
  Palu'e, 5:206
  Rotinese, 5:213
  Semang, 5:235
  Shan, 5:240

Marriage (cont'd)
  Shors, **6**:331
  Sundanese, **5**:247
  Tangu, **2**:311
  Tats, **6**:360
  Udis, **6**:377
  Ukrainian peasants, **6**:387
  Yakut, **6**:406
  Yugur, **6**:508
 as prime goal
  Peloponnesians, **4**:193
 processions to and from church
  Shetlanders, **4**:234
 procreation as primary function
  Highland Scots, **4**:141
 prohibitions. *See* Incest prohibitions
 property considerations
  Highland Scots, **4**:140, 141
 property constraints
  Saami, **4**:221
 property ownership maintained
  Cotopaxi Quichua, **7**:133
 provisional
  Gnau, **2**:81
 following puberty
  Sleb, **9**:315
 rape as means of
  Huarayo, **7**:177
 religious ceremony necessary
  Cypriots, **4**:80
 religious ceremony separate
  Russian peasants, **6**:312
 religious importance of ceremony
  Mennonites, **1**:218
 residency after. *See* Residence
 rice throwing at wedding
  Swiss, Italian, **4**:261
 ritual silence
  Armenians, **6**:30
 role of eldest brother
  Mingrelians, **6**:264
 role of godparents
  Moldovans, **6**:268
  Nahuat of the Sierra de Pueblo, **8**:192
  Romanians, **4**:213-214
  Tarascans, **8**:245, 246
 role of maternal uncle
  Mingrelians, **6**:264
 role of younger brother
  Chuvans, **6**:82
 royalty with commoner
  Mamprusi, **9**:212
 sacred bundle ownership importance
  Mandan, **1**:214
 sacrifice
  Buriats, **6**:68
 same gate forbidden
  Mamprusi, **9**:212
 same surname forbidden
  Poqomam, **8**:218
 self-mutilation
  Tongareva, **2**:340
 separate laws by group
  Antigua and Barbuda, **8**:9
 serial
  Circassians, **6**:88
  Tandroy, **9**:337
 serial between sibling sets

  Araweté, **7**:57
sexual consummation required
  Karaites, **9**:155
sexual intercourse in woman's house
  precedes
  Ute, **1**:361
sibling
  Koryaks and Kerek, **6**:209
sibling approval of bride
  Tiroleans, **4**:263
sibling exchange
  Ghorbat, **9**:107
sibling exchange preferred
  peripatetics of Afghanistan, Iran, and
   Turkey, **9**:275
sister exchange
  Abelam, **2**:5
  Aleuts, **6**:18
  Araweté, **7**:57
  Banaro, **2**:21
  Baniwa-Curripaco-Wakuenai, **7**:78
  Berbers of Morocco, **9**:50
  Boazi, **2**:30
  Candoshi, **7**:93
  Cubeo, **7**:140
  Desana, **7**:153
  Evenki (Northern Tungus), **6**:122
  Gainj, **2**:72
  Gebusi, **2**:78
  Gogodala, **2**:84
  Iatmul, **2**:99
  Kaluli, **2**:102
  Kariera, **2**:111
  Karihona, **7**:192
  Ka'wiari, **7**:199
  Keraki, **2**:113
  Lakalai, **2**:141
  Macuna, **7**:213
  Maisin, **2**:158
  Malekula, **2**:165
  Marind-anim, **2**:183
  Maring, **2**:186
  Mimika, **2**:207
  Miyanmin, **2**:210
  Mountain Arapesh, **2**:216
  Mundugumor, **2**:219
  Murik, **2**:222
  Nguna, **2**:243
  Nissan, **2**:250
  Sambia, **2**:285
  Selepet, **2**:294
  Sharanahua, **7**:299
  Taiwan aboriginal peoples, **5**:257, 258
  Tanimuka, **7**:319
  Tanna, **2**:314, 315
  Tatuyo, **7**:323
  Tauade, **2**:319
  Telefolmin, **2**:322
  Tor, **2**:343
  tropical-forest foragers, **9**:357
  Usino, **2**:362
  Wanano, **7**:350
  Wantoat, **2**:368
  Yanomamö, **7**:375
  Yukuna, **7**:387
with sister's daughter
  Akawaio, **7**:32
  Asurini, **7**:61

  Cinta Larga, **7**:128
  Guarayu, **7**:174
  Jivaro, **7**:183
  Pauserna, **7**:270
  Pemon, **7**:272
  Trio, **7**:336
  Wapisiana, **7**:355
  Yukpa, **7**:384
with sister's son
  Marubo, **7**:222
with sister's son's daughter
  Marubo, **7**:222
within small kinship circle
  Vlach Gypsies of Hungary, **4**:272
social importance of wedding celebration
  Orcadians, **4**:187
  Tiroleans, **4**:263
socially upward or equal. *See* Hypergamy
son-daughter exchange
  Gujar, **3**:89
  Pathan, **3**:232
  Tamil, **3**:277
spouse exchange
  Asmat, **2**:19, 21
  Chiquitano, **7**:118
  Copper Eskimo, **1**:78
  Daribi, **2**:47
  Namau, **2**:231
  Sirionó, **7**:310
  Waimiri-Atroari, **7**:344
standards
  Tamil, **3**:278, 2777
strong spousal solidarity
  Norwegians, **4**:181
substitute wife in case of infertility
  Ndebele, **9**:236
success dependant on producing
  children
  Luo, **9**:200
surreptitious
  Tory Islanders, **4**:265
tax
  Dargins, **6**:98
teenage, **1**:274
  Pima-Papago, **1**:289
  Pomaks, **4**:205
  Rominche, **4**:216
  Vlachs, **4**:274
temporary
  Amhara, **9**:19
timing of wedding
  Dani, **2**:44
as transaction between kin groups
  Basseri, **9**:42
transfer of cattle from groom's family to
  bride's
  Khoi, **9**:159
transfer of drink and money
  Akan, **9**:11
transfer rights from woman's lineage to
  groom's
  Suku, **9**:321
trial
  Awá Kwaiker, **7**:64
  Betsileo, **9**:56
  Central Yup'ik Eskimos, **1**:58
  Cook Islands, **2**:41
  Finns, **4**:103

Guambiano, **7:**172
Ifugao, **5:**100
Irula, **3:**106
Kewa, **2:**116
Lenca, **8:**156
Mataco, **7:**229
Montenegrins, **4:**173
Otavalo, **7:**254
Sagada Igorot, **5:**216
Saliva, **7:**292
Shipibo, **7:**305
Temiar, **5:**269
Tsimihety, **9:**358
Waimiri-Atroari, **7:**344
Warao, **7:**358
twins to twins
Mojo, **7:**242
as uniting families
Zoroastrians, **9:**408
virginity requirement. _See_ Virginity
"visiting" husband
Barbadians, **8:**22
Jamaicans, **8:**138
Montserratians, **8:**180
Saint Lucians, **8:**231
Tory Islanders, **4:**265
wedding customs
Amish, **1:**20
Central Yup'ik Eskimos, **1:**57
Hopi, **1:**149
Latinos, **1:**205
wedding held in winter
Kashubians, **4:**159
wedding house
Baggara, **9:**30
wife doesn't live with husband until she
bears child
Fipa, **9:**99
Turkana, **9:**372
wife doesn't speak to in-laws until she bears
child
Fipa, **9:**99
wife given as political reward
Mossi, **9:**229
wife sharing
Asiatic Eskimos, **6:**41
wife's religious conversion
Awakateko, **8:**16
wife's subserviency
Maasai, **9:**208
wife stealing
Abkhazians, **6:**8
Bajau, **5:**33
Hmong, **5:**93
Namau, **2:**231
Tasmanians, **2:**317
Tikopia, **2:**325
woman initiates courtship
Bouyei, **6:**422
woman must marry before brothers
Lango, **9:**180
woman retains own name
Kuna, **8:**148
woman returns to natal home when she
leaves husband
Sakalava, **9:**296
woman's choice
Sengseng, **2:**297

woman's choice following premarital
relations
Rukuba, **9:**290
woman's restrictions
German Swiss, **4:**126
woman-to-woman
Igbo, **9:**122
Kipsigis, **9:**164
Nandi and other Kalenjin peoples, **9:**233
woman wears gold or silver jewelry at
ceremony
Jews of Kurdistan, **9:**146
youth (prepuberty)
Albanians, **4:**5
Bhil, **3:**39
Copper Eskimo, **1:**78
Irish Travelers, **1:**163
Lakher, **3:**146
Lepcha, **3:**149
Maratha, **3:**169
Pahari, **3:**222
Reddi, **3:**250
see also Adultery; Common-law marriage;
Divorce; Premarital sex; Remarriage
Marriage circles
Kanbi, **3:**118
Marriage rate
declining
Walloons, **4:**277
high
Divehi, **3:**77
Greeks, **4:**132
low
Cubans, **8:**88
rising
Portuguese, **4:**207
Marriage variants. _See_ Marriage, irregular
forms of
Marriage within caste. _See_ Hypergamy
Marthoma Syrian Church
Syrian Christian of Kerala, **3:**274
Martial arts
Bugis, **5:**51
Malay, **5:**176
Truk, **2:**353
Mask carving
Central Yup'ik Eskimos, **1:**57, 59
Ingalik, **1:**158
Iroquois, **1:**167
Kwakiutl, **1:**200
Nootka, **1:**256, 257
Masked dancers
Havasupai, **1:**145
Keres Pueblo Indians, **1:**181
Nootka, **1:**257
Masks
Bakairi, **7:**74, 75
Cotopaxi Quichua, **7:**135
Dogon, **9:**73
Edo, **9:**82
Flemish, **4:**108
German Swiss, **4:**127
Igbo, **9:**121
Karajá, **7:**189, 191
Karihona, **7:**193
Kpelle, **9:**174
Lakalai, **2:**142
Lobi-Dagarti peoples, **9:**186

Luba of Shaba, **9:**193
Mehinaku, **7:**236
Modang, **5:**187
Namau, **2:**232
Ndembu, **9:**241
Orokolo, **2:**260
Pende, **9:**274
Tanaina, **1:**337
Tapirapé, **7:**321
tropical-forest foragers, **9:**357
Yukuna, **7:**390
Zuni, **1:**399
Maslennitsa (holiday)
Russian peasants, **6:**313
Masons. _See_ Freemasonry
Masta cult
Nepali, **3:**205
Mastamho (deity)
Mohave, **1:**241
Matamatam (ceremony)
Tolai, **2:**335
Material goods
disposal and repurchase
Gitanos, **4:**129
materialism
Czechs, **4:**84
Ingalik, **1:**157
Maternal line. _See_ Descent, matrilineal
Maternal uncle. _See_ Uncle, maternal
Mate selection. _See_ Courtship; Marriage
Matha. _See_ Monasticism
Mat making
Bhuiya, **3:**43
Klamath, **1:**191
Koya, **3:**140
Kwakiutl, **1:**198
Labbai, **3:**144
Lakher, **3:**145
Magar, **3:**156
Nagas, **3:**188
Nayaka, **3:**195
Santal, **3:**253
Matriarchy
Sakalava, **9:**296
Matriclan
Klingit, **1:**352
Toda, **3:**297
Tonkawa, **1:**354
Tsimshian, **1:**355
Matridemes
Ute, **1:**361
Matrifocal households. _See_ Family,
matrifocal
Matrilineal descent. _See_ Descent, matrilineal
Matrilocal residency. _See_ Residence,
matrilocal
Maulideen Nabi (celebration)
Tausug, **5:**264
Maulud (celebration)
Bajau, **5:**34
Madurese, **5:**168
Samal, **5:**221
Samal Moro, **5:**224
Sundanese, **5:**247
Maulut (ceremony)
Balkars, **6:**54
Mauza (revenue village)
Bengali, **3:**30

Maya belief
    Pahari, 3:222
Mayor
    Corsicans, 4:68
Mayordomo
    Boruca, Bribri, Cabécar, 8:30
    Chocho, 8:63
    Ch'ol, 8:65
    Cora, 8:76
    Lenca, 8:156
    Mazatec, 8:169
    Mixtec, 8:178
    Pame, 8:208
    Q'anjob'al, 8:225
    Q'eqchi,' 8:227
Mazdaism
    Svans, 6:346
Meal preparation. See Cooking
Measles
    Chipewyan, 1:67
Mecawetok (supreme deity)
    Menominee, 1:222
Mediation. See under Conflict resolution
Medical practices and treatments
    activity restrictions
        Apalai, 7:47
        Krikati/Pukobye, 7:206
    acupuncture
        Aleut, 1:16
        Chinese in Southeast Asia, 5:77
        Flemish, 4:109
        Han, 6:448
        Japanese, 5:110
        Kyrgyz, 6:232
        Zhuang, 6:511
    alcohol spraying
        Huarayo, 7:179
    allopathic medicine
        Austrians, 4:21
        Kota, 3:138
        Muslim, 3:185
        Oriya, 3:218
        Santal, 3:255
        Spanish Rom, 4:255
        Tamil, 3:279
        Tamil of Sri Lanka, 3:284
        Thakali, 3:292
    amulet use
        Bedouin, 9:46
        Krikati/Pukobye, 7:206
    ancestor invocation
        Garifuna, 8:115
        Ndembu, 9:240
    animal products
        Chimane, 7:113
        Mixtec, 8:178
        Sakalava, 9:298
        Turkana, 9:373
    animal sacrifice
        Betsileo, 9:57
    animals as payment
        Swazi, 9:333
    ayurvedic medicine
        Nayar, 3:200
        Oriya, 3:218
        Pahari, 3:223
        Sadhu, 3:252
        Sinhalese, 3:267

        Tamil, 3:279
        Tamil of Sri Lanka, 3:284
        Thakali, 3:292
        Vedda, 3:303
    balancing of forces
        Afro-Colombians, 7:18
    balm practitioners
        Jamaicans, 8:139
    bathing
        Belarussians, 6:61
        Germans, 4:124
        Tabasarans, 6:350
        Tasmanians, 2:317
        Tongareva, 2:341
        Ukrainians, 6:393
    baton use
        Noanamá, 7:252
    binding
        Easter Island, 2:55
        Tsakhurs, 6:368
    biomagnetics
        Yawalapití, 7:380
    biomedicine
        Germans, 4:123-124
    bleeding
        Aleut, 1:16
        Alur, 9:15
        Andamanese, 3:11
        Balkars, 6:54
        Boazi, 2:31
        Copper Eskimo, 1:79
        Dai, 6:428
        Dani, 2:45
        Hoti, 7:176
        Jews, Arabic-speaking, 9:136
        Jews of Kurdistan, 9:146
        Keraki, 2:114
        Montagnais-Naskapi, 1:246
        Murik, 2:223
        Tabasarans, 6:350
        Tasmanians, 2:317
        Tor, 2:344
        Torres Strait Islanders, 2:347
        Tsakhurs, 6:368
    blood stopping
        Saami, 4:222
    blowing
        Ache, 7:7
        Amahuaca, 7:36
        Asurini, 7:62
        Bugis, 5:51
        Chiriguano, 7:122
        Chorote, 7:126
        Cinta Larga, 7:129
        Cubeo, 7:142
        Desana, 7:154
        Hoti, 7:176
        Huarayo, 7:179
        Karihona, 7:193
        Ka'wiari, 7:200
        Macuna, 7:215
        Maká, 7:218
        Matsigenka, 7:232
        Mundurucu, 7:245
        Palikur, 7:264
        Paraujano, 7:268
        Paresí, 7:269
        Shipibo, 7:306

        Temiar, 5:273
        Toba, 7:333
        Tupari, 7:340
        Wapisiana, 7:356
        Yagua, 7:374
        Yawalapití, 7:380
        Yekuana, 7:381
        Yukuna, 7:390
    blowing smoke
        Quechan, 1:302
    body painting
        Marubo, 7:223
        Yuqui, 7:392
    bonesetting
        Baggara, 9:31
        Gusii, 9:110
        Itza,' 8:135
        Jews of Iran, 9:141
        Ladinos, 8:153
        Mazahua, 8:166
        Nahua of the Huasteca, 8:187
        Tz'utujil, 8:298
        Yakut, 6:407
        Zapotec, 8:313
    branding
        Bedouin, 9:46
        Yemenis, 9:390
    burning
        Boazi, 2:31
        Rotuma, 2:283
    bush
        Bahamians, 8:20
        Barbadians, 8:23
        Garifuna, 8:115
        Saint Lucians, 8:232
    cauterization
        Kiribati, 2:123
        Tabasarans, 6:350
        Tats, 6:360
    ceremonial
        Mandan, 1:215
        Navajo, 1:253
        Tzotzil and Tzeltal of Pantelhó, 8:278
        Tzotzil of Chamula, 8:281
        Western Apache, 1:373
    chanting
        Amahuaca, 7:36
        Ayoreo, 7:72
        Chácobo, 7:107
        Chimane, 7:113
        Chorote, 7:126
        Cinta Larga, 7:129
        Delaware, 1:86
        Desana, 7:154
        Huarayo, 7:179
        Kuna, 8:150
        Lengua, 7:211
        Macuna, 7:215
        Marubo, 7:223
        Mashco, 7:227
        Nambicuara, 7:247
        Nivaclé, 7:251
        Piaroa, 7:278
        Pomo, 1:295
        Shipibo, 7:306
        Suya, 7:317
        Toba, 7:333
        Wanano, 7:350

Yawalapití, **7:**380
Yekuana, **7:**381
Yuqui, **7:**394
charms
Shona, **9:**314
Swedes, **4:**258
clinics
Madeirans, **4:**166
Mescalero Apache, **1:**225
Slovaks, **4:**245
compress
Ukrainians, **6:**393
confession by patient
Goodenough Island, **2:**88
Tepehuan of Durango, **8:**258
Yurok, **1:**396
crystal gazing
Desana, **7:**154
crystals
Boruca, Bribri, Cabécar, **8:**30
curers. _See_ Healers
cutting
Rotuma, **2:**283
dancing
Chimila, **7:**114
Slav Macedonians, **4:**241
Toba, **7:**333
Tolowa, **1:**353
Ute, **1:**362
Yurok, **1:**395
dancing and singing
Mescalero Apache, **1:**225
dietary restrictions
Apalai, **7:**47
Apiaká, **7:**50
Baniwa-Curripaco-Wakuenai, **7:**80
Desana, **7:**154
Krikati/Pukobye, **7:**206
Pemon, **7:**273
Wayapi, **7:**363
Yukuna, **7:**390
distraction
Circassians, **9:**68
doll and long staff as diagnosis tools
Tanaina, **1:**337
dream interpretation
Desana, **7:**154
Sakalava, **9:**298
Tarahumara, **8:**242
Zoque, **8:**317
embodiment of illness as small bone to be
pulled out of body
Miami, **1:**232
emetics
Montagnais-Naskapi, **1:**246
Panare, **7:**267
exorcism
Cubeo, **7:**142
Ka'wiari, **7:**200
extraction of foreign matter
Bugis, **5:**51
Mailu, **2:**156
Marind-anim, **2:**184
Orokaiva, **2:**258
Tanaina, **1:**337
faith healing
Puerto Ricans, **8:**223
Swazi, **9:**332

firebrand use
Guajiro, **7:**170
folk
Acholi, **9:**6
Gaels (Irish), **4:**117
Haitians, **8:**122
Itza,' **8:**135
Jamaicans, **8:**139
Lango, **9:**182
Martiniquais, **8:**164
Mazahua, **8:**166
Montserratians, **8:**181
Otomí of the Valley of Mezquital, **8:**206
Sarakatsani, **4:**225
Slovaks, **4:**245
Swiss, Italian, **4:**262
Tory Islanders, **4:**266
Ukrainians of Canada, **1:**359
Washoe, **1:**370
Yuit, **1:**392, 393
food taboos
Tewa Pueblo, **1:**349
fumigation
Terena, **7:**327
Xikrin, **7:**369
Yekuana, **7:**381
gesticulating
Tupari, **7:**340
government-supported system
English, **4:**97
Gaels (Irish), **4:**117
Germans, **4:**123
Gitanos, **4:**130
Greeks, **4:**134
Highland Scots, **4:**142
Hungarians, **4:**145
Icelanders, **4:**148
Northern Irish, **4:**180
Norwegians, **4:**182
Orcadians, **4:**188
Pasiegos, **4:**191
Peloponnesians, **4:**194
Piemontese, **4:**199
Poles, **4:**204
Shetlanders, **4:**234
Welsh, **4:**280
ground stone
Nyakyusa and Ngonde, **9:**254
guilt relief
Awá Kwaiker, **7:**65
hallucinogens
Amahuaca, **7:**36
Desana, **7:**154
Guahibo-Sikuani, **7:**166
Itonama, **7:**179
Karihona, **7:**193
Marubo, **7:**223
Piaroa, **7:**278
Wayapi, **7:**363
Yanomamö, **7:**377
Yawalapití, **7:**380
healers. _See_ Healers; Medicine men;
Shamanism
healing clays
Chimane, **7:**113
healing invocations
Amahuaca, **7:**33
healing springs

Circassians, **6:**91
healing touch
Swedes, **4:**258
heat
Balkars, **6:**54
Dai, **6:**428
Easter Island, **2:**55
Telefolmin, **2:**323
Tsakhurs, **6:**368
heat/cold
Krikati/Pukobye, **7:**206
Xikrin, **7:**369
herbs. _See_ Herbal, plant, and root medicine
homeopathy
Austrians, **4:**21
Kanjar, **3:**121
Karelians, **6:**172
Oriya, **3:**218
Provencal, **4:**211
Qalandar, **3:**248
see also Herbal, plant, and root medicine
home remedies
Barbadians, **8:**23
Cape Coloureds, **9:**60
Hungarians, **4:**145
Peloponnesians, **4:**194
Romanians, **4:**214
honey
Sarakatsani, **4:**225
humoral
Mennonites, **1:**219
hunting/fishing restrictions
Wayapi, **7:**363
incantations
Tuareg, **9:**369
kneading
Yaqui, **8:**307
lamb's blood, **4:**225
laying on of hands
Cinta Larga, **7:**129
Jamaicans, **8:**139
Maká, **7:**218
Pomo, **1:**295
Tuareg, **9:**369
leaf beating
Wapisiana, **7:**356
leeches
Siberian Tatars, **6:**342
licensed rural visiting practictioners
Provencal, **4:**211
listening to blood flow
Tibetans, **6:**496
magic
Cape Coloureds, **9:**60
Kongo, **9:**168
Kpelle, **9:**174
Lango, **9:**182
Shahsevan, **9:**310
Songhay, **9:**320
Swedes, **4:**258
Tolowa, **1:**353
Tswana
Zande, **9:**364
Wolof, **9:**380
Zande, **9:**400
massage
Andamanese, **3:**11
Bau, **2:**24

Medical practices and treatments (cont'd)
  Chamacoco, **7:**110
  Chiriguano, **7:**122
  Chorote, **7:**126
  Dai, **6:**428
  Easter Island, **2:**55
  Futuna, **2:**67
  Hanunóo, **5:**91
  Hmong, **5:**95
  Hoti, **7:**176
  Huarayo, **7:**179
  Itza,' **8:**135
  Japanese, **5:**110
  Javanese, **5:**113
  Kapingamarangi, **2:**110
  Kiribati, **2:**123
  Kosrae, **2:**130
  Lao Isan, **5:**163
  Mailu, **2:**156
  Marshall Islands, **2:**194
  Nahua of the Huasteca, **8:**187
  Nambicuara, **7:**247
  Nivaclé, **7:**251
  North Alaskan Eskimos, **1:**261
  Palaung, **5:**203
  Pohnpei, **2:**269
  Pukapuka, **2:**273
  Quechan, **1:**302
  Rapa, **2:**276
  Rotuma, **2:**283
  Samoa, **2:**289
  Saraguro, **7:**295
  Shipibo, **7:**306
  Siona-Secoya, **7:**309
  Tabasarans, **6:**350
  Tasmanians, **2:**317
  Telefolmin, **2:**323
  Tepehuan of Durango, **8:**258
  Tewa Pueblos, **1:**349
  Tikopia, **2:**326
  Tokelau, **2:**333
  Tor, **2:**344
  Truk, **2:**353
  Tsakhurs, **6:**368
  Tuvalu, **2:**357
  Ukrainians, **6:**393
  Wape, **2:**372
  Wintun, **1:**383
  Woleai, **2:**384
  Yekuana, **7:**381
"medicalization" of everyday life
  Dutch, 94
medical team
  Cubans, **8:**90
medicine shrines
  Lobi-Dagarti peoples, **9:**185
midwives. See Midwives
minerals
  Qashqa'i, **9:**287
miracle cures
  Piemontese Sinti, **4:**200
moon water
  Meskhetians, **6:**261
moxibustion
  Han, **6:**448
  Japanese, **5:**110
  Khmer, **5:**138
mystical

  Swazi, **9:**332
native surgeons
  Suri, **9:**326
naturopathic
  Germans, **4:**124
noise making
  Karajá, **7:**191
painting sore part of body
  Marubo, **7:**223
patent remedies
  Guarijío, **8:**119
pilgrimages to holy sites
  Irish, **4:**153
pipe smoking
  Yurok, **1:**395
plants. See Herbal, plant, and root medicine
porridge
  Marubo, **7:**223
possession by "doctors"
  Swahili, **9:**329
poultices
  Calabrese, **4:**50
  Pemon, **7:**273
  Romanians, **4:**214
  Slovaks, **4:**245
  Tewa Pueblos, **1:**349
prayer
  Bulgarians, **4:**45
  Calabrese, **4:**50
  Cheyenne, **1:**66
  Delaware, **1:**86
  Flemish, **4:**109
  Micmac, **1:**235
  Toba, **7:**333
  Yurok, **1:**396
preventive
  Pokot, **9:**283
public health service
  Icelanders, **4:**147
  Seminole, **1:**314
pulse beat messages
  Tojolab'al, **8:**263
  Zoque, **8:**317
purification
  Rikbaktsa, **7:**288
  Salasaca, **7:**291
  Ticuna, **7:**330
  Yaqui, **8:**307
Quranic
  Bedouin, **9:**46
  Tuareg, **9:**369
rain medicine held by queen mother
  Swazi, **9:**332
rattle use
  Wayapi, **7:**363
  Yekuana, **7:**381
renaming
  Huichol, **8:**127
  Samal Moro, **5:**224
return of lost soul into body through
    wooden cylinder
  Menominee, **1:**222
roots/bark/leaves. See Herbal, plant, and
    root medicine
sacred bundles. See Sacred bundles
sacrifice
  Mixe, **8:**175
  Yuit, **1:**392

sauna
  Finns, **4:**104
scarification
  Sirionó, **7:**311
  Xikrin, **7:**369
séances
  Akawaio, **7:**33
  Chiriguano, **7:**122
  Hoti, **7:**176
  Karihona, **7:**193
  Tupari, **7:**340-341
  Yekuana, **7:**381
  Yuit, **1:**392
secret
  Mekeo, **2:**200
sexual restrictions
  Apalai, **7:**47
  Yukuna, **7:**390
shrine visits
  Jews, Arabic-speaking, **9:**136
  Lur, **9:**202
Siddha medicine
  Tamil, **3:**279
sleight-of-hand tricks
  Huarayo, **7:**179
  Mehinaku, **7:**239
song
  Ute, **1:**362
  Walapai, **1:**366
  Western Apache, **1:**373
sorcery and witchcraft
  Apiaká, **7:**50
  Pasiegos, **4:**191
  Portuguese, **4:**208
  Sherente, **7:**303
  Totonac, **8:**266
soul retrieval
  Araweté, **7:**57
  Lengua, **7:**211
  Mehinaku, **7:**239
  Mundurucu, **7:**245-246
  Nivaclé, **7:**251
  Wintun, **1:**383
spirit communication
  Khoi, **9:**160
  Pemon, **7:**273
spirit stones
  Wáiwai, **7:**348
spiritual
  Acholi, **9:**6
  Bamiléké, **9:**40
  Chinantec, **8:**55
  Ch'ol, **8:**66
  Chuj, **8:**74
  Kpelle, **9:**174
  Lunda, **9:**199
  Tzotzil of San Andrés Larraínzar, **8:**285
  Zarma, **9:**406
substance application
  Ache, **7:**7
  Amahuaca, **7:**36
  Nivaclé, **7:**251
sucking
  Angaité, **7:**44
  Asurini, **7:**62
  Chamacoco, **7:**110
  Chimane, **7:**113
  Chiquitano, **7:**118

Chiriguano, 7:122
Culina, 7:148
Desana, 7:154
Huarayo, 7:179
Karajá, 7:190-191
Karihona, 7:193
Lengua, 7:211
Macuna, 7:215
Maká, 7:218
Matsigenka, 7:232
Mundurucu, 7:245
Nambicuara, 7:247
Nivaclé, 7:251
Otavalo, 7:255
Panare, 7:267
Paraujano, 7:268
Piapoco, 7:274
Pomo, 1:295
Pume, 7:284
Quechan, 1:302
Sherente, 7:303
Shipibo, 7:306
Siona-Secoya, 7:309
Tanaina, 1:337
Tasmanians, 2:317
Terena, 7:327
Ticuna, 7:330
Toba, 7:333
Tolowas, 1:353
Tupari, 7:340
Ute, 1:362
Walapai, 1:366
Wape, 2:372
Western Shoshone, 1:375
Wintun, 1:383
Wiyot, 1:384, 385
Yagua, 7:374
Yawalapití, 7:380
Yekuana, 7:381
Yokuts, 1:389
Yukuna, 7:390
Yurok, 1:395
supernatural
Asmat, 2:21
Bai, 6:421
Balkars, 6:54
Chuvash, 6:85
Cook Islands, 2:42
Dolgan, 6:102
Easter Island, 2:55
Gayo, 5:90
Gebusi, 2:79
Guadalcanal, 2:91
Hmong, 5:95
Iatmul, 2:100
Javanese, 5:113
Kapauku, 2:107
Kapingamarangi, 2:110
Karachays, 6:162
Karelians, 6:172
Keraki, 2:114
Khanty, 6:192
Khevsur, 6:196
Kriashen Tatars, 6:212
Krymchaks, 6:215
Lahu, 5:154;6:463
Lakalai, 2:142
Mardudjara, 2:181

Melpa, 2:202
Minangkabau, 5:184
Nandi and other Kalenjin peoples, 9:234
Ngatatjara, 2:241
Nias, 5:197
Ogan-Besemah, 5:199
Old Believers, 6:294
Ossetes, 6:302
Palaung, 5:203
Palu'e, 5:209
Pintupi, 2:267
Qiang, 6:487
Rutuls, 6:321
Santa Cruz, 2:292
Siberian Estonians, 6:337
Tabasarans, 6:350
Tai Lue, 5:256
Tasmanians, 2:317
Torres Strait Islanders, 2:347
Tsakhurs, 6:368
Tujia, 6:499
Tuvalu, 2:357
Wa, 6:503
Yakut, 6:407
surgery
Huarayo, 7:178
Siwai, 2:304
Uighur, 6:385
sweatbath
Kiowa, 1:189
sweating
Montagnais-Naskapi, 1:246
"sweating out the evil"
Dalmatians, 4:87
talismans
Jews, Arabic-speaking, 9:136
tobacco
Fore, 2:65
tobacco juice
Barí, 7:85
Wayapi, 7:363
tobacco smoking
Mehinaku, 7:238
Ticuna, 7:330
Wáiwai, 7:348
Yawalapití, 7:380
toy cart to drive out plague
Bhil, 3:41
trance induction
Southern Paiute (and Chemehuevi),
   1:332
trancing
Khoi, 9:160
Tolowa, 1:353
trephination
Andis, 6:27
Avars, 6:46
Dargins, 6:98
unani medicine
Tamil, 3:279
urine analysis
Afro-Colombians, 7:18
Tibetans, 6:496
vegetable medicine
Nyakyusa and Ngonde, 9:254
vodun
Haitians, 8:122, 123
water cures

Germans, 4:124
water sprinkling/pouring
Desana, 7:154
Macuna, 7:215
weighing
Samal Moro, 5:224
whistling, 7:178
zar cult
Amhara, 9:20-21
Medicinal plants. _See_ Herbal, plant, and root
   medicine
Medicine bundles
Blackfoot, 1:42
Hidatsa, 1:147, 148
Kiowa, 1:188
Mandan, 1:214
Potawatomi, 1:297
Winnebago, 1:382
Medicine Dance
Ojibwa, 1:271
Medicine Hat (sacred object)
Cheyenne, 1:66
Medicine Lodge Society
Ojibwa, 1:271
Winnebago, 1:382
Medicine manufacture. _See_ Drugs,
   manufacture
Medicine men
Comanche, 1:75
Hare, 1:141, 142
Keres Pueblo Indians, 1:182
Kikuyu, 9:162
Kpelle, 9:173
Lunda, 9:199
Mbeere, 9:222
Menominee, 1:222
Northern Shoshone and Bannock, 1:267
Pawnee, 1:285
Teton, 1:346
Tewa Pueblos, 1:359
Zaramo, 9:402
Medicine Society
Tewa Pueblos, 1:349
Medicine women
Kpelle, 9:173
Meditation
Bengali Shakta, 3:35
Jain, 3:109
Japanese, 5:110
Mediums
Batak, 5:41
Bhil, 3:41
Bisaya, 5:43
Bonerate, 5:46
Chin, 3:64, 67
Chinese in Southeast Asia, 5:77
Hanunóo, 5:91
Hare, 1:142
Hill Pandaram, 3:100
Hungarians, 4:145
Kachin, 5:118
Kaluli, 2:103
Kiribati, 2:123
Lakher, 3:147, 148
Lao Isan, 5:162
Mae Enga, 2:151
Melanau, 5:180
Murut, 5:193

Mediums (cont'd)
  Ontong Java, 2:255
  Portuguese, 4:208
  Santa Cruz, 2:292
  Sora, 3:270
  Subanun, 5:245
  Telefolmin, 2:321, 323
  Temiar, 5:271, 272
  Tongareva, 2:341
  Ulithi, 2:360
  Vedda, 3:302
  Woleai, 2:384
  see also Sacred bundle; Séance
Megaliths
  Murut, 5:193
  Nias, 5:194
Melas (festivals)
  Baul, 3:26
Melkites
  Arab Americans, 1:24, 25
Melon growing
  Mohave, 1:240
  Potawatomi, 1:297
  Zuni, 1:397
Memorial feasts. See Feasting
  memorial
Memorial platforms
  Chin, 3:67
Memorial posts and stones. See Grave markers
Memorial services
  Badaga, 3:17
  Bavarians, 4:35
  Chin, 3:64
  Cretans, 4:71
  Kumeyaay, 1:195-196
  Parsi, 3:230
Men
  assertiveness
    Hidsata, 1:147
  chivalry rituals
    Dalmatians, 4:87
  domestic role proscriptions
    Andalusians, 4:11
    Castilians, 4:59
    see also Machismo
  dominance
    Abenaki, 1:5
    Ionians, 4:150
    Latinos, 1:205
  ear piercing
    Toda, 3:297
  emigration
    Azoreans, 4:27, 28
    Calabrese, 4:49
    Cape Verdeans, 4:55
    Ionians, 4:149
    Portuguese, 4:207
    see also Guest workers
  ideal
    Rom of Czechoslovakia, 4:219
  male heir importance
    Serbs, 4:231
  -only socialization
    Cyclades, 4:77
    Slovaks, 4:245
  saints
    Sidi, 3:260
  social centers

  Sindhi, 3:263
  status of
    Castilians, 4:59
    Chakma, 3:60
    Jatav, 3:114
    Magar, 3:158
    Nyinba, 3:210
    Pahari, 3:221
    Sinhalese, 3:266
    see also Patriarchal family structure;
      Primogeniture
  see also Gender roles; Gender-specific
    housing; Marriage; related subjects
Ménage. See Household
Mendicant. See Begging
Menluana. See Witch doctor
Mennonites
  Frisians, 4:112
  Germans, 6:138, 140
  Luxembourgeois, 4:163
  Mennonites, 1:216-220; 7:239-240
  Siberian Germans, 6:338, 339
Men's dormitories. See Dormitories
Men's houses
  Bororo, 7:87
  Gorotire, 7:162, 163
  Karajá, 7:190
  Kuikuru, 7:207
  Maxakali, 7:233
  Mehinaku, 7:236, 238
  Moré, 7:243
  Mundurucu, 7:244, 245
  Nivaclé, 7:248
  Paresí, 7:269
  Rikbaktsa, 7:287
  Suya, 7:315, 316
  Tapirapé, 7:321
  Tunebo, 7:337
  Waurá, 7:360
  Xikrin, 7:367, 368
  Yawalapití, 7:378, 379
  Yuracaré, 7:395
Men's societies. See under Associations, clubs,
    and societies
Menstruation
  Abelam, 2:5
  Abenaki, 1:5
  Ache, 7:7
  Achumawi, 1:10
  Ajië, 2:9
  Akawaio, 7:33
  Amuesha, 7:39
  Baiga, 3:19
  Brahman and Chhetri of Nepal, 3:53
  Bugle, 8:33
  Butonese, 5:67
  Chayahuita, 7:111
  Chimbu, 2:36
  Chinese in Southeast Asia, 5:77
  Chipewyan, 1:69
  Cinta Larga, 7:128
  Cree, 1:81
  Divehi, 3:78
  Eastern Shoshone, 1:104, 105
  Eipo, 2:56
  Emberá and Wounaan, 8:111
  Foi, 2:60
  Fore, 2:64, 63

  Fox, 1:129
  Garia, 2:75
  Gebusi, 2:78, 78
  Gogodala, 2:84
  Guahibo-Sikuani, 7:166
  Gururumba, 2:94
  Hare, 1:141
  Hill Pandaram, 3:100
  Huichol, 8:127
  Iatmul, 2:100
  Irula, 3:104
  Javanese, 5:112
  Jews of Iran, 9:141
  Jicarilla, 1:174
  Kagwahiv, 7:185
  Kapauku, 2:106, 106
  Karaites, 9:155
  Karihona, 7:193
  Karok, 1:177
  Ket, 6:184, 185
  Khanty, 6:190
  Khevsur, 6:193
  Kikapu, 8:144
  Kiwai, 2:127
  Klamath, 1:192
  Kond, 3:133
  Kurtatchi, 2:132
  Lakalai, 2:141
  Lesu, 2:146, 147
  Lithuanian Jews, 6:246
  Mae Enga, 2:150
  Magar, 3:158
  Maká, 7:217-218
  Malaita, 2:161, 163
  Mbeere, 9:222
  Mendi, 2:203
  Mohave, 1:241
  Nasioi, 2:234
  Ndebele, 9:237
  Nissan, 2:251
  Ojibwa, 1:270
  Páez, 7:257
  Paï-Tavytera, 7:260
  Paraujano, 7:268
  Parsi, 3:229
  Pauserna, 7:270
  Quechan, 1:301
  Rossel Island, 2:278
  Sambia, 2:284, 285
  San-speaking peoples, 9:303
  Santal, 3:254
  Sengseng, 2:296
  Sinhalese, 3:265
  Siona-Secoya, 7:308
  Slavey, 1:320
  Sumu, 8:239
  Suruí, 7:313
  Svans, 6:345
  Swazi, 9:331
  Tairora, 2:308, 310
  Tamil, 3:278, 278
  Tanaina, 1:337
  Tanna, 2:314
  Temiar, 5:270
  Ticuna, 7:330
  Tiwi, 2:328
  Usino, 2:361, 363
  Ute, 1:361

Vellala, 3:306
Wanano, 7:350
Warao, 7:358
Washoe, 1:370
Western Shoshone, 1:374
Winnebago, 1:380, 381
Wogeo, 2:381
Woleai, 2:383
Yangoru Boiken, 2:388, 390
Yekuana, 7:381
Yukuna, 7:388
Yuqui, 7:394
Yuracaré, 7:396
Zaramo, 9:402-403
Mental illness
    affective psychoses
        Hutterites, 1:155
    denial of
        Barbadians, 8:24
    as divorce ground
        Lakher, 3:146
    magico-religious cures
        Wolof, 9:380
    melancholia
        Highland Scots, 4:141, 142
    ritual specialists
        Pokot, 9:283
    sorcery as cause
        Swazi, 9:333
    spiritual healing
        Shona, 9:314
    supernatural cures
        Nandi and other Kalenjin peoples,
            9:234
    treatment
        Ewe and Fon, 9:88
Mercantile class
    Bania, 3:24-25
    Vaisyas, 3:222
    see also Shopkeeping; Traders
Mercenaries
    Don Cossacks, 6:104
    Gurung, 3:93, 94
    Pathan, 3:231
    Pima-Papgo, 1:290
Merchant marine. See Mariners
Merchants. See Mercantile class;
        Shopkeeping; Traders
Merit feasts
    Chin, 3:64, 66
    Kachin, 5:118
Mescal gathering
    Walapai, 1:364, 365
    Western Apache, 1:371
    Western Shoshone, 1:374
    Yavapai, 1:386
Mesquite pod gathering
    Western Shoshone, 1:374
Messenger service
    Mahar, 3:164
    peripatetics, 3:234
    Untouchable caste, 3:160
Messiah belief
    Ashkenazic Jews, 4:16
    Parsi, 3:230
    see also Ghost Dance; Millenarianism
Metabolic diseases
    Amish, 1:19

Metallurgy
    Tuscans, 4:269
Metalworking
    Acehnese, 5:3
    Achang, 6:418
    Armenians, 6:31
    Bonan, 6:422
    Bulgarians, 4:43
    Buriats, 6:68
    Croats, 4:75
    Dargins, 6:97
    Greeks, 4:134
    Gypsies, 6:146
    Ingilos, 6:150
    Kazakhs, 6:173, 177, 182
    Khasi, 3:126
    Kubachins, 6:217
    Kumyks, 6:221
    Lakher, 3:145
    Laks, 6:234
    Laz, 6:240
    Maguindanao, 5:169
    Maranao, 5:177
    Mongols, 6:474
    Naxi, 6:478
    Nepali, 3:202
    Newar, 3:206, 207
    Oriya, 3:216
    Osage, 1:277
    Ossetes, 6:299
    Pamir peoples, 6:305
    Rom, 1:304
    Romanians, 4:213
    Serbs, 4:230
    Shakers, 1:316
    Shors, 6:329, 330
    Sinhalese, 3:267
    Spanish Rom, 4:254, 255
    Talysh, 6:356
    Tamil, 3:277
    Tlingit, 1:351
    Tsakhurs, 6:366
    Turkmens, 6:370
    Ukrainian peasants, 6:386
    Ukrainians, 6:392
    Untouchable service caste, 3:159, 161
    Uzbeks, 6:397, 398
    Volga Tatars, 6:401
    Yakut, 6:405
    Zuni, 1:397
    see also Scrap trade; specific metals
Methodism
    Antigua and Barbuda, 8:10
    Assiniboin, 1:27
    Barbadians, 8:23
    Cape Coloureds, 9:60
    Chinese in Caribbean, 8:58
    Choiseul Island, 2:38, 39
    Cornish, 4:65
    Cubans, 8:90
    English, 4:97
    Grenadians, 8:116
    Japanese in Canada, 1:98
    Kittsians and Nevisians, 8:145
    Kurtatchi, 2:133
    Lakalai, 2:140
    Lau, 2:145
    Lesu, 2:146

Lumbee, 1:209
Mandak, 2:170, 171
Manx, 4:171
Montserratians, 8:181
Nahuat of the Sierra de Puebla, 8:193
Nasioi, 2:235
Northern Irish, 4:180
Polynesians, 1:292
Rossel Island, 2:278
Rotuma, 2:281, 283
Samoa, 2:287
Siwai, 2:302
Swazi, 9:332
Trobriand Islands, 2:348
Welsh, 4:279, 280
Mfundalai (rite of passage)
    African Americans, 1:12
Microcaste
    Sinhalese, 3:265, 266
    Tamil of Sri Lanka, 3:282
Mid-Autumn Festival
    Hakka, 6:439
    Hani, 6:451
    She, 6:491
Middlemen
    Ashkenazic Jews, 4:17
    Bulgarian Gypsies, 4:41
    Hidatsa, 1:146
    Kond use of, 3:132-133
    Kwakiutl, 1:198
    Mandan, 1:214
    Quechan, 1:301
    Rom, 1:304
    Vlach Gypsies of Hungary, 4:271
Midewiwin ceremony
    Ojibwa, 1:271
Midsummer's Eve (festival)
    Kashubians, 4:159
Midwives
    Acadian, 1:9
    Baggara, 9:31
    Balkars, 6:54
    Carpatho-Rusyns, 6:71
    Chatino, 8:52
    Ch'ol, 8:65, 66
    Danes, 4:90
    Itza,' 8:135
    Javanese, 5:113
    Jews of Iran, 9:141
    Khinalughs, 6:201
    Kiowa, 1:189
    Ladinos, 8:153
    Lenca, 8:156
    Madeirans, 4:166
    Malay, 5:176
    Maliseet, 1:212
    Mam, 8:160
    Mazahua, 8:166
    Nahua of the Huasteca, 8:187
    Nahuat of the Sierra de Puebla, 8:193
    Nandi and other Kalenjin peoples, 9:234
    Ndembu, 9:240
    Oneida, 1:275
    Otavalo, 7:255
    Otomí of the Valley of Mezquital, 8:206
    Ozarks, 1:282
    Pima Bajo, 8:214
    Pokot, 9:283

Midwives (cont'd)
    Qalandar, **3**:248
    Saraguro, **7**:295
    Selkup, **6**:327
    Selung/Moken, **5**:232
    Senoi, **5**:238
    Siona-Secoya, **7**:308
    Tats, **6**:360
    Tepehua, **8**:249
    Totonac, **8**:266
    Tsakhurs, **6**:368
    Tzotzil and Tzeltal of Pantelhó, **8**:278
    Tzotzil of Chamula, **8**:281
    Tzotzil of Zinacantan, **8**:293
    Tz'utujil, **8**:298
    Yemenis, **9**:390
    Zapotec, **8**:313
    Zoque, **8**:317
Migrant workers
    Calabrese, **4**:49
    Central Thai, **5**:70
    Chinantec, **8**:53
    Chinese in Southeast Asia, **5**:75
    Dusun, **5**:81
    Fore, **2**:62
    Futuna, **2**:66
    Goodenough Island, **2**:85
    Haitians, **1**:138
    Iban, **5**:97
    Irish Travellers, **4**:155
    Kédang, **5**:131, 132
    Kickapoo, **1**:183, 184
    Kikapu, **8**:144
    Korean, **5**:147
    Kwoma, **2**:134
    Lakalai, **2**:140
    Lamaholot, **5**:155
    Lao Isan, **5**:161
    Latinos, **1**:204
    Lobi-Dagarti peoples, **9**:184
    Lugbara, **9**:194
    Mimika, **2**:206
    Miyanmin, **2**:209
    Mountain Arapesh, **2**:216
    Mundugumor, **2**:218
    Ndebele, **9**:236
    Pentecost, **2**:261
    Pima Bajo, **8**:211
    Pima-Papago, **1**:288
    Rai, **3**:249
    Rominche, **4**:216
    Rotinese, **5**:212
    Russian peasants, **6**:311
    Santal, **3**:253
    Sardinians, **4**:226
    Sengseng, **2**:296
    Sicilians, **4**:236
    Siwai, **2**:302
    Svans, **6**:343
    Tabasarans, **6**:349
    Tangu, **2**:311
    Tanna, **2**:313
    Tauade, **2**:318
    Telefolmin, **2**:321
    Tojolab'al, **8**:261
    Tongareva, **2**:339
    Toraja, **5**:282
    Torres Strait Islanders, **2**:346
    Totonac, **8**:265
    Tswana, **9**:361
    Udis, **6**:377
    Wantoat, **2**:368
Migrant workers (as rite of passage)
    Dobu, **2**:50
    Goodenough Island, **2**:86
Migrant workers (seasonal)
    Bulgarian Gypsies, **4**:41
    Metis of Western Canada, **1**:228
    Santal, **3**:253
    see aslo Seminomads
    Slovensko Roma, **4**:250
    Tory Islanders, **4**:265
Migration
    Abor, **3**:3
    Aveyronnais, **4**:23-24
    Baluchi, **3**:22
    Basques, **1**:32
    Baweanese, **5**:42
    Blacks in Canada, **1**:43
    Black West Indians in the United Stats,
        1:45
    Bretons, **4**:37
    Bugis, **5**:50
    Bulgarian Gypsies, **4**:41
    Bunun, **5**:56
    Cajuns, **1**:48
    Canarians, **4**:51
    Cherokee, **1**:60
    Chiriguano, **7**:120
    Chocó, **7**:123
    Cochin Jews, **3**:71
    Cree, **1**:80
    Dalmatians, **4**:86
    Delaware, **1**:85
    East Asians of the United States, **1**:98-99
    Greeks, **4**:132
    Haitians, **1**:137
    Hindu, **3**:102
    Ionians, **4**:150
    Jat, **3**:110
    Kickapoo, **1**:182
    Koya, **3**:139
    Latinos, **1**:204
    Leonese, **4**:160
    Manus, **2**:175
    Mennonites, **1**:217
    Meskhetians, **6**:260
    Mizo, **3**:177
    Mohawk, **1**:242
    Mormons, **1**:247
    Muslim, **3**:184-185
    Nagas, **3**:187
    Nepali, **3**:201-202
    Occitans, **4**:184
    Ojibwa, **1**:268-269
    Oneida, **1**:275-276
    Ottawa, **1**:279
    Pahari, **3**:219
    Palu'e, **5**:206, 207
    Pasiegos, **4**:189, 190
    peripatetics, **4**:197
    Pintupi, **2**:265
    Punjabi, **3**:237, 238
    Purum, **3**:242
    Rotuma, **2**:282
    Russian peasants, **6**:310
    Russians, **6**:314, 316
    Santal, **3**:252
    Santee, **1**:307
    Sauk, **1**:308
    Sea Islanders, **1**:308, 309
    Seminole, **1**:311, 312
    Seminole of Oklahoma, **1**:314
    Senaca, **1**:315
    Sephardic Jews, **4**:229
    Serbs, **4**:230
    Swiss, Italian, **4**:260
    Tamil of Sri Lanka, **3**:280
    Thakali, **3**:292
    Tokelau, **2**:330
    Welsh, **4**:279
    Xikrin, **7**:367-368
    see also Diaspora; Refugees; Seminomads;
        Urban areas, migrants
Militant societies. *See* Aggressiveness; Warfare
Military service
    compulsory
        German Swiss, **4**:126
        Greeks, **4**:133
        Khinalughs, **6**:201
        Pamir peoples, **6**:305
        Peloponnesians, **4**:194
        Talysh, **6**:356
        Yuan, **5**:294
    importance in socialization
        German Swiss, **4**:126
    land grants in return
        Magar, **3**:154, 156
        Yi, **6**:506
    refusal to serve
        Yezidis, **6**:408
    skills and tradition
        Coorg, **3**:73-74
        Don Cossacks, **6**:104
        Gurkha, **3**:93
        Gurung, **3**:93, 94
        Jat, **3**:111
        Limbu, **3**:150
        Pathan, **3**:231
        Piemontese, **4**:199
    Warrior's Dance as protection from
        Menominee, **1**:222
    see also Warfare; Warrior
Milk
    high fat content
        Walloons, **4**:276
    retail sales
        Pasiegos, **4**:190
    wholesale sales
        Sardinians, **4**:226
Milk brotherhood
    Abkhazians, **6**:7
    Circassians, **6**:90
    Georgians, **6**:133
    Karachays, **6**:161
    Khevsur, **6**:195
    Laz, **6**:240
    Mingrelians, **6**:263
    Nogays, **6**:288
Millenarianism
    Karen, **5**:129
    Païsola-Tavytera, **7**:260
    Pomo, **1**:295

Shakers, **1:**316
see also Cargo cults; Ghost Dance
Millet
  alcoholic beverages
    Lunda, **9:**196
  beer
    Fipa, **9:**98
    Luba of Shaba, **9:**191
    Shona, **9:**313, 314
  cultivation by women
    Kikuyu, **9:**161
    Nuer, **9:**249
  religious/symbolic
    Lango, **9:**178
  stalks for houses
    Wolof, **9:**378
Millet growing
  Abkhazians, **6:**6, 7
  Alur, **9:**13
  Anuak, **9:**21
  Bagirmi, **9:**33
  Bemba, **9:**46
  Bilaan, **5:**42
  Circassians, **6:**88
  Daur, **6:**429
  Dinka, **9:**70
  Divehi, **3:**76
  Dogon, **9:**71
  Dong, **6:**431
  Fali, **9:**94
  Gelao, **6:**435
  Gusii, **9:**108
  Han, **6:**440
  Hausa, **9:**112
  Hmong, **5:**93
  Iraqw, **9:**125
  Irula, **3:**105
  Iteso, **9:**128
  Jingpo, **6:**456
  Kalasha, **3:**116
  Kanbi, **3:**118
  Kanuri, **9:**151
  Kazakhs, **6:**177
  Koya, **3:**140
  Lepcha, **3:**148, 149
  Lugbara, **9:**194
  Magar, **3:**160
  Manchu, **6:**467
  Moinba, **6:**473
  Mossi, **9:**228
  Nagas, **3:**188
  Nepali, **3:**202
  Nogays, **6:**287
  Nubians, **9:**246
  Ossetes, **6:**299
  Pahari, **3:**220
  Pamir peoples, **6:**304
  Pende, **9:**272
  Pokot, **9:**282
  Rotinese, **5:**213
  Rukuba, **9:**289
  Sakalava, **9:**294
  San-speaking peoples, **9:**302
  Santal, **3:**253
  Sara, **9:**305
  Sedang, **5:**230
  Shilluk, **9:**311
  Sunwar, **3:**271

Tabasarans, **6:**348
Tagbanuwa, **5:**251
Taiwan aboriginal peoples, **5:**257
Tamil, **3:**276
Thakur, **3:**293
T'in, **5:**278
Tonga, **9:**353
Ukrainian peasants, **6:**386
Vedda, **3:**301
Volga Tatars, **6:**401
Wolof, **9:**378
Zande, **9:**398
Zarma, **9:**404
Milpa plots. *See under* Agriculture
Mimes
  peripatetics, **3:**235
Mimía (ceremony)
  Kiwai, **2:**127
Mineral development
  Akan, **9:**11
  Cornish, **4:**64, 65
  Sikkimese, **3:**262
Mineral rights
  Osage, **1:**277
  Spokane, **1:**333
Mining
  Afro-Colombians, **7:**16
  Akawaio, **7:**31
  Altaians, **6:**21
  Apalai, **7:**45
  Barama River Carib, **7:**80-81
  Bashkirs, **6:**55
  Carpatho-Rusyn-Americans, **1:**108
  Chukchee, **6:**77
  Cypriots, **4:**80
  Dominicans, **8:**101
  East Asians of the United States, **1:**100
  English, **4:**96
  Finnish-Americans, **1:**110
  Friuli, **4:**113
  Galicians, **4:**119
  Georgians, **6:**132
  Greeks, **6:**143
  Hakka, **6:**437
  Hani, **6:**450
  Jamaicans, **8:**137, 138
  Kalingas, **5:**121
  Karelians, **6:**170
  Kazakhs, **6:**173
  Kédang, **5:**131
  Koreans, **6:**206
  Kyrgyz, **6:**229
  Ladin, **4:**160
  Lawa, **5:**163
  Lowland Scots, **4:**163
  Nauru, **2:**236
  Navajo, **1:**251
  Ningerum, **2:**245
  Ozarks, **1:**281
  Piaroa, **7:**276
  Pima Bajo, **8:**211
  Pueblo Indians, **1:**298
  Russian peasants, **6:**311
  Sardinians, **4:**226
  She, **6:**489
  Shors, **6:**329
  Siberiaki, **6:**333
  Silesians, **4:**238

Slav Macedonians, **4:**240
Tiroleans, **4:**263
Tujia, **6:**498
Tuvans, **6:**373
Uzbeks, **6:**396
Vietnamese, **5:**285
Vlachs, **4:**274
Wayapi, **7:**361
Welsh, **4:**279
Western Apache, **1:**372
Minstrels. *See* Bards
Miracle Church
  Western Apache, **1:**373
Miracles, belief in
  Andalusians, **4:**12
  Piemontese Sinti, **4:**201
Mirror embroidery
  Sindhi, **3:**261
Miscegenation. *See* Intermarriage;
    Intermarriage proscriptions; Mixed-
    race ancestry
Missions
  Gogodala, **2:**83
  Mailu, **2:**154
  Marshall Islands, **2:**192
  Pentecost, **2:**261
  Pohnpei, **2:**270
  Pukapuka, **2:**272
  Rapa, **2:**275
  Samoa, **2:**287
  Torres Strait Islanders, **2:**345, 347
  Tuvalu, **2:**355, 357
Mitakshara system of inheritance. *See*
    Inheritance, equally divided among
    sons only
Mixed-marriage proscriptions. *See*
    Intermarriage proscriptions
Mixed-race ancestry
  American Isolates, **1:**17-18
  Anglo Indian, **3:**12
  Black Creoles of Louisiana, **1:**36-40
  Black West Indians in the United States,
    1:44-46
  Cape Verdeans, **4:**53, 55, 56
  Latinos, **1:**205
  Mauritian, **3:**171, 172
  Metis of Western Canada, **1:**226-229
  Northern Metis, **1:**261-262
  see also Intermarriage
Mobility
  Abelam, **2:**3
  Dani, **2:**43
  Gebusi, **2:**77
  Greeks, **4:**132
  Makassar, **5:**172
  Mardudjara, **2:**179
  Mimika, **2:**208
  Ngatatjara, **2:**239
  see also Migration; Nomads
Mobility, social. *See* Class mobility
Moccasins. *See under* Footwear
Mocking. *See under* Social control measures
Modesty (as social value)
  Winnebago, **1:**382
Moguru (ceremony)
  Kiwai, **2:**126
Moieties
  Abelam, **2:**5

Moieties (cont'd)
Ambae, **2:**11
Asmat, **2:**20
Boazi, **2:**29, 30
Bororo, **7:**87
Chambri, **2:**32
Chickasaw, **1:**66
Choctaw, **1:**72
Craho, **7:**137
Creek, **1:**83
Dani, **2:**44
Dieri, **2:**49
Fox, **1:**129
Gogodala, **2:**83, 84
Goodenough Island, **2:**86, 87
Haida, **1:**136
Iatmul, **2:**98, 99
Kagwahiv, **7:**185
Kaingáng, **7:**186
Kamilaroi, **2:**104
Kapauku, **2:**106
Kariera, **2:**111
Kashinawa, **7:**195
Keraki, **2:**113
Khanty, **6:**189
Kiwai, **2:**125
Lak, **2:**138, 139
Lesu, **2:**146
Mandak, **2:**171
Mandan, **1:**214
Manihiki, **2:**172
Mansi, **6:**253
Marind-anim, **2:**183, 184
Mejbrat, **2:**196
Mekeo, **2:**199
Menominee, **1:**221
Miami, **1:**231
Miwok, **1:**240
Modang, **5:**185, 186
Mountain Arapesh, **2:**217
Mundurucu, **7:**245
Murngin, **2:**225
Namau, **2:**231
Niue, **2:**251
Osage, **1:**278
Pintupi, **2:**265
Pukapuka, **2:**271
Rikbaktsa, **7:**287
Rotinese, **5:**214
Santa Cruz, **2:**291
Shavante, **7:**301
Sherente, **7:**302
Sio, **2:**300
Suruí, **7:**313
Taiwan aboriginal peoples, **5:**257
Tanaina, **1:**336
Tanana, **1:**339
Tanna, **2:**314
Taos, **1:**342
Telefolmin, **2:**322, 323
Tewa Pueblos, **1:**348, 349
Ticuna, **7:**329
Tlingit, **1:**351, 352
Tolai, **2:**334
Warlpiri, **2:**374
Winnebago, **1:**381
Wogeo, **2:**381
Yip Yoront, **2:**395

Yokuts, **1:**388
see also Clan
Moksha (salvation)
Brahman and Chhetri of Nepal, **3:**53
Molenie Dom (community hall)
Doukhobors, **1:**90
Molenie (prayer)
Doukhobors, **1:**93
Molokany
Siberiaki, **6:**334
Moluccan Protestant Church
Ambonese, **5:**19
Molud (festival)
Gayo, **5:**89
Monarchy
ceremonial
Afro-Bolivians, **7:**10
constitutional
Danes, **4:**90
Dutch, **4:**93
English, **4:**97
Flemish, **4:**108
Luxembourgeois, **4:**163
Norwegians, **4:**182
Swedes, **4:**258
Walloons, **4:**277
parliamentary
Galicians, **4:**120
Monasticism
Basques, **4:**32
Buddhism, **5:**48
Burgundians, **4:**47
Burmese, **5:**65
Catalans, **4:**63
Copts, **9:**69
Dai, **6:**426
Lao Isan, **5:**162
Lingayat, **3:**151
Mahar, **3:**165
Mount Athos, **4:**174-177
Occitans, **4:**185
Palaung, **5:**203
Sadhu, **3:**251
Sherpa, **3:**259
Sinhalese, **3:**267
see also Ashrams
Money and wealth
beads
Hanunóo, **5:**91
Kenyah-Kayan-Kajang, **5:**134
Murut, **5:**193
cloth
Mejbrat, **2:**196
Trobriand Islands, **2:**349
competitive displays
Nguna, **2:**242
display considered immoral
Highland Scots, **4:**141
drums
Alorese, **5:**14, 15
feather
Santa Cruz, **2:**291
Tauade, **2:**318
fur
Selkup, **6:**326
Yakut, **6:**405
gold
Nias, **5:**196

gongs
Kenyah-Kayan-Kajang, **5:**134
Murut, **5:**193
inheritance of. *See* Inheritance
jars
Kenyah-Kayan-Kajang, **5:**134
Murut, **5:**193
jewelry
Lisu, **5:**166
land
Ifugao, **5:**100
livestock
Ifugao, **5:**100
Karen, **5:**128
management of
Suruí, **7:**312
obsession with amassing
Yurok, **1:**394
pigs
Alorese, **5:**14, 15
Melpa, **2:**201
Mendi, **2:**203
Murut, **5:**193
Nias, **5:**196
Nissan, **2:**249
political power based on. *See* Leadership
qualities, wealth
political power not linked with
Provencal, **4:**211
redistribution of
Parsi, **3:**228
rice
Karen, **5:**128
"richest people per capita in world"
Osage, **1:**277
shell
Abelam, **2:**4
Ajië, **2:**7
Choiseul Island, **2:**38
Divehi, **3:**76
Dobu, **2:**50
Garia, **2:**74
Guadalcanal, **2:**89, 90
Iatmul, **2:**99
Kapauku, **2:**105
Karok, **1:**176
Kosrae, **2:**128
Kumeyaay, **1:**194
Kurtatchi, **2:**131-132
Kwoma, **2:**136
Lak, **2:**139
Lesu, **2:**146
Malaita, **2:**161
Mandak, **2:**170
Manus, **2:**175
Melpa, **2:**201
Motu, **2:**214
Mundugumor, **2:**218
Muyu, **2:**228
Naagas, **3:**188
Nasioi, **2:**234
Ningerum, **2:**246
Nissan, **2:**249
Orokolo, **2:**259
Piapoco, **7:**274
Pomo, **1:**294
Rossel Island, **2:**278, 279
Saliva, **7:**292

San Cristobal, 2:289
Selepet, 2:294
Siwai, 2:302, 304
Tauade, 2:318
Tolai, 2:334
Trobriand Islands, 2:349
Wape, 2:371
Yangoru Boiken, 2:388, 389
Yurok, 1:394
slaves
Ifugao, 5:100
status linked with. _See_ Status, basis of,
wealth; Possessions
status not linked with
Northern Paiute, 1:264
stone
Sengseng, 2:296
Yap, 2:392, 394
teeth
Guadalcanal, 2:89
Kurtatchi, 2:131
Malaita, 2:161
Manus, 2:175
Ningerum, 2:246
wampum
Abenaki, 1:5
Money economy
Kwakiul, 1:198
Madeirans, 4:165
Mizo, 3:177-178
Pacific Eskimo, 1:283
Pasiegos, 4:190
Peloponnesians, 4:193
Sinhalese, 3:265
Tamil, 3:277
Tamil of Sri Lanka, 3:281
West Greenland Inuit, 1:377
Zuni, 1:397
Moneylending. _See_ Financial services
Monkey trainers
Gypsies and caravan dwellers in the
Netherlands, 4:137
peripatetics, 1:287
Qalandar, 3:245, 246, 247
Monogamy
Anambé, 7:42
Andamanese, 3:10
Apiaká, 7:49
Austrians, 4:20
Aymara, 7:67
Ayoreo, 7:70
Bakairi, 7:74
Barí, 7:84
Basques, 4:31
Bhuiya, 3:43
Burgundians, 4:47
Canela, 7:96
Canelos Quichua, 7:100
Catalans, 4:63
Chipaya, 7:116
Chiriguano, 7:121
Craho, 7:137
Cretans, 4:70
Croats, 4:73
Culina, 7:147
Cuna, 7:150
Danes, 4:89
Desana, 7:153

Emberá, 7:156
Friuli, 4:113
Galicians, 4:120
German Swiss, 4:126
Gorotire, 7:162
Greeks, 4:132
Hoti, 7:175
Kadiwéu, 7:183
Karajá, 7:189
Krikati/Pukobye, 7:205
Kuikuru, 7:208
Maká, 7:216
Makushi, 7:219
Maliseet, 1:211
Manx, 4:170
Marubo, 7:222
Mennonites, 4:218
Miami, 1:231
Micronesians, 1:237
Mocoví, 7:241
Moré, 7:243
Nagas, 3:189
Nambicuara, 7:247
Navajo, 1:252
Nepali, 3:203
Nivaclé, 7:249
North Alaskan Eskimos, 1:260
Northern Shoshone and Bannock,
1:267
Occitans, 4:185
Ojibwa, 1:270
Oriya, 3:217
Palikur, 7:262
Parsi, 3:228
Pathan, 3:232
Rikbaktsa, 7:287
Saami, 4:221
Saraguro, 7:294
Sardinians, 4:226
Siona-Secoya, 7:308
Sirionó, 7:310
Slovaks, 4:244
Sorbs, 4:253
Syrian Christian of Kerala, 3:273
Tanimuka, 7:319
Taos, 1:342
Tapirapé, 7:321
Telugu, 3:286
Terena, 7:326
Tewa Pueblos, 1:348
Ticuna, 7:329
Toba, 7:332
Tory Islanders, 4:265
Tunebo, 7:338
Vedda, 3:302
Wáiwai, 7:347
Walloons, 4:277
Waorani, 7:352
Washoe, 1:369
West Greenland Inuit, 1:377
Wiyot, 1:384
Yagua, 7:372
Yukuna, 7:387
Yuqui, 7:393
Monogamy, serial
Poles, 4:203
Monophysite Christianity
Amhara, 9:20

Monotheism
Bene Israel, 3:28
Bontok, 5:46
Endenese, 5:86
Jews, 1:171
Kamilaroi, 2:104
Lahu, 5:153
Lakalai, 2:142
Lakher, 3:147
Lingayat, 3:153
Manggarai, 5:176
Muong, 5:192
Muslim, 3:185, 186
Palu'e, 5:208
Parsi, 3:229
Sikh, 3:261
Wantoat, 2:369
Moon deity
Comanche, 1:75
Inughuit, 1:161
Mandan, 1:215
West Greenland Inuit, 1:378
Winnebago, 1:381
Moon Mother (deity)
Zuni, 1:399
Moon worship
Khoi, 9:160
Moose hunting
Cree, 1:80
Dogrib, 1:88
Maliseet, 1:211
Micmac, 1:233
Montagnais, 1:244
Ojibwa, 1:269
Tanaina, 1:335
Tanana, 1:338
Moots
Mardudjara, 2:181
Melpa, 2:202
Murngin, 2:226
Tairora, 2:309
Tolai, 2:335
see also Conflict resolution, moots
Moravians
Antigua and Barbuda, 8:10
Central Yup'ik Eskimo converts, 1:58
Creoles of Nicaragua, 8:86
Labrador Inuit, 1:201, 202
Miskito, 8:172
Nyakyusa and Ngonde, 9:254
Saramaka, 7:298
Sumu, 8:239
Morena (goddess of death)
Slovaks, 4:245
Mormons
Belau, 2:27
Catawba, 1:54
Danish-Americans, 1:109
Flemish, 4:108
Galicians, 4:120
Mormons, 1:246-2249
Northern Shoshone and Bannock,
1:267
Otavalo, 7:255
Polynesians, 1:292
Southern Paiute (and Chemehuevi), 1:332,
333
Western Apache, 1:373

Morning Star (spirit power)
  Pawnee, 1:285
  Winnebago, 1:382
Mortality rates. See Death rate; Infant and
    child mortality rates
Mortuary pole
  Haida, 1:136
Mortuary practices
  abandonment of deceased's house
    Akawaio, 7:33
    Apalai, 7:47
    Apiaká, 7:49, 51
    Asurini, 7:62
    Baniwa-Curripaco-Wakuenai, 7:78
    Barama River Carib, 7:82
    Bugle, 8:33
    Chamacoco, 7:110
    Colorado, 7:131
    Lengua, 7:211
    Matsigenka, 7:232-233
    Ngawbe, 8:196, 198
    Pemon, 7:272
    Siona-Secoya, 7:309
    Slovensko Roma, 4:251
    Suruí, 7:313
    Trio, 7:337
    Tunebo, 7:339
    Wayapi, 7:362
    Yagua, 7:373
    Yukuna, 7:390
    Yuracaré, 7:395
  abandonment of deceased's land
    Quechan, 1:301
  abandonment of deceased's possessions
    Irish Travellers, 4:156
  alcohol drinking
    Araucanians, 7:55
  ancestral shrine creation
    Lobi-Dagarti peoples, 9:185
  autopsy
    Araucanians, 7:55
    Gusii, 9:111
  avoidance of doing what deceased
      particularly loved
    Slovensko Roma, 4:251
  barren people left for scavengers
    Nandi and other Kalenjin peoples,
      9:234
  based on fears about ghost of deceased
    Rominche, 4:217
  belief that body lost before burial becomes
      troubled spirit
    Sakalava, 9:299
  bodies of criminals and disabled left in
      taboo areas
    Sakalava, 9:299
  body consumed by hyenas
    Nandi and other Kalenjin peoples, 9:234
  body covered with prayer rug
    Kurds, 9:177
  body dressed in fine clothes and wrapped in
      birchbark
    Ojibwa, 1:271
  body dressed in usual attire with personal
      accessories and seated in front yard
    Albanians, 4:8
  body dried
    Gnau, 2:82

body flexed with knees under chin
  Kaingáng, 7:186
  Kuikuru, 7:209
  Lozi, 9:190
body handled only by women
  Finns, 4:104
  Iatmul, 2:100
body left in wild
  Chipewyan, 1:69
  Kalmyks, 6:157
  Mongols, 6:476
body painted
  Ojibwa, 1:271
  Suya, 7:317
body painted and ornamented
  Suya, 7:317
body painted and wrapped in bison robe
  Pawnee, 1:286
body painted with soot and dentalium shell
    inserted through nose
  Yurok, 1:396
body placed on metal stretcher and grave
    cemented
  Zoroastrians, 9:410
body placed on platform
  Hare, 1:142
  Hidsata, 1:148
  Kewa, 2:117
  Kiwai, 2:127
  Mandan, 1:215
  Maring, 2:188
  Menominee, 1:222
  Miami, 1:232
  Miyanmin, 2:212
  Montagnais-Naskapi, 1:246
  Muyu, 2:230
  Orok, 6:297
  Sambia, 2:286
  Sarsi, 1:308
  Selung/Moken, 5:232
  Telefolmin, 2:323
  Temiar, 5:273
  Toba, 7:334
  Tor, 2:344
  Torres Strait Islanders, 2:348
  Warlpiri, 2:374
  Yankton, 1:386
body placed in rock crevices
  Northern Shoshone and Bannock, 1:268
body placed in tree
  Abkhazians, 6:9
  Hidatsa, 1:148
  Kwakiutl, 1:200
  Miami, 1:232
  Moinba, 6:473
  Saami, 4:223
  Senoi, 5:239
  Shors, 6:331
  Slavey, 1:320
  Tu, 6:497
  Yangoru Boiken, 2:390
body removed through hole in house
  Inughuit, 1:161
  Kikapu, 8:145
  Lozi, 9:190
body removed through hole in west side of
    wigwam
  Ojibwa, 1:271

body returned for burial on family home-
    land
  Micronesians, 1:239
body in sitting position in funerary well
  Fali, 9:97
body in sitting position in kashim
  Ingalik, 1:159
body smoked
  Kalingas, 5:123
  Malay, 5:176
  Wape, 2:372
body viewed at home for two days
  French Canadians, 1:133
body viewed by relatives
  Pame, 8:207
body washed
  Dungans, 6:111
  Finns, 4:104
  Goodenough Island, 2:88
  Karen, 5:129
  Kazakhs, 6:181
  Ket, 6:185
  Khevsur, 6:197
  Mailu, 2:157
  Palaung, 5:203
  Samal, 5:221
  Sasak, 5:227
  Talysh, 6:357
  Tausug, 5:264
  Tongareva, 2:341
  Udis, 6:378
  Uighur, 6:385
  Yao of Thailand, 5:293
  Yezidis, 6:411
body wrapped in skins
  Miami, 1:232
body wrapped in white shroud
  Frisians, 4:112
bone retrieval
  Asmat, 2:21
  Cocama, 7:130
  Craho, 7:138
  Cyclades, 4:78
  Goodenough Island, 2:88
  Greeks, 4:134
  Guahibo-Sikuani, 7:166
  Guajiro, 7:168, 169, 170
  Hanunóo, 5:91
  Kaluli, 2:104
  Karajá, 7:190
  Kiribati, 2:123
  Kiwai, 2:127
  Kwoma, 2:136
  Mafulu, 2:153
  Mailu, 2:157
  Maori, 2:178
  Miyanmin, 2:212
  Mojo, 7:242
  Mountain Arapesh, 2:218
  Palikur, 7:264
  Peloponnesians, 4:194
  Saliva, 7:292
  Sherente, 7:303
  Sirionó, 7:311
  Xikrin, 7:369
  Yekuana, 7:381
  Yuqui, 7:395
  see also subhead secondary burial below

bone retrieval and burning
  Pomo, 1:296
bones collected after cremation and fed
    ritually
  Santal, 3:255
broken object placed on grave
  Lozi, 9:190
burial above ground in elaborate grave
  Dalmatians, 4:87
burial above ground in sod-block tomb
  Chipaya, 7:117
burial after all-night wake
  Kickapoo, 1:186
burial at distance from village
  Nootka, 1:258
burial at sea
  Koryaks and Kerek, 6:210
  Nissan, 2:251
  Truk, 2:353
burial before first sunset
  Nubians, 9:248
burial below ground
  Abenaki, 1:6
  African Americans, 1:13
  Albanians, 4:8
  Aleut, 1:16
  Anambé, 7:43
  Bulgarians, 4:45
  Castilians, 4:61
  Chin, 3:67
  Cree, 1:82
  Divehi, 3:78
  Emerillon, 7:159
  Fox, 1:130
  Kanjar, 3:121
  Karajá, 7:188, 189
  Kiowa, 1:189
  Mizo, 3:179
  Mundurucu, 7:246
  Nagas, 3:191
  Qalandar, 3:248
  Saramaka, 7:298
  Shetlanders, 4:234
  Slovaks, 4:246
  Tamil, 3:279
  Tolowa, 1:353
  Tunebo, 7:339
  Winnebago, 1:382
  Xikrin, 7:369
  Yankton, 1:386
  Yukuts, 1:389
burial below ground in plank-lined grave
  Wiyot, 1:385
burial beneath logs on ground
  Menominee, 1:222
burial in canoe
  Warao, 7:359
  Yekuana, 7:381
burial in cattle kraals (men)
  Tswana, 9:364
burial in cave
  Aleut, 1:16
  Gros Ventre, 1:134
  Pima-Papago, 1:290
  Toradja, 5:281
  Western Shoshone, 1:375
burial of chicken head with body
  Tzotzil of Zinacantan, 8:294

burial close to house
  Tonga, 9:355
burial with coin
  Moldovans, 6:269
  Wa, 6:504
burial dressed in traditional clothing
  Altaians, 6:23
burial in extended position
  Ute, 1:363
burial facing east
  Akawaio, 7:33
  Canelos Quichua, 7:102
  Fox, 1:130
  Iroquois, 1:167
  Krikati/Pukobye, 7:206
  Nambicuara, 7:247
  Palikur, 7:264
  Pima-Papago, 7:264
  Waimiri-Atroari, 7:344
  Yukuna, 7:390
burial facing east (men)
  Lozi, 9:190
burial facing Mecca
  Berbers of Morocco, 9:52
  Kurds, 9:177
  Mappila, 3:167
  Nubians, 9:248
  Qashqa'i, 9:287
burial facing north
  Irula, 3:108-109
burial facing sun
  Lakandon, 8:154
burial facing west
  Montagnais-Naskapi, 1:246
  Pauserna, 7:270
  Terena, 7:327
  Toba, 7:334
burial facing west (women)
  Lozi, 9:190
burial facing west or northwest
  Yokuts, 1:389
burial of father by eldest son/mother by
    youngest son
  Kipsigis, 9:165
burial with feet facing Jerusalem
  Jews of Kurdistan, 9:146
burial with food
  Huarayo, 7:179
  Jivaro, 7:183
burial in front of deceased's house
  Yawalapití, 7:380
burial with gifts
  Temiar, 5:273
burial in graves lined with bark
  Delaware, 1:86
burial of headman at entrance to cattle
    enclosure
  Swazi, 9:333
burial in hollow tree
  Wolof, 9:380
burial in household fields (women)
  Mossi, 9:231
burial in hunting trails
  Araweté, 7:57
burial in hut
  Yukpa, 7:385
burial immediately
  Berbers of Morocco, 9:52

  Javanese, 5:113
  Jicarilla, 1:174
  Kurds, 9:177
  Mountain Jews, 6:274
  Rutuls, 6:321
  Tabasarans, 6:351
  Tangu, 2:312
  Tsakhurs, 6:368
  Wolof, 9:380
  Yörük, 9:396
burial islands
  Bajau, 5:33
burial in isolated place
  Delaware, 1:86
burial in Jerusalem preferred
  Palestinians, 9:266
burial in local graveyard
  Italian Mexicans, 8:132
burial in log
  Jivaro, 7:183
burial with money and valuables
  Wiyot, 1:385
burial with money, new clothes, and travel
    necessities
  Rom, 1:306
burial in natal village
  Kongo, 9:168
burial near deceased's house
  Temne, 9:345
burial only if sucessful
  Turkana, 9:373
burial only for infants and elders
  Nandi and other Kalenjin peoples, 9:234
burial in own compound
  Luyia, 9:206
burial with personal possessions
  Abor, 3:5
  Albanians, 4:8
  Apalai, 7:46
  Awá Kwaiker, 7:65
  Aymara, 7:68
  Baniwa-Curripaco-Wakuenai, 7:78
  Boazi, 2:30
  Bugle, 8:33
  Chácobo, 7:106
  Chinantec, 8:55
  Chiquitano, 7:118
  Copper Eskimo, 1:78, 79
  Cora, 8:77
  Cubeo, 7:142
  Delaware, 1:86
  Emerillon, 7:159
  Evenki (Northern Tungus), 6:122
  Gros Ventre, 1:134
  Ingalik, 1:157
  Inughuit, 1:161
  Jicarilla, 1:174
  Kalapuya, 1:175
  Karajá, 7:189
  Kashinawa, 7:196
  Ka'wiari, 7:200
  Ket, 6:185
  Khevsur, 6:197
  Kuikuru, 7:208
  Lozi, 9:190
  Lunda, 9:197
  Maliseet, 1:213
  Mansi, 6:255

Mortuary practices (cont'd)
    Mardudjara, **2:**181
    Menominee, **1:**222
    Micmac, **1:**234
    Montagnais-Naskapi, **1:**246
    Nagas, **3:**191
    Nayaga, **3:**195
    Ngawbe, **8:**196, 198
    Nicobarese, **3:**209, 210
    North Alaskan Eskimos, **1:**260, 261
    Northern Paiute, **1:**265
    Ojibwa, **1:**271
    Otavalo, **7:**255
    Paï-Tavytera, **7:**260
    Pame, **8:**207
    Panare, **7:**266
    Paresí, **7:**269
    Piaroa, **7:**277
    Pima-Papago, **1:**290
    Q'eqchi,' **8:**227
    Rominche, **4:**217
    Saramaka, **7:**298
    Sarsi, **1:**308
    Selkup, **6:**327
    Selung/Moken, **5:**232
    Seri, **8:**234
    Siona-Secoya, **7:**308
    Slavey, **1:**320
    Suruí, **7:**313
    Suya, **7:**316
    Tacana, **7:**318
    Tanaina, **1:**336
    Tangu, **2:**312
    Tapirapé, **7:**321
    Temiar, **5:**270, 273
    Terena, **7:**326
    T'in, **5:**279
    Tofalar, **6:**363
    Trio, **7:**336
    Triqui, **8:**272
    Wapisiana, **7:**356
    Wayapi, **7:**362, 364
    Western Apache, **1:**372
    West Greenland Inuit, **1:**377
    Yawalapití, **7:**380
    Yukpa, **7:**385
    Zhuang, **6:**512
  burial with pictures of afterlife
    Yukateko, **8:**310
  burial practice differs for men and women
    Gusii, **9:**110-111
  burial promptly without ceremony
    Navajo, **1:**253
  burial in remote place
    Kiowa, **1:**189
    Washoe, **1:**370
  burial on right side
    Pume, **7:**285
  burial rites last three to four days
    Lobi-Dagarti peoples, **9:**186
  burial in rock-covered grave
    Ute, **1:**363
  burial in seated position
    Fox, **1:**130
    Iroquois, **1:**167
  burial in shaft-tombs
    Páez, **7:**258
    Yukuna, **7:**390

  burial in shallow grave
    Ojibwa, **1:**271
  burial with simple and secular rites
    Herero, **9:**118
  burial site marked by rocks
    Amhara, **9:**21
  burial societies
    Portuguese, **4:**208
  burial as soon as possible
    Falasha, **9:**92
    Khoi, **9:**160
    Kipsigis, **9:**165
  burial in special structure
    Aleut, **1:**16
    Gros Ventre, **1:**134
    Kwakiutl, **1:**200
  burial with specific items
    Belarussians, **6:**61
    Catawba, **1:**55
    Even, **6:**119
    Koryaks and Kerek, **6:**210
    Lisu, **6:**466
    Maliseet, **1:**213
    Maris, **6:**258
    Muong, **5:**192
    Nganasan, **6:**282
    Salar, **6:**488
    Ukrainian peasants, **6:**388
    Wa, **6:**504
  burial in squatting position
    Maxakali, **7:**233
  burial in underground chamber
    Chocó, **7:**123
  burial under house
    Apalai, **7:**47
    Barama River Carib, **7:**82
    Cubeo, **7:**142
    Cuna, **7:**151
    Emberá, **7:**158
    Guajajára, **7:**167
    Guarayu, **7:**174
    Ka'wiari, **7:**200
    Macuna, **7:**215
    Maroni Carib, **7:**220
    Mundurucu, **7:**246
    Paresí, **7:**269
    Pauserna, **7:**270
    Shipibo, **7:**305
    Siona-Secoya, **7:**309
    Suya, **7:**317
    Tacana, **7:**318
    Tapirapé, **7:**321
    Trio, **7:**337
    Tswana, **9:**364
    Tunebo, **7:**339
    Tupari, **7:**341
    Wanano, **7:**350
    Yagua, **7:**374
    Yekuana, **7:**381
  burial under rock
    Tsimihety, **9:**359
  burial under small houselike structure
    Menominee, **1:**222
  burial in urns
    Jebero, **7:**181
  burial in urns under house
    Chiriguano, **7:**122
  burial vertically with head exposed

    Selepet, **2:**294
  burial in village plaza
    Kuikuru, **7:**209
    Mehinaku, **7:**239
  burial with water
    Mataco, **7:**229
  burial west of compound (men)
    Mossi, **9:**231
  burial within twenty-four hours
    Albanians, **4:**8
    Baggara, **9:**32
    Bamiléké, **9:**40
    Bedouin, **9:**46
    Greeks, **4:**134
    Jews, Arabic-speaking, **9:**136
    Jews of Iran, **9:**141
    Maltese, **4:**169
    Old Believers, **1:**275
    Pasiegos, **4:**191
    Peloponnesians, **4:**194
    Suku, **9:**323
    Syrian Christian of Kerala, **3:**275
    Turks, **9:**376
    Zuni, **1:**400
  buring of house
    Ndembu, **9:**241
  burning of beeswax
    Macuna, **7:**215
  burning of house
    Cinta Larga, **7:**128
    Guajajára, **7:**167
    Karihona, **7:**193
    Kikapu, **8:**145
    Lengua, **7:**211
    Lozi, **9:**190
    Matsigenka, **7:**232-233
    Mbeere, **9:**223
    Paï-Tavytera, **7:**260
    Pima-Papago, **1:**289
    Pomo, **1:**294, 296
    Shipibo, **7:**305
    Terena, **7:**327
    Toba, **7:**334
    Tupari, **7:**341
    Ute, **1:**362
    Wáiwai, **7:**347, 348
    Warlpiri, **2:**374
    Yagua, **7:**374
    Yekuana, **7:**381
  burning of personal possessions. *See subhead
    destruction of possessions below*
  burning of wagon or trailer
    Rominche, **4:**217
  burnt offerings of clothing
    Quechan, **1:**302
  cannibalism
    Fore, **2:**62, 65
    Iatmul, **2:**100
    Rossel Island, **2:**280
  captured bird released after burial
    Iroquois, **1:**167
  casket carried on bed of rose petals
    Sicilians, **4:**237
  caste and gender differences
    Telegu, **3:**287
  cattle horns placed on tomb
    Tandroy, **9:**338
  ceremonies

Araucanians, 7:55
Awá Kwaiker, 7:65
Aymara, 7:68
Guambiano, 7:173
Krikati/Pukobye, 7:206
Lengua, 7:211
Nivaclé, 7:251
Panare, 7:267
Piaroa, 7:278
Saramaka, 7:298
Sirionó, 7:311
Suya, 7:317
Tupari, 7:341
chanting
Dalmatians, 4:87
Kapingamarangi, 6:111
Kuna, 8:150
Maliseet, 1:213
Chasing the Dead
Cora, 8:77
chief mourner possessed by and imperson-
ates deceased
Santal, 3:255
chief's body placed on scaffold and burned
Powhatan, 1:297
for children
Afro-Colombians, 7:18
Afro-Hispanic Pacific Lowlanders, 7:23
Afro-Venezuelans, 7:28
Jivaro, 7:183
Mocoví, 7:241
Mojo, 7:242
Otomí of the Sierra, 8:203
Pemon, 7:273
Sagada Igorot, 5:217
Saraguro, 7:295
Shetlanders, 4:234
Tonga, 9:355
Tswana, 9:364
church bells tolling
Portuguese, 4:208
clan membership validated by attendance
Sara, 9:307
clan praises recited
Ndebele, 9:238
class differences
Swazi, 9:333
Temne, 9:345
Yoruba, 9:393
cleansing ritual for village
Lunda, 9:199
clocks stopped
Kashubians, 159
coffin carried around burial ground three
times
Frisians, 4:112
coffin used
Nagas, 3:191
commemorations on specific days after
death
Zoroastrians, 9:410
commemorations for year at designated
intervals
Bretons, 4:40
Peloponnesians, 4:194
Romanians, 4:215
commemorative gatherings held
periodically

Falasha, 9:93
commemorative masses
Portuguese, 4:208
commemorative rites after death
Yörük, 9:396
commemorative service at gravesite
Somalis, 9:318
commoners buried with closest kin
Sakalava, 9:298-299
communion with dead
Malaita, 2:163
community participation
Boruca, Bribri, Cabécar, 8:30
Leonese, 4:162
Orcadians, 4:188
condolence ceremonies
Iroquois, 1:167
corpse abandonment
Copper Eskimo, 1:79
corpse carried on plank to cemetery
Wiyot, 1:385
corpse disposed of promptly
Rukuba, 9:291
corpse dressed in inside-out clothing
Rominche, 4:217
corpse drying and storage
Candoshi, 7:94
corpse exposure
Parsi, 3:230
corpse-handling aversion
Rominche, 4:217
corpse painted red
Menominee, 1:222
corpse remains in house weeks to months
Tandroy, 9:338
corpse seen as contaminating
Yurok, 1:396
cremation. See Cremation
cremation ashes cast in river
Brahman and Chhetri of Nepal, 3:54
Pahari, 3:223
cremation only for accused witches
Northern Paiute, 1:265
"Cry" ceremony
Southern Paiute (and Chemehuevi),
1:332
dances and music
Vlachs, 4:275
dancing in circle around grave
Maliseet, 1:213
death anniversary commemoration
Bamiléké, 9:39, 40
Ingalik, 1:156
Kickapoo, 1:186
Pima-Papago, 1:290
Rom, 1:306
Yokuts, 1:388
death anniversary feast
Rom, 1:306
Vlach Gypsies of Hungary, 4:273
death announced to farm animals and
field
Kashubians, 4:159
death announced by gunshot
Yao of Thailand, 5:293
deceased welcomed back to community
year after death
Shona, 9:314

destruction of domestic animals and live-
stock
Luyia, 9:206
Panare, 7:266
Suri, 9:326-327
Suya, 7:316
Tandroy, 9:338
Tswana, 9:364
Wáiwai, 7:348
destruction of garden
Miyanmin, 2:212
Suya, 7:316
destruction of horse
Jicarilla, 1:174
Maricopa, 1:216
destruction of house. See subhead burning of
house above
destruction of personal possessions
Amahuaca, 7:36
Chácobo, 7:106
Chipewyan, 1:69
Cinta Larga, 7:128
Dogrib, 1:88
Guadalcanal, 2:90
Hare, 1:141, 142
Huarayo, 7:178
Kiowa, 1:188, 189
Klamath, 1:192
Kuikuru, 7:208
Kumeyaay, 1:195
Kurtatchi, 2:132
Kwakiutl, 1:199
Lengua, 7:211
Maká, 7:217
Mashco, 7:226
Mataco, 7:229
Matsigenka, 7:231
Mekeo, 2:199
Mohave, 1:241, 242
Mundurucu, 7:245, 246
Nasioi, 2:233
Nivaclé, 7:249
Northern Paiute, 1:265
Palu'e, 5:209
Panare, 7:266
Pemon, 7:272
Piemontese Sinti, 4:201
Pima-Papago, 1:289
Piro, 7:280
Pomo, 1:294, 296
Quechan, 1:301, 302
Rikbaktsa, 7:287
Rom, 1:305
Shipibo, 7:305
Siona-Secoya, 7:308
Slavey, 1:320
Slovensko Roma, 4:251
Tanaina, 1:336
Toba, 7:334
Tor, 2:343, 344
Trio, 7:336
Tubatulabal, 1:355
Tupari, 7:341
Ute, 1:361
ute, 1:362
Waimiri-Atroari, 7:344
Wáiwai, 7:347, 348
Walapai, 1:365, 366

Mortuary practices (cont'd)
    Washoe, **1:**370
    Wayapi, **7:**362
    Western Apache, **1:**372
    Yagua, **7:**373
    Yanomamö, **7:**376
    Yukuna, **7:**387, 390
    Yuqui, **7:**393, 395
  different customs for childless persons
    Akha, **5:**13
  dirges sung by women
    Peloponnesians, **4:**194
  disinternment of bones. *See subhead* bone
      retrieval *above; subhead* osteophagia;
      subhead secondary burial *below*
  disinternment forty days after death
    Vlachs, **4:**275
  display of body
    French Canadians, **1:**133
    Haida, **1:**136
  distribution of clothing
    Kazakhs, **6:**181
  distribution of food to the poor
    Castilians, **4:**60
  distribution of personal belongings
    Goodenough Island, **2:**87
    Tanana, **1:**339
    Telefolmin, **2:**322
    Tolai, **2:**335-336
  distribution of personal property to non-
      immediate family mourners
    Winnebago, **1:**381
  driving out the spirit
    Dai, **6:**428
  drumming
    Maliseet, **1:**213
  dual rituals
    Cahaitan, **8:**37
  elaborate funeral
    Balinese, **5:**37
    Belau, **2:**27
    Ewe and Fon, **9:**88
    Lozi, **9:**190
    North Alaskan Eskimos, **1:**261
    Nyakyusa and Ngonde, **9:**254
    Sea Islanders, **1:**311
    Tonga, **9:**355
    Toradja, **5:**281
    Toraja, **5:**283
    Tswana, **9:**364
    Wogeo, **2:**382
    Yakö, **9:**387
  eulogies
    Walloons, **4:**278
  exchange of personal belongings
    Seri, **8:**234
  exile of deceased's children
    Dobu, **2:**51, 52
  family funeral attendance important
    Welsh, **4:**280
  family tombs
    Betsileo, **9:**54
  fasting
    Yuqui, **7:**395
  feast. *See* Feasting, funerary; Feasting,
      memorial
  festivity of the dead after first month
    Fali, **9:**97

fiesta
    Guarijío, **8:**119
  financial contributions
    Belau, **2:**27
    Mingrelians, **6:**265
  food restrictions for mourners
    Lengua, **7:**211
    Limbu, **3:**150
    Ngawbe, **8:**198
    Okiek, **9:**262
    Yokuts, **1:**389
  food set out for deceased
    Bhil, **3:**42
    Romanians, **4:**215
    Tanaina, **1:**337
  fourth-day spirit-releasing rite
    Tewa Pueblos, **1:**350
  funeral arrangements made by opposite clan
      of deceased
    Tanaina, **1:**337
  funeral attended only by closest relatives
    Siberian Estonians, **6:**337
  funeral clubs
    Rapa, **2:**275
  funeral conducted by father's clan
    Mandan, **1:**215
  funeral conducted by household head
    Mossi, **9:**230
  funeral conducted by patrilineal members
    Mossi, **9:**231
  funeral conducted by son
    Brahman and Chhetri of Nepal, **3:**54
    Jatav, **3:**115
  funeral cortege
    Atoni, **5:**29
  funeral draws large gathering of mourners
    Latinos, **1:**206
  funeral draws large gathering of mourners
      from great distances for funeral
    Irish Travellers, **4:**156-157
  funeral held at homestead
    Gusii, **9:**110
  funeral as major life-cycle event
    Micronesians, **1:**239
    Peloponnesians, **4:**194
    Washoe, **1:**370
  funeral most important life-cycle event
    Badaga, **3:**18
    Basques, **4:**32
    Cahita, **8:**37
    Mount Athos, **4:**177
    Northern Paiute, **1:**265
  funeral prayers and feasts last forty days
    Vlachs, **4:**275
  funeral private
    Klamath, **1:**192
  funeral procession
    Shetlanders, **4:**234
  funeral procession accompanied by village
      band
    Slovaks, **4:**246
  funeral procession on foot
    Frisians, **4:**112
  funeral procession with jazz band
    Black Creoles of Louisiana, **1:**40
  funeral procession with songs of praise
    Lingayat, **3:**153
  funeral procession on winding path

Frisians, **4:**112
  funeral removes deceased from community
    Shona, **9:**314
  funeral rites last for ten days
    Oriya, **3:**218
  funeral rites for one week
    Dogon, **9:**73
  funeral rites to remove death pollution from
      mourners
    Nyinba, **3:**213
  funeral ritual held at place of death
    Nayaka, **3:**196
  funeral ritual lasts eleven days
    Badaga, **3:**18
  funeral ritual lasts five days
    Tepehuan of Durango, **8:**258
  funeral ritual lasts several days
    Kalingas, **5:**123
  funeral ritual lasts three days
    Gurung, **3:**95
  funeral ritual lasts three days minimum
    Hmong, **5:**95
  funeral ritual lengthy
    Kilenge, **2:**120
  funerals longest and most important life-
      cycle activity
    Sherpa, **3:**260
  funeral as wedding rite
    Ukrainian peasants, **6:**388
  game playing
    Salasaca, **7:**290
  gift exchange
    Mixtec, **8:**178
    Pomo, **1:**295-296
  gift giving
    Ambae, **2:**12
    Atoni, **5:**29
    Fore, **2:**65
    Lau, **2:**145
    Lesu, **2:**147
    Mae Enga, **2:**151
    Old Believers, **1:**275
    Pomo, **1:**295
    Wogeo, **2:**382
    Yakö, **9:**387
    Yap, **2:**394
  godfathers of death in charge
    Yaqui, **8:**307
  goods exchange
    Anuta, **2:**15
  grave decorated with deceased's favorite
      objects
    Sea Islanders, **1:**311
  grave dug immediately after death
    Acholi, **9:**6
  grave dug by neighbors
    Nyamwezi and Sukuma, **9:**258
  grave marked with objects
    Suku, **9:**323
  grave mound
    Dobu, **2:**50
  graveside rituals at designated intervals
      after burial
    Greeks, **4:**134
  "green" and "dry" funerals
    Kota, **3:**136, 138
  grief expressed hysterically
    Basmat, **2:**21

Easter Island, 2:55
grief expressed by painting body and tearing
	hair
	Kewa, 2:117
grief expressed by physically harming self
	Pintupi, 2:267
grief restrained
	Flemish, 4:109
	Kapingamarangi, 2:110
	Kickapoo, 1:186
gun fired to drive away deceased's spirit
	Cree, 1:82
hair burning by mourners
	Yokuts, 1:389
hair cutting by mourners
	Chamacoco, 7:110
	Krikati/Pukobye, 7:206
	Lengua, 7:211
	Lngua, 7:211
	Mocoví, 7:241
	Sumu, 8:239
	Ute, 1:362
handwritten obituary
	Chocho, 8:63
head shaving by mourner
	Bamiléké, 9:40
	Brahman and Chhetri of Nepal, 3:54
	Gusii, 9:111
	Irula, 3:108
	Luyia, 9:206
hired mourners
	Albanians, 4:8
	Balkars, 6:54
	Khevsur, 6:197
	Mountain Jews, 6:274
	Ossetes, 6:302
	Ukrainian peasants, 6:388
horse-drawn hearse
	Frisians, 4:112
house built over grave
	Kuna, 8:150
house cleaned
	Páez, 7:258
house door relocated
	Tacana, 7:318
	Terena, 7:327
house doors and windows opened
	Bretons, 4:40
	Kashubians, 4:159
house gates and doors opened
	Portuguese, 4:208
household rituals
	Iteso, 9:130
house inhabited until deceased is buried
	Micmac, 1:235
house purified
	Wiyot, 1:385
human sacrifice
	Ache, 7:6, 7
hut built above grave
	Ache, 7:4
infant not mourned
	Lobi-Dagarti peoples, 9:186
isolation of anyone touching corpse
	Falasha, 9:94
keening
	Andis, 6:27
	Avars, 6:46

Cretans, 4:71
	Karachays, 6:162
	Krikati/Pukobye, 7:206
killing of slaves
	Kalimantan Dayaks, 5:120
kin payments
	Daribi, 2:47
	Foi, 2:60
	Guadalcanal, 2:91
	Kwoma, 2:135
	Malaita, 2:163
	Melpa, 2:202
	Mendi, 2:205
	Miyanmin, 2:210-211
	Ningerum, 2:247
	Pentecost, 2:264
	Rossel Island, 2:279, 280
	Tanna, 2:315
	Telefolmin, 2:321
lamentations
	Finns, 4:104
	Greeks, 4:134
	Komi, 6:204
	Miami, 1:232
	Tats, 6:360
lying in state
	Abkhazians, 6:9
	Georgians, 6:136
	Greeks, 6:144
	Haida, 1:136
	Khevsur, 6:197
	Ojibwa, 1:271
	Slovenes, 4:249
male mourners forbidden to shave
	Armenians, 6:31
masked dancers
	Ndembu, 9:241
	tropical-forest foragers, 9:357
mass one year after death
	Itza,' 8:135
meeting with spirit of deceased
	Altaians, 6:23
men-only funerals
	Berbers of Morocco, 9:52
messenger announces death throughout
	area
	Ossetes, 6:302
	Tsakhurs, 6:368
mirrors covered
	Kashubians, 4:159
mirrors turned to wall
	Bretons, 4:40
mortuary pole
	Haida, 1:136
mourners abstain from fiestas
	Itza,' 8:135
mourners forbidden to bathe and groom
	selves
	Sakalava, 9:299
mourners remain inactive for four days
	Taos, 1:343
mourners restricted in activities
	Okiek, 9:262
	Ute, 1:362
mourners retreat from public life
	Kipsigis, 9:165
mourners self-inflict pain
	Sumu, 8:239

mourners' self-mutilation in grief
	Mardudjara, 2:182
	Ossetes, 6:302
	Tabasarans, 6:351
	Tats, 6:360
	Tongareva, 2:341
mourners sleep on ground seven days
	Zaramo, 9:402
mourners wear black
	Castilians, 4:61
	Dalmatians, 4:87
	Portuguese, 4:208
	Sicilians, 4:237
	Slovaks, 4:246
mourners wear dark clothing
	Bamiléké, 9:40
mourners wear skin cloaks inside out
	Lozi, 9:190
mourning
	Kikapu, 8:145
	Kiwai, 2:127
	Kurtatchi, 2:133
	Kwoma, 2:136
	Lau, 2:145
	Mae Enga, 2:151
	Mailu, 2:157
	Maisin, 2:160
	Malekula, 2:166
	Maori, 2:178
	Mardudjara, 2:181
	Mekeo, 2:200
	Melpa, 2:202
	Mendi, 2:205
	Mimika, 2:208
	Mountain Arapesh, 2:218
	Murik, 2:223
	Namau, 2:232
	Ontong Java, 2:255
	Orokolo, 2:260
	Tikopia, 2:326
mourning at house of family
	Konso, 9:172
mourning clothing
	Cyclades, 4:78
	Dungans, 6:111
	Georgians, 6:137
	Greeks, 6:144
	Karachays, 6:162
	Khinalughs, 6:202
	Lengua, 7:211
	Svans, 6:346
	Udis, 6:378
mourning duration
	Abkhazians, 6:9
	Albanians, 4:7-8
	Azoreans, 4:29
	Bania, 3:25
	Basques, 4:32
	Boazi, 2:31
	Brahman and Chhetri of Nepal, 3:54
	Bukharan Jews, 6:65
	Canarians, 4:53
	Cape Verdeans, 4:57
	Castilians, 4:61
	Central Thai, 5:72
	Chakma, 3:61
	Chechen-Ingush, 6:75
	Chitpavan Brahman, 3:70

Mortuary practices (cont'd)
    Circassians, **6**:91
    Cyclades, **4**:78, 78
    Delaware, **1**:86-87
    Dobu, **2**:52
    Dolgan, **6**:102
    Doukhobors, **1**:93
    Eipo, **2**:58
    Finns, **4**:104
    Fox, **1**:130
    Georgians, **6**:136, 137
    Gogodala, **2**:84
    Greeks, **6**:144
    Gujarati, **3**:92
    Iroquois, **1**:167
    Jews, **1**:171
    Jews of Iran, **9**:141
    Jews of Israel, **9**:144
    Kalapuya, **1**:175
    Karachays, **6**:162
    Karok, **1**:177
    Kazakhs, **6**:182
    Keraki, **2**:114
    Khevsur, **6**:197
    Khinalughs, **6**:202
    Lisu, **6**:466
    Lobi-Dagarti peoples, **9**:185
    Madeirans, **4**:166
    Magar, **3**:157
    Maris, **6**:258
    Mingrelians, **6**:265
    Mountain Jews, **6**:274
    Ojibwa, **1**:270
    Old Believers, **1**:275
    Oroquen, **6**:483
    Pahari, **3**:223
    Palestinians, **9**:266
    Palu'e, **5**:209
    Pathan, **3**:233
    Pohnpei, **2**:270
    Pomo, **1**:296
    Portuguese, **4**:208
    Qashqa'i, **9**:287
    Sagada Igorot, **5**:217
    Sambia, **2**:286
    Santal, **3**:255
    Senoi, **5**:239
    Siwai, **2**:304
    Suri, **9**:326
    Suya, **7**:317
    Svans, **6**:346
    Tats, **6**:360
    Tofalar, **6**:363
    Tokelau, **2**:333
    Torres Strait Islanders, **2**:348
    Trobriand Islands, **2**:351
    Tsakhurs, **6**:368
    Turkmens, **6**:371
    Udis, **6**:378
    Ulithi, **2**:360
    Ute, **1**:362
    Uzbeks, **6**:500
    Woleai, **2**:384
    Yawalapití, **7**:380
    Yukuna, **7**:390
  mourning songs
    Tanana, **1**:340
  mourning by spouse

    Apiaká, **7**:50-51
    Mocoví, **7**:241
  mummification
    Piaroa, **7**:278
  music and song
    African American, **1**:13
    Afro-Bolivians, **7**:10
    Afro-Venezuelans, **7**:28
    Emberá, **7**:158
    Mohave, **1**:242
  nine days of prayer and vigil
    Creoles of Nicaragua, **8**:86
    Jamaicans, **8**:140
    Lenca, **8**:156
    Mixtec, **8**:178
    Otomí of the Sierra, **8**:203
    Poqomam, **8**:219
    Saint Lucians, **8**:232
    Triqui, **8**:272
  novenas
    Chatino, **8**:52
    Chontal of Tabasco, **8**:69
    Italian Mexicans, **8**:132
    Puerto Ricans, **8**:224
  obstacles to prevent deceased's spirit from
    following survivors
    Karen, **5**:129
  osteophagia
    Amahuaca, **7**:36
    Luba of Shaba, **9**:193
    Marubo, **7**:223
    Yanomamö, **7**:377
  pacification of deceased's spirit
    Washoe, **1**:370
  paid mourners
    Castilians, **4**:60
  performance of deceased's favorite songs
    and tales
    Vlach Gypsies of Hungary, **4**:273
  periodic services to assist soul's journey
    Bretons, **4**:40
  personalized mourning
    Dutch, **4**:94
  pollution of mourners
    Murik, **2**:223
  postmortuary rites conducted by males
    Newar, **3**:208
  potlatch
    Tanaina, **1**:337
    Tanana, **1**:349
  prayer said on anniversary of death
    Jews of Israel, **9**:144
  prayer said at gravesite
    Jews of Israel, **9**:144
  prayers for forty days
    Old Believers, **1**:275
  prayers to spirit of deceased
    Southern Paiute (and Chemehuevi),
    1:333
  prohibition on discord at funeral
    Rominche, **4**:217
  prohibition on speaking name of deceased
    Shetlanders, **4**:234
    Washoe, **1**:370
  public mourning for one week
    Bamiléké, **9**:40
  purification rituals
    Khevsur, **6**:197

    Murngin, **2**:227
    Nandi and other Kalenjin peoples, **9**:234
    Nganasan, **6**:282
    Rotinese, **5**:214
    Suri, **9**:326
    T'in, **5**:279
    Usino, **2**:363
    Wogeo, **2**:382
  refusal to speak about deceased
    Piemontese Sinti, **4**:201
  return from gravesite by different route
    Jicarill1, **3**:174
  ritual consumption of remains. See *subhead*
    osteophagia *below*
  ritual crying
    Bonerate, **5**:46
  ritual dance
    Kumyks, **6**:224
  ritual punishment of survivors
    Pintupi, **2**:267
  ritual reenactments of warfare
    Mohave, **1**:242
  rituals to ensure deceased's spirit will not
    cause harm, **4**:145
  sacrifice
    Dani, **2**:45
    Konso, **9**:172
    Maring, **2**:188
    Marquesas Islands, **2**:191
  sale of personal property
    Piemontese Sinti, **4**:201
    Slovensko Roma, **4**:251
  scissors placed on chest of deceased
    Circassians, **9**:68
  séance
    Miyanmin, **2**:212
  seclusion
    Chamacoco, **7**:110
    Kiwai, **2**:127
    Lakalai, **2**:142
    Maisin, **2**:160
    Suruí, **7**:313
    Trobriand Islands, **2**:351
    Usino, **2**:363
  secondary burial
    Cham, **5**:74
    Kalimantan Dayaks, **5**:120
    Kwoma, **2**:136
    Maori, **2**:178
    Melanau, **5**:180
    Murut, **5**:193
    Ngatatjara, **2**:241
    Nicobarese, **3**:210
    Rossel Island, **2**:280
    Tagalog, **5**:251
    Tsimihety, **9**:359
    Vietnamese, **5**:287
    Zhuang, **6**:512
    see also subhead bone retrieval *above*
  second funeral
    Toda, **3**:298
  secret burial place
    Hawaiians, **2**:97
    Tahiti, **2**:307
  self-disfigurement by mourners
    Albanians, **4**:7
    Kiowa, **1**:189
  setting place for dead at table

Circassians, **6:**91
settlement taboo for five days
    Inughuit, **1:**161
shelters built for spirits
    Lozi, **9:**190
silk shroud for deceased
    Betsileo, **9:**57
"singing him or her out" Swedes, **4:**258
single-family burial plot
    Ionians, **4:**150
skeletons exhumed years after death
    Iteso, **9:**130
skull exhumed years after death
    Fali, **9:**97
skull mutilation
    Lengua, **7:**211
skulls exhumed one year after death
    Bamiléké, **9:**40
sky burial
    Tibetans, **6:**496
soul captured in crystal
    Huichol, **8:**128
soul farewell ceremony
    Huichol, **8:**128
soul released to make way to Land of Ever
        Summer
    Mescalero Apache, **1:**225
speeches
    Mohave, **1:**242
stilt walkers
    Ndembu, **9:**241
stoning or drubbing of corpse
    Maká, **7:**218
substitution of red objects for black
    Slovensko Roma, **4:**251
touching face of deceased
    Rominche, **4:**217
trumpet sounding
    tropical-forest foragers, **9:**357
veil wearing
    Gogodala, **2:**84
vigil
    Baggara, **9:**32
    Cora, **8:**77
    Guarijío, **8:**119
    Ifugao, **5:**100
    Leonese, **4:**162
    Moldovans, **6:**269
    Ndebele, **9:**238
    Puerto Ricans, **8:**224
    Samal, **5:**221
    Slovaks, **4:**246
    Tausug, **5:**264
vigil burial
    Castilians, **4:**61
vigil by postmenopausal women only
    Rominche, **4:**217
visiting networks for bereaved
    Yemenis, **9:**390
wailing
    Abkhazians, **6:**9
    Albanians, **4:**7
    Amhara, **9:**21
    Baggara, **9:**32
    Bakairi, **7:**75
    Bamiléké, **9:**40
    Circassians, **6:**90
    Cretans, **4:**71

Croats, **4:**75
Fox, **1:**130
Georgians, **6:**136
Gusii, **9:**111
Jews of Iran, **9:**141
Kumyks, **6:**224
Kuna, **8:**150
Lau, **2:**145
Lesu, **2:**147
Luyia, **9:**206
Mailu, **2:**157
Manam, **2:**169
Mohave, **1:**242
Ossetes, **6:**302
Pentecost, **2:**264
Portuguese, **4:**208
Seri, **8:**235
Svans, **6:**346
Tabasarans, **6:**351
Tasmanians, **2:**317
Tikopia, **2:**326
Tokelau, **2:**333
Torres Strait Islanders, **2:**348
Truk, **2:**353
Wáiwai, **7:**348
Wogeo, **2:**382
wake
    Acadian, **1:**9
    Afro-Colombians, **7:**18
    Afro-Hispanic Pacific Lowlanders, **7:**21,
        23
    Araucanians, **7:**55
    Arubans, **8:**14
    Awá Kwaiker, **7:**65
    Aymara, **7:**68
    Balkars, **6:**54
    Canelos Quichua, **7:**102
    Carib of Dominica, **8:**40
    Chatino, **8:**52
    Chipaya, **7:**117
    Chocho, **8:**63
    Ch'ol, **8:**66
    Colorado, **7:**131
    Costa Ricans, **8:**81
    Cotopaxi Quichua, **7:**135
    Creoles of Nicaragua, **8:**86
    Cretans, **4:**71
    Emberá, **7:**158
    Gaels (Irish), **4:**117
    Irish, **4:**154
    Jamaicans, **8:**140
    Kickapoo, **1:**186
    Lao, **5:**160
    Mam, **8:**160
    Manx, **4:**171
    Maroni Carib, **7:**220
    Melanau, **5:**180
    Mixe, **8:**175
    Orcadians, **4:**188
    Páez, **7:**258
    Popoloca, **8:**216
    Puerto Ricans, **8:**224
    Saint Lucians, **8:**232
    T'in, **5:**279
    Tory Islanders, **4:**266
    Vlach Gypsies of Hungary, **4:**272-273
    Winnebago, **1:**382
    Zoque, **8:**317

warrior killed in battle covered with
        branches where he fell
    Suri, **9:**326
water burial
    Moinba, **6:**473
white clay applied to human body during
        funeral
    Lobi-Dagarti peoples, **9:**186
white as mourning color
    Sorbs, **4:**254
widow expected to grieve longer than
        widower
    Swazi, **9:**333
widow homicide
    Bau, **2:**24
    Sengseng, **2:**296, 297, 298
widow purification, **2:**61-62
wind burial
    Oroquen, **6:**483
women buried in compound
    Tswana, **9:**364
women denied funerals
    Chechen-Ingush, **6:**75
women mourners
    Albanians, **4:**7-8, 8
    Greeks, **4:**134
    Pemon, **7:**273
    Sarakatsani, **4:**225
    Tupari, **7:**341
women prohibited from cemetery
    Kazakhs, **6:**181
as women's responsibility
    Ionians, **4:**150
see also Afterlife; Cemeteries; Cremation;
        Dead, the; Grave markers; Widowers;
        Widows
Moslems. _See_ Islam; Shia Muslims; Sunni
        Muslims
Mosque architecture
    Bengali, **3:**34
Mother
    conflict with daughters
        Ndembu, **9:**240
    importance of brother. _See_ Uncle,
        maternal
    matriarchy
        Sakalava, **9:**296
    sacredness in family
        Rom of Czechoslovakia, **4:**219
    strong ties with children
        Danes, **4:**90
    strong ties with daughter
        Andalusians, **4:**11, 12
        Burmese, **5:**65
        Chin, **3:**66, 67
        English, **4:**96
        Highland Scots, **4:**141
        Maltese, **4:**168
    strong ties with eldest son
        Aveyronnais, **4:**25
        Rom of Czechoslovakia, **4:**219
    strong ties with son
        Aveyronnais, **4:**25
        Jatav, **3:**114-115
    see also Childbirth; Family;
        Pregnancy
Mother Earth
    Taos, **1:**343

Mother-goddess worship
    Andalusians, **4:**12
    see also Madonna worship
Mother-in-law
    phobia
        Limbu, **3:**150
    power
        Brahman and Chhetri of Nepal, **3:**53
    power of
        Canarians, **4:**52
        Hutterites, **1:**154
    relationship with daughter-in-law
        Han, **6:**445
    relationship with son-in-law
        Tiwi, **2:**328
Mother-in-law avoidance
    Blackfoot, **1:**42
    Gros Ventre, **1:**134
    Mescalero Apache, **1:**224-225
    Sarsi, **1:**308
    Western Apache, **1:**372
Mother's brother's daughter marriage. *See*
        Cousin marriage, cross-cousin
Mother's brother. *See* Uncle, maternal
Mother of the Sea
    Inughuit, **1:**161
Motifs. *See* Symbolism
Mountaineering
    Sherpa, **3:**257-258
Mountain spirits
    Western Apache, **1:**373
Mourning Ceremony
    Southern Paiute (and Chemehuevi), **1:**332,
        333
Moutain Flower (festival)
    Miao, **6:**472
Movies. *See* Film industry
Mud-brick housing. *See under* Housing
Muharram (holiday)
    Samal Moro, **5:**224
    Talysh, **6:**357
Muharrem (ceremony)
    Azerbaijani Turks, **6:**50
Mulatsago (brotherhood gathering)
    Vlach Gypsies of Hungary, **4:**272
Mulatto. *See* Mixed-race ancestry
Mule trading
    Irish Travelers, **1:**162, 163
    peripatetics, **1:**287
Mullah
    Pathan, **3:**233
Multihousehold compounds. *See* Household,
        communal
Multiracial background. *See* Mixed-race
        ancestry
Mummification
    Aleut, **1:**16
Mumming
    Black Creoles of Louisiana, **1:**39-40
Mun religion
    Lepcha, **3:**149
Murals
    Latinos, **1:**206
    Ndebele, **9:**237-238
    Sardinians, **4:**227
    see also Wall paintings
Murder
    high rate

Agta, **5:**4
    Chatino, **8:**51-52
    Copper Eskimo, **1:**78
    Yörük, **9:**396
interfamily feuds
    North Alaskan Eskimos, **1:**260
none for past 120 years
    Orcadians, **4:**187
punishments
    Central Yup'ik Eskimos, **1:**58
    Cherokee, **1:**62
    Hidsata, **1:**148
    Ingalik, **1:**158
    Kumeyaay, **1:**195
    Kwakiutl, **1:**199
    Lakher, **3:**147
    see also Violent death, beliefs about
purification rites
    Ache, **7:**6
revenge for. *See* Conflict resolution, blood
        vengeance
site customs
    Albanians, **4:**8
of socially disruptive person
    Yokuts, **1:**388
widow
    Bau, **2:**24
as witch executions
    Western Apache, **1:**373
withdrawal to another tribe, then compen-
        sation for
    Tauade, **2:**320
of women
    Chamacoco, **7:**110
    see also Infanticide; Punishment, death
        compensation
Murugan (deity)
    Tamil, **3:**279
Murukan (deity)
    Tamil of Sri Lanka, **3:**283
Muscular dystrophy
    Amish, **1:**19
Musical instruments
    accordion
        Bretons, **4:**40
        Irish Travellers, **4:**156
        Saraguro, **7:**295
        Tory Islanders, **4:**266
    aerophones
        Croats, **4:**75
    bagpipes
        Bretons, **4:**40
        Galicians, **4:**120
        Sorbs, **4:**254
    banjo
        Tory Islanders, **4:**266
    bombarde
        Bretons, **4:**40
    bouzouki
        Greeks, **4:**134
    clarinet
        Greeks, **4:**134
    cordophones
        Croats, **4:**75
    drums
        Afro-Bolivians, **7:**10
        Afro-Venezuelans, **7:**28-29
        Araucanians, **7:**55

Awá Kwaiker, **7:**63, 65
        see also Drums and drumming
    dulcimer
        Greeks, **4:**134
        Ozarks, **1:**282
    fiddle
        Tory Islanders, **4:**266
    fiddle, three-fingered
        Serbs, **4:**254
    flutes. *See* Flute
    folk harp
        Bavarians, **4:**35
    gourd
        Kikuyu, **9:**162
    guitar
        Piemontese Sinti, **4:**201
    gusle
        Montenegrins, **4:**174
    harmonica
        Irish Travellers, **4:**156
    harp
        Bretons, **4:**40
    homemade
        Fipa, **9:**99
        Jews of Iran, **9:**141
        Pedi, **9:**270
        Swazi, **9:**333
        Tandroy, **9:**338
        Tepehuan of Chihuahua, **8:**254
        Tonga, **9:**355
        Tzotzil of San Andrés Larraínzar, **8:**285
    lute
        Greeks, **4:**134
    lute, one-stringed
        Dalmatians, **4:**87
    lyre
        Nandi and other Kalenjin peoples, **9:**234
    making
        Burgundians, **4:**47
        Chakma, **3:**61
        Garo, **3:**84
        Ghorbat, **9:**106, 107
        Klamath, **1:**192
        Kota, **3:**135
        Nagas, **3:**188
        Santal, **3:**253
    marimbas/xylophones
        Afro-Hispanic Pacific Lowlanders, **7:**23
        Awá Kwaiker, **7:**63, 65
        Mam, **8:**160
        Witoto, **7:**365
    musical bow
        Yokuts, **1:**389
    musical instruments
        rattles
            Mohave, **1:**241
    nail-piano
        Nyamwezi and Sukuma, **9:**258
    one-stringed viol
        Dalmatians, **4:**87
    panpipes
        Malaita, **2:**163
    percussion
        Afro-Bolivians, **7:**10
        Afro-Venezuelans, **7:**29
        Cubeo, **7:**142
        Ka'wiari, **7:**200
        Kongo, **9:**168

Otavalo, **7**:255
Paï-Tavytera, **7**:260
Suku, **9**:323
Wáiwai, **7**:348
see also Drums and drumming
pipe
Lozi, **9**:189
playing, gender proscription for
Sora, **3**:269
rattles
Ojibwa, **1**:271
Yokuts, **1**:389
rattles/maracas
Awá Kwaiker, **7**:63
Craho, **7**:138
Cubeo, **7**:142
Hoti, **7**:175
Karajá, **7**:191
Ka'wiari, **7**:200
Paï-Tavytera, **7**:260
Panare, **7**:265
Pume, **7**:285
Toba, **7**:333
Tupari, **7**:341
Waimiri-Atroari, **7**:345
Xikrin, **7**:369
repairs
Gypsies and caravan dwellers in the
Netherlands, **4**:137
sacred
Macuna, **7**:213, 214
Mundurucu, **7**:245
Paresí, **7**:269
Tatuyo, **7**:324
Yawalapití, **7**:378, 380
Yukuna, **7**:388, 389
shell
Cubeo, **7**:142
shepherd's flute
Slovaks, **4**:245
stringed
Afro-Venezuelans, **7**:29
Amahuaca, **7**:36
Aymara, **7**:68
Baul, **3**:26
Chiriguano, **7**:122
Greeks, **4**:134
Guarayu, **7**:174
Guarijío, **8**:119
Hoti, **7**:175
Lozi, **9**:189
Maká, **7**:218
Otavalo, **7**:255
Paï-Tavytera, **7**:260
Saraguro, **7**:295
Shetlanders, **4**:234
Siona-Secoya, **7**:309
Toba, **7**:333
Tupari, **7**:341
tambourines
Ojibwa, **1**:271
tin whistle
Tory Islanders, **4**:266
trumpets/horns
Araucanians, **7**:55
Salasaca, **7**:291
Tupari, **7**:341
Xikrin, **7**:369

whistles
Yokuts, **1**:389
wind/woodwind
Amahuaca, **7**:36
Araucanians, **7**:55
Asurini, **7**:62
Awá Kwaiker, **7**:63
Aymara, **7**:68
Baniwa-Curripaco-Wakuenai, **7**:79
Bretons, **4**:40
Bulgarian Gypsies, **4**:41
Chiriguano, **7**:122
Chocó, **7**:123
Cubeo, **7**:142
Culina, **7**:148
Guahibo-Sikuani, **7**:166
Guajiro, **7**:170
Hoti, **7**:175
Huarayo, **7**:178
Ka'wiari, **7**:200
Matsigenka, **7**:232
Otavalo, **7**:255
Paï-Tavytera, **7**:260
Panare, **7**:265
Pedi, **9**:270
Qashqa'i, **9**:287
Rikbaktsa, **7**:288
Saraguro, **7**:295
Shipibo, **7**:306
Shona, **9**:314
Siona-Secoya, **7**:309
Toba, **7**:333
Tupari, **7**:341
Waimiri-Atroari, **7**:345
Wáiwai, **7**:348
Xikrin, **7**:369
see also Flute
xylophone
Lobi-Dagarti peoples, **9**:186
zither
Bavarians, **4**:35
Music and song
Abkhazians, **6**:9
A-Bwe
Saint Lucians, **8**:232
Acadian, **1**:9
Ache, **7**:7
Acholi, **9**:6
African Americans, **1**:13
Afro-Bolivians, **7**:10
Afro-Brazilians, **7**:13
Afro-Colombians, **7**:18
Afro-Venezuelans, **7**:28
Agta, **5**:6
Aguaruna, **7**:30
Ainu, **5**:10
Akawaio, **7**:33
Akha, **5**:13
Albanians, **4**:7
alliterated
Somalis, **9**:318
Altaians, **6**:23
Alur, **9**:14
Ambonese, **5**:19
Amhara, **9**:19
Andamanese, **3**:11
Antigua and Barbuda, **8**:10
Anuta, **2**:15

Araucanians, **7**:55
Araweté, **7**:57
Ashkenazim, **6**:37
Asiatic Eskimos, **6**:42
Asmat, **2**:20, 21
Austrians, **4**:21
Avars, **6**:44, 45
Awá Kwaiker, **7**:65
Aymara, **7**:68
Azerbaijani Turks, **6**:50
Azoreans, **4**:29
Baggara, **9**:31
Bahamians, **8**:20
Bai, **6**:421
Bajau, **5**:35
Balinese, **5**:37
Balkars, **6**:54
Bamiléké, **9**:40
Baniwa-Curripaco-Wakuenai, **7**:79
Bashkirs, **6**:56
Basques, **4**:32
Bau, **2**:24
Baul, **3**:26
Bavarians, **4**:35
Bedouin, **9**:46
Belarussians, **6**:61
Bene Israel, **3**:28
Bengali, **3**:33, 34
Betsileo, **9**:57
Bhil, **3**:41
Bhuiya, **3**:44
Black Creoles of Louisiana, **1**:39-40
Blackfoot, **1**:42
Bondo, **3**:50-51
Bretons, **4**:40
Bugis, **5**:51
Bugle, **8**:34
Bulgarian Gypsies, **4**:41, 42
Bulgarians, **4**:45
Burakumin, **5**:63
Burusho, **3**:56
Cahita, **8**:35, 36, 37
Cajuns, **1**:50-51
Candoshi, **7**:94
Canela, **7**:97
Cape Verdeans, **4**:56
Caribou Inuit, **1**:51
Castilians, **4**:61
Catawba, **1**:55
cattle ranchers of Huasteca, **8**:44
Chakma, **3**:61
Cham, **5**:73
Chechen-Ingush, **6**:75
Cherokee, **1**:62
Cheyenne, **1**:66
Chilena
Chatino, **8**:52
Chimbu, **2**:37
Chimila, **7**:114
Chinese in Caribbean, **8**:58
Chiriguano, **7**:122
Chukchee, **6**:78, 79
Chuvans, **6**:83
Cinta Larga, **7**:129
Circassians, **6**:90
Cochin Jews, **3**:73
Cook Islands, **2**:42
Cotopaxi Quichua, **7**:133

Music and song (cont'd)
  Craho, 7:138
  Creoles of Nicaragua, 8:86
  Cretans, 4:71
  Crimean Tatars, 6:94
  Croats, 4:75
  Cubans, 8:90
  Cuiva, 7:145
  Culina, 7:148
  Desana, 7:154
  Dobu, 2:52
  Doukhobbors, 1:93
  Dungans, 6:111
  Eipo, 2:58
  Emberá, 7:158
  Endenese, 5:86
  Estonian, 6:115
  Even, 6:119
  Ewe and Fon, 9:86
  Falasha, 9:92
  Flemish, 4:108
  Foi, 2:61
  Fulani, 9:103
  Gaels (Irish), 4:117
  Galicians, 4:120
  Gebusi, 2:77
  Georgians, 6:136
  Gitanos, 4:131
  Gond, 3:87
  Goodenough Island, 2:88
  Greeks, 6:144
  Guahibo-Sikuani, 7:166
  Guajiro, 7:169-170
  Guarayu, 7:174
  Gurung, 3:95
  Gypsies, 6:146, 148
  Hakka, 6:439
  Hanunóo, 5:91
  Hausa
      Hausa, 9:114
  hijras, 3:96, 98
  Hill Pandaram, 3:100
  Hmong, 5:94
  Huarayo, 7:178
  Hui, 6:453
  Hungarians, 4:145
  Hutterites, 1:155
  Icelands, 4:148
  Ingalik, 1:158
  Irish Travellers, 4:156
  Irula, 3:106
  Itelmen, 6:154
  Jatav, 3:115
  Javanese, 5:113
  Jews, Arabic-speaking, 9:136
  Jews of Iran, 9:141
  Jews of Kurdistan, 9:147
  Jicarilla, 1:174
  Jingpo, 6:459
  Kalmyks, 6:157
  Kaluli, 2:103
  Kanjar, 3:119, 120, 121
  Kanuri, 9:152
  Kapingamarangi, 2:110
  Karachays, 6:162
  Karaites, 9:156
  Karakalpaks, 6:168
  Karen, 5:129

  Karok, 1:177
  Kazakhs, 6:182
  Khakas, 6:188
  Khasi, 3:126
  Khinalughs, 6:201
  Khmer, 5:138
  Kickapoo, 1:185
  Kilenge, 2:120
  Kipsigis, 9:165
  Kiribati, 2:123
  Kmhmu, 5:141
  Kogi, 7:203
  Komi, 6:204
  Kongo, 9:168
  Korean, 5:148
  Koryaks and Kerek, 6:210
  Kosrae, 2:130
  Kota, 3:135-136, 137, 138
  Koya, 3:140, 141
  Krikati/Pukobye, 7:205
  Krymchaks, 6:215
  Kubachins, 6:219
  Kumeyaay, 1:195
  Kumyks, 6:223, 223-224
  Kurtatchi, 2:133
  Kurumbas, 3:143
  Kyrgyz, 6:231
  Lahu, 5:154;6:463
  Lakalai, 2:142
  Lakher, 3:147
  Lamaholot, 5:156
  Lango, 9:181
  Lao, 5:159
  Lao Isan, 5:163
  Latinos, 1:206
  Latvians, 6:238
  Lau, 2:145
  Lingayat, 3:153
  Lisu, 5:166;6:466
  Lozi, 9:189
  Luba of Shaba, 9:193
  Mae Enga, 2:151
  Magar, 3:160
  Mahar, 3:165
  Mailu, 2:156
  Maká, 7:218
  Malaita, 2:163
  Maltese, 4:169
  Manam, 2:169
  Mansi, 6:255
  Maring, 2:188
  Maris, 6:258
  Marshall Islands, 2:194
  Matsigenka, 7:232
  Mauritian, 3:173
  Mbeere, 9:222
  Melpa, 2:202
  Mescalero Apache, 1:225
  Miao, 6:471, 472
  Mimika, 2:207
  Minangkabau, 5:184
  Mingrelians, 6:265
  Mizo, 3:179
  Modang, 5:187
  Mohave, 1:241, 242
  Moldovans, 6:268, 269
  Mongols, 6:476
  Montagnais-Naskapi, 1:246

  Moré, 7:243
  Mountain Arapesh, 2:217
  Mountain Jews, 6:272, 273
  Muong, 5:192
  Nagas, 3:191
  Nahua of the State of Mexico, 8:189
  Nambicuara, 7:247
  Nasioi, 2:235
  Navajo, 1:253
  Naxi, 6:480
  Nayaka, 3:196
  Nenets, 6:279
  Newar, 3:208
  Nganasan, 6:282
  Ngatatjara, 2:241
  Ngawbe, 8:198
  Nicobarese, 3:210
  Nivaclé, 7:251
  Nivkh, 6:285
  Nogays, 6:289
  North Alaskan Eskimos, 1:261
  Northern Paiute, 1:265
  Ogan-Besemah, 5:199
  Old Believers, 6:294
  Ontong Java, 2:255
  Oriya, 3:218
  Orochi, 6:295
  Orokaiva, 2:258
  Ossetes, 6:301
  Otavalo, 7:255
  Otomí of the Sierra, 8:202
  Ozarks, 1:282
  Pahari, 3:223
  Palaung, 5:203
  Palu'e, 5:209
  Pandit of Kashmir, 3:226
  Parsi, 3:229-230
  Pawnee, 1:285
  Pedi, 9:270, 271
  Piaroa, 7:278
  Piemontese Sinti, 4:201
  Pima-Papago, 1:290
  Pokot, 9:283, 283
  Pomo, 1:295
  Provencal, 4:211
  Puerto Ricans, 8:223
  Pukapuka, 2:272
  Pume, 7:285
  Purum, 3:244
  Qashqa'i, 9:287
  Qiang, 6:487
  Rastafarians, 8:229
  Rom, 1:306
  Rom of Czechoslovakia, 4:219
  Russian peasants, 6:313
  Saami, 4:222
  Sakalava, 9:298
  Salasaca, 7:291
  Samal, 5:221
  Samoa, 2:289
  Santal, 3:255
  Sara, 9:307
  Saramaka, 7:298
  Sasak, 5:227
  Sengseng, 2:298
  Seri, 8:235
  Shahsevan, 9:310
  Shakers, 1:316

Shavante, 7:301
She, 6:491
Sherpa, 3:259-260
Shors, 6:331
Siberiaki, 6:334
Siberian Estonians, 6:337
Siberian Germans, 6:339
Siberian Tatars, 6:342
Siona-Secoya, 7:309
Siwai, 2:304
Slav Macedonians, 4:241
Slovaks, 4:245
Sora, 3:270
Sorbs, 4:253-254
Sumu, 8:239
Suya, 7:317
Svans, 6:346
Swazi, 9:332
Tabasarans, 6:349
Tagalog, 5:251
Tai Lue, 5:256
Tajiks, 6:354
Tamil, 3:279
Tanaina, 1:336, 337
Tanana, 1:340
Tanna, 2:315
Tarahumara, 8:242
Tarascans, 8:246
Tasmanians, 2:317
Tats, 6:360
Tauade, 2:320
Temiar, 5:271, 272, 273
Temne, 9:345
Tepehua, 8:249
Tepehuan of Chihuahua, 8:254
Tepehuan of Durango, 8:258
Teton, 1:346
Ticuna, 7:330
Tigray, 9:349
Tiwi, 2:327, 329
Toda, 3:297, 298
Tofalar, 6:363
Tojolab'al, 8:263
Tokelau, 2:332
Tolai, 2:335
Tonga, 9:355
Tongareva, 2:341
Torres Strait Islanders, 2:347
Tory Islanders, 4:266
Trinidadians and Tobagonians, 8:269
Trobriand Islands, 2:351
tropical-forest foragers, 9:357
Truk, 2:353
Tsakhurs, 6:367
Tuareg, 9:369
Tujia, 6:499
Tupari, 7:341
Turkana, 9:373
Turks, 9:376
Tuvalu, 2:357
Tuvans, 6:374
Tzotzil and Tzeltal of Pantelhó, 8:278
Udmurt, 6:380
Uighur, 6:383, 385
Ukrainians, 6:393, 394
Ukrainians of Canada, 1:359
Ulithi, 2:360
Uzbeks, 6:398

Vedda, 3:303
Vlach Gypsies of Hungary, 4:271, 272
Volga Tatars, 6:402-403
Waimiri-Atroari, 7:345
Wáiwai, 7:348
Wape, 2:372
Warlpiri, 2:374
Washoe, 1:370
Wasteko, 8:303
Wayapi, 7:363
Welsh-Canadians, 1:127
West Greenland Inuit, 1:378
Woleai, 2:384
Yagua, 7:373
Yakan, 5:290
Yangoru Boiken, 2:390
Yao, 6:505
Yao of Thailand, 5:293
Yezidis, 6:411
Yörük, 9:396
Yuit, 1:92
Yukpa, 7:384
Zande, 9:399
Zarma, 9:406
Zhuang, 6:511
Zoque, 8:317
    see also Bards; Chanting; Dance; Musical
        instruments; Opera; Song duels
Musk-oxen hunting
    Copper Eskimo, 1:77
Muskrat hunting
    Maliseet, 1:211
Muslims. See Islam
Mustard production
    Burgundians, 4:46
    Santal, 3:253
Mutual-aid groups
    Aveyronnais, 4:24
    Nepali, 3:203
    see also Associations, clubs, and societies
Mutual assistance. See Exchange
    obligations
Myal
    African Americans, 1:13
Mysticism
    Baul, 3:26
    Bengali, 3:33, 34
    Jews, Arabic-speaking, 9:136
    Muslim, 3:185
    Nyinba, 3:213
Mythical ancestry
    Abor, 3:4
Mythology
    Labrador Inuit, 1:202
    Lillooet, 1:206
    Mataco, 7:227
    Slavey, 1:320
    Winnebago, 1:382
    see also Creation stories; Oral tradition
Myths (as socialization means)
    Kumeyaay, 1:195
    Ute, 1:362
    Western Apache, 1:373

Naguals
    Triqui, 8:272
Nahualism
    Amuzgo, 8:5, 6

Otomí of the Valley of Mezquital, 8:206
Pame, 8:208
Zapotec, 8:313
Nakwiari (ceremony)
    Tanna, 2:315
Naleoana (ceremony)
    Nguna, 2:244
Names
    age-set system
        Luyia, 9:206
        Okiek, 9:261
        Panare, 7:266
    ancestral
        Fipa, 9:100
        Luba of Shaba, 9:193
        Lunda, 9:198
        Munda, 3:184
        Pomo, 1:296
    ancestral by clan
        Luyia, 9:204
    animal nicknames
        Maliseet, 1:211
    avuncular-given
        Kagwahiv, 7:185
    biblical
        Syrian Christian of Kerala, 3:274
    changed after illness
        Chuvans, 6:83
    clan ownership
        Osage, 1:278
        Yuit, 1:391
        Zande, 9:401
    construction of
        Drung, 6:432
    for deceased
        Asurini, 7:62
        Baffinland Inuit, 1:30
        Central Yup'ik Eskimos, 1:57
        Inughuit, 1:161
        Jews, 1:169
        Kiowa, 1:189
        Macuna, 7:213, 215
        Sora, 3:270
        West Greenland Inuit, 1:379
        Yukuna, 7:388
    deceased's not mentioned
        Suruí, 7:314
        Washoe, 1:370
        Yawalapití, 7:380
        Yuqui, 7:395
        Zuni, 1:400
        see also Taboos, names
    delayed until child walks
        Nicobarese, 3:209
    depicting kin relations
        Bulgarian Gypsies, 4:41
    false name to deceive spirits
        Buriats, 6:68
    for family members
        Northern Irish (Protestant), 4:179
    for family member that infant resembles
        Pokot, 9:283
    first-name use
        Maltese, 4:168
    formal names not given
        Bribri-Cabécar, 8:29
    generational reversal of
        Frisians, 4:111

Names (cont'd)
  grandparent-given
    Guarayu, 7:174
    Wayapí, 7:363
  for grandparents
    Cyclades, 4:77
    Zaramo, 9:402
  Green Corn Ceremony
    Seminole of Oklahoma, 1:314
  in group identity
    Suyá, 7:316
  having own force
    Inughuit, 1:161
  Hindu-Muslim blended
    Meo, 3:174
  indicating birth order
    Osage, 1:278
  inheritance of ceremonial
    Nootka, 1:256
  inheritance of "great names"
    Khoi, 9:159
  inheritance ritual
    Ndembu, 9:240
  inherited
    Ashkenazim, 6:35
    Greeks, 6:143
    Kashinawa, 7:196
    Mayoruna, 7:234
    Shetlanders, 4:234
    Suyá, 7:316
    Welsh, 4:279
  kinship terms used in daily interactions
    West Greenland Inuit, 1:377
  marriage and
    Tikopia, 2:325
  multiple
    Ayoreo, 7:71
    Baffinland Inuit, 1:30
  naming as initiation rite
    Ndebele, 9:237
    Nubians, 9:248
    Suku, 9:322
    Tasmanians, 2:316
  naming ceremony
    Karen, 5:128
    Konso, 9:172
    Kota, 3:137
    Mashco, 7:226
    Nicobarese, 3:209
    Okiek, 9:261
    Rikbaktsa, 7:288
    Sherente, 7:303
    Sora, 3:270
    Suku, 9:322
    Xikrin, 7:369
    Yagua, 7:373
    Yukuna, 7:388
  naming group
    Kickapoo, 1:184
  nicknames
    Black Creoles of Louisiana, 1:38
    Faroe islanders, 4:100
    Greek-speaking Jews of Greece, 4:135
    Maliseet, 1:211
    Maltese, 4:168
    Manx, 4:170
    Portuguese, 4:207
    Welsh, 4:280

  praise name
    Luyia
      Bamiléké, 9:38
      Sakalava, 9:297
  of reincarnated persons
    Yuqui, 7:395
  renaming
    Cocama, 7:130
    Kagwahiv, 7:185
    Mashco, 7:226
    Mocoví, 7:241
    Panare, 7:266
    Sakalava, 9:296-297, 297
    Shavante, 7:301
    Sherente, 7:302, 303
    Yawalapití, 7:380
  for saints
    Northern Irish (Catholic), 4:179
  secret
    Asiatic Eskimos, 6:42
    Chambri, 2:32
    Iatmul, 2:100
  spouses alternate in choosing
    Highland Scots, 4:140
  taboos. See Taboos, names
  teknonymy
    Balinese, 5:37
    Bugis, 5:50
    Senoi, 5:237, 239
  tekonymy
    Danes, 4:89
  transmission of
    Craho, 7:137
    Marubo, 7:222
  true
    Ambae, 2:10
  version of father's as middle
    Old Believers, 1:273
  see also Surnames
Naojot rite (Zoroastrian)
  Parsi, 3:229
Napoleonic Code. See under Legal system
Naracotics. See Drugs; specific kinds
Nardughan (holiday)
  Kriashen Tatars, 6:212
Narrative poetry. See Bards; Epic
Narrators. See Storytelling
Natalocal residency
  Portuguese, 4:207
  Tory Islanders, 4:265
Natamate (ceremony)
  Nguna, 2:244
Nationalist movements
  Ashkenazic Jews, 4:16
  Baluchi, 3:23
  Basques, 4:30, 32
  Bengali, 3:29
  Cape Verdeans, 4:54, 56
  Chitpavan Brahman, 3:69
  Corsicans, 4:65, 66, 68
  Croat-Canadians, 1:120
  Croats, 4:72, 74
  French Canadians, 1:131
  Irish, 4:150, 151, 153
  Jurassians, 4:157-158
  Lowland Scots, 4:162
  Manx, 4:170
  Nagas, 3:187

  Pathan, 3:232
  Saami, 4:220
  Sikh, 3:261
  Slav Macedonians, 4:239, 241
  Slovaks, 4:242-243
  Slovenes, 4:247
  Tamil of Sri Lanka, 3:283
  Transylvanian ethnic groups, 4:269
  see also Civil war; Regionalist movements
Native American Church (Peyotism)
  Kiowa, 1:187, 188-189
  Northern Paiute, 1:265
  Northern Shoshone and Bannock, 1:267
  Osage, 1:278-279
  Ponca, 1:296
  Southern Paiute (and Chemehuevi), 1:332
  Taos, 1:343
  Teton, 1:346
  Ute, 1:362
  Washoe, 1:370
  Wichita, 1:379
  Winnebago, 1:380, 382
Natural phenomena totems
  Cocopa, 1:74
  Comanche, 1:75
  Eastern Shoshone, 1:106
  Kiowa, 1:188
  see also Animism
Nature spirits
  Anuta, 2:15
  Bai, 6:421
  Boazi, 2:30
  Bukidnon, 5:55
  Choiseul Island, 2:39
  Daribi, 2:48
  Eipo, 2:58
  Gainj, 2:73
  Guadalcanal, 2:91
  Hanunóo, 5:91
  Jingpo, 6:458
  Khmer, 5:137
  Kmhmu, 5:141
  Lahu, 5:153
  Lisu, 6:466
  Mansi, 6:254
  Mekeo, 2:200
  Miao, 6:472
  Mingrelians, 6:265
  Mnong, 5:184-185
  Orochi, 6:295
  Orokolo, 2:260
  Palu'e, 5:208
  Russian peasants, 6:313
  Saami, 6:324
  Shan, 5:241
  T'in, 5:279
  Toraja, 5:283
  Uighur, 6:384
  Ukrainian peasants, 6:388
  Ulithi, 2:360
  Usino, 2:363
  Wa, 6:503
  Wovan, 2:387
  Yakut, 6:406
  Yao of Thailand, 5:293
  Yi, 6:507
  see also Animism; Anthropomorphic
    beings

Nature worship
    Alur, 9:14-15
    Chiquitano, 7:118-119
    Huichol, 8:127
    Lobi-Dagarti peoples, 9:185
    Romanians, 4:214
    Suri, 9:326
    Tepehua, 8:249
    Washoe, 1:370
    Yukuna, 7:389
    Zoque, 8:317
Naturopathic medicine
    Germans, 4:124
    Provencal, 4:211
Nauruan Congregational Church
    Nauru, 2:237
Naval stores
    Finns, 4:102
Navigational skills
    Basques, 4:30
Nayar, 3:198
Necromancy
    Creoles of Nicaragua, 8:86
    Khasi, 3:126
Needlework
    appliqué
        Bukidnon, 5:55
        Lahu, 5:154
        Oriya, 3:218
    crochet
        Guajiro, 7:168
    needlepoint
        Azoreans, 4:27
        Zuni, 1:398
    openwork
        Canarians, 4:51
    see also Embroidery; Knitting; Tapestry
Neighbors
    as basic social unit
        Tiroleans, 4:263-264
    conflicts and feuds
        Pasiegos, 4:191
    obligations of
        Frisians, 4:111, 112
    social importance of
        English, 4:97
        Romanians, 4:214
    specific terms of address
        Frisians, 4:111
    see also Communal practices
Neolocal residency. See under Residence
    (newly married)
Nestorianism, 9:241-244
    Assyrians, 9:27
    Chaldeans, 9:63-64
    Uighur, 6:382, 384, 499, 500
    Yezidis, 6:410
Net bags
    Ngawbe, 8:195
Net fishing
    Vedda, 3:301
Newborns. See Infants
New religions
    Japanese in Canada, 1:98
    Japanese in the United States, 1:103
New Year (holiday)
    Abkhazians, 6:9
    Aleuts, 6:18

Andis, 6:27
Armenians, 6:31
Bukharan Jews, 6:65
Dai, 6:427
Dargins, 6:98
Georgians, 6:135
Hakka, 6:439
Hani, 6:451
Hmong, 5:94
Japanese, 5:109
Jingpo, 6:459
Jino, 6:460
Khmer, 5:137
Korean, 5:148
Kubachins, 6:219
Lao, 5:159
Lisu, 5:166;6:466
Maonan, 6:468
Miao, 6:472
Mountain Jews, 6:273
Orcadians, 4:188
Oroquen, 6:483
Pamir peoples, 6:304, 306
Russians, 6:317
Svans, 6:346
Tai Lue, 5:256
Tajiks, 6:354
Talysh, 6:357
Uighur, 6:384
Ukrainians, 6:394
Uzbeks, 6:398
Volga Tatars, 6:402
Yao of Thailand, 5:292
Yezidis, 6:410
Nhialac divinity
    Dinka, 9:71
Nichirenshu Buddhism
    Burakumin, 5:63
Nicknaming. See under Names
Nieri (ceremony)
    Tanna, 2:315
Night courting
    Danes, 4:89
    Finns, 4:103
Nighthawk Keetoowah movement
    Cherokee, 1:62
Nightworld (afterlife)
    Cherokee, 1:62
Nirvana belief
    Pahari, 3:222
Noah myth
    Wiyot, 1:385
Nobility
    Austrians, 4:20
    Nootka, 1:257
    Pacific Eskimo, 1:283
    Triqui, 8:271
    Tsimshian, 1:354
    Tuareg, 9:368
    see also Royalty; Status, basis of
Nogho Tilabwe (ceremony)
    Malekula, 2:166
Nomads
    Ache, 7:4
    Agta, 5:4
    Altaians, 6:21, 22
    Aranda, 2:16
    Arapaho, 1:26

Assiniboin, 1:27
Ayoreo, 7:69
Bajau, 5:30-35
Balkars, 6:52
Bashkirs, 6:55
Beaver, 1:35
Bedouins, 9:43
Blackfoot, 1:41
Bulgarian Gypsies, 4:41
Buriats, 6:66, 67, 68
Chimane, 7:112
Chimila, 7:114
Chukchee, 6:76
Chuvans, 6:81
Comanche, 1:75
Copper Eskimo, 1:76-77
Cree, 1:80, 81
Crow, 1:83
Cuiva, 7:143
Dolgan, 6:100
Even, 6:117
Evenki (Northern Tungus), 6:120
Ewenki, 6:433
Gagauz, 6:125
Gorotire, 7:162
Gypsies, 6:145
Havasupai, 1:145
Hill Pandaram, 3:99
Itelmen, 6:152
Jamináwa, 7:180
Jat, 3:110, 111, 113
Kalmyks, 6:155, 156
Kamilaroi, 2:104
Kanjar, 3:118-121
Kazak, 6:460
Kazakhs, 6:173, 174, 176
Khakas, 6:187
Khanty, 6:190
Kiowa, 1:187
Kirgiz, 6:461
Kolisuch'ok, 5:142, 144
Komi, 6:203
Koryaks and Kerek, 6:207, 208, 209
Kurds, 6:226
Kyrgyz, 6:228
Laz, 6:240
Mardudjara, 2:179
May, 5:177
Mayoruna, 7:234
Menominee, 1:220, 221
Mongols, 6:474
Nenets, 6:278
Nganasan, 6:280
Nivkh, 6:283
Nogays, 6:287, 289
Orok, 6:296
Pathan, 3:231, 232
Penan, 5:209
Saami, 4:220, 221, 222;6:323
sea nomads of the Andaman, 5:227-229
Selung/Moken, 5:230
Semang, 5:234
Slovensko Roma, 4:250, 251
Spanish Rom, 4:254, 255
Talysh, 6:355
Tasaday, 5:259-261
Tasmanians, 2:316
Tatars, 6:492

Nomads (cont'd)
  Teton, 1:344, 345
  Tibetans, 6:494
  Tofalar, 6:362, 363
  Tonkawa, 1:354
  Tor, 2:342
  Turkmens, 6:369, 371
  Tuvans, 6:373
  Uzbeks, 6:396
  Vlachs, 4:273-274, 274-275
  Xoraxané Romá, 4:281-283
  Yavapai, 1:386
  Yezidis, 6:408
  Yukagir, 6:412
  Yuqui, 7:391
  see also Itinerants; Seminomads
Nonc (avuncular figure)
  Black Creoles of Louisiana, 1:38
Nonconfrontation. See Avoidance
Noninheriting son
  Chin, 3:65
Noninterference (as social value)
  Slavey, 1:320
Nonmartial peoples. See Nonviolence
Nonpastoral nomads. See Itinerants
Nonrepresentational arts
  Chin, 3:67
Nonstratified society. See Egalitarianism
Nonviolence
  Akha, 5:13
  Amish, 1:18, 20
  Danes, 4:90
  Doukhobors, 1:90, 92
  Fipa, 9:99
  Hopi, 1:150
  Hutterites, 1:153
  Kongo, 9:168
  Luba of Shaba, 9:192
  Mennonites, 1:217, 219
  Shakers, 1:316
  Sherpa, 3:259
  Southern Paiute (and Chemehuevi),
    1:332
  Tewa Pueblos, 1:349
  Toda, 3:297
  Washoe, 1:367, 369
  see also Avoidance
North Star belief
  Tanaina, 1:336
Nosepieces
  Matsigenka, 7:232
Nose piercing and rings. See under Body
    piercing
Notxestoz (society)
  Cheyenne, 1:65
Novruz bairam [bayram] (holiday)
  Azerbaijani Turks, 6:50
  Tats, 6:360
Nuclear family. See under Family
Nudity
  as asceticism
    Sadhu, 3:251
  belt only (and cloak in cold weather)
    Kaingáng, 7:186
    Xokléng, 7:370
  body painting and ornamentation
    Chayahuita, 7:111
    Guarayu, 7:174

Hoti, 7:175
  Paresí, 7:269
  Sherente, 7:303
  Tanimuka, 7:319
  Waurá, 7:360
  Witoto, 7:365
  Yekuana, 7:381
breast-baring
  Noanamá, 7:252
  Pomo, 1:294
  Thakur, 3:293
buttock-baring
  Thakur, 3:293
ceremonial
  Pauserna, 7:270
children
  Itonama, 7:179
male nakedness
  Pomo, 1:294
nakedness until missionization
  Cashibo, 7:104
penis shield
  Apiaká, 7:48-49
  Ayoreo, 7:70
  Lobi-Dagarti peoples, 9:186
  Paresí, 7:269
  Shavante, 7:301
  Tapirapé, 7:321
pubic covers
  Hoti, 7:175
women
  Karihona, 7:192
  Shavante, 7:301
Numayams (descent groups)
  Kwakiutl, 1:198, 199
Numbers
  ritual
    Ingalik, 1:158
  symbolism
    Zaramo, 9:402
Number systems
  Divehi, 3:76
Nuns
  Basques, 4:32
  Nyinba, 3:213
  Sherpa, 3:259
Nursing (lactation). See Breast-feeding
Nursing profession
  Santal, 3:253
  Syrian Christian of Kerala, 3:273
Nut collection
  Amahuaca, 7:34
  Araweté, 7:56
  Asurini, 7:61
  Chácobo, 7:105
  Cinta Larga, 7:127
  Kaingáng, 7:188
  Moré, 7:242
  Paresí, 7:269
  Rikbaktsa, 7:287
  Tacana, 7:318
  Xikrin, 7:367
  Xokléng, 7:370
Nut production
  Old Believers, 1:273
  Sicilians, 4:236
  Sundanese, 5:247
Nuts. See specific kinds

Nyink (ceremony)
  Gainj, 2:73

Oath taking
  Albanians, 4:5, 6, 7
  Nagas, 3:190
  Thadou, 3:289
Oats growing
  Bavarians, 4:33
  Belarussians, 6:60
  Buriats, 6:67
  Daur, 6:429
  Gaels (Irish), 4:115
  Highland Scots, 4:139
  Hutterites, 1:153
  Latvians, 6:237
  Maris, 6:257
  Miao, 6:470
  Mongols, 6:474
  Nogays, 6:287
  Northern Irish, 4:178
  Orcadians, 4:186
  Poles, 4:203
  Serbs, 4:230
  Shetlanders, 4:233
  Shors, 6:330
  Tory Islander, 4:265
  Tuvans, 6:373
  Udmurt, 6:380
  Welsh, 4:279
Obeah
  Bahamians, 8:20
  Creoles of Nicaragua, 8:86
  Jamaicans, 8:139
  Montserratians, 8:181
  Saint Lucians, 8:231-232
Obedience (as social trait)
  Danes, 4:90
Oblation, 3:70
  Garo, 3:84
  Gond, 3:87
  Huichol, 8:126
  see also Sacrifice
Obligations. See under Exchange
Oboe playing
  Bretons, 4:40
  Bulgarian Gypsies, 4:41
Obscenity use
  Sidi, 3:261
Occult. See Mediums; Spirits, belief in;
    Supernatural
Occupations
  hereditary
    Koya, 3:140
    Luyia, 9:204
    Pahari, 3:220
    Rajput, 3:249
    Swazi, 9:330
    Swiss, Italian, 4:260
    Tonga, 2:337
    see also Castes; Itinerants; Priests,
      hereditary
  specialization
    castes, Hindu, 3:57
    Corsicans, 4:67
    Flemish, 4:106
    Mandan, 1:214
    Nepali, 3:202, 203

Newar, 3:206-208
Oraon, 3:214
Pahari, 3:220-221
Pandit of Kashmir, 3:224
peripatetics, 3:234
Punjabi, 3:239
Untouchables, 3:299
Zamindar, 3:307
see also specific occupations
Ocumo growing
Warao, 7:357
Offerings. See Oblation; Sacrifice
Oil (petroleum) industry
Arubans, 8:11, 12
Azerbaijani Turks, 6:49
Chechen-Ingush, 6:73
Curaçao, 8:96, 97
East Indians in Trinidad, 8:105
Edo, 9:79
Estonian, 6:113
Highland Scots, 4:140
Orcadians, 4:186-187
Persians, 9:279
Shetlanders, 4:233
Sicilians, 4:236
Welsh, 4:279
Oil (petroleum) rights ownership
Osage, 1:277
Seminole of Oklahoma, 1:315
Oils
marine animal
Kwakiutl, 1:198
pressing
Bene Israel, 3:27
see also Olive growing and processing; Palm
products
Ojha (healer)
Santal, 3:255
Okka (family unit)
Coorg, 3:74
Ok phansa (festival)
Lao Isan, 5:163
Old-age provisions. See Elderly; Elder respect;
Widow, care provisions; Ultimo-
geniture
Old Believers (Orthodox). See Russian Old
Rite
Older man-young woman marriage. See under
Marriage
Older people. See Elderly; Elder respect;
Household
Older woman-young man marriage. See under
Marriage
Oldest son inheritance. See Primogeniture
Old Lady Salt (deity)
Zuni, 1:399
Old Lady White Stone (supernatural)
Yavapai, 1:386
Old One (creator)
Shuswap, 1:318
Old Woman Who Never Dies (sacred
being)
Mandan, 1:215
Olive growing and processing
Andalusians, 4:10
Basques, 4:31
Calabrese, 4:49
Catalans, 4:62

Cretans, 4:70
Cyclades, 4:77
Dalmatians, 4:86
Ionians, 4:149
Montenegrins, 4:172
Occitans, 4:183, 184
Peloponnesians, 4:193
Provencal, 4:210
Sicilians, 4:236
Tuscans, 4:269
Omaha kinship terminology. See under
Kinship terminology
Ombudsman
Danes, 4:90
Omens, importance of
Albanians, 4:7
Gujarati, 3:92
Huron, 1:152
Karihona, 7:193
Khasi, 3:124
Krikati/Pukobye, 7:205
Otavalo, 7:255
Tamana, 1:340
Tanaina, 1:336-337
Zuni, 1:400
One-stringed viol
Dalmatians, 4:87
"Ones Who Hold Our Roads" (deities)
Zuni, 1:399
Only Man (culture hero)
Hidatsa, 1:147
Open-air markets. See Markets and fairs
"Opening of the Road" (ceremony)
Rom, 1:306
Openwork. See under Needlework
Opera
Azerbaijani Turks, 6:50
Chinese in Southeast Asia, 5:77, 77
Flemish, 4:108
Oriya, 3:218
Vietnamese, 5:287
Volga Tatars, 6:403
Yakut, 6:407
Zhuang, 6:511, 511
Opium growing
Bai, 6:419
Gelao, 6:435
Hmong, 5:93
Jingpo, 6:456
Lisu, 5:164, 165
Mejbrat, 2:195
Pahari, 3:220
Pamir peoples, 6:305
Pathan, 3:231
Qiang, 6:485
Wa, 6:502
Yao of Thailand, 5:291
Opium use
Hezhen, 6:452
Kota, 3:135
Oroquen, 6:482
Rajput, 3:249
Selung/Moken, 5:231
Optical products
Germans, 4:122
German Swiss, 4:125
Oracles
Dogon, 9:73

Frisians, 4:112
Nyinba, 3:213
Oral tradition
Abor, 3:5
Acadians, 1:9
Albanians, 4:6, 7
Aveyronnais, 4:26
Baiga, 3:21
Baluchi, 3:23, 24
Bedouin, 9:46
Bengali Shakta, 3:35-36
Bulgarian Gypsies, 4:41
Burusho, 3:56
Catawba, 1:54
Central Yup'ik Eskimos, 1:59
Copper Eskimo, 1:79
Cornish, 4:64
Corsicans, 4:68
Cree, 1:80, 82
Croats, 4:75
Doukhobor, 1:93
Fulani, 9:103
Hausa, 9:114
Iban, 5:98
Icelander-Canadians, 1:123
Ingalik, 1:158
Irish Travellers, 4:156
Jews of Kurdistan, 9:147
Karaites, 9:156
Karok, 1:176, 177
Khasi, 3:126
Kikuyu, 9:162
Kol, 3:131
Koya, 3:140
Kumeyaay, 1:195
Lakher, 3:147
Latinos, 1:206
Lepcha, 3:149
Lowland Scots, 4:163
Lumbee, 1:209
Mikir, 3:176
Mongo, 9:226
Montenegrins, 4:174
Nagas, 3:191
Northern Paiute, 1:264
Occitans, 4:185
Pokot, 9:283
Purum, 3:244
Rajput, 3:249
Rom, 1:306
Santal, 3:255
Sephardic Jews, 4:228
Serbs, 4:232
Somalis, 9:318
Sorbs, 4:253
Southern Paiute (and Chemehuevi), 1:332
Thadou, 3:289
Toda, 3:297, 298
Vlachs, 4:275
Washoe, 1:370
Western Apache, 1:373
Yuit, 1:392
see also Bards; Creation stories; Epic;
Storytelling
Oratorical skill
Cuiva, 7:145
Kwakiutl, 1:200
Maká, 7:217

Oratorical skill (cont'd)
  Mataco, **7**:229
  Mehinaku, **7**:238
  Mendi, **2**:205
  Rom, **1**:306
  Rotuma, **2**:283
  Samoa, **2**:289
  Shipibo, **7**:305
  Suya, **7**:316
  Truk, **2**:353
  Tupari, **7**:340
  Tuvalu, **2**:357
  Wapisiana, **7**:355
  Yangoru Boiken, **2**:390
  Yanomamö, **7**:377
  see also under Leadership qualities
Oraza (holiday)
  Tabasarans, **6**:351
Orchards. *See* Fruit growing; *specific fruits*
Ordeal, trials by. *See* Trial by ordeal
Organizations. *See* Associations, clubs, and
    societies
Organized crime. *See under* Crime
Orientation group
  Blackfoot, **1**:42
Origin myths. *See* Creation stories
Oriya kinship terminology. *See under* Kinship
    terminology
Ornamentation, body. *See* Body painting and
    ornamentation; Body piercing
Orthodox Christianity
  Abkhazians, **6**:9
  Ajarians, **6**:13, 15
  Albanians, **4**:7, 8
  Altaians, **6**:23
  Arab Americans, **1**:24, 25
  Avars, **6**:26
  Bashkirs, **6**:55
  Belarussians, **6**:59
  Bulgarian Gypsies, **4**:41, 42
  Bulgarians, **4**:45
  Carpatho-Rusyn-Americans, **1**:109
  Carpatho-Rusyns, **6**:71
  Chechen-Ingush, **6**:75
  Chuvans, **6**:80, 81, 82
  Chuvash, **6**:85
  Copts, **9**:68-69
  Dalmatians, **4**:87
  Dolgan, **6**:100, 102
  Estonian, **6**:111, 114
  Even, **6**:119
  Evenki (Northern Tungus), **6**:123
  Ewenki, **6**:434
  Gagauz, **6**:125, 126
  Gypsies, **6**:147, 148
  Ingilos, **6**:149, 150, 151
  Ionians, **4**:150
  Itelmen, **6**:152
  Kalmyks, **6**:157
  Karelians, **6**:169, 171
  Ket, **6**:183, 184
  Khakas, **6**:188
  Khanty, **6**:189, 192
  Khevsur, **6**:196
  Komi, **6**:203, 204
  Koreans, **6**:205, 206
  Kriashen Tatars, **6**:210, 211, 212
  Latvians, **6**:238

  Maris, **6**:256, 258
  Maronites, **9**:218-220
  Mingrelians, **6**:262, 265
  Moldovans, **6**:269
  Montenegrins, **4**:173
  Mount Athos, **4**:174-177
  Nenets, **6**:279
  Nivkh, **6**:285
  Palestinians, **9**:266
  Peloponnesians, **4**:194
  Poles, **4**:204
  Romanian-Canadians, **1**:125
  Romanians, **4**:214
  Saami, **6**:322, 324
  Sarakatsani, **4**:224
  Selkup, **6**:327
  Serbian-Canadians, **1**:126
  Siberiaki, **6**:334
  Slav Macedonians, **4**:241
  Svans, **6**:343, 346
  Tanaina, **1**:337
  Tigray, **9**:348
  Transylvanian ethnic groups, **4**:268
  Udis, **6**:375, 378
  Udmurt, **6**:379, 380, 381
  Ukrainian peasants, **6**:387
  Ukrainians, **6**:391, 394
  Ukrainians of Canada, **1**:358, 359
  Vlachs, **4**:275
  Yakut, **6**:404, 406
  see also Uniate Catholicism
Orthodox Christianity (Greek Orthodox)
  Albanians, **4**:7
  Arab Americans, **1**:25
  Cretans, **4**:68, 69, 71
  Cyclades, **4**:78
  Greek-Americans, **1**:112
  Greek-Canadians, **1**:122
  Greek Cypriots, **4**:81
  Greeks, **4**:132, 133, 134;**6**:141, 143,
      144
Orthodox Christianity (Russian Old Rite)
  Don Cossacks, **6**:106
  Old Believers, **1**:272-273, 274;**6**:290, 291,
      294
  Russians, **6**:315
  Siberiaki, **6**:334
Orthodox Christianity (Russian Orthodox)
  Aleuts, **1**:16;**6**:17, 18
  Buriats, **6**:68
  Central Yup'ik Eskimos, **1**:56, 58
  Don Cossacks, **6**:106
  Finns, **4**:104
  Georgians, **6**:129, 130, 135
  Pacific Eskimo, **1**:283
  Russian-Americans, **1**:116
  Russian Canadians, **1**:126
  Russian peasants, **6**:312, 312-313
  Russians, **6**:314, 317
Orthodox Christianity (Syrian Orthodox)
  Arab Americans, **1**:25
  Ssyrian Christian of Kerala, **3**:274
Orthodoxy markers
  Sikh, **3**:261
Ossuary. *See* Mortuary practices
Ostal (family unit)
  Aveyronnais, **4**:25
Ostracism. *See under* Social control measures

Ostrich hunting
  Sleb, **9**:315
Otak (male social center)
  Sindhi, **3**:263
Ots bay (festival)
  Avars, **6**:46
Our Grandmother (supreme being)
  Shawnee, **1**:317
Outcastes
  Burakumin, **5**:58-63
  Kolisuch'ok, **5**:141-144
Owl boards
  Frisians, **4**:111
Ox Birthday Festival
  Zhuang, **6**:511
Oxen raising
  Bai, **6**:419
  Belarussians, **6**:60
  Bugis, **5**:49
  Ewenki, **6**:433
  Karen, **5**:126
  Ket, **6**:183
  Khinalughs, **6**:198
  Lisu, **6**:465
  Mulam, **6**:476
  Ogan-Besemah, **5**:198
  Sasak, **5**:226
  Tagalog, **5**:249
  Yugur, **6**:508

Pacifism. *See* Aggressiveness, as undesirable
    trait; Avoidance; Nonviolence
Paddy growing. *See* Agriculture, wet
    cultivation; Rice growing
Pai (celebration)
  Tai Lue, **5**:256
Paint (as magical substance)
  Abelam, **2**:6
Painted glass
  Croats, **4**:75
Painted tilework
  Sindhi, **3**:263
Painting of body. *See* Body painting and
    ornamentation
Painting of face. *See* Face painting
Paintings
  Aranda, **2**:18
  Ashkenazim, **6**:36
  Belarussians, **6**:61
  Carpatho-Rusyns, **6**:71
  Chinese in Southeast Asia, **5**:77
  Dai, **6**:428
  Dutch, **4**:94
  Estonian, **6**:115
  Ewenki, **6**:434
  Flemish, **4**:108
  Georgians, **6**:136
  Greeks, **4**:133-134
  Han, **6**:448
  Japanese, **5**:110
  Khmer, **5**:138
  Korean, **5**:148
  Kwoma, **2**:136
  Mafulu, **2**:153
  Minangkabau, **5**:184
  Munda, **3**:184
  Mundugumor, **2**:220
  Murngin, **2**:224, 227

Navajo, 1:253
Ngatatjara, 2:241
Ossetes, 6:301
Pintupi, 2:267
Poles, 6:309
Russian peasants, 6:313
Siberian Tatars, 6:342
Sio, 2:301
Sora, 3:270
Svans, 6:346
Swedes, 4:258
Tai Lue, 5:256
Tiwi, 2:329
Volga Tatars, 6:402
Wa, 6:503
Walloons, 4:278
Warlpiri, 2:374
Wik Mungkan, 2:379
Yakut, 6:407
Zhuang, 6:511
see also Decorative arts; Icon painting;
    Murals; Rock art; Visual arts
Pajonalino (Campa group), 7:91
Pakhtunwali (honor code)
    Pathan, 3:232-233
Palm, sago. See Sago palm
Palm fruits
    Desana, 7:152
    Marubo, 7:222
    Moré, 7:243
    Nubians, 9:246, 247
    Panare, 7:265
    Pemon, 7:271
    Piapoco, 7:274
    Piaroa, 7:276
    Siona-Secoya, 7:307
    Tacana, 7:318
    Tuareg, 9:369
    Wáiwai, 7:346
    Waorani, 7:352
    Wayãpi, 7:361
    Witoto, 7:364
    Yagua, 7:372
    Yuqui, 7:392
Palm products
    Ache, 7:4
    Cape Verdeans, 4:55
    Ibibio, 9:119
    Igbo, 9:121
    Mongo, 9:226
    Nubians, 9:247
    Pende, 9:272
Palm products (wine)
    Mijikenda, 9:224
    Suku, 9:321
    Yakö, 9:383
    Zande, 9:398
Palm-reading
    Piemontese Sinti, 4:200
    Sadhu, 3:251
Palm weaving
    Chocho, 8:63
    Chontal of Tabasco, 8:68
    Emberá and Wounaan, 8:109
    Popoloca, 8:216
Panchayat. See Council
Pandanus
    Marshall Islands, 2:192

Raroia, 2:276
Tauade, 2:318
Tongareva, 2:340
Tuvalu, 2:355
Wamira, 2:365
Panludan (festival)
    Hanunóo, 5:91
Pano weaving
    Cape Verdeans, 4:55
Panpa (ceremony)
    Warlpiri, 2:374
Pantheism
    Bilaan, 5:42
    Irula, 3:104, 108
    Osage, 1:278
    Rotuma, 2:283
    see also Animism; Nature spirits; Polytheism
Pantomime
    Yagua, 7:373
Panulak Balah (ceremony)
    Tausug, 5:264
Papa belief
    Pandit of Kashmir, 3:226
Paper art
    Kwakiutl, 1:198
Papermaking industry
    Auvergnats, 4:22
    Slovenes, 4:247
Papier-mâché work
    Oriya, 3:218
Paradise. See Afterlife
Parallel-cousin marriage. See under Cousin
    marriage
Parapsychology
    Hare, 1:142
    kashubians, 4:159
    Russians, 6:317
Pardons (religious festival)
    Bretons, 4:39-40
Pargana (chief)
    Santal, 3:254
Parliamentary democracy. See Democratic
    political organization
Partible inheritance. See under Inheritance
Partitu (subgroup)
    Corsicans, 4:68
Partnerships
    Copper Eskimo, 1:78
    Ingalik, 1:157, 158
Parvati (female deity)
    Maratha, 3:170
Passing (racial)
    Black Creoles of Louisiana, 1:37-38
Passover (holiday)
    Ashkenazim, 6:36
    Bukharan Jews, 6:65
    Karaites, 6:165
    Lithuanian Jews, 6:246
    Mountain Jews, 6:273
Pastoralism. See Herding
Pastoral nomadism. See Seminomads
Paternal absences. See Father, absences; Men,
    emigration
Paternal aunt. See Aunt, paternal
Paternal uncle. See Uncle, paternal
Paternity. See Father
Pathen (creator deity)
    Thadou, 3:289

Patience (as social virtue)
    Hidsata, 1:147
    Montagnais-Naskapi, 1:245
Patriarchal family structure
    Abor, 3:4
    Acholi, 9:5
    Afar, 9:8
    Albanian-Americans, 1:107
    Amhara, 9:19
    Assyrians, 9:27
    Auvergnats, 4:22
    Bamiléké, 9:39
    Basseri, 9:41
    Bavarians, 4:34
    Bhuiya, 3:44
    Cape Verdeans, 4:55
    Corsicans, 4:67
    Cypriots, 4:80
    Garia, 3:81
    Gond, 3:85
    Greek-speaking Jews of Greece, 4:135
    Guarijío, 8:118
    Highland Scots, 4:141
    Hutterites, 1:154
    Italian Mexicans, 8:131
    Jews of Algeria, 9:138
    Jews of Kurdistan, 9:146
    Kanuri, 9:153
    Karaites, 9:155
    Latinos, 1:205
    Maasai, 9:208
    Magar, 3:158
    Mende, 9:223
    Nambudiri Brahman, 3:193
    Navajo, 1:252
    Old Believers, 1:274
    Pathan, 3:232
    Persians, 9:279
    Portuguese, 4:207
    Portuguese-Americans, 1:115
    Sarakatsani, 4:224
    Sinhalese, 3:265
    Slovenes, 4:248
    Slovensko Roma, 4:151
    South and Southeast Asians of Canada,
        1:323
    Spanish Rom, 4:255
    Swedes, 4:258
    Tamil of Sri Lanka, 3:281
    Telugu, 3:286
    Tlapanec, 8:259
    Toda, 3:296
    Tuscans, 4:270
    Vlachs, 4:274, 275
    Zoroastrians, 9:408
    see also Descent, patrilineal
Patriclan
    Albanians, 4:5, 6
    Cretans, 4:71
    Irula, 3:106, 107, 108
    Jat, 3:112
    Mauritian, 3:171
    Nepali, 3:203
    Toda, 3:297
Patrilineal descent. See Descent,
    patrilineal
Patrilocal residency. See under Residence
Patrimony. See Inheritance

Patriotic symbols
Hungarians, **4**:145
Patronage
Piemontese, **4**:199
Patron-client system
Albanians, **4**:5
Andalusians, **4**:12
Cretans, **4**:71
Hare, **1**:141
Jat, **3**:112
Madeirans, **4**:165
Mauritian, **3**:172
Oriya, **3**:217
Pahari, **3**:220, 221
Piemontese, **4**:199
Sarakatsani, **4**:224
Sardinians, **4**:227
Sherpa, **3**:259
Sicilians, **4**:237
Tamil of Sri Lanka, **3**:283
Tuscans, **4**:270
Vellala, **3**:304
see also Tenant farming
Patron saint
Auvergnats, **4**:23
Azoreans, **4**:28
Calabrese, **4**:50
Canarians, **4**:52
Cape Verdeans, **4**:56
Castilians, **4**:60, 61
Cyclades, **4**:78
Dalmatians, **4**:87
Galicians, **4**:119, 120
Latinos, **1**:206
Madeirans, **4**:166
Maltese, **4**:168, 169
Micmac, **1**:235
Montenegrins, **4**:173, 174
Portuguese, **4**:208
Serbs, **4**:231
Sicilians, **4**:237
Slav Macedonians, **4**:240
Tory Islanders, **4**:266
Welsh, **4**:280
Patronyms. *See* Surnames, patronymic
Pavula. *See* Microcaste
Pchum (ceremony)
Khmer, **5**:137
Peacefulness (as social trait). *See* Nonviolence
Peace lodge
Choctaw, **1**:72
Fox, **1**:129
Winnebago, **1**:382
Peach orchards
Zuni, **1**:397
Pea growing
Bahamians, **8**:18
Laks, **6**:234
Peanut growing
Maranao, **5**:177
Telugu, **3**:285
Wolof, **9**:378
Pear growing
Cretans, **4**:70
Pearls
Moluccans—South, **5**:188
Peasant carts
Sicilians, **4**:237

Peat
Frisians, **4**:110, 111
Gaels (Irish), **4**:115, 116
Highland Scots, **4**:139, 140
Irish, **4**:153
Orcadians, **4**:187
Shetlanders, **4**:233
Tory Islanders, **4**:265
Peddlers
Arab Americans, **1**:24
Bugis, **5**:49
Bulgarian Gypsies, **4**:41
Ghorbat, **9**:106
Gitanos, **4**:129
Irish Travelers, **1**:163
Irish Travellers, **4**:155
Jews, Arabic-speaking, **9**:135
Jews of Iran, **9**:140
Jews of Kurdistan, **9**:145
Kanjar, **3**:119, 120
Metis of Western Canada, **1**:226
Micmac, **1**:233
Pasiegos, **4**:189
peripatetics, **1**:287;**3**:235
peripatetics of Afghanistan, Iran, and
 Turkey, **9**:275
peripatetics of Iraq, Syria, Lebanon, Jordan,
 Israel, Egypt, Sudan, and Yemen,
 9:277
Piemontese Singi, **4**:200
Rom of Czechoslovakia, **4**:218, 219
Rominche, **4**:216
Sicilians, **4**:236
Tagalog, **5**:249
Peer pressure. *See* Social control measures,
 public opinion
Penis
incision (initiation)
 Wogeo, **2**:381
phallic symbolism
 Badaga, **3**:17
see also Circumcision
Penitence emphasis
Andalusians, **4**:12
Pentecost (holiday)
Carpatho-Rusyns, **6**:71
Old Believers, **6**:294
Pentecostalism
Anambé, **7**:42
Chipaya, **7**:116
Chorote, **7**:126
Germans, **6**:140
Gusii, **9**:110
Gypsies and caravan dwellers in the
 Netherlands, **4**:138
Jamaicans, **8**:139
Kongo, **9**:168
Maká, **7**:217
Mataco, **7**:229
Melpa, **2**:202
Montserratians, **8**:181
Nahuat of the Sierra de Puebla, **8**:193
Nyakyusa and Ngonde, **9**:254
Palikur, **7**:262, 263
Piemontese Sinti, **4**:201
Puerto Ricans, **8**:223
Rom, **1**:305, 306
Siberiaki, **6**:334

Tonga, **9**:355
Torres Strait Islanders, **2**:345, 347
Totonac, **8**:266
Transylvanian ethnic groups, **4**:268
Trinidadians and Tobagonians, **8**:269
Western Apache, **1**:373
Peppers growing
Loven, **5**:166
Peripatetics. *See* Itinerants
Personal god
Gond, **3**:86
Maratha, **3**:170
see also Guardian spirit
Personification. *See* Animism; Anthro-
 pomorphic beings
Person saints
Chatino, **8**:52
Petrochemical processing
Sardinians, **4**:226
Welsh, **4**:279
Petroglyphs. *See* Carved objects, rock
Petroleum. *See* Oil industry
Petty theft. *See* Theft
Pewter thread spinning
Saami, **4**:221
Peyote ritual
Huichol, **8**:127
Tarahumara, **8**:242
Washoe, **1**:370
see also Native American Church
Phallic symbol
Badaga, **3**:17
Pharmaceutical industry
Dutch, **4**:94
German Swiss, **4**:125
Pharmacopoeia
Santal, **3**:253, 255
Pheasant hunting
Highland Scots, **4**:140
Philanthropy. *See* Charitable giving
Photographs
arranged marriage by
 East Asians in Canada, **1**:96
 East Asians in the United States,
  1:99
bans
 Acadian, **1**:9
 Amish, **1**:20
Phratries
Baniwa-Curripaco-Wakuenai, **7**:77-78
Carrier, **1**:52
Crow, **1**:83
Delaware, **1**:86
Gururumba, **2**:93
Kapauku, **2**:106
Koya, **3**:140-141
Lakalai, **2**:141
Lau, **2**:144, 145
Marind-anim, **2**:183
Nenets, **6**:278
Osage, **1**:278
Rhadé, **5**:212
Sambia, **2**:285
Selepet, **2**:293
Siane, **2**:298
Tairora, **2**:309
Western Apache, **1**:372
Yangoru Boiken, **2**:389

Physical ordeals (initiation)
  Torres Strait Islanders, 2:346
  Usino, 2:363
Physical punishment. *See* Child discipline,
    corporal punishment; Punishment,
    corporal
Pictographic writing
  Han, 6:440
  Naxi, 6:480
  Shui, 6:491
  Yukagir, 6:411
Pictorial records. *See* Iconography
"Picture-bride" arrangements
  East Asians in Canada, 1:96
  East Asians in the United States, 1:99
Picture writing
  Cuna, 7:151
Piercing. *See* Body piercing
Pieve (village grouping)
  Corsicans, 4:68
Pig dealers
  Rom of Czechoslovakia, 4:218, 219
Pig fights
  Nicobarese, 3:210
Pig hunting
  Andamanese, 3:9, 10
Pigmentocracy
  Latinos, 1:205
Pig raising
  Abelam, 2:4
  Afro-Hispanic Pacific Lowlanders, 7:20
  Afro-Venezuelans, 7:26
  Alorese, 5:14
  Ata Tana 'Ai, 5:23
  Awá Kwaiker, 7:63
  Bai, 6:419
  Baiga, 3:19
  Bilaan, 5:42
  Bisaya, 5:42
  Bolaang Mongondow, 5:43
  Bontok, 5:46
  Cahita, 8:35
  Castilians, 4:59
  Central Thai, 5:70
  Chipaya, 7:115
  Corsicans, 4:66
  Dani, 2:43
  Drung, 6:432
  Dusun, 5:81
  Emberá, 7:155
  Endenese, 5:85
  Fore, 2:63
  Gahuku-Gama, 2:69
  Georgians, 6:132
  Greeks, 6:142
  Guahibo-Sikuani, 7:165
  Hani, 6:450
  Iban, 5:97
  Ilongot, 5:101
  Jingpo, 6:456
  Kalimantan Dayaks, 5:120
  Kalingas, 5:122
  Kaluli, 2:101
  Kapauku, 2:105
  Karen, 5:126
  Kashubians, 4:158
  Kédang, 5:131
  Kenyah-Kayan-Kajang, 5:133

  Khmer, 5:136
  Kmhmu, 5:139
  Kriashen Tatars, 6:211
  Lahu, 5:152;6:462
  Lak, 2:137
  Lamaholot, 5:155
  Lao, 5:158
  Lisu, 5:164
  Lithuanians, 6:250
  Mae Enga, 2:149
  Mafulu, 2:152
  Mailu, 2:154
  Malaita, 2:161
  Manchu, 6:467
  Mandak, 2:170
  Maring, 2:185
  Minahasans, 5:181
  Mingrelians, 6:263
  Miyanmin, 2:210
  Mnong, 5:184
  Mongols, 6:474
  Motu, 2:213
  Muong, 5:190
  Murut, 5:193
  Ndaonese, 5:194
  Ningerum, 2:246
  Orokaiva, 2:256
  Otavalo, 7:253
  Palaung, 5:201
  Pohnpei, 2:268
  Pukapuka, 2:271
  Pumi, 6:483
  Sagada Igorot, 5:216
  Sambia, 2:284
  Santa Cruz, 2:290
  Selepet, 2:293
  Siwai, 2:302
  Subanun, 5:244
  Svans, 6:344
  Tahiti, 2:305
  Tai Lue, 5:253
  Tairora, 2:308
  Taiwan aboriginal peoples, 5:257, 258
  Tangu, 2:311
  Tanna, 2:313
  Tauade, 2:318
  Telefolmin, 2:322
  Tetum, 5:276
  T'in, 5:278
  Tor, 2:342
  Toraja, 5:281, 282
  Tujia, 6:498
  Tuvalu, 2:355
  Vietnamese, 5:285
  Vlach Gypsies of Hungary, 4:271
  Wapisiana, 7:355
  Waropen, 2:376
  Wogeo, 2:380
  Woleai, 2:383
  Wovan, 2:385
  Yao of Thailand, 5:291
  Zhuang, 6:510
Pig ritual
  Nicobarese, 3:210
Pig sacrifice. *See* Sacrifice, pig
Pigs, as wealth. *See under* Money and wealth
Pilgrimages, 8:178
  Albanians, 4:7

  Azoreans, 4:28
  Baggara, 9:31
  Bedouin, 9:45
  Berbers of Morocco, 9:52
  Blue Lake
    Taos, 1:343
  Canarians, 4:52
  Costa Ricans, 8:81
  Cyclades, 4:78
  Galicians, 4:119, 120
  Huichol, 8:127
  Irish, 4:153
  Jews of Iran, 9:141
  Jews of Kurdistan, 9:146
  Lakandon, 8:154
  Lingayat, 3:153
  Maratha, 3:170
  Mauritian, 3:173
  Mazahua, 8:166
  Mount Athos, 4:174, 175, 176
  Muslim, 3:185
  Nubians, 9:248
  Pandit of Kashmir, 3:226
  Piemontese Sinti, 4:201
  Portuguese, 4:208
  Romanians, 4:214
  Sadhu, 3:251
  Shahsevan, 9:309
  Slovenes, 4:249
  Somalis, 9:318
  Tamil of Sri Lanka, 3:284
  Teda, 9:341
  Telugu, 3:286
  Toda, 3:297
  Tojolab'al, 8:263
  Tory Islanders, 4:266
  Turks, 9:376
  Tzotzil of San Bartolomé de los Llanos,
    8:290
  Vlach Gypsies of Hungary, 4:272
  Walloons, 4:277
  Yemenis, 9:390
  Yörük, 9:396
  Zoque, 8:317
  see also Shrines
Pilou pilou (ceremony)
  Ajië, 2:9
Pineapple growing
  East Asians of the United States, 1:99
  Mon, 5:189
Pine nut harvest
  Southern Paiute (and Chemehuevi),
    1:332
Pine resin production
  Castilians, 4:59
Pingna (supernatural)
  Caribou Inuit, 1:51
Piñon harvesting
  Northern Paiute, 1:263, 264
  Tubatulabal, 1:355
  Ute, 1:360
  Washoe, 1:367
  Western Apache, 1:371
  Western Shoshone, 1:374
Pipe making
  Iroquois, 1:165
  Maliseet, 1:211
  Northern Paiute, 1:263

Pipe-smoking ritual
  Miami, 1:232
  Teton, 1:346
  Yurok, 1:395
Piracy
  Bonerate, 5:44, 45
  Butonese, 5:67
  Cornish, 4:65
  Ilanon, 5:101
  Koreans in Japan, 5:149
  Laz, 6:239
  Palu'e, 5:205
  Samal, 5:220
  Selung/Moken, 5:231
  Tausug, 5:262, 264
  see also Brigandage
Pirism
  Bengali, 3:33
Pitri (ancestral spirit)
  Magar, 3:162
Plain living
  Amish, 1:18, 19
Plantain growing
  Afro-Bolivians, 7:8
  Afro-Colombians, 7:16
  Afro-Hispanic Pacific Lowlanders, 7:20
  Afro-Venezuelans, 7:26
  Aguaruna, 7:29
  Amuesha, 7:37
  Awá Kwaiker, 7:63
  Bamiléké, 9:38
  Barí, 7:83
  Bribri, Cabécar, 8:27
  Candoshi, 7:93
  Canelos Quichua, 7:99
  Cashibo, 7:104
  Chimila, 7:114
  Chocó, 7:122
  Chontal of Tabasco, 8:68
  Colorado, 7:131
  Culina, 7:146
  Edo, 9:79
  Emberá and Wounaan, 8:109
  Hoti, 7:175
  Huarayo, 7:177
  Jivaro, 7:182
  Kogi, 7:201
  Kuna, 8:147
  Macuna, 7:212
  Maisin, 2:158
  Marinahua, 7:220
  Maroni Carib, 7:220
  Marquesas Islands, 2:189
  Mashco, 7:225
  Matsigenka, 7:231
  Miskito, 8:171
  Noanamá, 7:251
  Páez, 7:257
  Panare, 7:265
  Pemon, 7:271
  Piro, 7:279
  Saramaka, 7:296
  Sharanahua, 7:299
  Shipibo, 7:304
  Siona-Secoya, 7:307
  Sirionó, 7:310
  Sumu, 8:237
  Tacana, 7:318

  Tahiti, 2:305
  Tanimuka, 7:318
  Ticuna, 7:328
  Waimiri-Atroari, 7:343
  Waorani, 7:352
  Witoto, 7:364
  Yagua, 7:372
  Yanomamö, 7:375
  Yuqui, 7:392
Plantation economy. *See* Agriculture,
    plantation; Agriculture, estate farm;
    products, e.g., Tea cultivation
Plants, medicinal. *See* Herbal, plant, and root
    medicine
Plant totems
  Cocopa, 1:74
Plasterers
  Black Creoles of Louisiana, 1:38
Plastics manufacture
  Welsh, 4:279
Plow agriculture. *See under* Agriculture
Plowshare taboo
  Kond, 3:133
Plutocracy
  Basques, 4:31
Pocamania (cult)
  Jamaicans, 8:139
Poetry
  Afro-Bolivians, 7:10
  Ainu, 5:10
  Andalusians, 4:12
  Ata Tana 'Ai, 5:26
  Atoni, 5:28
  Azerbaijani Turks, 6:48, 50
  Baggara, 9:31
  Bagobo, 5:29
  Baluchi, 3:24
  Basques, 4:32
  Bedouin, 9:46
  Bengali, 3:34
  Chechen-Ingush, 6:75
  Chimbu, 2:37
  Corsicans, 4:68
  Crimean Tatars, 6:94
  Dai, 6:427
  Daribi, 2:48
  Don Cossacks, 6:107
  Dungans, 6:111
  Evenki (Northern Tungus), 6:124
  Foi, 2:61
  Gaels (Irish), 4:117
  Galician, 4:121
  Gayo, 5:90
  Georgians, 6:136
  Han, 6:448
  Hausa, 9:114
  Japanese, 5:110
  Jatav, 3:115
  Jews, Arabic-speaking, 9:136
  Kalmyks, 6:157
  Karachays, 6:162
  Karaites, 6:165;9:156
  Karelians, 6:171, 172
  Kazakhs, 6:182
  Khakas, 6:188
  Khmer, 5:138
  Kiowa, 1:189
  Kmhmu, 5:141

  Komi, 6:203, 204
  Kumyks, 6:223
  Kurds, 6:227;9:177
  Kyrgyz, 6:231
  Laz, 6:240
  Mahar, 3:163, 165
  Makassar, 5:174
  Maratha, 3:170
  Minangkabau, 5:184
  Moldovans, 6:269
  Mongols, 6:476
  Nenets, 6:279
  Occitans, 4:185
  Ogan-Besemah, 5:199
  Ossetes, 6:301
  Palaung, 5:202, 203
  Pandit of Kashmir, 3:226
  Pathan, 3:233
  Persians, 9:280
  Poles, 6:309
  Provencal, 4:211
  Puerto Ricans, 8:223
  Punjabi, 3:242
  Russians, 6:314
  Rutuls, 6:321
  Santa Cruz, 2:292
  Sinhalese, 3:267
  Slovaks, 4:245
  Somalis, 9:318
  Svans, 6:346
  Swahili, 9:329
  Tagalog, 5:251
  Tajiks, 6:354
  Tats, 6:360
  Toda, 3:297, 298
  Truk, 2:353
  Tsakhurs, 6:367, 368
  Tuvans, 6:374
  Uighur, 6:384-385
  Ukrainians, 6:394
  Uzbeks, 6:396, 398
  Vietnamese, 5:287
  Welsh, 4:280
  Yörük, 9:396
  Zoque, 8:317
  see also Epic
Polar bear hunting
  Baffinland Inuit, 1:29
  Copper Eskimo, 1:77
  Yuit, 1:392
Polders
  Dutch, 4:93
  Flemish, 4:106
  Frisians, 4:110
Political organization
  absence of
    Yurok, 1:395
  age groups
    Afro-Colombians, 7:17
  coalitions
    Faroe Islanders, 4:99-100
  complex
    Hawaiians, 2:96
    Samoa, 2:288
  league
    iroquois, 1:164, 166
  male-only
    Sicilians, 4:237

peace and war divisions
  Shawnee, 1:317
theocracy
  Tewa Pueblos, 1:349
see also Council; Democratic political
    organization; Federalist political
    organization; Leadership; Monarchy;
    Socialism; Suffrage; Villages, as
    political units
Political succession. _See_ Leadership;
    Leadership qualities
Political violence
  Acholi, 9:6
  Basques, 4:30, 32
  Cypriotes, 4:81, 97
  English, 4:97
  Irish, 4:152
  Koya, 3:139
  Lakher, 3:147
  Montenegrins, 4:173
  Northern Irish, 4:180
  Serbs, 4:230, 231
  Sinhalese, 3:264-265, 266, 267
  Tamil of Sri Lanka, 3:281, 282, 283
  see also Civil war
Pollock fishing
  Shetlanders, 4:233
Pollution, environmental. _See_ Environmental
    degradation
Pollution beliefs. _See_ Purity and pollution
    codes
Pollution huts
  Irula, 3:104
Polyandry
  Ache, 7:5
  Akawaio, 7:32
  Aleuts, 6:18
  Eipo, 2:57
  Hare, 1:141
  Jat, 3:112
  Kapingamarangi, 2:109
  Lesu, 2:146
  Malekula, 2:165
  Mandak, 2:171
  Marquesas Islands, 2:190
  Marshall Islands, 2:193
  Moinba, 6:473
  Nayar, 3:199
  North Alaskan Eskimos, 1:260
  Northern Shoshone and Bannock, 1:267
  Pacific Eskimo, 1:283
  Pahari, 3:221, 222-223
  Semang, 5:235
  Tibetans, 6:495
  Waimiri-Atroari, 7:344
  Wáiwai, 7:347
  Waorani, 7:352
  Western Shoshone, 1:375
Polyandry (fraternal)
  Nepali, 3:203, 204
  Nyinba, 3:213
  Pahari, 3:221, 222-223
  Sherpa, 3:258
  Toda, 3:296
Polygamy
  Afro-Bolivians, 7:9
  Ajië, 2:8-9
  Aleut, 1:15

Asmat, 2:20
Baffinland Inuit, 1:30
Bhutanese, 3:45, 46
cattle ranchers of Huasteca, 8:43
Chukchee, 6:77
Cook Islands, 2:41
Delaware, 1:86
Dinka, 9:70
Edo, 9:80
Fali, 9:95
Gros Ventre, 1:134
Hani, 6:450
Itelmen, 6:153
Jews of Kurdistan, 9:146
Kalmyks, 6:156
Khanty, 6:191
Kipsigis, 9:164
Mafulu, 2:152
Makushi, 7:219
Manam, 2:168
Mazatec, 8:168
Mendi, 2:204
Mixe, 8:174
Nguna, 2:243
Nissan, 2:250
Pathan, 3:232
Pumi, 6:484
Tajiks, 6:353
Tanana, 1:339
Temiar, 5:269
Tuvans, 6:374
Volga Tatars, 6:401
Waimiri-Atroari, 7:344
Wáiwai, 7:347
Walapai, 1:365
Yao of Thailand, 5:292
Polygyny
  Abelam, 2:5
  Abenaki, 1:5
  Abor, 3:4
  Acehnese, 5:3
  Ache, 7:5
  Ainu, 5:8
  Akha, 5:12
  Aleut, 1:15
  Aleuts, 6:18
  Alur, 9:13
  Ambae, 2:12
  Anambé, 7:42
  Aranda, 2:17
  Arapaho, 1:26
  Asiatic Eskimos, 6:41
  Badaga, 3:16
  Baggara, 9:30-31
  Bagirmi, 9:34
  Bamiléké, 9:37, 39
  Barama River Carib, 7:81
  Bashkirs, 6:56
  Bau, 2:23
  Berbers of Morocco, 9:50
  Betsileo, 9:56
  Bhil, 3:39-40
  Bisaya, 5:43
  Blackfoot, 1:42
  Boazi, 2:30
  Bondo, 3:49
  Brahman of Nepal, 3:52
  Brahui, 3:54

Bugle, 8:32
Burusho, 3:56
Butonese, 5:67
Cahita, 8:36
Candoshi, 7:93
Caribou Inuit, 1:51
Central Thai, 5:70
Chácobo, 7:106
Chakma, 3:59
Cham, 5:73
Chambri, 2:32
Cherokee, 1:61
Chhetri of Nepal, 3:52
Chimbu, 2:36
Chin, 3:65
Chinantec, 8:54
Chuvash, 6:84
Cinta Larga, 7:128
Cora, 8:76
Cuicatec, 8:92
Cuna, 7:150
Dai, 6:425
Dani, 2:44, 46
Daribi, 2:47
Desana, 7:153
Dobu, 2:51
Dogon, 9:72
Dungans, 6:109
Dusun, 5:82
Dyula, 9:77
Eastern Shoshone, 1:105
Eipo, 2:57
Emberá, 7:156
Emerillon, 7:159
Evenki (Northern Tungus), 6:122
Ewe and Fon, 9:86
Foi, 2:60
Fore, 2:64
Fulani, 9:102
Gahuku-Gama, 2:69
Gainj, 2:72
Garia, 2:75
Garifuna, 8:114
Gogodala, 2:84
Gond, 3:85
Grasia, 3:88
Gros Ventre, 1:134
Guajajára, 7:167
Guajiro, 7:168
Guarayu, 7:174
Gusii, 9:109
Hausa, 9:113
Hawaiians, 2:96
Herero, 9:118
Hidatsa, 1:147
Hmong, 5:93
Hoti, 7:175
Huarayo, 7:177
Huichol, 8:126
Iraqw, 9:125
Iroquois, 1:166
Irula, 3:106
Iteso, 9:129
Jat, 3:111
Javanese, 5:112
Jicarilla, 1:81, 173
Jivaro, 7:183
Kachin, 5:117

Polygyny (cont'd)
Kalingas, 5:122
Kaluli, 2:102
Kanuri, 9:152
Kapauku, 2:106
Kapingamarangi, 2:109
Karihona, 7:192
Karok, 1:176
Kashinawa, 7:196
Kédang, 5:132
Keraki, 2:113
Kewa, 2:116
Kickapoo, 1:184
Kikuyu, 9:162
Kiowa, 1:187
Kiribati, 2:122
Kiwai, 2:126
Klamath, 1:191
Kogi, 7:202
Kol, 3:130
Konso, 9:170
Kosrae, 2:129
Kota, 3:136
Koya, 3:141
Kpelle, 9:173
Krikati/Pukobye, 7:205
Krymchaks, 6:215
Kuikuru, 7:208
Kumeyaay, 1:194
Kurds, 9:176
Kurtatchi, 2:132
Kwakiutl, 1:198
Kwoma, 2:135
Labrador Inuit, 1:201
Lak, 2:138
Lakandon, 8:154
Lango, 9:180
Lesu, 2:146
Lozi, 9:188
Luba of Shaba, 9:192
Lugbara, 9:194
Luo, 9:200
Luyia, 9:204
Maasai, 9:208
Macuna, 7:213
Mae Enga, 2:149, 150
Magar, 3:158
Mailu, 2:155
Malekula, 2:165
Mamprusi, 9:212, 213
Mandak, 2:171
Mandan, 4:214
Manihiki, 2:172
Maratha, 3:169
Mardudjara, 2:180
Maring, 2:186
Marshall Islands, 2:193
Matsigenka, 7:232
Mbeere, 9:221
Mejbrat, 2:196
Menominee, 1:221
Miami, 1:231
Micmacs, 1:234
Miskito, 8:171
Miyanmin, 2:209
Mohave, 1:241
Moinba, 6:473
Mojo, 7:242

Montagnais-Naskapi, 1:245
Montserratians, 8:180
Mormons, 1:246, 248
Mossi, 9:229
Mountain Arapesh, 2:216
Mundugumor, 2:219
Murngin, 2:225
Murut, 5:193
Muyu, 2:228
Nagas, 3:189
Namau, 2:231
Nambudiri Brahman, 3:193
Nandi and other Kalenjin peoples, 9:233
Navajo, 1:252
Ndembu, 9:240
Nenets, 6:279
Newar, 3:207
Nez Percé, 1:254
Ngatatjara, 2:240
Ngawbe, 8:196
Ningerum, 2:247
Noanamá, 7:251
Nogays, 6:288
North Alaskan Eskimos, 1:260
Nyakyusa and Ngonde, 9:253
Nyamwezi and Sukuma, 9:257
Nyinba, 3:212
Ojibwa, 1:270
Okiek, 9:261
Orokaiva, 2:257
Orokolo, 2:259
Pacific Eskimo, 1:283
Pahari, 3:221
Palu'e, 5:206
Pamir peoples, 6:305
Panare, 7:266
Paraujano, 7:268
Pauserna, 7:270
Pedi, 9:270
Pemon, 7:272
Penan, 5:210
Pende, 9:273
Pentecost, 2:263
peripatetics of Afghanistan, Iran, and
　　Turkey, 9:275
Piaroa, 7:277
Pima-Papago, 1:289
Pintupi, 2:266
Piro, 7:280
Popoluca, 8:217
Potawatomi, 1:297
Pume, 7:284
Purum, 3:243
Quechan, 1:301
Rennell Island, 2:277
Rikbaktsa, 7:287
Rotinese, 5:214
Saliva, 7:292
Sambia, 2:285
Samoa, 2:288
San Cristobal, 2:289
San-speaking peoples, 9:303
Santa Cruz, 2:291
Sara, 9:306
Saramaka, 7:296, 297
Sarsi, 1:308
Sasak, 5:226
Semang, 5:235

Senoi, 5:238
Shahsevan, 9:309
Shipibo, 7:305
Shona, 9:313
Siane, 2:299
Siona-Secoya, 7:308
Sirionó, 7:310
Siwai, 2:303
Slavey, 1:319
Sleb, 9:315
Somalis, 9:317
Subanun, 5:245
Suku, 9:322
Sundanese, 5:247
Suruí, 7:313
Suya, 7:316
Swahili, 9:328
Tairora, 2:309
Tanaina, 1:336
Tandroy, 9:337
Tanimuka, 7:319
Tatuyo, 7:323
Tauade, 2:319
Temne, 9:344
Terena, 7:326
Ternatan/Tidorese, 5:275
Ticuna, 7:329
Tikopia, 2:325
Tiv, 9:351
Toda, 3:296
Tolai, 2:335
Tonga, 9:353, 354
Tor, 2:343
Torres Strait Islanders, 2:346
Trio, 7:336
tropical-forest foragers, 9:357
Tuareg, 9:368
Tupari, 7:340
Turkana, 9:372
Tuvalu, 2:356
Tzotzil of Chamula, 8:280
Tzotzil of San Andrés Larraínzar, 8:285
Usino, 2:362
Ute, 1:361
Uvea, 2:364
Uzbeks, 6:397
Waimiri-Atroari, 7:344
Wantoat, 2:369
Waorani, 7:352
Wapisiana, 7:355
Warao, 7:358
Waropen, 2:376
Washoe, 1:369
Wayapi, 7:362
West Greenland Inuit, 1:377
Wiyot, 1:384
Wogeo, 2:381
Wolof, 9:379
Xoraxané Romá, 4:282
Yakan, 5:289
Yakö, 9:385
Yangoru Boiken, 2:389
Yawalapití, 7:379
Yekuana, 7:381
Yokuts, 1:388
Yoruba, 9:392
Yukpa, 7:384
Yukuna, 7:387

Yuracaré, **7**:396
Zande, **9**:398
Zaramo, **9**:402
Zarma, **9**:405
Zulu, **9**:411
  see also Concubinage
Polygyny (older/wealthier men)
  Pokot, **9**:282
  San-speaking peoples, **9**:303
  Yörük, **9**:395
  Zarma, **9**:405
Polygyny (one-fifth)
  Suku, **9**:321
Polygyny (preferred)
  Kpelle, **9**:173
  Shona, **9**:313
Polygyny (rare)
  Acholi, **9**:5
  Circassians, **9**:67
  Fipa, **9**:99
  Ghorbat, **9**:107
  Jews, Arabic-speaking, **9**:135
  Khoi, **9**:159
  Mbeere, **9**:221
  Nandi and other Kalenjin peoples, **9**:233
  peripatetics of Afghanistan, Iran, and
      Turkey, **9**:275
  Tsimihety, **9**:358
  Tswana, **9**:362
Polygyny (royal)
  Sakalava, **9**:295
Polygyny (serial)
  Afro-Colombians, **7**:17
Polygyny (sororal)
  Ahir, **3**:7
  Akawaio, **7**:32
  Amahuaca, **7**:35
  Apalai, **7**:46
  Araucanians, **7**:53
  Barí, **7**:84
  Bhil, **3**:39
  Cashibo, **7**:104
  Cheyenne, **1**:65
  Chimane, **7**:112
  Chipewyan, **1**:68
  Chiquitano, **7**:118
  Comanche, **1**:75
  Cree, **1**:81
  Emberá, **7**:156
  Kagwahiv, **7**:185
  Karajá, **7**:189
  Kashinawa, **7**:196
  Kiowa, **1**:187
  Klamath, **1**:191
  Mamprusi, **9**:212
  Mandan, **1**:214
  Maricopa, **1**:216
  Marubo, **7**:222
  Maxakali, **7**:233
  Mescalero Apache, **1**:224
  Mocoví, **7**:241
  Navajo, **1**:252
  Nivaclé, **7**:249
  Northern Paiute, **1**:264
  Northern Shoshone and Bannock, **1**:267
  Nyinba, **3**:212
  Osage, **1**:278
  Pahari, **3**:221

Paresí, **7**:269
Pawnee, **1**:284
Seminole, **1**:313
Shavante, **7**:301
Sherente, **7**:302
Slavey, **1**:319
Sora, **3**:269
Suya, **7**:316
Terena, **7**:326
Tunebo, **7**:338
Western Apache, **1**:372
Western Shoshone, **1**:375
Winnebago, **1**:381
Yagua, **7**:372
Yanomamö, **7**:375
Zulu, **9**:411
Polygyny (sororal prohibited)
  Mbeere, **9**:221
Polygyny (valued)
  Songhay, **9**:319
Polytheism
  Abkhazians, **6**:9
  Ahir, **3**:7
  Ainu, **5**:9
  Ajië, **2**:9
  Bagobo, **5**:29
  Baiga, **3**:21
  Bugis, **5**:51
  Chechen-Ingush, **6**:75
  Chinese in Southeast Asia, **5**:77
  Chitpavan Brahman, **3**:70
  Circassians, **6**:90
  Coorg, **3**:64
  Daur, **6**:429
  Dong, **6**:431
  Easter Island, **2**:55
  Garia, **2**:76
  Gond, **3**:86
  Han, **6**:447
  Hani, **6**:451
  Hawaiians, **2**:97
  Hindu, **3**:102
  Hmong, **5**:94
  Hopi, **1**:150
  Iban, **5**:98
  Ilongot, **5**:102
  Iroquois, **1**:167
  Irula, **3**:104, 108
  Kachin, **5**:118
  Kalingas, **5**:123
  Karachays, **6**:161
  Karen, **5**:128, 129
  Khanty, **6**:191-192
  Khasi, **3**:125, 126
  Kol, **3**:130
  Korean, **5**:148
  Kosrae, **2**:130
  Kota, **3**:137
  Lahu, **6**:463
  Lamaholot, **5**:156
  Limbu, **3**:150-151
  Lisu, **6**:466
  Magar, **3**:161
  Makassar, **5**:173
  Maori, **2**:178
  Maratha, **3**:170
  Marquesas Islands, **2**:190
  Marshall Islands, **2**:194

Mikir, **3**:176
Modang, **5**:187
Moluccans—South, **5**:188
Mulam, **6**:477
Muyu, **2**:229
Nagas, **3**:190-191
Nauru, **2**:237
Nepali, **3**:204-205
Newar, **3**:208
Nias, **5**:196
Niue, **2**:252
Nivkh, **6**:285
Orok, **6**:296
Oroquen, **6**:483
Pahari, **3**:222-223
Pandit of Kashmir, **3**:226
Piro, **7**:280
Pohnpei, **2**:269
Pukapuka, **2**:272
Purum, **3**:244
Raroia, **2**:276
Rennell Island, **2**:277
Rhadé, **5**:212
Rossel Island, **2**:279
Saami, **6**:324
Sadhu, **3**:251-252
Santal, **3**:254
Semang, **5**:235-237
She, **6**:490
Shui, **6**:491
Subanun, **5**:245
Tagbanuwa, **5**:251
Tahiti, **2**:306
Tamil, **3**:279
Tamil of Sri Lanka, **3**:283
Telugu, **3**:286-287
Tewa Pueblos, **1**:349
Thakur, **3**:293
Thompson, **1**:350
Tikopia, **2**:326
Toda, **3**:297
Tonga, **2**:338
Tongareva, **2**:341
Tor, **2**:344
Ukrainians, **6**:394
Ulithi, **2**:360
Uvea, **2**:364
Vedda, **3**:302-303
Vellala, **3**:306
Western Apache, **1**:373
Winnebago, **1**:382
Woleai, **2**:384
Xibe, **6**:504
Yakut, **6**:406
Yao of Thailand, **5**:292-293
Yi, **6**:507
Zhuang, **6**:511
Pomaks (Muslims)
  Bulgarians, **4**:45
  Pomaks, **4**:205
Populism
  Lingayat, **3**:151, 152
Porcelains
  Madeirans, **4**:165
Porcupine quill trade
  Tanaina, **1**:335
Porcupine quill work
  Blackfoot, **1**:42

Porcupine quill work (cont'd)
  Hidatsa, **1**:146
  Menominee, **1**:222
  Miami, **1**:232
  Micmac, **1**:235
  Ojibwa, **1**:271
  Tanaina, **1**:337
  Teton, **1**:345
Porpoise hunting
  Kwakiutl, **1**:198
Portents. *See* Omens, importance of
Possession rites and séance. *See* Divination;
    Exorcism; Mediums; Séance
Possessions
  death-related practices. *See* Mortuary
      practices, burial with personal
      possessions
  importance of
    Chin, **3**:64, 67
  unimportance of
    Hill Pandaram, **3**:100
    Nayaga, **3**:195
  see also Inheritance; Money and wealth
Potato famine
  Irish, **4**:152, 163
Potato growing
  Araucanians, **7**:52
  Aveyronnais, **4**:25
  Badaga, **3**:15
  Bavarians, **4**:33
  Belarussians, **6**:60
  Bretons, **4**:38
  Canarians, **4**:51
  Carpatho-Rusyns, **6**:70
  Chuvash, **6**:84
  Cinta Larga, **7**:127
  Cornish, **4**:65
  Dongxiang, **6**:432
  Faroe Islanders, **4**:99
  Gaels (Irish), **4**:115
  Georgians, **6**:132
  Guambiano, **7**:171
  Highland Scots, **4**:139
  Irish, **4**:152
  Kagwahiv, **7**:184
  Kashubians, **4**:158
  Khevsur, **6**:194
  Krikati/Pukobye, **7**:204
  Lezgins, **6**:242
  Lithuanians, **6**:250
  Maris, **6**:257
  Miao, **6**:470
  Micmac, **1**:233
  Nepali, **3**:202
  Newar, **3**:206
  Northern Irish, **4**:170
  Orcadians, **4**:186
  Otavalo, **7**:253
  Páez, **7**:257
  Poles, **4**:203
  Pomaks, **4**:205
  Portuguese, **4**:206
  Qiang, **6**:485
  Saami, **4**:221
  Salasaca, **7**:289
  Saraguro, **7**:294
  Sherpa, **3**:257, 258
  Shipibo, **7**:304

Siberiaki, **6**:333
  Sikkimese, **3**:262
  Slovaks, **4**:243
  Suruí, **7**:312
  Swedes, **4**:257
  Terena, **7**:325
  Toda, **3**:295
  Tory Islanders, **4**:264
  Ukrainians, **6**:392
  Walloons, **4**:276
  Welsh, **4**:279
  Yi, **6**:506
Potlatch
  Ahtna, **1**:14
  Alorese, **5**:15
  Carrier, **1**:52
  Comox, **1**:76
  Haida, **1**:136
  Ingalik, **1**:157
  Klallam, **1**:190
  Kwakiutl, **1**:199, 200
  Lillooet, **1**:206
  Lingit, **1**:353
  Nivaclé, **7**:251
  Nootka, **1**:257
  Tanaina, **1**:337
  Tanana, **1**:349
  Tsimshian, **1**:355
Pottery
  Abkhazians, **6**:7
  Bajau, **5**:32
  Belarussians, **6**:60, 61
  Canarians, **4**:51
  Canelos Quichua, **7**:99, 101
  Cashibo, **7**:104
  Catawba, **1**:53, 54, 55
  Chayahuita, **7**:111
  Cocama, **7**:130
  Croats, **4**:75
  Cuna, **7**:149
  Dai, **6**:424
  Dargins, **6**:97, 98
  Desana, **7**:152
  Garia, **2**:74
  Georgians, **6**:136
  Greeks, **4**:134
  Guahibo-Sikuani, **7**:165
  Hopi, **1**:149
  Hungarians, **4**:144, 145
  Iatmul, **2**:98
  Ingalik, **1**:158
  Jebero, **7**:181
  Karelians, **6**:170
  Keres Pueblo Indians, **1**:179, 180
  Khasi, **3**:123
  Korean, **5**:148
  Kota, **3**:135
  Kumyks, **6**:221
  Kurds, **6**:226
  Laks, **6**:234
  Lamaholot, **5**:155
  Lao Isan, **5**:161
  Latinos, **1**:206
  Lithuanians, **6**:251
  Mailu, **2**:154, 155
  Mandan, **1**:214
  Marubo, **7**:222
  Minangkabau, **5**:182

Mingrelians, **6**:263
  Mohave, **1**:241, 242
  Mojo, **7**:242
  Motu, **2**:215
  Mulam, **6**:476
  Nagas, **3**:188
  Navajo, **1**:251
  Newar, **3**:206, 207
  Nicobarese, **3**:209
  Noanamá, **7**:252
  Palikur, **7**:262
  Panare, **7**:265
  Pemon, **7**:273
  Pima-Papago, **1**:288
  Portuguese, **4**:208
  Provencal, **4**:210
  Pueblo Indians, **1**:298, 299
  Pume, **7**:283
  Quechan, **1**:301
  Rutuls, **6**:319
  Samal, **5**:219
  Shors, **6**:330
  Sio, **2**:300
  Siona-Secoya, **7**:307
  Slovaks, **4**:245
  Tabasarans, **6**:349
  Tamil, **3**:277
  Tangu, **2**:311
  Taos, **1**:342
  Terena, **7**:325
  Tewa Pueblos, **1**:348, 349
  Ticuna, **7**:328
  Tubatulabal, **1**:355
  Udis, **6**:377
  Ukrainian peasants, **6**:386
  Ukrainians, **6**:392
  Ukrainians of Canada, **1**:359
  Uzbeks, **6**:397, 398
  Volga Tatars, **6**:401
  Wáiwai, **7**:346
  Waurá, **7**:360
  Yakut, **6**:405
  Yawalapití, **7**:378
  Yukagir, **6**:412
  Yukuna, **7**:386
  Zuni, **1**:397, 398
  see also Ceramic manufacture
Poultry raising. *See* Chicken raising; Duck
    raising; Geese raising
Poverty
  Blackfoot, **1**:41
  Calabrese, **4**:48, 49, 50
  Cape Verdeans, **4**:55
  Cherokee, **1**:61
  Corsicans, **4**:65
  Mongo, **9**:227
  Ozarks, **1**:281
  Polynesians, **1**:291
  Washoe, **1**:367, 368
Powwows
  Catawba, **1**:55
Praderas (meadow clusters)
  Pasiegos, **4**:189
Pragmatism
  as desirable social trait
    Czechs, **4**:84
  religious
    Qalandar, **3**:248

Praise (as socialization)
  Mandan, 1:215
  Qalandar, 3:247
Praise house system
  Sea Islanders, 1:310
Praise songs
  Tuareg, 9:369
  Wolof, 9:380
Prarabdha beliefs
  Pandit of Kashmir, 3:226
Prawn fishing
  Manx, 4:170
  Vedda, 3:301
Prayer
  as central religious feature
    Yavapai, 1:386
    Zuni, 1:399
  curing
    Cheyenne, 1:66
    Delaware, 1:86
  to deceased to protect the living
    Southern Paiute (and Chemehuevi),
      1:333
  rituals
    Ashkenazim, 6:36
    Bukharan Jews, 6:65
    Calabrese, 4:50
    Chakma, 3:61
    Mount Athos, 4:176-177
    Muslim, 3:185
    Nagas, 3:190
    Washoe, 1:370
    Zamindar, 3:307
  see also Chanting
Prayer-maker (religious specialist)
  Chuj, 8:73
Prayer sticks
  Havasupai, 1:145
  Zuni, 1:399, 400
Preacher
  Hutterites, 1:154
Pregnancy
  ancestors foretell in dreams
    Luba of Shaba, 9:192
  bearing child for sister
    Sakalava, 9:296
  chief sleeps alone to protect
    Pende, 9:273
  conception myths
    Asurini, 7:61
  healing powers
    Lakandon, 8:154
  paternity acknowledged in seventh month
      by presenting woman with stylized bow
      and arrow
    Toda, 3:297
  reincarnated soul enters womb
    Rukuba, 9:291
  semen from multiple copulations help fetus
      grow
    Yukuna, 7:387
  taboos. See Taboos
  third, fifth, and seventh month celebrated
    Maratha, 3:169
  see also Childbirth
Pregnancy, unmarried. See Illegitimacy
Premarital sex
  Abor, 3:4

  Arubans, 8:12
  Ayoreo, 7:71
  Bahamians, 8:19
  Baiga, 3:20
  Balkars, 6:53
  Barí, 7:84
  Candoshi, 7:94
  Carib of Dominica, 8:39
  Chamorros, 2:34
  Cheyenne, 1:64-65
  Cocama, 7:130
  Dai, 6:425
  Danes, 4:89
  Dobu, 2:51
  Eastern Shoshone, 1:105
  Eipo, 2:57
  Finns, 4:103
  Frisians, 4:111
  Guambiano, 7:172
  Hani, 6:450
  Hmong, 5:93
  Ilongot, 5:102
  Jingpo, 6:457
  Jino, 6:460
  Kachin, 5:117
  Kapauku, 2:106
  Karen, 5:127
  Karihona, 7:193
  Kashubians, 4:159
  Khasi, 3:124
  Khevsur, 6:194-195
  Kmhmu, 5:140
  Lakalai, 2:141
  Lakher, 3:147
  Maisin, 2:158
  Maori, 2:177
  Mejbrat, 2:196
  Miao, 6:471
  Mizo, 3:178
  Moldovans, 6:268
  Mongols, 6:475
  Nagas, 3:190
  Naxi, 6:479
  Nganasan, 6:281
  Nicobarese, 3:209
  Nivaclé, 7:249
  Noanamá, 7:252
  Norwegians, 4:181
  Pasiegos, 4:190
  Piemontese, 4:200
  Rukuba, 9:290
  Russians, 6:316
  Saraguro, 7:294
  Sengseng, 2:297
  Sherente, 7:303
  Tangu, 2:312
  Temiar, 5:269
  Ternatan/Tidorese, 5:276
  Thadou, 3:288
  Tikopia, 2:325
  T'in, 5:278
  Truk, 2:352
  Ute, 1:361
  Wa, 6:503
  Yao of Thailand, 5:292
  Yawalapití, 7:379
  Yukagir, 6:413
  Yuqui, 7:393

  Yuracaré, 7:396
  see also Virginity, as marriage requirement
Prepuberty marriage. See Marriage, youth
Presbyterianism
  Chinese in Caribbean, 8:58
  Cubans, 8:90
  East Indians in Trinidad, 8:107
  Grenadians, 8:116
  Highland Scots, 4:141-142
  Koreans in Canada, 1:98
  Lowland Scots, 4:163
  Malekula, 2:164, 166
  Nguna, 2:242, 243, 244
  North Alaskan Eskimos, 1:261
  Northern Irish, 4:180
  Orcadians, 4:187
  Ottawa, 1:280
  Pentecost, 2:261
  Seminole of Oklahoma, 1:315
  Shetlanders, 4:234
  Tanna, 2:313
  Trinidadians and Tobagonians, 8:269
  Welsh, 4:280
Preschools. See under Education
Prestige distinctions. See Status, basis of
Prestige economy
  Chin, 3:64
Priesthood
  Albanians, 4:7
  Andalusians, 4:12
  Azoreans, 4:28
  Basques, 4:32
  Bau, 2:24
  Bavarians, 4:35
  Bhil, 3:41
  Bontok, 5:46
  Brahman, 3:51, 222, 223
  Brahman and Chhetri of Nepal, 3:52, 53
  Calabrese, 4:50
  Canarians, 4:52
  Castilians, 4:60
  Chaldeans, 9:63-64
  Chimila, 7:114
  Chin, 3:64, 67
  Copts
    9.169
  Cretans, 4:71
  Don Cossacks, 6:106
  Easter Island, 2:55
  Gaels (Irish), 4:117
  Gond, 3:86
  Greeks, 4:133
  Irula, 3:108
  Kali, 3:36
  Khasi, 3:125, 126
  Kiowa, 1:188
  Kiribati, 2:123
  Kogi, 7:202
  Kol, 3:130
  Kond, 3:133
  Kota, 3:135, 137-138
  Koya, 3:141
  Kumeyaay, 1:195
  Kurumbas, 3:143
  Lakher, 3:147
  Lau, 2:145
  Lingayat, 3:153
  Madeirans, 4:166

Priesthood (cont'd)
  Maltese, **4:**169
  Maori, **2:**178
  Maratha, **3:**170
  Marquesas Islands, **2:**190
  Mauritian, **3:**173
  Montenegrins, **4:**173
  Mormons, **1:**249
  Munda, **3:**184
  Navajo, **1:**253
  Nepali, **3:**205
  Newar, **3:**207, 208
  Nyinba, **3:**213
  Osage, **1:**279
  Pahari, **3:**220, 223
  Pandit of Kashmir, **3:**225, 226
  Parsi, **3:**229
  Pasiegos, **4:**191
  Peloponnesians, **4:**194
  Portuguese, **4:**208
  Rennell Island, **2:**277
  Romanians, **4:**214
  Santal, **3:**255
  Sicilians, **4:**237
  Slav Macedonians, **4:**241
  Slovenes, **4:**249
  Sora, **3:**269
  Syrian Christian of Kerala, **3:**274
  Tahiti, **2:**307
  Tamal of Sri Lanka, **3:**283
  Telugu, **3:**287
  Tikopia, **2:**325, 326
  Tonga, **2:**337
  Tuvalu, **2:**357
  Uvea, **2:**364
  Zuni, **1:**398-399, 400
  see also Women's priestly roles
Priests, circumvention of
  Vlach Gypsies of Hungary, **4:**272
  Vlachs, **4:**275
Priests, hereditary
  Bau, **2:**24
  Bhil, **3:**41
  Bontok, **5:**46
  Kiowa, **1:**188
  Lau, **2:**145
  Munda, **3:**184
  Nyinba, **3:**213
  Parsi, **3:**229
  Zoroastrians, **9:**409
Priests' wives
  Kota, **3:**138
  Santal, **3:**255
Primogeniture
  Acholi, **9:**5
  Austrians, **4:**20
  Auvergnats, **4:**22
  Aveyronnais, **4:**25
  Bahamians, **8:**19
  Basques, **4:**31
  Cape Verdeans, **4:**55
  Chin, **3:**65
  Dai, **6:**426
  Dogon, **9:**72
  Dutch, **4:**93
  Edo, **9:**80
  English, **4:**97
  Faroe Islanders, **4:**99

Flemish, **4:**108
German Swiss, **4:**126
Iatmul, **2:**99
Ibibio, **9:**120
Igbo, **9:**122
Kilenge, **2:**119
Korean, **5:**147
Kwakiutl, **1:**199
Lamaholot, **5:**156
Lango, **9:**180
Latinos, **1:**205
Lenca, **8:**156
Maasai, **9:**208
Manx, **4:**170
Marquesas Islands, **2:**189, 190
Mazatec, **8:**169
Mbeere, **9:**222
Mikir, **3:**176
Mongols, **6:**475
Motu, **2:**214
Muong, **5:**191
Murik, **2:**221, 222
Nambudiri Brahman, **3:**192, 193
Nguna, **2:**243
Nootka, **1:**256, 257
Nyakyusa and Ngonde, **9:**253
Occitans, **4:**184
Oriya, **3:**217
Palikur, **7:**263
Palu'e, **5:**207
Pawnee, **1:**285
Pentecost, **2:**263
Siberian Germans, **6:**338
Siwai, **2:**303
Slovenes, **4:**248
Swazi, **9:**331
Tahiti, **2:**306
Tai Lue, **5:**254
Taiwan aboriginal peoples, **5:**257, 258
Tajiks, **6:**353
Tandroy, **9:**337
Tibetans, **6:**495
Tiroleans, **4:**263
Tonga, **2:**338
Totonac, **8:**265
Tswana, **9:**363
Tujia, **6:**498
Xibe, **6:**504
Primogeniture (with compensation to other
    siblings)
  Norwegians, **4:**181
Printing shops
  Nayar, **3:**198
Print making
  Kwakiutl, **1:**200
Prison. *See* Punishment, incarceration
Processions
  folk
    Flemish, **4:**108
  funeral
    Shetlanders, **4:**234
    Sicilians, **4:**237
  religious associations
    Swiss, Italian, **4:**261
  religious festivals
    Flemish, **4:**108
    Ionians, **4:**150
    Kashubians, **4:**159

Maltese, **4:**169
Portuguese, **4:**208
Sicilians, **4:**237
Slovaks, **4:**246
Walloons, **4:**277
wedding
  Shetlanders, **4:**234
see also Carnival; Mortuary practices
Professional services
  Bosnian Muslims, **4:**36
  Chitpavan Brahman, **3:**69
  East Asians of the United States, **1:**100-101
  Jews, **1:**169
  Khoja, **3:**128
  Kota, **3:**134
  Kshatriya, **3:**142
  Mormons, **1:**247
  Nayar, **3:**197, 198
  Nepali, **3:**201
  Parsi, **3:**227-228
  Peloponnesians, **4:**194
  Syrian Christian of Kerala, **3:**274
  Tewa Pueblos, **1:**348
  see also Financial services; Medical practices
      and treatments
Prognosticators. *See* Diviners; Fortune-telling;
    Oracles
Property. *See* Inheritance; Landholding;
    Possessions
Property buried with dead. *See* Mortuary
    practices, burial with personal
    possessions
Property confiscation (as social control). *See
    under* Punishment
Property destruction (as social control). *See
    under* Punishment
Property destruction (at death). *See* Mortuary
    practices, destruction of deceased's
    property
Property disputes. *See under* Conflict causes
Property ownership. *See* Landholding;
    Women's property ownership
Property rights
  curtailed
    East Asians in the United States, **1:**100
  as stewardship for God
    Mennonites, **1:**219
  women's. *See* Women's property rights
Proselytizing. *See* Conversion
Prostitution
  Ayoreo, **7:**71
  hijra, **3:**96
  Kanjar, **3:**119, 120
  Nivaclé, **7:**250
  Ontong Java, **2:**254
  peripatetics, **3:**235
  peripatetics of Afghanistan, Iran, and
      Turkey, **9:**275
  peripatetics of the Maghreb, **9:**278
  Qalandar, **3:**246
  Santa Cruz, **2:**291
  Sleb, **9:**315
Protestant Church of the Nazarene
  Cape Verdeans, **4:**56
Protestantism (undifferentiated)
  Acholi, **9:**6
  Agta, **5:**6
  Akha, **5:**13

Alorese, 5:14
Ambonese, 5:16, 17, 19
Amish, 1:18
Amuzgo, 8:6
Appalachians, 1:22-23
Aquitaine, 4:14, 15
Armenians, 28
Arubans, 8:13
Atoni, 5:28
Awakateko, 8:16, 17
Batak, 5:41
Belarussians, 6:58
Bemba, 9:47
Betsileo, 9:57
Blacks in Canada, 1:44
Bolaang Mongondow, 5:43
Boruca, Bribri, Cabécar, 8:29, 30
Bukidnon, 5:55
Bulgarians, 4:45
Butonese, 5:68
Callahuaya, 7:90
Canelos Quichua, 7:100
Cape Verdeans, 4:55, 56
Catalans, 4:63
Chinantec, 8:54
Chontal of Tabasco, 8:69
Chuj, 8:73
Cornish, 4:65
Costa Ricans, 8:81
Creoles of Nicaragua, 8:85, 86
Czechs, 4:84
Danes, 4:90
Drung, 6:432
Dutch, 4:94
East Asians in Canada, 1:98
East Asians in the United States, 1:103
English, 4:97
Filipino, 5:87
Frisians, 4:112
Germans, 4:123;6:138
German Swiss, 4:127
Haitians, 8:122
Han, 6:448
Hawaiians, 2:97
Highland Scots, 4:141-142
Hungarians, 4:145
Ilongot, 5:102
Indian Christians, 3:103
Irish, 4:151, 152
Irish-Canadians, 1:123
Kachin, 5:118
Kapauku, 2:105
Karen, 5:128
Kiowa, 1:188
Kipsigis, 9:165
Kmhmu, 5:141
Kongo, 9:168
Korean, 5:148
Kuna, 8:150
Lahu, 5:152, 153, 154;6:463
Lakandon, 8:154
Lamaholot, 5:155, 156
Lisu, 6:466
Luo, 9:200
Makushi, 7:219
Manx, 4:171
Marind-anim, 2:184
Marquesas Islands, 2:189, 190

Mejbrat, 2:195
Micronesia, 1:238
Mixe, 8:175
Mixtec, 8:178
Mizo converts, 3:179
Moluccans—North, 5:188
Moluccans—South, 5:188
Mossi, 9:230
Mundurucu, 7:245
Nez Percé, 1:254
Nias, 5:195, 196
Nomoi, 2:252
Northern Irish, 4:177, 178, 179, 180
Northern Metis, 1:262
Nu, 6:481
Orcadians, 4:187-188
Ozarks, 1:281
Pentecost, 2:264
Pohnpei, 2:269
Polynesians, 1:292
Rapa, 2:275
Romanians, 4:214
Samoa, 2:288
Sara, 9:306
Shetlanders, 4:234
Sicilian converts, 4:237
Slovaks, 4:245
Subanun, 5:245
Suku, 9:322
Syrian Christian of Kerala, 3:274
Tagalog, 5:250
Tahiti, 2:305
Tamil of Sri Lanka converts, 3:283
Ticuna, 7:329
Tobelorese, 5:280
Toda converts, 3:297
Tojolab'al, 8:263
Tokelau, 2:332
Totonac, 8:265, 266
Transylvanian ethnic groups, 4:268
Truk, 2:351-352, 354
Tuvalu, 2:356, 357
Tzotzil and Tzeltal of Pantelhó, 8:277, 278
Tz'utujil, 8:297, 298
Welsh, 4:280
Yagua, 7:373
Yap, 2:394
Yi, 6:507
Yukateko, 8:310
Zande, 9:399
Zoque, 8:317
see also Fundamentalism, Christian; *specific sects*
Proverbs
Bania, 3:24, 25
Bretons, 4:39
Lakher, 3:147
Vlachs, 4:275
Provincialism
Aveyronnais, 4:24
Provo movement
Dutch, 4:94
Prüh (ceremony)
Palaung, 5:202
Psychics
Hare, 1:142
see also Mediums

Psychological disorders
Evenki (Northern Tungus), 6:123
Psychosomatic illness
Mauritian, 3:173
Psychotherapeutic rituals
Iban, 5:99
Puberty rites. See Coming of age; Initiation; Menstruation
Public assistance. See Government welfare assistance
Public esteem (social emphasis on)
Catalans, 4:63
Nayar, 3:199
Pandit of Kashmir, 3:226
Sarakatsani, 4:224
Sora, 3:270
see also Honor
Public opinion (as social control). See *under* Social control measures
Public schools. See Education
Pueblo
Hopi, 1:148-151
Hopi-Tewa, 1:151
Keres Pueblo Indians, 1:179-182
Taos, 1:341
Tewa Pueblos, 1:347, 349
Pueblo (nonurban settlement)
Andalusians, 4:10
Castilians, 4:59
Pumpkin growing
Anambé, 7:41
Angaité, 7:43
Arikara, 1:26
Cashibo, 7:104
Chiquitano, 7:118
Chorote, 7:124
Cocama, 7:130
Jivaro, 7:182
Kaingáng, 7:186
Lengua, 7:210
Maká, 7:216
Maricopa, 1:216
Maroni Carib, 7:220
Mashco, 7:225
Mataco, 7:228
Miami, 1:231
Mocoví, 7:240
Mohave, 1:240
Mojo, 7:242
Ndebele, 9:236
Ojibwa, 1:269
Panare, 7:265
Pawnee, 1:284
Pemon, 7:271
Powhatan, 1:297
Rikbaktsa, 7:287
Shavante, 7:300
Sirionó, 7:310
Usino, 2:361
Xokléng, 7:370
Punishment
by ancestors
Awakateko, 8:17
Garifuna, 8:115
Swazi, 9:333
ashes poured on head
Pashai, 9:267
banishment

Punishment (cont'd)
  Araucanians, 7:54
  Belau, 2:26
  Bhil, 3:40
  Burusho, 3:56
  Callahuaya, 7:89
  Candoshi, 7:94
  Chagga, 9:62
  Chamacoco, 7:109
  Culina, 7:147
  Evenki (Northern Tungus), 6:121, 122
  Huichol, 8:127
  Iraqw, 9:126
  Iteso, 9:130
  Karen, 5:128
  Khasi, 3:125
  Khevsur, 6:197
  Kipsigis, 9:165
  Konso, 9:171
  Koryaks and Kerek, 6:209
  Kumeyaay, 1:195
  Lango, 9:181
  Lisu, 5:166
  Matsigenka, 7:232
  Mixtec, 8:178
  Nyakyusa and Ngonde, 9:254
  Rutuls, 6:320
  Sakalava, 9:297
  Slavey, 1:320
  Svans, 6:345
  T'in, 5:279
  Ute, 1:362
  Washoe, 1:369
  see also subhead Excommunication below
  beating
    Kogi, 7:202
    Lakalai, 2:142
    Maori, 2:178
    Nandi and other Kalenjin peoples, 9:233
    Ndembu, 9:240
    Rennell Island, 2:277
    Rom of Czechoslovakia, 4:219
    Tanaina, 1:336
    Ternatan/Tidorese, 5:276
    Tongareva, 2:341
    Zuni, 1:399
  blood vengeance. See under Conflict
    resolution
  cannibalism
    Malaita, 2:162
  capital
    Ambae, 2:12
    Aranda, 2:18
    Araucanians, 7:54
    Bai, 6:420
    Baluchi, 3:23
    Candoshi, 7:94
    Chamacoco, 7:109
    Chinantec, 8:54
    Cotopaxi Quichua, 7:134 ·
    Cubeo, 7:141
    Don Cossacks, 6:106
    Easter Island, 2:55
    Even, 6:118
    Evenki (Northern Tungus), 6:121, 122
    Gebusi, 2:79
    Hasi, 3:125
    Hawaiians, 2:97

  Ifugao, 5:100
  Kapingamarangi, 2:110
  Karakalpaks, 6:168
  Khasi, 3:125
  Kilenge, 2:120
  Koryaks and Kerek, 6:209
  Kumeyaay, 1:195
  Kurtatchi, 2:133
  Lak, 2:139
  Maguindanao, 5:170
  Mailu, 2:156
  Makassar, 5:173
  Malaita, 2:162
  Maori, 2:178
  Montenegrins, 4:173
  murderous witch
    Zande, 9:399
  Nandi and other Kalenjin peoples, 9:234
  Naxi, 6:479
  Ojibwa, 1:270
  Palu'e, 5:207
  Pathan, 3:233
  Rennell Island, 2:277
  Selkup, 6:327
  Svans, 6:345
  Tolai, 2:334
  Uvea, 2:364
  Waorani, 7:353
  Western Apache, 1:373
  Yokuts, 1:388
  Zande, 9:399
community labor
  Kuna, 8:149
compensation payment
  Araucanians, 7:54
  Atoni, 5:28
  Gahuku-Gama, 2:70
  Guajiro, 7:168, 169
  Jingpo, 6:458
  Kiwai, 2:126
  Klingit, 1:352
  Krikati/Pukobye, 7:204, 205
  Malaita, 2:161
  Manam, 2:168
  Muyu, 2:229
  Pomo, 1:295
  Saramaka, 7:297
  Sio, 2:301
  Tanaina, 1:336
  Tauade, 2:319, 320
  Tolai, 2:335
  Truk, 2:353
  Wogeo, 2:381
  Wovan, 2:387
  Yurok, 1:394, 395
corporal
  Ambae, 2:12
  Anuta, 2:14
  Don Cossacks, 6:106
  Evenki (Northern Tungus), 6:122
  Fali, 9:96
  Jews, Arabic-speaking, 9:136
  Jews of Iran, 9:140
  Kalmyks, 6:157
  Karakalpaks, 6:168
  Mardudjara, 2:180
  Mixtec, 8:178
  Mohave, 1:241

  Mongols, 6:475
  Nandi and other Kalenjin peoples, 9:234
  Palu'e, 5:207
  Pende, 9:274
  Poles, 4:204
  Rom of Czechoslovakia, 4:219
  Tahiti, 2:306
  see also subhead beating above
death compensation
  Bagobo, 5:29
  Foi, 2:61
  Georgians, 6:135
  Kaluli, 2:103
  Karachays, 6:161
  Kewa, 2:117
  Khinalughs, 6:201
  Kipsigis, 9:164
  Mae Enga, 2:150
  Maguindanao, 5:170
  Mendi, 2:205
  Nivkh, 6:284, 285
  Nuristanis, 9:251
  Svans, 6:346
  Tats, 6:360
excommunication
  Baiga, 3:20
  Bohra, 3:47
  Cochin Jew, 3:72
  Mennonites, 1:219
  Old Believers, 1:274
  peripatetics, 3:236
  Rom of Czechoslovakia, 4:219
  Santal, 3:254
  Sinhalese, 3:266
  Tamil of Sri Lanka, 3:283
  Toda, 3:297
exile. See subhead banishment above
Family Code
  Costa Ricans, 8:80
fines
  Akha, 5:12-13
  Alorese, 5:15
  Avars, 6:46
  Baiga, 3:20
  Balinese, 5:37
  Baluchi, 3:23
  Batak, 5:40
  Belau, 2:26
  Berbers of Morocco, 9:51
  Bohra, 3:47
  Burusho, 3:56
  Chagga, 9:62
  Circassians, 6:90
  Cuna, 7:150
  Dusun, 5:82, 83
  Fali, 9:96
  Gnau, 2:82
  Hani, 6:450
  Hanunóo, 5:91
  Huichol, 8:127
  Ifugao, 5:100
  Kachin, 5:117
  Kalingas, 5:123
  Kalmyks, 6:157
  Karachays, 6:161
  Karen, 5:127
  Khasi, 3:125
  Konso, 9:171

Kubachins, **6:**219
Kuna, **8:**149
Lahu, **5:**153
Lak, **2:**139
Lakher, **3:**147
Lao Isan, **5:**162
Lisu, **5:**166
Lunda, **9:**198
Malekula, **2:**166
Mandak, **2:**171
Mejbrat, **2:**196
Mixtec, **8:**178
Munda, **3:**184
Murut, **5:**193
Nandi and other Kalenjin peoples,
  9:234
Nguna, **2:**244
Nias, **5:**196
Palaung, **5:**202
Palu'e, **5:**207
Pentecost, **2:**263
Purum, **3:**244
Rom, **1:**305
Sengseng, **2:**297, 298
Svans, **6:**345
Taiwan aboriginal peoples, **5:**257, 258
Thadou, **3:**289
T'in, **5:**279
Toda, **3:**297
Tolai, **2:**335
Tsakhurs, **6:**367
Wiyot, **1:**385
Woleai, **2:**384
Yao of Thailand, **5:**292
Yap, **2:**393
Zande, **9:**399
hard labor
  Kogi, **7:**202
incarceration
  Baiga, **3:**20
  Callahuaya, **7:**89
  Huichol, **8:**127
  Khasi, **3:**125
  Kuna, **8:**149
  Lunda, **9:**198
  Maguindanao, **5:**170
  Malekula, **2:**166
  Manam, **2:**168
  Mixtec, **8:**178
  Puerto Ricans, **8:**223
  Totonac, **8:**265
  Tzotzil and Tzeltal of Pantelhó, **8:**277
  Tzotzil of Chamula, **8:**281
mutilation
  Ojibwa, **1:**270
penance
  Old Believers, **1:**274
property confiscation
  Keres Pueblo Indians, **1:**181
  Maori, **2:**178
property destruction
  Fox, **1:**129, 130
  Hidsata, **1:**147
  Poles, **4:**204
property distribution
  Kwakiutl, **1:**199
public service
  Malekula, **2:**166

Tsakhurs, **6:**367
religious
  Curaçao, **8:**97
  Yezidis, **6:**410
restitution
  Georgians, **6:**135
retribution
  Tats, **6:**360
sacrifice of relative
  Kongo, **9:**168
scarification
  Ache, **7:**6
  Lango, **9:**181
shunning
  Acadians, **1:**8
  Amish, **1:**18, 20
  Dusun, **5:**82
  Gypsies, **6:**147
  Iraqw, **9:**126
  Javanese, **5:**113
  Karachays, **6:**161
  Kipsigis, **9:**165
  Latvians, **6:**238
  Lozi, **9:**189
  Mennonites, **1:**219
  Tarahumara, **8:**242
  Wogeo, **2:**381
spearing
  Aranda, **2:**18
  Kapauku, **2:**106
  Mardudjara, **2:**181
  Murut, **5:**193
  Ngatatjara, **2:**241
  Pintupi, **2:**266
  Sengseng, **2:**297
  Tasmanians, **2:**317
stocks
  Bugle, **8:**33
  Huichol, **8:**127
supernatural
  Atoni, **5:**28
  Bahamians, **8:**19
  Chatino, **8:**51
  Ch'ol, **8:**65
  Khmer, **5:**137
  Melanau, **5:**180
  Shona, **9:**313-314
  Wogeo, **2:**381
verbal
  Chinantec, **8:**54
whipping
  Keres Pueblo Indians, **1:**181
  Kumeyaay, **1:**195
withdrawal
  Canelos Quichua, **7:**101
  Central Yup'ik Eskimo, **1:**58
  Chiriguano, **7:**121
  Mataco, **7:**229
  Wapisiana, **7:**356
  Yagua, **7:**373
see also under Adultery; Child discipline;
    Social control measures
Punning
  Auvergnats, **4:**23
Punya belief
  Pandit of Kashmir, **3:**226
Puppetry
  Chinese in Southeast Asia, **5:**77

Flemish, **4:**108
Javanese, **5:**113
Mansi, **6:**255
Oriya, **3:**218
peripatetics, **3:**235, 236
Sicilians, **4:**237
Ukrainians, **6:**394
Walloons, **4:**278
Purdah
  Maratha, **3:**169
  Mogul, **3:**179
  Muslim, **3:**185
  Pathan, **3:**231, 232
  Sindhi, **3:**263
Purgatory. *See* Afterlife
Purification rites
  Ache, **7:**6
  Brahman and Chhetri of Nepal, **3:**53
  Parsi, **3:**229
  Purum, **3:**244
  Rikbaktsa, **7:**288
  Salasaca, **7:**291
  Ticuna, **7:**330
Purim (holiday)
  Karaites, **6:**165
  Mountain Jews, **6:**273
Purity and pollution codes
  Brahman and Chhetri of Nepal, **3:**53
  castes, Hindu, **3:**57
  Coorg, **3:**74
  Divehi, **3:**78
  Hindu castes, **3:**57
  Ingalik, **1:**157
  Irula, **3:**104, 109
  Jicarilla, **1:**174
  Kalasha, **3:**116
  Kanjar, **3:**121
  Kol, **3:**131
  Kolisuch'ok, **5:**142
  Kond, **3:**133
  Kurumbas, **3:**143
  Limbu, **3:**150, 151
  Luyia, **9:**205, 206
  Magar, **3:**157, 159
  Nayar, **3:**202
  Ndebele, **9:**238
  Nyinba, **3:**213
  Okkaliga, **3:**214
  Old Believers, **1:**274
  Pandit of Kashmir, **3:**225
  Parsi, **3:**229, 230
  Rom, **1:**305-306
  Rom of Czechoslovakia, **4:**219
  Rominche, **4:**217
  Sinhalese, **3:**265
  Tamil, **3:**278, 279
  Tamil of Sri Lanka, **3:**284
  Telugu, **3:**285
  Toda, **3:**297
  Untouchables, **3:**299
  Vellala, **3:**305, 306
  Vlach Gypsies of Hungary, **4:**272
  see also Castes; Ritual purification;
      Taboos
Purlapa (ceremony)
  Warlpiri, **2:**374
Purushartha beliefs
  Pandit of Kashmir, **3:**226

Pyrethrum growing
    Nandi and other Kalenjin peoples, 9:232
    Okiek, 9:259

Qama'its (female deity)
    Walapi, 1:36
Qingming [Qing Ming] (festival)
    Chinese in Southeast Asia, 5:77
    Hakka, 6:439
    Maonan, 6:468
    Zhuang, 6:511
Qorban (holiday)
    Uighur, 6:384
Quakers
    Iroquois, 1:167
    Osage, 1:279
Quarrying. See Stoneworking
Quezalcoatl symbol
    Triqui, 8:272
Quill work
    Blackfoot, 1:42
    Cheyenne, 1:65
    Delaware, 1:85
    Hidatsa, 1:146
    Maliseet, 1:211
    Mandan, 1:214
    Menominee, 1:222
    Miami, 1:232
    Micmac, 1:235
    Ojibwa, 1:271
    Tanaina, 1:337
    Teton, 1:345
Quilt making
    Amish, 1:20
    Cook Islands, 2:41
    Hidatsa, 1:146
    Ozarks, 1:282
    Teton, 1:345
Quinoa growing
    Araucanians, 7:52
    Aymara, 7:66
    Chipaya, 7:115
    Otavalo, 7:253
Quoits (stone tombs)
    Cornish, 4:64

Rabbi
    Hasidim, 1:143, 144
    Jews, 1:171
Rabbis
    Jews, Arabic-speaking, 9:136
Rabbit hunting
    Dogrib, 1:88
    Hare, 1:140
    Western Shoshone, 1:374
    Wintun, 1:383
    Yavapai, 1:386
Rabbit-skin blankets
    Taos, 1:342
Rabbit Society
    Kiowa, 1:188
Racial tensions. See Ethnic groups, tensions
Radha (female deity)
    Bengali Vaishnava, 3:36
Raiders
    Chin, 3:63
    Cretans, 4:71
    Ingalik, 1:158

Jicarilla, 1:172
Khasi, 3:125
Kickapoo, 1:183
Kiowa, 1:188
Lipan Apache, 1:207
Miami, 1:232
Nagas, 3:187, 190
Navajo, 1:252
North Alaskan Eskimos, 1:260
Northern Paiute, 1:264
Pathan, 3:231
Punjabi, 3:241
Slav Macedonians, 4:241
Thadou, 3:289
Thug, 3:294
Yurok, 1:395
Railroad building
    East Asians of Canada, 1:94, 95
    East Asians of the United States, 1:100
Rainmaking
    pilgrimages
        Tojolab'al, 8:263
        Tzotzil of San Bartolomé de los Llanos,
            8:290
    rituals
        Andis, 6:27
        Ayoreo, 7:72
        Lugbara, 9:194-195
        Mossi, 9:230
        Ojibwa, 1:272
        Santal, 3:255
        Tabasarans, 6:350
        Yukateko, 8:310
        Zapotec, 8:313
Rain priesthoods
    Zuni, 1:399, 400
Rakhelu. See Concubinage
Ramadan (holiday)
    Bajau, 5:34
    Crimean Tatars, 6:94
    Madurese, 5:168
    Maguindanao, 5:171
    Malay, 5:176
    Minangkabau, 5:184
    Samal, 5:221
    Samal Moro, 5:224
    Tajiks, 6:354
    Tausug, 5:264
    Ternatan/Tidorese, 5:276
    Trinidadians and Tobagonians, 8:269
    Turkish Cypriots, 4:81
    Uighur, 6:384
    Uzbeks, 6:398
Ramazan (holiday)
    Siberian Tatars, 6:342
Rancherias
    Quechan, 1:300-301, 302
Ranching
    Basques, 1:34
    Cajuns, 1:49
    Crow, 1:83
    Hidatsa, 1:146
    Hopi, 1:149
    Teton, 1:345
    see also Cattle raising
Ranch labor
    Washoe, 1:368
Ranga (deity). See Vaishnava Hindus

Rank. See Hierarchical society; Nobility;
    Royalty; Status, basis of
Rao San Ling (festival)
    Bai, 6:421
Rape
    Aranda, 2:18
    Chechen-Ingush, 6:75
    Trinidadians and Tobagonians, 8:268
Rastafarianism
    Barbadians, 8:23
    Blacks in Canada, 1:44
    Black West Indians in the United States,
        1:46
    Jamaicans, 8:139
    Montserratians, 8:181
Rattan
    Agta, 5:5
    Modang, 5:186
    Senoi, 5:237
    Temiar, 5:268, 272
Raven cult
    Itelmen, 6:153
    Koryaks and Kerek, 6:209
    Yukagir, 6:413
Raven messengers
    Kumeyaay, 1:195
Raven moiety
    Haida, 1:136
Raven trickster
    Tanaina, 1:336
    Tlingit, 1:353
    Yukagir, 6:413
Real estate agencies
    East Asians of Canada, 1:96
Rebellions. See Civil war; Political violence
Rebirth. See Reincarnation beliefs
Reciprocal labor. See Exchange, labor
Reciprocity. See Exchange
Recitatives. See Oral tradition
Red-Hat sect
    Bhutanese, 3:46
Red pottery
    Tewa Pueblos, 1:349
Red-tailed hawk messengers
    Kumeyaay, 1:195
Red war moiety
    Choctaw, 1:72
Reel (dance)
    Shetlanders, 4:234
Refugees
    Albanians, 4:3
    Basques, 1:32
    in England, 4:96
    Hmong, 5:94
    Latinos, 1:204, 206
    Mongo, 9:226
    Pathan, 3:230
    in Provencal, 4:209
    in South Asia, 3:250
    Tamil of Sri Lanka, 3:280, 281
Reggae
    Rastafarians, 8:229
Reggae music
    Black West Indians in the United States,
        1:46
Reincarnation beliefs
    Akawaio, 7:33
    Andamanese, 3:11

Bai, **6:**421
Baiga, 3:21
Balinese, **5:**37-38
Bengali, 3:34
Bondo, 3:50
Brahman, 3:53
Butonese, **5:**68
Callahuaya, 7:90
castes, Hindu, 3:57
Central Thai, 5:71
Central Yup'ik Eskimos, 1:59
Chhetri of Nepal, 3:53
Chinese in Southeast Asia, 5:78
Chipewyan, 1:69
Chuvans, 6:83
Cubeo, 7:142
Daur, 6:429
East Indians in Trinidad, 8:107
Edo, 9:82
Ewe and Fon, 9:88
Fipa, 9:100
Garia, 2:76
Gebusi, 2:79
Gujarati, 3:92
Haida, 1:136
Hare, 1:142
Hindu, 3:102
Hmong, 5:95
Ibibio, 9:120
Jain, 3:109
Jatav, 3:115
Javanese, 5:114
Karen, 5:129
Ka'wiari, 7:200
Kédang, 5:133
Ket, 6:185
Khanty, 6:192
Khasi, 3:126
Khmer, 5:138
Kipsigis, 9:165
Korean, 5:148
Lakher, 3:148
Lamaholot, 5:156
Lao, 5:159, 160
Lao Isan, 5:163
Macuna, 7:215
Mansi, 6:255
Mescalero Apache, 1:225
Mikir, 3:176
Munda, 3:184
Muong, 5:191-192
Nambudiri Brahman, 3:194
Nandi and other Kalenjin peoples, 9:234
Naxi, 6:480
Nayar, 3:200
Ndembu, 9:241
Nepali, 3:205
Newar, 3:208
North Alaskan Eskimos, 1:261
Nyinba, 3:213
Oriya, 3:218
Pahari, 3:222, 223
Pandit of Kashmir, 3:226
Pokot, 9:283
Rikbaktsa, 7:288
Rom of Czechoslovakia, 4:219
Rukuba, 9:291
Selkup, 6:328

Shan, 5:241
Sherpa, 3:259, 260
Sinhalese, 3:267
Tanaina, 1:337
Teton, 1:346
Thakali, 3:292
Tibetans, **6:**495, 496
Tlingit, 1:353
Toda, 3:298
Tuvans, 6:374
Uighur, 6:384
Vedda, 3:303
Winnebago, 1:382
Yakö, 9:387
Yezidis, 6:410
Yoruba, 9:393
Yuit, 1:392, 393
Yuqui, 7:395
see also Ceremonies, bear
Reindeer management
Central Yup'ik Eskimos, 1:57
Chukchee, **6:**76, 77
Chuvans, 6:81
Dolgan, 6:100
Even, 6:117
Evenki (Northern Tungus), 6:121
Ewenki, 6:433, 434
Ket, 6:184
Khanty, 6:190, 192
Komi, 6:203
Koryaks and Kerek, 6:207, 208
Mansi, 6:253
Nenets, 6:278
Nganasan, 6:280, 281
Nivkh, 6:284
North Alaskan Eskimos, 1:258, 259
Orok, 6:296
Saami, 4:220-221, 222;6:323, 324
Selkup, 6:325
Siberiaki, 6:333
Tofalar, 6:362
Yakut, 6:405
Yukagir, 6:412
Rejection. _See_ Shunning
Relay Race
Jicarilla, 1:174
Relic veneration
Mount Athos, 4:176
Occitans, 4:185
Sinhalese, 3:267
Religion
art
Canarians, 4:52-53
artifacts
Nyinba, 3:213
Catholic-Protestant conflict
Dutch, 4:94
confirmation ritual
Danes, 4:90
conversion. _See_ Conversion
decline in practice of
Walloons, 4:277
individual
Ute, 1:362
pluralism
Japanese, 5:109
schisms
Mennonites, 1:219

sexuality
Baul, 3:26
Bengali Vaishnava, 3:37
syncretic. _See_ Syncretism
see also specific religion
Religious ecstatics. _See_ Ecstasy
Religious healing. _See under_ Medical practices
and treatments; Shamanism
Religious practitioners. _See_ Priesthood;
Shamanism
Religious seekers
Europeans in South Asia, 3:79
Religious status
Chakma, 3:60
Religious syncretism. _See_ Syncretism
Religious warfare. _See_ Warfare (religious)
Reliquary mound
Sherpa, 3:258
Remarriage
after divorce
Afro-Bolivians, 7:9
Jews, Arabic-speaking, 9:135
Manx, 4:171
Maroni Carib, 7:220
Ojibwa, 1:270
Pima-Papago, 1:289
Sleb, 9:315
Slovaks, 4:244
Vlach Gypsies of Hungary, 4:272
Yawalapití, 7:379
after divorce unlikely
Ionians, 4:150
easy
Rominche, 4:216
following spouse's death
Manx, 4:171
Ojibwa, 1:270
Slav Macedonians, 4:240
low rate
Northern Irish, 4:179
Magar, 3:158
multiple
Western Shoshone, 1:375
Munda, 3:183
Nagas, 3:189
necessary for widower leader
Wáiwai, 7:347
Nepali, 3:204
Pahari, 3:221
Parsi, 3:228
Tamil, 3:278
widow discouraged
Bene Israel, 3:28
Bengali, 3:32
Irula, 3:107
Pandit of Kashmir, 3:225
Thakali, 3:291
widower as common practice
Macedonians, 4:240
widower with granddaughter
Pende, 9:273
widower sororate marriage. _See_ Sororate
marriage
widow inheritance marriage
Berbers of Morocco, 9:50
Igbo, 9:122
Sara, 9:306
Tonga, 9:354

Remarriage (cont'd)
    Turkana, **9**:372
    widow levirate marriage. *See* Levirate
        marriage
    widow levirate marriage not required
        Karaites, **9**:154
    widow limitations
        Bulgarians, **4**:44
    widow one-year delay
        Pacific Eskimo, **1**:282
    widow permitted
        Agaria, **3**:6
        Andamanese, **3**:10
        Awá Kwaiker, **7**:65
        Badaga, **3**:16
        Bhuiya, **3**:44
        Bondo, **3**:49
        Burusho, **3**:56
        Chiquitano, **7**:118
        Grasia, **3**:88
        Jat, **3**:112
        Jatav, **3**:114
        Jicarilla, **1**:173
        Koli, **3**:132
        Koya, **3**:141
        Mahar, **3**:164
        Mamprusi, **9**:213
        Meo, **3**:175
        Mocoví, **7**:241
        Nagas, **3**:189
        Nicobarese, **3**:209
        Pahari, **3**:221
        Parsi, **3**:228
        Santal, **3**:253
        Sleb, **9**:315
        Sora, **3**:269
    widow prohibited
        Bania, **3**:25
        Gond, **3**:85
        Kol, **3**:130
        Maasai, **9**:208
        Maratha, **3**:169
        Sarakatsani, **4**:224
        Tamil, **3**:278
        Vellala, **3**:305
    widow remarries as second wife
        Shahsevan, **9**:309
    widow's right to refuse levirate
        Fipa, **9**:99
    widow unlikely
        Dalmatians, **4**:87
    widow/widower as usual occurence
        Apiaká, **7**:49
        Awá Kwaiker, **7**:65
        Barí, **7**:84
        Cotopaxi Quichua, **7**:133
    see also Levirate marriage; Sororate
        marriage
Remittances
    Tonga, **2**:337
    Trobriand Islands, **2**:349
Renewing the world rite
    Karok, **1**:177
Rental of land. *See* Landholding,
    leaseholds
Reprocessed goods
    Piemontese Sinti, **4**:200
Reputation. *See* Honor

Reraya (festival)
    Gayo, **5**:90
Resepect
    as social value
        Tiroleans, **4**:263
Residence (newly married)
    ambilocal
        Iban, **5**:97
        Kenyah-Kayan-Kajang, **5**:134
        Taiwan aboriginal peoples, **5**:257
    avunculocal
        Siwai, **2**:303
        Tanaina, **1**:336
        Trobriand Islands, **2**:350
    bilocal
        Agta, **5**:5
        Bisaya, **5**:43
        Central Yup'ik Eskimos, **1**:57
        Chipewyan, **1**:68
        Dai, **6**:425
        Dobu, **2**:51
        Nganasan, **6**:281
        North Alaskan Eskimos, **1**:260
        Senoi, **5**:238
        Washoe, **1**:369
    matrilocal
        Acehnese, **5**:3
        Ajië, **2**:8
        Akawaio, **7**:32
        Amuesha, **7**:38
        Andalusians, **4**:11
        Apalai, **7**:46
        Apiaká, **7**:49
        Arapaho, **1**:26
        Araweté, **7**:57
        Ata Tana 'Ai, **5**:24
        Austrians, **4**:20
        Azoreans, **4**:28
        Baffinland Inuit, **1**:30
        Bagobo, **5**:29
        Bajau, **5**:32, 33
        Baniwa-Curripaco-Wakuenai, **7**:78
        Barama River Carib, **7**:81
        Bemba, **9**:46, 47
        Boazi, **2**:30
        Bonerate, **5**:45
        Bugis, **5**:50
        Bukidnon, **5**:54
        Butonese, **5**:67
        Cahita, **8**:36
        Canarians, **4**:52
        Canela, **7**:96
        Cariña, **7**:103
        Cashibo, **7**:104
        Castilians, **4**:60
        Catawba, **1**:54
        Central Thai, **5**:70
        Central Yup'ik Eskimos, **1**:57
        Cham, **5**:73
        Chamacoco, **7**:109
        Chamorros, **2**:34
        Cherokee, **1**:61
        Cheyenne, **1**:65
        Chipewyan, **1**:68
        Chiriguano, **7**:121
        Chocó, **7**:123
        Choctaw, **1**:72
        Chorote, **7**:125

        Chuvans, **6**:81, 82
        Comanche, **1**:75
        Craho, **7**:137
        Cree, **1**:81
        Cuiva, **7**:144
        Cuna, **7**:149, 150
        Dai, **6**:425
        Delaware, **1**:86
        Dogrib, **1**:88
        Fox, **1**:129
        Garo, **3**:83
        Gayo, **5**:89
        Gorotire, **7**:162
        Greeks, **4**:132
        Han, **6**:444
        Hanunóo, **5**:91
        Hidatsa, **1**:147
        Hopi, **1**:149
        Hopi-Tewa, **1**:151
        Ilongot, **5**:102
        Iroquois, **1**:166
        Jicarilla, **1**:173
        Kagwahiv, **7**:185
        Kalimantan Dayaks, **5**:120
        Kalingas, **5**:122
        Kapingamarangi, **2**:109
        Karaites, **6**:165
        Karen, **5**:127
        Karihona, **7**:192
        Kashinawa, **7**:196
        Kédang, **5**:132
        Khanty, **6**:191
        Khasi, **3**:124
        Kickapoo, **1**:184
        Klamath, **1**:192
        Kurtatchi, **2**:132
        Lahu, **5**:152
        Lao, **5**:158
        Lao Isan, **5**:161
        Lengua, **7**:210
        Lesu, **2**:146
        Maká, **7**:217
        Makushi, **7**:219
        Maliseet, **1**:211
        Maltese, **4**:168
        Mandan, **1**:214
        matrilocal
            Kuna, **8**:147
        Matsigenka, **7**:231
        Mejbrat, **2**:196
        Melanau, **5**:179
        Micronesians, **1**:237
        Mimika, **2**:207
        Minangkabau, **5**:183
        Mocoví, **7**:241
        Modang, **5**:186
        Mohave, **1**:241
        Moldovans, **6**:268
        Mundurucu, **7**:245
        Nasioi, **2**:234
        Navajo, **1**:252
        Nivaclé, **7**:249
        Nomatsiguenga, **7**:91
        Northern Paiute, **1**:264
        Norwegians, **4**:181
        Nyinba, **3**:212
        Ogan-Besemah, **5**:198
        Ontong Java, **2**:254

Osage, 1:278
Pacific Eskimo, 1:283
Pawnee, 1:285
Peloponnesians, 4:193
Penan, 5:210
Pintupi, 2:266
Piro, 7:280
Portuguese, 4:207
Qiang, 6:486
Rikbaktsa, 7:287
Romanians, 4:213
Rotuma, 2:282
Russians, 6:316
Samal Moro, 5:223
Santal, 3:253
Seminole, 1:313
Shan, 5:240
Sharanahua, 7:299
Shavante, 7:301
Sherente, 7:303
Sirionó, 7:310
Slavey, 1:319
Slovenes, 4:248
Southern Paiute (and Chemehuevi),
    1:331
Subanun, 5:245
Suya, 7:316
Taiwan aboriginal peoples, 5:257
Tanaina, 1:336
Tanana, 1:339
Tapirapé, 7:321
Temiar, 5:269
Ternatan/Tidorese, 5:275
T'in, 5:279
Tokelau, 2:331
Truk, 2:352
Ute, 1:361
Vlachs, 4:274
Waimiri-Atroari, 7:343-344
Waorani, 7:352
Western Apache, 1:372
Western Shoshone, 1:375
Winnebago, 1:381
Woleai, 2:383
Xikrin, 7:368
Yekuana, 7:381
Yokuts, 1:388
Yuit, 1:391
Yukagir, 6:413
Yukpa, 7:384
Zuni, 1:398
    see also Bride-service
matrilocal/neolocal
    Asurini, 7:61
    Bakairi, 7:74
    Culina, 7:147
    Guarayu, 7:174
    Mataco, 7:229
    Noanamá, 7:252
    Pauserna, 7:270
    Piapoco, 7:274
    Puinave, 7:281
    Saliva, 7:292
    Toba, 7:332
matrilocal/patrilocal
    Amahuaca, 7:35
    Ionians, 4:149
    Kuikuru, 7:208

Tatuyo, 7:323
Tunebo, 7:338-339
Tupari, 7:340
Yagua, 7:372
Yanomamö, 7:375
Yukuna, 7:387
natalocal
    Portuguese, 4:207
    Tory Islanders, 4:265
neolocal
    Alorese, 5:15
    Bai, 6:420
    Chipewyan, 1:68
    Copper Eskimo, 1:78
    Danes, 4:89
    Gelao, 6:435
    Guahibo-Sikuani, 7:165
    Iban, 5:97
    Javanese, 5:112
    Karaites, 6:165
    Korean, 5:147
    Latinos, 1:205
    Latvians, 6:237
    Madurese, 5:167
    Malay, 5:175
    Manx, 4:170
    Miami, 1:231
    Micmac, 1:234
    Northern Metis, 1:262
    Norwegians, 4:181
    Orcadians, 4:187
    Otavalo, 7:254
    Ozarks, 1:281
    Páez, 7:257
    Paraujano, 7:268
    Peloponnesians, 4:193
    Poles, 4:203
    Saami, 4:221
    Santa Cruz, 2:291
    Sardinians, 4:226
    Sasak, 5:226
    Shetlanders, 4:234
    Slovaks, 4:244
    Sorbs, 4:253
    Sundanese, 5:247
    Taos, 1:342
    Toraja, 5:282
    Torres Strait Islanders, 2:346
patrilocal
    Abkhazians, 6:6, 7
    Acadians, 1:8
    Ajië, 2:8
    Akha, 5:12
    Albanians, 4:4, 5
    Aleuts, 6:18
    Alorese, 5:15
    Altaians, 6:22
    Ambae, 2:12
    Ambonese, 5:18
    Andis, 6:26
    Apiaká, 7:49
    Armenians, 6:29
    Atoni, 5:28
    Auvergnats, 4:22
    Avars, 6:45
    Awá Kwaiker, 7:64
    Ayoreo, 7:70
    Azerbaijani Turks, 6:49

Badaga, 3:16
Bai, 6:420
Baiga, 3:20
Balinese, 5:37
Balkars, 6:54
Baluchi, 3:23
Baniwa-Curripaco-Wakuenai, 7:78
Batak, 5:40
Bau, 2:23
Bavarians, 4:34
Belarussians, 6:61
Bene Israel, 3:28
Bengali, 3:32
Bhil, 3:39
Bhuiya, 3:44
Bosnian Muslims, 4:36
Brahman and Chhetri of Nepal, 3:53
Bulgarian Gypsies, 4:41
Bulgarians, 4:44
Bunun, 5:57
Burgundians, 4:47
Canelos Quichua, 7:100
Cariña, 7:103
Carpatho-Rusyns, 6:70
Chakma, 3:59
Chatino, 8:51
Chayahuita, 7:111
Chimbu, 2:36
Chin, 3:65
Chinese in Southeast Asia, 5:76
Chocó, 7:123
Circassians, 6:88
Corsicans, 4:67
Cotopaxi Quichua, 7:133
Cree, 1:81
Croats, 4:73
Cubeo, 7:140
Dani, 2:44
Dargins, 6:97
Daribi, 2:47
De'ang, 6:430
Desana, 7:153
Dolgan, 6:101
Don Cossacks, 6:105
Drung, 6:432
East Greenland Inuit, 1:106
Eipo, 2:57
Endenese, 5:85
Ewenki, 6:434
Gainj, 2:72
Gayo, 5:89
Georgians, 6:133
Gitanos, 4:129
Goodenough Island, 2:86
Greeks, 4:132;6:143
Greek-speaking Jews of Greece, 4:135
Guambiano, 7:172
Gujar, 3:89
Gurung, 3:94
Gururumba, 2:93
Gypsies, 6:147
Han, 6:444
Hungarians, 4:144
Hutterites, 1:154
Iatmul, 2:99
Itza,' 8:134
Japanese, 5:107
Jingpo, 6:457

Residence (newly married) (cont'd)
 Kachin, 5:117
 Kalmyks, 6:156
 Kanbi, 3:118
 Kapauku, 2:106
 Kapingamarangi, 2:109
 Karachays, 6:161
 Karakalpaks, 6:167
 Karelians, 6:171
 Kariera, 2:111
 Karok, 1:176
 Ka'wiari, 7:199
 Kazakhs, 6:180
 Kewa, 2:116
 Khanty, 6:191
 Kikapu, 8:144
 Kilenge, 2:119
 Kiowa, 1:187
 Kirgiz, 6:461
 Kiribati, 2:122
 Klamath, 1:192
 Kol, 3:130
 Korean, 5:147
 Kota, 3:136, 137
 Koya, 3:141
 Kriashen Tatars, 6:212
 Krymchaks, 6:215
 Kyrgyz, 6:230
 Labrador Inuit, 1:201
 Lakalai, 2:141
 Lakkher, 3:146
 Lamaholot, 5:156
 Lau, 2:144
 Laz, 6:240
 Lisu, 5:165;6:465
 Macuna, 7:213
 Mae Enga, 2:150
 Mafulu, 2:152
 Magar, 3:158
 Maguindanao, 5:170
 Malaita, 2:161, 162
 Malekula, 2:165
 Manam, 2:168
 Manchu, 6:467
 Manihiki, 2:172
 Manus, 2:174
 Maori, 2:177
 Mardudjara, 2:180
 Marquesas Islands, 2:190
 Maxakali, 7:233
 Mazatec, 8:168
 Mekeo, 2:199
 Melpa, 2:201
 Mendi, 2:204
 Meskhetians, 6:260
 Miao, 6:471
 Mikir, 3:175
 Mingrelians, 6:263, 264
 Mixe, 8:174
 Mohave, 1:241
 Mojo, 7:242
 Mongols, 6:475
 Montenegrins, 4:173
 Motu, 2:214
 Mountain Arapesh, 2:216
 Mundugumor, 2:219
 Murut, 5:193
 Muslim, 3:185

 Muyu, 2:228
 Namau, 2:231
 Nambicuara, 7:247
 Naxi, 6:479
 Nepali, 3:204
 Newar, 3:207
 Ngatatjara, 2:240
 Nguna, 2:243
 Nias, 5:196
 Nivkh, 6:284
 Nogays, 6:289
 Norwegians, 4:181
 Nuer, 9:250
 Nyinba, 3:212
 Ogan-Besemah, 5:198
 Old Believers, 1:274;6:293
 Oriya, 3:217
 Orokaiva, 2:257
 Ossetes, 6:300
 Páez, 7:257
 Pahari, 3:221
 Palaung, 5:202
 Palikur, 7:262
 Palu'e, 5:206
 Pandit of Kashmir, 3:225
 Peloponnesians, 4:193
 Pentecost, 2:263
 peripatetics, 3:235
 Piemontese Sinti, 4:200
 Pima-Papago, 1:289
 Poles, 4:203
 Pumi, 6:484
 Punjabi, 3:240
 Purum, 3:243
 Quechan, 1:301
 Rennell Island, 2:277
 Rom, 1:305
 Romanians, 4:213
 Rom of Czechoslovakia, 4:219
 Rossel Island, 2:279
 Russian peasants, 6:312
 Russians, 6:316
 Salar, 6:488
 Samoa, 2:288
 San Cristobal, 2:289
 Santa Cruz, 2:291
 Santal, 3:253, 254
 Sarakatsani, 4:224
 Sea Islanders, 1:310
 Selung/Moken, 5:232
 Serbs, 4:231
 She, 6:490
 Siane, 2:299
 Siberiaki, 6:333
 Sio, 2:300
 Siwai, 2:303
 Slav Macedonians, 4:240, 241
 Slovaks, 4:244
 Slovenes, 4:248
 South and Southeast Asians of Canada,
   1:323
 Syrian Christian of Kerala, 3:273
 Tabasarans, 6:349
 Tairora, 2:309
 Tajiks, 6:353
 Tamil, 3:277
 Tanimuka, 7:319
 Tanna, 2:314

 Tarascans, 8:245
 Tauade, 2:319
 Teluga, 3:286
 Thadou, 3:288
 Thakali, 3:291
 Tibetans, 6:495
 Toda, 3:296
 Tolai, 2:335
 Tongareva, 2:340
 Trobriand Islands, 2:350
 Tsakhurs, 6:367
 Tsimshian, 1:355
 Tu, 6:497
 Tujia, 6:498
 Tuscans, 4:270
 Tuvalu, 2:356
 Tuvans, 6:374
 Ulithi, 2:359
 Usino, 2:362
 Uvea, 2:364
 Uzbeks, 6:397
 Vellala, 3:305
 Vietnamese, 5:285
 Vlach Gypsies, 4:272
 Vlachs, 4:274
 Wa, 6:502
 Wamira, 2:366
 Wape, 2:371
 West Greenland Inuit, 1:377
 Wiyot, 1:384
 Wogeo, 2:381
 Wovan, 2:386
 Xoraxané Romá, 4:280
 Yakut, 6:406
 Yangoru Boiken, 2:389
 Yao, 6:505
 Yao of Thailand, 5:292
 Yap, 2:393
 Yawalapití, 7:379
 Yugur, 6:509
 Yuit, 1:391
 Yukagir, 6:413
 Yuqui, 7:393
 Yurok, 1:395
 Zhuang, 6:511
 uxorilocal. *See subhead* matrilocal
   above
 virilocal. *See subhead* patrilocal *above*
Resource redistribution
 Ajië, 2:9
 Bisaya, 5:43
 Chechen-Ingush, 6:73
 Circassians, 6:90
 Dolgan, 6:102
 Iatmul, 2:98
 Kiribati, 2:121, 123
 Kosrae, 2:128
 Lak, 2:138
 Maisin, 2:159
 Mardudjara, 2:180
 Nganasan, 6:282
 Ningerum, 2:248
 Nomoi, 2:252
 Orokaiva, 2:257-258
 Sio, 2:301
 Tiwi, 2:328
 Turkmens, 6:370
 Woleai, 2:383

Respect
  for in-laws
    Yawalapití, 7:379
  mutual
    Aymara, 7:67
    Chimane, 7:113
  for others
    Fi:.ns, 4:103
    Winnebago, 1:382
  for own kind
    Chamacoco, 7:109
  as social value
    Apiaká, 7:49
    Aymara, 7:67
    Hungarians, 4:144
    Kogi, 7:202
    Maltese, 4:168
    Micronesians, 1:237
    Serbs, 4:231
    Vlachs, 4:274
  see also Honor
Restaurants. See Food, restauranteurs
Restraint (as admired trait)
  Kiowa, 1:188
Resurrection beliefs
  Austrians, 4:21
  Jews, Arabic-speaking, 9:136
  Mount Athos, 4:177
  Parsi, 3:230
Retail stores. See Service industry;
    Shopkeeping
Retirees
  Cape Verdeans, 4:55
  Europeans in South Asia, 3:79
  French of India, 3:80
Retribution fears. See under Social control
    measures
Revenge. See Conflict resolution, blood
    vengeance
Revenge fears. See under Social control
    measures
Revenue collecting. See Tax collectors
Revivalism. See Evangelicalism
Ribbon work
  Delaware, 1:85-86
  Fox, 1:130
  Osage, 1:277
Rice
  harvesting wild
    Ojibwa, 1:269
  prohibition
    Palu'e, 5:205
  spirits
    Kmhmu, 5:141
  as wealth
    Karen, 5:128
  as wedding fertility symbol
    Swiss, Italian, 4:261
Rice goddess
  Lao, 5:159
  Sasak, 5:227
  Sundanese, 5:247
Rice growing
  Abor, 3:4
  Acehnese, 5:3
  Achang, 6:417
  Afro-Hispanic Pacific Lowlanders, 7:20
  Agta, 5:5

Aguaruna, 7:29
Akha, 5:11
Alak, 5:13
Ambonese, 5:17
Anambé, 7:41
Anavil Brahman, 3:7
Apiaká, 7:48
Araweté, 7:56
Asháninca, 7:91
Assamese, 3:13-14
Ata Sikka, 5:20
Ata Tana 'Ai, 5:23
Atoni, 5:27
Bagobo, 5:29
Bai, 6:419
Bajau, 5:32
Bakairi, 7:74
Balantak, 5:35
Balinese, 5:36
Barí, 7:84
Batak, 5:39
Baweanese, 5:41
Bengali, 3:30
Betsileo, 9:54, 55
Bilaan, 5:42
Bisaya, 5:42
Blang, 6:421
Bolaang Mongondow, 5:43
Bontok, 5:46
Bororo, 7:86
Bouyei, 6:422
Brao, 5:47
Bugis, 5:49, 50
Bugle, 8:32
Bukidnon, 5:53
Burmese, 5:64
Butonese, 5:67
Cajuns, 1:49
Campa del Pichis, 7:91
Candoshi, 7:93
Canela, 7:96
Cashibo, 7:104
Central Thai, 5:70
Cham, 5:72
Chamorros, 2:34
Chayahuita, 7:111
Chin, 3:63
Chiquitano, 7:118
Chocó, 7:122
Chontal of Tabasco, 8:68
Cinta Larga, 7:127
Colorado, 7:131
Coorg, 3:74
Cotabato Manobo, 5:79
Craho, 7:136
Cuna, 7:149
Dai, 6:423, 424
De'ang, 6:430
Dong, 6:431
Dungans, 6:109
Dusun, 5:79, 80, 81
East Asians of the United States, 1:100
East Indians in Trinidad, 8:105
Emberá, 7:155
Endenese, 5:85
Garia, 3:81
Gayo, 5:88
Gorontalese, 5:90

Gorotire, 7:162
Guajajára, 7:166
Guarayu, 7:174
Hakka, 6:437
Han, 6:440, 442, 443
Hani, 6:450
Hanunóo, 5:91
Hausa, 9:112
Hmong, 5:93
Huarayo, 7:177
Hui, 6:453
Ibaloi, 5:95
Iban, 5:96, 97
Ifugao, 5:99
Ilanon, 5:101
Ilongot, 5:101
Indonesian, 5:102, 103
Irula, 3:105
Isneg, 5:103
Itonama, 7:179
Japanese, 5:105, 106
Javanese, 5:111
Jing, 6:454
Jingpo, 6:456
Jino, 6:460
Kachin, 5:116
Kalimantan Dayaks, 5:120
Kalingas, 5:122
Karajá, 7:188
Karakalpaks, 6:167
Karen, 5:126
Kasseng, 5:130
Kattang, 5:131
Katu, 5:131
Kédang, 5:131
Kenyah-Kayan-Kajang, 5:133
Kerintji, 5:134
Khmer, 5:135, 136
Kmhmu, 5:139
Kond, 3:132
Korean, 5:146
Koreans, 6:206
Koya, 3:140
Kpelle, 9:173
Krikati/Pukobye, 7:204
Kui, 5:150
Lahu, 5:151, 152;6:462
Laki, 5:154
Lamaholot, 5:155
Lamet, 5:157
Lao, 5:158
Lao Isan, 5:161
Lawa, 5:163
lepcha, 3:148
Li, 6:464
Limbu, 3:150
Lisu, 5:164
Ma, 5:167
Madurese, 5:167
Magar, 3:155, 160
Maguindanao, 5:169
Makassar, 5:172
Malay, 5:175
Mamprusi, 9:211
Mande, 9:215
Manggarai, 5:176
Maranao, 5:177
Mayoruna, 7:234

Rice growing (cont'd)
  Melanau, **5:**178
  Mende, **9:**223
  Mijikenda, **9:**224
  Mikir, **3:**175
  Minahasans, **5:**181
  Minangkabau, **5:**182
  Mizo, **3:**178
  Mnong, **5:**184
  Modang, **5:**186
  Moinba, **6:**473
  Mon, **5:**189
  Mountain Jews, **6:**272
  Mulam, **6:**476
  Mundurucu, **7:**244
  Muong, **5:**190
  Murut, **5:**193
  Nagas, **3:**188
  Namburdiri Brahman, **3:**192
  Naxi, **6:**478
  Nayar, **3:**197, 198
  Nepali, **3:**202
  Newar, **3:**206
  Ngeh, **5:**194
  Nias, **5:**195
  Nicobarese, **3:**209
  Nyakyusa and Ngonde, **9:**253
  Nyamwezi and Sukuma, **9:**256
  Ogan-Besemah, **5:**198
  Okkaliga, **3:**214
  Oriya, **3:**216
  Pahari, **3:**220
  Paï-Tavytera, **7:**259
  Pak Thai, **5:**200
  Palaung, **5:**201
  Palawan, **5:**204
  Panare, **7:**265
  Pandit of Kashmir, **3:**224
  Pashai, **9:**267
  Pauserna, **7:**270
  Philippine Negritos, **5:**211
  Portuguese, **4:**206
  Pumi, **6:**483
  Punjabi, **3:**238
  P'u Noi, **5:**211
  Rai, **3:**249
  Rhadé, **5:**212
  Rikbaktsa, **7:**287
  Rotinese, **5:**213
  Sagada Igorot, **5:**216
  Sakalava, **9:**293, 294
  Saliva, **7:**292
  Saluan, **5:**217
  Samal, **5:**219
  Santal, **3:**253
  Saramaka, **7:**296
  Sasak, **5:**226
  Sedang, **5:**230
  Semang, **5:**234
  Senoi, **5:**237
  Shan, **5:**240
  Shavante, **7:**300
  She, **6:**489
  Shui, **6:**491
  Sinhalese, **3:**264, 265
  Sirionó, **7:**310
  Sora, **3:**268
  Stieng, **5:**243

  Subanun, **5:**243, 244
  Sulod, **5:**246
  Sundanese, **5:**247
  Sunwar, **3:**271
  Suruí, **7:**312
  Swahili, **9:**327
  Syrian Christian of Kerala, **3:**272-273
  Tagalog, **5:**248, 249
  Tagbanuwa, **5:**251
  Tai Lue, **5:**253
  Taiwan aboriginal peoples, **5:**257
  Taiwanese, **5:**259
  Talysh, **6:**355
  Tamil, **3:**276, 277
  Tamil of Sri Lanka, **3:**281
  Tapirapé, **7:**320
  Tau-Oi, **5:**261
  Tausug, **5:**262
  Tay, **5:**265
  Telugu, **3:**285
  Temiar, **5:**267
  Temne, **9:**342
  Terena, **7:**325
  Ternatan/Tidorese, **5:**274
  Tetum, **5:**276
  Tharu, **3:**293
  T'in, **5:**278
  Toala, **5:**280
  Tobelorese, **5:**280
  Tomini, **5:**280
  Toraja, **5:**281, 282
  Trio, **7:**335
  Tsimihety, **9:**358
  Tujia, **6:**498
  Ucayalino, **7:**91
  Udis, **6:**376
  Vedda, **3:**301
  Vietnamese, **5:**285
  Visayan, **5:**287
  Wa, **6:**502
  Wapisiana, **7:**355
  Warao, **7:**357
  Xibe, **6:**504
  Xikrin, **7:**367
  Yakan, **5:**288, 290
  Yakö, **9:**383
  Yao of Thailand, **5:**291
  Yuqui, **7:**392
  Zaramo, **9:**401
  Zhuang, **6:**510
  see also Agriculture, wet cultivation
Richman (leader)
  Tanaina, **1:**336, 337
Riddle telling
  Craho, **7:**135
  Vlachs, **4:**275
Ridicule (as social control). *See under* Child
    discipline; *under* Social control
    measures
Rights of the eldest. *See* Primogeniture
Ring shouts (dance)
  Sea Islanders, **1:**310
Rites of passage
  African American, **1:**12
  Albanians, **4:**6, 7
  Andamanese, **3:**11
  Azoreans, **4:**28
  Bene Israel, **3:**28

  Bosnian Muslims, **4:**36
  Brahman and Chhetri of Nepal, **3:**53
  Castilians, **4:**60
  Cherokee, **1:**62
  Choctaw, **1:**70
  Coorg, **3:**74
  Danes, **4:**90
  Hutterites, **1:**155
  Jat, **3:**112
  Jews, **1:**169
  Jicarilla, **1:**173
  Kikuyu, **9:**162
  Klamath, **1:**192
  Kota, **3:**137
  Luiseño, **1:**208
  Lunda, **9:**199
  Luyia, **9:**206
  Magar, **3:**158-159
  Maratha, **3:**170
  Mauritian, **3:**173
  Mbeere, **9:**222
  Ndembu, **9:**241
  Nepali, **3:**204, 205
  Nubians, **9:**248
  Pandit of Kashmir, **3:**226
  Pathan, **3:**232, 233
  Pokot, **9:**283
  Purum, **3:**244
  Santal, **3:**254
  Temne, **9:**345
  Toda, **3:**297
  Tuareg, **9:**369
  Yoruba, **9:**393
  see also Coming of age; Initiation; Marriage;
    Mortuary practices
Ritual dances. *See* Dance, ceremonial
Ritual fire. *See* Fire, sacralization
Ritual hunting. *See* Ceremonies, hunting
Ritual kinship. *See* Fictive kinship
Ritual objects
  Manx, **4:**171
Ritual offerings. *See* Oblation; Sacrifice
Ritual purification
  Cherokee, **1:**62
  Cheyenne, **1:**66
  Choctaw, **1:**73
Ritual purity. *See* Purity and pollution codes
Rituals. *See* Ceremonies
Ritual self-torture
  Hidsata, **1:**147
Ritual specialists
  Sidi, **3:**260
  see also Priesthood
Riverbank, death rituals at
  Brahman and Chhetri of Nepal, **3:**54
  Nepali, **3:**205
  Pahari, **3:**223
Riverine communities. *See* Villages, waterway
    locations
Rizalianism
  Bukidnon, **5:**54, 55
Robe trade
  Metis of Canada, **1:**226, 227-228
Rock art
  Kumeyaay, **1:**195
  Ngatatjara, **2:**241
  Tanaina, **1:**337
Rock carving. *See under* Carved objects

Rocket Festival
    Lao Isan, 5:162, 163
Rock spirits
    Yuit, 1:392
Rodnaya Ukrainskaya Natsional'naya Vera
    Ukrainians, 6:394
Roman Catholicism
    Acadians, 1:9
    Acholi, 9:6
    Afro-Bolivians, 7:9-10
    Afro-Brazilians, 7:12
    Afro-Colombians, 7:18
    Afro-Venezuelans, 7:27
    Agta, 5:6
    Akha, 5:13
    Albanian-Americans, 1:107
    Albanians, 4:7
    Alorese, 5:14
    Alsatians, 4:8
    Ambonese, 5:17
    Amuzgo, 8:5, 6
    Anambé, 7:42
    Andalusians, 4:12
    Apiaká, 7:50
    Aquitaine, 4:15
    Arubans, 8:12, 13, 14
    Assyrians, 9:27
    Ata Sikka, 5:22
    Ata Tana 'Ai, 5:23
    Atoni, 5:28
    Austrians, 4:21
    Auvergnats, 4:23
    Aveyronnais, 4:24, 26
    Awakateko, 8:16, 17
    Awá Kwaiker, 7:65
    Aymara, 7:68
    Azoreans, 4:27, 28-29
    Bamiléké, 9:39
    Baniwa-Curripaco-Wakuenai, 7:79, 80
    Barbadians, 8:23
    Barí, 7:85
    Basques, 1:34;4:32
    Bavarians, 4:33, 34, 35
    Belau, 2:27
    Bemba, 9:47
    Betsileo, 9:57
    Black Creoles of Louisiana, 1:39
    Blacks in Canada, 1:44
    Boazi, 2:29
    Boruca, Bribri, Cabécar, 8:29-30
    Bretons, 4:38, 39-40
    Bukidnon, 5:54, 55
    Burgundians, 4:47
    Butonese, 5:68, 69
    Cahita, 8:36
    Cajuns, 1:48, 50
    Calabrese, 4:49, 50
    Callahuaya, 7:89
    Canarians, 4:52, 53
    Canelos Quichua, 7:100
    Cape Coloureds, 9:60
    Cape Verdeans, 4:55, 56
    Carib of Dominica, 8:40
    Cariña, 7:102
    Carrier, 1:52
    Castilians, 4:58, 60-61
    Catalans, 4:63
    cattle ranchers of Huasteca, 8:44

Central Yup'ik Eskimos, 1:56, 58
Chambri, 2:31, 32
Chatino, 8:51, 52
Chimbu, 2:35
Chinantec, 8:54
Chinese of Costa Rica, 8:62
Chipaya, 7:116
Chipewyan, 1:68, 69
Chiquitano, 7:118
Choiseul Island, 2:38, 39
Ch'ol, 8:65
Chontal of Tabasco, 8:68-69
Chuj, 8:73
Colorado, 7:131
Comox, 1:76
Cora, 8:77
Corsicans, 4:68
Costa Ricans, 8:81
Cotopaxi Quichua, 7:134
Creoles of Nicaragua, 8:86
Croats, 4:74
Cubans, 8:88, 90
Cuicatec, 8:93
Curaçao, 8:97
Cyclades, 4:78
Czech-Canadians, 1:120
Czechs, 4:84
Dalmatians, 4:87
Dinka, 9:70
Dogrib, 1:87, 88, 89
Dominicans, 8:103
Dutch, 4:94
Dutch-Americans, 1:110
Easter Island, 2:53, 54, 55
East Indians in Trinidad, 8:107
English, 4:97
Filipino, 5:86, 87
Filipinos in Canada, 1:97, 98
Filipinos in the United States, 1:102, 103
Fipa, 9:99
Flemish, 4:107, 108, 109
French-Americans, 1:111
French Canadians, 1:132, 133
Friuli, 4:113
Futuna, 2:67
Gaels (Irish), 4:117
Galicians, 4:120
Garifuna, 8:115
Germans, 4:123;6:140
German Swiss, 4:126, 127
Gitanos, 4:130
Grenadians, 8:115
Gros Ventre, 1:134
Guadeloupians, 8:116
Guarayu, 7:174
Gusii, 9:110
Gypsies, 6:148
Gypsies and caravan dwellers in the
    Netherlands, 4:138
Haitians, 1:138;8:122
Han, 6:448
Hare, 1:141, 142
Hawaiians, 2:97
Highland Scots, 4:141, 142
Hungarians, 4:145
Indian Christians, 3:103
Irish, 4:151, 152, 153
Irish-Americans, 1:113

Irish-Canadians, 1:123
Irish Travelers, 1:162, 164
Irish Travellers, 4:156
Italian-Americans, 1:113
Italian-Canadians, 1:124
Italian Mexicans, 8:131, 132
Iteso, 9:130
Itza,' 8:135
Jing, 6:454
Kachin, 5:118
Kapauku, 2:105
Karen, 5:128, 129
Kédang, 5:131, 132
Keres Pueblo Indians, 1:180, 181, 182
Kewa, 2:117
K'iche,' 8:142
Kilenge, 2:119, 120
Kiribati, 2:123
Kittsians and Nevisians, 8:145
Kmhmu, 5:141
Kongo, 9:168
Korean, 5:148
Kumeyaay converts, 1:195
Kuna, 8:150
Kurtatchi, 2:133
Ladin, 4:160
Ladinos, 8:153
Lahu, 5:152, 153, 154;6:463
Lakalai, 2:140
Lamaholot, 5:154, 155, 156
Latinos, 1:205, 206
Latvians, 6:236, 238
Lenca, 8:156
Leonese, 4:162
Lesu, 2:146, 147
Lisu, 6:466
Lithuanian-Americans, 1:114
Lithuanians, 6:250, 251
Lobi-Dagarti peoples, 9:185
Lowland Scots, 4:163
Luba of Shaba, 9:192
Lugbara, 9:195
Lunda, 9:198
Luo, 9:200
Luxembourgeois, 4:163
Madeirans, 4:166
Mafulu, 2:153
Makushi, 7:219
Malaita, 2:163
Maliseet, 1:211, 212, 213
Maltese, 4:167, 169
Mam, 8:159
Manam, 2:167, 169
Mandak, 2:170, 171
Mandan, 1:215
Manggarai, 5:176
Manus, 2:173
Marind-anim, 2:184
Marquesas Islands, 2:189, 190
Marshall Islands, 2:192
Martiniquais, 8:163
Mashco, 7:227
Mauritian converts, 3:173
Mazahua, 8:166
Mazatec, 8:169
Mbeere, 9:222
Mejbrat, 2:195
Mekeo, 2:199, 200

Roman Catholicism (cont'd)
Melpa, 2:202
Mendi, 2:205
Micmac, 1:234, 235
Micronesia, 1:238
Miskito, 8:172
Mixe, 8:175
Mixtec, 8:178
Moluccans—South, 5:188
Montenegrins, 4:173
Montserratians, 8:181
Mossi, 9:230
Mundugumor, 2:219
Mundurucu, 7:245
Murik, 2:221
Muyu, 2:228, 229, 230
Nahua of the Huasteca, 8:186
Nahua of the State of Mexico, 8:190
Nahuat of the Sierra de Puebla, 8:193
Nasioi, 2:233, 235
Nauru, 2:237
Ngawbe, 8:197
Nias, 5:196
Ningerum, 2:247
Nissan, 2:249, 250, 251
Noanamá, 7:252
Nomoi, 2:252
Northern Irish, 4:177, 178, 179, 180
Northern Metis, 1:262
Northern Shoshone and Bannock, 1:267
Nu, 6:481
Nyakyusa and Ngonde, 9:254
Occitans, 4:185
Ojibwa, 1:270
Osage, 1:279
Otavalo, 7:255
Otomí of the Sierra, 8:201
Otomí of the Valley of Mezquital, 8:206
Ottawa, 1:280
Oy, 5:200
Páez, 7:257, 258
Palestinians, 9:266
Palikur, 7:263
Palu'e, 5:205, 206
Pame, 8:208
Pasiegos, 4:191
Pentecost, 2:261, 262, 264
Philippine Negritos, 5:210
Piemontese, 4:199
Piemontese Sinti, 4:201
Pima Bajo, 8:213
Piro, 7:280
Pohnpei, 2:269
Poles, 4:201, 202, 204;6:307, 308
Polish-Americans, 1:115
Polish-Canadians, 1:125
Portuguese, 4:208
Provencala, 4:211
Puerto Ricans, 8:223
Pukapuka, 2:272
Q'anjob'al, 8:225
Q'eqchi,' 8:227
Rapa, 2:275
Raroia, 2:276
Rom, 1:305, 306
Rossel Island, 2:278, 279
Rotuma, 2:281, 283
Saint Lucians, 8:231

Sakalava, 9:298
Salasaca, 7:290, 291
Saliva, 7:292
Samal Moro, 5:222
Samoa, 2:287, 288
Saraguro, 7:295
Saramaka, 7:298
Sardinians, 4:227
Sengseng, 2:296
Shui, 6:491
Siberian Germans, 6:339
Sicilians, 4:236, 237
Sinhalese converts, 3:267
Sirionó, 7:311
Siwai, 2:302, 304
Slovak-Americans, 1:117
Slovaks, 4:245
Slovene-Americans, 1:117
Slovene-Canadians, 1:127
Slovenes, 4:249
Slovensko Roma, 4:251
Sorbs, 4:253
Spanish Rom, 4:255
Subanun, 5:245
Suku, 9:322, 323
Sumu, 8:239
Swazi, 9:332
Swiss, Italian, 4:261, 262
Syrian Christian of Kerala, 3:272, 274
Tagalog, 5:248, 250
Tamil of Sri Lanka converts, 3:283
Tanna, 2:313
Taos, 1:342, 343
Tarahumara, 8:242
Tarascans, 8:246
Tauade, 2:318
Tepehua, 8:249
Tepehuan of Chihuahua, 8:253
Terena, 7:327
Tetum, 5:276
Tewa Pueblos, 1:347, 349
Ticuna, 7:329, 330
Tiroleans, 4:264
Tiwi, 2:327, 329
Tlapanec, 8:259
Tokelau, 2:332
Tolai, 2:333
Tory Islanders, 4:265, 266
Totonac, 8:265, 266
Transylvanian ethnic groups
Triqui, 8:272
Trobriand Islands, 2:348
Truk, 2:352, 354
Tu, 6:496
Tuscans, 4:269
Tzotzil and Tzeltal of Pantelhó, 8:277-278
Tzotzil of San Andrés Larraínzar, 8:285
Tzotzil of San Bartolomé de los Llanos,
    8:289, 290
Tzotzil of Zinacantan, 8:293-294
Tz'utujil, 8:297, 298
Ulithi, 2:358, 359
Vietnamese, 5:286
Visayan, 5:287
Vlach Gypsies of Hungary, 4:272
Vlachs, 4:275
Walloons, 4:276, 277, 278
Wanano, 7:350

Wape, 2:370
Wapisiana, 7:356
Warao, 7:359
Wasteko, 8:303
Wayapi, 7:363
Western Apache, 1:373
Wogeo, 2:380
Woleai, 2:384
Yagua, 7:373
Yap, 2:393-394
Yaqui, 8:306, 307
Yi, 6:507
Yukateko, 8:310
Yukpa, 7:384
Zande, 9:399
Zapotec, 8:313
Zaramo, 9:403
Zoque, 8:317
Zuni, 1:399
  see also Syncretism; Uniate Catholicism
Romanesque architecture
Bretons, 4:40
Romanian Orthodox. See Orthodox
    Christianity
Romeiros (pilgrims)
Azoreans, 4:28
Roofing trade
peripatetics, 1:287
Root crops
Akan, 9:11
Lugbara, 9:194
Shetlanders, 4:233
Sumu, 8:237
Root medicines. See Herbal, plant, and root
    medicine
Root weaving
Saami, 4:221
Rope making
Divehi, 3:76
Iroquois, 1:165
Santal, 3:253
Rope-sliding ceremony
Pahari, 3:223
Rope tying
Yap, 2:394
Rose painting
Norwegians, 4:182
Rosh Hashanah (holiday)
Bukharan Jews, 6:65
Mountain Jews, 6:273
Royalty
Akan, 9:12
Bamiléké, 9:37, 39
Ganda, 9:104-105
Hausa, 9:113
Kanuri, 9:152
Lakher, 3:146
Lozi, 9:189
Mamprusi, 9:213
Mossi, 9:229
Ndebele, 9:237
Parsi, 3:228
Rajput, 3:249
Sakalava, 9:297
Shilluk, 9:311
Swazi, 9:331-332
Tsimshian, 1:354
Yoruba, 9:392

Zulu, **9**:411
see also Nobility
Rubber growing
  Kalimantan Dayaks, **5**:120
  Kenyah-Kayan-Kajang, **5**:133-134
  Malay, **5**:175
  Ogan-Besemah, **5**:198
  Senoi, **5**:237
  Sinhalese, **3**:265
  Syrian Christian of Kerala, **3**:273
Rubber industry
  Edo, **9**:79
Rubber processing
  Syrian Christian of Kerala, **3**:273
Rubber tapping
  Campa del Pichis, **7**:91
  Chácobo, **7**:105-106
  Cinta Larga, **7**:127
  Culina, **7**:146
  Pauserna, **7**:270
  Puinave, **7**:282
  Rikbaktsa, **7**:287
  Tatuyo, **7**:323
  Ucayalino, **7**:91
Ru (bone) kinship concept
  Nyinba, **3**:211
Rug hooking
  Acadians, **1**:8
Rug weaving
  Azoreans, **4**:27
  Baluchi, **3**:23
  Bulgarians, **4**:43
  Finns, **4**:102
  Jews of Kurdistan, **9**:145
  Navajo, **1**:251, 253
  Nepali, **3**:202
  Nyinba, **3**:213
  Portuguese, **4**:208
  Qashqa'i, **9**:285
  Romanians, **4**:214
  Shahsevan, **9**:308
  Turks, **9**:376
Rune song
  Finns, **4**:104
Russian Old Rite
  Don Cossacks, **6**:106
  Karelians, **6**:171
  Old Believers, **1**:272-273, 274;**6**:290, 291
  Russians, **6**:315
  Siberiaki, **6**:334
Russian Orthodox Church. _See_ Orthodox
    Christianity
Rye growing
  Aghuls, **6**:11
  Aveyronnais, **4**:25
  Bavarians, **4**:33
  Belarussians, **6**:60
  Bonan, **6**:422
  Buriats, **6**:67
  Chuvash, **6**:84
  Dargins, **6**:96
  Don Cossacks, **6**:104
  Kashubians, **4**:158
  Kazakhs, **6**:177
  Kriashen Tatars, **6**:211
  Leonese, **4**:161
  Lezgins, **6**:242
  Montenegrins, **4**:172

Poles, **4**:203
Pomaks, **4**:205
Portuguese, **4**:206
Russian peasants, **6**:311
Rutuls, **6**:319
Slovaks, **4**:243
Svans, **6**:344
Tabasarans, **6**:348
Tiroleans, **4**:263
Udmurt, **6**:380
Ukrainian peasants, **6**:386

Sabantui [Savantuy] festival
  Kriashen Tatars, **6**:212
  Siberian Tatars, **6**:342
Sachem
  Cayuga, **1**:55
  Iroquois, **1**:166, 167
  Mohawk, **1**:242
  Oneida, **1**:276
  Onondaga, **1**:276
  Senaca, **1**:315
Sacred animals. _See_ Animal reverence
Sacred Arrows (Cheyenne sacred object),
    1:66
Sacred Ball Game
  Teton, **1**:346
Sacred band
  Cheyenne, **1**:65
Sacred bundles
  Fox, **1**:130
  Kickapoo, **1**:185
  Mandan, **1**:214, 215
  Pawnee, **1**:285
  Zuni, **1**:399
  see also Medicine bundles
Sacred clowns
  Zuni, **1**:399
Sacred dairy cult
  Toda, **3**:296-297, 298
Sacred fire. _See_ Fire, sacralization
Sacred grove
  Santal, **3**:254, 255
Sacred land areas
  Kumeyaay, **1**:194
Sacred packs. _See_ Sacred bundles
Sacred pole
  Omaha, **1**:275
Sacred thread
  Maratha, **3**:169
  Parsi, **3**:229
  Tamil, **3**:278
  Vaisya, **3**:300
Sacrifice
  for ancestors
    Igbo, **9**:123
    Kpelle, **9**:174
    Lugbara, **9**:194
    Pedi, **9**:270
    Shona, **9**:314
    Swazi, **9**:332
    Xhosa, **9**:381
  animal
    Abkhazians, **6**:9
    Agaria, **3**:6
    Alak, **5**:13
    Ata Tana 'Ai, **5**:23, 25
    Bhutanese, **3**:46

Chipaya, **7**:117
Chukchee, **6**:77
Cinta Larga, **7**:129
Circassians, **6**:90
Dyula, **9**:77
East Indians in Trinidad, **8**:106, 107
Gagauz, **6**:125
Garifuna, **8**:115
Garo, **3**:84
Gelao, **6**:435
Gond, **3**:86, 87
Hani, **6**:451
Hmong, **5**:94
Iban, **5**:97
Ilongot, **5**:102
Irula, **3**:108
Itelmen, **6**:153
Jingpo, **6**:456, 458, 458-459
Jino, **6**:460
Kachin, **5**:116, 118
Kalingas, **5**:123
Karachays, **6**:161
Karelians, **6**:172
Karen, **5**:128, 129
Kazakhs, **6**:182
Khanty, **6**:190, 191-192
Khasi, **3**:125, 126
Khevsur, **6**:196
Kikuyu, **9**:162
Kond, **3**:132, 133
Koryaks and Kerek, **6**:208, 209
Koya, **3**:140, 141
Kriashen Tatars, **6**:211, 212
Lahu, **5**:152
Lakher, **3**:147, 148
Lepcha, **3**:148, 149
Limbu, **3**:150
Magar, **3**:157, 160-161, 161, 162
Mamprusi, **9**:214
Mansi, **6**:254
Maonan, **6**:468-469
Maris, **6**:258
Miami, **1**:231
Miao, **6**:472
Mikir, **3**:176
Mnong, **5**:185
Mountain Jews, **6**:273
Munda, **3**:184
Muong, **5**:192
Murut, **5**:193
Nambudiri Brahman, **3**:194
Nias, **5**:197
Nivkh, **6**:285
Pahari, **3**:221, 222, 223
Palu'e, **5**:207, 208, 209
Pathan, **3**:233
Pedi, **9**:270
Pokot, **9**:283
Popoloca, **8**:216
Purum, **3**:244
Rotinese, **5**:214
Sagada Igorot, **5**:216, 217
Santal, **3**:253
Sarakatsani, **4**:224
Shui, **6**:491
Siberiaki, **6**:333, 334
Sora, **3**:270
Svans, **6**:346

Sacrifice (cont'd)
    Taiwan aboriginal peoples, 5:257
    Thadou, 3:289
    T'in, 5:278, 279
    Toda, 3:298
    Tonga, 9:335
    Toraja, 5:281, 282, 283
    Triqui, 8:272
    Tzotzil of San Bartolomé de los Llanos,
        8:291
    Tzotzil of Zinacantan, 8:294
    Wa, 6:501, 503
    Yakan, 5:290
    Yakut, 6:407
    Zhuang, 6:511
    see also subhead livestock *below; subhead*
      pig *below*
  at burial groves of chiefs
    Nyakyusa and Ngonde, 9:254
  blood
    Lugbara, 9:195
    Qiang, 6:487
  blood (own)
    Santal, 3:255
    Temiar, 5:272
  bloodless
    Orok, 6:296
  by bridegroom
    Buriats, 6:68
  chickens
    Mossi, 9:230
    Nyamwezi and Sukuma, 9:257
  for deities
    Lobi-Dagarti peoples, 9:185
    Pokot, 9:283
  Easter
    Falasha, 9:92
  feasts as
    Nuristanis, 9:251
  for fertility
    Mossi, 9:230
  fingers of girls
    Dani, 2:45
  food
    Miami, 1:232
    Miao, 6:472
  funerary
    Dogon, 9:73
    Iteso, 9:130
    Lugbara, 9:195
  haoma drink
    Zoroastrians, 9:410
  for healing
    Betsileo, 9:57
    Dogon, 9:74
    Mixe, 8:175
    Tzotzil and Tzeltal of Pantelhó, 8:278
  human
    Ache, 7:6, 7
    Apiaká, 7:50
    Bilaan, 5:42
    Bukidnon, 5:54
    Khanty, 6:189
    Kond, 3:132, 133
    Kongo, 9:168
    Maori, 2:178
    Marquesas Islands, 2:191
    Nias, 5:196, 197

    Oraon, 3:214
    Pawnee, 1:285
    San Cristobal, 2:289
    Tahiti, 2:306, 307
    Wa, 6:503
  for land needs
    Lobi-Dagarti peoples, 9:184
  livestock
    Berbers of Morocco, 9:52
    Betsileo, 9:57
    Khoi, 9:159
    Lugbara, 9:194
    Rukuba, 9:291
    Shilluk, 9:311
    Suri, 9:326-327
    Tandroy, 9:338
    Tsimihety, 9:359
    Tuareg, 9:369
    Turks, 9:376
    Xhosa, 9:381
  pig
    Malaita, 2:163
    Melpa, 2:202
    Mendi, 2:205
    Nguna, 2:244
    Orokaiva, 2:257-258
    Sio, 2:301
    Telefolmin, 2:323
  for rain
    Mossi, 9:230
    Zapotec, 8:313
  rituals
    Konso, 9:171
    Tandroy, 9:338
  tobacco
    Miami, 1:232
  valuable possessions
    Yuit, 1:392
  for village guardian spirit
    Alorese, 5:16
  white dog
    Iroquois, 1:167
  see also Oblation
Sacrifice to Heaven (ceremony)
  Naxi, 6:480
Sagamore
  Abenaki, 1:5
Sagas
  Icelander-Canadians, 1:123
Sago palm
  Asmat, 2:19
  Banaro, 2:21
  Boazi, 2:29
  Bolaang Mongondow, 5:43
  Chambri, 2:31
  Daribi, 2:46
  Foi, 2:59, 60
  Gebusi, 2:77
  Gnau, 2:80
  Iatmul, 2:98
  Kaluli, 2:101
  Kwoma, 2:134
  Laki, 5:154
  Manus, 2:173
  Marind-anim, 2:183
  Melanau, 5:178-179
  Mimika, 2:206
  Minahasans, 5:181

    Miyanmin, 2:210
    Mountain Arapesh, 2:216
    Mundugumor, 2:218
    Murik, 2:221
    Namau, 2:231
    Nasioi, 2:233
    Ningerum, 2:245, 246
    Orokolo, 2:259
    Penan, 5:210
    Saluan, 5:217
    Ternatan/Tidorese, 5:274
    Tikopia, 2:325
    Tomini, 5:280
    Tor, 2:342
    Wape, 2:371
    Waropen, 2:376
    Yangoru Boiken, 2:388
    see also Palm *headings*
Sahajiya Vaishnavism
  Baul, 3:26
Sailors. *See* Mariners
Sainday (trickster). *See* Sendeh
Saint Ann's Day
  Micmac, 1:235
Saint David's Day
  Welsh, 4:280
Saint Demetrius Day
  Sarakatsani, 4:224
Saint George's Day
  Carpatho-Rusyns, 6:71
  Ingilos, 6:151
  Sarakatsani, 4:224
  Slav Macedonians, 4:241
Saint Gerasimos Day
  Ionians, 4:150
Saint John's Day
  Carpatho-Rusyns, 6:71
Saint John's Eve
  Siberiaki, 6:334
Saint John the Baptist (holiday)
  Belarussians, 6:61
  Siberian Estonians, 6:337
  Siberian Germans, 6:339
  Tagalog, 5:251
  Ukrainian peasants, 6:387
Saint Joseph Day
  Sicilians, 4:237
Saint Lazarus's Day
  Slav Macedonians, 4:241
Saint Nicholas Day
  Frisians, 4:112
Saint Spiros Day
  Ionians, 4:150
Saint veneration
  Afro-Colombians, 7:18
  Afro-Hispanic Pacific Lowlanders,
    7:22-23
  Afro-Venezuelans, 7:28
  Albanians, 4:7
  Aquitaine, 4:15
  Auvergnats, 4:23
  Azoreans, 4:28
  Bretons, 4:39, 40
  Cahita, 8:37
  Calabrese, 4:50
  Canarians, 4:52
  Cape Berdeans, 4:56
  Castilians, 4:60, 61

Catalans, 4:63
Cyclades, 4:78
Gaels (Irish), 4:117
Galicians, 4:120
Ionians, 4:150
Irish, 4:153
Latinos, 1:206
Lenca, 8:156
Madeirans, 4:166
Maratha, 3:170
Mazahua, 8:166
Mount Athos, 4:176
Occitans, 4:185
Otomí of the Valley of Mezquital, 8:206
Pame, 8:208
Portuguese, 4:208
Puerto Ricans, 8:223
Sarakatsani, 4:224
Sicilians, 4:237
Sidi, 3:260
Slav Macedonians, 4:241
Slovensko Roma, 4:251
Tharu, 3:293
Totonac, 8:266
Tzeltal, 8:274
Tzotzil of San Andrés Larraínzar, 8:285
Tzotzil of Zinacantan, 8:294
Yaqui, 8:307
Zapotec, 8:313
Zoque, 8:317
see also Patron saint
Sakti (spiritual power)
Lingayat, 3:153
Sales jobs
East Asians of the United States, 1:101
Sallah festival
Hausa, 9:114
Salmon canneries
Pacific Eskimo, 1:282, 283
Tanaina, 1:335
Salmon ceremony
Karok, 1:176
Tanaina, 1:337
Yurok, 1:395
Salmon fishing
Ahtna, 1:14
Carrier, 1:52
Central Yup'ik Eskimos, 1:57
Chinook, 1:67
Comox, 1:76
Highland Scots, 4:140
Iglulik Inuit, 1:155
Ingalik, 1:157
Karok, 1:176
Kashubians, 4:158
Kawkiutl, 1:198
Klallam, 1:190
Lillooet, 1:206
Nez Percé, 1:254
Nootka, 1:256
Northern Shoshone and Bannock, 1:266, 267
Okanagon, 1:272
Pacific Eskimo, 1:282, 283
Tanaina, 1:335, 337
Tanana, 1:338
Thompson, 1:350

Tlingit, 1:351
Tolowa, 1:353
Tsimshian, 1:354, 355
Wintun, 1:383
Wiyot, 1:384
Yurok, 1:394, 395
Salsa music
Afro-Colombians, 7:18
Latinos, 1:206
Salt
as seasoning and preserving
Tubatulabal, 1:355
taboo after death of adult
Magar, 3:157
Salt exchange
Nyakyusa and Ngonde, 9:253
Salt production and trade
Alur, 9:13
Cape Verdeans, 4:55
Cherokee, 1:61
Kalapalo, 7:187
Luba of Shaba, 9:191
Mehinaku, 7:237
Nagas, 3:187, 188
Paraujano, 7:267
Sleb, 9:315
Tewa Pueblos, 1:348
Thakali, 3:290, 292
Tigray, 9:347
Yukateko, 8:309
Zuni, 1:398
Salvation beliefs
Brahman and Chhetri of Nepal, 3:53
castes, Hindu, 3:57
see also Afterlife, immortality of soul
Samsara
Bengali, 3:34
Pahari, 3:222
Pandit of Kashmir, 3:226
see also Reincarnation beliefs
Sanctuary customs
Baluchi, 3:23
Winnebago, 1:382
Sandal making
Pume, 7:283
Sanga (ceremony)
Ontong Java, 2:255
Sangha (Buddhist monastic organizations)
Sinhalese, 3:267
Sangha (festival)
Dai, 6:427
Sansari Mari (female deity)
Magar, 3:161
Sanskritization
castes, Hindu, 3:57
Jatav, 3:115
see also Class mobility
Santeria [Santería] religion
African Americans, 1:13
Afro-Venezuelans, 7:27
Cubans, 8:90
Dominicans, 8:103
Latinos, 1:206
Saraswati (female deity)
Bengali, 3:34
Pandit of Kashmir, 3:224
Satdinna (prayer)
Chakma, 3:61

Sauna
Finns, 4:104
Maris, 6:258
Savior, future. See Messiah belief
Sayyeds
Pathan, 3:233
Scaffold burial. See Mortuary practices
Scallop fishing
Manx, 4:170
Scalp Dance
Northern Shoshone and Bannock, 1:267
Scalp Society
Tewa Pueblos, 1:349
Scalp taking
Algonkin, 1:17
Chorote, 7:126
Lengua, 7:211
Maká, 7:217
Moantagnais-Naskapi, 1:246
Nivaclé, 7:250, 251
Northern Shoshone and Bannock, 1:267
Scarification. See Body scarification; Face scarification
Scavengers
Rom of Czechoslovakia, 4:218, 219
Rominche, 4:216
Slovensko Roma, 4:250
Untouchables, 3:299
Vlach Gypsies of Hungary, 4:271
see also Scrap trade
Scholars. See Education
Schooling. See Education; Literacy
Scientific knowledge
Muslim, 3:185
Scientific medicine. See Medical practices and treatments, allopathic medicine
Scolding (as social control). See under Social control measures
Scrap trade
Gitanos, 4:129
Irish Travellers, 4:155
Piemontese Sinti, 4:200
Rom of Czechoslovakia, 4:218, 219
Rominche, 4:216
Slovensko Roma, 4:250
see also Scavengers
Scribes
Jews of Yemen, 9:149
Sculpture
Ashkenazim, 6:36
Belarussians, 6:61
Bretons, 4:40
Buriats, 6:68
Circassians, 6:91
Dai, 6:428
Dolgan, 6:102
Estonian, 6:115
Flemish, 4:108
Iatmul, 2:100
Japanese, 5:110
Khmer, 5:138
Korean, 5:148
Kwakiutl, 1:200
Malekula, 2:166
Maori, 2:178
Mundugumor, 2:220
Nootka, 1:257
Northern Paiute, 1:263

Sculpture (cont'd)
  Poles, 6:309
  Santa Cruz, 2:292
  Senoi, 5:237
  Siberian Tatars, 6:342
  Tibetans, 6:496
  Tiwi, 2:329
  Volga Tatars, 6:402
  Warlpiri, 2:374
  Yakut, 6:407
  see also Carved objects
Sea bird catching
  West Greenland Inuit, 1:377
Seafarers. See Mariners
Seal hunting
  Aleut, 1:15
  Baffinland Inuit, 1:29, 30
  Copper Eskimo, 1:76, 77, 78
  East Greenland Inuit, 1:106
  Iglulik Inuit, 1:155
  Inughuit, 1:160
  Kwakiutl, 1:198
  Labroador Inuit, 1:201
  Netsilik Inuit, 1:254
  Nootka, 1:256
  Pacific Eskimo, 1:283
  Tanaina, 1:335
  West Greenland Inuit, 1:377, 378
  Yuit, 1:390
Sea mammal hunting. See Marine animal
    hunting
Seana (camp of the dead)
  Cheyenne, 1:66
Séance
  Agta, 5:6
  Akawaio, 7:33
  Asiatic Eskimos, 6:42
  Bajau, 5:34
  Chiriguano, 7:122
  Chukchee, 6:78
  Gebusi, 2:77, 79
  Han, 6:447
  Hoti, 7:176
  Karihona, 7:193
  Ket, 6:185
  Khanty, 6:192
  Nivkh, 6:285
  Siberiaki, 6:334
  Subanun, 5:245
  Tupari, 7:340-341
  Yekuana, 7:381
  Yuit, 1:392
  see also Mediums
Sea otter hunting
  Aleut, 1:15
  Baffinland Inuit, 1:29
  Pacific Eskimo, 1:283
Seasonal housing. See under Houses and
    housing
Seasonal migration. See Herding; Hunting
    and gathering; Migrant workers
    (seasonal); Seminomads
Seasonal villages. See Houses and housing,
    seasonal
Sea tenure
  Icelanders, 4:147
Sea Woman (deity)
  West Greenland Inuit, 1:378

Seclusion (as initiation rite)
  Abenaki, 1:5
  Butonese, 5:67-68
  Chipewyan, 1:69
  Cree, 1:81
  Eastern Shoshone, 1:104, 105
  Haida, 1:136
  Keraki, 2:114
  Khoi, 9:16160
  Kilenge, 2:119
  Kwoma, 2:135
  Lau, 2:144
  Lesu, 2:147
  Mafulu, 2:153
  Marind-anim, 2:183
  Miami, 1:231
  Namau, 2:231
  Orokolo, 2:259, 260
  Tangu, 2:312
  Tanna, 2:314
  Tauade, 2:319, 320
  Thompson, 1:350
  Tor, 2:344
  Torres Strait Islanders, 2:346
  Usino, 2:363
  Warlpiri, 2:374
  Winnebago, 1:381
  Woleai, 2:383
  see also Childbirth, seclusion; Menstrua-
      tion; Mortuary practices, seclusion;
      Vision quest
Seclusion of women. See Gender separation;
    Menstruation; Purdah; Women's
    activity curtailment
Second coming. See Millenarianism beliefs;
    Messiah belief
Second sight beliefs. See Parapsychology
Secret societies. See under Associations, clubs,
    and societies
Secularism
  Herero, 9:118
Security circle
  Garia, 2:75, 76
  Ningerum, 2:247
Seed packaging
  Shakers, 1:316
Seer. See Diviners; Fortune-telling; Mediums;
    Oracles
Séga (musical form)
  Mauritian, 3:173
Segregation
  African Americans, 1:10
  Jatav, 3:113
  Tamil, 3:278
  Untouchables, 3:299
  see also Closed community; Gender
      separation
Self-choice marriage. See Marriage, free
    choice
Self-control (as valued trait)
  German Swiss, 4:127
  Menominee, 1:221
  West Greenland Inuit, 1:377-378
  Wiyot, 1:385
Self-employment
  Flemish, 4:129
  Gitanos, 4:129
  Rominche, 4:216

  see also Entrepreneurs; Informal economy;
      Shopkeeping; Small businesses
Self-purification. See Asceticism
Self-reliance (as valued trait)
  Hidsata, 1:147
  Ozarks, 1:281
  Poles, 4:203
  Yuit, 1:391
Self-sufficiency. See Individual autonomy
Self-torture
  Hidsata, 1:147
Seminomads
  Afar, 9:7
  Albanians, 4:4, 5
  Baluchi, 3:22-24
  Bedouin, 9:43
  Berbers of Morocco, 9:49
  Brahui, 3:54
  Chipewyan, 1:68
  Corsicans, 4:66
  Cretans, 4:70, 71
  Delaware, 1:85
  Fox, 1:128-129
  Fulani, 9:101
  Gujar, 3:89
  Iglulik Inuit, 1:155
  Jicarilla, 1:172
  Kickapoo, 1:182, 183, 184
  Klamath, 1:191
  Kohistani, 3:128
  Kurds, 9:175
  Labroador Inuit, 1:201
  Lur, 9:201-202
  Mandan, 1:214
  Montagnais-Naskapi, 1:244, 245
  Navajo, 1:251
  Nayaka, 3:195
  North Alaskan Eskimos, 1:259
  Northern Shoshone and Bannock, 1:266
  Ojibwa, 1:269
  Okanagon, 1:272
  Omaha, 1:344
  Ottawa, 1:279-280
  Pasiegos, 4:188, 189, 190, 191
  Pawnee, 1:284
  Peloponnesians, 4:193
  peripatetics of Afghanistan, Iran, and
      Turkey, 9:275
  Qashqa'i, 9:285
  Rom, 1:303
  Saami, 4:220
  Sarakatsani, 4:223-224
  Shahsevan, 9:308
  Somalis, 9:316
  Southern Paiute and (Chemehuevi), 1:330
  Swiss, Italian, 4:260
  Tanana, 1:338
  Tandroy, 9:336
  Teda, 9:340
  Thakali, 3:292
  Thompson, 1:350
  Tuareg, 9:367
  Tubatulabal, 1:355
  Ute, 1:360
  Walapai, 1:364
  Western Apache, 1:371
  Western Shoshone, 1:374
  West Greenland Inuit, 1:376

Wichita, 1:379
Yörük, 9:394
see also Herding; Hunting and gathering;
        Itinerants
Semiseclusion of women. See Women's
        activity curtailment
Semisubterranean housing. See under Houses
        and housing
Senawahv (creator)
    Ute, 1:362
Sendeh (culture hero/trickster)
    Kiowa, 1:188
Seniority. See Elder respect
Separatism (political). See Nationalist
        movements
Separatist sects. See Closed community
Septum piercing. See Body piercing, nose
Serfdom
    Bulgarian Gypsies, 4:41
Servants. See Domestic service; Labor,
        bonded; Slavery
Service industry
    Basques, 1:33
    Bene Israel, 3:27
    Black West Indians in the United States,
        1:45
    Bulgarian Gypsies, 4:41
    Catalans, 4:62
    Chinese of South Asia, 3:68
    Danes, 4:88
    East Asians of Canada, 1:96
    East Asians of the United States, 1:100,
        101
    English, 4:96
    Madeirans, 4:165
    Meo, 3:174
    Micronesians, 1:237
    Moor of Sri Lanka, 3:180, 181
    Pahari, 3:220-221
    peripatetics, 3:234, 235
    Provencal, 4:210
    Rom, 1:304
    Rom of Czechoslovakia, 4:218
    Rominche, 4:216
    Sardinians, 4:226
    Sea Islanders, 1:310
    Sicilians, 4:236
    Slovensko Roma, 4:250
    Syrian Christian of Kerula, 3:273
    Tamil of Sri Lanka, 3:281
    Thakali, 3:290
    see also Shopkeeping; Tourism
Sesame growing
    Anuak, 9:21
    Baggara, 9:30
    Guarijío, 8:117
    Kachin, 5:116
    Mazatec, 8:168
    Persians, 9:279
    Rukuba, 9:289
    Shilluk, 9:311
    Telugu, 3:285
Setsubun (ceremony)
    Japanese, 5:109
Settlements. See Villages
Seventh-Day Adventists
    Bamiléké, 9:39
    Barbadians, 8:23

Belau, 2:27
    Choiseul Island, 2:38, 39
    Germans, 6:140
    Gusii, 9:110
    Kurtatchi, 2:133
    Maisin, 2:159
    Malaita, 2:163
    Manam, 2:169
    Manus, 2:173
    Martiniquais, 8:163
    Melpa, 2:202
    Micronesians, 1:238
    Murik, 2:221
    Nasioi, 2:235
    Nyakyusa and Ngonde, 9:254
    Pemon, 7:273
    Pentecost, 2:261
    Piro, 7:280
    Pukapuka, 2:272
    Rotuma, 2:283
    Sambia, 2:286
    Transylvanian ethnic groups, 4:268
    Turks and Caicos Islanders, 8:273
    Zoque, 8:317
Sex ratio, disproportionate
    Andamanese, 3:8
    Ionians, 4:148
Sex roles. See Gender roles
Sex separation. See Dormitories; Gender
        separation; Gender-specific housing;
        Purdah; Women's activity curtailment
Sexual ambiguity. See Transsexuality
Sexual assault. See Rape
Sexuality
    children's free expression of
        Araweté, 7:57
    culture denial of that children have
        Rominche, 4:217
    freedom until puberty
        Pawnee, 1:285
    infantile manifestations punished, 7:202
    initiation manipulation to develop genitalia
        Luba of Shaba, 9:192
    joking relationship
        Winnebago, 1:381
    puritanical mores
        Malaita, 2:162
    religious experience
        Baul, 3:26
    religious experience link
        Bengali Vaishnava, 3:37
    separation of sexes until marriage
        Pawnee, 1:285
Sexual jealousy
    Blackfoot, 1:42
Sexually transmitted disease. See Veneral
        disease
Sexual offense litigation
    Santal, 3:254
Sexual relations
    abstinence at male initiation
        Puinave, 7:282
    abstinence before calendrical ceremonial
        occasions
        Chatino, 8:52
    abstinence before hunting
        Pende, 9:273
    abstinence before hunting certain animals

Guahibo-Sikuani, 7:166
    abstinence before prescribed activities
        Kagwahiv, 7:185
        Pende, 9:273
    access to fictive brother's wife
        Yuit, 1:391
    adolescent
        Jamaicans, 8:138
        Mohave, 1:241
        Norwegians, 4:181
    avoided during planting
        Abelam, 2:4
    chief's symbolic behavior
        Pende, 9:273
    early age
        Ewe and Fon, 9:86
    extamarital. See Adultery
    forbidden to enter synagogue after
        Karaites, 9:155
    forbidden on Sabbath
        Karaites, 9:156
    forbidden in village
        Tor, 2:342
    free expression
        Danes, 4:89, 90
        Hawaiians, 2:96
        Qiang, 6:486
    initiation customs
        Santal, 3:254
    instruction at puberty
        Kiwai, 2:127
    interracial forbidden
        Afrikaners, 9:9
    male valuation of prowess
        Ionians, 4:150
    in manioc fields
        Yukuna, 7:387
    maternal uncle's wife initiates unmarried
        youth
        Pawnee, 1:285
    matrimonial fidelity expected
        Tewa Pueblos, 1:348
    planting ritual
        Q'eqchi,' 8:227
    postpartum taboo. See under Childbirth
    premarital. See Premarital sex
    prohibited
        Kagwahiv, 7:185
        Yukuna, 7:389
    ritualized group
        Marind-anim, 2:183
    taboo during breast-feeding years
        Suku, 9:322
    "visiting" relationships
        Barbadians, 8:22
        Jamaicans, 8:138
        Nayar, 3:199, 200
    see also Adultery; Concubinage; Incest
        prohibitions; Premarital sex;
        Prostitution; Virginity
Sexual segregation. See Dormitories; Food,
        sexually segregated eating; Gender
        separation; Gender-specific housing;
        Purdah; Women's activity
curtailment
Shades. See Ghost beliefs
Shad fishing
    Delaware, 1:85

Shadow
  as real world
    Mescalero Apache, 1:225
Shadow play
  Javanese, 5:113
  Malay, 5:176
  Oriya, 3:218
  Sasak, 5:227
Shadows. *See* Afterlife
Shaivism. *See* Shiva (deity)
Shaking tent ritual
  Cree, 1:82
  Montagnais-Naskapi, 1:246
Shaktism
  Baul, 3:26
  Bengali Shakta, 3:35-36
  Magar, 3:160
Shalako ceremony
  Zuni, 1:399
Shamanism
  Abenaki, 1:5
  Acehnese, 5:4
  Achumawi, 1:10
  Afro-Colombians, 7:18
  Agta, 5:6
  Aguaruna, 7:30
  Ainu, 5:8, 9
  Akawaio, 7:33
  Akha, 5:13
  Aleut, 1:16
  Altaians, 6:22
  Amuesha, 7:39
  Angaité, 7:44
  Apalai, 7:47
  Apiaká, 7:50
  Aranda, 2:18
  Araucanians, 7:54
  Araweté, 7:57
  Asiatic Eskimos, 6:38-39, 41, 42
  Asmat, 2:21
  Asurini, 7:61, 62
  Awakateko, 8:16-17
  Awá Kwaiker, 7:65
  Ayoreo, 7:71, 72
  Azerbaijani Turks, 6:50
  Baffinland Inuit, 1:31
  Bai, 6:421
  Bakairi, 7:75
  Baniwa-Curripaco-Wakuenai, 7:79, 80
  Barama River Carib, 7:82
  Baure, 7:86
  Bella Coola, 1:36
  Bengali Shakta, 3:35
  Bhutanese, 3:46
  Bisaya, 5:43
  Blackfoot, 1:42
  Bondo, 3:50, 51
  Bororo, 7:87
  Brahman and Chhetri of Nepal, 3:53
  Bribri-Cabécar, 8:29, 30
  Bugle, 8:33
  Buriats, 6:68
  Candoshi, 7:94
  Canela, 7:97
  Canelos Quichua, 7:99, 100, 101
  Cariña, 7:103
  Central Yup'ik Eskimos, 1:59
  Chácobo, 7:107

Chimane, 7:113
Chinook, 1:67
Chipaya, 7:117
Chipewyan, 1:69
Chiquitano, 7:118
Chiricahua, 1:70
Chiriguano, 7:121, 122
Chocó, 7:123
Choctaw, 1:73
Ch'ol, 8:65, 66
Chorote, 7:126
Chukchee, 6:77, 77-78
Chumash, 1:73
Colorado, 7:131
Comox, 1:76
Copper Eskimo, 1:78, 79
Cora, 8:76, 77
Cotopaxi Quichua, 7:135
Cree, 1:81, 82
Crow, 1:83
Cubeo, 7:141-142
Cuicatec, 8:93
Culina, 7:148
Cuna, 7:150, 151
Daur, 6:429
Desana, 7:153
Divehi, 3:78
Dolgan, 6:102
Drung, 6:432
Emberá, 7:156, 157, 158
Emberá and Wounaan, 8:110, 111
Emerillon, 7:159
Even, 6:119
Evenki (Northern Tungus), 6:122, 123
Ewenki, 6:434
Finns, 4:104
Garifuna, 8:115
Georgians, 6:136
Gond, 3:86
Gorotire, 7:163
Guajiro, 7:168, 169, 170
Guambiano, 7:173
Guarijío, 8:119
Han, 6:447
Hare, 1:141, 142
Havasupai, 1:145
Hezhen, 6:452
Hidsata, 1:148
Hmong, 5:93, 94, 95
Hopi, 1:151
Huarayo, 7:178
Huichol, 8:126, 127, 128
Huron, 1:152
Iban, 5:98
Iglulik Inuit, 1:155
Ilongot, 5:102
Ingalik, 1:158
Inughuit, 1:161
Iroquois, 1:167
Itelmen, 6:153
Itonama, 7:179
Japanese, 5:110
Jatav, 3:115
Jebero, 7:181
Jicarilla, 1:174
Jing, 6:454
Jino, 6:460
Kagwahiv, 7:185

Kalimantan Dayaks, 5:120
Kalingas, 5:122, 123
Karajá, 7:190-191
Karelians, 6:172
Karihona, 7:193, 194
Karok, 1:177
Kashinawa, 7:197
Ka'wiari, 7:200
Kazakhs, 6:181
Ket, 6:183, 184, 185
Khakas, 6:188
Khanty, 6:191-192
Khevsur, 6:196
K'iche,' 8:142
Kiowa, 1:189
Klamath, 1:192
Kmhmu, 5:141
Komi, 6:204
Koreans, 5:148;6:206
Koryaks and Kerek, 6:209
Koya, 3:141, 142
Kpelle, 9:173, 174
Kuikuru, 7:209
Kwakiutl, 1:199, 200
Kyrgyz, 6:231
Labrador Inuit, 1:201
Ladinos, 8:153
Lahu, 5:154
Lengua, 7:211
Lisu, 5:166
Macuna, 7:214, 215
Magar, 3:161-162
Maká, 7:217
Makushi, 7:219
Maliseet, 1:211, 212-213
Manchu, 6:467
Maonan, 6:469
Maris, 6:258
Martiniquais, 8:164
Marubo, 7:223
Mashco, 7:226, 227
Mataco, 7:229
Matsigenka, 7:232
Mayoruna, 7:234
Mazatec, 8:169
Mehinaku, 7:238, 239
Miami, 1:232
Miao, 6:472
Miskito, 8:172
Miwok, 1:240
Mixe, 8:175
Mixtec, 8:178
Mnong, 5:185
Mohave, 1:241, 242
Moinba, 6:473
Mojo, 7:242
Mongols, 6:476
Montagnais-Naskapi, 1:246
Mulam, 6:477
Munda, 3:184
Mundurucu, 7:245
Muong, 5:192
Nahua of the Huasteca, 8:187
Nambicuara, 7:247
Nanai, 6:276
Navajo, 1:253
Naxi, 6:479
Nenets, 6:279

Nepali, **3**:204, 205
Netsilik Inuit, **1**:254
Newar, **3**:208
Nez Percé, **1**:254
Nganasan, **6**:282
Nivaclé, **7**:249, 250, 251
Nivkh, **6**:284, 285
Noanamá, **7**:251, 252
Nomoi, **2**:252-253
Nootka, **1**:257
North Alaskan Eskimos, **1**:261
Northern Paiute, **1**:264, 265
Northern Shoshone and Bannock, **1**:267
Nuristanis, **9**:252
Ojibwa, **1**:270, 271
Okanagon, **1**:272
Oriya, **3**:218
Orochi, **6**:295
Orok, **6**:297
Otomí of the Sierra, **8**:202
Pacific Eskimo, **1**:283
Páez, **7**:258
Pahari, **3**:223
Palikur, **7**:263-264
Panare, **7**:267
Paraujano, **7**:268
Paresí, **7**:269
Pawnee, **1**:286
Pemon, **7**:272, 273
Penan, **5**:210
Piapoco, **7**:274
Piaroa, **7**:277, 278
Pima-Papago, **1**:289, 290
Piro, **7**:280
Pomo, **1**:295
Potawatomi, **1**:297
Pume, **7**:284
Qiang, **6**:487
Rikbaktsa, **7**:288
Saami, **4**:222, 258
Saliva, **7**:292
Sambia, **2**:286
Santee, **1**:307
Saraguro, **7**:295
Selkup, **6**:327, 328
Selung/Moken, **5**:232
Semang, **5**:236
Seri, **8**:234, 235
She, **6**:491
Sherente, **7**:303
Sherpa, **3**:259, 260
Shors, **6**:331
Shui, **6**:491
Shuswap, **1**:318
Siona-Secoya, **7**:308
Slavey, **1**:320
Sora, **3**:269, 270
Southern Paiute (and Chemehuevi), **1**:332
Sumu, **8**:238, 239
Suruí, **7**:312, 313
Tairora, **2**:310
Taiwan aboriginal peoples, **5**:257
Tanaina, **1**:337
Tanana, **1**:340
Tanimuka, **7**:319-320
Tapirapé, **7**:321-322
Tasmanians, **2**:317
Tatuyo, **7**:324

Temiar, **5**:273
Tepehua, **8**:249
Tepehuan of Chihuahua, **8**:253-254
Tepehuan of Durango, **8**:258
Terena, **7**:327
Ternatan/Tidorese, **5**:276
Thakali, **3**:291, 292
Tharu, **3**:293
Thompson, **1**:350
Ticuna, **7**:330
Toba, **7**:333
Tofalar, **6**:363
Tolowa, **1**:353
Trio, **7**:336
Tu, **6**:497
Tubatulabal, **1**:355
Tunebo, **7**:338, 339
Tupari, **7**:340-341
Tuvans, **6**:374
Tzeltal, **8**:274
Tzotzil of Zinacantan, **8**:294
Tz'utujil, **8**:298
Udmurt, **6**:380
Uighur, **6**:384
Ute, **1**:361, 362
Vietnamese, **5**:286
Waimiri-Atroari, **7**:344, 345
Wáiwai, **7**:348
Walapai, **1**:366
Wanano, **7**:350
Wape, **2**:372
Warao, **7**:358, 359
Waropen, **2**:376
Washoe, **1**:369, 370
Wasteko, **8**:304
Wayapi, **7**:363
Western Apache, **1**:372, 373
Western Apaches, **1**:373
Western Shoshone, **1**:375
West Greenland Inuit, **1**:378
Winnebago, **1**:382
Wintun, **1**:383
Witoto, **7**:365
Wiyot, **1**:384, 385
Wolof, **9**:380
Xibe, **6**:504
Xikrin, **7**:369
Yagua, **7**:373
Yakan, **5**:290
Yakut, **6**:406
Yanomamö, **7**:376, 377
Yao of Thailand, **5**:293
Yavapai, **1**:386
Yawalapití, **7**:380
Yekuana, **7**:381
Yokuts, **1**:388, 389
Yugur, **6**:509
Yuit, **1**:392
Yukagir, **6**:413
Yukateko, **8**:310
Yukpa, **7**:384
Yukuna, **7**:386, 388, 389, 390
Yurok, **1**:394, 395
Zhuang, **6**:511
see also Healers; Women shamans
Shame
Kwakiutl, **1**:199
see also Honor code

Shaming (as social control). _See under_ Child
    discipline; _under_ Social control
    measures
Shaobaichai (ceremony)
    Dai, **6**:427
Sharecropping
    Afro-Colombians, **7**:16
    Akan, **9**:11
    Amhara, **9**:18
    Canarians, **4**:52
    Chimila, **7**:114
    Madeirans, **4**:165
    Montserratians, **8**:180
    Pasiegos, **4**:190
    Provencal, **4**:210
    Sicilians, **4**:236
    see also Tenant farming
Shared resource rights. _See_ Communal
    practices
Sharia law
    Divehi, **3**:78
Sharing (as social virtue)
    Northern Paiute, **1**:264
    Nyakyusa and Ngonde, **9**:253
    Southern Paiute (and Chemehuevi),
        1:331
    Toba, **7**:332
    Tokelau, **2**:331
    Wapisiana, **7**:356
    Wayapi, **7**:362
    West Greenland Inuit, **1**:378
    Winnebago, **1**:382
    Yuit, **1**:391, 392
    see also Communal practices; Exchange;
        Food sharing
Shaving. _See_ Head shaving
Shavuot (holiday)
    Bukharan Jews, **6**:65
    Lithuanian Jews, **6**:246, 247
Sheep breeding
    Vlachs, **4**:274
Sheepherding
    Khoi, **9**:158
    Maasai, **9**:207
    Nuer, **9**:249
Sheep hunting
    Western Shoshone, **1**:374
Sheep raising
    Aghuls, **6**:11
    Aimaq, **9**:10
    Ajarians, **6**:13
    Altaians, **6**:21
    Andalusians, **4**:10
    Andis, **6**:25
    Avars, **6**:44
    Aveyronnais, **4**:25
    Azerbaijani Turks, **6**:49
    Bakhtiari, **9**:36
    Balkars, **6**:53
    Basques, **1**:32-33, 34
    Berbers of Morocco, **9**:49
    Bosnian Muslims, **4**:36
    Buriats, **6**:66
    Callahuaya, **7**:88
    Carpatho-Rusyns, **6**:70
    Castilians, **4**:59
    Chechen-Ingush, **6**:73
    Chipaya, **7**:115

Sheep raising (cont'd)
  Circassians, **6:**88
  Cornish, **4:**65
  Cotopaxi Quichua, **7:**133
  Cretans, **4:**70, 71
  Daur, **6:**429
  Fulani, **9:**101
  Gagauz, **6:**125
  Georgians, **6:**132
  Greeks, **6:**142
  Guajiro, **7:**168
  Jicarilla, **1:**172
  Kalmyks, **6:**155
  Karachays, **6:**159
  Karakalpaks, **6:**167
  Karelians, **6:**170
  Kazak, **6:**460
  Kazakhs, **6:**177
  Khevsur, **6:**194
  Khinalughs, **6:**198
  Kirgiz, **6:**461
  Kriashen Tatars, **6:**211
  Kumyks, **6:**221
  Kurds, **6:**226
  Kyrgyz, **6:**229
  Laks, **6:**234
  Laz, **6:**240
  Lengua, **7:**210
  Lezgins, **6:**242
  Lisu, **6:**465
  Lowland Scots, **4:**162
  Madurese, **5:**167
  Mansi, **6:**253
  Manx, **4:**170
  Miao, **6:**470
  Mingrelians, **6:**263
  Mocoví, **7:**240
  Moldovans, **6:**266
  Mongols, **6:**474
  Montenegrins, **4:**172
  Mountain Jews, **6:**272
  Navajo, **1:**251
  Naxi, **6:**478
  Nogays, **6:**287
  Northern Irish, **4:**178
  Nu, **6:**481
  Orcadians, **4:**186, 187
  Ossetes, **6:**299
  Otavalo, **7:**253
  Ozarks, **1:**281
  Palu'e, **5:**205
  Pamir Peoples, **6:**304
  Pashai, **9:**267
  Peloponnesians, **4:**193
  Pumi, **6:**483
  Qashqa'i, **9:**285
  Rotinese, **5:**213
  Rutuls, **6:**319
  Salar, **6:**488
  Sarakatsani, **4:**223-224
  Sardinians, **4:**226
  Shahsevan, **9:**308
  Shetlanders, **4:**233
  Siberian Germans, **6:**338
  Somalis, **9:**316
  Suri, **9:**324
  Tabasarans, **6:**348
  Tats, **6:**358

  Tibetans, **6:**494
  Tsakhurs, **6:**365
  Tswana, **9:**361
  Tu, **6:**496
  Turkana, **9:**371
  Turkmens, **6:**369
  Tzotzil of Chamula, **8:**280
  Tzotzil of Zinacantan, **8:**292
  Udis, **6:**376
  Uzbeks, **6:**396
  Vlachs, **4:**274-275
  Volga Tatars, **6:**401
  Welsh, **4:**279
  West Greenland Inuit, **1:**377
  Yezidis, **6:**409
  Yi, **6:**506
  Yörük, **9:**394
  Yugur, **6:**508
  Zuni, **1:**397
Sheep sacrifice. *See* Sacrifice, livestock
Shell
  amulets and charms
    Walapai, **1:**366
  carved
    Wiyot, **1:**384
  currency. *See under* Money and wealth
  embroidery
    Tanaina, **1:**337
  jewelry
    Kumeyaay, **1:**194
    Walapai, **1:**366
    Washoe, **1:**370
  tools, **2:**38
  trade
    Northern Paiute, **1:**263
Shifting cultivation. *See* Agriculture, slash-
    and-burn
Shiite Muslims. *See* Islam (Shia)
Shinshu Buddhism
  Burakumin, **5:**63
Shinto
  Japanese, **5:**104, 105, 109
Shipbuilding industry
  Basques, **4:**30, 31
  Curaçao, **8:**96
  Lowland Scots, **4:**163
  Maltese, **4:**167
  see also Boat building
Shipping. *See* Mariners; Traders
Shipping, inland
  Frisians, **4:**111
Shiva (deity)
  Badaga, **3:**17
  Bengali, **3:**33, 34
  Bengali Shakta, **3:**35
  Chitpavan Brahman, **3:**70
  hijra, **3:**97, 98
  Hindu, **3:**102
  Irula, **3:**108
  Lingayat, **3:**151, 153
  Maratha, **3:**170
  Nepali, **3:**204
  Pandit of Kashmir, **3:**226
  Rajput, **3:**249
  Sadhu, **3:**251-252
  Tamil of Sri Lanka, **3:**283
  Telegu, **3:**287
  Vellala, **3:**305

Shivah (mourning period)
  Jews, **1:**171
Shoemaking. *See under* Footwear
Shopkeeping
  Arab Americans, **1:**24
  Catalans, **4:**62
  Greek-speaking Jews of Greece, **4:**135
  Ionians, **4:**149
  Jews, **1:**169
  Latinos, **1:**204
  Nayar, **3:**198
  Newar, **3:**206, 207
  Parsi, **3:**228
  Syrian Christian of Kerala, **3:**273
  Tetons, **1:**345
  Vlachs, **4:**274
  see also Service industry
Shopping centers
  Bretons, **4:**38
  Hungarians, **4:**144
  Provencal, **4:**210
  Serbs, **4:**230
  Welsh, **4:**279
Shotgun houses
  Black Creoles of Louisiana, **1:**40
Shri (female deity)
  Bengali Shakta, **3:**35
Shrimp farming
  Afro-Colombians, **7:**16
  Afro-Hispanic Pacific Lowlanders, **7:**20-21
Shrimp fishing
  West Greenland Inuit, **1:**377
Shrine maintenance
  Sidi, **3:**260
Shrines
  Bhil, **3:**41
  Cotopaxi Quichua, **7:**134-135
  Jews of Iran, **9:**141
  Jews of Kurdistan, **9:**146
  Magar, **3:**161
  Maratha, **3:**170
  Sadhu, **3:**251
  Sikh, **3:**261
  see also Pilgrimages
Shrovetide (holiday)
  Ukrainians, **6:**394
Shuffling Dance. *See* Ghost Dance
Shunning. *See under* Punishment
Siblings
  adult solidarity
    Irish, **4:**153
    Northern Irish, **4:**179
    Tory Islanders, **4:**265
  approval of bride needed
    Tiroleans, **4:**263
  brother-sister avoidance
    Boruca, Bribri, Cabécar, **8:**29
  brother-sister relations
    Belau, **2:**26
    Bugis, **5:**50
    Futuna, **2:**66
    Georgians, **6:**134
    Magar, **3:**159
    Nissan, **2:**250
    Tokelau, **2:**331
    see also Uncle, maternal
  care of younger siblings. *See* Child care, by
    older siblings

close ties
  Northern Irish, **4**:179
cousins as semisiblings
  Saami, **4**:221
deference relationships
  Winnebago, **1**:381
dissension
  Piemontese, **4**:198
fictive brothers
  Yuit, **1**:391
as godparents
  Old Believers, **1**:273
inheritance
  Blackfoot, **1**:42
inheritance by man's sister's children,
    1:245
linguistic differentiation between elder and
    younger brothers or sisters, **4**:144
married brothers in common household
    until father's death
  Serbs, **4**:231
maternal cousins included
  Mescalero Apache, **1**:224
Mejbrat, **2**:196
milk brotherhood. _See_ Milk brotherhood
paired marriages
  Cree, **1**:81
  Faroe Islanders, **4**:99
  Hutterites, **1**:154
  Qiang, **6**:486
relations
  Magar, **3**:159
relations take precedence
  Arapaho, **1**:26
  Kiowa, **1**:188
ritual
  Georgians, **6**:133
  Ossetes, **6**:300
  Svans, **6**:345
  Tabasarans, **6**:349
rivalry discouraged
  Faroe Islanders, **4**:99
sworn
  Khinalughs, **6**:201
  Mingrelians, **6**:263-264
  Tsakhurs, **6**:366
  Yap, **2**:393
  see also Blood brotherhood
Sickle use. _See under_ Agriculture
Siddha medicine
  Tamil, **3**:279
Sieve manufacture
  Bulgarian Gypsies, **4**:41
  Ghorbat, **9**:106
Sign language
  Warlpiri, **2**:373
Signs. _See_ Omens, importance of
Sikhism
  Jat, **3**:111, 112-113
  Punjabi, **3**:241, 242
  Sikh, **3**:261
  South and Southeast Asians of Canada,
    1:324
  South Asians in Southeast Asia, **5**:243
Silks
  Azerbaijani Turks, **6**:49
  Dai, **6**:424
  Han, **6**:442, 444

Ingilos, **6**:150
Karakalpaks, **6**:167
Koreans, **6**:206
Mingrelians, **6**:263
Moldovans, **6**:266
Piemontese, **4**:198
Talysh, **6**:355, 356
Udis, **6**:376
Uighur, **6**:382
Uzbeks, **6**:397
Silk work
  Canarians, **4**:51
Silkworm farming
  Cyclades, **4**:77
  Irula, **3**:105
Silversmithing
  Achang, **6**:417
  Araucanians, **7**:53
  Bonan, **6**:422
  Dai, **6**:424
  Dargins, **6**:98
  De'ang, **6**:430
  Fox, **1**:130
  Hani, **6**:450
  Hmong, **5**:93
  Hopi, **1**:150
  Jino, **6**:460
  Kiowa, **1**:189
  Kota, **3**:135
  Lisu, **5**:165
  Mongols, **6**:474
  Navajo, **1**:251
  Ndaonese, **5**:194
  Orcadians, **4**:187, 188
  Osage, **1**:277
  Pahari, **3**:223
  Shan, **5**:241
  Shetlanders, **4**:234
  Sora, **3**:270
  Swedes, **4**:258
  Tamil, **3**:277
  Tewa Pueblos, **1**:349
  Zuni, **1**:398
Silviculture. _See_ Forest products
Simplicity (as social virtue)
  Shakers, **1**:316
Singers (religious practictioners)
  Navajo, **1**:253
Singing. _See_ Chanting; Choral singing; Music
    and song; Opera
Singing contests
  Yuit, **1**:391
Single-men's dormitory. _See_ Dormitories
    (single male and female)
Single motherhood. _See_ Household, single-
    parent; Illegitimacy
Single people
  agricultural bachelorhood
    Finns, **4**:103
    Gaels (Irish), **4**:116
  bachelerhood
    Welsh, **4**:280
  bachelor communities
    East Asians of Canada, **1**:96
    East Asians of the United States, **1**:101,
      102
  bachelor housing. _See_ Dormitories; _under_
    Houses and housing

female-headed households. _See_ Household,
    women as heas
girls' spinning evening
  Sorbs, **4**:253
increasing rate of
  Germans, **4**:122
living with parents
  Flemish, **4**:107
  Maltese, **4**:168
  Sardinians, **4**:226
living with siblings
  Irish, **4**:153
  Sardinians, **4**:226
negatively viewed after early twenties
  Hungarians, **4**:144
as noninheriting siblings
  Tiroleans, **4**:263
pitied
  Peloponnesians, **4**:193
spinsterhood
  Azoreans, **4**:28
  Highland Scots, **4**:141
  Portuguese, **4**:207
  see also Virginity
subtle social sanctions
  Finns, **4**:107
  see also Dormitories; _under_ Household
Sisters, marriage to several at same time. _See_
    Polygyny (sororal)
Skiing
  Ewenki, **6**:434
  Saami, **6**:324
  Shors, **6**:330
  Siberian Tatars, **6**:341
  Yukagir, **6**:412
Skilled crafts. _See_ Decorative arts; _specific
    crafts_
Skin color
  Black Creoles of Louisiana, **1**:37-38
  Cape Verdeans, **4**:55, 56
  Latinos, **1**:205
Skins. _See_ Hides
Skyland (cosmology)
  Central Yup'ik Eskimos, **1**:59
Sky world. _See_ Cosmology; Dual worlds
Slametan (ceremonial meal)
  Javanese, **5**:113
Slash-and-burn agriculture. _See under_
    Agriculture
Slate mining
  Welsh, **4**:279
Slave owners
  Aleut, **1**:16
  Cherokee, **1**:62
  Chickasaw, **1**:66
  Chin, **3**:66
  Chinook, **1**:67
  Chiriguano, **7**:121
  Cocama, **7**:130
  Emerillon, **7**:159
  Haida, **1**:135, 136
  Kadiwéu, **7**:183
  Klamath, **1**:192
  Kwakiutl, **1**:198, 199
  Maliseet, **1**:212
  Mocoví, **7**:241
  Mongo, **9**:226
  Nootka, **1**:257

Slave owners (cont'd)
Nyinba, 3:212
Pawnee, 1:285
Piro, 7:279
Shuswap, 1:318
Tanaina, 1:336
Tanimuka, 7:319
Tsimshian, 1:354, 355
Yuqui, 7:392, 394
Yurok, 1:395
Slavery
African Americans, 1:11, 12
Afro-South Americans, 7:24
Akan, 9:11-12
Aleuts, 6:18
Altaians, 6:22
Andis, 6:26
Antigua and Barbuda, 8:8, 9
Ata Sikka, 5:22
Atoni, 5:27, 28
Bagirmi, 9:33
Bahnar, 5:30
Bai, 6:419
Bajau, 5:31, 34
Balkars, 6:54
Batak, 5:39, 40
Betsileo, 9:56
Bilaan, 5:42
Black Creoles of Louisiana, 1:37
Blacks in Canada as, 1:43
Bolaang Mongondow, 5:43
Bonerate, 5:44
Bugis, 5:50
Bukidnon, 5:54
Butonese, 5:67, 68
Cape Verdeans, 4:55
Circassians, 6:89
decendants
African Mexicans, 8:3
Don Cossacks, 6:105
Drung, 6:432
Easter Island, 2:53
Endenese, 5:85
Ewe and Fon, 9:87
Georgians, 6:135
Gypsies, 6:145
Haitians, 8:121, 122
Iban, 5:96, 98
Ilanon, 5:101
Jamaicans, 8:137, 138
Kalimantan Dayaks, 5:120
Kalmyks, 6:155
Karen, 5:128
Kédang, 5:132
Khanty, 6:189
Kolisuch'ok, 5:142
Kumyks, 6:223
Kyrgyz, 6:230
Laks, 6:234
Lamaholot, 5:156
Laz, 6:240
Lhoba, 6:464
Lisu, 5:164, 166;6:465
Maguindanao, 5:169
Makassar, 5:173
Mande, 9:215
Manggarai, 5:176
Maori, 2:178

Mejbrat, 2:195, 196
Mende, 9:223
Modang, 5:186
Murut, 5:193
Nias, 5:194
Nivkh, 6:284
Nu, 6:481
Nyinba as, 3:212, 213
Palu'e, 5:205, 207
Pende, 9:272-273
peripatetics as, 4:196
Pumi, 6:484
Russians, 6:315
Sakalava, 9:294
Samal, 5:218
Santa Cruz, 2:291
Sea Islanders as, 1:308, 309
second-class
Somalis, 9:317
Sedang, 5:230
Selkup, 6:327
Selung/Moken, 5:231
Semang, 5:233
Senoi, 5:237, 238
Sidi as, 3:260
Somalis, 9:317
Subanun, 5:244
Swahili, 9:327, 327-328, 328
Tagalog, 5:248
Tausug, 5:262, 263, 264
Teda, 9:340
Temiar, 5:266
Tetum, 5:276
Tokelau, 2:330
Tongareva, 2:339
Toraja, 5:281, 282
Tuareg, 9:368
Turkmens, 6:371
Waropen, 2:376
Yakut, 6:406
Yemenis, 9:390
Yi, 6:506, 507
Yuan, 5:294
Zarma, 9:405
see also Labor, forced
Slave trading
Baure, 7:86
Cape Verdeans, 4:53-54, 55
Cariña, 7:102
Klamath, 1:191
Mescalero Apache, 1:223
Osage, 1:277
Piapoco, 7:274
Pima-Papago, 1:290
Slayer of Monsters (deity)
Western Apache, 1:373
Sleds. See Dogsled use; Toboggans
Sleeping sickness
Sara, 9:305
Small businesses
Basques, 1:33
Black West Indians in the United States,
1:45
East Asians of Canada, 1:96, 97
East Asians of the United States, 1:100,
101
Estonian-Canadians, 1:121
Flemish, 4:106-107

Greeks, 4:132
Jews, 1:169
Metis of Western Canada, 1:228, 229
Slav Macedonians, 4:240
see also Entrepreneurs; Service industry;
Shopkeeping
Smallpox. See Epidemics
Smarta sect (Hindu)
Chitpavan Brahman, 3:70
Smelt fishing
Klallam, 1:190
Tolowa, 1:353
Smoking
ceremonial herbs
Rastafarians, 8:229
cigarette use
Kota, 3:135
Rajput, 3:249
to gain favor from spirits
Fox, 1:130
Miami, 1:232
Teton, 1:346
heavy
Azoreans, 4:29
Madeirans, 4:166
prohibition
Doukhobors, 1:92
Mormons, 1:248
Sikh, 3:261
see also Opium use; Pipe-smoking ritual
Smuggling
Bajau, 5:32
Cape Verdeans, 4:54
Cornish, 4:65
Garifuna, 8:114
Manx, 4:170
Pathan, 3:231
Samal Moro, 5:222
Tai Lue, 5:253
Snow house
Caribou Inuit, 1:51
Copper Eskimo, 1:76-77
Labrador Inuit, 1:201
Snowshoe hare hunting
Dogrib, 1:88
Snowshoe making
Dogrib, 1:88
Maliseet, 1:211
Montagnais-Naskapi, 1:244
Tanana, 1:339
Thompson, 1:350
Snowshoe use
Ingalik, 1:156
Snuff and snuffboxes
Kashubians, 4:159
Soapstone carving
Baffinland Inuit, 1:29
Callahuaya, 7:88
Gusii, 9:110
Social appearances, emphasis on. See Public
esteem
Social class. See Class mobility; Egalitar-
ianism; Hierarchical society; Status,
basis of
Social clubs. See Associations, clubs, and
societies
Social control measures
age-set pressure

Canela, **7**:97
aggressive humor
  Murik, **2**:222
avoidance behavior
  Circassians, **9**:67
  Itza,' **8**:135
  Siwai, **2**:304
  Tanna, **2**:314
  Tauade, **2**:319
  Telefolmin, **2**:323
  see also Punishment, shunning; _subhead_
    withdrawal of support _below_
backbiting
  Siona-Secoya, **7**:308
"catching sense"
  Sea Islanders, **1**:310
coercion
  Yuqui, **7**:394
coercion frowned upon
  Spanish Rom, **4**:255
collective oath
  Berbers of Morocco, **9**:51
collective responsibility
  Navajo, **1**:252
  Vietnamese, **5**:286
communal ceremony encouraging
    compliance
  Kmhmu, **5**:141
community closeness
  Icelanders, **4**:147
community honor code
  Yemenis, **9**:390
community meetings
  Baniwa-Curripaco-Wakuenai, **7**:79
  Huarayo, **7**:178
community pressure. _See subhead_ public
    opinion _below_
complaining
  Warao, **7**:358
  Yekuana, **7**:381
credit withdrawal
  Kapauku, **2**:106-107
criticism
  Canela, **7**:97
  Garifuna, **8**:115
  Guahibo-Sukuani, **7**:165
  Kashinawa, **7**:196
  Otavalo, **7**:255
  Panare, **7**:266
curse
  Atoni, **5**:28
  Khasi, **3**:125
  Kipsigis, **9**:165
  Maasai, **9**:209
  Mbeere, **9**:222
  Pokot, **9**:283
  Yoruba, **9**:393
deference to elders
  Tlingit, **1**:352
deference to rank
  Bugis, **5**:51
  Tlingit, **1**:352
defined rights and obligations
  Yukpa, **7**:384
derision
  Jamaicans, **8**:139
derision singing
  Copper Eskimo, **1**:78

disfavor of chief
  Canela, **7**:97
envy
  Tz'utujil, **8**:298
  Zapotec, **8**:313
ethical principles
  Rom of Czechoslovakia, **4**:219
ethnic pride
  Welsh, **4**:280
etiquette
  Circassians, **6**:89
  Evenki (Northern Tungus), **6**:122
face-to-face encounters
  Canelos Quichua, **7**:101
  Mataco, **7**:229
  Nootka, **1**:257
fairness appealed to
  Icelanders, **4**:147
by family
  Palestinians, **9**:266
family blessing
  Manus, **2**:175
family honor
  Chechen-Ingush, **6**:74-75
  Falasha, **9**:92
family's good name
  Navajo, **1**:252
family unity
  North Alaskan Eskimos, **1**:260
fear
  Bretons, **4**:39
  Nambudiri Brahman, **3**:193
fear of being different
  Wanano, **7**:350
fear of causing disease
  Semang, **5**:235
  Temiar, **5**:271
fear of divine sanctions
  Araweté, **7**:57
  Karamojong, **9**:157
fear of illness or misfortune
  Luba of Shaba, **9**:192
  Nyakyusa and Ngonde, **9**:254
  Tswana, **9**:363
fear of punishment
  Yoruba, **9**:393
fear of retribution
  Central Yup'ik Eskimo, **1**:58
  Cherokee, **1**:62
  Ingalik, **1**:158
  Maliseet, **1**:212
  Micmac, **1**:234
fear of sorcery and witchcraft
  Afro-Hispanic Pacific Lowlanders, **7**:22
  Baniwa-Curripaco-Wakuenai, **7**:79
  Batak, **5**:40
  Canela, **7**:97
  Chácobo, **7**:106
  Chamacoco, **7**:109
  Chiriguano, **7**:121
  Craho, **7**:138
  Culina, **7**:147
  Cuna, **7**:150
  Daribi, **2**:48
  Dobu, **2**:51
  Eipo, **2**:58
  Emberá, **7**:157
  Foi, **2**:61

Fore, **2**:64
Gainj, **2**:73
Gnau, **2**:82
Goodenough Island, **2**:87
Guahibo-Sikuani, **7**:165
Jamaicans, **8**:139
Ka'wiari, **7**:199
Keraki, **2**:114
Kilenge, **2**:120
Krikati/Pukobye, **7**:205
Kuikuru, **7**:208
Kurtatchi, **2**:133
Lakalai, **2**:142
Maisin, **2**:159
Maká, **7**:217
Mandak, **2**:171
Maori, **2**:178
Marind-anim, **2**:184
Mataco, **7**:229
Mehinaku, **7**:238
Menominee, **1**:221
Mixtec, **8**:178
Nahua of the Huasteca, **8**:186
Nasioi, **2**:235
Ningerum, **2**:247
Pemon, **7**:273
Piaroa, **7**:277
Pima-Papago, **1**:289
Quechan, **1**:302
Rikbaktsa, **7**:288
Rossel Island, **2**:279
Salasaca, **7**:290
Santa Cruz, **2**:292
Siona-Secoya, **7**:308
Siwai, **2**:304
Suya, **7**:316-317
Telefolmin, **2**:323
Ticuna, **7**:329
Toba, **7**:333
Usino, **2**:362
Wáiwai, **7**:347
Wanano, **7**:350
Wape, **2**:372
Wapisiana, **7**:356
Warao, **7**:358
Warlpiri, **2**:374
Wasteko, **8**:303
Yagua, **7**:373
Yangoru Boiken, **2**:390
Zapotec, **8**:313
fear of supernatural retribution
  Kickapoo, **1**:185
  Kumeyaay, **1**:195
  Maliseet, **1**:212
  Washoe, **1**:369
fear of witchcraft accusation. _See subhead_
    sorcery accusation _below_
fear of witch's envy
  Winnebago, **1**:382
formal visits by officials
  Tewa Pueblos, **1**:349
gossip
  Afro-Hispanic Pacific Lowlanders, **7**:22
  Aleut, **1**:16
  Amahuaca, **7**:35
  Ambonese, **5**:19
  Andalusians, **4**:12
  Araweté, **7**:57

Social control measures (cont'd)
    Arubans, 8:13
    Asmat, 2:20
    Austrians, 4:20
    Aymara, 7:67
    Azoreans, 4:28
    Bagirmi, 9:34
    Bakairi, 7:75
    Balinese, 5:37
    Baluchi, 3:23
    Bau, 2:24
    Bavarians, 4:35
    Bisaya, 5:43
    Blackfoot, 1:42
    Bonerate, 5:45
    Boruca, Bribri, Cabécar, 8:29
    Bulgarians, 4:45
    Cahita, 8:36
    Calabrese, 4:50
    Callahuaya, 7:89
    Canela, 7:97
    Canelos Quichua, 7:101
    Carib of Dominica, 8:40
    Castilians, 4:60
    Central Thai, 5:71
    Central Yup'ik Eskimos, 1:58
    Chatino, 8:51
    Cherokee, 1:62
    Cheyenne, 1:65
    Chinantec, 8:54
    Chiriguano, 7:121
    Choctaw, 1:72
    Cinta Larga, 7:128
    Corsicans, 4:68
    Costa Ricans, 8:81
    Cotopaxi Quichua, 7:134
    Craho, 7:138
    Cretans, 4:71
    Cubeo, 7:141
    Culina, 7:147
    Cuna, 7:150
    Dalmatians, 4:87
    Daribi, 2:48
    Dogrib, 1:89
    Dusun, 5:82
    Eipo, 2:58
    Faroe Islanders, 4:100
    Frisians, 4:112
    Gaels (Irish), 4:117
    Gainj, 2:72
    Gurung, 3:95
    Hare, 1:141
    Hidsata, 1:147
    Hmong, 5:94
    Hopi, 1:150
    Hungarians, 4:144
    Ionians, 4:150
    Itza,' 8:135
    Jamaicans, 8:139
    Javanese, 5:113
    Kaluli, 2:103
    Kashinawa, 7:196
    Ka'wiari, 7:199
    Keres Pueblo Indians, 1:181
    Khmer, 5:137
    Kickapoo, 1:185
    Kilenge, 2:120
    Kiribati, 2:123

    Kmhmu, 5:141
    Lahu, 5:153
    Lao Isan, 5:162
    Mafulu, 2:153
    Maisin, 2:159
    Maká, 7:217
    Maliseet, 1:212
    Maori, 2:178
    Mataco, 7:229
    Matsigenka, 7:232
    Mehinaku, 7:238
    Mekeo, 2:199
    Mescalero Apache, 1:225
    Miskito, 8:172
    Mixtec, 8:178
    Miyanmin, 2:211
    Montenegrins, 4:173
    Montserratians, 8:181
    Mountain Arapesh, 2:217
    Murik, 2:222
    Nahua of the Huasteca, 8:186
    Nasioi, 2:235
    Naxi, 6:479
    Ngatatjara, 2:241
    Nivaclé, 7:250
    North Alaskan Eskimos, 1:260
    Osage, 1:278
    Pasiegos, 4:190
    Pemon, 7:272
    Piaroa, 7:277
    Pima-Papago, 1:289
    Poles, 4:204
    Quechan, 1:302
    Rapa, 2:275
    Rikbaktsa, 7:288
    Rom, 1:305
    Rotuma, 2:282
    Sakalava, 9:297
    Salasaca, 7:290
    Samal Moro, 5:223
    Samoa, 2:288
    Saraguro, 7:295
    Sardinians, 4:227
    Sasak, 5:227
    Seminole, 1:313
    Shan, 5:241
    Sicilians, 4:237
    Sinhalese, 3:266
    Slavey, 1:320
    Slovenes, 4:248
    Sora, 3:270
    Tai Lue, 5:255
    Tamil of Sri Lanka, 3:283
    Tanaina, 1:336
    Tandroy, 9:338
    Taos, 1:342
    Tarahumara, 8:242
    Temiar, 5:270
    Tewa Pueblos, 1:349
    Ticuna, 7:329
    Tonga, 2:338;9:354
    Toraja, 5:282
    Tuvalu, 2:356
    Tzotzil of Chamula, 8:281
    Tz'utujil, 8:298
    Usino, 2:362
    Vietnamese, 5:286
    Wáiwai, 7:347

    Warao, 7:358
    Welsh, 4:280
    Western Apache, 1:373
    Winnebago, 1:382
    Wogeo, 2:381
    Yagua, 7:373
    Yangoru Boiken, 2:390
    Yekuana, 7:381
    Yoruba, 9:393
    Yörük, 9:396
    Yuit, 1:392
    Yukpa, 7:384
    Yuqui, 7:394
    Zapotec, 8:313
    Zuni, 1:399
  group solidarity
    Japanese, 5:108
    Qalandar, 3:247-248
    Washoe, 1:369
  guilt
    Danes, 4:90
  gun carrying
    Slovensko Roma, 4:251
  humiliation
    Gujarati, 3:91
    Pashai, 9:267
    Pende, 9:274
    Yuqui, 7:394
  ignoring
    Choctaw, 1:72
  indirect criticism
    Western Apache, 1:373
  in-law respect
    Yawalapití, 7:379
  innuendo. *See subhead* gossip
  internal harmony emphasis
    Mandan, 1:215
  isolation. *See subhead* ostracism *below*
  joking
    Frisians, 4:112
  kinship system
    Betsileo, 9:57
    Pomo, 1:295
  lack of privacy
    Samoa, 2:288
  laughter
    Ndembu, 9:240
  law. *See* Law
  lecturing
    Krikati/Pukobye, 7:205
  loss of face
    Ewenki, 6:434
    Han, 6:447
  loss of rights and property
    Lozi, 9:189
  maleness and seniority
    Dalmatians, 4:87
  mocking
    Chamacoco, 7:109
    Costa Ricans, 8:81
    Faroe Islanders, 4:100
    Hopi, 1:150
    Tewa Pueblos, 1:349
    see also subhead ridicule *below*
  mocking songs
    Mbeere, 9:222
  negative language
    Apalai, 7:47

Yukateko, 8:310
nicknames
 Faroe Islanders, 4:100
nonviolence
 Danes, 4:90
open-sided houses
 Lao Isan, 5:162
oracles
 Bamiléké, 9:39
ostracism
 Agta, 5:6
 Ambonese, 5:19
 Amuesha, 7:39
 Apalai, 7:47
 Avars, 6:46
 Aymara, 7:67
 Bagirmi, 9:34
 Baniwa-Curripaco-Wakuenai, 7:79
 Barama River Carib, 7:82
 Bau, 2:24
 Bhil, 3:40
 Bohra, 3:47
 Bulgarians, 4:45
 Canarians, 4:52
 Catawba, 1:54
 Central Yup'ik Eskimos, 1:58
 Cherokee, 1:61, 62
 Cheyenne, 1:65
 Chiriguano, 7:121
 Cinta Larga, 7:128
 Fipa, 9:99
 Goodenough Island, 2:87
 Gypsies, 6:147
 Hidsata., 1:147
 Ingalik, 1:158
 Irish Travelers, 1:164
 Jamaicans, 8:139
 Jews, Arabic-speaking, 9:136
 Kaluli, 2:103
 Kashinawa, 7:196
 Keres Pueblo Indians, 1:181
 Khevsur, 6:195
 Khmer, 5:137
 Kickapoo, 1:185
 Konso, 9:171
 Maliseet, 1:212
 Marshall Islands, 2:194
 Mataco, 7:229
 Matsigenka, 7:232
 Metis of Western Canada, 1:228
 Micmac, 1:234, 235
 Mossi, 9:230
 Mountain Arapesh, 2:217
 Nahua of the Huasteca, 8:186
 Newar, 3:207
 Nivaclé, 7:250
 Ojibwa, 1:270
 Osage, 1:278
 Pemon, 7:272
 Piaroa, 7:277
 Piemontese Sinti, 4:201
 Poles, 4:204
 Rikbaktsa, 7:288
 Rom, 1:305
 Romanians, 4:214
 Sakalava, 9:297
 Santal, 3:254
 Sasak, 5:227

 Seminole, 1:313
 Slovenes, 4:248
 Tabasarans, 6:349
 Tagalog, 5:250
 Tanaina, 1:336
 Ticuna, 7:329
 Toba, 7:333
 Tor, 2:344
 Tujia, 6:498
 Ulithi, 2:359
 Wamira, 2:367
 West Greenland Inuit, 1:377
 Xikrin, 7:368
 Yagua, 7:373
 Yoruba, 9:393
 Yukpa, 7:384
 see also Shunning
peer evaluation
 English, 4:97
peer pressure. _See subhead_ public opinion
  below
personal honor
 Bugis, 5:51
 Makassar, 5:173
personal reputation
 Lao, 5:159
 Shan, 5:241
physical attacks
 Mijikenda, 9:225
police constables
 Gaels (Irish), 4:117
press publicity
 Swiss, Italian, 4:262
public confession
 Kogi, 7:202
public denunciation
 Asmat, 2:20
 Awá Kwaiker, 7:64
 Dobu, 2:51
 Fore, 2:64
 Goodenough Island, 2:87
 Kapauku, 2:107
 Keraki, 2:114
 Murik, 2:222
 Pasiegos, 4:191
 Tuvalu, 2:356
 Wape, 2:372
public discussion
 Wáiwai, 7:347
 Yukuna, 7:388
public embarrassment
 Ambonese, 5:19
 Pohnpei, 2:269
 Tasmanians, 2:317
public opinion
 Ache, 7:6
 Agta, 5:6
 Andis, 6:26, 27
 Azerbaijani Turks, 6:49
 Balinese, 5:37
 Basques, 1:34;4:32
 Bulgarian Gypsies, 4:41
 Chipaya, 7:116
 Chuvans, 6:82
 Dogon, 9:73
 English, 4:97
 Ewenki, 6:434
 Hidsata, 1:147

 Hungarians, 4:144
 Inughuit, 1:161
 Iraqw, 9:126
 Jews of Iran, 9:141
 Krymchaks, 6:215
 Kwakiutl, 1:199
 Manx, 4:171
 Nganasan, 6:282
 Old Believers, 6:293
 Ontong Java, 2:255
 Orokaiva, 2:257
 Orokolo, 2:260
 Pawnee, 1:285
 Piemontese Sinti, 4:201
 Pume, 7:284
 Sardinians, 4:227
 Serbs, 4:232
 Sicilians, 4:237
 Sio, 2:301
 Sora, 3:270
 Syrian Christian of Kerala, 3:274
 Tai Lue, 5:255
 Tangu, 2:312
 Tikopia, 2:326
 Tongareva, 2:341
 Tor, 2:344
 Torres Strait Islanders, 2:347
 Tuvalu, 2:356
 Uighur, 6:383
 Ulithi, 2:359
 Uzbeks, 6:398
 Wáiwai, 7:347
 Waorani, 7:353
 Wape, 2:372
 Warlpiri, 2:374
 Zarma, 9:405
 see also subhead gossip _above_
public oratory
 Mandan, 1:215
 Suya, 7:317
reciprocity laws
 Awá Kwaiker, 7:64
 Zoque, 8:316
rejection
 Acadians, 1:8
religious
 Bau, 2:24
 Irish, 4:153
 Khmer, 5:137
 Kogi, 7:202
 Kosrae, 2:130
 Lakalai, 2:142
 Lao Isan, 5:162
 Marshall Islands, 2:194
 Mennonites, 1:218
 Old Believers, 2:274;6:293
 Palaung, 5:203
 Puerto Ricans, 8:223
 Rapa, 2:275
 Samal Moro, 5:223
 Tahiti, 2:306
 Welsh, 4:280
respect
 Kipsigis, 9:165
 Luba of Shaba, 9:192
 Zapotec, 8:313
respect for elders
 Circassians, 6:89

Social control measures (cont'd)
  respect for individual autonomy
    Senoi, 5:238
  retribution fears
    Central Yup'ik Eskimo, 1:58
    Cherokee, 1:62
    Ingalik, 1:158
    Maliseet, 1:212
    Micmac, 1:234
  ridicule
    Ache, 7:6
    Aleut, 1:16
    Alorese, 5:15
    Amahuaca, 7:35
    Araweté, 7:57
    Bisaya, 5:43
    Blackfoot, 1:42
    Bonerate, 5:45
    Catawba, 1:54
    Central Yup'ik Eskimos, 1:58
    Cherokee, 1:61
    Cheyenne, 1:65
    Choctaw, 1:72
    Copper Eskimo, 1:78
    Cretans, 4:71
    Dogon, 9:73
    Dusun, 5:82
    Frisians, 4:112
    Hare, 1:141
    Inughuit, 1:161
    Keres Pueblo Indians, 1:181
    Mbeere, 9:222
    Mixtec, 8:178
    Navajo, 1:252
    Nivaclé, 7:250
    North Alaskan Eskimos, 1:260
    Northern Paiute, 1:264
    Ojibwa, 1:270
    Osage, 1:278
    Pemon, 7:272
    Poles, 4:204
    Pukapuka, 2:272
    Rom, 1:305
    San-speaking peoples, 9:303
    Seminole, 1:313
    Sicilians, 4:237
    Sinhalese, 3:266
    Tagalog, 5:250
    Tamil of Sri Lanka, 3:283
    Tanaina, 1:336
    Teton, 1:345
    Toba, 7:333
    Tor, 2:344
    Tz'utujil, 8:298
    Ulithi, 2:359
    Ute, 1:361, 362
    Vietnamese, 5:286
    Wamira, 2:367
    Wanano, 7:350
    Warao, 7:358
    Winnebago, 1:382
    Xikrin, 7:368
    Yagua, 7:373
    Yoruba, 9:392
    Zuni, 1:399
  ritual-caused misfortune
    Callahuaya, 7:89
  ritual reciprocity

    Zoque, 8:316
  ritual restrictions
    Canela, 7:97
    Desana, 7:153
    Mazatec, 8:169
    Tsimihety, 9:359
  scolding
    Chuj, 8:73
    Cubeo, 7:141
    Ka'wiari, 7:199
    Tarahumara, 8:242
  self-help
    Sara, 9:306
  shaman cures
    Bakairi, 7:75
    Baniwa-Curripaco-Wakuenai, 7:79
  shaming
    Alorese, 5:15
    Blackfoot, 1:42
    Candoshi, 7:93
    Chinese in Southeast Asia, 5:77
    Dusun, 5:82
    Emberá, 7:157
    Gahuku-Gama, 2:70
    Garia, 2:75
    Gayo, 5:89
    Guadalcanal, 2:91
    Hopi, 1:149, 150
    Kashinawa, 7:196
    Kiribati, 2:123
    Kumeyaay, 1:195
    Lakalai, 2:141, 142
    Mae Enga, 2:150
    Mafulu, 2:153
    Mailu, 2:156
    Makassar, 5:173
    Malekula, 2:165
    Manam, 2:168
    Matsigenka, 7:232
    Mekeo, 2:199
    Metis of Western Canada, 1:228
    Nambudiri Brahman, 3:193
    Nasioi, 2:235
    Navajo, 1:252
    Nayar, 3:199
    Nissan, 2:250
    Nootka, 1:256
    Northern Paiute, 1:264
    Ogan-Besemah, 5:199
    Pokot, 9:283
    Rom of Czechoslovakia, 4:219
    Rotuma, 2:282
    Suya, 7:317
    Tandroy, 9:338
    Tanna, 2:314
    Tausug, 5:263
    Telefolmin, 2:323
    Toraja, 5:282
    Tuvalu, 2:356
    Tzotzil of Chamula, 8:281
    Wáiwai, 7:347
    Wanano, 7:350
  shaming by food-giving
    Goodenough Island, 2:87
  shared value system
    German Swiss, 4:127
  shunning. See under Punishment
  slander

    Canela, 7:97
    Kuikuru, 7:208
    Mataco, 7:229
  socialist ideology
    Cubans, 8:89
  social pressure. See subhead public opinion
    above
  social withdrawal. See subhead withdrawal
    of support below
  sorcery accusation
    Ajië, 2:9
    Boazi, 2:30
    Canelos Quichua, 7:101
    Chimbu, 2:37
    Gainj, 2:73
    Gebusi, 2:78
    Hmong, 5:94
    Lak, 2:139
    Lao, 5:159
    Lisu, 5:165
    Malaita, 2:162
    Mekeo, 2:199
    Ningerum, 2:247
    Sakalava, 9:297
    Tai Lue, 5:255
    T'in, 5:279
    Tlingit, 1:352
    Torres Strait Islanders, 2:347
    Western Apache, 1:372
    Winnebago, 1:382
    Zuni, 1:399
  sorcery and witchcraft
    Bagirmi, 9:34
    Kipsigis, 9:165
    Kpelle, 9:174
    Lango, 9:181
    Mbeere, 9:222
    Mijikenda, 9:225
    Nyakyusa and Ngonde, 9:253, 254
    Tonga, 9:354
  supernatural
    Ambonese, 5:19
    Berbers of Morocco, 9:51
    Central Yup'ik Eskimo, 1:58
    Ch'ol, 8:65
    Dogon, 9:73
    Ewe and Fon, 9:87
    Iban, 5:98
    Kaluli, 2:103
    Keraki, 2:114
    Lahu, 5:153
    Manus, 2:175
    Marshall Islands, 2:194
    Ontong Java, 2:255
    Orokaiva, 2:257
    Orokolo, 2:260
    Palu'e, 5:207
    Rotuma, 2:282
    Samal Moro, 5:223
    Selepet, 2:294
    Sio, 2:301
    T'in, 5:279
    Ulithi, 2:359
    Warlpiri, 2:374
    Yoruba, 9:393
    Zoque, 8:316
  surveillance of activities
    Salasaca, 7:290

taboos. _See_ Taboos
taunting
   Baluchi, 3:23
teasing
   Central Yup'ik Eskimos, 1:58
   Cheyenne, 1:65
   Hopi, 1:150
   Kumeyaay, 1:195
   Samal Moro, 5:223
   Santal, 3:254
   Tewa Pueblos, 1:349
threat of abandonment
   Central Yup'ik Eskimos, 1:58
threat of evil spell
   Mixtec, 8:178
threat of external forces
   Cherokee, 1:61
   Choctaw, 1:72
   Copper Eskimo, 1:78
   Eastern Shoshone, 1:105
   Ingalik, 1:157
   Maliseet, 1:212
threat of gang rape
   Mundurucu, 7:245
threat of imprisonment
   Tandroy, 9:338
   Zande, 9:399
threat of poisoning
   Cinta Larga, 7:128-129
   Rikbaktsa, 7:288
threat of revenge. _See subhead_ retribution
   fears _above_
threat of violence
   cattle ranchers of Huasteca, 8:44
threats
   Cretans, 4:71
   Cyclades, 4:78
   Pomo, 1:294
   West Greenland Inuit, 1:377
threats by males
   Bakairi, 7:75
tradition
   English, 4:97
   Mandan, 1:215
   Serbs, 4:232
unarmed police
   Yukateko, 8:310
value system
   Ghorbat, 9:107
vandalization of property
   Russian peasants, 6:312
verbal abuse
   San-speaking peoples, 9:303
village group armed with bows and arrows
   Nyamwezi and Sukuma, 9:257
violence
   Boazi, 2:30
   Keraki, 2:114
   Mae Enga, 2:150
   Manam, 2:168
   Miyanmin, 2:211
   Montenegrins, 4:173
   Mundugumor, 2:219
   Murngin, 2:226
   Ngatatjara, 2:241
   Santa Cruz, 2:292
   Tor, 2:344
   Usino, 2:362

War Clan
   Winnebago, 1:382
witchcraft. _See subhead_ fear of sorcery and
   witchcraft _above; subhead_ sorcery and
   witchcraft _above_
withdrawal of support
   Garia, 2:75
   Lao, 5:159
   Mae Enga, 2:150
   Maliseet, 1:212
   Pukapuka, 2:272
   Telefolmin, 2:323
   Woleai, 2:384
withholding of food/sex
   Yuqui, 7:394
women's group sanctions for "crimes against
   women"
   Nandi and other Kelenjin peoples, 9:234
xenophobia
   Samal Moro, 5:223
see also Child discipline; Conflict
   resolution; Court system; Law;
   Punishment; Taboos
Social dancing. _See_ Dance, social
Socialism
   Albanians, 4:4, 5, 6
   Bulgarian Gypsies, 4:40, 41, 42
   Bulgarians, 4:42, 44, 45, 214
   Cape Verdeans, 4:54
   Croats, 4:73-74
   Cubans, 8:89
   Romanians, 4:213
   Serbs, 4:231, 232
   Slav Macedonians, 4:239, 240, 241
   Slovaks, 4:244, 245
   Slovenes, 4:247, 248
   Swedes "middle way," 4:258
Socially equal/upward marriage. _See_
   Hypergamy
Social mobility. _See_ Class mobility;
   Sanskritization
Social separateness. _See_ Closed community
Social status. _See_ Castes; Status, basis of;
   Wealth and status
Social stratification. _See_ Hierarchical society
Societal violence. _See_ Violence, societal
Societies. _See_ Associations, clubs, and
   societies
Sod houses. _See under_ Houses and housing
Son-daughter marriage exchange. _See under_
   Marriage
Song. _See_ Choral singing; Music and song
Song Cycle
   Mohave, 1:241
   Southern Paiute (and Chemehuevi),
   1:332
Song duels
   Maltese, 4:169
   Nivaclé, 7:250
   West Greenland Inuit, 1:378
   Yuit, 1:392
Songkran (festival)
   Lao Isan, 5:163
Songsarek (followers of native faith)
   Garo, 3:84
Son's inheritance (oldest). _See_ Primogeniture
Son's inheritance (shared). _See_ Inheritance,
   equally shared

Son's inheritance (youngest). _See_ Ultimo-
   geniture
Sorcery and witchcraft, beliefs about
   Acadians, 1:9
   Acholi, 9:6
   Afro-Colombians, 7:18
   Afro-Hispanic Pacific Lowlanders, 7:23
   Afro-Venezuelans, 7:28
   Agta, 5:6
   Akawaio, 7:33
   Alak, 5:13
   Albanians, 4:7
   Alur, 9:14, 15
   Ambae, 2:12
   Amuzgo, 8:5, 6
   Apiaká, 7:50
   Aquitaine, 4:15
   Araucanians, 7:54
   Avars, 6:46
   Aymara, 7:68
   Bagirmi, 9:34, 35
   Bamiléké, 9:39, 40
   Berbers of Morocco, 9:52
   Betsileo, 9:57
   Bhil, 3:41
   Bondo, 3:50
   Bororo, 7:87
   Boruca, Bribri, Cabécar, 8:29
   Calabrese, 4:50
   Callahuaya, 7:90
   Cape Coloureds, 9:60
   Cape Verdeans, 4:56
   Carib of Dominica, 8:40
   Chambri, 2:32
   Chickasaw, 1:66
   Chinantec, 8:54
   Chinese in Southeast Asia, 5:77
   Choctaw, 1:72, 73
   Ch'ol, 8:66
   Chuj, 8:73
   Circassians, 6:90
   Copper Eskimo, 1:78
   Corsicans, 4:68
   Costa Ricans, 8:81
   Craho, 7:138
   Cree, 1:82
   Croats, 4:74
   Dalmatians, 4:87
   Dani, 2:45-46
   Dobu, 2:51
   Dogon, 9:73
   Don Cossacks, 6:107
   Eipo, 2:58
   Emberá and Wounaan, 8:111
   Endenese, 5:86
   Estonian, 6:115
   Fipa, 9:100
   Foi, 2:61
   Gainj, 2:73
   Garifuna, 8:115
   Gebusi, 2:77, 78
   Georgians, 6:136
   Gond, 3:87
   Guadalcanal, 2:91
   Gurung, 3:95
   Gusii, 9:110
   Hawaiians, 2:97
   Hopi, 1:150, 151

Sorcery and witchcraft, beliefs about (cont'd)
Iatmul, 2:100
Ingilos, 6:151
Iraqw, 9:126
Iroquois, 1:166
Irula, 3:109
Iteso, 9:130
Jamaicans, 8:139
Kachin, 5:119
Kaluli, 2:103
Kapauku, 2:107
Kapingamarangi, 2:108
Karok, 1:177
Kashubians, 4:159
Kédang, 5:133
Keraki, 2:114
Ket, 6:185
Kewa, 2:117
Khasi, 3:126
Khoi, 9:160
Kickapoo, 1:185
Kiwai, 2:126
Kongo, 9:168
Koya, 3:141
Kpelle, 9:174
Kubachins, 6:219
Kumeyaay, 1:195
Kurumbas, 3:143
Kwakiutl, 1:199, 200
Lamaholot, 5:156
Lango, 9:181
Lesu, 2:147
Lozi, 9:189
Luba of Shaba, 9:192
Lugbara, 9:195
Lunda, 9:199
Luyia, 9:203, 205-206
Maasai, 9:209
Madurese, 5:168
Mae Enga, 2:150-151
Mafulu, 2:153
Magar, 3:161
Maguindanao, 5:170
Mailu, 2:156
Maisin, 2:159
Makassar, 5:174
Malekula, 2:166
Maliseet, 1:212, 213
Manam, 2:168
Manus, 2:175
Manx, 4:171
Maring, 2:187
Maris, 6:258
Marquesas Islands, 2:190, 191
Martiniquais, 8:163-164
Mashco, 7:227
Matsigenka, 7:232
Mauritian, 3:173
Mazatec, 8:169
Mbeere, 9:222
Mekeo, 2:198, 199, 200
Mendi, 2:205
Menominee, 1:221
Meskhetians, 6:261
Micmac, 1:235
Mikir, 3:176
Mixtec, 8:178
Miyanmin, 2:211

Mnong, 5:185
Mongo, 9:227
Motu, 2:215
Mountain Arapesh, 2:217
Mundugumor, 2:220
Mundurucu, 7:245
Muong, 5:192
Murngin, 2:227
Muyu, 2:230
Nandi and other Kalenjin peoples, 9:234
Ndebele, 9:237
Ndembu, 9:240
Nepali, 3:205
Newar, 3:208
Nguna, 2:244
Ningerum, 2:247
Noanamá, 7:251
Nyakyusa and Ngonde, 9:253, 254
Nyamwezi and Sukuma, 9:257
Nyinba, 3:213
Ojibwa, 1:270
Oriya, 3:218
Orokolo, 2:260
Otomí of the Sierra, 8:202
Palaung, 5:203
Palikur, 7:263, 264
Palu'e, 5:208
Pasiegos, 4:191
Pawnee, 1:285
Pohnpei, 2:269
Popoloca, 8:216
Popoluca, 8:217
Portuguese, 4:208
Puerto Ricans, 8:223
Q'eqchi,' 8:227
Romanians, 4:214
Russian peasants, 6:313
Saint Lucians, 8:231
Sakalava, 9:298
Samal Moro, 5:224
Santal, 3:254
Sengseng, 2:298
Seri, 8:234
Sherente, 7:303
Shona, 9:314
Siberian Estonians, 6:337
Sora, 3:270
Suku, 9:322
Sumu, 8:239
Swahili, 9:329
Swazi, 9:332, 333
Tairora, 2:309
Tangu, 2:312
Tanna, 2:315
Taos, 1:343
Tauade, 2:320
Temne, 9:345
Tigray, 9:347
Tlingit, 1:352
Toda, 3:298
Tolai, 2:335
Tonga, 9:354
Tor, 2:343, 344
Torres Strait Islanders, 2:347
Totonac, 8:266
Trobriand Islands, 2:350
Truk, 2:353
Tubatulabal, 1:355

Tupari, 7:340
Tzeltal, 8:274
Tzotzil and Tzeltal of Pantelhó, 8:277
Tzotzil of San Bartolomé de los Llanos,
    8:291
Usino, 2:363
Vlachs, 4:275
Wamira, 2:367
Wape, 2:372
Warlpiri, 2:374
Waropen, 2:376
Wasteko, 8:303
Western Apache, 1:373
West Greenland Inuit, 1:378
Wik Mungkan, 2:379
Winnebago, 1:382
Wolof, 9:379, 380
Wovan, 2:386, 387
Yangoru Boiken, 2:390
Yoruba, 9:393
Yurok, 1:395
Zande, 9:399, 400
Zapotec, 8:313
Zarma, 9:406
Zoque, 8:317
Zulu, 9:412
Zuni, 1:399
see also under Death, causes of; under Illness,
    causes of; under Social control
    measures; Witch doctors
Sorghum
  as ancestral offering
    Pende, 9:272
  beer
    Lobi-Dagarti peoples, 9:183
    Luba of Shaba, 9:191
    Lunda, 9:196
    Mossi, 9:228
  diseased
    Pende, 9:272
  as religious symbol
    Lango, 9:178
Sorghum growing
  Amhara, 9:18
  Baggara, 9:30
  Bagirmi, 9:33
  Fali, 9:94
  Han, 6:440
  Iraqw, 9:125
  Iteso, 9:128
  Kanuri, 9:151
  Karakalpaks, 6:167
  Karamojong, 9:137
  Konso, 9:169
  Korean, 5:146
  Lisu, 6:465
  Lugbara, 9:194
  Manchu, 6:467
  Maonan, 6:468
  Mijikenda, 9:224
  Ndebele, 9:236
  Nyamwezi and Sukuma, 9:256
  Pokot, 9:282
  Rukuba, 9:289
  San-speaking peoples, 9:302
  Sara, 9:305
  Somalis, 9:316
  Suri, 9:325, 326

Swahili, **9:**327
Swazi, **9:**330
Tandroy, **9:**336
Tigray, **9:**347
Tonga, **9:**353
Tswana, **9:**361
Xhosa, **9:**381
Zarma, **9:**404
Sorohabora (ceremony)
 Foi, **2:**61
Sororal polygyny. _See_ Polygyny (sororal)
Sororate marriage
 Akawaio, **7:**32
 Amahuaca, **7:**35
 Araucanians, **7:**53
 Araweté, **7:**57
 Asiatic Eskimos, **6:**41
 Bisaya, **5:**43
 Buriats, **6:**67
 Chuvash, **6:**84
 Cree, **1:**81
 Ewenki, **6:**434
 Fox, **1:**129
 Gros Ventre, **1:**134
 Huarayo, **7:**178
 Ilongot, **5:**102
 Karajá, **7:**189
 Kazakhs, **6:**180
 Keraki, **2:**113
 Kiribati, **2:**122
 Konso, **9:**170
 Kumeyaay, **1:**194
 Lakalai, **2:**141
 Maká, **7:**216
 Mansi, **6:**253
 Mossi, **9:**229
 Mountain Jews, **6:**272
 Muong, **5:**191
 Nomoi, **2:**252
 Osage, **1:**278
 Pima-Papago, **1:**289
 Pomo, **1:**294
 Qiang, **6:**486
 Rapa, **2:**274
 Rutuls, **6:**320
 Sarsi, **1:**308
 Senoi, **5:**238
 Shipibo, **7:**305
 Slavey, **1:**319
 Southern Paiute (and Chemehuevi), **1:**331
 Subanun, **5:**245
 Swazi, **9:**331
 Tabasarans, **6:**349
 Tajiks, **6:**353
 Tatuyo, **7:**323
 Terena, **7:**326
 Tibetans, **6:**495
 Toba, **7:**332
 Truk, **2:**352
 Tsakhurs, **6:**367
 Ute, **1:**361
 Waimiri-Atroari, **7:**344
 Warao, **7:**358
 Washoe, **1:**369
 Wayapi, **7:**362
 Western Apache, **1:**372
 Western Shoshone, **1:**375
 Winnebago, **1:**381

Wolof, **9:**379
Yanomamö, **7:**375
Soul
 in afterlife
  Achumawi, **1:**10
  Angaité, **7:**44
  Araucanians, **7:**55
  Araweté, **7:**57-58
  Asurini, **7:**62
  Aymara, **7:**68
  Ayoreo, **7:**72
  Baniwa-Curripaco-Wakuenai, **7:**80
  Canela, **7:**97-98
  Canelos Quichua, **7:**102
  Chiriguano, **7:**122
  Craho, **7:**138-139
  Cuiva, **7:**145
  Culina, **7:**148
  Guajiro, **7:**170
  Guarayu, **7:**174-175
  Huarayo, **7:**179
  Karajá, **7:**190, 191
  Kashubians, **4:**159
  Kogi, **7:**203
  Kuikuru, **7:**209
  Lengua, **7:**211
  Macuna, **7:**215
  Maká, **7:**218
  Marubo, **7:**223
  Mashco, **7:**227
  Matsigenka, **7:**232-233
  Mohave, **1:**242
  Nambicuara, **7:**247
  Nivaclé, **7:**251
  Otavalo, **7:**255
  Païtavytera, **7:**260
  Panare, **7:**267
  Paresí, **7:**269
  Pemon, **7:**273
  Piaroa, **7:**278
  Powhatan, **1:**297
  Quechan, **1:**302
  Sherente, **7:**303
  Shipibo, **7:**306
  Siona-Secoya, **7:**309
  Suruí, **7:**314
  Tanaina, **1:**337
  Toba, **7:**333-334
  Trio, **7:**337
  Tupari, **7:**340
  Waimiri-Atroari, **7:**345
  Wáiwai, **7:**348
  Wayapi, **7:**364
  Yagua, **7:**374
  Yanomamö, **7:**377
 Ainu, **5:**8
 Akha, **5:**13
 in all animate and inanimate objects
  Micmac, **1:**235
  Teton, **1:**346
 in all natural phenomena
  Inughuit, **1:**161
 animals possessing
  West Greenland Inuit, **1:**378
 breath
  Yuit, **1:**392
 Cherokee, **1:**62
 children

Daribi, **2:**47
Dani, **2:**45
Daribi, **2:**47
Delaware, **1:**87
Doukhobors, **1:**93
dual
 Gond, **3:**87
 Micmac, **1:**235
 Munda, **3:**184
feared
 Ute, **1:**362
Flathead, **1:**128
four aspects of
 Mandan, **1:**215
 Teton, **1:**346
Gahuku-Gama, **2:**70
Gururumba, **2:**94
Haida, **1:**136
of handicapped persons
 Svan, **6:**347
Iglulik Inuit, **1:**155
illness and
 Chamacoco, **7:**110
 Craho, **7:**138
 Maká, **7:**218
 Mehinaku, **7:**239
 Mundurucu, **7:**245-246
 Nivaclé, **7:**251
 Paraujano, **7:**268
 Trio, **7:**336
immortal. _See under_ Afterlife; Reincarna-
 tion beliefs
Ingalik, **1:**158
Inughuit, **1:**161
Iroquois, **1:**167
Japanese, **5:**110
Keraki, **2:**114
Kilenge, **2:**120
lacked by commoners
 Tonga, **2:**339
Lakalai, **2:**142
as life force
 Inughuit, **1:**161
 Mimika, **2:**208
 Mountain Arapesh, **2:**217
multiple
 Abelam, **2:**6
 Alorese, **5:**15
 Aranda, **2:**18
 Bukidnon, **5:**55
 Bunun, **5:**57
 Iban, **5:**99
 Jingpo, **6:**459
 Ket, **6:**185
 Khanty, **6:**192
 Kriashen Tatars, **6:**212
 Lahu, **5:**153
 Lamaholot, **5:**156
 Lau, **2:**145
 Mailu, **2:**156
 Mansi, **6:**255
 Miao, **6:**472
 Muong, **5:**192
 Nasioi, **2:**235
 Ngatatjara, **2:**241
 Nomoi, **2:**253
 Palaung, **5:**203
 Sea Islanders, **1:**311

Soul (cont'd)
    Senoi, 5:238
    Taiwan aboriginal peoples, 5:257
    Tausug, 5:264
    Temiar, 5:271
    Truk, 2:353
    Wik Mungkan, 2:379
    Winnebago, 1:382
    Wovan, 2:387
    Yakut, 6:407
    Yuit, 1:392
  Murik, 2:223
  Murngin, 2:227
  name
    Yuit, 1:392, 393
  Ningerum, 2:248
  Orokaiva, 2:258
  Pukapuka, 2:273
  rebirth of. See Reincarnation beliefs
  in religious beliefs
    Canela, 7:97
    Canelos Quichua, 7:101
    Maká, 7:217
    Marubo, 7:223
    Maxakali, 7:233
    Mehinaku, 7:238
    Nivaclé, 7:250
    Pemon, 7:273
    Terena, 7:326-327
    Yanomamö, 7:376
    Yuqui, 7:395
  reservoir of
    Siane, 2:299
    Wantoat, 2:370
  Samal Moro, 5:224
  Samoa, 2:289
  single
    Hindu, 3:102
    Jain, 3:109
    see also Reincarnation beliefs
  stealing of
    Lakher, 3:148
  Tangu, 2:312
  Tasmanians, 2:317
  Wamira, 2:367
  wandering
    Bondo, 3:51
    Brahman and Chhetri of Nepal, 3:54
    Bretons, 4:40
    Iroquois, 1:167
    Khasi, 3:126
    Lakher, 3:148
    Purum, 3:244
    Sinhalese, 3:267
    Slav Macedonians, 4:241
    Tamil of Sri Lanka, 3:284
  see also Spirits, belief in
Soul loss
  death caused by
    Tarahumara, 8:242
    Tzotzil of Chamula, 8:281
    Tzotzil of Zinacantan, 8:294
  fright causing
    Tzotzil of Zinacantan, 8:294
  illness caused by
    Cuicatec, 8:93
    Kwakiutl, 1:200
    Popoluca, 8:217

    Tzotzil of San Andrés Larraínzar, 8:285
    Zapotec, 8:313
  as punishment
    Tzotzil of Zinacantan, 8:294
"Soul-loss" doctors
  Wiyot, 1:384
South Sea Evangelical Church
  Malaita, 2:163
Soybean growing
  Sasak, 5:226
Speaking in tongues
  Appalachians, 1:23
Specialty-product farming
  Aveyronnais, 4:25
Speech making. See Oratorical skill
Spell casting
  Baniwa-Curripaco-Wakuenai, 7:79, 80
  Kashubians, 4:159
  Sarakatsani, 4:224
  Yanomamö, 7:377
Spice growing
  Q'eqchi,' 8:226
Spice trade
  Grenadians, 8:116
  Nayar, 3:198
Spider Woman (culture hero)
  Kiowa, 1:188
  Navajo, 1:253
  Western Apache, 1:373
Spinning
  Bulgarians, 4:43
  Purum, 3:243
  see also Weaving
Spinning Evening (event)
  Sorbs, 4:253, 254
Spinsterhood. See under Single people
Spirit
  female helper
    Frisians, 4:112
  interaction with the living
    Bhil, 1:42
    Koya, 1:142
    Rom of Czechoslovakia, 4:219
    Sea Islanders, 1:311
    Sora, 3:270
    Vedda, 3:303
  mortal and immortal
    Klingit, 1:353
  need to propriate
    Kickapoo, 1:186
  shadow of self
    Kaluli, 2:103
  wandering
    Hidsata, 1:148
  see also Afterlife; Ancestral spirits; Ghosts;
      Guardian spirit; Soul
Spirit doctors
  Ndembu, 9:240
  Swahili, 9:329
  Tandroy, 9:338
  Tlingit, 1:353
Spirit husband
  Sora, 3:270
Spirit posts
  T'in, 5:277
Spirits, ancestral. See Ancestral spirits
Spirits, animal. See Animals, as protectors or
    spirits

Spirits, anthropomorphic. See Animism;
    Anthropomorphic beings
Spirits, belief in
  Abelam, 2:6
  Abor, 3:5
  Ache, 7:6
  Acholi, 9:6
  Achumawi, 1:10
  Afro-Colombians, 7:18
  Afro-Hispanic Pacific Lowlanders, 7:22-23
  Afro-Venezuelans, 7:27
  Agta, 5:6
  Ajië, 2:10
  Akan, 9:12
  Aleut, 1:16
  Alorese, 5:16
  Altaians, 6:22
  Amahuaca, 7:36
  Ambae, 2:13
  Amuesha, 7:39
  Andamanese, 3:11
  Andis, 6:27
  Anuak, 9:22
  Apiaká, 7:50
  Arabs, 9:24
  Araucanians, 7:54
  Araweté, 7:57
  Asiatic Eskimos, 6:42
  Ata Sikka, 5:22
  Ata Tana 'Ai, 5:25
  Aymara, 7:68
  Bajau, 5:34
  Balinese, 5:37
  Bamiléké, 9:39
  Baniwa-Curripaco-Wakuenai, 7:79
  Barama River Carib, 7:82
  Batak, 5:41
  Bemba, 9:47
  Bhil, 3:41
  Bhuiya, 3:44
  Blackfoot, 1:42
  Bonerate, 5:46
  Bugis, 5:51
  Bukidnon, 5:54
  Burmese, 5:65
  Candoshi, 7:94
  Canelos Quichua, 7:101
  Cariña, 7:103
  Carrier, 1:52
  Catawba, 1:54, 55
  Central Yup'ik Eskimos, 1:59
  Chácobo, 7:107
  Chagga, 9:62
  Chakma, 3:60
  Chamacoco, 7:110
  Cherokee, 1:62
  Cheyenne, 1:65
  Chimane, 7:113
  Chin, 3:64, 66, 67
  Chinese in Southeast Asia, 5:77
  Chinook, 1:67
  Chipaya, 7:116, 117
  Chipewyan, 1:69
  Chiriguano, 7:121
  Chocó, 7:123
  Choctaw, 1:72
  Chorote, 7:126
  Chuj, 8:73, 74

Cinta Larga, **7**:129
Comanche, **1**:75
Copper Eskimo, **1**:78-79
Corsicans, **4**:68
Cotopaxi Quichua, **7**:135
Cree, **1**:82
Crow, **1**:83
Cubeo, **7**:142
Culina, **7**:148
Cyclades, **4**:78
Dai, **6**:428
Delaware, **1**:86
Desana, **7**:153
Dinka, **9**:71
Divehi, **3**:78
Dobu, **2**:52
Dogon, **9**:73
Dolgan, **6**:102
Dusun, **5**:83
Edo, **9**:81-82
Emberá and Wounaan, **8**:111
Endenese, **5**:86
Ewe and Fon, **9**:87
Falasha, **9**:92
Filipino, **5**:87
Fox, **1**:130
Gaels (Irish), **4**:117
Ganda, **9**:105
Garo, **3**:84
Gebusi, **2**:79
Gond, **3**:85, 86
Gorotire, **7**:163
Grasia, **3**:88
Guahibo-Sikuani, **7**:165
Guambiano, **7**:173
Gujarati, **3**:92
Hausa, **9**:114
Hidsata, **1**:147
Hill Pandaram, **3**:100
Huarayo, **7**:178
Huron, **1**:152
Ibibio, **9**:120
Ifugao, **5**:100
Iglulik Inuit, **1**:155
Ingalik, **1**:158
Ingilos, **6**:151
Iraqw, **9**:126
Iroquois, **1**:167
Irula, **3**:108, 109
Iteso, **9**:130
Itza,' **8**:135
Jews of Iran, **9**:141
Kachin, **5**:118
Kagwahiv, **7**:185-186
Kalimantan Dayaks, **5**:120
Kalingas, **5**:123
Kamilaroi, **2**:104
Kapauku, **2**:107
Kapingamarangi, **2**:110
Karen, **5**:128
Kashinawa, **7**:197
Kazakhs, **6**:181
Ket, **6**:185
Khakas, **6**:188
Khanty, **6**:191-192
Khasi, **3**:125, 126
Khoi, **9**:160
Kickapoo, **1**:185, 186

Kiwai, **2**:126
Klamath, **1**:192
Kmhmu, **5**:141
Kogi, **7**:202
Konso, **9**:171
Kpelle, **9**:174
Krikati/Pukobye, **7**:205
Kuikuru, **7**:209
Kumeyaay, **1**:195
Kwakiutl, **1**:199
Kwoma, **2**:136
Labrador Inuit, **1**:202
Lahu, **5**:153, 154
Lakher, **3**:147
Lango, **9**:181
Lao, **5**:159
Lepcha, **3**:149
Lisu, **5**:165
Lozi, **9**:189
Luba of Shaba, **9**:192
Lugbara, **9**:195
Magar, **3**:161
Maisin, **2**:160
Maká, **7**:217
Malekula, **2**:166
Maliseet, **1**:212-213
Mam, **8**:160
Manam, **2**:169
Mandak, **2**:171, 172
Mansi, **6**:254
Maratha, **3**:170
Mardudjara, **2**:181
Marubo, **7**:223
Matsigenka, **7**:232
Maxakali, **7**:233
Mbeere, **9**:222
Mehinaku, **7**:238
Melanau, **5**:180
Menominee, **1**:222
Micronesians, **1**:239
Mijikenda, **9**:225
Miskito, **8**:172
Mixe, **8**:175
Mizo, **3**:179
Mountain Jews, **6**:273
Munda, **3**:184
Mundugumor, **2**:220
Muong, **5**:191-192
Murik, **2**:222
Murngin, **2**:226
Nagas, **3**:190-191
Namau, **2**:232
Nambicuara, **7**:247
Nandi and other Kalenjin peoples,
    9:234
Nauru, **2**:237
Navajos, **1**:253
Nayaka, **3**:196
Ndebele, **9**:237
Nenets, **6**:279
Nepali, **3**:204, 205
Newar, **3**:208
Nganasan, **6**:282
Nguna, **2**:244
Nicobarese, **3**:210
Ningerum, **2**:247
Nissan, **2**:251
Nogays, **6**:289

Nootka, **1**:257
Nyamwezi and Sukuma, **9**:257
Nyinba, **3**:211, 213
Okiek, **9**:261
Orok, **6**:297
Otavalo, **7**:255
Ottawa, **1**:280
Pacific Eskimo, **1**:283
Páez, **7**:258
Paï-Tavytera, **7**:260
Palaung, **5**:202
Palikur, **7**:263
Paresí, **7**:269
Parsi, **3**:229
Pathan, **3**:233
Pawnee, **1**:285
Pemon, **7**:273
Piaroa, **7**:278
Piro, **7**:280
Pume, **7**:284
Purum, **3**:244
Rhadé, **5**:212
Rom, **1**:306
Romanians, **4**:214
Saami, **4**:222
Sakalava, **9**:297-298
Salasaca, **7**:291
Samal, **5**:221
Samal Moro, **5**:224
Sambia, **2**:286
Santa Cruz, **2**:292
Santal, **3**:254-255
Saraguro, **7**:295
Sarakatsani, **4**:224
Saramaka, **7**:298
Selepet, **2**:295
Selkup, **6**:327
Selung/Moken, **5**:232
Semang, **5**:235-236
Senoi, **5**:238-239
Seri, **8**:235
Shahsevan, **9**:310
Sherente, **7**:303
Shilluk, **9**:311
Shipibo, **7**:306
Shona, **9**:314
Sinhalese, **3**:267
Siona-Secoya, **7**:309
Siwai, **2**:304
Sora, **3**:270
Stieng, **5**:243
Sundanese, **5**:247
Suruí, **7**:313
Swahili, **9**:329
Tagbanuwa, **5**:251
Tai Lue, **5**:255
Tanaina, **1**:336, 337
Tangu, **2**:312
Tanimuka, **7**:319-320
Tanna, **2**:315
Tapirapé, **7**:321
Tauade, **2**:320
Tausug, **5**:264
Telefolmin, **2**:323
Telegu, **3**:287
Ticuna, **7**:330
Tigray, **9**:348-349
Tiv, **9**:351

Spirits, belief in (cont'd)
  Tolai, **2:**335
  Tonga, **9:**355
  Trio, **7:**336
  Truk, **2:**353
  Tuareg, **9:**369
  Tubatulabal, **1:**355
  Udmurt, **6:**380
  Uzbeks, **6:**398
  Vedda, **3:**302-303
  Vietnamese, **5:**286
  Wáiwai, **7:**348
  Wamira, **2:**367
  Wanano, **7:**350
  Wantoat, **2:**369
  Waorani, **7:**353
  Warao, **7:**359
  Wogeo, **2:**381
  Wolof, **9:**380
  Yagua, **7:**373
  Yakan, **5:**290
  Yakö, **9:**386, 387
  Yangoru Boiken, **2:**390
  Yanomamö, **7:**376
  Yap, **2:**394
  Yawalapití, **7:**380
  Yuit, **1:**392
  Zaramo, **9:**402
  Zarma, **9:**406
  Zulu, **9:**412
  see also Animism; Death, causes of; Evil
      spirits; Ghosts; Guardian spirit; Illness,
      causes of; Polytheism; Shamanism
Spiritualists
  Black Creoles of Louisiana, **1:**39
  Callahuaya, **7:**90
Spiritual kinship. *See* Fictive kin
Splint baskets
  Abenaki, **1:**4
  Maliseet, **1:**211
Sponsorship roles. *See* Fictive kin
Sports
  club fights
    Ache, **7:**5, 6, 7
  cricket
    Antigua and Barbuda, **8:**10
  football
    Orcadians, **4:**188
  lacrosse
    Pomo, **1:**295
  log racing
    Shavante, **7:**301
    Sherente, **7:**303
  running races
    Canela, **7:**97
  soccer
    Yawalapití, **7:**379
  stickball
    Choctaw, **1:**73
  upward mobility via
    Afro-Brazilians, **7:**13-14
  varied
    Seminoles of Oklahoma, **1:**315
  wrestling
    Mehinaku, **7:**236, 238, 239
    Waurá, **7:**360
    Yagua, **7:**373
    Yawalapití, **7:**379

Yuit, **1:**392
Yuqui, **7:**394
Spousal abuse. *See* Domestic violence
Spouse exchange. *See under* Marriage
Spouse selection. *See* Marriage
Spray painters
  Irish Travelers, **1:**163
Spring festival
  She, **6:**491
  Slav Macedonians, **4:**241
  Tabasarans, **6:**350
Spruce root products
  Haida, **1:**135
Squash growing
  Alkongin, **1:**17
  Arikara, **1:**26
  Choctaw, **1:**71
  Ch'ol, **8:**64
  Cocopa, **1:**74
  Creek, **1:**83
  Hidatsa, **1:**146
  Hopi-Tewa, **1:**151
  Iroquois, **1:**165
  Lenca, **8:**155
  Mam, **8:**158
  Mandan, **1:**214
  Miami, **1:**231
  Nahuat of the Sierra de Puebla, **8:**191
  Ojibwa, **1:**269
  Omaha, **1:**275
  Osage, **1:**277
  Ottawa, **1:**279
  Pame, **8:**207
  Pawnee, **1:**284
  Popoluca, **8:**216
  Potawatomi, **1:**297
  Q'anjob'al, **8:**225
  Quechan, **1:**300
  Santee, **1:**307
  Shawnee, **1:**317
  Taos, **1:**341
  Tepehuan of Chihuahua, **8:**252
  Tepehuan of Durango, **8:**256
  Tewa Pueblos, **1:**348
  Tzotzil of Chamula, **8:**279
  Tzotzil of San Bartolomé de los Llanos,
      8:287
  Tzotzil of Zinacantan, **8:**292
  Walapai, **1:**364
  Wichita, **1:**379
  Winnebago, **1:**380
  Yukateko, **8:**309
  Zapotec, **8:**312
  Zoque, **8:**315
  Zuni, **1:**397
Squatters
  Dutch, **4:**94
Stainless steel
  design
    Swedes, **4:**258
  production
    Burgundians, **4:**47
Star gods
  Pawnee, **1:**285
Star powers
  Pawnee, **1:**285
Star quilts
  Teton, **1:**345

Star Society
  Gros Ventre, **1:**134
Starvation. *See* Famine
State-owned land. *See* Landholding, state
State Religion
  Han, **6:**447
Statis, basis of
  class
    Persians, **9:**279-280
  royalty vs. commoner
    Alur, **9:**14
Status, basis of
  ability
    Bukidnon, **5:**54
    Maranao, **5:**177
    Rom, **1:**305
  achievement
    German Swiss, **4:**126
    Tlingit, **1:**352
  age
    Awakateko, **8:**16
    Blackfoot, **1:**42
    Callahuaya, **7:**89
    Central Thai, **5:**71
    Chorote, **7:**125
    Cuiva, **7:**144
    Dusun, **5:**82
    Edo, **9:**81
    Fipa, **9:**99
    Gorotire, **7:**162, 163
    Gros Ventre, **1:**134
    Hidsata, **1:**147
    Hmong, **5:**94
    Iatmul, **2:**99
    Igbo, **9:**122
    Iraqw, **9:**126
    Karamojong, **9:**157
    Kikuyu, **9:**162
    Kipsigis, **9:**165
    Konso, **9:**170-171
    Lunda, **9:**198
    Maasai, **9:**208-209
    Mbeere, **9:**222
    Mijikenda, **9:**224-225
    Nandi and other Kalenjin peoples, **9:**233
    Northern Paiute, **1:**264
    Okiek, **9:**261
    Osage, **1:**278
    Palikur, **7:**263
    Piro, **7:**280
    Pokot, **9:**283
    Rom, **1:**305
    Samoa, **2:**288
    Saraguro, **7:**294
    Saramaka, **7:**297
    Suri, **9:**326
    Suya, **7:**316
    Tapirapé, **7:**321
    Tonga, **2:**337
    Trio, **7:**336
    Turkana, **9:**372
    Xikrin, **7:**368-369
    Yakö, **9:**386
    Yoruba, **9:**392
    Zapotec, **8:**313
  behavior
    Peloponnesians, **4:**194
  bilaterally determined

Hawaiians, 2:96
birth order
    Altaians, 6:22
    Bau, 2:23
    Osage, 1:278
bride-price
    Yurok, 1:395
civil-religious
    Cuicatec, 8:92
    Lenca, 8:156
    Poqomam, 8:218
    Q'anjob'al, 8:225
    Q'eqchi,' 8:227
    Tzeltal, 8:274
    Tz'utujil, 8:298
clan ranking
    Bau, 2:23
    Woleai, 2:383-384
class
    Afar, 9:7
    Bagirmi, 9:34
    Cape Verdeans, 4:56
    Castilians, 4:60
    Catalans, 4:62, 63
    Cherokee, 1:62
    Chickasaw, 1:66
    Chinook, 1:67
    Comox, 1:76
    Dutch, 4:93
    English, 4:97
    Flemish, 4:107
    French Canadians, 1:132
    Haida, 1:136
    Haitians, 1:138
    Hare, 1:141
    Hidsata, 1:147
    Kanuri, 9:152
    Kiowa, 1:188
    Klallam, 1:190
    Kumeyaay, 1:195
    Kwakiutl, 1:199
    Maliseet, 1:212
    Pawnee, 1:285
    Saint Lucians, 8:231
    Swazi, 9:331
cofradía
    Tz'utujil, 8:298
    Zoque, 8:316
dream power
    Quechan, 1:302
education
    Austrians, 4:20
    Chakma, 3:60
    Greeks, 4:133
    Palestinians, 9:266
    Tonga, 9:354
ejido
    Pima Bajo, 8:212
    Tojolab'al, 8:262
    Yukateko, 8:310
elite class
    Bengali, 3:29, 34
ethnicity
    Manx, 4:171
family prestige
    Flemish, 4:107
    Osage, 1:278
fiesta sponsorship

Cotopaxi Quichua, 7:134
    Otavalo, 7:255
    Salasaca, 7:291
freeman or slave descendancy
    Somalis, 9:317-318
    Zarma, 9:405
gender
    Hausa, 9:113
    Iraqw, 9:126
    Mijikenda, 9:224-225
    Yoruba, 9:392
gender as divider
    Flemish, 4:108
heading large family
    Pima-Papago, 1:289
herbal medicine knowledge
    Huarayo, 7:178
    Shipibo, 7:305
heredity
    Maguindanao, 5:169
    Malaita, 2:162
    Manam, 2:168
    Nootka, 1:257
    San-speaking peoples, 9:303
    Tonga, 2:337
    Wiyot, 1:384
    Yemenis, 9:389
honorable behavior
    Greeks, 4:133
house roofing
    Nagasa, 3:190
housing location
    Central Thai, 5:71
    Maltese, 4:167
    Yap, 2:393
hunting and fishing skill
    Ache, 7:6
    Ambae, 2:12
    Shipibo, 7:305
    Yuracaré, 7:395
husband's status
    Flemish, 4:108
jaguar killing
    Mojo, 7:242
kinship
    Corsicans, 4:67
knowledge
    Kogi, 7:202
landholding, 4:270
    Azoreans, 4:26, 27, 28
    Bavarians, 4:34
    Provencal, 4:211
lineages
    Acholi, 9:5
    Ibibio, 9:120
    peripatetics of Afghanistan, Iran, and
        Turkey, 9:276
    Somalis, 9:317
    Tiv, 9:351
linguistic
    Azoreans, 4:28
magicoreligious ceremonies
    Purum, 3:244
mana
    Maori, 2:178
marginality. _See_ Marginality
marriage
    Flemish, 4:107

marriage and well-behaved children
    Peloponnesians, 4:194
marrying upward. _See_ Hypergamy
mobility. _See_ Class mobility; Sanscritization
noble vs. commoner
    Abkhazians, 6:8
    Aleuts, 6:18
    Altaians, 6:22
    Bajau, 5:34
    Batak, 5:40
    Bolaang Mongondow, 5:43
    Bonerate, 5:44
    Bugis, 5:50
    Dai, 6:426
    Georgians, 6:135
    Iban, 5:98
    Javanese, 5:112-113
    Jingpo, 6:457-458
    Kachin, 5:117
    Kenyah-Kayan-Kajang, 5:134
    Korean, 5:146
    Kosrae, 2:129
    Kumyks, 6:223
    Laki, 5:154
    Lisu, 5:166
    Makassar, 5:173
    Melanau, 5:179
    Modang, 5:186
    Muong, 5:191
    Nias, 5:196
    Rotinese, 5:214
    Samal Moro, 5:223
    Svans, 6:343
    Tahiti, 2:306
    Tai Lue, 5:254-255
    Taiwan aboriginal peoples, 5:257
    Talysh, 6:356
    Tausug, 5:263-264
    Tetum, 5:276
    Tibetans, 6:494
    Toraja, 5:282
    Trobriand Islands, 2:350
    Uvea, 2:364
number of enemies slain
    Ayoreo, 7:71
number of wives
    Shipibo, 7:305
occupation
    Bashkirs, 6:56
    Central Thai, 5:71
    Dogon, 9:73
    Easter Island, 2:54
    Manx, 4:171
    Mingrelians, 6:264
    Palestinians, 9:266
    Pashai, 9:267
    Persians, 9:279
    Yemenis, 9:389
occupational power
    Croats, 4:74
oratorical skills
    Huarayo, 7:178
    Shipibo, 7:305
    Yanomamö, 7:376
parenting success
    Mescalero Apache, 1:224
patron-client
    Madeirans, 4:165

Status, basis of (cont'd)
  personal conduct
    Osage, 1:278
  professionalism
    Peloponnesians, 4:194
  property ownership
    Aveyronnais, 4:26
  race
    Afrikaners, 9:9
    Asians of Africa, 9:26
    Bermudians, 8:25
    Cape Verdeans, 4:56
    Creoles of Nicaragua, 8:85
    Nahua of the Huasteca, 8:186
    Trinidadians and Tobagonians, 8:269
  ranking
    Jews of Iran, 9:141
    Swazi, 9:331
    Tanaina, 1:336
    Tzotzil of Zinacantan, 8:293
  religion
    Saraguro, 7:294, 295
  religious practictioners
    Azoreans, 4:26, 27
    Nagas, 3:190-191
    Toda, 3:297
  religious practitioners
    Jews, Arabic-speaking, 9:136
  reputation
    Peloponnesians, 4:194
  rigid system
    Shetlanders, 4:234
  scalp-taking skill
    Nivaclé, 7:250
  shaman role
    Piaroa, 7:277
    Yanomamö, 7:376
  skin color
    Black Creoles of Louisiana, 1:37-38
    Latinos, 1:205
    Martiniquais, 8:163
  social
    Belau, 2:26
  subclan membership
    Osage, 1:278
  terms of address
    Highland Scots, 4:141
  title
    Tlingit, 1:352
  tribal
    Aimaq, 9:10
    Baggara, 9:31
    Bagirmi, 9:34
    Bedouin, 9:45
    Fali, 9:96
    Khoi, 9:160
    Kurds, 9:176
    Lur, 9:202
    Ndebele, 9:237
    Qashqa'i, 9:286
  urban divisions
    Norwegians, 4:182
  urban dwelling
    Frisians, 4:111
  valor
    Yanomamö, 7:376
  warrior power
    Niue, 2:251

    Quechan, 1:302
  wealth
    Aquitaine, 4:14-15
    Austrians, 4:20
    Bai, 6:420
    Central Thai, 5:71
    Chakma, 3:60
    Chin, 3:64, 66
    Croats, 4:74
    Divehi, 3:77-78
    German Swiss, 4:126
    Greeks, 4:133
    Hupa, 1:152
    Ifugao, 5:100
    Ingalik, 1:157
    Kapauku, 2:105
    Karok, 1:177
    Khasi, 3:125
    Khmer, 5:137
    Kiowa, 1:187, 188
    Klallam, 1:190
    Klamath, 1:192
    Kwakiutl, 1:199
    Lakher, 3:146
    Lamaholot, 5:156
    Lillooet, 1:206
    Lingayat, 3:153
    Mongo, 9:226
    osage, 1:278
    Pumi, 6:484
    Rom, 1:305
    Saraguro, 7:294
    Tanaina, 1:336
    Tlingit, 1:352
    Tolowa, 1:353
    Wiyot, 1:384
    Yoruba, 9:392
    Yurok, 1:395
  see also Cargo system; Castes; Egalitarian-
    ism; Hierarchical society; Marginality;
    Outcastes
Status sources
  Kumeyaay, 1:195
"Staying sickness"
  Pima-Papago, 1:290
Steam baths
  Aleuts, 6:16
Stem family. See Household, three-genera-
    tional stem
Sterility. See Infertility
Stomp Dance
  Seminole of Oklahoma, 1:314
Stone-age
  Tasaday, 5:259-261
Stone-blade knives
  West Greenland Inuit, 1:377
Stone carving. See Carved objects, stone
Stone chipping
  Yurok, 1:394
Stone housing. See under Houses and housing
Stone pipe. See Pipe making
Stone quarrying
  Landin, 4:160
Stones
  placement on graves
    Albanians, 4:8
    Chin, 3:67
  spirit-inhabited

    Irula, 3:109
  as wealth
    Sengseng, 2:296
    Yap, 2:392, 394
Stone tombs
  Cornish, 4:64
Stone tools
  Ainu, 5:8
  Ajië, 2:7
  Boazi, 2:29
  Chambri, 2:31
  Choiseul Island, 2:38
  Dani, 2:44
  Dobu, 2:50
  Eipo, 2:56
  Gnau, 2:80
  Kiwai, 2:125
  Marind-anim, 2:183
  Melpa, 2:201
  Mountain Arapesh, 2:216
  Muyu, 2:228
  Tanaina, 1:335
  Tanna, 2:313
  Tasmanians, 2:316
  Tauade, 2:318
Stoneworking
  Avars, 6:45
  Dai, 6:428
  Dargins, 6:97, 98
  Easter Island, 2:54, 55
  Hakka, 6:437
  Hani, 6:450
  Ingilos, 6:150
  Kubachins, 6:217
  Kumyks, 6:221, 223
  Ladin, 4:160
  Laks, 6:234
  Maonan, 6:468
  Rutuls, 6:321
  Shan, 5:241
  Taiwan aboriginal peoples, 5:257
  Toradja, 5:281
  Tujia, 6:498
  Tuvans, 6:374
  Volga Tatars, 6:401
  Wiyot, 1:384
  Yap, 2:392
  see also Carved objects, stone
Storeowners. See Shopkeeping
Storytelling
  Afro-Venezuelans, 7:29
  Ainu, 5:10
  Ajië, 2:9
  Altaians, 6:23
  Andamanese, 3:11
  Andis, 6:27
  Angaité, 7:44
  Anuta, 2:15
  Araucanians, 7:55
  Asiatic Eskimos, 6:42
  Balkars, 6:54
  Baniwa-Curripaco-Wakuenai, 7:79
  Chimbu, 2:37
  Chukchee, 6:79
  Chuvash, 6:85
  Circassians, 6:90
  Dai, 6:427
  Daribi, 2:48

Desana, 7:154
Dolgan, 6:102
Evenki (Northern Tungus), 6:124
Gaels (Irish), 4:117
Georgians, 6:136
Goodenough Island, 2:88
Guahibo-Sikuani, 7:166
Gypsies, 6:148
Iban, 5:99
Irish Travellers, 4:156
Itelmen, 6:154
Iteso, 9:129, 130
Jews of Kurdistan, 9:146, 147
Jingpo, 6:459
Kapingamarangi, 2:110
Karachays, 6:162
Kazakhs, 6:182
Khakas, 6:188
Kmhmu, 5:141
Kogi, 7:203
Koryaks and Kerek, 6:210
Kumyks, 6:223
Kurds, 6:227;9:177
Kyrgyz, 6:231
Laz, 6:240
Lithuanians, 6:251
Lozi, 9:189
Mansi, 6:255
Maris, 6:258
Menominee, 1:221
Miao, 6:472
Nandi and other Kalenjin peoples, 9:234
Nenets, 6:279
Nganasan, 6:282
Ngatatjara, 2:241
Nguna, 2:244
Nivkh, 6:285
Nogays, 6:289
North Alaskan Eskimos, 1:261
Northern Paiute, 1:265
Ogan-Besemah, 5:199
Old Believers, 6:294
Orcadians, 4:187
Orochi, 6:295
Ossetes, 6:301
Pemon, 7:273
peripatetics, 3:235
Rom of Czechoslovakia, 4:219
Rutuls, 6:321
Saramaka, 7:298
Shahsevan, 9:310
Shavante, 7:301
Shipibo, 7:306
Siberiaki, 6:334
Siberian Estonians, 6:337
Siberian Tatars, 6:342
Sicilians, 4:237
Southern Paiute (and Chemehuevi), 1:332
Svans, 6:346
Tabasarans, 6:350
Tairora, 2:309
Temiar, 5:272
Temne, 9:345
Tory Islanders, 4:266
Truk, 2:353
Tsakhurs, 6:367
Udmurt, 6:380
Ukrainian peasants, 6:388

Western Apache, 1:373
West Greenland Inuit, 1:378
Winnebago, 1:381
Yanomamö, 7:377
Yuit, 1:392
Yukpa, 7:384
Zhuang, 6:511
see also Oral tradition
Stratified society. _See_ Hierarchical society
Straw work
  Bahamians, 8:20
  Swedes, 4:258
  Swiss, Italian, 4:260
Street gangs
  African American, 1:12
Stress avoidance
  Delaware, 1:86
Stringed instruments. _See under_ Musical
      instruments
String work
  Mataco, 7:228, 229
  Tunebo, 7:338
  Yuit, 1:392
Student protests. _See_ Youth revolt
Sturgeon fishing
  Winnebago, 1:381
Subincision (as initiation rite)
  Aranda, 2:18
  Cashibo, 7:104
Sudanese-type kinship terminology. _See under_
      kinship terminology
Suffrage
  compulsory
    Flemish, 4:108
  male head of household
    Balinese, 5:37
  property qualifictions
    Antigua and Barbuda, 8:10
  Shaker abstention, 1:316
  universal adult
    Greeks, 4:133
  women (delayed)
    German Swiss, 4:127
    Swiss, Italian, 4:261
Sufism
  Afar, 9:8
  Baul, 3:26
  Bengali, 3:33, 34
  Butonese, 5:68
  Hui, 6:453
  Kanuri, 9:153
  Kyrgyz, 6:231
  Laks, 6:233, 234
  Maranao, 5:177
  Muslim, 3:185
  Ogan-Besemah, 5:199
  Tajiks, 6:354
  Turkmens, 6:371
  Uighur, 6:384
  Wolof, 9:380
  Yezidis, 6:410
Sugar beet growing
  Bavarians, 4:33
  Castilians, 4:59
  Dungans, 6:109
  Lithuanians, 6:250
  Poles, 4:203
  Portuguese, 4:206

Slovaks, 4:243
Ukrainians, 6:392
Walloons, 4:276
Sugarcane growing
  Acehnese, 5:3
  Achang, 6:417
  Afro-Colombians, 7:16
  Afro-Hispanic Pacific Lowlanders, 7:20
  Akawaio, 7:31
  Amuzgo, 8:4
  Anambé, 7:41
  Antigua and Barbuda, 8:8
  Asurini, 7:61
  Awá Kwaiker, 7:63
  Bakairi, 7:74
  Cajuns, 1:49
  Cape Verdeans, 4:55
  Cariña, 7:102
  Cashibo, 7:104
  Chácobo, 7:105
  Chimila, 7:114
  Chocó, 7:122
  Colorado, 7:131
  Cuna, 7:149
  Dominicans, 8:101
  East Asians of the United States, 1:98, 100
  East Indians in Trinidad, 8:105
  Emberá, 7:155
  Emerillon, 7:159
  Guadeloupians, 8:116
  Guahibo-Sikuani, 7:164
  Guarayu, 7:174
  Hoti, 7:175
  Huarayo, 7:177
  Jebero, 7:181
  Jivaro, 7:182
  Karihona, 7:192
  Kikuyu, 9:161
  Kpelle, 9:173
  Krikati/Pukobye, 7:204
  Macuna, 7:212
  Madeirans, 4:164, 165
  Maroni Carib, 7:220
  Mauritian, 3:171
  Mayoruna, 7:234
  Mazatec, 8:168
  Mojo, 7:242
  Muna, 5:189
  Nahua of the Huasteca, 8:185
  Noanamá, 7:251
  Nubians, 9:247
  Palikur, 7:262
  Panare, 7:265
  Pemon, 7:271
  Puerto Ricans, 8:221, 222
  Rikbaktsa, 7:287
  Saliva, 7:292
  Saramaka, 7:296
  Sharanahua, 7:299
  Shavante, 7:300
  Suya, 7:315
  Tanimuka, 7:318
  Telugu, 3:285
  Tequistlatec, 8:259
  Terena, 7:325
  Totonac, 8:264
  Trio, 7:335
  Triqui, 8:270

Sugarcane growing (cont'd)
Tupari, 7:339
Virgin Islanders, 8:300
Waimiri-Atroari, 7:343
Wapisiana, 7:355
Warao, 7:357
Witoto, 7:364
Xikrin, 7:367
Yagua, 7:372
Yekuana, 7:381
Yuqui, 7:392
Sugar industry
Jamaicans, 8:137, 138
Kittsians and Nevisians, 8:146
Sugarloaf manufacture
Nahua of the Huasteca, 8:185
Suicide
beliefs about
Ayoreo, 7:71
Bhil, 3:41, 42
Cheyenne, 1:66
Dobu, 2:51
Evenki (Northern Tungus), 6:124
Foi, 2:61
Hmong, 5:94
Itelmen, 6:154
Kewa, 2:117
Khevsur, 6:195
Koryaks and Kerek, 6:210
Mafulu, 2:153
Micronesians, 1:239
Naxi, 6:479, 480
Qiang, 6:486
Russian peasants, 6:313
Russians, 6:317
Tairora, 2:309
Tausug, 5:264
Xibe, 6:504
Yuracaré, 7:396
Zuni, 1:400
burial proscriptions
Bene Israel, 3:28
causes for
Sora, 3:270
Tamil of Sri Lanka, 3:282, 283
high rates of
Austrians, 4:21
West Greenland Inuit, 1:378
Su Jeddim (holiday)
Azerbaijani Turks, 6:50
Suki relationship
Tagalog, 5:249
Sukkoth [Sukkes] (festival)
Ashkenazim, 6:36
Bukharan Jews, 6:65
Karaites, 6:165
Summer houses. *See* Houses and housing,
second or summer houses
Sun
as creator representation
Mescalero Apache, 1:225
daily prayer to
Northern Paiute, 1:264
Wintun, 1:383
in religious beliefs
Akawaio, 7:32
Amuesha, 7:39
Desana, 7:153

Sun Dance
Arapaho, 1:26
Assiniboin, 1:27
Blackfoot, 1:41, 42
Crow, 1:83
Eastern Shoshone, 1:104, 106
Gros Ventre, 1:134
Kiowa, 1:187, 188, 189
Northern Paiute, 1:265
Northern Shoshone and Bannock, 1:266
Ojibwa, 1:269, 271
Okanagon, 1:272
Sarsi, 1:308
Teton, 1:344, 346
Ute, 1:362
Sun deities
Bhuiya, 3:44
Bondo, 3:50
Comanche, 1:75
Kiowa, 1:188
Mandan, 1:215
Navajo, 1:253
Zuni, 1:399
Sunflower growing
Andalusians, 4:10
Arikara, 1:26
Burgundians, 4:46
Hidatsa, 1:146
Mandan, 1:214
Sunni Muslims. *See* Islam (Sunni)
Superincision (as initiation rite)
Lau, 2:144
Supermarkets. *See* Shopping centers
Supernatural beliefs
Abenaki, 1:5
Aleut, 1:16
Apalai, 7:47
Araucanians, 7:54
Araweté, 7:57
Arubans, 8:13
Asurini, 7:62
Azoreans, 4:28
Baiga, 3:21
Bamiléké, 9:39
Bedouin, 9:45
Berbers of Morocco, 9:51, 52
Betsileo, 9:57
Bhil, 3:41
Bhuiya, 3:44
Bondo, 3:50
Bretons, 4:40
Bulgarians, 4:45
Burusho, 3:56
Cahita, 8:37
Calabrese, 4:50
Cape Verdeans, 4:56
Carib of Dominica, 8:40
Caribou Inuit, 1:51
Cherokee, 1:62
Chipewyan, 1:69
Chiricahua, 1:70
Choctaw, 1:72
Ch'ol, 8:65
Corsicans, 4:68
Croats, 4:74
Curaçao, 8:98
Cyclades, 4:78
Dalmatians, 4:87

Dogon, 9:73
Eastern Shoshone, 1:105, 106
Ewe and Fon, 9:87
Falasha, 9:92
Fali, 9:97
Finns, 4:104
Fipa, 9:99, 100
Fox, 1:130
Friuli, 4:113
Gaels (Irish), 4:117
Galicians, 4:120
German Swiss, 4:127
ghost belief
Khoi, 9:160
Gond, 3:86-87
Grasia, 3:88
Greeks, 4:133
Guajiro, 7:169, 170
Haida, 1:136
Hare, 1:141
Hidsata, 1:147, 148
Hill Pandaram, 3:100
Hopi, 1:150
Iglulik Inuit, 1:155
Ingalik, 1:158
Irish Travellers, 4:156
Iroquois, 1:166-167
Jat, 3:113
Karajá, 7:190
Karok, 1:177
Kashubians, 4:159
Keres Pueblo Indians, 1:181
Khoi, 9:160
Kiowa, 1:188, 189
Koya, 3:141
Kurumbas, 3:143
Kutchin, 1:196
Kwakiutl, 1:199, 200
Lobi-Dagarti peoples, 9:185
Lozi, 9:189
Lunda, 9:198, 199
Luyia, 9:206
Maliseet, 1:212-213
Mandan, 1:215
Mangbetu, 9:217
Manx, 4:171
Mataco, 7:229
Mbeere, 9:222-223
Menominee, 1:221
Mikir, 3:176
Montagnais-Naskapi, 1:246
Montenegrins, 4:173, 174
Mossi, 9:230
Nagas, 3:190, 191
Nandi and other Kalenjin peoples, 9:234
Navajo, 1:253
Ndebele, 9:238
Newar, 3:208
Noanamá, 7:251
Nootka, 1:257
Northern Paiute, 1:264-265
Nyinba, 3:213
Ojibwa, 1:270
Osage, 1:278
Páez, 7:258
Pahari, 3:222-223
Pame, 8:208
Pandit of Kashmir, 3:226

Paniyan, **3:**227
Paraujano, **7:**268
Pathan, **3:**233
Pomo, **1:**295
Ponca, **1:**296
Popoluca, **8:**217
Poqomam, **8:**219
Purum, **3:**244
Rikbaktsa, **7:**288
Rom, **1:**305
Saliva, **7:**292
Sara, **9:**306
Seminole of Oklahoma, **1:**314-315
Seri, **8:**235
Shuswap, **1:**318
Sicilians, **4:**237
Slovaks, **4:**245
Tanaina, **1:**336
Tanana, **1:**340
Tarahumara, **8:**242
Tatuyo, **7:**324
Teton, **1:**346
Tewa Pueblos, **1:**349
Thadou, **3:**289
Tharu, **3:**293
Toba, **7:**333
Toda, **3:**297, 298
Tory Islanders, **4:**266
Totonac, **8:**266
tropical-forest foragers, **9:**357
Tswana, **9:**364
Tupari, **7:**340
Turks, **9:**376
Tzotzil of San Bartolomé de los Llanos,
    8:291
Ute, **1:**362
Vedda, **3:**303
Waimiri-Atroari, **7:**344
Western Apaches, **1:**373
Western Shoshone, **1:**375
Wichita, **1:**379
Winnebago, **1:**382
Yavapai, **1:**386
Yoruba, **9:**393
Yukuna, **7:**389
Yuqui, **7:**394
Zapotec, **8:**313
Zoque, **8:**316
Zuni, **1:**399
    see also Animism; Evil eye; Ghosts;
        Shamanism; Spirits; _specific types of
        beliefs_
Supernatural powers. _See_ Evil eye; Second
    sight
Supernatural retribution, fear of. _See under_
    Social control measures
Superstitions
    Chinese of Costa Rica, **8:**62
    see also Evil eye; Supernatural beliefs
Supreme being
    Algonkin, **1:**17
    Bondo, **3:**50
    Candoshi, **7:**94
    Cheyenne, **1:**65, 66
    Chickasaw, **1:**66
    Chiriguano, **7:**121
    Cuna, **7:**151
    Hidsata, **1:**147

Hutterites, **1:**154
Iroquois, **1:**166-167
Islam, **1:**25
Jews, **1:**171
Kickapoo, **1:**185
Kumeyaay, **1:**195
Menominee, **1:**222
Nambicuara, **7:**247
Ojibwa, **1:**270
Oriya, **3:**217-218
Ottawa, **1:**280
Pende, **9:**273-274
Shawnee, **1:**317
Tanaina, **1:**336
Walapai, **1:**364
Warao, **7:**359
Wayapi, **7:**363
Wintun, **1:**383
Wiyot, **1:**385
Yagua, **7:**373
Yankton, **1:**386
Yekuana, **7:**381
Yuit, **1:**392
Zuni, **1:**399
see also Creator; Monotheism; _specific
    religions_
Supreme being, female. _See_ Woman supreme
    being
Surnames
    clan as
        Mossi, **9:**229
        Nenets, **6:**279
        Temne, **9:**343
        Tonga, **9:**353
        Zaramo, **9:**401
    combined "household" name
        Flemish, **4:**107
    Dai, **6:**425
    dominant joint families
        Slovenes, **4:**248
    from enslavement period
        African Americans, **1:**12
    father's given name as
        Micronesians in United States, **1:**237
    fluid choice between maternal or paternal
        family
        Mescalero Apache, **1:**224
    geographic referents
        Frisians, **4:**111
    Lao, **5:**158
    lineal
        Vlachs, **4:**274
    lineal ancestors
        Tory Islanders, **4:**265
    married woman keeping own
        Dutch, **4:**93
        Galicians, **4:**120
        Georgians, **6:**133
        Koreans, **6:**206
    maternal and paternal
        Azoreans, **4:**28
        Galicians, **4:**120
    maternal-paternal hyphenated
        English, **4:**96
        Flemish, **4:**107
        German Swiss, **4:**126
    matronymic
        Chuvans, **6:**82

natal homestead
    Faroe Islanders, **4:**99
nicknames used as
    Greek-speaking Jews of Greece, **4:**135
occupational
    Frisians, **4:**111
patrilineal
    Appalachians, **1:**22
    Arab American, **1:**24
    Bavarians, **4:**34
    Danes, **4:**89
    Dutch, **4:**93
    Greek-speaking Jews of Greece, **4:**135
    Jews, **1:**169
    Manx, **4:**170
    Ndembu, **9:**239
    Piemontese Sinti, **4:**200
    Serbs, **4:**231
    Sharanahua, **7:**299
    Swiss, Italian, **4:**261
patrilineal (reflecting generations of)
    Gaels (Irish), **4:**116
patronymic
    Acadians, **1:**8
    Ashkenazim, **6:**35
    Avars, **6:**45
    Bretons, **4:**39
    Chukchee, **6:**77
    Circassians, **6:**88
    Cyclades, **4:**77
    Czechs, **4:**83
    Faroe Islanders, **4:**99
    Friuli, **4:**113
    Occitans, **4:**185
    Ossetes, **6:**300
personal association emphasis
    Rominche, **4:**216
shared by clan
    Mossi, **9:**229
use of "O'" and "N'"
    Gaels (Irish), **4:**116
vironymic
    Bretons, **4:**39
see also Names
Surrealistic painting
    Walloons, **4:**278
Suspiciousness of foreigners. _See_ Xenophobia
Suttee
    Chitpavan Brahman, **3:**70
Sweat bath
    Cree, **1:**82
    Hidsata, **1:**148
    Kiowa, **1:**189
    Mam, **8:**158
    Q'anjob'al, **8:**225
Sweat lodge
    Cheyenne, **1:**66
    Hidsata, **1:**148
    Hupa, **1:**152
    Karok, **1:**176
    Maliseet, **1:**212
    Nez Percé, **1:**254
    Northern Paiute, **1:**265
    Okanagon, **1:**272
    Teton, **1:**346
    Thompson, **1:**350
    Tubatulabal, **1:**355
    Western Shoshone, **1:**374

Sweat lodge (cont'd)
  Winnebago, **1**:380
  Wiyot, **1**:384
  Yurok, **1**:394
Sweet Medicine (sacred being)
  Mandan, **1**:215
Sweet potato growing
  Abelam, **2**:4
  Afro-Venezuelans, **7**:26
  Ajië, **2**:7-8
  Akawaio, **7**:31
  Amahuaca, **7**:34
  Ambae, **2**:11
  Ambonese, **5**:17
  Amuesha, **7**:37
  Angaité, **7**:43
  Apiaká, **7**:48
  Asurini, **7**:61
  Ata Tana 'Ai, **5**:23
  Bagobo, **5**:29
  Bakairi, **7**:74
  Balantak, **5**:35
  Banaro, **2**:21
  Banggai, **5**:38
  Bolaang Mongondow, **5**:43
  Bunun, **5**:56
  Candoshi, **7**:93
  Canela, **7**:95
  Cariña, **7**:102
  Cashibo, **7**:104
  Central Thai, **5**:70
  Chácobo, **7**:105
  Chamorros, **2**:34
  Chimane, **7**:112
  Chimbu, **2**:35
  Chimila, **7**:114
  Chiriguano, **7**:120
  Choiseul Island, **2**:38
  Cinta Larga, **7**:127
  Cocama, **7**:130
  Colorado, **7**:131
  Cuna, **7**:149
  Dani, **2**:43
  Daribi, **2**:46, 47
  Dobu, **2**:50
  Dong, **6**:431
  Dusun, **5**:81
  Easter Island, **2**:54
  Edo, **9**:79
  Eipo, **2**:56
  Emerillon, **7**:159
  Ewe and Fon, **9**:85
  Filipino, **5**:87
  Fore, **2**:63
  Futuna, **2**:66
  Gahuku-Gama, **2**:69
  Gainj, **2**:71
  Ganda, **9**:104
  Garia, **2**:74
  Gelao, **6**:435
  Gogodala, **2**:83
  Goodenough Island, **2**:86
  Gorontalese, **5**:90
  Gorotire, **7**:162
  Guadalcanal, **2**:89
  Guahibo-Sikuani, **7**:164
  Gururumba, **2**:92
  Hakka, **6**:437

  Hoti, **7**:175
  Ibibio, **9**:119
  Igbo, **9**:121
  Isneg, **5**:103
  Jing, **6**:454
  Jivaro, **7**:182
  Kamilaroi, **2**:104
  Kapauku, **2**:105
  Karajá, **7**:188
  Karihona, **7**:192
  Kenyah-Kayan-Kajang, **5**:133
  Keraki, **2**:112
  Kewa, **2**:115
  Kikuyu, **9**:161
  Kilenge, **2**:118
  Kiwai, **2**:125
  Kuikuru, **7**:207
  Kurtatchi, **2**:131
  Kwoma, **2**:134, 136
  Lak, **2**:137
  Lakalai, **2**:140
  Lau, **2**:143
  Lengua, **7**:210
  Lesu, **2**:146
  Loven, **5**:166
  Macuna, **7**:212
  Mae Enga, **2**:149
  Mafulu, **2**:152
  Maguindanao, **5**:169
  Mailu, **2**:154
  Maisin, **2**:158
  Makushi, **7**:218
  Malaita, **2**:161
  Malekula, **2**:164
  Manam, **2**:167
  Mandak, **2**:170
  Manus, **2**:173
  Maori, **2**:177
  Maring, **2**:185
  Maroni Carib, **7**:220
  Maxakali, **7**:233
  Mayoruna, **7**:234
  Mejbrat, **2**:195, 197
  Melpa, **2**:201
  Mendi, **2**:203
  Mocoví, **7**:240
  Mojo, **7**:242
  Mon, **5**:189
  Mongo, **9**:226
  Moré, **7**:242
  Motu, **2**:213
  Mountain Arapesh, **2**:216
  Muna, **5**:189
  Muyu, **2**:228
  Namau, **2**:231
  Nasioi, **2**:233
  Nguna, **2**:242
  Nias, **5**:195
  Nissan, **2**:249
  Orokolo, **2**:259
  Palikur, **7**:262
  Panare, **7**:265
  Paresí, **7**:269
  Pauserna, **7**:270
  Pemon, **7**:271
  Pentecost, **2**:262
  Piapoco, **7**:274
  Piaroa, **7**:276

  Pohnpei, **2**:268
  Rennell Island, **2**:277
  Rikbaktsa, **7**:287
  Rossel Island, **2**:278
  Rotuma, **2**:281
  Sagada Igorot, **5**:216
  Sambia, **2**:284
  Samoa, **2**:287
  San Cristobal, **2**:289
  Santa Cruz, **2**:290
  Selepet, **2**:293
  Semang, **5**:234
  Shavante, **7**:300
  She, **6**:489
  Sherente, **7**:302
  Shui, **6**:491
  Siane, **2**:298
  Sio, **2**:300
  Sirionó, **7**:310
  Siwai, **2**:302, 303
  Sulod, **5**:246
  Sundanese, **5**:247
  Suruí, **7**:312
  Suya, **7**:315
  Tahiti, **2**:305
  Tairora, **2**:308
  Tangu, **2**:311
  Tanimuka, **7**:318
  Tanna, **2**:313
  Tapirapé, **7**:320
  Tauade, **2**:318
  Toba, **7**:331
  Tolai, **2**:334
  Tonga, **2**:337
  Torres Strait Islanders, **2**:346
  Trio, **7**:335
  Trobriand Islands, **2**:349, 350
  Tunebo, **7**:337
  Tupari, **7**:339
  Uvea, **2**:364
  Vietnamese, **5**:285
  Waimiri-Atroari, **7**:343
  Wamira, **2**:365
  Wantoat, **2**:368
  Waorani, **7**:352
  Wape, **2**:371
  Wapisiana, **7**:355
  Waurá, **7**:360
  Wayapi, **7**:361
  Wik Mungkan, **2**:377
  Witoto, **7**:364
  Wovan, **2**:386
  Xikrin, **7**:367
  Yagua, **7**:372
  Yangoru Boiken, **2**:388
  Yekuana, **7**:381
  Yoruba, **9**:391
  Yuracaré, **7**:395
  Zhuang, **6**:510
Swidden agriculture. *See* Agriculture, slash-
    and-burn
Swine. *See* Pig *headings*
Symbolism
  amulets
    Galicians, **4**:120
    Badaga, **3**:17
  black
    Zaramo, **9**:402

clan
    Klingit, **1:**353
    Tsimshian, **1:**355
cross
    Q'anjob'al, **8:**225
death and resurrection
    Austrians, **4:**21
design motifs
    Ata Sikka, **5:**21
    Slovenes, **4:**249
designs
    Hungarians, **4:**145
    Kiowa, **1:**189
    Menominee, **1:**222
    Sarakatsani, **4:**225
    Slav Macedonians, **4:**241
of footwashing
    Mennonites, **1:**219
maize as resurrection
    Cuicatec, **8:**93
number
    Zaramo, **9:**402
patriotic
    Hungarians, **4:**145
pentagrams against evil spirits
    Kashubians, **4:**159
phallic
    Badaga, **3:**17
Quezalcoatl
    Triqui, **8:**272
Santal, **3:**255
vermillion for married woman
    Kol, **3:**130
wedding rituals
    Croats, **4:**75
see also Iconography; Totems
Syncretism
    Acholi, **9:**6
    African Americans, **1:**13
    Afro-Venezuelans, **7:**27
    Ajarians, **6:**14
    Albanians, **4:**7
    Ambonese, **5:**19
    Amuzgo, **8:**6
    Awakateko, **8:**16
    Bagirmi, **9:**34
    Batak, **5:**41
    Bengali, **3:**33
    Bonerate, **5:**46
    Bugis, **5:**51
    Bulgarian Gypsies, **4:**42
    Buriats, **6:**68
    Cahita, **8:**37
    Cape Coloureds, **9:**60
    Chagga, **9:**62
    Chatino, **8:**52
    Chinantec, **8:**54
    Chinese in Southeast Asia, **5:**77
    Ch'ol, **8:**65
    Chuj, **8:**73
    Circassians, **9:**67
    Cora, **8:**77
    Cubans, **8:**90
    Cuicatec, **8:**93
    Dalmatians, **4:**87
    Dargins, **6:**98
    Dogon, **9:**73
    Dominicans, **8:**103

Even, **6:**119
Evenki (Northern Tungus), **6:**123
Filipino, **5:**87
Finns, **4:**104
Frisians, **4:**112
Friuli, **4:**113
Gaels (Irish), **4:**117
Galicians, **4:**120
Gorontalese, **5:**90
Guarayu, **7:**174
Han, **6:**447, 448
Huichol, **8:**127
Jamaicans, **8:**139
Javanese, **5:**113
Karelians, **6:**172
Karen, **5:**129
Kashubians, **4:**159
Khakas, **6:**188
Khanty, **6:**192
Khevsur, **6:**196
Khmer, **5:**137
K'iche,' **8:**142
Kumeyaay, **1:**195
Kurds, **9:**176
Kyrgyz, **6:**231
Latinos, **1:**205, 206
Lenca, **8:**156
Lobi-Dagarti peoples, **9:**185
Luba of Shaba, **9:**192
Madurese, **5:**168
Maguindanao, **5:**170
Makassar, **5:**174
Malay, **5:**176
Maliseet, **1:**212, 212-213, 213
Maris, **6:**258
Mende, **9:**223
Metis of Western Canada, **1:**229
Micmac, **1:**235
Micronesians, **1:**238, 239
Mixe, **8:**175
Montagnais-Naskapi, **1:**246
Montenegrins, **4:**173
Nahua of the Huasteca, **8:**186
Nahuat of the Sierra de Puebla, **8:**193
Northern Paiute, **1:**265
Northern Shoshone and Bannock, **1:**267
Ojibwa, **1:**270
Ossetes, **6:**301
Pame, **8:**208
Pima-Pago, **1:**290
Pomaks, **4:**205
Pomo, **1:**295
Popoloca, **8:**216
Pueblo Indians, **1:**298
Q'anjob'al, **8:**225
Q'eqchi,' **8:**227
Quechan, **1:**302
Rom, **1:**305, 306
Romanians, **4:**214
Saami, **4:**222
Sarakatsani, **4:**224
Sasak, **5:**225, 226, 227
Seminole, **1:**314
Siberiaki, **6:**334
Sidi, **3:**260
Slav Macedonians, **4:**241
Slovaks, **4:**245
Slovenes, **4:**249

Sundanese, **5:**247
Svans, **6:**346
Swazi, **9:**332
Tajik, **6:**492
Tarascans, **8:**246
Tepehuan of Chihuahua, **8:**253
Tewa Pueblos, **1:**349, 350
Thakali, **3:**291
Tibetans, **6:**495-496
Tojolab'al, **8:**263
Tory Islanders, **4:**266
Totonac, **8:**265-266
Tzeltal, **8:**274
Tzotzil of Chamula, **8:**281
Tzotzil of San Bartolomé de los Llanos,
    8:290-291
Tzotzil of Zinacantan, **8:**294
Tz'utujil, **8:**298
Udmurt, **6:**380
Ukrainian peasants, **6:**387
Vietnamese, **5:**286
Vlachs, **4:**275
Western Apache, **1:**373
Winnebago, **1:**382
Yakan, **5:**290
Yakut, **6:**406
Yaqui, **8:**307
Yoruba, **9:**393
Yukateko, **8:**310
Zapotec, **8:**313
Zarma, **9:**406
Zhuang, **6:**511
Zuni, **1:**399
see also Hindu influences
Syndicates
    Afro-Bolivians, **7:**9
    Callahuaya, **7:**89
Syrian Antiochian Orthodoxy
    Arab Americans, **1:**25
Syrian Catholics
    Assyrians, **9:**27
Syrian Orthodox Church
    Syrian Christian of Kerala, **3:**274

Tabancas (religious celebrations)
    Cape Verdeans, **4:**56
Taboos
    activity
        Krikati/Pukobye, **7:**205
    agricultural
        Dobu, **2:**51
        Kond, **3:**133
        Yuracaré, **7:**395
    animal
        Hare, **1:**141
        Ingalik, **1:**158
        Arapaho, **1:**26
        Baffinland Inuit, **1:**31
        Bania, **3:**24, 25
        Caribou Inuit, **1:**51
        castes, Hindu, **3:**57
        Catawba, **1:**55
    ceremonial
        Albanians, **4:**7
        Cherokee, **1:**62
    childbirth
        Boazi, **2:**31
        Eastern Shoshone, **1:**104

Taboos (cont'd)
    Guajajára, 7:167
    Kaingáng, 7:186
    Karen, 5:128
    Karihona, 7:192
    Kazakhs, 6:180
    Malaita, 2:163
    Melanau, 5:180
    Melpa, 2:202
    Mundugumor, 2:219
    Nenets, 6:279
    Palaung, 5:203
    Pemon, 7:273
    Senoi, 5:239
    Suruí, 7:313
    Tapirapé, 7:321
    Vellala, 3:306
    Xokléng, 7:371
    see also Childbirth, couvade observed
  clerically influenced
    Dutch, 4:94
  color
    Yezidis, 6:409, 411
  Comanche, 1:75
  conservation
    Uvea, 2:364
  deep-water swimming
    Itonama, 7:179
  deity propitiation
    Netsilik Inuit, 1:254
  Eastern Shoshone, 1:104, 106
  food
    Ache, 7:4, 7
    Apalai, 7:47
    Ashkenazim, 6:34
    Baniwa-Curripaco-Wakuenai, 7:80
    Bukharan Jews, 6:64
    Chocó, 7:123
    Dani, 2:44
    Dieri, 2:49
    Eipo, 2:56
    Emerillon, 7:159
    Foi, 2:61
    Garia, 2:75
    Georgian Jews, 6:128
    Gnau, 2:82
    Gogodala, 2:83
    Guadalcanal, 2:91
    Guajajára, 7:167
    Guarayu, 7:174
    Gururumba, 2:92
    Hawaiians, 2:97
    Kachin, 5:116
    Kagwahiv, 7:185
    Kaingáng, 7:186
    Kalingas, 5:123
    Kaluli, 2:103
    Karaites, 6:165
    Karakalpaks, 6:168
    Karihona, 7:192, 193
    Keraki, 2:114
    Krikati/Pukobye, 7:205
    Lakalai, 2:141, 142
    Lengua, 7:211
    Lunda, 9:199
    Maring, 2:188
    Mayoruna, 7:234
    Mehinaku, 7:237

    Namau, 2:232
    Nissan, 2:250
    Pauserna, 7:270
    Pemon, 7:273
    Piaroa, 7:278
    Rikbaktsa, 7:287
    Sengseng, 2:296
    Sherente, 7:303
    Suruí, 7:312, 313
    Tapirapé, 7:320, 321
    Telefolmin, 2:321, 323
    Temiar, 5:272
    Tewa Pueblos, 1:349
    Torres Strait Islanders, 2:346
    Trobriand Islands, 2:350
    Ulithi, 2:358
    Ute, 1:361
    Waimiri-Atroari, 7:344
    Wáiwai, 7:346
    Xokléng, 7:371
    Yezidis, 6:411
    Yukuna, 7:389
    Yuqui, 7:391, 394
    Yuracaré, 7:395
    see also Food, dietary laws and
      restrictions
  Gond, 3:85
  groom choice
    Spanish Rom, 4:255
  Haida, 1:136
  hair
    Mojo, 7:242
  Hare, 1:141, 142
  Hill Pandaram, 3:100
  hunting
    Asiatic Eskimos, 6:42
    Chiquitano, 7:118
    Guajajára, 7:167
    Kalapalo, 7:187
    Moré, 7:243
    Pende, 9:273
    Rikbaktsa, 7:287
    Somalis, 9:316
    Suruí, 7:312
    West Greenland Inuit, 1:378
  Iban, 5:98
  imposed by individuals
    Tongareva, 2:341
  incest. See Incest prohibitions
  Ingalik, 1:158, 159
  in-law
    Arapaho, 1:26
    Barama River Carib, 7:81
    Chamacoco, 7:109
    Yawalapití, 7:379
  interpersonal behaviors
    Mejbrat, 2:196
  Inughuit, 1:161
  Karok, 1:176, 177
  Ket, 6:185
  Kiowa, 1:187, 188, 189
  Klamath, 1:192
  Lepcha, 3:149
  Lesu, 2:147
  Limbu, 3:150
  Marshall Islands, 2:194
  medicine
    Evenki (Northern Tungus), 6:124

  menstruation
    Malaita, 2:163
    Nenets, 6:279
    Yuqui, 7:394
  Modang, 5:185, 187
  mortuary, 1:370
    Balkars, 6:54
    Bau, 2:24
    Easter Island, 2:55
    Georgians, 6:137
    Goodenough Island, 2:88
    Greeks, 6:144
    Guadalcanal, 2:91
    Hill Pandaram, 3:100
    Itelmen, 6:153, 154
    Kaluli, 2:104
    Karachays, 6:162
    Karaites, 9:155
    Keraki, 2:114
    Lau, 2:145
    Lesu, 2:147
    Miami, 1:232
    Mingrelians, 6:265
    Mohave, 1:242
    Navajo, 1:253
    Nomoi, 2:252
    North Alaskan Eskimos, 1:261
    Ojibwa, 1:270
    Sambia, 2:286
    Sengseng, 2:297
    Senoi, 5:239
    Telefolmin, 2:323
    Ulithi, 2:360
    Warlpiri, 2:373
    West Greenland Inuit, 1:379
    Wiyot, 1:385
    Wogeo, 2:382
    Woleai, 2:384
  Mountain Arapesh, 2:217
  Muong, 5:192
  names
    Asiatic Eskimos, 6:42
    Chechen-Ingush, 6:74
    Inguhuit, 1:161
    Kiowa, 4:189
    Mailu, 2:155
    Nganasan, 6:281
    Oroquen, 6:483
    Pemon, 7:272
    Pomo, 1:294
    Sengseng, 2:297
    Temiar, 5:273
    West Greenland Inuit, 1:379
  naming the dead
    Mardudjara, 2:180
    Sambia, 2:286
    Tasmanians, 2:317
  Nenets, 6:279
  Nepali, 3:203
  occupational
    Swazi, 9:330
    Tolai, 2:334
    Truk, 2:353
  Orok, 6:296
  Oroquen, 6:483
  parental possessions
    Lau, 2:144
  pregnancy

Karen, **5**:128
Kashubians, **4**:159
Senoi, **5**:238
speech
  Warlpiri, **2**:373
spirit placating
  North Alaskan Eskimos, **1**:261
Taiwan aboriginal peoples, **5**:258
Tanana, **1**:340
Temiar, **5**:272
T'in, **5**:279
totemic
  Gond, **3**:85
  Kapauku, **2**:106
  Namau, **2**:232
Tuvalu, **2**:357
Ulithi, **2**:360
violation
  Anuta, **2**:15
  Easter Island, **2**:55
  Garia, **2**:75
  Hawaiians, **2**:97
  Kaluli, **2**:103
  Makassar, **5**:173
  Maring, **2**:187
  Pima-papago, **2**:289
  Pomo, **1**:295
  Sengseng, **2**:297
  Taiwan aboriginal peoples, **5**:258
  West Greenland Inuit, **1**:358
West Greenland Inuit, **1**:378
women
  Saami, **6**:324
words
  Yezidis, **6**:410
work
  Rom, **1**:304
Yao of Thailand, **5**:292
see also Gender separation; Purity and
    pollution codes
Tailoring
  Bulgarians, **4**:43
  Minangkabau, **5**:182
  Tatars, **6**:492
  Untouchable service caste, **3**:159
  Vlachs, **4**:274
Taime (anthropomorphic effigy)
  Kiowa, **1**:188
Talismans. _See_ Amulets
Tali-tying marriage ceremony
  Nayar, **3**:198-199
Tall Men (supernatural)
  Seminole of Oklahoma, **1**:315
Talysh, **6**:355, 356
Tambaran (ceremony)
  Mountain Arapesh, **2**:217
Tanners. _See_ Leather work
Tantric influences
  Baul, **3**:26
  Bengali Shakta, **3**:35
  Bengali Vaishnava, **3**:17
Taoism. _See_ Daoism
Tapestry
  Bretons, **4**:40
  Flemish, **4**:106, 108
  Madeirans, **4**:165
Tapioca growing
  Rotuma, **2**:281

Tapu
  Futuna, **2**:67
  Maori, **2**:178
  Marquesas Islands, **2**:189
  Niue, **2**:252
  Tikopia, **2**:326
  Uvea, **2**:364
Tara (female deity)
  Bengali Shakta, **3**:35;**4**:166
Taravad house
  Nayar, **3**:198, 199
Tari (female deity)
  Kond, **3**:133
Taro growing
  Abelam, **2**:4
  Afro-Hispanic Pacific Lowlanders, **7**:20
  Ajië, **2**:7
  Akawaio, **7**:31
  Ambae, **2**:11
  Ambonese, **5**:17
  Anuta, **2**:14
  Apiaká, **7**:48
  Balantak, **5**:35
  Banaro, **2**:21
  Banggai, **5**:38
  Bau, **2**:22
  Belau, **2**:25
  Bikini, **2**:27
  Cariña, **7**:102
  Cashibo, **7**:104
  Choiseul Island, **2**:38
  Eipo, **2**:56
  Futuna, **2**:66
  Garia, **2**:74
  Gogodala, **2**:83
  Goodenough Island, **2**:86
  Gorotire, **7**:162
  Gururumba, **2**:92
  Hawaiians, **2**:96
  Hoti, **7**:175
  Ibibio, **9**:119
  Ifugao, **5**:99
  Igbo, **9**:121
  Isneg, **5**:103
  Jing, **6**:454
  Jivaro, **7**:182
  Kapingamarangi, **2**:108
  Kilenge, **2**:118
  Kiribati, **2**:121
  Kiwai, **2**:125
  Kosrae, **2**:128
  Kurtatchi, **2**:131
  Kwoma, **2**:134
  Lak, **2**:137
  Lakalai, **2**:140
  Lesu, **2**:146
  Mafulu, **2**:152
  Mailu, **2**:154
  Maisin, **2**:158
  Malaita, **2**:161
  Malekula, **2**:164
  Manam, **2**:167
  Mandak, **2**:170
  Mangareva, **2**:172
  Manihiki, **2**:172
  Manus, **2**:173
  Maring, **2**:185
  Maroni Carib, **7**:220

Mejbrat, **2**:195, 197
Melpa, **2**:201
Mentaweian, **5**:181
Miyanmin, **2**:210
Mountain Arapesh, **2**:216
Namau, **2**:231
Nasioi, **2**:233
Nguna, **2**:242
Nissan, **2**:249
Niue, **2**:251
Nomoi, **2**:252
Ontong Java, **2**:254, 255
Orokaiva, **2**:256
Orokolo, **2**:259
Pentecost, **2**:262
Pohnpei, **2**:268
Pukapuka, **2**:270, 271
Rapa, **2**:274
Raroia, **2**:276
Rennell Island, **2**:277
Rossel Island, **2**:278
Rotuma, **2**:281
Samoa, **2**:287
San Cristobal, **2**:289
Santa Cruz, **2**:290
Saramaka, **7**:296
Selepet, **2**:293
Sengseng, **2**:296
Siane, **2**:298
Sio, **2**:300
Siwai, **2**:302
Tagbanuwa, **5**:251
Tairora, **2**:308
Tangu, **2**:311
Tanna, **2**:313
Telefolmin, **2**:321
Tikopia, **2**:325
Tolai, **2**:334
Tonga, **2**:337
Trobriand Islands, **2**:349
Truk, **2**:352
Usino, **2**:361
Uvea, **2**:364
Wamira, **2**:365
Wantoat, **2**:368
Wogeo, **2**:380
Woleai, **2**:383
Wovan, **2**:386
Yangoru Boiken, **2**:388
Yap, **2**:392
Yekuana, **7**:381
Tattooing
  Abor, **3**:5
  Angaité, **7**:43
  Anuta, **2**:15
  Apiaká, **7**:50
  Baiga, **3**:21
  Bedouin, **9**:45
  Bhil, **3**:41
  Bondo, **3**:51
  Central Thai, **5**:71
  Colorado, **7**:131
  Cook Islands, **2**:42
  Copper Eskimo, **1**:79
  Cree, **1**:82
  Drung, **6**:432
  Dusun, **5**:83
  Ghorbat, **9**:107

Tattooing (cont'd)
Guarayu, 7:174
Gujarati, 3:92
Haida, 1:136
Hawaiians, 2:97
Ingalik, 1:158
Irula, 3:108
Japanese, 5:105
Kalimantan Dayaks, 5:120
Karen, 5:129
Kond, 3:133
Kota, 3:137
Lakher, 3:147
Lamaholot, 5:156
Lao Isan, 5:163
Luba of Shaba, 9:192
Mailu, 2:155
Maisin, 2:159
Marquesas Islands, 2:191
Marshall Islands, 2:194
Mayoruna, 7:235
Mekeo, 2:200
Miami, 1:232
Mikir, 3:176
Mohave, 1:242
Motu, 2:215
Nivaclé, 7:251
Ontong Java, 2:255
Palaung, 5:203
Paresí, 7:269
Pauserna, 7:270
peripatetics of Iraq, Syria, Lebanon, Jordan,
    Israel, Egypt, Sudan, and Yemen,
    9:277
peripatetics of the Maghreb, 9:278
Pohnpei, 2:269
Pomo, 1:295
Rikbaktsa, 7:287, 288
Rotuma, 2:283
Samoa, 2:287, 289
Santal, 3:254
Sleb, 9:315
Suruí, 7:313
Taiwan aboriginal peoples, 5:257
Thadou, 3:289
Tigray, 9:348
Tonga, 2:337, 339
Tor, 2:344
Truk, 2:353
Vlachs, 4:275
Washoe, 1:370
Woleai, 2:384
Xikrin, 7:369
Yuan, 5:293
Taunting (as social control)
Baluchi, 3:23
Tax collectors
Sherpa, 3:259
Zamindar, 3:306
Tea
herbal
    Tewa Pueblos, 1:348, 349
medicinal
    Provencal, 4:212
    Romanians, 4:214
    Slovaks, 4:245
ritual preparation
    Spanish Rom, 4:255

yerba maté specialty
    Paï-Tavytera, 7:295
Tea cultivation
Azerbaijani Turks, 6:49
Badaga, 3:15
Blang, 6:421
Dai, 6:424
De'ang, 6:430
Georgians, 6:132
Greeks, 6:142
Gusii, 9:108
Hani, 6:450
Jingpo, 6:456
Jino, 6:460
Karen, 5:126
Kipsigis, 9:164
Kota, 3:135
Lahu, 6:462
Laz, 6:239, 240
Mingrelians, 6:263
Nandi and other Kalenjin peoples, 9:232
Nyakyusa and Ngonde, 9:253
Palaung, 5:201
Portuguese, 4:206
Sinhalese, 3:265
Syrian Christian of Kerala, 3:273
Talysh, 6:355
Tea dance
Cree, 1:82
Dogrib, 1:89
Teasing (as social control). See under Social
    control measures
Teasing relationship
Winnebago, 1:381
Technological borrowings
Seminole of Oklahoma, 1:315
Shakers, 1:316
Technological resistance
Sinhalese, 3:265
Teeth
blackening
    Dai, 6:423
    Kédang, 5:132
    Sengseng, 2:298
    Taiwan aboriginal peoples, 5:257
ceremony for first
    Zaramo, 9:402
filing
    Kalimantan Dayaks, 5:120
    Kédang, 5:132
inlayed
    Dai, 6:423
pointing in adolescence
    tropical-forest foragers, 9:357
relic veneration
    Sinhalese, 3:267
removal at marriage
    Gelao, 6:435
removal ceremony in childhood
    Lugbara, 9:194
    Luyia, 9:206
as wealth. See under Money and wealth
Teff grain
Falasha, 9:91
Teknonymy
Betsileo, 9:56
Cashibo, 7:103
Cuna, 7:150

Hare, 1:141
Lengua, 7:211
Maasai, 9:208
Piaroa, 7:277
Slavey, 1:319
Telecommunications industry
Swedes, 4:257
Television
Tagalog, 5:251
Temperment control (as social value)
Piaroa, 7:277
Temples
Newar, 3:208
Nyinba, 3:211, 213
Oriya, 3:218
Rajput, 3:249
Sinhalese, 3:267
Sudra, 3:271
Tamal of Sri Lanka, 3:283
Tamil, 3:276, 279
Telugu, 3:286, 287
Toda dairies, 3:297
Vellala, 3:305, 306
Tenant farming
Andalusians, 4:11
Auvergnats, 4:22
Azoreans, 4:27
Canarians, 4:52
Cape Verdeans, 4:54, 55
Irish, 4:153
Lumbee, 1:209
Nayar, 3:198, 199
Oriya, 3:217
Pathan, 3:231
Sinhalese, 3:265
Swiss, Italian, 4:260
Tamil, 3:277
Tuscans, 4:270
see also Sharecropping
Tents. See under Houses and housing
Terhope (religious practitioner)
Nagas, 3:190
Terms of address
Highland Scots, 4:141
Terraced agriculture. See under Agriculture
Terra-cotta
buildings
    Bengali, 3:34
manufacture
    Nagas, 3:188
toy manufacture
    Kanjar, 3:119, 120
Territorial disputes. See Conflict causes
Terrorist movements. See Political violence
Tet (holiday)
Muong, 5:192
Textile decoration
Bulgarians, 4:45
Jat, 3:113
Tewa Pueblos, 1:349
see also Beadwork; Embroidery
Textile design
Finns, 4:104
Textiles
Achang, 6:417
Balkars, 6:53
Batak, 5:41
Bulgarians, 4:43, 45

Canarians, **4**:51
Cape Verdeans, **4**:55
Catalans, **4**:62
Czechs, **4**:83
Finns, **4**:102
Flemish, **4**:106
Greek-speaking Jews of Greece, **4**:135
Han, **6**:443
Karakalpaks, **6**:167
Kumyks, **6**:221
Kyrgyz, **6**:229
Laks, **6**:234
Mongols, **6**:474
Nyinba, **3**:213
Orcadians, **4**:187
Ossetes, **6**:299
Piemontese, **4**:198
Portuguese, **4**:206
Romanians, **4**:213
Shui, **6**:491
Slav Macedonians, **4**:240
Slovenes, **4**:247, 248
Swedes, **4**:257, 258
Tiroleans, **4**:263
Tuscans, **4**:269
Zhuang, **6**:510
see also Batik; Clothing; Cotton _headings_;
    Felt; Needlework; Silks; Spinning;
    Weaving; Woolen products
Thanksgiving festivals. See under Ceremonies
Thatched roof housing. See under Houses and
    housing
Theater. See Drama; Entertainers; Opera;
    Puppetry
Theft
Chechen-Ingush, **6**:73
Chin, **3**:64
Easter Island, **2**:55
Ndembu, **9**:249
Selkup, **6**:327
Xoraxané Romá, **4**:281, 282
"Theft" marriages. See Elopment
Themuma (religious practitioner)
Nagas, **3**:190
Theocracy
Tewa Pueblos, **1**:349
Theravada Buddhism. See Buddhism
    (Theravada)
Thirst Dance
Assiniboin, **1**:27
Threads, sacred. See Sacred thread
Threats. See under Child discipline; under
    Social control measures
Three-generational family. See Household,
    three-generational stem family
Thule culture
Baffinland Inuit, **1**:28
Copper Eskimo, **1**:76
Thunder and lightning significance
Thadou, **3**:289
Zuni, **1**:400
Thunder Clan
Winnebago, **1**:382
Tibetan Buddhism. See Buddhism (Tibetan)
Tie-dyed textiles
Nyinba, **3**:213
Tika (auspicious spot)
Magar, **3**:157, 159

Tile work
Azoreans, **4**:27, 28-29
Frisians, **4**:110, 111, 112
Madeirans, **4**:165
Sindhi, **3**:263
Syrian Christian of Kerala, **3**:273
Timbering. See Forest products; Forestry
Tinkers. See Peripatetics; Tinsmithing
Tin mining
Cornish, **4**:64, 65
Tinsmithing
Bulgarian Gypsies, **4**:41
Gypsies and caravan dwellers in the
    Netherlands, **4**:137
Irish Travellers, **4**:154, 155, 156
peripatetics, **1**:287
Rom, **1**:304
Vlachs, **4**:274
Tipis. See under Houses and housing
Tirawa (creator)
Pawnee, **1**:285
Title-holders
Kwakiutl, **1**:199
Tiyospayes (grouping)
Teton, **1**:345, 346
Toasting
Georgians, **6**:134
Mountain Jews, **6**:272
Tobacco cultivation
Acehnese, **5**:3
Achang, **6**:417
Afro-Hispanic Pacific Lowlanders, **7**:20
Aguaruna, **7**:29
Amahuaca, **7**:34
Anambé, **7**:41
Angaité, **7**:43
Asurini, **7**:61
Ayoreo, **7**:70
Batak, **5**:39
Betsileo, **9**:54
Bororo, **7**:86
Canelos Quichua, **7**:99
Cashibo, **7**:104
Chin, **3**:63
Chiquitano, **7**:118
Cocama, **7**:130
Cretans, **4**:70
Crimean Tatars, **6**:93
Daribi, **2**:47
Delaware, **1**:84
Desana, **7**:152
Dyula, **9**:76
Eipo, **2**:56
Emerillon, **7**:159
Greeks, **6**:142
Hoti, **7**:175
Ingilos, **6**:150
Iteso, **9**:128
Itonama, **7**:179
Jivaro, **7**:182
Karihona, **7**:192
Karok, **1**:176
Koya, **3**:140
Krikati/Pukobye, **7**:204
Kuikuru, **7**:207
Kurds, **6**:226;**9**:175
Lahu, **6**:462
Lengua, **7**:210

Mbeere, **9**:221
Miami, **1**:231
Mimika, **2**:206, 207
Mocoví, **7**:240
Mojo, **7**:242
Mountain Jews, **6**:272
Mundugumor, **2**:218
Muyu, **2**:228
Nambicuara, **7**:247
Nissan, **2**:249
Nyamwezi and Sukuma, **9**:256
Ozarks, **1**:281
Panare, **7**:265
Paresí, **7**:269
Persians, **9**:279
Pomaks, **4**:205
Portuguese, **4**:206
Puerto Ricans, **8**:221
Saliva, **7**:292
Santal, **3**:253
Selkup, **6**:326
Shilluk, **9**:311
Shona, **9**:312
Sirionó, **7**:310
Slav Macedonians, **4**:240
Suruí, **7**:312
Tanimuka, **7**:318
Telugu, **3**:285
Tepehuan of Chihuahua, **8**:252
Trio, **7**:335
Tunebo, **7**:337
Tupari, **7**:339
Wapisiana, **7**:355
Waurá, **7**:360
Wichita, **1**:379
Winnebago, **1**:380
Witoto, **7**:364
Yawalapití, **7**:378
Yekuana, **7**:381
Yuracaré, **7**:395
Tobacco medicine. See under Medical
    practices and treatments
Tobacco offering
Fox, **1**:130
Iroquois, **1**:167
Miami, **1**:232
Tobacco processing
Slav Macedonians, **4**:240
Tobacco smoking. See Pipe-smoking ritual;
    Smoking
Tobacco snuff and snuffboxes
Kashubians, **4**:159
Tobacco Society
Crow, **1**:83
Tobacco use. See Pipe-smoking ritual;
    Smoking
Toboggans
Dogrib, **1**:88
Ingalik, **1**:156
Toe rings
Irula, **3**:108
Toilet training
early
Austrians, **4**:20
Santal, **3**:254
Tamil, **3**:278
Toda, **3**:296
methods

Toilet training (cont'd)
    Toda, 3:296
  relaxed
    Tamil of Sri Lanka, 3:282
    Yuit, 1:391
Tomato growing
  Canarians, 4:51
  Cretans, 4:70
Tomb stone. See Grave markers
Tongs (secret societies)
  East Asians of the United States, 1:102
Tools
  Ache, 7:4-5
  Akawaio, 7:31
  Amahuaca, 7:35
  Amuesha, 7:38
  Anambé, 7:41, 42
  Apalai, 7:45
  Apiaká, 7:49
  Araweté, 7:56
  Ayoreo, 7:70
  Chin, 3:63
  Cotopaxi Quichua, 7:133
  Cuiva, 7:143
  Finns, 4:102
  Galicians, 4:119
  Garo, 3:82
  Guambiano, 7:171
  Huarayo, 7:177
  Jebero, 7:181
  Kashinawa, 7:195
  Kogi, 7:201
  Mashco, 7:225
  Mizo, 3:178
  Nagas, 3:188
  Nambicuara, 7:247
  Palikur, 7:262
  Saramaka, 7:296
  Sirionó, 7:310
  Tamil prohibitions, 3:277
  Tupari, 7:340
  Vedda, 3:301
  Wapisiana, 7:355
  Yanomamö, 7:375
  see also Agriculture; Carved objects; specific
    tools
Tooth customs. See Teeth
Torch Festival
  Bai, 6:421
  Lisu, 6:466
Totemic taboos. See Tatoos, totemic
Totem poles
  Comox, 1:76
  Haida, 1:135, 136
  Lillooet, 1:206
  Tsimshian, 1:355
Totems
  Abenaki, 1:4
  Ajië, 2:9
  Aranda, 2:18
  Bau, 2:24
  Boazi, 2:29
  Cham, 5:73
  Chambri, 2:32
  Cocopa, 1:74
  Dani, 2:44
  Dieri, 2:49
  Dobu, 2:50

Eipo, 2:57
Ewenki, 6:434
Foi, 2:60
Gogodala, 2:83, 84
Goodenough Island, 2:86
Kamilaroi, 2:104
Kapauku, 2:106
Kazakhs, 6:177
Keraki, 2:113
Kiwai, 2:124, 126
Kmhmu, 5:140
Kwoma, 2:134
Kyrgyz, 6:231
Lau, 2:145
Lesu, 2:146
Lingayat, 3:151, 153
Luyia, 9:204
Maratha, 3:169
Mardudjara, 2:181
Mejbrat, 2:196
Mossi, 9:229
Munda, 3:182
Namau, 2:231, 232
Ndebele, 9:236
Nguna, 2:243
Nu, 6:481
Ojibwa, 1:270
Orokolo, 2:259
Osage, 1:278
Ossetes, 6:301
Pintupi, 2:266
Quechan, 1:301
Rossel Island, 2:278
Santa Cruz, 2:291
Temne, 9:343
Tsakhurs, 6:367
Ukrainians, 6:394
Wik Mungkan, 2:379
Yip Yoront, 2:395
Zuni, 1:398
  see also Animal totems; Iconography
Tourist industry
  Abkhazians, 6:7
  Akan, 9:11
  Alabama, 1:14
  Antigua and Barbuda, 8:8
  Arubans, 8:11, 12
  Austrians, 4:19
  Auvergnats, 4:22
  Azoreans, 4:27
  Baffinland Inuit, 1:29
  Bahamians, 8:18
  Bai, 6:419
  Barbadians, 8:22
  Bavarians, 4:33-34
  Bermudians, 8:25
  Bretons 4.38
    Bretons, 4:40
  Cajuns, 1:49
  Canarians, 4:51, 52
  Catalans, 4:62
  Cayman Islanders, 8:46
  Cherokee, 1:60, 61
  Chinese in the United States, 1:100
  Corsicans, 4:66, 67
  Costa Ricans, 8:79
  Cretans, 4:70
  Crow, 1:83

Cubans, 8:90
Curaçao, 8:96
Cyclades, 4:77;5:78
Dalmatians, 4:86
Dominicans, 8:101
Emberá and Wounaan, 8:109
English, 4:96
French Antillians, 8:112
Frisians, 4:111
Gaels (Irish), 4:115, 117
Galicians, 4:119
Georgians, 6:132
German Swiss, 4:125, 127
Guadeloupians, 8:116
Highland Scots, 4:140
Indonesian, 5:103
Ionians, 4:148, 149, 150
Irish, 4:152
Itza,' 8:134
Jamaicans, 8:137
Japanese, 5:109
Jews of Israel, 9:143
Kittsians and Nevisians, 8:146
Kuna, 8:147
Madeirans, 4:164-165, 166
Maltese, 4:167, 168
Manx, 4:169, 170
Mauritian, 3:171
Montserratians, 8:180
Navajo, 1:251
Netherlands Antillians, 8:194
Nias, 5:195
Occitans, 4:184
Okinawans, 5:200
Peloponnesians, 4:193
Portuguese, 4:206
Provencal, 4:210
Pueblo Indians, 1:298, 299
Saami, 4:222
Saint Lucians, 8:230
Sea Islanders, 1:308, 309
Sea Nomads of the Andaman, 5:227, 229
Seminole, 1:312, 313
Shakers, 1:316
Sherpa, 3:258
Swiss, Italian, 4:260, 261
Tai Lue, 5:255
Temiar, 5:268
Tiroleans, 4:263
Tlingits, 1:351
Tonga, 9:353
Toraja, 5:281, 283
Turks, 9:375
Turks and Caicos Islanders, 8:273
Virgin Islanders, 8:300
Western Apache, 1:372
Yakan, 5:289
Towers of Silence (Zoroastrianism)
  Parsi, 3:230
Toy making
  Friuli, 4:113
  Kanjar, 3:119
  Orcadians, 4:187
Trade (individual). See Barter; Exchange; Gift
    exchange
Trade fairs. See Markets and fairs
Traders (commercial)
  Andalusians, 4:9-10

Aquitaine, **4**:13, 14
Auvergnats, **4**:22
Azoreans, **4**:27
Bania, **3**:24-25
Basques, **4**:31
Bavarians, **4**:33
Bengali, **3**:30, 31
Bretons, **4**:38
Bulgarians, **4**:43
Canarians, **4**:51
Cape Verdeans, **4**:53-54, 55
Flemish, **4**:106
Frisians, **4**:111
Gujarati, **3**:90
haggling
   Piemontese Sinti, **4**:200
Hidatsa, **1**:146
Hill Pandaram, **3**:98-99
Hopi, **1**:149
Huron, **1**:152
Ingalik, **1**:157
Iroquois, **1**:165-166
Khasi, **3**:123-124
Khoja, **3**:127, 128
Kickapoo, **1**:184
Kiowa, **1**:187
Klamath, **1**:191
Kwakiutl, **1**:198
Labbai, **3**:144
Labrador Inuit, **1**:201
Lillooet, **1**:206-207
Malayali, **3**:165
Mandan, **1**:214
Mennonites, **1**:218
Metis of Western Canada, **1**:226, 227
Miami, **1**:231
Mohave, **1**:241
Montagnais-Naskapi, **1**:244
Nagas, **3**:187, 188-189
Navajo, **1**:251
Nayar, **3**:198
Nepali, **3**:202-203
Newar, **3**:206
Nootka, **1**:256
North Alaskan Eskimos, **1**:259, 261
Northern Shoshone and Bannock, **1**:267
Nyinba, **3**:211
Ojibwa, **1**:269
Osage, **1**:277
Otavalo, **7**:253
Pathan, **3**:231
Piaroa, **7**:276
Rom, **1**:304
Romanians, **4**:213
Sherpa, **3**:257, 258, 259
Tamil, **3**:277
Telugu, **3**:285
Thakali, **3**:290-291, 292
Tiroleans, **4**:263
Tubatulabal, **1**:355
Vaisya, **3**:300
Vaisyas, **3**:222
Vlach Gypsies of Hungary, **4**:271
Walloons, **4**:277
   see also Fur trade; Peddling; Slave trade
Trading activities
  among tribes
    Akawaio, **7**:31

Amuesha, **7**:38
Apalai, **7**:45-46
Baniwa-Curripaco-Wakuenai, **7**:77
Canelos Quichua, **7**:99
Chiriguano, **7**:120
Chorote, **7**:125
Desana, **7**:152
Guahibo-Sikuani, **7**:165
Karajá, **7**:189
Karihona, **7**:192
Kashinawa, **7**:195
Ka'wiari, **7**:198
Klingit, **1**:351-352
Kuikuru, **7**:207
Macuna, **7**:213
Mataco, **7**:228
Mehinaku, **7**:237
Nivaclé, **7**:249
Panare, **7**:265
Pemon, **7**:272
Piaroa, **7**:276
Piro, **7**:279
Suya, **7**:315
Tanaina, **1**:335, 336
Tatuyo, **7**:323
Tewa Pueblos, **1**:348
Ticuna, **7**:329
Toba, **7**:332
Trio, **7**:335
Wáiwai, **7**:346
Walapai, **1**:365
Wayapi, **7**:361
Wiyot, **1**:384
Yagua, **7**:372
Yawalapití, **7**:378
Yokuts, **1**:388
Yukpa, **7**:383
Zuni, **1**:398
based on rank
   Chamacoco, **7**:108
exploitative
   Piemontese Sinti, **4**:200
in-law networks
   Wanano, **7**:349
with nontribal groups
   Araucanians, **7**:53
   Aymara, **7**:66-67
   Baniwa-Curripaco-Wakuenai, **7**:77
   Canelos Quichua, **7**:99
   Cubeo, **7**:140
   Culina, **7**:146
   Cuna, **7**:149
   Emberá, **7**:156
   Emerillon, **7**:158
   Guajiro, **7**:168
   Huarayo, **7**:177
   Karajá, **7**:189
   Ka'wiari, **7**:198
   Kogi, **7**:201
   Macuna, **7**:213
   Marubo, **7**:222
   Mashco, **7**:225-226
   Mataco, **7**:228
   Palikur, **7**:262
   Panare, **7**:265
   Suya, **7**:315
   Tatuyo, **7**:323
   Yawalapití, **7**:378

with potential enemies
   Candoshi, **7**:93
within tribe
   Amahuaca, **7**:35
   Araucanians, **7**:53
   Asháninca, **7**:91
   Baniwa-Curripaco-Wakuenai, **7**:77
   Barama River Carib, **7**:81
   Emberá, **7**:156
   Karajá, **7**:189
   Kashinawa, **7**:195
   Kuikuru, **7**:207
   Nambicuara, **7**:247
   Piaroa, **7**:276
   Piro, **7**:279
   Shipibo, **7**:304
   Wapisiana, **7**:355
   Yukpa, **7**:383
   see also Barter; Exchange; Gift
    exchange
Traditional healers. *See* Healers; Shaminism
Trance-dancing ceremonies
   Temiar, **5**:271, 272
Trance state. *See* Mediums; Séance
Transcendency
   Muslim, **3**:186
Transfiguration of the dead. *See* Resurrection
   beliefs
Transhumance. *See* Herding; Seminomads
Transmigration of souls. *See* Reincarnation
   beliefs; Samsara
Transsexuality
   hijra, **3**:96
   Miami, **1**:231
   Winnebago, **1**:381
Transvestism
   Bugis, **5**:51
   Khanty, **6**:192
   Ontong Java, **2**:254
   Toraja, **5**:283
Travel, fear of
   Mardudjara, **2**:181
Travelers. *See* Itinerants
Trees
  holy
    Talysh, **6**:357
  ownership
    Choiseul Island, **2**:38
    Daribi, **2**:47
    Gahuku-Gama, **2**:69
    Gainj, **2**:72
    Kurtatchi, **2**:132
    Lakalai, **2**:141
    Lesu, **2**:146
    Manam, **2**:168
    Marind-anim, **2**:183
    Mimika, **2**:207
    Semang, **5**:234
    Temiar, **5**:268
    Tor, **2**:343
    see also Forest products; Forestry
Trespass conflicts
   Kumeyaay, **1**:195
Trial by ordeal
   Bhil, **3**:40, 41
   Lakher, **3**:147
Trial marriage. *See under* Marriage
Trials. *See* Court system; Jural system

"Triangular trade"
  Cape Verdeans, 4:55
Tribute payment
  Bau, 2:23
  Yurok, 1:394
Trickster culture hero
  Algonkin, 1:17
  Cree, 1:82
  Crow, 1:83
  Kiowa, 1:188
  Klamath, 1:192
  Northern Shoshone and Bannock,
    1:267
  Piro, 7:280
  Pomo, 1:295
  Shuswap, 1:318
  Sorbs, 4:253
  Tanaina, 1:336
  Teton, 1:346
  Tlingit, 1:353
  Yukagir, 6:413
Trinity (holiday)
  Russian peasants, 6:313
  Siberian Estonians, 6:337
Trinity (Jesus, Mary, Joseph)
  syncretic deities
    Western Apache, 1:373
  worship
    Gaels (Irish), 4:117
Tro religious order
  Ewe and Fon, 9:87
Troubadours
  Occitans, 4:185
  Provencal, 4:211
Trousseau
  Castilians, 4:60
  Kashubians, 4:159
  Old Believers, 1:274
  Sicilians, 4:236
Trout fishing
  Iglulik Inuit, 1:155
  Klallam, 1:190
  Wintun, 1:383
Trucking industry
  Tamil, 3:277
Tsahan Sara (holiday)
  Kalmyks, 6:157
Tsakro (religious practitioner)
  Nagas, 3:190
Tuak Bala' (ceremony)
  Samal, 5:221
Tuberculosis
  Baffinland Inuit, 1:28
  Chipewyan, 1:67
  Jicarilla, 1:172
Tuber-eating prohibitions
  Bania, 3:25
Tugurada (ceremony)
  Guarijío, 8:119
Tulak bala' (ceremony)
  Bajau, 5:34
Tule use
  Yokuts, 1:387, 388
Tuna fishing
  Basques, 4:31
Tupan (two-headed drum)
  Bulgarian Gypsies, 4:41
Turquoise jewelry

Navajo, 1:251
  Zuni, 1:397
Turquoise Man (deity)
  Zuni, 1:399
Turtle egg collection
  Kagwahiv, 7:185
  Mashco, 7:225
  Moré, 7:243
  Saliva, 7:292
  Sirionó, 7:310
  Tacana, 7:318
  Yekuana, 7:381
Turtle fishing
  Creoles of Nicaragua, 8:84
  Seri, 8:233, 235
Turtle hunting
  Andamanese, 3:9, 10
Twelfth Night (holiday)
  Kashubians, 4:159
Twined basketry
  Achumawi, 1:10
Twine making
  Koya, 3:140
Twin Heroes (culture heroes)
  Kiowa, 1:188
Twins
  abandonment of
    Comanche, 1:75
  birth as unlucky event for village
    Hani, 6:451
  cleansing ceremony
    Pokot, 9:283
  fear of
    Bhil, 3:41
  kinship
    Chuj, 8:72
  must marry other twins
    Mojo, 7:242
  mythology
    Mixe, 8:175
  one set adrift in river for shaman to rescue
    Cocama, 7:130
  special pre-existence of
    Teton, 1:346
  welcomed
    Seri, 8:234
Twin War Gods (culture heroes)
  Mescalero Apache, 1:225
Two-part singing
  Ndembu, 9:241
  Pomo, 1:295
Tyeff seeds
  Amhara, 9:18
Tynwald Day (holiday)
  Manx, 4:171

Ulebuorden (decorated gables)
  Frisians, 4:110, 111, 112
Ultimogeniture
  Abkhazians, 6:8
  Abor, 3:4
  Achang, 6:418
  Altaians, 6:22
  Amish, 1:20
  Andis, 6:26
  Armenians, 6:30
  Badaga, 3:16
  Bulgarians, 4:44

Burakumin, 5:62
  Burusho, 3:56
  Chakma, 3:59
  Cherokee, 1:61
  Chin, 3:65
  Chinantec, 8:54
  Chiriguano, 7:121
  Ch'ol, 8:65
  Cretans, 4:70
  Cyclades, 4:78
  De'ang, 6:430
  Germans, 6:140
  Gond, 3:86
  Iraqw, 9:125
  Irula, 3:107
  Jingpo, 6:457
  Kachin, 5:117
  Ket, 6:184
  Khasi, 3:124-125, 125, 126
  Korean, 5:147
  Kota, 3:137
  Kumeyaay, 1:195
  Kumyks, 6:223
  Miao, 6:471
  Mizo, 3:178
  Mongols, 6:475
  Nagas, 3:189
  Ndebele, 9:236, 237
  Nganasan, 6:282
  Northern Irish, 4:179
  Nu, 6:481
  Old Believers, 1:274
  Pedi, 9:270
  peripatetics, 3:235
  peripatetics of Afghanistan, Iran, and
    Turkey, 9:275
  Pumi, 6:484
  Purum, 3:243
  Romanians, 4:214
  Saami, 4:221, 222
  Sherpa, 3:259
  Siberiaki, 6:333
  Sora, 3:269
  Syrian Christian of Kerula, 3:273
  Tarascans, 8:245
  Thakali, 3:291
  Tofalar, 6:363
  Turkmens, 6:370
  Tzotzil and Tzeltal of Pantelhó, 8:276
  Welsh, 4:280
  Xoraxané Romá, 4:282
  Yi, 6:507
  Yörük, 9:395
  Zapotec, 8:312
  Zhuang, 6:511
Umiak travel
  Labrador Inuit, 1:201
Unani medicine
  Tamil, 3:279
Uncle
  reciprocity with nieces and newphews
    Winnebago, 1:381
Uncle, fictive
  Black Creoles of Louisiana, 1:38
Uncle, maternal
  as child discipliner
    Konso, 9:170
    Seminole, 1:331

Zuni, 1:398
incest taboo
    Xoraxané Romá, 4:282
marriage arrangement by
    Pawnee, 1:284
matrilineal system
    Winnebago, 1:381
niece marriage. _See_ Marriage, avuncular
role in sister's childbirth
    Ata Sikka, 5:21
roles with sister's children
    Abkhazians, 6:7
    Akha, 5:12
    Ata Sikka, 5:21
    Atoni, 5:28
    Balkars, 6:53
    Bau, 2:23
    Belau, 2:26
    Bunun, 5:57
    Chambri, 2:32
    Choiseul Island, 2:39
    Circassians, 6:88
    Daribi, 2:47
    Daur, 6:429
    Gnau, 2:81, 82
    Gogodala, 2:84
    Goodenough Island, 2:87
    Guadalcanal, 2:90
    Gururumba, 2:93
    Jino, 6:460
    Kachin, 5:117
    Ket, 6:184
    Khinalughs, 6:200-201
    Khoi, 9:159
    Lakalai, 2:141
    Lisu, 6:465
    Marind-anim, 2:183
    Mejbrat, 2:196
    Minangkabau, 5:183, 184
    Miyanmin, 2:211
    Murik, 2:222
    Nissan, 2:250
    Nivkh, 6:284
    Pamir peoples, 6:305
    Rotinese, 5:213, 214
    Selepet, 2:294
    Sio, 2:300
    Tangu, 2:312
    Tikopia, 2:325
    Tor, 2:343
    Torres Strait Islanders, 2:346
    Tujia, 6:498
    Woleai, 2:383
    Yagua, 7:373
    Zhuang, 6:511
social control by
    Seminole, 1:313
Uncle, paternal
    Khinalughs, 6:200
Underground burial. _See_ Mortuary practices,
    burial below ground
Underworld. _See under_ Afterlife
Unemployment
    Dutch, 4:92, 93
    English, 4:96
    Gaels (Irish), 4:115
    Irish, 4:152
    Jamaicans, 8:138

Malayali, 3:166
Mappila, 3:167
Martiniquais, 8:162
Ndembu, 9:239
Northern Irish, 4:178
Polynesians, 1:291
Sicilians, 4:236
Uzbeks, 6:397
Walloons, 4:277
see also Migrant workers
Unfaithfulness. _See_ Adultery
Uniate Catholicism
    Arab Americans, 1:25
    Belarussians, 6:58, 59
    Poles, 4:204
    Romanians, 4:214
    Transylvanian ethnic groups, 4:268
    Ukrainian peasants, 6:387
    Ukrainians, 6:391, 394
    Ukrainians of Canada, 1:358, 359
    see also Chaldeans; Maronites; Melkites
Unigeniture. _See_ Inheritance, equally shared
Unilineal descent. _See_ Descent, matrilinea;
    Descent, patrilineal
Unitarianism
    Transylvanian ethnic groups, 4:268
    Welsh, 4:280
United Church
    Cayman Islanders, 8:47
    Koreans in Canada, 1:97, 98
    Mendi, 2:205
    Rossel Island, 2:278, 279
    Siwai, 2:304
    Trobriand Islands, 2:348
Uniting Church
    Murngin, 2:226
Universal conscription. _See_ Military service,
    compulsory
Universities. _See_ Education
Up-Helly-Aa (secular ritual)
    Shetlanders, 4:234
Uraza-bairam (holiday)
    Kubachins, 6:2197
Uraza Bäyram (holiday)
    Volga Tatars, 6:402
Urban areas
    artistic views of
        Austria, 21
    conurbations
        English, 4:96
    dwellers
        Aquitaine, 4:14
        Catalans, 4:62, 63
        Corsicans, 4:66
        Cretans, 4:69-70, 71
        Finns, 4:102
        Gitanos, 4:129
        Indian Christians, 3:103
        Jains, 3:110
        Newar, 3:206
        Pandit of Kashmir, 3:226
        Parsi, 3:227, 228
        Poles, 4:202
        Provencal, 4:210
        Rom, 1:303
        Tamil, 3:276, 278
        Thakali, 3:290
        Walloons, 4:276

Welsh, 4:278
    dwellers on edges of
        Piemontese Sinti, 4:200
    dwellers' status
        Frisians, 4:111
    dwellers' ties with rural culture
        Irish, 4:153
    ethnic communities
        Croat-Canadian, 1:120
        East Asians of Canada, 1:95
        East Asians in the United States, 1:99,
            100, 101
        Estonian-Canadians, 1:121
        Haitians, 1:137-138
        Irish-Americans, 1:113
        Italian-Americans, 1:113
        Italian-Canadians, 1:124
        Jews, 1:168
        Latinos, 1:203, 204
        Polish-Americans, 1:115
        Polish-Canadians, 1:125
        Polynesians, 1:291
        Romanian-Americans, 1:115
        Russian-Americans, 1:116
        South and Southeast Asians of Canada,
            1:321
        Ukrainians of canada, 1:357
    migrants
        African Americans, 1:10
        Aveyronnais, 4:23-24
        Black Creoles of Louisiana, 1:37
        Blacks in Canada, 1:43
        Bretons, 4:37
        Bulgarians, 4:42
        castes, Hindu, 3:57
        Cyclades, 4:77
        Finns, 4:101
        German Swiss, 4:126
        Greeks, 4:132
        Irish, 4:151
        Irish Travellers, 4:155, 156
        Lumbee, 1:209
        Nepali, 3:201
        Ojibwa, 1:269
        Ottawa, 1:280
        Peloponnesians, 4:192
        Saami, 4:220
        Slav Macedonians, 4:239
        Swiss, Italian, 4:259
        Walloons, 4:277
    population concentration
        English, 4:96
Usane habora (ceremony)
    Foi, 2:61
Usufruct. _See under_ Landholding
Uxorilocal residency. _See_ Residence (newly
    married), matrilocal

Vacanas
    Lingyat, 3:153
Vaishnava Hindus. _See_ Hinduism
    (Vaishnava)
Vajrayana. _See_ Buddhism (Mahayana)
Vampires
    Albanians, 4:7, 8
    Croats, 4:74
    Dalmatians, 4:87
    Xoraxané Romá, 4:283

Vanilla bean growing
    Totonac, 8:264-265
    Tsimihety, 9:358
Varna. See Castes
Vegetable growing
    Bretons, 4:38
    Bulgarians, 4:43
    Canarians, 4:51
    Chin, 3:63
    Hidatsa, 1:146
    Mandan, 1:214
    Santal, 3:253
    Sherpa, 3:258
    Tuscans, 4:269
    see also specific vegetables
Vegetarianism. See under Food
Veiling of women
    Crimean Tatars, 6:93
    face covered in presence of strange men
        Shahsevan, 9:309
        Turks, 9:376
    face half-covered with kerchief
        Khinalughs, 6:201
        Udis, 6:376
    half-veiled at engagement and fully covered
        at wedding
        Khinalughs, 6:200
    married women before husband's kinsmen
        and neighbors
        Jatav, 3:114
    veil not worn
        Somalis, 9:318
    veil worn
        Talysh, 6:355
        Yemenis, 9:390
    veil worn rarely
        Jews of Kurdistan, 9:146
    veil worn strictly
        Sindhi, 3:263
    see also Purdah
Vendetta. See Blood feud
Venereal disease
    Baiga, 3:21
Vengeance. See Conflict resolution, blood
    vengeance
Ventriloquism
    Copper Eskimo, 1:79
Verbal arts. See Drama; Oral tradition;
    Storytelling
Verbal threats. See Threats
Verdzin (perpetual virgin)
    Albanians, 4:5, 6
Versifiers
    Basques, 4:32
Vesak (ceremony)
    Tai Lue, 5:256
Vestoz (camp)
    Cheyenne, 1:65
Veterinary medicine
    Baggara, 9:31
Village deities
    Coorg, 3:74
    Sicilians, 4:235
    Telegu, 3:287
Village green
    Badaga, 3:15
Villages
    absence of

Carib of Dominica, 8:38
    absence of of
        Gainj, 2:71
        Mendi, 2:203
        Pohnpei, 2:268
        Rennell Island, 2:277
    agglomerated
        Serbs, 4:230
    central focus
        Badaga, 3:15
        Gaels (Irish), 4:115
        Galicians, 4:119
        German Swiss, 4:125
        Ionians, 4:149
        Maltese, 4:167
        Miami, 1:230
        Occitans, 4:184
        Seminoles, 1:312
        Shawnee, 1:317
        Sicilians, 4:235
    clan
        Tlingit, 1:351
    cluster
        Montenegrins, 4:172
        Serbs, 4:230
    commercial specialization
        Romanians, 4:213
    commercial specializations
        English, 4:96
    conurbations
        English, 4:96
    cooperative
        Jews of Israel, 9:150
        Jews of Yemen, 9:150
    councils. See Councils
    cross-road
        Serbs, 4:230
    dispersed
        Montenegrins, 4:172
    ethnically exclusive
        Cypriots, 4:80
    extended family
        Winnebago, 1:381
    fortified
        Aghuls, 6:10
        Albanians, 4:4
        Austrians, 4:19
        Avars, 6:44
        Bau, 2:22
        Butonese, 5:67
        Chechen-Ingush, 6:73
        Corsicans, 4:66
        Gururumba, 2:92
        Hidatsa, 1:146
        Kachin, 5:115
        Kalimantan Dayaks, 5:120
        Karen, 5:126
        Khakas, 6:187
        Khevsur, 6:193
        Lakher, 3:145
        Lau, 2:143
        Manggarai, 5:176
        Maori, 2:177
        Melanau, 5:180
        Nagas, 3:187-188
        Ngeh, 5:194
        Ossetes, 6:299
        Palaung, 5:201

Palu'e, 5:205
        Punjabi, 3:237-238
        Rapa, 2:273
        Sambia, 2:284
        Santa Cruz, 2:290
        Selkup, 6:325
        Svans, 6:344
        Tabasarans, 6:348
        Tairora, 2:308
        Taiwan aboriginal peoples, 5:257
        Tauade, 2:318
        Vietnamese, 5:285
    governmental systemization of
        Romanians, 4:213
    grid plan
        Mormons, 1:247
    hillside
        Occitans, 4:184
    immaculately clean
        Miami, 1:230
    infield setting
        Faroe Islanders, 4:99
    mountainside
        German Swiss, 4:125
        Ionians, 4:149
        Madeirans, 4:164
        Swiss, Italian, 4:260
        Vlachs, 4:274
        Washoe, 1:367;3:168
    open field system
        Danes, 4:89
    palisaded
        Miami, 1:230
        Ottawa, 1:279
    as political units
        Potawatomi, 1:297
        Tanaina, 1:336
        Tsimshian, 1:354-355
        Wintun, 1:383
        Yurok, 1:395
    promenade
        Sicilans, 4:235
    puebelo
        Keres Pueblo Indians, 1:179-182
    pueblo
        Hopi, 1:148-151
        Taos, 1:341
        Tewa Pueblos, 1:347, 349
    satellite
        North Alaskan Eskimos, 1:259
    savanna
        Makushi, 7:218
        Mundurucu, 7:244
        Pemon, 7:271
        Saliva, 7:292
        Shavante, 7:300
        Sherente, 7:302
    as social units
        Bhuiya, 3:44
        Bondo, 3:50
        Brahman and Chhetri of Nepal,
            3:53
        Coorg, 3:73, 74
        Corsicans, 4:68
        Gujarati, 3:90
        Irula, 3:107
        Kanbi, 3:118
        Klamath, 1:192

Kota, **3:**136, 137
Koya, **3:**141
Lakher, **3:**146, 147
Nagas, **3:**187-188
Nyinba, **3:**212-213
Okkaliga, **3:**214
Oriya, **3:**217
Punjabi, **3:**239, 241
Purum, **3:**244
Santal, **3:**254
Serbs, **4:**230
Tamang, **3:**275
Tamil, **3:**278
Vedda, **3:**302
Yurok, **1:**394
specific layouts and boundaries
Austrians, **4:**19
Baiga, **3:**19
Basques, **4:**30
Bhil, **3:**39
Bhuiya, **3:**43
Bondo, **3:**48
Bulgarians, **4:**43
Burusho, **3:**55
Castilians, **4:**59
Chakma, **3:**58
Chenchu, **3:**61
Chin, **3:**63, 64-65
Cretans, **4:**69
Croats, **4:**72
Cyclades, **4:**76
Fox, **1:**128-29
Garo, **3:**82
Highland Scots, **4:**139
Iroquois, **1:**165
Kanbi, **3:**118
Khasi, **3:**123
Korku, **3:**133-134
Koya, **3:**139, 140
Lakher, **3:**145
Leonese, **4:**160
Lingayat, **3:**151
Maltese, **4:**167
Maratha, **3:**168-169
Mizo, **3:**177
Mormons, **1:**247
Nagas, **3:**187-188
Nayar, **3:**197
Nyinba, **3:**211
Okkaliga, **3:**214
Old Believers, **1:**273
Oriya, **3:**216-217
Osage, **1:**277
Pahari, **3:**219, 220
Pathan, **3:**231
Pima-Papago, **1:**288
Punjabi, **3:**237-238
Seminole, **1:**312
Sherpa, **3:**258
Slovenes, **4:**247
Sora, **3:**268
Tamil, **3:**276
Telugu, **3:**285
Thadou, **3:**288
Yurok, **1:**394
see also Fortification
walled
Flemish, **4:**106

Occitans, **4:**184
Serbs, **4:**230
see also subhead palisaded _above_
walled (sod)
Pawnee, **1:**284
waterway locations
Anambé, **7:**41
Apalai, **7:**45
Apiaká, **7:**48
Araweté, **7:**56
Arikara, **1:**26
Austrians, **4:**19
Baniwa-Curripaco-Wakuenai, **7:**76
Barama River Carib, **7:**80
Basques, **4:**30
Bulgarians, **4:**43
Chiriguano, **7:**120
Cocama, **7:**130
Flemish, **4:**106
Hidatsa, **1:**146
Kagwahiv, **7:**184
Karajá, **7:**188
Kashinawa, **7:**195
Kuikuru, **7:**206-207
Maliseet, **1:**210
Mataco, **7:**228
Matsigenka, **7:**231
Metis of Western Canada, **1:**228
Miami, **1:**230
Mundurucu, **7:**244
Nambicuara, **7:**246
Nivaclé, **7:**248
Ottawa, **1:**279
Panare, **7:**264
Piro, **7:**279
Quechan, **1:**300-301
Rikbaktsa, **7:**287
Saami, **4:**220
Saramaka, **7:**296
Shipibo, **7:**304
Siona-Secoya, **7:**307
Slav Macedonians, **4:**239
Tanaina, **1:**335
Tanana, **1:**338
tanana, **1:**338
Tatuyo, **7:**322
Tubatulabal, **1:**355
Wanano, **7:**349
Warao, **7:**357
West Greenland Inuit, **1:**376
Xikrin, **7:**367
Yagua, **7:**372
Yanomamö, **7:**375
Yekuana, **7:**381
Yukuna, **7:**386
Yurok, **1:**394
Village of the dead
Thadou, **3:**289
Violence, societal
Montenegrins, **4:**173
Sicilians, **4:**237
Sora, **3:**270
Tamil of Sri Lanka, **3:**283
Vlachs, **4:**275
see also Blood feud; Conflict sources; Political violence; Warfare
Violence, societal (censorship)
Danes, **4:**90

Violent death, beliefs about
Bhil, **3:**41, 42
Chin, **3:**67
Lakher, **3:**148
see also Suicide
Virginity
annulment in absence of bridal
Piemontese, **4:**198
bloodied sheets as proof of
Greeks, **6:**143
Gypsies, **6:**147
as bonus in divorce settlement
Krymchaks, **6:**215
bride-price lower in absence of
Ewe and Fon, **9:**86
Ket, **6:**185
burial in white dress
Moldovans, **6:**269
defloration ritual
Huarayo, **7:**178
Toda, **3:**297
as marriage requirement
Bhil, **3:**39
Calabrese, **4:**49, 50
Cape Verdeans, **4:**55
Castilians, **4:**60
Georgians, **6:**133
Gitanos, **4:**129
Mingrelians, **6:**264
Montenegrins, **4:**173
Swahili, **9:**328
more ideal than reality
Piemontese Sinti, **4:**200
no ritual for public proof of
Pamir peoples, **6:**306
not valued
Otavalo, **7:**254
oaths
Albanians, **4:**5, 6
premarital test
Gitanos, **4:**129
public proof of
Kiribati, **2:**122
rituals
Magar, **3:**157-158
valuation
Chechen-Ingush, **6:**75
Cheyenne, **1:**64-65
Cypriots, **4:**80
Dalmatians, **4:**87
Guajiro, **7:**168
Persians, **9:**279
Samoa, **2:**288
Sherente, **7:**303
Tuareg, **9:**369
Western Apache, **1:**372
Virgin of Juquila (fiesta)
Chatino, **8:**50
Virgin Mary. _See_ Madonna worship; Trinity
Virgin of Valbanuz worship
Pasiegos, **4:**191
Virilocal residency. _See_ Residence (newly married), patrilocal
Vishnu (deity). _See_ Hindus (Vaishnava)
Visible deities
Magar, **3:**161
Vision quest
Algonkin, **1:**17

Vision quest (cont'd)
 Comanche, 1:75
 Crow, 1:83
 Eastern Shoshone, 1:106
 Fox, 1:129, 130
 Hidsata, 1:147
 Kalapuya, 1:175
 Klamath, 1:192
 Lillooet, 1:207
 Miami, 1:231, 232
 Nez Percé, 1:254
 Nootka, 1:257
 Northern Shoshone and Bannock, 1:267
 Ojibwa, 1:270, 271
 Okanagon, 1:272
 Ottawa, 1:280
 Potawatomi, 1:297
 Shuswap, 1:318
 Teton, 1:346
 Winnebago, 1:381
Visions
 experiences
  Kiowa, 1:188, 189
 individual reenactment of
  Teton, 1:346
 power of
  Cree, 1:82
  Crow, 1:83
  Flathead, 1:128
  Northern Shoshone and Bannock, 1:267
  Ojibwa, 1:270
  Sarsi, 1:308
  Ute, 1:362
  Western Shoshone, 1:375
  see also Guardian spirits
 predictive
  Frisians, 4:112
 in religious beliefs
  Omaha, 1:275
  Spokane, 1:333
"Visiting" husband
 Barbadians, 8:22
 Jamaicans, 8:138
 Nayar, 3:199, 200
Visual arts
 Austrians, 4:21
 Azerbaijani Turks, 6:48
 Basques, 4:32
 Bretons, 4:40
 Canarians, 4:52-53
 Castilians, 4:61
 Catalans, 4:64
 Cheyenne, 1:67
 Eastern Shoshone, 1:104
 Futuna, 2:67
 Greeks, 4:133-134
 Haida, 1:136
 Hidatsa, 1:146
 Hopi, 1:150-151
 Ingalik, 1:158
 Jicarilla, 1:174
 Keres Pueblo Indians, 1:180
 Kiowa, 1:189
 Kumeyaay, 1:195
 Kwakiutl, 1:198, 200
 Lakher, 3:147
 Lao Isan, 5:163
 Latinos, 1:206

 Mauritian, 3:173
 Mizo, 3:179
 Munda, 3:184
 Nagas, 3:191
 Newar, 3:208
 Ngatatjara, 2:241
 Oriya, 3:218
 Pahari, 3:223
 Santal, 3:255
 Sardinians, 4:227
 Sherpa, 3:259
 Sinhalese, 3:267
 Sora, 3:270
 Tanaina, 1:337
 Tibetans, 6:496
 see also Architecture; Decorative arts;
   Paintings; Sculpture
Visualization
 Bengali Shakta, 3:35
Viticulture. See Grape growing; Wine making
Vodun
 African Americans, 1:13
 Black Creoles of Louisiana, 1:39
 Blacks in Canada, 1:44
 Dominicans, 8:103
 Haitians, 1:138;8:122
Vodu religious order
 Ewe and Fon, 9:87
Voice of God within
 Doukhobors, 1:90
Voice of guardian spirit
 Quechan, 1:302
Voluntary associations. See Associations,
   clubs, and societies
Vomiting (as initiation)
 Fore, 2:65
Voodoo. See Vodun

Waffles
 Walloons, 4:276
Wage labor
 Ache, 7:4
 Akha, 5:11
 Alak, 5:13
 Angaité, 7:43
 Austrians, 4:19
 Aymara, 7:66
 Baggara, 9:31
 Bhil, 3:38
 Bulgarian Gypseis, 4:41
 Calabrese, 4:49
 Carrier, 1:52
 Cashibo, 7:104
 Cherokee, 1:61
 Choctaw, 1:71
 Copper Eskimo, 1:77
 Cotopaxi Quichua, 7:133
 East Asians in the United States, 1:99, 100
 East Asians of Canada, 1:94
 Emberá, 7:155
 Fipa, 9:99
 Guajiro, 7:168
 Hare, 1:140
 hired
  Swahili, 9:327
 Hopi, 1:149
 Jatav, 3:114
 Jivaro, 7:182

 Kalagan, 5:119
 Karihona, 7:192
 Kickapoo, 1:183
 Kol, 3:129
 Kongo, 9:167
 Kpelle, 9:173
 Lamet, 5:157
 Lozi, 9:188
 Makushi, 7:219
 Maliseet, 1:210, 211
 Manx, 4:171
 Mescalero Apache, 1:224
 Micmac, 1:233
 Micmacs, 1:234
 Micronesians, 1:237
 Navajo, 1:251
 Nayaka, 3:194, 195
 Newar, 3:206
 Nomoi, 2:252
 Northern Paiute, 1:263
 Ontong Java, 2:254
 Pacific Eskimos, 1:282
 Pedi, 9:269-270
 Piaroa, 7:276
 Pima-Papago, 1:288
 Pomo, 1:294
 Provencal, 4:210
 Pume, 7:283
 Quechan, 1:301
 Rom of Czechoslovakia, 4:218
 Saami, 4:221
 Salasaca, 7:290
 Saliva, 7:292
 Santee, 1:307
 Saramaka, 7:297
 Semang, 5:234
 Serbs, 4:230, 231
 Shahsevan, 9:308
 Sherpa, 3:258
 Shona, 9:313
 Sicilians, 4:236
 Southern Paiute (and Chemehuevi),
   1:331
 Taos, 1:342
 Terena, 7:325
 Tewa Pueblos, 1:348
 Ticuna, 7:329
 Tolai, 2:334
 Tory Islanders, 4:265
 Trio, 7:335
 Trobriand Islands, 2:348
 Tswana, 9:362
 Vedda, 3:301
 Vlach Gypsies of Hungary, 4:271
 Warao, 7:357
 Warlpiri, 2:373
 Washoe, 1:368
 Wayapi, 7:361
 Yanomamö, 7:375
 Yap, 2:392
Wagons
 Irish Travellers, 4:155, 156
 Piemontese Sinti, 4:200
 Rominche, 4:216
Wailing. See under Mourning
Wakánda (creator)
 Ponca, 1:296
Wake. See under Mortuary practices

Wakonda (creator)
  Omaha, **1:**275
Wa-kon-tah (life force)
  Osage, **1:**278
Waldensians
  Piemontese, **4:**199
Walkabout. _See_ Journey
Walled villages. _See_ Villages, fortified
Wall paintings
  Munda, **3:**184
  Sora, **3:**270
  Swedes, **4:**258
  see also Murals
Walrus hunting
  Baffinland Inuit, **1:**29
  Iglulik Inuit, **1:**155
  Inughuit, **1:**160
  Labrador Inuit, **1:**201
  Yuit, **1:**390, 392
Wampum
  Abenaki, **1:**5
Wanderers. _See_ Itinerants; Nomads
Wandering Souls (festival)
  Vietnamese, **5:**287
War bundles
  Winnebago, **1:**382
War chief
  Huron, **1:**152
  Kickapoo, **1:**185
  Miami, **1:**231, 232
  Mohave, **1:**241
  Okanagon, **1:**272
  Quechan, **1:**302
  Shawnee, **1:**317
Warfare
  Abkhazians, **6:**8
  Ache, **7:**6
  Afar, **9:**8
  Ajië, **2:**9
  Akan, **9:**12
  Aleuts, **1:**16;**6:**16
  Ambonese, **5:**19
  Andis, **6:**25
  Angaité, **7:**44
  Asiatic Eskimos, **6:**38
  Assiniboin, **1:**27
  Atoni, **5:**28
  Ayoreo, **7:**71
  Bagirmi, **9:**34
  Bakhtiari, **9:**36
  Balinese, **5:**37
  Batak, **5:**41
  Bavarians, **4:**35
  Bisaya, **5:**43
  Blackfoot, **1:**41
  Bretons, **4:**39
  Butonese, **5:**68
  Central Yup'ik Eskimos, **1:**58
  Chechen-Ingush, **6:**73
  Cherokee, **1:**62
  Cheyenne, **1:**65
  Chin, **3:**66
  Choctaw, **1:**72
  Circassians, **6:**89
  Corsicans, **4:**66
  Desana, **7:**153
  Dogon, **9:**73
  Don Cossacks, **6:**106

Dyula, **9:**77
Easter Island, **2:**55
Eipo, **2:**58
Emerillon, **7:**159
Evenki (Northern Tungus), **6:**120, 123
Ewenki, **6:**433
Fore, **2:**64
Gahuku-Gama, **2:**70
Gainj, **2:**72, 73
Georgians, **6:**135
Gnau, **2:**82
Gogodala, **2:**84
Gururumba, **2:**94
Gusii, **9:**110
Hawaiians, **2:**97
Ifugao, **5:**100
Ilongot, **5:**102
Itelmen, **6:**153
Jamináwa, **7:**180
Jebero, **7:**181
Jicarilla, **1:**172
Jingpo, **6:**455
Jivaro, **7:**182-183
Kachin, **5:**118
Kaingáng, **7:**186
Kalmyks, **6:**157
Karakalpaks, **6:**168
Karelians, **6:**171
Kashmiri, **3:**122
Kenyah-Kayan-Kajang, **5:**133
Kewa, **2:**116
Khoi, **9:**160
Kilenge, **2:**120
Kiribati, **2:**123
Klamath, **1:**192
Kwoma, **2:**135
Kyrgyz, **6:**229
Latvians, **6:**238
Lau, **2:**144
Lesu, **2:**147
Lithuanians, **6:**250, 251
Luiseño, **1:**208
Mae Enga, **2:**150
Mafulu, **2:**153
Maguindanao, **5:**169
Mailu, **2:**156
Maisin, **2:**159
Malekula, **2:**164, 166
Manam, **2:**168
Mandak, **2:**171
Manus, **2:**175
Maori, **2:**178
Marind-anim, **2:**183
Maring, **2:**187
Marquesas Islands, **2:**189, 190
Mejbrat, **2:**196
Melanau, **5:**178, 179
Melpa, **2:**202
Mendi, **2:**205
Mescalero Apache, **1:**223
Metis of Western Canada, **1:**226-227, 229
Miami, **1:**231, 232
Miao, **6:**470
Mimika, **2:**208
Mingrelians, **6:**264
Mocoví, **7:**241
Mongols, **6:**474
Mossi, **9:**230

Motu, **2:**215
Mountain Arapesh, **2:**216, 217
Mundugumor, **2:**219
Murik, **2:**222
Nagas, **3:**190
Navajo, **1:**251
Naxi, **6:**479
Nez Percé, **1:**254
Nganasan, **6:**282
Nias, **5:**196
Nissan, **2:**249, 250
Noanamá, **7:**251
Nootka, **1:**257
North Alaskan Eskimos, **1:**260
Northern Shoshone and Bannock, **1:**267
Ojibwa, **1:**269
Orokolo, **2:**260
Osage, **1:**277
Palu'e, **5:**205, 206, 208
Pentecost, **2:**263
Pima-Papago, **1:**289-1290
Pohnpei, **2:**269
Qiang, **6:**485, 486
Quechan, **1:**301
Rapa, **2:**274
Rotinese, **5:**214
Rotuma, **2:**283
Russians, **6:**315
Sambia, **2:**284, 285
Samoa, **2:**288
Selkup, **6:**327
Seminole, **1:**312, 313
Sengseng, **2:**296, 297
Serbs, **4:**232
Shan, **5:**241
Siane, **2:**299
Siwai, **2:**304
Slav Macedonians, **4:**241
Somalis, **9:**318
Tahiti, **2:**306
Tai Lue, **5:**255
Tairora, **2:**309
Taiwan aboriginal peoples, **5:**257, 258
Tangu, **2:**312
Tasmanians, **2:**316
Tausug, **5:**264
Telefolmin, **2:**322, 323
Tofalar, **6:**363
Tongareva, **2:**341
Torres Strait Islanders, **2:**347
Trobriand Islands, **2:**350
Truk, **2:**353
Tubatulabal, **1:**355
Turkmens, **6:**371
Tuvalu, **2:**357
Udmurt, **6:**379
Ulithi, **2:**359
Uzbeks, **6:**398
Vietnamese, **5:**285
Walapai, **1:**364, 365
Wamira, **2:**365, 367
Wantoat, **2:**368
Waorani, **7:**353
Waropen, **2:**376
Winnebago, **1:**382
Witoto, **7:**365
Woleai, **2:**384
Yakut, **6:**406

Warfare (cont'd)
 Yangoru Boiken, 2:390
 Yuan, 5:294
 Yurok, 1:394
 Zande, 9:399
 see also Civil war; Raiders
Warfare (rare)
 Kapauku, 2:107
 Malaita, 2:162
 Nasioi, 2:235
Warfare (religious)
 Kashmiri, 3:122
Warfare (ritual)
 Asmat, 2:20, 21
 Choctaw, 1:70
 Dani, 2:45
 Gebusi, 2:78
 Maring, 2:187
 Namau, 2:232
 Tiwi, 2:329
Warfare (suprise and stage battles)
 Wiyot, 1:385
Warfare motivations. See Conflict causes
War Gods
 Zuni, 1:399
War group
 Choctaw, 1:72
 Fox, 1:129
War-related population decimation
 Bretons, 4:37, 39
 Burgundians, 4:46
 Corsicans, 4:66
 Walapai, 1:364
Warrior
 initiation
  Nandi and other Kalenjin peoples, 9:233
  Pima-Papago, 1:290
  Sambia, 2:285
 leadership
  Choctaw, 1:72
  Creek, 1:83
  Eastern Shoshone, 1:105
 mortuary practices
  Mohave, 1:242
  Sarsi, 1:308
 tradition
  Arapaho, 1:26
  Assiniboin, 1:27
  Baluchi, 3:23
  Haida, 1:136
  Kshatriya, 3:142, 222
  Nayar, 3:196, 197, 198
  Rajput, 3:249
  Winnebago, 1:382
 traditions
  Gurkha, 3:93
 war society
  Yakö, 9:386
 women
  Quechan, 1:301
Warrior Clan
 Winnebago, 1:382
Warrior's Dance
 Menominee, 1:222
Washing. See Bathing; Foot washing
Watchmaking. See Clocks and watches
Watchman
 Kurumbas, 3:143

Watchtowers
 Garo, 3:82
Water babies (anthropomorphic beings)
 Northern Paiute, 1:264
 Southern Paiure (and Chemehuevi), 1:332
 Ute, 1:362
Water-based world
 Yurok, 1:395
Water buffalo domestication
 Cham, 5:72
Water buffalo hunting
 Bontok, 5:46
Water buffalo raising
 Acehnese, 5:3
 Bai, 6:419
 Bajau, 5:32
 Balinese, 5:36
 Batak, 5:39
 Bisaya, 5:42
 Bolaang Mongondow, 5:43
 Bugis, 5:49
 Bukidnon, 5:53
 Central Thai, 5:70
 Dai, 6:424
 Dusun, 5:80, 81
 Gayo, 5:88
 Gujar, 3:89
 Jat, 3:111, 112
 Jingpo, 6:456
 Kalingas, 5:122
 Karen, 5:126
 Khmer, 5:136
 Kmhmu, 5:139
 Lao, 5:158
 Lao Isan, 5:161
 Makassar, 5:172
 Mnong, 5:184
 Mulam, 6:476
 Muong, 5:190
 Ogan-Besemah, 5:198
 Pahari, 3:220
 Rotinese, 5:213
 Sagada Igorot, 5:216
 Sasak, 5:226
 Tagalog, 5:249
 Tai Lue, 5:253
 Taiwan aboriginal peoples, 5:257
 Tats, 6:358
 Telugu, 3:285
 Tetum, 5:276
 Toda, 3:295, 297
 Toraja, 5:281, 282
 Vietnamese, 5:285
 Yakan, 5:288, 289
Water cures
 Germans, 4:124
Water Festival
 Khmer, 5:137
Water jar manufacture
 Western Apache, 1:372
Waterman (mythical creature)
 Sorbs, 4:253
Watermelon growing
 Walapai, 1:364
Water power
 Dalmatians, 4:86
 Slave Macedonians, 4:240
 Swedes, 4:257

Water rights
 Madeirans, 4:165
Water rituals
 Nicobarese, 3:209
 Pahari, 3:223
 see also Bathing, ceremonial
Wax modeling
 Karajá, 7:188, 189
Wealth. See Money and wealth; under Leadership qualities; under Status, basis of
Weaning. See Breast-feeding
Weapons industry
 German Swiss, 4:125
 Khasi, 3:126
 Lakher, 3:145
Weaving
 Acadians, 1:8
 Acehnese, 5:3
 Ainu, 5:10
 Altaians, 6:21
 Armenians, 6:31
 Atoni, 5:27, 28
 Azerbaijani Turks, 6:49
 Bajau, 5:34
 Bedouin, 9:45
 Belarussians, 6:60, 61
 Betsileo, 9:57
 Bondo, 3:51
 Bugis, 5:49
 Bulgarians, 4:43, 45
 Callahuaya, 7:88, 90
 Cape Verdeans, 4:55
 Chakma, 3:61
 Chechen-Ingush, 6:75
 Chin, 3:64, 67
 Chipaya, 7:116, 117
 Chiriguano, 7:120
 Chocho, 8:63
 Chontal of Tabasco, 8:63
 Cotopaxi Quichua, 7:133
 Cretans, 4:70, 71
 Dai, 6:424
 Dargins, 6:98
 De'ang, 6:430
 Drung, 6:432
 elaborate
  Dyula, 9:76, 77-78
 Emberá and Wounaan, 8:109
 by farmers
  Konso, 9:169
 Garo, 3:82
 Greeks, 4:134
 Guajiro, 7:168
 Guarayu, 7:174
 Gurung, 3:94
 Hakka, 6:437
 Hani, 6:450
 Hanunóo, 5:91
 Highland Scots, 4:140
 Hopi, 1:149
 Iban, 5:97, 98, 99
 Ibibio, 9:119
 ikat designs
  Sakalava, 9:294
 Itonama, 7:179
 Japanese, 5:105
 Jebero, 7:181
 Jingpo, 6:456, 459

Karajá, **7:**188-189
Karakalpaks, **6:**167
Karelians, **6:**170
Karen, **5:**126, 129
Kashinawa, **7:**195
kente cloth
    Ewe and Fon, **9:**88
Kewa, **2:**115
Khasi, **3:**123
Khinalughs, **6:**199, 201
Kiribati, **2:**123
Klingit, **1:**353
Kogi, **7:**201
Kosrae, **2:**130
Kriashen Tatars, **6:**211
Kubachins, **6:**217
Kumyks, **6:**221
Kurds, **6:**226
Kwakiutl, **1:**198
Lahu, **6:**462
Laks, **6:**234
Lamaholot, **5:**156
Lao Isan, **5:**161
Latinos, **1:**204
Lepcha, **3:**149
Lezgins, **6:**242
Li, **6:**464
Lisu, **5:**165
Maguindanao, **5:**169
Maonan, **6:**468
Maranao, **5:**177
Maris, **6:**257
Miao, **6:**471, 472
Minangkabau, **5:**182
Mingrelians, **6:**263
Mizo, **3:**178, 179
Mnong, **5:**184
Modang, **5:**187
Mojo, **7:**242
Moluccans—South, **5:**188
Mossi, **9:**231
Mundurucu, **7:**244
Muong, **5:**190
Murik, **2:**221, 223
Nagas, **3:**188, 189
Navajo, **1:**251, 253
Naxi, **6:**478
Nepali, **3:**202
Newar, **3:**206
Nguna, **2:**243
Nootka, **1:**256, 257
Nyinba, **3:**213
Ogan-Besemah, **5:**198
Oriya, **3:**216
Otavalo, **7:**253
Palaung, **5:**202
Pamir peoples, **6:**305
Panare, **7:**265
Piaroa, **7:**276
Pima-Papago, **1:**288
Piro, **7:**279
Pomaks, **4:**205
Popoloca, **8:**216
Purum, **3:**243
Romanians, **4:**213, 214
Rotinese, **5:**213, 214
Rotuma, **2:**283
Rutuls, **6:**319, 321

Salasaca, **7:**290
Samal, **5:**219
Santa Cruz, **2:**290-291
Saraguro, **7:**295
Selkup, **6:**326
Shakers, **1:**316
Shan, **5:**241
She, **6:**490, 491
Siberian Estonians, **6:**336
Siona-Secoya, **7:**307
Slovaks, **4:**245
Swedes, **4:**258
Swiss, Italian, **4:**260
Tabasarans, **6:**349
Tai Lue, **5:**253
Tajiks, **6:**354
Talysh, **6:**356
Tamil, **3:**277
Taos, **1:**342
Tats, **6:**359, 360
Tetum, **5:**276
Tewa Pueblos, **1:**348
Tiv, **9:**350
Tlingit, **1:**351
Trobriand Islands, **2:**349
Truk, **2:**352, 353
Tsakhurs, **6:**366, 367
Tsimshian, **1:**355
Tujia, **6:**498
Tunebo, **7:**338
Turkmens, **6:**370, 371
Tuvalu, **2:**355
Ukrainian peasants, **6:**386
Ukrainians of Canada, **1:**359
Ute, **1:**361
Uzbeks, **6:**397
Warao, **7:**358
Wayapi, **7:**361
Yagua, **7:**372
Yakan, **5:**289
Yao, **6:**505
Yukpa, **7:**383
Yukuna, **7:**386
Zuni, **1:**397, 398
see also Basketry; Mat making; Rug
    weaving; Textile production
Wedding ceremonies and festivities. _See_
    Feasting, wedding; Marriage
Wedding gifts. _See_ Marriage, gift giving
Welfare assistance. _See_ Government welfare
    assistance
Welfare state
    Austrians, **4:**19
    Danes, **4:**89, 90
    Germans, **4:**122
    Mauritian, **3:**171
    Norwegians, **4:**182
    Swedes, **4:**258
    see also Government welfare assistance
Werewolves
    Kashubians, **4:**159
Wesleyan religious movement. _See_ Methodism
Western classical music
    Parsi, **3:**229-230
Wet cultivation. _See under_ Agriculture
Wet nursing
    Khevsur, **6:**195
Whalebone carving. _See under_ Carved objects

Whaling
    Baffinland Inuit, **1:**28, 29
    Basques, **1:**32, 33;**4:**30
    Cape Verdeans, **4:**54
    Faroe Islanders, **4:**100
    Iglulik Inuit, **1:**155
    Labrador Inuit, **1:**201
    Nootka, **1:**255, 256, 257
    North Alaskan Eskimos, **1:**259, 261
    Norwegians, **4:**181
    Pacific Eskimo, **1:**283
    Portuguese, **4:**206
    West Greenland Inuit, **1:**377
    Yuit, **1:**390, 392
Wheat growing
    Aghuls, **6:**11
    Azerbaijani Turks, **6:**49
    Bai, **6:**419
    Basques, **4:**31
    Bavarians, **4:**33
    Berbers of Morocco, **9:**49
    Bonan, **6:**422
    Bouyei, **6:**422
    Buriats, **6:**67
    Calabrese, **4:**49
    Castilians, **4:**59
    Chuvash, **6:**84
    Circassians, **6:**88
    Cornish, **4:**65
    Crimean Tatars, **6:**93
    Cyclades, **4:**77
    Cypriots, **4:**80
    Dargins, **6:**96
    Don Cossacks, **6:**104
    Dong, **6:**431
    Dongxiang, **6:**432
    Drung, **6:**432
    Dungans, **6:**109
    Falasha, **9:**91
    Han, **6:**440
    Hazara, **9:**115
    Hidatsa, **1:**146
    Hui, **6:**453
    Hutterites, **1:**153
    Ionians, **4:**149
    Kalasha, **3:**116
    Kalmyks, **6:**156
    Karakalpaks, **6:**167
    Kashubians, **4:**158
    Kazakhs, **6:**177
    Konso, **9:**169
    Kriashen Tatars, **6:**211
    Kurds, **9:**175
    Kyrgyz, **6:**229
    Laks, **6:**234
    Leonese, **4:**161
    Lezgins, **6:**242
    Limbu, **3:**150
    Lur, **9:**202
    Maonan, **6:**468
    Maris, **6:**257
    Mennonites, **1:**217-218
    Moldovans, **6:**266
    Mongols, **6:**474
    Mulam, **6:**476
    Nandi and other Kalenjin peoples,
        9:232
    Naxi, **6:**478

Wheat growing (cont'd)
  Nepali, 3:202
  Newar, 3:206
  Nogays, 6:287
  Nubians, 9:246
  Nyinba, 3:211
  Opata, 8:199
  Ossetes, 6:299
  Ozarks, 1:281
  Pahari, 3:220
  Pamir peoples, 6:304
  Pandit of Kashmir, 3:224
  Pashai, 9:267
  Pathan, 3:231
  Persians, 9:279
  Piemontese, 4:198
  Poles, 4:203
  Portuguese, 4:206
  Pumi, 6:483
  Punjabi, 3:238
  Qashqa'i, 9:285
  Rutuls, 6:319
  Salar, 6:488
  Serbs, 4:230
  She, 6:489
  Shors, 6:329, 330
  Shui, 6:491
  Sicilians, 4:236
  Slovaks, 4:243
  Sunwar, 3:271
  Svans, 6:344
  Tabasarans, 6:348
  Tajik, 6:492
  Talysh, 6:355
  Taos, 1:341
  Tats, 6:358
  Thakali, 3:290
  Tibetans, 6:494
  Tigray, 9:347
  Tiroleans, 4:263
  Tujia, 6:498
  Tuscans, 4:269
  Tuvans, 6:373
  Udis, 6:376
  Udmurt, 6:380
  Ukrainian peasants, 6:386
  Volga Tatars, 6:401
  Walapai, 1:364
  Walloons, 4:276
  Welsh, 4:279
  Xibe, 6:504
  Zuni, 1:397
  see also Buckwheat growing
Whipping (ritual)
  Karihona, 7:193
  Saliva, 7:292
  Waimiri-Atroari, 7:345
  Yekuana, 7:381
Whippings (as punishment)
  Keres Pueblo Indians, 1:181
  Kumeyaay, 1:195
Whiskey. See Alcohol
Whistle courtship
  Kickapoo, 1:184
White Anglo-Saxon Protestants
  English-Americans, 1:110
White Buffalo Calf Woman (deity)
  Teton, 1:346

White Buffalo Cow Society
  Mandan, 1:215
White-collar crime
  Austrians, 4:21
White Deerskin Dance
  Yurok, 1:395
Whitefish fishing
  Ingalik, 1:157
White ladies (vindictive ghosts)
  Frisians, 4:112
  Gaels (Irish), 4:117
White moiety
  Choctaw, 1:72
  Fox, 1:129
White Painted Woman (culture heroine)
  Mescalero Apache, 1:225
White Shell Woman (deity)
  Zuni, 1:399
White wedding garments
  Nicobarese, 3:209
Wickerwork
  Madeirans, 4:165
  Magar, 3:156
Widow
  black mourning garments. See under
        Mourning
  may rent land
    Konso, 9:170
  pays death-dues to in-laws
    Lunda, 9:199
  pollution
    Luyia, 9:205, 206
    Ndebele, 9:238
  property rights
    Baiga, 3:20
    Montenegrins, 4:173
    Nagas, 3:189
    Oriya, 3:217
    Toda, 3:296
  responsibility for husband's death
    Telugu, 3:286
  returns to natal home
    Palestinians, 9:265
  status
    Chin, 3:64
  subordinate to sons
    Maasai, 9:208
  wears husband's clothes until inherited by
        his brother
    Luyia, 9:206
  year-long rites to separate from deceased
    Lobi-Dagarti peoples, 9:186
Widow-care provisions
  Basseri, 9:42
  Chagga, 9:62
  Falasha, 9:92
  Galicians, 4:120
  Garo, 3:83
  Korku, 3:134
  Lakher, 3:146
  Leonese, 4:161
  Mamprusi, 9:213
  Mikir, 3:176
  Nyakyusa and Ngonde, 9:253
  Okiek, 9:261
  Purum, 3:244
  Sardinians, 4:226
  see also Ultimogeniture

Widower
  lives alone
    Sardinians, 4:227
  lives with eldest married son
    Falasha, 9:92
  pays death-dues to in-laws
    Luba of Shaba, 9:192
    Lunda, 9:199
  year-long rites to separate from deceased
    Lobi-Dagarti peoples, 9:186
Widower remarriage. See under Remarriage
Widower remarriage to wife's sister. See
        Sororate marriage
Widow immolatation
  Chitpavan Brahman, 3:70
Widow remarriage to husband's brother. See
        Levirate marriage
Wife beating. See Domestic violence
Wills and trusts
  Parsi, 3:228
Windigo (supernatural)
  Algonkin, 1:17
  Ojibwa, 1:270
Wind instruments. See under Musical
        instruments
Wine making
  Andalusians, 4:10
  Aquitaine, 4:13, 14
  Armenians, 6:29
  Ata Tana 'Ai, 5:23
  Azoreans, 4:27
  Burgundians, 4:46
  Castilians, 4:59
  Corsicans, 4:67
  Cretans, 4:70
  Cyclades, 4:77
  Georgians, 6:132
  German Swiss, 4:125
  Ionians, 4:149
  Madeirans, 4:164, 165
  Mingrelians, 6:263
  Moldovans, 6:266
  Occitans, 4:183, 184
  Portuguese, 4:206
  Provencal, 4:210
  Romanians, 4:213
  Sardinians, 4:226
  Slovaks, 4:243
  Swiss, Italian, 4:261
  Tuscans, 4:269
  Vlachs, 4:274
Wine making (palm)
  Mijikenda, 9:224
  Suku, 9:321
  Yakö, 9:383
  Zande, 9:398
Winter Solstice (holiday)
  Hakka, 6:439
  Slav Macedonians, 4:241
Wisaaka (Kickapoo culture heroo),
        1:185
Wisaka bucha (festival)
  Lao Isan, 5:163
Wisdom (as admired trait)
  Kiowa, 1:188
  Tanana, 1:339
  see also under Leadership qualities
Witchcraft. See Sorcery and witchcraft

Witch doctor
  Bhil, **3**:41
  Lozi, **9**:189
  Nicobarese, **3**:210
  Salasaca, **7**:290, 291
  Zande, **9**:399
Withdrawal. _See under_ Conflict resolution
Withdrawal of support. _See under_ Social
    control measures
Wohpekumew (creator)
  Yurok, **1**:395
Wolf (mythological figure)
  Northern Shoshone and Bannock, **1**:267,
    268
  Ute, **1**:362
Wolf Dance
  Nootka, **1**:257
Wolf protector
  Tanaina, **1**:336
Wolf Society
  Gros Ventre, **1**:134
Woman's Dance
  Kickapoo, **1**:185
Woman supreme being
  Khasi, **3**:125
  Shawnee, **1**:317
Women
  astronomical observation by
    Winnebago, **1**:381
  beaten by husbands. _See_ Domestic violence
  careers
    Bengali, **3**:31
    Czech, **4**:83-84
    Jews of Algeria, **9**:138
    Jews of Israel, **9**:143
    Piemontese, **4**:198
    Syrian Christian of Kerala, **3**:274
    Walloons, **4**:277
  chastity importance. _See_ Virginity
  decision making by
    Ata Tana 'Ai, **5**:24, 25
    Mejbrat, **2**:196
    Northern Paiute, **1**:264
    Norwegians, **4**:181
    Piemontese, **4**:198
    Sardinians, **4**:226
    Tewa Pueblos, **1**:349
  deities. _See_ Women deities
  descent line from. _See_ Descent, matrilineal
  economic control by
    Hopi, **1**:149
  economic importance of
    Irish Travellers, **4**:155
    Portuguese, **4**:207
  economic importance but low status of
    Montenegrins, **4**:172
  education and literacy
    Mahar, **3**:165
    Nayar, **3**:199
    Parsi, **3**:228
  enduring worst fate possible
    Nambudiri Brahman, **3**:193
  equality. _See_ Gender equality
  equal rights within marriage
    Chenchu, **3**:62
  as expert specialists
    Washoe, **1**:369
  female infanticide

Jat, **3**:112
  Sinhalese, **3**:266
  Toga, **3**:296
fertility ceremonies. _See_ Ceremonies,
    fertility
fighting over men
  Micmac, **1**:235
finances kept separately from men
  Yoruba, **9**:392
financial control by
  Khmer, **5**:136
  Kmhmu, **5**:140
  Mejbrat, **2**:196
  Piemontese, **4**:198
  Siberian Germans, **6**:339
  Vietnamese, **5**:285
forbidden from ritual
  Ainu, **5**:8
  Svans, **6**:346
  Tahiti, **2**:307
forced to stay at home. _See_ Women's
    activity curtailment
freedom in mate selection
  Andalusians, **4**:11
  Nagas, **3**:189
  Sora, **3**:269
generative power
  hijra, **3**:98
healers. _See_ Women medical practitioners
high status of. _See under_ Women, status of
home linkage
  Cyclade, **4**:77
housebuilders and owners
  Khoi, **9**:159
  Mandan, **1**:214
  Mescalero Apache, **1**:225
household deities
  Limbu, **3**:151
as household heads. _See under_ Household
hunting ceremony
  Oraon, **3**:215
ideal
  Rom of Czechoslovakia, **4**:219
intercession by
  Baluchi, **3**:23
as inventors and sustainers of culture
  Tauade, **2**:320
kinship bonds
  Azoreans, **4**:28
known by husband's or father's age-set
  Okiek, **9**:261
landholding by. _See_ Women's property
    rights
landless day labor
  Portuguese, **4**:207
low rate of modern labor participation
  Dutch, **4**:92
low status of. _See under_ Women, status of
maintenance rights
  Punjabi, **3**:240
  Purum, **3**:244
market monopoly
  Ewe and Fon, **9**:84, 85
markets for
  Berbers of Morocco, **9**:49
marriage between
  Igbo, **9**:122
  Nandi and other Kalenjin peoples, **9**:233

medical professionals
  Bengali, **3**:31
  see also Women medical practitioners
natal clan ties
  Yuit, **1**:391
own leaders
  Shahsevan, **9**:309
as peacemakers
  Andamanese, **3**:10-11
political participation
  Belau, **2**:26
  Igbo, **9**:123
  Kalingas, **5**:122
  Samoa, **2**:288
  Ute, **1**:362
  see also Women political leaders
political power
  Belau, **2**:26
  Kapauku, **2**:106
  Portuguese, **4**:207
pollution by
  Bhil, **3**:41
  Rom, **1**:306
  Sinhalese, **3**:265
  see also Chidbirth; Menstruation
price paid for bride. _See_ Bride-price
primary role in royal ritual
  Sakalava, **9**:297
property control and ownership by. _See_
    Women's property rights
puberty. _See_ Initiation; Menstruation
religious knowledge not expected
  Jews of Yemen, **9**:150
religious orders. _See_ Nuns
religious roles
  Corsicans, **4**:68
  Cretans, **4**:71
  Cyclades, **4**:77-78
  see also Women clergy; Women
    magicoreligious practitioners;
    Women's priestly roles
ritual homicide of
  Chamacoco, **7**:110
ritual lore held exclusively by
  Pintupi, **2**:266
sacred drum for extracting fees
  Mijikenda, **9**:225
sanctions against men
  Nandi and other Kalenjin peoples, **9**:234
seclusion. _See_ Gender separation; Purdah
shortage of
  Albanians, **4**:5-6
  Copper Eskimo, **1**:78
  Finns, **4**:103
  Gaels (Irish), **4**:116
single head of household. _See_ Household
social groups
  Sorbs, **4**:253
supernatural powers
  Kashubians, **4**:159
  Rom, **1**:306
  see also Women shamans
traders
  Iatmul, **2**:98
  Tonga, **9**:353
valuation of. _See_ Women, status of, high
valued equally. _See_ Gender equality
veiling of. _See_ Veiling of women

Women (cont'd)
  wage discrimination
    Icelanders, **4:**147
    Lowland Scots, **4:**163
    Swiss, Italian, **4:**261
    Walloons, **4:**277
  wage labor by
    Tory Islanders, **4:**265
  work more than men
    Suri, **9:**325
  work outside home
    Nubians, **9:**247
  see also Childbirth; Gender *headings*
      Marriage; Pregnancy; Sexual relations
Women, status of
  based on husband's
    Osage, **1:**278
  considered inviolable
    Tongareva, **2:**341
  dominance
    Kanjar, **3:**120, 121
    Khasi, **3:**124, 125
  high
    Aimaq, **9:**10
    Drung, **6:**432
    Druze, **9:**74
    Hopi, **1:**149, 150
    Jino, **6:**460
    Kanjar, **3:**120-121
    Mohave, **1:**241
    Moinba, **6:**473
    Navajo, **1:**252
    Orochi, **6:**295
    Sio, **2:**300
    Yemenis, **9:**389
    Zuni, **1:**398
  increasing with age
    Rom of Czechoslovakia, **4:**218
  increasing with children
    Fulani, **9:**102
  independence and self-sufficiency
    Kyrgyz, **6:**230
  as inferior to men
    Kanuri, **9:**152
  low
    Chipewyan, **1:**68
    Mijikenda, **9:**225
    Mongo, **9:**226
    Montenegrins, **4:**172
    Munda, **3:**183
    Nambudiri Brahman, **3:**193
    Sinhalese, **3:**266
    Tamil of Sri Lanka, **3:**281
  more freedom than neighbors
    Jews of Kurdistan, **9:**146
  power within family
    Ionians, **4:**150
    Mamprusi, **9:**213
  as property
    Albanians, **4:**5
  respect for
    Black Creoles of California, **1:**39
    Kiowa, **1:**188
    Maliseet, **1:**212
    see also Madonna worship
  restricted from knowledge
    Lesu, **2:**146
  rights restrictions

German Swiss, **4:**126
  societal freedom
    Kalasha, **3:**116
    Lakher, **3:**145
    Pahari, **3:**221
    Parsi, **3:**228
  as traveling or married
    Pende, **9:**272
Women ascetics
  Sadhu, **3:**251
Women beggars
  Qalandar, **3:**247
  Sadhu, **3:**251
  Slovensko Roma, **4:**250
  Xoraxané Romá, **4:**281-282
Women changers
  Chácobo, **7:**107
Women chiefs. *See* Women political leaders
Women clergy
  Jews, **1:**171
  Shakers, **1:**316
  Swedes, **4:**258
  Tanana, **1:**340
  see also Women's priestly roles
Women deities
  Andalusians, **4:**12
  Baul, **3:**26
  Bella Coola, **1:**36
  Bengali, **3:**34
  Bengali Shakta, **3:**35;**4:**166
  Bengali Vaishnava, **3:**36
  Bhil, **3:**41
  Bhuiya, **3:**44
  Brahman and Chhetri of Nepal, **3:**53
  Caribou Inuit, **1:**51
  Chitpavan Brahman, **3:**70
  Gond, **3:**86, 87
  Haida, **1:**136
  hijra, **3:**96, 97, 98
  Inughuit, **1:**161
  Irula, **3:**108
  Kond, **3:**133
  Koya, **3:**141
  Labrador Inuit, **1:**202
  Lao, **5:**159
  Magar, **3:**161
  Mahar, **3:**165
  Netsilik Inuit, **1:**254
  Oraon, **3:**215
  Pandit of Kashmir, **3:**224
  Paniyan, **3:**227
  Sasak, **5:**227
  Slovaks, **4:**245
  Sundanese, **5:**247
  Tamil, **3:**279
  Telegu, **3:**287
  Teton, **1:**346
  Thug, **3:**294
  Walapi, **1:**36
  Zuni, **1:**399
  see also Woman supreme being
Women healers. *See* Women medical
      practitioners
Women impersonators. *See* Transsexuality
Women magicoreligious practitioners
  Calabrese, **4:**50
  Kashubians, **4:**159
  Micmac, **1:**235

Mijikenda, **9:**225
Mikir, **3:**176
Tigray, **9:**348-349
see also Sorcery and witchcraft; Women
      shamans
Women medical practitioners
  Bengali, **3:**31
  Daribi, **2:**48
  Greeks, **4:**134
  Ojibwa, **1:**271
  Santal, **3:**253
  Sea Islanders, **1:**310-311
  Slovaks, **4:**245
  Southern Paiute (and Chemehuevi), **1:**332
  Syrian Christian of Kerala, **3:**273
  Teton, **1:**346
  Tewa Pueblos, **1:**350
  Vlach Gypsies of Hungary, **4:**272
  Yurok, **1:**395-396
  see also Midwives; Women shamans
Women mourners. *See* Mortuary practices;
      Mourning
Women political leaders
  Ata Tana 'Ai, **5:**25
  Blackfoot, **1:**42
  Bulgarian Gypsies, **4:**41
  Chin, **3:**64
  Hmong, **5:**94
  Kumeyaay, **1:**195
  Lipan Apache, **1:**208
  Maliseet, **1:**212
  Mejbrat, **2:**196, 196
  Nicobarese, **3:**210
  Norwegians, **4:**182
  Quechan, **1:**302
  Shahsevan, **9:**309
  Shawnee, **1:**317
  Tanana, **1:**339
  Waorani, **7:**353, 353
  Washoe, **1:**369
  Western Apache, **1:**372
  see also Women, political role
Women professionals
  Bengali, **3:**31
  Syrian Christian of Kerala, **3:**274
  see also Women, careers
Women's activity curtailment
  Bengali, **3:**32
  Chin, **3:**64
  Cypriots, **4:**80
  Muslim, **3:**185
  Nambudiri Brahman, **3:**193
  Sicilians, **4:**235-236
  Sinhalese, **3:**265
  Tamil of Sri Lanka, **3:**281
  Telugu, **3:**285
  Thakali, **3:**291
  Zorastrians, **9:**408
  see also Gender separation; Menstruation;
      Purdah
Women saints
  Sidi, **3:**260
Women's ceremonies
  Chitpavan Brahman, **3:**70
  Toda, **3:**297
Women's equality. *See* Gender equality
Women shamans
  Abenaki, **1:**5

Achumawi, 1:10
Chin, 3:67
Chiricahua, 1:70
Cree, 1:81
Ingalik, 1:158
Karok, 1:177
Labrador Inuit, 1:202
Montagnais-Naskapi, 1:246
Munda, 3:184
Northern Paiute, 1:265
Pahari, 3:223
Pomo, 1:295
Saami, 4:222
Santee, 1:307
Sora, 3:269, 270
Tanaina, 1:337
Tanana, 1:349
Tolowa, 1:353
Tubatulabal, 1:355
Ute, 1:361, 362
Western Apache, 1:372
Western Shoshone, 1:375
West Greenland Inuit, 1:378
Yurok, 1:394, 395
see also Midwives
Women's inheritance proscriptions
Albanians, 4:6
Burusho, 3:56
Grasia, 3:88
Gusii, 9:109
Highland Scots, 4:141
Korku, 3:134
Lakher, 3:146
Munda, 3:182
Pandit of Kashmir, 3:225
Pathan, 3:232
Pawnee, 1:285
Punjabi, 3:240
Purum, 3:244
Shahsevan, 9:309
Toda, 3:2296
Zamindar, 3:307
Women's inheritance rights
Azoreans, 4:28
Bretons, 4:39
Cretans, 4:70
Divehi, 3:77
Garia, 3:81
Garo, 3:83
Gujarati, 3:91
Gurung, 3:94
Khasi, 3:124-125
Kol, 3:130
Magar, 3:158
Maltese, 4:168
Mandan, 1:215
Mizo, 3:178
Nagas, 3:189-190
Nayar, 3:199
Nepali, 3:204
Nyinba, 3:212
Oriya, 3:217
Parsi, 3:228
Pasiegos, 4:190
Sardinians, 4:227
Sinhalese, 3:266
Slovenes, 4:248
Sora, 3:269-270

Swedes, 4:257-258
Syrian Christian of Kerala, 3:273
Tamil of Sri Lanka, 3:282
Vedda, 3:302
see also Dowry; Inheritance, equal distribution; Women's property rights
Women's life-cycle events. _See_ Childbirth; Coming of age; Initiation; Menstruation; Marriage; Mortuary practices
Women spirits. _See_ Women deities
Women's political power. _See_ Women, political power; Women political leadership
Women's priestly roles
Khasi, 3:125, 126
Kota, 3:138
Kurumbas, 3:143
Lingayat, 3:153
Santal, 3:255
see also Women clergy
Women's property rights
Abelam, 2:5
Ambae, 2:11
Choctaw, 1:71, 72
Goodenough Island, 2:87
Hopi, 1:149
Huarayo, 7:177
Kashinawa, 7:195
Khoi, 9:159
Kickapoo, 1:185
Kumeyaay, 1:195
Kwakiutl, 1:199
Kyrgz, 6:230
Latinos, 1:205
Magar, 3:158
Mailu, 2:155
Mandan, 1:214
Mescalero Apache, 1:225
Mimika, 2:207
Nepali, 3:204
Newar, 3:207
Pasiegos, 4:190
Pawee, 1:285
Portuguese, 4:207
Rhadé, 5:212
Tanaina, 1:336
Teton, 1:345
Tory Islanders, 4:265
Yawalapití, 7:379
Yokuts, 1:388
Women's restrictions. _See_ Gender separation; Veiling of women; Women's activity curtailment
Women's seclusion. _See_ Childbirth, seclusion; Menstruation; Purdah
Women's societies. _See under_ Associations, clubs, and societies
Women's Society
Tewa Pueblos, 1:349
Women warriors
Quechan, 1:301
Wood. _See_ Forest products; Forestry
Wood-apple collection
Kol, 3:129
Wood-burn etching
Slovaks, 4:245
Wood carving. _See under_ Carved objects
Woodcutters. _See_ Forestry

Wooden shoes
Burgundians, 4:47
Pasiegos, 4:190
Wood gatherers
Kol, 3:129
Magar, 3:156
Wood sculpture. _See under_ Carved objects
Wood shaping
Iroquois, 1:165
Klallam, 1:190
Woodworking
Armenians, 6:31
Avars, 6:45
Bai, 6:419
Bisaya, 5:42
Bulgarian Gypsies, 4:41
Bulgarians, 4:43
Dai, 6:424
Dargins, 6:97, 98
drum making
Pedi, 9:270
Even, 6:119
Finns, 4:102
Gypsies, 6:146
Ingalik, 1:157
Ingilos, 6:150
Karelians, 6:170
Kazakhs, 6:177, 178, 182
Kenyah-Kayan-Kajang, 5:133
Kickapoo, 1:184
Konso, 9:170
Kumyks, 6:221
Kwakiutl, 1:198
Kyrgyz, 6:229
Latinos, 1:206
Lau, 2:143
Lhoba, 6:464
Lisu, 5:165
Madeirans, 4:165
Minangkabau, 5:182
Mingrelians, 6:263
Mongols, 6:474
Nootka, 1:256
Ogan-Besemah, 5:198
Ojibwa, 1:269
Old Believers, 1:273
Ossetes, 6:299
Pamir Peoples, 6:305
Rennell Island, 2:277
Romanians, 4:213
Serbs, 4:230
Siberian Germans, 6:339
Swedes, 4:258
Tabasarans, 6:349, 350
Talysh, 6:356
Ticuna, 7:328
Toba, 7:332
Trio, 7:335
Truk, 2:352, 353
Tsakhurs, 6:366
Tujia, 6:498
Turkmens, 6:370
Ukrainian peasants, 6:386
Ukrainians, 6:392
Volga Tatars, 6:401
Wiyot, 1:384
Yukuna, 7:386
Yurok, 1:394

Woodworking (cont'd)
  see also Carpentry; Carved objects, wood
    carving
Woolen products
  Bulgarians, 4:43
  Dargins, 6:97
  Karachays, 6:160
  Kurds, 6:226
  Navajo, 1:251
  Pamir peoples, 6:305
  Romanians, 4:213
  Shetlanders, 4:233, 234
  Swedes, 4:258
  Tory Islanders, 4:265
  Tsakhurs, 6:366
  Vlachs, 4:274
  see also Knitting; Rug weaving
Work ethic
  Old Believers, 1:274
World concept
  on animal's back
    Semang, 5:235
  dual
    Albanians, 4:7
    Mataco, 7:226-227
    Menominee, 1:222
    Toda, 3:297, 298
  multi-level
    Kédang, 5:133
    Melanau, 5:180
    Modang, 5:187
    Muong, 5:192
    Palu'e, 5:208
  multiple spheres
    Toraja, 5:283
  nine-level
    Circassians, 6:90
  three-level
    Evenki (Northern Tungus), 6:123
    Karelians, 6:172
    Mansi, 6:254
    Selkup, 6:328
  see also Cosmology
Wormwood, medicinal use of
  Romanians, 4:214
"Wreckers"
  Cornish, 4:65
Writing, pictographic. See Pictographic
    writing
Wrought-iron work
  Madeirans, 4:165

Xenophobia
  Samal Moro, 5:223
  Santal, 3:254

Yaks raising
  Tibetans, 6:494
Yam gathering
  Hill Pandaram, 3:99
  Irula, 3:105
  Nayaka, 3:195
Yam growing. See Sweet potato growing
Yarn dyeing
  Bukharan Jews, 6:64
Yawulyu (ceremony)
  Warlpiri, 2:374
Yehasuri ("wild Indians')
  Catawba, 1:54
Yerba maté (tea)
  Païz-Tavytera, 7:259
Yeti. See Abominable Snowman legend
Yezidis
  Kurds, 6:227
  Yezidis, 6:408, 410
Yhyak (festival)
  Yakut, 6:407
Yodeling
  German Swiss, 4:127
  tropical-forest foragers, 9:357
Yoga
  Bengali Shakta, 3:35
  Santal, 3:255
Yogurt production
  Bavarians, 4:33
Yoik (musical form)
  Saami, 4:222
Yom Kippur (holiday)
  Bukharan Jews, 6:65
  Lithuanian Jews, 6:246
  Mountain Jews, 6:273
Younger sons' marriage prohibitions
  Nambudiri Brahman, 3:193
Youngest son inheritance. See Ultimogeniture
Young men's house. See Dormitories (single
    male or female)
Youth clubs and groups. See under
    Associations, clubs, and societies
Youth initiation rites. See Initiation
Youth (prepuberty) marriage. See under
    Marriage
Youth revolt
  Auvergnats, 4:23
  Basques, 4:30, 32

Cape Verdeans, 4:56
Tamil of Sri Lanka, 3:282, 283
  see also Political violence
Yule holiday. See Christmas
Yuppies (young urban professionals)
  English, 4:96
Yuri day (holiday)
  Belarussians, 6:61

Zadrugas (corporate family unit)
  Bulgarians, 4:44
  Croats, 4:73
  Dalmatians, 4:86
  Slav Macedonians, 4:240-241
  Slovenes, 4:248
Zhevo (religious practitioner)
  Nagas, 3:190
Zhongyuan (festival)
  Maonan, 6:468
Zhumma (religious practitioner)
  Nagas, 3:190
Zinc mining
  Slav Macedonians, 4:240
Zion Christian Church
  Ndebele, 9:237
  Swazi, 9:332
Zionism
  Ashkenazic Jews, 4:16
Zion Revival
  Jamaicans, 8:139
Zither
  Bavarians, 4:35
Zootheism
  Cherokee, 1:62
  Cheyenne, 1:65
  Chipewyan, 1:69
  Haida, 1:136
  Zuni, 1:399
Zoroastrianism
  Kubachins, 6:219
  Kyrgyz, 6:228
  Parsi, 3:227, 228, 229
  South Asians in Southeast Asia, 5:243
  Uighur, 6:382, 384
  Uzbeks, 6:398
  Yezidis, 6:410
  Zarma, 9:406-410
Zurna (oboe)
  Bulgarian Gypsies, 4:41
Zydeco music
  Black Creoles of Louisiana, 1:39-40
  Cajuns, 1:51